# SAS Activity-Based Costing (ABC) Software Integration

Activity-Based Costing (ABC) is a cost accounting method used by leading firms to accurately determine the costs of their product lines, service lines, distribution channels, and customers. SAS's Activity-Based Costing (ABC) software is then used to identify the firm's most profitable products and customers, their inefficient operations, and their most effective and ineffective management methods.

The increasing complexity of manufacturing and service operations, together with increasingly competitive business conditions, has caused many organizations to adopt improved cost accounting systems, such as ABC costing. These organizations typically use software such as SAS Institute's ABC system to perform the data organizing and calculations required by ABC. Blocher/Stout/Juras/Cokins' learning resources includes SAS ABC software, together with class-tested case materials and tutorials that utilize the SAS ABC software.

The SAS ABC software (formerly called OROS) maintains and processes information about the activities within a company. OROS Quick, a simplified version of the fully functional software, includes all the steps of developing an ABC system, including:

- Creating the necessary files of information about cost resources, activities, and cost objects
- Creating the cost driver assignments
- Data entry
- Calculating ABC costs
- Comparing ABC costs to traditional cost calculations

The OROS Quick software and a related tutorial are available for download at **www.mhhe.com/blocher6e,** the Online Learning Center (OLC) that accompanies Blocher/Stout/Juras/Cokins *Cost Management: A Strategic Emphasis, 6e.* The software and tutorial are designed for those new to ABC as well as the more experienced user.

The Blocher/Stout/Juras/Cokins *Cases and Readings Supplement* and OLC include three short cases that can be used with the tutorial and software to build a simplified ABC model. The objective of each case and tutorial is to illustrate how a comprehensive ABC software system such as SAS can be used. While the cases are greatly simplified, the software is capable of running large scale, complex applications. In this way, the cases provide insight into actual applications of ABC that go well beyond the typical textbook examples. Additional cases will be added to the OLC as they become available.

# Cost Management

A Strategic Emphasis

# Cost Management

**A Strategic Emphasis**

*Sixth Edition*

**Edward J. Blocher**
*University of North Carolina at Chapel Hill*
*Kenan-Flagler Business School*

**David E. Stout**
*Youngstown State University*
*Williamson College of Business Administration*

**Paul E. Juras**
*Babson College*
*Accountancy and Law Division*

**Gary Cokins**
*Strategist, Performance Management Solutions*
*SAS/Worldwide Strategy*

McGraw-Hill
Irwin

COST MANAGEMENT: A STRATEGIC EMPHASIS, SIXTH EDITION

Published by McGraw-Hill/Irwin, a business unit of The McGraw-Hill Companies, Inc., 1221 Avenue of the Americas, New York, NY, 10020. Copyright © 2013 by The McGraw-Hill Companies, Inc. All rights reserved. Printed in the United States of America. Previous editions © 2010, 2008, and 2005. No part of this publication may be reproduced or distributed in any form or by any means, or stored in a database or retrieval system, without the prior written consent of The McGraw-Hill Companies, Inc., including, but not limited to, in any network or other electronic storage or transmission, or broadcast for distance learning.

Some ancillaries, including electronic and print components, may not be available to customers outside the United States.

This book is printed on acid-free paper.

1 2 3 4 5 6 7 8 9 0 DOW/DOW 1 0 9 8 7 6 5 4 3 2

ISBN   978-0-07-802553-2
MHID 0-07-802553-2

Senior Vice President, Products & Markets: *Kurt L. Strand*
Vice President, General Manager, Products & Markets: *Brent Gordon*
Vice President, Content Production & Technology Services: *Kimberly Meriwether David*
Director: *Tim Vertovec*
Brand Manager: *Donna M. Dillon*
Executive Director of Development: *Ann Torbert*
Editorial Coordinator: *Danielle Andries*
Director of Digital Content: *Patricia Plumb*
Senior Marketing Manager: *Kathleen Klehr*
Senior Project Manager: *Diane L. Nowaczyk*
Content Project Manager: *Ravi Raj Adukambarai*
Senior Buyer: *Michael R. McCormick*
Senior Designer: *Matt Diamond*
Cover Designer: *Gino Cieslik*
Cover Image: *Alamy Images*
Typeface: *10/12 Times New Roman MT Std.*
Compositor: *Laserwords Private Limited*
Printer: *R. R. Donnelley*

All credits appearing on page or at the end of the book are considered to be an extension of the copyright page.

**Library of Congress Cataloging-in-Publication Data**

Cost management : a strategic emphasis / Edward J. Blocher . . . [et al.]. — 6th ed.
    p. cm.
    Includes index.
    ISBN 978-0-07-802553-2 (alk. paper) — ISBN 0-07-802553-2 (alk. paper)
    1. Cost accounting. 2. Managerial accounting. I. Blocher, Edward.
    HF5686.C8B559 2013
    658.15'52—dc23

                                    2012013249

The Internet addresses listed in the text were accurate at the time of publication. The inclusion of a website does not indicate an endorsement by the authors or McGraw-Hill, and McGraw-Hill does not guarantee the accuracy of the information presented at these sites.

We dedicate this edition . . .

To my wife, Sandy, and our sons, Joseph and David

Ed Blocher

To my wife, Anne, and our sons, David and Kevin

David Stout

To my wife, Colleen, and my children, Stephen and Kate

Paul Juras

To my wife, Pam Tower, and my mentor, Robert A. Bonsack—a true craftsman in the field of cost management

Gary Cokins

# Meet the Authors

**Edward J. Blocher** is professor of accounting at the Kenan-Flagler Business School at the University of North Carolina at Chapel Hill. His undergraduate degree (economics) is from Rice University, his MBA from Tulane University, and his Ph.D. from the University of Texas at Austin. Professor Blocher presents regularly on strategic cost management at the national meetings of both the American Accounting Association (AAA) and the Institute of Management Accountants (IMA).

While he is involved in a number of accounting organizations, Professor Blocher has been most continually active in the IMA, where he is now a member of the IMA's Research Foundation. He is a certified management accountant (CMA), has taught review courses for the CMA exam, and has served on the IMA's national education committee. Professor Blocher is also the author or co-author of several articles in management accounting and in other areas of accounting and has served as associate editor and reviewer for a number of accounting journals. Recently he published an article in *Issues in Accounting Education* (February 2009) on the topic of teaching strategic cost management.

Putting research and teaching into practice is important to Professor Blocher, who has worked closely with other firms and organizations in developing products, publications, and teaching materials. He was a member of the task force for the IMA that developed a new definition of management accounting in 2008. He currently serves on the IMA's Research Foundation to review academic research proposals for possible funding by the IMA. Also, he has provided expert testimony and has consulted with a number of organizations regarding cost management matters.

**David E. Stout** is the John S. and Doris M. Andrews Professor of Accounting, Williamson College of Business Administration, Youngstown State University. Previously, he held the position of the John M. Cooney Professor of Accounting, School of Business, Villanova University. David earned his Ph.D. in accounting (1982) from the Katz Graduate School of Business, University of Pittsburgh, and teaches in the cost/managerial accounting area. He served previously as editor of *Issues in Accounting Education* and serves currently as editor-in-chief of the *Journal of Accounting Education* and as a member of the editorial board of each of the following journals: *Journal of International Accounting, Auditing & Taxation; China Finance and Accounting Review; IMA Educational Case Journal;* and *Management Accounting Quarterly/Strategic Finance.* Professor Stout has published over 80 articles in numerous professional and academic journals including *Advances in Accounting Education, Issues in Accounting Education,* the *Journal of Accounting Education, The Accounting Educators' Journal, Advances in International Accounting, Behavioral Research in Accounting (BRIA), The CPA Journal, Educational and Psychological Measurement,* the *IMA Educational Case Journal, Managerial Finance, Management Accounting, Management Accounting Quarterly, Financial Practice and Education, Strategic Finance,* and *Advances in Accounting.* David is past president of the Teaching, Learning & Curriculum (TLC) Section of the AAA, past president of the Academy of Business Education (ABE), and past president of the Ohio Region, American Accounting Association (AAA). During the period 2011–2014, he served as a member of the AAA Board of Directors. In 2007, he was the recipient of the R. Lee Brummet Award for Distinguished Accounting Educators, Institute of Management Accountants (IMA), and the Ohio Outstanding Accounting Educator Award, which is cosponsored by the Ohio Society of CPAs and the AAA's Ohio Region. In 2008, David received the Distinguished Achievement in Accounting Education Award from the AICPA, and the Distinguished Service Award for Educators given by the IMA. Also in 2008, David was inducted into the Hall of Honor, TLC Section of the AAA and was selected by *Ohio Magazine* as one of Ohio's Outstanding College and University Teachers.

In 2012, he was a co-recipient of the Jim Bulloch Award for Innovations in Management Accounting Education, an award given annually by the Management Accounting Section (MAS) of the AAA and sponsored by the Institute of Management Accountants (IMA).

**Paul E. Juras** is a professor of accountancy at Babson College. Previously he was a professor of accountancy at Wake Forest University. He earned both his BBA and MBA at Pace University and his Ph.D. from Syracuse University. He is a certified management accountant (CMA) and has a certified public accountant (CPA) license from New York. Professor Juras has expertise in strategic management accounting. He has published articles and cases in many journals, including the *Journal of Corporate Accounting and Finance, Issues in Accounting Education, The CPA Journal,* and *Strategic Finance.* He has made numerous presentations at meetings of both the American Accounting Association (AAA) and the Institute of Management Accountants (IMA).

Professor Juras teaches managerial accounting and strategic cost management courses and has taught in the undergraduate program, the Masters of Science in Accountancy program, and the MBA program at Wake Forest University. He currently teaches in the full-time MBA program, the evening MBA program, and the blended-learning fast track MBA program at Babson College.

While he is active in CAM-I, the Consortium for Advanced Management-International, and has served in leadership roles in the Management Accounting Section of the AAA, Professor Juras has dedicated most of his efforts outside the classroom to the IMA. He is currently a member of the IMA Global Board of Directors and recently served as a Regent of the Institute of Certified Management Accountants, the organization responsible for the CMA certification. In addition, Professor Juras served a three-year term as the chair of the IMA Research Foundation and is an associate editor of the *IMA Educational Case Journal.*

**Gary Cokins** is a principal consultant involved with performance-management solutions with SAS, a leading provider of business analytics software. Gary is an internationally recognized expert, speaker, and author in advanced cost management and performance-improvement systems. He received a BS degree in industrial engineering/operations research (with honors) from Cornell University in 1971 and an MBA from Northwestern University's Kellogg School of Management in 1974. Gary began his career as a strategic planner with FMC Corporation and then served as a financial controller and operations manager. In 1981 he began his management consulting career with Deloitte Consulting and continued with KPMG Peat Marwick. He then headed the National Cost Management Consulting Services for Electronic Data Systems (EDS). Gary was the lead author of the acclaimed *A Manager's Primer on ABC Costing,* published by the IMA. He also has four successful books in *Activity-Based Costing and Enterprise Performance Management.* Gary participates and serves on professional society committees including: The American Institute of Certified Public Accountants (AICPA), the Consortium for Advanced Management-International (CAM-I), the Supply Chain Council, the IMA, and the International Federation of Accountants (IFAC). He is also a member of *Journal of Cost Management* Editorial Advisory Board. Gary is a regular writer and blogger for websites including **www.businessfinance.com**, **www.smartdatacollective.com**, and **www.iianalytics.com**.

**The Author Team:** Selected to provide a leading book in cost management based on leadership in teaching experience, commitment to learning, and a connection to practice that provides them with up-to-date knowledge of real-world management accounting issues and practices.

### Welcome to Students:

We have written this book to help you understand the role of cost management in helping an organization succeed. Unlike many books that aim to teach you *about* accounting, we aim to show you how an important area of accounting, cost management, is *used* by managers to help organizations achieve their goals.

An important aspect of cost management in our text is the strategic focus. By strategy we mean the long-term plan the organization has developed to compete successfully. Most organizations strive to achieve a competitive edge through the execution of a specific strategy. For some firms it is low cost, and for others it might be high quality, customer service, or some unique feature or attribute of its product or service. We know in these competitive times that an organization does not succeed by being ordinary. Rather, it develops a strategy that will set it apart from competitors and ensure its attractiveness to customers and other stakeholders into the future. The role of cost management is to help management of the organization attain and maintain success through strategy implementation. Thus, for every major topic covered in our text there is a larger issue, which is: "How does this organization compete? What type of cost-management information does it need?" We do *not* cover a cost-management method simply to become proficient at it. We want you to know why, when, and how the technique is used to help the organization succeed.

A strategic understanding of cost management today is so important that many senior financial managers and many CPAs—both in public and in private practice—are coming back to school to learn more about strategy, competitive analysis, and new cost-management techniques. Knowing how to do the accounting alone, no matter how well you do it, is by itself no longer sufficient. Cost management with a strategic emphasis is one way to enhance your career and to add value to your employer, whatever type of organization it might be.

## Key Text Features that Integrate the Strategy Emphasis

**Real-World Focus** *Cost Management, 6e*, provides extensive real-world examples of how accounting systems can add value to the organization. The **Real-World Focus** boxes throughout the text take real organizations and demonstrate strategy in action and the role that cost management plays in supporting the organization's strategy.

To augment this coverage, the Blocher team encourages students to further explore real-world companies through **Cost Management in Action** boxes that appear throughout the text. This feature poses important questions that make students think critically about the relationship between cost management and management strategy. At the end of each chapter, the authors then supply their comments for the **Cost Management in Action** boxes.

**Problem Material** The Blocher team has taken great care to develop assignment material that effectively reinforces concepts, procedures, and strategic issues presented in each chapter. In addition, each chapter has one or more end-of-chapter assignments that focus on strategic or ethical issues, or that deal with an international context or a service (i.e., nonmanufacturing) setting. New to the sixth edition, and covered throughout the text, are exercises and problems that relate topical coverage to the general issue of sustainability. Many chapters have assignments based on readings from periodicals such as the *Harvard Business Review* (*HBR*). The attempt of these assignments is to link topical material in the chapter to the broader, strategic issues that organizations face. Other end-of-chapter assignments require the consideration of sustainability or ethical issues for the topic at hand. All such assignments are marked appropriately for easy identification, as follows:

 Strategy  International  Service  Ethics  Sustainability

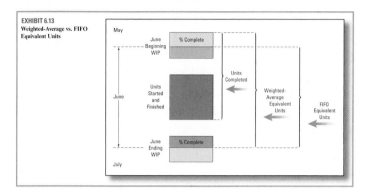

EXHIBIT 6.13
Weighted-Average vs. FIFO Equivalent Units

**Text Illustrations** Clear and concise exhibits help illustrate basic and complicated topics throughout the book.

**Excel Solutions Manual** The *Excel Solutions Manual* has been revised and updated for the sixth edition. This unique supplement consists of an Excel workbook for each chapter and comes in two versions: one for the instructor, the other for students.

Each workbook provides for the instructor the solution to *every* exercise and problem in the chapter, each in its own worksheet in the workbook. Each solution has three components: background information, data, and solution/model-building. The *Excel Solutions Manual* provides the basis for the instructor to guide students through the use of Excel in solving problems and is a useful tool for generating new problems.

The *Excel Solutions Manual* also has a student version that differs from the instructor's version in only one respect: worked-out solutions are available for only half of the end-of-chapter exercises and problems. The remaining assignments (without solutions) can be used for Excel assignments. In other respects the student version of the manual is identical to the instructor version. Because all pertinent information for each exercise and problem, including background information and data, is included in each worksheet, the *Excel Solutions Manual* is self-contained and easy to use. In short, the student version of the *Excel Solutions Manual* is a unique resource designed to enhance the learning process.

**Cases and Readings Supplement** The *Cases and Readings Supplement,* available in electronic form, challenges students to think about and use cost-management information in a real-world setting. The longer articles provide a basis for more comprehensive and in-depth discussions about the role of *cost management* in helping an organization successfully execute its strategy. We have found the *Cases and Readings Supplement* to be particularly useful for upper-level undergraduate courses and for MBA course offerings.

**Assurance of Learning Ready** Many educational institutions today are focused on the notion of assurance of learning, an important element of some accreditation standards. *Cost Management* is designed specifically to help support your assurance of learning initiatives with a simple, yet powerful solution.

Test bank questions for *Cost Management* map to a specific chapter learning outcome/objective listed in the text. You can use our test bank and EZ Test Online to easily query for the learning objectives specified at the beginning of each chapter.

**AACSB Statement** The McGraw-Hill Companies is a proud corporate member of AACSB International. Understanding the importance and value of AACSB accreditation, Cost Management, 6e, *recognizes the guidelines detailed in the AACSB standards by connecting selected questions in the test bank to the six general knowledge and skill areas in the AACSB standards.*

*The statements contained in* Cost Management, 6e, *are provided only as a guide for the users of this textbook.* The AACSB leaves content coverage and assessment within the purview of individual schools, the mission of the school, and the faculty.

**Excel Tutorials** The fourth and fifth editions of *Cost Management* made available accompanying Excel tutorials, one for each chapter and in Microsoft Word. The sixth edition maintains the Word version of these Excel tutorials but also provides them in a narrated, step-by-step video animation format. The tutorials are tied to one of the main topics covered in the chapter. Thus, students can hone their Excel-based skills using either version of the tutorials, while working to reinforce major topics covered in the text.

**A Framework to Integrate Strategy: The Five Steps of Strategic Decision Making**

The first edition of *Cost Management* introduced a five-step framework for decision making with a strategic emphasis. The framework shows that each decision starts and ends with a consideration of the organization's strategy. To extend and integrate the strategic emphasis, the sixth edition continues the tradition of including this five-step framework throughout the text. In all but a few chapters there is a short section that uses the five-step framework to show how a consideration of the organization's strategy plays a key role in making the decision that will address the business-related problems presented in that chapter.

**The Current Economic Downturn Increases the Importance of Reviewing and Executing Strategy**

The current economic downturn is addressed in the text, both in the chapters and in the end-of-chapter exercises and problems. The downturn requires firms to place an even greater emphasis on the successful execution of an organization's strategy. Moreover, the economic difficulties may require an organization to review and modify its strategy to compete more effectively in the changed economic conditions.

## The Online Learning Center (OLC)

*Cost Management: A Strategic Emphasis, 6e,* by **Blocher/Stout/Juras/Cokins** offers a wide array of supplements to instructors and students. Key to the *Cost Management* learning resources is the **Online Learning Center (OLC): www.mhhe.com/blocher6e**. Here instructors and students will find valuable course-preparation materials, study tools, and links to important web resources.

The password-protected portion of the *Cost Management* OLC—meant for instructors—contains solution files (in Word format and in both student and instructor versions) to all of the end-of-chapter items in the book, along with an **Excel-based solutions manual.** As noted earlier, the Excel solution files are available in two forms: one for the instructor, the other for students. Both are available in the password-protected portion of the OLC for *Cost Management*.

On the student portion of the OLC, students have access to many resources to assist them in their cost management course, including the *Cases and Readings Supplement,* check figures for the end-of-chapter material, and PowerPoint presentations. See the full list below for the resources available!

The OLC is a one-stop resource for essential course resources for students and instructors:

## For STUDENTS:

- Chapter Objectives
- Chapter Overview
- 20 Excel Tutorials (one for each chapter) in Word format
- 20 Animated, Narrated Excel Tutorials (one for each chapter)
- Animated, Narrated Tutorials for Solving End-of-Chapter Self-Study Problems
- Cases and Readings Supplement
- Online Quizzes
- PowerPoint Presentations

## For INSTRUCTORS (and password protected):

- Sample Syllabi
- Instructor's Resource Guide
- Solutions Manual (in Word format and in both student and instructor versions)
- Excel-based Solutions Manual (in both student and instructor versions)
- PowerPoint Presentations
- Solutions and Teaching Notes for ABC-SAS Software Cases

*(Continued on next page)*

*(Continued from previous page)*

- Links to Professional Resources
- Text Updates
- Check Figures for End-of-Chapter Exercises and Problems
- ABC-SAS Software and Tutorial
- Cases for use with ABC-SAS Software
- Regression Analysis Supplement

- Teaching Notes for Cases and Readings Supplement
- Test Bank: Word Format and EZ Test Online
- Text Updates

> **Excel Tutorials and Self-Study Problems are now available as Camtasia files, which provide narrated, step-by-step video animation that walks the student through the Tutorials and Self-Study Problems!**

## Excel Tutorials

Free to adopters of the sixth edition is a set of 20 Excel tutorials, one for each chapter. This resource provides a context-based means for students to hone their Excel skills. In many cases, the Excel tutorial is linked to one or more of the Self-Study Problem(s) included at the end of the chapter. The tutorials cover a wide variety of Excel topics, from elementary to the intermediate level, and some at the advanced level. The tutorials are an easy way for students to learn more about Excel without having to ask the instructor. For the sixth edition, these tutorials are available in two formats: Word files and Camtasia files (new to the sixth edition). This learning resource is available free to adopters of the text via the Online Learning Center.

## Integration of Important Topics throughout the Text

Key topic areas for the course are integrated across the chapters. As previously noted, strategy is integrated throughout the text. In addition, accounting for "lean" is included in four chapters as it relates to the subject matter of that chapter. Similarly, time-driven activity-based costing (TDABC) is covered in the ABC chapter and also in the chapter on budgeting. ABC appears in most of the chapters in Part Two, as it has a key role in planning and decision making. Nonfinancial performance measures and the balanced scorecard (BSC) are introduced in Part One and then covered as part of the operational and management control chapters included in Parts Three and Four. Resource consumption accounting (RCA) is covered both in Chapter 5 and again in Chapter 15. The topic of capacity resource planning is covered in Chapters 10 and 15. These are just examples of the efforts the authors have made to integrate key topics throughout the text.

## New Features throughout the Sixth Edition

- Paul E. Juras of Babson College, who has published numerous articles and cases in management accounting, joins the 6th edition as a coauthor.
- A strong focus on improving end-of-chapter exercises and problems—for clarity, clear linkage to chapter learning objectives, and an appropriate level of challenge.
- Each end-of-chapter exercise and problem is tagged with the chapter learning objective(s) examined in that exercise or problem.
- *Sustainability* is now integrated into each chapter, and exercises and problems that involve sustainability are marked with a distinctive icon.
- The self-study problems at the end of all chapters are now available as Camtasia files (accessible at **www.mhhe.com/blocher6e**). Students can use the Camtasia files to understand the solution by viewing a video that takes them through the problem on a step-by-step basis and in an animated, narrated fashion.
- Selected chapters offer increased use of specialized features in Excel.
- Excel tutorials (one for each chapter) are now available in Camtasia file form, which provides narrated, step-by-step video animation, as well as Word form.

# Important Changes in Each Chapter of the Sixth Edition

## Part One: Introduction to Strategy, Cost Management, and Cost Systems

### Chapter 1: Cost Management and Strategy

- Two new Real-World Focus items reporting on recent surveys on strategy and ethics.
- Several revised and four new exercises and problems with a focus on ethics, risk management, and the recent economic downturn.

### Chapter 2: Implementing Strategy: The Value Chain, the Balanced Scorecard, and the Strategy Map

- New Real-World Focus item on the balanced scorecard.
- New Cost Management in Action item on strategy implementation.
- The section on sustainability has been updated and enhanced.
- Six revised exercises and problems and an additional six new exercises and problems, including two research problems, one on the value chain and one on sustainability. Research articles are available on the text website.

### Chapter 3: Basic Cost-Management Concepts

- New Real-World Focus item involving costs in the airline industry.
- Twelve new or revised exercises and problems, three of which include sustainability.
- A new section on periodic and perpetual inventory systems.

### Chapter 4: Job Costing

- New Real-World Focus item involving costs in apparel manufacturing.

- A new section on errors in overhead application, with reference to applicable academic research.
- Completely revised example for job costing in a service industry.
- Ten new or revised exercises and problems with a focus on global issues and sustainability.

### Chapter 5: Activity-Based Costing and Customer Profitability Analysis

- Two new Real-World Focus items.
- Enhanced coverage of resource consumption accounting (RCA).
- Enhanced coverage of time-driven activity-based costing, including an additional problem at the end of the chapter.
- Two new research problems, one on customer lifetime value and one on sustainability.

### Chapter 6: Process Costing

- New section on normal and standard process costing.
- Sixteen new or revised exercises and problems.

### Chapter 7: Cost Allocation: Departments, Joint Products, and By-Products

- Real-World Focus items updated to include coverage of new cost allocation issues, particularly in Medicare cost reimbursement.
- Fourteen new or revised exercises and problems with a focus on strategy, ethics, and sustainability.

## Part Two: Planning and Decision Making

### Chapter 8: Cost Estimation

- New Real-World Focus item explaining an application of

regression analysis in the context of predictive analytics.
- New Cost Management in Action item about cost estimation in the construction industry.
- Revised chapter introduction to reflect the recent economic downturn.
- To streamline the presentation of this chapter, the appendix on regression analysis has been moved to the text website where any student can access it. The coverage of regression analysis in the printed text remains comprehensive and complete. The 5th edition appendix is now a Regression Analysis Supplement that is available for instructors and students who want a more in-depth coverage of regression. No exercises or problems in the text require information from this supplement.
- Ten new or revised exercises and problems include a focus on sustainability, the recent economic downturn, and the application of regression analysis to practical current business issues.

### Chapter 9: Short-Term Profit Planning: Cost-Volume-Profit (CVP) Analysis

- Expanded coverage of dealing with uncertainty (including degree of operating leverage [DOL], decision tables, expected value analysis, and use of the built-in Excel function NORMDIST).
- Inclusion of alternative formulas (sales basket approach and weighted-average contribution margin per unit) in conjunction with profit planning for the multiproduct firm.
- Six new Real-World Focus items covering the following topics: operating leverage, choice of cost

structure, assessing the financial viability of academic departments/majors, pricing decisions in the steel industry, managing profitability under different cost structures, and GM IPO—breakeven pricing.

- Five new exercises and problems, including a comprehensive problem that deals with sustainability.
- Increased use of Excel's *Goal Seek* function throughout the assignment material.
- Many enhancements to existing exercises and problems.

## Chapter 10: Strategy and the Master Budget

- Three totally new exercises and problems, covering kaizen budgeting, resource capacity planning (with ABC), and sustainability.
- Reduction in length of the chapter, with shorter, crisper explanations of the budgeting process.
- Expanded coverage of uncertainty and the budgeting process, including a new discussion of scenario analysis.
- Two new Real-World Focus items regarding the importance of accurate sales forecasts to the master budgeting process and rolling financial forecasts.

## Chapter 11: Decision Making with a Strategic Emphasis

- Three new exercises (sell-or-process-further decision, determining the optimum product mix, and sustainability) and three new problems (sustainability, sell-or-process-further decision, and a research-based assignment based on a *Harvard Business Review* [HBR] article).
- Increased use of Goal Seek function from Excel in exercises and problems.

- Three new Real-World Focus items, all of which deal in some manner with sustainability.
- Expanded discussion of the topic of short-term product planning (i.e., determining the optimum short-term product/service mix), including optional reports generated by the Solver function in Excel.

## Chapter 12: Strategy and the Analysis of Capital Investments

- Improved explanation and coverage of tax effects associated with asset-replacement decisions (including expanded coverage of the topic in Appendix A).
- Two new Real-World Focus items regarding sustainability/green architecture investments and the application of real-options analysis to supply-chain and plant-expansion investment decisions.
- Incorporation of two new Excel-based functions (viz., using the array function to calculate the NPV of a proposed investment, and creating both one-variable and two-variable data tables for sensitivity analysis purposes).
- New exercises and problems regarding the equipment-replacement decision, sensitivity analysis, and sustainability.

## Chapter 13: Cost Planning for the Product Life-Cycle: Target Costing, Theory of Constraints, and Strategic Pricing

- Inclusion of peak load pricing in the discussion of pricing methods.
- Three new Real-World Focus items.
- Updated Cost Management in Action item.
- One new research assignment that deals with sustainability.

## Part Three: Operational-Level Control

## Chapter 14: Operational Performance Measurement: Sales, Direct-Cost Variances, and the Role of Nonfinancial Performance Measures

- Three new problems, including a *Harvard Business Review* (*HBR*)-based reading dealing with service-based innovation and another *HBR*-based reading dealing with transparency across a company's supply chain.
- One updated Real-World Focus (RWF) item and two entirely new RWF items that deal with managing JIT supply-chain risks and sustainability and the bottom line.

## Chapter 15: Operational Performance Measurement: Indirect-Cost Variances and Resource Capacity-Management

- Three new problems, including an *HBR*-based reading dealing with strategies for reducing administrative costs and a *Journal of Accounting Education* paper that provides new insights into the decomposition of the production volume variance.
- Continued emphasis on exercises and problems regarding the topic of capacity-resource planning and the financial reporting requirements of FASB ASC 330-10-30.
- Two new Real-World Focus items: one dealing with expensing the cost of idle capacity (based on a recent article in *Strategic Finance*), and the other dealing with managing capacity in the airline industry (based on a recent article in *The Wall Street Journal*).
- In the appendix, explicit consideration of the expected value of perfect information (Variance-Investigation Decisions under Uncertainty).

## Chapter 16: Operational Performance Measurement: Further Analysis of Productivity and Sales

- New Real-World Focus regarding the new ways organizations are improving productivity.

- New Cost Management in Action item with a focus on the difficulties in measuring productivity.

- Completely revised chapter introduction that reflects changes in the auto industry since 2008.

- Sixteen new or revised exercises and problems with a focus on strategy and sustainability.

## Chapter 17: The Management and Control of Quality

- Repositioning of Taguchi quality loss function material from the appendix into the body of the chapter.

- Inclusion of new Exhibit (17.2) that depicts two primary dimensions of quality: *design quality* and *performance quality.*

- Four new Real-World Focus items dealing with: the high cost (and risk) of external failures (J&J example); implementing Six Sigma projects successfully and learning from failures; lean and Six Sigma principles and the health care sector; and, airline quality ratings and competitive benchmarking.

- Two new problems: one that deals with the concept of net promoter score (as a nonfinancial, external measure of quality), and one (based on a recent *Harvard Business Review* article) that attempts to apply lean principles to knowledge-based work.

## Part Four: Management-Level Control

## Chapter 18: Strategic Performance Measurement: Cost Centers, Profit Centers, and the Balanced Scorecard

- Two new Real-World Focus items that illustrate changes in outsourcing practices and the findings of academic research about management control in the retail industry.

- Completely new section on the impact of international financial reporting standards (IFRS) on the management accountant's role in management control.

- Ten new or revised exercises and problems with a focus on sustainability and ethics; one of the new problems is a research problem on sustainability. The research article is available on the text website.

## Chapter 19: Strategic Performance Measurement: Investment Centers

- Three new Real-World Focus (RWF) items dealing with strategic applications of the return on investment (ROI) metric (viz., evaluating the return from investments in employee training programs, pursuing a doctorate in accounting, and employee wellness programs [based on a *Harvard Business Review* article]). Two of the three new RWF items require Internet-based research on the part of the student.

- Three new problems (all of which deal with sustainability-related issues).

- Expanded discussion of the transfer-pricing decision in an international context.

## Chapter 20: Management Compensation, Business Analysis, and Business Valuation

- Four new Real-World Focus items regarding current trends in CEO pay; new regulations in executive pay; a review of academic research on the question of the link between CEO pay and company financial performance; and a commentary on the relevance of the price-earnings ratio.

- Eleven new or revised exercises and problems that include a look at international accounting standards and bonus compensation, ethics, and the link between CEO pay and financial performance. One of the problems is a research assignment on business valuation; the research article is available on the text website.

# Supplements

## For Instructors...

### Online Learning Center (OLC): www.mhhe.com/blocher6e.

The Instructor Edition of the *Cost Management: A Strategic Emphasis, 6e,* OLC is password-protected and a convenient place for instructors to access course supplements. Resources for professors include: the Instructor and Student Solutions Manual (in both Word and Excel formats), the Test Bank (both Word and EZ Test Online), the Instructor's Resource Guide, teaching notes for the casebook, links to professional resources, sample syllabi, text updates, and the set of Excel tutorials (both Word and Camtasia files).

## For Students...

**Cost Management**
A Strategic Emphasis
Sixth Edition

Chapter 5
Activity-Based Costing and
Customer Profitability Analysis
**Guided Example Self-Study Problem Series**

|  | Production Department A | Production Department B | Total |
|---|---|---|---|
| Machine-hours | 4,000 | 16,000 | 20,000 |
| Relative % | 20% | 80% |  |
| Overhead | 200,000 | 800,000 | 1,000,000 |
| Direct labor-hours | 20,000 | 10,000 |  |
| Cost per hour | $ 10.00 | $ 80.00 |  |
| Deluxe |  |  |  |
| Labor hours per unit | 2 | 1 |  |
| Overhead rate | 10 |  |  |

### Problem Takeaways

- Determined product costs under a
  - ✓ volume-based method and
  - ✓ activity-based method
- Contrasted the two methods
- Described activity-based costing (ABC),
  - – the steps in developing an ABC system
  - – the benefits of an ABC system

### Camtasia Files available with Excel Tutorials and End-of-Chapter Self-Study Problems.

New with the 6th edition are Camtasia files for the set of 20 Excel tutorials and the end-of-chapter self-study problems. The solutions to the self-study problems are provided using videos that take an animated, narrated approach and walk through each problem and its solution step by step. The Excel tutorials cover a wide range of topics that allow students to learn more about Excel. These learning resources are available at **www.mhhe.com/blocher6e**.

### Cases and Readings for use with *Cost Management: A Strategic Emphasis, 6e.*

This supplement (available free to adopters) contains cases and readings covering a variety of important topics. The case scenarios put students in situations that allow them to think strategically and to apply concepts they've learned in the course. Key readings have been chosen to give students more background into the evolution of strategic cost management topics as well as to contemporary controversies in the field.

### Online Learning Center (OLC): www.mhhe.com/blocher6e.

The Student Edition of the *Cost Management: A Strategic Emphasis, 6e,* OLC contains many tools designed to help students study, including: the *Cases and Readings Supplement,* check figures, text updates, links to professional resources, chapter overviews, chapter objectives, multiple-choice quizzes, Excel tutorials, and PowerPoint® presentations.

**SAS Software.** SAS's Activity-Based Costing (ABC) software is used worldwide for performance management functions and analysis. *Cost Management* incorporates SAS software in its ABC case material to prepare students for calculating ABC costs, creating cost-driver assignments, and organizing cost information using real-world software. Visit the Blocher OLC (**www.mhhe.com/blocher6e**) today to learn more about the software and the cases available for use. Both the cases and the software are available free to adopters.

# Acknowledgments

**Our Sincerest Thanks . . .**

In writing this book, we were fortunate to have received extensive feedback from a number of accounting educators. We want to thank our colleagues for their careful and complete review of our work. The comments that we received were invaluable in helping us to shape the manuscript. We believe that this collaborative development process helped us to create a text that will truly meet the needs of today's students and instructors. We are sincerely grateful to the following individuals for their participation in the process:

**Reviewers for 6e:**

Michele Chwastiak, *University of New Mexico–Albuquerque*

Karen Farmer, *Texas A&M University*

Michael Flores, *Wichita State University*

Ralph Greenberg, *Temple University–Philadelphia*

James Higgins, *Holy Family University*

Il-Woon Kim, *University of Akron*

Jamshed Mistry, *Suffolk University*

Kay Poston, *University of Indianapolis*

Steve Swirsky, *Florida A&M University*

**Previous Edition Reviewers:**

Wagdy Abdallah, *Seton Hall University*

Nas Ahadiat, *California State Polytechnic University–Pomona*

Vidya N. Awasthi, *Seattle University*

K. R. Balachandran, *New York University*

Mohamed E. Bayou, *School of Management, University of Michigan–Dearborn*

Marvin L. Bouillon, *Iowa State University*

Wayne Bremser, *Villanova University*

Wede E. Brownell, *University of Central Oklahoma*

Dennis Caplan, *Oregon State University*

Bea Chiang, *The College of New Jersey*

Jeffrey Cohen, *Boston College*

Cheryl Corke, *Genesee Community College*

Alan B. Czyzewski, *Indiana State University*

Robert J. DePasquale, *Saint Vincent College*

Joe Dowd, *Eastern Washington University*

Robert W. Duron, *Chadron State College*

David Eichelberger, *Austin Peay State University*

Rafik Elias, *California State University–Los Angeles*

James M. Emig, *Villanova University*

Sidney Ewer, *Missouri State University*

Jerry W. Ferry, *University of North Alabama*

Michael Flores, *Wichita State University*

Jay D. Forsyth, *Central Washington University*

Mike Grayson, *Jackson State University*

Olen L. Greer, *Southwest Missouri State University*

Donald C. Gribbin, *Southern Illinois University*

Sanjay Gupta, *Valdosta State University*

Betty Harper, *Middle Tennessee State University*

Jeannie Harrington, *Middle Tennessee State University*

Judith A. Harris, *Nova Southeastern University*

Aleecia Hibbets, *University of Louisiana–Monroe*

Jay Holmen, *University of Wisconsin–Eau Claire*

Linda Holmes, *University of Wisconsin–Whitewater*

Norma C. Holter, *Towson University*

David R. Honodel, *University of Denver*

Bambi Hora, *University of Central Oklahoma*

Todd Jensen, *California State University–Sacramento*

Sanford R. Kahn, *University of Cincinnati*

Larry N. Killough, *Virginia Polytechnic Institute and State University*

Mehmet C. Kocakulah, *University of Southern Indiana*

Laura Jean Kreissl, *University of Wisconsin–Parkside*

Leslie Kren, *University of Wisconsin–Milwaukee*

Sandra S. Lang, *McKendree College*

Randall E. LaSalle, *West Chester University of Pennsylvania*

Dan Law, *Gonzaga University*

Stephen Makar, *University of Wisconsin–Oshkosh*

Joetta Malone, *Strayer University*

Man C. Maloo, *Towson University*

Linda Marquis, *Northern Kentucky University*

John McGowan, *St. Louis University*

Brian L. McGuire, *University of Southern Indiana*

Laurie B. McWhorter, *Mississippi State University*

Michael Morris, *University of Notre Dame*

Yaw M. Mensah, *Rutgers University*

Cheryl E. Mitchem, *Virginia State University*

Ann Murphy, *Metropolitan State College of Denver*

Jennifer Niece, *Assumption College*

Margaret O'Reilly-Allen, *Rider University*

Lisa Owens, *Clemson University*

Chei M. Paik, *George Washington University*

Hugh Pforsich, *University of Idaho*

Shirley Polejewski, *University of St. Thomas*

Jenice Prather-Kinsey, *University of Missouri–Columbia*

Martha L. Sale, *Sam Houston State University*

Marsha Scheidt, *University of Tennessee–Chattanooga*

Dennis Shanholtzer, *Metropolitan Slate University*

Shiv Sharma, *Robert Morris University*

Kenneth P. Sinclair, *Lehigh University*

John L. Stancil, *Florida Southern College*

Ronald A. Stunda, *Birmingham–Southern College*

Jerry Thorne, *North Carolina A&T State University*

Rich White, *Florida Metro University*

Finally, we are most appreciative of the outstanding assistance and support provided by the professionals of McGraw-Hill/Irwin: Tim Vertovec, our director, and Donna Dillon, our brand manager, for their guidance; our editorial coordinator, Danielle Andries, for her invaluable suggestions; Kathleen Klehr, our senior marketing manager, for her significant promotional efforts; Diane Nowaczyk, our project manager, for her attention to detail; and Matt Diamond, for the outstanding presentation of the text. An added thanks to Ilene Leopold Persoff for her significant contributions to the accuracy of our text.

*Ed Blocher*

*David Stout*

*Paul Juras*

*Gary Cokins*

# Brief Contents

# Contents

# Introduction to Strategy, Cost Management, and Cost Systems

The objective of the first seven chapters is to introduce the strategic approach to cost management and to cover the basic concepts of cost accounting systems.

**Chapter 1** is an introduction to cost management—how companies plan for success and the management accountant's role in implementing strategy. The chapter includes coverage of the Institute of Management Accountants's recently revised definition of management accounting. It is also an introduction to the current environment of business, including contemporary management techniques and professional responsibilities.

**Chapter 2** focuses on some of the principal means that organizations use to implement strategy. The chapter introduces a strategic management system known as the balanced scorecard (BSC), the strategy map, and the value chain, and shows how these tools can be used to help the organization implement its strategy. These tools are foundational tools that appear throughout the text; this is why they are covered in this chapter.

**Chapter 3** defines the key terms that management accountants use to describe product cost systems and cost information for planning, decision making, and control. This terminology is important for both accountants and managers alike. The chapter also introduces the differences in management accounting between service, manufacturing, and merchandising companies.

**Chapters 4–7** cover costing systems and their role in strategy implementation.

**Chapter 4** provides an introduction to costing systems by defining the elements of cost and how these elements are combined to determine the cost of a product or service. There are a number of variations on this basic cost system, each of which is designed to fit a particular manufacturing or service environment. These variations are explained in Chapters 5, 6, and 7.

**Chapter 5** covers a strategically important advance in product costing called activity-based costing (ABC). Rather than using the volume-based approach (explained in Chapter 4), the ABC approach incorporates the details of all the activities that are needed to provide the product or service. The result is much more accurate, and therefore more strategically useful, cost information regarding the resource demands of an organization's outputs.

**Chapter 6** introduces process costing, a costing system that is applicable for firms that have relatively homogeneous products passing through similar processing steps, often in a continuous flow. Commodity-based industries are of this nature: food processing, chemical, and consumer products firms.

**Chapter 7** covers cost-allocation issues associated with costing systems—departmental cost allocation and joint cost allocation. The chapter begins with an overview of the objectives and strategic role of cost allocation and then shows how departmental costs and joint costs are allocated to products.

# CHAPTER ONE

# Cost Management and Strategy

**After studying this chapter, you should be able to . . .**

LO 1-1    Explain the use of cost management information in each of the four functions of management and in different types of organizations, with emphasis on the strategic management function

LO 1-2    Explain the contemporary business environment and how it has influenced cost management

LO 1-3    Explain the contemporary management techniques and how they are used in cost management to respond to the contemporary business environment

LO 1-4    Explain the different types of competitive strategies

LO 1-5    Describe the professional environment of the management accountant, including professional organizations and professional certifications

LO 1-6    Understand the principles and rules of professional ethics and explain how to apply them

Talk about a success story! Walmart has grown from its first discount store in 1962 to become the world's largest company, with over $400 billion in sales. It has achieved this through clear day-to-day attention to accomplishing its business strategy and to living up to its motto of "Save Money, Live Better." Walmart achieves success through extensive use of technology and aggressive efforts to grow the business globally. And the environment is very competitive! A key competitor, Target, with a different strategy and a different motto ("Expect More, Pay Less") has challenged Walmart with aggressive advertising campaigns and new stores. During the 2004–2006 period, Target was outpacing Walmart in sales growth and stock price growth. This reversed in the 2006–2008 period, as the global economic outlook weakened for many consumers and the low-cost strategy of Walmart proved to be more successful. Since 2008 both Walmart and Target have been facing the heat of increased competition from both **Amazon.com** and Costco as well as other retailers such as Dollar General.[1] The stakes are high and the competition is fierce. Imagine yourself as a manager for one of these companies; how would you help your company be more competitive?

This book is about how managers use cost management to build a successful company as those at Walmart and Target have done. Everyone wants to be a winner, and so it is in business and accounting. We are interested in how the management accountant can play a key role in making a firm or organization successful. Now you might be asking, Don't we have to know what you mean by *success*? Absolutely! A firm must define clearly what it means by success in its mission statement. Then it must develop a road map to accomplish that mission, which we call *strategy*. Briefly, strategy is a plan to achieve competitive success. In Walmart's case, the mission is to achieve customer value, and the strategy involves the extensive use of technology to reduce cost, a management structure that welcomes change, and a constant focus on customer service. For Target, the competitive focus is the promise of value through brand recognition, customer service, store location, differentiated offerings, quality, fashion, and price.

Because we are interested in how the management accountant can help a company be successful, we take a strategic approach throughout the book, beginning with an introduction to strategy in this chapter. The key idea is that success comes from developing and implementing

[1] Kelly Evans, "To Gauge Walmart, Watch Its Flanks," *The Wall Street Journal,* May 25, 2011, p. C1; John Jannarone, "Retailers Struggle in Amazon Jungle," *The Wall Street Journal,* February 22, 2011, p. C8; Karen Talley, "Walmart Sticks to Low Prices," *The Wall Street Journal,* November 16, 2011, p. B3;

an effective strategy aided by management accounting methods. These management accounting methods are covered in this text chapter by chapter; we include them in the text because we know they have helped companies succeed.

---

> The most successful man in life is the man who has the best information.
>
> *Benjamin Disraeli, a 19th-century prime minister of England*

---

**LO 1-1**

*Explain the use of cost management information in each of the four functions of management and in different types of organizations, with emphasis on the strategic management function.*

As Disraeli knew in the 19th century, having the best information is the key to success. In today's business environment, the development and use of cost management information have important strategic roles in an organization's success.

## Management Accounting and the Role of Cost Management

**Cost management information** is developed and used to implement the organization's strategy. It consists of financial information about costs and revenues and nonfinancial information about customer retention, productivity, quality, and other key success factors for the organization.

**Cost management** is the development and use of cost management information.

**Management accounting** is a profession that involves partnering in management decision making, devising planning and performance management systems, and providing expertise in financial reporting and control to assist management in the formulation and implementation of an organization's strategy.

Management accountants are the accounting and finance professionals who develop and use cost management information to assist in implementing the organization's strategy. **Cost management information** consists of financial information about costs and revenues and nonfinancial information about customer retention, productivity, quality, and other key success factors for the organization. **Cost management** is the development and use of cost management information.

The strategic role of the management accountant in an organization is explained in the definition of management accounting provided by the Institute of Management Accountants (IMA). Relevant additional information on the definition can be found in the IMA's Statement on Management Accounting: *Definition of Management Accounting.*

---

> **Management accounting** is a profession that involves partnering in management decision making, devising planning and performance management systems, and providing expertise in financial reporting and control to assist management in the formulation and implementation of an organization's strategy.

---

Management accountants use their unique expertise (decision making, planning, performance management, and more), working with the organization's managers, to help the organization succeed in formulating and implementing its strategy. Cost management information is developed and used within the organization's information value chain, from stage 1 through stage 5, as shown below:

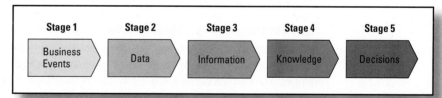

At lower stages of the value chain, management accountants gather and summarize data (stage 2) from business events (stage 1) and then transform the data to information (stage 3) through analysis and use of the management accountant's expertise. At stage 4 the information is combined with other information about the organization's strategy and competitive environment to produce actionable knowledge. At stage 5 management accountants use this knowledge to participate with management teams in making strategic decisions that advance the organization's strategy.

In a typical organization (illustrated in Exhibit 1.1) management accountants report to the controller, a key accounting professional in the firm. The controller, assisted by management accountants, has a wide range of responsibilities, including cost management, financial reporting, maintaining financial information systems, and other reporting functions. The chief financial officer (CFO) has the overall responsibility for the financial function, the treasurer manages investor and creditor relationships, and the chief information officer (CIO) manages the firm's use of information technology, including computer systems and communications.

**EXHIBIT 1.1**
**A Typical Organization Chart Showing the Functions of the Controller**

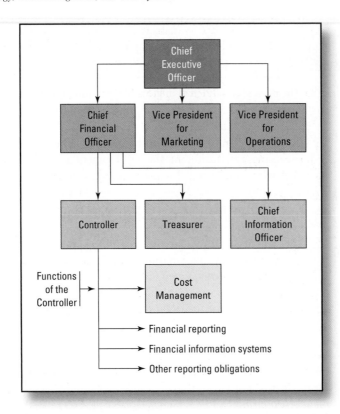

In contrast to the cost management function, the financial reporting function involves preparing financial statements for *external users* such as investors and government regulators. These financial accounting reports require compliance with certain external requirements. Cost management information is developed for use *within* the firm to facilitate management and is not needed to meet those requirements. The main focus of cost management information therefore must be *usefulness* and *timeliness;* the focus of financial reports must be *accuracy* and *compliance* with reporting requirements. However, strict adherence to accuracy can compromise the usefulness and timeliness of the information. The function of the financial information systems department is to develop and maintain the financial reporting system and related systems such as payroll, financial security systems, and tax preparation. The challenge for the controller is to reconcile these different and potentially conflicting roles.

### The Four Functions of Management

The management accountant develops cost management information for the CFO, other managers, and employee teams to use to manage the firm and make the firm more competitive and successful. Cost management information is provided for each of the four major management functions: (1) strategic management, (2) planning and decision making, (3) management and operational control, and (4) preparation of financial statements. (See Exhibit 1.2.) The most important function is **strategic management,** which is the development and implementation of a sustainable competitive position in which the firm's competitive advantage provides continued success. A strategy is a set of goals and specific action plans that, if achieved, provide the desired competitive advantage. Strategic management involves identifying and implementing these goals and action plans. Next, management is responsible for **planning and decision making,** which involve budgeting and profit planning, cash flow management, and other decisions related to the firm's operations, such as deciding when to lease or buy a facility, when to repair or replace a piece of equipment, when to change a marketing plan, and when to begin development of a new product.

The third area of responsibility, control, consists of two functions, operational control and management control. **Operational control** takes place when mid-level managers (e.g., site managers, product managers, regional managers) monitor the activities of operating-level

**Strategic management**
is the development and implementation of a sustainable competitive position.

**Planning and decision making**
involve budgeting and profit planning, cash flow management, and other decisions related to operations.

**Operational control**
takes place when mid-level managers monitor the activities of operating-level managers and employees.

Our unique approach in this book is to demonstrate cost management from a strategic emphasis. Every cost management method we cover is linked to the firm's strategy, that is, how the method helps the firm to be successful. Why emphasize the strategic approach? Managers tell us why . . .

A recent survey of 1,054 chief financial officers (CFOs) by the consulting firm Accenture revealed that the CFOs were ". . . getting more deeply involved in business strategy, deciding where to invest capital and even looking at a company's product mix." Similarly, a recent study by the accounting firm, PricewaterhouseCoopers (PWC) found that in 2010 ". . . 78% of survey respondents reported that their finance function now plays a key role in strategic planning, compared to 63% in 2009." *CFO* magazine did a similar survey in 2009 and found that 90% of the CFOs surveyed indicated that they had a significant role in the company's strategy.

A 2008 survey of 250 chief executive officers by the public accounting firm Ernst & Young indicated that more than 84% agreed or strongly agreed with the statement, "The Chief Financial Officer (CFO) in our company is seen as a business partner of the CEO." Similarly, a 2005 IBM Corporation study of 900 CFOs found that most agreed that the most important areas for the CFO were "measuring and monitoring business performance" and "partnering with the organization to identify and execute growth strategies."

A 2003 survey of 1,995 members of the Institute of Management Accountants (the IMA is an international professional organization for management accountants) reported "Cost management plays a significant role at companies; 81% of all respondents reported that cost management was important to their organization's overall strategic goals."

The Society of the Management Accountants of Canada has developed a competency framework for certified management accountants in Canada, which has the following introduction:

Certified Management Accountants (CMAs) do more than just measure value—they create it. As the leaders in management accounting, CMAs apply a unique mix of financial expertise, strategic insight, innovative thinking and a collaborative approach to help grow successful businesses.

**Sources:** Robert A. Howell, "CFOs: Not Just for Finance Anymore," *The Wall Street Journal,* February 27, 2012, p. R7; Dana Mattioli, "Finance Chiefs Expand Roles," *The Wall Street Journal,* January 31, 2011, p. B7; John Lynes, "Cost Control: An Issue for Major Businesses, PWC Finds," *Accountancy News,* March 28, 2011; Alix Stuart, "Are You Strategic," *CFO,* November 2009, pp. 45–48; "Competency Map of the CMA Profession," The Society of Management Accountants of Canada, www.cma-canada.org; Ashish Garg, Debashis Gosh, James Hudick, and Chuen Nowacki, "Roles and Practices in Management Accounting Today," *Strategic Finance,* July 2003, pp. 30–35; Ernst & Young, *What's Next for the CFO? Where Ambition Meets Reality,* 2008; IBM Corporation, *The Agile CFO: Acting on Business Insight,* 2005, www-935.ibm.com/services/us/imc/pdf/ge510-6239-agile-cfo-full.pdf; Gary Siegel, James E. Sorensen, and Sandra Richtermeyer, "Are You a Business Partner? Parts 1 and 2," *Strategic Finance,* September and October 2003.

---

**EXHIBIT 1.2**

**Cost Management Information Is Needed for Each of the Four Management Functions**

1. **Strategic Management.** Cost management information is needed to make sound strategic decisions regarding choice of products, manufacturing methods, marketing techniques and distribution channels, assessing customer profitability and other long-term issues.
2. **Planning and Decision Making.** Cost management information is needed to support recurring decisions regarding replacing equipment, managing cash flow, budgeting raw materials purchases, scheduling production, and pricing.
3. **Management and Operational Control.** Cost management information is needed to provide a fair and effective basis for identifying inefficient operations and to reward and motivate the most effective managers.
4. **Preparation of Financial Statements.** Cost management information is needed to provide accurate accounting for inventory and other assets, in compliance with reporting requirements, for the preparation of financial reports and for use in the three other management functions.

---

**Management control**
is the evaluation of mid-level managers by upper-level managers.

**Preparation of financial statements**
requires management to comply with the financial reporting requirements of regulatory agencies.

managers and employees (e.g., production supervisors and various department heads). In contrast, **management control** is the evaluation of mid-level managers by upper-level managers (the controller or the CFO).

In the fourth function, **preparation of financial statements,** management complies with the reporting requirements of relevant groups (such as the Financial Accounting Standards Board) and relevant federal government authorities (for example, the Internal Revenue Service and the Securities and Exchange Commission). The financial statement preparation role has recently received a renewed focus as countries throughout the world have adopted International Financial Reporting Standards (IFRS), and the United States is expected to adopt these standards by 2015. The financial statement information also serves the other three management functions, because this information is often an important part of planning and decision making, control, and strategic management.[2]

[2] The professional groups and the accountant's professional responsibility are identified and explained at the end of this chapter.

The first three management functions are covered in this text. Strategic management and the design of the costs systems upon which strategic decisions rely are covered in Part One. Part Two covers planning and decision making, Part Three covers operational control, and Part Four covers management control. Financial reporting for inventory and cost of sales is covered in Part One.

## Strategic Management and the Strategic Emphasis in Cost Management

Effective strategic management is critical to the success of the firm or organization and is thus a pervasive theme of this book. The growing pressures of economic recession, global competition, technological innovation, and changes in business processes have made cost management much more critical and dynamic than ever before. Managers must think *competitively;* doing so requires a strategy.

Strategic thinking involves anticipating changes; products, services, and operating processes are designed to accommodate expected changes in customer demands. Flexibility is important. The ability to make fast changes is critical as a result of the demands of the new management concepts of e-commerce, speed-to-market, and flexible manufacturing. Product life cycles—the time from the introduction of a new product to its removal from the market—is expected to become shorter and shorter. Success in the recent past days or months is no longer a measure of ultimate success; the manager must be "driving" the firm by using the windshield, not the rear-view mirror.

The strategic emphasis also requires creative and integrative thinking, that is, the ability to identify and solve problems from a cross-functional view. The business functions are often identified as marketing, production, finance, and accounting/controllership. Instead of viewing a problem as a production problem, a marketing problem, or a finance and accounting problem, cross-functional teams view it from an integrative approach that combines skills from all functions simultaneously. The integrative approach is necessary in a dynamic and competitive environment. The firm's attention is focused on satisfying the customers' needs; all of the firm's resources, *from all functions,* are directed to that goal.

## Types of Organizations

Cost management information is useful in all organizations: business firms, governmental units, and not-for-profit organizations. Business firms are usually categorized by industry, the main categories being merchandising, manufacturing, and service. Merchandising firms purchase goods for resale. Merchandisers that sell to other merchandisers are called *wholesalers;* those selling directly to consumers are called *retailers.* Examples of merchandising firms are the large retailers, such as Walmart, Target, and **Amazon.com**.

Manufacturing firms use raw materials, labor, and manufacturing facilities and equipment to produce products. They sell these products to merchandising firms or to other manufacturers as raw materials to make other products. Examples of manufacturers are Ford, General Electric, and Cisco Systems.

Service firms provide a service to customers that offers convenience, freedom, safety, or comfort. Common services include transportation, health care, financial services (banking, insurance, accounting), personal services (physical training, hair styling), and legal services. In the United States, service industries are growing at a much faster rate than manufacturing or merchandising, in part because of the increased demand for leisure and convenience and society's increased complexity and need for information.

Governmental and not-for-profit organizations provide services, much like the firms in service industries. However, these organizations provide the services for which no direct relationship exists between the amount paid and the services provided. Instead, both the nature of these services and the customers that receive them are determined by government or philanthropic organizations. The resources are provided by governmental units and/or charities. The services provided by these organizations are often called *public goods* to indicate that no typical market exists for them. Public goods have a number of unique characteristics, such as the impracticality of limiting consumption to a single customer (clean water and police and fire protection are provided for *all* residents).

Most firms and organizations use cost management information. For example, manufacturing firms use it to manage production costs. Similarly, retail firms such as Walmart use cost management information to manage stocking, distribution, and customer service. Firms in the service industries, such as those providing financial services or other professional services, use cost management information to identify the most profitable services and to manage the costs of providing those services.

Cost management information is used in a wide variety of ways. Whatever the business, a firm must know the cost of new products or services, the cost of making improvements in existing products or services, and the cost of finding a new way to produce the products or provide the services. Cost management information is used to determine prices, to change product or service offerings to improve profitability, to update manufacturing facilities in a timely fashion, and to determine new marketing methods or distribution channels. For example, manufacturers such as Toyota study the cost implications of design options for each new product. The design study includes analysis of projected manufacturing costs as well as costs to be incurred after the product is completed, which include service and warranty costs. Service and warranty costs are often called *downstream costs* because they occur after manufacturing. By analyzing both manufacturing and downstream costs, a company is able to determine whether product enhancements might cause manufacturing and downstream costs to be out of line with expected increases in customer value and revenue for that feature.

Both large and small firms in all types of industries use cost management information. A firm's degree of reliance on cost management depends on the nature of its competitive strategy. Many firms compete on the basis of being the low-cost provider of the industry's goods or services; for these firms, cost management is critical. Other firms, such as cosmetics, fashion, and pharmaceutical firms, compete on the basis of product leadership, in which the unusual or innovative features of the product make the firm successful. For these firms, the critical management concern is maintaining product leadership through product development and marketing. The role of cost management is to support the firm's strategy by providing the information managers need to succeed in their product development and marketing efforts, such as the expected cost of adding a new product feature, the defect rate of a new part, or the reliability of a new manufacturing process.

Not-for-profit and governmental organizations also must have a strategy to accomplish their mission and satisfy their constituents. Historically, governmental units and not-for-profit agencies have tended to focus on their responsibility to spend in approved ways rather than to spend in efficient and effective ways. Increasingly, however, these types of organizations are using cost management for efficient and effective use of their financial resources.

## The Contemporary Business Environment

**LO 1-2**

*Explain the contemporary business environment and how it has influenced cost management.*

Many changes in the business environment in recent years have caused significant modifications in cost management practices. The primary changes are (1) increase in global competition; (2) lean manufacturing; (3) advances in information technologies, the Internet, and enterprise resource management; (4) greater focus on the customer; (5) new forms of management organization; and (6) changes in the social, political, and cultural environment of business. The current global economic challenges (high public debt, high unemployment rates, and slow economic growth, among others) will surely have a significant effect on each of these six changes. It is likely there will be an even greater rate of change in each of these six areas as firms search for new ways to compete and governmental regulations adapt to the difficult economic times.

### The Global Business Environment

A key development that drives the extensive changes in the contemporary business environment is the growth of international markets and trade due to the rise of economies throughout the world and the decline of trade barriers. Businesses and not-for-profit

The following table indicates the percentage of sales coming from outside the home market for the listed companies.

|  | 1993 | 2007 | 2010 |
|---|---|---|---|
| General Electric | 17% | 50% | 60% |
| Walmart | 0.0 | 22 | 50 |
| McDonald's | 47 | 65 | 67 |

**Source:** Company annual reports.

organizations, as well as consumers and regulators, are all significantly affected by the rapid growth of economic interdependence and increased competition from other countries. The North American Free Trade Agreement (NAFTA), the Central America Free Trade Agreement (CAFTA), the World Trade Organization (WTO), the European Union (EU), and the growing number of alliances among large multinational firms clearly indicate that the opportunities for growth and profitability lie in global markets. Most consumers benefit as low-cost, high-quality goods are traded worldwide. Managers and business owners know the importance of pursuing sales and operating activities in foreign countries, and investors benefit from the increased opportunities for investment in foreign firms.

The increasing competitiveness of the global business environment means that firms increasingly need cost management information to be competitive. Firms need financial and nonfinancial information about doing business and competing effectively in other countries.

> The winning companies in the global competition will be those companies that can put together the best of research, engineering, design, manufacturing, distribution—wherever they can get it, anywhere in the world—and the best of each of these will not come from one country or from one continent.
>
> *Jack Welch, former CEO of General Electric*

## Lean Manufacturing

To remain competitive in the face of the increased global competition and decreased economic growth, firms around the world are adopting new manufacturing technologies. These include just-in-time inventory methods to reduce the cost and waste of maintaining large levels of raw materials and unfinished product. Also, many firms are adopting the lean methods applied in Japanese manufacturing that have produced significant cost and quality improvements through the use of quality teams and statistical quality control. Other manufacturing changes include flexible manufacturing techniques developed to reduce setup times and allow fast turnaround of customer orders. A key competitive edge in what is called *speed-to-market* is the ability to deliver the product or service faster than the competition.

## Use of Information Technology, the Internet, and Enterprise Resource Management

Perhaps the most fundamental of all business changes in recent years has been the increasing use of information technology, the Internet, and performance management systems. This *new economy* is reflected in the rapid growth of Internet-based firms (companies such as Amazon, eBay, and Google); the increased use of the Internet for communications, sales, and business data processing; and the use of enterprise management systems. These technologies have fostered the growing strategic focus in cost management by reducing the time required for processing transactions and by expanding the individual manager's access to information within the firm, the industry, and the business environment around the world.

## Focus on the Customer

A key change in the business environment is increased *consumer expectation* for product functionality and quality. The result has been a shorter product life cycle, as firms seek to add new features and new products as quickly as possible, thereby increasing the overall intensity of competition.

In past years, a business typically succeeded by focusing on only a relatively small number of products with limited features and by organizing production into long, low-cost, and high-volume production runs aided by assembly-line automation. The new business process focuses instead on customer satisfaction. Producing value for the customer changes the orientation of managers from low-cost production of large quantities to *quality, service, timeliness of delivery, and the ability to respond to the customer's desire for specific features.* Today many of the critical success factors (discussed later) are customer oriented. Cost management practices are also changing; cost management reports now include specific measures of customer preferences and customer satisfaction.

## Management Organization

Management organization is changing in response to the changes in technology, marketing, and manufacturing processes. Because of the focus on customer satisfaction and value, the emphasis has shifted from financial and profit-based measures of performance to customer-related, nonfinancial performance measures such as quality, time to delivery, and service. Similarly, the hierarchical command-and-control type of organization is being replaced by a more flexible organizational form that encourages teamwork and coordination among business functions. In response to these changes, cost management practices are also changing to include reports that are useful to cross-functional teams of managers; the reports reflect the multifunctional roles of these teams and include a variety of operating and financial information: product quality, unit cost, customer satisfaction, and production bottlenecks, for example. The changes in manufacturing, marketing, and management in organizations are summarized in Exhibit 1.3.

**EXHIBIT 1.3** **Comparison of Prior and Contemporary Business Environments**

| Manufacturing | Prior Business Environment | Contemporary Business Environment |
|---|---|---|
| Basis of competition | Economies of scale, standardization | Quality, functionality, customer satisfaction |
| Manufacturing process | High volume, long production runs, significant levels of in-process and finished inventory; this is called the "push" approach | Low volume, short production runs, focus on reducing inventory levels and other non-value-added activities and costs; this is called the "pull" approach |
| Manufacturing technology | Assembly line automation, isolated technology applications | Robotics, flexible manufacturing systems, integrated technology applications connected by networks |
| Required labor skills | Machine-paced, low-level skills | Individually and team-paced, high-level skills |
| Emphasis on quality | Acceptance of a normal or usual amount of waste | Goal of zero defects |
| **Marketing** | | |
| Products | Relatively few variations, long product life cycles | Large number of variations, short product life cycles |
| Markets | Largely domestic | Global |
| **Management Organization** | | |
| Type of information recorded and reported | Almost exclusively financial data | Financial and operating data, the firm's strategic success factors |
| Management organizational structure | Hierarchical, command and control | Network-based organization forms, teamwork focus—employee has more responsibility and control, coaching rather than command and control |
| Management focus | Emphasis on the short term, short-term performance measures and compensation, concern for sustaining the current stock price, short tenure and high mobility of top managers | Increased emphasis on the long term, focus on critical success factors, commitment to the long-term success of the firm, including shareholder value |

### Social, Political, and Cultural Considerations

In addition to changes in the business environment, significant changes have taken place in the social, political, and cultural environments that affect business. Although the nature and extent of these changes vary a great deal from country to country, they include a more ethnically and racially diverse workforce, and a renewed sense of ethical responsibility among managers and employees.

The new business environment requires firms to be flexible and adaptable and to place greater responsibility in the hands of a more highly skilled workforce. Additionally, the changes tend to focus the firm on factors *outside* the production of its product or provision of its service to the ultimate consumer and the global society in which the consumer lives.

## The Strategic Focus of Cost Management

The competitive firm incorporates the emerging and anticipated changes in the contemporary environment of business into its business planning and practices. The competitive firm is customer driven, uses advanced manufacturing and information technologies when appropriate, anticipates the effect of changes in regulatory requirements and customer tastes, and recognizes its complex social, political, and cultural environment. Guided by strategic thinking, the management accountant focuses on the factors that make the company successful rather than relying only on costs and other financial measures. We are reminded of the story of the Scottish farmer who had prize sheep to take to market. When asked why his sheep were always superior to those of his neighbors, the farmer responded, "While they're weighing their sheep, I'm fattening mine." Similarly, cost management focuses not on the measurement per se but on the *identification of those measures that are critical* to the firm's success. Robert Kaplan's classification of the stages of the development of cost management systems describes this shift in focus:[3]

> **Stage 1.** Cost management systems are basic transaction reporting systems.
>
> **Stage 2.** As they develop into the second stage, cost management systems focus on external financial reporting. The objective is reliable financial reports; accordingly, the usefulness for cost management is limited.
>
> **Stage 3.** Cost management systems track key operating data and develop more accurate and relevant cost information for decision making; cost management information is developed.
>
> **Stage 4.** Strategically relevant cost management information is an integral part of the system.

The first two stages of cost system development focus on the management accountant's measurement and reporting role, and the third stage shifts to operational control. In the fourth stage, the ultimate goal, the management accountant is an integral part of management, not a reporter but a full business partner, working on management teams to implement the firm's strategy. This requires the identification of the firm's critical success factors and the use of analytical, forward-looking decision support. **Critical success factors (CSFs)** are measures of those aspects of the firm's performance essential to its competitive advantage and, therefore, to its success. Many of these critical success factors are financial, but many are nonfinancial. The CSFs for any given firm depend on the nature of the competition it faces.

**Critical success factors (CSFs)** are measures of those aspects of the firm's performance that are essential to its competitive advantage and, therefore, to its success.

## Contemporary Management Techniques: The Management Accountant's Response to the Contemporary Business Environment

**LO 1-3**

*Explain the contemporary management techniques and how they are used in cost management to respond to the contemporary business environment.*

Management accountants, guided by a strategic focus, have responded to the six changes in the contemporary business environment with 13 methods that are useful in implementing strategy in these dynamic times. The first six methods focus directly on strategy implementation: the balanced scorecard/strategy map, value chain, activity-based costing, business

[3] Robert S. Kaplan, "The Four-Stage Model of Cost System Design," *Management Accounting,* February 1990, pp. 22–26.

intelligence, target costing, and life-cycle costing. The next seven methods help to achieve strategy implementation through a focus on process improvement: benchmarking, business process improvement, total quality management, lean accounting, the theory of constraints, sustainability, and enterprise risk management. Each of these methods is covered in one or more of the chapters of the text.

## The Balanced Scorecard (BSC) and Strategy Map

Strategic information using critical success factors provides a road map for the firm to use to chart its competitive course and serves as a benchmark for competitive success. Financial measures such as profitability reflect only a partial, and frequently only a short-term, measure of the firm's progress. Without strategic information, the firm is likely to stray from its competitive course and to make strategically wrong product decisions, for example, choosing the wrong products or the wrong marketing and distribution methods.

To emphasize the importance of using strategic information, *both financial and nonfinancial,* accounting reports of a firm's performance are now often based on critical success factors in four different perspectives. One perspective is financial; the other three are nonfinancial:

1. **Financial performance.** Measures of profitability and market value, among others, as indicators of how well the firm satisfies its owners and shareholders.
2. **Customer satisfaction.** Measures of quality, service, and low cost, among others, as indicators of how well the firm satisfies its customers.
3. **Internal processes.** Measures of the efficiency and effectiveness with which the firm produces the product or service.
4. **Learning and growth.** Measures of the firm's ability to develop and utilize human resources to meet its strategic goals now and into the future.

The **balanced scorecard (BSC)** is an accounting report that includes the firm's critical success factors in four areas: (1) financial performance, (2) customer satisfaction, (3) internal processes, and (4) learning and growth.

The **strategy map** is a method, based on the balanced scorecard, that links the four perspectives in a cause-and-effect diagram.

An accounting report based on the four perspectives is called a **balanced scorecard (BSC).** The concept of balance captures the intent of broad coverage, financial and nonfinancial, of all factors that contribute to the firm's success in achieving its strategic goals. The balanced scorecard provides a basis for a more complete analysis than is possible with financial data alone. The use of the balanced scorecard is thus a critical ingredient of the overall approach that firms take to become and remain competitive. An example of a balanced scorecard is shown in Exhibit 1.4.

The **strategy map** is a method, based on the balanced scorecard, that links the four perspectives in a cause-and-effect diagram. For many companies, high achievement in the learning and growth perspective contributes directly to higher achievement in the internal

**EXHIBIT 1.4**
**The Balanced Scorecard: Financial and Nonfinancial Measures of Success**

| Financial Measures of Success | Nonfinancial Measures of Success |
|---|---|
| Sales growth | **Customer** |
| Earnings growth | Market share and growth in market share |
| Dividend growth | Customer service (e.g., based on number of complaints) |
| Bond and credit ratings | On-time delivery |
| Cash flow | Customer satisfaction (customer survey) |
| Increase in stock price | Brand recognition (growth in market share) |
| | |
| | **Internal Processes** |
| | High product quality |
| | High manufacturing productivity |
| | Cycle time (the time from receipt of a customer's order to delivery) |
| | Product yield and reduction in waste |
| | |
| | **Learning and Growth** |
| | Competence of managers (education attained) |
| | Morale and firmwide culture (employee survey) |
| | Education and training (training hours) |
| | Innovation (number of new products) |

process perspective, which in turn causes greater achievement in the customer satisfaction perspective, which then produces the desired financial performance. The strategy map is therefore a useful means in understanding how improvement in certain critical success factors contributes to other goals and to the ultimate financial results. We cover the balanced scorecard throughout the text; particularly in Chapters 2, 12, 18, and 20.

## The Value Chain

The **value chain** is an analysis tool organizations use to identify the specific steps required to provide a competitive product or service to the customer. In particular, an analysis of the firm's value chain helps management discover which steps or activities are not competitive, where costs can be reduced, or which activity should be outsourced. Also, management can use the analysis to find ways to increase value for the customer at one or more steps of the value chain. For example, companies such as General Electric, IBM, U-Haul, and Harley-Davidson have found greater overall profits by moving downstream in the value chain to place a greater emphasis on high-value services and less emphasis on lower-margin manufactured products. A key idea of the value-chain analysis is that the firm should carefully study each step in its operations to determine how each step contributes to the firm's profits and competitiveness. The value chain is covered in Chapters 2, 13, and 17.

## Activity-Based Costing and Management

Many firms have found that they can improve planning, product costing, operational control, and management control by using **activity analysis** to develop a detailed description of the specific activities performed in the firm's operations. The activity analysis provides the basis for activity-based costing and activity-based management. **Activity-based costing (ABC)** is used to improve the accuracy of cost analysis by improving the tracing of costs to products or to individual customers. **Activity-based management (ABM)** uses activity analysis and activity-based costing to help managers improve the value of products and services, and to increase the organization's competitiveness. ABC and ABM are key strategic tools for many firms, especially those with complex operations or diverse products and services. ABC and ABM are explained in Chapter 5 and then applied in several of the chapters that follow.

## Business Intelligence

**Business intelligence** (also called *business analytics or predictive analytics*) is an approach to strategy implementation in which the management accountant uses data to understand and analyze business performance. Business intelligence (BI) often uses statistical methods such as regression or correlation analysis to predict consumer behavior, to measure customer satisfaction, or to develop models for setting prices, among other uses. BI is best suited for companies that have a distinctive capability which can be derived from measurable critical success factors. BI is similar to the BSC because it focuses on critical success factors; the difference is that BI uses analytical tools to develop predictive models of core business processes. BI is covered in Chapter 8.

## Target Costing

Target costing is a method that has resulted directly from the intensely competitive markets in many industries. **Target costing** determines the desired cost for a product on the basis of a given competitive price, such that the product will earn a desired profit. Cost is thus determined by price. The firm using target costing must often adopt strict cost reduction measures or redesign the product or manufacturing process to meet the market price and remain profitable.

Target costing forces the firm to become more competitive, and, like benchmarking, it is a common strategic form of analysis in intensely competitive industries where even small price differences attract consumers to the lower-priced product. The camera manufacturing industry is a good example of an industry where target costing is used. Camera manufacturers such as Canon know the market price for each line of camera they

---

The **value chain** is an analysis tool firms use to identify the specific steps required to provide a product or service to the customer.

**Activity analysis** is used to develop a detailed description of the specific activities performed in the firm's operations.

**Activity-based costing (ABC)** is used to improve the accuracy of cost analysis by improving the tracing of costs to products or to individual customers.

**Activity-based management (ABM)** uses activity analysis and activity-based costing to help managers improve the value of products and services and increase the organization's competitiveness.

**Business intelligence** is an approach to strategy implementation in which the management accountant uses data to understand and analyze business performance.

**Target costing** determines the desired cost for a product on the basis of a given competitive price so that the product will earn a desired profit.

manufacture, so they redesign the product (add/delete features, use less expensive parts and materials) and redesign the production process to get the manufacturing cost down to the predetermined target cost. The automobile industry also uses target costing. Target costing is covered in Chapter 13.

## Life-Cycle Costing

**Life-cycle costing**
is a method used to identify and monitor the costs of a product throughout its life cycle.

**Life-cycle costing** is a method used to identify and monitor the costs of a product throughout its life cycle. The life cycle consists of all steps from product design and purchase of raw materials to delivery and service of the finished product. The steps include (1) research and development; (2) product design, including prototyping, target costing, and testing; (3) manufacturing, inspecting, packaging, and warehousing; (4) marketing, promotion, and distribution; and (5) sales and service. Cost management has traditionally focused only on costs incurred at the third step, manufacturing. Thinking strategically, management accountants now manage the product's full life cycle of costs, including upstream and downstream costs as well as manufacturing costs. This expanded focus means careful attention to product design, since design decisions lock in most subsequent life-cycle costs. See Chapter 13 for coverage of life-cycle costing.

## Benchmarking

**Benchmarking**
is a process by which a firm identifies its critical success factors, studies the best practices of other firms (or other business units within a firm) for achieving these critical success factors, and then implements improvements in the firm's processes to match or beat the performance of those competitors.

**Benchmarking** is a process by which a firm identifies its critical success factors, studies the best practices of other firms (or other business units within a firm) for achieving these critical success factors, and then implements improvements in the firm's processes to match or beat the performance of those competitors. Benchmarking was first implemented by Xerox Corporation in the late 1970s. Today many firms use benchmarking. Some firms are recognized as leaders, and therefore benchmarks, in selected areas—for example, Nordstrom in retailing, Ritz-Carlton Hotels in service, The Boeing Company in manufacturing, and Apple Computer in innovation, among others.

Benchmarking efforts are facilitated today by cooperative networks of noncompeting firms that exchange benchmarking information. For example, the International Benchmarking Clearinghouse (**www.apqc.org**) and the International Organization for Standardization (ISO) (**www.iso.org**) assist firms in strategic benchmarking.

## Business Process Improvement

> Whether you think you can or whether you think you can't—you're right.
>
> *Henry Ford*

**Business process improvement (BPI)**
is a management method by which managers and workers commit to a program of continuous improvement in quality and other critical success factors.

Henry Ford realized that the right attitude is important to success. That belief is what continuous improvement is all about. **Business process improvement (BPI)** is a management method by which managers and workers commit to a program of continuous improvement in quality and other critical success factors. Continuous improvement is very often associated with benchmarking and total quality management as firms seek to identify other firms as models to learn how to improve their critical success factors. While BPI is an incremental method, business process reengineering (BPR) is more radical. BPR is a method for creating competitive advantage in which a firm reorganizes its operating and management functions, often with the result that positions are modified, combined, or eliminated.

## Total Quality Management

**Total quality management (TQM)**
is a method by which management develops policies and practices to ensure that the firm's products and services exceed customers' expectations.

**Total quality management (TQM)** is a method by which management develops policies and practices to ensure that the firm's products and services exceed customers' expectations. This approach includes increased product functionality, reliability, durability, and serviceability. Cost management is used to analyze the cost consequences of different design choices and to measure and report the many aspects of quality including, for example, production breakdowns and production defects, wasted labor or raw materials, the number of service calls, and the nature of complaints, warranty costs, and product recalls.

## Lean Accounting

**Lean accounting**
uses value streams to measure the financial benefits of a firm's progress in implementing lean manufacturing.

Firms that have adopted lean manufacturing, which is one of the six key aspects of the contemporary business environment (see page 8), will also typically use lean accounting. **Lean accounting** uses value streams to measure the financial benefits of a firm's progress in implementing lean manufacturing. Lean accounting places the firm's products and services into value streams, each of which is a group of related products or services. For example, a company manufacturing consumer electronics might have two groups of products (and two value streams)—digital cameras and video cameras—with several models in each group. Accounting for value streams can help the firm to better understand the impact on profitability of its lean manufacturing improvements. TQM and lean accounting are covered in Chapters 17 and 18.

## The Theory of Constraints

The **theory of constraints (TOC)** is used to help firms effectively improve the rate at which raw materials are converted to finished products.

The **theory of constraints (TOC)** is used to help firms effectively improve a very important critical success factor: cycle time, the rate at which raw materials are converted to finished products. The TOC helps identify and eliminate bottlenecks—places where partially completed products tend to accumulate as they wait to be processed in the production process. In the competitive global marketplace common to most industries, the ability to be faster than competitors is often a critical success factor. Many managers argue that the focus on speed in the TOC approach is crucial. They consider speed in product development, product delivery, and manufacturing to be paramount as global competitors find ever-higher customer expectations for rapid product development and prompt delivery. TOC is covered in Chapter 13.

## Sustainability

**Sustainability**
means the balancing of the company's short- and long-term goals in all three dimensions of performance—social, environmental, and financial.

**Sustainability** means the balancing of the organization's short- and long-term goals in all three dimensions of performance—social, environmental, and financial. We view it in the broad sense to include identifying and implementing ways to reduce cost and increase revenue as well as to maintain compliance with social and environmental regulations and expectations. This can be accomplished through technological innovation and new product development as well as common-sense measures to improve the social and environmental impacts of the company's operations. Ford Motor saves money through improvements in its storm water draining system at its River Rouge, Michigan, plant; other leaders in sustainability include Toyota and Honda motor companies, McDonald's, and Walmart, among many others. The Dow Jones Sustainability Indexes (**www.sustainability-indexes. com/07_htmle/sustainability/corpsustainability.html**) identify and rank companies according to their sustainability performance. Sustainability is a key topic and is covered in each chapter; look for the sustainability icon next to problems involving sustainability.

## Enterprise Risk Management

**Enterprise risk management (ERM)**
is a framework and process that firms use to manage the risks that could negatively or positively affect the company's competitiveness and success.

**Enterprise risk management (ERM)** is a framework and process that organizations use to manage the risks that could negatively or positively affect the company's competitiveness and success. Risk is considered broadly to include (1) hazards such as fire or flood; (2) financial risks due to foreign currency fluctuations, commodity price fluctuations, and changes in interest rates; (3) operating risk related to customers, products, or employees; and (4) strategic risk related to top management decisions about the firm's strategy and implementation thereof. For financial service firms particularly, ERM has become a much more important topic since the passage of the Dodd-Frank Wall Street Reform and Consumer Protection Act (2010), which requires new regulations for these firms. To indicate how widely used ERM has become, a 2010 survey of 1,541 executives by the Deloitte Consulting firm, reported that 80% of their organizations either had an ERM program in place or were currently implementing one.[4] The text explains the role of ERM in Chapters 10, 11, and 12.

---

[4] Russ Banham, "Disaster Averted?" *CFO*, April 2011, pp. 57–60.

**EXHIBIT 1.5**
**Mission Statements of Selected Companies**

**Procter & Gamble** (pg.com)

To provide branded products and services of superior quality and value that improve the lives of the world's consumers, now and for generations to come.

**IBM** (ibm.com)

To lead in the creation, development, and manufacture of the industry's most advanced information technologies, and to translate these into value for our customers.

**Google** (google.com)

To organize the world's information and make it universally accessible and useful.

**Walt Disney** (disney.com)

To make people happy.

**Merck** (merck.com)

To preserve and improve human life.

**Sara Lee** (saralee.com)

To simply delight you . . . every day.

**EXHIBIT 1.6**
**Sara Lee Corporate Strategy**

Source: Sara Lee Corporation (saralee.com and 2010 annual report).

The company is focused on building sustainable, profitable growth over the long term by achieving share leadership in its core categories: innovating around its core products and product categories; expanding into high opportunity geographic markets and strategic joint venture/partnerships; delivering superior quality and value to our customers; and driving operating efficiencies.

## How a Firm Succeeds: The Competitive Strategy

If you do not know where you are going, you will probably get there.

*Anonymous*

**A strategy**
is a plan for using resources to achieve sustainable goals within a competitive environment.

A firm succeeds by implementing a **strategy,** that is, a plan for using resources to achieve sustainable goals within a competitive environment. Finding a strategy begins with determining the purpose and long-range direction, and therefore the mission, of the company. Exhibit 1.5 lists excerpts from the mission statements of several companies. The mission is developed into specific performance objectives, which are then implemented by specific corporate strategies, that is, specific actions to achieve the objectives that will fulfill the mission. See the Sara Lee corporate strategy in Exhibit 1.6. Note that Sara Lee's broad mission statement is explained in terms of more specific objectives, which are in turn operationalized through specific corporate strategies.

Firms also are using cost management to support their strategic goals. Cost management has shifted away from a focus on the stewardship role, that is, product costing and financial reporting. The new focus is on a management-facilitating role: developing cost and other information to support the management of the firm and the achievement of its strategic goals (Exhibit 1.7).

**EXHIBIT 1.7**
**Cost Management Focus in Prior and Contemporary Business Environments**

|  | **Prior Business Environment** | **Contemporary Business Environment** |
| --- | --- | --- |
| Cost management focus | Financial reporting and cost analysis; common emphasis on standardization and standard costs; the accountant as financial accounting expert and financial scorekeeper | Cost management as a tool for the development and implementation of business strategy; the accountant as business partner |

**EXHIBIT 1.8**
**Consequences of Lack of Strategic Information**

- Decision making based on intuition instead of accurate and timely information
- Lack of clarity about direction and goals
- Lack of a clear and favorable perception of the firm by customers and suppliers
- Incorrect investment decisions; choosing products, markets, or manufacturing processes inconsistent with strategic goals
- Inability to effectively benchmark competitors, resulting in lack of knowledge about more effective competitive strategies
- Failure to identify most profitable products, customers, and markets

Without strategic information, the firm is likely to stray from its competitive course, to make strategically wrong manufacturing and marketing decisions: to choose the wrong products or the wrong customers. Some of the consequences of a lack of strategic information are shown in Exhibit 1.8.

## Developing a Competitive Strategy

**LO 1-4**

*Explain the different types of competitive strategies.*

In developing a sustainable competitive position, each firm purposefully or as a result of market forces arrives at one of the two competitive strategies: cost leadership or differentiation.[5]

### Cost Leadership

**Cost leadership**
is a competitive strategy in which a firm outperforms competitors in producing products or services at the lowest cost.

**Cost leadership** is a competitive strategy in which a firm outperforms competitors in producing products or services at the lowest cost. The cost leader makes sustainable profits at lower prices, thereby limiting the growth of competition in the industry through its success at reducing price and undermining the profitability of competitors, which must meet the firm's low price. The cost leader normally has a relatively large market share and tends to avoid niche or segment markets by using the price advantage to attract a large portion of the broad market. While most firms make strong efforts to reduce costs, the cost leader may focus almost exclusively on cost reduction, thereby ensuring a significant cost and price advantage in the market.

Cost advantages usually result from productivity in the manufacturing process, in distribution, or in overall administration. For example, technological innovation in the manufacturing process and labor savings from overseas production are common routes to competitive productivity. Firms known to be successful at cost leadership are typically very large manufacturers and retailers, such as Walmart, Texas Instruments, and Hewlett-Packard.

A potential weakness of the cost leadership strategy is the tendency to cut costs in a way that undermines demand for the product or service, for example, by deleting key features. The cost leader remains competitive only so long as the consumer sees that the product or service is (at least nearly) equivalent to competing products that cost somewhat more.

### Differentiation

**Differentiation**
is a competitive strategy in which a firm succeeds by developing and maintaining a unique value for the product or service as perceived by consumers.

The **differentiation** strategy is implemented by creating a product or service that is unique in some important way, usually higher quality, customer service, product features, or innovation. Sometimes a differentiation strategy is called *product leadership* to refer to the innovation and features in the product. In other cases the strategy might be called a *customer-focused* or *customer-solution* strategy, to indicate that the organization succeeds

[5] This section is adapted from Michael Porter, *Competitive Advantage*, The Free Press, 1985. The Porter concept of strategy is widely used. See for example, Michael E. Porter, "The Five Forces that Shape Strategy," *Harvard Business Review*, January 2008, pp. 79–93. Porter makes the point that strategy is even more important in times of broad economic crisis, in his article, "Why America Needs an Economic Strategy," *BusinessWeek*, November 10, 2008, pp. 39–42. There are many articles and books on strategy. For another important view on strategy, see John K. Shank and Vijay Govindarajan, *Cost Management*, The Free Press, 1993; Robert S. Kaplan and David P. Norton, *Strategy Maps*, Harvard Business School Press, 2007; and Robert S. Kaplan and David P. Norton, "Mastering the Management System," *Harvard Business Review*, January 2008, pp. 63–77. A recent framework for strategy is the resource-based view of the organization, as explained by David J. Collis and Cynthia A. Montgomery, "Competing on Resources," *Harvard Business Review*, July–August 2008, pp. 140–150.

**EXHIBIT 1.9**
**Distinctive Aspects of the Two Competitive Strategies**

| Aspect | Cost Leadership | Differentiation |
|---|---|---|
| Strategic target | Broad cross section of the market | Focused section of the market |
| Basis of competitive advantage | Lowest cost in the industry | Unique product or service |
| Product line | Limited selection | Wide variety, differentiating features |
| Production emphasis | Lowest possible cost with high quality and essential product features | Innovation in differentiating products |
| Marketing emphasis | Low price | Premium price and innovative, differentiating features |

on some dimension(s) of customer service. This perception allows the firm to charge higher prices and outperform the competition in profits without reducing costs significantly. Most industries, including consumer electronics and clothing, have differentiated firms. The appeal of differentiation is especially strong for product lines for which the perception of quality and image is important, as in cosmetics, jewelry, and automobiles. Tiffany, Bentley, Rolex, Maytag, and BMW are good examples of firms that have a differentiation strategy.

A weakness of the differentiation strategy is the firm's tendency to undermine its strength by attempting to lower costs or by ignoring the necessity of having a continual and aggressive marketing plan to reinforce the differentiation. If the consumer begins to believe that the difference is not significant, then lower-cost rival products will appear more attractive.

## Other Strategic Issues

A firm succeeds, then, by adopting and effectively implementing one of the strategies explained earlier (and summarized in Exhibit 1.9). Recognize that although one strategy is generally dominant, a firm is most likely to work hard at process improvement throughout the firm, whether cost leader or differentiator, and on occasion to employ both of the strategies at the same time. However, a firm following both strategies is likely to succeed only if it achieves one of them significantly. A firm that does not achieve at least one strategy is not likely to be successful. This situation is what Michael Porter calls "getting stuck in the middle." A firm that is stuck in the middle is not able to sustain a competitive advantage. For example, giant retailer Kmart/Sears has been stuck in the middle between trying to compete with Walmart on cost and price and with style-conscious Target on differentiation. In 2008–2009 some analysts suggested that Kmart/Sears might find success by abandoning the suburban locations where Target and Walmart are strong and instead focusing on their many urban locations where they offer convenience to the urban shopper. On December 27, 2011, Sears announced the closing of 120 stores, most of which were in suburban or rural locations with fewer than 80 employees.

Developing a competitive strategy is the first step for a successful business. The critical next step is to implement that strategy, and this is where the management accountant comes in. The management accountant works to implement strategy as a part of the management team, by contributing the management accountant's specific expertise (cost management methods). We cover these methods in each of the chapters as we go through the text. Our focus in each chapter, then, will be to show how the method we are covering in that chapter is used in implementing strategy. We will use the following five-step framework to show how the method demonstrated in the chapter can be used to help the organization achieve its strategy by solving a particular problem.

## The Five Steps of Strategic Decision Making

The five steps for decision making with a strategic emphasis are listed below, together with a short illustration of how the steps could be used by Walmart to help the company deal with the problem of rising fuel prices that affect the cost of the firm's use of trucks to deliver products from Walmart's warehouses to its retail stores.

The first step is to determine the strategic issues surrounding the problem, because the solution of any problem must fit the organization's strategy. A good decision is one that makes the organization more competitive and successful. By starting with the strategic issues, we ensure that the decision fits the organization's strategic goals.

1. **Determine the strategic issues surrounding the problem.** Fuel costs are critical to Walmart because it competes on low cost and low prices. So this problem will get close management attention. In contrast, the effect of a rise in fuel prices will likely not be as critical for a differentiated company, such as a high-end retailer like Nordstrom.

2. **Identify the alternative actions.** In one alternative, Walmart considers the use of smaller and more fuel-efficient trucks together with a relocation of its warehouses, to reduce travel time and fuel usage. Another option would be to outsource all of Walmart's delivery needs to other trucking firms.

3. **Obtain information and conduct analyses of the alternatives.** Walmart collects relevant cost information and calculates the expected cost of each alternative and finds that the use of other truckers would provide significantly lower total fuel cost. Considering the problem strategically, Walmart projects on the one hand that it can more effectively compete with Target by providing more rapid delivery of fast-moving items to its stores, and that this could be accomplished with the use of smaller trucks. On the other hand, Walmart also knows that it competes on cost and that lower cost is critical to its success.

4. **Based on strategy and analysis, choose and implement the desired alternative.** After considering the options, Walmart chooses to outsource the delivery function to other trucking firms, in order to maintain or perhaps improve its low cost position. In contrast, a high-end retailer such as Nordstrom might have chosen the option with more rapid delivery and higher cost, because its strategy is based on quality of product and customer satisfaction. Knowing the strategic context for the decision can make a big difference!

5. **Provide an ongoing evaluation of the effectiveness of implementation in step 4.** To provide an ongoing review of delivery costs, Walmart top management instructs operational managers in the firm to present an updated review of the decision to top management once every quarter. In this way, changes in costs or strategic objectives will be reviewed on a regular basis.

Look for these five steps for the topics in the chapters ahead.

## The Professional Environment of Cost Management

**LO 1-5**

*Describe the professional environment of the management accountant, including professional organizations and professional certifications.*

Personally, I'm always ready to learn, although I do not always like being taught.

*Winston Churchill*

If I had eight hours to chop down a tree, I would spend six sharpening my axe.

*Abraham Lincoln*

Winston Churchill, the former prime minister of the United Kingdom, and Abraham Lincoln, the 16th president of the United States, understood the importance of continuous learning. Their words apply equally well to the management accountant. Management accountants must continuously improve their technical and other skills and maintain a constant high level of professionalism, integrity, and objectivity about their work. Many professional organizations, such as the Institute of Management Accountants (IMA) and the American Institute of Certified Public Accountants (AICPA), encourage their members to earn relevant professional certifications, participate in professional development programs, and continually reflect on the professional ethics they bring to their work.

### Professional Organizations

The professional environment of the management accountant is influenced by two types of organizations: one that sets guidelines and regulations regarding management accounting practices and one that promotes the professionalism and competence of management accountants.

The first group of organizations includes a number of federal agencies, such as the Internal Revenue Service, which sets product costing guidelines for tax purposes, and the Federal Trade Commission (FTC), which, to foster competitive practices and protect trade, restricts pricing practices and requires that prices in most circumstances be justified on the basis of cost. In addition, the Securities and Exchange Commission (SEC) provides guidance, rules, and regulations regarding financial reporting.

The role of the SEC has been strengthened by the Sarbanes-Oxley Act of 2002, which created the Public Company Accounting Oversight Board (PCAOB) to establish rules for "auditing, quality control, ethics, independence, and other professional standards relating to the preparation of audit reports for issuers." Of particular importance to management accountants is that the SEC, in implementing the act, now requires each public company to disclose in its annual report whether it has a code of ethics covering its chief financial executives, including high-level management accountants such as the controller.

The Dodd-Frank Wall Street Reform and Consumer Protection Act (2010) includes a variety of new regulations for the financial services industry. The Act also created the Consumer Financial Protection Bureau (CFPB), the goal of which is to detect and prevent unfair lending practices. Under this Act, management accountants in the financial services industry now have increased responsibilities.

In the private sector, the Financial Accounting Standards Board (FASB), an independent organization, and the AICPA supply additional guidance regarding financial reporting practices. The AICPA also provides educational opportunities in the form of newsletters, magazines, professional development seminars, and technical meetings for management accountants.

Congress established the Cost Accounting Standards Board (CASB) in 1970 (Public Law 91–379), which operates under the Office of Federal Procurement Policy "to make, promulgate, amend and rescind cost accounting standards and interpretations thereof designed to achieve uniformity and consistency in the cost accounting standards governing measurement, assignment, and allocation of cost to contracts with the United States federal government." The CASB's objective is to achieve uniformity and consistency in the cost accounting standards used by government suppliers to reduce the incidence of fraud and abuse. Twenty standards cover a broad range of issues in cost accounting.

In addition, to enhance cost accounting standards and financial reporting by federal governmental entities, Congress established in 1990 the Federal Accounting Standards Advisory Board. The FASAB publishes reports and documents on cost accounting concepts and standards that are comparable to those used in business firms.

Another group of organizations supports the growth and professionalism of management accounting practice. The Institute of Management Accountants (IMA) is the principal organization devoted primarily to management accountants in the United States. The IMA provides journals, newsletters, research reports, management accounting practice reports, professional development seminars, and technical meetings that serve the broad purpose of providing continuing education opportunities for management accountants. An especially important service of the IMA is its 39 Statements on Management Accounting (SMAs) which cover a broad range of practice areas for the management accountant: leadership strategies, ethics, technology enablement, cost management, business performance management, and enterprise risk management. In the United Kingdom, the Chartered Institute of Management Accountants (CIMA) performs a similar role, as does the Society of Management Accountants in Canada (CMA-Canada), the Spanish Management Accounting Association, the French Accounting Association, and the Institutes of Chartered Accountants in Ireland, Australia, Scotland, and India. Similar organizations are present in most other countries around the world.

Walmart and Target are two of the most successful retailers in the United States. Walmart bears the slogan, "Save Money, Live Better," while Target stores say "Expect More, Pay Less." If you have shopped at either of these stores you will likely have formed an opinion about the stores and how they compete.

**Required**

1. Based on your experience, explain what you think are the competitive strategies of these retailers. Are they key competitors, targeting the same customers? Do you think each firm has adopted the most effective strategy? Why or why not?

2. While customers are pleased with Walmart's low prices, there is ongoing controversy about the firm's employment practices, including alleged discrimination against women in promotion and pay policies. What are your thoughts on the controversy? Are the ethical principles and standards of the management accountant relevant in this context?

In areas related to the management accounting function, the Financial Executives International (FEI) provides services much like those provided by the IMA for financial managers, including controllers and treasurers.

Because one of the management control responsibilities of the management accountant is to develop effective systems to detect and prevent errors and fraud in the accounting records, the management accountant commonly has strong ties to control-oriented organizations such as the Institute of Internal Auditors (IIA).

---

Even if you're on the right track, you'll get run over if you just sit there.

*Will Rogers*

---

## Professional Certifications

The role of professional certification programs is to provide a distinct measure of experience, training, and performance capability for the management accountant. Certification is one way in which the management accountant shows professional achievement and stature. Two types of certification are relevant for management accountants. The first is the Certified Management Accountant (CMA) designation administered by the Institute of Management Accountants, which is achieved by passing a qualifying exam and satisfying certain background and experience requirements. The exam has two parts: (1) financial planning, performance, and control, and (2) financial decision making. Four of the five topics of part (1) (representing 85% of part (1) of the exam) are covered in this text: (a) planning, budgeting, and forecasting, (b) performance management, (c) cost management, and (d) professional ethics. Three of the five topics of part (2) (representing about 45% of the content in that part of the exam) are covered in this text: (a) decision analysis, (b) investment decisions, and (c) professional ethics (professional ethics is included in both parts of the exam).

The second certification is the Certified Public Accountant (CPA) designation. Like the CMA, the CPA is earned by passing a qualifying exam, and by satisfying certain background, education, and experience requirements. Unlike the CMA, which is an international designation, the CPA certificate is a professional license monitored in the United States by each state and territorial jurisdiction which has its own set of criteria. While the CPA license is critical for those accountants who practice auditing, the CMA designation is widely viewed as the most relevant for those dealing with cost management issues. Many countries have certificates that are similar to the CPA and CMA, and many management accountants have both the CMA and the CPA certification. In addition, the AICPA and CIMA have recently partnered to offer a credential for professional accountants called the Chartered Global Management Accountant (CGMA).

**LO 1-6**

*Understand the principles and rules of professional ethics and explain how to apply them.*

## Professional Ethics

Ethics is an important aspect of the management accountant's work and profession. Professional ethics can be summed up as the commitment of the management accountant to provide a useful service for management. This commitment means that the management accountant has the competence, integrity, confidentiality, and credibility to serve management effectively.

### The IMA Statement of Ethical Professional Practice

The ethical behavior of the management accountant is guided by the code of ethics of the Institute of Management Accountants (IMA). The IMA Statement of Ethical Professional Practice specifies *minimum* standards of behavior that are intended to guide the management accountant and to inspire a very high overall level of professionalism. By complying with these standards, management accountants enhance their profession and facilitate the development of a trusting relationship in which managers and others can confidently rely on their work.

The IMA Statement of Ethical Professional Practice contains four main standards: (1) competence, (2) confidentiality, (3) integrity, and (4) credibility (see Exhibit 1.10). The standard of competence requires the management accountant to develop and maintain the skills necessary for her or his area of practice and to continually reassess the adequacy of those skills as their firm grows and becomes more complex. The standard of confidentiality requires adherence to the firm's policies regarding communication of data to protect its trade secrets and other confidential information. Integrity refers to behaving in a professional manner (e.g., refraining from activities that would discredit the profession, such as unfair hiring practices) and to avoiding conflicts of interest (e.g., not accepting a gift from a supplier or customer). Finally, credibility refers to the need to

**EXHIBIT 1.10**
**Institute of Management Accountants Statement of Ethical Professional Practice**

Source: **www.imanet.org**

**1. Competence**

Each member has a responsibility to:
1. Maintain an appropriate level of professional expertise by continually developing knowledge and skills.
2. Perform professional duties in accordance with relevant laws, regulations, and technical standards.
3. Provide decision support information and recommendations that are accurate, clear, concise, and timely.
4. Recognize and communicate professional limitations or other constraints that would preclude responsible judgment or successful performance of an activity.

**2. Confidentiality**

Each member has a responsibility to:
1. Keep information confidential except when disclosure is authorized or legally required.
2. Inform all relevant parties regarding appropriate use of confidential information. Monitor subordinates' activities to ensure compliance.
3. Refrain from using confidential information for unethical or illegal advantage.

**3. Integrity**

Each member has a responsibility to:
1. Mitigate actual conflicts of interest. Regularly communicate with business associates to avoid apparent conflicts of interest. Advise all parties of any potential conflicts.
2. Refrain from engaging in any conduct that would prejudice carrying out duties ethically.
3. Abstain from engaging in or supporting any activity that might discredit the profession.

**4. Credibility**

Each member has a responsibility to:
1. Communicate information fairly and objectively.
2. Disclose all relevant information that could reasonably be expected to influence an intended user's understanding of the reports, analyses, or recommendations.
3. Disclose delays or deficiencies in information, timeliness, processing, or internal controls in conformance with organization policy and/or applicable law.

maintain impartial judgment (e.g., not developing analyses to support a decision that the management accountant knows is not correct). The guiding principles behind these standards are honesty, fairness, objectivity, and responsibility. IMA members are expected to behave in accordance with these principles and standards.

### *How to Apply the Statement of Ethical Professional Practice*

Handling situations in which an ethical issue arises can be very challenging and frustrating. To effectively resolve an ethical issue, it is crucial to understand the firm's business and strategy. Determining whether a particular action is ethical requires an understanding of the business context to understand the intent of the act—is it for a business purpose or is it intended to mislead or disguise fraud? An example is Sherron Watkins, an Enron Corporation employee, who is credited with bringing that firm's 2001 accounting fraud to light. She wrote a letter to the CEO about financial accounting practices at Enron that did not appear to fit the firm's business or strategy. In contrast, Betty Vinson at first rejected and then agreed to make false accounting entries that were part of the accounting scandal at WorldCom in 2001–2002. As noted by the U.S. attorney prosecuting the case against Ms. Vinson, ". . . just following orders" is not an excuse for breaking the law.

## Summary

The central theme of this book is that cost management information includes all the information that managers need to manage effectively to lead their firms to competitive success. Cost management information includes both financial and nonfinancial information critical to the firm's success. The specific role of cost management in the firm differs depending on the firm's competitive strategy, its type of industry and organization (manufacturing firm, service firm, merchandising firm, not-for-profit organization, or governmental organization), and the management function to which cost management is applied (the functions are strategic management, planning and decision making, management and operational control, and preparation of financial statements).

Changes in the business environment have altered the nature of competition and the types of techniques managers use to succeed in their businesses. These changes include (1) an increase in global competition; (2) lean manufacturing; (3) advances in information technologies, the Internet, and enterprise resource management; (4) a greater focus on the customer; (5) new forms of management organization; and (6) changes in the social, political, and cultural environment of business.

Management accountants have responded to the above six changes in the contemporary business environment with 13 methods that are useful in implementing strategy in these dynamic times. The first six methods focus directly on strategy implementation—the balanced scorecard/strategy map, value chain, activity-based costing, business intelligence, target costing, and life-cycle costing. The next seven methods focus on strategy implementation through a focus on process improvement—benchmarking, business process improvement, total quality management, lean accounting, the theory of constraints, sustainability, and enterprise risk management.

To apply new management methods effectively, it is crucial that the management accountant understand the firm's strategy. Strategy is the set of plans and policies that a firm employs to develop a sustainable competitive advantage. Using Michael Porter's framework, a firm can compete effectively either as a cost leader or through differentiation.

A variety of professional organizations supports management accounting, including the Institute of Management Accountants (IMA), the American Institute of Certified Public Accountants (AICPA), and the Financial Executives International (FEI), among others. Several relevant certification programs recognize competence and experience in management accounting; they include the Certified Management Accountant (CMA) and the Certified Public Accountant (CPA).

The management accountant is responsible to the firm and to the public for maintaining a high standard of performance and ethical responsibility, as set forth in the IMA Statement of Ethical Professional Practice. The professional ethics standards of the management accountant include competence, confidentiality, integrity, and credibility.

## Key Terms

activity analysis, *12*

activity-based costing (ABC), *12*

activity-based management (ABM), *12*

balanced scorecard (BSC), *11*

benchmarking, *13*

business intelligence, *12*

business process improvement (BPI), *13*

cost leadership, *16*

cost management, *3*

cost management information, *3*

critical success factors (CSFs), *10*

differentiation, *16*

enterprise risk management (ERM), *14*

lean accounting, *14*

life-cycle costing, *13*

management accounting, *3*

management control, *5*

operational control, *4*

planning and decision making, *4*

preparation of financial statements, *5*

strategic management, *4*

strategy, *15*

strategy map, *11*

sustainability, *14*

target costing, *12*

theory of constraints (TOC), *14*

total quality management (TQM), *13*

value chain, *12*

## Comments on Cost Management in Action

### A Case in Competitive Strategy: Walmart and Target

These questions are intended for open discussion and expression of differences of opinion. Here we have an outline of some thoughts on these competitive issues, combined with some of the most recent news reports available at the time of publication.

1. Most would argue that Walmart is a cost leader because of its focus on low prices. Its operating efficiencies and persistent pursuit of low costs from its suppliers help Walmart to achieve these low prices; the slogan says it all about that firm, "Save Money, Live Better."

   Target also values low prices, but competes somewhat differently. As the company website states, the firm has a "promise of differentiation and value" and "upscale, fashion forward." Moreover, the Target financial report to the SEC (10K) states that, for Target, the competitive focus is "brand recognition, customer service, store location, differentiated offerings, value, quality, fashion, price, advertising, depth of selection, and credit availability." These statements point to a differentiated firm, even though low price is an element of the contribution. Another difference is that Target's advertising budget is somewhat larger, at 3% of sales, relative to 1% at Walmart.

Perhaps another indicator: where do the richest 10% of Americans shop? For these wealthy Americans, Home Depot, Target, and Costco are the three most popular retailers (Costco is another low-cost retailer, with fewer customers—and a different customer base).

|  | **Men** | **Women** |
|---|---|---|
| Target | 46% | 61% |
| Home Depot | 69 | 60 |
| Costco | 46 | 54 |

At the time of this writing, July 2011, Walmart has had a stock price increase of 15% over July 2009, while Target's stock price has risen by 40% in the same period. Why? In 2009, Walmart began a strategy of raising prices and adding more expensive items (for example, organic foods and trendy jeans). The strategy did not work, and same-store sales fell for two years until February 2011, when Walmart returned to its core strategy of "Every Day Low Prices." In the meantime, Target retained its strategy of "differentiation and value" and continued to prosper.

2.  The controversy over Walmart's competitive and labor practices has drawn a lot of comment in the press, and opinions are divided. One line of argument would say that, as for any large business, Walmart must compete in an increasingly competitive global economy, while others would say that its values are in conflict with this type of competition. The role of the management accountant in this context is to help the firm succeed, and to do so in an ethical manner, as set out in the IMA principles and standards—competence, confidentiality, integrity, and credibility.

A particularly important controversy for Walmart in recent years has been the class-action suit by approximately 1.5 million female workers of Walmart, which alleges discrimination in promotion and pay practices. In June 2011, the U.S. Supreme Court ruled that the case could not be tried as a class, but would have to proceed by individual claimant. The ruling undermines the ability of the female workers to collect damages from Walmart.

**Sources:** Miguel Bustillo, "Walmart Tries to Recapture Mr. Sam's Winning Formula," *The Wall Street Journal,* February 22, 2011; Miguel Bustillo, "With Sales Flabby, Walmart Turns to Its Core," *The Wall Street Journal,* March 21, 2011, p. B1; "Where Do the Rich Shop?" *The Wall Street Journal,* February 19, 2004, p. 13; Adam Liptak, "Justices Rule for Walmart in Class-Action Bias Case," *The New York Times,* June 20, 2011; Miguel Bustillo, Ann Zimmerman, "In Cities That Battle Walmart, Target Gets a Welcome," *The Wall Street Journal,* October 15, 2010, p. B1; Michelle Conlin, "Look Who's Stalking Walmart," *BusinessWeek,* December 7, 2009, pp. 30–33. Also, the firms' websites: Walmart at **www.Walmart.com** and Target at **www.target.com**

## Self-Study Problem

(For solution, please turn to the end of the chapter.)

### Strategy: An Ethical Issue

Frank Sills, the CEO and founder of ENVIRO-WEAR, is facing the first big challenge of his young company. Frank began the company on the principle of environmental consciousness in the manufacture of sports and recreation wear. His idea was to develop clothing that would appeal to active people who were concerned about quality, about waste in manufacturing and packaging, and the environmental impact of the manufacture of the goods they purchased. Starting with a small shop in Zebulon, North Carolina, Frank was able to develop his small business through strategic alliances with mail-order merchandisers, and by effective public relations about his environmentally concerned processes. A special advantage for the young firm was Frank's knowledge of accounting and his prior experience as a CPA in a major public accounting firm and as a controller (and CMA) of a small manufacturing firm.

ENVIRO-WEAR had reached $25,000,000 in sales in its sixth year, when a disastrous set of events put the firm and its prospects in a tail spin. One of the key sales managers was overheard by a news reporter telling jokes about the poor quality of the firm's clothing, and the news of it spread quickly. Also, rumors (largely unfounded) spread at the same time that the firm was not really as environmentally conscious in its manufacturing and packaging as it claimed. The result was an immediate falloff in sales, and some retailers were returning the goods.

Frank intends to fire the manager and deny publicly any association with the manager's comments, as well as to defend the firm's environmental record.

**Required**

1. On the basis of Porter's analysis of strategic competitive advantage, what type of competitive strategy has ENVIRO-WEAR followed? What type of strategy should it follow in the future?

2. What are the ethical issues involved in the case, and how would you resolve them?

*Please visit* **http://www.mhhe.com/blocher6e** *to access a narrated, animated tutorial for solving this problem.*

## Questions

1-1   Give four examples of firms you believe would be significant users of cost management information and explain why.

1-2   Give three examples of firms you believe would *not* be significant users of cost management information and explain why.

1-3   What does the term *cost management* mean? Who in the typical firm or organization is responsible for cost management?

1-4   Name three professional cost management organizations and explain their roles and objectives.

1-5   What type of professional certification is most relevant for the management accountant and why?

1-6   List the four functions of management. Explain what type of cost management information is appropriate for each.

1-7   Which is the most important function of management? Explain why.

1-8   Identify the different types of business firms and other organizations that use cost management information, and explain how the information is used.

1-9   Name a firm or organization you know of that you are reasonably sure uses cost management and explain why it does so. Does it use cost leadership or differentiation, and why?

1-10  As firms move to the Internet for sales and customer service, how do you expect their competitive strategies will change?

1-11  As firms move to the Internet for sales and customer service, how do you expect their need for cost management information will change?

1-12  What are some factors in the contemporary business environment that are causing changes in business firms and other organizations? How are the changes affecting the way those firms and organizations use cost management information?

1-13  Contrast past and present business environments with regard to the following aspects: basis of competition, manufacturing processes and manufacturing technology, required labor skills, emphasis on quality, number of products, number of markets, types of cost management information needed, management organizational structure, and management focus.

1-14  Name the 13 contemporary management techniques and describe each briefly.

## Brief Exercises

1-15  Identify what you think is a very successful firm and explain why. How did it become successful?

1-16  Do you think there is value to the firm and to its shareholders of a strong ethical climate in the firm? Why or why not?

1-17  In 2004 the drug VIOXX was removed from the market by the pharmaceutical giant, Merck & Co. The drug was used to relieve arthritis pain and was especially beneficial for patients who needed a medication that was easy on the stomach. But research reports showed there was a risk of strokes and heart attacks after taking VIOXX for 18 months. Evaluate Merck's decision on business and ethics grounds.

1-18  What would you consider to be the strategy of The Coca-Cola Company, cost leadership or differentiation, and why?

1-19  What is a commodity? Give some examples of what you consider to be commodities and explain whether you think the company making the commodity product or service is a cost leader or a differentiator and why.

1-20  Take as an example the bank where you have your account(s) and say whether you think it is a cost leader or a differentiator and why.

1-21 Consider the three broad categories of firms: manufacturers, retailers, and service firms. Give an example of a cost leader and a differentiator in each of the three categories. Do there tend to be more cost leaders relative to differentiators in one or more of these categories?

1-22 Michael Porter argues a firm cannot be at the same time a cost leader and a differentiator. Do you think a firm could be a cost leader and then become a differentiator, or vice versa?

1-23 What is the difference between strategy and planning?

## Exercises

[LO 1-1, 1-6]   1-24 **Strategy; Real Estate Services**   As a management accountant in a small real estate services firm, you have become aware of a strategic initiative in your firm to promote its services to a new class of customers. Currently, most of your firm's customers lease space in large office buildings where they might occupy three or more floors of the building. Your firm provides maintenance, security, and cleaning services for the office space leased by these customers. The strategic initiative you have discovered is to seek out smaller firms that occupy as small a space as a few thousand square feet. You know that most of these smaller firms are now serviced in a haphazard manner, with part-time help for which turnover is very high; some of the smaller office buildings might not employ security of any kind. You expect that the demand for your company's services among firms of this smaller size will be good, but you are worried about the profitability of these new customers. In fact, although you cannot prove it with hard numbers, you are sure that this new strategy will cause big losses for your firm. You have not been consulted about this new strategy by the firm's owners because you are not viewed as part of the management decision-making team. You would like very much, however, to be more involved in the company's strategy development and decision making.

**Required**   What should you do or say about this new strategic initiative?

[LO 1-2]   1-25 **Impact of the Recession on the Role of Cost Management**   The impact of the 2007–2009 recession and financial crisis continues to linger in most countries and in most industries. From what you have read in this chapter and heard or read in other sources of business news, consider the potential effect of the financial crisis on the role of the management accountant.

**Required**   How has the financial crisis affected the management accountant's role in the organization, if at all?

[LO 1-3]   1-26 **Risk Management; Enterprise Sustainability; and Lean Accounting**   Jane Englehard is a feature writer for *National Business Weekly.* Her assignment is to develop a feature article on enterprise risk management. Her editor has asked her to research the available literature and to write an informative article that would be useful to those who are not familiar with the topic.

**Required**
1. What are some of the key points that Jane should integrate into her article on enterprise risk management? What are the main ideas she would want to communicate in her article?
2. Same as (1) above, but assume Jane's topic is enterprise sustainability.
3. Same as (1) above, but assume Jane's topic is lean accounting.

[LO 1-3]   1-27 **Contemporary Management Techniques**   Tim Johnson is a news reporter and feature writer for *The Wall Street Review,* an important daily newspaper for financial managers. Tim's assignment is to develop a feature article on target costing, including interviews with chief financial officers and operating managers. Tim has a generous travel budget for research into company history, operations, and market analysis for the firms he selects for the article.

**Required**
1. Tim has asked you to recommend industries and firms that would be good candidates for the article. What would you advise? Explain your recommendations.
2. Assume that Tim's assignment is a feature article on life-cycle costing. Answer as you did for requirement (1).
3. Assume that Tim's assignment is a feature article on the theory of constraints. Answer as you did for requirement (1).
4. Assume Tim's assignment is a feature article on business intelligence. Answer as you did for requirement (1).

[LO 1-3]   1-28   **Balanced Scorecard**   Johnson Industrial Controls, Inc. (JIC), is a large manufacturer of specialized instruments used in automated manufacturing plants. JIC has grown steadily over the past several years on the strength of technological innovation in its key product lines. The firm now employs 3,500 production employees and 450 staff and management personnel in six large plants located across the United States. In the past few years, the growth of sales and profits has declined sharply because of the entrance into the market of new competitors. As part of a recent strategic planning effort, JIC identified its key competitive strengths and weaknesses. JIC's management believes that the critical strengths are in the quality of the product and that the weakness in recent years has been in customer service, particularly in meeting scheduled deliveries. The failure to meet promised delivery dates can be quite costly to JIC's customers, because it is likely to delay the construction or upgrading of the customers' plants and therefore delay the customers' production and sales.

JIC's management believes that the adoption of the balanced scorecard for internal reporting might help the firm become more competitive.

**Required**

1. Explain how the balanced scorecard might help a firm like JIC.

2. Develop a brief balanced scorecard for JIC. Give some examples of the items that might be included in each of these four parts of the scorecard: (a) customer satisfaction, (b) financial performance, (c) manufacturing and business processes, and (d) learning and growth.

[LO 1-3, 1-5, 1-6]   1-29   **Banking, Strategy; Skills**   A large U.S.–based commercial bank with global operations recently initiated a new program for recruiting recent college graduates into the financial function of the bank. These new hires will initially be involved in a variety of financial functions, including transactions processing, control, risk management, business performance reporting, new business analysis, and financial analysis. Recognizing that they are competing with many other banks for the relatively small number of qualified graduates, the bank has assigned you to develop a skills statement to be used in college recruiting as well as an in-house training program for new hires. You have some old training manuals and recruiting guides to assist you, but your boss advises you not to use them but to start with a fresh page. The reason for developing new materials is that the bank recently reorganized based on new management methods.

**Required**

1. Briefly explain 8 to 10 critical success factors for this bank. Consider how a bank of this size remains competitive and successful.

2. Develop a one-page outline of the skills statement and training program that your boss requested. Be brief and specific about the proper job description of a new employee in the finance area of the bank. What is the role of professional ethics, if any, in the job description? *Hint:* Use a balanced scorecard approach.

[LO 1-3, 1-5]   1-30   **Consulting; Skills**   A consulting firm offering a broad range of services will soon visit your college to recruit graduates. This firm has more than 20,000 professional staff in 275 offices of 11 different countries. Most of its clients are large corporations in a variety of different industries. Because of the opportunity for the experience and travel, you are very interested in getting a job with this firm. You have an interview in two weeks, and you're planning to do some research about the firm and the job to be as well prepared as you can be for the interview.

**Required**   Write a brief, one-half page statement of what you think the job description for this employer is. What skills would you need to succeed as a consultant in this firm?

[LO 1-3]   1-31   **Activity Analysis in a Bank**   Mesa Financial is a small bank located in west Texas. As a small bank, Mesa has a rather limited range of services: mortgage loans, installment (mostly auto) loans, commercial loans, checking and savings accounts, and certificates of deposit. Mesa's management has learned that activity analysis could be used to study the efficiency of the bank's operations.

**Required**

1. Explain how activity analysis might help a bank like Mesa.

2. Give six to eight examples of activities you would expect to identify in Mesa's operations.

[LO 1-5]   1-32   **Professional Organizations and Certification**   Ian Walsh has just been hired as a management accountant for a large manufacturing firm near his hometown of Canton, Ohio. The firm manufactures a wide variety of plastic products for the automobile industry, the packaging industry, and other customers. At least initially, Ian's principal assignments have been to develop product costs for new product lines. His cost accounting professor has suggested to Ian that he begin to consider professional organizations and professional certifications that will help him in his career.

**Required**  Which organizations and certifications would you suggest for Ian, and why?

**[LO 1-6]**  1-33  **Ethics; Product Quality**  HighTech, Inc., manufactures computer chips and components. HighTech has just introduced a new version of its memory chip, which is far faster than the previous version. Because of high product demand for the new chip, the testing process has been thorough but hurried. As the firm's chief of operations, you discover after the chip has been on the market for a few months and is selling very well that it has a minor fault that will cause hard-to-discover failures in certain, very unusual circumstances.

**Required**  Now that you know of the chip's faults, what should you disclose and to whom should you disclose it?

## Problems

**[LO 1-2, 1-4]**  1-34  **Strategy; Calvin Klein**  For many, the name Calvin Klein (CK) is synonymous with high-fashion clothing and accessories, super models, and fashion shows. It has an image of quality and style. In reality, a significant amount of CK products are sold by discount retailers such as Costco. How can this be? The answer is that the designer Calvin Klein licensed Warnaco Group and other manufacturers to produce his products. Under this arrangement, CK receives a royalty based on Warnaco's sales. As it turns out, Warnaco found that it could be more successful with the brand through a broad strategy involving a number of retailers, including discounters.

**Required**  What type of strategy (cost leadership or differentiation) is Calvin Klein following at this time? Comment on how effective you think the relationship with Warnaco is likely to be.

**[LO 1-2]**  1-35  **Current Economic Information; Use of the Internet**  There are a number of sources of economic and demographic information that can assist the management accountant. The information includes financial information such as interest rates, employment, income, international trade, output of goods and services, consumer price levels, and market values of stocks and bonds. The management accountant uses this information to better understand the environment in which his or her firm competes. For example, when interest rates are moving up (or down) rapidly, the management accountant will want to consider the effect of the interest cost changes on his or her analysis and recommendations regarding managing cash flow, introducing new products, improving or expanding production facilities, and so on. There are many sources for this information; one useful sources is shown below:

Federal Reserve Board Statistics: **http://www.federalreserve.gov/apps/fof/FOFTables.aspx**

**Required**  Review the Federal Reserve Board statistics for gross domestic product and home mortgages statistics. Comment on the current state of the economy that you see in these statistics, in 200 words or less.

**[LO 1-2, 1-4]**  1-36  **Strategy; Innovation**  One common measure of a firm's efforts in innovation is the amount the firm spends on research and development and capital spending (new plant and equipment) relative to other expenditures. Based on U.S. firms in the Standard and Poor's 500 stock index, innovation measured in this way differs significantly among industries. The highest rates of innovation are in software and services, semiconductors, drugs, biotech, and technology hardware. Somewhat lower levels of innovation are seen in the food and beverage, consumer goods, household products, and automobile industries.

**Required**
1. Comment on the differences observed above from a strategic point of view.
2. When compared to large non-U.S. firms in the Standard and Poor's database, the highest innovators have a similar rate of innovation in the U.S. and non-U.S. firms for the household products industry and the food and beverage industry. However, the rate of innovation is somewhat higher for non-U.S. firms in the auto industry and consumer goods industry, but somewhat higher in the United States for firms in the software and services, drug, biotech, and semiconductor industries. Comment on these differences from strategic and global competitive points of view.

**[LO 1-2, 1-4]**  1-37  **Strategy; Analyzing a Commodity Business**  SanDisk Corp, the Sunnyvale, California, firm, is the world's largest manufacturer of removable memory disks used in digital cameras, cell phones, music players, and game consoles. Like many electronic components of this type, the business is very cyclical and price competitive. Most analysts view the product as a commodity, and thus vulnerable to global low-cost competition. SanDisk has adopted a new strategy to attempt to distinguish itself based on innovation and increased advertising. The firm has developed waterproof memory cards and cards with a security feature—the owner's fingerprint is needed to operate the device.

**Required**   What type of strategy did SanDisk follow at this time? What strategy was intended in SanDisk's new plans? Comment on how successful you think the new strategy will be.

[LO 1-3]   1-38   **Enterprise Risk Management**   Enterprise risk management (ERM) is a management technique that provides a systematic way for companies to identify and manage the wide variety of risks in their business environment. Any one of these risks, if not properly managed, could cause the company to fail to meet its strategic goals. As an example, United Health Group (UHG; **united-healthgroup.com**) has adopted ERM to manage the risks in its business environment, which includes a variety of health care businesses, from health insurance to health care claims processing services. UHG classifies its risks into six categories (external environment, business strategies and policies, business process execution, people, analysis and reporting, and technology and data). UHG has identified four to five key risks in each of these categories.

| External Environment | Business Strategies and Policies | Business Process Execution | People | Analysis and Reporting | Technology and Data |
|---|---|---|---|---|---|
| Competitor | Strategy and innovation | Operations planning | Leadership | Performance management | Technology infrastructure |
| Legal & regulatory | Business/product portfolio | Customer satisfaction | Skills and competencies | Budgeting and financial planning | Reliability |
| Catastrophic loss | Organization structure | Regulatory compliance | Communications | External reporting | System security |
| Medical loss/ utilization trend | Organization policies | Intellectual capital | Fraud and abuse | Market intelligence | |

**Required**   Review the risks identified above and consider a company in a different industry, a manufacturer of auto parts. Identify and explain three or four ways that the ERM for an auto parts manufacturer would differ from that of United Health Group.

[LO 1-4]   1-39   **Strategy; Service Company**   Full Frame is a family-owned company that operates five custom framing stores. Each store offers a variety of services: matting and mounting prints; framing photos, paintings, posters, and prints; and sales of posters and prints. About 85% of the business is the service of matting, mounting, and framing photos, prints, and paintings. The main goals of Clyde Fuller, the founder, are growth and profitability: growth now, and profitability later. He sees the business as a commodity-service business, in which other frame shops provide essentially the same service, and the competition is on price and customer service. From his seven years in the business he knows that any frame store's work has to be high quality or it will quickly lose customers, so he maintains quality as a necessary component of his business and uses price and customer service to succeed in competing with other shops. The strategy has worked well for Clyde as he has been able to grow from a single store seven years ago to five stores at the present time. The additional stores are managed by members of Clyde's extended family.

To achieve a competitive price, Clyde watches his costs carefully and limits the amount of profit margin that he expects from each customer transaction. He looks for only an 8% markup over the total costs of the service. This policy has meant that initially his take-home profits were not great, but the low price has enabled him to attract customers and to grow the business. Total profits have increased as the business has grown. To enhance his low-price approach, he has devised efficient techniques to provide his service, and he instructs his employees to follow his techniques to be very efficient with their time and use of materials. He also has a profit-sharing plan that rewards each store employee when cost-per-service declines at that store.

**Required**
1. What strategy does Clyde use in the business? Briefly explain your choice.
2. Do you think Clyde's pricing and employee-incentive policies support this strategy? Why or why not?

[LO 1-4]   1-40   **Strategy; Auto Tire Manufacturing**   Michelin, the 121-year-old French manufacturer of tires, is a worldwide leader in tire sales. But there are plenty of challenges. One is the growth of low-cost tire producers in Southeast Asia and elsewhere. Michelin knows that most tire buyers are shopping primarily for price, viewing tires primarily as a commodity. This is true even though the problems at some tire makers in recent years have brought consumer attention to tire safety. To help differentiate his firm's product, Edouard Michelin (Michelin's former CEO) pushed development of technologically advanced tires that, for example, provide blowout protection and are more suited for high-performance use.

**Required**  Is the auto tire a commodity? Would you consider Michelin to be a cost leader or a differentiator, and why?

[LO 1-4]  1-41  **Strategy; Brand Value**  Each year, *Bloomberg Businessweek* reports the 100 top brands in the world. The leading brands are determined from a calculation by Interbrand Corp., an independent rater. The calculation is based on an analysis to determine what portion of the firm's sales and earnings can be credited to the firm's brand. For 2009 (reported in the September 28, 2009, issue), the top 10 brands were, in order:

1. Coca-Cola
2. IBM
3. Microsoft
4. General Electric
5. Nokia
6. McDonald's
7. Google
8. Toyota
9. Intel
10. Disney

In 2010, *Bloomberg Businessweek* (April 25, 2010) also reported a survey by the Boston Consulting Group of 1,590 senior executives to determine the world's most innovative companies. The top 10 in order were:

1. Apple
2. Google
3. Microsoft
4. IBM
5. Toyota
6. **Amazon.com**
7. LG Electronics
8. BVD (maker of gas-powered cars in China)
9. General Electric
10. Sony

**Required**  Which of the above firms would you classify as a cost leader and which would you classify as a differentiator, and why?

[LO 1-4]  1-42  **Strategy and Balance Scorecard; Customer Service**  In its ranking of firms on the basis of customer service, *Bloomberg Businessweek* (March 1, 2010) collaborated with J.D. Power & Associates (a global marketing information firm that conducts independent surveys of customer satisfaction) to develop a list of the top companies. The ranking was based in part on ratings by J.D. Power and also by a survey of 5,000 readers of *Bloomberg Businessweek*. The top 10 firms are listed in order:

1. L.L Bean
2. USAA, a financial services firm for military families
3. Apple
4. Four Seasons Hotels & Resorts
5. Publix Super Markets
6. Nordstrom
7. Lexus
8. The Ritz-Carlton
9. Barnes & Noble
10. Ace Hardware

**Required**  Which of the above firms would you classify as a cost leader and which as a differentiator, and why?

**[LO 1-4]**   1-43   **Strategy; Discounting, Differentiating, and Contract Manufacturing**   Contract manufacturing refers to a process in which one company, the contract manufacturer, produces the same or very similar products for other manufacturers or retailers. As an example, headquartered in Singapore, Flextronics is a large electronics manufacturing services company providing design, engineering, and manufacturing services to automotive, computing, consumer digital, industrial, and health care product companies. Microsoft is one of Flextronics's customers, among many others. Another example is High Tech Company (HTC), a Taiwan-based company that manufacturers cell phones and other products for the consumer electronics industry. Acer is another Taiwan-based computer manufacturer, the fourth largest in the world, but not a well-known brand. To change that image, Acer purchased Gateway Computer in October 2007 and is shedding its contract manufacturing business. Both HTC and Acer are now embarked on a strategy to gain brand recognition and to move away from the contract manufacturing business.

In a related instance, Menu Food, Inc. of Ontario, Canada, a contract manufacturer, produces pet food for Procter & Gamble (Iams brand), Colgate-Palmolive (Science Diet brand), and Walmart (the O'Roy brand). While Menu Food says it has 1,300 recipes, it may be hard to distinguish one product from another except for the branding due to advertising and promotion by the manufacturers and retailers who purchase the product from Menu and differing prices.

In a final example, home products and fashion apparel by such well-known designers as Martha Stewart, the Italian fashion house Missoni, and Vera Wang are appearing in discount retail stores. Vera Wang has developed a line of clothing for Kohl's, Martha Stewart for Kmart and Macy's, and Missoni for Target.

**Required**   For each of these cases of contract manufacturing, consider the strategic and competitive implications of the buyer-seller arrangement.

1. For the Taiwan-based companies HTC and Acer
2. For Menu Food
3. For Vera Wang

**[LO 1-5]**   1-44   **Different Professional Certification Programs**   There are several professional certificate programs that are of interest to management accountants. Each certificate is awarded based on the results of a comprehensive exam plus other education and experience requirements. Perhaps the best known is the CPA, which is administered by each of the 50 states and five other jurisdictions in the United States. The CPA certificate represents achievement of a broad knowledge of the accounting profession, including auditing, tax accounting, and governmental accounting, among others. Information about the CPA is available at the American Institute of Certified Public Accountants (AICPA) website.

The Institute of Management Accountants (IMA) has a professional certification program leading to the Certificate in Management Accounting (CMA). The CMA exam has a framework similar to that of the CPA exam except that its focus is on broad business knowledge, strategy implementation, and competence in management accounting, rather than taxation and auditing.

American Institute of Certified Public Accountants: **www.aicpa.org/index.htm**

Institute of Management Accounting: **www.imanet.org/**

**Required**   Review the AICPA and IMA websites and, in 200 words or less, explain how the two certificate programs differ, and which certificate program (if any) might be most appropriate for you given your current career interests. Use specific examples that you notice in reviewing the websites.

**[LO 1-5]**   1-45   **Learning about Different Professional Organizations; Using the Internet**   There are a number of professional organizations throughout the world that represent the interests of the management accountant professional, providing educational materials and other services to the management accountant. A partial list of some of these organizations is provided below.

Institute of Management Accounting: **www.imanet.org/**

Society of Management Accountants (CMA-Canada) **www.cma-Canada.org/**

Chartered Institute of Management Accountants (CIMA, UK): **www.cimaglobal.com**

American Institute of Certified Public Accountants: **www.aicpa.org/index.htm**

Financial Executives International: **www.financialexecutives.org**

**Required**  In 200 words or less, explain how the different organizations support the profession of management accountant, that is, the nature and extent of the publications they offer, educational programs, and other services. Use specific examples that you notice in reviewing the websites.

[LO 1-6]  1-46  **Ethics; Product Quality**  Green Acres, Inc., is a large U.S.-based multinational producer of canned fruits and vegetables. While Green Acres has a reputation of traditionally using only organic suppliers for its fruits and vegetables, it has recently experimented with produce from farmers known to have genetically modified crops. These genetically modified fruits and vegetables are often cheaper than their organic counterparts because farmers are able to achieve greater yields than with organic crops, and they have provided the firm with a way to cut its production costs. As Green Acres's chief of operations, the firm's marketing researchers have informed you that consumers continue to view Green Acres's products as organic despite the fact that Green Acres has never placed the word *organic* on its product labels. Moreover, the marketing researchers have discovered that Green Acres's sales and profits have dramatically increased due to this misperception in the wake of debates over the health and environmental consequences of genetically modified organisms.

**Required**  Now that you know of your consumers' misperception about your product, should you disclose your use of genetically modified crops to the public?

[LO 1-6]  1-47  **Ethics; Who, What, and How?; Use of Internet**  Occupational fraud is defined by the Association of Certified Fraud Examiners (ACFE) as "the use of one's occupation for personal enrichment through the deliberate misuse or misapplication of the employing organization's resources or assets." This means that the perpetrator of the fraud steals assets from the employer, in contrast to financial fraud in which the firm's financial statements are misrepresented. For example, the Enron fraud is a case of financial fraud, while the theft of the company's inventory by an employee would be occupational fraud. The ACFE's 2010 Report to the Nation on occupational fraud is shown at **http://www.acfe.com/rttn/2010-rttn.asp**. The study shows some distinct patterns to these fraud cases.

**Required**  Go to the ACFE link shown above and review the study to determine the following.

1. What are the three most common behavioral indicators (red flags) of fraud?
2. What are the three most commonly used anti-fraud measures to detect and prevent fraud?
3. Are small companies or larger companies more vulnerable to fraud, and why?
4. What was the dollar amount of the median annual loss to the companies in the ACFE's study of occupational fraud?
5. List the three top means by which occupational fraud is usually detected.
6. How important in detecting fraud is the use of "hotlines," which employees can use to report fraud?

## Solution to Self-Study Problem

### An Ethical Problem

1. ENVIRO-WEAR's strategy to this point is best described as the differentiation strategy, wherein Frank has been able to succeed by differentiating his product as environmentally sound. This has appealed to a sufficient number of customers of sports wear, and ENVIRO-WEAR has grown accordingly. However, given the unfortunate jokes made by the sales manager and the rumors, the differentiation strategy is unlikely to continue to work, since the offense of the jokes and the disclosure of some discrepancies in the manufacturing methods will undermine the appeal of environmentally sound manufacturing. Frank will have to work quickly to maintain differentiation, perhaps through a quick response that effectively shows the firm's commitment to quality and environmental issues. Failing that, Frank should quickly decide what change in strategy will be necessary for his firm to survive and continue to succeed. Frank should consider a new strategy, perhaps based on cost leadership. The cost leadership strategy would bring Frank into competition with different types of firms, and the question for Frank would be whether his firm could successfully compete in that type of market.

2. There are a number of ethical issues in the case, which are especially important to Frank as a CMA and a CPA with previous experience in public accounting practice where ethics are very important. Frank should try to identify and understand the different options and the ethical aspects of the consequences of those options. For example, should Frank deny all charges against the company? Should he undertake an investigation to determine what his other sales managers think (do they have the same view as the offensive sales manager)? Do the manufacturing processes of the firm really live

up to the claimed quality and environmental standards? It seems the relevant ethical issue requires communicating unfavorable as well as favorable information and disclosing fully all relevant information that could reasonably be expected to influence a consumer's understanding of the situation. To disguise or mislead consumers and others would be in conflict with the professional standards Frank is very familiar with.

Also at issue is whether it is appropriate to fire the offensive sales manager. Most would probably agree that the firing is appropriate, since the sales manager has publicly put himself at odds with the strategic goals of the firm. However, others might want to consider the consequences of the firing and its fairness to the employee.

*Please visit* **http://www.mhhe.com/blocher6e** *to access a narrated, animated tutorial for solving this problem.*

# CHAPTER TWO

# Implementing Strategy:
## The Value Chain,
## the Balanced Scorecard,
## and the Strategy Map

**After studying this chapter, you should be able to . . .**

LO 2-1   Explain how to implement a competitive strategy by using strengths-weaknesses-opportunities-threats (SWOT) analysis

LO 2-2   Explain how to implement a competitive strategy by focusing on the execution of goals

LO 2-3   Explain how to implement a competitive strategy using value-chain analysis

LO 2-4   Explain how to implement a competitive strategy using the balanced scorecard and strategy map

LO 2-5   Explain how to expand the balanced scorecard by integrating sustainability

**Amazon.com** typifies successful competition in the new economy far more than many firms. Some would say that Amazon invented the Internet retailing business model that all other dot-coms are struggling to copy. Amazon understands well the strategy of developing and maintaining customer loyalty, which is the key to success in retail e-business, and implements it effectively.

Amazon has a loyal and growing customer base because of its reliable service and low cost. Recently it has been cited as a major factor in the bankruptcies of Borders and Circuit City. Amazon also presents a competitive threat to Walmart, OfficeMax, and other retailers. The reason: Shoppers find the same product at lower prices and enjoy the convenience of online shopping. A recent study showed that, on average, the Walmart product is 19% more expensive than at Amazon. The savings come from the following: Amazon customers do not pay sales tax, a real savings in most states. Consider also that many states are raising sales tax rates to balance state budgets. Also, Amazon avoids the costs to maintain retail facilities such as the Walmart stores. On the other hand, Amazon does require shipping costs that must be paid by the customer, and shipping costs (because of fuel prices) are on the increase. Also, some states are challenging Amazon and other online retailers on their avoidance of state sales tax. So the competitive environment for Amazon may be in for change.[1] Whatever the future holds, Amazon must adapt its strategy to the competitive environment and then implement this strategy. The implementation of strategy is critical; Success follows not just the development of a strategy but the implementation of an effective strategy. This chapter covers the key tools in strategy implementation: (1) SWOT analysis, (2) focus on execution, (3) value-chain analysis, and (4) the balanced scorecard and the strategy map.

The chapter concludes with an introduction to sustainability, which we present as an extension of the balanced scorecard. The value chain, balanced scorecard, and strategy map are foundational concepts that will appear again throughout the remaining chapters.

[1] John Jannarone, "Retailers Struggle in Amazon Jungle," *The Wall Street Journal*, February 22, 2011, p. C8.

If you don't set goals, you can't regret not reaching them.

*Yogi Berra*

# Strengths-Weaknesses-Opportunities-Threats (SWOT) Analysis

**LO 2-1**

*Explain how to implement a competitive strategy by using strengths-weaknesses-opportunities-threats (SWOT) analysis.*

**SWOT analysis**
is a systematic procedure for identifying a firm's critical success factors: its internal strengths and weaknesses and its external opportunities and threats.

Skills or competencies that the firm employs especially well are called **core competencies.**

One of the first steps in implementing strategy is to identify the critical success factors that the firm must focus on to be successful. **SWOT analysis** is a systematic procedure for identifying a firm's critical success factors: its *internal* strengths and weaknesses and its *external* opportunities and threats. Strengths are skills and resources that the firm has more abundantly than other firms. Skills or competencies that the firm employs especially well are called **core competencies.** The concept of core competencies is important because it points to areas of significant competitive advantage for the firm; core competencies can be used as the building blocks of the firm's overall strategy. In contrast, weaknesses represent a lack of important skills or competencies relative to the presence of those resources in competing firms.

Strengths and weaknesses are most easily identified by looking inside the firm at its specific resources:

- **Product lines.** Are the firm's products and services innovative? Are the product and service offerings too wide or too narrow? Are there important and distinctive technological advances?
- **Management.** What is the level of experience and competence?
- **Research and development.** Is the firm ahead of or behind competitors? What is the outlook for important new products and services?
- **Operations.** How competitive, flexible, productive, and technologically advanced are the current operations? What plans are there for improvements in facilities and processes?
- **Marketing.** How effective is the overall marketing approach, including promotion, selling, and advertising?
- **Strategy.** How clearly defined, communicated, and effectively implemented is corporate strategy?

Opportunities and threats are identified by looking outside the firm. Opportunities are important favorable situations in the firm's environment. Demographic trends, changes in regulatory matters, and technological changes in the industry might provide significant advantages or disadvantages for the firm. For example, the gradual aging of the U.S. population represents an advantage for firms that specialize in products and services for the elderly. In contrast, threats are major unfavorable situations in the firm's environment. These might include the entrance of new competitors or competing products, unfavorable changes in government regulations, and technological change that is unfavorable to the firm.

Opportunities and threats can be identified most easily by analyzing the industry and the firm's competitors:[2]

- **Barriers to entry.** Do certain factors, such as capital requirements, economies of scale, product differentiation, and access to selected distribution channels, protect the firm from newcomers? Do other factors, including the cost of buyer switching or government regulations and licensing restrictions, restrict competition?
- **Intensity of rivalry among competitors.** Intense rivalry can be the result of high entry barriers, specialized assets (and therefore limited flexibility for a firm in the industry), rapid product innovation, slow growth in total market demand, or significant overcapacity in the industry. How intense is the overall industry rivalry facing the firm?
- **Pressure from substitute products.** Will the presence of readily substitutable products increase the intensity level of the firm's competition?

[2] The five forces of industry competition are adapted from Michael E. Porter, "The Five Competitive Forces that Shape Strategy," *Harvard Business Review,* January 2008, pp. 79–93.

- **Bargaining power of customers.** The greater the bargaining power of the firm's customers, the greater the level of competition facing the firm. The bargaining power of customers is likely higher if switching costs are relatively low and if the products are not differentiated.

- **Bargaining power of suppliers.** The greater the bargaining power of a firm's suppliers, the greater the overall level of competition facing the firm. The bargaining power of suppliers is higher when a few large firms dominate the group of suppliers and when these suppliers have other good outlets for their products.

SWOT analysis guides the strategic analysis by focusing attention on the strengths, weaknesses, opportunities, and threats critical to the company's success. By carefully identifying the critical success factors in this way, executives and managers can discover differences in viewpoints. For example, what some managers might view as a strength others might view as a weakness. SWOT analysis therefore also serves as a means for obtaining greater understanding and perhaps consensus among managers regarding the factors that are crucial to the firm's success.

A final step in the SWOT analysis is to identify quantitative measures for the critical success factors (CSFs). Critical success factors are sometimes called *value propositions,* that is, the CSF represents the critical process in the firm that delivers value to the customer. At this final step the firm converts, for example, the CSF of customer service to a quantitative measure, such as the number of customer complaints or a customer satisfaction score.

Identifying critical processes and developing measures for the CSFs involves a careful study of the firm's business processes. Product development, manufacturing, marketing, management, and financial functions are investigated to determine in which specific ways these functions contribute to the firm's success. The objective at this step is to determine the specific measures that will allow the firm to monitor its progress toward achieving its strategic goals. Exhibit 2.1 lists sample CSFs and ways in which they might be measured.

## Execution

It is very hard to develop a unique strategy, and even harder, should you develop one, to keep it proprietary. Sometimes a company does have a unique cost advantage or a unique patented position. Brand position can also be a powerful competitive position—a special advantage that competitors strive to match. However, these advantages are rarely permanent barriers to others. . . . So, execution is really the critical part of a successful strategy. Getting it done, getting it done right, getting it done better than the next person is far more important than dreaming up new visions of the future.

*Louis V. Gerstner, Jr.*

Source: Louis V. Gerstner, Jr., *Who Says Elephants Can't Dance?* (New York: Harper Business, 2002), pp. 229–230.

**EXHIBIT 2.1**
**Measuring Critical**
**Success Factors**

| Critical Success Factor | How to Measure the CSF |
| --- | --- |
| **Financial Factors** | |
| • Profitability | Earnings from operations, earnings trend |
| • Liquidity | Cash flow, trend in cash flow, interest coverage, asset turnover, inventory turnover, receivables turnover |
| • Sales | Level of sales in critical product groups, sales trend, percent of sales from new products, sales forecast accuracy |
| • Market value | Share price |
| **Customer Factors** | |
| • Customer satisfaction | Customer returns and complaints, customer survey |
| • Dealer and distributor | Coverage and strength of dealer and distributor channel relationships; e.g., number of dealers per state or region |
| • Marketing and selling | Trends in sales performance, training, market research activities; measured in hours or dollars |
| • Timeliness of delivery | On-time delivery performance, time from order to customer receipt |
| • Quality | Customer complaints, warranty expense |
| **Internal Business Processes** | |
| • Quality | Number of defects, number of returns, customer survey, amount of scrap, amount of rework, field service reports, warranty claims, vendor quality defects |
| • Productivity | Cycle time (from raw materials to finished product); labor efficiency; machine efficiency; amount of waste, rework, and scrap |
| • Flexibility | Setup time, cycle time |
| • Equipment readiness | Downtime, operator experience, machine capacity, maintenance activities |
| • Safety | Number of accidents, effects of accidents |
| **Learning and Growth** | |
| • Product innovation | Number of design changes, number of new patents or copyrights, skills of research and development staff |
| • Timeliness of new product | Number of days over or under the announced ship date |
| • Skill development | Number of training hours, amount of skill performance improvement |
| • Employee morale | Employee turnover, number of complaints, employee survey |
| • Competence | Rate of turnover, training, experience, adaptability, financial and operating performance measures |
| **Other** | |
| • Governmental and community relations | Number of violations, community service activities |

**LO 2-2**

*Explain how to implement a competitive strategy by focusing on the execution of goals.*

Lou Gerstner is credited with the remarkable success of IBM in the 1990s. He became CEO of IBM at a very troubled time for the company. He rejected the notion that he could save the company with some high vision, but instead he determined that the company needed to focus on execution. This meant determining the critical success factors and putting in place the processes to develop, achieve, and regularly inspect these processes. At IBM this meant a focus on the customer: beginning with a careful understanding of the customer's needs, then working on "faster cycle times, faster delivery times, and a higher quality of service." The service focus has served IBM well as its profits have grown to $15.9 billion in 2011 compared to the $8 billion loss in 1993, the year Gerstner took over at IBM. Following Gerstner, and IBM's CEO through 2011, Samuel J. Palmisano continued Gerstner's focus on execution. When referring to an earnings shortfall in the first quarter of 2005, he noted that the company had trouble closing deals at the end of the quarter, and "we attribute most of that to our (lack of) execution." IBM's stock fell sharply in the first quarter of 2005 but recovered quickly and has been increasing ever since. In fact, the value of a share of IBM stock has more than doubled since 2005.

Effective execution requires a concise statement of strategy that is clearly communicated within the organization. It requires a business process approach to management, in which

**EXHIBIT 2.2**
**Effects of Competitive Strategy on Required Resources and Execution**

| Strategy | Required Resources | Execution |
|---|---|---|
| Cost leadership | • Substantial capital investment and access to capital<br>• Process engineering skills<br>• Intense supervision of labor<br>• Products designed for ease of manufacturing | • Tight cost control<br>• Frequent, detailed control reports<br>• Structured organization and policies<br>• Incentives based on meeting strict quantitative targets |
| Differentiation | • Strong marketing capability<br>• Product engineering<br>• Corporate reputation for quality or technological leadership<br>• Long tradition in the industry or unique skills drawn from other businesses | • Strong coordination among functions: research, product development, manufacturing, and marketing |

the CSFs are clearly identified, communicated, and acted upon. It means aligning strategy with action, or as the saying goes, "plan your work and then work your plan."

The nature of the types of CSFs that the manager executes depends, of course, on the type of strategy. For cost leadership firms, the CSFs are likely to relate to operational performance and quality, while differentiated firms are more likely to focus on the customer or innovation. Exhibit 2.2 summarizes the differences between the two types of competition, the nature of the required skills and resources, and the focus of efforts in execution. Also, while most topics we cover in the text are applicable to executing strategy for both cost leadership and differentiated firms, the topics in Part Three (Operational-Level Control) are particularly relevant for the cost leadership firm, while those in Part Two (Planning and Decision Making) and Part Four (Management-Level Control) are useful for both types of firms.

Looking more closely at differentiated firms, the key CSFs and execution issues are in marketing and product development—developing customer loyalty and brand recognition, emphasizing superior and unique products, and developing and using detailed and timely information about customer needs and behavior. This is where the marketing and product development functions within the firm provide leadership, and the management accountants support these efforts by gathering, analyzing, and reporting the relevant information. Firms that excel in the execution of these functions include Coca-Cola, Microsoft, and IBM, which have been the top three global brands for the last seven years.[3]

Both cost leadership and differentiation firms also can improve on execution through benchmarking and total quality improvement. The Malcolm Baldrige National Quality Program (U.S. Department of Commerce; **www.quality.nist.gov**) sets forth improvement criteria and awards firms that excel on these criteria. The criteria include a wide variety of business functions, including leadership, strategic planning, marketing, information and analysis, human resources, process management, and business results. Another resource for benchmarking is the International Organization for Standardization, a network of national standards institutes from 145 countries (**www.iso.org**).

## Value-Chain Analysis

**LO 2-3**

*Explain how to implement a competitive strategy using value-chain analysis.*

Because execution is so important in implementing strategy, managers must know how the firm's strategy and its CSFs are implemented *in each and every phase of the firm's operations.* In other words, managers must implement their firm's strategy at the detail level of operations. This sequence of activities must include all the steps necessary to satisfy customers. Value-chain analysis is a means to reach this detail level of analysis.[4]

[3] "The 100 Top Brands," *BusinessWeek,* September 28, 2009.

[4] This section is based on John K. Shank and Vijay Govindarajan, *Cost Management* (New York: The Free Press, 1993). See also the Institute of Management Accountants Statement on Management Accounting, "Value Chain Analysis for Assessing Competitive Advantage," Institute of Management Accountants (**www.imanet.org**).

**Value-chain analysis**
is a strategic analysis tool used
to better understand the firm's
competitive advantage, to
identify where value to
customers can be increased or
costs reduced, and to better
understand the firm's linkages
with suppliers, customers, and
other firms in the industry.

**Value-chain analysis** is a strategic analysis tool used to better understand the firm's competitive advantage, to identify where value to customers can be increased or costs reduced, and to better understand the firm's linkages with suppliers, customers, and other firms in the industry. The activities include all steps necessary to provide a competitive product or service to the customer. For a manufacturer, this starts with product development and new product testing, then raw materials purchases and manufacturing, and finally sales and service. For a service firm, the activities begin with the concept of the service and its design, purpose, and demand and then move to the set of activities that provide the service to create a satisfied customer. Although the value chains are sometimes more difficult to describe for a service firm or a not-for-profit organization, the approach is applied in all types of organizations. An organization might break its operations into dozens or hundreds of activities; in this chapter, it is sufficient to limit the analysis to no more than six to eight activities.

The term *value chain* is used because each activity is intended to add value to the product or service for the customer. Management can better understand the firm's competitive advantage and strategy by separating its operations according to activity. If the firm succeeds by cost leadership, for example, management should determine whether each individual activity in the value chain is consistent with that overall strategy. A careful consideration of each activity should also identify those activities in which the firm is most and least competitive.

 The value chain can be thought of as three main phases, in sequence: (1) upstream, (2) operations, and (3) downstream. The *upstream phase* includes product development and the firm's linkages with suppliers; *operations* refers to the manufacturing operations or, for a retailer or service firm, the operations involved in providing the product or service; the *downstream phase* refers to linkages with customers, including delivery, service, and other related activities. Some have referred to the analysis of the upstream phase as *supply chain management* and to the analysis of the downstream phase as *customer relationship management.*

The determination of which part or parts of the value chain an organization should occupy is a strategic analysis based on the consideration of comparative advantage for the individual firm, that is, where the firm can best provide value to the ultimate consumer at the lowest possible cost. For example, some firms in the computer manufacturing industry focus on the manufacture of chips (Texas Instruments) while others primarily manufacture processors (Intel), hard drives (Seagate), or monitors (Acer). Some manufacturers (Hewlett-Packard) combine purchased and manufactured components to manufacture the complete computer; others (Dell) depend primarily on purchased components. In the sport-shoe industry, Reebok manufactures its shoes and sells them to large retailers; Nike concentrates on design, sales, and promotion, contracting out all manufacturing. In effect, each firm establishes itself in one or more parts of the value chain on the basis of a strategic analysis of its competitive advantage.

Value-chain analysis has two steps:

**Step 1.** *Identify the Value-Chain Activities.* The firm identifies the specific value activities that firms in the industry must perform in the processes of designing, manufacturing, and providing customer service. For example, see the value chain for the computer manufacturing industry in Exhibit 2.3.

The development of a value chain depends on the type of industry. For example, the focus in a service industry is on operations and on advertising and promotion rather than on raw materials and manufacturing. An example of a service industry value chain is shown in Self-Study Problem 1 at the end of the chapter.

**Step 2.** *Develop a Competitive Advantage by Reducing Cost or Adding Value.* In this step, the firm determines the nature of its current and potential competitive advantage by studying the value activities and cost drivers identified earlier. In doing so, the firm must consider the following:

**Value activities**
are activities that firms in the
industry must perform in the
process of designing,
manufacturing, and providing
customer service.

1. **Identify competitive advantage (cost leadership or differentiation).** The analysis of value activities can help management better understand the firm's strategic competitive advantage

**EXHIBIT 2.3**
Value Chain for the Computer
Manufacturing Industry

| Step in the Value Chain | Activities | Expected Output of Activities |
| --- | --- | --- |
| Step 1: Design | Performing research and development | Completed product design |
| Step 2: Raw materials acquisition | Purchasing, receiving, and stocking | Various parts and materials |
| Step 3: Materials assembled into components | Converting raw materials into components and parts used to manufacture the computer | Desired components and parts |
| Step 4: Intermediate assembly | Converting, assembling, finishing, testing, and grading | Boards, higher-level components |
| Step 5: Computer manufacturing | Final assembling, packaging, and shipping the final product | Completed computers |
| Step 6: Wholesaling, warehousing, and distribution | Moving products to retail locations and warehouses, as needed | Rail, truck, and air shipments |
| Step 7: Retail sales | Making retail sales | Cash receipts |
| Step 8: Customer service | Processing returns, inquiries, and repairs | Serviced and restocked computers |

and its proper positioning in the overall industry value chain. For example, IBM, Boeing, General Electric, and other firms have increased emphasis on services for their customers, as many of these services are more profitable than the sale of their basic products or services.

2. **Identify opportunities for added value.** The analysis of value activities can help identify activities in which the firm can add significant value for the customer. For example, food-processing plants and packaging plants are now commonly located near their largest customers to provide faster and cheaper delivery. Similarly, large retailers such as Walmart use computer-based technology to coordinate with suppliers to efficiently and quickly restock each of their stores. In banking, ATMs (automated teller machines) were introduced to provide improved customer service and to reduce processing costs. Banks have begun to develop on-line computer technologies to further enhance customer service and to provide an opportunity to reduce processing costs further.

3. **Identify opportunities for reduced cost.** A study of its value activities can help a firm determine those parts of the value chain for which it is *not* competitive. For example, firms in the electronics business, such as Flextronics International Ltd. and Sanmina-SCI, have become large suppliers of parts and subassemblies for computer manufacturers and other electronics manufacturers such as Hewlett-Packard, Sony, Apple, and Microsoft, among others. The brand-name manufacturers have found that outsourcing some of the manufacturing to firms such as Flextronics reduces total cost and can improve speed, quality, and competitiveness.

### Value-Chain Analysis in Computer Manufacturing

The computer industry provides an opportunity to show value-chain analysis in action. To illustrate, we will refer to the Computer Intelligence Company (CIC), which manufactures high quality computers for small businesses. CIC has an excellent reputation for customer service, product innovation, and quality. CIC is able to compete with the larger manufacturers of computers because it designs the product specially for each customer and has superior service. CIC has a growing list of customers who are willing to pay a small premium for these advantages. The manufacturing process consists primarily of assembling components purchased from various electronics firms plus a small amount of metalworking and finishing. The manufacturing operations cost $250 per unit. The purchased parts cost CIC $500, of which $300 is for parts that CIC could manufacture in its existing facility for $190 in materials for each unit plus an investment in labor and equipment that would cost $55,000 per month. CIC is considering whether to make or continue to buy these parts.

**EXHIBIT 2.4**

**Value-Chain Analysis for CIC, a Manufacturing Company**

| Value Activity | Option 1: Continue Current Operations | Option 2: Manufacture Components and Contract Out Marketing, Distributing, and Servicing Functions |
|---|---|---|
| Acquiring raw materials | CIC is not involved at this step in the value chain. | CIC is not involved at this step in the value chain. |
| Manufacturing computer chips and other parts | CIC is not involved at this step in the value chain; the cost of these parts is $200 to CIC. | CIC is not involved at this step in the value chain; the cost of these parts is $200 to CIC. |
| Manufacturing components, some of which CIC can make | CIC purchases $300 of parts for each unit. | CIC manufactures these parts for $190 per unit plus monthly costs of $55,000. |
| Assembling | CIC's costs are $250. | CIC's costs are $250. |
| Marketing, distributing, and servicing | CIC's costs are $175,000 per month. | CIC contracts out servicing to JBM Enterprises for $130 per unit sold. |

CIC can contract out the marketing, distributing, and servicing of its units to another firm, JBM Enterprises. This would save CIC $175,000 in monthly materials and labor costs. The cost of the contract would be $130 per machine sold for the average of 600 units sold per month. CIC uses value-chain analysis to study the effect of these options on its strategy and costs. The analysis for CIC is summarized in Exhibit 2.4.

## The Five Steps of Strategic Decision Making for CIC Manufacturing

1. **Determine the strategic issues surrounding the problem.** CIC competes as a differentiator based on customer service, product innovation, and reliability; customers pay more for the product as a result.

2. **Identify the alternative actions.** CIC faces two decisions, the first of which is whether to make or buy certain parts, which CIC currently buys for $300 but could manufacture for $190 per unit plus an additional $55,000 monthly cost.

The second decision is whether to continue marketing, distributing, and servicing its products or to outsource that set of activities to JBM Enterprises for $130 per unit sold and save $175,000 per month in materials and labor costs.

3. **Obtain information and conduct analyses of the alternatives.** First decision: CIC calculates that the monthly cost to buy the part is $180,000 (=600 × $300) while the monthly cost to manufacture the part is only $169,000 (= [600 × $190] + $55,000); thus, making the part saves $11,000 per month.

Second decision: CIC calculates that the monthly cost of the contract with JBM Enterprises would be $78,000 (= 600 × $130) per month. This is a $97,000 savings over the in-house cost of $175,000 per month.

4. **Based on strategy and analysis, choose and implement the desired alternative.** First decision: As a differentiator based on product quality and innovation, CIC considers the importance of the quality of the part in question and decides to manufacture the part. Note that while this would save CIC $11,000 per month, the key reason for the decision is to control the quality of the part and thereby improve overall quality and to support the firm's differentiation strategy. Note, however, that if CIC believes that the supplier can provide the part at a higher level of quality than can CIC, the decision is reversed; it is now better to continue to buy, even if the costs are higher, in order to support quality, a critical success factor.

Second decision: As a differentiator based on customer service, CIC considers the continued high level of service from in-house personnel as critical to the company's success and continues to maintain these personnel, even if it means the loss of monthly savings of $97,000.

5. **Provide an ongoing evaluation of the effectiveness of implementation in Step 4.** Management of CIC realize that the quality of the product and customer service is critical to the company's success. So, CIC will continue to review the quality of product and service provided internally. If the quality of the part purchased outside or the service provided internally is inferior, then a change would be desirable.

## The Balanced Scorecard and Strategy Map

**LO 2-4**

*Explain how to implement a competitive strategy using the balanced scorecard and strategy map.*

The balanced scorecard (BSC) and strategy map, introduced in Chapter 1, are key tools for the implementation of strategy. The BSC implements strategy by providing a comprehensive performance measurement tool that reflects the measures critical for the success of the firm's strategy and thereby provides a means for aligning the performance measurement in the firm to the firm's strategy. Thus, managers and employers within the firm have the awareness of the firm's CSFs (through the balanced scorecard) and an incentive to achieve these CSFs in moving the firm forward to its strategic goals. The strategy map is also used to implement strategy, but in contrast to the focus on performance measurement in the BSC, the main role of the strategy map is to develop and communicate strategy throughout the organization. The strategy map links the perspectives of the BSC in a causal framework that shows systematically how the organization can succeed by achieving specific critical success factors in the learning and growth perspective, thereby leading to desired performance in internal processes, and thus to desired performance in the customer perspective, and finally to the ultimate goal, financial performance and, for a public firm, shareholder value. In sum, the BSC provides the structure of performance measures and the strategy map provides the road map the firm can use to execute the strategy.

### The Balanced Scorecard

Prior to the wide use of the BSC in the late 1990s, firms tended to focus only on financial measures of performance, and as a result, some of their critical nonfinancial measures were not sufficiently monitored and achieved. In effect, the BSC enables the firm to employ a strategy-centered performance measurement system, one that focuses managers' attention on critical success factors and rewards them for achieving these critical factors.

Now a rapidly increasing number of firms, not-for-profit organizations, and governmental units use the BSC to assist them in implementing strategy. As noted in Chapter 1, the balanced scorecard consists of four perspectives, or groupings of critical success factors: (1) the *financial perspective* includes financial performance measures such as operating income and cash flow; (2) the *customer perspective* includes measures of customer satisfaction; (3) the *internal process perspective* includes measures of productivity and speed, among others; and (4) *learning and growth* includes such measures as employee training hours and the number of new patents or new products. The BSC provides five key potential benefits:

### Benefits of the BSC

- A means for tracking progress toward achievement of strategic goals.
- A means for implementing strategy by drawing managers' attention to strategically relevant critical success factors and rewarding them for achievement of these factors.
- A framework firms can use to achieve a desired organizational change in strategy, by drawing attention to and rewarding achievement on factors that are part of a new strategy. The BSC makes the nature and direction of the desired change clear to all.
- A fair and objective basis for firms to use in determining each manager's compensation and advancement.
- A framework that coordinates efforts within the firm to achieve critical success factors. BSC enables managers to see how their activity contributes to the success of others and motivates teamwork.

### Implementing the BSC

To be implemented effectively, the balanced scorecard should:

- Have the strong support of top management.
- Accurately reflect the organization's strategy.
- Communicate the organization's strategy clearly to all managers and employees, who understand and accept the scorecard.
- Have a process that reviews and modifies the scorecard as the organization's strategy and resources change.
- Be linked to reward and compensation systems; managers and employees have clear incentives linked to the scorecard.
- Include processes for assuring the accuracy and reliability of the information in the scorecard.
- Ensure that the relevant portions of the scorecard are readily accessible to those responsible for the measures and that the information is also secure, available only to those authorized to have the information.[5]

Because of its emphasis on performance measurement, we will again cover the BSC when we cover operational-level control (Part Three) and management-level control (Part Four) in later chapters.

### The Balanced Scorecard Reflects Strategy

The BSC can be viewed as a two-way street. Since it is designed to help implement strategy, it also should reflect strategy. One should be able to infer a firm's strategy by a careful study of the firm's BSC. For example, consider the BSC of an electronics manufacturer shown in Exhibit 2.5. Does this firm follow a cost leadership strategy or a differentiation strategy, and why?

---

[5] The above is based on information from: Robert S. Kaplan and David P. Norton, *Strategy Maps* (Boston: Harvard Business School Press, 2007); Robert S. Kaplan and David P. Norton, "The Future of the Balanced Scorecard," *CGMA Magazine,* January 31, 2012; Raef Lawson, Toby Hatch, and Denis Desroches, *Scorecard Best Practices* (New York: Wiley, 2008); Robert S. Kaplan and David P. Norton, "Mastering the Management System," *Harvard Business Review,* January 2008, pp. 63–70.

## The Key Role of the Customer in the Balanced Scorecard and Strategy Map

The balanced scorecard (BSC) and strategy map are key tools for strategy execution. The BSC shows the key categories of critical success factors for the organization, and the strategy map shows the roadmap by which these success factors lead to the ultimate goal of financial performance. Note that the strategy map places the customer perspective next to financial performance—success in the customer perspective is the gateway to financial success. Recently, two studies of the giant retailers Johnson & Johnson and Procter & Gamble have shown how these companies' focus on the customer has produced

superior financial returns. Similarly, a refocus on the customer at GM by the new CEO, Dan Akerson, produced increased market share for the automaker in 2009.

**Sources:** Roger Martin, "The Age of Customer Capitalism," *Harvard Business Review,* January–February, 2010, pp. 58–65; Susan C. Borkowski, Mary Jeanne Welsh, and Kristin Wentzel, "Johnson & Johnson: A Model for Sustainability Reporting," *Strategic Finance,* September 2010, pp. 29–37; David Welch, "For Dan Akerson, A Magic Moment to Remake GM," *Bloomberg Businessweek,* January 24, 2011, pp. 21–22.

**EXHIBIT 2.5** The Balanced Scorecard for an Electronics Firm

Source: Chee W. Chow, Kamal M. Haddad, James W. Williamson, "Applying the Balanced Scorecard to Small Companies," *Management Accounting,* August 1997, pp. 21–27.

| | Measures |
|---|---|
| **Customer Perspective** | |
| Quality | Number of defects; delivered product quality |
| Price | Low price relative to competitive market price; sales volume |
| Delivery | Number of on-time deliveries |
| Shipments | Sales growth; number of customers that make up 90% of shipments |
| New products | Number of new products; percent of sales from new products |
| Support | Response time; customer satisfaction surveys |
| **Internal Capabilities** | |
| Efficiency of manufacturing | Manufacturing cost; output per hour; rate of increase in use of automation |
| New product introduction | Rate of new product introductions |
| New product success | New products' sales; number of orders |
| **Innovation** | |
| Technology leadership | Product performance compared to competition; number of new products with patented technology |
| Cost leadership | Manufacturing cost as a percent of sales; rate of decrease in cost of quality |
| Market leadership | Market share in all major markets; |
| Research and development | Number of new products; number of patents |
| **Financial Perspective** | |
| Sales | Annual growth in sales and profits |
| Cost of sales | Gross margin percent |
| Profitability | Operating profit |
| Liquidity | Cash flows |
| **Employees and Community Perspective** | |
| Competitive benefits and salaries | Salaries compared to norm in local area |
| Opportunity | Individual contribution; personal satisfaction in job |
| Citizenship | Company contributions to community and the institutions that support the environment |

Exhibit 2.5 shows that the electronics firm places the customer perspective at the top of the scorecard. Also, while price is mentioned, note that the emphasis is on customer satisfaction, through quality, innovation, and service. A strong theme through the entire scorecard is the importance of innovation and new products. This firm succeeds through

differentiation based on quality and innovation, and the scorecard reflects that. Cost control is mentioned in the innovation perspective, but as supportive of the differentiation strategy, rather than in conflict with it. Note also the inclusion of an "employees and community" perspective that reflects this firm's strategic emphasis and desire to achieve in these areas.

### Timing, Cause-and-Effect, and Leading Measures in the BSC

Another look at the BSC for the electronics firm in Exhibit 2.5 will reveal that some of the measures are likely to be taken daily or weekly (sales or number of defects) and some monthly or less frequently (cash flow, operating profit). So, the BSC is not a single document that is presented on a given weekly or monthly cycle, but the measures will be updated on their appropriate time line. Also, some of these measures are known to have a cause-and-effect relationship with other measures. For example, improved quality should increase sales and customer satisfaction. So, some measures are in effect "leading indicators" of what will happen to other measures in later periods. The insights to be gained from understanding these cause-and-effect relationships are captured in the strategy map.

## The Strategy Map

While the electronics firm in Exhibit 2.5 placed the customer perspective at the top of the BSC to show its priority, it is also possible to create a strategy map by linking the perspectives in the order they contribute to the overall success of the firm. A strategy map is a cause-and-effect diagram of the relationships among the BSC perspectives. Managers use it to show how the achievement of goals in each perspective affect the achievement of goals in other perspectives, and finally the overall success of the firm.

For most firms, the ultimate goal is stated in financial performance, and for public firms in particular, in shareholder value. So, the financial perspective of the BSC is the target in the strategy map. The other BSC perspectives contribute to financial performance in a predictable, cause-and-effect way. For many firms, the learning and growth perspective is the base upon which the firm's success is built. The reason is that learning and growth—resulting in great products and great employees—drive performance in the internal processes perspective and also the customer perspective. Similarly, great performance in the internal processes perspective drives performance in the customer perspective; better operations mean more satisfied customers. Finally, satisfied customers lead directly to improved financial performance.

### An Illustration of the Strategy Map: The Martin & Carlson Co.

To illustrate how the strategy map and the balanced scorecard can be used to implement strategy, we take an example, Martin & Carlson Co., a manufacturer of high-end furniture. Janet Martin and Jack Carlson, both highly skilled in woodworking, started a small business in Graham, North Carolina, in 1990 to produce handmade furniture. First customers were friends and acquaintances; because of the very high quality and distinctive style of their furniture, the list of customers grew quickly, and Jack and Janet moved into a larger space and hired and trained additional woodworking employees. At present the company has grown to become a nationally recognized manufacturer with annual sales of $200 million. Because of their distinctive brand, Jack and Janet have never experienced price competition, but in recent years the costs of the commodities they require, including fuel, have risen sharply, and it has become more difficult to maintain their profitable growth. A consultant has been called in to help them assess their strategy going forward.

The assessment began with the consideration of the firm's mission and strategy. Owning a privately held business, Janet and Jack felt that their strategy should reflect their personal values as well as the need to provide a successful business. The consultant took them through the sequence of steps. First, determine the mission of the company and its competitive strategy (see Chapter 1 for coverage of mission and strategy). Second, use SWOT analysis and value-chain analysis to further develop the strategy. Third, determine a balanced scorecard and strategy map for the company, which requires identifying and linking goals, management techniques, and critical success factors.

In the first step, Jack and Janet chose their firm's mission, which they based on personal values that they knew were shared by their employees: "To be the highest-rated brand in crafted furniture." The strategy then followed: "To differentiate the firm based

**EXHIBIT 2.6**  **A Strategy Map for Martin & Carlson**

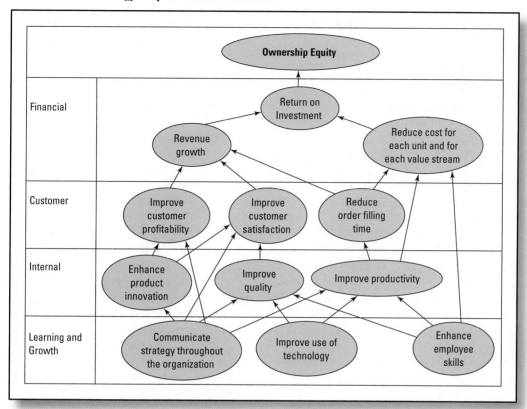

on innovation, style, quality, and customer service (with an emphasis on short lead time, the time from receipt of an order to delivery of the customer's order)." They chose as the firm's tagline, "To delight with our product, and impress with our speed."

The second step (SWOT and value chain) provided further insights which are reflected in the BSC and strategy map. The third step was to develop the strategy map, shown in Exhibit 2.6. The financial goals are revenue growth, cost reduction, and increased return on investment (which would be achieved by the revenue growth and cost reduction). Similarly, goals were set for the other three perspectives of the BSC, being careful to ensure that the goals were consistent with the firm's mission and strategy. Note how the goals are linked to show the causal relationships among the goals. For example, improved customer satisfaction (a customer goal) should positively affect revenue growth (a financial goal). The strategy map is a key tool for Janet and Jack to better understand their road to success and, importantly, a way to communicate to their employees where and how the firm needs to perform to achieve the firm's strategy and mission.

The next step was to determine how to achieve and measure these goals. The techniques, shown in the middle column of Exhibit 2.7, are the contemporary management techniques covered in Chapter 1. They are tried and true tools for achieving the goals. The final step was to determine the measures that, when achieved, would show progress on the desired goals. For brevity, we show a small number of measures here, though in practice there may be 100 or more measures. Also, the strategy map and scorecard could be integrated with the concepts of lean accounting or enterprise risk management, which we have not attempted here.[6] These measures are what constitute the BSC for Martin & Carlson Co. Janet and Jack now have the tools they need to understand their strategy, to communicate it to employees, and to measure performance and strategic success. What would happen if they had not developed these strategic tools? The answer is shown in Exhibit 1.8 on page 16.

[6] "Lean Enterprise Fundamentals," Statement on Management Accounting (**www.imanet.org**); Mark Beasley, Al Chen, Karen Nunez, and Lorraine Wright, "Working Hand in Hand: Balanced Scorecards and Enterprise Risk Management," *Strategic Finance*, March 2006, pp. 49–54; Mark L. Frigo, "When Strategy and ERM Meet," *Strategic Finance*, January 2008, pp. 45–49.

**EXHIBIT 2.7** Goals, Techniques, and Measures for Martin & Carlson's Balanced Scorecard

| | Goals | Techniques | Balanced Scorecard: Measures |
|---|---|---|---|
| Financial | • Increase return on investment<br>• Revenue growth<br>• Reduce cost for each unit and each value stream | | • Return on investment<br>• Percentage increase in sales, by product line<br>• Cost per unit, by product line |
| Customer | • Improve customer profitability | • Activity-based costing used to determine the profitability of customers and distribution channels, used with business intelligence to manage customer relationships | • Customer profitability by distribution channel and customer groups |
| | • Improve customer satisfaction | | • Survey customer satisfaction |
| | • Reduce order-filling time | • Theory of constraints and lean manufacturing | • Lead time, the time between when the order is received and delivered |
| Internal Processes | • Enhance product innovation<br>• Improve quality<br>• Improve productivity | • Target costing<br>• Total quality management<br>• Lean accounting, business process improvement | • Number of profitable new products or product features<br>• Number of defects detected<br>• Inventory level, process speed |
| Learning and Growth | • Communicate strategy throughout the organization<br>• Improve use of technology<br>• Enhance employee skills | • Strategy map and balanced scorecard<br>• Business intelligence, enterprise risk management | • Percentage of employees trained on the firm's strategy map<br>• Number of business risks discovered and analyzed<br>• Training hours in skill development |

## Expanding the Balanced Scorecard and Strategy Map: Sustainability

> Sustainable growth seeks to make more of the world's people our customers—and to do so by developing markets that promote and sustain economic prosperity, social equity, and environmental integrity.
>
> *Charles O. Holliday, Jr, CEO of DuPont*

The growing concerns worldwide about climate change, volatile gasoline prices, high commodity prices, and corporate social and environmental responsibility have created new expectations that organizations adopt the triple bottom line—social, economic, and environmental performance (or, "people, planet, and profits"). The triple bottom line has come to be known as sustainability, that is, the balancing of short- and long-term goals in all three dimensions of performance. Economic performance is measured in traditional ways, while social performance relates to the health and safety of employees and other stakeholders. The environmental dimension refers to the impact of the firm's operations on the environment.

Many companies manage sustainability in a strategic manner, through sustainability reports to shareholders. Some, such as Nike and Ford Motor Co., integrate sustainability into their balanced scorecards, both as a separate perspective and as additional measures in the internal process, customer, or learning and growth perspectives. Business intelligence firms such as IBM, Oracle, and SAS Institute offer sustainability scorecard software. The following shows why and how a number of global organizations are adapting to the challenge of sustainability.

**LO 2-5**

*Explain how to expand the balanced scorecard by integrating sustainability.*

This chapter covers the set of tools that are used to implement strategy: SWOT analysis, the value chain, and the balanced scorecard/strategy map. Apart from these effective tools, managers have learned that certain organizational policies are key to successful implementation. A recent research report based on the responses of 26,000 managers in 31 companies identified the top five policies of effective implementation:

1. Everyone has a good idea of the decisions and actions for which he or she is responsible.
2. Important information about the competitive environment gets to headquarters quickly.
3. Once made, decisions are rarely second-guessed.
4. Information flows freely across organizational boundaries.
5. Field and line employees usually have the information they need to understand the bottom-line impact of the day-to-day choices.

**Required**

Summarize briefly and explain what you consider to be the main takeaway from this research.

(Refer to Comments on Cost Management in Action at the end of the chapter.)

### *Indicators of the Concern about Sustainability*

The concern for sustainability has many dimensions. One is climate change, which was highlighted by former vice president Al Gore's documentary, *An Inconvenient Truth.* Climate change is a responsibility for all organizations and consumers; this dimension views sustainability as a "green issue." Others concern labor, health, and safety issues in organizations around the world, and these issues would place sustainability as a part of enterprise risk management.

Corporations are under pressure from regulators and shareholders to adopt sustainable practices. Being rated on sustainability, for example, by the Dow Jones Sustainability Index (**www.sustainability-indexes.com**), places additional pressure on companies. Some companies, including Home Depot, Nike, Procter & Gamble, Nissan, Toyota, and Walmart, have adopted sustainability to improve profits. As a result of these developments, recent surveys show that the majority of chief executives see sustainability as playing a key role in their corporate strategy.[7]

### *How Companies Have Responded*

In 2010, the Boston Consulting Group (BCG) and the MIT *Sloan Management Review* completed a survey of more than 3,000 executives and managers and conducted dozens of interviews to determine how fast businesses were adopting sustainability-driven management. Among the findings were that, even in the economic downturn, 60% of the companies had increased their investments in sustainability in 2010, and 70% planned to increase their investment in 2011. Many executives indicated that the economic downturn had actually caused them to increase their investment in sustainability, as a means to add "brand trust and reputation" and to reduce cost.

The five reasons most frequently cited in the BCG/MIT survey for choosing to embrace a sustainability strategy were (a) improved brand reputation, (b) increased competitive advantage, (c) access to new markets, (d) increased margins or market share, and (e) reduced costs due to energy efficiency. Many executives also thought that the sustainability strategy would improve perceptions of how well the company was managed, improve the company's ability to attract and retain top talent, enhance stakeholder relationships, and increase employee productivity.

---

[7] "How Sustainability Has Expanded the CFO's Role" (2011), Ernst & Young (**http://www.ey.com/publication/vwLUAssets/ Sustainability_extends_CFO_role/$FILE/CFOSustain.pdf**); Mark J. Epstein, Adriana Rejc Buhovac, and Kristi Yuthas, "Implementing Sustainability," *Strategic Finance,* April 2010, pp. 41–47; Karen Weise, "Who's the Greenest of Them All?" *Bloomberg Businessweek,* November 28, 2011, pp. 59–61; Marc J. Epstein, *Making Sustainability Work: Best Practices in Managing and Measuring Corporate Social, Environmental and Economic Impacts* (San Francisco: Berrett Koehler Publishers, 2008); Stephanie Rosenbloom and Michael Barbaro, "Green-Light Specials, Now at Walmart," *The New York Times,* January 25, 2009, Business Section, p 1; Yuliya Chernova and Sari Krieger, "How to Go Green in Hard Times," *The Wall Street Journal,* February 9, 2009, p. R1.

Patagonia, maker of clothing and gear for the outdoors enthusiast, is known for its focus on environmental issues in its manufacturing and company strategy. As an example of its commitment to the environment, the company studies the environmental impact of planned new products. One new product, a wool shirt, would be made from wool from New Zealand, processed in a factory in Japan, sewn in Los Angeles, and then packaged in Reno for distribution to retail locations worldwide. Patagonia figured the following would be the impact on the environment for a single shirt:

| | |
|---|---|
| Miles traveled | 16,280 |
| Pounds of carbon emitted | 47 |
| Waste generated (oz) | 9 (for a 7 oz shirt) |
| Energy consumption (megajoules) | 89 (This is enough electric power for an average household for 20 hours.) |

Patagonia verdict: Not sustainable; the product was not produced.

**Source:** *National Geographic Adventures,* February 2008, p. 40; www.Patagonia.com. See also a short biographical sketch of Patagonia's founder (Yvon Chouinard): Seth Stevenson, "America's Most Unlikely Guru," *The Wall Street Journal Magazine,* April 26, 2012, pp. 85–89. http://online.wsj.com/article/SB10001424052702303 51340457735222146598612.html

Based on the results of this survey, the industries with the greatest commitment to sustainability included automakers, large retailers, energy and utilities, chemicals, construction, industrial goods, and consumer products. These industries are leading the way in corporate environmental and social responsibility. For example, three firms frequently mentioned in corporate responsibility include Toyota, GM, and Ford from the auto industry. Toyota rates highly for its hybrid gas–electric vehicles and its efforts to promote environmental management systems and waste reduction efforts. Ford and GM are included because of their efforts in developing hybrid and electric cars, fuel economy, and vehicle safety. Other recognized companies include General Electric, which works on reducing the emissions of the jet engines it produces and on developing solar energy. Home Depot is recognized for its community service—allowing employees time off to participate in important community activities. PepsiCo and Walmart are recognized for having adopted electric vehicles and for using lighter shipping containers to reduce shipping costs. Google, Apple, and IBM are also highly rated in the BCG/MIT study.[8]

### Sustainability Measures for the Balanced Scorecard

Environmental performance indicators (EPIs) are the CSFs in a sustainability perspective; they are defined in three categories by the World Resources Institute (www.wri.org):

1. Operational indicators measure potential stresses to the environment; for example, fossil fuel use, toxic and nontoxic waste, and pollutants.

2. Management indicators measure efforts to reduce environmental effects; for example, hours of environmental training.

3. Environmental condition indicators measure environmental quality; for example, ambient air pollution concentrations.

Social performance indicators (SPIs), another important area for sustainability, include the following three categories:

1. Working conditions indicators that measure worker safety and opportunity; for example, training hours and number of injuries.

2. Community involvement indicators that measure the firm's outreach to the local and broader community; for example, employee volunteering and participation in Habitat for Humanity

3. Philanthropy indicators that measure the direct contribution by the firm and its employees to charitable organizations

[8] Knut Haanaes, David Arthur, Balu Balagopal, Ming Teck Kong, Martin Reeves, Ingrid Velken, Michael S. Hopkins, and Nino Kruschwitz, "Sustainability: The 'Embracers' Seize Advantage," *Sloan Management Review,* Winter 2011, pp. 1–27; Duane Stanford, "Sustainability Meets the Profit Motive," *Bloomberg Businessweek,* April 4, 2011, pp. 25–26.

The role of the management accountant, in developing the sustainability perspective of the BSC, is to make these EPIs and SPIs an integral part of management decision making, not only for regulatory compliance but also for product design, purchasing, strategic planning, and other management functions.[9] As for the BSC, there are a number of implementation issues, including measurement problems and confidentiality issues. For example, the Global Reporting Initiative (**www.globalreporting.org**), an independent global institution in partnership with the United Nations and other groups, has a goal of developing generally accepted standards for sustainability reporting.

---

### Summary

This chapter has discussed the four cost management resources for implementing strategy: SWOT analysis, a focus on execution, value-chain analysis, and the balanced scorecard and the strategy map. The first, SWOT analysis, helps management to implement strategy by providing a system and structure in which to identify the organization's critical success factors. The second, execution, is a management focus on making priorities and achieving these CSFs. The third, value-chain analysis, helps management to implement strategy by breaking the organization down into a sequence of value-providing activities; management can identify the CSFs at each step in the value chain and ask the question, How do we add value at this step in the value chain? The final step, the balanced scorecard and strategy map, provides a means to collect, report, and analyze the CSFs; the BSC helps management to measure progress toward strategic goals and to align employees' performance efforts, incentives, and rewards with these strategy goals.

An important supplement to the balanced scorecard is the organization's performance in the area of sustainability. Because of climate change, increases in commodity prices, and other factors, expectations for corporate social and environmental responsibility have increased significantly in recent years.

[9] See for example, Curtis C. Verschoor, "Should Sustainability Reporting Be Integrated?" *Strategic Finance,* December 2011, pp. 13–15; Janet Butler, Sandra Henderson, and Cecily Raiborn, "Sustainability and the Balanced Scorecard: Integrating Green Measures into Business Reporting," *Management Accounting Quarterly,* Winter 2011, pp. 1–10; and Evangeline Elijido-Ten, "The Impact of Sustainability and Balanced Scorecard Disclosures on Market Performance: Evidence from Australia's Top 100," *JAMAR* (the research journal of the Institute of Certified Management Accountants, Australia), 9, no. 1 (2011), pp. 59–73.

---

### Key Terms

core competencies, *36*          value activities, *40*
SWOT analysis, *36*              value-chain analysis, *40*

### Comments on Cost Management in Action

The main take-away from this research is that information flow must support the implementation of strategy. Each of the five key policies is related in some way to information flow. For the strategy to be implemented effectively, everyone in the organization needs to know how the organization competes and what their role is in making the organization successful.

**Source:** Gary L. Neilson, Karla L. Martin, and Elizabeth Powers, "The Secrets to Successful Strategy Execution," *Harvard Business Review,* June 2008, pp. 61–70.

### Self-Study Problems

(For solutions, please turn to the end of the chapter.)

#### 1. Value-Chain Analysis

The Waynesboro Bulls are a Class-AA baseball team and farm club for the Atlanta Braves. The Bulls' league consists of eight teams that are all located within a 150-mile radius of Waynesboro. The Bulls ranked sixth of eight last year, but have high hopes for the coming season in part because of the acquisition at the end of the last season of a great new pitcher, Wing Powers. Wing had the next to best ERA last season. Wing is also a popular player, seen frequently in the community, using his humor and occasionally outrageous behavior to develop a local fan club called the "Wingers." None of the other players come close to Wing in popularity. Head Coach Bud Brown, a 15-year veteran of the Bulls, is optimistic for the coming season, noting the team's luck has "got to change." The Bulls have had only 2 winning seasons in the last 10 years. The Waynesboro baseball park is somewhat typical of AA parks, though somewhat older and a bit smaller. It serves a variety of sodas and beers and nachos to its fans on game days.

Also in a 150-mile radius of Waynesboro are 3 NASCAR venues, 2 outdoor concert venues, 12 colleges with competitive sports teams, 1 major league football team, 1 major league basketball team, but no major league baseball team.

Jack Smith, a consultant for the Waynesboro Bulls, has been asked to complete a value-chain analysis of the franchise with a particular focus on a comparison with a nearby competing team, the Durham Buffaloes. Jack has been able to collect selected cost data as follows for each of the six steps in the value chain. Single-ticket prices range from $4.50 to $8.00, and average paying attendance is approximately 2,200 for Waynesboro and 3,400 for Durham.

**Average Cost per Person at Scheduled Games**

| Waynesboro Bulls | Activities in the Value Chain | Durham Buffaloes |
|---|---|---|
| $0.45 | Advertising and general promotion expenses | $0.50 |
| 0.28 | Ticket sales: At local sporting goods stores and the ballpark | 0.25 |
| 0.65 | Ballpark operations | 0.80 |
| 0.23 | Management compensation | 0.18 |
| 0.95 | Players' salaries | 1.05 |
| 0.20 | Game-day operations: security, special entertainment, and game-day promotions | 0.65 |
| $2.76 | Total Cost | $3.43 |

**Required** Analyze the value chain to help Jack better understand the nature of the competition between the Bulls and the Buffaloes and to identify opportunities for adding value and/or reducing cost at each activity.

### 2. SWOT Analysis

**Required** Refer to the information in Self-Study Problem 1, regarding the Waynesboro Bulls. Prepare a SWOT analysis for the Bulls.

### 3. The Balanced Scorecard

**Required** Refer to the information in Self-Study Problem 1, regarding the Waynesboro Bulls. Prepare a balanced scorecard for the Bulls.

*Please visit http://www.mhhe.com/blocher6e to access a narrated, animated tutorial for solving these problems.*

## Questions

2-1 Identify and explain the two types of competitive strategy.

2-2 Identify three or four well-known firms that succeed through cost leadership.

2-3 Identify three or four well-known firms that succeed through product differentiation.

2-4 How are the four strategic resources—SWOT analysis, execution, the value chain, and the balanced scorecard—linked in a comprehensive strategic analysis?

2-5 What is a strategy map and how is it used?

2-6 What is SWOT analysis? For what is it used?

2-7 What is the role of the management accountant regarding nonfinancial performance measures such as delivery speed and customer satisfaction?

2-8 What is a critical success factor? What is its role in strategic management and in cost management?

2-9 Identify four or five potential critical success factors for a manufacturer of industrial chemicals. Explain why you consider those factors critical for the firm to be successful.

2-10 Identify four or five potential critical success factors for a large savings and loan institution.

2-11 Identify four or five potential critical success factors for a small chain of retail jewelry stores.

2-12 Identify four or five potential critical success factors for a large retail discount store that features a broad range of consumer merchandise.

2-13 Identify four or five potential critical success factors for an auto-repair shop.

2-14 What is a balanced scorecard? What is its primary objective?

2-15 Contrast using the balanced scorecard with using only financial measures of success.

2-16 What is sustainability and what does it mean for a business?

2-17 Explain the uses of value-chain analysis.

**Brief Exercises**

2-18 Think of an example of a firm that succeeds on cost leadership and give some examples of its strengths and weaknesses that would be included in a SWOT analysis.

2-19 Think of an example of a firm that succeeds on differentiation and give some examples of its strengths and weaknesses that would be included in a SWOT analysis.

2-20 What industries do you think are most suited for the value-chain analysis and why?

2-21 How would you explain the relationship between value-chain analysis and the use of the balanced scorecard for a firm that uses both? You can use a hospital as an example.

2-22 Suppose you are a large firm in a service business and you think that by acquiring a certain competing firm, you can generate growth and profits at a greater rate for the combined firm. You have asked some financial analysts to study the proposed acquisition/merger. Do you think value-chain analysis would be useful to them? Why or why not?

2-23 Consider the question in 2-22 above. How would your answer differ if the firm were a manufacturer?

2-24 What are some of the key issues to consider in effectively implementing a balanced scorecard?

2-25 How many measures are usually on the balanced scorecard?

2-26 1. Consider a commodity business such as building materials, many types of food products, and many types of electronics products. A good example of a commodity is gasoline. Are these companies likely to compete on cost leadership or differentiation, and why?

   2. Consider professional service firms such a law firms, accounting firms, and medical practices. Are these firms likely to compete on cost leadership or differentiation, and why?

2-27 Many would argue that the TV manufacturing business has become largely a commodity business, and competition is based on price, with many good brands offered at low prices at retailers such as Walmart. The manufacturers of TVs are said to have a barrier to entry from other potential competitors because the existing manufacturers (Phillips, Sony, Samsung, etc.) have spent huge sums to develop their brands and manufacturing facilities. In recent years there has been a large growth in the number of contract manufacturers (such as Flextronics) that manufacture TVs for the large firms. How does this affect the competition within the industry? Are there now new opportunities for smaller manufacturers of TVs?

**Exercises**

[LO 2-1, 2-2, 2-3, 2-4] 2-28 **Strategy; Execution**   Joel Deaine, CEO of Deaine Enterprises, Inc. (DEI), is considering a special offer to manufacture a new line of women's clothing for a large department store chain. DEI has specialized in designer women's clothing sold in small, upscale retail clothing stores throughout the country. To protect the very elite brand image, DEI has not sold clothing to the large department stores. The current offer, however, might be too good to turn down. The department store is willing to commit to a large order, which would be very profitable to DEI, and the order would be renewed automatically for two more years, presumably to continue after that point.

**Required**
1. Determine Joel's competitive strategy (cost leadership or differentiation) and use this strategy to analyze the choice Joel faces.
2. Explain two means Joel can use to implement his strategy.

[LO 2-1, 2-2, 2-3] 2-29 **Strategy; Execution**   In recent years, a large retailer of auto parts, Best Parts, Inc. (BPI), was looking for ways to invest an accumulation of excess cash. BPI's success was built on a carefully developed inventory control system that guaranteed the availability of a desired part on demand 99% of the time and within one business day for the remaining 1%. The speed and quality of service set BPI apart from other parts dealers, and the business continued to grow.

   On the advice of close friends and consultants, BPI's owner and CEO decided to invest a significant portion of the excess cash in a small chain of gift and craft stores in shopping malls.

**Required**
1. Determine BPI's competitive strategy (cost leadership or differentiation) in the auto-parts business. Assess whether this competitive advantage will or will not facilitate success in the new venture.
2. Explain two means that BPI can use to implement its strategy.

[LO 2-3] 2-30 **Value Chain; Currency Fluctuations**   In early 2011 Brazil's economy was flourishing in many dimensions, except for a significant and worsening trade deficit with China. The root of the problem was that the value of the Brazilian currency (the real) had increased by 10% over the

Chinese currency (the yuan) over the prior year. The increased value of the real meant that Chinese imports were relatively cheap and Brazilian exports were relatively expensive, in currency fluctuation terms. The excess of imports over exports thus heightened the trade deficit. An analysis of the matter identified the relatively high Brazilian interest rates (at almost 11%) that attracted foreign investors and the Chinese government's ongoing efforts to keep the value of the yuan stable versus other currencies as the causes of the increasing value of the real relative to the Yuan.

**Required**   Briefly explain how you would expect the currency fluctuation issues facing Brazil to affect the value chains of Brazilian companies.

[LO 2-3, 2-4]   2-31   **Value Chain; Strategy Map; Role in Corporate Alliances**   A recent report of the consulting firm McKinsey & Company indicates that about one-half of all corporate alliances fail. These alliances are partnerships in which two corporations jointly participate in one or more of the activities in the industry value chain. A good example, provided by Robert S. Kaplan and David Norton (founders of the balanced scorecard and strategy map; see *Harvard Business Review,* January 2010) is the alliance between the European pharmaceutical company, Solvay, and U.S.-based Quintiles, a company that specializes in the conduct of clinical trials for testing potential new drugs. Solvay's strategy is to employ its research-driven organization to develop and market new drugs. One of the steps in Solvay's value chain is to complete the testing required by the U.S. Food and Drug Administration. Rather than divert its operations from research, Solvay has partnered with Quintiles. Realizing that they both benefit from the success and growth of Solvay's products, the two companies have developed a joint strategy map and identified the critical drivers for the joint success of the alliance.

**Required**   Considering the Solvay-Quintiles collaboration, we know that about 50% of such alliances fail. Explain briefly how you think the strategy map and value-chain analysis can help this alliance to succeed.

[LO 2-3, 2-4, 2-5]   2-32   **Value Chain; Sustainability**   One way the value chain can be helpful is to provide a basis for a company to determine the full cost of its product or service, over the entire value chain. Often companies tend to focus only on manufacturing costs and ignore the upstream (design and testing, etc.) and downstream (marketing, distribution, etc.) costs of the product or service. Full value-chain analysis of this type is useful to the consumer as well as the manufacturer. For example, a product might be inexpensive to buy, but the operating costs may be higher than expected. Lockhart et al. (*Strategic Finance,* January 2011) illustrate this example with the case of a company, CleanTech, which provides a cleaning service to owners of large storage tanks that often contain hazardous liquids such as fuel oil or toxic chemicals. CleanTech is considering the purchase of a new system for cleaning tanks that is somewhat more expensive than its current equipment, but one which could reduce both operating costs and the amount of environmentally harmful waste product that must be disposed of after the cleaning process is complete.

**Required:**
1. What is the role of the value chain in CleanTech's purchase decision?
2. In its analysis, how should CleanTech include the disposal of the environmentally harmful waste product?
3. Consider how CleanTech might use a balanced scorecard with a sustainability perspective and what the measures in this sustainability scorecard might include. Give two or three examples of possible sustainability measures.

[LO 2-5]   2-33   **Strategy; Sustainability**   Seventh Generation, Inc. (SGI) manufactures environmentally friendly cleaning products, including laundry detergent, soap, and all-purpose cleaners. Prior to 2008, SGI would not do business with Walmart, because of the perception of a poor environmental record at the large retailer. In 2008, SGI realized that, despite the perception of Walmart's environmental record, it was important to partner with the big retailer in order to have the largest possible impact on consumers—to bring environmentally friendly products into the mainstream. In August 2010, the partnership was arranged and SGI's products started to appear in Walmart's stores. While most cleaning products sold at Walmart are offered at a lower price than SGI's products, the difference is not significant, and the Walmart prices compare well to SGI product prices at supermarkets where these products are also sold.

**Required**   Is this partnership is a good strategy for (a) Walmart? (b) Seventh Generation, Inc.? Explain why or why not.

**[LO 2-5]**   2-34 **Ethics; Sustainability**   Like myself, perhaps you love a good cup of coffee. Suppose that you do, and you have the following information about the company that makes the coffee you are considering. You are selecting a one-pound bag of coffee and you can choose to pay anywhere from $5 to $15 for the bag of coffee. In each of these cases, we mean ethical standards to refer to business practices and labor relations; an example of an unethical business practice would be price fixing, and an example of unethical labor relations would be discrimination in hiring practices.

**Required:**   Report the dollar figure asked for in each part of the four cases, and for each case, explain briefly your rationale for the price differences.

**Case A:**   How much would you pay for the bag of coffee if (a) you know with certainty the company has high ethical standards, (b) you know with certainty the company has low ethical standards, and (c) you do not know anything about the company's ethical standards?

**Case B:**   Similar to Case A, except that you only know what the company says about its ethical standards; however, you have for some time had high expectations that the company has high standards. How much would you pay for the bag of coffee if (a) you now find out with certainty the company has high ethical standards, or (b) you now find out with certainty the company has low ethical standards?

**Case C:**   Same as Case B, except that you have for some time had low expectations that the company has high ethical standards. How much would you pay for the bag of coffee if (a) you now find out with certainty the company has high ethical standards, or (b) you now find out with certainty the company has low ethical standards?

Now suppose that with your cup of coffee you like to relax in a comfortable all-cotton shirt. You have the option to purchase a 100% organic cotton shirt, a 50% organic shirt, a 25% organic, or a totally nonorganic shirt. Organic production is more environmentally safe, using no toxic dyes and no harmful cleaning or processing materials.

**Case D:**   What price would you pay for the cotton shirt, from a low of $15 to a high of $30?

1. For the 100% organic shirt
2. For the 50% organic shirt
3. For the 25% organic shirt
4. For the nonorganic shirt
5. How much would you pay if you had no idea how much organic content was in the shirt?

## Problems

**[LO 2-2, 2-4]**   2-35 **Strategy; Balanced Scorecard: Health Care**   Consumers, employers, and governments at all levels are very concerned about the rising costs of health care. As a result, health care systems nationwide are experiencing an ongoing demand to improve the efficiency of their operations. The health care industry faces significant challenges due to changing patient needs, reduced reimbursement, and the fierce competitive environment. The industry is experiencing consolidations through systemwide mergers and acquisitions as a way to reduce operating costs. Patients and payors are demanding a one-stop shopping approach. While improving operations is necessary, the quality of the health care delivered must not be jeopardized. The Medical University of Greenbelt is feeling the impact of the increasing penetration of its market by managed care companies. As a result, management has been asked to develop a strategic plan to ensure that its funding sources will continue to meet the demands of its patients.

Because it is an academic medical center, the Medical University of Greenbelt's mission encompasses three components: clinical care, education, and research. Management must consider these competing objectives in the proposed plan:

**Required**

1. What should the Medical University of Greenbelt's strategy emphasize?
2. Do you think a balanced scorecard could help ensure the success of the Medical University of Greenbelt? What advantages does a balanced scorecard have over a traditional approach?
3. Determine three or four critical success factors for each of the four areas within the balanced scorecard.
4. What types of challenges is management likely to face in implementing a balanced scorecard? How can employee buy-in be increased?

**[LO 2-2]    2-36    Strategic Positioning**    Fowler's Farm is a 1,000-acre dairy and tobacco farm located in southern Virginia. Jack Fowler, the owner, has been farming since 1982. He initially purchased 235 acres and has made the following purchases since then: 300 acres in 1985, 150 acres in 1988, dairy equipment and buildings worth $350,000 in 1988, and 315 acres in 1998. The cost of farmland has inflated over the years so that, although Jack has a total investment of $1,850,000, the land's current market value is $2,650,000. The current net book value of his buildings and equipment is $300,000, with an estimated replacement cost of $1,250,000. Current price pressures on farm commodities have affected Fowler's Farm as well as others across the country. Jack has watched as many of his neighbors either have quit farming or have been consolidated into larger, more profitable farms.

Fowler's Farm consists of three different operating segments: dairy farming, tobacco, and corn and other crops intended for livestock feed. The dairy farm consists of 198 milk-producing cows that are grazed on 250 acres of farmland. The crop farm consists of the remaining acreage that covers several types of terrain and has several types of soil. Some of the land is high and hilly, some of it is low and claylike, and the rest is humus-rich soil. Jack determines the fertilizer mix for the type of soil and type of crop to be planted by rules of thumb based on his experience.

The farm equipment used consists of automated milking equipment, six tractors, two tandem-axle grain bed trucks, and numerous discs, plows, wagons, and assorted tractor and hand tools. The farm has three equipment storage barns, an equipment maintenance shed, and a 90,000-bushel grain elevator/drier. The equipment and buildings have an estimated market value of $1,500,000.

Jack employs five full-time farmhands, a mechanic, and a bookkeeper and has contracted part-time accounting/tax assistance with a local CPA. All employees are salaried; the farmhands and the bookkeeper make $25,000 a year, and the mechanic makes $32,000 annually. The CPA contract costs $15,000 a year.

In 2013, the farm produced 256,000 gallons of raw milk, 23,000 bushels of tobacco, and 75,300 bushels of corn. Jack sells the tobacco by contract and auction at the end of the harvest. The revenue in 2013 was $1,345,000, providing Jack a net income after taxes of $233,500.

Jack's daughter Kelly has just returned from college. She knows that the farm is a good business but believes that the use of proper operating procedures and cost management systems could increase profitability and improve efficiency, allowing her father to have more leisure time. She also knows that her father has always run the farm from his experience and rules of thumb and is wary of scientific concepts and management principles. For example, he has little understanding of the accounting procedures of the farm, has not participated in the process, and has adopted few, if any, methods to maintain control over inventories and equipment. He has trusted his employees to maintain the farm appropriately without using any accounting or operating procedures over inventories or equipment, preventive maintenance schedules, or scientific application of crop rotation or livestock management.

**Required**    Identify and describe briefly the competitive strategy for Fowler's Farm and explain your choice.

**[LO 2-1]    2-37    SWOT Analysis**

**Required**    Develop a SWOT analysis for Fowler's Farm based on Problem 2-36. The analysis should include two to three items in each category: strengths, weaknesses, opportunities, and threats.

**[LO 2-3]    2-38    Value-Chain Analysis**

**Required**    Develop a value chain of six to nine activities for Fowler's Farm based on Problem 2-36.

**[LO 2-5]    2-39    The Balanced Scorecard**

**Required**    Develop a balanced scorecard with three or more groups of CSFs for Fowler's Farm based on Problem 2-36. Explain your choice of groups and identify four to five CSFs in each group. Make sure that your CSFs are quantitative and can be measured.

**[LO 2-2]    2-40    Strategic Positioning**    Tartan Corporation has been manufacturing high-quality home lighting systems for more than 90 years. The company's first products in the 1920s—the Classic line—were high-quality floor lamps and table lamps made of the highest-quality materials with features that other manufacturers did not attempt: multiple switches, adjustable heights, and stained glass. In the 1950s and 1960s, the company introduced a number of new products that were in demand at the time, including track lighting and lava lamps, which became the company's Modern line. In keeping with its brand image, Tartan ensured that these new products also met the highest standards of quality in the industry. A new customer style emerged in the 1960s and 1970s, which resulted in another new line of products, Contemporary. It was followed in more recent years by two new product lines, Margaret Stewart and Western.

Jess Jones, the company's chief financial officer, had become concerned about the performance of some of the product lines in recent years. Although total sales were growing at an acceptable rate, approximately 10% per year, the sales mix was changing significantly, as shown in the following product line sales report. Jess was particularly concerned about the Classic line because of its sharp drop in sales and its high costs. Because of the high level of craftsmanship required for the Classic line, it always had higher than average costs for labor and materials. Furthermore, attracting and retaining the highly skilled workers necessary for this product line were becoming more and more difficult. The workers in the Classic line in 2013 were likely to be older and very loyal employees who were paid well because of their skill and seniority. These workers displayed the highest level of workmanship in the company and, some would argue, in the entire industry. Few newer employees seemed eager to learn the skills required in this product line.

Moreover, manufacturing capacity was experiencing an increasing strain. The sharper than expected increase in sales for the Western styles had created a backlog of orders for them, and plant managers had been scrambling to find the plant capacity to meet the demand. Some plant supervisors suggested shutting down the Classic line to make capacity for the Western line. Some managers of the Margaret Stewart line argued the same thing. However, eliminating the Classic line would make obsolete about $233,000 worth of raw materials inventory that is used only in the manufacture of Classic line products.

Tom Richter, the firm's sales manager, acknowledged that sales of the Classic line were more and more difficult to find and that demand for the new styles was increasing. He also noted that the sales of these products reflected significant regional differences. The Western line was popular in the south and west, and the Contemporary, Modern, and Stewart styles were popular nationally. The Classic line tended to have strong support only in the northeast states. In some sales districts in these states, Classic sales represented a relatively high proportion of total sales.

Kelly Arnold, the firm's CEO, is aware of these concerns and has decided to set up a task force to consider the firm's options and strategy in regard to these problems.

**Product Line Sales Report**

|      | Classic | Contemporary | Margaret Stewart | Modern | Western |
|------|---------|--------------|------------------|--------|---------|
| 2010 | 20%     | 33%          | 5%               | 40%    | 2%      |
| 2011 | 16      | 35           | 11               | 34     | 4       |
| 2012 | 14      | 33           | 14               | 33     | 6       |
| 2013 | 9       | 31           | 18               | 31     | 11      |

**Required**   Describe Tartan's competitive strategy. On the basis of this competitive strategy, what recommendation would you make to the task force?

[LO 2-1]   **2-41   SWOT Analysis**

**Required**   Develop a SWOT analysis for Tartan Corporation based on Problem 2-40. The analysis should include two to three items in each category: strengths, weaknesses, opportunities, and threats.

[LO 2-3]   **2-42   Value-Chain Analysis**

**Required**   Develop a value chain of six to eight items for Tartan Corporation as described in Problem 2-40. Why would the value chain be useful to a firm like Tartan?

[LO 2-4]   **2-43   The Balanced Scorecard**

**Required**   Develop a balanced scorecard with three or more groups of CSFs for Tartan Corporation described in Problem 2-40. Explain your choice of groups and identify four to five CSFs in each group. Make sure that your CSFs are quantitative and can be measured.

[LO 2-2, 2-4]   **2-44   Strategy Map**

**Required**   Based on your analysis of Tartan Corporation, create a strategy map for the company.

[LO 2-2, 2-4]   2-45   The following are critical success factors for Dell Inc.
- Product manufacturing time
- Customer perception of order-taking convenience and accuracy

- Revenue growth
- Selling expense to sales ratio
- Number of new manufacturing processes developed
- Order processing time
- Raw materials inventory
- Training dollars per employee
- Number of emerging technologies evaluated
- Customer retention
- Manufacturing defects
- Number of new manufacturing processes under development
- Customer satisfaction with speed of service
- Gross margin
- Operating cost ratio

**Required**

1. Using the four BSC perspectives of learning and growth, internal processes, customer, and financial, sort these CSFs into the appropriate perspective.

2. Create a simple strategy map for Dell Inc.

[LO 2-2] 2-46 **Strategic Analysis** Jim Hargreave's lifelong hobby is racing small sailboats. Jim has been successful both at the sport and in the design of new equipment to be used on small sailboats to make them easier to sail and more effective in racing. Jim is now thinking about starting an Internet business in his garage to sell products he favors as well as some he has designed himself. He plans to contract out most of the manufacturing for the parts and equipment to machine shops and other small manufacturers in his area.

**Required** Develop a strategic analysis for Jim's new business plan. What should be his competitive position; that is, how should he choose to compete in the existing market for sailboat supplies and equipment? How is he likely to use cost management information in building his business?

[LO 2-2] 2-47 **Strategic Analysis** Consider the following companies, each of which is your consulting client:

1. Performance Bicycles, a company that supplies bicycles, parts, and bicycling equipment and clothing from its website.
2. The Oxford Omni, a downtown hotel that primarily serves convention and business travelers.
3. The Orange County Public Health Clinic, which is supported by tax revenues of Orange County and public donations.
4. The Harley-Davidson motorcycle company.
5. The Merck pharmaceutical company.
6. St. Sebastian's College, a small, private liberal arts college.

**Required** Determine each client's competitive strategy and related critical success factors.

[LO 2-2, 2-3] 2-48 **Strategic Analysis: The Camera Industry** Olympus, Canon, and other firms in the market for low-cost cameras have experienced significant changes in recent years. The rate of introduction of new products has increased significantly. Entirely new products, such as the digital camera, are coming down in cost, so they are likely to be a factor in the low-cost segment of the market in the coming years. Additionally, product life cycles have fallen from several years to several months. The new products in this market are introduced at the same price as the products they replace, but the new products have some significant advances in functionality. Thus, there are price points at which the customer expects to purchase a camera of a given functionality. In effect, the camera manufacturers compete to supply distinctive and therefore competitive functionality at the same cost as that of the previous models.

The manufacturing process for Olympus, one of the key firms in the industry, is representative of the others. Olympus makes extensive use of suppliers for components of the camera. Working closely with the suppliers, not only in a supplier's manufacturing process but also in the supplier's design of the parts, ensures the quality of the parts. Each supplier is, in effect, part of a team that includes the other suppliers and Olympus's own design and manufacturing operations.

**Required**

1.   Explain what you think is the competitive strategy of Olympus.

2.   Develop a value chain for Olympus. What are the opportunities for cost reduction and/or value enhancement for Olympus?

[LO 2-2, 2-3, 2-4]   2-49   **Strategic Analysis; the Balanced Scorecard; and Value-Chain Analysis: The Packaging Industry**
Dana Packaging Company is a large producer of paper and coated-paper containers with sales worldwide. The market for Dana's products has become very competitive in recent years because of the entrance of two large European competitors. In response, Dana has decided to enter new markets where the competition is less severe. The new markets are principally the high end of the packaging business for products that require more technological sophistication and better materials. Food and consumer products companies use these more advanced products to enhance the appeal of their high-end products. In particular, more sturdy, more colorful, more attractive, and better-sealing packaging has some appeal in the gourmet food business, especially in coffees, baked goods, and some dairy products. As a consequence of the shift, Dana has had to reorient its factory to produce the smaller batches of product associated with this new line of business. This change has required additional training for plant personnel and some upgrading of factory equipment to reduce setup time.

Dana's manufacturing process begins with pulp paper, which it produces in its own mills around the world. Some of the pulp material is purchased from recycling operators when price and availability are favorable. The pulp paper is then converted into paperboard, which is produced at Dana's own plants or purchased at times from outside vendors. In most cases, the paperboard plants are located near the pulp mills. At this point in the manufacturing process, the paperboard might be coated with a plastic material, a special embossing, or some other feature. This process is done at separate plants owned by Dana. On occasion, but infrequently, when Dana's plants are very busy, the coating and embossing process is outsourced to other manufacturers. The final step in the process is filling the containers with the food product or consumer product. This step is done exclusively at Dana-owned plants. Dana has tried to maintain a high reputation for the quality of the filling process, stressing safety, cleanliness, and low cost to its customers.

**Required**

*outsourcing*

1.   Describe Dana Company's new strategic competitive position.

2.   Develop a value chain for Dana. What are its opportunities for cost reduction and/or value enhancement?

3.   Dana's management is considering the use of a balanced scorecard for the firm. For each of the four areas within the balanced scorecard, list two or three examples of measurable critical success factors that should be included.

[LO 2-2, 2-4]   2-50   **Strategy Requirements under the Baldrige National Quality Program**   The Baldrige National Quality Program was established by the U.S. Congress in 1987 to promote quality awareness and to enhance the competitiveness of U.S. businesses. The program is under the National Institute of Standards and Technology (NIST), a nonregulatory federal agency within the Commerce Department, and is administered by the American Society for Quality (**www.asq.org/**) under contract to the NIST. The program has seven categories of performance criteria including leadership, strategic planning, customer focus, information and analysis, human resources, process management, and business results. The last category, business results, includes four parts: customer-focused results, financial and market results, human resources results, and organizational effectiveness results. Recipients of the prestigious Malcolm Baldrige National Quality Award are recognized annually for the firms' achievements in meeting these performance criteria.

**Required**

1.   Go to the NIST website that shows the Baldrige Program's Criteria for Performance Excellence (**www.quality.nist.gov/Business_Criteria.htm**) and review the performance criteria. Comment on the degree to which the program stresses strategy development and strategy implementation.

2.   How would you compare the process within a firm to develop a balanced scorecard versus developing the performance measures to compete in the Baldrige program?

[LO 2-2, 2-4, 2-5]   2-51   **Value Chain: The Oil and Gas Industry; Internet Research**   The oil and gas industry is often in the news these days as consumers look for ways to deal with the large increases in fuel prices in recent years. Some concerns have been expressed about the profits of these firms. We will use the value chain to study the industry and find out where the profits are. At a relatively high level, the value chain of the oil and gas industry would look like the following.

| | |
|---|---|
| 1 | Exploration: Oil and natural gas leasing; purchasing rights to explore, drill, and extract crude oil and natural gas from privately or publicly owned land |
| 2 | Drilling |
| 3 | Oil and gas equipment and services |
| 4 | Transport of unrefined oil and unprocessed gas: oil and gas pipelines |
| 5 | Oil and gas refining |
| 6 | Oil and gas marketing |
| 7 | Transport of refined product to retailer or distributor; oil and gas pipelines; trucks |
| 8 | Purchase and use by customer |

Step one of the value chain is to identify the land where oil and/or gas are likely to be present, followed by drilling to obtain the product, and then additional steps until the product is delivered to the customer, usually in a convenience store or a retail outlet of one of the large integrated oil firms such as Exxon Mobil or BP.

Steps one and two are often combined into what is called a *sector* for oil and gas exploration and drilling. Also, refining and marketing are often combined into a sector, oil and gas refining and marketing. Thus, there are four sectors:

1. Oil and gas drilling and exploration.
2. Oil and gas equipment and services.
3. Oil and gas pipelines (transportation of unrefined oil or refined product).
4. Oil and gas refining and marketing.

There are a number of companies that operate in just one of the sectors. Some operate in two or more. There is also a fifth group of companies, integrated oil and gas producers, that operates throughout the value chain.

In addition to the four sectors, there are the last two steps in the value chain that involve delivery and purchase of product. The delivery of the product to the customer is often by truck, but could also be by pipeline. Integrated oil and gas producers are involved in these last steps as well as independent truckers and distributors.

**Required**   Go to the Yahoo link for Industries—Basic Materials (biz.yahoo.com/p/1conameu.html) and research the four sectors of the industry.
1. For each of the four sectors, determine (a) the size of the sector as measured by the total market cap of the sector (this is the value of all of the outstanding shares of a firm at the date you do the research, for all firms in the sector) and (b) the profitability of the sector, as measured by return on equity (ROE: ROE is earnings divided by total shareholder equity) and net profit margin (profit to sales) of the sector. Put the information in a table so that you can readily compare the sectors on the three measures. Interpret the table of measures in terms of where the profits are in the oil and gas industry. Which part of the industry would a company like to be in and why?
2. What are some of the critical success factors for each of the first seven steps in the value chain for this industry?
3. Explain the nature of the sustainability risks in the industry, from the perspective of the BP oil spill of April 2010.

[LO 2-2]   2-52   **Strategy; Critical Success Factors; Martial Arts Training**   Martial Arts of Cincinnati (MAC) provides karate training and practice services in three locations in Cincinnati, Ohio. MAC is known for its quality of training and has grown rapidly in recent years due to its solid reputation and the growing interest in martial arts, particularly karate. George Moody, the owner of MAC, is a retired police officer who has been training and teaching martial arts for almost 20 years. He has a plan to grow his business to 10 locations in the Cincinnati area in the coming 5 to 10 years. George thinks that by careful attention to customer service, and by choosing his locations wisely, he can achieve this goal. He plans to locate his new studios in strip malls where rental costs are relatively low. This way he can keep his prices down, perhaps lower than other competitors, and thereby attract more customers.

George has developed a list of indicators that he uses to manage the business. The indicators are targeted to George's two key concerns—sales growth and teacher performance.

---

**Sales Indicators**

Number of introductory lessons
Number of new students
Number of students attending classes
Total number of enrolled students
Class size by teacher and age group

---

The first four indicators are obtained on a daily basis, while the last is obtained weekly

---

**Teacher performance indicators (for each teacher; data collected on a monthly basis)**

Number of classes taught
Average number of students per class
Average retention percentage
Student progress in martial arts skills

---

**Required**

1. How would you describe George's competitive strategy?

2. George has listed some of his CSFs. Critically review these indicators, and explain which CSFs you would add or change, and why.

[LO 2-2, 2-4]   2-53   **Balanced Scorecard and Strategy: Food Ingredients Company**   The balanced scorecard for a small food ingredients company is shown below. The information is based on an actual company, and detailed information about its operations and strategy is confidential. You may assume that the firm's products and services are used by a diverse set of customers, including different types of food processors (Kraft, Heinz, Unilever, . . .), restaurant chains, bakeries, supermarkets, and the like. The company is located in a large city.

**BALANCED SCORECARD FOR A FOOD INGREDIENTS COMPANY**

| Goals | Scorecard Measures |
| --- | --- |
| **Financial Perspective** | |
| Capture an increasing share of industry growth | Company growth versus industry growth |
| Secure the base business while remaining the preferred supplier to our customers | Volume trend by line of business; revenue trend by line of business; gross margin |
| Expand aggressively in global markets | Ratio of North American sales to international sales |
| Commercialize a continuous stream of profitable new ingredients and services | Percentage of sales from products launched within the past five years; gross profit from new products |
| **Customer Perspective** | |
| Become the lowest-cost supplier | Total cost of using our products and services relative to total cost of using competitive products and services |
| Tailor products and services to meet local needs | |
| Expand those products and services that meet customers' needs better than competitors | Percent of products in R & D pipeline that are being test-marketed by our customers |
| Customer satisfaction | Customer survey |
| **Internal Perspective** | |
| Maintain lowest cost base in the industry | Our total costs relative to number one competitor; inventory turnover; plant utilization |
| Maintain consistent, predictable production processes | First-pass success rate |

*(Continued)*

| | |
|---|---|
| Continue to improve distribution efficiency | Percentage of perfect orders |
| Build capability to screen and identify profitable customers | Change in customer profitability |
| Integrate acquisitions and alliances efficiently | Revenues per acquired company and allied company |

**Learning and Growth Perspective**

| | |
|---|---|
| Link the overall strategy to reward and recognition system | Net income per dollar of variable pay |
| Foster a culture that supports innovation and growth | Annual preparedness assessment; quarterly report |

**Source:** Chee W. Chow, Kamal M. Haddad, and James W. Williamson, "Applying the Balanced Scorecard to Small Companies," *Management Accounting,* August 1997, pp. 21–27.

**Required**    Based on the information provided, determine what you think is the competitive strategy of the company. Does the balanced scorecard shown above reflect this strategy? Why or why not?

[LO 2-2, 2-3]    **2-54 Value-Chain Analysis**

**Required**    Develop a value chain for the airline industry. Identify areas in which any given airline might find a cost advantage by modifying the value chain in some way. Similarly, identify areas of the value chain in which the airline might be able to develop additional value for the airline customer. For example, consider ways the ticketing operation might be reconfigured for either cost or value-added advantage.

[LO 2-2, 2-3]    **2-55 Value-Chain Analysis**    Sheldon Radio manufactures yacht radios, navigational equipment, and depth-sounding and related equipment from a small plant near New Bern, North Carolina. One of Sheldon's most popular products, making up 40% of its revenues and 35% of its profits, is a marine radio, model VF4500, which is installed on many of the new large boats produced in the United States. Production and sales average 500 units per month. Sheldon has achieved its success in the market through excellent customer service and product reliability. The manufacturing process consists primarily of the assembly of components purchased from various electronics firms plus a small amount of metalworking and finishing. The manufacturing operations cost $110 per unit. The purchased parts cost Sheldon $250, of which $130 is for parts that Sheldon could manufacture in its existing facility for $80 in materials for each unit plus an investment in labor and equipment that would cost $35,000 per month.

Sheldon is considering outsourcing the marketing, distributing, and servicing for its units to another North Carolina firm, Brashear Enterprises. This would save Sheldon $125,000 in monthly materials and labor costs. The cost of the contract would be $105 per radio.

**Required**
1. Prepare a value-chain analysis for Sheldon to assist in deciding whether to purchase or manufacture the parts and whether to contract out the marketing, distributing, and servicing of the units.
2. Should Sheldon (a) continue to purchase the parts or manufacture them and (b) continue to provide the marketing, distributing, and servicing or outsource these activities to Brashear? Explain your answer.

[LO 2-2, 2-3]    **2-56 Value Chain; Harley-Davidson**    Harley-Davidson Inc. (HD) is one of the most recognized brands worldwide. The motorcycle manufacturer has one of the most loyal owner groups of any company. Unfortunately, the firm's success has come at a price. Harley has a reputation that drives some customers away and a "this is for a different generation" effect on some potential younger customers. Other potential customers are simply intimidated at the idea of riding a 400+ pound Harley-Davidson. To deal with these concerns, and to try to encourage new owners, HD developed the Rider's Edge program in which anyone who could pass the Motorcycle Safety Foundation's written test and driving test would be eligible for instructions on how to ride a Harley. The instructions are provided by local dealers. Another new program at HD is intended to attract women. HD publishes *Harley Women* magazine and has introduced a new bike, the SuperLow, which has a lower seat height, sells for a lower price, and is more than 150 pounds lighter than the usual Harley.

**Required** Where do these two new programs fit in the Harley-Davidson value chain? From a value-chain perspective, how do these programs support the firm's strategy?

[LO 2-2, 2-4]    2-57   **The Balanced Scorecard; Strategy Map; Banking**   Carlos Aguilar, a CMA and consultant in Los Angeles, has been asked to help develop a balanced scorecard for a local medium-sized commercial bank. Carlos is familiar with the area around the bank and he knows that the bank has succeeded in part because of good community ties and customer service. The bank managers also realize that employee morale is an important factor in the success of the bank.

Here are some examples of critical success factors that might appear for one or more of the balanced scorecard perspectives of the bank:

Net interest income; noninterest income

Number of problem loans

Number of complaints

Sales volume

Customer surveys to measure customer satisfaction

Training for employees

**Required**

1. Carlos has asked you to help him in the initial phases of this project. Specifically, he has asked you to identify the balanced scorecard perspectives you would use for this bank and provide a short list of two or three critical success factors that you would include in each perspective.

2. Also, Carlos is interested in knowing how the concept of a strategy map might be applicable for this client. Prepare a brief report for Carlos.

3. Explain how the balanced scorecard for a bank could be linked to an incentive compensation plan for the managers and employees of the bank.

[LO 2-3]    2-58   **Value Chain; Multiple Industries**   Generally, the value chains involved in providing a given product or service can be from multiple industries that can be interconnected in complex ways. One example is the auto industry where the primary consumer, the purchaser of an auto, is served by many different industries. The figure below shows five industries that support the auto purchaser directly: the manufacturer of the auto, the bank or financial institution that finances the loan for the car buyer, the insurance company, auto repair, and at some point, a company that purchases the car and resells it. The arrows show the links of service in this multiple industry value chain.

The value chain for the manufacturer is shown in the center column, and the steps in the chain are shown as design, purchase of materials, purchase of components (brake systems, seats, dashboard, carpeting, etc.), assembly, and delivery to the auto dealer. To the right of the

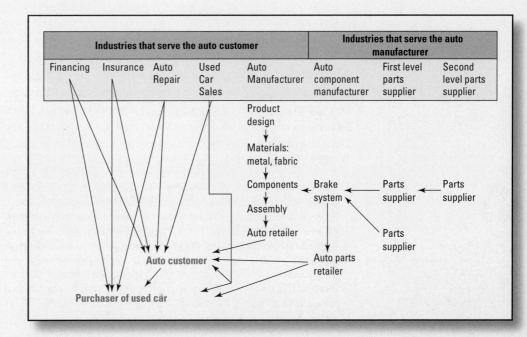

figure we show one of the suppliers of components for the auto manufacturer, an auto parts manufacturer that provides brake systems. This manufacturer also requires supplies from other companies, which in turn require parts or materials from other companies. So there are two or more levels, or "tiers," to the supply chain for the manufacturer. A thorough understanding of the value chain for the auto industry requires consideration of the full complexity of all the different suppliers and industries involved.

**Required** Using the above figure as a guide, create a multiple-industry value chain for a boat manufacturer, including financing, repair, used sales, and parts suppliers.

[LO 2-3] **2-59 Follow-up to Problem 2-58; Value Chain for Financing Auto Purchases**

**Required** Consider the comprehensive value chain in Problem 2-58 and complete a value chain for the financing portion of the value chain only. Use a value chain with four to six steps, beginning with the application for a loan by the car buyer and ending with the car buyer completing the loan and purchase.

[LO 2-3] **2-60 Foreign Currency Exchange Rates** The websites shown below provide historical information on the exchange rates of currencies used throughout the world. Review the changes in exchange rates for the last few years.

www.federalreserve.gov/releases/H10/hist/

http://www.xe.com/ucc/

**Required (choose 1, 2, or 3):**

1. Which Asian countries have experienced changing exchange rates relative to the U.S. dollar in the recent few years, and what are the implications of this trend for global companies such as General Electric?

2. Most European countries now use the euro as the currency for international exchange. Study the recent trends in the euro and determine the implications of this trend for global companies such as Walmart.

3. Which North American countries (other than the United States) have experienced changing exchange rates relative to the U.S. dollar in the recent year, and what are the implications of this trend for global companies such as Ford Motor Company?

[LO 2-3] **2-61 Research Assignment; Value Chain** To complete this assignment, read the article by Noah P. Barsky and Anthony H. Catanach Jr., titled, "Every Manager Can Be an Innovator" (*Strategic Finance*, August 2011, pp. 22–29). The article provides a comprehensive discussion of how companies can use the value chain as a tool to help guide their efforts to provide ongoing innovation in their companies.

The article is available in the Cases and Readings book that comes with the text and which has a link on the text website.

**Required**

1. Explain briefly the difference between disruptive and sustaining innovation.

2. What are the five activities in the value chain depicted in the article?

3. What is the role of strategy in looking for innovation in each of the activities in the value chain?

4. Describe an example of an opportunity for innovation in market analysis.

5. Describe an example of an opportunity for innovation in product development and design.

6. Describe an example of an opportunity for innovation in sales and marketing.

7. Describe an example of an opportunity for innovation in procurement, production, and distribution.

8. Describe an example of an opportunity for innovation in after-sale customer service.

[LO 2-4, 2-5] **2-62 Research Assignment; Sustainability** To complete this assignment, read the article by Janet B. Butler, Sandra Cherie Henderson, and Cecily Raiborn, titled, "Sustainability and the Balanced Scorecard: Integrating Green Measures into Business Reporting" (*Management Accounting Quarterly*, Winter 2011, pp. 1–10). The article explains three ways that sustainability can be incorporated into the BSC. Also, the article explains key issues in developing and using sustainability metrics.

The article is available in the Cases and Readings book that comes with the text and which has a link on the text website.

**Required**

1. What are the three options for incorporating sustainability into the BSC? Explain briefly the advantages and disadvantages of each.

2. Explain briefly each of the seven BSC measurement considerations identified by the authors.

## Solutions to Self-Study Problems

### 1. Value-Chain Analysis

The cost figures Jack has assembled suggest that the two teams' operations are generally quite similar, as expected in AA baseball. However, an important difference is the amount the Durham team spends on game-day operations, more than three times that of the Waynesboro Bulls. That difference has, in part, built a loyal set of fans in Durham where gate receipts average more than twice that of Waynesboro ($28,500 versus $12,350). The Buffaloes appear to have found an effective way to compete by drawing attendance to special game-day events and promotions.

To begin to compete more effectively and profitably, Waynesboro might consider additional value-added services, such as game-day activities similar to those offered in Durham. Waynesboro's costs per person are somewhat lower than Durham's, but its cost savings are probably not enough to offset the loss in revenues.

On the cost side, the comparison with Durham shows little immediate promise for cost reduction; Waynesboro spends on the average less than Durham in every category except ticket sales and management compensation. Perhaps this also indicates that instead of reducing costs, Waynesboro should spend *more* on fan development. The next step in Jack's analysis might be to survey Waynesboro fans to determine the level of satisfaction and to identify desired services that are not currently provided.

### 2. SWOT Analysis

Your SWOT analysis for the Waynesboro Bulls might look as follows:

---

**Strengths:**

- Not much local competition for baseball; note that the 150-mile radius is probably irrelevant anyway as the Bulls' customers are local (within 20 miles); the main issue is local competition
- Wing, the new pitcher; an opportunity for more wins, and increased fan interest

**Weaknesses:**

- Lots of losing records, which hinders fan interest
- Not much to offer by way of game-day promotions and special attractions
- What appears to be a lackluster team and coaching staff

**Opportunities:**

- More new players like Wing, especially those that can create some fan excitement; it seems there is little personality to the current team
- New coach
- Improve the baseball park; add some improvements, such as better parking, seats, etc.
- Increase the quality and variety of food and beverages beyond soda, beer, and nachos
- Lower the ticket prices; offer free tickets to those who have attended a certain number of games
- Offer special promotions, in which groups (employees of a given company; those over 65, etc.) get a free or low-price admission

**Threats:**

- Only the closest of the other venues (NASCAR, outdoor concerts, etc.) would be a threat to this basically local audience.

---

### 3. The Balanced Scorecard

While the key to growth and profitability is probably increasing fan interest, this will probably come about most directly through improvements in operations and personnel. Here is a partial list of examples.

---

**Operations (at the Bulls' park, and on travel days):**

- Cleanliness of park and restrooms as measured by a survey of fans or regular review by management
- Parking, problems measured by number of complaints
- Timeliness and comfort for players and coaching staff on away-days; player and staff survey

**Personnel (coaching and players):**

- Players' performance statistics
- Average player salary (benchmark to other teams)
- Average player age
- Player satisfaction as measured by multiple question survey

**Customers (the ticket-buying fans):**

- Survey of customer satisfaction
- Number of paying customers to number of free admissions

**Financial:**

- Ticket sales revenue
- Revenue; food and beverages
- Other revenue (parking, etc)
- Ballpark maintenance cost, by category
- Travel costs for away games

---

*Please visit **http://www.mhhe.com/blocher6e** to access a narrated, animated tutorial for solving these problems.*

# CHAPTER THREE

# Basic Cost Management Concepts

After studying this chapter, you should be able to . . .

LO 3-1   Understand the strategic role of basic cost management concepts

LO 3-2   Explain the cost driver concepts at the activity, volume, structural, and executional levels

LO 3-3   Explain the cost concepts used in product and service costing

LO 3-4   Demonstrate how costs flow through the accounts, and prepare an income statement for both a manufacturing and a merchandising company

**LO 3-1**

*Understand the strategic role of basic cost management concepts.*

As we will see in this chapter, irrespective of their competitive strategy, successful firms find that they need to apply cost management effectively and, in doing so, to understand the key concepts and terms of cost management. We begin with an example firm that illustrates the importance of understanding the complexity of a firm's operations—the number and diversity of its products, production processes and locations, distribution networks, and types of customers. Complexity on any of these dimensions will have consequences for costs, and the management accountant has developed the necessary vocabulary to identify and describe these effects.

A good example of a firm that deals effectively with complexity is Procter & Gamble (P&G), one of the world's leading consumer products companies, maker of such well-known products as Tide detergent and Crest toothpaste. P&G has achieved success through product excellence and continuous improvement. One key area of continuous improvement is the firm's emphasis on cost reduction through product and process simplification. To accomplish this, P&G uses a concept that we study in this chapter: the influence of product and process complexity on overall costs. P&G has had as many as 50 different varieties of some of its brands, including different size containers and flavors. In addition to variety, the number of trade promotions, discounts, rebates, and coupons that affected P&G's net price were complex. The high complexity in products and pricing increased manufacturing costs, inventory holding costs, selling and distribution costs, customer service costs, administrative and accounting costs, and other operating costs. In recent years, P&G has reduced its product variety significantly, and as a result, it has experienced improved overall sales and profits. At the same time, P&G has improved its supply chain—the process of managing its suppliers—to reduce supply chain cost and to improve product quality and product innovation. Overall, what P&G has accomplished is to effectively manage its sales and costs through careful attention to its brand strategy and to minimize product complexity.[1]

## Costs, Cost Drivers, Cost Objects, and Cost Assignment

**LO 3-2**

*Explain the cost driver concepts at the activity, volume, structural, and executional levels.*

A critical step in achieving a competitive advantage is to identify the key costs and cost drivers in the company or organization. In P&G's case, product complexity is one of those key cost drivers.

[1] Ellen Byron, "Whitens, Brightens, and Confuses," *The Wall Street Journal,* February 23, 2011, pp. D1–2; Barry Berman, "Products, Products, Everywhere," *The Wall Street Journal,* August 23, 2010, p. R8; Emily Nelson, "Too Many Choices," *The Wall Street Journal,* April 20, 2011, p. B1.

**A cost**
is incurred when a resource is used for some purpose.

**Cost pools**
are the meaningful groups into which costs are often collected.

**A cost driver**
is any factor that causes a change in total cost.

**A cost object**
is any product, service, customer, activity, or organizational unit to which costs are assigned for some management purpose.

**A value stream**
is a group of related products.

**Cost assignment**
is the process of assigning costs to cost pools or from cost pools to cost objects.

**A direct cost**
can be conveniently and economically traced directly to a cost pool or a cost object.

**An indirect cost**
cannot be conveniently or economically traced to a cost pool or cost object.

A company incurs a cost when it uses a resource for some purpose. For example, a company producing kitchen appliances uses certain resources, the costs of materials (such as sheet metal and bolts for the enclosure), costs of manufacturing labor, and other costs. Often costs are assigned into meaningful groups called cost pools. Costs can be grouped in many different ways, including by type of cost (labor costs in one pool, material costs in another), by source (department 1, department 2), or by responsibility (manager 1, manager 2). For example, an assembly department or a product engineering department might be treated as a cost pool.

A cost driver is any factor that has the effect of changing the amount of total cost. For a firm that competes on the basis of cost leadership, management of the key cost drivers is essential. For example, to achieve its low-cost leadership in manufacturing, P&G carefully watches the design and manufacturing factors that drive the costs of its products. It makes design improvements when necessary, and the manufacturing plants are designed and automated for the highest efficiency in using materials, labor, and equipment. For firms that are not cost leaders, the management of cost drivers may not be so critical, but attention to the key cost drivers contributes directly to the firm's success. For example, because an important cost driver for retailers is loss and damage to merchandise, most retailers establish careful procedures for handling, displaying, and storing their merchandise.

A cost object is any product, service, customer, activity, or organizational unit to which costs are assigned. Products, services, and customers are generally cost objects; manufacturing departments are considered either cost pools or cost objects, depending on whether management's main focus is on the costs for the products or for the manufacturing departments. The concept of cost objects is a broad concept. It includes products, groups of products (called value streams), services, projects, and departments; it can also apply to customers or vendors, among many other possibilities. Cost objects play a key role in decision making, performance measurement, and strategy implementation, as well as financial statement preparation and tax preparation.

### Cost Assignment and Cost Allocation: Direct and Indirect Costs

Cost assignment is the process of assigning resource costs to cost pools and then from cost pools to cost objects. There are two types of assignment—direct tracing and allocation. Direct tracing is used for assigning direct costs and allocation is used for indirect costs. Any cost is either a direct or indirect cost, relative to the cost pool or cost object. A direct cost can be conveniently and economically traced directly to a cost pool or a cost object. For example, the cost of materials required for a particular product is a direct cost because it can be traced directly to the product.

In a manufacturing company, the materials cost is accumulated in cost pools (manufacturing departments) and then is traced to each product manufactured, which is the cost object. Similarly, an airline's cost of preparing a passenger's beverage is a direct cost that can be traced to each passenger. For a direct cost, the cost driver is the number of units of that object, for example, the number of cartons of Tide produced by P&G, or the number of passengers on Flight 617 for Delta Airlines. Total direct cost increases directly in proportion to the number of cartons or passengers.

In contrast, there is no convenient or economical way to trace an indirect cost from the cost to the cost pool or from the cost pool to the cost object. The cost of supervising manufacturing employees and the cost of handling materials are good examples of costs that generally cannot be traced to individual products and therefore are considered indirect costs. Similarly, the cost of fueling an aircraft is an indirect cost when the cost object is the airline passenger since the aircraft's use of fuel cannot be traced directly to that passenger. In contrast, if the cost object for the airline is the flight, the cost of fuel is a direct cost that can be traced directly to the aircraft's use of fuel for that flight.

Since indirect costs cannot be traced to the cost pool or cost object, the assignment for indirect costs is made by using cost drivers. For example, if the cost driver for materials

**EXHIBIT 3.1**

**Relationships between Costs, Cost Pools, and Cost Objects, in Appliance Manufacturing**

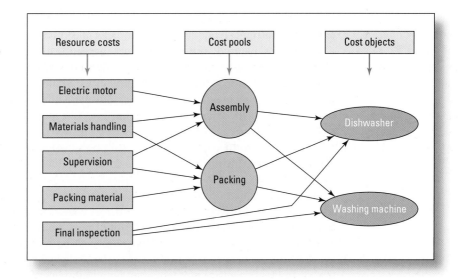

handling cost is the number of parts, the total cost of materials handling can be assigned to each product on the basis of each product's number of parts relative to the total number of parts in all products. The result is that costs are assigned to the cost pool or cost object that caused the cost in a manner that is fairly representative of the way the cost is incurred. For example, a product with a large number of parts should bear a larger portion of the cost of materials handling than a product with fewer parts. Similarly, a department with a large number of employees should bear a larger portion of the cost of supervision provided for all departments.

The assignment of indirect costs to cost pools and cost objects is called **cost allocation,** a form of cost assignment in which direct tracing is not economically feasible, so cost drivers are used instead. The cost drivers used to allocate costs are often called **allocation bases**. The relationships between costs, cost pools, cost objects, and cost drivers in appliance manufacturing are illustrated in Exhibit 3.1 and Exhibit 3.2. This simplified example includes

**Cost allocation**

is the assignment of indirect costs to cost pools and cost objects.

**Allocation bases**

are the cost drivers used to allocate costs.

**EXHIBIT 3.2**

**Selected Examples of Costs, Cost Pools, Cost Objects, and Cost Drivers in Appliance Manufacturing**

## The Flow of Cost Assignment

| Resource Cost | Cost Driver | Cost Pool | Cost Driver | Cost Object |
|---|---|---|---|---|
| **Direct Costs** | | | | |
| Electric motor | Direct trace | Assembly department | Direct trace | Dishwasher and washing machine |
| Packing material | Direct trace | Packing department | Direct trace | Dishwasher and washing machine |
| Final inspection | Direct trace | → | | Dishwasher and washing machine |
| **Indirect Costs** | | | | |
| Supervision | Allocation base: Number of employees in the department | Assembly and packing departments | Allocation base: Direct labor hours for each product | Dishwasher and washing machine |
| Materials handling | Allocation base: Weight of materials | Assembly and packing departments | Allocation base: Number of parts in the product | Dishwasher and washing machine |

two cost objects (dishwasher, washing machine), two cost pools (assembly department, packing department), and five cost resources (electric motor, materials handling, supervision, packing material, and final product inspection). The electric motor is traced to the assembly department and from there directly to the two products, assuming for simplicity that the same motor is used in both appliances. Similarly, the packing material is traced directly to the packing department and from there directly to the two products. Each finished product, dishwasher or washing machine, is inspected, so the cost of final inspection is traced directly to each of the two products. The two indirect costs, supervision and materials handling, are allocated to the two cost pools (assembly and packing departments) and are then allocated from the cost pools to the products (the allocation bases are shown in Exhibit 3.2).

Exhibit 3.2 illustrates the differences between direct and indirect costs and the different types of cost drivers for each. The direct costs—motor, packing material, and final inspection—are traced directly to the final cost objects, the dishwasher and washing machine. In contrast, the indirect costs cannot be traced directly to the products and instead are allocated to the products using an allocation base. The details of the allocation of indirect costs are not explained here but are covered in Chapters 4 and 5.

### Direct and Indirect Materials Costs

**Direct materials cost** includes the cost of materials in the product or other cost object (less purchase discounts but including freight and related charges) and usually a reasonable allowance for scrap and defective units (e.g., if a part is stamped from strip steel, the material lost in the stamping is ordinarily included as part of the product's direct materials).

On the other hand, the cost of materials used in manufacturing that are not part of the finished product is **indirect materials cost.** Examples include supplies used by manufacturing employees, such as rags and small tools, or materials required by the machines, such as lubricant. For convenience and economic feasibility, direct materials that are a very small part of materials cost, such as glue and nails, are often not traced to each product but are included instead in indirect materials.

### Direct and Indirect Labor Costs

**Direct labor cost** includes the labor used to manufacture the product or to provide the service plus some portion of non-value-added time that is normal and unavoidable, such as coffee breaks and personal time. Other types of nonproductive labor that are discretionary and planned, such as downtime, payroll taxes, fringe benefits (vacation, etc.), and training usually are included not as direct labor but as indirect labor.

**Indirect labor costs** include supervision, quality control, inspection, purchasing and receiving, materials handling, janitorial labor, downtime, training, and cleanup. Note that an element of labor can sometimes be both direct and indirect, depending on the cost object; for example, labor for the maintenance and repair of equipment might be direct to the manufacturing department where the equipment is located but indirect to the products manufactured in that department.

Although these examples of direct and indirect costs are from a manufacturing setting, the concepts also apply to service companies. For example, in a restaurant where the cost object is each meal served, the food and food preparation costs are direct costs for each meal served, but the costs of purchasing, handling, and storing food items are indirect costs. Similarly, in professional services firms such as law firms or accounting firms, the professional labor and materials costs for providing client services are direct costs, but the costs of research materials, nonprofessional support staff, and training are indirect costs. An example of cost drivers at a service company, Pennsylvania Blue Shield, is shown in Exhibit 3.3.

### Other Indirect Costs

In addition to labor and materials, other types of indirect costs are necessary to manufacture the product or provide the service. They include the costs of facilities, the equipment used to manufacture the product or provide the service, and any other support equipment, such as that used for materials handling.

---

**Direct materials cost** includes the cost of the materials in the product and a reasonable allowance for scrap and defective units.

**Indirect materials cost** refers to the cost of materials used in manufacturing that are not physically part of the finished product.

**Direct labor cost** includes the labor used to manufacture the product or to provide the service.

**Indirect labor cost** includes supervision, quality control, inspection, purchasing and receiving, and other manufacturing support costs.

**EXHIBIT 3.3**
**Resource Costs, Cost Pools, Cost Objects, and Cost Drivers at Pennsylvania Blue Shield**

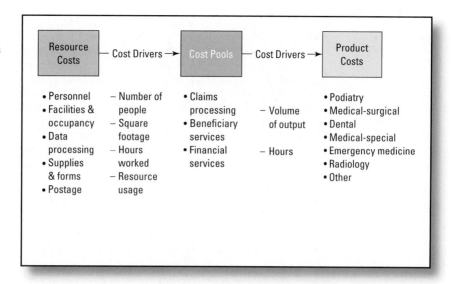

All indirect costs are commonly combined into a single cost pool called **overhead** or, in a manufacturing firm, **factory overhead.**

**Prime costs**
refer to direct materials and direct labor that are combined into a single amount.

**Conversion cost**
refers to direct labor and overhead combined into a single amount.

All indirect costs—for indirect materials, indirect labor, and other indirect items—are commonly combined into a cost pool called **overhead.** In a manufacturing firm, it is called **factory overhead.**

The three types of costs—direct materials, direct labor, and overhead—are sometimes combined for simplicity and convenience. Direct materials and direct labor are sometimes considered together and called **prime costs.** Similarly, direct labor and overhead are often combined into a single amount called **conversion cost.** The labor component of total manufacturing costs for many firms that have highly automated operations is relatively low, and these firms often choose to place their strategic focus on materials and facilities/overhead costs by combining labor costs with overhead.

## Cost Drivers and Cost Behavior

Cost drivers provide two important roles for the management accountant: (1) enabling the assignment of costs to cost objects, as we saw in the above discussion and in Exhibits 3.1 and 3.2, and (2) explaining cost behavior: how total costs change as the cost driver changes. Generally, an increase in a cost driver will cause an increase in total cost. Occasionally, the relationship is inverse; for example, assume the cost driver is degree of temperature, then in the colder times of the year, increases in this cost driver will decrease total heating cost. Cost drivers can be used to provide both the cost assignment and cost behavior roles at the same time. In the remainder of this section, we focus on the cost behavior role of cost drivers.

Most firms, especially those following the cost leadership strategy, use cost management to maintain or improve their competitive position. Cost management requires a good understanding of how the total cost of a cost object changes as the cost drivers change. The four types of cost drivers are activity-based, volume-based, structural, and executional. Activity-based cost drivers are developed at a detailed level of operations and are associated with a given manufacturing activity (or activity in providing a service), such as machine setup, product inspection, materials handling, or packaging. In contrast, volume-based cost drivers are developed at an aggregate level, such as an output level for the number of units produced. Structural and executional cost drivers involve strategic and operational decisions that affect the relationship between these cost drivers and total cost.

## Activity-Based Cost Drivers

Activity-based cost drivers are identified by using activity analysis—a detailed description of the specific activities performed in the firm's operations. The activity analysis includes each step in manufacturing the product or in providing the service. For each activity, a cost driver is determined to explain how the costs incurred for that activity change. Example activities and cost drivers for a bank are illustrated in Exhibit 3.4. The total cost to the bank is affected by changes in the cost drivers for each activity.

**EXHIBIT 3.4**
**Bank Activities and Cost Drivers**

| Activity | Cost Drivers |
|---|---|
| Provide ATM service | Number of ATM transactions; number of customers |
| Provide cashier service | Number of customers |
| Open and close customer accounts | Number of accounts opened or closed |
| Advise customers on banking services | Number of customers |
| Prepare applications for new loans | Number of loan applications prepared |
| Process loan applications | Number of loan applications processed |
| Prepare approved loans and disburse funds | Number of loans approved |
| Mail customer statements | Number of accounts by customer type and size |

The detailed description of the firm's activities helps the firm achieve its strategic objectives by enabling it to develop more accurate costs for its products and services. The activity analysis also helps improve operational and management control in the firm since performance at the detailed level can be monitored and evaluated, for example, by (1) identifying which activities are contributing value to the customer and which are not and (2) focusing attention on those activities that are most costly or that differ from expectations. Activity-based costing and activity-based management are explained in Chapter 5.

## Volume-Based Cost Drivers

Many types of costs are volume-based, that is, the cost driver is the amount produced or quantity of service provided. Management accountants commonly call this volume, or volume of output, or simply output. Good examples of volume-based costs are direct materials cost and direct labor cost—these costs increase with each unit of the volume of output. Note that the three cost drivers—the output of complete units, the quantity (in pounds, etc.) of direct materials, and the hours of direct labor—are all volume-based cost drivers and are proportional to each other.

The total of a volume-based cost increases at the rate of increase in volume, and over short ranges of output, the relationship is approximately linear. Over a very broad range of output, say, from output of zero up to plant capacity and beyond, the relationship between volume of output and cost tends to be nonlinear. As illustrated in Exhibit 3.5, at low values for the cost driver, costs increase at a decreasing rate, due in part to factors such as more efficient use of resources and higher productivity through learning. The pattern of increasing costs at a decreasing rate is often referred to as *increasing marginal productivity*, which means that the inputs are used more productively or more efficiently as manufacturing output increases.

At higher levels of the cost driver, costs begin to increase at an increasing rate, due in part to inefficiency associated with operating nearer the limit of capacity; the less efficient resources are now being used, overtime may be required, and so on. This cost behavior in the higher levels of the cost driver is said to satisfy the *law of diminishing marginal productivity*.

**EXHIBIT 3.5**
**Total Cost over a Wide Range of Output**

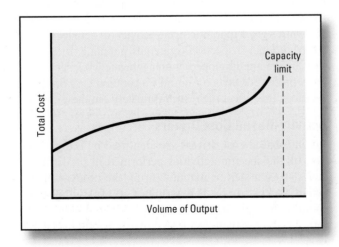

**EXHIBIT 3.6** Total Cost and the Relevant Range

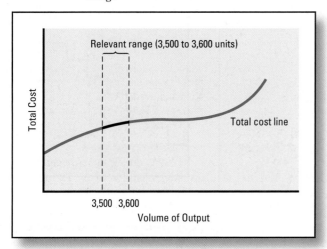

**EXHIBIT 3.7** Linear Approximation for Actual Cost Behavior, within the Relevant Range

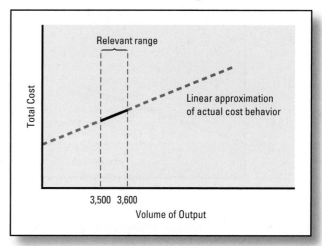

The nonlinear cost relationships depicted in Exhibit 3.5 present some difficulties in estimating costs and in calculating total costs since relatively simple, linear relationships cannot be used. Fortunately, we are often interested in only a relatively small range of activity for the cost driver. For example, we might know in a certain instance that the *volume-based* cost driver will fall somewhere between 3,500 and 3,600 units of product output. We observe that within this range, the total cost curve is approximately linear. The range of the cost driver in which the actual value of the cost driver is expected to fall and for which the relationship to total cost is assumed to be approximately linear is called the **relevant range.**

This simplification process is illustrated in Exhibit 3.6 and Exhibit 3.7. Exhibit 3.6 shows the curved actual total cost line and the relevant range of 3,500 to 3,600 units; Exhibit 3.7 shows the linear approximation of actual total cost; within the relevant range, the behavior of total cost approximates that shown in Exhibit 3.6. Note that the cost line above 3,600 and below 3,500 in Exhibit 3.7 is a dotted line to indicate that this portion of the line is not used to approximate total cost because it is outside the relevant range. Chapter 8 explains the methods management accountants use for estimating total cost.

### Fixed and Variable Costs

Total cost is made up of variable costs and fixed costs. **Variable cost** is the change in total cost associated with each change in the quantity of the cost driver. The cost driver can be activity-based or volume-based, though typically management accountants in practice use the term *variable costs* in connection with volume-based cost drivers. Common examples of variable costs are costs of direct materials and direct labor. In contrast, **fixed cost** is that portion of the total cost that does not change with the volume of output within the relevant range. *Total* fixed costs and *unit* variable costs are expected to remain approximately constant within the relevant range. Fixed cost is illustrated as the horizontal dashed line at $3,000 in Exhibit 3.8. Variable cost is $1 per unit, total cost is the upward-sloping line, and total variable cost is the difference between total cost and fixed cost. Total cost of $6,500 at 3,500 units is made up of fixed cost ($3,000) plus total variable cost (3,500 × $1 = $3,500); similarly, total cost at 3,600 units is $6,600 ($3,000 fixed cost plus 3,600 × $1 = $3,600 variable cost).

Fixed costs include many indirect costs, especially facility costs (depreciation or rent, insurance, taxes on the plant building), production supervisors' salaries, and other manufacturing support costs that do not change with the number of units produced. However, some indirect costs that are not traceable to a cost object are nevertheless variable since they change

**Relevant range**
is the range of the cost driver in which the actual value of the cost driver is expected to fall and for which the relationship to total cost is assumed to be approximately linear.

**Variable cost**
is the change in total cost associated with each change in the quantity of the cost driver.

**Fixed cost**
is the portion of the total cost that does not change with a change in the quantity of output within the relevant range.

**EXHIBIT 3.8**   **Total Cost, Total Variable Cost, and Fixed Cost**

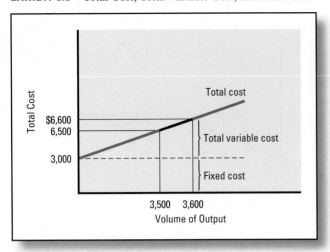

**EXHIBIT 3.9**   **A Step Cost**

**Mixed cost**
is the term used to refer to
total cost when total cost
includes both variable and
fixed cost components.

with the number of units produced. An example is lubricant for machines. The term **mixed cost** is used to refer to total cost that includes costs for both variable and fixed components as illustrated.

The determination of whether a cost is variable depends on the nature of the cost object. In manufacturing firms, the cost object is typically the product. In service firms, however, the cost object is often difficult to define because the service can have a number of qualitative as well as quantitative dimensions. Let's develop cost objects for one type of service firm, a hospital, which could use a number of measures of output including the number of patients served, the number successfully treated, and so on. However, a common approach in hospitals is to use the number of patient-days since this measure most closely matches the way the hospital incurs costs.

It has sometimes been said that all costs are variable in the long run; that is, with enough time, any cost can be changed. While it is true that many fixed costs do change over time (for example, the cost of rent might increase from year to year), that does not mean these costs are variable. A variable cost is a cost for which *total costs change with changes in the volume of output.* Fixed costs are defined for a period of time rather than in relationship to volume of output, and it is assumed that fixed costs will not change during this period of time which is usually taken to be a year. For example, rent is a fixed cost that is normally the same amount *per year* and does not vary with volume. Strategically, especially for a cost leader type of firm, the important point is that both fixed and variable costs can be managed, but variable costs are managed in the very short term, as each unit is produced, while fixed costs are managed over a period of time. Some fixed costs cannot be changed for a relatively long period of time (for example, depreciation on the plant building) while others can be changed more quickly (for example, equipment with a one-year lease).

To summarize, when we want to understand the cost behavior of a certain cost object, we have to have clearly in mind the following three questions: (1) what is the cost driver (or cost drivers if there are two or more) for this cost object? (2) what is the relevant range of the cost driver for which we are developing the cost estimate? and (3) what time horizon are we using for fixed costs (usually one year is used)?

### *Step Costs*

A cost is said to be a **step cost**
when it varies with the cost
driver but in steps.

A cost is said to be a **step cost** when it varies with the cost driver but does so in steps (Exhibit 3.9). Step costs are characteristic of certain clerical tasks, such as order filling and claims processing. For example, if a warehouse clerk can fill 100 orders in a day, 10 clerks will be needed to process approximately 1,000 orders; as demand exceeds 1,000 orders, an eleventh clerk must be added. The steps correspond to specific levels of the cost driver for

**EXHIBIT 3.10**
**Illustration of Fixed Cost and Variable Cost per Unit**

|  | Fixed Cost | | Variable Cost | |
|---|---|---|---|---|
| Units of output | 10,000 | 20,000 | 10,000 | 20,000 |
| Per unit | $10 | $5 | $8 | $8 |
| Total | $100,000 | $100,000 | $80,000 | $160,000 |

which an additional clerk is required; in effect, each step corresponds to one additional clerk. The steps will be relatively narrow if clerks are added for relatively small increases in the cost driver; the steps will be wider for large increases.

### Unit Cost

**Unit cost** (or **average cost**) is the total manufacturing cost (materials, labor, and overhead) divided by the number of units of output.

**Unit cost** (or **average cost**) is the total manufacturing cost (materials, labor, and overhead) divided by the number of units of output. It is a useful concept in setting prices and in evaluating product profitability, but it can be subject to some misleading interpretations. To properly interpret unit cost, we must distinguish *unit variable* costs, which do not change as output changes, from *unit fixed costs,* which do change as output changes. See Exhibit 3.10. For example, an automobile driver's cost per mile is likely lower for a person who drives a car 20,000 miles/year than it is for a person who drives a car only 5,000 miles/year because the fixed costs for the person driving 20,000 miles are spread over more miles. An increase in volume does not increase total cost by the amount of the increase in volume multiplied by total unit cost; total cost increases by the increase in volume multiplied by the unit variable cost. These relationships are illustrated graphically in Exhibit 3.11. The management accountant is careful in using the term *average cost* because of the potential for misleading interpretations.

### Capacity vs. Usage of Costs

It is important to distinguish between costs that provide capacity for operations (e.g., plant building and equipment) and costs that are consumed during operations (e.g., direct materials and labor). The former are fixed costs, while the latter are variable costs. In practice, the management accountant uses care in making the distinctions because sometimes capacity-type costs are treated as variable costs. For example, compare the cost of two types of direct labor employees who work in the assembly of a product: one is a salaried worker who is paid by the month and another is a worker paid by the hour. The former is a capacity (fixed) cost, while the latter is a variable cost. While both workers might be considered direct labor because they work in product assembly, if volume of output falls and the salaried worker is idle, the total cost of labor does not change, while the total cost of labor would fall for a wage worker who has fewer hours. On the other hand, effective managers try to schedule production and labor carefully by using part-time help and by other means, so that no workers are idle; then, all assembly work can be considered a direct and

**EXHIBIT 3.11**
**Average Variable Cost and Average Fixed Cost**

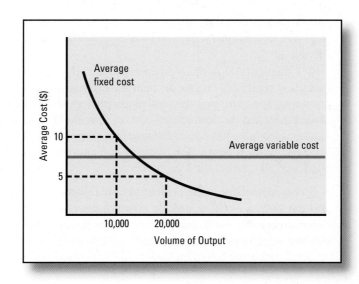

variable cost. When idle time is present, some management accountants measure the cost of the unused capacity. Note that the cost of unused capacity would potentially apply to many types of fixed costs.

## Structural and Executional Cost Drivers

Structural and executional cost drivers are used to facilitate strategic decision making. **Structural cost drivers** are strategic in nature because they involve decisions that have long-term effects on the firm's total costs. Here are four examples of structural decisions.

**Structural cost drivers** are strategic in nature and involve plans and decisions that have a long-term effect with regard to issues such as scale, experience, technology, and complexity.

1. Scale. Larger firms have lower overall costs as a result of economies of scale. For example, a retail firm such as Walmart or Target must determine how many new stores to open in a given year to achieve its strategic objectives and compete effectively as a retailer.

2. Experience. Firms having employees with greater manufacturing and sales experience will likely have lower development, manufacturing, and distribution costs. For example, a manufacturer such as Hewlett-Packard uses existing manufacturing methods as much as possible for new products to reduce the time and cost necessary for workers to become pro-ficient at manufacturing the new product.

3. Technology. New technologies can reduce design, manufacturing, distribution, and customer service costs significantly. For example, manufacturers such as Procter & Gamble use computer technology to monitor the quantities of their products that their customers (typically, large retailers) have on hand so that they can promptly restock these products as needed.

4. Complexity. How many different products does the firm have? As noted in the opening discussion regarding Procter & Gamble, firms with many products have higher costs of scheduling and managing the production process, as well as the upstream costs of product development and the downstream costs of distribution and service. In particular, the current economic recession has caused firms to trim their brand offerings; for example, in 2009 Kraft Foods dropped its South Beach entrees and announced that it would be pulling its Handi-Snacks puddings from the U.S. market.

Strategic analyses using structural cost drivers help the firm improve its competitive position. These analyses include value-chain analysis and activity-based management. Value-chain analysis can help the firm assess the long-term consequences of its current or planned commitment to a structural cost driver. For example, the growth in size and

The following data are provided by the U.S. Department of Agriculture (USDA) regarding the cost of soybean production in the U.S. Heartland (Minnesota, Iowa, South Dakota, Indiana, and Illinois and parts of Ohio, Missouri, Nebraska, and Kentucky) and the Mato Grosso region in western Brazil. The data are used to analyze the cost competitiveness of soybean production in the United States and Brazil.

**Required**

1. What can you learn from the information below about the cost competitiveness of the United States and Brazil in soybean production?
2. Critically evaluate the cost information.

**Source:** Data from U.S. Department of Agriculture (USDA), Economic Research Service (Refer to Comments on Cost Management in Action at the end of the chapter.)

| Cost per Acre and per Bushel of Soybeans | | |
|---|---|---|
| | U.S. Heartland | Brazil's Mato Grosso |
| Variable costs (per acre) | | |
| Seed | $ 19.77 | $ 11.23 |
| Fertilizers | 8.22 | 44.95 |
| Chemicals | 27.31 | 39.97 |
| Machinery | 20.19 | 18.22 |
| Labor | 1.29 | 5.58 |
| Other | 1.81 | 12.11 |
| Total variable costs | $ 78.59 | $132.06 |
| Fixed costs (per acre) | | |
| Equipment depreciation | $ 47.99 | $ 8.97 |
| Land costs (rental rate) | 87.96 | 5.84 |
| Taxes, insurance | 6.97 | .55 |
| Farm overhead | 13.40 | 14.65 |
| Total fixed costs | $156.32 | $ 30.01 |
| **Total production cost (per acre)** | **$234.91** | **$162.07** |
| Total cost per bushel | | |
| Average yield per acre | 46.00 | 41.65 |
| Variable costs | $ 1.71 | $ 3.17 |
| Fixed costs | 3.40 | .72 |
| **Total costs per bushel** | **$ 5.11** | **$ 3.89** |

capability of parts manufacturers for automakers should cause the automakers to reassess whether they should outsource the manufacture of certain parts that they are currently manufacturing. Activity-based management is covered in Chapter 5.

**Executional cost drivers** are factors the firm can manage in short-term, operational decision making to reduce costs. They include the following:

**Executional cost drivers**
are factors the firm can manage in the short term to reduce costs, such as workforce empowerment, design of the production process, and supplier relationships.

1. Workforce empowerment. Are the employees dedicated to continual improvement and quality? This workforce commitment will lower costs. Firms with strong employee relationships, such as Federal Express, can reduce operating costs significantly.

2. Design of the production process. Speeding up the flow of product through the firm can reduce costs. Innovators in manufacturing technology, such as Hewlett-Packard and General Electric, can reduce manufacturing costs significantly.

3. Supplier relationships. Can the cost, quality, or delivery of materials and purchased parts be improved to reduce overall costs? Walmart and Toyota, among other firms, maintain a low-cost advantage partially by agreements with their suppliers that they will provide products or parts that meet the companies' explicit requirements as to their quality, timeliness of delivery, and other features.

Plant managers study executional cost drivers to find ways to reduce costs. Such studies are done as a part of operational-level control, which is covered in Part Three.

## Cost Concepts for Product and Service Costing

**LO 3-3**

*Explain the cost concepts used in product and service costing.*

Accurate information about the cost of products and services is important in each management function: strategic management, planning and decision making, management and operational control, and financial statement preparation. Cost accounting systems differ significantly between firms that manufacture products and merchandising firms that resell those products. Merchandising firms include both retailers, which sell the final product to the consumer, and wholesalers, which distribute the product to retailers. Service firms often have little or no inventory, so their costing systems are relatively simple. Costing systems are introduced here and covered in detail in the remaining chapters of Part One. First, we have to define product costs.

### Product Costs and Period Costs

**Cost of goods sold**
is the cost of the product transferred to the income statement when inventory is sold.

**Product costs**
for a manufacturing firm include *only* the costs necessary to complete the product: direct materials, direct labor, and factory overhead.

Product inventory for both manufacturing and merchandising firms is treated as an asset on their balance sheets. As long as the inventory has market value, it is considered an asset until the inventory is sold; then the cost of the inventory is transferred to the income statement as **cost of goods sold**. It is helpful in understanding product costs for a manufacturer to consider the value chain. The value chain of a manufacturer begins with the upstream activities of design, product development, and new product testing and then moves to manufacturing, followed by the downstream activities of distribution, sales, and customer service. The costs of the upstream and downstream activities are *not* product costs.

**Product costs** for a manufacturing firm include *only* the costs necessary to complete the product at the manufacturing step in the value chain:

1. Direct materials. The materials used to manufacture the product, which become a physical part of it.
2. Direct labor. The labor used to manufacture the product.
3. Factory overhead. The indirect costs for materials, labor, and facilities used to support the manufacturing process.

Product costs for a merchandising firm include the cost to purchase the product plus the transportation costs paid by the retailer or wholesaler to get the product to the location from which it will be sold or distributed.

**Period costs**
are all nonproduct expenditures for managing the firm and selling the product.

All other costs for managing the firm and selling the product are not product costs. They are expensed in the period in which they are incurred; for that reason, they are also called **period costs**. Period costs (nonproduct costs) include the general, selling, and administrative costs that are necessary for the management of the company but are *not* involved directly or indirectly in the manufacturing process (or, for a retailer, in the purchase of the products for resale). Advertising costs, data processing costs, and executive and staff salaries are good examples of period costs. In a manufacturing or a merchandising firm, period costs are also sometimes referred to as *operating expenses* or *selling and administrative expenses*. In a service firm, these costs are often referred to as *operating expenses*. Exhibit 3.12 summarizes the previous sections with an illustration showing examples of variable and fixed, direct and indirect, and product and period costs for a furniture manufacturer.

### Manufacturing, Merchandising, and Service Costing

**LO 3-4**

*Demonstrate how costs flow through the accounts, and prepare an income statement for both a manufacturing and a merchandising company.*

The cost flows in manufacturing, retail, and service firms are illustrated in Exhibits 3.13, 3.14, 3.15A, and 3.15B. The left-hand side of Exhibit 3.13 presents a graphic representation of the flow of costs for a manufacturing company. The first step of the manufacturing process is to purchase materials. The second step involves adding the three cost elements—materials used, labor, and overhead—to work-in-process. In the third step, as production is completed, the production costs that have been accumulating in the Work-in-Process account are transferred to the Finished Goods Inventory account and from there to the Cost of Goods Sold account when the products are sold.

In the merchandising company, shown on the right-hand side of Exhibit 3.13, the process is somewhat simpler. The merchandising company purchases merchandise and places

**EXHIBIT 3.12**
**Furniture Manufacturing Costs: Variable/Fixed, Direct/Indirect, and Product/Period Costs**

The following case illustration of a furniture manufacturer is used to provide examples of costs for each cost concept: variable/fixed, direct/indirect, and product/period. The furniture manufacturer has organized its manufacturing by product line: dining table sets, upholstered chairs, sofas, bedroom furniture, end tables, and outdoor furniture. Each product line has its own manufacturing team although much of the equipment in the plant is shared among product lines (e.g., multiple product lines use the table saws). The company owns its retail sales outlets, each of which offers all of the firm's products. The cost object in this illustration is the *product line* for dining table sets (*not* each dining set produced).

**Variable/Fixed, Direct/Indirect, and Product/Period Costs for the Product Line, Dining Table Sets**

|  | Product Cost | | Period (Nonproduct) Cost |
|---|---|---|---|
|  | **Direct** | **Indirect** |  |
| **Variable** | Wood and fabric | Power for table saws | Sales commissions |
| **Fixed** | Salary of manufacturing supervisor for dining table sets product line | Depreciation on table saws used for all product lines | Insurance and depreciation on company-owned sales outlets |

Note: This illustration is based on the *cost object,* the product line for dining table *sets.* The examples would not change if we had chosen instead to have the cost object be *each set* manufactured except that the manufacturing supervisor's salary would no longer be a direct fixed product cost. It would become an *indirect* fixed product cost because the salary can be traced to the product line but not to each table set manufactured.

the merchandise in the Product Inventory account. When sold, it is transferred to the Cost of Goods Sold account. The merchandising and manufacturing companies in Exhibit 3.13 are shown side by side to emphasize the difference: The merchandising company purchases inventory but the manufacturing company manufactures inventory using materials, labor, and overhead.

**EXHIBIT 3.13**
**Cost Flows in Manufacturing and Merchandising Firms**

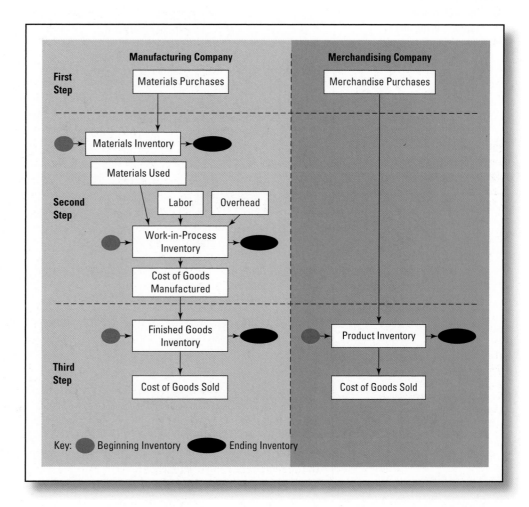

**Materials Inventory**
is the cost of the supply of materials used in the manufacturing process or to provide the service.

**Work-in-Process Inventory**
contains all costs put into the manufacture of products that are started but not complete at the financial statement date.

**Finished Goods Inventory**
is the cost of goods that are ready for sale.

Manufacturing companies use three inventory accounts: (1) **Materials Inventory,** which contains the cost of the supply of materials to be used in the manufacturing process; (2) **Work-in-Process Inventory,** which contains all costs put into the manufacture of products that are started but not complete at the financial statement date; and (3) **Finished Goods Inventory,** which holds the cost of goods that are ready for sale. Each account has its own beginning and ending inventory balance.

An inventory formula relates the inventory accounts, as follows:

Beginning inventory + Cost added = Cost transferred out + Ending inventory

The terms *cost added* and *cost transferred out* have different meanings, depending on which inventory account is being considered:

| Inventory Account | Cost Added | Cost Transferred Out |
|---|---|---|
| Materials Inventory | Purchases of materials | Cost of materials used in production |
| Work-in-Process Inventory | 1. Cost of materials used<br>2. Labor cost<br>3. Overhead cost | Cost of goods manufactured |
| Finished Goods Inventory | Costs of goods manufactured | Cost of goods sold |

The inventory formula is a useful concept to show how materials, labor, and overhead costs flow into Work-in-Process Inventory, then into Finished Goods Inventory, and finally into Cost of Goods Sold. Exhibit 3.14 illustrates the effects of the cost flows on the accounts

**EXHIBIT 3.14**
**Account Relationships for Manufacturing and Merchandising Companies**

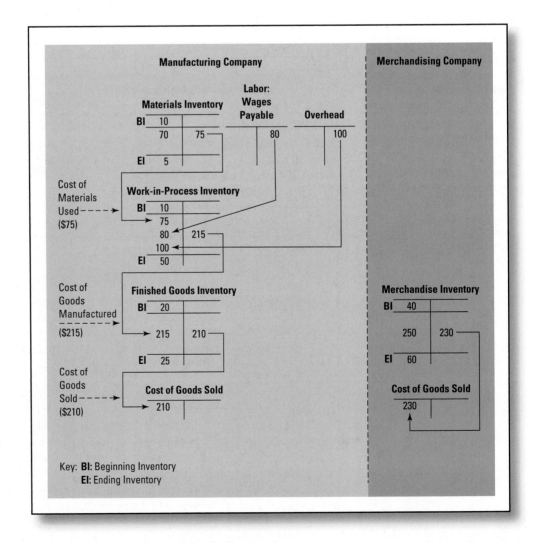

involved when the manufacturing company converts materials into finished products and then sells them and when the merchandising company sells merchandise inventory.

The illustration in Exhibit 3.14 shows the accounts for a manufacturing company that begins the period with $10 in Materials Inventory, $10 in Work-in-Process Inventory, and $20 in Finished Goods Inventory. During the period, it purchases $70 of materials, uses $75 of materials and $80 of direct labor, and spends $100 for factory overhead. The sum of materials used, labor, and overhead ($255 = $75 + $80 + $100) is called **total manufacturing cost** for the period. Also during the period, $215 of goods are completed and transferred from the Work-in-Process Inventory account to the Finished Goods Inventory account, and $210 of goods are sold. These events leave ending inventories of $5 in the Materials account, $50 in the Work-in-Process account, and $25 in the Finished Goods account. The merchandising company purchased merchandise of $250 and had sales of $230, and its Merchandise Inventory account increases from $40 to $60.

Exhibit 3.15A shows how the accounting relationships are represented in the income statements for the two types of companies. Note that the manufacturing company requires a two-part calculation for cost of goods sold: the first part combines the cost flows affecting the Work-in-Process Inventory account to determine the amount of **cost of goods manufactured,** that is, the cost of the goods finished and transferred out of Work-in-Process during this period. The second part combines the cost flows for the Finished Goods Inventory account to determine the amount of the cost of the goods sold and operating income, assuming $50 of selling expense for the manufacturing firm and $40 of operating expense for the merchandising firm. Operating expenses for a merchandising company include all the nonproduct costs—facilities cost, advertising, staffing, and so on.

Exhibit 3.15B shows the relatively simple income statement for a service firm with $300 in sales, $10 in materials costs, $90 in labor costs, and $100 in other operating expenses for an operating income of $100. Exhibit 3.15 provides an introduction to cost flows in the three types of firms. The process is shown in greater detail in Chapter 4.

## Attributes of Cost Information

### *Accuracy*

The experienced decision maker does not use accounting information without considering the potential for inaccuracy. Inaccurate data can mislead, resulting in potentially costly mistakes. A primary way to ensure accurate data for decision making is to design and monitor an effective system of internal accounting controls. The system of **internal accounting controls** is a set of policies and procedures that restrict and guide activities in the processing of financial data with the objective of preventing or detecting errors and fraud. The emphasis on effective internal controls has increased significantly in recent years in response to Securities and Exchange Commission (SEC) requirements imposed by the Sarbanes-Oxley Act of 2002.

### *Timeliness*

Cost management information must be available to the decision maker in a timely manner to facilitate effective decision making. The cost of delay can be significant in many decisions, such as in filling rush orders that may be lost if the necessary information is not timely. The cost of identifying quality defects *early* in a manufacturing process can be far less than the cost of materials and labor wasted when a defect is detected later in the process.

### *Cost and Value of Cost Information*

Thinking of cost management information as having a certain cost and value emphasizes that the management accountant is an information specialist, very much like other financial professionals, such as tax advisers, financial planners, and consultants. The management accountant provides an information service that has both a preparation cost and a value to the user. The preparation costs for cost management information should be controlled as should any other service provided within the firm. These preparation costs are likely influenced by the desired accuracy, timeliness, and level of aggregation; when increased accuracy, timeliness, and detail are desired, the preparation costs are higher.

---

**Total manufacturing cost** is the sum of materials used, labor, and overhead for the period.

**Cost of goods manufactured** is the cost of goods finished and transferred out of the Work-in-Process Inventory account this period.

The system of **internal accounting controls** is a set of policies and procedures that restrict and guide activities in the processing of financial data with the objective of preventing or detecting errors and fraudulent acts.

**EXHIBIT 3.15A**   **Income Statements for Manufacturing and Merchandising Companies**

### MANUFACTURING, INC.
**Statement of Cost of Goods Manufactured**
**For the Year Ended December 31, 2013**

(No need for a Cost of Goods Manufactured Statement for Merchandising, Inc.)

| | | |
|---|---|---|
| Direct Materials | | |
| Beginning Inventory | $ 10 | |
| Purchases | 70 | |
| Direct Materials Available | 80 | |
| Less: Ending Direct Materials Inventory | 5 | |
| Direct Materials Used | | $ 75 |
| Direct Labor | | 80 |
| Factory Overhead | | 100 |
| Total Manufacturing Cost | | 255 |
| Add: Beginning Work-in-Process Inventory | | 10 |
| Total Manufacturing Cost to Account for | | 265 |
| Less: Ending Work-in-Process Inventory | | 50 |
| Cost of Goods Manufactured | | $215 |

### MANUFACTURING, INC.
**Income Statement For the Year Ended December 31, 2013**

| | | |
|---|---|---|
| Sales | | $300 |
| Cost of Goods Sold | | |
| Beginning Finished Goods Inventory | $ 20 | |
| Cost of Goods Manufactured | 215 | |
| Cost of Goods Available for Sale | 235 | |
| Less: Ending Finished Goods Inventory | 25 | 210 |
| Gross Margin | | 90 |
| Selling and Administrative Expenses | | 50 |
| Operating Income | | $ 40 |

### MERCHANDISING, INC.
**Income Statement For the Year Ended December 31, 2013**

| | | |
|---|---|---|
| Sales | | $300 |
| Cost of Goods Sold | | |
| Beginning Finished Goods Inventory | $ 40 | |
| Purchases | 250 | |
| Cost of Goods Available for Sale | 290 | |
| Less: Ending Finished Goods Inventory | 60 | 230 |
| Gross Margin | | $ 70 |
| Operating Expenses | | 40 |
| Operating Income | | $ 30 |

**EXHIBIT 3.15B**
**Income Statement for**
**a Service Firm**

### SERVICE, INC.
**Income Statement**
**For the Year Ended December 31, 2013**

| | | |
|---|---|---|
| Sales | | $300 |
| Operating Expenses | | |
| Materials | $ 10 | |
| Labor | 90 | |
| Other Operating Expenses | 100 | 200 |
| Operating Income | | $100 |

The **perpetual inventory system** updates the Finished Goods Inventory account for each sales transaction.

The **periodic inventory system** involves a count of inventory at the end of each accounting period to determine the ending balance in inventory.

## Periodic and Perpetual Inventory Systems

Most large retailers and manufacturers use a point-of-sale or transaction-based computer system for recording sales and changes in inventory. In these systems each sale updates the amount in the inventory account, so that the inventory balance is always current. This is called the **perpetual inventory system**. Another method, called the **periodic inventory system,** involves a count of inventory at the end of each accounting period to determine the ending balance in inventory. Often a company will use both methods. The perpetual system keeps the accounts current and the periodic system detects the amount of lost, stolen, obsolete, or damaged inventory that must be written off at the end of the accounting period. As our focus in this text is on the flow of costs, we will assume throughout that the ending inventory value is given; as such, it is not necessary to know whether the system is a periodic or perpetual system.

## Summary

There are several important concepts for the management accountant, which Chapter 3 presents in two groups: (1) cost objects, cost drivers, cost pools, and cost assignment and (2) product and service costing for the preparation of financial statements.

The first group of concepts includes the four types of cost drivers: activity-based, volume-based, structural, and executional. Activity-based cost drivers are at the detail level of operations: equipment setup, materials handling, and clerical or other tasks. In contrast, volume-based cost drivers are at the aggregate level: usually the number of units produced. Structural cost drivers involve plans and decisions having long-term effects; executional cost drivers have short-term effects. The most important volume-based concepts are variable costs, which change according to a change in the level of output, and fixed costs, which do not. Direct costs are defined as costs that can be traced directly to a cost object in contrast to indirect costs, which cannot.

The important concepts in product costing are product costs, which are the costs of direct materials, direct labor, and indirect manufacturing (called *overhead*) required for the product and production process. Nonproduct costs (also called *period costs*) are the selling, administrative, and other costs not involved in manufacturing. The inventory formula is used to determine the cost of materials used in production, the cost of goods manufactured, and the cost of goods sold for a given period.

## Key Terms

| | | |
|---|---|---|
| allocation bases, *69* | direct materials cost, *70* | periodic inventory system, *82* |
| average cost, *75* | executional cost drivers, *77* | perpetual inventory |
| conversion cost, *71* | factory overhead, *71* | system, *82* |
| cost, *68* | Finished Goods Inventory, *80* | prime costs, *71* |
| cost allocation, *69* | fixed cost, *73* | product costs, *78* |
| cost assignment, *68* | indirect cost, *68* | relevant range, *73* |
| cost driver, *68* | indirect labor cost, *70* | step cost, *74* |
| cost object, *68* | indirect materials cost, *70* | structural cost drivers, *76* |
| cost of goods manufactured, *81* | internal accounting controls, *81* | total manufacturing cost, *81* |
| cost of goods sold, *78* | Materials Inventory, *80* | unit cost, *75* |
| cost pools, *68* | mixed cost, *74* | value stream, *68* |
| direct cost, *68* | overhead, *71* | variable cost, *73* |
| direct labor cost, *70* | period costs, *78* | Work-in-Process Inventory, *80* |

## Comments on Cost Management in Action

### Cost per Bushel of Soybeans: United States and Brazil

The data are taken from an October 2001 Report of the Economic Research Service of the U.S. Department of Agriculture, based on 1998–1999 data. The report can be viewed at the following website: **http://www.ers.usda.gov/Briefing/SoybeansOilcrops/pdf/SBProdExpCompOCS2001.pdf**

1. Of particular value here is that the report distinguishes variable and fixed costs, which is not common in reports of this type. The distinction gives the reader an opportunity to better understand how cost production costs behave in the two countries. A wide number of observations are possible. In particular, we see the relatively high cost of land and equipment in the United States, partly balanced by relatively high labor and fertilizer and chemical costs in Brazil. Is the high labor cost a result of a substitution of labor for equipment or does it represent poorly trained or supervised workers? Similarly, does the high cost of chemicals and fertilizer in Brazil indicate that U.S. farmers have superior land use practices, or are the fertilizers and chemicals more expensive in Brazil for other reasons?

   While the figures clearly show that Brazil has a total cost advantage over the United States in the production of soybeans, other nonproduction, downstream costs are likely to be higher in

Brazil—transportation (including fuel costs), marketing, and sales—because of its more remote location from world markets. Also, the United States has a cost advantage in variable costs, showing clearly the importance of the cost of land and farm equipment in the United States.

Since the significance of the data is for understanding international competitiveness in global soybean production, it is also important to note that the above analysis does not include data on fluctuations in currency exchange rates, import restrictions, government subsidies, taxes, and other factors that are critical in global trade (see, for example, a discussion of Brazil's exchange rate fluctuations in Exercise 2-30 at the end of Chapter 2). Some of the strongest controversies among the World Trade Organization (WTO) countries at this time are the restrictions and subsidies involved in agricultural trade.

2. A number of potential questions arise about the way the data have been collected and presented. Here are some ideas to start with. First, what about the size of the farm: should this affect the fixed cost-per-acre calculations, since fixed costs are driven in part by the number of acres farmed but also by the fact that certain pieces of equipment are necessary for a farm of any size? Farm equipment might be more of a step cost than a fixed cost. If this is the case, the relatively low equipment cost per acre might simply be due to the fact that farm sizes are larger in Brazil. Are the fixed costs computed annually or monthly? And if land can be rented by the acre, is it not a variable cost?

## Self-Study Problem
(For solution, please turn to the end of the chapter.)

The following data pertain to Spartan Products Company:

| | |
|---|---:|
| Sales revenue | $1,000,000 |
| Direct materials inventory, Jan. 1, 2013 | 20,000 |
| Direct labor—wages | 350,000 |
| Depreciation expense—plant and equipment | 80,000 |
| Indirect labor—wages | 5,000 |
| Heat, light, and power—plant | 12,000 |
| Supervisor's salary—plant | 40,000 |
| Finished goods inventory, Jan. 1, 2013 | 35,000 |
| Work-in-process inventory, Dec. 31, 2013 | 25,000 |
| Supplies—administrative office | 6,000 |
| Property taxes—plant | 13,000 |
| Finished goods inventory, Dec. 31, 2013 | 40,000 |
| Direct materials inventory, Dec. 31, 2013 | 30,000 |
| Sales representatives' salaries | 190,000 |
| Work-in-process inventory, Jan. 1, 2013 | 35,000 |
| Direct materials purchases | 100,000 |
| Supplies—plant | 4,000 |
| Depreciation—administrative office | 30,000 |

**Required**  Prepare a statement of cost of goods manufactured and an income statement for Spartan Products Company for the year ended December 31, 2013, similar to the one in Exhibit 3.15A.

*Please visit* **http://www.mhhe.com/blocher6e** *to access a narrated, animated tutorial for solving this problem.*

## Questions

3-1   What is the difference between cost allocation and cost assignment?

3-2   Distinguish between direct and indirect costs and give several examples of each.

3-3   Are all direct costs variable? Explain.

3-4   Are all fixed costs indirect? Explain.

3-5   Define *cost driver.*

3-6   What is the difference between variable and fixed costs?

3-7   Explain step costs and give an example.

3-8   Define *relevant range* and explain its use.

3-9   What is a conversion cost? What are prime costs?

3-10  Why might the term *average cost* be misleading?

3-11  How do total variable costs, total fixed costs, average variable costs, and average fixed costs react to changes in the cost driver?

3-12  What does the term *unit cost* mean?

3-13  Distinguish between product costs and period costs.

3-14  Explain the difference between cost of goods sold and cost of goods manufactured.

3-15  What are the three types of inventory in a manufacturing firm?

3-16  Cost management information should be timely and accurate. Which of these attributes is most important? Why?

3-17  Provide an example of an executional cost driver.

3-18  Provide an example of a structural cost driver.

3-19  Provide an example of an indirect materials cost.

3-20  Provide an example of an indirect labor cost.

## Brief Exercises

3-21  Identify what are likely to be variable costs for an airline such as Southwest Airlines. Also, what are the fixed costs likely to be?

3-22  Identify what are likely to be variable costs for a discount retailer such as Walmart. Also, what are the fixed costs likely to be?

3-23  Identify what are likely to be variable costs for a movie theater. Also, what are the fixed costs likely to be?

3-24  Identify what are likely to be variable costs for a brewery such as Molson Coors or Heineken. Also, what are the fixed costs likely to be?

3-25  Identify what variable costs are likely to be for a company that provides personal trainers. The personal trainers are paid a small salary plus a commission for each lesson. Also, what are the company's fixed costs?

3-26  Womble, Inc. has beginning inventory of $200 and an ending inventory of $400 for a given period in which it purchased $13,400 of materials. What is the dollar amount of materials used in this period?

3-27  Jordan Sports, Inc. has labor costs and overhead totaling $2.6 million during a given period. The company purchased $10.5 million of materials during the period and used $10 million of this amount. What is the amount of total manufacturing cost for the period?

3-28  Lucas Diving Supplies Company, in its first year of business, had labor costs of $66,000, overhead costs of $98,000, materials purchases of $22,000, and ending materials and work-in-process inventories of $1,000 and $2,000, respectively. What is the amount of cost of goods manufactured in the first year of operations?

3-29  If a merchandising company has a beginning finished goods inventory of $400,000 and a finished goods ending inventory of $200,000, and the company purchased $1,600,000 of inventory during the month, what is the company's cost of goods sold?

3-30  The Walden Manufacturing Corp. has interest expense of $4,000, factory supplies of $1,000, indirect labor of $6,000, direct materials of $16,000, advertising expense of $2,500, office expense of $14,000, and direct labor of $20,000. What is the total period cost?

## Exercises

[LO 3-1]   3-31  **Fares and Fees in the Airline Industry**   Navigating the various websites for low fares, avoiding fees for checked bags and priority seating, and finding the right flight schedule can be a real challenge for the average airline passenger. The complexity of options and sources for purchasing a ticket have expanded significantly in recent years. And the outlook for the future is for more complexity, as new search sites (Google, Hipmunk, etc.) become available and some airlines seek more control over where and how tickets on their flights are purchased. According to Forrester Research, an independent research company, the airlines want passengers to buy tickets based on value and not on low prices. They do not want passengers to comparison shop. For example, American Airlines recently announced that it wanted to deliver fare information directly to customers and to bypass search systems such as Expedia or Travelocity.

**Required**

1. Explain why you think competition in the airline industry is a cost leadership or a differentiated type of competition.

2. Give an example or two of how you think the complexity of fares and fees in the airline industry affects the sales and costs of the airlines.

[LO 3-1]    3-32    **Complexity of Operations and the Effect on Cost**    In the mid-1990s, a large consumer goods manufacturer moved its customer-based department and specialty stores to mass merchandising in a variety of retail stores, large and small. The strategic change required it to increase significantly the complexity of its operations—the number of products, prices, discounts, patterns, colors, and sizes. After noticing the firm's expense beginning to rise, the company hired a consultant to study the firm's cost structure. The findings:

- As many as 10 different vendors provided certain purchased items.
- Of the firm's customers after the strategic shift, 98% were responsible for only 7% of total sales volume.
- The wide variety of prices and discounts and promotional programs added complexity to the accounts receivable collection process because of increased disputes over pricing and customer balances.
- Seventy-five percent of the company sales involved products with five or more color combinations.
- Customer demands for fast delivery of new orders had caused a shift in manufacturing to smaller batch sizes and more frequent equipment setups. Thus, total setup-related costs increased.

**Required**    What would you advise the company to do?

[LO 3-2, 3-3]    3-33    **Classification of Costs**    The following are the costs incurred by a printing company.

1. Print machine setup costs
2. Cost of complexity; the number and variety of products
3. Training costs for new staff
4. Ink
5. Customer service costs
6. Paper
7. Redesign of the print process to improve efficiency
8. Machine operation labor
9. Order taking
10. Purchasing and stocking paper and other supplies

**Required**
1. Identify the above costs as (a) activity-based costs, (b) volume-based costs, (c) structural costs, or (d) executional costs.
2. Identify each cost as either a product cost or a period cost.
3. Identify which, if any, of these costs has a potential harmful environmental impact.

[LO 3-2, 3-3]    3-34    **Classification of Costs**    The following costs were taken from the accounting records of the Barnwell Manufacturing Company:

1. State income taxes
2. Insurance on the manufacturing facilities
3. Supplies used in manufacturing
4. Wages for employees in the assembly department
5. Wages for employees who deliver the product
6. Interest on notes payable
7. Materials used in the production process
8. Rent for the sales outlet in Sacramento
9. Electricity for manufacturing equipment
10. Depreciation expense on delivery trucks
11. Wages for the sales staff
12. Factory supervisors' salaries
13. Company president's salary
14. Advertising expense

**Required**    Classify each item as either a product cost or a period cost. Also, classify all product costs as direct or indirect, assuming that the cost object is each unit of product manufactured.

[LO 3-2, 3-3]  3-35  **Classification of Costs**  Following is a list of costs from Oakland Company, a furniture manufacturer:

1. Wood used in chairs
2. Salaries of inspectors
3. Lubricant used in machinery
4. Factory rent
5. Wages of assembly workers
6. Factory workers' compensation insurance
7. Sandpaper
8. Fabric used for upholstery
9. Property taxes on manufacturing plant
10. Depreciation on machinery

**Required**  Classify each cost as direct or indirect assuming that the cost object is each item manufactured. Also indicate whether each cost is a variable or fixed cost.

[LO 3-2]  3-36  **Classification of Costs**  The following is a list of costs from the accounting records of Sunshine Pool Management, Inc. Each of Sunshine's 77 customers is a swim club. Sunshine maintains each customer's pool by providing lifeguards, supplies, cleaning, and repairs.

1. Lifesaving supplies
2. Salaries of Sunshine's managers
3. Pool chemicals
4. Sunshine's office rental expense
5. Wages of lifeguards
6. Workers' compensation insurance
7. Training for lifeguards
8. pH testing supplies
9. Office expense, including bookkeeping and clerical
10. Depreciation on cleaning and testing equipment

**Required**  Classify each item as direct or indirect assuming that the cost objects are each of the 77 swim clubs.

[LO 3-2]  3-37  **Activity Levels and Cost Drivers**  Zeller Manufacturing Company produces four lines of high-quality lighting fixtures in a single manufacturing plant. Products are built to specific customer specifications. All products are made-to-order. Management of the plant lists the following as the key activities at the plant:

1. Product design
2. Product testing
3. Developing marketing plan for new products
4. Purchasing, receiving, and inspecting materials for production
5. Manufacturing labor
6. Setups for machine
7. Product inspection, done for each product before packaging for shipment
8. Packaging and shipping
9. Sales calls for new orders from existing customers
10. Processing customer orders
11. Maintenance of plant and equipment
12. Plant security

**Required**  Identify a cost object and a cost driver for each activity.

[LO 3-2]  3-38  **Application of the Direct Cost Concept in the Fashion Industry**  Jane Wilson is the production manager for a company that produces high-fashion designer clothing for women. The product is made in small batches that are presold to high-end retailers, based on specific orders. In effect, Jane manages the flow of small batches of product through the company's design/production shop in New York. The materials and labor for each batch are purchased and scheduled well in advance of the time of production. The materials are unique to the job, and the employees assigned to the job will work on it until the job is done. The company has found that dedicating specific employees to each batch improves employee satisfaction, and most important, product quality.

**Required**   Apply what you have just learned about the direct cost concept and explain its specific application with regard to this unique firm.

[LO 3-2]   **3-39   Manufacturing Direct Labor: Fixed or Variable?**

To retain skilled employees instead of letting them go when demand falls, Lincoln Electric trains employees for other tasks in the company. The Cleveland-based manufacturer of welding and cutting parts has integrated the approach in all its operations, so that it can guarantee employment for all employees who have been with the company for 3 or more years. This policy has worked for more than 60 years.

Other companies such as Nestle and Apex Precision Technology accomplish the same goal of keeping their employees as demand fluctuates by using part-time arrangements with the employees.

**Required**   Discuss whether manufacturing labor should be considered a fixed or a variable cost at these companies.

[LO 3-2]   **3-40   Average and Total Costs**   The Accounting Club wants to have a party for its members. The cost of renting space is $1,500, and the cost of refreshments will be $15 per person.

**Required**
1. What is the total cost if 100 people attend? What is the average cost?
2. What is the total cost if 200 people attend? What is the average cost?
3. Explain why average total cost differs with changes in total attendance.

[LO 3-2]   **3-41   Classification of Costs**   Jan Holliday Dance Studios is a chain of 45 wholly owned dance studios that offer private lessons in ballroom dancing. The studios are located in various cities throughout the southern and southeastern states. Holliday offers a set of 12 private lessons; students may pay for the lessons one at a time, but each student is required to enroll for at least a 12-lesson plan. The 20-, 40-, and 100-lesson plans offer savings. Each dance instructor is paid a small salary plus a commission based on the number of dance lessons provided.

**Required**
1. Holliday's owner is interested in a strategic analysis of the business. The owner wants to understand why overall profitability has declined slightly in the most recent year while other studios in the area seem to be doing well. What is the proper cost object to begin this analysis? Explain your choice.
2. For each of the cost elements, determine the cost classification from the following list for the cost object you chose in requirement 1. (In some cases, two or more classifications may apply.)

**Cost Elements**

1. Each dancing instructor's salary
2. Manager's salary
3. Music tapes used in instruction
4. Utilities for the studio
5. Part-time studio receptionist
6. Planning and development materials sent from the home office
7. Free lessons given by each studio as a promotion
8. Regional TV and radio advertisements placed several times a year

**Cost Classifications**

a. Direct
b. Indirect
c. Variable
d. Fixed

[LO 3-2]   **3-42   Relevant Range**   PhotoGraphicImages, Inc. (PGI) is an international supplier of graphic and photo images that are used in the publishing business and by a variety of firms that need graphic images for their annual reports, sales brochures, and other documents. PGI purchases the rights to these images from other sources, including photographers, publishers, and graphic artists. PGI then pays the provider of the image a royalty based on the number of times the image will be used (for example, the number of sales brochures that will be printed with that image). PGI operates in 16 countries, with small marketing and customer service offices located in each country. PGI's operating headquarters is located in Austin, Texas, where company management is located as well as a significant portion of the computer operations that are the backbone of the company's operations. Because of increased demand, PGI has just opened an operations center in Paris. All European and U.K. area business is now handled out of Paris, while the rest of the world's demand is handled out of Austin. The company foresees that it may be necessary to locate another operations center in China, if Asian demand continues to grow.

The computer operations at each of the operating locations consist of both large and small computer servers where the images are stored, the company website is maintained, and the business records are kept. There is capacity at each location to increase the number of servers as demand increases, though the capacity for expansion is limited in the current facility in Austin.

**Required**

1. Assuming PGI's output volume is measured by the number of customer orders, give some examples of the volume-based costs of this company.
2. How does the relevant range apply within this company?
3. How does the growth of PGI globally affect the firm's total costs (consider also foreign currency fluctuations)?

[LO 3-2]    3-43   **Fixed; Variable; and Mixed Costs**   Adams Manufacturing's five manufacturing departments had the following operating and cost information for the two most recent months of activity:

|  | May | June |
|---|---|---|
| Units produced | 10,000 | 20,000 |
| Costs in each department |  |  |
|   Department A | $10,000 | $10,000 |
|   Department B | 25,000 | 50,000 |
|   Department C | 35,000 | 45,000 |
|   Department D | 18,000 | 64,000 |
|   Department E | 22,000 | 44,000 |

**Required**   Identify whether the cost in each department is fixed, variable, or mixed.

[LO 3-2]    3-44   **Fixed; Variable; and Mixed Costs**   Habib Manufacturing has five manufacturing departments and operating and cost information for the most recent two months of activity.

|  | April | May |
|---|---|---|
| Units produced | 4,000 | 6,000 |
| Costs in each department: |  |  |
|   Department 1 | $16,000 | $18,000 |
|   Department 2 | 16,000 | 26,000 |
|   Department 3 | 20,000 | 20,000 |
|   Department 4 | 32,000 | 48,000 |
|   Department 5 | 16,000 | 24,000 |

**Required**   Identify whether the cost in each department is fixed, variable, or mixed.

[LO 3-2]    3-45   **Strategy; Variable and Fixed Costs**

Zipcar (**www.zipcar.com**) is a car-sharing club founded in Cambridge, Massachusetts, in 1999. The club members pay an annual fee and then have the opportunity to rent a small car (usually a subcompact; the models include the Toyota Prius) for a fixed hourly rate. Zipcar is located largely in select metropolitan areas such as Boston, San Francisco, and Washington, D.C. Members, called "Zipsters," make reservations for a car on the Zipcar website, and then use an access card to open the vehicle. The vehicle has a "home base" parking spot where the driver picks up and returns the vehicle. The club, with over 500,000 members and 8,000 vehicles, had its initial public offering of stock for public purchase on April 14, 2011, and has great plans for the future, subject to potential competition from the existing car rental companies such as Hertz and Enterprise.

**Required**
1. What are the fixed and variable costs for Zipcar?
2. What are some of the competitive advantages and challenges of the Zipcar concept?

[LO 3-2]    3-46 **Interpreting Average Cost**   Concern for gas emissions and depletion of nonrenewable resources has caused environmentalists and others to push for higher fuel-efficiency standards for new cars. The current Corporate Automotive Fuel Efficiency (CAFE) standards require automakers to produce an overall fuel efficiency of 27.5 miles per gallon for all autos produced. Currently the U.S. government supports the development of hybrid autos that combine gas and electric power as the solution to the problem. Others propose simply raising the CAFE standards for auto manufacturers. To study the issue, the American Council for an Energy-Efficient Economy (ACEEE) conducted research to determine the cost for raising fuel efficiency for the different proposals. Their findings are as follows:

| Option to Reduce Emissions and Provide Better Fuel Economy | Fuel Efficiency (mpg) | Cost for Each Gallon of Gas Saved |
|---|---|---|
| Current mileage standards | 26.2 | — |
| Moderate increase in CAFE | 40.8 | $0.57 |
| Significant increase in CAFE | 45.8 | $0.60 |
| Partial hybrid (15% of power from electricity) | 52.6 | $1.38 |
| Full hybrid (40% of power from electricity) | 59.3 | $1.80 |

The increase in fuel economy required by higher CAFE standards would require automakers to use conventional technology to improve engines and transmissions. The hybrid vehicles require newer technology and electric motors.

**Required**   Give a brief critical review of the ACEEE's research results. What questions would you have for the researchers who presented these results?

[LO 3-2]    3-47 **Interpreting Average Cost**   The American Institute of Certified Public Accountants (AICPA) and the Hackett Group, a consulting firm, partnered to study the trends in the nature and amount spent on the accounting function in corporations. A key finding was that the world's best accounting departments were able to function effectively at relatively low cost; these departments' total costs were only about 1% of their firm's total revenues. In contrast, less efficient accounting departments required on the average 1.4% of total revenue, 40% higher. The world-class accounting departments were also faster in preparing regular financial reports (less than two days for the best departments, compared to five to eight days for the others). The study also found that larger firms spent less on accounting:

| Manufacturing Firms | Finance Cost as a Percent of Total Revenue |
|---|---|
| Firms with less than $1 billion in revenues | 1.6% |
| $1 billion to $5 billion | 1.4% |
| More than $5 billion | 1% |
| **Service Firms** | |
| Less than $1 billion in revenues | 2.1% |
| More than $1 billion | 1.6% |

**Required**   Give a brief critical review of these research results. What questions would you have for the researchers who presented these results?

[LO 3-2]    3-48 **Average Cost**   Company A has 50% of its total variable manufacturing cost in labor and the other 50% in fuel. Company B has 80% of its total variable manufacturing cost in labor and the remainder in fuel. Suppose in a given year labor costs rise 5% and fuel costs rise 10%.

**Required**   Which company has the higher percentage increase in total variable cost?

[LO 3-2]    3-49 **Classification of Costs; Customer Profitability**

Pet Partner is a small company that provides pet boarding, grooming, and minor medical services for dogs and cats. The company has been successful for its first three years because of its careful attention to customer expectations. The staff knows the names of each customer's pet, their food preferences, and their individual preferences. The company is now studying the profitability of the business, using each customer as a cost object. In the business, there are a number of costs:

1. Staff salaries
2. Rent on office and work space used by the company
3. Licenses and fees
4. Supplies; grooming supplies and related items
5. Medications
6. Legal fees
7. Accounting services provided part time by practicing accountant
8. Pet food
9. Utilities for office and work space
10. Fire insurance for office and work space and its contents
11. Liability insurance for the company business

**Required**
1. For each cost category, indicate whether it is direct or indirect relative to the company's cost object.
2. Describe how Pet Partner could use the information in (1) to assess the profitability of each customer.

**[LO 3-2]**   3-50  **Classification of Costs**   Papa's Pizza Heaven serves take-out pizza from three locations in Columbus, Maryland. Papa's considers each pizza delivered (even if the order is for two or more pizzas) as the cost object for the company. The company incurs the following costs:

1. Food costs including pizza dough, olive oil, tomato sauce, mozzarella cheese, mushrooms, bell peppers, Italian sausage, chopped fresh basil, pesto, pepperoni, onions, and ham
2. Salaries for drivers
3. Salaries for telephone operators
4. Salaries for cooks
5. Insurance for drivers
6. Utilities; water and electricity
7. Advertising
8. Discount coupons offered in local newspapers to attract customers
9. Food handling licenses, inspections, and fees
10. Accounting and payroll services
11. Cooking supplies
12. Cleaning supplies
13. Mortgage payments on the three locations owned by Papa's Pizza Heaven
14. Insurance on facilities

**Required**
1. For each cost item, indicate whether it is fixed or variable relative to the cost object.
2. For each cost item, indicate whether it is a product or a period cost.
3. Which of the above costs could have potentially harmful environmental effects, and why?

**[LO 3-2]**   3-51  **Classification of Costs**

Speedy Auto Service provides oil changes, tire repair/replacement, and minor repairs from 12 different locations in Wadesborough, Pennsylvania. The technicians who replace the oil and parts (mostly windshield wipers, air filters, and the like) are paid for an eight-hour day, irrespective of the number of customers in a given day. The cost object for Speedy is each customer visit. The cost elements for Speedy include:

1. Technicians who change the oil and replace parts
2. Parts
3. Purchase of oil and tires
4. Supplies, rags, cleanup equipment
5. Tools
6. Rental of each location
7. Advertising

    8. Utilities

    9. Licenses and fees

   10. Employee training; 10 hours at time of hiring and 2 hours per month thereafter

   11. Security service to watch the locations during closing hours

   12. Online software system for managing sales, costs, and financial reports, including tax returns and employee payroll

   13. Disposal of waste oil and used tires

**Required**

1. For each cost item, indicate whether it is fixed or variable relative to the cost object.

2. For each cost item, indicate whether it is a product or a period cost.

3. Which of the above costs could have potentially harmful environmental effects, and why?

## Problems

[LO 3-2]    **3-52  Executional Cost Drivers; Internet Retailer**   Assume that you are a consultant for a start-up Internet retailer, **Bikes.com**, which provides a variety of bicycle parts and accessories in a convenient and effective customer service approach. The firm operates from an office building and nearby warehouse located in Danville, Virginia. Currently, the firm has 10 permanent administrative staff, 6 customer service representatives who respond to customer inquiries, and 12 employees who pick, pack, and ship customer orders. All orders are placed over the firm's website. An 800 telephone number is available for customer service. The firm's sales increased at about 20% per year in the last two years, a decline from the 50% rate in its first three years of operation. Management is concerned that the decline will delay the firm's first expected profit, which had been projected to occur in the next two years. The firm is privately held and has been financed with a combination of bank loans, personal investments of top managers, and venture capital funding.

**Required**   What specific executional cost drivers are important in this business? How should the firm use them to improve its sales rate?

[LO 3-2]    **3-53  Structural Cost Drivers**

   **Case A.**   Food Fare is a small chain of restaurants that has developed a loyal customer base by providing fast-food items with more choices (e.g., how the hamburger should be cooked; self-serve toppings) and a more comfortable atmosphere. The menu has a small number of popular items, including several different hamburgers, grilled chicken sandwiches, and salads. Recently, to broaden its appeal, Food Fare added barbecue, seafood, and steak to its menu.

   **Case B.**   Gilman Heating and Air Conditioning, Inc., provides a broad range of services to commercial and residential customers, including installation and repair of several different brands of heating and air conditioning systems. Gilman has a fleet of 28 trucks, each operated by one or more service technicians, depending on the size of a job. A recurrent problem for Gilman has been coordinating the service teams during the day to determine the status of a job and the need for parts not kept in the service vehicle as well as to identify which team to send on emergency calls. Gilman's service area is spread over an urban/rural area of approximately 50 square miles. The company has developed cost and price sheets so that the service technicians accurately and consistently price the service work they perform.

**Required**   For each case, identify the important structural cost drivers for the company and the related strategic issues that it should address to be competitive.

[LO 3-4]    **3-54  Cost of Goods Manufactured and Sold**   Hamilton Company produces women's clothing. During 2013, the company incurred the following costs:

| | |
|---|---:|
| Factory rent | $380,000 |
| Direct labor | 310,000 |
| Utilities—factory | 38,000 |
| Purchases of direct materials | 555,000 |
| Indirect materials | 66,000 |
| Indirect labor | 70,000 |

Inventories for the year were as follows:

|  | January 1 | December 31 |
|---|---|---|
| Direct materials | $ 25,000 | $40,000 |
| Work-in-process | 45,000 | 40,000 |
| Finished goods | 135,000 | 75,000 |

**Required**

1. Prepare a statement of cost of goods manufactured.

2. Calculate cost of goods sold.

[LO 3-4]  3-55  **Cost of Goods Manufactured**  The following data pertain to Blazek Company for the year ended December 31, 2013:

|  | December 31, 2012 | December 31, 2013 |
|---|---|---|
| Purchases of direct materials |  | $165,000 |
| Direct labor |  | 115,000 |
| Indirect labor |  | 45,000 |
| Factory insurance |  | 8,000 |
| Depreciation—factory |  | 33,000 |
| Repairs and maintenance—factory |  | 11,000 |
| Marketing expenses |  | 145,000 |
| General and administrative expenses |  | 86,000 |
| Direct materials inventory | $22,000 | 55,000 |
| Work-in-process inventory | 13,000 | 16,000 |
| Finished goods inventory | 17,000 | 24,000 |

Sales in 2013 were $625,000.

**Required**  Prepare a schedule of cost of goods manufactured and an income statement for 2013 for Blazek Company similar to those in Exhibit 3.15A.

[LO 3-4]  3-56  **Cost of Goods Manufactured; Income Statement**  Consider the following information for Household Furnishings, Inc., for the year ended December 31, 2013:

| | |
|---|---|
| Depreciation expense—administrative office | $ 33,000 |
| Depreciation expense—plant and equipment | 88,000 |
| Direct labor—wages | 487,000 |
| Direct materials inventory, Dec. 31, 2013 | 25,000 |
| Direct materials inventory, Jan. 1, 2013 | 18,000 |
| Direct materials purchases | 155,000 |
| Finished goods inventory, Dec. 31, 2013 | 38,000 |
| Finished goods inventory, Jan. 1, 2013 | 15,000 |
| Heat, light, and power—plant | 44,000 |
| Indirect labor | 25,000 |
| Property taxes—plant | 34,000 |
| Sales representatives' salaries | 145,000 |
| Sales revenue | 1,500,000 |
| Factory supervisor's salary | 66,000 |
| Supplies—administrative office | 16,000 |
| Supplies—plant | 29,000 |
| Work-in-process inventory, Dec. 31, 2013 | 9,000 |
| Work-in-process inventory, Jan. 1, 2013 | 23,000 |

**Required**  Prepare a statement of cost of goods manufactured and an income statement for Household Furnishings for the year ended December 31, 2013, similar to the one in Exhibit 3.15A.

[LO 3-4]  3-57  **Cost of Goods Manufactured; Income Statement**  Consider the following information for Fair Wind Yachts, Inc., a manufacturer of sailboat rigging, blocks, and cordage.

| | |
|---|---:|
| Advertising expenses | $ 150,000 |
| Depreciation expense—admin. office | 75,000 |
| Depreciation expense—plant and equip. | 320,000 |
| Depreciation expense—delivery trucks | 45,000 |
| Direct materials inventory, beginning | 16,000 |
| Direct materials inventory, ending | 18,000 |
| Direct materials purchases | 410,000 |
| Direct labor | 512,000 |
| Indirect labor | 269,000 |
| Finished goods inventory, beginning | 55,000 |
| Finished goods inventory, ending | 43,000 |
| Insurance on plant | 32,000 |
| Heat and light for plant | 22,000 |
| Repairs on plant building | 36,000 |
| Supervisor's salary—plant | 98,000 |
| Supplies—plant | 132,000 |
| Supplies—administrative office | 78,000 |
| Work-in-process inventory, beginning | 31,000 |
| Work-in-process inventory, ending | 39,000 |
| Sales representatives' salaries | 325,000 |
| Sales revenue | 2,885,000 |

**Required**   Prepare a statement of cost of goods manufactured and an income statement for Fair Wind Yachts, Inc. for the year ended December 31, 2013.

[LO 3-4]   3-58   **Cost of Goods Manufactured; Income Statement**   Norton Industries, a manufacturer of cable for the heavy construction industry, closes its books and prepares financial statements at the end of each month. The statement of cost of goods sold for April 2013 follows:

**NORTON INDUSTRIES**
**Statement of Cost of Goods Sold**
**For the Month Ended April 30, 2013**
**($000 omitted)**

| | |
|---|---:|
| Inventory of finished goods, March 31 | $ 50 |
| Cost of goods manufactured | 790 |
| Cost of goods available for sale | $840 |
| Less inventory of finished goods, April 30 | 247 |
| Cost of goods sold | $593 |

**Additional Information**

- Of the utilities, 80% relates to manufacturing the cable; the remaining 20% relates to the sales and administrative functions.
- All rent is for the office building.
- Property taxes are assessed on the manufacturing plant.
- Of the insurance, 60% is related to manufacturing the cable; the remaining 40% is related to the sales and administrative functions.
- Depreciation expense includes the following:

| | |
|---|---:|
| Manufacturing plant | $20,000 |
| Manufacturing equipment | 30,000 |
| Office equipment | 4,000 |
| | $54,000 |

- The company manufactured 7,825 tons of cable during May 2013.
- The inventory balances at May 31, 2013, follow:
  - Direct materials inventory $23,000
  - Work-in-process inventory $220,000
  - Finished goods inventory $175,000

**NORTON INDUSTRIES**
**Preclosing Account Balances**
**May 31, 2013**
**($000 omitted)**

| | |
|---|---:|
| Cash and marketable securities | $ 54 |
| Accounts and notes receivable | 210 |
| Direct materials inventory (4/30/2013) | 28 |
| Work-in-process inventory (4/30/2013) | 150 |
| Finished goods inventory (4/30/2013) | 247 |
| Property, plant, and equipment (net) | 1,140 |
| Accounts, notes, and taxes payable | 70 |
| Bonds payable | 600 |
| Paid-in capital | 100 |
| Retained earnings | 930 |
| Sales | 1,488 |
| Sales discounts | 20 |
| Other revenue | 2 |
| Purchases of direct materials | 510 |
| Direct labor | 260 |
| Indirect factory labor | 90 |
| Office salaries | 122 |
| Sales salaries | 42 |
| Utilities | 135 |
| Rent | 9 |
| Property tax | 60 |
| Insurance | 20 |
| Depreciation | 54 |
| Interest expense | 6 |
| Freight-in for materials purchases | 15 |

**Required**   Based on Exhibit 3.15A, prepare the following:
1. Statement of cost of goods manufactured for Norton Industries for May 2013.
2. Income statement for Norton Industries for May 2013.

**(CMA Adapted)**

**Solution to Self–Study Problem**

**SPARTAN PRODUCTS COMPANY**
**Statement of Cost of Goods Manufactured**
**For the Year Ended December 31, 2013**

| | | |
|---|---:|---:|
| Direct materials | | |
| Direct materials inventory, Jan. 1, 2013 | $ 20,000 | |
| Purchases of direct materials | 100,000 | |
| Total direct materials available | $120,000 | |
| Less: Direct materials inventory, Dec. 31, 2013 | 30,000 | |
| Direct materials used | | $ 90,000 |
| Direct labor | | 350,000 |
| Factory overhead | | |
| Depreciation expense—plant and equipment | 80,000 | |
| Indirect labor—wages | 5,000 | |
| Heat, light, and power—plant | 12,000 | |
| Supervisor's salary—plant | 40,000 | |
| Property taxes—plant | 13,000 | |
| Supplies—plant | 4,000 | |
| Total factory overhead | | 154,000 |

*(Continued)*

| | |
|---|---:|
| Total manufacturing costs | $594,000 |
| Add: Beginning work-in-process inventory, Jan. 1, 2013 | 35,000 |
| Total manufacturing costs to account for | $629,000 |
| Less: Ending work-in-process, Dec. 31, 2013 | 25,000 |
| Cost of goods manufactured | $604,000 |

**SPARTAN PRODUCTS COMPANY**
**Income Statement**
**For the Year Ended December 31, 2013**

| | | |
|---|---:|---:|
| Sales revenue | | $1,000,000 |
| Cost of goods sold | | |
| Finished goods inventory, Jan. 1, 2013 | $ 35,000 | |
| Cost of goods manufactured | 604,000 | |
| Total goods available for sale | $639,000 | |
| Finished goods inventory, Dec. 31, 2013 | 40,000 | |
| Cost of goods sold | | 599,000 |
| Gross margin | | $ 401,000 |
| Selling and administrative expenses | | |
| Sales representatives' salaries | $190,000 | |
| Supplies—administrative office | 6,000 | |
| Depreciation expense—administrative office | 30,000 | |
| Total selling and administrative expenses | | 226,000 |
| Operating income | | $ 175,000 |

*Please visit* **http://www.mhhe.com/blocher6e** *to access a narrated, animated tutorial for solving this problem.*

# CHAPTER FOUR

# Job Costing

After studying this chapter, you should be able to . . .

LO 4-1   Explain the types of costing systems

LO 4-2   Explain the strategic role of costing

LO 4-3   Explain the flow of costs in a job costing system

LO 4-4   Explain the application of factory overhead costs in a job costing system

LO 4-5   Calculate underapplied and overapplied overhead and show how it is accounted for

LO 4-6   Explain an operation costing system

LO 4-7   Explain how to handle spoilage, rework, and scrap in a job costing system (appendix)

Determining the accurate cost of a product or service plays a critical role in the success of firms in most industries. For example, Smith Fabrication Inc. of Kent, Washington (**www.smithfabinc.com**), uses a product costing system to estimate costs and to charge customers for the sheet metal products it provides to other manufacturers in the aviation, computer, telecom, and medical products industries. The product costing method it uses provides a competitive edge by providing accurate cost information in a form that customers can easily understand. Similarly, Hammert's Iron Works of St. Louis, Missouri (**http://www.hammertsiron.com**), uses job costing with a real-time labor and materials reporting system to provide the ability to account for materials and labor accurately at any point in the production process—important for managing the process of the job and for improving customer service. What these and many companies have found is that a simple yet accurate method for determining product cost is crucial to their competitive success. Another example is home construction and remodeling, where product costing plays a key role in cost estimating and pricing the work (**www.housingzone.com**).

Smith Fabrication, Hammert's Iron Works, and most home builders use a type of product costing called *job costing,* which is explained in this chapter.

The following section explains all the different choices a management accountant must make in choosing a cost system, with job costing as one of the possibilities.

## Costing Systems

**LO 4-1**

*Explain the types of costing systems.*

**Costing**

is the process of accumulating, classifying, and assigning direct materials, direct labor, and factory overhead costs to products, services, or projects.

**Costing** is the process of accumulating, classifying, and assigning direct materials, direct labor, and factory overhead costs to products, services, or projects.

In developing the particular costing system to fit a specific firm, the management accountant must make three choices, one for each of the three following characteristics of costing methods: (1) the cost accumulation method—job costing, process costing, or joint costing; (2) the cost measurement method—actual, normal, or standard costing; and (3) the overhead application method—volume-based or activity-based. Each product costing system will reflect these three choices. For example, a company may choose to use job costing, normal costing, and activity-based costing, because that combination of choices best fits the firm's operations and strategic goals. Another firm might be better served by a product costing system based on process cost, standard cost, and volume-based costing.

The choice of a particular system depends on the nature of the industry and the product or service, the firm's strategy and management information needs, and the costs and benefits of acquiring, designing, modifying, and operating a particular system. Here are the three choices.

## Cost Accumulation: Job or Process Costing?

Costs can be accumulated by tracing costs to a specific product or service, or by accumulating costs at the department level and then allocating these costs from the departments to the products or services. The first type is called *job costing* and the latter is *process costing.* In a job costing system the jobs consist of individual products or batches of products or services. A job costing system is appropriate when most costs incurred for the job can be readily identified with a specific product, batch of product, customer order, contract, or project. Types of companies that use job costing include those in construction, printing, special equipment manufacturing, shipbuilding, custom furniture manufacturing, professional services, medical services, advertising agencies, and others. Examples of companies using job costing systems include FedEx (**www.fedex.com**), Paramount Pictures (**www.paramount.com**), Jiffy Lube International (**www.jiffylube.com**), and Accenture (**www.accenture.com**). In job costing the job might consist of a single product or multiple products in a batch. For example, a batch might consist of 20 units of a product planned for distribution to a warehouse for future sale. Alternatively, a job could consist of the quantity of products ordered by a particular customer. The first approach is often called the *push* method because it fills the warehouse, while the latter is called the *pull* method because it is based on direct customer demand. The significance of the difference between these methods will be a recurring topic in later chapters.

In contrast, process costing is likely to be found in a firm that produces one or a few homogenous products or services. These firms often have continuous mass production. In this case, it is economically impractical to trace most costs to individual products. Industries where process costing is common include the chemical industry, bottling companies, plastics, food products, and paper products. Examples of companies using process costing systems include The Coca-Cola Company (**www.coca-cola.com**) and International Paper (**www.internationalpaper.com**). This chapter describes job costing systems and operation costing, a variation of job costing. Chapter 6 explains process costing systems, and Chapter 7 covers a variation of process costing in which there is joint processing of multiple products.

## Cost Measurement: Actual, Normal, or Standard Costing?

Costs in either a job or process costing system can be measured in their actual, normal, or standard amount. An *actual costing system* uses actual costs incurred for all product costs including direct materials, direct labor, and factory overhead.

A *normal costing system* uses actual costs for direct materials and direct labor and normal costs for factory overhead. Normal costing involves estimating a portion of overhead to be assigned to each product as it is produced. A normal costing system provides a timely estimate of the cost of producing each product or job.

A *standard costing system* uses standard costs and quantities for all three types of manufacturing costs: direct materials, direct labor, and factory overhead. Standard costs are expected costs the firm should attain. Standard costing systems provide a basis for cost control, performance evaluation, and process improvement. This chapter explains actual costing and normal costing systems; Chapters 14 and 15 explain standard costing systems. The different cost measurement systems are summarized in Exhibit 4.1.

## Overhead Application under Normal Costing: Volume-Based or Activity-Based?

Volume-based product costing systems allocate overhead to products or jobs using a volume-based cost driver, such as units produced. This approach relies heavily on the assumption

**EXHIBIT 4.1**
**Cost Measurement Systems**

| Costing System | Direct Materials | Direct Labor | Factory Overhead |
|---|---|---|---|
| | | Types of Cost Used for | |
| Actual costing | Actual cost | Actual cost | Actual cost |
| Normal costing | Actual cost | Actual cost | Estimated overhead cost (using predetermined rate(s)) |
| Standard costing | Standard cost | Standard cost | Standard cost |

that each product uses the same amounts of overhead, since each product is charged the same amount. Many accountants argue that instead of an equal amount, the overhead in each product should be proportional to the direct labor-hours needed to manufacture that unit, because more labor time also means increased overhead costs for equipment, supervision, and other facilities costs. Generally, neither of these assumptions turns out to be sufficiently accurate in many companies, so many firms use an activity-based approach.

Activity-based costing (ABC) systems allocate factory overhead costs to products using cause-and-effect criteria with multiple cost drivers. ABC systems use both volume-based and nonvolume-based cost drivers to more accurately allocate factory overhead costs to products based on resource consumption during various activities. Chapter 5 explains ABC systems.

## The Strategic Role of Costing

**LO 4-2**

*Explain the strategic role of costing.*

To compete successfully, firms need accurate cost information, regardless of their competitive strategies. This is even more likely to be true for cost leadership firms that rely on a high level of manufacturing efficiency and quality to succeed. Effective management of manufacturing costs requires timely and accurate cost information. Getting this timely and accurate information requires that the firm choose a cost system that is a good match for its competitive strategy. For example, a cost leadership firm that produces a commodity product is also likely to be in a process industry, such as food or chemical processing, or assembly line manufacturing. Thus, process costing systems are likely to be a good fit. Because accurate costs are important, such firms are likely to use activity-based costing, which is more accurate than the volume-based method for overhead assignment. And finally, this type of firm is likely to choose a standard costing system to provide the cost targets and regular reports on meeting these targets. In sum, the commodity/cost leadership type of firm might very well use a cost system that combines elements of process costing (Chapter 6), activity-based costing (Chapter 5), and standard costing (Chapters 14 and 15).

Many firms' competitive environments are changing rapidly, especially in the current economic recession. To provide useful information, a costing system must keep up with the constantly changing environment. To be competitive, the firm needs accurate cost information—for product pricing, profitability analysis of individual products, profitability analysis of individual customers, evaluation of management performance, and refinement of strategic goals.

## Job Costing: The Cost Flows

**LO 4-3**

*Explain the flow of costs in a job costing system.*

**Job costing**
is a product costing system that accumulates costs and assigns them to specific jobs, customers, projects, or contracts.

**A job cost sheet**
records and summarizes the costs of direct materials, direct labor, and factory overhead for a particular job.

**Job costing** is a costing system that accumulates costs and assigns them to specific jobs, customers, projects, or contracts. The basic supporting document (usually in electronic form) in a job costing system is the **job cost sheet**. It records and summarizes the costs of direct materials, direct labor, and factory overhead for a particular job.

An example of a job cost sheet for Thomasville Furniture Industries (TFI) of Thomasville, North Carolina, with disguised information, is shown in Exhibit 4.2. TFI (**www.thomasville .com**) is a large, global furniture manufacturer whose core values are quality and innovation. Its products are sold through 150 TFI retail stores and more than 400 independent retailers. The job cost sheet in Exhibit 4.2 shows the materials, labor, and overhead required for the production of a batch of 20 end tables by TFI. The example is presented in the form of a Microsoft Access software application to emphasize that job costing is typically done by a database software system that collects all relevant job cost data and then prepares a variety of reports, such as the job cost sheet, reports of cost by department, listing of jobs by customer, and many others, including the firm's financial statements and tax return. Database software systems are used because of the large amounts of data that manufacturing firms such as TFI must maintain and use for a variety of purposes, such as the reports listed above. Often the software system is designed specifically for the industry (CYMA and Sage are among many companies that provide software for the furniture industry). Microsoft Access is used here as a generic database system; the system used by a company like TFI could be any of a variety of the software systems available today.

**EXHIBIT 4.2** **Job Cost Sheet**

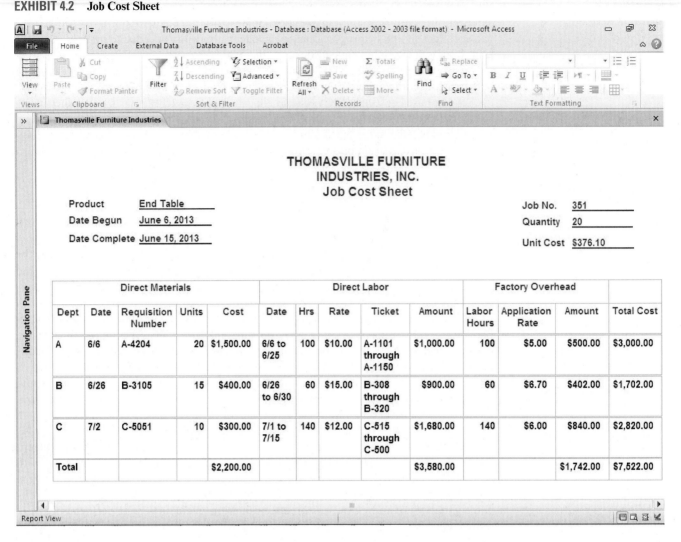

### THOMASVILLE FURNITURE INDUSTRIES, INC.
### Job Cost Sheet

Product     End Table

Date Begun    June 6, 2013

Date Complete June 15, 2013

Job No.   351

Quantity   20

Unit Cost   $376.10

| | Direct Materials | | | | Direct Labor | | | | | Factory Overhead | | | |
|---|---|---|---|---|---|---|---|---|---|---|---|---|---|
| Dept | Date | Requisition Number | Units | Cost | Date | Hrs | Rate | Ticket | Amount | Labor Hours | Application Rate | Amount | Total Cost |
| A | 6/6 | A-4204 | 20 | $1,500.00 | 6/6 to 6/25 | 100 | $10.00 | A-1101 through A-1150 | $1,000.00 | 100 | $5.00 | $500.00 | $3,000.00 |
| B | 6/26 | B-3105 | 15 | $400.00 | 6/26 to 6/30 | 60 | $15.00 | B-308 through B-320 | $900.00 | 60 | $6.70 | $402.00 | $1,702.00 |
| C | 7/2 | C-5051 | 10 | $300.00 | 7/1 to 7/15 | 140 | $12.00 | C-515 through C-500 | $1,680.00 | 140 | $6.00 | $840.00 | $2,820.00 |
| Total | | | | $2,200.00 | | | | | $3,580.00 | | | $1,742.00 | $7,522.00 |

A job cost sheet includes all three cost elements (materials, labor, overhead) as well as other detailed data required by management. The job cost sheet follows the product as it goes through the production process; all costs are recorded on the sheet as materials and labor are added. On completion of production, the overhead is added based usually on a certain dollar amount per labor hour, as shown in Exhibit 4.2. The total of all costs recorded on the job cost sheet is the total cost of the job.

### Direct and Indirect Materials Costs

As part of the preparation for the job, TFI purchases materials that are needed for the job. These purchases include both direct materials (lumber, fabric, and other direct materials ) and indirect materials (glue, nails, and other indirect materials). The purchase, for $2,200, is illustrated with the following journal entry.

| (1) | Materials Inventory | 2,200 | |
| | Accounts Payable | | 2,200 |

A **materials requisition** is an online data entry or a source document that the production department supervisor uses to request materials for production.

The purchased materials are used as TFI produces the job. A **materials requisition** is an online data entry or a source document that the production department uses to request materials for production. The materials requisition indicates the specific job charged with the materials used. An example of a materials requisition for TFI is shown in Exhibit 4.3. The example shows that part of the Department A $1,500 materials requisition for the job

**EXHIBIT 4.3**
**Materials Requisition**

| MATERIALS REQUISITION | | No. A–4024 |
|---|---|---|

Job Number _____ 351 _____    Date _____ June 6, 2013 _____
Department _____ A _____    Received by _____ Tom Chan _____
Authorized by _____ Juanita Perez _____    Issued by _____ Ted Mercer _____

| Item Number | Description | Quantity | Unit Cost | Total Cost |
|---|---|---|---|---|
| MJI 428 | Drawer Pull | 20 | $.75 | $15 |

shown in Exhibit 4.2 includes a drawer pull for each of the 20 end tables in the job, for a total cost of $15. A detailed listing of all the materials needed for a given job is often developed in what is called a bill of materials. For example, the bill of materials used by Thomasville Furniture Industries, Inc., in the manufacture of the end table is shown in Exhibit 4.4.

**EXHIBIT 4.4**   **Bill of Materials for End Table for Thomasville Furniture Industries, Inc.**

Thomasville Furniture Industries, Inc.
Bill of Materials
CHANGES FOR 14521–211

PLANT ___ "T" ___
STYLE ___ 14531–210 ___    ARTICLE ___ GEORGIAN END TABLE ___    DATE ___ 1–19–12 ___    SHEET ___ 1 ___ OF ___ 2 ___

| LINE | | NO. PCS. | DESCRIPTION | FINISH SIZE | | | | MULTI | ROUGH SIZE | | | FOOTAGE | SKETCH |
|---|---|---|---|---|---|---|---|---|---|---|---|---|---|
| | | | | L | W | T | BS | | L | W | T | | |
| 1 | 14531–210 ONLY | 1 | TOP | 26 | 20 | 13/16 | | 1 | 27 | 21 | 9/16 | | |
| 2 | | 1/2 | TOP CORE | | | | | 1 | 17 | 47½ | 3/4 | | |
| 3 | | 1 | TOP CORE SIDE BANDS | 47½ | 2 | 3/4 | | 1 | 47½ | 2 | 4/4 | | |
| 4 | | 2 | TOP CORE FRT. & BK. BANDS | 21 | 2 | 3/4 | | 1 | 21 | 2 | 4/4 | | |
| 5 | | | | | | | | | | | | | |
| 6 | | 2 | SIDE PANELS | 22³/8 | 4¹⁵/16 | 3/4 | 21³/8 | 4 | 23⁷/8 | 21³/4 | 5/8 | | 4/4 POP CORE |
| 7 | | 2 | SIDE APRON RAIL | 22³/8 | 1⁷/8 | 1⁷/16 | 21³/8 | 1 | 23³/8 | 2⅛ | 8/4 | | |
| 8 | | 1 | BACK PANEL | 16³/8 | 4¹⁵/16 | 3/4 | 15³/8 | 4 | 17⁷/8 | 21³/4 | 5/8 | | 4/4 POP CORE |
| 9 | | 1 | BACK APRON RAIL | 16³/8 | 1⁷/8 | 1⁷/16 | 15³/8 | 1 | 17³/8 | 2⅛ | 8/4 | | |
| 10 | | 2 | FRONT POST | 22³/4 | 2½ | 2½ | | 1 | 23³/4 | 2³/4 | 3 pcs 5/4 | | |
| 11 | | 2 | BACK POST | 22³/4 | 2½ | 2½ | | 1 | 23³/4 | 2³/4 | 3 pcs 5/4 | | |
| 12 | | | | | | | | | | | | | |
| 13 | 14531–210 ONLY | 1 | DRAWER FRONT | 14⁷/8 | 3⁷/8 | 3/4 | | 3 | 16⁷/16 | 16⁵/16 | 5/8 | | 4/4 POP CORE |
| 14 | | 2 | DWR. SIDES | 20 | 3 | 7/16 | | 1 | 21 | 3¼ | 5/8 | | |
| 15 | | 1 | DWR. BACK | 14¹¹/16 | 2⁷/8 | 7/16 | | | | | | | |
| 16 | | 1 | DWR. BOTTOM | 14¼ | 19¹³/16 | 3/16 | | 1 | 15³/4 | 20⁷/8 | R.C. | | |
| 17 | | 1 | DWR. GUIDE—FEMALE | 20½ | 13³/32 | 9/16 | 19¹³/16 | 1 | 21½ | 2¼ | 4/4 | | |
| 18 | | 1 | DWR. GUIDE—MALE | 22½ | 1 | ½ | | 1 | 23½ | 1¼ | 4/4 | | |
| 19 | | 1 | DWR. HOWE PULL | | | | | | | | | | |
| 20 | | | | | | | | | | | | | |

Thomasville Furniture Industries' Department A used a total of $1,500 in direct materials for Job 351. These costs are charged to work-in-process inventory until the job is completed, as shown in the following entry.

| (2) | Work-in-Process Inventory | 1,500 | |
| | Materials Inventory | | 1,500 |

Indirect materials are treated as part of the total factory overhead cost. Typical indirect materials are glue, nails, and factory supplies. The journal entry to record the use of indirect materials of $50 is

| (3) | Factory Overhead | 50 | |
| | Materials Inventory | | 50 |

## Direct and Indirect Labor Costs

Direct labor costs are recorded on the job cost sheet by means of a time ticket (an online data entry or source document) prepared for each employee. A **time ticket,** usually part of a costing software system, shows the amount of time an employee worked on each job, the pay rate, and the total labor cost chargeable to each job. Analysis of the time tickets provides information for assigning direct labor costs to individual jobs. The total cost of the $1,000 direct labor incurred in TFI's Department A for Job 351 is recorded by the following journal entry:

| (4) | Work-in-Process Inventory | 1,000 | |
| | Accrued Payroll | | 1,000 |

Indirect labor costs are treated as part of the total factory overhead cost. Indirect labor includes items such as salaries or wages for supervisors, inspectors, and warehouse clerks. The following is a journal entry to record the $100 indirect labor cost incurred:

| (5) | Factory Overhead | 100 | |
| | Accrued Payroll | | 100 |

## Factory Overhead Costs

**Overhead application** is a process of allocating factory overhead costs to jobs. Allocation is necessary because overhead costs are not traceable to individual jobs. The two approaches to allocating overhead costs are actual costing and normal costing. A third approach, standard costing, is covered in Chapters 14 and 15.

### *Actual Costing*

An **actual costing system** uses actual costs incurred for direct materials and direct labor and records actual factory overhead for the jobs.

Actual factory overhead costs are incurred each month for indirect materials, indirect labor, and other indirect factory costs, including factory rent, insurance, property tax, depreciation, repairs and maintenance, power, light, heat, and employer payroll taxes for factory personnel. Different firms use terms such as *manufacturing overhead, indirect manufacturing cost,* or *overhead* in referring to factory overhead.

Generally, the total amount of actual overhead costs is not known until the end of the accounting period when total expenses are determined. Thus, the actual costing system

**EXHIBIT 4.5**
**Monthly per-Unit Fixed Factory Overhead Cost Fluctuations under Actual Costing**

Steece Machine Tools, Inc., has a monthly total actual fixed factory overhead of $60,000 and actual variable manufacturing costs per unit of $10 for its only product. The firm produced 50,000 units in January but only 10,000 units in February because it had a large inventory of unsold products at the end of January. The unit costs would be as follows if actual costing were used to determine the manufacturing cost per unit:

| Month | Production Units | Variable Cost per Unit | Fixed Cost per Unit | Total Unit Cost |
|---|---|---|---|---|
| January | 50,000 | $10 | $60,000/50,000 = $1.20 | $11.20 |
| February | 10,000 | 10 | 60,000/10,000 = 6.00 | 16.00 |

This fluctuation in unit cost arises under actual costing because total fixed costs do not change, so unit costs change as volume changes. These changes are not desirable for cost estimation, budgeting, pricing, or product profitability analysis. Predetermined overhead rates, used in normal costing, are easy to apply and reduce monthly fluctuations in job costs caused by changes in the production volume and/or overhead costs throughout the year.

is often recorded for all of the company's jobs at the end of the accounting period. Revenues from all jobs and the actual expenses for materials, labor, and overhead are used to calculate overall profitability at that time. Using actual costing, the company could not know the cost or the profitability of each job when it is completed during the period, but only at the end of the period, and then the company would know the profitability of all the jobs combined. Most companies, like TFI, need to know for management planning and control purposes the cost and profitability of each job as it is completed, so they use normal rather than actual costing.

### *Normal Costing*

**Normal costing system**
uses actual costs for direct materials and direct labor and applies factory overhead to jobs using a predetermined allocation rate.

In practice, most firms adopt a **normal costing system** that uses actual costs for direct materials and direct labor and applies factory overhead to jobs by adding to the job an amount of overhead for each unit of product in the job.

Normal costing avoids the fluctuations in cost per unit under actual costing resulting from changes in the month-to-month volume of units produced and changes in overhead costs from month to month. Using a predetermined *annual* factory overhead rate normalizes overhead cost fluctuations, hence, the term *normal costing*. The fluctuations in unit cost under actual costing are illustrated in Exhibit 4.5.

## The Application of Factory Overhead in Normal Costing

**LO 4-4**

*Explain the application of factory overhead costs in a job costing system.*

The **predetermined factory overhead rate**
is an estimated rate used to apply factory overhead cost to a specific job.

**Factory overhead applied**
is the amount of overhead assigned to a job using a predetermined factory overhead rate.

The **predetermined factory overhead rate** is an estimated rate used to apply factory overhead cost to a specific job. The amount of overhead applied to a job using a predetermined factory overhead rate is called **factory overhead applied.**

The predetermined overhead rate is so-called because it is determined from estimates of overhead costs and cost drivers for the upcoming operating period, usually the coming fiscal year. To obtain the predetermined overhead rate, use these four steps:

1. Estimate total factory overhead costs for the upcoming operating period, usually a year.
2. Select the most appropriate cost driver for applying the factory overhead costs.
3. Estimate the total amount of the chosen cost driver for the upcoming operating period.
4. Divide the estimated factory overhead costs by the estimated amount of the chosen cost driver to obtain the predetermined overhead rate.

### Cost Drivers for Factory Overhead Application

The cost driver selected for applying a predetermined overhead rate (step 2 above) can be either a volume- or activity-based cost driver. This chapter explains the use of volume-based cost drivers, and Chapter 5 explains activity-based cost drivers.

Direct labor-hours, direct labor costs, and machine-hours are among the most frequently used volume-based cost drivers for applying factory overhead. The proper bases or cost drivers for a labor-intensive firm are probably direct labor-hours, direct labor costs, or some labor-related measure. In contrast, if factory overhead costs are predominantly related to the equipment operation, the proper cost driver is probably machine-hours or a related measure. Surveys of practice show that direct labor (hours or dollars) and machine-hours are the most commonly used cost drivers for overhead application.

## Applying Factory Overhead Costs

The predetermined overhead rate usually is calculated at the beginning of the year and is used throughout the year.

$$\text{Predetermined factory overhead rate} = \frac{\text{Estimated total factory overhead amount for the year}}{\text{Estimated total amount of cost driver for the year}}$$

For example, suppose TFI budgets, that is, estimates factory overhead cost of $200,070 for the coming year. TFI's cost system uses labor-hours as the cost driver for overhead application. TFI has the following budgeted (i.e., estimated) and actual data.

| | |
|---|---|
| Budgeted annual overhead for all departments | $200,070 |
| Budgeted annual labor-hours for all departments | 34,200 |
| Actual labor-hours for Job 351 for all departments (100 + 60 + 140 hrs; from Exhibit 4.2) | 300 |

Thus, the predetermined overhead rate is

$$\frac{\text{Budgeted factory overhead}}{\text{Budgeted number of labor-hours}} = \frac{\$200,070}{34,200} = \$5.85 \text{ per labor-hour}$$

The overhead cost applied to Job 351 is $1,755 (=300 hours × $5.85 per labor-hour). This amount would be recorded using the following journal entry

| (6) | Work-in-Process Inventory | 1,755 | |
| | Factory Overhead | | 1,755 |

This approach is called the *plantwide method of normal costing,* since total overhead for all departments is used to determine the overhead rate. An alternative approach, and the one used by TFI, is to determine the overhead rate for each production department. Departmental overhead rates are explained in the next section.

Quality Printing Company (QPC) is profitable in a very competitive market within a large urban area. QPC attributes its success to customer service, especially quick turn-around on urgent print jobs. Jim Bernard, QPC's operating manager, is very effective at scheduling jobs so that customer order due dates are met, and urgent orders are handled expeditiously. As QPC has grown, it has developed a reputation for its ability to handle a wide range of print jobs, from simple tri-fold mailings to multiple page color brochures. For costing the jobs, QPC uses a job costing system that applies overhead based on operating hours, as follows, where BHR (budgeted hourly cost rate , which is determined from total estimated overhead costs and operating hours for the year) is the overhead rate:

Job cost = Materials costs + Any outside purchases necessary for the order + (BHR × Job hours)

Pricing is based in part on job cost and Jim's knowledge of the printing competition in his area, so that some jobs are more profitable than others. Jim is interested in finding out more about job profitability. He wants to know which customers are really profitable and which are not.

**Required**

What would you suggest to Jim?

(Refer to Comments on Cost Management in Action at the end of the chapter.)

## Departmental Overhead Rates

When the production departments in the plant are very similar as to the amount of overhead in each department and the usage of cost drivers in the departments, then the use of a plantwide rate (one rate for all production departments taken as a whole) is appropriate. In many cases, however, the various production departments differ significantly in the amount of cost and cost drivers. Assume, as in Exhibit 4.2, that TFI has three production departments (A, B, and C), and that the total overhead costs and labor-hours in the three departments are shown below.

|  | Department A | Department B | Department C | Total |
|---|---|---|---|---|
| Overhead | $60,600 | $65,670 | $73,800 | $200,070 |
| Labor-hours | 12,100 | 9,800 | 12,300 | 34,200 |

Note that the total overhead of $200,070 and total labor-hours of 34,200 hours are the same as in our above calculations for the plantwide rate.

Using TFI's departmental approach, the rates are calculated as follows:

**Overhead Rate for Department A**

$60,600/12,100 labor-hours = $5.00 per labor-hour

**Overhead Rate for Department B**

$65,670/9,800 labor-hours  = $6.70 per labor-hour

**Overhead Rate for Department C**

$73,800/12,300 labor-hours = $6.00 per labor-hour

Using TFI's departmental approach, the overhead applied to Job 351 is $1,742 as shown in Exhibit 4.2. The amount for the plantwide rate shown above, $1,755, differs by only $13 from the amount determined by the departmental approach, a very small difference. This means the usage of resources in the three departments by Job 351 is similar to that for the other TFI jobs, so that the plantwide rate and the departmental rate have a similar total cost. When the usage of resources in the three departments differs significantly from one job to another, then the departmental approach is considered the more appropriate and accurate since job cost is based on the actual usage of the different departments, not an overall average.

## Disposition of Underapplied and Overapplied Overhead

Using a predetermined factory overhead rate to apply overhead cost to products can cause total overhead applied to the units produced to exceed the actual overhead incurred in periods when production is higher than expected. Alternatively, applied overhead might

**Overapplied overhead**
is the amount of factory overhead applied that exceeds actual factory overhead cost.

**Underapplied overhead**
is the amount by which actual factory overhead exceeds factory overhead applied.

**LO 4-5**

*Calculate underapplied and overapplied overhead and show how it is accounted for.*

exceed incurred (actual) overhead if the amount incurred is less than estimated. **Overapplied overhead** is the amount of factory overhead applied that exceeds the actual factory overhead cost incurred.

On the other hand, it is possible that applied overhead will be less than the incurred amount of overhead, due either to the fact that the actual amount of incurred overhead was greater than expected and/or the actual production level was smaller than expected. **Underapplied overhead** is the amount by which actual factory overhead exceeds factory overhead applied. If the predetermined overhead rate has been determined carefully, and if actual production is similar to expected production, the overapplied or underapplied difference should be small.

What do we do with the difference between factory overhead applied and the actual amount of overhead incurred? Since actual production costs should be reported in the period they were incurred, total product costs at the end of the accounting period should be based on actual rather than applied overhead.

Underapplied or overapplied overhead can be disposed of in two ways:

1.  Adjust the Cost of Goods Sold account.
2.  Adjust the production costs of the period; that is, allocate (often called "prorate") the underapplied or overapplied overhead among the ending balances of Work-in-Process Inventory, Finished Goods Inventory, and Cost of Goods Sold.

When the amount of underapplied or overapplied overhead is not significant, it generally is adjusted to Cost of Goods Sold. On the other hand, if the amount is significant, it is often prorated. The proration method is explained in Chapter 15.

### *Adjustment to Cost of Goods Sold*

Suppose that TFI applied $200,000 overhead but found at the end of the year that the actual total amount of overhead incurred was $205,000. The $5,000 difference represents underapplied overhead. The appropriate adjusting entry to the Cost of Goods Sold account is:

| (7) | Cost of Goods Sold | 5,000 | |
| | Factory Overhead | | 5,000 |
| | To record the disposition of underapplied overhead | | |

At the time of the adjusting entry, the Factory Overhead account had a debit balance of $5,000; the applied amount was credited to the account for $200,000 and the incurred amount was debited for $205,000, leaving a debit balance of $5,000. The entry removes this debit balance and transfers it to Cost of Goods Sold.

No matter which method is used (adjust cost of goods sold or prorate), underapplied or overapplied overhead is usually adjusted only at the end of a year. Nothing needs to be done during the year because the predetermined factory overhead rate is based on annual figures. A variance is expected between the actual overhead incurred and the amount applied in a particular month or quarter because of seasonal fluctuations in the firm's operating cycle. Furthermore, underapplied factory overhead in one month is likely to be offset by an overapplied amount in another month (and vice versa).

## Potential Errors in Overhead Application

The application of overhead is a critical step in costing, and since it is based on estimates, it is subject to potential errors in determining the cost of a product or service. There are three types of potential errors:

1.  Aggregation error. This costing error arises when, for example, a single plantwide rate is used instead of departmental rates. The departmental rates are more accurate when the departments differ significantly in the amount of cost or the amount of the cost drivers. ABC costing, which we explain in Chapter 5, also addresses aggregation errors.

2. Specification error. This error arises when the wrong cost driver is used in the application rate. For example, in a plant where labor costs are relatively small and machine costs are relatively large, a rate based on machine-hours is a better choice for overhead application than one based on labor-hours.

3. Measurement error. This is a common type of error that arises when the amounts used for estimated overhead or estimated cost drivers are incorrect. Measurement error is a combination of estimation error and potential error in calculating the overhead and cost driver amounts.

The management accountant uses care to develop a cost system that minimizes these potential errors. The management accountant also tries to balance the cost of improving the accuracy of the cost system with the benefits of improved accuracy.[1]

## Job Costing in Service Industries; Project Costing

Job costing is used extensively in service industries such as advertising agencies, hospitals, and repair shops, as well as consulting, architecture, accounting, and law firms. Instead of using the term *job,* accounting and consulting firms use the term *client* or *project;* hospitals and law firms use the term *case,* and advertising agencies use the term *contract* or *project.* Many firms use the term *project costing* to indicate the use of job costing in service industries. Project costing is also used to track the costs and progress of nonrecurring tasks that take place within companies, for example, projects to develop a new marketing plan or to improve operating efficiency, projects to implement a new strategic direction for the company, or projects to introduce a new software system. These projects also have the characteristics that are suitable for job costing.

Job costing in service industries uses recording procedures and accounts similar to those illustrated earlier in this chapter except for direct materials involved (there could be none or an insignificant amount). The primary focus is on direct labor. The overhead costs are usually applied to jobs based on direct labor cost.

Suppose the law firm, Sandings and Midgett LLP, provides legal services to a wide range of clients in the Chicago area. The firm has two main costs: (1) compensation for professional staff, and (2) all other costs, which include support staff, facilities costs, and other costs. The costs of professional staff are considered direct costs for the purposes of billing clients and assessing the profitability of each client job; all other costs are considered overhead. The firm determines an overhead rate for client billing based on the number of professional staff hours used for the job. Professional staff time is billed at $250 per hour. The firm estimates the following total costs for the coming year, 2013:

| | |
|---|---|
| Estimated cost of professional staff | $ 6,000,000 (40,000 hours of staff time) |
| Estimated other costs (overhead) | 5,000,000 |
| Total estimated costs | $11,000,000 |

Suppose Abby Johnson was a client of the firm in 2013 and that the job for Abby required 100 hours of professional staff time. The cost to be billed to Abby for the job is determined in three steps.

1. Determine the overhead rate:

$$\frac{\text{Estimated total overhead}}{\text{Estimated total hours}} = \frac{\$5,000,000}{40,000} = \$125 \text{ per hour}$$

2. Determine applied overhead for the job:

$$100 \text{ hours for the Abby Johnson job} \times \$125 \text{ per hour} = \$12,500$$

[1] For a more complete explanation of costing errors, see the IMA publication by Ramji Balakrishnan, Stephen Hansen, and Eva Labro, "Designing an Effective Cost System," The Institute of Management Accountants, 2011 (**http://imanet.org.cn/userfiles/file/FAR%20report/Designing%20an%20Effective%20Cost%20System.pdf**).

3. Determine the total billing for the job:

| | |
|---|---|
| Total billing for professional staff ($250 per hour × 100) | $25,000 |
| Total overhead applied to the job | 12,500 |
| Total billing for the Abby Johnson job | $37,500 |

The job cost of the Abby Johnson job can be determined in a similar manner, by replacing the billing rate of $250 per hour with the cost of compensation for professional staff, $150 per hour (= $6,000,000/40,000 hours).

| | |
|---|---|
| Total cost for professional staff ($150 per hour × 100) | $15,000 |
| Total overhead applied to the job | 12,500 |
| Total cost for the Abby Johnson job | $27,500 |

The profit on the Abby Johnson job is $37,500 − $27,500 = $10,000.

The above costing can also be adapted to account for differences in billing rates for different levels of professional staff (partners, associates) and for differences in overhead rates for different professional staff levels, if desired. For example, if partners are billed at $350 and associates are billed at $150, and if $2,000,000 of the $5,000,000 total overhead could be attributed to partners and $3,000,000 could be attributed to associates in the law firm, and if 10,000 of the 40,000 annual hours of professional time were partner hours and 30,000 were for associates, and if 10 of the 100 hours of professional time for the Abby Johnson job were partner hours and the remaining 90 hours were associates' time, then the following could be calculated for billing purposes:

1. Determine the overhead rates:

Partners: $2,000,000/10,000 = $200 per hour
Associates: $3,000,000/30,000 = $100 per hour

2. Determine applied overhead:

Partners: 10 × $200 = $2,000
Associates: 90 × $100 = $9,000

3. Determine total billing for the job:

| | |
|---|---|
| Partners: | |
| Professional time: $350 per hour × 10 | $ 3,500 |
| Overhead: $200 per hour × 10 | 2,000 |
| Associates: | |
| Professional time: $150 per hour × 90 | 13,500 |
| Overhead: $100 per hour × 90 | 9,000 |
| Total billing for the Abby Johnson job | $28,000 |

The job cost of the Abby Johnson job can be determined in a similar manner, by replacing the billing rates of $350 and $150 per hour with the cost of compensation for professional staff. If we assume that of the $6,000,000 compensation cost, one-half is attributed to partners and the other one-half is attributed to associates, then the cost rate for a partner is $300 (= $3,000,000/10,000 hours) and the cost rate for an associate is $100 (= $3,000,000/30,000 hours). The job cost determination is:

| | |
|---|---|
| Partners: | |
| Professional time: $300 per hour × 10 | $ 3,000 |
| Overhead: $200 per hour × 10 | 2,000 |
| Associates: | |
| Professional time: $100 per hour × 90 | 9,000 |
| Overhead: $100 per hour × 90 | 9,000 |
| Total cost for the Abby Johnson job | $23,000 |

The profit for the Abby Johnson job is $28,000 − $23,000 = $5,000.

The differences between the two billing statements and the two job costs are significant; the second approach based on partner and associate time is more accurate and therefore likely to be more fair and appropriate. The second approach reflects the fact that most of the professional hours for the Abby Johnson job were for associates, who have lower billing rates and costs. The difference between the two approaches is very much like the difference between the plantwide and departmental overhead rates explained earlier.

## Operation Costing

**LO 4-6**

*Explain an operation costing system.*

**Operation costing**
is a hybrid costing system that uses job costing to assign direct materials costs to jobs and process costing to assign conversion costs to products or services.

**Operation costing** is a hybrid costing system that uses a job costing approach to assign direct materials costs to jobs and a process costing approach to assign conversion costs to products or services.

Manufacturing operations whose conversion activities are very similar across several product lines, but whose direct materials used in the various products differ significantly, use operation costing. After direct labor and factory overhead conversion costs have been accumulated by operations or departments, these costs are then assigned to products. On the other hand, direct materials costs are accumulated by jobs or batches, and job costing assigns these costs to products or services.

Industries suitable for applying operation costing include food processing, textiles, shoes, furniture, metalworking, jewelry, and electronic equipment. For example, a glass manufacturing company that makes multiple products from a basic clear glass would be a potential user of operation costing.

Suppose that Irvine Glass Company manufactures two types of glass: clear glass and tinted glass. Department 1 produces clear glass sheets, some of which are sold as finished goods. Others are transferred to Department 2, which adds metallic oxides to clear glass sheets to form tinted glass sheets, which are then sold as finished goods. The company uses operation costing.

Irvine Glass Company finished two jobs: Job A produced 10,000 sheets of clear glass and Job B produced 5,000 sheets of tinted glass. Manufacturing operations and costs applied to these products follow.

| Direct materials | | |
|---|---|---|
| Job A (10,000 clear glass sheets) | | $400,000 |
| Job B (5,000 tinted glass sheets) | | |
|   Materials for clear glass sheets in Department 1 | $200,000 | |
|   Materials added to clear glass sheets in Department 2 | 100,000 | 300,000 |
| Total direct materials | | $700,000 |
| Conversion costs | | |
|   Department 1 | | $180,000 |
|   Department 2 | | 50,000 |
| Total conversion costs | | $230,000 |
| Total costs | | $930,000 |

Notice in this table that operation costing identifies direct materials by job; in contrast, it identifies conversion costs with each of the two production departments.

The product cost for each type of glass sheet is computed as follows:

| | Clear Glass | Tinted Glass |
|---|---|---|
| Direct materials | | |
|   Job A ($400,000/10,000) | $40 | |
|   Job B ($300,000/5,000) | | $60 |
| Conversion: Department 1 ($180,000/15,000) | 12 | 12 |
| Conversion: Department 2 ($50,000/5,000) | | 10 |
| Total product cost per sheet | $52 | $82 |

Notice in this table that each glass sheet receives the same conversion costs in Department 1 since this operation is identical for the two products. Total product costs are calculated as follows:

| | |
|---|---:|
| Clear glass sheets ($52 per sheet $\times$ 10,000) | $520,000 |
| Tinted glass sheets ($82 per sheet $\times$ 5,000) | 410,000 |
| Total | $930,000 |

The following journal entries record Irvine Glass Company's flow of costs. Department 1 makes the first entry by recording the requisition of direct materials when Job A enters production:

| (1) | Work-in-Process Inventory: Department 1 | 400,000 | |
|---|---|---|---|
| | Materials Inventory | | 400,000 |

Department 1 makes the following entry to record the requisition of direct materials when Job B enters production:

| (2) | Work-in-Process Inventory: Department 1 | 200,000 | |
|---|---|---|---|
| | Materials Inventory | | 200,000 |

Conversion costs are applied in Department 1 with the following journal entry:

| (3) | Work-in-Process Inventory: Department 1 | 180,000 | |
|---|---|---|---|
| | Conversion Costs Applied | | 180,000 |

The following entry records the transfer of completed clear glass sheets to finished goods:

| (4) | Finished Goods Inventory | 520,000 | |
|---|---|---|---|
| | Work-in-Process Inventory: Department 1 | | 520,000 |

Direct materials of $400,000 + Conversion ($12 per sheet $\times$ 10,000) = $520,000

The following entry records the transfer of partially completed clear glass sheets to Department 2 for completion as tinted glass:

| (5) | Work-in-Process Inventory: Department 2 | 260,000 | |
|---|---|---|---|
| | Work-in-Process Inventory: Department 1 | | 260,000 |

Direct materials of $200,000 + Conversion($12 $\times$ 5,000) = $260,000

The following entry records the requisition of materials by Department 2 when job B enters production:

| (6) | Work-in-Process Inventory: Department 2 | 100,000 | |
|---|---|---|---|
| | Materials Inventory | | 100,000 |

Conversion costs are applied in Department 2 with the following journal entry.

| (7) | Work-in-Process Inventory: Department 2 | 50,000 | |
| | Conversion Costs Applied | | 50,000 |

The completed tinted glass sheets are transferred to finished goods.

| (8) | Finished Goods Inventory | 410,000 | |
| | Work-in-Process Inventory: Department 2 | | 410,000 |

Department 2 work-in-process $260,000 + Materials for tinted glass of $100,000 + Conversion($10 × 5,000) = $410,000

## Summary

Product costing is the process of accumulating, classifying, and assigning direct materials, direct labor, and factory overhead costs to products or services. Product costing provides useful cost information for both manufacturing and nonmanufacturing companies. Accurate cost information helps a company make better decisions and compete more effectively.

Several different product costing systems are available and can be classified on three dimensions: (1) cost accumulation method—job or processing costing systems, (2) cost measurement method—actual, normal, or standard costing systems, and (3) overhead application method—volume- or activity-based costing systems. The choice of a particular system depends on the nature of the industry and the product or service; the firm's strategy and its management information needs; and the costs and benefits to acquire, design, modify, and operate a particular system.

Job costing uses several accounts to control the product cost flows. Direct materials costs are debited to the Materials Inventory account at time of purchase and debited to the Work-in-Process Inventory account when a production department requests materials. Direct labor costs are debited to the Work-in-Process Inventory account when they are incurred. Actual factory overhead costs are debited to the Factory Overhead account when they are incurred. Factory overhead applied using the predetermined factory overhead rate in normal costing is debited to the Work-in-Process Inventory account and credited to the Factory Overhead account. When a job is complete, the cost of goods manufactured is transferred from the Work-in-Process Inventory account to the Finished Goods Inventory account.

The predetermined factory overhead rate is an estimated factory overhead rate used to apply factory overhead cost to a specific job. The application of a predetermined overhead rate has four steps: (1) estimate factory overhead costs for an upcoming operating period, usually a year, (2) select the most appropriate cost driver for charging the factory overhead costs, (3) estimate the total amount of the chosen cost driver for the upcoming operating period, and (4) divide the estimated factory overhead costs by the estimated amount of the chosen cost driver to obtain the predetermined factory overhead rate.

The difference between the actual factory overhead cost and the amount of the factory overhead applied is the overhead variance; it is either underapplied or overapplied. It can be disposed of in two ways: (1) adjust the Cost of Goods Sold account or (2) prorate the difference among the Work-in-Process Inventory, the Finished Goods Inventory, and the Cost of Goods Sold accounts.

Job costing is used extensively in service industries such as advertising agencies, construction companies, hospitals, repair shops, and consulting, architecture, accounting, and law firms.

Operation costing is used when most of the plant's products have a similar conversion cycle, but materials costs may differ significantly between jobs. In this case, materials costs are traced to jobs, while conversion costs are traced to departments and then to jobs.

# Appendix

## Spoilage, Rework, and Scrap in Job Costing

**LO 4-7**

*Explain how to handle spoilage, rework, and scrap in a job costing system.*

**Spoilage**
refers to an unaccepted unit that is discarded or sold for disposal value.

**Rework**
is a produced unit that must be reworked into a good unit that can be sold in regular channels.

**Scrap**
is the material left over from the manufacture of the product; it has little or no value.

**Normal spoilage**
is waste that occurs under normal operating conditions.

**Abnormal spoilage**
is waste that should not arise under normal operating conditions.

In today's manufacturing environment, firms adopt various quality-improvement programs to reduce spoilage, rework units, and scrap. **Spoilage** refers to unacceptable units that are discarded or sold for disposal value. **Rework** units are units produced that must be reworked into good units that can be sold in regular channels. **Scrap** is the material left over from the manufacture of the product; it has little or no value.

### SPOILAGE

The two types of spoilage are normal and abnormal. **Normal spoilage** occurs under normal operating conditions; it is uncontrollable in the short term and is considered a normal part of production and product cost. That is, the cost of spoiled unit costs is absorbed by the cost of good units produced. **Abnormal spoilage** is in excess over the amount of normal spoilage expected under normal operating conditions; it is charged as a loss to operations in the period detected.

Normal spoilage is of two types: (1) specific normal spoilage, which is particular to a given job and is not due to factors related to other jobs, and (2) common normal spoilage, which is due to factors that affect two or more jobs, such as a machine malfunction that affected parts used in several jobs. Normal spoilage that is specific to a job is treated as a cost of that job, so that in effect the cost of spoilage is spread over the cost of the good units in the job. Normal spoilage that is common to two or more jobs is charged to factory overhead and, in this way, affects the costs of all jobs. Abnormal spoilage is charged to a special account, such as Loss from Abnormal Spoilage, so that management attention can be given to spoilage of this type, and because product cost should not include abnormal elements such as abnormal spoilage.

Suppose a furniture manufacturer spoiled 1 sofa from an order of 100 sofas (job #1233) because of stains and tears in the fabric and that the spoilage was normal and particular to this job. At the time the spoilage was detected, a total of $500 had been incurred in the manufacture of the sofa. Suppose further that the spoiled sofa could be disposed of—sold as-is for $100, then the net cost of the spoilage is now $500 − $100 = $400. This means that $400 of work-in-process cost for the spoiled sofa will be spread over the remaining 99 sofas. The accounting treatment would be as follows:

| | | |
|---|---|---|
| Inventory of spoiled sofa for sale | 100 | |
| Work-in-process for job #1233 | | 100 |

Suppose the same information as above, except that the spoiled sofa described above was spoiled by a hard-to-detect malfunction in a fabric cutting machine that was also involved in other jobs in the plant and had affected other jobs. The spoilage is now considered common normal spoilage, and the accounting treatment is:

| | | |
|---|---|---|
| Inventory of spoiled sofa for sale | 100 | |
| Factory overhead | 400 | |
| Work-in-process for job #1233 | | 500 |

Finally, assume again the same information as above except that the malfunction in the fabric cutting machine is due to controllable operator error and is now considered to be abnormal spoilage. The accounting treatment is now:

| | | |
|---|---|---|
| Inventory of spoiled sofa for sale | 100 | |
| Loss from abnormal spoilage | 400 | |
| Work-in-process for job #1233 | | 500 |

## REWORK

Like spoilage, there are three types of rework: (1) rework on normal defective units for a particular job, (2) rework on normal defective units common with all jobs, and (3) rework on abnormal defective units not falling within the normal range. The cost of rework units is charged to one of three accounts depending on its nature. Normal rework for a particular job is charged to that specific job's Work-in-Process Inventory account. Normal rework common to all jobs is charged to the Factory Overhead account and abnormal rework is charged to the Loss from Abnormal Rework account.

## SCRAP

Scrap can be classified according to (1) a specific job and (2) common to all jobs. Suppose that the furniture manufacturer above incurred and sold the scrap from a specific job for $100 cash and sold the scrap common to all jobs for $200 cash. The proper journal entries follow:

| | | |
|---|---|---|
| Cash | 100 | |
| Work-in-Process Inventory | | 100 |
| Cash | 200 | |
| Factory Overhead | | 200 |

**Comments on Cost Management in Action**

**Job Costing in a Printing Company**

Quality Printing Company has succeeded on the competitive knowledge of the manager, Jim Bernard, and on his ability to effectively manage operations. But the costing system stands in the way of Jim's further progress to profitability. One problem with the costing system is that it uses a plantwide rate. The BHR system uses a rate derived from all of the firm's equipment and facilities. Since some print jobs are more complex (more colors, etc.) and must run on more expensive equipment while others are relatively simple, QPC needs overhead rates for each piece of equipment. The National Association for Printing Leadership (NAPL) publishes hourly cost rates (BHRs) for different types of machines, and these rates are updated twice a year. Using the NAPL rates would give Jim a more accurate basis for job costing; it is very much like the departmental approach mentioned in the chapter, except in this case the department is the printing machine.

Other issues Jim should consider in his analysis of customer profitability is that the customers who demand very quick turnaround are likely to increase operating costs by incurring overtime charges, delaying or interrupting other jobs, and so on. These additional costs should be considered in pricing these expedited jobs.

Jim can use job costing to measure the profitability of each job and, by extension, of each customer. This information can help him set prices and manage costs.

**Source:** Lisa Cross, "Benefiting from Costing and Pricing Tools," *Graphic Arts Monthly,* July 2004, pp. 32–34.

## Self-Study Problem

(For solution, please turn to the end of the chapter.)

### Journal Entries and Accounting for Overhead

Watkins Machinery Company uses a normal job costing system. The company has this partial trial balance information on March 1, 2013, the last month of its fiscal year:

| | |
|---|---:|
| Materials Inventory (X, $3,000; Y, $2,000; Indirect materials, $5,000) | $10,000 |
| Work-in-Process Inventory—Job 101 | 6,000 |
| Finished Goods Inventory—Job 100 | 10,000 |

These transactions relate to the month of March:

a.  Purchased direct materials and indirect materials with the following summary of receiving reports:

| | |
|---|---:|
| Material X | $10,000 |
| Material Y | 10,000 |
| Indirect materials | 5,000 |
| Total | $25,000 |

b.  Issued direct materials and indirect materials with this summary of requisitions:

| | Job 101 | Job 102 | Total |
|---|---:|---:|---:|
| Material X | $5,000 | $3,000 | $ 8,000 |
| Material Y | 4,000 | 3,000 | 7,000 |
| Subtotal | $9,000 | $6,000 | $15,000 |
| Indirect materials | | | 8,000 |
| Total | | | $23,000 |

c.  Factory labor incurred is summarized by these time tickets:

| | |
|---|---:|
| Job 101 | $12,000 |
| Job 102 | 8,000 |
| Indirect labor | 5,000 |
| Total | $25,000 |

d.  Factory utilities, factory depreciation, and factory insurance incurred is summarized as follows:

| | |
|---|---:|
| Utilities | $ 500 |
| Depreciation | 15,000 |
| Insurance | 2,500 |
| Total | $18,000 |

e.  Factory overhead costs were applied to jobs at the predetermined rate of $15 per machine-hour. Job 101 incurred 1,200 machine-hours; Job 102 used 800 machine-hours.

f.  Job 101 was completed; Job 102 was still in process at the end of March.

g.  Job 100 and Job 101 were shipped to customers during March. Both jobs had gross margins of 20% based on manufacturing cost.

The company closed the overapplied or underapplied overhead to the Cost of Goods Sold account at the end of March.

**Required**

1. Prepare journal entries to record the transactions for the events from a to g.
2. Compute the ending balance of the Work-in-Process Inventory account.
3. Compute the overhead variance and indicate whether it is overapplied or underapplied.
4. Close the overhead variance to the Cost of Goods Sold account.

*Please visit* **http://www.mhhe.com/blocher6e** *to access a narrated, animated tutorial for solving this problem.*

## Questions

4-1 What is the strategic role of a costing system?

4-2 Identify the three characteristics of costing systems.

4-3 Distinguish between job costing and process costing.

4-4 Explain when companies are likely to use a job costing system or a process costing system. Provide examples.

4-5 Which costing system is extensively used in the service industry for hospitals, law firms, or accounting firms? Explain why.

4-6 What document is prepared to accumulate costs for each separate job in a job costing system? What types of costs are recorded in the document?

4-7 Explain how predetermined factory overhead rates are computed and why they are used to apply factory overhead to units of products instead of actual overhead costs.

4-8 What is the role of materials requisitions in a job costing system? Time tickets? Bills of materials?

4-9 What does the statement "Accounting for overhead involves an important cost-benefit issue" mean? Why is that issue important?

4-10 Describe the flow of costs through a job costing system from materials through finished product.

4-11 What do *underapplied overhead* and *overapplied overhead* mean? How are these amounts disposed of at the end of a period?

4-12 Why would a manufacturing firm switch from direct labor-hours to machine-hours as the cost driver for factory overhead application?

4-13 Explain why overhead might be overapplied in a given period.

4-14 Distinguish between an actual costing system and a normal costing system. What are the components of the actual manufacturing costs and the components of the normal manufacturing costs?

4-15 What is the best way to choose an appropriate cost driver when applying factory overhead?

4-16 What is the difference between normal and abnormal spoilage?

## Brief Exercises

4-17 How is job costing in a service firm different from job costing in a manufacturer?

4-18 If the overhead rate is $10 per machine-hour, and there are 20 labor-hours, 16 machine-hours, and 2 personnel on the job, how much overhead should be applied to the job?

4-19 Nieto Machine Shop has 4,000 labor-hours and 8,000 machine-hours used in May. Total budgeted overhead for May is $80,000. What is the overhead rate using labor-hours and also using machine-hours? Which would you pick and why?

4-20 Assume that actual overhead is $613,000 in a given year and the overhead rate is $10 per unit, 60,000 units were sold, and 59,000 units were produced. For the end of the year, is overhead underapplied or overapplied, and by how much?

4-21 If the end-of-period balance for cost of goods sold is $90,000 and underapplied overhead is $10,000, what is the ending balance in cost of goods sold, after adjusting for the underapplied overhead?

4-22 A small consulting firm has an overhead rate of 200% of direct labor charged to each job. The materials cost (including travel and other direct costs) for a particular job is $10,000 and the direct labor is $20,000. What is the total job cost for this job?

4-23 Company A has a number of jobs that are processed through similar manufacturing processes. However, most jobs have labor-hour requirements ranging from 100 to 130 hours, while these jobs differ significantly in the number of machine-hours required for each job—some as low as 50, others as high as 5,000 hours. One reason for this is a well-trained labor pool that has the ability to work cross-functionally and perform a variety of duties. What do you think is the best overhead rate basis for this firm—labor-hours, machine-hours, or some other rate basis? Explain your answer.

4-24    When overhead is overapplied, is the balance of cost of good sold, before adjustment, too low or too high? Why?

4-25    Some firms pool overhead into a single plantwide overhead pool, while others collect overhead costs into manufacturing departments, each of which has an overhead cost pool and overhead cost application rate. Which approach is likely to provide more accurate cost numbers for cost estimating, pricing, and performance evaluation?

4-26    Assume the following for White Top, Inc., for 2013. White Top applies overhead on the basis of units produced.

| | |
|---|---|
| Budgeted overhead | $200,000 |
| Actual overhead | $222,000 |
| Actual labor-hours | 15,000 |
| Actual number of units sold | 43,000 |
| Underapplied overhead | $20,000 |
| Budgeted production (units) | 50,000 |

**Required**    How many units were produced in 2013?

4-27    Assume the following for Round Top, Inc., for 2013. Round Top applies overhead on the basis of units produced.

| | |
|---|---|
| Budgeted overhead | $350,000 |
| Actual overhead | $360,000 |
| Actual labor-hours | 22,000 |
| Actual number of units sold | 650,000 |
| Overapplied overhead | $30,000 |
| Budgeted production (units) | 700,000 |

**Required**    How many units were produced in 2013?

4-28    What are the three types of potential errors in overhead application?

## Exercises

[LO 4-1, 4-2]    **4-29    Choice of Costing System**

**Required**    The following is a list of websites for a number of companies. Briefly describe each company and indicate whether it is more likely to use job costing or process costing. Explain why in each case. Also explain why you think each company (a) is or is not a global company, and (b) has significant environmental issues in its operations.

1. New Century Software Inc. at **www.newcenturysoftware.com**.
2. FedExOffice at **www.fedex.com**.
3. TXI Cement (TXI) at **www.txi.com**.
4. Paramount Pictures at **www.paramount.com**.
5. Coca-Cola at **www.coca-cola.com**.

[LO 4-1, 4-2]    **4-30    Choice of Costing System**

**Required**    The following is a list of websites for a number of companies. Briefly describe each company and indicate whether it is more likely to use job costing or process costing. Explain why in each case. Also explain why you think each company (a) is or is not a global company, and (b) has significant environmental issues in its operations.

1. Zurich Financial Services Group at **www.zurich.com**.
2. Reichhold Chemical Co. at **www.reichhold.com**.
3. Nestle S.A. at **www.nestle.com**.
4. Evian at **www.evian.com**.

[LO 4-3, 4-4]   4-31 **Cost Flows; Applying Overhead**   Erkens Company uses a job costing system with normal costing and applies factory overhead on the basis of machine-hours. At the beginning of the year, management estimated that the company would incur $1,980,000 of factory overhead costs and use 66,000 machine-hours.

Erkens Company recorded the following events during the month of April:

a. Purchased 180,000 pounds of materials on account; the cost was $5.00 per pound.
b. Issued 120,000 pounds of materials to production, of which 15,000 pounds were used as indirect materials.
c. Incurred direct labor costs of $240,000 and $40,000 of indirect labor costs.
d. Recorded depreciation on equipment for the month, $75,700.
e. Recorded insurance costs for the manufacturing property, $3,500.
f. Paid $8,500 cash for utilities and other miscellaneous items for the manufacturing plant.
g. Completed Job H11 costing $7,500 and Job G28 costing $77,000 during the month and transferred them to the Finished Goods Inventory account.
h. Shipped Job G28 to the customer during the month. The job was invoiced at 35% above cost.
i. Used 7,700 machine-hours during April.

**Required**
1. Compute Erkens Company's predetermined overhead rate for the year.
2. Prepare journal entries to record the events that occurred during April.
3. Compute the amount of overapplied or underapplied overhead and prepare a journal entry to close overapplied or underapplied overhead into cost of goods sold on April 30.

[LO 4-4, 4-5]   4-32 **Application of Overhead**   Alles Company uses a job costing system that applies factory overhead on the basis of direct labor dollars. No job was in process on February 1. During the month of February, the company worked on these three jobs:

|  | Job Number | | |
|---|---|---|---|
|  | **B10** | **C44** | **G15** |
| Direct labor ($8/hour) | $34,000 | ? | $10,000 |
| Direct materials | 42,000 | 61,000 | ? |
| Overhead applied | ? | 20,750 | 6,000 |

During the month, the company completed and transferred Job B10 to the finished goods inventory. Jobs C44 and G15 were not completed and remain in work in process at the cost of $148,650 at the end of the month. Actual factory overhead costs during the month totaled $38,500.

**Required**
1. What is the predetermined factory overhead rate?
2. Compute the amount of underapplied or overapplied overhead for February.

[LO 4-4, 4-5]   4-33 **Job Costing**   Johnson Inc. is a job-order manufacturing company that uses a predetermined overhead rate based on direct labor-hours to apply overhead to individual jobs. For 2013, estimated direct labor-hours are 95,000 and estimated factory overhead is $617,500. The following information is for September 2013. Job A was completed during September, and Job B was started but not finished.

| September 1, 2013, inventories | |
|---|---:|
| Materials inventory | $ 7,500 |
| Work-in-process inventory (All Job A) | 31,200 |
| Finished goods inventory | 67,000 |
| Material purchases | 104,000 |
| Direct materials requisitioned | |
| Job A | 65,000 |
| Job B | 33,500 |
| Direct labor-hours | |
| Job A | 4,200 |
| Job B | 3,500 |
| Labor costs incurred | |
| Direct labor ($8.50/hour) | 65,450 |
| Indirect labor | 13,500 |
| Supervisory salaries | 6,000 |
| Rental costs | |
| Factory | 7,000 |
| Administrative offices | 1,800 |
| Total equipment depreciation costs | |
| Factory | 7,500 |
| Administrative offices | 1,600 |
| Indirect materials used | 12,000 |

**Required**

1. What is the total cost of Job A?
2. What is the total factory overhead applied during September?
3. What is the overapplied or underapplied overhead for September?

[LO 4-4, 4-5]    4-34 **Application of Overhead**   Whitley Construction Company is in the home remodeling business. Whitley has three teams of highly skilled employees, each of whom has multiple skills involving carpentry, painting, and other home remodeling activities. Each team is led by an experienced employee who coordinates the work done on each job. As the needs of different jobs change, some team members may be shifted to other teams for short periods of time. Whitley uses a job costing system to determine job costs and to serve as a basis for bidding and pricing the jobs. Direct materials and direct labor are easily traced to each job, using Whitley's cost tracking software. Overhead consists of the purchase and maintenance of construction equipment, some supervisory labor, the cost of bidding for new customers, and administrative costs. Whitley uses an annual overhead rate based on direct labor-hours.

Whitley has recently completed work for three clients: Harrison, Barnes, and Tyler. The cost data for each of the three jobs are summarized below.

| Job | Direct Materials | Direct Labor-Hours | Direct Labor Cost |
|---|---|---|---|
| Harrison | $ 6,753 | 45 | $15,367 |
| Barnes | 13,229 | 88 | 22,184 |
| Tyler | 42,338 | 133 | 49,654 |

Budgeted direct materials cost and direct labor cost for the year are estimated at $450,000 and $600,000, respectively. Direct labor-hours are budgeted at 22,500 hours, and total overhead is budgeted at $495,000.

**Required**

1. Calculate the total cost of each of the three jobs.
2. Suppose that for the entire year, Whitley used 23,800 labor-hours and total actual overhead was $525,000. What is the amount of underapplied or overapplied overhead?
3. Whitley's business is very seasonal, with summer the period of high activity and winter the low period. How would seasonality potentially affect the job costing at the company?
4. What are some of the potential sustainability issues for Whitley?
5. Whitley has chosen direct labor-hours as the cost-driver base for applying overhead. What are some alternative cost drivers, and how would you choose among them?

[LO 4-4, 4-5]    4-35 **Application of Overhead**   Tomek Company uses a job costing system that applies factory overhead on the basis of direct labor-hours. The company's factory overhead budget for 2013 included the following estimates:

| | |
|---|---|
| Budgeted total factory overhead | $568,000 |
| Budgeted total direct labor-hours | 71,000 |

At the end of the year, the company shows these results:

| | |
|---|---|
| Actual factory overhead | $582,250 |
| Actual direct labor-hours | 71,500 |

**Required**

1. Compute the firm's predetermined factory overhead rate for 2013.
2. Calculate the amount of overapplied or underapplied overhead.
3. Prepare a journal entry to transfer the underapplied or overapplied overhead to the Cost of Goods Sold account.

**[LO 4-4]  4-36  Application of Overhead**  Norton Associates is an advertising agency in Austin, Texas. The company's controller estimated that it would incur $325,000 in overhead costs for 2013. Because the overhead costs of each project change in direct proportion to the amount of direct professional hours incurred, the controller decided that overhead should be applied on the basis of professional hours. The controller estimated 25,000 professional hours for the year. During October, Norton incurred the following costs to make a 20-second TV commercial for Central Texas Bank:

| | |
|---|---|
| Direct materials | $32,000 |
| Direct professional hours ($50/hour) | 1,200 |

The industry customarily bills customers at 150% of total cost.

**Required**

1. Compute the predetermined overhead rate.
2. What is the total amount of the bill that Norton will send Central Texas Bank?

**[LO 4-4]  4-37  Application of Overhead**  Progressive Painting Company (PPC) is a successful company in commercial and residential painting. PPC has a variety of jobs: new construction, repair and repainting existing structures, and restoration of very old buildings and homes. The company is known for the quality and reliability of its work, and customers expect to pay a little more for those benefits. One of the company's core values is sustainability, and it insists on using the most environmentally friendly paints and materials in its work; it has refused jobs where the client required a more environmentally harmful paint than PPC thought was appropriate for the application. The company's commitment to sustainability has lost PPC some jobs, but it has also attracted a loyal and growing customer base.

The company uses job costing and applies overhead on the basis of direct labor-hours. Overhead for the company consists of painting equipment, trucks, supervisory labor, supplies, and administrative operation costs. The total budgeted costs for the year are shown below.

| | Budgeted Data |
|---|---|
| Direct materials | $2,900,000 |
| Direct labor-hours | 33,500 |
| Direct labor dollars | $750,000 |
| Gallons of paint | 20,000 |
| Total overhead | $360,125 |

PPC has just completed two jobs:

| Job | Direct Materials | Gallons of Paint | Direct Labor-Hours | Direct Labor Cost |
|---|---|---|---|---|
| Prevette | $3,800 | 24 | 42 | $ 855 |
| Harmon | 4,600 | 38 | 66 | 1,366 |

**Required**

1. Determine the total cost of each job.
2. The Prevette job required oil-based paint and the clean-up after the job required the use of chemicals that, after use, had to be disposed of in an environmentally appropriate way. In contrast, the Harmon job required water-based paint and the job clean-up was very quick and simple and involved no harmful chemicals. Does the job costing in part 1 above capture the difference between

the two jobs in regard to the types of paint used? Do you think the costing system should capture this difference, if any, and if so, how do you think the costing system should be changed?

**[LO 4-7]**   4-38   **Spoilage and Scrap (appendix)**   Lexan Textile Company's Job X12 had one of its 20 units spoiled. The cost incurred on the unit was $600. It was specific normal spoilage with an estimated disposal price of $300 for the spoiled unit. Job Y34 had common normal spoilage with the estimated cost of $400 from the general production process failure and abnormal spoilage of $200. The company also incurred scrap due to Job Y34 and sold it for $80. It also sold the scrap common to all jobs for $120 cash in May.

**Required**
1. Make the necessary journal entries to record normal and abnormal spoilage costs.
2. Make the necessary journal entries to record both types of scrap sold.

## Problems

**[LO 4-2]**   4-39   **Overhead Rates Used for Each Machine in a Printing Plant**   Ennis Inc.'s Forms Solutions Group (http://www.ennis.com/) is a Texas-based machine-intensive printing company that produces business forms. The resources demanded by a specific job depend on the type and amount of paper used and the composition and the construction of the business form. All jobs are constrained by the time necessary on a press and on a collator capable of producing forms at the required size.

Ennis Inc.'s Forms Solutions (EFS) uses job costing for pricing and bidding decisions. EFS uses a separate factory overhead rate for each machine. Costs of machine operator, support personnel, and supplies are identified directly with presses and collators. Other factory overhead costs—including insurance, supervision, and office salaries—are allocated to machines based on their processing capacity (cost driver is the number of feet of business forms per minute), weighted by the maximum paper width and complexity (the cost driver is the number of colors and other features) that they are capable of handling.

When EFS receives a request for a bid on a particular job, the company uses computer software to determine direct materials costs based on the type and quantity of paper. Then it identifies the least expensive press and collator that are capable of handling the specifications for the business form ordered. The third step is to estimate the total press and collator processing costs by using specific cost-driver rates per machine time multiplied by the estimated processing time. The bid price is calculated by adding a standard markup to the total press, collator, and direct materials costs. A higher markup is used for rush jobs and jobs requiring special features.

**Required**   Discuss the strengths and weaknesses of the EFS costing system and its strategic implications.

**[LO 4-2, 4-4, 4-5]**   4-40   **Plantwide vs. Departmental Overhead Rate**   Rose Bach was recently hired as controller of Empco Inc., a sheet metal manufacturer. Empco has been in the sheet metal business for many years and is currently investigating ways to modernize its manufacturing process. At the first staff meeting Rose attended, Bob Kelley, chief engineer, presented a proposal for automating the drilling department. He recommended that Empco purchase two robots that could replace the eight direct labor workers in the department. The cost savings outlined in Bob's proposal included eliminating direct labor cost and reducing factory overhead cost to zero in the drilling department because Empco charges factory overhead on the basis of direct labor dollars using a plantwide rate.

Empco's president was puzzled by Kelley's explanation of cost savings, believing it made no sense. Rose agreed, explaining that as firms become more automated, they should rethink their factory overhead systems. The president then asked her to look into the matter and prepare a report for the next staff meeting.

**Required**
1. Describe the shortcomings of Empco's current system for applying overhead.
2. Explain the misconceptions in Bob Kelley's statement that the factory overhead cost in the drilling department would be reduced to zero if the automation proposal were implemented.
3. How would you improve the allocation of overhead costs?

**[LO 4-2, 4-4, 4-5]**   4-41   **Plantwide vs. Departmental Overhead Rate**   Adams Corporation manufactures auto steering systems. Cost estimates for one unit of the product for the year 2013 follow:

| | |
|---|---|
| Direct materials | $200 |
| Direct labor ($12/hour) | 240 |
| Machine-hours | 20 |

This product requires 12 hours of direct labor in department A and 8 hours in department B. Also, it requires 5 machine-hours in department A and 15 machine-hours in department B. The factory overhead costs estimated in these two departments follow:

|  | A | B |
|---|---|---|
| Variable cost | $146,000 | $ 77,000 |
| Fixed cost | 94,000 | 163,000 |

Management expects the firm to produce 1,000 units during 2013.

**Required**

1. Assume that factory overhead was applied on the basis of direct labor-hours. Compute the predetermined factory overhead rate.

2. If factory overhead were applied on the basis of machine-hours, what would be the plantwide overhead rate?

3. If the company produced 1,000 units during the year, what was the total amount of applied factory overhead in each department in requirements 1 and 2?

4. If you were asked to evaluate the performance of each department manager, which allocation basis (cost driver) would you use? Why?

5. Compute the departmental overhead rates for each department.

[LO 4-3, 4-4, 4-5]   4-42  **Application of Overhead**   Work in process inventory for Carston Inc. at the beginning of the year was a single job, Job T114:

| Job # | Materials | Labor | Overhead | Total |
|---|---|---|---|---|
| T114 | $31,500 | $16,250 | $28,750 | $76,500 |

The company's budgeted costs for the year are as follows:

| | |
|---|---|
| Budgeted overhead | |
| Variable | |
|     Indirect materials | $ 68,000 |
|     Indirect labor | 56,000 |
|     Employee benefits | 28,000 |
| Fixed | |
|     Supervision | 13,000 |
|     Depreciation | 15,000 |
| Total | $180,000 |
| Budgeted direct labor dollars | $ 90,000 |
| Rate per direct labor dollar | 200.00% |

The company's actual costs incurred during the year are as follows:

| | | Incurred by Jobs | | |
|---|---|---|---|---|
| Job # | Materials | Labor | Other | Total |
| T114 | $ 2,000 | $10,000 | $  – | $ 12,000 |
| T119 | 24,000 | 18,000 | – | 42,000 |
| T133 | 8,000 | 34,000 | – | 42,000 |
| T136 | 1,000 | 16,000 | – | 17,000 |
| | $35,000 | $78,000 | | $113,000 |

| Overhead | | | | |
|---|---|---|---|---|
| Indirect materials and supplies | 60,000 | – | – | 60,000 |
| Indirect labor | – | 50,000 | – | 50,000 |
| Employee benefits | – | – | 33,000 | 33,000 |
| Depreciation | – | – | 15,000 | 15,000 |
| Supervision | – | 12,000 | – | 12,000 |
| Total | $60,000 | $62,000 | $48,000 | $170,000 |

**Required**

1. What was the actual factory overhead for Carston Inc. for the year?
2. What was overapplied or underapplied overhead for the year?
3. Job T114 was the only job completed and sold in the year. What amount was included in the cost of the goods sold for this job?
4. What was the amount of work-in-process inventory at the end of the year?

[LO 4-4, 4-5]   4-43  **Quarterly and Annual Overhead Application**   The Mansfield Machine Shop is a family-owned business with 25 employees. The founding brothers, Steve and George, started the business in 1974 with a single milling machine, a grinder, and a lathe. The brothers now own a business with 27 machines and operating revenues of more than $5 million per year. The brothers have noticed that they are losing business to new competitors and they have heard from some of their customers that their competitors have better prices. So they have asked you to study their operations and summary financial reports for the prior year and to make recommendations.

The information available to you includes:

1. The business is very seasonal, as it reflects the seasonality of the businesses of its major customers in the manufacturing and construction industries. The first and third quarters of the year have relatively low demand, while their busiest periods are the second and fourth quarters. George and Steve measure the volume of their business in machine-hours, since they charge by the machine-hour and the materials costs are negligible. The machine-hours demand for last year was 5,000 hours in the first quarter, 12,500 in the second quarter, 7,500 in the third quarter, and 11,250 in the fourth quarter.

2. Mansfield has 27 machines in the plant, and while some are newer and more technologically advanced than others, the differences are not great. Because of this, the brothers charge the same price for machining on each of the machines. George and Steve realize that their business is very seasonal and that their machines and operators will be busier at times, but to keep the machines in good shape and operators rested, they try to limit the work to approximately 150 hours per month per machine.

3. Because of the seasonality of the business, George and Steve have always recalculated the overhead rate for each quarter. The overhead rate is determined at the end of each quarter based on actual total overhead costs for the quarter (which are $450,000 per quarter) and the actual machine-hours for that quarter. This machine-hours-based rate is then used in the following quarter and is revised accordingly at the end of each quarter.

4. Mansfield's variable costs are $45 per machine-hour. The firm charges a 50% markup over full cost, the sum of variable costs and overhead charges per unit. Mansfield uses $85 full cost in pricing for the first quarter.

5. In addition to $450,000 fixed operating costs per quarter, Mansfield has $25,000 administrative fixed costs per quarter.

**Required**

1. Calculate the overhead rates and machine-hour pricing rates using the quarterly overhead system now used by the firm.
2. Recalculate the overhead rates and machine-hour pricing rates using an annual overhead rate.
3. Calculate total contribution and operating income for the year and for each quarter under both the quarterly and annual rates.
4. Interpret your findings in parts 1 through 3. How does the choice of a quarterly overhead rate affect pricing for Mansfield? Which overhead rate, quarterly or annual, do you think Mansfield should use and why? What are the strategic implications of the choice of overhead rates for the company?

[LO 4-3, 4-4, 4-5]   4-44  **Application of Overhead**   The following information applies to the O'Donnell Company for March production. There are only two jobs (X and Y) in production in March.

a. Purchased direct materials and indirect materials with the following summary of receiving reports:

| | |
|---|---|
| Material A | $16,000 |
| Material B | 12,000 |
| Indirect materials | 3,000 |
| Total | $31,000 |

b. Issued direct materials and indirect materials with this summary of requisitions:

|  | Job X | Job Y | Total |
|---|---|---|---|
| Material A | $ 8,000 | $16,000 | $24,000 |
| Material B | 3,000 | 8,000 | 11,000 |
| Subtotal | $11,000 | $24,000 | $35,000 |
| Indirect materials |  |  | 39,000 |
| Total |  |  | $74,000 |

c. Factory labor incurred is summarized by these time tickets:

| | |
|---|---|
| Job X | $22,000 |
| Job Y | 15,000 |
| Indirect labor | 28,000 |
| Total | $65,000 |

d. Factory utilities, factory depreciation, and factory insurance incurred is summarized as follows:

| | |
|---|---|
| Utilities | $ 3,000 |
| Depreciation | 18,000 |
| Insurance | 2,500 |
| Total | $23,500 |

e. Factory overhead costs were applied to jobs at the predetermined rate of $46 per machine-hour. Job X incurred 1,100 machine-hours; Job Y used 800 machine-hours.

f. Job X was completed; Job Y was still in process at the end of March.

The company closed the overapplied or underapplied overhead to the Cost of Goods Sold account at the end of March.

**Required**

1. Calculate the total manufacturing cost for Job X and Job Y for March.
2. Calculate the amount of overapplied or underapplied overhead and state whether the cost of goods sold account will be increased or decreased by the adjustment.

**[LO 4-3, 4-4, 4-5]**   4-45 **Application of Overhead**   The following information is for Punta Company for July 2013:

a. Applied factory overhead costs to jobs at the predetermined rate of $42.50 per labor-hour. Job S incurred 6,175 labor-hours; Job T used 4,275 labor-hours.

b. Shipped Job S to customers during July. Job S had a gross margin of 24% based on manufacturing cost.

c. Job T was still in process at the end of July.

d. Closed the overapplied or underapplied overhead to the Cost of Goods Sold account at the end of July.

e. Factory utilities, factory depreciation, and factory insurance incurred are summarized as follows:

| | |
|---|---|
| Utilities | $14,250 |
| Depreciation | 45,000 |
| Insurance | 18,000 |
| Total | $77,250 |

f. Direct materials and indirect materials used are as follows:

| | Job S | Job T | Total |
|---|---|---|---|
| Material A | $28,500 | $ 71,250 | $ 99,750 |
| Material B | 12,000 | 35,000 | 47,000 |
| Subtotal | $40,500 | $106,250 | $146,750 |
| Indirect materials | | | 211,000 |
| Total | | | $357,750 |

g. Factory labor incurred for the two jobs and indirect labor are as follows:

| | |
|---|---|
| Job S | $ 55,500 |
| Job T | 45,000 |
| Indirect labor | 133,000 |
| Total | $233,500 |

**Required**

1. Calculate the total manufacturing cost for Job S and Job T for July 2013.
2. Calculate the amount of overapplied or underapplied overhead and state whether the Cost of Goods Sold account will be increased or decreased by the adjustment.

[LO 4-3, 4-4, 4-5] 4-46 **Cost Flows; Application of Overhead** Apex Corporation manufactures reproductions of eighteenth-century, classical-style furniture. It uses a job costing system that applies factory overhead on the basis of direct labor-hours. Budgeted factory overhead for the year 2013 was $1,235,475, and management budgeted 86,700 direct labor-hours. Apex had no materials, work-in-process, or finished goods inventory at the beginning of August 2013. These transactions were recorded during August:

a. Purchased 5,000 square feet of oak on account at $25 per square foot.
b. Purchased 50 gallons of glue on account at $36 per gallon (indirect material).
c. Requisitioned 3,500 square feet of oak and 30.5 gallons of glue for production.
d. Incurred and paid payroll costs of $187,900. Of this amount, $46,000 were indirect labor costs; direct labor personnel earned $22 per hour.
e. Paid factory utility bill, $15,230 in cash.
f. August's insurance cost for the manufacturing property and equipment was $3,500. The premium had been paid in March.
g. Incurred $8,200 depreciation on manufacturing equipment for August.
h. Recorded $2,400 depreciation on an administrative asset.
i. Paid advertising expenses in cash, $5,500.
j. Incurred and paid other factory overhead costs, $13,500.
k. Incurred miscellaneous selling and administrative expenses, $13,250.
l. Applied factory overhead to production on the basis of direct labor-hours.
m. Completed goods costing $146,000 manufactured during the month.
n. Sales on account in August were $132,000. The cost of goods sold was $112,000.

**Required**

1. Compute the firm's predetermined factory overhead rate for the year.
2. Prepare journal entries to record the August events. Letter your entries from a to n.
3. Calculate the amount of overapplied or underapplied overhead to be closed to the Cost of Goods Sold account on August 31, 2013.
4. Prepare a schedule of cost of goods manufactured and sold.
5. Prepare the income statement for August.

[LO 4-3, 4-4, 4-5] 4-47 **Cost Flows; Application of Overhead** Platinum Wish is a small manufacturer of gold and platinum jewelry. It uses a job costing system that applies overhead on the basis of direct labor-hours. Budgeted factory overhead for the year 2013 was $443,800, and management budgeted

31,700 direct labor-hours. The company had no materials, work-in-process, or finished goods inventory at the beginning of April. These transactions were recorded during April:

a. April insurance cost for the manufacturing property and equipment was $1,600. The premium had been paid in January.

b. Recorded $1,025 depreciation on an administrative asset.

c. Purchased 21 pounds of high-grade polishing materials at $15 per pound (indirect material).

d. Paid factory utility bill, $6,510 in cash.

e. Incurred 4,000 hours and paid payroll costs of $160,000. Of this amount, 1,000 hours and $20,000 were indirect labor costs.

f. Incurred and paid other factory overhead costs, $5,770.

g. Purchased $24,500 of materials. Direct materials included unpolished semiprecious stones and gold. Indirect materials included supplies and polishing materials.

h. Requisitioned $18,500 of direct materials and $1,500 of indirect materials from materials inventory.

i. Incurred miscellaneous selling and administrative expenses, $5,660.

j. Incurred $3,505 depreciation on manufacturing equipment for April.

k. Paid advertising expenses in cash, $2,350.

l. Applied factory overhead to production on the basis of direct labor-hours.

m. Completed goods costing $65,000 manufactured during the month.

n. Made sales on account in August, $56,410. The cost of goods sold was $47,860.

**Required**
1. Compute the firm's predetermined factory overhead rate for the year.
2. Prepare journal entries to record the April events.
3. Calculate the amount of overapplied or underapplied overhead to be closed to the Cost of Goods Sold account on April 30.
4. Prepare a schedule of cost of goods manufactured and sold.
5. Prepare the income statement for April.

[LO 4-4]    4-48    **Application of Overhead**    The Terry CPA firm has the following overhead budget for 2013:

| Overhead | |
|---|---:|
| Indirect materials | $ 250,000 |
| Indirect labor | 1,350,000 |
| Depreciation—Building | 293,000 |
| Depreciation—Furniture | 25,000 |
| Utilities | 285,000 |
| Insurance | 34,000 |
| Property taxes | 28,000 |
| Other expenses | 135,000 |
| Total | $2,400,000 |

The firm estimates total direct labor cost in 2013 to be $1,600,000. The firm uses direct labor cost as the cost driver to apply overhead to clients.

During January, the firm worked for many clients; data for two of them follow:

| | |
|---|---:|
| Barry account | |
| Direct labor | $2,200 |
| Miles account | |
| Direct labor | $8,400 |

**Required**
1. Compute the firm's budgeted overhead rate.
2. Compute the amount of overhead to be charged to the Barry and Miles accounts using the predetermined overhead rate calculated in requirement 1.
3. Compute total job cost for the Barry account and the Miles account.

**[LO 4-4]** **4-49** **Job Cost; Spreadsheet Application; Pivot Tables in Excel (see Excel tutorial on text website)** Decker Screw Manufacturing Company produces special screws made to customer specifications. During June, the following data pertained to these costs:

### Summary of Direct Materials Requisitions

| Department Number | Job Number | Requisition Number | Quantity | Cost per Unit |
|---|---|---|---|---|
| 1 | 2906 | B9766 | 4,550 | $ 1.34 |
| 2 | 2907 | B9767 | 110 | 22.18 |
| 1 | 2908 | B9768 | 1,000 | 9.00 |
| 1 | 2906 | B9769 | 4,430 | 1.35 |
| 2 | 2908 | B9770 | 23 | 48.00 |

### Summary of Direct Labor Time Tickets

| Department Number | Job Number | Ticket Number | Hours | Cost per Hour |
|---|---|---|---|---|
| 1 | 2906 | 1056-1168 | 1,102 | $6.50 |
| 2 | 2907 | 2121-2130 | 136 | 8.88 |
| 1 | 2908 | 1169-1189 | 151 | 6.50 |
| 2 | 2908 | 2131-1239 | 32 | 8.88 |
| 1 | 2906 | 1190-1239 | 810 | 6.50 |

### Summary of Factory Overhead Application Rates

| Department Number | Basis of Application Rates |
|---|---|
| 1 | $3 per direct labor-hour |
| 2 | 150% of direct labor cost |

Decker had no beginning work-in-process inventory for June. Of the jobs begun in June, Job 2906 was completed and sold on account for $30,000, Job 2907 was completed but not sold, and Job 2908 was still in process.

**Required**
1. Calculate the direct materials, direct labor, factory overhead, and total costs for each job started in June, using Excel.
2. Perform the same calculations as in requirement (1), but assume that the direct labor-rate per hour increased by 10% in Department 1 and 25% in Department 2.
3. Perform the same calculations in part (1) except that you should use Pivot Tables in Excel to arrive at the answer. The Excel Tutorial for Chapter 4, on the text website, explains how to use Pivot Tables.
4. Perform the same calculations in part (2) except that you should use Pivot Tables in Excel to arrive at the answer.

**[LO 4-4, 4-5]** **4-50** **Application of Overhead; Schedule of Cost of Goods Manufactured**

Haughton Company uses a job costing system for its production costs and a predetermined factory overhead rate based on direct labor costs to apply factory overhead to all jobs. During the month of July, the firm processed three jobs: X13, X14, and X15, of which X13 was started in June.

| Inventories | July 1 | July 31 |
|---|---|---|
| Direct materials | $36,500 | ? |
| Work in process | 41,000 | ? |
| Finished goods | 0 | 0 |
| Cost of Goods Sold, July | $ ? | |
| Direct materials purchased in July | 55,000 | |
| Issued to production: | | |
| X13 | 16,380 | |
| X14 | 24,220 | |
| X15 | 14,000 | |

Factory labor-hours used ($30/hour):

| | |
|---|---|
| X13 | 3,500 |
| X14 | 2,800 |
| X15 | 1,600 |
| Indirect labor | 6,900 |

Other factory overhead costs incurred:

| | |
|---|---|
| Rent | $131,500 |
| Utility | 180,600 |
| Repairs and maintenance | 188,500 |
| Depreciation | 131,100 |
| Other | 56,000 |

As of July 31, Job X13 was sold and Jobs X14 and X15 were still in processing. Total factory overhead applied in July was $900,600.

**Required**

1. Compute the predetermined factory overhead rate.
2. Compute the amount of materials inventory at the end of July.
3. Compute the actual factory overhead cost incurred during the month of July.
4. Compute the ending balance of the work-in-process inventory account for July.
5. Prepare the statement cost of goods manufactured for July.
6. Compute the amount of over- or underapplied overhead.
7. What is the cost per unit of Job X13 if it has a total of 100 units?
8. Prepare the statement of cost of goods sold for July.

[LO 4-4]   4-51   **Application of Overhead; Ethics**   Aero Systems is a manufacturer of airplane parts and engines for a variety of military and commercial aircraft. It has two production departments. Department A is machine-intensive; Department B is labor-intensive. Aero Systems has adopted a traditional plantwide rate using the direct labor-hour-based overhead allocation system. The company recently conducted a pilot study using a departmental overhead rate costing system. This system used two overhead allocation bases: machine-hours for Department A and direct labor-hours for Department B. The study showed that the system, which will be more accurate and timely, will assign lower costs to the government jobs and higher costs to the company's nongovernmental jobs. Apparently, the current (less accurate) direct labor-based costing system has overcosted government jobs and undercosted private business jobs. On hearing of this, top management has decided to scrap the plans for adopting the new departmental overhead rate costing system because government jobs constitute 40% of Aero Systems' business and the new system will reduce the price and thus the profit for this part of its business.

**Required**   As the management accountant participating in this pilot study project, what is your responsibility when you hear of top management's decision to cancel the plans to implement the new departmental overhead rate costing system? What would you do?

[LO 4-6]   4-52   **Operation Costing**   Brian Canning Co., which sells canned corn, uses an operation costing system. Cans of corn are classified as either sweet or regular, depending on the type of corn used. Both types of corn go through the separating and cleaning operations, but only regular corn goes through the creaming operation. During January, two batches of corn were canned from start to finish. Batch X consisted of 800 pounds of sweet corn and batch Y consisted of 700 pounds of regular corn. The company had no beginning or ending work-in-process inventory. The following cost information is for the month of January:

| | Batch | Cost | Batch Size |
|---|---|---|---|
| Raw sweet corn | X | $5,200 | 800 lb. |
| Raw regular corn | Y | 2,450* | 700 lb. |
| Separating department costs | | 1,500 | |
| Cleaning department costs | | 900 | |
| Creaming department costs | | 210 | |

*Includes $300 for cream.

**Required**

1. Compute the unit cost for sweet corn and regular corn.

2. Record appropriate journal entries.

[LO 4-7] 4-53 **Spoilage, Rework, and Scrap (appendix)** Richport Company manufactures products that often require specification changes or modifications to meet customer needs. Consequently, Richport employs a job costing system for its operations.

Although the specification changes and modifications are commonplace, Richport has been able to establish a normal spoilage rate of 2.5% of good units produced (before spoilage). The company recognizes normal spoilage during the budgeting process and classifies it as a component of factory overhead. Thus, the predetermined overhead rate used to apply factory overhead costs to jobs includes an allowance for net spoilage cost for normal spoilage. If spoilage on a job exceeds the normal rate, it is considered abnormal and then must be analyzed and the cause of the spoilage must be submitted to management.

Randa Duncan, one of Richport's inspection managers, has been reviewing the output of Job N1192-122 that was recently completed. A total of 122,000 units had been started for the job, and 5,000 units were rejected at final inspection, meaning that the job yielded 117,000 good units.

Randa noted that 900 of the first units produced were rejected due to a very unusual design defect that was corrected immediately; no more units were rejected for this reason.

Randa was unable to identify a pattern for the remaining 4,100 rejected units. They can be sold at a salvage value of $7 per unit.

The total costs accumulated for all 122,000 units of Job N1192-122 follow. Although the job is completed, all of these costs are still in the Work-in-Process Inventory account (i.e., the cost of the completed job has not been transferred to the Finished Goods Inventory account).

| | |
|---|---|
| Direct materials | $2,196,000 |
| Direct labor | 1,830,000 |
| Applied factory overhead | 2,928,000 |
| Total cost of job | $6,954,000 |

**Required**

1. Explain the distinction between normal and abnormal spoilage.

2. Distinguish between spoiled units, rework units, and scrap.

3. Review the results and costs for Job N1192-122.

  a. Prepare an analysis separating the spoiled units into normal and abnormal spoilage by first determining the normal input required to yield 117,000 good units.

  b. Prepare the appropriate journal entries to account for Job N1192-122.

## Solution to Self-Study Problem

### Journal Entries and Accounting for Overhead

1. Journal entries:

| (a) | Materials Inventory | 25,000 | |
|---|---|---|---|
| |     Accounts Payable | | 25,000 |
| | To record the purchase of direct materials and indirect materials. | | |
| (b) | Work-in-Process Inventory | 15,000 | |
| | Factory Overhead | 8,000 | |
| |     Materials Inventory | | 23,000 |
| | To record direct and indirect materials issued. | | |
| (c) | Work-in-Process Inventory | 20,000 | |
| | Factory Overhead | 5,000 | |
| |     Accrued Payroll | | 25,000 |
| | To record factory labor incurred. | | |

| (d) | Factory Overhead | 18,000 | |
| |     Accounts Payable | | 500 |
| |     Accumulated Depreciation—Factory | | 15,000 |
| |     Prepaid Insurance | | 2,500 |
| |     To record actual overhead costs incurred, including factory utilities, depreciation, and insurance. | | |
| (e) | Work-in-Process Inventory | 30,000 | |
| |     Factory Overhead | | 30,000 |
| |     To record the application of factory overhead to jobs. | | |

---

**Summary of factory overhead applied**

| | |
|---|---|
| Job 101($15 per machine hour × 1,200 hours.) | $18,000 |
| Job 102($15 per machine hour × 800 hours) | 12,000 |
| Total | $30,000 |

---

| (f) | Finished Goods Inventory | 45,000 | |
| |     Work-in-Process Inventory | | 45,000 |
| |     To record the completion of Job 101. | | |

---

**Total manufacturing cost for Job 101**

| | |
|---|---|
| Beginning inventory | $ 6,000 |
| Direct materials added | 9,000 |
| Direct labor incurred | 12,000 |
| Factory overhead applied | 18,000 |
| Total | $45,000 |

---

| (g) | Accounts Receivable | 66,000 | |
| |     Sales | | 66,000 |
| |     To record the total sales revenue of jobs 100 and 101. | | |
| | Cost of Goods Sold | 55,000 | |
| |     Finished Goods Inventory | | 55,000 |
| |     To record the total cost of goods sold. | | |

---

**Summary of the total cost in shipping orders**

| | |
|---|---|
| Job 100 | $10,000 |
| Job 101 | 45,000 |
| Total | $55,000 |

Sales = $55,000 × 120% = $66,000

---

2. Ending balance of the Work-in-Process Inventory account for Job 102:

| | |
|---|---|
| Direct materials ($3,000 material X, $3,000 material Y) | $ 6,000 |
| Direct labor | 8,000 |
| Factory overhead applied (800 machine hours × $15) | 12,000 |
| Total ending balance | $26,000 |

3. Factory overhead variance:

| Actual factory overhead | | |
|---|---|---|
| Indirect materials | $ 8,000 | |
| Indirect labor | 5,000 | |
| Utilities | 500 | |
| Depreciation | 15,000 | |
| Insurance | 2,500 | $31,000 |
| Less: Applied factory overhead (e) | | 30,000 |
| Underapplied factory overhead | | $ 1,000 |

4. To record the disposition of underapplied factory overhead by closing the Factory Overhead account to the Cost of Goods Sold account:

| (h) | Cost of Goods Sold | 1,000 | |
|---|---|---|---|
| | Factory Overhead | | 1,000 |

*Please visit* **http://www.com/blocher6e** *to access a narrated, animated tutorial for solving this problem.*

# CHAPTER FIVE

# Activity-Based Costing and Customer Profitability Analysis

---

Beware of little expenses. A small leak will sink a great ship.

*Benjamin Franklin*

---

This chapter has a lot to do with implementing the spirit of Benjamin Franklin's observation—in cost management terms—that it really does matter how accurately you calculate a cost. Why? Having accurate costs is important for a variety of reasons: a company might find that it has a difficult time determining which of its products is most profitable. Alternatively, it finds its sales increasing but profits declining and cannot understand why. Perhaps the company keeps losing competitive bids for products and services and does not understand why. In many cases, accurate cost information is the answer to these questions. Improved understanding of the use of resources and the assignment of their related costs provides a competitive advantage. It helps a company or organization to develop and to execute its strategy by providing accurate information about the cost of its products and services, the cost of serving its customers, the cost of dealing with its suppliers, and the cost of supporting business processes within the company.

## The Strategic Role of Activity-Based Costing

**LO 5-1**

*Explain the strategic role of activity-based costing.*

Activity-based costing (ABC) is a method for improving the accuracy of cost determination. While ABC is a relatively recent innovation in cost accounting, it has been adopted by companies in varying industries and within government and not-for-profit organizations. Here is a quick example of how it works, and why it is important. Suppose you and two friends (Joe and Al) have gone out for dinner. You each order a personal-size pizza, and Al suggests ordering a plate of appetizers for the table. You and Joe figure you will have a bite or two of the appetizers, so you say OK. Dinner is great, but at the end Al is still hungry, so he orders another plate of appetizers, but this time, eats all of it. When it is time for the check, Al suggests the three of you split the cost of the meal equally. Is this fair? Perhaps Al should offer to pay more for the two appetizer plates. The individual pizzas are direct costs for each of you so that an equal share is fair, but while the appetizer plates were intended to be shared equally, it turns out that Al consumed most of them.

There are similar examples in manufacturing. Suppose you and Joe and Al are also product managers at a plant that manufactures furniture. There are three product lines. Al is in charge of sofa manufacturing, Joe of dining room tables and chairs, and you are in charge of bedroom furniture. The direct materials and labor costs are traced directly to each product line. Also, there are indirect manufacturing costs (overhead) that are associated with activities that cannot be traced to a single product, including: materials acquisition, materials storage and handling, product inspection, manufacturing supervision, job scheduling, equipment maintenance, and fabric cutting. What if the company decides to charge each of the three product managers a "fair share" of the total indirect cost using the proportion of units produced in a manager's area relative to the total units produced? This approach is described in Chapter 4 and is commonly referred to as *volume-based costing.* Note that whether the proportions used are based on units of product, direct labor-hours, or machine-hours, each of these is volume-based.

But if, as is often the case, the usage of these activities is not proportional to the number of units produced, then some managers will be overcharged and others undercharged under the volume-based approach. For example, suppose Al insists on more frequent inspections of his production; then he should be charged a higher proportion of overhead (inspection) than that based on units alone. Moreover, why should you pay any portion of fabric cutting if your bedroom furniture does not require fabric?

Another consideration is that the volume-based method provides little incentive for the manager to control indirect costs. Unfortunately, the only way you could reduce your share of the indirect costs is to reduce your units produced (or hope that Joe and/or Al increase production)—not much of an incentive. On reflection, the approach that charges indirect costs to product based on units produced does not provide very accurate product costs and certainly does not provide the appropriate incentives for managing the indirect costs. The solution is to use activity-based costing to charge these indirect costs to the products, using detailed information on the activities that make up the indirect costs—inspection, fabric cutting, and materials handling. This chapter shows how to do it.

A good example of one of many success stories for ABC is the application of ABC at the U.S. Postal Service (USPS). The ABC application at the USPS originated from the Postmaster General's directive to develop a costing system that would help the USPS become more competitive and serve as a basis for comparing performance among the various mail- processing facilities. The initial ABC system used 58 work activities and nine cost objects. The cost objects included handling of letters, flats, small parcels, large parcels, priority mail, express mail, registered mail, large mail containers, and small mail containers. In the initial application at a single mail-processing facility, there was a reduction of 13% in total cost as a result of the improved understanding of cost behavior in the facility. The USPS also used ABC to determine the cost differences in processing payments from customers who used cash, checks, or credit cards and from this analysis determined that the low-cost approach was to encourage the use of credit cards. The ABC-based analyses have helped the USPS to implement an effective, cost-competitive strategy.

## Role of Volume-Based Costing

Volume-based costing can be a good strategic choice for some firms. It is generally appropriate when common costs are relatively small or when activities supporting the production of the product or service are relatively homogenous across different product lines. This may be the case, for example, for a firm that manufactures a limited range of paper products or a firm that produces a narrow range of agricultural products. Similarly, a professional service firm (law firm, accounting firm) may not need ABC because labor costs for the professional staff are the largest cost of the firm, and labor is also easily traced to clients (the cost object). For firms other than these, the ABC approach may be preferred to avoid the distortions from overcosting or undercosting that may occur using a volume-based approach.

## Activity-Based Costing

**LO 5-2**

*Describe activity-based costing (ABC), the steps in developing an ABC system, and the benefits of an ABC system.*

To develop a costing system we need to understand relationships among resources, activities, and products or services. Resources are spent on activities, and products or services are a result of activities. Many of the resources used in an operation can be traced to individual products or services and identified as direct materials or direct labor costs. Most overhead costs relate only indirectly to final products or services. A costing system identifies costs with activities that consume resources and assigns resource costs to cost objects such as products, services, or intermediate cost pools based on activities performed for the cost objects.

### Resources, Activities, Resource Consumption Cost Drivers, and Activity Consumption Cost Drivers

Before discussing activity-based costing, several important terms must be understood: *activity, resource, cost driver, resource consumption cost driver,* and *activity consumption cost driver.*

An **activity**
is some specific task or action of work done.

An **activity** is a specific task or action of work done. An activity can be a single action or an aggregation of several actions. For example, moving inventory from workstation A to workstation B is an activity that may require only one action. Production setup is an activity that may include several actions. Activities are often listed in what is called an *activity dictionary.* An illustration of key activities in a firm's internal supply chain is shown by the Supply Chain Council in what is called the SCOR® (Supply Chain Operations Reference) on the Council's website (**www.supply-chain.org/**).

A **resource**
is an economic element needed or consumed in performing activities.

A **resource** is an economic element needed or consumed in performing activities. Labor and supplies, for example, are resources needed or used in performing manufacturing activities.

A **cost driver**
is a factor that causes or relates to a change in the cost of an activity.

A **cost driver** is a factor that causes or relates to a change in the cost of an activity. Because cost drivers cause or relate to cost changes, measured or quantified amounts of cost drivers are excellent bases for assigning resource costs to activities and for assigning the cost of activities to cost objects.

A **resource consumption cost driver**
is a measure of the amount of resources consumed by an activity.

A cost driver is either a *resource consumption cost driver* or an *activity consumption cost driver.* A **resource consumption cost driver** is some measure of the demand for resources by an activity. It is the basis for assigning resource costs to a particular activity or cost pool. Examples of resource consumption cost drivers are the number of items in a purchase or sales order, changes in product design, and square feet to occupied space.

An **activity consumption cost driver**
measures how much of an activity a cost object uses.

An **activity consumption cost driver** measures the amount of an activity performed for a cost object. It is used to assign activity cost pool costs to cost objects. Examples of activity consumption cost drivers are the number of machine-hours in the manufacturing of product X, or the number of batches used to manufacture product Y.

### What Is Activity-Based Costing?

**Activity-based costing (ABC)**
is a costing approach that assigns resource costs to cost objects based on activities performed for the cost objects.

**Activity-based costing (ABC)** is a costing approach that assigns resource costs to cost objects such as products, services, or customers based on activities performed for the cost objects. The premise of this costing approach is that a firm's products or services are the result of activities and activities require resources, which have costs. Costs of resources are assigned to activities based on the activities that use or consume resources (resource consumption drivers), and costs of activities are assigned to cost objects based on activities performed for the cost objects (activity consumption drivers). ABC recognizes the causal or direct relationships between resource costs, cost drivers, activities, and cost objects in assigning costs to activities and then to cost objects.

**EXHIBIT 5.1**
**The Volume-Based Two-Stage Procedure**

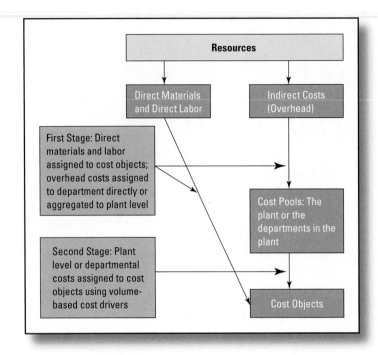

ABC assigns factory overhead costs to cost objects such as products or services by identifying the resources and activities as well as their costs and amounts needed to produce output. Using resource consumption cost drivers, a firm determines the resource costs consumed by activities, calculates the cost of a unit of activity, and then assigns the cost of an activity to cost objects by multiplying the cost of each activity by the amount of the activity consumed by each of the cost objects.

## The Two-Stage Cost Assignment Procedure

A **two-stage cost assignment** assigns resource costs to activity cost pools and then to cost objects.

A **two-stage cost assignment** procedure assigns resource costs such as factory overhead costs to activity cost pools and then to cost objects to determine the amount of resource costs for each of the cost objects. Volume-based costing systems assign factory overhead costs first to plant or departmental cost pools and second to products or services (see Exhibit 5.1). In the first stage of volume-based costing the factory overhead costs are combined into a single plant cost pool or several departmental cost pools. This approach is convenient and simple, because many accounting systems in use today accumulate cost information by department, which is easily aggregated to the plant level. In the second stage, a volume-based rate (based on units produced or hours used in production) is then used to apply overhead to each of the cost objects. The volume-based approach is used in Chapter 4 in job costing. A strictly volume-based cost assignment procedure, however, is likely to distort product or service costs. This is true especially in the second stage where the volume-based costing system uses a cost driver such as direct labor-hours or output units to assign factory overhead costs. Because all products or services do not usually consume factory overhead resources in proportion to the volume-based measure the firm uses to assign factory overhead costs, a volume-based system often leads to inaccurate measures for the costs of support activities in its operations. This distortion becomes more serious when the firm manufactures a diverse mix of products with differences in volumes, sizes, or complexities and a substantial portion of the allocated costs are not related to output volume.

ABC systems differ from volume-based costing systems by linking uses of resources to activities and linking activity costs to products, services, or customers (see Exhibit 5.2). The first stage assigns factory overhead costs to activities by using appropriate resource consumption cost drivers. The second stage assigns the costs of activities to cost objects using appropriate activity consumption cost drivers that measure the demands cost objects

**EXHIBIT 5.2**
**The Activity-Based Two-Stage Procedure**

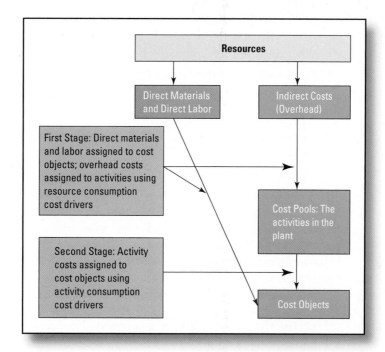

have for the activities. By using cost drivers in both the first and second stage cost assignments, activity-based costing systems provide more accurate measures of product or service costs for the cost of activities that are not proportional to the volume of outputs produced.

In summary, ABC systems differ from volume-based costing systems in two ways. First, the ABC system defines cost pools as activities rather than production plant or department cost centers. Second, the cost drivers that the ABC system uses to assign activity costs to cost objects are drivers based on an activity or activities performed for the cost object. The volume-based approach uses a volume-based cost driver that often bears little or no relationship to the consumption of resources by the cost objects.

## Steps in Developing an Activity-Based Costing System

Developing an activity-based costing system entails three steps: (1) identifying resource costs and activities, (2) assigning resource costs to activities, and (3) assigning activity costs to cost objects. Steps 1 and 2 constitute stage 1 from Exhibit 5.2, and step 3 is equivalent to stage 2 from that exhibit.

## Step 1: Identify Resource Costs and Activities

Most firms record resource costs in specific accounts in the accounting system. These accounts are often based upon the underlying function of the resources that are included, such as purchasing, marketing, and office supplies. The first step in the ABC process is to determine which of the resources in each of the accounts is consumed by the identified activities. The costs of the resources consumed for a particular activity may be only a small part of the costs in a particular account. For example, a single factory supplies account may include the cost of resources consumed by several different manufacturing operations. Also, the resources to perform an activity may come from several accounts. For example, order fulfillment might require resources from warehousing, shipping, and billing accounts.

An activity analysis identifies the work performed to carry out a firm's operations. It includes gathering data from existing documents and records, as well as collecting additional data using questionnaires, observations, or interviews of key personnel. Questions that ABC project team members typically ask employees or managers in gathering activity data include:

- What work or activities do you do?
- How much time do you spend performing these activities?
- What resources are required to perform these activities?
- What value does the activity have for the product, service, customer, or organization?

With the help of industrial engineers and management accountants, the team also collects activity data by observing the work performed and making a list of all the activities involved.

### *Levels of Activities*

To identify resource costs for various activities, a firm classifies all activities according to the way in which the activities consume resources.

A **unit-level activity** is performed for each unit of the cost object.

1. A **unit-level activity** is performed for each individual unit of product or service of the firm. Consider the activity of inserting a component. This activity is required for each unit produced, so the activity level varies in direct proportion to the quantity of the cost object produced. As a result, unit-level activities are said to be volume-based. The resource consumption driver and the activity consumption driver are likely to be the same for unit-level activities.

A **batch-level activity** is performed for each batch or group of products or services.

2. A **batch-level activity** is performed for each batch or group of units of products or services. Examples of batch-level activities are setting up machines, placing purchase orders, scheduling production, conducting inspections by batch, handling materials, and expediting production.

A **product-level activity** supports the production of a specific product or service.

3. A **product-level activity** supports the production of a specific product or service. Examples of product-level activities include designing products, purchasing parts required for products, and engaging in engineering changes to modify products.

A **facility-level activity** supports operations in general.

4. A **facility-level activity** supports operations in general. These activities are not caused by products or customer service needs and cannot be traced to individual units, batches, or products. Examples of facility-level activities include providing security for the plant, performing maintenance of general purpose machines, and incurring factory property taxes and insurance. Some firms refer to these activities as business or infrastructure-sustaining activities.

Note that a unit-level activity can always be traced to a batch (one of the units in the batch), and a batch-level activity can always be traced to a product (one batch of this particular product), and a product-level activity can usually be traced to a manufacturing facility; but, the reverse is not possible. Exhibit 5.3 illustrates activity-level classifications at Siemens Electric Motor Works.

## Step 2: Assign Resource Costs to Activities

Activities drive the consumption of resources, so the next step is to use resource consumption drivers to assign resource costs to activities. A firm should choose resource consumption cost drivers based on cause-and-effect relationships. Typical resource consumption

**EXHIBIT 5.3**

**Activities and Activity Levels at Siemens Electric Motor Works**

| Activity | Activity Level |
|---|---|
| Using direct materials | Unit |
| Using direct labor-hours | Unit |
| Using machine-hours | Unit |
| Starting production orders | Batch |
| Adding special components | Batch |

**EXHIBIT 5.4**

**Resource and Resource Consumption Cost Drivers at AT&T's New River Valley Plant**

| Resource | Resource Consumption Cost Driver |
|---|---|
| Personnel | Number of workers |
| Storeroom | Number of items picked for an order |
| Engineers | Time worked |
| Materials management | Time worked |
| Accounting | Time worked |
| Research and development | Number of new codes developed |
| Quality | Time worked |
| Utilities | Square-footage |

cost drivers include the number of (1) labor-hours for labor intensive activities; (2) employees for payroll-related activities; (3) setups for batch-related activities; (4) moves for materials-handling activities; (5) machine-hours for machine repair and maintenance; and (6) square feet for general maintenance and cleaning activities.

Ideally, the cost of resources is directly traced or assigned to activities, which requires measuring the actual usage of resources by an activity. For example, power used to operate a machine can be traced directly to that machine's operation by reading the meter attached to the machine. When direct tracing is not available, department managers and supervisors need to estimate the amount or percentage of time (or effort) employees spend on each identified activity. Exhibit 5.4 illustrates resources and resource consumption drivers for factory overhead costs at AT&T's New River Valley plant.

### Step 3: Assign Activity Costs to Cost Objects

The final step is to assign costs of activities to items of interest, generically called cost objects, based on the appropriate activity consumption cost drivers. The cost objects are the outputs resulting from the firm's activities, and typically are products or services; however, customers, projects, and even business units can be cost objects. For example, the cost objects of an insurance company may be individual insurance policies sold to customers, claims processed, types of policies offered, insurance agents, or divisions or subunits of the company.

## Benefits of Activity-Based Costing

Since the 1980s an increasing number of firms have adopted an activity-based costing system. As previously noted, many firms found ABC reduced the distortions that resulted from using a volume-based system. ABC clearly shows the effect of differences in activities and changes in products or services on costs. Among the major benefits of activity-based costing that many firms have experienced from the improved information are:

1. **Better profitability measures.** ABC provides more accurate and informative product costs, leading to more accurate product and customer profitability measurements.

2. **Better decision making.** ABC provides more accurate measurements of activity-driving costs, helping managers to improve product and process value by making better product design decisions and better customer support decisions and fostering value-enhancement projects.

3. **Process improvement.** The ABC system provides the information to identify areas where process improvement is needed.

4. **Improved planning.** Improved product costs lead to better estimates of costs for budgeting and planning.
5. **Cost of unused capacity.** Since many firms have seasonal and cyclical fluctuations in sales and production, there are times when plant capacity is supplied but not used. This can mean that costs are *incurred* at the batch-, product-, and facility-level activities but are *not used.* ABC systems provide better information to identify the cost of unused capacity and maintain a separate accounting for this cost. For example, if a plant manager decides to add capacity in expectation of future increases in sales and production, then the cost of that additional capacity should not be charged to current production but charged as a lump-sum in the plant's costs. Overall, the goal is to manage capacity levels to reduce the cost of underutilization of capacity and to price products and services properly.

Each of these benefits can contribute significantly to a company's competitiveness by helping the company make better decisions and implement its strategy.

## A Comparison of Volume-Based and Activity-Based Costing

**LO 5-3**

*Determine product costs under both the volume-based method and the activity-based method and contrast the two.*

The following example contrasts the volume-based costing system using only direct labor-hours as the cost driver with an activity-based costing system that uses both volume-based and activity-based cost drivers. Since this illustration shows only step 3 of the ABC method, we also show an illustration (AIRCO Ltd) that includes all three steps of the ABC method in the section, "Real-World Activity-Based Costing/Management Applications," on page 145.

Haymarket BioTech Inc. (HBT) produces and sells two secure communications systems, AW(Anywhere) and SZ (SecureZone). AW uses satellite technology and allows customers to communicate anywhere on the earth. SZ uses similar technology but only allows communication between two parties that are within 10 miles of each other. HBT's customers are governmental and corporate customers for which these products are critical; the customers rely on HBT's ability to quickly adapt its products to threats from devices that would compromise the security of the products. SZ has been successful for nearly 10 years and has undergone a number of improvements in this time; sales are expected to continue to grow at 8–10% per year. AW, a more recent product, has also been successful, but demand has not been as strong and sales growth is expected to be 3–5% per year. Because of the higher profitability of the AW system (Exhibit 5.5), HBT is considering an extensive advertising campaign to boost sales of AW and is making plans for reallocating manufacturing facilities from SZ to AW to make this possible. HBT has the following operating data for the two products.

| | AW | SZ |
|---|---|---|
| Production volume | 5,000 | 20,000 |
| Selling price | $400.00 | $200.00 |
| Unit direct materials and labor | $200.00 | $80.00 |
| Direct labor-hours | 25,000 | 75,000 |
| Direct labor-hours per unit | 5 | 3.75 |

## Volume-Based Costing

The volume-based costing system assigns factory overhead (FOH) based on direct labor-hours (DLH). The firm has total budgeted FOH of $2,000,000. Since the firm budgeted 100,000 direct labor-hours for the year, the FOH rate is $20 per direct labor-hour.

| Total overhead | | $2,000,000 |
|---|---|---|
| Total DLH | 25,000 + 75,000 = | 100,000 |
| Overhead rate per DLH | | $    20.00 |

Since the firm uses 25,000 direct labor-hours to manufacture 5,000 units of AW, the FOH assigned to AW is $500,000 in total and $100 per unit:

| Total overhead assigned to AW | $20 × 25,000 = $500,000 |
|---|---|
| Number of units of AW | 5,000 |
| Factory overhead per unit of AW | $ 100.00 |

The FOH for SZ is $1,500,000 in total and $75 per unit since the firm spent 75,000 direct labor-hours to manufacture 20,000 units of SZ:

| Total overhead assigned to SZ | $20 × 75,000 = $1,500,000 |
|---|---|
| Number of units of SZ | 20,000 |
| Factory overhead per unit of SZ | $    75.00 |

Exhibit 5.5 shows a product profitability analysis using the firm's volume-based costing system.

## Activity-Based Costing

To be able to assign activity costs to cost objects, HBT identified the following activities, budgeted costs, and activity consumption cost drivers:

| Activity | Budgeted Cost | Activity Consumption Cost Driver |
|---|---|---|
| Engineering | $  125,000 | Engineering hours |
| Setups | 300,000 | Number of setups |
| Machine operation | 1,500,000 | Machine-hours |
| Packing | 75,000 | Number of packing orders |
| Total | $2,000,000 | |

**EXHIBIT 5.5**
**Product Profitability Analysis under Volume-Based Costing**

| | AW | | SZ | |
|---|---|---|---|---|
| Unit selling price | | $400 | | $200 |
| Unit manufacturing cost: | | | | |
| Direct materials and labor | $200 | | $80 | |
| Factory overhead | 100 | | 75 | |
| Cost per unit | | 300 | | 155 |
| Profit margin | | $100 | | $ 45 |

HBT also gathered the following operating data pertaining to each of its products:

|  | AW | SZ | Total |
|---|---|---|---|
| Engineering hours | 5,000 | 7,500 | 12,500 |
| Number of setups | 200 | 100 | 300 |
| Machine hours | 50,000 | 100,000 | 150,000 |
| Number of packing orders | 5,000 | 10,000 | 15,000 |

Using the above data, the cost driver rate for each activity consumption cost driver is calculated as follows:

| (1) Activity Consumption Cost Driver | (2) Budgeted Cost | (3) Budgeted Activity Consumption | (4) = (2) ÷ (3) Activity Consumption Rate |
|---|---|---|---|
| Engineering hours | $ 125,000 | 12,500 | $   10 per hour |
| Number of setups | 300,000 | 300 | 1,000 per setup |
| Machine hours | 1,500,000 | 150,000 | 10 per hour |
| Number of packing orders | 75,000 | 15,000 | 5 per order |

Factory overhead costs are assigned to both products by these calculations:

| AW (5,000 units) | | | | |
|---|---|---|---|---|
| (1) Activity Consumption Cost Driver | (2) Activity Consumption Rate | (3) Activity Consumption | (4) = (2) × (3) Total Overhead | (5) Overhead per Unit |
| Engineering hours | $   10 | 5,000 | $ 50,000 | $ 10 |
| Number of setups | 1,000 | 200 | 200,000 | 40 |
| Machine hours | 10 | 50,000 | 500,000 | 100 |
| Number of packing orders | 5 | 5,000 | 25,000 | 5 |
| Overhead cost per unit | | | $775,000 | $155 |

| SZ (20,000 units) | | | | |
|---|---|---|---|---|
| (1) Activity Consumption Cost Driver | (2) Activity Consumption Rate | (3) Activity Consumption | (4) = (2) × (3) Total Overhead | (5) Overhead per Unit |
| Engineering hours | $   10 | 7,500 | $   75,000 | $ 3.75 |
| Number of setups | 1,000 | 100 | 100,000 | 5.00 |
| Machine hours | 10 | 100,000 | 1,000,000 | 50.00 |
| Number of packing orders | 5 | 10,000 | 50,000 | 2.50 |
| Overhead cost per unit | | | $1,225,000 | $61.25 |

Exhibit 5.6 presents a product profitability analysis under the ABC system and Exhibit 5.7 compares product costs and profit margins under the two costing systems. The comparison shows that the volume-based product costing system significantly under-costs AW and overcosts SZ when considering the actual overhead consumption of the two products. This overcosting/undercosting is sometimes called *cross-subsidization.* Often the cross-subsidization is in the direction of undercosting the low-volume products (small batch size, as for AW) and overcosting the high-volume products (large batch size, as for SW) using the volume-based approach. The reason is that with ABC the batch-level costs are averaged over a larger number of units for high-volume products, thus bringing the costs of these products down, and vice-versa for the low-volume products.

**EXHIBIT 5.6**
**Product Profitability Analysis**
**under the ABC Costing System**

|  | AW | | SZ | |
|---|---|---|---|---|
| Unit selling price | | $400 | | $200.00 |
| Unit manufacturing cost | | | | |
| Direct materials and labor | | $200 | | $80.00 |
| Factory overhead: | | | | |
| Engineering | $ 10 | | $ 3.75 | |
| Setups | 40 | | 5.00 | |
| Machine running | 100 | | 50.00 | |
| Packing | 5 | 155 | 2.50 | 61.25 |
| Cost per unit | | 355 | | 141.25 |
| Profit margin | | $ 45 | | $ 58.75 |

**EXHIBIT 5.7**
**Comparison of Alternative**
**Costing Approaches**

|  | AW | SZ |
|---|---|---|
| Unit overhead cost | | |
| Volume-based | $100 | $75.00 |
| Activity-based | 155 | 61.25 |
| Difference | $ 55 | $13.75 |
| Profit margin | | |
| Volume-based | $100 | $45.00 |
| Activity-based | 45 | 58.75 |
| Difference | $ 55 | $13.75 |

For a short additional example, assume that product A is produced in a batch of 10 units, while product B is produced in a batch of 100 units, and that batch-level costs are $100 per batch. The ABC method would calculate the cost per unit of batch costs as $100 ÷ 10 = $10 per unit for the low-volume batch and $100 ÷ 100 = $1 per unit for the high-volume batch. In contrast, the volume-based method would calculate the cost of two batches and spread this equally to the 110 units produced; $200 ÷ 110 = $1.82 per unit. Using the volume-based method, the high-volume product is overcosted ($1.82 vs. $1) and the low-volume product is undercosted ($1.82 vs. $10). Distorted or inaccurate product costing can lead to inappropriate inventory valuations, unrealistic pricing, ineffective resource allocations, misplaced strategic focus, misidentified critical success factors, and lost competitive advantage.

## The Five Steps of Strategic Decision Making for Haymarket BioTech Inc.

We can see how inaccurate costs under the volume-based method can affect HBT's success by considering the five steps of strategic decision making.

1. **Determine the strategic issues surrounding the problem.** HBT, the maker of AW and SZ, competes on product leadership (differentiation) as its customers rely on the ability of these products to provide secure communications. Because innovation is a key customer-buying criteria, HBT must take a long-term focus on developing innovations that meet expected future customer expectations and implement these innovations into successful, profitable products.

2. **Identify the alternative actions.** HBT is considering an advertising campaign and re-allocation of manufacturing facilities to favor the AW product line.

3. **Obtain information and conduct analyses of the alternatives.** The information available to HBT under the volume-based cost system shows a unit margin of $100 for AW and $45 for SZ, while the ABC-based cost system shows unit margins for AW and SZ of $45 and $58.75, respectively. As the ABC system provides more comprehensive and accurate cost information, HBT should rely on the latter figures, which show that on a unit basis the SZ product is more profitable.

4. **Based on strategy and analysis, choose and implement the desired alternative.** Considering the ABC cost information and the higher margins for SZ relative to AW, the plans to

promote AW and reallocate manufacturing facilities from SZ to AW are not consistent with HBT's long-term growth and profitability. The firm's best advantage for future growth and profitability would be to put resources behind SZ rather than AW.

5. **Provide an ongoing evaluation of the effectiveness of implementation in Step 4.** HBT should continue to review the ABC-based costs and profit margins of existing and new products, together with long-term projections of sales and customer expectations for these products, to choose the products with the best advantage for long-term growth and profitability.

## Calculating the Cost of Capacity in ABC

The ABC application illustrated above uses activity-consumption rates based on total budgeted activity costs and budgeted activity consumption. Since budgets are plans, budgeted activity costs are the planned level of spending, and budgeted activity consumption is based on planned usage. The ABC costs assigned to cost objects are, therefore, based on planned levels of spending and usage of capacity. What if we want to know the cost of maintaining idle or excess capacity for planning capacity utilization? Perhaps the unused capacity can be used by other business units in the firm to expand their operations, or alternatively, the excess capacity can be sold or leased. Information on excess capacity allows the firm to manage and reduce these costs when appropriate.

A straightforward adaptation of the ABC method provides the desired additional information—the cost of capacity. For example, suppose for simplicity that of the four activities for HBT we consider only the engineering activity. Engineering cost for HBT is budgeted at $125,000 as currently shown, but suppose that instead of a budgeted activity consumption of 12,500 hours, HBT were to use the practical capacity of the engineering staff, which is 15,625 hours. Practical capacity is the capacity available with the current resources of people, equipment, and facilities—the reasonable level of output if the resource is fully utilized. Using practical capacity, the activity consumption rate would be $8 per engineering hour (= $125,000 ÷ 15,625). If only 12,500 hours were used, as shown in the example, then the overhead cost charged to AW and SZ would be reduced because of the lower rate ($8 instead of the original rate of $10). AW overhead would be reduced by $10,000 (5,000 hours × $2) and SZ overhead would be reduced by $15,000 (7,500 hours × $2). The total reduction for the two products, $25,000 (= $10,000 + $15,000) is the cost of unused capacity. The cost of unused capacity can also be calculated directly by taking the hours of unused capacity—3,125 hours (15,625 − 12,500)—and multiplying by the $8 activity consumption rate for engineering.

Determining the cost of capacity is a strategically important feature of ABC because it helps managers plan the short- and longer-term use of the available operating resources. Also, the cost of capacity plays a central role in two methods that extend the basic ABC model; these are resource consumption accounting and time-driven activity-based costing. Both methods are explained at the end of the chapter.[1]

## Activity-Based Management

**LO 5-4**

*Explain activity-based management (ABM).*

Benefits of activity-based costing systems are not limited to improved assignment of product costs. The information from the ABC system can also help management increase both the value customers receive and the profits to the firm through the use of activity-based management.

---

[1] Generally accepted accounting principles (FASB ASC 330-10-30) for "Inventory Costs" requires the costs associated with an abnormally low production level to be treated as a period cost and not assigned to product. The authoritative accounting literature notes that some variation in production level from period to period is expected and that these variances should not affect the accounting for inventory, but when in the accountant's judgment the amount of expense is for an abnormally low production level, then the amount should be separated from inventory costs, as we have done in the above example, and charged against current income.

When finding themselves in financially dire straits, hospital managers, like managers from other industries, often yield to their first impulse: lay off staff. At one level, this solution makes sense. However, management may benefit from taking a step back and examining their processes. A thorough examination of how things work from beginning to end can help identify inefficiencies that exist in end-to-end processes and result in staggering savings and improvements to their bottom line.

Many inefficiencies in a process come from handoffs from one department to another, but these handoffs are often not analyzed, meaning the opportunities for improvement are missed. In one example, a hospital found such inefficiency through an analysis of its admitting

process. The underlying problem was simply that the admitting department lacked a fax machine, and this was revealed by simply walking through the admitting process from end to end. The observation showed that in order to receive the eight or nine admitting orders that came from physicians each day, staff would take an elevator up several floors, pull the orders from the fax machine in the nursing unit, and then go back downstairs to preregister patients. This was a massive inefficiency that was easily remedied.

**Source:** John Ortiz, "Cutting Hospital Costs without Cutting Staff," *Healthcare Financial Management* 65, no. 10 (Oct. 2011), pp. 46–48.

**EXHIBIT 5.8**
**The Role of ABC/M Tools**

| Critical Questions | ABC/M Tools |
| --- | --- |
| What do we do? | Activity analysis |
| How much does it cost? | Activity-based costing |
| How well do we do it? | Performance measurement, including the balanced scorecard |
| How can we do it better? | Benchmarking, total quality management, business process improvement, and business intelligence |

## What Is Activity-Based Management?

*Activity-based management (ABM)* manages resources and activities to improve the value of products or services to customers and increase the firm's competitiveness and profitability. ABM draws on ABC as its major source of information and focuses on the efficiency and effectiveness of key business processes and activities. Using ABM, management can identify ways to improve operations, reduce costs, or increase value to customers, all of which can enhance the firm's competitiveness.

ABM applications can be classified into two categories: operational ABM and strategic ABM. Operational ABM enhances operational efficiency and asset utilization and lowers costs; its focuses are on doing things right and performing activities more efficiently. Operational ABM applications use management techniques such as activity analysis, business process improvement, total quality management, and performance measurement.

Strategic ABM focuses on choosing appropriate activities for the operation, eliminating nonessential activities, and selecting the most profitable customers. Strategic ABM applications use management techniques such as process design, customer profitability analysis, and value-chain analysis, all of which can alter the demand for activities and increase profitability through improved activity efficiency.

Exhibit 5.8 illustrates questions that strategic and operational ABC/ABM (ABC/M) can help to answer and the tools that are used. Some of the key tools of ABC/M are activity analysis, activity-based costing, performance measurement (covered in Chapters 18 and 19), and several contemporary management techniques explained in Chapter 1: benchmarking, total quality management, business process improvement, and others. Another technique, value-added analysis, is explained here.

## Activity Analysis

To be competitive a firm must assess each of its activities based on its need by the product or customer, its efficiency, and its value content. Ideally, a firm performs an activity for one of the following reasons:

- It is required to meet the specification of the product or service or satisfy customer demand.

**EXHIBIT 5.9**  **Example of an Activity Analysis**

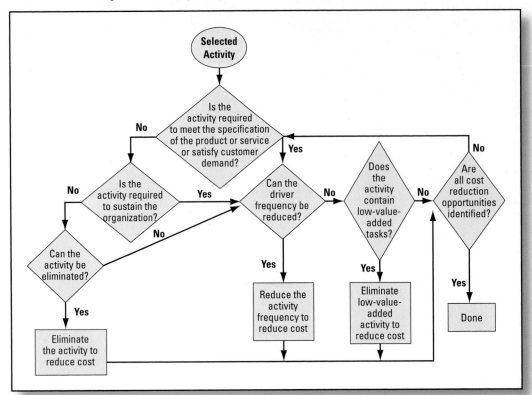

- It is required to sustain the organization.
- It is deemed beneficial to the firm.

Examples of activities required to sustain the organization are providing plant security and compliance with government regulations. Although these activities have no direct effect on the product or service or customer satisfaction, they cannot be eliminated. Examples of discretionary activities deemed beneficial to the firm include a holiday party and free coffee. Exhibit 5.9 depicts an activity analysis. Some activities, however, may not adequately meet any of the above criteria, making them candidates for elimination.

## Value-Added Analysis

Eliminating activities that add little or no value to customers reduces resource consumption and allows the firm to focus on activities that increase customer satisfaction. Knowing the values of activities allows employees to see how work really serves customers and which activities may have little value to the ultimate customers and should be eliminated or reduced.

> A **high-value-added activity** increases the value of the product or service to the customers.

   A **high-value-added activity** increases significantly the value of the product or service to the customers. Removal of a high-value-added activity decreases perceptively the value of the product or service to the customer. Inserting a flange into a part, pouring molten metal into a mold, and preparing a field for planting are examples of high-value-added activities, as are designing, processing, and delivering products and services. Exhibit 5.10 illustrates high-value-added activities of a television news broadcasting firm. The exhibit also includes examples of low-value-added activities.

> A **low-value-added activity** consumes time, resources, or space, but adds little to satisfying customer needs.

   A **low-value-added activity** consumes time, resources, or space, but adds little in satisfying customer needs. If eliminated, customer value or satisfaction decreases imperceptively or remains unchanged. Moving parts between processes, waiting time, repairing, and rework are examples of low-value-added activities.

**EXHIBIT 5.10**
Television News Broadcasting Firm's High-Value-Added and Low-Value-Added Activities

A *high-value-added activity* is one that, if eliminated, would affect the accuracy and effectiveness of the newscast and decrease total viewers as well as ratings for that time slot.
1. Activities that augment accuracy
   • Verification of story sources and acquired information.
2. Activities that augment effectiveness
   • Efficient electronic journalism to ensure effective taped segments.
   • Newscast story order planned so that viewers can follow from one story to the next.
   • Field crew time used to access the best footage possible.
   • Meaningful news story writing.
   • Contents of the newscast planned so that viewers get the best possible package of stories.
A *low-value-added activity* is one that, if eliminated, would not affect the accuracy and effectiveness of the newscast. The activity contributes nothing to the quest for viewer retention and improved ratings.
   • Developing stories not used in a newscast.
   • Assigning more than one person to develop each facet of the same news story.
   • Newscast not completed on time because of one or more inefficient processes.
   • Too many employees on a particular shift or project.

**EXHIBIT 5.11**
A Classification of High-Value-Added and Low-Value-Added Activities

| Activity | High-Value-Added | Low-Value-Added |
|---|---|---|
| Designing product | X | |
| Setting up | | X |
| Waiting | | X |
| Moving | | X |
| Processing | X | |
| Reworking | | X |
| Repairing | | X |
| Storing | | X |
| Inspecting | | X |
| Delivering product | X | |

Reduction or elimination of low-value-added activities reduces cost. *Low-value-added activities* are those that:

• Can be eliminated without affecting the form, fit, or function of the product or service.
• Begin with prefix "re" (such as rework or returned goods).
• Result in waste and add little or no value to the product or service.
• Are duplicated in another department or add unnecessary steps to the business process.
• Produce an unnecessary or unwanted output.

Additional examples of high- and low-value-adding activities are shown in Exhibit 5.11.

## Real-World Activity-Based Costing/Management Applications

**LO 5-5**
*Describe how ABC/M is used in manufacturing companies, service companies, and governmental organizations.*

Activity-based costing/management (ABC/M) applications are quite common and this section provides an application example in manufacturing and within government.

### ABC/M Application in Manufacturing: Industrial Air Conditioner Units

AIRCO Ltd (**www.airco.co.za**) of Johannesburg and Cape Town, South Africa, is a manufacturer of industrial air conditioning units. The units range in size and power from 5 to 20 tons.[2] Each unit has more than 200 parts, including holding tanks, electronic controllers,

[2] Heather Nachtmann and Mohammad Hani Al-Rifai, "An Application of Activity-Based Costing in the Air Conditioner Manufacturing Industry," *The Engineering Economist* 49 (2001), pp. 221–236. Used with permission. For simplicity, for the remainder of the chapter we will refer to resource consumption cost drivers as resource cost drivers and we will refer to activity consumption cost drivers as activity cost drivers.

**EXHIBIT 5.12**
**AIRCO Overhead Cost Resources**

| Overhead Resource | Cost |
|---|---|
| Indirect labor | $2,786,900 |
| Computer and software | 731,405 |
| Product transportation | 319,800 |
| Energy | 170,600 |
| Facility and vehicle rent | 165,870 |
| Business and training travel | 66,000 |
| Miscellaneous | 65,480 |
| Maintenance | 60,000 |
| Depreciation | 48,200 |
| Advertising | 40,000 |
| Office and utilities | 4,355 |
| | $4,458,610 |

metal sheets, cooling coils, wires, and insulation material. Almost 90% of manufacturing workers are hourly workers, and the company operates two shifts. The organization of the manufacturing process is conventional, with separate departments for purchasing, engineering, job scheduling, materials handling, shipping, accounting, and human resources. AIRCO developed an ABC system to assist in the analysis of product profitability. Its first step was to identify the resource cost pools that make up total overhead of $4,458,610 at the plant (Exhibit 5.12). The resource costs are from the firm's accounting system, which collects resources costs in the 11 categories noted in the exhibit.

The next step is to identify production activities and to use resource consumption cost drivers to assign the resource costs to the activity cost pools, which are shown in column 1 of Exhibit 5.13. The activity cost pools are machines; data record maintenance; materials handling; production changeover (setup); scheduling and production preparation; materials receiving and handling; product shipment; and customer service. The assignment of resources to activities typically uses resource cost drivers. Instead of using cost drivers, AIRCO determined the estimated contribution of each resource to each activity based on managers' and employees' experience. For example, the resource, maintenance costs of $60,000, was assigned entirely to the activity, machines. To illustrate, the cost of the machine activity was determined from the resources as follows (other activities were obtained in a similar way):

$$
\begin{aligned}
\text{Machine activity cost} = {} & 20\% \text{ of the computer and software costs} \\
& + 100\% \text{ of energy costs} + 15\% \text{ of miscellaneous expense} \\
& + 100\% \text{ of maintenance expense} + 100\% \text{ of depreciation expense} \\
& + 12\% \text{ of office and utilities expense} \\
= {} & (.2 \times \$731,405) + \$170,600 + (.15 \times \$65,480) + \$60,000 \\
& + \$48,200 + (.12 \times \$4,355) \\
= {} & \$435,425
\end{aligned}
$$

The machine activity cost and the cost of other activities is shown in column 2 of Exhibit 5.13. The use of estimated percentages in place of other types of resource consumption cost drivers is a practical and convenient approach that is often used in implementing ABC costing.

The next step in ABC is to identify activity cost drivers, to identify the total amounts for these cost drivers, and then to determine the ABC-based application rate. This is shown in Exhibit 5.13, columns 3, 4, and 5, respectively. Thus, the cost of machine time is assigned to each of the products based on machine-hours used by that product times the rate of $5.89 per machine-hour ($5.89 = $435,425 ÷ 73,872). This same process is done for the other activities. The determination of ABC cost and profitability analysis for AIRCO's key product lines is the final step and is shown in Exhibit 5.14. Note that this analysis shows that the 5-ton, 6-ton, and 12.5-ton products are not profitable.

**EXHIBIT 5.13**    **AIRCO Resource Consumption Cost Pools Assigned to Activities, Activity Cost Drivers, and Activity-Based Rates**

| (1)<br><br>Activity Cost Pool | (2)<br>Budgeted<br>Activity Cost | (3)<br><br>Activity Cost Driver | (4)<br>Budgeted<br>Activity | (5) = (2) ÷ (4)<br>Activity-Based<br>Application Rate |
|---|---|---|---|---|
| Machines | $ 435,425 | Number of machine-hours | 73,872 | $    5.89 per hour |
| Data record maintenance | 132,596 | Number of products lines | 14 | 9,471 per line |
| Materials handling | 1,560,027 | Number of products | 16,872 | 92.46 per product |
| Production changeover<br>(setup) | 723,337 | Setup time (hours) | 72 | 10,046 per hour |
| Scheduling and production<br>preparation | 24,876 | Number of production runs | 2,788 | 8.92 per run |
| Materials receiving and<br>handling | 877,106 | Number of receipts | 2,859 | 307 per receipt |
| Product shipment | 561,013 | Distance (miles) | 13,784,015 | .041 per mile |
| Customer service | 144,230 | Number of customer contacts | 2,533 | 56.94 per contact |
| Total | $4,458,610 | | | |

**EXHIBIT 5.14**    **AIRCO: Overhead Allocation and Product Profitability under ABC Costing**

| | 5-ton | 6-ton | 7.5-ton | 10-ton | 12.5-ton | 15-ton | 20-ton |
|---|---|---|---|---|---|---|---|
| Direct labor | $   342.20 | $   342.20 | $   342.20 | $   410.64 | $   410.64 | $   410.64 | $   410.64 |
| Direct material | 665.00 | 665.00 | 665.00 | 1,957.00 | 1,957.00 | 2,510.00 | 2,510.00 |
| Overhead<br>(ABC-based) | 174.63 | 404.27 | 160.26 | 172.62 | 1,029.52 | 343.95 | 309.90 |
| Total manufacturing<br>cost | $ 1,181.83 | $1,411.47 | $1,167.46 | $2,540.26 | $3,397.16 | $3,264.59 | $3,230.54 |
| Selling price | 1,000.00 | 1,300.00 | 1,750.00 | 2,560.00 | 3,200.00 | 4,572.00 | 5,450.00 |
| Product margin | $ (181.83) | $ (111.47) | $ 582.54 | $   19.74 | $ (197.16) | $1,307.41 | $2,219.46 |

The ABC analysis can be compared to the volume-based approach that AIRCO used prior to ABC, in which overhead costs were assigned to products based on a rate of $12.02 per direct labor-hour. The results of the volume-based approach are shown in Exhibit 5.15 and a comparison of those results to the ABC results is shown in Exhibit 5.16. Note that the ABC and volume-based methods show significantly different results for some of the products, particularly the 6-ton and 12.5-ton models. While the detailed calculations of the ABC costs for these products are not shown, the company reports that the 12.5-ton model required significantly more raw materials receipts (the cost driver for materials receiving and handling) than other products, and it also required more setup time and customer service contacts. Thus, the ABC costs for the 12.5-ton model are significantly higher than for volume-based costs. Similarly, the 6-ton product has higher costs under

**EXHIBIT 5.15**    **AIRCO: Overhead Allocation and Product Profitability under Volume-Based Costing**

| | 5-ton | 6-ton | 7.5-ton | 10-ton | 12.5-ton | 15-ton | 20-ton |
|---|---|---|---|---|---|---|---|
| Direct labor | $   342.20 | $   342.20 | $   342.20 | $   410.64 | $   410.64 | $   410.64 | $   410.64 |
| Direct material | 665.00 | 665.00 | 665.00 | 1,957.00 | 1,957.00 | 2,510.00 | 2,510.00 |
| Overhead<br>(volume-based) | 240.41 | 240.41 | 240.41 | 288.49 | 288.49 | 288.49 | 288.49 |
| Total product<br>cost | $1,247.61 | $1,247.61 | $1,247.61 | $2,656.13 | $2,656.13 | $3,209.13 | $3,209.13 |
| Selling price | 1,000.00 | 1,300.00 | 1,750.00 | 2,560.00 | 3,200.00 | 4,572.00 | 5,450.00 |
| Product margin | $ (247.61) | $   52.39 | $ 502.39 | $  (96.13) | $ 543.87 | $1,362.87 | $2,240.87 |

## The Cost of Complexity and the Role of ABC: Lego, Nike, and GM

In three companies (Nike, General Motors, and the Lego Group), the strong influence of the design staff created a proliferation of products that created additional complexity and costs without improving profits.

Nike, a leader in the sports apparel industry, discovered in 2006 that it had 30 different styles of the basic T-shirt. The company knew, however, that 95% of the company's apparel sales came from 40% of its apparel products. Over several months a design team was assigned to bring this to one design that would be available in a variety of colors and fabrics. This was part of a companywide effort to reduce complexity. The goal was to reduce costs and improve overall profitability.

The same could be said for GM and the Lego Group. GM found that car models that sold less than 2,000 units (such as the Saturn Astra and the Pontiac G8) were unprofitable. Even if the vehicle shared most parts with other vehicles, there were incremental costs of engineering, sales, brochures, owner manuals, and the like. So GM as well as Ford and Chrysler are simplifying their model lineups. In the Lego Group, the concern arose when sales were increasing but profits were falling.

This is a common sign of a company that could use ABC costing, to identify those products that might have sales growth but are unprofitable. Lego found that it, like GM and Nike, had become a design-driven company, and there was a proliferation of products. The solution for Lego was to place more emphasis on costs and to reduce the number of products and color variety; this was accomplished in part by requiring closer coordination between operations and design.

The cost of complexity as illustrated in the above examples is a key reason that ABC costing can play a strategic role for these firms—it provides a way to accurately determine the cost of product variety and other operating complexities, so the firm can identify the most profitable products and operations.

**Source:** Kaj Grichnik and Conrad Winkler, *Make or Break: How Manufacturers Can Leap from Decline to Revitalization* (New York: McGraw-Hill, 2008), pp. 52–56; Stephanie Kang, "Nike Gets Back to Basics, Reinventing the T-Shirt," *The Wall Street Journal,* April 2, 2007, p. B1; Sharon Terlep and Neal E. Boudette, "Unpopular Models Slow Down GM," *The Wall Street Journal,* September 9, 2008, p. B1.

**EXHIBIT 5.16**

**AIRCO: Comparison of Product Profit Margins under Volume-Based and ABC Costing**

|  | ABC Product Margin | Volume-Based Product Margin | Difference |
|---|---|---|---|
| 5-ton | $ (181.83) | $ (247.61) | $  65.78 |
| 6-ton | (111.47) | 52.39 | (163.86) |
| 7.5-ton | 582.54 | 502.39 | 80.15 |
| 10-ton | 19.74 | (96.13) | 115.87 |
| 12.5-ton | (197.16) | 543.87 | (741.03) |
| 15-ton | 1,307.41 | 1,362.87 | (55.46) |
| 20-ton | 2,219.46 | 2,240.87 | (21.41) |

ABC because of its relatively high use of setup time and customer service contact. The ABC information provides the company a useful basis for becoming more competitive, for example, by reconsidering the pricing of certain products and looking for ways to increase efficiency in the use of its activities.

### ABC/M Applications in Government

ABC/M is used widely in government, as illustrated by the U.S. Postal Service example that introduced this chapter (see page 132). Another example is the U.S. Patent and Trademark Office (PTO), which uses ABC to better understand its cost structure. The PTO is not taxpayer supported; rather, it relies on user fees, and the volume of applications has been rising, making the determination of accurate costs and the setting of appropriate user fees for its different services critical. The ABC model at the PTO used 29 activities and the cost objects included utility patents, design patents, plant patents, reissues, reexaminations, trademarks, and appeals. One finding of the ABC implementation was that the cost of trademark processing was higher than expected.[3]

There are many other examples because the U.S. federal government encourages the use of ABC within its various units. In 1990, three officials responsible for federal financial reporting established the Federal Accounting Standards Advisory Board (FASAB) as a federal advisory committee (**www.fasab.gov**). The officials were the Secretary of the

[3] For additional examples: Gary Cokins, *Activity-Based Cost Management in Government,* Management Concepts, Inc., 2001.

Treasury, the Director of the Office of Management and Budget, and the Comptroller General of the United States. They created FASAB to develop accounting standards and principles for the U.S. government. *FASAB Standard Number 4,* "Managerial Cost Accounting Concepts and Standards for the Federal Government," explains the advantages of ABC for use in governmental units.

## Customer Profitability Analysis

---

The customer is the most important part of the assembly line.

*W. Edwards Deming*

---

ABC/M is best known for its application in computing product costs, but firms also find it useful in determining the cost of serving customers and as a basis for evaluating the profitability of a specific customer or group of customers. Why is this important? Most managers agree that 80% of their profits come from the top 20% of their customers, and most important, the bottom 20% of their customers are unprofitable! For example, to better compete with Walmart, Best Buy works hard to attract profitable customers (it calls them *angels*) and equally hard to discourage the unprofitable customers (the *devils*)—those that are price shopping and looking for discounts and promotions and comparing prices to Walmart. Best Buy studies demographic and sales data for each store location to identify angels and devils. Similarly, the large food distributor, CONCO, studies its customer base (mostly restaurants) to identify profitable and unprofitable customers. CONCO found that certain food products and smaller customers tended to be unprofitable.[4]

**Customer profitability analysis**
identifies customer service activities, cost drivers, and the profitability of individual customers or customer group.

**Customer profitability analysis** identifies customer service activities and cost drivers and determines the profitability of each customer or customer group. Here, customer service includes all activities to complete the sale and satisfy the customer, including advertising, sales calls, delivery, billing, collections, service calls, inquiries, and other forms of customer service. Customer profitability analysis allows managers to:

- Identify most profitable customers.
- Manage each customer's costs-to-serve.
- Introduce profitable new products and services.
- Discontinue unprofitable products, services, or customers.
- Shift a customer's purchase mix toward higher-margin products and service lines.
- Offer discounts to gain more volume with low costs-to-serve customers.
- Choose types of after-sale services to provide.

A good understanding of the profitability of a firm's current and potential customers can help firms improve overall profits and become more competitive. This begins with an analysis of the cost to serve the customer.

### Customer Cost Analysis

**LO 5-6**

*Use an activity-based approach to analyze customer profitability.*

Not all customers require similar activities either before or after the sale. Examples of customer-specific activities include:

- Order processing costs.
- Billing, collection, and payment processing costs.
- Accounts receivable and carrying costs.
- Customer service costs.
- Selling and marketing costs.

[4] Stephen Schulist, "Using ABC to Manage and Improve at CONCO Foods," *The Journal of Corporate Accounting & Finance,* March/April 2004, pp. 29–34; Gary McWilliams, "Analyzing Customers, Best Buy Decides Not All Are Welcome," *The Wall Street Journal,* November 8, 2004, p. 1; Jaclyne Badal, "A Reality Check for the Sales Staff," *The Wall Street Journal,* October 16, 2006, p. B3.

Loyal customers are not necessarily desirable customers. The common practice of trying to retain customers by discounting or providing a loyalty program may no longer be an affordable way to do business. In fact, the customer that needs such incentives may be what Kumar and Rajan call "barnacles." It does not necessarily mean the customers should be abandoned, just that the level of resources dedicated to supporting these customers may need to be altered. However, a weak economy is causing some businesses to, in fact, stop servicing customers. Customers that continue to ask for more discounts or concessions and extend out their payments put tremendous pressure on businesses. Tying up resources to support unprofitable customers hurts the company's ability to take advantage of other, more profitable opportunities. Websmith Group, LLC is an example. The owner decided to eliminate 5% of the group's clients; they were taking up 20% of the resources. By redeploying the resulting freed-up resources, the group's revenues were on track to rise over 10% from the prior year. The bottom line is that maybe a company will reach a point where it makes no sense to continue to service customers on which money with every transaction.

**Sources:** V. Kumar and Bharath Rajan, "Nurturing the Right Customers," *Strategic Finance*, September 2009, pp. 27–33; and Raymund Flandez, "It Just Isn't Working? Some File for Customer Divorce," *The Wall Street Journal*, November 10, 2009, p. B7.

**Customer cost analysis** identifies activities and cost drivers related to servicing customers.

**Customer cost analysis** is the process of identifying the activities and cost drivers related to servicing customers. Traditionally these costs are hidden in the customer support, marketing, and sales function. ABC/M can help managers to understand their costs to serve customers.

Different activities often have different cost drivers. Based on the activities and cost drivers involved in services performed to acquire and complete a transaction, customer costs can be classified into the following categories:

- *Customer unit-level cost*—resources consumed for each unit sold to a customer. Examples include sales commissions based on the number of units sold or sales dollars, shipping cost when the freight charge is based on the number of units shipped, and cost of restocking each returned unit.

- *Customer batch-level cost*—resources consumed for each sales transaction. Examples include order-processing costs, invoicing costs, and recording of sales returns or allowances every time a return or allowance is granted.

- *Customer-sustaining cost*—resources consumed to service a customer regardless of the number of units or batches sold. Examples are salespersons' travel costs to visit customers, monthly statement processing costs, and collection costs for late payments.

- *Distribution-channel cost*—resources consumed in each distribution channel the firm uses to service customers. Examples are operating costs of regional warehouses that serve major customers and centralized distribution centers that serve small retail outlets.

- *Sales-sustaining cost*—resources consumed to sustain sales and service activities that cannot be traced to an individual unit, batch, customer, or distribution channel. Examples are general corporate expenditures for sales activities, and the salary, fringe benefits, and bonus of the general sales manager.

Exhibit 5.17 shows customer-related activities, cost drivers and their rates, and the cost category of each of the activities of Winsome Office Supply. These activities are based on the results of a careful study of the firm's selling, administrative, and general expenditures, as well as customer transactions for the last three years. Exhibit 5.18 shows the detailed customer-related activities that Winsome experienced for the sales to the firm's three major customers GereCo., HomeServ Inc., and Advance Tek.

Both customer activity costs, cost categories, and their cost drivers illustrated in Exhibit 5.17 and the detailed customer-related activities reported in Exhibit 5.18 provide the basis for analyzing customer costs. Exhibit 5.19 shows customer cost analyses for Winsome's three customers.

As illustrated in Exhibits 5.18 and 5.19, while these three customers purchased about equal amounts from Winsome, the costs to serve these customers ranged from $1,555 to $20,395. The costs to service these customers differ because they do not place similar demands on the service-related resources of the firm.

**EXHIBIT 5.17**
Customer-Related Activity,
Cost Driver, Cost Rate, and
Cost Category: Winsome Office
Supply

| Activity | Cost Driver and Rate | Cost Category |
|---|---|---|
| Order taking | $30 per order | Customer batch-level |
| Order processing | $20 per order, | Customer batch-level |
| | and $1 per item | Customer unit-level |
| Delivery | $100 per trip, and | Customer batch-level |
| | $1 per mile | Customer batch-level |
| Expedited order taking, | | |
|    processing, and delivery | $800 per order | Customer batch-level |
| Customer visit | $200 per visit | Customer-sustaining |
| Monthly billing: | | |
|    First statement | $5 per statement | Customer-sustaining |
|    Subsequent reminder | $25 per notice | Customer-sustaining |
| Sales returns | $100 per occurrence | Customer batch-level |
| Restocking | $5 per item returned | Customer unit-level |

**EXHIBIT 5.18**
Customer-Related Activity for
Selected Customers: Winsome
Office Supply

| | GereCo. | HomeServ Inc. | Advance Tek |
|---|---|---|---|
| Net sales | $463,917 | $477,600 | $472,576 |
| Number of orders and deliveries | 2 | 20 | 80 |
| Average number of items per order | 400 | 38 | 8 |
| Delivery miles | 10 | 15 | 20 |
| Number of expedited orders | 0 | 0 | 5 |
| Number of visits by salesperson | 1 | 2 | 5 |
| Sales returns | | | |
|    Number of requests | 2 | 1 | 10 |
|    Average units per return | 3 | 4 | 2 |
| Billing reminder | 0 | 0 | 2 |

**EXHIBIT 5.19**
Customer Cost Analysis:
Winsome Office Supply

| | GereCo. | HomeServ Inc. | Advance Tek |
|---|---|---|---|
| Customer unit-level cost | | | |
|    Order processing | 400 × 2 × $1 = $800 | 38 × 20 × $1 = $760 | 8 × 80 × $1 = $640 |
|    Restocking | 2 × 3 × $5 = 30 | 1 × 4 × $5 = 20 | 10 × 2 × $5 = 100 |
| Customer batch-level cost | | | |
|    Order taking | 2 × $30 = 60 | 20 × $30 = 600 | 80 × $30 = 2,400 |
|    Order processing | 2 × $20 = 40 | 20 × $20 = 400 | 80 × $20 = 1,600 |
|    Delivery | | | |
|      Trips | 2 × $100 = 200 | 20 × $100 = 2,000 | 80 × $100 = 8,000 |
|      Miles | 10 × 2 × $1 = 20 | 15 × 20 × $1 = 300 | 20 × 80 × $1 = 1,600 |
|      Expedited orders | — | — | $800 × 5 = 4,000 |
|      Sales returns | 2 × $100 = 200 | 1 × $100 = 100 | 10 × $100 = 1,000 |
| Customer-sustaining costs | | | |
|    Sales visits | 1 × $200 = 200 | 2 × $200 = 400 | 5 × $200 = 1,000 |
|    Monthly billings | 1 × $5 = 5 | 1 × $5 = 5 | 1 × $5 = 5 |
|    Subsequent reminders | — | — | 2 × $25 = 50 |
| Sales-sustaining costs | — | — | — |
| Total | $1,555 | $4,585 | $20,395 |

## Customer Profitability Analysis

Customer profitability analysis combines customer revenues and customer cost analyses to assess customer profitability and helps identify actions to improve customer profitability. Exhibit 5.20 illustrates customer profitability analysis for Winsome.

The reasons that GereCo. is not as profitable as HomeServ relate to sales activities. Winsome granted GereCo. much more favorable sales terms than the terms granted to HomeServ. GereCo. also had a high amount of sales returns and allowances; it returned twice as often as HomeServ did.

# Cost Management in Action

## How to Validate Your Customer Profitability Strategy: Data or Expertise?

Harrah's Casinos, the Royal Bank of Canada, and Capital One have a special ability to understand customer profitability. In recent years, these companies have used their customer profitability strategy effectively to improve revenues and profits. Some would say their success has been due to hard work, or to good judgment, or just dumb luck.

Perhaps you are a customer of one of these companies; how do you think they have been successful?

(Refer to Comments on Cost Management in Action at the end of the chapter.)

**EXHIBIT 5.20**
**Customer Profitability Analysis: Winsome Office Supply**

|  | GereCo. | HomeServ Inc. | Advance Tek |
|---|---|---|---|
| Total sales | $500,000 | $480,000 | $540,000 |
| Less: Sales discounts | 25,000 | — | 27,000 |
| Net invoice amount | $475,000 | $480,000 | $513,000 |
| Less: Sales returns and allowances | 4,750 | 2,400 | 30,780 |
| Less: Cash discounts | 6,333 | — | 9,644 |
| Net sales | $463,917 | $477,600 | $472,576 |
| Cost of goods sold | 408,620 | 384,720 | 432,014 |
| Gross margin | $ 55,297 | $ 92,880 | $ 40,562 |
| Customer costs |  |  |  |
| Order processing | $ 800 | $ 760 | $ 640 |
| Restocking | 30 | 20 | 100 |
| Order taking | 60 | 600 | 2,400 |
| Order processing | 40 | 400 | 1,600 |
| Delivery |  |  |  |
| Trips | 200 | 2,000 | 8,000 |
| Miles | 20 | 300 | 1,600 |
| Expedited orders | — | — | 4,000 |
| Sales returns | 200 | 100 | 1,000 |
| Sales visits | 200 | 400 | 1,000 |
| Monthly billings | 5 | 5 | 5 |
| Subsequent reminders | — | — | 50 |
| Total customer costs | $ 1,555 | $ 4,585 | $ 20,395 |
| Net customer profit | $ 53,742 | $ 88,295 | $ 20,167 |

Although Advance Tek had the highest total sales, it generated the lowest profit of the three customers. Winsome should be concerned about Advance Tek's high returns and its frequency of orders and number of expedited orders. Winsome needs to look into the reasons for these high levels of activity, as it may potentially lose this customer. Late payments also add to the cost to serve Advance Tek; they might indicate Advance Tek's dissatisfaction with Winsome's sales and services or weakness of Advance Tek's financial condition.

Customer profitability analysis provides valuable information to the assessment of customer value. In addition, firms must weigh other relevant factors before determining the action appropriate for each customer. The following are among these relevant factors:

- Growth potential of the customer, the customer's industry, and its cross-selling potential.
- Possible reactions of the customer to changes in sales terms or services.
- Importance of having the firm as a customer for future sales references, especially when the customer could play a pivotal role in bringing in additional business.

## Customer Lifetime Value

Exhibit 5.20 shows how to determine the profitability of a customer at a given point in time. Many companies now see the importance of looking at the long-term value of the customer, the expected contribution to profit during the full period the company retains

Sunil Gupta and Valerie Zeithaml have summarized the research that has examined the relationship between a variety of customer metrics and profitability. They integrated this large amount of knowledge into the following generalizations which they argue are supported by the research. These generalizations are important because they help us to understand the role of customer lifetime value (CLV).

1. Improvement in customer satisfaction has a significant and positive impact on firms' financial performance—shown by many studies

2. The link between customer satisfaction and profitability is asymmetric and nonlinear—an increase in satisfaction has less of a positive effect on profitability than the negative effect of declines in satisfaction; increases in satisfaction have a greater than linear effect on profits.

3. The strength of the satisfaction-profitability link varies across industries as well as across firms within an industry

4. There is a strong positive relationship between customer satisfaction and customer retention.

5. While customer satisfaction and service quality are strongly correlated with behavioral intentions, behavioral intentions imperfectly predict actual (buying) behavior.

6. The relationship between observable and unobservable metrics is nonlinear—as the relationship between satisfaction and profitability is nonlinear, so is the relationship between satisfaction and repurchase intention (an unobservable).

7. Marketing decisions based on observable customer metrics, such as CLV, improve a firm's financial performance.

8. Customer retention is one of the key drivers of CLV and firm profitability.

**Source:** Sunil Gupta and Valerie Zeithaml, "Customer Metrics and Their Impact on Financial Performance," *Marketing Science,* November–December 2006, pp. 718–739.

---

**Customer lifetime value (CLV)** is the net present value of estimated future profits from the customer.

the customer. This concept is called **customer lifetime value (CLV)**, and it is calculated as the net present value of estimated future profits from the customer for a specified time, which may be three to five years. Present value is used because the profits from the customer are expected to occur over a number of years. To provide a more comprehensive and strategically relevant measure of the value of the customer, CLV takes into account the company's expectations about the future potential growth in profits for a customer. The following example illustrates the calculation of CLV. Assume MidTown Medical Clinic purchases medical supplies from Johnson Medical Supply Company. Johnson calculates the CLV of the medical clinic by projecting profits from the clinic. Suppose the forecast is for $20,000 profit per year for the next three years. Further, suppose Johnson uses a discount rate of 6% (the relevant discount factor is 2.673 from the present value Table 2 at the end of Chapter 12 on page 498), then

$$\text{CLV} = \$53,460 = \$20,000 \times 2.673$$

CLV can be used to measure the value of a customer or group of customers and to determine how marketing and support services should be allocated to these customers to improve the firm's overall profitability. Since there is a significant level of judgment involved in estimating the variables in the calculation, it is also important to compare different calculations of CLV made with different assumptions about profit forecasts and discount rates.

## Implementation Issues and Extensions

**LO 5-7**

*Identify key factors for successful ABC/M implementation.*

---

If you want to make enemies, try to change something.

*Woodrow Wilson*

---

A successful ABC/M implementation requires close cooperation among management accountants, engineers, and manufacturing and operating managers. They need to act as a team in identifying activities, cost drivers, and requisite information, both financial and nonfinancial.

Following are processes found in many successful implementations of ABC/M:

| Implementation Process | Why This Leads to Success |
| --- | --- |
| Involve management and employees in creating an ABC system | Allows them to become familiar with ABC/M. They could then be more willing to implement the system because they feel included and share in ownership of the new system. |
| Use ABC/M on a job that will succeed | Shows how and why the process works. Successfully completing one job enables individuals to see the benefits of ABC/M more clearly. |
| Keep the initial ABC/M design simple | Avoids overwhelming users and holds costs down; also reduces implementation time. |

Extensions of the ABC model are becoming more common. We discuss three of these below: multistage ABC, resource consumption accounting (RCA), and time-driven activity-based costing (TDABC). All three respond directly to the inherent complexity of resource and activity cost assignments in actual applications, noted as one of the implementation issues above. The latter two take a resource-focused approach to ABC.

## Multistage Activity-Based Costing

In practice, you may find some activities are intermediate cost objects for other activities while others are assigned directly to cost objects. To capture and calculate accurately the costs for this situation, some firms use multistage activity-based costing rather than two-stage ABC described earlier in the chapter. In **multistage ABC,** resource costs are assigned to certain activities which in turn are assigned to other activities before being assigned to the final cost objects. Exhibit 5.21 illustrates such a case. The activity labeled "support activities" provides service to other activities later in the value chain—product/service activities, customer activities, and infrastructure-sustaining activities. The exhibit illustrates how a total of $70 of resource costs are assigned in multistage ABC costing. After multistage allocations, $25 is assigned to products, $20 is assigned to customer-related activities, and $25 is assigned to infrastructure-related costs (computer equipment and software, buildings, and other equipment, etc.).

In **multistage ABC,** resource costs are assigned to certain activities which in turn are assigned to other activities before being assigned to the final cost objects.

**EXHIBIT 5.21**
**Multistage Activity Cost Flows**

**ABC as a total system in this example begins with $70. It then reassigns and accumulates the costs into the final cost objects.**

*Intermediate activity drivers reassign each activity's cumulative input costs plus its own cost.

**Cost of product, Customer activities + Sustaining costs = Total costs to recover = $70**

## Resource Consumption Accounting (RCA)

**Resource consumption accounting (RCA)**
is a comprehensive and fully integrated management accounting approach that provides managers with decision support information based on an operational view of the organization.

**Resource consumption accounting (RCA)** is relatively new to the field of cost management and is an integration of principle from the German costing system Grenzplankostenrechnung (GPK) and ABC. On the RCA Institute website (**www.rcainstitute.org**), RCA is formally defined as "a dynamic, fully integrated, principle-based, and comprehensive management accounting approach that provides managers with decision support information for enterprise optimization."[5] Like ABC, RCA uses an activity/process view but integrates marginal costs and a detailed resource consumption analysis to generate information for decision support. Another notable feature of RCA is that depreciation expense is based on an estimated replacement cost for the asset rather than historical acquisition cost.

RCA's emphasis is on being able to attribute costs, both fixed and proportional, to cost objects for decision support, and there are three foundational concepts for RCA:

- The view of resources—resources are the suppliers of capacity, meaning that capacity is a function of the resources available.
- The quantity-based model—an operational view of the organization based on the concept that there is a causal relationship that can be expressed in terms of input and output units.
- Cost behavior—the characteristics of the cost are inherent to the underlying resource and the consumption of those resources by value-creating operations.

The RCA approach relies heavily on the concept of an attributable cost, which is a concept of attaching costs to a cost object only when causality exists. This concept helps ensure that decisions are not made on the basis of arbitrary allocations. Understanding and modeling causality allows for the modeling of cost behavior based on responsiveness, which is the level of correlation between a particular output quantity and the input quantity needed to produce the output.

RCA offers tremendous potential benefits, but like any system, management must decide if the benefits exceed the cost of implementation. Additionally, the collection, storage, and processing of the underlying data for an effective RCA implementation requires its own use of resources, which could be quite extensive. For large organizations, this may mean an enterprise resource planning (ERP) system needs to be in place. However, medium and smaller sized organizations are not out of luck. There is an open source application for RCA available called ROSA, making RCA possible for those organizations that have less sophisticated cost management systems.

## Time-Driven Activity-Based Costing (TDABC)

Another resource-centric approach to the implementation of large ABC costing systems is based on the idea that the common element in the utilization of activities is the unit of time. ABC traces and reassigns resource expenses to the activities that consume them and then further reassigns them proportionately to the final cost objects based on the quantity of each activity's cost driver. When a substantial amount of the cost of a company's activities are in a highly repetitive process, the cost assignment can be based on the average time required for each activity. **Time-driven activity-based costing (TDABC)** assigns resource costs directly to cost objects using the cost per time unit of supplying the resource, rather than first assigning costs to activities and then from activities to cost objects.[6]

**Time-driven activity-based costing (TDABC)**
assigns resource costs directly to cost objects using the cost per time unit of supplying the resource, rather than first assigning costs to activities and then from activities to cost objects.

TDABC provides a direct way to measure unused capacity. To illustrate, assume there is a credit card processing facility and one of its activities is validation of mailing addresses. Traditional ABC would first pool the costs associated with the various activities of the facility and then select cost drivers to come up with costs per activity. The cost of activities associated with validating mailing addresses would be assigned to the cost object "mailing list validation" and that pool of costs would be divided by the number of

[5] In RCA, resource cost pools are called cost centers. Useful references for RCA include Kip Krumwiede and Augustin Suessmair, "Getting Down to Specifics on RCA," *Strategic Finance* (June 2007); and the Resource Consumption Accounting Institute website **www.rcainstitute.org**.

[6] Robert S. Kaplan and Steven R. Anderson, *Time-Driven Activity-Based Costing* (Boston: Harvard Business School Press, 2007).

validations to determine a cost per validation. Assume there were 10,000 validations for the year and the ABC rate was $10 per validation.

In contrast, TDABC considers the standard time for each validation, which we assume is 17 minutes. TDABC computes the cost per minute of the resources performing the work activity. In this example we assume that two clerical workers, each paid $45,000 annually, work only on validations. TDABC calculates the total cost as $45,000 × 2 employees = $90,000; then TDABC calculates the total time available for the activity. Assuming each employee has 30 productive hours per week and actually works 50 weeks per year, the time available is 2 employees × 50 weeks × 30 hours per week × 60 minutes per hour = 180,000 minutes. The TDABC rate is $90,000 ÷ 180,000 minutes = $0.50 per minute. The cost of a validation can now be estimated to be 17 minutes × $0.50 per minute = $8.50 per validation.

TDABC can then calculate the unused capacity cost by determining the activity cost and netting it from the total expense. In this example the TDABC activity cost is calculated as $85,000 (i.e., 17 minutes × 10,000 validations × $.50 per validation). This means that $5,000 (or 10,000 minutes at $.50 per minute) unused capacity is potentially available to be used for other work.

TDABC can be expanded to include complexities in the activity, in what is called a time equation. For example, we assume the time to validate an address is significantly increased for an international address—each requires an additional 22 minutes. Then the time equation can be determined as follows:

Time to validate address = 17 minutes + 22 minutes (if it is an international address)

The determination of the cost per minute is done in the same manner, but with the addition of the expected time for international addresses.

A difference between TDABC and ABC is that TDABC is capacity-sensitive and computes a standard activity cost using standard rates, meaning activity driver rates remain constant. In contrast, ABC might not include capacity, as in the HBT and AIRCO Ltd cases presented earlier. ABC computes the activity cost each period as actual and therefore the final cost object's unit cost fluctuates each period. TDABC requires an upfront investment to measure activity times and to continuously maintain them.

Note that traditional ABC may use amount of time for an activity. For example, setup time might be used rather than number of setups. Of course, it will be necessary to determine budgeted time for the activity and the actual time for each setup. Note however, that this approach to ABC is still different from TDABC; TDABC uses the time to drive costs directly from resources to cost objects—there is no assignment of resource costs to activities and then from activities to cost objects.

The following is an example illustrating the use of time as a driver. Consider that the three activities—machine setup, inspection, and packaging—require an average of 80 minutes, 15 minutes, and 20 minutes, respectively. Under ABC the activity consumption cost drivers for these activities are based on the total activity cost divided by the number of minutes available for that activity. For example, if the total cost of setup is $50,000, and there is a capacity of 1,250 minutes of setup time, then the activity rate is $50,000 ÷ 1,250 = $40 per minute. This approach can improve the ABC application since actual time is used to assign costs. For example, if setup time for a special customer order requires an additional 15 minutes, the assigned setup cost would be based on $40 per minute times the total time of 95 minutes: 95 minutes × $40 = $3,800.

A disadvantage of TDABC is its reliance on the accuracy of the time estimates; also, the effort to determine these time estimates could be very time-consuming and costly. Some activities are not time-driven and should not be included in a comprehensive TDABC; for example, in a chemical company, the cost of the setup and cleanup activities involves significant materials costs, apart from the cost of the time involved. However, these materials costs could be included in a modified TDABC where pounds of materials could be used rather than minutes of setup or cleanup; this is then a combination of time- and pounds-driven ABC. Finally, because of its distinction of resources and activities, traditional ABC can in some cases provide a better framework for identifying opportunities for cost savings, while TDABC can provide a better framework for identifying unused capacity.

## Summary

Many companies have replaced their volume-based costing systems with activity-based costing systems for more accurate product costing and better decision making.

Volume-based costing systems use a volume-based overhead rate, either a single rate for the entire plant or departmental rates. These volume-based overhead rates typically use measures such as direct labor-hours, machine-hours, or direct labor costs for all products or services, even if the firm has diverse products, manufacturing processes, and volumes. For firms with more than one product or process, these overhead rates often generate inaccurate and significantly distorted product costs.

Activity-based costing systems recognize that products and services consume indirect costs in a manner that follows the usage of activities rather than the volume of output. ABC costing improves on costing accuracy because it identifies the detail-level activities which cause the consumption of resources; ABC costing assigns these activity-based costs to the products or services using activity-consumption cost drivers, rather than volume-based cost drivers.

Activity-based management manages resource costs and activities to improve the value of products or services to the customer by reducing product cost and/or increasing value-adding activities.

Customer profitability analysis and customer lifetime value are methods, enabled by activity-based costing, which provide important tools for determining the profitability of product lines, customer groups, or individual customers.

Multistage ABC, resource consumption accounting (RCA), and time-driven ABC (TDABC) are new tools which have been developed in recognition of the complexity of cost relationships in many organizations.

## Key Terms

activity, *133*
activity-based costing (ABC), *133*
activity consumption cost driver, *133*
batch-level activity, *136*
cost driver, *133*
customer cost analysis, *150*
customer lifetime value (CLV), *153*

customer profitability analysis, *149*
facility-level activity, *136*
high-value-added activity, *144*
low-value-added activity, *144*
multistage ABC, *154*
product-level activity, *136*
resource, *133*
resource consumption accounting (RCA), *155*

resource consumption cost driver, *133*
time-driven activity-based costing (TDABC), *155*
two-stage cost assignment, *134*
unit-level activity, *136*

## Comments on Cost Management in Action

Admittedly, the answer to this question requires some guesswork. However, it has been proven time after time that data win over perceived expertise, experience, or unaided judgment. Each of these companies uses business analytics, a key form of business intelligence. Business analytics involves the use of computer-based models, statistical analysis, or simulations to test hypotheses about what drives customer loyalty and profitability.

Harrah's is a company that uses a model to predict when a customer is about to change to another casino. At Harrah's, the model predicts when customers are reaching their threshold of "too much" gambling losses; a "luck ambassador" is sent to encourage them to take a break and have a free meal, on Harrah's. Its model is based on extensive data obtained about customers. Harrah's system is based on information from a loyalty program, a program in which customers use a swipeable card whenever they use the firm's services and receive "rewards," while the company receives vital data about the customers. Capital One uses the same approach to determine the best ways to recruit and retain credit card customers. And the Royal Bank of Canada uses customer data extensively, in combination with ABC costing, to assess customer profitability for each of its banking customers.

**Sources:** Thomas H. Davenport and Jeanne G. Harris, *Competing on Analytics* (Boston: Harvard Business School Press, 2007); and Ian Ayres, *Super Crunchers: Why Thinking-by-Numbers Is the New Way to Be Smart* (New York: Bantam, 2007).

## Self–Study Problem

(For solution, please turn to the end of the chapter.)

### Volume-Based Costing versus ABC

Carter Company manufactures two products, Deluxe and Regular, and uses a traditional two-stage cost allocation system. The first stage assigns all factory overhead costs to two production departments, A and B, based on machine-hours. The second stage uses direct labor-hours to allocate overhead to individual products.

For 2013, the firm budgeted $1,000,000 total factory overhead cost for these operations.

|  | Production Department A | Production Department B |
|---|---|---|
| Machine-hours | 4,000 | 16,000 |
| Direct labor-hours | 20,000 | 10,000 |

The following information relates to the firm's operations for the month of January:

|  | Deluxe | Regular |
|---|---|---|
| Units produced and sold | 200 | 800 |
| Unit cost of direct materials | $100 | $50 |
| Hourly direct labor wage rate | $25 | $20 |
| Direct labor-hours in Department A per unit | 2 | 2 |
| Direct labor-hours in Department B per unit | 1 | 1 |

Carter Company is considering implementing an activity-based costing system. Its management accountant has collected the following information for activity cost analysis for 2013.

| Activity | Budgeted Overhead | Cost Driver | Budgeted Quantity | Driver Consumption Deluxe | Driver Consumption Regular |
|---|---|---|---|---|---|
| Material movement | $ 7,000 | Number of production runs | 350 | 15 | 20 |
| Machine setups | 400,000 | Number of setups | 500 | 25 | 50 |
| Inspections | 588,000 | Number of units | 19,600 | 200 | 800 |
| Shipment | 5,000 | Number of shipments | 250 | 50 | 100 |
|  | $1,000,000 |  |  |  |  |

### Required

1. Calculate the unit cost for each of the two products under the existing volume-based costing system.
2. Calculate the overhead per unit of the cost driver under the proposed ABC system.
3. Calculate the unit cost for each of the two products if the proposed ABC system is adopted.

*Please visit **http://www.mhhe.com/blocher6e** to access a narrated, animated tutorial for solving this problem.*

## Questions

5-1 "Undercosting a product increases the profit from the product and benefits the firm." Do you agree? Why?

5-2 Firms sell products with high costs at high prices. High selling prices increase revenues and profits. Why then should managers worry about product overcosting?

5-3 Explain why a costing system that uses a volume-based rate is likely to produce distorted product costs.

5-4 What is activity-based costing, and how can it improve an organization's costing system?

5-5 Describe general levels of cost hierarchy in activity-based costing systems.

5-6 What is the second-stage procedure in assigning costs to products when using an activity-based costing system?

5-7 What type of company needs an activity-based costing system?

5-8 What are unit-level activities? Give two examples of unit-level activities.

5-9 What are batch-level activities? Give two examples of batch-level activities.

5-10 What are product-level activities? Give two examples of product-level activities.

5-11 What are facility-level activities? Give two examples of facility-level activities.

5-12 Why do product-costing systems using a single, volume-based cost driver tend to overcost high-volume products? Will there be any undesirable strategic effects from such product cost distortion?

5-13 What is activity-based management?

5-14 How can activity-based costing and management be used in service organizations?

5-15 Identify opportunities afforded by performing a customer profitability analysis.

## Brief Exercises

5-16 Tasty Beverage Co. produces soft drinks, specializing in fruit drinks. Tasty produces 5,000 cans of product per batch. Setup cost for each batch is $50 and each drink $0.10 to produce. What is the total cost per batch? How much would it cost to fill an order for 100,000 cans?

5-17 Montross Lumber processes wood to be shipped to construction companies. In order to keep its products uniform, Montross conducts inspections on 20% of the boards produced. Inspections cost the company $10 per hour and it takes one minute to inspect each board. How much would it cost to fill an order for 30,000 boards?

5-18 Orange Inc. grows cabbage. Each package shipped contains 20 vegetables. It costs Orange $5 to put together each package and $0.10 to clean and process each vegetable. How much more does it cost to produce an order for 60 heads of cabbage than an order of 50 heads?

5-19 Williams Performance Co. manufactures sports cars. After making a sale, the salesperson sends the car to be detailed before the customer takes it home. Detailing the car takes 30 minutes at a cost of $15 per hour for direct labor and $5 per car for materials. If the average salesperson sells five cars per day, what is the average cost per five-day week for detailing cars?

5-20 Stackhouse Computing produces high performance desktop computers. Labor cost data shows that the company spent $1,000,000 for 5,000 computers produced, and each computer requires two technician hours and five hours of direct labor. Direct labor is paid $10 per hour by the company. What is the cost of one technician hour?

5-21 Haywood Printing is processing a job with the following activity rates:

| Activity | Cost Driver | Driver Rate |
|---|---|---|
| Direct labor | Number of hours | $8 |
| Copying | Number of copies | $0.05 |

If this job requires five hours for the 1,000 copies, what is the activity-based cost of the job?

5-22 Locke Data Processing reported expenses of $5 million for indirect labor, of which $3 million was for data analysis and $2 million was for data entry. Locke recorded 30,000 hours of data analysis and 100,000 hours of data entry. What are the activity-based rates for each area of direct labor?

5-23 The materials handling charge for ABC Corp. is $.50 per pound of finished product. What is the materials handling charge for a job that produced 10,000 units at a weight of 6 pounds per unit?

## Exercises

[LO 5-1] 5-24 **Role of Activity-Based Costing in Implementing Strategy**  Laurent Products is a manufacturer of plastic packaging products with plants located throughout Europe and customers worldwide. During the past 10 years Laurent Products has successfully developed a line of packaging materials and a unique bagging system that present an important opportunity to increase the productivity of checkout counters in grocery stores. The plastic bags manufactured by Laurent are produced in several sizes and different plastic film colors and may have attractive multicolor printed designs on one or both sides to meet the specification of a particular grocery store. The advantages provided by the Laurent bagging system include the lower cost of bags and labor at the checkout counter as well as improved customer service. The system has contributed to a significant growth in Laurent's sales in recent years.

Laurent's success in the grocery chain market has attracted an increasing number of competitors into the market. While the company had been very successful in bringing out a series of new product types with innovative labor-saving features for the grocery stores, the competitors have eventually been able to develop quite similar products. The result has been increased competition with a substantial reduction in Laurent's prices.

As a result of the increased competition in the grocery chain market, Laurent is planning to begin to focus on the small independent grocery stores that purchase bags from large wholesale distributors. The potential sales for this wholesaler segment is about the same size as the grocery chain market but includes a much larger number of independent store customers.

Investments in manufacturing equipment in recent years have been to support two principal objectives: to increase capacity and to reduce costs. The cost reduction initiatives principally concerned material costs and reduced processing times. Over the years Laurent has chosen to invest in machines that are similar to existing equipment in order to capitalize on the fact that the process is relatively simple and that products can, with relatively few exceptions, be processed on any machine in the plant. The only major restriction is the number of colors that a machine can accommodate on a single pass. Future investment proposals now being considered are based on this rationale.

**Required**   What are the key strategic issues facing Laurent, and how can ABC costing assist in resolving these issues?

**[LO 5-2, 5-3]   5-25   Activity-Based Costing in the Fashion Apparel Industry**   Fleet Street Inc., a manufacturer of high-fashion clothing for women, is located in South London. Its product line consists of trousers (45%), skirts (35%) , dresses (15%), and other (5%). Fleet Street Inc. has been using a volume-based rate to assign overhead to each product; the rate it uses is £2.25 per unit produced. The results for the trousers line, using the volume-based approach are as follows:

| | |
|---|---:|
| Number of units produced | 10,000 |
| Price (all figures in £) | 20.525 |
| Total revenue | 205,250 |
| Direct materials | 33,750 |
| Direct labor | 112,500 |
| Overhead (volume-based) | 22,500 |
| Total product cost | 168,750 |
| Nonmanufacturing expenses | 31,500 |
| Total cost | 200,250 |
| Profit margin for trousers | 5,000 |

Recently, it has conducted a further analysis of the trousers line of product, using ABC. In the study, eight activities were identified, and direct labor was assigned to the activities. The total conversion cost (labor and overhead) for the eight activities, after allocation to the trousers line, is as follows:

| | |
|---|---:|
| Pattern cutting | £22,000 |
| Grading | 19,000 |
| Lay planning | 18,500 |
| Sewing | 21,000 |
| Finishing | 14,300 |
| Inspection | 6,500 |
| Boxing up | 3,500 |
| Storage | 7,000 |

**Required**   Determine the profit margin for trousers using ABC and comment on the difference in comparison to the volume-based calculations. Is Fleet Street more likely to use ABC as a U.K. company than a similar company in France or the United States (refer to real-world focus boxes in the chapter)?

**[LO 5-3]   5-26   Activity Levels and Cost Drivers**   Steve's Slop Shop, a small hamburger shop, has identified the resources used in its operations (assume each customer's order is a batch for this example):

a. Bread

b. Hourly help

c. Store rent

d. Ground beef

e. Catsup

f. Advertising for Triple-Burger special

g. Salary for the store managers

h. Utilities

i. $1-off-coupon for each order

j. Bags for each order

**Required**

1. Classify its costs as unit-level, batch-level, product-level, or facility-level costs.

2. Suggest a proper driver for each of the above items.

**[LO 5-3]**   5-27  **Activity Levels and Cost Drivers**   Shroeder Machine Shop has the following activities:

a. Machine operation

b. Machine setup

c. Production scheduling

d. Materials receiving

e. Research and development

f. Machine maintenance

g. Product design

h. Parts administration

i. Final inspection

j. Materials handling

**Required**

1. Classify each of the activities as a unit-level, batch-level, product-level, or facility-level activity.

2. Identify a proper cost driver for each activity in requirement 1.

**[LO 5-3]**   5-28  **Activity-Based Costing**   Hakara Company has been using direct labor costs as the basis for assigning overhead to its products. Under this allocation system product A has been assigned overhead of $46.88 per unit while product B has been assigned $15.63 per unit. Management feels that an ABC system will provide a more accurate allocation of the overhead costs and has collected the following cost pool and cost driver information:

| Cost Pools | Activity Costs | Cost Driver | Driver Consumption |
|---|---|---|---|
| Machine setup | $360,000 | Setup hours | 4,000 |
| Materials handling | 100,000 | Pounds of materials | 20,000 |
| Electric power | 40,000 | Kilowatt-hours | 40,000 |

The following cost information pertains to the production of two of its products, A and B:

| | A | B |
|---|---|---|
| Number of units produced | 4,000 | 20,000 |
| Direct materials cost | $42,000 | $54,000 |
| Direct labor cost | $24,000 | $40,000 |
| Number of setup hours | 200 | 240 |
| Pounds of materials used | 1,000 | 3,000 |
| Kilowatt-hours | 2,000 | 4,000 |

**Required**

1. Use activity-based costing to determine a unit cost for each product.

2. Comment on management's belief that the ABC system will generate an overhead allocation that is more accurate than the volume-based system currently in use.

**[LO 5-3]**   5-29  **ABC and Job-Costing Working with Unknowns**   North Company designs and manufactures machines that facilitate DNA sequencing. Depending on the intended purpose of each machine and its functions, each machine is likely to be unique. The job-order costing system in its Norfolk plant has five activity cost pools, in addition to direct materials and direct labor. Job TPY–2306 requires 1,000 printed-circuit boards. The cost per board that passes the final inspection is $240. On average, only 50% of the completed units pass the final inspection. The prime costs per completed board are direct materials $25 and direct labor $5. Information pertaining to manufacturing overhead for printed-circuit boards follows:

| Activity Cost Pool | Cost Driver | Activity Driver Rate | Unit of Cost Driver per Board | Factory Overhead per Board |
|---|---|---|---|---|
| Axial insertion | Number of axial insertions | $0.20 | $ 30 | $  A? |
| Hardware insertion | Number of hardware insertions | 2.00 | B? | 37.00 |
| Hand load | Boothroyd time | C? | 5 | 35.50 |
| Masking | Number of points masked | 0.12 | 100 | D? |
| Final test | Test time | E? | 10 | 6.00 |

**Required**   Fill in the unknowns identified as A through E.

[LO 5-4]  5-30  **High-Value-Added and Low-Value-Added Activities**  The Lindex General Hospital has determined the activities of a nurse including the following:

    a. Report for duty and review patient charts h

    b. Visit each patient and take her/his temperature h

    c. Update patients' records h

    d. Coordinate lab and radiology works L

    e. Wait for the attending physician to arrive L

    f. Accompany attending physician L

    g. Explain treatments to patients h

    h. Call kitchen to have the wrong meal tray replaced L

    i. Perform CPR h

**Required**  Classify each item as a high-value-added or a low-value-added activity.

[LO 5-5]  5-31  **Applications of ABC in Government**  Activity-based costing is used widely within the U.S. government. One example is the Department of Agriculture's Animal and Plant Health Inspection Service (APHIS). APHIS helps to protect U.S. agriculture from exotic pests and diseases, to minimize wildlife/agriculture conflicts, and to protect the welfare of animals used for research or sold wholesale for pets. APHIS performs its services for a variety of users, some of whom pay a user fee. ABC was adopted to provide an accurate basis for determining these fees, and also for analysis of the effectiveness and efficiency of its programs in meeting the service's overall goals. The National Institute of Health and the U.S. Mint also use ABC/M to achieve their missions effectively and efficiently.

**Required**
1. Identify an example or two of a governmental entity that you think could benefit from the application of activity-based costing, and explain why.
2. Identify some of the resources, activities, and cost drivers you would expect to see in this application.

[LO 5-1, 5-3, 5-5]  5-32  **Product-Line Profitability; ABC**  Supermart Food Stores (SFS) has experienced net operating losses in its frozen food products line in the last few periods. Management believes that the store can improve its profitability if SFS discontinues frozen foods. The operating results from the most recent period are:

|  | Frozen Food | Baked Goods | Fresh Produce |
| --- | --- | --- | --- |
| Sales | $120,000 | $91,000 | $158,175 |
| Cost of goods sold | 105,000 | 67,000 | 110,000 |

SFS estimates that store support expenses, in total, are approximately 20% of revenues.

    The controller says that not every sales dollar requires or uses the same amount of store support activities. A preliminary analysis reveals store support activities for these three product lines are:

| Activity (cost driver) | Frozen Food | Baked Goods | Fresh Produce |
| --- | --- | --- | --- |
| Order processing (number of purchase orders) | 10 | 45 | 100 |
| Receiving (number of deliveries) | 12 | 55 | 120 |
| Shelf-stocking (number of hours per delivery) | 2 | 0.5 | 4 |
| Customer support (total units sold) | 30,000 | 40,000 | 86,000 |

The controller estimates activity-cost rates for each activity as follows:

| | |
| --- | --- |
| Order processing | $ 80 per purchase order |
| Receiving | 110 per delivery |
| Shelf-stocking | 15.25 per hour |
| Customer support | 0.21 per item |

**Required**
1. Prepare a product-line profitability report for SFS under the current costing system.
2. Prepare a product-line profitability report for SFS using the ABC information the controller provides.

3. What new insights does the ABC system in requirement 2 provide to SFS managers?

4. It is not clear what measure of activity was used to determine the activity-cost rates above. Comment on the impact of using the expected driver consumption versus the practical capacity of the driver when computing the activity-cost rates.

**[LO 5-1, 5-3, 5-5]** 5-33 **Product Line Profitability Analysis** Studemeir Paint & Floors (SPF) has experienced net operating losses in its Other Flooring Products line during the last few periods. SPF's management team thinks that the store will improve its profitability if it discontinues the Other Flooring Products line. The operating results from the most recent period are:

| | Paint & Paint Supplies | Carpet | Other Flooring Products |
| --- | --- | --- | --- |
| Sales | $295,000 | $214,900 | $167,900 |
| Cost of goods sold | 165,000 | 150,000 | 135,250 |

SPF estimates that store support expenses are approximately 24% of revenues.

Harish Rana, SPF's controller, states that not every sales dollar requires or uses the same amount of store support activities. He conducts a preliminary investigation and his results and analysis are as follows:

| Activity (cost driver) | Paint & Paint Supplies | Carpet | Other Flooring Products |
| --- | --- | --- | --- |
| Order processing (number of purchase orders) | 425 | 150 | 100 |
| Receiving (number of deliveries) | 50 | 120 | 60 |
| Customer support (hours required per sale) | 0.50 | 8.0 | 0.75 |

Harish estimates activity-cost rates for each activity as follows:

| | |
| --- | --- |
| Order processing | $140 per purchase order |
| Receiving | 180 per delivery |
| Customer support | 18 per hour |

**Required**
1. Prepare a product-line profitability report for SPF under the current costing system.
2. Prepare a product-line profitability report for SPF using the ABC information the controller provides.
3. What new insights does the ABC system in requirement 2 provide to SPF managers?

**[LO 5-6]** 5-34 **Customer Profitability Analysis; Luxury Hotel Industry** The luxury hotel chain Ritz-Carlton introduced a system called "Mystique" that collects information about its customers from employees and staff at the hotel. The information is used to personalize the services provided to each guest. For example, a bottle of the guest's favorite type of wine would be placed in the room without the guest having to request it. Similarly, the type of fruit a guest prefers will be waiting in the room on arrival. The information is available throughout the Ritz system so that when the guest checks into any Ritz-Carlton hotel, the special treatment is available. Other hotel chains such as Marriott, Hilton, and Hyatt have similar programs

**Required**
1. How do these information-gathering programs help the hotels become more competitive? What is the strategic role of these programs?
2. Do you see a role for activity-based accounting for these firms, as it relates to their information gathering and customer service?
3. What ethical issues, if any, do you see in the information-gathering systems?

**[LO 5-6]** 5-35 **Customer Profitability Analysis** Colleen Company has gathered the following data pertaining to activities it performed for two of its major customers.

| | Jerry Inc. | Kate Co. |
| --- | --- | --- |
| Number of orders | 5 | 30 |
| Units per order | 1,000 | 200 |
| Sales returns: | | |
| Number of returns | 2 | 5 |
| Total units returned | 40 | 175 |
| Number of sales calls | 12 | 4 |

Colleen sells its products at $200 per unit. The firm's gross margin ratio is 25%. Both Jerry and Kate pay their accounts promptly and no accounts receivable is over 30 days. After a careful analysis using a business intelligence software on the operating data for the past 30 months the firm has determined the following activity costs:

| Activity | Cost Driver and Rate |
|---|---|
| Sales calls | $ 1,000 per visit |
| Order processing | 300 per order |
| Deliveries | 500 per order |
| Sales returns | 100 per return and $5 per unit returned |
| Sales salary | 100,000 per month |

**Required**

1. Classify activity costs into cost categories (unit, batch, etc.) and compute the total cost for Colleen Company to service Jerry Inc. and Kate Co.

2. Compare the profitability of these two customers.

[LO 5-6] 5-36 **Customer Profitability Analysis** Garner Industries manufactures precision tools. The firm uses an activity-based costing system. CEO Deb Garner is very proud of the accuracy of the system in determining product costs. She noticed that since the installment of the ABC system 10 years earlier the firm had become much more competitive in all aspects of the business and earned an increasing amount of profits every year.

In the last two years the firm sold 1 million units to 4,100 customers each year. The manufacturing cost is $600 per unit. In addition, Garner has determined that the order-filling cost is $100.50 per unit. The $784.56 selling price per unit includes 12% markup to cover administrative costs and profits.

The order-filling cost per unit is determined based on the firm's costs for order-filling activities. Order-filling capacity can be added in blocks of 60 orders. Each block costs $60,000. In addition, the firm incurs $1,500 order-filling costs per order.

Garner serves two types of customers designated as PC (Preferred Customer) and SC (Small Customer). Each of the 100 PCs buys, on average, 5,000 units in two orders. The firm also sells 500,000 units to 4,000 SCs. On average each SC buys 125 units in 10 orders. Ed Cheap, a buyer for one PC, complains about the high price he is paying. Cheap claims that he has been offered a price of $700 per unit and threatens to take his business elsewhere. Garner does not give in because the $700 price Cheap demands is below cost. Besides, she has recently raised the price to SC to $800 per unit and experienced no decline in orders.

**Required**

1. Demonstrate how Garner arrives at the $100.50 order-filling cost per unit.

2. What would be the amount of loss (profit) per unit if Garner sells to Cheap at $700 per unit?

3. What is the amount of loss (profit) per unit at the $800 selling price per unit for units sold to SC?

[LO 5-7] 5-37 **Tools for Successful ABC/M Implementation** The Consortium for Advanced Management, International (CAM-I) and the American Productivity and Quality Center (APQC) collaborated in the survey of 166 manufacturing and service firms to assess the implementation of ABC/M in these firms. Sixty-eight percent of the respondents were in manufacturing and 25% in service companies. The results showed that the majority of senior managers reported "very successful" implementations of the ABC/M system, while department managers were somewhat evenly split between "very successful" and "moderately successful." Line personnel tended to vote "moderately successful." So, the higher the level in the organization, the more perceived benefit of the ABC/M system.

Interviews with selected respondents and further data analysis showed that the three most common characteristics of successful systems were (1) a high level of top-management support and commitment, (2) technical competence of the implementation team, and (3) effective change management, that is, companies driven by competitive pressures to strive to better understand their internal capabilities and external competition. Some of the responding companies made strategic changes, including changes in the supply chain and changes in target customers. These results are similar to those reported in prior studies of ABC/M implementation.

**Required** In addition to the three characteristics of successful ABC/M implementation noted above, list two or three other guidelines or tips for ABC/M implementation.

# Problems

[LO 5-1, 5-3]   5-38 **Activity-Based Costing; Value-Chain Analysis**   Hoover Company uses activity-based costing and provides this information:

| Manufacturing Activity | Cost Driver | Overhead Rate |
|---|---|---|
| Materials handling | Number of parts | $ 0.50 |
| Machinery | Number of machine-hours | 51.00 |
| Assembly | Number of parts | 2.85 |
| Inspection | Number of finished units | 30.00 |

Hoover has just completed 80 units of a component for a customer. Each unit required 105 parts and 3 machine-hours. The prime cost is $1,250 per finished unit. All other manufacturing costs are classified as manufacturing overhead.

**Required**

1. Compute the total manufacturing costs and the unit costs of the 80 units just completed using ABC costing.

2. In addition to the manufacturing costs, the firm has determined that the total cost of upstream activities including research and development and product design is $180 per unit. The total cost of downstream activities, such as distribution, marketing, and customer service is $250 per unit. Compute the full product cost per unit, including upstream, manufacturing, and downstream activities. What are the strategic implications of this new cost result?

3. Explain to Hoover Company the usefulness of calculating the total value-chain cost and of knowing costs of different value-creating activities.

[LO 5-1, 5-3]   5-39 **Resource and Activity-Based Cost Drivers**   EyeGuard Equipment Inc. (EEI) manufactures protective eyewear for use in commercial and home applications. The product is also used by hunters, home woodworking hobbyists, and in other applications. The firm has two main product lines—the highest-quality product is called Safe-T, and a low-cost, value version is called Safe-V. Information on the factory conversion costs for EEI is as follows:

| | Factory Costs |
|---|---|
| Salaries | $ 850,000 |
| Supplies | 150,000 |
| Factory expense | 550,000 |
| | $1,550,000 |

EEI uses ABC costing to determine the unit costs of its products. The firm uses resource consumption cost drivers based on rough estimates of the amount that each activity consumes, as shown below. EEI has four activities: job setup, assembly, inspecting and finishing, and packaging.

| | Setup | Assembly | Inspect & Finishing | Packaging | |
|---|---|---|---|---|---|
| Salaries | 15% | 55% | 20% | 10% | 100% |
| Supplies | 20 | 60 | 20 | | 100 |
| Factory expense | | 80 | 20 | | 100 |

The activity cost drivers for the two products are summarized below.

| Activities | Activity Driver |
|---|---|
| Setup | Batch |
| Assembly | Units |
| Inspect and finishing | Hours |
| Packaging | Hours |

| | Safe-V | Safe-T |
|---|---|---|
| Batches | 250 | 600 |
| Units | 60,000 | 72,000 |
| Finishing hours, per unit | 0.2 | 0.3 |
| Packaging hours, per unit | 0.1 | 0.15 |
| Materials per unit | $ 3.50 | $ 6.00 |

**Required**
1. Determine the amount of the cost pool for each of the four activities.
2. Determine the activity-based rates for assigning factory costs to the two products.
3. Determine the activity-based unit cost for each of the products.
4. What is the strategic role of the information obtained in requirement 3?
5. The quantities of resource consumption cost drivers used were based on rough estimates. Under what conditions would you recommend that more accurate cost driver data be collected?

[LO 5-1, 5-3, 5-6]   5-40   **Activity-Based Costing; Customer Group Cost Analysis**   Lenngton Furniture, Inc. (LFI) manufactures bedroom furniture in sets (a set includes a dresser, two queen-size beds, and one bedside table) for use in motels and hotels. LFI has three customer groups, which it calls the value, quality, and luxury groups. The value products are targeted to low-price motels that are looking for simple furniture, while the luxury furniture is targeted to the very best hotels. The value line is attractive to a variety of hotels and motels that appreciate the combination of quality and value. Currently there has been a small increase in the low-cost and value lines, and an appreciable increase in demand in the luxury line, reflecting cyclical changes in the marketplace. Luxury hotels are now in more demand for business travel, while a few years ago, the value segment was the most popular for business travelers. LFI wants to be able to respond to the increased demand with increased production but worries about the increased production cost and about price setting as its mix of customers and production change. LFI has used a volume-based rate based on direct labor-hours for some time. Direct labor cost is $12 per hour.

| | Budgeted Cost | Cost Driver |
|---|---|---|
| Materials handling | $ 349,600 | Number of parts |
| Product scheduling | 160,000 | Number of production orders |
| Setup labor | 216,000 | Number of setups |
| Automated machinery | 1,750,000 | Machine-hours |
| Finishing | 619,500 | Direct labor-hours |
| Pack and ship | 290,400 | Number of orders shipped |
| | $3,385,500 | |
| General, selling, and adm. costs | $5,000,000 | |

The budgeted production data for the three product lines follows.

| Product Lines | Value | Quality | Luxury |
|---|---|---|---|
| Units produced | 15,000 | 5,000 | 500 |
| Price | $650 | $900 | $1,200 |
| Direct materials cost per unit | $80 | $50 | $110 |
| Number of parts per unit | 30 | 50 | 120 |
| Direct labor-hours per unit | 4 | 5 | 7 |
| Machine-hours per unit | 3 | 7 | 15 |
| Production orders | 50 | 70 | 200 |
| Production setups | 20 | 50 | 50 |
| Orders shipped | 1,000 | 2,000 | 300 |
| Number of inspections | 2 | 6 | 14 |

**Required**   (Round all rates to two decimal places)
1. Determine the cost per set and the total production cost of each of the three customer groups using activity-based costing.
2. Determine the production cost for each of the three customer groups using LFI's current volume-based approach.
3. The activity usage data given in the problem reflects current usage of the various cost drivers to manufacture the firm's product lines. Suppose you are given the following information regarding the firm's practical capacity for each of these activities, as follows:

| Cost Driver | Practical Capacity |
|---|---|
| Number of parts | 990,000 |
| Number of production orders | 800 |
| Number of setups | 200 |
| Machine-hours | 100,000 |
| Direct labor-hours | 123,900 |
| Number of orders shipped | 5,000 |

Comment on how you would use this additional information for costing the firm's products and assisting in strategic planning.

4. Compare the two approaches and discuss the strategic and competitive issues of using each of the two methods.

[LO 5-1, 5-3, 5-4]     5-41  **Volume-Based Costing versus ABC**   West Chemical Company produces three products. The operating results of 2013 are:

| Product | Sales Quantity | Target Price | Actual Price | Difference |
|---|---|---|---|---|
| A | 1,000 | $279.00 | $280.00 | $  1.00 |
| B | 5,000 | 294.00 | 250.00 | <44.00> |
| C | 500 | 199.50 | 300.00 | $100.50 |

The firm sets the target price of each product at 150% of the product's total manufacturing cost. Recognizing that the firm was able to sell Product C at a much higher price than the target price of the product and lost money on Product B, Tom Watson, CEO, wants to promote Product C much more aggressively and phase out Product B. He believes that the information suggests that Product C has the greatest potential among the firm's three products since the actual selling price of Product C was almost 50% higher than the target price while the firm was forced to sell Product B at a price below the target price.

Both the budgeted and actual factory overheads for 2013 are $493,000. The actual units sold for each product also are the same as the budgeted units. The firm uses direct labor dollars to assign manufacturing overhead costs. The direct materials and direct labor costs per unit for each product are:

| | Product A | Product B | Product C |
|---|---|---|---|
| Direct materials | $50.00 | $114.40 | $65.00 |
| Direct labor | 20.00 | 12.00 | 10.00 |
| Total prime cost | $70.00 | $126.40 | $75.00 |

The controller noticed that not all products consumed factory overhead similarly. Upon further investigations, she identified the following usage of factory overhead during 2013:

| | Product A | Product B | Product C | Total Overhead |
|---|---|---|---|---|
| Number of setups | 2 | 5 | 3 | $  8,000 |
| Weight of direct materials (pounds) | 400 | 250 | 350 | 100,000 |
| Waste and hazardous disposals | 25 | 45 | 30 | 250,000 |
| Quality inspections | 30 | 35 | 35 | 75,000 |
| Utilities (machine-hours) | 2,000 | 7,000 | 1,000 | 60,000 |
| Total | | | | $493,000 |

**Required**

1. Determine the manufacturing cost per unit for each of the products using the volume-based method.
2. What is the least profitable and the most profitable product under both the current and the ABC costing systems?

3. What is the new target price for each product based on 150% of the new costs under the ABC system? Compare this price with the actual selling price.

4. Comment on the result from a competitive and strategic perspective. As a manager of West Chemical, describe what actions you would take based on the information provided by the activity-based unit costs.

[LO 5-2, 5-3] 5-42 **Activity-Based Costing** Miami Valley Architects Inc. provides a wide range of engineering and architectural consulting services through its three branch offices in Columbus, Cincinnati, and Dayton, Ohio. The company allocates resources and bonuses to the three branches based on the net income of the period. The results of the firm's performance for the year 2013 follows ($ in thousands):

|  | Columbus | Cincinnati | Dayton | Total |
|---|---|---|---|---|
| Sales | $1,500 | $1,419 | $1,067 | $3,986 |
| Less: Direct labor | 382 | 317 | 317 | 1,016 |
| Direct materials | 281 | 421 | 185 | 887 |
| Overhead | 710 | 589 | 589 | 1,888 |
| Net income | $ 127 | $ 92 | $ (24) | $ 195 |

Miami Valley accumulates overhead items in one overhead pool and allocates it to the branches based on direct labor dollars. For 2013, this predetermined overhead rate was $1.859 for every direct labor dollar incurred by an office. The overhead pool includes rent, depreciation, and taxes, regardless of which office incurred the expense. Some branch managers complain that the overhead allocation method forces them to absorb a portion of the overhead incurred by the other offices.

Management is concerned with the 2013 operating results. During a review of overhead expenses, management noticed that many overhead items were clearly not correlated to the movement in direct labor dollars as previously assumed. Management decided that applying overhead based on activity-based costing and direct tracing wherever possible should provide a more accurate picture of the profitability of each branch.

An analysis of the overhead revealed that the following dollars for rent, utilities, depreciation, and taxes could be traced directly to the office that incurred the overhead ($ in thousands):

|  | Columbus | Cincinnati | Dayton | Total |
|---|---|---|---|---|
| Direct overhead | $180 | $270 | $177 | $627 |

Activity pools and their corresponding cost drivers were determined from the accounting records and staff surveys as follows:

| | |
|---|---|
| General administration | $ 409,000 |
| Project costing | 48,000 |
| Accounts payable/receiving | 139,000 |
| Accounts receivable | 47,000 |
| Payroll/Mail sort and delivery | 30,000 |
| Personnel recruiting | 38,000 |
| Employee insurance processing | 14,000 |
| Proposals | 139,000 |
| Sales meetings/Sales aids | 202,000 |
| Shipping | 24,000 |
| Ordering | 48,000 |
| Duplicating costs | 46,000 |
| Blueprinting | 77,000 |
| | $1,261,000 |

| | Volume of Cost Drivers by Location | | |
|---|---|---|---|
| Cost Driver | Columbus | Cincinnati | Dayton |
| Direct labor cost | $ 382,413 | $ 317,086 | $317,188 |
| Timesheet entries | 6,000 | 3,800 | 3,500 |
| Vendor invoices | 1,020 | 850 | 400 |
| Client invoices | 588 | 444 | 96 |
| Employees | 23 | 26 | 18 |

| | | | |
|---|---|---|---|
| New hires | 8 | 4 | 7 |
| Insurance claims filed | 230 | 260 | 180 |
| Proposals | 200 | 250 | 60 |
| Contracted sales | 1,824,439 | 1,399,617 | 571,208 |
| Projects shipped | 99 | 124 | 30 |
| Purchase orders | 135 | 110 | 80 |
| Copies duplicated | 162,500 | 146,250 | 65,000 |
| Blueprints | 39,000 | 31,200 | 16,000 |

**Required**   (Round all answers to thousands)

1. What overhead costs should be assigned to each branch based on ABC concepts?
2. What is the contribution of each branch before subtracting the results obtained in requirement 1?
3. What is the profitability of each branch office using ABC?
4. Evaluate the concerns of management regarding the volume-based cost technique currently used.

**[LO 5-2, 5-4]**   5-43   **Volume-Based Costing versus ABC**   Coffee Bean Inc. (CBI) processes and distributes a variety of coffee. CBI buys coffee beans from around the world and roasts, blends, and packages them for resale. Currently the firm offers 15 coffees to gourmet shops in one-pound bags. The major cost is direct materials; however, a substantial amount of factory overhead is incurred in the predominantly automated roasting and packing process. The company uses relatively little direct labor.

Some of the coffees are very popular and sell in large volumes; a few of the newer brands have very low volumes. CBI prices its coffee at full product cost, including allocated overhead, plus a markup of 30%. If its prices for certain coffees are significantly higher than the market, CBI lowers its prices. The company competes primarily on the quality of its products, but customers are price conscious as well.

Data for the 2013 budget include factory overhead of $3,000,000, which has been allocated by its current costing system on the basis of each product's direct labor cost. The budgeted direct labor cost for 2013 totals $600,000. The firm budgeted $6,000,000 for purchases and use of direct materials (mostly coffee beans).

The budgeted direct costs for one-pound bags of two of the company's products are as follows:

| | Mona Loa | Malaysian |
|---|---|---|
| Direct materials | $4.20 | $3.20 |
| Direct labor | 0.30 | 0.30 |

CBI's controller, Mona Clin, believes that its current product costing system could be providing misleading cost information. She has developed this analysis of the 2013 budgeted factory overhead costs:

| Activity | Cost Driver | Budgeted Activity | Budgeted Cost |
|---|---|---|---|
| Purchasing | Purchase orders | 1,158 | $ 579,000 |
| Materials handling | Setups | 1,800 | 720,000 |
| Quality control | Batches | 720 | 144,000 |
| Roasting | Roasting-hours | 96,100 | 961,000 |
| Blending | Blending-hours | 33,600 | 336,000 |
| Packaging | Packaging-hours | 26,000 | 260,000 |
| Total factory overhead cost | | | $3,000,000 |

Data regarding the 2010 production of two of its lines, Mona Loa and Malaysian, follow. There is no beginning or ending direct materials inventory for either of these coffees.

| | Mona Loa | Malaysian |
|---|---|---|
| Budgeted sales | 100,000 pounds | 2,000 pounds |
| Batch size | 10,000 pounds | 500 pounds |
| Setups | 3 per batch | 3 per batch |
| Purchase order size | 25,000 pounds | 500 pounds |
| Roasting time | 1 hour per 100 pounds | 1 hour per 100 pounds |
| Blending time | 0.5 hour per 100 pounds | 0.5 hour per 100 pounds |
| Packaging time | 0.1 hour per 100 pounds | 0.1 hour per 100 pounds |

**Required**

1. Using Coffee Bean Inc.'s current product costing system,

   a. Determine the company's predetermined overhead rate using direct labor cost as the single cost driver.

   b. Determine the full product costs and selling prices of one pound of Mona Loa coffee and one pound of Malaysian coffee.

2. Using an activity-based costing approach, develop a new product cost for one pound of Mona Loa coffee and one pound of Malaysian coffee. Allocate all overhead costs to the 100,000 pounds of Mona Loa and the 2,000 pounds of Malaysian. Compare the results with those in requirement 1.

3. What are the implications of the activity-based costing system with respect to CBI's pricing and product mix strategies? How does ABC add to CBI's competitive advantage?

**(CMA Adapted)**

[LO 5-2, 5-3, 5-4]   **5-44   Cost of Capacity (Continuation of Problem 5-43)**   Use the same information as above for Coffee Bean Inc. (CBI) except assume now that Mona Loa and Malaysian are the only two products at CBI. Also, now include the following additional information about the practical capacity Coffee Bean has in each of its activities. For example, currently Coffee Bean has total practical capacity for processing 1,400 purchase orders, 2,400 setups, etc. These are the levels of activity work that are sustainable.

| Activity | Practical Capacity |
|---|---|
| Purchasing | 1,400 |
| Materials handling | 2,400 |
| Quality control | 1,200 |
| Roasting | 100,000 |
| Blending | 36,000 |
| Packaging | 30,000 |

**Required**

1. Determine the activity rates based on practical capacity and the cost of unused capacity for each activity.

2. Explain the strategic role of the information you have developed in part (1) above.

3. Assume the same information used in parts (1) and (2) above, but now assume also that the cost in the purchasing activity consists entirely of the cost of 8 employees; the cost in materials handling consists entirely of the cost of 20 employees; the cost of quality control consists entirely of the cost of 4 employees; the cost of roasting and blending consists entirely of the costs of machines—10 roasting machines and 10 blending machines; and the cost of packaging consists entirely of the cost of 3 employees. Based on this additional information, what can you now advise management about the utilization of capacity?

[LO 5-2, 5-7]   **5-45   Ethics; Cost System Selection**   Aero Dynamics manufactures airplane parts and engines for a variety of military and civilian aircraft. The company is the sole provider of rocket engines for the U.S. military that it sells for full cost plus a 5% markup.

   Aero Dynamics's current cost system is a direct labor-hour-based overhead allocation system. Recently, the company conducted a pilot study on the feasibility of using an activity-based costing system. The study shows that the new ABC system, while more accurate and timely, will result in the assignment of lower costs to the rocket engines and higher costs to the company's other products. Apparently, the current direct labor-based costing system overcosts the rocket engines and undercosts the other products. On hearing of this, top management has decided to scrap the plans to adopt the ABC system because its rocket engine business with the military is significant and the reduced cost would lower the price and, thus, the profit for this part of Aero Dynamics's business.

**Required**   As the management accountant participating in this ABC pilot study project, what is your responsibility when you learn that top management has decided to cancel the plans for the ABC system? Can you ignore your professional ethics code in this case? What would you do?

[LO 5-3, 5-7]   **5-46   Time-Driven Activity-Based Costing (TDABC) in a Call Center**   Marketing Specialists Inc. (MSI) provides a range of services to its retail clients—customer service for inquiries, order taking, credit checking for new customers, and a variety of related services. Auto Supermarket (AS) is a large auto dealer that provides financing for the autos and trucks that it sells. AS has approached MIS to manage the inquiries that come in regarding these loans. AS is not satisfied with the performance of the call center it currently uses for handling inquiries on these loans and is considering a change to MSI. MSI has been asked to estimate the cost of providing the service for the coming year.

There are two types of loans at AS, one for autos and SUVs and another for light trucks. The loans for auto and truck buyers typically have different types of customers and loan terms, so the nature and volume of the inquiries are expected to differ. MSI would use its own call center to handle the AS engagement. The MSI call center's annual costs are as follows:

| | |
|---|---|
| Call center costs | |
| Salaries | $4,223,555 |
| Utilities | 2,387,446 |
| Leasing of facilities | 1,983,063 |
| Other expenses | 801,036 |
| | $9,395,100 |

MSI's call center is staffed 12 hours per day with 60 call staff always available. Each staff has a paid 10-minute break for each hour worked, and an unpaid 1-hour break for a lunch/dinner during their 12-hour shift. Thus, the call center has 12,045,000 minutes (11 hrs. × 50 min. × 60 staff × 365 days) available for calls during the year.

AS and MSI work together to estimate the number of calls and time required for each call, based on AS's prior experience with its current call center.

| Inquiries | Total Calls Answered | Average Number of Minutes/Call | Total Time (minutes) |
|---|---|---|---|
| Inquire re: rates and terms | | | |
| Autos | 96,000 | 5 | 480,000 |
| Trucks | 32,000 | 7 | 224,000 |
| Inquire re: loan application status | | | |
| Autos | 37,500 | 6 | 225,000 |
| Trucks | 6,750 | 11 | 74,250 |
| Inquire re: payment status | | | |
| Autos | 39,000 | 3 | 117,000 |
| Trucks | 12,000 | 4 | 48,000 |
| Inquire re: other matters | | | |
| Autos | 29,000 | 11 | 319,000 |
| Trucks | 8,500 | 15 | 127,500 |
| | | | 1,614,750 |

**Required**

1. Determine the amount that MSI should propose to charge AS for the coming year using TDABC, assuming MSI desired a profit of 25% of incurred cost.

2. Suppose that AS wants the proposal broken down by type of loan (auto, truck). What would the proposal look like now?

[LO 5-3, 5-4, 5-7]   5-47  **TDABC (Continuation of Problem 5-46)**   Suppose that in addition to the call center engagement outlined above, AS also provides the following annual service to 10 other clients:

| | Total Calls Answered | Average Number of Minutes/Call |
|---|---|---|
| Platinum Regional Bank | 234,000 | 6.0 |
| Healthwise Software Inc. | 66,788 | 5.0 |
| Johnson Manufacturing | 122,665 | 4.0 |
| Lesco Online Shopping | 233,756 | 6.0 |
| Babcock Insurance Service | 55,455 | 5.5 |
| Garcia Electric Supply and Service | 38,956 | 3.4 |
| Gilbert's Online Garden Supplies | 145,902 | 4.0 |
| Financial Planning Services Inc. | 68,993 | 11.0 |
| Porter's Camera and Optical | 198,440 | 6.0 |
| Jordan Auto World Inc | 965,887 | 3.0 |

**Required**

1. What is the unused capacity at MSI, **not** assuming that AS becomes a customer? What are the implications for the operating and marketing strategies at AS?

2. Assume that AS comes back to MSI with a revised proposal. The revised proposal includes call center activity as described in Problem 5-46, but in addition, AS wants MSI to provide error-checking services for those who apply for loans at AS. MSI would use some of the call center staff, after appropriate training, to complete the processing of the credit checks. AS expects the following service to be needed:

| Processing Credit Checks | Requests | Min./request |
|---|---|---|
| Auto | 45,600 | 10 |
| Truck | 12,500 | 18 |

What would be the unused capacity with the revised proposal? What would be the cost of the unused capacity?

[LO 5-3, 5-5, 5-7]   5-48   **Personnel Planning; TDABC**   Recent competitive pressures have caused National Insurance Company to examine policies regarding personnel planning. As a start, the company has decided to experiment with and develop a time-driven ABC model for its claims processing center.

A study of this support center indicates the following three primary activities: remote processing of customer claims, 0.5 hour; onsite processing of customer claims, 1.0 hour; and, updating/maintaining customer records, 0.2 hour. Onsite processing is required for larger claims, while remote processing is done for smaller claims. (For onsite processing, assume—for simplicity—that the claims processors use their own automobiles.) All claims will require that the customers' records be updated.

The claims processing center currently employs three full-time employees. Total annual cost of the center (salaries, depreciation, utilities, etc.) is estimated at $255,000. The net amount of available personnel time per year for this department is approximately 5,000 hours.

**Required**

1. Why are service organizations, such as the present example, particularly well-suited to apply activity-based costing for cost and resource planning purposes?

2. What estimates are needed to implement a time-driven activity-based costing (TDABC) model? In this regard, what is the budgeted resource cost rate for the present example?

3. Assume that the budgeted number of offsite (i.e., remote) claims is 1,900 for the year. What is the budgeted claims-processing support cost to serve this subset of customers? (Show calculation.)

4. Assume that the budgeted number of onsite (i.e., large) claims for the coming year is 2,900. What is the budgeted claims-processing support cost for this subset of customers? (Show calculation.)

5. Assume now that the customer mix reflected above in requirements 2 and 3 were to change as follows: number of remote cases, 2,700; number of onsite claims, 2,000. How much labor processing time would be needed to service this revised level of service demand? What support cost would be budgeted for each class of customer?

6. In response to the projected shift in customer mix reflected above in requirement 5, why might the company not experience an immediate financial improvement? Put another way, will National's resource spending necessarily decrease in response to the shift in customer demand?

7. Finally, why do most proponents of ABC (both traditional and time-driven) recommend the use of practical capacity when calculating cost rates for planning purposes?

[LO 5-6]   5-49   **Research Assignment; Assessing Customer Lifetime Value**   How important to profitability are customer referrals? What customers feel about your company (and you) and what they are prepared to tell others about you can be just as important as what your customers do themselves. The authors of the following article hypothesize overall customer value, what they call *customer lifetime value,* as consisting of two components: the amount a customer brings in from purchases and the value of referrals. See V. Kumar, J. A. Petersen, and R. P. Leone, "How Valuable Is Word of Mouth?" *Harvard Business Review,* October 2007, pp. 139–146, prior to answering the following questions.

**Required**

1. What is the primary managerial question or issue that the authors of this article are addressing?

2. Define the terms *customer lifetime value (CLV)* and *customer referral value (CRV).* Which of these values do the authors believe is more important for financial success? Why?

3. Which of the two components of value, CLV or CRV, is the more difficult to estimate? Why?

4. Explain the *customer value matrix* developed by the authors and presented on page 144 of their article. Of what strategic importance is this matrix?

5. In what way can the management accountant aid in the estimation of CLV and CRV (and, by extension, the creation of the customer value matrix)?

**[LO 5-1, 5-2, 5-3, 5-5]**   5-50   **Volume-Based Costing versus ABC**   ADA Pharmaceutical Company produces three drugs— Diomycin, Homycin, and Addolin—belonging to the analgesic (pain-killer) family of medication. Since its inception four years ago, ADA has used a direct labor-hour-based system to assign manufacturing overhead costs to products.

Eme Weissman, the president of ADA Pharmaceutical, has just read about activity-based costing in a trade journal. With some curiosity and interest, she asked her financial controller, Takedo Simon, to examine differences in product costs between the firm's current costing and activity-based costing systems.

ADA has the following budget information for the year:

|  | Diomycin | Homycin | Addolin |
|---|---|---|---|
| Cost of direct materials | $ 205,000 | $265,000 | $258,000 |
| Cost of direct labor | 250,000 | 234,000 | 263,000 |
| Number of direct labor-hours | 7,200 | 6,800 | 2,000 |
| Number of capsules | 1,000,000 | 500,000 | 300,000 |

ADA has identified the following activities as cost drivers and has allocated them to total overhead cost of $200,000 as follows:

| Activity | Cost Driver | Budgeted Overhead Cost | Budgeted Cost Driver Volume |
|---|---|---|---|
| Machine setup | Setup hours | $ 16,000 | 1,600 |
| Plant management | Workers | 36,000 | 1,200 |
| Supervision of direct labor | Direct labor-hours | 46,000 | 1,150 |
| Quality inspection | Inspection-hours | 50,400 | 1,050 |
| Expediting orders | Customers served | 51,600 | 645 |
| Total overhead |  | $200,000 |  |

Takedo selected the cost drivers with the following justifications:

**SETUP HOURS:**   The cost driver of setup hours is used because the same product takes about the same amount of setup time regardless of size of batch. For different products, however, the setup time varies.

**NUMBER OF WORKERS:**   Plant management includes plant maintenance and corresponding managerial duties that make production possible. This activity depends on the number of workers. The more workers involved, the higher the cost.

**SUPERVISION OF DIRECT LABOR:** Supervisors spend their time supervising production. The amount of time they spend on each product is proportional to the direct labor-hours worked.

**QUALITY INSPECTION:** Inspection involves testing a number of units in a batch. The time varies for different products but is the same for all similar products.

**NUMBER OF CUSTOMERS SERVED:** The need to expedite production increases as the number of customers served by the company increases. Thus, the number of customers served by ADA is a good measure of expediting production orders.

Takedo gathered the following information about the cost driver volume for each product:

|  | Diomycin | Homycin | Addolin |
|---|---|---|---|
| Machine setups | 200 | 600 | 800 |
| Plant management | 200 | 400 | 600 |
| Supervision of direct labor | 200 | 300 | 650 |
| Quality inspection | 150 | 200 | 700 |
| Expediting production orders | 45 | 100 | 500 |

**Required**

1. Use the firm's current costing system to calculate the unit cost of each product.

2. Use the activity-based cost system to calculate the unit cost of each product.

3. The two cost systems provide different results; give several reasons for this. Why might these differences be strategically important to ADA Pharmaceutical? How does ABC add to ADA's competitive advantage?

4. How and why may firms in the pharmaceutical industry use ABC? What is the strategic advantage?

[LO 5-1, 5-7]   5-51   **Research Assignment; Environmental Costing**   Environmental sustainability is not only a potential competitive advantage to an organization, but might also be a regulatory requirement. The creation of business processes to support environmental sustainability requires the expenditure of resources and management is faced with evaluating the costs and benefits of such efforts. See the article, "An Activity Based Management Methodology for Evaluating Business Processes for Environmental Sustainability," by Joseph Sarkis, Laura Meade, and Adrien Presley, *Business Process Management Journal* 12, no. 6 (2006), pp. 751–766, for some advice on how managers can deal with these issues. Read the article and then answer the following questions.

**Required**

1. What is the purpose of environmental cost accounting and why is it important?

2. What are some of the obvious and what are some of the "hidden" environmental costs?

3. The authors reference a categorization developed by the EPA, which classifies costs based on the ease of measurement. Difficulty of measurement does not relieve management of the responsibility to adequately evaluate the costs of a proposed course of action (or inaction). How might the concepts of ABC and ABM be applied to help managers evaluate environmental costs?

## Solution to Self-Study Problem

### Volume-Based Costing versus ABC

1. Volume-based costing system

| Stage 1 Allocation: Machine Hours |
| --- |
| Total overhead allocated to Department A |
| $1,000,000 × (4,000 ÷ 20,000) = $200,000 |
| Total overhead allocated to Department B |
| $1,000,000 × (16,000 ÷ 20,000) = $800,000 |

| Stage 2 Allocation: Labor Hours | | |
| --- | --- | --- |
| | **Per Unit Cost** | |
| | **Deluxe** | **Regular** |
| Overhead allocated to | | |
| Department A | | |
| ($200,000 ÷ 20,000) × 2 = | $ 20 | |
| ($200,000 ÷ 20,000) × 2 = | | $ 20 |
| Department B | | |
| ($800,000 ÷ 10,000) × 1 = | 80 | |
| ($800,000 ÷ 10,000) × 1 = | | 80 |
| Total | $100 | $100 |

Product cost per unit

| | **Deluxe** | **Regular** |
| --- | --- | --- |
| Direct materials | $100 | $ 50 |
| Direct labor | | |
| $25 × (2 + 1) = | 75 | |
| $20 × (2 + 1) = | | 60 |
| Factory overhead | 100 | 100 |
| Unit cost | $275 | $210 |

2. Budgeted overhead rates for cost drivers:

| Cost Driver | Budgeted Overhead | Budgeted Cost Driver Quantity | Budgeted Overhead Rate |
|---|---|---|---|
| Number of production runs | $ 7,000 | 350 | $ 20 per run |
| Number of setups | 400,000 | 500 | 800 per setup |
| Number of units | 588,000 | 19,600 | 30 per unit |
| Number of shipments | 5,000 | 250 | 20 per shipment |
| | $1,000,000 | | |

3. ABC system

| | Deluxe | Regular |
|---|---|---|
| Overhead allocated to | | |
| Material movement | | |
| $20 × 15 = | $ 300 | |
| $20 × 20 = | | $ 400 |
| Machine setups | | |
| $800 × 25 = | 20,000 | |
| $800 × 50 = | | 40,000 |
| Inspections | | |
| $30 × 200 = | 6,000 | |
| $30 × 800 = | | 24,000 |
| Shipment | | |
| $20 × 50 = | 1,000 | |
| $20 × 100 = | | 2,000 |
| Total | $27,300 | $66,400 |
| Unit overhead cost | $136.50 | $ 83 |
| Product cost per unit | | |
| Direct materials | $100 | $ 50 |
| Direct labor | 75 | 60 |
| Factory overhead | 136.50 | 83 |
| Unit cost | $311.50 | $ 193 |

Note that the volume-based costing system overcosts the high-volume regular product and undercosts the low-volume deluxe product.

*Please visit* **http://www.mhhe.com/blocher6e** *to access a narrated, animated tutorial for solving this problem.*

# CHAPTER SIX

# Process Costing

**After studying this chapter, you should be able to . . .**

LO 6-1  Identify the types of firms or operations for which a process costing system is most suitable

LO 6-2  Explain and calculate equivalent units

LO 6-3  Describe the five steps in process costing

LO 6-4  Demonstrate the weighted-average method of process costing

LO 6-5  Demonstrate the FIFO method of process costing

LO 6-6  Analyze process costing with multiple departments

LO 6-7  Prepare journal entries to record the flow of costs in a process costing system

LO 6-8  Explain how process costing systems are implemented and enhanced in practice

LO 6-9  Account for spoilage in process costing (appendix)

The Coca-Cola Company (**www.coca-cola.com**) is the world's leading manufacturer, marketer, and distributor of soft drink concentrates, syrups, and soft drinks. Coca-Cola's strategy focuses on both price and differentiation.

Coca-Cola's differentiation strategy is apparent in its positioning. It positions itself as a unique and special product with a young, fresh image equal to none in the soft drink segment; it is a permanent reminder of classic values, of American culture inside and outside the country, and of all things American: entertainment, sports, and youth. Furthermore, its brand is recognized in practically every country in the world. Its exclusive formula makes it unique.

Coca-Cola uses process costing to track product and customer costs such as direct materials, direct labor, and factory overhead costs incurred in three major processes: (1) concentrate and syrup manufacturing, (2) blending, and (3) packaging. During the first process, mixing water with sugar, colorings, and other ingredients produces concentrates, and adding sweeteners and water to the concentrates produces syrups. In the second process, pure carbon dioxide is added to the blend of syrups and water to produce the beverage. In the third process, a filler injects a precise amount of the blended beverage into plastic bottles or cans, and a metal crown or plastic closure seals the package.

*Process costing* is a product costing system that accumulates costs according to processes or departments and assigns them to a large number of nearly identical products. The typical firm that uses process costing employs a standardized production process to manufacture homogeneous products. Process costing provides information for managers to analyze product and customer profitability and to make pricing, product-mix, and process improvement decisions.

In today's globally competitive environment, managers must know product costs to be able to make good decisions. Imagine a large corporation's top manager trying to decide whether to discontinue a product without knowing what it costs. Managers need cost information for setting goals; forming strategy; developing long- and short-term plans; and for control, performance measurement, and decision-making purposes. For example, Milliken & Co. (**www.milliken.com**) uses an activity-based costing type of process costing to help managers focus on the actual costs in each process and to reduce non-value-added work in each process.

## Characteristics of Process Costing Systems

**LO 6-1**

*Identify the types of firms or operations for which a process costing system is most suitable.*

Firms having homogeneous products that pass through a series of similar processes or departments use process costing. These firms usually engage in continuous mass production of a few similar products. Manufacturing costs are accumulated in each process. The management accountant uses a production cost report to track production quantity and cost information for each department. Unit product cost is calculated by dividing process costs in each department by the number of equivalent units produced during the period.

The process cost system is used in many industries such as chemicals, oil refining, textiles, paints, flour, canneries, rubber, steel, glass, food processing, mining, automobile production lines, electronics, plastics, drugs, paper, lumber, leather goods, metal products, and sporting goods. Process costing can also be used by service organizations with homogeneous services and repetitive processes such as check processing in a bank or mail sorting by a courier. Companies using process costing include Coca-Cola (**www.coca-cola.com**) and International Paper (**www.internationalpaper.com**).

### Equivalent Units

**LO 6-2**

*Explain and calculate equivalent units.*

A manufacturing firm typically has partially completed units (work-in-process) at the end of an accounting period. Under the job costing system, these partially completed units are not difficult to account for because job costs are available on job cost sheets.

In a process costing system, however, product costs for partially completed units are not readily available. Because the focus in cost accounting has shifted from jobs to processes or departments, the interest is in the unit cost of performing a certain *process* for a given period. The goal is to find the combined unit cost of all product units processed in that period, including those that are partially complete at *either* the beginning or the end of the accounting period. Note that by *partially complete,* we mean partially complete for that department; a unit could be complete for a given department but still be in the Work-in-Process Inventory for a department that follows in the sequence of manufacturing processes.

With both complete and partially complete units, we need a way to measure the proper amount of production work performed during a period. An equivalent unit is the measure commonly used.

**Equivalent units**
are the number of the same or similar complete units that could have been produced given the amount of work actually performed on both complete and partially complete units.

**Equivalent units** are the number of the same or similar complete units that could have been produced given the amount of work actually performed on both complete and partially complete units. Equivalent units are not the same as physical units. For example, suppose in a given month a chemical company had in process 30,000 gallons of a chemical, of which 20,000 gallons were complete at the end of the month but the remaining 10,000 gallons were only 50% complete. The equivalent units would be 25,000 gallons [20,000 + (10,000 × 50%)]. The percentage of completion is usually measured by percentage of total cost that has already been incurred in the production of the product.

The equivalent units should be calculated separately for direct materials, direct labor, and factory overhead because the proportion of the total work performed on the units in the work-in-process inventories is not always the same for each cost element. Partially complete units are often complete for direct materials but incomplete for direct labor and factory overhead. Examples include chemical or brewing processes that add direct materials at the beginning but are not complete until the completion of processing, which can extend over hours or days. Because overhead is often applied on the basis of labor hours, some firms use the two categories—direct materials and conversion cost. *Conversion costs* are the sum of direct labor and factory overhead costs.

### *Conversion Costs*

Because of the relatively small direct labor content in many process industries, such as the oil refining, aluminum, paper, chemical, and pharmaceutical industries, factory overhead and direct labor costs are sometimes combined and called conversion costs for the purpose of computing equivalent units of production. Linking these two cost elements is practical because direct labor cost is not a significant cost element in these process industries.

**EXHIBIT 6.1**  Equivalent Units for Direct Materials in Work-in-Process Ending Inventory

| | | | Equivalent Units in Ending Work-in-Process Inventory for Direct Materials | | | |
| Type of Inventory | Physical Units Partially Complete | Percentage of Completion for Conversion | Materials Added Gradually | All Materials Added at the Beginning | All Materials Added at the 40% Point | All Materials Added at the End |
| --- | --- | --- | --- | --- | --- | --- |
| Ending work-in-process inventory | 1,500 | 60% | 1,500 × 60% = 900 | 1,500 × 100% = 1,500 | 1,500 × 100% = 1,500 | 0 |

Many manufacturing operations incur conversion costs uniformly throughout production. The equivalent units of conversion costs are therefore the result of multiplying the percentage of work that is complete during the period by the number of units on which work is partially complete. For example, for 1,000 units estimated to be 30% complete in the work-in-process ending inventory, the equivalent units of conversion in the period are 300 (30% × 1,000 units).

Firms using nonlabor-based cost drivers (such as machine-hours or the number of setups) for factory overhead costs find that calculating separate equivalent units of production for factory overhead and direct labor costs is more appropriate.

### Direct Materials

Direct materials can be added at discrete points or continuously during production. If the materials are added uniformly, the proportion used for computing equivalent units of direct materials is the same as the proportion for conversion costs. However, if the materials are added all at once, the proportion used in the computation depends on whether the point in the process where the materials are added has been reached.

Exhibit 6.1 illustrates the determination of equivalent units in direct materials for ending work-in-process (WIP) inventory. The example assumes that ending WIP inventory has 1,500 product units that are 60% complete for conversion. Exhibit 6.1 has four materials-adding situations: (1) materials are added gradually throughout the process, (2) all materials are added at the beginning of the process, (3) all materials are added at the 40% point (since ending WIP is 60% complete for conversion, with materials added at the 40% point, ending WIP is thus complete for materials), and (4) all materials are added at the end of the process. Note that the equivalent units of materials in ending work-in-process inventory would be 900 (1,500 × .6) equivalent units under assumption (1).

### Flow of Costs in Process Costing

In process costing, costs flow through different processes or departments. Exhibit 6.2 is a T-account model of direct materials, direct labor, and factory overhead cost flows in a two-department process costing system. Note four key points in this exhibit. First, a separate Work-in-Process Inventory account is used to record costs of each production department. Second, when Department A finishes its work, the costs of the goods completed are transferred to Department B's Work-in-Process Inventory account for further work. After this further work, the costs of goods completed are then transferred to the Finished Goods Inventory account. Third, direct materials, direct labor, and factory overhead costs can be entered directly into either production department's Work-in-Process Inventory account, not just that of the first department. Finally, starting with the second department (Department B), an additional cost element, *transferred-in-costs,* appears. These are costs of the goods completed in the prior department and transferred into this department during the period.

**LO 6-3**

*Describe the five steps in process costing.*

A **production cost report** summarizes the physical units and equivalent units of a department, the costs incurred during the period, and the costs assigned to both units completed and ending work-in-process inventories.

### Steps in Process Costing

The key document in a typical process costing system is the production cost report, prepared at the end of each period for each production process or department. The **production cost report** summarizes the number of physical units and equivalent units of a department, the costs incurred during the period, and the costs assigned to both units completed (and transferred out) and ending work-in-process inventories. The preparation of a production cost report includes the five steps in Exhibit 6.3.

**EXHIBIT 6.2** **Flow of Costs for Two Departments in Process Costing**

### Step 1: Analyze the Physical Flow of Production Units

The first step determines the number of units on hand in beginning work-in-process, the number of units started into production (or received from a prior department), the number of units completed, and the number of units in ending work-in-process inventory.

The analysis of physical units includes accounting for both input and output units. *Input units* include beginning work-in-process inventory and all units that enter a production department during an accounting period. *Output units* include units that are complete and transferred out from a production department and units in the ending work-in-process inventory.

### Step 2: Calculate Equivalent Units for Each Manufacturing Cost Element

The purpose of calculating equivalent units of production for direct materials, direct labor, and factory overhead is to measure the total work expended on production during an accounting period. The partially complete physical units are converted into the equivalent number of whole units.

### Step 3: Determine Total Costs for Each Manufacturing Cost Element

The total manufacturing costs for each cost element (materials, labor, and overhead) include the current costs incurred and the prior period costs of the units in work-in-process beginning inventory. The amount of these costs is obtained from material requisitions, labor time cards, and factory overhead allocation. The total manufacturing cost for each cost element is also called *total cost to account for*. The total cost determined in step three must agree with the total cost assigned in step 5.

### Step 4: Compute Cost per Equivalent Unit for Each Manufacturing Cost Element

The purpose of computing direct materials, direct labor, and factory overhead costs per equivalent unit of production is to have a proper product costing and income determination for an accounting period, which includes both complete and incomplete units.

**EXHIBIT 6.3**
**Five Steps in Process Costing**

1. Analyze the physical flow of production units.
2. Calculate equivalent units for each manufacturing cost element (materials, labor, overhead).
3. Determine total costs for each manufacturing cost element.
4. Compute cost per equivalent unit for each manufacturing cost element.
5. Assign total manufacturing costs to units completed and ending work-in-process (WIP).

Many process industries such as paper manufacturing, chemical production, oil refining, and steel processing create environmentally sensitive waste products. Many of these firms use a sustainability scorecard as explained in Chapter 2. A critical cost management goal for these firms is to find cost-effective means to manage these waste products. For example, a steel plating facility in the United States recently faced the need to redesign its plant to meet U.S. environmental standards. The firm sought bids from environmental engineering firms for the redesign work. The average bid was $800,000, each requiring a significant rebuilding of the plant and extensive downtime at the plant. To avoid the cost and disruption of such a plant redesign, the company used cost management methods based in part on process cost information to develop a plan to reduce cost within the

plant's current facilities. The plan involved several changes in operations, including new ways to handle raw materials, changes in product mix and scheduling, segregating wastewater flows, and treating some wastes within the plant rather than off-site. The cost of the plan was less than 25% of the cost of the plant redesign and it also was projected to have lower operating costs. Moreover, the plan offered a better integration of day-to-day decision making with environmental compliance, in comparison to the redesign plan of the consulting environmental engineers. Can you think of other examples of how a process industry could save money and also improve environmental sustainability?

(Refer to Comments on Cost Management in Action at the end of the chapter.)

### Step 5: Assign Total Manufacturing Costs to Units Completed and Ending WIP

The objective of the production cost report is to assign total manufacturing costs incurred to the units completed during the period and the units that are still in process at the end of the period. The total costs assigned in step 5 should equal the total costs to be accounted for in step 3.

Companies generally divide the five-step production cost report into three parts: (1) production quantity information, (2) unit cost determination, and (3) cost assignment. The first part includes step 1, analyze the flow of physical units, and step 2, calculate equivalent units. The second part includes step 3, determine total costs to account for, and step 4, compute equivalent unit cost. The third part includes step 5, assign total manufacturing costs (total costs accounted for).

## Process Costing Methods

The **weighted-average method** includes both current period and prior period costs in calculating unit cost.

The **FIFO method** includes only costs incurred and work performed during the current period in calculating the unit cost.

The two methods used to prepare the departmental production cost report when the firm uses process costing are the weighted-average method and the first-in, first-out (FIFO) method. The **weighted-average method** includes all costs in calculating the unit cost, including both costs incurred during the current period and costs incurred in the prior period that are shown as the beginning work-in-process inventory of the current period. In this method, prior period costs and current period costs are averaged; hence, the name *weighted average.* The **FIFO method** includes only costs incurred and work performed during the current period in calculating the unit cost. FIFO considers the beginning inventory as a batch of goods separate from the goods started and completed within the period. FIFO assumes that the first work done is to complete the beginning work-in-process inventory. Thus, all beginning work-in-process inventories are assumed to be completed before the end of the current period.

## Illustration of Process Costing

To illustrate these two process costing methods, assume that Naftel Toy Company has two production departments, molding and finishing. The molding department places a direct material (plastic vinyl) into production at the beginning of the process. Direct labor and factory overhead costs are incurred gradually throughout the process with different proportions.

Exhibit 6.4 summarizes the molding department's units and costs during June.

**LO 6-4**

*Demonstrate the weighted-average method of process costing.*

## Weighted-Average Method

The weighted-average method makes no distinction between the cost incurred prior to the current period and the cost incurred during the current period. As long as a cost is on the current period's cost sheet for a production department, it is treated as any other

**EXHIBIT 6.4**
**Basic Data for Naftel Toy Company—Molding Department**

| | |
|---|---|
| Work-in-process inventory, June 1 | 10,000 units |
|    Direct materials: 100% complete | $10,000 |
|    Direct labor: 30% complete | 1,060 |
|    Factory overhead: 40% complete | 1,620 |
|    Beginning work-in-process inventory | $12,680 |
| Units started during June | 40,000 units |
| Units completed during June and transferred out of the molding department | 44,000 units |
| Work-in-process inventory, June 30 | 6,000 units |
|    Direct materials: 100% complete | |
|    Direct labor: 50% complete | |
|    Factory overhead: 60% complete | |
| Costs added during June | |
|    Direct materials | $ 44,000 |
|    Direct labor | 22,440 |
|    Factory overhead | 43,600 |
| Total costs added during June | $110,040 |

cost regardless of when it was incurred. Consequently, the average cost per equivalent unit includes costs incurred both during the current period and in the prior period that carry over into this period through beginning work-in-process inventory. We use the five-step procedure to assign direct materials, direct labor, and factory overhead costs to the cost object, the molding department, for the month of June.

### *Step 1: Analyze the Physical Flow of Production Units*

The first step is to analyze the flow of all units through production. Exhibit 6.5 presents the procedures for this step.

The two sections in Exhibit 6.5 show the two aspects of physical units flowing through production, *input units* and *output units*. This procedure ensures that all units in production are accounted for. Input units include all units that enter a production department during an accounting period or that entered during the prior period but were incomplete at the beginning of the period. These units come from two sources: (1) beginning work-in-process inventory started in a previous period that was partially complete at the end of the preceding period, which is 10,000 units in our example, and (2) work started or received in the current period, which is 40,000 units in our example. The sum of these two sources, 50,000 units, is referred to as the number of **units to account for,** which is the sum of beginning inventory units and the number of units started during the period.

Output units include those that have been completed and transferred out and those not yet complete at the end of a period. These units can be in one of two categories: the 44,000 units completed or the 6,000 units in the ending work-in-process inventory. The sum of these two categories, 50,000 units, is referred to as the *number of units accounted for.* This number should match the number of units to account for. **Units accounted for** includes the sum of units completed and transferred out plus ending inventory units.

**Units to account for** refers to the sum of the beginning inventory units and the number of units started during the period.

**Units accounted for** refers to the sum of the units completed and transferred out plus ending inventory units.

**EXHIBIT 6.5**
**Step 1: Analyze the Physical Flow of Units—Molding Department**

| Input | Physical Units |
|---|---|
| Work-in-process inventory, June 1 | 10,000 |
| Units started during June | 40,000 |
| Total units to account for | 50,000 |
| **Output** | |
| Units completed and transferred out during June | 44,000 |
| Work-in-process inventory, June 30 | 6,000 |
| Total units accounted for | 50,000 |

**EXHIBIT 6.6**
Step 2: Calculate Equivalent
Units—Molding Department:
Weighted-Average Method

|  | Physical Units | Completion Percentage | EQUIVALENT UNITS | | |
|---|---|---|---|---|---|
|  |  |  | Direct Materials | Direct Labor | Factory Overhead |
| Work-in-process, June 1 | 10,000 |  |  |  |  |
| Direct materials |  | 100% |  |  |  |
| Direct labor |  | 30 |  |  |  |
| Factory overhead |  | 40 |  |  |  |
| Units started | 40,000 |  |  |  |  |
| Units to account for | 50,000 |  |  |  |  |
| Units completed | 44,000 | 100% | 44,000 | 44,000 | 44,000 |
| Work-in-process, June 30 | 6,000 |  |  |  |  |
| Direct materials |  | 100% | 6,000 |  |  |
| Direct labor |  | 50 |  | 3,000 |  |
| Factory overhead |  | 60 |  |  | 3,600 |
| Units accounted for | 50,000 |  |  |  |  |
| Total equivalent units |  |  | 50,000 | 47,000 | 47,600 |

The primary purpose of this first step is to ensure that all units in production are accounted for before we compute the number of equivalent units of production for each production element.

### Step 2: Calculate Equivalent Units for Each Manufacturing Cost Element

The second step in the process costing procedure is to calculate the number of equivalent units of production activity for direct materials, direct labor, and factory overhead. A table of equivalent units, presented in Exhibit 6.6, is based on the table of physical units prepared in step 1 (Exhibit 6.5).

The weighted-average method computes the total equivalent units produced to date. The number of units in production in the current period for each manufacturing production element includes both (1) the units from previous periods that are still in production at the beginning of the current period and (2) the units placed into production in the current period.

In Exhibit 6.6, 44,000 physical units were complete and transferred out of the molding department. These units were 100% complete. Thus, they represent 44,000 equivalent units for direct materials, direct labor, and factory overhead. Note that the 44,000 units include 10,000 units placed into production prior to June and completed in June, and 34,000 units (44,000 units − 10,000 units) started and completed in June.

The 6,000 units in ending work-in-process inventory are complete with respect to direct materials because direct materials are added at the beginning of the process. Thus, they represent 6,000 equivalent units of direct materials. However, they are only 50% and 60% complete for direct labor and factory overhead, respectively. Therefore, the ending work-in-process inventories represent 3,000 equivalent units of direct labor (6,000 physical units × 50% complete) and 3,600 equivalent units of factory overhead (6,000 physical units × 60% complete).

From Exhibit 6.6, we calculate the total number of equivalent units for each cost element as follows:

$$\frac{\text{Completed and transferred out units} + \text{Ending work-in-process equivalent units}}{= \text{Total equivalent units of production}}$$

Combining completed units and ending work-in-process equivalent units, the equivalent units of production for the molding department under the weighted-average method are 50,000 units of direct materials, 47,000 units of direct labor, and 47,600 units of factory overhead.

### Step 3: Determine Total Costs for Each Manufacturing Cost Element

The third step determines the amount spent both in the beginning work-in-process inventory and current production for direct materials, direct labor, and factory overhead.

**EXHIBIT 6.7**
**Step 3: Determine Total Costs—Molding Department**

| Beginning work-in-process inventory | | |
|---|---|---|
| Direct materials | $10,000 | |
| Direct labor | 1,060 | |
| Factory overhead | 1,620 | |
| Total | | $ 12,680 |
| Costs added during June | | |
| Direct materials | $44,000 | |
| Direct labor | 22,440 | |
| Factory overhead | 43,600 | |
| Total costs added | | 110,040 |
| Total costs to account for | | $122,720 |

**EXHIBIT 6.8**
**Step 4: Compute Cost per Equivalent Unit—Molding Department: Weighted-Average Method**

| | Direct Materials | Direct Labor | Factory Overhead | Total |
|---|---|---|---|---|
| Costs (from Exhibit 6.7) | | | | |
| Work-in-process, June 1 | $10,000 | $ 1,060 | $ 1,620 | $ 12,680 |
| Costs added during June | 44,000 | 22,440 | 43,600 | 110,040 |
| Total costs to account for | $54,000 | $23,500 | $45,220 | $122,720 |
| Divide by equivalent units (from Exhibit 6.6) | 50,000 | 47,000 | 47,600 | |
| Equivalent unit costs | $ 1.08 + | $ 0.50 + | $ 0.95 = | $ 2.53 |

Exhibit 6.7 summarizes the total manufacturing costs to account for. As given in our example data, total manufacturing costs ($122,720) consist of the beginning work-in-process inventory balance, $12,680, plus the costs added during June, $110,040.

### Step 4: Compute Cost per Equivalent Unit

For the fourth step in the process costing procedure, we compute the equivalent unit costs of production for direct materials, direct labor, and factory overhead; see Exhibit 6.8. The cost per equivalent unit for direct materials ($1.08) is computed by dividing the total direct materials cost ($54,000), including the cost of the beginning work-in-process ($10,000) and the cost added during June ($44,000), by the total equivalent units (50,000). Similar procedures are used for direct labor and factory overhead costs. The total equivalent unit cost of $2.53 can be determined by adding the unit direct materials cost of $1.08, the unit direct labor cost of $0.50, and the unit factory overhead cost of $0.95.

### Step 5: Assign Total Manufacturing Costs to Units Completed and Ending WIP

The final step of the process costing procedure is to assign total manufacturing costs to units completed and to units in the ending work-in-process inventory. Exhibit 6.9 summarizes the cost assignment schedule. Various unit information comes directly from Exhibit 6.6; various unit costs come from Exhibit 6.8. Note that the total costs accounted for in this step ($122,720) equal the total costs to account for in step 3 (Exhibit 6.7).

**EXHIBIT 6.9**
**Step 5: Assign Total Manufacturing Costs—Molding Department: Weighted-Average Method**

| | Completed and Transferred out | Ending Work-in-Process | Total |
|---|---|---|---|
| Goods completed and transferred out (44,000 × $2.53) | $111,320 | | $111,320 |
| Ending work-in-process: | | | |
| Direct materials (6,000 × $1.08) | | $ 6,480 | 6,480 |
| Direct labor (3,000 × $0.50) | | 1,500 | 1,500 |
| Factory overhead (3,600 × $0.95) | | 3,420 | 3,420 |
| Total costs accounted for | $111,320 | $11,400 | $122,720 |

## Cost Reconciliation

After finishing the five-step procedure, we need to determine whether the total manufacturing costs to account for in step 3 (i.e., total input costs) agree with the total costs accounted for in step 5 (i.e., total output costs). This checking procedure is called the *cost reconciliation*. For example, for the Naftel Toy Company's molding department, the $122,720 total manufacturing costs accounted for in step 3 equal the total costs accounted for in step 5.

## Production Cost Report

Steps 1 through 5 provide all of the information needed to prepare a production cost report for the molding department for June. This report is shown in Exhibit 6.10.

**EXHIBIT 6.10**
**Production Cost Report—Molding Department: Weighted-Average Method**

| Production Quantity Information | | | | | |
|---|---|---|---|---|---|
| | Step 1: Analyze Flow of Physical Units | | Step 2: Calculate Equivalent Units | | |
| | Physical Units | Completion Percentage | Direct Materials | Direct Labor | Factory Overhead |
| **Input** | | | | | |
| Work-in-process, June 1 | 10,000 | | | | |
| Direct materials | | 100% | | | |
| Direct labor | | 30 | | | |
| Factory overhead | | 40 | | | |
| Units started | 40,000 | | | | |
| Units to account for | 50,000 | | | | |
| **Output** | | | | | |
| Units completed | 44,000 | 100% | 44,000 | 44,000 | 44,000 |
| Work-in-process, June 30 | 6,000 | | | | |
| Direct materials | | 100% | 6,000 | | |
| Direct labor | | 50 | | 3,000 | |
| Factory overhead | | 60 | | | 3,600 |
| Units accounted for | 50,000 | | | | |
| Total equivalent units | | | 50,000 | 47,000 | 47,600 |

| Unit Cost Determination | | | | |
|---|---|---|---|---|
| **Step 3: Determine Total Costs** | Direct Materials | Direct Labor | Factory Overhead | Total |
| Work-in-process, June 1 | $10,000 | $ 1,060 | $ 1,620 | $ 12,680 |
| Costs added during June | 44,000 | 22,440 | 43,600 | 110,040 |
| Total costs to account for | $54,000 | $23,500 | $45,220 | $122,720 |
| **Step 4: Compute Cost per Equivalent Unit** | | | | |
| Divide by equivalent units | 50,000 | 47,000 | 47,600 | |
| Equivalent unit costs | $ 1.08 | $ 0.50 | $ 0.95 | $ 2.53 |

| Cost Assignment | | | |
|---|---|---|---|
| **Step 5: Assign Total Manufacturing Costs** | Completed and Transferred out | Ending Work-in-Process | Total |
| Goods completed and transferred out (44,000 × $2.53) | $111,320 | | $111,320 |
| Ending work-in-process | | | |
| Direct materials (6,000 × $1.08) | | $ 6,480 | 6,480 |
| Direct labor (3,000 × $0.50) | | 1,500 | 1,500 |
| Factory overhead (3,600 × $0.95) | | 3,420 | 3,420 |
| Total costs accounted for | $111,320 | $11,400 | $122,720 |

**LO 6-5**

*Demonstrate the FIFO method of process costing.*

## First-In, First-Out (FIFO) Method

Another way to account for inventory in a process costing application is the first-in, first-out (FIFO) method, which assumes that the first units to enter a production process are the first units to be completed and transferred out.

Our illustration of the FIFO method of process costing again uses Naftel Toy Company's molding department data (see Exhibit 6.4). Unlike the weighted-average method, the FIFO method does not combine beginning inventory costs with current costs when computing equivalent unit costs. The costs from each period are treated separately. We follow the same five steps as in the weighted-average method, however, in determining product costs.

### Step 1: Analyze the Physical Flow of Production Units

The physical flow of product units is unaffected by the process costing method used. Therefore, step 1 for the FIFO method is the same as the weighted-average method in Exhibit 6.5.

### Step 2: Calculate Equivalent Units for Each Manufacturing Cost Element

The FIFO method considers the beginning inventory as a batch of goods separate from the goods started and completed within the same period. The equivalent units in the beginning work-in-process—work done in the prior period—are not counted as part of the FIFO method equivalent units. Only the equivalent units of the beginning work-in-process to be completed this period are counted.

Two equivalent, alternative procedures are used to calculate equivalent units of production under the FIFO method.

### Step 2, Alternative A

One way to calculate FIFO equivalent units is to subtract the equivalent units in beginning work-in-process from the weighted-average equivalent units to obtain the FIFO method equivalent units, as shown in the last three rows of Exhibit 6.11. The 10,000 physical units in June 1 work-in-process have 100% of direct materials, so these units have 10,000 equivalent units of direct materials prior to the current period. However, these units are only 30% and 40% complete for direct labor and factory overhead, respectively, so they contribute only 3,000 equivalent units of direct labor (10,000 × 30%) and 4,000 equivalent units of factory overhead (10,000 × 40%) prior to the current period.

To calculate the total number of FIFO equivalent units, the following equation is used for each cost element:

$$
\begin{aligned}
&\text{Completed and transferred out units} \\
+\ &\underline{\text{Ending work-in-process equivalent units}} \\
=\ &\text{Weighted-average equivalent units} \\
-\ &\underline{\text{Beginning work-in-process equivalent units}} \\
=\ &\text{FIFO equivalent units of work done during this period}
\end{aligned}
$$

Exhibit 6.11 shows that Naftel Toy Company must account for a total of 50,000 units. Of these, 44,000 units are completed and 6,000 units are ending work-in-process inventory that is 100% complete for direct materials. The total equivalent units for the period for direct materials under the weighted-average method is 50,000. Of the 44,000 units completed during the period, 10,000 were in the beginning work-in-process inventory. These 10,000 units already had all direct materials added in the prior period. Subtracting 10,000 units from the 50,000 total equivalent units for the period, the FIFO equivalent units for work done only in June for direct materials is 40,000 units. Following the same procedure, equivalent units of production for the molding department using the FIFO method are 44,000 units of direct labor and 43,600 units of factory overhead.

The difference between the weighted-average method and the FIFO method is that under the weighted-average method, the equivalent units of production completed prior to the current period are not subtracted from the total completed units, so equivalent units under the weighted-average method are always as large or larger than those under the FIFO method.

**EXHIBIT 6.11**
Step 2: Calculate Equivalent
Units—Molding Department:
FIFO Method—Alternative A

| | Physical Units | Completion Percentage | Equivalent Units | | |
|---|---|---|---|---|---|
| | | | Direct Materials | Direct Labor | Factory Overhead |
| **Input** | | | | | |
| Work-in-process, June 1 | 10,000 | | | | |
|   Direct materials | | 100% | 10,000 | | |
|   Direct labor | | 30 | | 3,000 | |
|   Factory overhead | | 40 | | | 4,000 |
| Units started | 40,000 | | | | |
| Units to account for | 50,000 | | | | |
| **Output** | | | | | |
| Units completed | 44,000 | 100% | 44,000 | 44,000 | 44,000 |
| Work-in-process, June 30 | 6,000 | | | | |
|   Direct materials | | 100% | 6,000 | | |
|   Direct labor | | 50 | | 3,000 | |
|   Factory overhead | | 60 | | | 3,600 |
| Units accounted for | 50,000 | | | | |
| Total equivalent units (weighted-average method) | | | 50,000 | 47,000 | 47,600 |
| Less: equivalent units in June 1 work-in-process | | | (10,000) | (3,000) | (4,000) |
| Equivalent units for work done in June only (FIFO method) | | | 40,000 | 44,000 | 43,600 |

### Step 2, Alternative B

An alternative way to determine the equivalent units using the FIFO method is to add equivalent units of work performed in the current period for each of the three components: (1) equivalent units added to complete the beginning work-in-process inventory, (2) units started and completed during the period, and (3) equivalent units of the ending work-in-process inventory. Exhibit 6.12 presents the FIFO equivalent units computation using this second alternative procedure. Notice that under the FIFO method, the equivalent units in the beginning work-in-process inventory from last month's work effort are not added to equivalent units of work performed this month.

For example, the 10,000 units of beginning work-in-process inventory were 30% complete for direct labor. Naftel Toy Company completed the beginning work-in-process inventory by adding the remaining 70% of the direct labor during the current period to complete production. In addition, the firm started another 40,000 units in production during the period. Of these 40,000 units, the firm started and completed production of 34,000, and the remaining 6,000 were still in the manufacturing process at the end of the period. The firm has completed only 50% of the total direct labor in ending work-in-process inventory, or an equivalent of 3,000 units. To summarize the direct labor spent during the period, the firm spent an equivalent of 7,000 units of direct labor to complete the beginning work-in-process inventory on hand, started and completed 34,000 units, and spent an equivalent of 3,000 units to complete 50% of the 6,000 units of ending work-in-process inventory. The total direct labor of the period is equivalent to production of 44,000 FIFO units. Exhibit 6.13 graphically illustrates the difference between weighted-average and FIFO equivalent units.

### Step 3: Determine Total Costs for Each Manufacturing Cost Element

The total costs incurred to manufacture product units are unaffected by the process costing method used. Therefore, step 3 is the same as the weighted-average method in Exhibit 6.7. It shows that Naftel Toy Company's molding department has $122,720 total manufacturing costs to account for.

**EXHIBIT 6.12** Step 2: Calculate Equivalent Units—Molding Department:    FIFO Method—Alternative B

| | Physical Units | Completion Percentage | Equivalent Units (FIFO) | | |
|---|---|---|---|---|---|
| | | | Direct Materials | Direct Labor | Factory Overhead |
| Input | | | | | |
| Work-in-process, June 1 | 10,000 | | | | |
| Direct materials | | 100% | 10,000 | | |
| Direct labor | | 30 | | 3,000 | |
| Factory overhead | | 40 | | | 4,000 |
| Units started | 40,000 | | | | |
| Units to account for | 50,000 | | | | |
| Output | | | | | |
| Completed and transferred out | | | | | |
| from work-in-process, June 1 | 10,000 | | | | |
| Direct materials    10,000 × (1 − 100%) | | | 0 | | |
| Direct labor        10,000 × (1 − 30%) | | | | 7,000 | |
| Factory overhead  10,000 × (1 − 40%) | | | | | 6,000 |
| Started and completed (44,000 − 10,000) | 34,000 | 100% | 34,000 | 34,000 | 34,000 |
| Work-in-process, June 30 | 6,000 | | | | |
| Direct materials | | 100% | 6,000 | | |
| Direct labor | | 50 | | 3,000 | |
| Factory overhead | | 60 | | | 3,600 |
| Units accounted for | 50,000 | | | | |
| Equivalent units of work for June (FIFO method) | | | 40,000 | 44,000 | 43,600 |

**EXHIBIT 6.13**
**Weighted-Average vs. FIFO Equivalent Units**

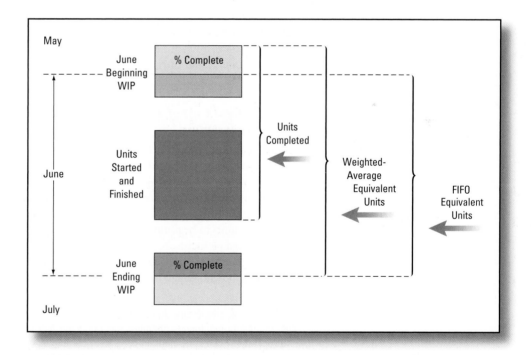

### *Step 4: Compute Cost per Equivalent Unit for Each Manufacturing Cost Element*

Under the FIFO method, equivalent unit costs are calculated by dividing the costs added during the current period by the equivalent units for work completed only during the current period. No cost in the work-in-process beginning inventory is included in determining equivalent unit costs for cost elements. Exhibit 6.14 presents the calculations. The equivalent unit cost for direct materials ($1.10) is computed by dividing the direct materials cost added during June ($44,000) by the equivalent units for work done in June only (40,000).

**EXHIBIT 6.14**
**Step 4: Compute Cost per Equivalent Unit—Molding Department: FIFO Method**

| | Direct Materials | | Direct Labor | | Factory Overhead | | Total |
|---|---|---|---|---|---|---|---|
| Costs (from Exhibit 6.7) | | | | | | | |
| Work-in-process, June 1 | | | | | | | $ 12,680 |
| Costs added during June | $44,000 | | $22,440 | | $43,600 | | 110,040 |
| Total costs to account for | | | | | | | $122,720 |
| Divide by equivalent units (from Exhibit 6.11) | 40,000 | | 44,000 | | 43,600 | | |
| Equivalent unit costs | $ 1.10 | + | $ 0.51 | + | $ 1.00 | = | $ 2.61 |

Similar procedures are used for direct labor and factory overhead costs. Notice that the total equivalent unit cost of $2.61 is determined by adding the unit direct materials cost of $1.10, the unit direct labor cost of $0.51, and the unit factory overhead cost of $1.00.

### Step 5: Assign Total Manufacturing Costs to Units Completed and Ending WIP

The final step of the process costing procedure is to assign total manufacturing costs to units completed and to units in the ending work-in-process inventory. As for the weighted-average method, the FIFO method assigns the total costs of a period to the units completed and the units still in process at the end of the period. Unlike the weighted-average method, however, the FIFO method accounts separately for current and prior period costs.

The manufacturing process for units in the beginning work-in-process overlaps two periods. Thus, units completed from beginning work-in-process inventory incurred costs prior to the current period as well as during the current period. This fact makes the assignment of total manufacturing costs to units completed during a period a two-part process. In the first part, the total manufacturing cost for units completed from beginning work-in-process is determined. In the second part, the total manufacturing costs for units started and completed during the manufacturing process in the current period are calculated.

### Step 5, Part A: Total Cost of Units Completed from Beginning Work-in-Process Inventory

To determine the total manufacturing costs for the units completed from beginning work-in-process, the firm adds the manufacturing costs assigned to the units during the current period to the costs of the beginning work-in-process inventory ($12,680).

The total additional cost incurred in the current period to complete these units is the sum of the equivalent units of each cost element added to complete the element. These are assigned to the units in beginning work-in-process and multiplied by the current period's unit cost for the cost element.

The costs assigned to the 10,000 units of the beginning work-in-process inventory that were completed and transferred out during the current period are calculated as follows:

| | |
|---|---|
| Work-in-process inventory, June 1, 10,000 units | $12,680 |
| Costs added during June to complete the beginning WIP inventory | |
| Direct labor 7,000 equivalent units × $0.51 per equivalent unit | 3,570 |
| Factory overhead 6,000 equivalent units × $1.00 per equivalent unit | 6,000 |
| Total for beginning inventory | $22,250 |

### Step 5, Part B: Total Cost for Units Started and Completed

The production cost of units started and completed in the current period can be computed by multiplying the number of units started and completed by the total cost per equivalent unit of the period.

The number of units started and completed in the period is the difference between the units completed and the number of units in beginning work-in-process. In the molding department example, we compute the number of units started and completed as follows:

$$\text{Units completed} - \text{Units in beginning work-in-process} = \text{Units started and completed}$$
$$44{,}000 \text{ units} - 10{,}000 \text{ units} = 34{,}000 \text{ units}$$

Then the cost assigned to units started and completed is

$$34{,}000 \text{ units} \times \$2.61 = \$88{,}740$$

The total costs transferred out are the sum of the total cost from the beginning inventory and the total cost for units started and completed; that is

$$\$22{,}250 + \$88{,}740 = \$110{,}990$$

### *Ending Work-in-Process Inventory*

The cost assigned under FIFO to ending work-in-process units is derived by multiplying the current period's cost per equivalent unit of each manufacturing cost element by the equivalent units of the ending work-in-process inventory.

The cost of 6,000 units in ending work-in-process inventory of the molding department is computed as follows:

| | |
|---|---|
| Direct materials, 6,000 equivalent units $\times$ $1.10/equivalent unit | $ 6,600 |
| Direct labor, 3,000 equivalent units $\times$ $0.51/equivalent unit | 1,530 |
| Factory overhead, 3,600 equivalent units $\times$ $1.00/equivalent unit | 3,600 |
| Total ending work-in-process inventory | $11,730 |

Exhibit 6.15 shows that the sum of the costs assigned to goods transferred out and in ending work-in-process inventory equals the total costs accounted for of $122,720.

### *Cost Reconciliation*

Now we need to determine whether the total manufacturing costs to account for in step 3 agree with the total costs accounted for in step 5. Again, step 3 accounts for $122,720 total manufacturing costs; this equals the total costs of $122,720 accounted for in step 5.

### *Production Cost Report*

Steps 1 through 5 provide all of the information needed to prepare a production cost report for the molding department for June (Exhibit 6.16).

**EXHIBIT 6.15**
**Step 5: Assign Total Manufacturing Costs—Molding Department: FIFO Method**

| | Completed and Transferred out | Ending Work-in-Process | Total |
|---|---|---|---|
| Goods completed and transferred out | | | |
| Beginning work-in-process | $ 12,680 | | $ 12,680 |
| Current cost to complete | | | |
| Direct materials | 0 | | 0 |
| Direct labor (7,000 $\times$ $0.51) | 3,570 | | 3,570 |
| Factory overhead (6,000 $\times$ $1.00) | 6,000 | | 6,000 |
| Total for beginning inventory | $ 22,250 | | $ 22,250 |
| Started and completed | | | |
| (34,000 $\times$ $2.61) | 88,740 | | 88,740 |
| Total costs transferred out | $110,990 | | $110,990 |
| Ending work-in-process | | | |
| Direct materials (6,000 $\times$ $1.10) | | $ 6,600 | $ 6,600 |
| Direct labor (3,000 $\times$ $0.51) | | 1,530 | 1,530 |
| Factory overhead (3,600 $\times$ $1.00) | | 3,600 | 3,600 |
| Total costs accounted for | $110,990 | $11,730 | $122,720 |

**EXHIBIT 6.16**
**Production Cost Report—**
**Molding Department: FIFO**
**Method**

### Production Quantity Information

| | Step 1: Analyze Flow of Physical Units | | Step 2: Calculate Equivalent Units | | |
| | Physical Units | Completion Percentage | Direct Materials | Direct Labor | Factory Overhead |
|---|---|---|---|---|---|
| **Input** | | | | | |
| Work-in-process, June 1 | 10,000 | | | | |
| Direct materials | | 100% | 10,000 | | |
| Direct labor | | 30 | | 3,000 | |
| Factory overhead | | 40 | | | 4,000 |
| Units started | 40,000 | | | | |
| Units to account for | 50,000 | | | | |
| **Output** | | | | | |
| Units completed | 44,000 | 100% | 44,000 | 44,000 | 44,000 |
| Work-in-process, June 30 | 6,000 | | | | |
| Direct materials | | 100% | 6,000 | | |
| Direct labor | | 50 | | 3,000 | |
| Factory overhead | | 60 | | | 3,600 |
| Units accounted for | 50,000 | | | | |
| Total equivalent units (weighted-average method) | | | 50,000 | 47,000 | 47,600 |
| Less: equivalent units in June 1 work-in-process | | | (10,000) | (3,000) | (4,000) |
| Equivalent units for work performed in June only (FIFO method) | | | 40,000 | 44,000 | 43,600 |

### Unit Cost Determination

| Step 3: Determine Total Costs | Direct Materials | Direct Labor | Factory Overhead | Total |
|---|---|---|---|---|
| Work-in-process, June 1 | | | | $ 12,680 |
| Costs added during June | $44,000 | $22,440 | $43,600 | 110,040 |
| Total costs to account for | $44,000 | $22,440 | $43,600 | $122,720 |

| Step 4: Compute Cost per Equivalent Unit | | | | |
|---|---|---|---|---|
| Divide by equivalent units (from Step 2) | 40,000 | 44,000 | 43,600 | |
| Equivalent unit costs | $ 1.10 | $ 0.51 | $ 1.00 | $ 2.61 |

### Cost Assignment

| Step 5: Assign Total Manufacturing Costs | Completed and Transferred out | Ending Work-in-Process | Total |
|---|---|---|---|
| Goods completed and transferred out | | | |
| Beginning work-in-process | $ 12,680 | | $ 12,680 |
| Current cost to complete | | | |
| Direct labor (7,000 × $0.51) | 3,570 | | 3,570 |
| Factory overhead (6,000 × $1.00) | 6,000 | | 6,000 |
| Total for beginning inventory | $ 22,250 | | $ 22,250 |
| Started and completed (34,000 × $2.61) | 88,740 | | 88,740 |
| Total costs transferred out | $110,990 | | $110,990 |

*(Continued; Ending work-in-process on next page)*

**EXHIBIT 6.16**
**(Continued)**

| Ending work-in-process | | | |
|---|---|---|---|
| Direct materials (6,000 × $1.10) | | $ 6,600 | $ 6,600 |
| Direct labor (3,000 × $0.51) | | 1,530 | 1,530 |
| Factory overhead (3,600 × $1.00) | | 3,600 | 3,600 |
| Total costs accounted for | $110,990 | $11,730 | $122,720 |

## Comparison of Weighted-Average and FIFO Methods

**LO 6-6**

*Analyze process costing with multiple departments.*

Both the weighted-average and the FIFO methods produce the same total costs accounted for (compare Exhibits 6.10 and 6.16). The key difference between the two methods is the handling of partially completed beginning work-in-process inventory units. The FIFO method separates the units in the beginning inventory from the units started and completed during the period. In contrast, the weighted-average method makes no separate treatment of the units in the beginning work-in-process inventory. Thus, there is a difference between the cost of goods completed under the weighted-average and FIFO methods. Similarly, there is a difference between ending work-in-process inventory under the two methods.

The weighted-average method generally is easier to use because the calculations are simpler. This method is most appropriate when work-in-process is relatively small, or direct materials prices, conversion costs, and inventory levels are stable. The FIFO method is most appropriate when direct materials prices, conversion costs, or inventory levels fluctuate significantly.

Some firms prefer the FIFO method over the weighted-average method for purposes of cost control and performance evaluation because the cost per equivalent unit under FIFO represents the cost for the current period's efforts only. Firms often evaluate department managers' performance on only current period costs without mixing in the effects of performance during different periods. Under the weighted-average method, the costs of the prior period and the current period are mixed, and deviations in performance in the current period could be concealed by interperiod variations in unit costs.

## Process Costing with Multiple Departments

Most manufacturing firms have multiple departments or use several processes that require a number of steps. As the product passes from one department to another, the cost passes from department to department. The costs from the prior department are called *transferred-in costs* or *prior department costs*. This section explains the concept of transferred-in costs and describes the weighted-average and FIFO methods of cost flow assumptions for firms with multiple departments.

### Transferred-In Costs

**Transferred-in costs**
are costs of work performed in the earlier department that are transferred into the present department.

**Transferred-in costs** are costs of work performed in the earlier department that are transferred into the present department. Including these costs is a necessary part of process costing because we treat each department as a separate entity, and each department's production cost report includes all costs added to the product up to that point. If transferred-in costs were not included, each completed unit transferred out of a department would include only the value of the work performed by that department. It might help to think of transferred-in costs as similar to the direct materials introduced at the beginning of the production process. The equivalent units of production of transferred-in costs can be computed in the same manner as direct materials that are added at the beginning of a process. The difference between the direct materials cost and the transferred-in cost is that the former comes from the storeroom while the latter comes from another production department.

The equivalent units of the transferred-in cost for ending work-in-process inventory is always assumed to be the same as the number of units in ending work-in-process inventory. Because

**EXHIBIT 6.17**
**Basic Data for Naftel Toy Company—Finishing Department**

| | |
|---|---:|
| Work-in-process, June 1: | 14,000 units |
| Transferred-in: 100% complete | $ 34,250 |
| Direct materials: 0% complete* | 0 |
| Conversion: 50% complete | 7,000 |
| Beginning work-in-process inventory | $ 41,250 |
| Units transferred in during June | 44,000 units |
| Transferred-in costs during June | |
| Weighted-average method (From Exhibit 6.10) | $111,320 |
| FIFO method (From Exhibit 6.15) | 110,990 |
| Units completed | 50,000 units |
| Work-in-process, June 30 | 8,000 units |
| Transferred-in: 100% complete | |
| Direct materials: 0% complete | |
| Conversion: 50% complete | |
| Costs added by the finishing dept. during June | |
| Direct materials | $ 25,000 |
| Conversion | 47,000 |

*Materials are added at the *end* of the process.

all units in process are complete for prior departments' costs, by definition the number of equivalent units transferred in is the same as the number of physical units transferred in.

Suppose that Naftel Toy Company's molding department transfers its production units to the finishing department. In the finishing department, direct materials are added at the end of the process. Conversion costs (direct labor and factory overhead) are applied evenly throughout the finishing department's process. The finishing department uses direct labor cost as the cost driver to apply factory overhead costs.

Data for the finishing department for June are shown in Exhibit 6.17.

## Weighted-Average Method

Follow the five-step procedure as we illustrate the weighted-average method for process costing with multiple departments.

### Steps 1 and 2: Analyze Flow of Physical Units and Calculate Equivalent Units

The first step is to analyze the physical units of production. The second step is to calculate equivalent units. Exhibit 6.18 summarizes the computation of physical units and equivalent units. Note that because overhead is charged to the product based on direct labor cost in the finishing department, direct labor and overhead are combined into a single element, conversion.

The 8,000 units in ending work-in-process inventory are 100% complete with respect to transferred-in costs because they were 100% complete in the preceding department. There is no direct materials component because materials are added at the end of the finishing process. Because ending work-in-process inventory is only 50% complete with respect to conversion costs, ending work-in-process inventories represent 4,000 equivalent units of conversion costs (8,000 physical units × 50% complete).

As Exhibit 6.18 shows, the total number of equivalent units is calculated as follows:

Completed units
+ Ending work-in-process equivalent units
= Total equivalent units of production

That is, under the weighted-average method, the equivalent units of production for the finishing department include 58,000 units transferred in, 50,000 units of direct materials, and 54,000 units of conversion.

### Steps 3 and 4: Determine Total Costs and Compute Unit Costs

The third step is to determine the total manufacturing costs to account for, and the fourth step is to compute equivalent unit costs for transferred-in, direct materials, and conversion costs.

<br>

<br>

<br>

<br>

<table>
<tr><td>REAL-WORLD FOCUS</td><td>Process Costing in Practice at the U.S. Department of Agriculture (USDA)</td></tr>
</table>

The USDA's accounting standards manual urges the use of activity-based costing in conjunction with process costing. The USDA also suggests that process costing be used in situations involving a large volume of similar goods or services. An example is the use of process costing to account for the cost of the process for the payment of unemployment benefits. The payment of unemployment benefits involves a series of processes: reviewing applications, computing the amount of benefits, and issuing checks. Process costing is well suited for this context.

Based on information in *U.S. Department of Agriculture Financial and Accounting Standards Manual,* Version 2.0, Chapter 5, Section 5.9 (U.S. Department of Agriculture, www.ocfo.usda.gov/acctpol/pdf/fasm.pdf). Activity-based process costing is covered on page 197 later in this chapter.

**EXHIBIT 6.18**

**Steps 1 and 2: Analyze Physical Flow of Units and Calculate Equivalent Units—Finishing Department: Weighted-Average Method**

| | Step 1 | | Step 2 | | |
| --- | --- | --- | --- | --- | --- |
| | | | **Equivalent Units** | | |
| | **Physical Units** | **Completion Percentage** | **Transferred-in Costs** | **Direct Materials** | **Conversion Costs** |
| Input | | | | | |
| Work-in-process, June 1 | 14,000 | | | | |
| Transferred-in | | 100% | | | |
| Direct materials | | 0 | | | |
| Conversion | | 50 | | | |
| Transferred-in | 44,000 | 100% | | | |
| Units to account for | 58,000 | | | | |
| Output | | | | | |
| Units completed | 50,000 | 100% | 50,000 | 50,000 | 50,000 |
| Work-in-process, June 30 | 8,000 | | | | |
| Transferred-in | | 100% | 8,000 | | |
| Direct materials | | 0 | | | |
| Conversion | | 50 | | | 4,000 |
| Units accounted for | 58,000 | | | | |
| Total equivalent units | | | 58,000 | 50,000 | 54,000 |

Exhibit 6.19 summarizes the total manufacturing costs to account for and unit costs for all cost components. Total manufacturing costs to account for ($224,570) consist of the beginning work-in-process inventory balance, $41,250, plus the current costs added during June, $183,320 ($111,320 + $25,000 + $47,000).

The equivalent unit cost for units transferred in ($2.5098) is computed by dividing the total transferred-in cost ($145,570), including the cost of beginning work-in-process ($34,250) and the cost added during June ($111,320), by the total equivalent units transferred in (58,000). Similar procedures are used for direct materials and conversion costs.

**EXHIBIT 6.19**

**Steps 3 and 4: Determine Total Costs and Compute Cost per Equivalent Unit—Finishing Department: Weighted-Average Method**

| Step 3 | Transferred-in Costs | Direct Materials | Conversion Costs | Total |
| --- | --- | --- | --- | --- |
| Work-in-process, June 1 | $ 34,250 | $ 0 | $ 7,000 | $ 41,250 |
| Costs added during June | 111,320 | 25,000 | 47,000 | 183,320 |
| Total costs to account for | $145,570 | $25,000 | $54,000 | $224,570 |
| **Step 4** | | | | |
| Divide by equivalent units (from Exhibit 6.18) | 58,000 | 50,000 | 54,000 | |
| Equivalent unit costs | $ 2.5098 + | $ 0.50 + | $ 1.00 = | $ 4.0098 |

**EXHIBIT 6.20**
Step 5: Assign Total Manufacturing Costs—Finishing Department: Weighted-Average Method

| Step 5 | Completed and Transferred out | Ending Work-in-Process | Total |
|---|---|---|---|
| Goods completed and transferred out (50,000 × $4.0098) | $200,490 | | $200,490 |
| Ending work-in-process | | | |
| Transferred-in (8,000 × $2.5098) | | $20,078 | 20,078 |
| Conversion (4,000 × $1.00) | | 4,000 | 4,000 |
| Total costs accounted for | $200,490 | $24,078 | $224,568 |

### Step 5: Assign Total Manufacturing Costs to Completed Units and Ending WIP

The final step of the process costing procedure is to assign total manufacturing costs to units completed and to units in ending work-in-process inventory. Exhibit 6.20 summarizes the cost assignment schedule with $224,568 total costs in step 5.

### Cost Reconciliation

The small difference between the total cost accounted for in step 5 and the total cost in step 3 is due to a very small rounding error. *To avoid unacceptable large rounding errors, at least four significant digits or more should be used in calculating the cost per equivalent unit in step 4.*

## The FIFO Method

Now we illustrate the FIFO method of process costing for multiple departments using data from the Naftel Toy Company's finishing department (see Exhibit 6.17).

### Steps 1 and 2: Analyze Flow of Physical Units and Calculate Equivalent Units

Exhibit 6.21 summarizes the physical flow units and equivalent units of production for the finishing department.

The physical flow of product units is unaffected by the process costing method used. Therefore, step 1 is the same as with the weighted-average method.

The 14,000 physical units in the June 1 work-in-process inventory have 100% of transferred-in costs, so they represent 14,000 equivalent units of transferred-in work. Because the materials are added at the end of the process in the finishing department, zero equivalent units of direct materials for work-in-process inventory are on hand on June 1. The beginning work-in-process inventory is only 50% complete with respect to conversion, so this department has 7,000 equivalent units of conversion costs (14,000 × 50%).

As Exhibit 6.21 indicates, the total number of equivalent units is calculated as follows:

> Completed units
> + Ending work-in-process equivalent units
> − Beginning work-in-process equivalent units
> ───────────────────────────────
> = Equivalent units of work completed during this period (FIFO)

That is, equivalent units of production for the finishing department using the FIFO method are 44,000 transferred-in units, 50,000 direct materials units, and 47,000 conversion units.

### Steps 3 and 4: Determine Total Costs to Account for and Compute Unit Costs

Exhibit 6.22 shows the computation of total costs to account for and equivalent unit costs for the finishing department.

The beginning work-in-process inventory has a cost of $41,250. The $182,990 total costs added during June include $110,990 transferred-in costs from the molding department, $25,000 direct materials costs, and $47,000 conversion costs incurred in the finishing department as shown in Exhibit 6.22.

**EXHIBIT 6.21**

**Steps 1 and 2: Analyze Flow of Physical Units and Calculate Equivalent Units—Finishing Department: FIFO Method**

| | Step 1 | | Step 2 | | |
|---|---|---|---|---|---|
| | | | Equivalent Units | | |
| | Physical Units | Completion Percentage | Transferred-in Costs | Direct Materials | Conversion Costs |
| **Input** | | | | | |
| Work-in-process, June 1 | 14,000 | | | | |
|    Transferred-in | | 100% | 14,000 | | |
|    Direct materials | | 0 | | 0 | |
|    Conversion | | 50 | | | 7,000 |
| Transferred-in | 44,000 | 100% | | | |
| Units to account for | 58,000 | | | | |
| **Output** | | | | | |
| Units completed | 50,000 | 100% | 50,000 | 50,000 | 50,000 |
| Work-in-process, June 30 | 8,000 | | | | |
|    Transferred-in | | 100% | 8,000 | | |
|    Direct materials | | 0 | | 0 | |
|    Conversion | | 50 | | | 4,000 |
| Units accounted for | 58,000 | | | | |
| Total equivalent units (weighted-average method) | | | 58,000 | 50,000 | 54,000 |
| Less: equivalent units in June 1 work-in-process | | | (14,000) | (0) | (7,000) |
| Equivalent units for work done in June only (FIFO method) | | | 44,000 | 50,000 | 47,000 |

**EXHIBIT 6.22**

**Steps 3 and 4: Determine Total Costs to Account for and Compute Unit Costs—Finishing Department: FIFO Method**

| Step 3 | Transferred-in Costs | Direct Materials | Conversion Costs | Total |
|---|---|---|---|---|
| Work-in-process, June 1 | | | | $ 41,250 |
| Costs added during June* | $110,990 | $25,000 | $47,000 | 182,990 |
| Total costs to account for | | | | $224,240 |
| | | | | |
| **Step 4** | | | | |
| Divide by equivalent units (from Exhibit 6.21): | 44,000 | 50,000 | 47,000 | |
| Equivalent unit costs | $ 2.5225 + | $ 0.50 + | $ 1.00 = | $ 4.0225 |

*Note: The transferred-in cost of $110,990 is taken from the FIFO report of the molding department, Exhibit 6.16.

The equivalent unit cost for transferred-in units ($2.5225) is computed by dividing the transferred-in cost during June ($110,990) by the equivalent units for work completed only in June (44,000). Similar procedures are used for direct materials and conversion costs. Notice that the costs of beginning inventory are excluded from this calculation. The calculations use only current costs added in June.

### Step 5: Assign Total Manufacturing Costs

The final step of the process costing procedure is to assign total manufacturing costs to units completed and to units in the ending work-in-process inventory. Exhibit 6.23 summarizes the cost assignment schedule.

**EXHIBIT 6.23**
**Step 5: Assign Total Costs—Finishing Department: FIFO Method**

| | Completed and Transferred out | Ending Work-in-Process | Total |
|---|---|---|---|
| Goods completed and transferred out | | | |
| Beginning work-in-process | $ 41,250 | | $ 41,250 |
| Current cost to complete | | | |
| Direct materials (14,000 × $0.50) | 7,000 | | 7,000 |
| Conversion (7,000 × $1.00) | 7,000 | | 7,000 |
| Total from beginning WIP inventory | $ 55,250 | | $ 55,250 |
| Started and completed (36,000 × $4.0225) | 144,810 | | 144,810 |
| Total costs completed and transferred out | $200,060 | | $200,060 |
| Ending work-in-process | | | |
| Transferred-in (8,000 × $2.5225) | | $20,180 | 20,180 |
| Conversion costs (4,000 × $1.00) | | 4,000 | 4,000 |
| Total costs accounted for | $200,060 | $24,180 | $224,240 |

The total manufacturing cost associated with the 14,000 units of beginning work-in-process inventory is calculated as follows:

| | |
|---|---|
| Work-in-process, June 1, 14,000 units | $41,250 |
| Costs added during June to complete the beginning inventory: | |
| Direct materials (14,000 equivalent units × $0.50) | 7,000 |
| Conversion costs (7,000 equivalent units × $1.00) | 7,000 |
| Total for beginning inventory | $55,250 |

The costs assigned to the 36,000 units started and completed during June are calculated:

$$50,000 \text{ units} - 14,000 \text{ units} = 36,000 \text{ units}$$

$$36,000 \text{ units} \times \$4.0225 = \$144,810$$

The total costs for units completed are the sum of the total costs from beginning inventory and the total costs for units started and completed, that is,

$$\$55,250 + \$144,810 = \$200,060$$

The cost of the finishing department's 8,000 units in ending work-in-process inventory is computed as follows:

| | |
|---|---|
| Transferred-in: 8,000 equivalent units × $2.5225 | $20,180 |
| Conversion: 4,000 equivalent units × $1.00 | 4,000 |
| Total ending work-in-process inventory | $24,180 |

In Exhibit 6.23, the sum of the costs assigned to goods completed and ending work-in-process inventory is $224,240. Note that the amount of total costs accounted for in step 5 should equal the total costs to account for in step 3 (as shown in Exhibit 6.22).

## Journal Entries for Process Costing

**LO 6-7**

*Prepare journal entries to record the flow of costs in a process costing system.*

Process costing uses the same general ledger manufacturing accounts as job costing explained in Chapter 4. However, instead of assigning product costs to specific jobs, we accumulate costs in production departments. Each department has a separate Work-in-Process Inventory account. These journal entries for Naftel Toy Company use the weighted-average method data from steps 3 and 5 of both Exhibit 6.10 (molding department) and Exhibits 6.19 and 6.20 (finishing department). Assume that 50% of the conversion costs in the finishing department are direct labor ($47,000 × 50% = $23,500).

The following direct materials were requisitioned and used:

| (1) | Work-in-Process Inventory—Molding Department | 44,000 | |
| | Work-in-Process Inventory—Finishing Department | 25,000 | |
| |     Materials Inventory | | 69,000 |
| | To record direct materials costs added during June. | | |

The direct labor incurred follows:

| (2) | Work-in-Process Inventory—Molding Department | 22,440 | |
| | Work-in-Process Inventory—Finishing Department | 23,500 | |
| |     Accrued Payroll | | 45,940 |
| | To record direct labor costs incurred during June. | | |

Factory overhead applied is as follows:

| (3) | Work-in-Process Inventory—Molding Department | 43,600 | |
| | Work-in-Process Inventory—Finishing Department | 23,500 | |
| |     Factory Overhead | | 67,100 |
| | To record the application of factory overhead to departments. | | |

Transferred-in costs from the molding department are as follows (using weighted-average):

| (4) | Work-in-Process Inventory—Finishing Department | 111,320 | |
| |     Work-in-Process Inventory—Molding Department | | 111,320 |
| | To record the weighted-average method of the cost of goods completed in the molding department and transferred out to the finishing department. | | |

Product units finished are as follows (using weighted-average):

| (5) | Finished Goods Inventory | 200,490 | |
| |     Work-in-Process Inventory—Finishing Department | | 200,490 |
| | To record the weighted-average method of the cost of goods completed in the finishing department. | | |

## Implementation and Enhancement of Process Costing

**LO 6-8**

*Explain how process costing systems are implemented and enhanced in practice.*

### Activity-Based Costing and the Theory of Constraints

Process costing systems are appropriate where there are one or a few homogeneous products, as in many process industries such as chemical or paper manufacturing. The goal of the costing system is to account for production costs in the cost of work-in-process units and finished products in the production cost report. There is little need for cost information to identify the cost of *different products* or *different customer jobs,* because there are only one or a few products and they all go through the same processing and thus have the same unit cost. But sometimes the process-based manufacturer has very different products going through different processes, making the process costing system by itself inadequate. For example, Reichhold Inc. (**www.reichhold.com**), a manufacturer of industrial chemicals, adhesives, and other products, is a process company that uses processing costing, but it has adapted the system to include activity-based costing, because of its product variety. While most of its products go through similar processing steps (cleaning, reacting, filtration, and blending), some products require much more time in some steps than other products. For example, one Reichhold product requires careful cleanup of the vat where it is processed, because even very small quantities of the chemical can contaminate other products that are later processed in the vat. So, activity-based costing is used to properly charge the extra cleanup costs to this product.[1] Activity-based costing is an important enhancement to process costing when product and process variety arises.

Similarly, process costing information is not intended to help the firm determine the most profitable product mix or to identify the most profitable use of the plant. These questions require analyses that utilize the products' contribution margins and the location of production constraints in the plant. To determine the most profitable product mix, the process firm would use the contribution methods explained in Chapter 11 and the theory of constraints method explained in Chapter 13. For example, Reichhold could use the theory of constraints to identify the process that is a bottleneck in the manufacture of its products. After determining which process (such as cleaning or reacting) is the bottleneck, Reichhold could adjust production schedules to most profitably use this process.

## Just-in-Time Systems and Backflush Costing

Firms use the just-in-time (JIT) method to minimize inventory and improve quality by carefully coordinating the receipt of raw materials and the delivery of product with the manufacturing processes in the plant. The goal is to have little or no raw material, work-in-process, or finished goods inventory in the plant. This saves costs that arise from holding inventory, including the risk of damage, theft, loss, or failure to find a customer for the finished product. Since inventory is minimal in an effective JIT system, there is no need for a system such as process costing to determine equivalent units and to account for production costs in work-in-process and finished goods. Simpler methods such as **backflush costing** can be used instead. These methods charge current production costs (using standard unit costs) directly to finished goods inventory, without accounting for the flows in and out of the Work-in-Process account. Any difference between these standard unit costs and actual costs is typically very small and is charged to cost of goods sold at the end of the year. While not in compliance with generally accepted accounting principles (because the small amount of work-in-process inventory is not valued and placed on the balance sheet), the backflush method is reasonable and convenient for a JIT production environment.

A brief illustration of backflush costing follows. Assume that a company has the following information for a given month of activity:

**Backflush costing**
is a method that charges current production costs (using standard costs) directly to finished goods inventory without accounting for the flows in and out of work-in-process.

| | |
|---|---|
| Purchase of direct materials | $100,000 |
| Actual cost of materials used | $92,000 |
| Conversion cost incurred | $145,000 |
| Direct materials standard cost | $5 per unit |
| Conversion cost at standard | $8 per unit |
| Total standard cost | $13 per unit |
| Units produced | 18,000 units |
| Units sold | 17,000 units |

[1] "Edward Blocher, Betty Wong, and Christopher T. McKittrick, "Making Bottom-Up ABC Work at Reichhold, Inc," *Strategic Finance*, April 2002, pp. 51–55. Also, activity-based costing together with process costing has been used in health care applications: William N. Zelman, "Animated-Simulation Modeling Facilitates Clinical Process Costing, *Healthcare Financial Management*, September 2001.

The cost of production using the backflush method is $13 \times 18,000 = \$234,000$, of which \$90,000 ($= \$5 \times 18,000$) is materials and \$144,000 ($= \$8 \times 18,000$) is conversion. The following journal entries show how the costs are applied and cost of goods sold is determined using the following five steps.

1. Materials inventory is increased for the amount of purchases, \$100,000.
2. The conversion cost account is increased for the amount of conversion costs incurred, \$145,000.
3. Finished goods are shown at the standard cost for 18,000 units completed, \$234,000; this includes \$90,000 of materials cost and \$144,000 of applied conversion cost.
4. Cost of goods sold are shown for sales of 17,000 units, \$221,000 (17,000 $\times$ \$13).
5. At the end of the accounting period, the difference (\$1,000) between incurred (\$145,000) and applied (\$144,000) conversion costs is closed to the Cost of Goods Sold account. Also, the \$2,000 difference between the actual usage of materials (\$92,000) and the standard (\$90,000) is closed to Cost of Goods Sold.

| (1) | Materials Inventory | 100,000 | |
| | Accounts Payable, Cash | | 100,000 |

| (2) | Conversion Cost Incurred | 145,000 | |
| | Wages Payable, Other Accounts | | 145,000 |

| (3) | Finished Goods | 234,000 | |
| | Materials inventory (for actual usage) | | 90,000 |
| | Conversion Cost Applied | | 144,000 |

| (4) | Cost of Goods Sold | 221,000 | |
| | Finished Goods | | 221,000 |

| (5a) | Conversion Cost Applied | 144,000 | |
| | Cost of Goods Sold | 1,000 | |
| | Conversion Cost Incurred | | 145,000 |

| (5b) | Cost of Goods Sold | 2,000 | |
| | Materials Inventory | | 2,000 |

The final amount for cost of goods sold is therefore \$221,000 + \$1,000 + \$2,000 = \$224,000. The above presents a simple approach that is used when work-in-process is negligible. The use of standard costs means that product costs can be quickly and conveniently calculated for both production and sales; the differences between actual and standard costs are usually small and are closed to Cost of Goods Sold at the end of the period. A full explanation of standard costs and standard cost variances is provided in Chapters 14 and 15.

## Normal and Standard Process Costing

Process cost reports illustrated in this chapter have taken a normal costing approach, that is, labor and materials are added to product at actual cost and overhead is determined and applied to product using a predetermined overhead rate. Normal costing is explained on page 103 and illustrated throughout Chapter 4. An alternative approach is standard costing, in which all three cost elements—materials, labor, and overhead—are added to product at a standard cost rather than actual cost. As noted in Chapter 4, both job costing (covered in Chapter 4) or process costing (covered in Chapter 6) can be applied using either the normal costing or the standard costing approach. For simplicity and brevity, Chapters 4 and 6 are based on normal costing only, and standard costing is presented in Chapters 14 and 15.[2]

## Summary

Process costing is a product costing system that accumulates costs in processing departments and allocates them to all units processed during the period, including both completed and partially completed units. It is used by firms producing homogeneous products on a continuous basis to assign manufacturing costs to units in production during the period. Firms that use process costing include paint, chemical, oil-refining, and food-processing companies.

Process costing systems provide information so managers can make strategic decisions regarding products and customers, manufacturing methods, pricing options, overhead allocation methods, and other issues.

Equivalent units are the number of the same or similar completed units that could have been produced given the amount of work actually performed on both complete and partially completed units.

The key document in a typical process costing system is the production cost report that summarizes the physical units and equivalent units of a production department, the costs incurred during the period, and the costs assigned to goods both completed and transferred out as well as to ending work-in-process inventories. The preparation of a production cost report includes five steps: (1) analyze physical units, (2) calculate equivalent units, (3) determine total costs to account for, (4) compute unit costs, and (5) assign total manufacturing costs.

The two methods of preparing the departmental production cost report in process costing are the weighted-average method and the first-in, first-out (FIFO) method. The weighted-average method includes costs incurred in both current and prior periods that are shown as the beginning work-in-process inventory of this period. The FIFO method includes only costs incurred during the current period in calculating unit cost.

Most manufacturing firms have several departments or use processes that require several steps. As the product passes from one department to another, the costs from the prior department are transferred-in costs or prior department costs. Process costing with multiple departments should include the transferred-in cost as the fourth cost element in addition to direct materials, direct labor, and factory overhead costs.

## Appendix

## Spoilage in Process Costing

**LO 6-9**

*Account for spoilage in process costing.*

In this appendix we explain the two types of spoilage—normal and abnormal. *Normal spoilage* occurs under normal operating conditions. It is uncontrollable in the short term and is considered a part of product cost. That is, the costs of lost units are absorbed by the good units produced. *Abnormal spoilage* exceeds expected losses under efficient operating conditions and is charged as a loss to operations in the period detected.

Two approaches are used to account for normal spoilage in process costing systems. The first approach is to count the number of spoiled units, prepare a separate equivalent unit computation with the cost per unit of the spoiled goods, and then allocate the cost to the good units produced. The second approach is to omit the spoiled units in computing

---

[2] Jennifer Dosch and Joel Wilson explain the advantages of applying the standard costing approach to process costing and comment on its application in three companies in, "Process Costing and Management Accounting in Today's Business Environment," *Strategic Finance,* August 2010, pp. 37–43.

the equivalent units of production; the spoilage cost is thus included as part of total manufacturing costs. The first approach provides more accurate product costs because it computes the costs associated with normal spoilage and spreads them over the good units produced. The second approach is less accurate because it spreads the costs of normal spoilage over all units—good completed units, units in ending work-in-process inventory, and abnormal spoiled units. This appendix discusses only the first approach.

Consider Weatherly Company, which has the following data for the current period:

|  | Units | Cost |
|---|---|---|
| Beginning work-in-process inventory | 2,000 | |
|     Direct materials (100%complete) | | $100,000 |
|     Conversion costs (75% complete) | | 80,000 |
| Units started in the period | 8,000 | |
| Costs incurred during the period | | |
|     Direct materials | | 300,000 |
|     Conversion costs | | 405,000 |
| Ending work-in-process inventory | 2,000 | |
|     Direct materials (100% complete) | | |
|     Conversion costs (80% complete) | | |
| Completed and transferred out (good units produced) | 7,000 | |
| Normal spoilage is 10% of good units produced | 700 | |
| Abnormal spoilage | 300 | |

Weatherly Company inspects all products at the completion point. Inspection at the completion point means that all costs incurred to the completion point are spoiled; the unit cost of spoilage is thus the total cost per equivalent unit. If the inspection point is earlier, then spoilage cost can be reduced; the cost of spoilage is then adjusted accordingly.

Using the five-step procedure described in the chapter, we need only add normal spoilage and abnormal spoilage components in calculations.

### Step 1. Analyze Physical Flow of Production Units

With 7,000 good production units completed in May, the normal spoiled units total 700 (7,000 × 10%). Abnormal spoilage is 300 spoiled units.

### Step 2. Calculate Equivalent Units

Equivalent units for spoilage are calculated in the same way as good units. Normal and abnormal spoiled units are included in the calculation of equivalent units. Since the company inspects all products at the completion point, the same amount of work is performed on each completed good unit and each spoiled unit.

### Step 3. Determine Total Costs

These costs include all costs in the beginning work-in-process inventory and all costs added during the period. The detail of this step is the same as for the process costing procedure without spoilage incurred.

### Step 4. Compute Cost per Equivalent Unit

The detail of this step is the same as for the process costing procedure without any spoilage.

### Step 5. Assign Total Manufacturing Costs to Units Completed, Ending WIP, and Abnormal Spoilage

Exhibit 6A.1 summarizes the five-step procedure for the weighted-average process costing method, including both normal and abnormal spoilage. Exhibit 6A.2 is the production cost report under the FIFO process costing method.

**EXHIBIT 6A.1**
**Weatherly Company's**
**Production Cost Report:**
**Weighted-Average Method**

| Production Quantity Information | | | | |
|---|---|---|---|---|
| | Step 1:<br>Analyze Flow of Physical Units | | Step 2:<br>Calculate Equivalent Units | |
| | Physical<br>Units | Completion<br>Percentage | Direct<br>Materials | Conversion<br>Costs |
| **Input** | | | | |
| Work-in-process, May 1 | 2,000 | | | |
|    Direct materials | | 100% | | |
|    Conversion | | 75 | | |
| Number started | 8,000 | | | |
| Units to account for | 10,000 | | | |
| **Output** | | | | |
| Units completed | 7,000 | 100% | 7,000 | 7,000 |
|    Normal spoilage (10%) | 700 | | 700 | 700 |
|    Abnormal spoilage | 300 | | 300 | 300 |
|    Work-in-process, May 31 | 2,000 | | | |
|    Direct materials | | 100% | 2,000 | |
|    Conversion | ____ | 80 | | 1,600 |
| Units accounted for | | | | |
| Total equivalent units | 10,000 | | 10,000 | 9,600 |

| Unit Cost Determination | | | |
|---|---|---|---|
| **Step 3: Determine Total Costs** | Direct<br>Materials | Conversion<br>Costs | Total |
| Work-in-process, May 1 | $100,000 | $ 80,000 | $ 180,000 |
| Costs added during period | 300,000 | 405,000 | 705,000 |
| Total costs to account for | $400,000 | $ 485,000 | $ 885,000 |
| **Step 4: Compute Cost per Equivalent Unit** | | | |
| Divide by number of equivalent units | 10,000 | 9,600 | |
| Equivalent unit costs | $ 40.00 | $ 50.5208 | $ 90.5208 |

| Cost Assignment | | | |
|---|---|---|---|
| **Step 5: Assign Total<br>Manufacturing Costs** | Completed and<br>Transferred out | Ending<br>Work-in-Process | Total |
| Goods completed and transferred out<br>  [(Good units 7,000 +<br>  Normal spoilage 700)<br>  × $90.5208] | $697,011 | | $697,011 |
| Abnormal spoilage<br>(300 × $90.5208) | | | 27,156 |
| Work-in-process, May 31<br>  Direct materials<br>  (2,000 × $40.00) | | $ 80,000 | 80,000 |
| Conversion<br>  (1,600 × $50.5208) | | 80,833 | 80,833 |
| Total costs accounted for | $697,011 | $160,833 | $885,000 |

**EXHIBIT 6A.2**
**Weatherly Company's FIFO Production Cost Report**

| Production Quantity Information | | | |
|---|---|---|---|
| | Step 1: Analyze Flow of Physical Units | Step 2: Calculate Equivalent Units | |
| | Physical Units | Direct Materials | Conversion Costs |
| Input | | | |
| Work-in-process | | | |
| beginning inventory | 2,000 | (100%) | (75%) |
| Started this period | 8,000 | | |
| Units to account for | 10,000 | | |
| Output | | | |
| Completed | 7,000 | 7,000 | 7,000 |
| Normal spoilage (10%) | 700 | 700 | 700 |
| Abnormal spoilage | 300 | 300 | 300 |
| Work-in-process | | | |
| ending inventory | 2,000 (80%) | 2,000 | 1,600 |
| Units accounted for | 10,000 | | |
| Total work done to date | | 10,000 | 9,600 |
| Work-in-process | | | |
| beginning inventory | | (2,000) | (1,500) |
| Total work done this period (total equivalent units) | | 8,000 | 8,100 |

| Unit Cost Determination | | | |
|---|---|---|---|
| Step 3: Determine Total Costs for | Direct Materials | Conversion Costs | Total |
| Work-in-process | | | |
| Beginning inventory | $100,000 | $ 80,000 | $180,000 |
| Current cost | 300,000 | 405,000 | 705,000 |
| Total costs to account for | $400,000 | $485,000 | $885,000 |

| Step 4: Compute Cost per Equivalent Unit | | | |
|---|---|---|---|
| | ($300,000/ 8,000) = | ($405,000/ 8,100) = | |
| Cost per equivalent unit | $ 37.50 | $ 50.00 | $ 87.50 |

| Cost Assignment | | | |
|---|---|---|---|
| Step 5: Assign Total Manufacturing Costs | Completed and Transferred out | Ending Work-in-Process | Total |
| Units completed and transferred out (7,000) | | | |
| Beginning work-in-process | $180,000 | | $180,000 |
| Current cost to complete | | | |
| Conversion (500 × $50) | 25,000 | | 25,000 |
| Total from beginning work-in-process | $205,000 | | $205,000 |
| Units started & finished (5,000 × $87.50) | 437,500 | | 437,500 |
| Normal spoilage (700 × $87.50) | 61,250 | | 61,250 |
| Total cost completed and transferred out | $703,750 | | $703,750 |
| Abnormal spoilage (300 × $87.50) | | | 26,250 |
| Ending work-in-process (2,000) | | | |
| Materials (2,000 × $37.50) | | $ 75,000 | 75,000 |
| Conversion (1,600 × $50) | — | 80,000 | 80,000 |
| Total costs accounted for | $703,750 | $155,000 | $885,000 |

| Key Terms | backflush costing, *198* | production cost report, *178* | units to account for, *181* |
|---|---|---|---|
| | equivalent units, *177* | transferred-in costs, *191* | weighted-average method, *180* |
| | FIFO method, *180* | units accounted for, *181* | |

## Comments on Cost Management in Action

Achieving sustainability requires a carefully planned and executed policy for reducing the firm's environmental and social footprint. This could be measured in a number of ways, such as the amount of waste products, workplace injuries, carbon and sulfur emissions, and other social and environmental indicators.

Marc Epstein notes that Royal Dutch Shell and Alcoa, two large process firms, employ review processes to assess human rights risks, health, safety, and other environmental issues before investing in a new location. Other initiatives include those by Walmart in recent years to redesign its product distribution system to reduce fuel usage by over 30%. Other companies are using solar energy, some to the extent that they can sell energy back to the energy grid provided by the energy companies. In other initiatives in agriculture, genetic engineering and improved seed and planting methods have reduced the need for fertilizer and other soil treatments, saving the cost and also the environmental impact of these chemicals. There are many other examples that you may know of. The Epstein publications cited below provide additional examples.

**Source:** Marc J. Epstein, "Implementing Corporate Sustainability: Measuring and Managing Social and Environmental Impacts," *Strategic Finance,* January 2008, pp. 25–31; Marc J. Epstein, *Making Sustainability Work: Best Practices in Managing and Measuring Corporate Social, Environmental and Economic Impacts* (San Francisco: Berrett-Koehler, 2008).

## Self-Study Problems

(For solutions, please turn to the end of the chapter.)

### 1. Weighted-Average Method versus FIFO Method

Smith Electronic Company's chip-mounting production department had 300 units of unfinished product, each 40% complete on September 30. During October of the same year, this department put another 900 units into production and completed 1,000 units and transferred them to the next production department. At the end of October, 200 units of unfinished product, 70% completed, were recorded in the ending work-in-process inventory. Smith Electronic introduces all direct materials when the production process is 50% complete. Direct labor and factory overhead (i.e., conversion) costs are added uniformly throughout the process.

Following is a summary of production costs incurred during October:

| | Direct Materials | Conversion Costs |
|---|---|---|
| Beginning work-in-process | | $2,202 |
| Current costs | $9,600 | 6,120 |
| Total costs | $9,600 | $8,322 |

**Required**

1. Calculate each of the following amounts using weighted-average process costing:
   a. Equivalent units of direct materials and conversion.
   b. Unit costs of direct materials and conversion.
   c. Cost of goods completed and transferred out during the period.
   d. Cost of work-in-process inventory at the end of the period.
2. Prepare a production cost report for October using the weighted-average method.
3. Repeat requirement 1 using the FIFO method.
4. Repeat requirement 2 using the FIFO method.

### 2. Weighted-Average Method versus FIFO Method with Transferred-In Cost

Reed Company has two departments, a machining department and a finishing department. The following information relates to the finishing department: work-in-process, November 1, was 10 units, 40% completed, consisting of $100 transferred-in costs, $80 direct materials, and $52 conversion costs. Production completed for November totaled 82 units; work-in-process, November 30, is 8 units, 50% completed. All finishing department direct materials are introduced at the start of the process; conversion costs are incurred uniformly throughout the process. Transferred-in costs from the machining department during November were $800; direct materials added were $720; conversion costs incurred were $861. Following is the summary data of Reed Company's finishing department:

| Work-in-process, November 1, 10 units: | |
|---|---|
| Transferred-in: 100% complete | $ 100 |
| Direct materials: 100% complete | 80 |
| Conversion: 40% complete | 52 |
| Balance in work-in-process, November 1 | $ 232 |
| Units transferred in from machining department during November | 80 units |
| Units completed during November and transferred out to finished goods inventory | 82 units |
| Work-in-process, November 30 | 8 units |
| Transferred-in: 100% complete | |
| Direct materials: 100% complete | |
| Conversion: 50% complete | |
| Costs incurred during November | |
| Transferred-in | $ 800 |
| Direct materials | 720 |
| Conversion | 861 |
| Total current costs | $2.381 |

**Required**

1. Prepare a production cost report for November using the weighted-average method.
2. Prepare a production cost report for November using the FIFO method.

*Please visit* **http://www.mhhe.com/blocher6e** *to access a narrated, animated tutorial for solving these problems.*

**Questions**

6-1    What are the typical characteristics of a company that should use a process costing system?

6-2    List three types of industries that would likely use process costing.

6-3    Explain the primary differences between job costing and process costing.

6-4    What does the term *equivalent units* mean?

6-5    How is the equivalent unit calculation affected when direct materials are added at the beginning of the process rather than uniformly throughout the process?

6-6    What is a production cost report? What are the five key steps in preparing a production cost report?

6-7    What is the distinction between equivalent units under the FIFO method and equivalent units under the weighted-average method?

6-8    Identify the conditions under which the weighted-average method of process costing is inappropriate.

6-9    Specify the advantage of the weighted-average method of process costing in contrast to the FIFO method.

6-10    From the standpoint of cost control, why is the FIFO method superior to the weighted-average method? Is it possible to monitor cost trends using the weighted-average method?

6-11    What are transferred-in costs?

6-12    Suppose that manufacturing is performed in sequential production departments. Prepare a journal entry to show a transfer of partially completed units from the first department to the second department. Assume the amount of cost transferred is $50,000.

6-13    Under the weighted-average method, all units transferred out are treated the same way. How does this differ from the FIFO method of handling units transferred out?

6-14    Under the FIFO method, only current period costs and work are included in unit costs and equivalent units computation. Under the weighted-average method, what assumptions are made when unit costs and equivalent units are computed?

6-15    What is the main difference between journal entries in process costing and in job costing?

6-16    What is the difference between process costing and backflush costing?

6-17    Explain activity-based process costing, and give an example of a company that uses it.

**Brief Exercises**

**Required**    For problems 6-18 to 6-21, fill in the missing amount.

6-18    

| Work-in-process inventory, February 1 | 80,000 units |
|---|---|
| Work-in-process inventory, February 28 | ? |
| Units started during February | 60,000 |
| Units completed during February | 75,000 |

6-19  Work-in-process inventory, June 1                    ?
      Work-in-process inventory, June 30               55,000 gallons
      Units started during June                        75,000 gallons
      Units completed during June                      83,000 gallons

6-20  Work-in-process inventory, September 1            5,500 tons
      Work-in-process inventory, September 30           3,400 tons
      Units started during September                   ?
      Units completed during September                 7,300 tons

6-21  Work-in-process inventory, November 1             45,000 units
      Work-in-process inventory, November 30            23,000 units
      Units started during November                    57,000 units
      Units completed during November                  ?

6-22  Beginning work-in-process is 2,000 units; units completed is 44,000 units, and ending work-in-process is 3,000 units, which are 100% complete for materials and 50% complete for conversion costs. The beginning work-in-process inventory is 100% complete for materials and 50% complete for conversion.

   a.  What are the equivalent units for materials and conversion using the weighted average method?

   b.  What are the equivalent units for materials and conversion using the FIFO method?

6-23  Cost per equivalent unit is $2 for materials and $3 for conversion. There are no transferred-in costs and no spoilage. What is the cost of goods completed if 10,000 units are completed and 1,000 are in ending inventory?

6-24  Abnormal spoilage is 100 units and normal spoilage is 400 units. Beginning work-in-process inventory consisted of 5,000 units; 20,000 units were started; and 22,000 units were completed this period. How many units are in ending work-in-process?

6-25  The number of abnormal spoiled units is 300 and the cost per equivalent unit is $2 for materials and $3 for conversion. The inspection point is at the end of processing. There are 600 units in ending work-in-process and 200 normal spoiled units. What is the cost of spoilage shown separately on the cost report?

6-26  There is no spoilage, the beginning work-in-process inventory is 6,000 units, and the ending work-in-process inventory is 4,000 units for the second department in a two department process. What is the number of units transferred in to the second department if good output of the second department is 35,000 units?

## Exercises

[LO 6-1]  6-27  **Process Costing in Process Industries**  Process costing is a good fit for companies in process industries in which costs are more easily traced to production departments than to individual products. The products are generally produced on a continuous, mass production basis. Process industries often involve the production of a commodity product, and the companies in these industries usually have a small number of relatively homogeneous products.

**Required**  Give some examples of companies that would use process costing, and explain why.

[LO 6-1, 6-2, 6-4]  6-28  **Equivalent Units; Weighted-Average Method**  Washington State Fisheries, Inc., processes salmon for various distributors. Two departments, processing and packaging, are involved. Data relating to tons of salmon sent to the processing department during May follow:

(Note: Many of the problems in this chapter require a series of calculations and rounding errors can affect totals unless each calculation is carried to a recommended four or more significant digits. An excellent way to avoid rounding errors is to use Excel to set up and solve these problems.)

|  | | Percent Completed | |
| --- | --- | --- | --- |
|  | Tons of Salmon | Materials | Conversion |
| Work-in-process inventory, May 1 | 1,000 | 80% | 70% |
| Work-in-process inventory, May 31 | 2,000 | 50 | 30 |
| Started processing during May | 7,000 | | |

**Required**
1. Calculate the number of tons completed and transferred out during the month.
2. Calculate the number of equivalent units for both materials and conversion for the month of May, assuming that the company uses the weighted-average method.

3. How would your answer in part 2 change if the percentage of completion in ending inventory were as follows: materials 30%, conversion 40%?

4. Explain briefly why process costing is appropriate in the fish processing industry.

**[LO 6-1, 6-3, 6-4, 6-5, 6-6, 6-8, 6-9]**

**6-29 Process Costing in Sugar Manufacturing** The food-processing industry, like most process industries, is a common user of process costing. Consider, for example, the sugar manufacturing industry. The processes in sugar manufacturing can differ depending on the agricultural product used to produce sugar. When sugar cane is used, the sequence of processes looks something like this:

**First: Cane shredding** The sugar cane is shredded into small pieces to facilitate its movement through the milling machine.

**Second: Milling** The shredded cane is crushed between the rollers in the milling machine to produce the cane juice.

**Third: Heating and adding lime** In this step, the cane juice is heated to concentrate the juice, and lime is added to reduce acidity.

**Fourth: Clarifying** Impure elements are removed from the juice.

**Fifth: Evaporating and separating** Here the juice is heated, vacuum is applied, and the liquid is centrifuged to remove the molasses and to produce what is called raw sugar.

**Sixth: Crystallizing** The raw sugar is melted and carbon-filtered to produce the refined sugar.

**Seventh: Drying** The refined sugar is dried and made ready for packaging.

Due to the nature of the seven processes, there is a relatively large amount of work-in-process inventory at any point in time. Also, sugar cane and raw sugar commodity prices can be stable for a period of time but there are periods of high volatility caused by, for example, India's mandate in 2007 to develop ethanol fuel; or the supply/demand imbalance in 1980 that sent prices up. Also, government price supports, import restrictions, and quotas affect the price of sugar cane. For example, as part of its development policy, the European Union (EU) in recent years paid above-market rates for sugar from a number of African, Caribbean, and Pacific countries, many of them former colonies of European countries.

**Required**

1. Are firms that produce sugar likely to incur transferred-in costs? Why or why not?

2. Should a sugar producer use the FIFO or the weighted-average method for the process cost report? Explain your answer.

3. Identify and explain any sustainability issues for the production of sugar.

4. Identify and interpret the significance of any global issues for the production of sugar.

**[LO 6-2, 6-4]**

**6-30 Equivalent Units; Weighted-Average Method** Northern Washington Lumber Company grows, harvests, and processes timber for use as building lumber. The following data pertain to the company's sawmill:

| | |
|---|---|
| Work-in-process inventory, January 1 (materials: 60% conversion: 40%) | 30,000 units |
| Work-in-process inventory, December 31 (materials: 70% conversion: 60%) | 15,000 units |

During the year the company started 180,000 units in production.

**Required** Prepare a physical flow schedule and compute the number of equivalent units of both direct materials and conversion for the year, using the weighted-average method.

**[LO 6-2, 6-4, 6-5]**

**6-31 Equivalent Units; Weighted-Average and FIFO Methods** Murray Chemical Company refines a variety of petrochemical products. These data are from the firm's Houston plant:

| | |
|---|---|
| Work-in-process inventory, September 1 | 4,000,000 gallons |
| Direct materials | 50% completed |
| Conversion | 20% completed |
| Units started in process during September | 4,850,000 gallons |
| Work-in-process inventory, September 30 | 2,400,000 gallons |
| Direct materials | 40% completed |
| Conversion | 60% completed |

**Required**    Compute the equivalent units of direct material and conversion for the month of September. Use both the weighted-average and the FIFO methods.

[LO 6-2, 6-4, 6-5]    6-32    **Equivalent Units; Weighted-Average and FIFO Methods**    Holly Company has the following information for December 1 to December 31. All direct materials are 100% complete.

| Work-in-Process | | |
|---|---|---|
| Beginning balance | | Completed 800 units and |
| December 200 units, | | transferred to finished |
| 20% complete | | goods inventory |
| for conversion | $14,000 | $140,000 |
| Direct materials | 54,000 | |
| Direct labor | 34,000 | |
| Factory overhead | | |
| Property taxes | 6,000 | |
| Depreciation | 32,000 | |
| Utilities | 18,000 | |
| Indirect labor | 4,000 | |
| Ending balance December 31, | | |
| 300 units, 40% complete | 22,000 | |

**Required**    Calculate equivalent units using the weighted-average and FIFO methods.

[LO 6-2, 6-3, 6-4]    6-33    **Equivalent Units; Weighted-Average Unit Cost**    Perrette Motor Company rebuilds automobile engines that have been damaged or are in need of extensive repair. The rebuilt engine has a 100,000-mile warranty and is purchased by auto shops, large motor pools in companies and governmental units, and some individual auto owners. The Dayton plant at Perrette specializes in the Ford V6 engine. Approximately 600 to 800 engines are rebuilt each month, and the costs of the plant are assigned to monthly production using weighted-average process costing. The current month began with a work-in-process inventory of 100 engines which were 50% complete for materials and 50% complete for conversion costs. The materials cost in beginning work-in-process was $50,000, while the conversion cost was $60,000. A total of 500 engines were completed and shipped out during the month, and total materials cost of $550,000 and conversion cost of $640,000 were incurred during the month. The ending work-in-process of 200 units was 50% complete for materials and 30% complete for conversion costs.

**Required**    Compute the cost per equivalent unit for materials and conversion for the month.

[LO 6-2, 6-3, 6-4, 6-5]    6-34    **Equivalent Units; Weighted-Average and FIFO Unit Cost**    Pablo Company calculates the cost for an equivalent unit of production using process costing.

| Data for June | |
|---|---|
| Work-in-process inventory, June 1: 30,000 units | |
| Direct materials: 100% complete | $ 60,000 |
| Conversion: 40% complete | 24,000 |
| Balance in work-in-process, June 1 | $ 84,000 |
| Units started during June | 70,000 |
| Units completed and transferred out | 70,000 |
| Work-in-process inventory, June 30 | 30,000 |
| Direct materials: 100% complete | |
| Conversion: 80% complete | |
| Cost incurred during June | |
| Direct materials | $120,000 |
| Conversion costs | |
| Direct labor | 120,000 |
| Applied overhead | 180,000 |
| Total conversion costs | $300,000 |

**Required**
1. Compute cost per equivalent unit for both the weighted-average and FIFO methods.
2. Explain the difference between the FIFO and weighted-average unit costs.

[LO 6-2, 6-3, 6-5]   6-35  **FIFO Method**   Taxes R Us (TRU), an income tax preparation firm, uses the FIFO method of process costing for the monthly reports. TRU has no materials cost in the preparation of the returns. The following shows its March information:

| | |
|---|---:|
| Returns in process, March 1 (30% complete) | 100 |
| Returns started in March | 1,600 |
| Returns in process, March 31 (90% complete) | 200 |
| Labor and overhead costs for returns in process, March 1 | $2,500 |
| Labor and overhead costs incurred in March | $173,250 |

**Required**   Calculate the following amounts for conversion costs using the FIFO method:
1. Equivalent units.
2. Cost per equivalent unit.
3. Cost of completed tax returns for the month of March.
4. Cost of tax returns in process as of March 31.

## Problems

[LO 6-2, 6-3, 6-4]   6-36  **Weighted-Average Method**   Gifford Inc. produces a single model of a popular cell phone in large quantities. A single cell phone moves through two departments, assembly and testing. The manufacturing costs in the assembly department during March follow:

| | |
|---|---:|
| Direct materials added | $187,500 |
| Conversion costs | 165,410 |
| | $352,910 |

The assembly department has no beginning work-in-process inventory. During the month, it started 25,000 cell phones, but only 22,000 were fully completed and transferred to the testing department. All parts had been made and placed in the remaining 3,000 cell phones, but only 60% of the conversion had been completed. The company uses the weighted-average method of process costing to accumulate product costs.

**Required**
1. Compute the equivalent units and cost per equivalent unit for March in the assembly department.
2. Compute the costs of units completed and transferred to the testing department.
3. Compute the costs of the ending work-in-process.

[LO 6-2, 6-3, 6-4]   6-37  **Weighted-Average Method**   Weatherly Lumber Company processes wood pulp for manufacturing various paper products. The company employs a process costing system for its manufacturing operations. All direct materials are added at the beginning of the process, and conversion costs are incurred uniformly throughout the process. This is the company's production schedule for May:

| | | Percent Completed | |
|---|---|---|---|
| | **Tons of Pulp** | **Materials** | **Conversion** |
| Work-in-process inventory, May 1 | 5,000 | 100% | 50% |
| Started during May | 15,000 | | |
| Units to account for | 20,000 | | |
| | | | |
| Units from beginning work-in-process, which were completed and transferred out during May | 5000 | | |
| Started and completed during May | 12,000 | | |
| Work-in-process inventory, May 31 | 3,000 | 100% | 50% |
| Total units accounted for | 20,000 | | |

The following cost data are available:

| | |
|---|---:|
| Work-in-process inventory, May 1 | |
| Direct materials | $ 94,000 |
| Conversion | 133,000 |
| Costs incurred during May | |
| Direct materials | 230,000 |
| Conversion | 376,000 |

**Required**

1. Calculate equivalent units of direct materials and conversion during May. Use the weighted-average method.
2. Calculate the cost per equivalent unit for both direct materials and conversion during May. Use the weighted-average method.

[LO 6-2, 6-3, 6-5]    6-38 **FIFO Method**    Refer to the information in Problem 6-37.

**Required**    Complete Problem 6-37 using the FIFO method.

[LO 6-2, 6-3, 6-4]    6-39 **Weighted-Average Method**    Cuevas Company manufactures a single product that goes through two processes, mixing and cooking. These data pertain to the mixing department for August:

| | |
|---|---:|
| Work-in-process inventory, August 1 | |
| Conversion: 80% complete | 33,000 units |
| Work-in-process inventory, August 31 | |
| Conversion: 40% complete | 27,000 units |
| Units started into production | 54,000 |
| Units completed and transferred out | ? |
| Costs | |
| Work-in-process inventory, August 1 | |
| Material X | $ 64,800 |
| Material Y | 89,100 |
| Conversion | 119,880 |
| Costs added during August | |
| Material X | 152,700 |
| Material Y | 135,900 |
| Conversion | 304,920 |

Material X is added at the beginning of work in the mixing department. Material Y is also added in the mixing department, but not until product units are 60% complete with regard to conversion. Conversion costs are incurred uniformly during the process. The company uses the weighted-average cost method.

**Required**

1. Calculate equivalent units of material X, material Y, and conversion for the mixing department.
2. Calculate costs per equivalent unit for material X, material Y, and conversion.
3. Calculate the cost of units transferred out.
4. Calculate the cost of ending work-in-process inventory.

[LO 6-2, 6-3, 6-4]    6-40 **Weighted-Average Method**    R. Chen Company manufactures a variety of natural fabrics for the clothing industry in a suburb of Shanghai. The following data in Chinese currency called *yuan* pertain to the month of October.

| | |
|---|---:|
| Work-in-process inventory, October 1 | 40,000 units |
| Direct materials: 60% complete | 57,000 yuan |
| Conversion: 30% complete | 45,000 yuan |
| Cost incurred during October | |
| Direct materials | 820,000 yuan |
| Conversion | 1,350,000 yuan |

During October, 180,000 units were completed and transferred out. At the end of the month, 30,000 units (direct materials 80% and conversion 40% complete) remain in work-in-process inventory.

**Required** Calculate each of the following amounts using weighted-average process costing.
1. Equivalent units of direct materials and conversion.
2. Unit costs of direct materials and conversion.
3. Cost of goods completed and transferred out during October.
4. Cost of the work-in-process inventory at October 31.
5. Check the most recent issue of *The Wall Street Journal* or go to **http://www.federalreserve.gov/releases/H10/hist/** to learn the exchange rate between the U.S. dollar and the Chinese yuan.

[LO 6-2, 6-3, 6-4, 6-6] **6-41 Weighted-Average Method; Transferred-in Costs** McCallum Tool Company has two departments, assembly and finishing. The assembly department takes purchased parts and assembles the final product. The finishing department performs testing and adds other materials and packages the product. Direct materials are added at the end of the process in the finishing department. The following summarizes the finishing department's operations for the month of July.

|  | Number of Units |
|---|---|
| Work-in-process, July 1, 50% complete for conversion costs | 4,000 |
| Transferred in during July | 28,000 |
| Completed during July | 27,000 |
| Work-in-process, July 31, 50% complete for conversion costs | 5,000 |

|  | Costs |
|---|---|
| Work-in-process, July 1 (transferred-in costs: $50,000; conversion costs: $30,000) | $ 80,000 |
| Transferred-in from assembly department during July | 150,000 |
| Direct materials added during July | 60,000 |
| Conversion added during July | 110,000 |
| Total to account for | $400,000 |

**Required** Calculate each of the following amounts for the finishing department using the weighted-average process costing method:
1. Equivalent units of transferred-in, direct materials, and conversion.
2. Unit costs of transferred-in, direct materials, and conversion.
3. Cost of goods completed and transferred out during July.
4. Cost of work-in-process inventory at July 31.

[LO 6-2, 6-3, 6-4] **6-42 Reconditioning Service; Weighted-Average Method** Golf World Inc. (GWI) sells products and services for the sport of golf. One of its key business units specializes in the repair and reconditioning of golf carts. GWI enters into contracts with a number of golf clubs throughout the U.S. in which the clubs send their carts to GWI for a complete recondition: motor, frame repair where necessary, and replacement of seat covers and canvas tops. The clubs usually will cycle 10–15% of their carts through this process each year. Because GWI's business has been growing steadily, it is very important to complete the reconditioning of the carts within a budgeted time and cost. The firm uses weighted-average process costing to keep track of the costs incurred in the reconditioning process.

GWI's golf cart repair and reconditioning unit has the following information for the month of November, in which 1,200 carts were started for reconditioning:

Beginning WIP: 150 units, 50% complete for materials ($15,000) and 30% complete for conversion ($20,000)

Current costs:
  Materials: $200,000
  Conversion: $385,000 (conversion costs for GWI usually average about $250 to $320 per unit, based on an average of 1,000–1,300 units completed each month)
Ending WIP: 300 units, 30% complete for materials and 20% complete for conversion

**Required**
1. Complete the cost report for the month of November.
2. GWI is scheduled to start another batch of 1,500 carts for reconditioning in December. Comment on the information the cost report contains regarding planning for December's work.

**[LO 6-2, 6-3, 6-4]**    6-43  **Weighted-Average Method**   Bellisario Company has a department that manufactures wood trusses (wood frames used in the construction industry). The following information is for the production of these trusses for the month of February:

| | |
|---|---|
| Work-in-process inventory, February 1 | 4,000 trusses |
| Direct materials cost: 100% complete | $100,000 |
| Conversion: 20% complete | $135,000 |
| Units started during February | 13,000 trusses |
| Units completed during February and transferred out | 12,000 trusses |
| Work-in-process inventory, February 29 | |
| Direct materials: 100% complete | |
| Conversion cost: 40% complete | |
| Costs incurred during February | |
| Direct materials | $ 44,500 |
| Conversion | $ 92,500 |

**Required**   Using the weighted-average method, calculate the following:

1. Costs per equivalent unit.

2. Cost of goods completed and transferred out.

3. Cost remaining in the ending work-in-process inventory.

4. Assume that you are the company's controller. The production department's February unit cost is higher than standard cost. If the manager of the first department asks you to do him a favor by increasing the ending inventory completion percentage from 40 to 60% to lower the unit costs, what should you do? How much would unit cost be affected by this request?

**[LO 6-2, 6-3, 6-5]**    6-44  **FIFO Method**   Refer to the information in problem 6-43.

**Required**   Repeat Problem 6-43 using the FIFO method.

**[LO 6-2, 6-3, 6-4, 6-6]**    6-45  **Weighted-Average Method; Transferred-in Costs**   Sanyo Corporation manufactures a popular model of business calculators in a suburb of Seoul, South Korea. The production process goes through two departments, assembly and testing. The following information (in thousands of South Korean currency, the *won*) pertains to the testing department for the month of July.

| | | |
|---|---|---|
| Work-in-process inventory, July 1 | | 6,000 units |
| Transferred-in costs | 57,800 won | (100% complete) |
| Costs added by the department | | |
| Direct materials | 23,400 won | (100% complete) |
| Conversion | 23,360 won | (80% complete) |

During the month of July, 15,000 units were transferred in from the assembly department at the cost of 141,700 won, and the testing department added costs of 201,820 won, as follows:

| | |
|---|---|
| Direct materials | 92,520 won |
| Conversion | 109,300 won |

During the month, 18,000 units were completed and transferred to the warehouse. At July 31, the completion percentage of work-in-process was as follows:

| | |
|---|---|
| Direct materials | 90% |
| Conversion | 60% |

**Required**

1. Prepare the production report of the testing department for the month of July using weighted-average process costing.

2. Check the most recent issue of *The Wall Street Journal* or **www.federalreserve.gov/releases/H10/hist/** to learn the exchange rate between the U.S. dollar and the South Korean won.

**[LO 6-2, 6-3, 6-5, 6-6]** 6-46 **FIFO Method; Two Departments** Bhatti Company produces plastic photo frames. Two departments, molding and finishing, are involved in the manufacturing. The molding department fills the molds with hot liquid plastic that is left to cool and then opens them. The finishing department removes the plastic frame from the mold and strips the edges of the frames of extra plastic.

The following information is available for the month of January:

| | January 1 | | January 31 | |
| Work-in-Process Inventory | Quantity (pounds) | Cost | Quantity (pounds) | Cost |
| --- | --- | --- | --- | --- |
| Molding department | None | — | None | — |
| Finishing department | 5,000 | $15,000 | 2,000 | ? |

The work-in-process inventory in the finishing department is estimated to be 40% complete for conversion both at the beginning and end of January. Costs of production for January follow:

| Costs of Production | Materials Used | Conversion |
| --- | --- | --- |
| Molding department | $450,000 | $90,000 |
| Finishing department | — | 80,000 |

The molding department started 50,000 pounds of product in January. The firm uses the FIFO method of process costing.

**Required** Prepare a report for both the molding and finishing departments for the month of January. The report should include equivalent units of production (in pounds), total manufacturing costs, cost per equivalent unit (pounds), cost of ending work-in-process inventory, and cost of goods completed and transferred out.

**[LO 6-2, 6-3, 6-4, 6-6]** 6-47 **Weighted-Average Method; Two Departments** Porter Company manufactures its one product by a process that requires two departments. The production starts in department A and is completed in department B. Materials are added at the beginning of the process in department A. Additional materials are added when the process is 50% complete in department B. Conversion costs are incurred proportionally throughout the production processes in both departments.

On April 1, department A had 500 units in work-in-process estimated to be 30% complete for conversion; department B had 300 units in work-in-process estimated to be 40% complete for conversion. During April, department A started 1,500 units and completed 1,600 units; department B completed 1,400 units. The work-in-process ending inventory on April 30 in department A is estimated to be 20% complete for conversion, and the work-in-process ending inventory in department B is estimated to be 70% complete for conversion.

The cost sheet for department A shows that the units in the work-in-process beginning inventory had $3,000 in direct materials costs and $1,530 in conversion costs. The production costs incurred in April were $12,000 for direct materials and $10,710 for conversion. Department B's work-in-process beginning inventory on April 1 was $6,100, of which $4,200 was transferred-in costs; it incurred $38,000 in direct materials costs and $24,350 in conversion costs in April.

Porter Company uses the weighted-average method for departments A and B.

**Required**
1. Prepare a production cost report for department A.
2. Prepare a production cost report for department B.

**[LO 6-2, 6-3, 6-4, 6-6, 6-9]** 6-48 **Weighted-Average Process Costing; Spoilage (Appendix)** Alexander Paint Company, which manufactures quality paint to sell at premium prices, uses a single production department. Production begins by blending the various chemicals that are added at the beginning of the process and ends by filling the paint cans. The gallon cans are then transferred to the shipping department for crating and shipment. Labor and overhead are added continuously throughout the process. Factory overhead is applied at the rate of $3 per direct labor dollar. The company combines labor and overhead in computing product cost.

Prior to May, when a change in the manufacturing process was implemented, work-in-process inventories were insignificant. The changed manufacturing process, which has resulted in increased equipment capacity, allows increased production but also results in considerable amounts of work-in-process inventory. Also, the company had 1,000 spoiled gallons in May—one-half of which was normal spoilage and the rest abnormal spoilage. The product is inspected at the end of the production process.

These data relate to actual production during the month of May:

| | Costs |
|---|---|
| Work-in-process inventory, May 1 | |
| Direct materials | $ 52,500 |
| Direct labor ($10 per hour) | 8,500 |
| May costs added: | |
| Direct materials | 332,500 |
| Direct labor ($10 per hour) | 38,500 |

| | Units |
|---|---|
| Work-in-process inventory, May 1 | |
| (30% complete) | 2,000 |
| Sent to shipping department | 25,500 |
| Started in May | 30,000 |
| Work-in-process inventory, May 31 | |
| (70% complete) | 5,500 |

**Required**

1. Prepare a production cost report for May using the weighted-average method.

2. Was the change in the manufacturing process to increase capacity an appropriate strategic move for the company? Why or why not?

3. How does the change in manufacturing process potentially affect the company's sustainability performance?

**(CMA Adapted)**

[LO 6-2, 6-3, 6-4, 6-6, 6-9]   6-49   **Spoilage; Weighted-Average Method; Transferred-in Costs (Appendix)**   APCO Company manufactures various lines of bicycles. Because of the high volume of each line, the company employs a process cost system using the weighted-average method to determine unit costs. Bicycle parts are manufactured in the molding department and then are consolidated into a single bike unit in the molding department and transferred to the assembly department where they are assembled. After assembly, the bicycle is sent to the packing department.

Annual cost and production figures for the assembly department are presented in the schedules that follow the requirements.

Defective bicycles are identified at the inspection point when the assembly labor process is 70% complete; all assembly materials have been added at this point. The normal rejection for defective bicycles is 5% of the bicycles reaching the inspection point. Any defective bicycles above the 5% quota are considered to be abnormal. All defective bikes are removed from the production process and destroyed.

**Required**

1. Compute the number of defective, or spoiled, bikes that are considered to be
   a. Normal.
   b. Abnormal.

2. Compute the equivalent units of production for the year for
   a. Bicycles transferred in from the molding department.
   b. Bicycles produced with regard to assembly material.
   c. Bicycles produced with regard to assembly conversion.

3. Compute the cost per equivalent unit for the fully assembled bike.

4. Compute the amount of the total production cost of $1,672,020 that will be associated with the following items:
   a. Normal spoiled units.
   b. Abnormal spoiled units.
   c. Good units completed in the assembly department.
   d. Ending work-in-process inventory in the assembly department.

5. Describe how to present the applicable dollar amounts for the following items in the financial statements:

a. Normal spoiled units.

b. Abnormal spoiled units.

c. Completed units transferred in to the packing department.

| | **Assembly Department Cost Data** | | | |
| --- | --- | --- | --- | --- |
| | **Transferred in from Molding Department** | **Assembly Materials** | **Assembly Conversion Cost** | **Total Cost of Bike through Assembly** |
| Prior period costs | $ 82,200 | $ 6,660 | $ 11,930 | $ 100,790 |
| Current period costs | 1,237,800 | 96,840 | 236,590 | 1,571,230 |
| Total costs | $1,320,000 | $103,500 | $248,520 | $1,672,020 |

| | **Assembly Department Production Data** | | | |
| --- | --- | --- | --- | --- |
| | | **Percentage Complete** | | |
| | **Bicycles** | **Transferred in** | **Assembly Materials** | **Assembly Conversion** |
| Beginning inventory | 3,000 | 100% | 100% | 80% |
| Transferred in from molding during year | 45,000 | 100 | — | — |
| Transferred out to packing during year | 40,000 | 100 | 100 | 100 |
| Ending inventory | 4,000 | 100 | 50 | 20 |

**(CMA Adapted)**

[LO 6-2, 6-3, 6-4, 6-6, 6-8]  6-50  **Process Costing and Activity-Based Costing**  Hampton Chemical Specialties, Inc. (HCS) is a manufacturer of specialty chemicals sold to manufacturers, hospitals, and other users. HCS produces 10 to 15 million gallons of its main product HCS-22 each month. The data for July follows (in thousands of gallons). The chemical raw materials are added at the beginning of processing.

| | |
| --- | --- |
| Beginning work-in-process inventory (60% complete for conversion; materials $55,000, conversion $7,250) | 200 gallons |
| Units started | 1,000 gallons |
| Good units finished (no spoilage) | 800 gallons |
| Ending work-in-process inventory (30% complete for conversion) | 400 gallons |

| Current manufacturing costs | |
| --- | --- |
| Materials | $176,000 |
| Conversion | 66,900 |

Each month HCS averages 100 batches of product with approximately 12,000 gallons per batch, though some batches are as large as 50,000 gallons or more, and some are as small as a few hundred gallons. Also, the pattern of customer orders is that large orders come in at all times of the month, while small orders tend to cluster around the last few days of the month. The small orders are due to salespersons trying to meet monthly sales quotas and the buying patterns of smaller customers who want their shipments early in the following month. As a result, in the average month three-fourths of the total orders are started in the last few days of the month, and most are not completed until early in the following month. For example, in July, 100 batches were produced, and 75 were still in the ending work-in-process inventory at the end of the month. Ted Brown, plant controller for HCS, thinks that the current costing method, using weighted-average process costing, underestimates the cost of the ending work-in-process inventory as well as the cost of smaller jobs.

**Required**

1. Prepare the production cost report using the weighted-average method.

2. Assume that $28,500 of the $66,900 current conversion costs could be traced to batch-related activities such as equipment setup. Further, assume that these batch-related costs are all incurred when the batch is started. Ted has asked you to recalculate the production cost report to separate the batch-related costs from total conversion costs. How do the results differ from the method in requirement 1? Is Ted right about underestimating the cost of ending work-in-process inventory?

[LO 6-2, 6-3, 6-5]   6-51   **FIFO Method and Rising Prices**   Healthy Selections Cereals Inc. (HSC) is a large food-processing company specializing in whole-grain, high-energy, low-calorie, and low-fat cereals that appeal to the health-conscious consumer. HSC has a premium image in the market and most of its customers are loyal and willing to pay a bit extra to get the healthy choice that HSC offers. HSC's cereals are made in a series of processes which begin with sorting, cleaning, preparing, and inspecting the raw materials (grains, nuts, and other ingredients). The materials are then mixed and processed for consistency, cooked, given a final inspection, and packaged. Raw materials are added only at the beginning of the first process. The inspections in the first and final processes are made at the end of those respective processes, so all materials and conversion costs are lost for waste detected at the inspection point. The company uses weighted-average process costing and accounts for all waste as normal spoilage.

Currently commodity prices are rising sharply, affecting the costs of many of the ingredients in HSC's products. The CFO, noting the sharp rise in the cost of the company's raw materials (the ingredients for its products), has considered using the FIFO method.

The following data are for the first process for the current month. All output is measured in pounds.

| | |
|---|---|
| Beginning work-in-process | 14,000 pounds, 25% complete for conversion |
| Ending work-in-process | 12,000 pounds, 40% complete for conversion |
| Normal spoilage | 1,000 pounds |
| Pounds added this month | 33,000 pounds |

The cost information for the first process is as follows:

| | Materials | Conversion | Total |
|---|---|---|---|
| Beginning WIP | $ 3,500 | $ 3,400 | $ 6,900 |
| Current costs | 66,000 | 104,000 | 170,000 |

**Required**

1. Calculate a process cost report for the first process using the weighted-average method.

2. Calculate a process cost report for the first process using the FIFO method.

3. Explain which of the two methods you would recommend to the CFO, considering the firm's competitive environment.

[LO 6-2, 6-3, 6-4]   6-52   **Weighted-Average Method; Two Departments**   Benoit Chemical Company (BCC) produces a variety of specialty chemicals used in the pharmaceutical industry and construction industry. BCC spends almost 20% of its net revenues on research, product development, and customer development to achieve its reputation as a high-quality producer of chemicals, a reliable supplier, and a great provider of customer service. BCC has a small number of large customers, each of which typically has one or more large orders being processed at BCC at any given point in time. These orders are typically completed over one to three months or longer. BCC uses job costing to keep track of total job costs over the duration of each order and process costing to keep track of monthly costs, department by department. The processing departments include mixing, reacting (in which chemicals are heated and sometimes vacuum is applied), cleaning, inspecting, packaging, and distribution. Much of the total product cost is accumulated in the first two processes, mixing and reacting. The following information is for activity and costs in the first two departments during the current month.

The mixing department started 74,000 gallons this month. No spoilage is measured in the mixing department, but a careful measure of the loss of material in reacting is taken after the completion of the reacting process. No materials are added in the reacting process. The number of gallons lost (spoilage) is considered normal spoilage and is considered to have lost the full cost of processing up to that point of inspection. BCC uses the weighted-average method for process costing.

Work-in-process for the two departments is as follows. Percentage completion for conversion costs is 60% in the mixing department for both beginning and ending inventory. The percentage completion for conversion costs for the reacting department for beginning and ending inventory is 30% and 40%, respectively.

| | Mixing Department (gallons) | Reacting Department (gallons) |
|---|---|---|
| Beginning work-in-process units | 28,000 | 16,500 |
| Ending work-in-process units | 26,000 | 18,250 |
| Normal spoilage (lost gallons) | 0 | 2,250 |

Costs in the mixing department:

| | Materials | Conversion |
|---|---|---|
| Beginning work-in-process | $ 56,480 | $282,400 |
| Current costs | 288,500 | 989,400 |

Transferred-in beginning work-in-process costs are $242,150 and conversion costs in the reacting department are as follows:

| | Conversion |
|---|---|
| Beginning work-in-process | $ 412,510 |
| Current costs | 1,245,320 |
| | $1,657,830 |

**Required**

1. Prepare the production cost report for the mixing department.
2. Prepare the production cost report for the reacting department.
3. What comments and observations do you have about the two departments' cost reports?
4. What is Benoit's competitive strategy, based on Michael Porter's framework? Explain whether or not you think the company's costing system supports this strategy.

[LO 6-8] 6-53 **Backflush Costing** Grand Marine Inc. (GMI) manufactures sailcloth used by sailmakers that produce sails for sailboats. GMI's sailcloth is the conventional polyester-based sail material and is used widely in recreational boating. Sailmakers throughout the world use GMI's sailcloth. The manufacture of sailcloth has a small number of processes, and GMI integrates them carefully so that there is very little work-in-process inventory. The product is measured in yards of cloth, which is prepared in rolls 42 inches wide. Because it has little work-in-process inventory, GMI also uses backflush accounting to simplify the accounting for its operations. GMI has the following information for the most recent accounting period. The beginning inventory of polyester fiber was $142,000 and the ending inventory was $147,000.

| | |
|---|---|
| Polyester fiber purchased | $690,000 |
| Conversion cost incurred | $1,300,000 |
| Direct materials standard cost | $4.35 per yard of cloth |
| Conversion standard cost | $8.50 per yard of cloth |
| Units produced | 155,000 yards of cloth |

**Required**

1. Show the entries for manufacturing costs, completion of 155,000 yards of product, and the closing entries.
2. Under what conditions is backflush costing used in practice?

## Solutions to Self-Study Problems

### 1. Weighted-Average Method versus FIFO Method

1. Weighted-average method

   a. Equivalent units

     Direct materials: $1,000 + (200 \times 100\%)$          1,200

     Conversion: $1,000 + (200 \times 70\%)$          1,140

   b. Cost per equivalent unit

     Direct materials: ($9,600/1,200)          $8.00

     Conversion: ($2,202 + $6,120)/1,140          $7.30

     Total unit costs: $8.00 + $7.30          $15.30

   c. Cost of goods completed and transferred out:      $15.30 \times 1,000$      $15,300

   d. Cost of work-in-process, 10/31

     Direct materials: $8 \times 200 \times 100\%$          $1,600

     Conversion: $7.30 \times 200 \times 70\%$          $1,022

     Total: $1,600 + $1,022          $2,622

2. Weighted-average method production cost report

**SMITH ELECTRONIC COMPANY**
**Chip-Mounting Production Department**
**Weighted-Average Production Cost Report**

### Production Quantity Information

| | Step 1: Analyze Flow of Physical Units | | Step 2: Calculate Equivalent Units | |
| --- | --- | --- | --- | --- |
| | **Physical Units** | **Completion Percentage** | **Direct Materials** | **Conversion Costs** |
| **Input** | | | | |
| Work-in-process beginning inventory | 300 | | | |
| Completion percentage | | | | |
| Direct materials | | 0% | | |
| Conversion | | 40% | | |
| Started this period | 900 | | | |
| Total to account for | 1,200 | | | |
| **Output** | | | | |
| Completed | 1,000 | 100% | 1,000 | 1,000 |
| Work-in-process ending inventory | 200 | | | |
| Completion percentage | | | | |
| Direct materials | | 100% | 200 | |
| Conversion | | 70% | | 140 |
| Total accounted for | 1,200 | | | |
| Total work done to date (Total equivalent units) | | | 1,200 | 1,140 |

### Unit Cost Determination

| Step 3: Determine Costs to Account for | Total Direct Materials | Conversion Costs | Total |
| --- | --- | --- | --- |
| Work-in-process beginning inventory | | $2,202 | $ 2,202 |
| Current cost | $9,600 | $6,120 | 15,720 |
| Total costs to account for | $9,600 | $8,322 | $17,922 |

### Step 4: Compute Unit Costs

| | Total Direct Materials | Conversion Costs | Total |
| --- | --- | --- | --- |
| Cost per equivalent unit | ($9,600/1,200) = $ 8.00 | ($8,322/1,140) = $ 7.30 | $ 15.30 |

*(Continued)*

**Cost Assignment**

| Step 5: Assign Total Manufacturing Costs | Completed and Transferred out | Ending Work-in-Process | Total |
|---|---|---|---|
| Units completed and transferred out (1,000 × $15.30) | $15,300 | | $15,300 |
| Ending work-in-process (200) | | | |
| Materials (200 × $8) | | $1,600 | 1,600 |
| Conversion (140 × $7.30) | — | 1,022 | 1,022 |
| Total costs accounted for | $15,300 | $2,622 | $17,922 |

3. FIFO method

   a. Equivalent units:

| | |
|---|---|
| Direct materials: (300 × 100%) + (1,000 − 300) + (200 × 100%) | 1,200 |
| or 1,000 + (200 × 100%) − (300 × 0%) | 1,200 |
| Conversion: [300 × (1 − 40%)] + (1,000 − 300) + (200 × 70%) | 1,020 |
| or 1,000 + (200 × 70%) − (300 × 40%) | 1,020 |

   b. Cost per equivalent unit

| | |
|---|---|
| Direct materials: $9,600/1,200 | $ 8 |
| Conversion: $6,120/1,020 | $ 6 |
| Total unit costs | $14 |

   c. Cost of goods completed and transferred out

     From beginning work-in-process inventory:

| | |
|---|---|
| Direct materials: $0 + $8 × 300 × (1 − 0%) | $ 2,400 |
| Conversion: $2,202 + $6 × 300 × (1 − 40%) | $ 3,282 |
| Total | $ 5,682 |
| Started and completed: $14 × (1,000 − 300) | $ 9,800 |
| Total cost of goods completed: $5,682 + $9,800 | $15,482 |

   d. Cost of work in process, 10/31

| | |
|---|---|
| Direct materials: $8 × 200 × 100% | $1,600 |
| Conversion: $6 × 200 × 70% | $ 840 |
| Total | $2,440 |

4. FIFO method production cost report

---

**SMITH ELECTRONIC COMPANY**
**Chip-Mounting Production Department**
**FIFO Production Cost Report**

---

**Production Quantity Information**

---

| | Step 1: Analyze Flow of Physical Units | Step 2: Calculate Equivalent Units | |
|---|---|---|---|
| | Physical Units | Direct Materials | Conversion Costs |
| Input | | | |
| Work-in-process beginning inventory | 300 | | |
| Completion percentage | | | |
| Direct materials 0% | | 0 | |
| Conversion 40% | | | 120 |
| Started this period | 900 | | |
| Total units to account for | 1,200 | | |

*(Continued)*

Output
|  | | | |
|---|---|---|---|
| Completed | 1,000 | 1,000 | 1,000 |
| Work-in-process ending inventory | 200 | | |
| Completion percentage Direct materials 100% | | 200 | |
| Conversion 70% | | | 140 |
| Total units accounted for | 1,200 | 1,200 | 1,140 |

Total work performed to date
Work-in-process

|  | | | |
|---|---|---|---|
| beginning inventory | 300 | 0 | (120) |
| Total work performed this period | | 1,200 | 1,020 |

(FIFO equivalent units)

### Unit Cost Determination

| **Step 3: Determine Total Costs to Account for Flow** | **Direct Materials** | **Conversion Costs** | **Total** |
|---|---|---|---|
| Work-in-process beginning inventory | | $2,202 | $ 2,202 |
| Current cost | $9,600 | 6,120 | 15,720 |
| Total costs to account for | $9,600 | $8,322 | $17,922 |

| **Step 4: Compute Unit Costs** | ($9,600/1,200) = | ($6,120/1,020) = | |
|---|---|---|---|
| Cost per equivalent unit | $8 | $6 | $14 |

### Cost Assignment

| **Step 5: Assign Total Manufacturing Costs** | **Completed and Transferred out** | **Ending Work-in-Process** | **Total** |
|---|---|---|---|
| Units completed and transferred out (1,000) | | | |
| Beginning work-in-process | $ 2,202 | | $ 2,202 |
| Current cost to complete | | | |
| Materials (300 × $8) | 2,400 | | 2,400 |
| Conversion (180 × $6) | 1,080 | | 1,080 |
| Total from beginning work-in-process | $ 5,682 | | $ 5,682 |
| Units started and finished (700 × $14) | 9,800 | | 9,800 |
| Total cost completed and transferred out | $15,482 | | $15,482 |
| Ending work-in-process (2,000) | | | |
| Materials (200 × $8) | | $1,600 | 1,600 |
| Conversion (140 × $6) | — | 840 | 840 |
| Total costs accounted for | $15,482 | $2,440 | $17,922 |

### 2. Weighted-Average Method vs. FIFO Method with Transferred-In Cost

1. Weighted-average method

---

**REED COMPANY**
**Finishing Department**
**Weighted-Average Production Cost Report**

---

#### Production Quantity Information

| | Step 1: Analyze Flow of Physical Units | | Step 2: Calculate Equivalent Units | |
|---|---|---|---|---|
| | **Physical Units** | **Transferred in** | **Direct Materials** | **Conversion Costs** |
| Input | | | | |
| Work-in-process, November 1 | 10 (40%) | | | |
| Started this month | 80 | | | |
| Total units to account for | 90 | | | |
| Output | | | | |
| Completed | 82 | 82 | 82 | 82 |
| Work-in-process, November 30 | 8 (50%) | 8 | 8 | 4 |
| Total accounted for | 90 | | | |
| Total work done to date | | | | |
| (Total equivalent units) | | 90 | 90 | 86 |

#### Unit Cost Determination

| Step 3: Determine Total Costs to Account for | Transferred in | Direct Materials | Conversion Costs | Total |
|---|---|---|---|---|
| Work-in-process, November 1 | $100 | $ 80 | $ 52 | $ 232 |
| Current costs | 800 | 720 | 861 | 2,381 |
| Total costs to account for | $900 | $800 | $913 | $2,613 |
| **Step 4: Compute Unit Costs** | ($900/90) = | ($800/90) = | ($913/86) = | |
| Cost per unit | $10.00 | $8.89 | $10.62 | $29.51 |

#### Cost Assignment

| Step 5: Assign Total Manufacturing Costs | Completed and Transferred out | Ending Work-in-Process | Total |
|---|---|---|---|
| Units completed and transferred out (82 × $29.51) | $2,420 | | $2,420 |
| Ending work-in-process (8) | | | |
| Transferred-in (8 × $10) | | $80 | 80 |
| Materials (8 × $8.89) | | 71 | 71 |
| Conversion (4 × $10.62) | | 42 | 42 |
| Total costs accounted for | $2,420 | $193 | $2,613 |

2. FIFO method

**REED COMPANY**
**Finishing Department**
**FIFO Production Cost Report**

### Production Quantity Information

| | Step 1: Analyze Flow of Physical Units | | Step 2: Calculate Equivalent Units | |
| --- | --- | --- | --- | --- |
| | Physical Units | Transferred in | Direct Materials | Conversion Costs |
| **Input** | | | | |
| Work-in-process, November 1 | 10 (40%) | | | |
| Started this month | 80 | | | |
| Total units to account for | 90 | | | |
| **Output** | | | | |
| Completed | 82 | 82 | 82 | 82 |
| Work-in-process, November 30 | 8 (50%) | 8 | 8 | 4 |
| Total accounted for | 90 | | | |
| Total work done to date | | 90 | 90 | 86 |
| Work-in-process, November 1 | | (10) | (10) | (4) |
| Total work done this month— FIFO equivalent units | | 80 | 80 | 82 |

### Unit Cost Determination

| Step 3: Determine Total Costs to Account for | Transferred in | Direct Materials | Conversion Costs | Total |
| --- | --- | --- | --- | --- |
| Work-in-process, November 1 | | | | $ 232 |
| Current costs | $800 | $720 | $861 | 2,381 |
| Total costs to account for | | | | $2,613 |

| Step 4: Compute Unit Costs | ($800/80) = | ($720/80) = | ($861/82) = | |
| --- | --- | --- | --- | --- |
| Cost per unit | $10.00 | $9.00 | $10.50 | $29.50 |

### Cost Assignment

| Step 5: Assign Total Manufacturing Costs | Completed and Transferred out | Ending Work-in-Process | Total |
| --- | --- | --- | --- |
| Units completed and transferred out (82) | | | |
| Beginning work-in-process | $232 | | $232 |
| Current cost to complete conversion (6 × $10.50) | 63 | | 63 |
| Total from beginning work-in-process | $295 | | $295 |
| Units started & finished (72 × $ 29.50) | 2,124 | | 2,124 |
| Total cost completed and transferred out | $2,419 | | $2,419 |
| Ending work-in-process (8) | | | |
| Transferred-in (8 × $10) | | $ 80 | 80 |
| Materials (8 × $9) | | 72 | 72 |
| Conversion (4 × 10.50) | — | 42 | 42 |
| Total costs accounted for | $2,419 | $194 | $2,613 |

*Please visit **http://www.mhhe.com/blocher6e** to access a narrated, animated tutorial for solving these problems.*

# CHAPTER SEVEN

# Cost Allocation: Departments, Joint Products, and By-Products

**After studying this chapter, you should be able to . . .**

LO 7-1    Identify the strategic role and objectives of cost allocation

LO 7-2    Explain the ethical issues of cost allocation

LO 7-3    Use the three steps of departmental cost allocation

LO 7-4    Explain the implementation issues of the different departmental cost allocation methods

LO 7-5    Explain the use of cost allocation in service firms

LO 7-6    Use the three joint product costing methods

LO 7-7    Use the four by-product costing methods (appendix)

In keeping with their firms' mission of continual improvement in their products and services, General Electric (GE) and many other firms such as Ford Motor Company, Johnson & Johnson, IBM, and Marriott have sought improved methods of providing administrative services within their firms. These administrative services are often called *shared services* because they are shared among the company's operating units. Shared services generally include such transaction-processing services as payroll processing, claims processing, human resources, and many accounting services, among others. The firms above have studied the cost to provide the services and have been alarmed at the relatively high costs, such as $10 or more to process a single vendor invoice. Some firms have chosen to outsource these services or to have the operating units provide the services locally, but, like GE, most firms are centralizing these services to reduce cost, provide a high and standardized level of service quality, and provide a single base of technology for easy use, communication, and future modification.

With the growth of these centralized services, the need for effective methods to allocate the shared costs to the operating units has increased. Generally, the allocation issue arises when cost is shared because of a shared facility, program, production process, or service. The methods used to allocate these common costs to products are explained in this chapter.

This chapter explains methods for allocating common costs to products for two broad types of common costs: (1) the costs of production and service departments shared by two or more individual products and (2) the joint manufacturing costs for products that are not separately identifiable until later in the manufacturing process. An example of the latter is the cost of refining crude oil (the joint cost) into the individual products: gasoline, heating oil, and other products.

We take a strategic perspective in developing these allocation methods and ask key strategic questions. How do the allocation methods we have chosen affect the motivations and behaviors of those in the operating units as well as the service units? Can we use ABC costing principles to develop more accurate methods of cost allocation? Does this service add value or should it be outsourced? The firm's answers to these questions can have a significant impact on its competitiveness and success.

Recording artists Courtney Love, LeAnn Rimes, Clint Black, and others have sued the music industry for millions of dollars of unpaid royalties. The artists claim that the music industry unfairly cut into their royalties by improperly accounting for expenses. At issue lies the often complex recording contracts between the artists and the music companies that contain the details of how the expenses of producing and distributing the artist's work are to be calculated and charged to the artist's account. The artists think they are being cheated, while an industry spokesperson says that the contracts reflect a "complex business relationship where both the artists and the label understandably angle to secure the best possible contract—in negotiations or renegotiations—while still preserving a mutually beneficial relationship." In other words, both sides should be well represented by management accountants who understand how the costs are to be calculated and allocated.

**Source:** David Byrne, "David Byrne's Survival Strategies for Emerging Artists and Megastars," *Wired Magazine*, December 18, 2007; Jennifer Ordonez, "Rockers vs. Bean Counters," *The Wall Street Journal*, September 24, 2002, p. B1.

## The Strategic Role and Objectives of Cost Allocation

The strategic role of cost allocation has four objectives:

1. Determine *accurate departmental and product costs* as a basis for the evaluation of the cost efficiency of departments and the profitability of different products, for financial reporting, and for tax compliance.
2. *Motivate* managers to exert a high level of effort to achieve the goals of top management.
3. Provide the right *incentive* for managers to make decisions that are consistent with the goals of top management.
4. *Fairly determine the rewards* earned by the managers for their effort and skill and for the effectiveness of their decision making.

**LO 7-1**

*Identify the strategic role and objectives of cost allocation.*

The first and most important objective requires the cost allocation method to be sufficiently accurate to support effective management decision making about products and departments. The cost allocation methods must also comply with the financial reporting standards of FASB (and ultimately, the International Financial Reporting Standards of the International Accounting Standards Board, as the SEC moves to convergence of U.S. and international standards) and the Internal Revenue Service. The management accountant recognizes that the desired cost allocation method might differ for the three objectives: cost management, financial reporting, and tax compliance.

The second objective, motivating managers, means that, to be effective, the cost allocation must reward department managers for reducing costs as desired. A key motivation issue is whether the manager *controls* the allocated cost. For example, when a department's cost allocation for equipment maintenance is based on the number of the department's machine breakdowns, the manager has an incentive to reduce breakdowns and therefore reduce the maintenance costs. On the other hand, when the cost of maintenance is allocated on the basis of a department's square feet of floor space, the manager—who cannot affect the amount of floor space—is not motivated.

The third objective, providing the incentive for decision making, is achieved when cost allocation effectively provides the incentives for the individual manager to act autonomously in a manner that is consistent with top management's goals. For example, a major advantage of cost allocation methods is that they draw managers' attention to shared facilities. The cost allocation provides an incentive for individual and joint efforts to manage these costs and to encourage the managers to use these facilities to improve the performance of their units.

The fourth objective, fairness, is met when the cost allocation is clear, objective, and consistently applied. The most objective basis for cost allocation exists when a *cause-and-effect relationship* can be determined. For example, the allocation of maintenance costs on the basis of the number of equipment breakdowns is more objective and fair than an allocation based on square feet, the number of products produced, or labor costs in the department.

The reason is that a cause-and-effect relationship exists between maintenance costs and the number of breakdowns; square feet or labor costs, however, do not have a clear relationship to maintenance costs.

In some situations, cause-and-effect bases are not available and alternative concepts of fairness are used. One such concept is *ability-to-bear,* which is commonly employed with bases related to size, such as total sales, total assets, or the profitability of the user departments. Other concepts of fairness are based on equity perceived in the circumstance, such as *benefit received,* which often is measured in a nonquantitative way. For example, the cost of a firm's computer services might be allocated largely or entirely to the research and development department because the computer is more critical to this department's functioning and this department uses it more than other departments.

## The Ethical Issues of Cost Allocation

**LO 7-2**

*Explain the ethical issues of cost allocation.*

A number of ethical issues are important in cost allocation. First, ethical issues arise when costs are allocated to products or services that are produced for both a competitive market and a public agency or government department. Although government agencies very often purchase on a cost-plus basis, products sold competitively are subject to price competition. The incentive in these situations is for the manufacturer, using cost allocation methods, to shift manufacturing costs from the competitive products to the cost-plus products.

A second ethical issue in implementing cost allocation methods is the equity or fair share issue that arises when a governmental unit reimburses the costs of a private institution or when it provides a service for a fee to the public. In both cases, cost allocation methods are used to determine the proper price or reimbursement amount. Although no single measure of equity exists in these cases, the objectives of cost allocation identified at the beginning of the chapter are a useful guide.

A third important ethical issue is the effect of the chosen allocation method on the costs of products sold to or from foreign subsidiaries. The cost allocation method usually affects the cost of products traded internationally and therefore the amount of taxes paid in the domestic and the foreign countries. Firms can reduce their worldwide tax liability by increasing the costs of products purchased in high-tax countries or in countries where the firm does not have favorable tax treatment. For this reason, international tax authorities closely watch the cost allocation methods used by multinational firms. The methods most acceptable to these authorities are based on sales and/or labor costs.[1]

## Cost Allocation to Service and Production Departments

**LO 7-3**

*Use the three steps of departmental cost allocation.*

The preceding chapters on job costing (Chapter 4), activity-based costing (Chapter 5), and process costing (Chapter 6) provide a useful context for introducing cost allocation. Chapter 4 illustrated how overhead costs could be allocated to products in a single step, using a single overhead pool and single overhead rate in what we called the volume-based approach. Chapter 4 then showed an enhancement of the volume-based approach in which overhead was allocated to products in two steps, first to departments and then to products, in what we called the departmental approach. The departmental approach is an improvement over the single-step, volume-based approach because it takes into account differences in costs incurred in the different departments and differences in consumption of the departments' resources by the products, thus leading to more accurate product costs.

The activity-based approach, explained in Chapter 5, follows a two-step approach like the departmental approach, with the difference that it assigns costs at a much more detailed level—that of the operating activity rather than the department. Because of the greater level of detail, the activity-based approach captures more accurately the usage of resources by the different products; therefore it provides more accurate product costs.

[1] See Joanna Faith, "Transfer Pricing Helps Tax Avoidance, Says GAO Study," *International Tax Review,* September 2008; "Comparison of Tax Liabilities of Foreign- and U.S-Controlled Corporations, 1998–2005," United States Government Accountability Office (GAO), July 2008, at: **www.gao.gov/products/GAO-08-957**. Taxation issues in transfer pricing are covered in Chapter 19.

**EXHIBIT 7.1**
**Three Types of Overhead Allocation**

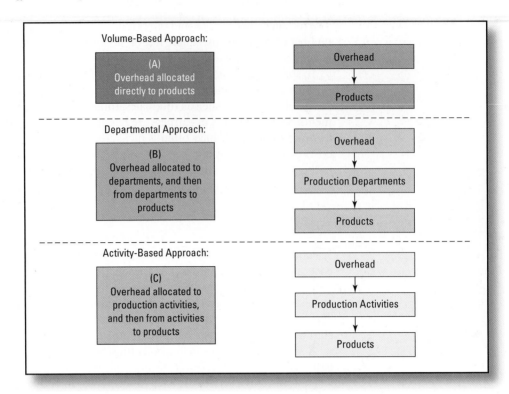

Because of the increased accuracy, the activity-based approach is generally preferred. However, the activity-based approach is not preferred in all situations, such as those in which the company has homogeneous products and processes. Then the departmental approach is preferred because it is simpler, less costly, and produces results comparable to the activity-based approach. Also, there are some organizations that are required by law or regulation to use the departmental approach for cost reporting and cost reimbursement; a health care provider affected by the U.S. Medicare law is one such example. The three types of overhead allocation are illustrated in Exhibit 7.1.

The departmental allocation approach recognizes that the typical manufacturing operation involves two types of manufacturing departments: production departments and service departments. Service departments provide human resources, maintenance, engineering, and other support to the production departments; production departments directly assemble and complete the product. The departmental allocation approach has three phases: (1) trace all direct manufacturing costs and allocate manufacturing overhead costs to both the service departments and the production departments, (2) allocate the service department costs to the production departments, and finally (3) allocate the production department costs to the products.

Direct manufacturing costs are wages and materials that can be directly traced to a department; for example, direct materials and direct labor costs would be traced to the production departments where they are used. Direct labor and materials used in a service department would be traced to that service department. Indirect costs (manufacturing overhead) are the indirect materials and indirect labor costs that are allocated by means of a predetermined cost driver to the departments that use those resources. For example, the indirect labor cost of the plant supervisor who oversees all production and support departments would be allocated to all departments, while the indirect labor for inspection of the output of the two production departments would be allocated only to those two production departments.

The cost drivers commonly used include labor-hours, machine-hours, head count (number of personnel in the department), and square feet of space in the department, among others. For example, the cost of the plant supervisor might be allocated to all departments based on the proportion of total labor-hours in the departments. The cost of the inspection in the production departments might be allocated based on the number of units of output in those two departments. In practice, a variety of cost drivers are used; the goal is to use a cost driver such that the cost allocation reflects the usage of the resource in the departments.

The three phases are illustrated in Exhibit 7.2.

**EXHIBIT 7.2**  **The Three Phases in Departmental Cost Allocation**

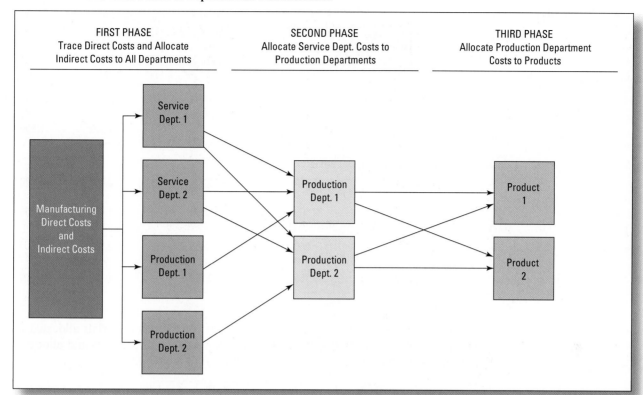

## First Phase: Trace Direct Costs and Allocate Indirect Costs to All Departments

The first phase in the departmental allocation approach traces the direct costs and allocates the indirect manufacturing costs in the plant to each service and production department.

For the first-phase allocation, see the information for Beary Company in Exhibit 7.3. Beary manufactures two products and has two manufacturing departments and two service departments. As shown in Exhibit 7.3, $36,000 direct cost can be traced to each department, and an indirect cost of $30,000 ($25,000 labor and $5,000 materials) is common to all departments but cannot be traced directly to each department. Beary uses labor-hours for allocating indirect labor cost and machine-hours for allocating indirect materials cost.

The first-phase allocation for Beary Company is shown in Exhibit 7.4. Total direct costs of $36,000 are traced to the four departments, and the overhead costs are allocated using labor-hours (for indirect labor) and machine-hours (for indirect materials). The exhibit presents the allocation base for labor-hour and machine-hour usage as a percent of total usage. The $25,000 of indirect labor is allocated to the four departments using the labor-hours allocation base. For example, the amount of indirect labor allocated to service department 1 is $3,750 (service department 1's share of total indirect labor, or 15% × $25,000). The allocations of indirect labor costs to the other departments are made in the same way. Similarly, the $5,000 of indirect materials cost is allocated to the

**EXHIBIT 7.3**
**Data for Beary Company**

| | Service Department 1 | Service Department 2 | Production Department 1 | Production Department 2 | Total Hours | Total Amount |
|---|---|---|---|---|---|---|
| Labor-hours | 1,800 | 1,200 | 3,600 | 5,400 | 12,000 | |
| Machine-hours | 320 | 160 | 1,120 | 1,600 | 3,200 | |
| Direct costs | $1,600 | $5,500 | $15,500 | $13,400 | | $36,000 |
| Indirect labor | | Not traceable | | | | 25,000 |
| Indirect materials | | Not traceable | | | | 5,000 |
| | | | | | | $66,000 |

**EXHIBIT 7.4   Departmental Allocation, First Phase: Beary Company**

| Departmental Allocation Bases | All Departments | | | | |
| --- | --- | --- | --- | --- | --- |
| | Service Department 1 | Service Department 2 | Production Department 1 | Production Department 2 | Total |
| Direct labor-hours | 1,800 | 1,200 | 3,600 | 5,400 | 12,000 |
| Percent | 15% | 10% | 30% | 45% | 100% |
| Machine-hours | 320 | 160 | 1,120 | 1,600 | 3,200 |
| Percent | 10% | 5% | 35% | 50% | 100% |
| **First Phase: Trace Direct Costs and Allocate Indirect Costs to All Departments** | | | | | |
| Direct costs | $1,600 | $5,500 | $15,500 | $13,400 | $36,000 |
| Allocate indirect costs to departments: | | | | | |
| Indirect labor | 3,750 | 2,500 | 7,500 | 11,250 | 25,000 |
| | = 15% × $25,000 | = 10% × $25,000 | = 30% × $25,000 | = 45% × $25,000 | |
| Indirect materials | 500 | 250 | 1,750 | 2,500 | 5,000 |
| | = 10% × $5,000 | = 5% × $5,000 | = 35% × $5,000 | = 50% × $5,000 | |
| Totals for all departments | **$5,850** | **$8,250** | **$24,750** | **$27,150** | **$66,000** |

four departments using machine-hours. The amount of indirect materials allocated to service department 1 is $500 (10% × $5,000). The totals for direct costs and allocated indirect costs are $66,000, the same as total cost from Exhibit 7.3.

| | |
| --- | --- |
| Service department 1 | $ 5,850 |
| Service department 2 | 8,250 |
| Production department 1 | 24,750 |
| Production department 2 | 27,150 |
| Total | $66,000 |

## Allocation Phases Two and Three

The second phase allocates service department costs to the producing departments. This is the most complex of the allocation phases because services can flow back and forth between the service departments. These are often called **reciprocal flows.** For example, assume that 40% (720 hours) of service department 1's 1,800 labor-hours are spent serving service department 2. Also assume that 10% of service department 2's time is spent serving service department 1. You can see these two reciprocal flows for Beary Company in Exhibit 7.5.

**Reciprocal flows** represent the flow of services back and forth between service departments.

The percentage of service relationships is commonly determined by reference to labor-hours, units processed, or some other allocation base that best reflects the service provided in the departments. At Beary Company, the service flow percentages for each service department are determined according to the labor-hours used for services provided to the other service department and to the production departments. Beary's first service department spends 40% of its labor time serving service department 2 and 30% serving each of the two production departments. Service department 2 serves service department 1 10% of the time, the first production department 30% of the time, and the second production department 60% of the time.

Accountants can choose among three common methods to allocate costs for the second phase: (1) the direct method, (2) the step method, and (3) the reciprocal method.

**EXHIBIT 7.5**
**Reciprocal Relationships in Beary Company**

| From | To | | | |
| --- | --- | --- | --- | --- |
| | Service Department 1 | Service Department 2 | Production Department 1 | Production Department 2 |
| Service Department 1 | — | 40% | 30% | 30% |
| Service Department 2 | 10% | — | 30 | 60 |

### The Direct Method

The **direct method**
of departmental cost allocation
is accomplished by using the
service flows *only to production
departments* and determining
each production department's
share of that service.

The **direct method** of departmental cost allocation is the simplest of the three methods because it ignores the reciprocal flows. The cost allocation is accomplished by using the service flows *only to production departments* and determining each production department's share of that service. For example, for service department 1, the share of time for each production department is 50% of the total production department service, determined as follows (frp, Exhibit 7.5).

For service department 1:

---

Net service to both production departments from service department 1:
  30% + 30% = 60%
Production department 1's share: 30%/60% = <u>50%</u>
Production department 2's share: 30%/60% = <u>50%</u>

---

For service department 2 (note that we use 4 significant digits after the decimal in order to reduce rounding error):

---

Net service to both production departments from service department 2:
  30% + 60% = 90%
Production department 1's share: 30%/90% = <u>33.3333%</u>
Production department 2's share: 60%/90% = <u>66.6667%</u>

---

These percentage shares are used to allocate the costs from service departments to production departments, as shown in the second-phase section at the top of Exhibit 7.6. In that

---

**EXHIBIT 7.6**  **Departmental Allocation Second and Third Phases, Using the Direct Method: Beary Company**

**Second Phase: Allocate Service Department Costs to Production Departments**

| Direct Method | | Production 1 Department | Production 2 Department | Total |
|---|---|---|---|---|
| Service Department 1 | Service % to producing dept. | 30% | 30% | |
| | Allocation % per direct method | 50% = 30/(30 + 30) | 50% = 30/(30 + 30) | |
| | Allocation amount | **$2,925** | **$2,925** | **$ 5,850** |
| | | = 50% × $5,850 | = 50% × $5,850 | |
| Service Department 2 | Service % to producing dept. | 30% | 60% | |
| | Allocation % per direct method | 33.3333% = 30/(30 + 60) | 66.6667% = 60/(30 + 60) | |
| | Allocation amount | **2,750** | **5,500** | **8,250** |
| | | = 33.3333% × $8,250 | = 66.6667% × $8,250 | |
| Plus: First-phase allocation | | 24,750 | 27,150 | 51,900 |
| Totals for production departments | | **$30,425** | **$35,575** | **$66,000** |

**Third Phase: Allocate Production Department Costs to Products**

| 1. Allocation Base | Product 1 | Product 2 | |
|---|---|---|---|
| Base: labor-hours | | | |
|   Hours | 1,800 | 1,800 | 3,600 |
|   Percent | 50% | 50% | |
| Machine-hours | | | |
|   Hours | 400 | 1,200 | 1,600 |
|   Percent | 25% | 75% | |

| 2. Cost Allocation to Products | Product 1 | Product 2 | |
|---|---|---|---|
| Production Department 1 (labor-hours basis) | **$15,212.50** | **$15,212.50** | |
| | = 50% × $30,425 | = 50% × $30,425 | |
| Production Department 2 (machine-hours basis) | **8,893.75** | **26,681.25** | |
| | = 25% × $35,575 | = 75% × $35,575 | |
| Totals for each product | **$24,106.25** | **$41,893.75** | **$66,000** |

## COST ALLOCATION AND MEDICARE REIMBURSEMENT IN HOSPITALS

A recent study of 105 hospitals found evidence of bias in their cost allocation practices. Since 1983, Medicare has reimbursed hospitals for inpatient services on the basis of specific, prospective rates and for outpatient services on the basis of cost. This reimbursement plan motivates hospitals to allocate as much common cost as possible to outpatient departments instead of inpatient services. A study examined the ratio of cost allocated to outpatient departments relative to total allocated cost for the period 1977 to 1991. Using regression analysis and data for each hospital, the study found a significant upward shift in costs allocated to outpatient departments after 1983.

This cost shifting has apparently continued for 30 years. A recent study by the U.S. Chamber of Commerce estimates that Medicare reimburses approximately 78% of the hospital's costs in providing patient care. In contrast, a recent study by an independent organization, the Medicare Payment Advisory Committee, showed that the rates charged by hospitals to private patients were influenced largely by competition in the industry, including the decline in the early 2000s of the managed-care industry, after which the hospitals had more leverage in obtaining higher reimbursement rates from private insurers.

## COST DRIVERS USED IN HOSPITAL COST ALLOCATION FOR MEDICARE

Some examples of cost drivers used for allocating services to outputs in hospitals for the purpose of Medicare reimbursement include:

| Cost Element | Cost Driver |
| --- | --- |
| Buildings and fixtures | Square footage |
| Equipment | Square footage |
| Maintenance and repairs | Square footage |
| Housekeeping | Square footage |
| Employee benefits | Salaries |
| Nursing administration | Nursing salaries |
| Laundry and linen | Patient days |
| Dietary | Patient days |

## DETERMINING THE COST OF HEALTH CARE PROCEDURES

A recent report by Cooper and Kramer shows that a common method used by providers of health care (hospitals, nursing homes, etc.) to calculate the cost of procedures (electrocardiogram, echocardiogram, cardiovascular stress test, etc.) based on revenue is equivalent to a method that produces equal profit margin for each procedure and each provider. The method is hailed as a useful way to determine cost information for making decisions, while it is simply a variation on the simple revenue-based methods once more commonly used, and thus does not actually provide the accurate cost information needed for decision making. ABC costing is one method that would provide more accurate cost information, but a recent study found that the rate of adoption of ABC in the health care industry has fallen from 16% in 1994 to 14% in 2004, and the rate of adoption in hospitals has fallen from 21% to 8% in the same period.

Based on information in: James Sasseen and Catherine Arnst, "Why Business Fears the Public Option," *BusinessWeek,* October 12, 2009, pp. 26–27; "Cost Report for Electronic Filing of Hospitals," Centers for Medicare and Medicaid (CMS) Services, May 1, 2005, pp. 36–75 at CMS.gov; Leslie Eldenburg and Sanjay Kallapur, "Changes in Hospital Service Mix and Cost Allocations in Response to Changes in Medicare Reimbursement Schemes," *Journal of Accounting and Economics,* May 1997, pp. 31–51; Robin Cooper and Theresa R. Kramer, "RBRVS Costing: The Inaccurate Wolf in Expensive Sheep's Clothing," *Journal of Health Care Finance,* Spring 2008, pp. 6–18; Robert M. Dowless, "What's the Procedure? Your Guide to Costing Methods and Terminology," *Nursing Management,* April 2007, pp. 52–56.

panel, for example, $5,850 of service department 1's costs are allocated equally to the production departments, so that each production department is responsible for $2,925, or 50%, of the costs. The $8,250 of service department 2's costs are allocated as follows: 33.3333% or $2,750 to production department 1 and 66.6667% or $5,500 to production department 2. Total costs in production departments 1 and 2 at the end of the second phase allocations are $30,425 and $35,575, respectively.

The third and final phase is much like the first phase. The allocation from production departments to products typically is based on the number of labor-hours or machine-hours used in the production departments that produce the products. For Beary Company, using the direct method, costs are allocated to production department 1 on the basis of labor-hours and to production department 2 on the basis of machine-hours; see the third-phase panel of Exhibit 7.6. Assume that the production of product 1 requires 1,800 hours of production and that department 1's total labor time is 3,600 hours; thus product 1 is allocated 50% (1,800/3,600) of the total cost in production department 1. Similarly, assume that product 1 requires 400 of the 1,600 machine-hours used in production department 2, and thus is allocated 25% (400/1,600) of the costs of production department 2. Product 2's costs are determined in a similar manner, as shown in Exhibit 7.6. The total cost of $66,000 is allocated as $24,106.25 to product 1 and $41,893.75 to product 2.

### *The Step Method*

The **step method**

uses a sequence of steps in allocating service department costs to production departments.

The second method to allocate service department costs is the **step method,** so-called because it uses a sequence of steps in allocating service department costs to production departments. In the first step, one service department is selected to be allocated fully, that is, to the other service department as well as to each production department. The department to be allocated first usually is chosen because it provides the most service to other service departments. At Beary Company, service department 1 provides more service (40%) and it goes first in the allocation. Service department 2 is allocated only to the production departments, in the same manner as the direct method. Overall, this means that the step method may provide more accurate allocations because one of the reciprocal flows between the two service departments (the one in the first step) is considered in the allocation, unlike the direct method, which ignores all reciprocal flows.

The first phase of the step method (tracing direct costs and initial allocation of indirect costs) is the same as for the direct method as shown in Exhibit 7.4. However, in the second phase (Exhibit 7.7), service department 1, which is in the first step, is allocated to service department 2 and the two production departments. The allocation to service department 2

**EXHIBIT 7.7**   **Departmental Allocation, Second and Third Phases, Using the Step Method**

| Second Phase: Allocate Service Department Costs to Production Departments: Using the Step Method | | | | |
|---|---|---|---|---|
| | Service Department 2 | Production Department 1 | Production Department 2 | Total |
| **First Step** | | | | |
| Service Department 1 | | | | |
|   Service percent | 40% | 30% | 30% | |
|   Amount | $2,340 | $ 1,755 | $ 1,755 | $ 5,850 |
| | = 40% × $5,850 | = 30% × $5,850 | = 30% × $5,850 | |
| **Second Step** | | | | |
| Service Department 2 | | | | |
|   Service percent | | 30% | 60% | |
|   Allocation percent per direct method | | 33.3333 | 66.6667 | |
|   Amount | 10,590 | 3,530 | 7,060 | 8,250 |
| | = $8,250 + $2,340 | = 33.3333% × $10,590 | = 66.6667% × $10,590 | (= 3,530 |
| | | | | + 7,060 − 2,340) |
| Plus: First-phase allocation | | 24,750 | 27,150 | 51,900 |
| Totals for production departments | | $30,035 | $35,965 | $66,000 |
| **Third Phase: Allocate Production Department Costs to Products** | | | | |
| **1. Allocation Base** | | Product 1 | Product 2 | |
| Labor-hours | | | | |
|   Hours | | 1,800 | 1,800 | 3,600 |
|   Percentage | | 50% | 50% | |
| Machine-hours | | | | |
|   Hours | | 400 | 1,200 | 1,600 |
|   Percentage | | 25% | 75% | |
| **2. Cost Allocation to Products** | | | | |
| Production Department 1 (labor-hours basis) | | $ 15,017.50 | $15,017.50 | |
| | | = 50% × $30,035 | = 50% × $30,035 | |
| Production Department 2 (machine-hours basis) | | 8,991.25 | 26,973.75 | |
| | | = 25% × $35,965 | = 75% × $35,965 | |
| Totals for each product | | $ 24,008.75 | $41,991.25 | $66,000 |

Since the advent of Medicare in 1966 to cover medical expenses of aged, blind, and disabled individuals, health care providers have been required to use cost allocation methods to receive reimbursement from the federal government for services covered by Medicare. The costs of health care service activities are allocated to the patient revenue-generating services. Some examples of service activities and patient revenue-generating services in a hospital are shown on the right.

Which of the three allocation methods (direct, step, or reciprocal) would you recommend a hospital use in determining its cost of revenue-generating services for Medicare purposes? Explain your choice briefly.

(Refer to Comments on Cost Management in Action at the end of the chapter.)

**Patient Revenue-Generating Services**

| | |
|---|---|
| Intensive care unit | Laboratory |
| Psychiatric care | Radiology |
| Coronary care | Emergency room |
| Surgery | Pharmacy |
| Anesthesia | |

**Service Activities**

| | |
|---|---|
| Dietary | Operation of hospital |
| Laundry and linen | Administrative and general |
| Admissions | Housekeeping |
| Social services | |
| Nursing administration | |

is $2,340 (40% × $5,850). The allocations for the two production departments are determined in a similar manner. Then, in the second step, service department 2 is allocated to the two production departments in the same manner as the direct method in Exhibit 7.6. The only difference is that the total cost in service department 2 ($10,590) now includes the original cost in service department 2 ($8,250) plus the cost allocated from service department 1 in the first step ($2,340).

The third phase of the step method is completed in the same manner as in Exhibit 7.6. Using the step method, the total cost allocated to product 1 is $24,008.75 and the total cost allocated to product 2 is $41,991.25, for a total of $66,000.

### The Reciprocal Method

The **reciprocal method** considers *all* reciprocal flows between service departments through simultaneous equations.

The **reciprocal method** is the preferred of the three methods because, unlike the others, it considers *all* reciprocal flows between the service departments. This is accomplished by using simultaneous equations; the reciprocal flows are simultaneously determined in a system of equations.

An equation for each service department represents the cost to be allocated, consisting of the first-phase allocation costs plus the cost allocated from the other department. For Beary Company, the equation for service department 1 is as follows, using the symbol S1 to represent service department 1 costs and the symbol S2 to represent costs in service department 2.

**Allocated S1 Costs = Initial allocation + Cost allocated from S2**

$$S1 = \$5,850 = (10\% \times S2)$$

Similarly, the equation for the second service department is as follows:

**Allocated S2 Costs = Initial allocation + Cost allocated from S1**

$$S2 = \$8,250 + (40\% \times S1)$$

These two equations can be solved for S1 and S2 by substituting the second equation into the first as follows:

$$S1 = \$5,850 + 10\% \times [\$8,250 + (40\% \times S1)]$$

$$S1 = \$6,953.13$$

And substituting S1 back into the second equation:

$$S2 = \$11,031.25$$

These values for S1 and S2 are allocated to the producing departments using the percentage service amounts for each department. We illustrate the process for Beary Company

**EXHIBIT 7.8**   **Departmental Allocation Second and Third Phases, Using the Reciprocal Method**

**Second Phase: Allocate Service Department Costs to Production Departments Using the Reciprocal Method**

First: Solve the simultaneous equations for Service Department 1 and Service Department 2 (see text):

| | | | | |
|---|---|---|---|---|
| Amount allocated from service department 1 | $ 6,953.13 | | | |
| Amount allocated from service department 2 | $11,031.25 | | | |

| | Production Department 1 | Production Department 2 | Total |
|---|---|---|---|
| **Second: Allocate to producing departments** | | | |
| **Service Department 1** | | | |
| Service % | 30% | 30% | |
| Allocated amount | **$2,086** | **$2,086** | **$ 4,172** |
| | = 30% × $6,953 | = 30% × $6,953 | |
| **Service Department 2** | | | |
| Service % | 30% | 60% | |
| Allocated amount | **3,309** | **6,619** | **9,928** |
| | = 30% × $11,031 | = 60% × $11,031 | |
| Plus: Costs allocated in first phase | 24,750 | 27,150 | 51,900 |
| Totals for production departments | **$30,145** | **$35,855** | **$66,000** |

**Third Phase: Allocate Production Department Costs to Products**

| **1. Allocation Base** | Product 1 | Product 2 | |
|---|---|---|---|
| Base: Direct labor-hours | | | |
| Hours | 1,800 | 1,800 | 3,600 |
| Percent | 50% | 50% | |
| Machine-hours | | | |
| Hours | 400 | 1,200 | 1,600 |
| Percent | 25% | 75% | |

| **2. Cost Allocation to Products** | | | |
|---|---|---|---|
| Production Department 1 (direct labor-hours basis) | **$15,072.50** | **$15,072.50** | |
| | = 50% × $30,145 | = 50% × $30,145 | |
| Production Department 2 (machine-hours basis) | 8,963.75 | 26,891.25 | |
| | = 25% × $35,855 | = 75% × $35,855 | |
| Totals for each product | **$24,036.25** | **$41,963.75** | **$66,000** |

in Exhibit 7.8. Note that since the reciprocal method has considered all reciprocal service department activities, the allocation in the second phase is based on the actual service percentages for each production department. For example, production department 1, which receives 30% of service department 1's work, is allocated 30% of service department 1's cost, $2,086 (30% × $6,953.13). The allocation of service department 2's costs to production departments is done in a similar manner.

A simple and accurate way to calculate the reciprocal costs for S1 and S2 is to use the Solver function in Excel. Exhibit 7.9 illustrates how to use Solver for this purpose.

The third phase analysis in Exhibit 7.8 is done in the same manner as in Exhibits 7.6 and 7.7. The total cost allocated to product 1 is $24,036.25 and for product 2, $41,963.75.

## Implementation Issues

**LO 7-4**

*Explain the implementation issues of the different departmental cost allocation methods.*

The key implementation issue is the choice of the most accurate allocation method. Briefly review Exhibits 7.6, 7.7, and 7.8. Note that although total costs are the same ($66,000), the amounts allocated to the two products vary. Although these amounts do not vary greatly for Beary Company, wide variations can occur in practice. When significant differences exist, a management accountant should consider the value of the reciprocal method, which is more complete and accurate than the others because it fully considers the reciprocal flows between service departments.

**EXHIBIT 7.9** Solving for the Reciprocal Allocation Method Using the Solver Function in Microsoft Excel

Solving reciprocal departmental allocation problems can become tedious if three or more departments are involved. In this case, we suggest the use of software programs such as the Solver tool in Excel. The following screen capture illustrates how the Solver tool can be used to solve the Beary Company example in the text. The column for "Allocated Cost" in the spreadsheet contains the cost in each service department, while the columns for "Service Rates to" contain the reciprocal service rates. The column for "Initial Allocation to" contains the product of the "Allocated Cost" and "Service Rates" columns, using cell-based formulas. Cells E7 and F7 contain the formula-based sums of these columns. After

selecting "Solver" from the Data menu, the dialog box in Exhibit 7.9 panel A appears and must be completed as shown. For example, the Target Cell (E7) must be set to a value of $5,850 (the cost of the first service department). Make sure to select the "Value of" button. Also, the "changing cells" are B5:B6; the three constraints are: B5 > or = 0, B6 > or = 0, and F7 = 8250. Then, select "Solving Method" as GRG Nonlinear. When the dialog box is complete, select Solve, and the solution will appear in cells B5 and B6 (overwriting the amounts originally entered in the Allocated Cost column). The solution is $6,953.13 in cell B5 and $11,031.25 in cell B6. The solution is shown in panel B.

**Panel A: Solver Dialog Box**

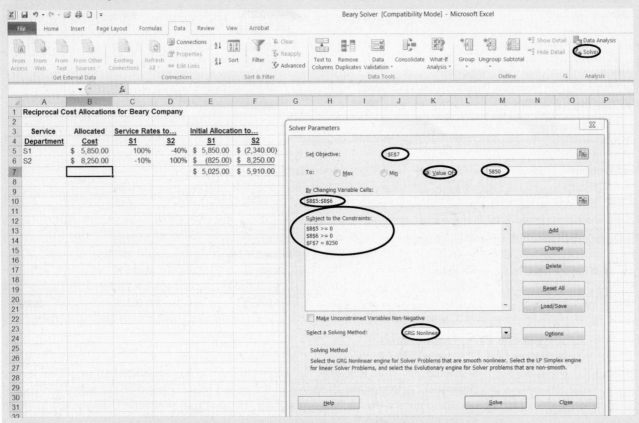

**Panel B: Solver Solution for Beary Example**

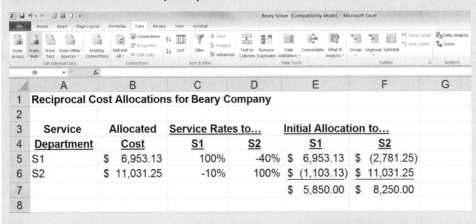

**EXHIBIT 7.10** **Disincentive Effects When the Allocation Base Is Unrelated to Usage**

| | Department A | Department B | Total Maintenance Cost |
|---|---|---|---|
| **Panel 1:** Basic information | | | |
| Square feet of floor space | 5,000 | 5,000 | |
| Average number of maintenance requests | 50 | 50 | |
| Total maintenance costs | | | $200,000 |
| **Panel 2:** Maintenance cost allocation in an average month using square feet of floor space or number of requests: | | | |
| Allocated maintenance cost | $100,000 | $100,000 | $200,000 |
| **Panel 3:** Here we consider maintenance cost allocation based on square feet for a month when department A increases usage of maintenance from 50 to 80 maintenance requests, while department B's usage remains the same at 50 requests. For simplicity, assume that maintenance costs are variable with the number of maintenance requests, or $2,000 per request [$200,000/(50 + 50)], so that total maintenance costs increase to $260,000 [$2,000 × (50 + 80)]. The allocation based on square feet and number of requests is compared below: | | | |
| Number of maintenance requests | 80 | 50 | |
| Allocation of maintenance costs based on square feet | $130,000 | $130,000 | $260,000 |
| Allocated maintenance cost based on number of maintenance requests | $2,000 × 80 = $160,000 | $2,000 × 50 = $100,000 | $260,000 |

Three additional issues to consider when implementing the departmental allocation approach are (1) disincentive effects when the allocation base is unrelated to usage, (2) disincentive effects when the allocation base is actual usage, and (3) disincentive effects when allocated costs exceed external purchase cost.

### Disincentive Effects When the Allocation Base Is Unrelated to Usage

Determining an appropriate allocation base and a percentage amount for service provided by the service departments is often difficult. For example, using labor-hours could be inappropriate in an automated plant where labor is a small part of total cost. Similarly, square feet of floor space could be inappropriate to allocate certain costs when a great deal of idle space exists. Furthermore, the use of square feet of floor space can have undesirable motivational consequences. For example, if we are allocating plantwide maintenance costs to production departments using floor space as a base, a department has inadequate incentive to limit its use of maintenance expense. Since the actual use of maintenance is unrelated to floor space, if a given department increases its use of maintenance, then the other departments pay for the increase as well, as illustrated in Exhibit 7.10. Here, department A increases its use of maintenance from 50 to 80 maintenance requests (panel 3 in Exhibit 7.10), while department B's usage stays the same. The effect of department A's increased usage (when allocation is based on square feet) is that department B pays one-half of the increased cost ($60,000), which is likely to be perceived as unfair and therefore a disincentive for department B. In contrast, using the number of requests as a base allocates to department A the full cost of its increased usage of maintenance ($60,000), while department B's allocated cost remains the same.

### Disincentive Effects When the Allocation Base Is Actual Usage

When the cost allocation base is determined from actual usage, disincentives can arise because the usage of the resource by one department will affect the cost allocation to other departments, as illustrated in Exhibit 7.11. We continue with the same example as Exhibit 7.10 except we now assume that the cost to be allocated is made up of $100,000 fixed cost and $1,000 variable cost per maintenance request. Panel 2 shows that the amount of cost allocated will be the same for both departments if the usage is the same. Panels 3 and 4 illustrate

**EXHIBIT 7.11** **Disincentive Effects When the Allocation Base Is Actual Usage**

| | Department A | Department B | Total Maintenance Cost |
|---|---|---|---|
| **Panel 1:** Basic information | | | |
| Actual number of maintenance requests | 50 | 50 | |
| Total maintenance costs | | | $200,000 |

**Panel 2:** Assume that maintenance costs are $100,000 fixed cost and $1,000 variable costs per request. The allocation base is $2,000 per request; $100,000 + (50 + 50) × $1,000 = $200,000; $200,000/100 = $2,000 per request

| | Department A | Department B | Total Maintenance Cost |
|---|---|---|---|
| Allocated maintenance cost: | $100,000 | $100,000 | |
| | = $2,000 × 50 | = $2,000 × 50 | $200,000 |

**Panel 3:** Department A increases its usage to 80 requests, while department B continues to use 50 requests. Now total maintenance costs = $100,000 fixed cost plus $1,000 × 130 requests = $230,000; $230,000/130 = $1,769.23 per request

| | Department A | Department B | Total Maintenance Cost |
|---|---|---|---|
| Allocated maintenance cost based on requests: | $1,769.23 × 80 | $1,769.23 × 50 | |
| | = $141,538 | = $88,462 | $230,000 |

The outcome is that, while department B has not changed its usage of maintenance, its allocated costs have decreased; and department A's allocation has increased, but not at the rate of the increase in number of requests. Department B benefits from the fact that increased usage of maintenance reduces the per-request charge from $2,000 to $1,769.23—variable costs are the same per request, but the $100,000 fixed cost is allocated over more requests. The result may not be satisfying to department A, which sees department B benefit from department A's increased usage.

**Panel 4:** Similar to Panel 3, except that department A **reduces** its usage of maintenance to 30 requests. Now total maintenance costs = $100,000 + $1,000 × (30 + 50) = $180,000; $180,000/80 = $2,250 per request

| | Department A | Department B | Total Maintenance Cost |
|---|---|---|---|
| Allocated maintenance costs based on requests: | $2,250 × 30 | $2,250 × 50 | |
| | = $67,500 | = $112,500 | $180,000 |

The outcome is that, while department B has not changed its usage of maintenance, its allocated costs have increased; and department A's allocation has decreased, but not at the rate of the decrease in number of requests. Department B suffers from the fact that decreased usage of maintenance in department A increases the per-request charge from $2,000 to $2,250. While department B has not changed its usage, its cost increases because of department A's decreased usage.

how the cost allocation changes if the usage of one of the departments changes. If the usage in department A increases (Panel 3) while department B's usage remains the same, then department B has an unexpected reduction in allocated cost from $100,000 to $88,462. The reason is that the fixed costs per maintenance request are now smaller due to the increase in total maintenance requests. Department A is unlikely to see this allocation as fair. In contrast, Panel 4 shows the outcome if department A reduces it usage of maintenance, while department B again maintains the same level of usage. Now department B's allocated cost increases from $100,000 to $112,500. The increase is due to the fact that fixed cost per maintenance request is now larger due to the overall reduction in maintenance requests. Now department B is unlikely to see that the allocation is fair.

**Dual allocation**

separates fixed and variable costs and traces variable costs to the departments based on actual usage; fixed costs are allocated based on either equal share among departments or a predetermined budgeted proportion.

*Dual Allocation*    The disincentives illustrated in Exhibit 7.11 can be resolved by using dual allocation. **Dual allocation** separates fixed and variable costs and traces variable costs to the departments based on actual usage; fixed costs are allocated based on either equal share among departments or a predetermined budgeted proportion. Exhibit 7.12 illustrates how dual allocation works. Again, Panels 1 and 2 follow the example from Exhibit 7.11. Panel 3 illustrates dual allocation in which fixed costs are equally shared among the departments. The reason for the equal-share approach is that each department pays in effect a fee for the right to receive future services from the maintenance department, irrespective of the amount of service to be used. This concept is similar to the minimum monthly charge on a checking account at the bank or a cell phone. Note that the effect of separating the fixed and variable costs is that department A pays for its increased usage, measured at variable cost, and department B's allocated cost does not change—a result that is likely to be satisfactory to both departments.

**EXHIBIT 7.12**   **Dual Allocation**

| | Department A | Department B | Total Maintenance Cost |
|---|---|---|---|
| **Panel 1:** Basic information | | | |
| Actual number of maintenance requests | 50 | 50 | |
| Total maintenance costs | | | $200,000 |
| **Panel 2:** Assume that maintenance costs are mixed; $100,000 fixed and $1,000 variable per request. The allocation base is $2,000 per request; $100,000 + (50 + 50) × $1,000 = $200,000; $200,000/100 = $2,000 per request. | | | |
| Allocated maintenance cost: | $100,000 | $100,000 | $200,000 |
| | = $2,000 × 50 | = $2,000 × 50 | |
| **Panel 3 (Dual allocation; fixed costs shared equally):** Department A increases its usage to 80 requests, while department B continues to use 50 requests. Now total maintenance costs = $100,000 fixed cost plus $1,000 × 130 requests = $230,000. This method allocates fixed costs equally between the departments and variable cost based on usage. | | | |
| Allocated maintenance cost: | $50,000 + ($1,000 × 80) | $50,000 + ($1,000 × 50) | $230,000 |
| | = $130,000 | = $100,000 | |
| The outcome is that department B's cost has not changed and department A's increase is in proportion to its increased usage. The result should be satisfying to both department A and department B. | | | |
| **Panel 4: (Dual allocation; budget-based allocation of fixed costs)** Assume, as in Panel 3 above, that department A increases its usage to 80 requests, while department B continues to use 50 requests. Now total maintenance costs = $100,000 fixed cost plus $1,000 × 130 requests = $230,000. Budget-based allocation uses a predetermined budgeted amount of usage to allocate the fixed costs; in this example we budget 60 requests for department A and 40 requests for department B. Thus, fixed costs are allocated $60,000 to department A and $40,000 to department B. | | | |
| Allocated maintenance cost: | $60,000 + ($1,000 × 80) | $40,000 + ($1,000 × 50) | $230,000 |
| | = $140,000 | = $90,000 | |
| This outcome could be preferred to that of Panel 3 above, if the actual usage of the department were to fluctuate from period to period, but the long-term average usage of the resources by department A and department B is 60% and 40%, respectively. | | | |

Panel 4 of Exhibit 7.12 illustrates the dual allocation method when fixed costs are allocated on the basis of a predetermined budget. This approach is used when usage differs significantly between departments and over time; the rationale is that the allocation of fixed costs should reflect the long-term average usage by each department. In this example, we assume that the long-term rate of usage is 60% for department A and 40% for department B.

### *Disincentive Effects When Allocated Costs Exceed External Purchase Cost*

Another limitation of the three departmental allocation methods is that sometimes they can allocate a higher cost for the service than the department would pay were it to purchase the service from an outside supplier. Should the department pay more for a service internally than an outside vendor would charge? To motivate managers to be efficient and for fairness, the allocation should be based on the cost of obtaining the service outside the firm. Consider the data in Exhibit 7.13 for a firm with four departments that share a common data processing service costing $1,000. Data processing costs are allocated using direct labor-hours in each department as shown in columns (B), (C), and (D) of Exhibit 7.13. The data processing service can also be obtained from an outside firm at the cost shown in column (E).

The direct labor-hours allocation base in this example penalizes department D, which can obtain the service outside the firm for $80 less than the inside cost ($200 − $120), perhaps because of the simplified nature of the requirements in department D. In contrast, department B can obtain the service outside only at a much higher price ($600 versus $400 inside), perhaps because of the specialized nature of the service. In this case, the allocation based on the *outside price* (column G in Exhibit 7.13) is fair to both departments B and D. It is a better reflection of the competitive cost of the service. The question of whether, and under what conditions, the department should be allowed to purchase outside the firm is a different issue, which is addressed in the coverage of management control in Chapters 18 and 19.

**EXHIBIT 7.13** Cost Allocation Using External Prices

| (A)<br>User<br>Department | (B)<br>Direct<br>Labor-Hours | (C)<br>Direct<br>Labor-Hours<br>Allocation Base | (D)<br>Cost Allocation<br>Based on<br>Labor-Hours | (E)<br>Outside<br>Price | (F)<br>Allocation Base<br>for Outside<br>Price | (G)<br>Allocation Based<br>on Outside<br>Price |
|---|---|---|---|---|---|---|
| A | 3,000 | 30%<br>(3,000/10,000) | $ 300<br>(30% × $1,000) | $ 360 | 30%<br>(360/1,200) | $ 300<br>(30% × $1,000) |
| B | 4,000 | 40%<br>(4,000/10,000) | 400<br>(40% × $1,000) | 600 | 50%<br>(600/1,200) | 500<br>(50% × $1,000) |
| C | 1,000 | 10%<br>(1,000/10,000) | 100<br>(10% × $1,000) | 120 | 10%<br>(120/1,200) | 100<br>(10% × $1,000) |
| D | 2,000 | 20%<br>(2,000/10,000) | 200<br>(20% × $1,000) | 120 | 10%<br>(120/1,200) | 100<br>(10% × $1,000) |
| Total | 10,000 | | $1,000 | $1,200 | | $1,000 |

## Cost Allocation in Service Industries

**LO 7-5**

*Explain the use of cost allocation in service firms.*

The concepts presented in this chapter apply equally well to manufacturing, service, or not-for-profit organizations that incur joint costs. For example, financial institutions such as commercial banks also use cost allocation. To illustrate, we use the Community General Bank (CGB), which provides a variety of banking services, including deposit accounts, mortgage loans, installment loans, investment services, and other services. Currently, CGB is analyzing the profitability of its mortgage loan unit, which has two main businesses, commercial construction loans and residential loans. An important part of the analysis of these loan businesses is determining how to trace or allocate costs to the two businesses.

The cost allocation begins by identifying which departments directly support the two loan businesses, the loan operations department and the marketing department. The *operations department* handles the processing of loan applications, safekeeping of appropriate documents, billing, and maintaining accounts for both commercial and residential loans. The *marketing department* provides direct advertising, promotions, and customer service for both types of loans. The operations and marketing departments in this illustration are comparable to the production departments in the Beary Company example used earlier in the chapter.

Other departments support the operations and marketing departments. Two important support departments are the administrative services department and the accounting department. The *administrative services department* provides legal and technical support. The *accounting department* provides financial services, including regular financial reports and the maintenance of customer records. The administrative services and accounting departments provide services to each other as well as to the operations and marketing departments, as illustrated in Exhibit 7.14. Each of the four departments has labor and certain supplies costs that can be traced directly to the departments. In addition, CGB's human resources and computer services departments provide services to all four departments. In this example, human resources and computer services are assumed to be part of the larger set of services

**EXHIBIT 7.14**
**Cost Flows in Community General Bank**

| From | To | | | |
|---|---|---|---|---|
| | Accounting<br>Department | Administrative<br>Services<br>Department | Operations<br>Department | Marketing<br>Department |
| Accounting Department (Service) | — | 25% | 35% | 40% |
| Administrative Services Department (Service) | 20% | — | 40 | 40 |

that CGB provides to all of its business units; the mortgage loan unit is only one of these. Thus, human resources and computer services can be compared to the use of indirect labor and indirect materials in the Beary Company example earlier in the chapter; the accounting and administrative services departments provide service only to the loan unit and are comparable to the service departments used in the Beary Company example.

To summarize, the mortgage loan unit in CGB has two service departments (accounting and administrative services), two operations departments (marketing and operations), and two products (commercial loans and residential loans). The indirect costs in the mortgage loan unit consist of $1,560,000 labor costs and $33,000 supplies cost which can be traced directly to the two service departments and the two operations departments. In addition, there are indirect costs of $80,000 human services cost and $66,000 computer service costs which must be allocated to the two service and two operations departments.

CGB uses the step method to allocate costs from support departments to the loan businesses. See the step method in Exhibit 7.15, which follows the same approach as for

**EXHIBIT 7.15** **Cost Allocation at Community General Bank, Using the Step Method**

| Departmental Allocation Bases | Departments Accounting | Administrative Services | Operations | Marketing | | Total |
|---|---|---|---|---|---|---|
| Human resources | | | | | | |
| Head count | 80 | 100 | 160 | 60 | | 400 |
| | 20% | 25% | 40% | 15% | | 100% |
| Computer services | | | | | | |
| Number of computers | 60 | 60 | 150 | 30 | | 300 |
| | 20% | 20% | 50% | 10% | | 100% |

**First Phase: Trace Direct Costs and Allocate Overhead Costs to Departments**

| | | | | | | |
|---|---|---|---|---|---|---|
| Direct costs (given) | | | | | | |
| Labor | $221,000 | $339,500 | $554,500 | $445,000 | | $1,560,000 |
| Supplies | 3,500 | 8,800 | 4,200 | 16,500 | | 33,000 |
| Indirect costs | | | | | | |
| Human resources | 16,000 | 20,000 | 32,000 | 12,000 (e.g., $12,000 = 15% × $80,000) | | 80,000 |
| Computer services | 13,200 | 13,200 | 33,000 | 6,600 (e.g., $ 6,600 = 10% × $66,000) | | 66,000 |
| Totals for all departments | $253,700 | $381,500 | $623,700 | $480,100 | | $1,739,000 |

**Second Phase: Allocate Service Department Costs to Operations and Marketing, Using the Step Method**

First step

| Accounting department | Service percent | 25% | 35% | 40% | | |
|---|---|---|---|---|---|---|
| | Amount | $63,425 | $88,795 | $101,480 (e.g., $101,480 = 40% × $253,700) | | |

Second step

| Administrative services | Service percent | | 40% | 40% | | |
|---|---|---|---|---|---|---|
| | Allocation percent (per direct method) | | 50% | 50% | | |
| | Amount | | $222,462.50 | $222,462.50 [e.g., $222,462.50 = 50% × ($381,500 + $63,425)] | | |
| Totals for production departments | | | $934,957.50 | $804,042.50 | | $1,739,000 |

**Third Phase: Allocate Operations and Marketing Costs to Commercial and Residential Loan Businesses**

| | Commercial Loans | Residential Loans | |
|---|---|---|---|
| Base: Number of banking transactions | 15,000 | 10,000 | 25,000 |
| Percent | 60% | 40% | |
| Number of loans | 900 | 3,600 | 4,500 |
| Percent | 20% | 80% | |
| Operations (number of transactions basis) [e.g., $934,957.50 × 60% = $560,974.50] | $560,974.50 | $ 373,983 | |
| Marketing (number of loans basis) [e.g., $804,042.50 × 20% = $160,808.50] | 160,808.50 | 643,234 | |
| Totals for commercial and residential loans | $ 721,783 | $1,017,217 | $1,739,000 |

Beary Company in Exhibit 7.7. The top of Exhibit 7.15 shows the allocation bases that CGB uses to allocate human resources costs and computer services costs to each department. The allocation base for human resources costs is the number of employees, or the head count, in each department, and the allocation of computer services costs is based on the number of computers in each department. The number of employees and the number of computers in each department are given.

The first phase of the allocation in Exhibit 7.15 traces the totals of $1,560,000 of direct labor and $33,000 for supplies costs to each department and allocates the human resources costs ($80,000) and computer services costs ($66,000), using the allocation bases head count and number of computers, respectively. The result is that the total cost of $1,739,000 is allocated as follows:

| | |
|---|---|
| Accounting department | $  253,700 |
| Administrative services department | 381,500 |
| Operations department | 623,700 |
| Marketing department | 480,100 |
| Total cost | $1,739,000 |

In the second phase, the accounting and administrative services department costs are allocated to the operations and marketing departments using the step method and the service percentages in Exhibit 7.14. The accounting department goes first since it has a higher percentage service to the administrative services department (25%) than the service percentage from administrative services to accounting (20%). The result is that the $1,739,000 of total cost is now allocated to the operations department ($934,957.50) and the marketing department ($804,042.50).

In the third and final phase, the costs from the operations and marketing departments are allocated to the two businesses, commercial and residential loans. The base that CGB uses to allocate operations department costs is the number of banking transactions handled within operations (15,000 for commercial loans and 10,000 for residential loans); to allocate marketing costs CGB uses the number of loans of either type (900 commercial loans and 3,600 residential loans). The result of the final allocation is that the total cost of $1,739,000 is allocated to the commercial loans department ($721,783) and the residential loans department ($1,017,217), as illustrated for the third phase in Exhibit 7.15.

Cost allocation provides CGB a basis for evaluating the cost and profitability of its services. By taking the allocated operating costs just determined, the cost of funds provided, and the revenue produced by both commercial and residential loans, a profitability analysis of commercial and residential loans can be completed. Assume that the commercial and residential loan businesses have revenues of $2,755,455 and $2,998,465, respectively, and direct cost of funds of $1,200,736 and $1,387,432, respectively.

The profitability analysis in Exhibit 7.16 shows that the relatively high allocated operating costs of the residential loan unit are an important factor in its overall poor performance (only 19.8% operating profit per dollar of revenue in contrast to more than 30% for the commercial loan unit). In contrast, the cost of funds appears to be comparable for both types of loans (43.58% of revenues for commercial loans and 46.27% of revenues for residential loans). The analysis indicates that the bank should investigate the profitability of residential loans and, in particular, the cost of operations and marketing for these loans.

**EXHIBIT 7.16**
**Profitability Analysis of Commercial and Residential Loans for Community General Bank**

| | Commercial Loans | Residential Loans |
|---|---|---|
| Revenues | $2,755,455 | $2,998,465 |
| Less expenses | | |
| Cost of funds | 1,200,736 | 1,387,432 |
| Allocated operating costs (Exhibit 7.15) | 721,783 | 1,017,217 |
| Operating profit | $  832,936 | $  593,816 |
| Key ratios | | |
| Operating profit/revenue | 30.23% | 19.80% |
| Cost of funds/revenue | 43.58% | 46.27% |

## Joint Product Costing

**LO 7-6**

*Use the three joint product costing methods.*

Many manufacturing plants yield more than one product from a joint manufacturing process. For example, the petroleum industry processes crude oil into multiple products: gasoline, kerosene, fuel oils, and residual heavy oils. Similarly, the semiconductor industry processes silicon wafers into a variety of computer memory chips with different speeds, temperature tolerances, and life expectancies. Other industries that yield joint products include lumber production, food processing, soap making, grain milling, dairy farming, and fishing.

Joint products and by-products are derived from processing a single input or a common set of inputs. **Joint products** are products from the same production process that have relatively substantial sales values. Products whose total sales values are minor in comparison to the sales value of the joint products are classified as **by-products**.

Joint products and by-products both start their manufacturing life as part of the same raw material. Until a certain point in the production process, no distinction can be made between the products. The point in a joint production process at which individual products can be separately identified for the first time is called the **split-off point**. Thereafter, separate production processes can be applied to the individual products. At the split-off point, joint products or by-products might be salable or require further processing to be salable, depending on their nature.

Joint costs include all manufacturing costs incurred prior to the split-off point (including direct materials, direct labor, and factory overhead). For financial reporting purposes, these costs are allocated among the joint products. Additional costs incurred after the split-off point that can be identified directly with individual products are called **separable processing costs**.

Other outputs of joint production include scrap, waste, spoilage, and defective units. Scrap is the residue from a production process that has little or no recovery value. Waste, such as chemical waste, is a residual material that has no recovery value and must be disposed of by the firm as required. In addition to waste and scrap, some products do not meet quality standards and can be reworked for resale. Defective units are reworked to become salable units. Spoiled units are not reworked for economic reasons.

**Joint products**
are products from the same production process that have relatively substantial sales values.

**By-products**
are products whose total sales values are minor in comparison with the sales value of the joint products.

The **split-off point**
is the point in a joint production process at which individual products can be separately identified.

**Separable processing costs**
or separable costs
are those that occur after the split-off point and can be identified directly with individual products.

### Methods for Allocating Joint Costs to Joint Products

Joint costs are most frequently allocated to joint products using (1) the physical measure, (2) the sales value at split-off, and (3) the net realizable value methods.

### *The Physical Measure Method*

The **physical measure method**
uses a physical measure such as pounds, gallons, yards, or units of volume produced at the split-off point to allocate the joint costs to joint products.

The **average cost method**
uses units of output to allocate joint costs to joint products.

The **physical measure method,** naturally enough, uses a physical measure such as pounds, gallons, yards, or units of volume produced at the split-off point to allocate the joint costs to joint products. The first step is to select the proper physical measure as the basis for allocation. We can use units of input or units of output. For example, if we are costing tuna products, the production of 100 pounds of tuna into quarter-pound cans would have an input measure of 100 pounds and an output measure of 400 cans. When units of output are used, this also is called the **average cost method**. Assume that Johnson Seafood produces tuna filets and canned tuna for distribution to restaurants and supermarkets in the southeastern United States. The cost of 14,000 pounds of raw, unprocessed tuna plus the direct labor and overhead for cutting and processing the tuna into filets and canned tuna is the joint cost of the process. The flow of production is illustrated in Exhibit 7.17.

The production process starts at point 1. A total $16,000 joint cost ($7,000 direct materials, $5,000 direct labor, and $4,000 overhead) is incurred. Point 2 is the split-off point where two joint products are separated: 2,000 pounds of tuna filets and 8,000 pounds of canned tuna. The remaining 4,000 pounds of by-products, scrap, and waste are not accounted for. (The appendix to the chapter explains how to account for by-products.) If we use a physical measure method, the joint cost of $16,000 is allocated as shown in Exhibit 7.18.

**EXHIBIT 7.17**
**Diagram of Two Joint Product Cost Flows for Johnson Seafood**

**EXHIBIT 7.18**
**Physical Measure Method**

| Product | Physical Measure | Proportion | Allocation of Joint Cost | Cost per Pound |
|---|---|---|---|---|
| Tuna filets | 2,000 lbs | 0.20 | $16,000 × 20% = $ 3,200 | $1.60 |
| Canned tuna | 8,000 lbs | 0.80 | 16,000 × 80% = 12,800 | 1.60 |
| Total | 10,000 lbs | 1.00 | $16,000 | |

Based on the physical measure method (pounds in this example), when the joint products reach the split-off point, we can compute the relationship of each of the joint products to the sum of the total units. The joint cost allocated to the products is the average cost per pound of the joint cost, which is $1.60 per pound.

The physical measure used to determine the relative weights for allocating the joint cost should be the measure of the products at the *split-off point*, not the measure when the production of the products is completed. Thus, the relevant measure in the example is the 2,000 pounds of filets and 8,000 pounds of canned tuna.

The production costs per pound for both products follow:

Filets          $1.60 per pound = $3,200/2,000 pounds
Canned tuna     $1.60 per pound = $12,800/8,000 pounds

***Advantages and Limitations***   Among the advantages of the physical measure method are that (1) it is easy to use and (2) the criterion for the allocation of the joint costs is objective. This method, however, ignores the revenue-producing capability of individual products that can vary widely among the joint products and have no relationship at all to any physical measure. Each product can also have a unique physical measure (gallons for one, pounds for another) and, hence, the physical measure method might not be applicable. The following method addresses these limitations.

### The Sales Value at Split-Off Method

**The sales value at split-off method** allocates joint costs to joint products on the basis of their relative sales values at the split-off point.

The sales value at split-off method is an alternative and widely used method. The **sales value at split-off method** (or more simply, *sales value method*) allocates joint costs to joint products on the basis of their relative sales values at the split-off point. This method can be used only when joint products can be sold at the split-off point. If we assume that Johnson can sell a pound of filets for $2.20 and a pound of canned tuna for $1.65 and that Johnson has produced 2,000 pounds of filets and 8,000 pounds of canned tuna, the $16,000 joint cost should be allocated between the products as shown in Exhibit 7.19.

The first step in the sales value method (Exhibit 7.19) is to compute the total sales value of the joint products at the split-off point. Note that the sales value is the sales price multiplied by the number of production units, *not the actual number of sales units*. Determining the proportion of the sales value of each joint product to the total sales value is the second step. The final operation allocates the total joint cost among the joint products based on those proportions.

## JOINT COSTS OF PUBLIC EDUCATION AND FUND-RAISING IN CHARITIES

Most large charities incur costs of fund-raising and public education/outreach as part of their mission. The charities also have programs they support with funds they have raised. For program evaluation and for regulatory reporting requirements, the charities then must allocate some portion of their joint costs of public education and fund-raising to the charities' programs. The practice of allocating public education/fund-raising costs is viewed as reasonable in this context, as for example in the case of a charity that describes the symptoms of a disease and explains the actions the individual should take if those symptoms occur.

These costs can be allocated to the related programs of the charity. The cost allocation is important because it affects the total amounts the charity shows for fund-raising versus program delivery. The relationship between these costs is important because some governmental regulations restrict the "administrative cost ratio" to some maximum amount, and the relationship is also important for donors who would like to see most of their donations going to programs rather than fund-raising.

**Source:** U.S. Office of Management and Budget, Circular No. A-122, "Cost Principles for Non-Profit Organizations," http://www.whitehouse.gov/omb/circulars_a122_2004/; Andrea Alston Roberts, "The Implications of Joint Cost Standards for Charity Reporting," *Accounting Horizons,* March 2005, pp. 11–23.

**EXHIBIT 7.19**
**Sales Value at Split-Off Method**

| Product | Units | Price per unit | Sales Value | Proportion | Joint Cost Allocated | Cost per Pound |
|---------|-------|---------------|-------------|------------|---------------------|----------------|
| Filets | 2,000 lbs | $2.20 | $ 4,400 | 0.25 | $16,000 × 25% = $ 4,000 | $2.00 |
| Canned tuna | 8,000 lbs | 1.65 | 13,200 | 0.75 | 16,000 × 75% = 12,000 | 1.50 |
| Total | | | $17,600 | 1.00 | $16,000 | |

In the Johnson Seafood example, the sales value of filets and canned tuna is $4,400 and $13,200, respectively, a total of $17,600. The proportion of the individual sales values of the products to the total sales value are 0.25 ($4,400/$17,600) for filets and 0.75 ($13,200/$17,600) for canned tuna. The allocated costs are $4,000 to filets and $12,000 to canned tuna.

The production costs per pound for both products are calculated as follows:

| | |
|---|---|
| Filets | $2.00 per pound = $4,000/2,000 |
| Canned tuna | $1.50 per pound = $12,000/8,000 |

Note that filets have a higher unit cost under the sales value method than under the physical measure method. The reason is that filets have a higher sales value. If the sales prices are estimated accurately and no separable processing costs are involved, the sales value at split-off method generates the same gross margin percentage for both filets and canned tuna, as shown in Exhibit 7.20.

***Advantages and Limitations***   The advantages of the sales value method are that it (1) is easy to calculate and (2) is allocated according to the individual product's revenues. This method is superior to the physical measure method because it allocates the joint costs in proportion to the products' ability to absorb these costs. This is an application of the ability-to-bear concept of fairness included in the objectives of cost allocation at the beginning of the chapter.

One limitation of the sales value method is that market prices for some industries change constantly. Also, the sales price at split-off might not be available because separable processing is necessary before the product can be sold.

**EXHIBIT 7.20**
**Product-Line Profitability Analysis**

| | Tuna Filets | Canned Tuna |
|---|---|---|
| Sales | $2.20 × 2,000 = $4,400 | $1.65 × 8,000 = $13,200 |
| Cost of goods sold | $2.00 × 2,000 = 4,000 | $1.50 × 8,000 = 12,000 |
| Gross margin | $ 400 | $ 1,200 |
| Gross margin percent | 9.09% | 9.09% |

**EXHIBIT 7.21**   **Diagram of Three Joint Product Cost Flows for Johnson Seafood**

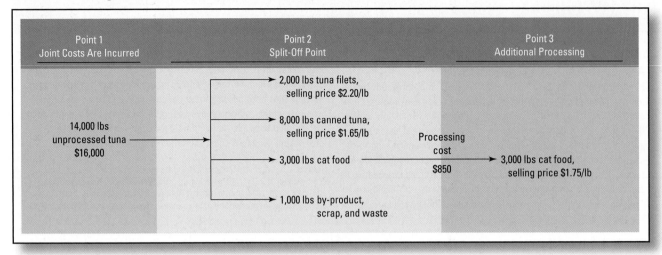

### The Net Realizable Value Method

The **net realizable value (NRV)** of a product is the estimated sales value of the product at the split-off point; it is determined by subtracting the separable processing and selling costs beyond the split-off point from the ultimate sales value of the product.

Not all joint products can be sold at the split-off point; some require additional processing before the product can be sold. Thus, there is no market price to attach to some products at the split-off point. In these cases, the concept of net realizable value is used. The **net realizable value (NRV)** of a product is the product's *estimated sales value* at the split-off point; it is determined by subtracting the separable processing and selling costs beyond the split-off point from the estimated ultimate sales value for that product.

$$\text{NRV} = \text{Ultimate sales value} - \text{separable processing and selling cost}$$

In the Johnson Seafood example, assume that in addition to filets and canned tuna, the firm processes cat food from raw, unprocessed tuna. Assume also that, at the split-off point, 14,000 pounds of tuna yield 2,000 pounds of filets and 8,000 pounds of canned tuna, as before. However, now assume that an additional 3,000 pounds of cat food is also produced. The remaining 1,000 pounds are scrap, waste, and by-products. For cat food, the tuna must be processed further for sale to pet food distributors. The separable processing cost is $850 for minerals and other supplements that are important for cat nutrition but that add no weight to the product. The pet food distributors buy the prepared cat food from Johnson at $1.75 per pound and package it into 5.5-ounce cans for sale to pet stores and supermarkets. Exhibit 7.21 is a diagram of this situation.

Exhibit 7.22 shows the joint cost allocation calculation using the net realizable value method.

If Johnson Seafood sold all of the products it produced during the period, its gross margin amounts for the products would be as shown in Exhibit 7.23. Note that the gross margin percentage is lower for cat food than for filets because of the separable processing cost of $850.

***Advantages and Limitations***   The NRV method is superior to the physical measure method because, like the sales value at split-off method, it produces an allocation that yields a predictable, comparable level of profitability among the products. The physical measure method might provide misleading guidance to top management regarding product profitability.

**EXHIBIT 7.22**   **Joint Cost Allocation Using the Net Realizable Value Method**

| Product | Pounds | Price | Sales Value | Separable Processing | Net Realizable Value | Percent of NRV | Allocated Cost | Total Cost | Cost per Pound |
|---|---|---|---|---|---|---|---|---|---|
| Filets | 2,000 | $2.20 | $ 4,400 | — | $ 4,400 | 20% | $ 3,200 | $ 3,200 | $1.60 |
| Canned tuna | 8,000 | 1.65 | 13,200 | — | 13,200 | 60 | 9,600 | 9,600 | 1.20 |
| Cat food | 3,000 | 1.75 | 5,250 | $850 | 4,400 | 20 | 3,200 | 4,050 | 1.35 |
| Total | 13,000 | | $22,850 | $850 | $22,000 | 100% | $16,000 | $16,850 | |

**EXHIBIT 7.23**
**Johnson Seafood's Product-Line Profitability Analysis**

|  | Tuna Filets | Canned Tuna | Cat Food |
|---|---|---|---|
| Sales | $2.20 × 2,000 = $4,400 | $1.65 × 8,000 = $13,200 | $1.75 × 3,000 = $5,250 |
| Cost of goods sold | $1.60 × 2,000 = 3,200 | $1.20 × 8,000 = 9,600 | $1.35 × 3,000 = 4,050 |
| Gross margin |  $1,200 |  $ 3,600 |  $1,200 |
| Gross margin percent | 27.27% | 27.27% | 22.86% |

## Summary

This chapter introduces the objectives, concepts, and methods of cost allocation. There are two main cost allocation applications—departmental cost and joint product costing. Most important, the objectives and methods for cost allocation are determined based on the firm's strategy. Cost allocation is concerned with strategy in four key ways: (1) to determine accurate departmental and product costs as a basis for evaluating each department's cost efficiency and the profitability of different products, (2) to motivate managers to work hard, (3) to provide the proper incentive for managers to achieve the firm's goals, and (4) to provide a fair basis for rewarding managers for their effort.

Ethical issues often arise in cost allocation when managers must choose between alternative allocation methods. The manager must choose between methods that might decrease the cost of one product, customer, or business unit at the expense of increased costs for another product, customer, or unit.

Departmental cost allocation is performed in three phases: (1) trace all direct costs and allocate overhead to service and production departments, (2) allocate service department costs to production departments, and (3) allocate production department costs to products. The second phase is the most complex. Service department costs can be allocated to production departments using three methods—the direct method, the step method, and the reciprocal method. The three methods differ in the way they include service flows among service departments. The direct method ignores these flows, the step method includes some of them, and the reciprocal method includes all. For this reason, the reciprocal method is preferred.

A number of implementation issues arise when applying cost allocation methods, including the strategic and ethical issues of the cost allocation. It is also important to allocate variable and fixed costs separately (in a process called *dual allocation*), to use budgeted rather than actual amounts in the allocation, and to consider alternative allocation methods when the result of an allocation to a department is a cost that is greater than what the department would pay to purchase the service from an outside entity.

The need for joint product costing arises when two or more products are made simultaneously in a given manufacturing process. The three methods for costing joint products are the (1) physical measure method, (2) sales value at split-off method, and (3) net realizable value method. The physical measure method is the simplest to use but also has a significant disadvantage. Because the allocation ignores sales value, the gross margins of joint products determined using the physical measure method can differ in significant and unreasonable ways. In contrast, the sales value and net realizable value methods tend to result in similar gross margins among the joint products. The sales value at split-off method is used when sales value at split-off is known; otherwise the net realizable value is used.

## Appendix

# By-Product Costing

**LO 7-7**

*Use the four by-product costing methods.*

A by-product is a product of relatively small sales value that is produced simultaneously with one or more joint products. Two approaches are used for by-product costing: (1) the asset recognition approach and (2) the revenue approach. The main difference between these approaches lies in whether they assign an inventoriable value to by-products at the split-off point. The asset recognition approach records by-products as inventory at net realizable values; the by-product is therefore recognized as inventory when the by-product is produced. In contrast, the revenue approach does not assign values to the by-products in the period of production but recognizes by-product revenue in the period sold.

Each of the two approaches contain two alternative methods, depending on the way in which by-products are reported in the income statement. The two asset recognition methods follow:

---

**Net Realizable Value Method.** This method shows the net realizable value of by-products on the balance sheet as inventory and on the income statement as a deduction from the total manufacturing cost of the joint products. This is done in the *period in which the by-product is produced.*

**Other Income at Production Point Method.** This method shows the net realizable value of by-products on the income statement as other income or other sales revenue. This is done in the *period in which the by-product is produced.*

---

The two revenue methods follow:

---

**Other Income at Selling Point Method.** This method shows the net sales revenue from a by-product sold at time of sale on the income statement as other income or other sales revenue.

**Manufacturing Cost Reduction at Selling Point Method.** This method shows the net sales revenue from a by-product sold *at time of sale* on the income statement as a reduction of total manufacturing cost.

---

In Exhibit 7A.1 we summarize the four major by-product costing methods.

## ASSET RECOGNITION METHODS

To illustrate the asset recognition methods, assume that Johnson Seafood believes that it can make additional profit by taking a portion of the 1,000 pounds of scrap and waste in each batch of unprocessed tuna and reprocessing them to produce a high-quality garden fertilizer. However, the selling price of the fertilizer is expected to be relatively low, 50 cents per pound. Moreover, additional, separable processing and selling costs of 30 cents per pound would be necessary for preparing, packaging, and distributing the product. Since the sales value of fertilizer is relatively low, the firm decides to treat tuna filets, canned tuna, and cat food as joint products and fertilizer as a by-product. Suppose that Johnson sold all production of filets, canned tuna, and cat food, but sold only 400 of the 500 pounds of the fertilizer produced. Exhibit 7A.2 shows the cost flows of the three joint products and one by-product.

From Exhibit 7.22, the total sales value of filets, canned tuna, and cat food is $22,850 ($4,400 + $13,200 + $5,250) and the total cost of the goods sold is $16,850 ($3,200 + $9,600 + $4,050). The net realizable value (NRV) of the 500 pounds of fertilizer produced is

$$\text{NRV} = \text{Sales value} - \text{Separable processing cost}$$
$$= (\$0.50 \times 500) - (\$0.30 \times 500)$$
$$= \$100$$

**EXHIBIT 7A.1**
**A Summary of By-Product Costing Methods**

| | Place in Income Statement | |
| --- | --- | --- |
| **Time to Recognize** | **As Other Income** | **As a Deduction of Manufacturing Cost** |
| At time of production (asset recognition methods) | Other income at time of production | Net realizable value method; reduction in joint product cost at time of production |
| At time of sale (revenue methods) | Other income at time of sale | Reduction in cost of joint products at time of sale |

**EXHIBIT 7A.2**
**Diagram of Three Joint Products and One By-Product Cost Flows for Johnson Seafood**

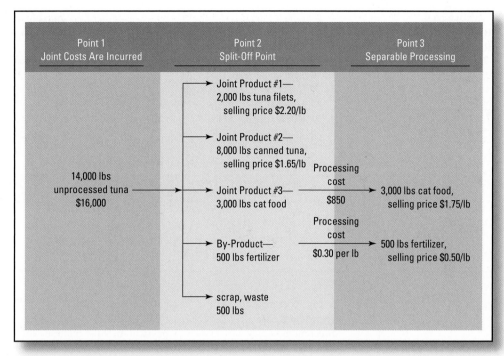

**EXHIBIT 7A.3**
**By-Product Costing—Asset Recognition Methods**

|  | Net Realizable Value Method | Other Income at Production Method |
|---|---|---|
| Sale of joint products (Exhibit 7.22) | $22,850 | $22,850 |
| Cost of joint products sold (Exhibit 7.22) | $16,850 | $16,850 |
| Less net realizable value of by-product | (100) | — |
| Cost of goods sold | $16,750 | $16,850 |
| Gross margin | $ 6,100 | $ 6,000 |
| Other income at production | — | 100 |
| Income before tax | $ 6,100 | $ 6,100 |

Johnson's accounting for the by-product using the asset recognition methods (the net realizable value method and the other income at production point method) appears in Exhibit 7A.3.

Asset recognition methods are based on the financial accounting concepts of asset recognition, matching, and materiality. By-products are *recognized* as assets with probable future economic benefits because a market exists for them. Asset recognition methods also have the preferred effect of *matching* the value of the by-product with its manufacturing cost; when the by-product is sold, its inventory cost is shown as the cost of sales. If the net realizable value of a by-product is *material* (that is, it will have a significant effect on inventory or profit), the asset recognition methods should be used because of the matching concept.

## REVENUE METHODS

Revenue methods recognize by-products at the time of sale. Exhibit 7A.4 illustrates the two methods. Note that Exhibit 7A.4 shows the 400 pounds of by-product sold, not the 500 pounds of by-product produced.

Revenue methods are justified on the financial accounting concepts of revenue realization, materiality, and cost benefit. These methods are consistent with the argument that by-product net revenue should be recorded at the time of sale because this is the *point revenue is realized.* Revenue methods are also appropriate when the value of the by-product is *not material,* that is, very small in relation to net income.

**EXHIBIT 7A.4**
**By-Product Costing—Revenue Recognition Methods**

|  | Other Income at Selling Point Method | Manufacturing Cost Reduction Method |
|---|---|---|
| Sale of joint products | $22,850 | $22,850 |
| Cost of goods sold |  |  |
| Cost of joint products sold | $16,850 | $16,850 |
| Less net sales revenue of by-product sold ($0.50 − $0.30) × 400 | — | (80) |
| Cost of goods sold | $16,850 | $16,770 |
| Gross margin | $ 6,000 | $ 6,080 |
| By-product revenue | 80 | — |
| Income before tax | $ 6,080 | $ 6,080 |

## Key Terms

average cost method, *241*
by-products, *241*
direct method, *229*
dual allocation, *236*
joint products, *241*

net realizable value (NRV), *244*
physical measure method, *241*
reciprocal flows, *228*
reciprocal method, *232*

sales value at split-off method, *242*
separable processing costs, *241*
split-off point, *241*
step method, *231*

## Comments on Cost Management in Action

### Health Care Providers Allocate Cost for Medicare Reimbursement

The direct method of the departmental approach to cost allocation explained in this chapter has never been permitted for Medicare cost reports. The only permissible method is the step method, which must be performed under Medicare guidelines and audited by a private intermediary (e.g., Blue Cross). A hospital chooses the order in which the step method occurs and the allocation bases (e.g., square feet, pounds of laundry, time spent, number of meals served). The order of the step method and the choice of allocation base are widely recognized to have a significant effect on allocated costs. Hospitals naturally choose methods that favor them in cost reimbursement. Many consultants, authors, and policymakers have called for improved guidance regarding the allocation of costs for Medicare reimbursement. Some have argued that since software tools are readily available to allocate costs using the reciprocal method, Medicare should require this more accurate method.

Marianne L Muise and Bonnie A Amoia, "Step Up to the Step-Down Method," *Healthcare Financial Management*, May 2006, pp. 72–77; William N. Zelman, Michael J. McCue, and Noah Glick, *Financial Management of Health Care Organizations*," Third Edition (Wiley, 2009). Also, the relevant guidance on Medicare costing is provided by the Centers for Medicare and Medicare Services, a U.S. federal agency to administer Medicare and Medicaid (www.cms.hhs.gov/). Medicare cost report information can be found at www.cms.hhs.gov/CostReports/.

## Self-Study Problem

(For solution, please turn to the end of the chapter.)

### Joint Product Costing

Northern Company processes 100 gallons of raw materials into 75 gallons of product GS-50 and 25 gallons of GS-80. GS-50 is further processed into 50 gallons of product GS-505 at a cost of $5,000, and GS-80 is processed into 50 gallons of product GS-805 at a cost of $2,000. Exhibit 1 depicts this manufacturing flow.

**EXHIBIT 1**
**Joint Cost Flows for Northern Company**

| Point 1 | Point 2 | Separable Processing Cost | Point 3 |
|---|---|---|---|
| 100 gallons of raw material processed at a cost of $20,000 | 75 gallons of GS-50 Price = $300 | $5,000 | 50 gallons of GS-505 Price = $500 |
| | 25 gallons of GS-80 Price = $60 | $2,000 | 50 gallons of GS-805 Price = $140 |

The production process starts at point 1. A total of $20,000 in joint manufacturing costs are incurred in reaching point 2. Point 2 is the split-off point of the process that manufactures GS-50 and GS-80. At this point, GS-50 can be sold for $300 a gallon, and GS-80 can be sold for $60 a gallon. The process is completed at point 3—products GS-505 and GS-805 have a sales price of $500 a gallon and $140 a gallon, respectively.

**Required**    Allocate the joint product costs using each of the three methods: (1) physical measure, (2) sales value at split-off, and (3) net realizable value.

*Please visit* **http://www.mhhe.com/blocher6e** *to access a narrated, animated tutorial for solving this problem.*

## Questions

7-1    What are the four objectives in the strategic role of cost allocation? Explain each briefly.

7-2    Explain the difference between joint products and by-products.

7-3    What does the term *reciprocal* mean in the context of departmental cost allocation?

7-4    What are the three methods of departmental cost allocation? Explain how they differ, which is the most preferred, and why.

7-5    What are the three phases of the departmental allocation approach? What happens at each phase?

7-6    Give two or three examples of the use of cost allocation in service industries and not-for-profit organizations.

7-7    What are the four methods used in by-product costing, and how do they differ? Which is the preferred method and why?

7-8    What are the limitations of joint product cost allocation?

7-9    What are the implementation issues of departmental cost allocation?

7-10    What are some of the ethical issues of cost allocation?

## Brief Exercises

**Brief Exercises 7-11 through 7-14 involve departmental cost allocation with two service departments and two production departments. Use the following information for these four exercises:**

| Department | Cost | Percentage Service Provided to | | | |
|---|---|---|---|---|---|
| | | S1 | S2 | P1 | P2 |
| Service 1 (S1) | $ 30,000 | 0% | 30% | 35% | 35% |
| Service 2 (S2) | 20,000 | 20 | 0 | 20 | 60 |
| Production 1 (P1) | 100,000 | | | | |
| Production 2 (P2) | 150,000 | | | | |

7-11    What is the amount of service department cost allocated to P1 and P2 using the direct method?

7-12    What is the total cost in P1 and in P2 after allocation using the direct method?

7-13    What is the amount of service department cost allocated to P1 and P2 using the step method with S1 going first?

7-14    How does your answer to 7-11 change if the cost in P1 is changed from $100,000 to $120,000?

**Brief Exercises 7-15 and 7-16 require the following information:**

| Department | Cost | Percentage Service Provided to | | | |
|---|---|---|---|---|---|
| | | S1 | S2 | P1 | P2 |
| Service 1 | $ 112,000 | 0% | 40% | 40% | 20% |
| Service 2 | 44,000 | 20 | 0 | 40 | 40 |
| Production 1 | 345,000 | | | | |
| Production 2 | 216,000 | | | | |
| | $ 717,000 | | | | |

7-15    What portion of service department 1's costs are allocated to P1 and to P2 under the direct method?

7-16    What portion of service department 2's costs are allocated to P1 and to P2 under the direct method?

**Brief Exercises 7-17 through 7-20 require the following information about a joint production process for three products, with a total joint production cost of $100,000. There are no separable processing costs for any of the three products.**

| Product | Sales Value at Split-Off | Units at Split-Off |
|---------|--------------------------|---------------------|
| 1 | $130,000 | 240 |
| 2 | 50,000 | 960 |
| 3 | 20,000 | 1,200 |
|  | $200,000 | 2,400 |

7-17    What amount of joint cost is allocated to each of the three products using the relative sales value method?

7-18    What amount of joint cost is allocated to each of the three products using the physical units method?

7-19    Assume that the total sales value at the split-off point for product 1 is $50,000 instead of $130,000 and the sales value of product 3 is $2,000 instead of $20,000. Assume also that, because of its relatively low sales value, the firm treats product 3 as a by-product and uses the net realizable value method for accounting for joint costs. There are no separable processing costs for product 3. What amount of joint cost would be allocated to the three products?

7-20    Assume the same as in 7-19 above except that product 3 is treated as a joint product. What amount of joint costs would be allocated to the three products using the relative sales value method?

## Exercises

[LO 7-1]    7-21    **Cost Allocation; General Concepts**    An organization's service and administrative costs can be substantial, and some or all of these costs usually are allocated to cost objects. Thus, the allocations of service and administrative costs can have a significant impact on product cost and pricing, asset valuation, and segment profitability.

**Required**
1. What are service and administrative costs?
2. When service and administrative costs are allocated, they are grouped into homogeneous pools and then allocated to cost objects according to some allocation base.
   a. Compare and contrast the benefit and cost criteria for selecting an allocation base.
   b. Explain what the ability-to-bear criterion means in selecting an allocation base.

**(CMA Adapted)**

[LO 7-1, 7-7]    7-22    **By-Products and Decision-Making; Strategy**    Lowman Gourmet Products produces a wide variety of gourmet coffees (sold in pounds of roasted beans), jams, jellies, and condiments such as spicy mustard sauce. The firm has a reputation as a high-quality source of these products. Lowman sells the products through a mail-order catalog that is revised twice a year. Joe, the president, is interested in developing a new line of products to complement the coffees. The manufacture of the jams and jellies presently produces an excess of fruit liquid that is not used in these products. The firm is now selling excess liquid to other firms as flavoring for canned fruit products. Joe is planning to refine the liquid and add other ingredients to it to produce a coffee-flavoring product instead of selling the liquid. He figures that the cost of producing the jams and jellies, and therefore the fruit liquid, is irrelevant; the only relevant concern is the lost sales to the canneries and the cost of the additional ingredients, processing, and packaging.

**Required**    Does this plan make financial and strategic sense?

[LO 7-1, 7-2, 7-5]    7-23    **Federal Reserve Banks; Cost Allocation**    The Monetary Control Act of 1980 (**www.federalreserve .gov/paymentsystems/pricing/pricingpol.htm**) requires the Federal Reserve (the Fed) to charge explicitly for certain services, in effect placing Federal Reserve banks in direct competition with large commercial banks for these services. The act also requires the Fed to price these services based on full cost, including allocated indirect costs. Recent research indicates that the Fed responded to the act by both improving the efficiency with which it provides these services and reallocating indirect costs to the less price-competitive services.

**Required**    Describe briefly how the allocation of indirect costs could have made the Fed's most price-sensitive services more competitive. Are there ethical or professional issues involved in this case?

[LO 7-1, 7-2, 7-5]   7-24 **Cost Allocation and Taxation at Nonprofit Organizations**   Nonprofit organizations are exempt from federal income tax except for income from any activities that are unrelated to the nonprofit's charitable purpose. An example is the use of a laboratory for both tax-exempt basic medical research and for testing a taxable product for commercial pharmaceutical firms. A concern in these cases is that tax-exempt nonprofit organizations will be able to compete unfairly with for-profit firms because of their tax-exempt status. The key argument is that common costs for the nonprofit's exempt and business activities will be used to "subsidize" the for-profit business (in this case, the taxable product testing).

**Required**   How would cost allocation play a role in affecting the operating results of a nonprofit organization which has both business and charitable activities?

[LO 7-1, 7-5]   7-25 **Fuel Surcharges: Allocating the Increased Cost of Fuel**   U.S. railroads, including Burlington Northern Santa Fe Corp (BNSF) and CSX Corp., began using fuel surcharges in 2001 to recapture some of the additional costs due to the sharp rise in fuel costs in late 1999, continuing into 2000. Fuel costs have continued to increase and the fuel surcharges have continued to increase as well, accounting for approximately 12% of BNSF's revenues in the third quarter of 2008. Companies that use the railroads for shipping agricultural, chemical, and other commodities have been critical of the allocation methods the railroads use to apply the surcharges. The railroads have used surcharges based on a percentage of charges for the shipment. Shippers have argued that an allocation based on miles traveled in the shipment or other usage-based measure would be preferable. To resolve the conflict, the Surface Transportation Board (STB) in January 2007 prohibited the use of a surcharge based on shipping rates. Though it did not require the use of mileage, it required that railroads must use a method to allocate fuel surcharges that correlates with actual fuel costs. The STB is an economic regulatory agency within the Department of Transportation that Congress charged with the fundamental missions of resolving railroad rate and service disputes and reviewing proposed railroad mergers. After spiking in 2008, the cost of fuel fell in 2009 and 2010, but it has risen substantially in early 2012 to near the peak levels of 2008. While the increase in fuel costs has put pressure on railroads to raise rates (BSNF, one of the large rail shippers, doubled its surcharge in January 2011), rising fuel costs have helped increase rail traffic, as some shippers switch from less fuel efficient trucks to more fuel efficient rail transportation.

**Required**
1. How would you propose that the increased cost of fuel be charged to shippers by the railroads?
2. Do you think the STB ruling should solve the problem?
3. What are the key sustainability issues for a consumer of rail transport?

[LO 7-2]   7-26 **Cost Allocation and Legal Disputes**   Cost allocation is often the centerpiece of conflict that is resolved in court cases. The litigation usually involves the dispute over how costs are allocated to a product or product line that is of interest to the plaintiff. This is particularly an issue when a company produces some products or services for a price-competitive market while other products or services are produced for a governmental unit on a cost-plus or reimbursement basis.

The following cost allocation disputes involve an organization (Nursing Care Inc., or NCI) that operates both a nursing home and an apartment building for retirees (retirement home). A single kitchen is used to provide meals to both the nursing home and retirement home. Also, certain labor costs and utilities costs of the kitchen are shared by the two homes. Many of those living in the nursing home are indigent and are on Medicaid. The state Department of Health and Family Services (DHFS) reimburses NCI at Medicaid-approved cost reimbursement rates. The Medicaid reimbursement rates are based on cost information supplied by the organization, in this case NCI, and are assumed to be accurate; cost allocations are assumed to be reasonable. DHFS has examined the cost report of NCI and has raised the following issues which are now being litigated.

**Required**   (The above is based upon an actual case, with names disguised.)

For each issue, consider whether you think the defendant (NCI) or the plaintiff (DHFS) has the valid position, based on your understanding of cost allocation.
1. DHFS alleges that NCI charged specific milk, condiments, and paper products to the nursing home, without following the usual 60% (nursing home) and 40% (retirement home) sharing for food costs. NCI asserts that these items are used in the nursing home to counteract the greater danger of spread of disease in the nursing home. DHFS claims that NCI's documentation to support charging these costs directly to the nursing home is inadequate.

2. DHFS alleges that nourishments (liquid supplements, cookies, and some puree foods) that are consumed by nursing home residents at bedtime for their special health needs are akin to "seconds" at meals and should be allocated to both the nursing home and the retirement home.

3. Three kitchen employees not involved in meal preparation are involved in service to both the nursing home and the retirement home; NCI asks the three employees to keep track of how much time they spend on the nursing home versus the retirement home. These time reports are then sent to management and are used as a basis for allocating the cost of the employees to the two homes. DHFS alleges that the practice is not sufficiently accurate, and relies largely on unsupported, self-reported information.

4. NCI allocates utility costs to the two homes using an industrial engineering study performed by the power company on five days in June four years ago. DHFS disputes that this allocation base is valid and says that NCI must use a square footage base rate.

5. NCI argues that because it competes on cost leadership in both the nursing home and retirement home businesses, the cost allocations must be fair for strategic reasons as well as to satisfy DHFS requirements.

**[LO7-2]**   7-27   **Cost Allocation; Cost Shifting**   In the last several years, airlines have succeeded in boosting profits by adding fees for previously free services such as in-flight snacks and meals, checked baggage, priority boarding, and other services. These fees have caused some shifts in customer behavior, as more airline passengers bring their own snacks on the airline and pack a smaller bag that is acceptable for "carry-on." By using the carry-on luggage, the airline customer can save $25 or more in baggage-checking fees. This situation has resulted in a cost shifting for passengers, airlines, and airport security. As the number of checked bags decreases, the cost of baggage handling for the airlines decreases (and revenues increase for those bags that are checked). In contrast, the costs and delays in security checkpoints increase as security personnel must check additional carry-on bags, causing delays for passengers and the need for additional security personnel to handle the increased number of carry-on bags. Transportation Security Administration (TSA) officials explain that there has been a "huge" increase in the number of carry-on bags. In response, the Department of Homeland Security has proposed an increase in the passenger security fee each passenger pays for each flight from $2.50 in 2011 to $4.00 in 2012. Alternatively, as suggested by the U.S. Travel Association, TSA could simply require each airline to include one free checked bag as part of the ticket price. The airline industry has objected to this proposal on the grounds that it "diminishes customer choice and competitive differentiation among carriers."

**Required**

1. Explain the nature of the cost-shifting taking place currently in the airline industry.

2. What are the ethical issues, if any, in this case?

3. Explain how you think airlines compete, on cost leadership or differentiation, and explain whether the current "fees for services" approach is or is not consistent with the airlines' strategy.

**[LO 7-3, 7-5]**   7-28   **Departmental Cost Allocation**   HomeLife Life Insurance Company has two service departments (actuarial and premium rating) and two production departments (advertising and sales). The distribution of each service department's efforts (in percentages) to the other departments is

| | | To | | |
|---|---|---|---|---|
| **From** | **Actuarial** | **Premium Rating** | **Advertising** | **Sales** |
| Actuarial | — | 80% | 10% | 10% |
| Premium | 20% | — | 20 | 60 |

The direct operating costs of the departments (including both variable and fixed costs) are

| | |
|---|---|
| Actuarial | $80,000 |
| Premium rating | 15,000 |
| Advertising | 60,000 |
| Sales | 40,000 |

**Required**

1. Determine the total cost allocated to the advertising and sales departments using the direct method.

2. Determine the total cost allocated to advertising and sales using the step method.

3. Determine the total cost allocated to advertising and sales using the reciprocal method.

[LO 7-3] 7-29 **Departmental Cost Allocation** Robinson Products Company has two service departments (S1 and S2) and two production departments (P1 and P2). The distribution of each service department's efforts (in percentages) to the other departments is

| From | To | | | |
|------|------|------|------|------|
| | **S1** | **S2** | **P1** | **P2** |
| S1 | — | 10% | 20% | ?% |
| S2 | 10% | — | ? | 30 |

The direct operating costs of the departments (including both variable and fixed costs) are

| | |
|------|------|
| S1 | $180,000 |
| S2 | 60,000 |
| P1 | 50,000 |
| P2 | 120,000 |

**Required**
1. Determine the total cost of P1 and P2 using the direct method.
2. Determine the total cost of P1 and P2 using the step method.
3. Determine the total cost of P1 and P2 using the reciprocal method.

[LO 7-6] 7-30 **Joint Products; Blood Donation** Donation of blood through the American Red Cross and other organizations is an important way to maintain the blood supplies which are critical to patient treatment in hospitals.

Three blood products are produced from blood received from donors: (1) red cells, used primarily in surgery; (2) platelets, used to prevent spontaneous bleeding in leukemia patients; and (3) plasma, used after further processing, for the treatment of protein deficiency.

The joint cost of producing the three products consists of the blood collection costs, the safety testing costs, and further processing in a laboratory to split off the three joint products. Commonly the joint costs are allocated to the three products on the basis of physical units produced. The National Blood Authority (NBA) in the U.K. observed the unfavorable effect of this approach in that the cost of each blood product could change significantly from time to time, as the demand for the products varied; the demand for the platelets was particularly volatile. In response, the NBA decided to allocate all joint costs to red cells, on the basis, in part, that plasma was routinely discarded to minimize the risk of Creutzfeldt-Jakob Disease.

**Required** What are the advantages and disadvantages of the allocation approach proposed by the NBA? What allocation method would you suggest as an alternative, if any?

[LO 7-6] 7-31 **Joint Products** Tango Company produces joint products M, N, and T from a joint process. This information concerns a batch produced in April at a joint cost of $120,000:

| Product | Units Produced and Sold | After Split-Off | |
|---------|-------------------------|-----------------|--|
| | | **Total Separable Costs** | **Total Final Sales Value** |
| M | 10,000 | $10,000 | $160,000 |
| N | 4,000 | 10,000 | 140,000 |
| T | 5,000 | 5,000 | 25,000 |

**Required** How much of the joint cost should be allocated to each joint product using the net realizable value method?

[LO 7-6] 7-32 **Joint Products** Arkansas Corporation manufactures liquid chemicals A and B from a joint process. It allocates joint costs on the basis of sales value at split-off. Processing 5,000 gallons of product A and 1,000 gallons of product B to the split-off point costs $5,600. The sales value at split-off is $2 per gallon for product A and $30 for product B. Product B requires an additional separable process beyond split-off at a cost of $2.50 per gallon before it can be sold.

**Required** What is the company's cost to produce 1,000 gallons of product B?

[LO 7-6, 7-7] 7-33 **Joint and By-Product Costing (Appendix)** Webster Company produces 25,000 units of product A, 20,000 units of product B, and 10,000 units of product C from the same manufacturing process at a cost of $340,000. A and B are joint products, and C is regarded as a by-product. The unit selling prices of the products are $30 for A, $25 for B, and $1 for C. None of the products require separable processing. Of the units produced, Webster Company sells 18,000 units of A, 19,000 units of B, and 10,000 units of C. The firm uses the net realizable value method to allocate joint costs and by-product costs. Assume no beginning inventory.

**Required**
1. What is the value of the ending inventory of product A?
2. What is the value of the ending inventory of product B?

# Problems

**[LO 7-3]**

Note regarding Rounding Error: Problems 34 through 41 involve a series of calculations in which rounding errors can become significant. Use either Excel or use 4 decimal places in your calculations to minimize rounding errors.

**7-34 Departmental Cost Allocation; Outsourcing** Levy Company produces two software products (WebX and WebY) in two separate departments (A and B). These products are highly regarded network maintenance programs. WebX is used for small networks and WebY is used for large networks. Levy is known for the quality of its products and its ability to meet dates promised for software upgrades.

Department A produces WebX, and department B produces WebY. The production departments are supported by two support departments, systems design and programming services. The source and use of the support department time are summarized as follows:

| | | To | | | Total |
| From | Design | Programming | Department A | Department B | Labor-Hours |
|---|---|---|---|---|---|
| Design | — | 5,000 | 1,000 | 9,000 | 15,000 |
| Programming | 200 | — | 200 | 600 | 1,000 |

The costs in the two service departments are as follows:

| | Design | Programming |
|---|---|---|
| Labor and materials (all variable) | $30,000 | $25,000 |
| Depreciation and other fixed costs | 40,000 | 25,000 |
| Total | $70,000 | $50,000 |

**Required**
1. What are the costs allocated to the two production departments from the two service departments using (a) the direct method, (b) the step method (design department goes first), and (c) the reciprocal method?
2. The company is considering outsourcing programming services to DDB Services, Inc., for $45 per hour. Should Levy do this?

**[LO 7-3]**

**7-35 Departmental Cost Allocation** Marshfield Manufacturing has two production departments—assembly and finishing. These are supported by two service departments—sourcing (purchasing and handling of raw materials and human resources) and operations (work scheduling, supervision, and inspection). Marshfield has the following labor-hours devoted by each of the service departments to the other departments.

| | Total Labor-Hours Used by Departments | | | |
| | Sourcing | Operations | Assembly | Finishing |
|---|---|---|---|---|
| Sourcing | | 25,000 | 45,000 | 70,000 |
| Operations | 10,000 | — | 50,000 | 40,000 |

The costs incurred in the plant are as follows:

| Departments | Departmental Costs |
|---|---|
| Sourcing | $134,000 |
| Operations | 189,000 |
| Assembly | 398,500 |
| Finishing | 266,000 |
| Total | $987,500 |

**Required** Use 4 decimal places (e.g., 33.3333%) in your calculations.

1. What are the costs allocated to the two production departments using (a) the direct method, (b) the step method (with the sourcing department going first), and (c) the reciprocal method?

2. What are the total costs in the production departments after allocation?

[LO 7-3, 7-4] 7-36 **Departmental Cost Allocation; Outsourcing; Outside Price** McKeoun Enterprises is a large machine tool company now experiencing alarming increases in maintenance expense in each of its four production departments. Maintenance costs are currently allocated to the production departments on the basis of labor-hours incurred in the production department. To provide pressure for the production departments to use less maintenance, and to provide an incentive for the maintenance department to become more efficient, McKeoun has decided to investigate new methods of allocating maintenance costs. One suggestion now being evaluated is a form of outsourcing: The producing departments could purchase maintenance service from an outside supplier. That is, they could choose either to use an outside supplier of maintenance or to be charged an amount based on their use of labor-hours. The following table shows the labor-hours in each department, the allocation of maintenance cost based on labor-hours, and the cost to purchase the equivalent level of maintenance service from an outside maintenance provider.

| Production Department | Direct Labor-Hours Allocation Base (Percent) | Direct Labor-Hours Allocation Cost | Outside Price |
|---|---|---|---|
| A | 20% | $ 90,000 | $115,000 |
| B | 30 | 135,000 | 92,000 |
| C | 10 | 45,000 | 69,000 |
| D | 40 | 180,000 | 184,000 |
| Total | 100% | $450,000 | $460,000 |

**Required** Use 4 decimal places (e.g., 33.3333%) in your calculations.

1. As a first step in moving to the outsourcing approach, McKeoun is considering an allocation based on the price of the outside maintenance supplier for each department. Calculate the cost allocation on this basis and compare it to the current labor-hours basis.

2. If McKeoun follows the proposed plan, what is likely to happen to the overall use of maintenance? How will each department manager be motivated to increase or decrease the use of maintenance? What will be the overall effect of going to the new plan?

[LO 7-3, 7-5] 7-37 **Departmental Cost Allocation** Ravenscraft Corporation prepares business plans and marketing analyses for start-up companies in the Boston area. Ravenscraft has been very successful in recent years in providing effective service to a growing number of clients. The company provides its service from a single office building in Boston and is organized into two main client-service groups: one for market research and the other for financial analysis. The two groups are treated as cost centers with budgeted annual costs of $1,000,000 and $1,500,000, respectively. In addition, Ravenscraft has a support staff that is organized into two main functions; one for clerical, facilities, and logistical support (called the CFL group) and another for computer-related support. The CFL group is also a cost center with budgeted annual costs of $450,000, while the annual cost of the computer group is $750,000.

Tom Miggs, CFO of Ravenscraft, plans to prepare a departmental cost allocation for his four groups, and he assembles the following information:

Percentage of estimated dollars of work and time by CFL:

> 20%—service to the computer group
> 60%—service to market research
> 20%—service to financial analysis

Percentage of estimated dollars of work and time by the computer group:

> 12%—service to the CFL group
> 48%—service to market research
> 40%—service to financial analysis

**Required** Use 4 decimal places (e.g., 33.3333%) in your calculations. Determine the total cost in the financial analysis and market research groups, after departmental allocation, using (a) the direct method, (b) the step method, and (c) the reciprocal method.

[LO 7-3]    7-38    **Departmental Cost Allocation**    Solexx Corporation distributes its service department overhead costs to product departments. This information is for the month of June:

|  | Service Departments | |
| --- | --- | --- |
|  | **Maintenance** | **Utilities** |
| Overhead costs incurred | $115,000 | $65,000 |
| Service provided to departments |  |  |
|    Maintenance | — | 15% |
|    Utilities | 25% | — |
|    Producing—A | 25 | 40 |
|    Producing—B | 50 | 45 |
| Totals | 100% | 100% |

**Required**    Use 4 decimal places (e.g., 33.3333%) in your calculations. What is the amount of maintenance and utility department costs distributed to producing departments A and B for June using (1) the direct method, (2) the step method, and (3) the reciprocal method?

[LO 7-3, 7-4]    7-39    **Departmental Cost Allocation**    Computer Intelligence, a computer software consulting company, has three major functional areas: computer programming, information systems consulting, and software training. Carol Bingham, a pricing analyst in the accounting department, has been asked to develop total costs for the functional areas. These costs will be used as a guide in pricing a new contract. In computing these costs, Carol is considering three different methods of the departmental allocation approach to allocate overhead costs: the direct method, the step method, and the reciprocal method. She assembled the following data from the two service departments, information systems and facilities:

|  | Service Departments | | Production Departments | | | |
| --- | --- | --- | --- | --- | --- | --- |
|  | **Information Systems** | **Facilities** | **Computer Programming** | **Information Systems Consulting** | **Software Training** | **Total** |
| Budgeted overhead | $80,000 | $45,000 | $150,000 | $190,000 | $135,000 | $600,000 |
| Information systems (hours)* |  | 200 | 1,200 | 600 | 1,000 | 3,000 |
| Facilities (square feet)† | 200 |  | 400 | 600 | 800 | 2,000 |

*Allocated on the basis of hours of computer usage.
†Allocated on the basis of floor space.

**Required**    Use 4 decimal places (e.g., 33.3333%) in your calculations.
1. Using as the application base computer usage time for the information systems department and square feet of floor space for the facilities department, apply overhead from these service departments to the production departments, using these three methods.
   a. Direct method.
   b. Step method.
   c. Reciprocal method.
2. Rather than allocate costs, how might Computer Intelligence better assign the information systems department's costs?

**(CMA Adapted)**

[LO 7-3, 7-5]    7-40    **Departmental Cost Allocation; Not-for-Profit**    The Fleming Foundation is a charitable organization founded by Gaylord Fleming and Sandy Fleming. The Flemings intended for the charity to provide programs in health care for the elderly, particularly those in poverty. The two main program divisions of the foundation are mental health for the elderly and housing for the elderly. In addition to these programs, the Foundation also provides health care educational programs and has a significant fund-raising effort to help the Foundation grow and accomplish the goals of the founders. The Foundation is organized into two main departments—education and program management. These departments are supported by two service departments—information technology (IT) and administration.

There are $418,000 of costs directly traceable to each of the four departments. An additional $65,000 of indirect costs are shared among the four departments—$50,000 of which is allocated to the departments based on direct labor-hours and $15,000 to the departments based on the number of personnel (head count) in the departments.

The cost, labor-hours, and head count in these departments in the most recent year are as follows:

|  | Direct Cost | Labor-Hours | No. of Personnel |
|---|---|---|---|
| Information technology | $ 6,000 | 2,000 | 2 |
| Administration | 122,000 | 6,000 | 3 |
| Education | 100,000 | 4,000 | 3 |
| Program management | 190,000 | 4,000 | 4 |
|  | $418,000 | | |

IT serves Education, Administration, and Program Management 20%, 20%, and 60% of its time, respectively. Administration serves Education, IT, and Program Management 30%, 10%, and 60%, respectively.

The costs of the two main departments (Education and Program Management) are allocated to the two programs (Mental Health and Housing) as follows: the costs in education are allocated on the basis of labor-hours in the programs, while the costs in program management are allocated using the head count used in the two programs. The following table shows the labor-hours and head count consumption by the two programs.

|  | Labor-Hours | Head Count |
|---|---|---|
| Mental health | 2,000 | 1 |
| Housing | 2,000 | 3 |
| Labor-hours in education | 4,000 | |
| Head count in program management | | 4 |

**Required**   Use 4 decimal places (e.g., 33.3333%) in your calculations. Determine the costs allocated to the mental health and housing programs using the (a) direct method, (b) the step method (assuming that IT goes first), and (c) the reciprocal method.

[LO 7-3, 7-4, 7-5]   7-41   **Departmental Cost Allocation; Insurance Company**   CareMark Insurance Company has two product lines: health insurance and auto insurance. The two product lines are served by three operating departments which are necessary for providing the two types of services: claims processing, administration, and sales. These three operating departments are supported by two departments: information technology and facilities. The support provided by information technology and facilities to the other departments is shown below.

|  | Support Departments | | Operating Departments | | |
|---|---|---|---|---|---|
|  | Information Technology | Facilities | Claims Processing | Administration | Sales |
| Information Technology | — | 30% | 30% | 20% | 20% |
| Facilities | 10% | — | 20 | 40 | 30 |

The total costs incurred in the five departments are:

| Information technology | $ 600,000 |
|---|---|
| Facilities | 1,800,000 |
| Claims processing | 345,000 |
| Administration | 875,000 |
| Sales | 555,000 |
| Total costs | $4,175,000 |

**Required**   Use 4 decimal places (e.g., 33.3333%) in your calculations. Allocate the $4,175,000 total departmental costs to the three operating departments using (a) the direct method, (b) the step method (once for information technology and once for facilities going first in the allocation), and (c) the reciprocal method.

**[LO 7-3, 7-4]** **7-42 Joint Product Costing** Choi Company manufactures two skin care lotions, Smooth Skin and Silken Skin, from a joint process. The joint costs incurred are $420,000 for a standard production run that generates 180,000 pints of Smooth Skin and 120,000 pints of Silken Skin. Smooth Skin sells for $2.40 per pint, while Silken Skin sells for $3.90 per pint.

**Required**

1. Assuming that both products are sold at the split-off point, how much of the joint cost of each production run is allocated to Smooth Skin on the sales value basis?

2. If no separable costs are incurred after the split-off point, how much of the joint cost of each production run is allocated to Silken Skin on the physical measure method basis?

3. If separable processing costs beyond the split-off point are $1.40 per pint for Smooth Skin and $0.90 per pint for Silken Skin, how much of the joint cost of each production run is allocated to Silken Skin on a net realizable value basis?

4. If separable processing costs beyond the split-off point are $1.40 per pint for Smooth Skin and $0.90 per pint for Silken Skin, how much of the joint cost of each production run is allocated to Smooth Skin on a physical measure method basis?

**(CMA Adapted)**

**[LO 7-6]** **7-43 Joint Product Costing** Northwest Building Products (NBP) manufactures two lumber products from a joint milling process: residential building lumber (RBL) and commercial building lumber (CB). A standard production run incurs joint costs of $450,000 and results in 80,000 units of RBL and 120,000 units of CB. Each RBL sells for $10 per unit and each CB sells for $12 per unit.

**Required**

1. Assuming that no further processing occurs after the split-off point, how much of the joint costs are allocated to commercial lumber (CB) on a physical measure method basis?

2. If no further processing occurs after the split-off point, how much of the joint cost is allocated to the residential lumber (RBL) on a sales value basis?

3. Assume that the CB is not marketable at split-off but must be planed and sized at a cost of $300,000 per production run. During this process, 10,000 units are unavoidably lost and have no value. The remaining units of CB are salable at $14 per unit. The RBL, although salable immediately at the split-off point, is coated with a tarlike preservative that costs $200,000 per production run. The RBL is then sold for $12 each. Using the net realizable value basis, how much of the completed cost should be assigned to each unit of CB?

4. Based on information in part 3 above, should NBP choose to process RBL beyond split-off?

**(CMA Adapted)**

**[LO 7-6]** **7-44 Joint Products** The Salinas Company produces three products, X, Y, and Z, from a joint process. Each product can be sold at the split-off point or processed further. Additional separable processing requires no special facilities, and the production costs of further processing are entirely variable and traceable to the products involved. Last year all three products were processed beyond split-off. Joint production costs for the year were $80,000. Sales values and costs needed to evaluate Salinas's production policy follow:

| Product | Units Produced | Sales Value at Split-Off | If All Units Processed Further | |
| --- | --- | --- | --- | --- |
| | | | Sales Value | Separable Costs |
| X | 5,000 | $25,000 | $55,000 | $9,000 |
| Y | 4,000 | 41,000 | 45,000 | 7,000 |
| Z | 1,000 | 24,000 | 30,000 | 8,000 |

**Required**

1. Determine the unit cost and gross profit for each product if Salinas allocates joint production costs in proportion to the relative physical volume of output.

2. Determine unit costs and gross profit for each product if Salinas allocates joint costs using the sales value method.

3. Should the firm sell any of its products after further processing?

4. Salinas has been selling all of its products at the split-off point. Selling any of the products after further processing will entail direct competition with some major customers. What strategic factors does the firm need to consider in deciding whether to process any of the products further?

**[LO 7-6]**   7-45   **Joint Products**   Mumbai Chemical makes three widely used industrial adhesives: M10, M15, and M18. Sales and production information for a gallon of each of the three adhesives are shown in the following table. Most of Mumbai's customers ask for a special blend of the three products which improves heat-resistance. The additional separable processing requires additional time and materials, and the price is increased accordingly, as shown in the table. Assume that Mumbai produces only for specific customer orders, so there is no beginning or ending inventory. Assume also that all of Mumbai's customers requested the heat-resistant version of the product, so that all production required additional separable processing. Total joint cost for the three products is $3,500,000.

|  | M10 | M15 | M18 |
| --- | --- | --- | --- |
| Units sold | 150,000 | 125,000 | 125,000 |
| Price (after additional separable processing) | $    20 | $    10 | $    15 |
| Price at split-off | 10 | 5 | 10 |
| Separable processing cost | $550,000 | $125,000 | $625,000 |

**Required**

1. Calculate the product cost and gross margin for each of the three product lines using the following methods:

   (a) physical unit method, (b) sales value at split-off method, and (c) the net realizable value method.

2. Which of the three methods do you think would be preferred in this case? Why?

**[LO 7-6, 7-7]**   7-46   **Joint Products; By-Products (Appendix)**   Multiproduct Corporation is a chemical manufacturer that produces two main products (Pepco–1 and Repke–3) and a by-product (SE–5) from a joint process. If Multiproduct had the proper facilities, it could process SE-5 further into a main product. The ratio of output quantities to input quantity of direct material used in the joint process remains consistent with the processing conditions and activity level.

Multiproduct currently uses the physical measure method of allocating joint costs to the main products. The by-product is inventoried at its net realizable value, which is used to reduce the joint production costs before they are allocated to the main products.

Jim Simpson, Multiproduct's controller, wants to implement the sales value method of joint cost allocation. He believes that inventory costs should be based on each product's ability to contribute to the recovery of joint production costs. Multiproduct uses an asset recognition approach in accounting for by-products.

Data regarding Multiproduct's operations for November are presented in the following report. The joint cost of production totaled $2,640,000 for November.

|  | Main Products | | By-Product |
| --- | --- | --- | --- |
|  | Pepco–1 | Repke–3 | SE–5 |
| November sales in gallons | 800,000 | 700,000 | 200,000 |
| November production in gallons | 900,000 | 720,000 | 240,000 |
| Sales value per gallon at split-off point | $2.00 | $1.50 | $0.55* |
| Separable process costs after split-off | $1,800,000 | $720,000 | — |
| Final sales value per gallon | $5.00 | $4.00 | — |

*Selling costs of 5 cents per gallon are incurred to sell the by-product.

**Required**

1. Describe the sales value method and explain how it would accomplish Jim's objective.

2. Assuming Multiproduct adopts the sales value method for internal reporting purposes, calculate the allocation of the joint production cost for November.

3. Multiproduct plans to expand its production facilities to further process SE–5 into a main product. Discuss how the allocation of the joint production costs under the sales value method would change when SE–5 becomes a main product.

**(CMA Adapted)**

**[LO 7-6, 7-7]**   7-47   **Joint Products; By-Products (Appendix)**   Texchem manufactures chemicals for various purposes. Texchem produces PX-105, a chemical used in swimming pools; GZ-233, a chemical used in pesticides; and M-13, a by-product sold to fertilizer manufacturers. Texchem uses the net realizable value of its main products to allocate joint production costs. The by-product is inventoried at its net realizable value, which is used to reduce the joint production costs before they are allocated to the main products.

Data regarding Texchem's operations for the month of November follow. During this month, Texchem incurred joint production costs of $1,800,000 in the manufacture of its three products.

|  | PX-105 | GZ-233 | M-13 |
|---|---|---|---|
| November sales in gallons | 450,000 | 225,000 | 50,000 |
| November production in gallons | 600,000 | 300,000 | 100,000 |
| Sales value per gallon at split-off | $2.00 | $4.00 | $0.70* |
| Separable processing costs | $550,000 | $633,000 | |
| Final sales value per gallon | $8.50 | $7.00 | $— |

*Selling costs of 15 cents per gallon are incurred to sell the by-product.

**Required**

1. Determine Texchem's allocation of joint production costs for the month of November. Be sure to present appropriate supporting calculations.
2. Texchem has an opportunity to sell GZ-233 at the split-off point for $4.00 per gallon. Prepare an analysis showing whether Texchem should sell GZ-233 at the split-off point or process further.
3. As a production supervisor for Texchem, you have learned that small quantities of the critical chemical compound in GZ-233 might be present in PX-105. What should you do?

**(CMA Adapted)**

[LO 7-6, 7-7]   7-48   **Joint Products; By-Products (Appendix)**   The Marshall Company has a joint production process that produces two joint products and a by-product. The joint products are Ying and Yang, and the by-product is Bit. Marshall accounts for the costs of its products using the net realizable value method. The two joint products are processed beyond the split-off point, incurring separable processing costs. There is a $1,000 disposal cost for the by-product. A summary of a recent month's activity at Marshall is shown below.

|  | Ying | Yang | Bit |
|---|---|---|---|
| Units sold | 50,000 | 40,000 | 10,000 |
| Units producted | 50,000 | 40,000 | 10,000 |
| Separable processing costs—variable | $140,000 | $42,000 | $— |
| Separable processing costs—fixed | $10,000 | $8,000 | $— |
| Sales price | $6.00 | $12.50 | $1.60 |

Total joint costs for Marshall in the recent month are $265,000, of which $115,000 is a variable cost.

**Required**

1. Calculate the manufacturing cost per unit for each of the three products.
2. Calculate the gross margin for each product.

[LO 7-6]   7-49   **Joint Products**   Yonica Petroleum is a global manufacturer of specialty chemicals that are made from the waste products of the petroleum industry. Yonica in effect recycles a good portion of the waste from the refineries used by the large oil companies. The specialty chemicals are used as cleaning solvents and lubricants in industrial applications. Yonica has three products—Y64, G22, and X17—and total joint production cost of $356,000. Yonica plans to process all three products beyond the split-off point in order to be able to sell the product at the higher price after separable processing.

|  | Y64 | G22 | X17 |
|---|---|---|---|
| Gallons produced and sold | 22,000 | 45,500 | 18,000 |
| Sales price at split-off point | $2.24 | $2.88 | $0.44 |
| Separable processing cost | $65,500 | $34,250 | $55,400 |
| Sales price after separable processing | $10.50 | $6.75 | $4.22 |
| Number of customers | 22 | 3 | 46 |

**Required**

1. Calculate the product cost of each of the three product lines using the following methods:
   (a) physical unit method, (b) sales value at split-off method, and (c) net realizable value method.

2. Which of the three methods do you think would be preferred in this case? Why?

3. While Yonica chose to process all three products beyond the split-off point, do you think this is the correct decision? Which products, if any, do you think should have been processed beyond the split-off point, and why?

4. Since Yonica is involved in the recycling of waste chemicals, it is able to purchase its raw materials at greatly reduced cost. However, its manufacturing costs are slightly higher than some of its competitors because of the relatively high cost of recycling. Yonica plans to bring these recycling costs down in the next 18 months. Yonica has been able to compete successfully by maintaining lower margins than its competitors and because some of its customers are willing to pay more for a product that has been manufactured from recycled material. Comment on Yonica's strategy and why (or why not) you think it will continue to be successful.

5. What are some of the global issues that Yonica should consider in effectively executing its strategy?

6. What should Yonica do, if anything, to improve the overall effect of its operations on the environment?

[LO 7-6]  7-50  **Joint Cost Allocation: Managerial Incentives**  Cameron Manufacturing produces auto parts for auto manufacturers and parts wholesalers. The business is very competitive, and productivity measures are used throughout its eight manufacturing plants. Jill Owens, the manufacturing vice president, explains to her plant managers the importance of reducing cycle time, improving throughput, and reducing waste. One type of waste she keeps close track of is waste due to accidents and injuries on the job. Jill believes that a safe workplace also contributes to productivity. A reduction in accidents and injuries can also lead to a reduction in the insurance the firm pays to cover its liability in these incidents. The premium for this insurance coverage is a single policy and is a joint cost shared by all eight plants. One of the plant managers, Mike Griffin, notes that the current procedure for allocating the cost of insurance, which is based on total plant output, does not provide plant managers with the desired incentive to reduce accidents. It just means that the larger plants get charged more. Mike suggests that the insurance cost should be charged to the plants based on the number of manufacturing personnel in each plant.

**Required**  What do you think of Mike's suggestion? What alternative would you suggest, if any, for allocating the cost of insurance to the plants?

## Solution to Self-Study Problem

### Joint Product Costing

**The Physical Measure Method**  If we use a physical measure method, the joint cost of $20,000 is allocated as shown in Exhibit 1.

The production costs per gallon for both products are the same:

$$\text{Product GS-50: } \$15,000/75 = \$200$$
$$\text{Product GS-80: } \$5,000/25 = \$200$$

**The Sales Value at Split-Off Method**  Assume that Northern Company sold 60 gallons of GS-50 and 20 gallons of GS-80. Then the $20,000 joint cost should be allocated among the products as shown in Exhibit 2.

Note that the gallons sold do not figure in the analysis, which is based on units produced only. The production costs per gallon for both products are calculated:

$$\text{Product GS-50: } \$18,750/75 = \$250$$
$$\text{Product GS-80: } \$1,250/25 = \$50$$

**EXHIBIT 1**
**Physical Measure Method**

| Product | Physical Measure | Proportion | Allocation of Joint Cost |
|---|---|---|---|
| GS-50 | 75 gallons | 75% | $20,000 × 75% = $15,000 |
| GS-80 | 25 gallons | 25 | 20,000 × 25% = 5,000 |
| | 100 gallons | 100% | $20,000 |

**EXHIBIT 2**
**Sales Value at Split-Off Method**

| Product | Units | Price | Sales Value | Proportion | Joint Cost Allocated |
|---|---|---|---|---|---|
| GS-50 | 75 | $300 | $22,500 | 93.75% | $20,000 × 93.75% = $18,750 |
| GS-80 | 25 | 60 | 1,500 | 6.25 | 20,000 × 6.25% = 1,250 |
| Total | | | $24,000 | 100% | $20,000 |

**EXHIBIT 3** Net Realizable Value Method

| Product | Production Units | Sales Price | Sales Value | Separable Cost | Net Realizable Value | Weight | Joint Cost Allocated |
|---------|------------------|-------------|-------------|----------------|----------------------|--------|----------------------|
| GS-50 | 50 | $500 | $25,000 | $5,000 | $20,000 | 80% | $20,000 × 80% = $16,000 |
| GS-80 | 50 | 140 | 7,000 | 2,000 | 5,000 | 20 | 20,000 × 20% = 4,000 |
| Total | 100 | | $32,000 | $7,000 | $25,000 | 100% | $20,000 |

**The Net Realizable Value Method**   The net realizable values of GS-50 and GS-80 are $20,000 and $5,000, respectively, as shown in Exhibit 3. The allocated costs are $16,000 to GS-50 and $4,000 to GS-80. The costs per gallon for products GS-505 and GS-805 are calculated:

Product GS-505: ($16,000 + $5,000)/50 = $420

Product GS-805: ($4,000 + $2,000)/50 = $120

*Please visit http://www.mhhe.com/blocher6e to access a narrated, animated tutorial for solving this problem.*

# PART TWO

# Planning and Decision Making

The objective of these six chapters is to show how cost management information can be used strategically to support management planning and decision making. A key idea that ties these chapters together is that planning and decision making require a good understanding of cost drivers, that is, the activities or transactions that cause changes in costs, both from a short-term and a long-term perspective. There are both volume-based cost drivers (explained in Chapter 4) and activity-based cost drivers (explained in Chapter 5); both types of cost drivers are important in planning and decision making.

Because of this importance, the first chapter in this part, Chapter 8, is about cost estimation—how cost estimation equations are used to predict costs using cost drivers. We cover both statistical and nonstatistical approaches to cost estimation equations. This foundational material is followed by a discussion of a short-run profit-planning tool, cost-volume-profit analysis, also called CVP, in Chapter 9.

Chapter 10 explains the master budget, which is one of the key planning tools that management accountants develop for their organizations. The master budget is often referred to as the most commonly used tool in management accounting for coordinating operations and for providing a set of financial targets to guide management. Linkages in Chapter 10 are made to some important topics covered earlier in the text, for example, budgeting for sustainability, preparation of activity-based budgets, and the impact of time-based activity-based costing on budgeting systems.

Chapter 11 shows how the management accountant uses cost calculations and a strategic understanding of the competitive context of an organization to address decisions such as whether to make or buy a component of a manufactured product or service, when to add features to a product, and when to accept one-time orders from customers. In each of these decisions, competitive context is crucial. For example, suppose that a company competes on the basis of *cost leadership* and is looking for ways to reduce manufacturing cost. The management accountant determines that it is cheaper to make rather than buy a part in the product; independently, the plant engineer figures out how to do away with the part while retaining the product's functionality. This accountant's analysis is flawed because it does not consider that the company can become more competitive by a redesign of the product.

Chapter 12 covers the topic of allocating capital (funds) to long-term projects, that is, those investments that require substantial amounts of capital and that provide financial returns over an extended period of time. As such, we extend the framework covered in Chapter 11 to include the analysis of decisions that have a long-term effect on the organization. The tools for decision making in this context incorporate the time value of money and are called *discounted cash flow (DCF)* decision models. The chapter shows how to deal with uncertainty in capital budgeting, including the use of a real options approach.

Chapter 13 applies the concepts of the value chain and life-cycle analysis as cost-planning and cost-reduction tools. The value chain begins with the idea for a product or service; this is followed by market research, testing sample products, manufacturing, and finally, sales and customer service. The chapter comprises four main parts: target costing at the front end of the value chain, the theory of constraints for the operational portion of the value chain, life-cycle costing for the full value chain, and strategic pricing.

# CHAPTER EIGHT

# Cost Estimation

**After studying this chapter, you should be able to . . .**

LO 8-1  Understand the strategic role of cost estimation

LO 8-2  Understand the six steps of cost estimation

LO 8-3  Use each of the cost estimation methods: the high-low method and regression analysis

LO 8-4  Explain the implementation issues of the cost estimation methods

LO 8-5  Use learning curves in cost estimation when learning is present (appendix)

**LO 8-1**

*Understand the strategic role of cost estimation.*

Cost management information is critical in cost planning and decision making, for example, planning a new product or plant expansion, analyzing product or customer profitability, or developing a new manufacturing and marketing strategy. A basic requirement for cost effective planning is to use *accurate cost estimates* in the planning process. This chapter describes the methods that can be used to develop accurate estimates.

An example where cost estimation is particularly important is the construction industry. Large construction projects are often obtained on the basis of competitive bids. The contractors that bid on these projects must have accurate cost estimation methods to win their share of the bids and to be profitable. Cost estimation methods for contractors develop detailed analyses of the material and labor costs that are directly traceable to the project, as well as projections of the indirect costs, preferably using activity analysis as described in Chapter 5. Cost estimation in the construction industry has become particularly important in recent years because of the recession in the commercial and residential real estate markets. Estimating the cost of construction materials, gasoline for equipment, and other commodities used in construction has become more difficult as the prices of these materials and commodities have fluctuated widely in recent years.

## Strategic Role of Cost Estimation

Carnegie's success can be attributed to another lesson he had learned on the way up: the value of meticulous cost accounting . . . As a result, when Union Iron or Keystone Bridge submitted a bid on a project, there was no guesswork involved. If Carnegie chose to undercut a rival's figure, he did so with absolute confidence that he could deliver what he promised and make a profit, for his was the only firm in the field with a near-fanatical devotion to cost accounting. As Charles Schwab would later put it, "Carnegie never wanted to know the profits. He always wanted to know the costs."[1]

**Cost estimation**

is the development of a well-defined relationship between a cost object and its cost drivers for the purpose of predicting the cost.

As Carnegie understood, a critical starting point for strategic cost management is having accurate cost estimates. The strategic approach is forward looking, and thus cost estimation is an essential element of it. **Cost estimation** is the development of a well-defined relationship between a cost object and its cost drivers for the purpose of predicting the cost.

Cost estimation facilitates strategic management in two important ways. First, it helps predict future costs using previously identified activity-based, volume-based, structural, or executional cost drivers. Second, cost estimation helps identify the key cost drivers for a cost object and which of these cost drivers are most useful in predicting cost.

[1] Les Standiford, *Meet You in Hell* (New York: Crown Publishers, 2005), pp. 47–48, writing about Andrew Carnegie, business leader and philanthropist.

## Using Cost Estimation to Predict Future Costs

Strategic management requires accurate cost estimates for many applications, including these:

1. **To facilitate strategy development and implementation.** Cost estimates are particularly important for firms competing on the basis of cost leadership. Cost estimates guide management in determining which management techniques, such as business intelligence, target costing, or total quality management, the firm should employ to succeed in its chosen strategy. A recent survey of the Hackett Group showed that forecasting (including cost estimation) was listed as the most "strategic" and "critical" to the company's success, ahead of cash management, decision support, and four other highly rated management tools.[2]

2. **To facilitate value-chain analysis.** Cost estimates help the firm identify potential opportunities for cost reduction by reconfiguring the value chain. For example, cost estimates are useful in determining whether overall costs and value to the product can be improved by manufacturing one of its components in-house or by purchasing it from a supplier. Value chain analysis in decision making is covered in Chapters 2 and 11.

3. **To facilitate target costing and pricing.** Cost estimates are an integral part of target costing and pricing. Management uses cost estimates of different product designs as part of the process of selecting the particular design that provides the best value to the customer while reducing manufacturing and other costs. Target costing and pricing are covered in Chapter 13.

4. **To facilitate effective performance measurement, evaluation, and compensation.** Cost estimates play a key role in determining costs in business units, which affect division managers' financial performance and opportunity for promotion and compensation and the ability to attract capital investment to their division. Accurate cost estimates play a crucial role in performance measurement, which is covered in Chapters 18 through 20.

### *Cost Estimation for Different Types of Cost Drivers*

The cost estimation methods explained in this chapter can be used for any of the four types of cost drivers: activity-based, volume-based, structural, or executional. The relationships between costs and activity-based or volume-based cost drivers often are best fit by the linear cost estimation methods explained in this chapter because these relationships are at least approximately linear within the relevant range of the firm's operations.

Structural cost drivers involve plans and decisions that have a long-term and therefore strategic impact on the firm. Such decisions include manufacturing experience, scale of product, product or production technology, and product or production complexity. Technology and complexity issues often lead management to use activity-based costing and linear estimation methods. In contrast, experience and scale often require nonlinear methods. As a cost driver, experience represents the reduction in unit cost due to learning. The effect on total cost of experience is nonlinear: that is, costs decrease with increased manufacturing experience. The learning effect is explained in the appendix to the chapter. Similarly, the relationship between the structural cost driver, scale, and total cost is nonlinear. *Scale* is the term used to describe the manufacture of similar products that differ in size—for example, pipe valves of different capacity. A common effect of scale is that total manufacturing cost increases more rapidly than the increase in the size of the product. For example, the manufacture of a 22-inch industrial valve requires more than twice the cost of an 11-inch valve.

## Using Cost Estimation to Identify Cost Drivers

Often the most practical way to identify cost drivers is to rely on the judgment of product designers, engineers, and manufacturing personnel. Those who are most knowledgeable about the product and production processes have the most useful information on cost drivers. Cost estimation sometimes plays a discovery role and at other times a collaborative role to validate and confirm the judgments of the designers and engineers. For example, Hewlett-Packard uses cost estimation to confirm the usefulness of cost drivers selected by teams of engineers and production personnel.

[2] Kate O'Sullivan, "From Adversity, Better Budgets," *CFO,* June 2010, pp. 45–48.

## Six Steps of Cost Estimation

**LO 8-2**

*Understand the six steps of cost estimation.*

The six steps of cost estimation are (1) define the cost object for which the related costs are to be estimated, (2) determine the cost drivers, (3) collect consistent and accurate data on the cost object and the cost drivers, (4) graph the data, (5) select and employ an appropriate estimation method, and (6) evaluate the accuracy of the cost estimate.

### Step 1: Define the Cost Object to Be Estimated

Although it might seem elementary, defining the particular cost to be estimated requires care. For example, if the goal is to estimate product costs to improve product pricing, the relevant cost objects are the products manufactured in the plant. In contrast, if the goal is to reward managers for reducing cost, the most appropriate cost objects are the individual manufacturing departments in the plant since costs are most directly controllable by department managers.

### Step 2: Determine the Cost Drivers

Cost drivers are the causal factors used in the estimation of the cost. Some examples of estimated costs and their related cost drivers follow:

| Cost to Be Estimated | Cost Driver |
| --- | --- |
| Fuel expense for a delivery truck | Miles driven |
| Heating expense for a building | Temperature outside the building |
| Maintenance cost in a manufacturing plant | Machine-hours, labor-hours |
| Product design cost | Number of design elements, design changes |

Identifying cost drivers is the most important step in developing the cost estimate. A number of relevant drivers might exist, yet some might not be immediately obvious. Fuel expense for a large delivery truck, for example, might be primarily a function of miles traveled, but it is also affected by the average weight delivered, the number of hours of operation, and the nature of the delivery area.

### Step 3: Collect Consistent and Accurate Data

Once the cost drivers have been selected, the management accountant collects data on the cost object and cost drivers. The data must be consistent and accurate. *Consistent* means that each period of data is calculated using the same accounting basis (for example, all periods use accrual accounting rather than cash-basis accounting) and all transactions are properly recorded in the period in which they occurred. For example, using biweekly data for some variables and monthly data for other variables causes errors in estimates. Similarly, mismatch between periods occurs when data for one variable are based on the calendar month while data for another variable are based on four consecutive weekly periods that do not match the calendar month. Difficulties also arise when supplies purchased during the month are used instead of supplies consumed.

The period used in cost estimating can vary from daily to weekly or annually. If the period is too short, the chance of mismatch between variables increases because of recording lags. On the other hand, if the period is too long, important short-term relationships in the data might be averaged out, and the estimate will not be as accurate. Moreover, a longer period reduces the number of data points available to improve the accuracy of the estimate. Management accountants must determine which time period best satisfies the competing objectives for accurate estimation.

Also the accuracy of the data depends on the source. Sometimes data developed within the firm are very reliable, as a result of management policies and procedures to ensure accuracy. External sources of data, including governmental sources, trade and industry publications, universities, and other sources, have varying degrees of accuracy. The choice of cost drivers requires trade-offs between the relevance of the drivers and the consistency and accuracy of the data.

## Step 4: Graph the Data

The objective of graphing data is to identify unusual patterns. Any shift or nonlinearity in the data must be given special attention in developing the estimate. For example, a week's downtime to install new equipment causes unusual production data for that week; such data should be excluded when developing a cost estimate. Any unusual occurrences can be detected easily by studying a graph.

## Step 5: Select and Employ the Estimation Method

The two estimation methods presented in the next section of the chapter differ in their ability to provide superior accuracy in cost estimation relative to the cost of the expertise and resources required. The management accountant chooses the method with the best precision/cost trade-off for the estimation objectives.

## Step 6: Assess the Accuracy of the Cost Estimate

A critical final step in cost estimation is to consider the potential for error when the estimate is prepared. This involves considering the completeness and appropriateness of cost drivers selected in step 2, the consistency and accuracy of data selected in step 3, the study of the graphs in step 4, and the precision of the method selected in step 5.

A common approach for assessing the accuracy of an estimation method is to compare the estimates to the actual results over time. For example, when a firm predicts annual overhead costs each year, over a 10-year period there are 10 estimation errors to evaluate. These errors can be evaluated using the **mean absolute percentage error (MAPE)**. MAPE is calculated by taking the absolute value of each error, and then averaging these 10 errors.

> The **mean absolute percentage error (MAPE)** is calculated by taking the absolute value of each error, and then averaging these errors and converting the result to a percentage of the actual values.

## Cost Estimation Methods

**LO 8-3**

*Use each of the cost estimation methods: the high-low method and regression analysis.*

The two estimation methods we will study in this chapter are the high-low method and regression analysis. The high-low method is the least accurate but easiest to apply and regression analysis is the most accurate and most costly, requiring more time, data collection, and expertise. In choosing the best estimation method, management accountants seek a balance between the level of accuracy desired and any limitations on cost, time, effort, and expertise.

### An Illustration of Cost Estimation

To illustrate the two methods, we use the example of a management accountant, Ben Garcia, who is developing cost estimates of maintenance costs for a manufacturing plant. Garcia has the following data on maintenance costs:

|  | January | February | March | April | May | June | July |
|---|---|---|---|---|---|---|---|
| Maintenance cost ($) | 22,843 | 22,510 | 22,706 | 23,030 | 22,413 | 22,935 | 23,175 |

As a first step, Garcia graphs the data (Exhibit 8.1) and observes that maintenance costs are increasing, although not steadily. Based only on a visual study of the graph, he also predicts that maintenance costs will be between $22,500 and $23,500 in the coming month, August. Since this prediction is rough and he wants to improve its accuracy, he turns to the cost estimation methods, beginning with the high-low method.

### High-Low Method

> The **high-low method** uses algebra to determine a *unique* estimation line between representative high and low points in the data.

The **high-low method** uses algebra to determine a *unique* estimation line between representative high and low points in the data. The high-low method accomplishes two important objectives for Garcia. First, it is based on a unique cost line rather than a rough estimate based on a view of the graph. Second, it permits him to add information that might be useful in predicting maintenance costs. For example, he knows that total maintenance costs are likely to include both variable and fixed costs. The fixed cost portion is the planned (preventive) maintenance that is performed regardless of the plant's volume of activity. Also, a part of maintenance cost varies with the number of operating hours; more

**EXHIBIT 8.1**
**Graph of Maintenance Costs**

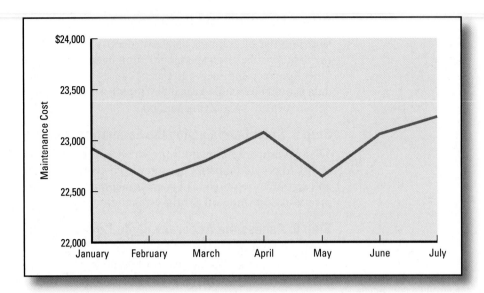

operating hours mean more wear on the machines and thus more maintenance costs. Garcia collects the additional operating-hours information as follows:

| | January | February | March | April | May | June | July |
|---|---|---|---|---|---|---|---|
| Total operating hours | 3,451 | 3,325 | 3,383 | 3,614 | 3,423 | 3,410 | 3,500 |
| Maintenance costs ($) | 22,843 | 22,510 | 22,706 | 23,030 | 22,413 | 22,935 | 23,175 |

To use the high-low method, Garcia enters the data into a graph, as shown in Exhibit 8.2; note that operating hours are on the horizontal axis, and each data point is the location of the cost and operating hours for a particular month. Ben then selects two points from the data, one representative of the lower points and the other representative of the higher points. Often these can be simply the lowest and highest points in the data. However, if either the highest or lowest point is a great distance from the other points around it, a biased estimation can result. Both points must be representative of the data around them.

**EXHIBIT 8.2**
**Ben Garcia's Data on**
**Maintenance Cost and Hours**

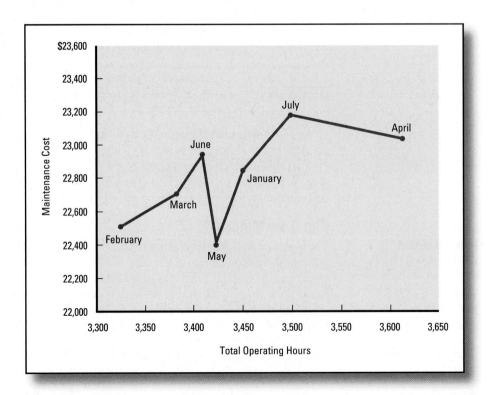

The high-low estimate is represented as follows:

$$Y = a + (b \times X)$$

where: $Y$ = the value of the estimated maintenance cost

$a$ = a fixed quantity that represents the value of $Y$ when $X$ = zero

$b$ = the slope of the line (in the plant maintenance example, it is the unit variable cost for maintenance cost per operating hour).

$X$ = the cost driver, the number of operating hours of operation for the plant

To obtain the high and low points, Garcia draws a freehand line through the data to help select the high and low points (try this yourself on Exhibit 8.2). He then chooses a high and a low point reasonably close to the freehand line. Suppose that he has chosen the points for February and April. Then he calculates the value for $b$:

$b$ = Variable cost per hour

$$= \frac{\text{Difference between } \textit{costs} \text{ for high and low points}}{\text{Difference for the value of the } \textit{cost driver} \text{ for the high and low points}}$$

$$b = \frac{\$23,030 - \$22,510}{3,614 - 3,325} = \$1.80 \text{ per hour}$$

Next, the value for $a$ (the fixed quantity) can be calculated using either February or April data:

**Using April Data**

$$a = Y - (b \times X) = \$23,030 - (\$1.80 \times 3,614) = \$16,525$$

Using February data gives the same value for $a$ because fixed cost is the same at both levels of operating hours; only total variable costs for the two levels differ:

**Using February Data**

$$a = Y - (b \times X) = \$22,510 - (\$1.80 \times 3,325) = \$16,525$$

So the estimation equation using the high-low method is:

$$Y = \$16,525 + (\$1.80 \times X)$$

This equation can be used to estimate maintenance cost for August. Suppose that 3,600 operating hours are expected in August. Then maintenance costs are estimated as follows:

$$\text{Maintenance cost in August} = \$16,525 + (\$1.80 \times 3,600)$$

$$= \$23,005$$

Recall our discussion of the relevant range in Chapter 3. The data used to obtain the above cost equation were operating hours in the range of 3,325 to 3,614 hours, which is the relevant range for this equation. Thus, the management accountant is careful to rely only on predictions for which the operating hours fall in this range. Since the operating hours for August (3,600 hours) fall in the relevant range, the estimate of $23,005 is useful.

The key advantage of the high-low method is that it provides a unique cost equation—once the high and low points are chosen, there is only one possible cost estimation equation. However, the high-low method is limited; it can represent only the best possible line for the two selected points, and the selection of the two points requires judgment. The next method, regression analysis, is generally more accurate because it uses statistical estimation, which provides greater mathematical precision.

## Regression Analysis

**Regression analysis** is a statistical method for obtaining the unique cost-estimating equation that best fits a set of data points. Regression analysis fits the data by *minimizing the sum of the squares* of the estimation errors. Each error is the distance measured from the regression line to one of the data points. Because regression analysis systematically minimizes the estimation errors in this way, it is sometimes called **least squares regression.**

**Regression analysis** is a statistical method for obtaining the unique cost-estimating equation that best fits a set of data points.

**Least squares regression,** which minimizes the sum of the squares of the estimation errors, is widely viewed as one of the most effective methods for estimating costs.

**The dependent variable** is the cost to be estimated.

**The independent variable** is the cost driver used to estimate the value of the dependent variable.

A regression analysis has two types of variables. The **dependent variable** is the cost to be estimated.[3] The **independent variable** is the cost driver used to estimate the value of the dependent variable. When one cost driver is used, the analysis is called a *simple regression.* When two or more cost drivers are used, it is called *multiple regression.*

The regression equation has both an intercept and a slope term, much like the high-low method. In contrast to the high-low method, the amount of the estimation error is considered explicitly in the simple regression estimate, which is

$$Y = a + bX + e$$

where: $Y$ = the amount of the *dependent variable,* the cost to be estimated

$a$ = a *fixed quantity,* also called the *intercept* or *constant term,* which represents the amount of $Y$ when $X = 0$

$b$ = the *unit variable cost,* also called the *coefficient* of the independent variable, that is, the increase in $Y$ (cost) for each unit increase in $X$ (cost driver)

$X$ = the value for the *independent variable,* the cost driver for the cost to be estimated; there may be one or more cost drivers

$e$ = the *estimation error,* which is the amount by which the regression prediction $(y = a + bX)$ differs from the data point.

To illustrate the regression method, the following table and Exhibit 8.3A show three months of data on supplies expense and production levels. (To simplify the presentation, only three data points are used; applications of regression usually involve at least 12 data points.) The management accountant's task is to estimate supplies expense for month 4, in which the production level is expected to be 125 units.

| Month | Supplies Expense (*Y*) | Production Level (*X*) |
|---|---|---|
| 1 | $250 | 50 units |
| 2 | 310 | 100 |
| 3 | 325 | 150 |
| 4 | ? | 125 |

The regression for the data is determined by a statistical procedure that finds the unique line through the three data points that minimizes the sum of the squared error distances. The regression line (see Exhibit 8.3B) is[4]

$$Y = \$220 + \$0.75X$$

Thus, the estimated value for supplies expense in month 4 is

$$Y = \$220 + (\$0.75 \times 125) = \$313.75$$

Regression analysis gives management accountants an objective, statistically precise method to estimate supplies expense. Its principal advantage is a unique estimate that produces the least estimation error for the data. On the other hand, since the errors are squared to find the best fitting line, the regression analysis can be influenced strongly by unusual data points called **outliers,** with the result that the estimation line is not representative of most of the data. Such a situation is illustrated in Exhibit 8.4. To prevent this type of distortion, management accountants often prepare a graph of the data prior to using regression and determine whether any outliers are present. Each outlier is reviewed to determine whether it is due to a data-recording error, normal operating condition, or unique and nonrecurring event. Guided by the objective of developing the regression that is most representative of the data, the accountant then decides whether to correct or remove the outlier.

**Outliers** are unusual data points that strongly influence a regression analysis.

[3] Although the dependent variable is a cost in most of the cases we consider, the dependent variable also could be a revenue or some other type of financial or operating data.

[4] The derivation of the intercept ($220) and coefficient ($0.75) for this regression line is done in Excel or other software, as illustrated later in this chapter. For those looking for advanced coverage of regression analysis, there is a Regression Analysis Supplement on the text website under Course Wide Content. This supplement covers some of the common modeling problems in using regression analysis, such as nonlinearity, nonconstant variance, and other modeling issues. The supplement also includes a brief discussion of how to detect and resolve these modeling issues.

**EXHIBIT 8.3A**   Supplies Expense Data for Regression Application

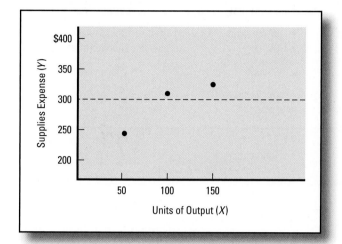

**EXHIBIT 8.3B**   The Regression Line for Supplies Expense with Units of Output as the Cost Driver (i.e., independent variable)

**EXHIBIT 8.4**

**The Effect of Outliers on Regression**

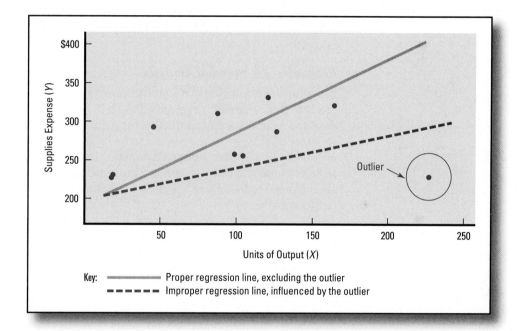

### Choosing the Dependent Variable

Development of a regression analysis begins with the choice of the cost object, the dependent variable. The dependent variable might be at a very aggregate level, such as total maintenance costs for the entire firm, or at a detail level, such as maintenance costs for each plant or department. The choice of aggregation level depends on the objectives for the cost estimation, data availability and reliability, and cost/benefit considerations. When a high level of accuracy is desired, a detail level of analysis is preferred.

### Choosing the Independent Variable(s)

To identify the independent variables, management accountants consider all financial, operating, and other economic data that might be relevant for estimating the dependent variable. The goal is to choose variables that (1) are relevant, that is, they change when the dependent variable changes, and (2) do not duplicate other independent variables. As an example, Exhibit 8.5 presents some dependent and independent variables that might be appropriate for the study of costs in a retail store.

**EXHIBIT 8.5**
Selected Independent Variables
and Dependent Variables for
Costs in a Retail Store

| Selected Dependent Variables | Independent Variables | |
|---|---|---|
| | **Financial Data** | **Operating Data** |
| • Labor expense | • Wage rates<br>• Sales | • Hours worked<br>• Number of employees |
| • Utilities expense | • Sales | • Average daily temperature<br>• Number of hours store is open |
| • General expenses: office supplies, cleaning, security, and repairs | • Sales<br>• Total expense<br>• Net fixed assets | • Number of employees |

Most often the data in a regression analysis are numerical amounts in dollars or units. Another type of variable, called a **dummy variable,** represents the presence or absence of a condition. For example, dummy variables can be used to indicate seasonality. If the management accountant is estimating costs of production, and if production is always high in March, a dummy variable with a value of 1 for March and 0 for the other months could be used.

**A dummy variable**
is used to represent the presence or absence of a condition.

### Evaluating a Regression Analysis

In addition to a cost estimate, regression analysis also provides quantitative measures of its precision and reliability. *Precision* refers to the accuracy of the estimates from the regression, and *reliability* indicates whether the regression reflects actual relationships among the variables; that is, is the regression model likely to continue to predict accurately? These measures can aid management accountants in assessing the usefulness of the regression. Four key (and related) measures are explained here. These and other statistical measures are explained more fully in a regression analysis supplement available on the text website (see footnote 4).

1. $R$-squared, also called the *coefficient of determination.*
2. The $t$-value.
3. The standard error of the estimate (SE).
4. The $p$-value

$R$-squared, the $t$-value, and the $p$-value are used to measure the reliability of the regression; the standard error is a useful measure of the precision, or accuracy, of the regression.

**$R$-squared**
is a number between zero and 1 and often is described as a measure of the explanatory power of the regression; that is, the degree to which changes in the dependent variable can be predicted by changes in the independent variable(s).

**$R$-squared** is a number between zero and 1 and often is described as a measure of the explanatory power of the regression; that is, the degree to which changes in the dependent variable can be predicted by changes in the independent variable(s). The higher the $R$-squared, the more reliable the regression model is for cost estimation; in fact if $R$-squared equals one, then SE must equal zero. When viewed graphically, regressions with high $R$-squared show the data points lying near the regression line; in low $R$-squared regressions, the data points are scattered about, as demonstrated in Exhibit 8.6A (high $R$-squared) and 8.6B (low $R$-squared). Most regression analyses involving financial data have $R$-squared values above 0.5, and many have values in the 0.8 to 0.9 range.[5]

**The $t$-value**
is a measure of the reliability of each independent variable; that is, the degree to which an independent variable has a valid, stable, long-term relationship with the dependent variable.

The **$t$-value** is a measure of the statistical reliability of each independent variable. *Reliability* is the degree to which an independent variable has a valid, stable, long-term relationship with the dependent variable. A relatively small $t$-value (generally, the $t$-value should be

[5] The square root of $R$-squared, or simply $R$, is called the *correlation coefficient* and is interpreted in the same manner as $R$-squared. The correlation coefficient is a number between $-1$ and $+1$; a value near zero is interpreted as a lack of relationship between the independent and dependent variables. When $R$ is positive, the relationship is direct; that is, when one variable increases, so does the other. When $R$ is negative, the relationship is inverse; that is, when one variable increases, the other decreases.

**EXHIBIT 8.6A** Regression with High *R*-Squared

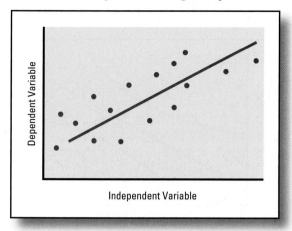

**EXHIBIT 8.6B** Regression with Low *R*-Squared

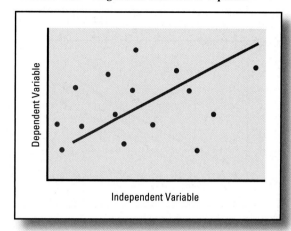

**Multicollinearity**
means that two or more independent variables are highly correlated with each other.

**Correlation**
means that a given variable tends to change predictably in the same (or opposite) direction for a given change in the other, correlated variable.

The **standard error of the estimate (SE)**
is a measure of the dispersion of the actual observations around the regression line, and as such provides a measure of the accuracy of the regression's estimates.

A **confidence interval**
is a range around the regression line within which the management accountant can be confident the actual value of the predicted cost will fall.

more than 2) indicates little or no statistical relationship between the independent and dependent variables. A variable with a low *t*-value should be removed from the regression to simplify the model and to lead to more accurate cost estimates.[6]

When two or more independent variables exist, the presence of a low *t*-value for one or more of these variables is a possible signal of **multicollinearity,** which means that two or more independent variables are highly correlated with each other. As suggested by the name, independent variables are supposed to be independent of each other, not correlated. **Correlation** among variables means that a given variable tends to change predictably in the same (or opposite) direction of a given change in the other variable. For example, the number of machine-hours used in manufacturing is often correlated with the number of labor-hours because both are affected by the same factor, the number of units produced. Moreover, because a common trend tends to affect many types of financial data, accounting and operating data are often highly correlated.

The effect of multicollinearity is that the regression estimates of the coefficients for the independent variables are unreliable. The cost estimates of the regression will be reliable, but the amount of the coefficient could not be reliably interpreted as the per-unit cost driver for the related independent variable. For example, if the independent variable is labor-hours, the coefficient for this variable does not give a reliable estimate of the labor cost per hour when multicollinearity is present. When practical, one or more of the correlated variables should be removed from the model.

The **standard error of the estimate (SE)** is a measure of the dispersion of the actual observations around the regression line, and as such provides a measure of the accuracy of the regression's estimate. The SE can be used to determine a range around the regression estimate in which the unknown actual value for the estimate can reasonably be expected to fall.

This range is called a **confidence interval** and is used to measure the accuracy of the prediction at any point for the independent variable, as illustrated in Exhibits 8.7A and 8.7B. A 67% confidence interval is determined by taking the regression line and identifying a range that is a 1 standard-error distance on either side of the regression line; a 95% confidence interval would be determined from 2 standard-error distances. Confidence intervals are useful tools for management accountants to describe the degree of precision obtained from the regression prediction. To illustrate, if the regression prediction is $4,500 and the SE is $500, then the 67% confidence interval is $4,500 +/− $500; one can be 67% confident that the unknown true value of the dependent variable lies between $4,000 and $5,000. An equivalent interpretation is to say that there is a 67% probability that the unknown true

---

[6] The *t*-value can be a positive or negative number, just as the correlation coefficient (see footnote 5) can be positive or negative. A positive *t*-value means that the relationship between the dependent and independent variable is direct (when one variable increases, the other variable increases), while a negative *t*-value indicates an inverse relationship (when one variable increases, the other variable decreases).

**EXHIBIT 8.7A** The Confidence Interval for a Regression with a Relatively Small (Good) Standard Error

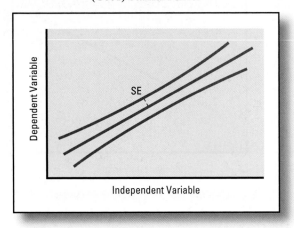

**EXHIBIT 8.7B** The Confidence Interval for a Regression with a Relatively Large (Poor) Standard Error

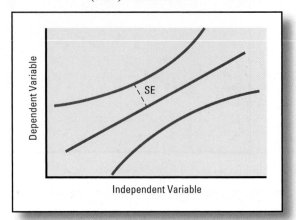

value of the dependent variable lies between $4,000 and $5,000. The confidence range for 95% would be $4,500 +/− (2 × $500), a range of $3,500 to $5,500.[7]

Because it is used to measure a confidence range, the SE must be interpreted by its relationship to the average size of the dependent variable. If the SE is small relative to the dependent variable, the precision of the regression can be assessed as relatively good. How small the SE value must be for a favorable precision evaluation is a matter of judgment, but a threshold of approximately 5 to 10% of the average of the dependent variable can be used. The confidence ranges for two regressions are illustrated in Exhibit 8.7A (good precision) and 8.7B (relatively poor precision).

**The *p*-value**
measures the risk that a particular independent variable has only a chance relationship to the dependent variable.

The **p-value** measures the risk that a particular independent variable has only a chance relationship to the dependent variable, and there is no significant statistical relationship. A small *p*-value (small risk) is desirable; a *p*-value of .05 or less is often used as a guide in practice. The *R*-squared, *t*-value, SE, and *p*-value are illustrated in the following example and are shown in the Excel spreadsheet for this example (Exhibit 8.9, p. 277). Note that the *t*-values greater than 2 have low *p*-values. Also, there is a *p*-value for the regression as a whole, which is labeled "Significance *F*" in Exhibit 8.9. As for the *p*-values for each independent variable, the significance of *F* should be less than approximately .05 for a statistically reliable regression.

### An Example: Using Regression to Estimate Maintenance Costs

We continue the case developed earlier, Ben Garcia's estimation of maintenance costs. Following the six steps outlined in the first section of the chapter, Garcia defined the cost object and the relevant cost driver as maintenance cost and operating hours, respectively. He also collected and graphed the data (Exhibit 8.2). The next step is to solve the regression using regression software such as Excel with the following findings (*Y* represents maintenance cost and *X* represents operating hours):

$$Y = \$15,843 + (\$2.02 \times X)$$

Garcia expects approximately 3,600 operating hours in August, so the amount of maintenance cost for August is estimated to be

$$Y = \$15,843 + (\$2.02 \times 3,600) = \$23,115$$

[7] Note that the confidence intervals shown in Exhibits 8.7A and 8.7B are curved and move away from the regression line at low and high values for the independent variable. The reason is that *for a given value, or "point," of the independent variable (let's call the point "p"),* the standard error of that point, $SE_p$, can be calculated from two factors: the value of SE and the distance of the point *p* from the mean of the independent variable. $SE_p$ is smallest at the mean of the independent variable and increases the further the point *p* is away from the mean. The calculation of $SE_p$ is beyond the scope of this text but can be found in introductory statistics texts.

The statistical measures are:

$R$-squared $= .461$

$t$-value $= 2.07$     ($p = .09$)

Standard error of the estimate $= \$221.71$

Garcia notes that $R$-squared is less than 0.5, the $t$-value is greater than 2.0, and the SE is approximately 1% of the mean of the dependent variable. The SE value is very good. However, since the $t$-value is marginally greater than two (and has a weak $p$ value of .09) and since $R$-squared is low, Garcia asks his accounting assistant, Jan, to review the regression.

Jan looks at the regression and the related graphs and notices immediately that in May maintenance cost dropped significantly and operating hours experienced a modest drop. Garcia observes that the drop in May was probably due to the unusually poor economic conditions that month; thus, output was reduced and operating hours and maintenance fell accordingly. Recalling that dummy variables can be used to correct for isolated variations and seasonal or other patterns, Jan suggests that Garcia run the regression again with a dummy variable having a value of 1 in May and a value of zero otherwise (the symbol $D$ represents the dummy variable). The new regression result is as follows:

$$Y = \$16{,}467 + (\$1.856 \times X) - (\$408.638 \times D)$$

The coefficients in the revised equation indicate that the poor performance in May reduced estimated costs by $408.638, and that each operating hour increases maintenance cost by $1.856. With the revised regression, the estimate of maintenance costs for August is as follows (assuming no unusual unfavorable event in August, and thus $D = 0$):

$$Y = \$16{,}467 + (\$1.856 \times 3{,}600) - (\$408.638 \times 0)$$
$$= \$23{,}149$$

The construction industry uses cost estimation extensively, and in many cases a project cost is estimated directly based on projected labor-hours, materials, and other elements of the project. Alternatively, the construction cost for a project can be estimated based upon the actual costs incurred for similar projects already completed. In this approach the management accountant identifies the key cost driver of construction cost, which might be square feet of space or a similar measure of capacity. A regression is then used to develop a cost estimation equation to predict project cost based upon the cost driver. This approach has been used to estimate the cost of building waste

recycling plants based on the capacity of each plant measured in tons per day (TPD). Regression analyses for TPD versus construction costs for a variety of completed waste recycling plants have shown a very good fit, with an R-squared of .88.

**Required:**

How would a construction contractor use the information in the regression analysis for TPD versus construction costs?

(Refer to comments on Cost Management in Action at the end of the chapter.)

The statistical measures are as follows:

$R$-squared $= .772$

$t$-values:

   Hours: 2.60 ($p = .05$)

   Dummy variable: $-2.33$ ($p = .07$)

Standard error of the estimate (SE) = \$161.27

Garcia observes that the inclusion of the dummy variable improves $R$-squared, the $t$-values, the $p$-values, and the SE of the regression. For this reason, he relies on the estimate from the latter regression.

## A Second Example: Using Excel for Regression Analysis

Taking a new example, suppose that WinDoor Inc. is developing a regression cost equation for the indirect costs in its plant. WinDoor manufactures windows and doors used in home construction; both products are made in standard and custom sizes. Occasionally, a very large order substantially increases the direct and indirect costs in a given month. The indirect costs primarily consist of supplies, quality control and testing, overtime, and other indirect labor. Regression is used to budget indirect costs for the coming year, primarily for cash management purposes. The management accountant, Charlotte Williams, knows from prior years that both direct labor-hours and machine-hours in the plant are good independent variables for estimating indirect costs. She gathers the data in Exhibit 8.8 for the most recent 12 months.

Williams develops the regression for these data using Excel. To use Excel, she selects the Regression option from the Data/Data Analysis tab, then selects the $X$ and $Y$ ranges for the independent and dependent variables, and obtains the regression results in Exhibit 8.9 (where $L$ represents labor-hours and $M$ represents machine-hours):

$$Y = \$35,070 + (\$5.090 \times L) + (\$40.471 \times M)$$

**EXHIBIT 8.8**

**Indirect Costs, Labor-Hours, and Machine-Hours for WinDoor Inc.**

| Date | Total Indirect Costs | Direct Labor-Hours | Machine-Hours |
|------|---------------------|--------------------|---------------|
| June 2012 | $274,500 | 26,940 | 2,009 |
| July | 320,000 | 35,690 | 3,057 |
| August | 323,200 | 32,580 | 3,523 |
| September | 219,900 | 24,580 | 1,856 |
| October | 232,100 | 19,950 | 2,168 |
| November | 342,300 | 34,330 | 3,056 |
| December | 427,800 | 43,180 | 3,848 |
| January 2013 | 231,000 | 21,290 | 1,999 |
| February | 257,300 | 28,430 | 2,290 |
| March | 248,700 | 24,660 | 1,894 |
| April | 248,400 | 27,870 | 2,134 |
| May | 338,400 | 31,940 | 3,145 |

**EXHIBIT 8.9   Excel Regression Results for WinDoor Data, Showing Regression Dialog Box**

This exhibit shows both the regression results and the dialog box used to produce the regression results shown in the exhibit. Note that the independent variables (*X* Range) and dependent variable (*Y* Range) are entered into the dialog box. Labels are used in the top row of each column of data. The output is presented in the cells to the right and below the selected cell, F1. The dialog box is accessed by choosing **Data Analysis** at the right end of the ribbon under the DATA tab in Excel 2010. If Data Analysis is not on the ribbon, then it needs to be installed by clicking the **File** tab at the top left of the Excel spreadsheet and then clicking Excel Options. In the next screen click Add-ins on the left of the screen and then choose Analysis-ToolPak, which contains a number of statistical methods including regression. The location of Data Analysis and the key data entry in the regression dialog box are marked on the spreadsheet in Exhibit 8.9.

The statistical measures follow:

*R*-squared = .935

*t*-values:

Labor-hours: 2.976 (*p* = .0155)

Machine-hours: 2.505 (*p* = .0336)

Standard error of the estimate (SE) = $17,480

**Multiple linear regression** is used to describe regression applications having two or more independent variables.

A **simple linear regression** has a single independent variable.

The regression satisfies our statistical criteria: *R*-squared is relatively high, and the *t*-values and SE are good. The *p*-value for the regression ("significance of F" in Excel on the right-hand side of Exhibit 8.9) is 4.44221E-06, or .0000044, a very low and very good *p*-value. Thus, WinDoor can use the estimates with a reasonable degree of confidence.

The WinDoor example is an application of **multiple linear regression**, because it involves two or more independent variables. In contrast, the original Ben Garcia example, which used a single independent variable, operating hours, is an application of **simple linear regression**.

## Illustration of the Use of Regression Analysis in the Gaming Industry

Harrah's owns many large casinos throughout the world, but particularly in Las Vegas, where it operates Flamingo Las Vegas, Caesars Palace, and Paris Las Vegas. Harrah's competes in a business that is very focused on customer satisfaction and customer loyalty.

To be more competitive, Harrah's uses regression analysis to predict customer satisfaction. The approach is used by many other companies, including UPS and Google. The five-step model below explains how and why Harrah's uses regression analysis.[8]

### The Five Steps of Strategic Decision Making for Harrah's

1. **Determine the strategic issues surrounding the problem.** Since it operates in a very customer-focused business, Harrah's strategy is to develop and maintain customer loyalty (a differentiation strategy) and to improve customer profitability.

2. **Identify the alternative actions.** Harrah's knows that its customers have a "pain point," the amount of gaming losses at which the customer leaves the casino. The casinos have customer service representatives, called "luck ambassadors" who are responsible for maintaining customer satisfaction and, in particular, to make sure the customer does not reach the pain point.

3. **Obtain information and conduct analyses of the alternatives.** To obtain information about the pain points of individual customers, Harrah's began a "Total Rewards" program that involved a swipeable electronic card that provides certain rewards to customers but also provides data on the customers gaming in the casino. Harrah's uses this information together with other information provided by the Rewards customers to develop a regression analysis to predict the individual customer's pain point.

4. **Based on strategy and analysis, choose and implement the desired alternative.** Harrah's has implemented the regression-based system, so that when a given customer is gaming in the casino (Harrah's computer system lets it know real-time what the customer is gaming and the gains or losses for that day), the customer service representatives can be alerted when a given customer is approaching his or her predicted pain point and can be dispatched to urge that customer to take a break, and perhaps enjoy a free meal at Harrah's expense.

5. **Provide an ongoing evaluation of the effectiveness of implementation in step 4.** Harrah's system requires continuous updating for new customers and changes in customer behavior, so that the regression analyses can be kept current.

## Implementation Problems: Nonlinearity

**LO 8-4**

*Explain the implementation issues of the cost estimation methods.*

The cost estimation methods considered in this chapter, the high-low method and linear regression, assume a linear relationship between the variables, and the regression estimates are unreliable when the data relationships are nonlinear. Nonlinearity most often happens because of certain time-series patterns to the data such as trend and/or seasonality, an outlier in the data, and data shift. The high-low method cannot be adapted for nonlinearity but regression analysis can be adapted for nonlinear relationships. The following explains a few of the ways regression can be adapted to a variety of nonlinear situations. Also, an example of a nonlinear regression is shown in Self-Study Problem 4 at the end of the chapter.

1. **Trend and/or seasonality.** A common characteristic of accounting data is a significant trend that results from changing prices and/or seasonality. When trend or seasonality is present, a linear regression is not a good fit to the data, and the management accountant should use a method to deseasonalize or to detrend a variable. The most common methods to do this follow:

**A trend variable**
is a variable that takes on values of 1, 2, 3, . . . for each period in sequence.

- Use of a price change index to adjust the values of each variable to some common time period.
- Use of a trend variable. A **trend variable** takes on values of 1, 2, 3, . . . for each period in sequence.

[8] The story is described in the book, *Super Crunchers,* by Ian Ayres, Bantam Books, 2007, pp. 30–32. There is a similar description of the use of analytics such as regression analysis to predict consumer behavior in a 2011 McKinsey research report, "Big Data: The Next Frontier for Innovation, Competition, and Productivity," as reported by Steve Lohr, "New Ways to Exploit Raw Data May Bring Surge of Innovation, A Study Says," *The New York Times,* May 13, 2011, p. B3. See also, Carol Eisenberg, "Drugmakers Mine Data for Trial Patients," *Bloomberg Businessweek,* November 7, 2011, pp. 21–22; Scott Thurm, "Data Mining Your Mind: The Next Frontier Is Predicting Personal Behavior; The 'Ability to Pay' Index," *The Wall Street Journal,* October 27, 2011, p. B1.

**EXHIBIT 8.10**
**Adjusting for Trend and Seasonality Using First Difference or a Price Index**

| Supplies Expense | First Difference | Price Index Adjustment | |
|---|---|---|---|
| | | Hypothetical Price Index for Supplies Expense | Supplies Expense Adjusted for Price Index |
| $250 | — | 1.00 | $250/1.00 = $250 |
| 310 | $60 | 1.08 | 310/1.08 = 287 |
| 325 | 15 | 1.12 | 325/1.12 = 290 |

- Replacement of the original values of each of the variables with the first differences. First difference for each variable is the difference between each value and the succeeding value in the time series.

The index approach and the first difference approach are shown in Exhibit 8.10 using the supplies expense data from Exhibit 8.3.

Trend is present in virtually all financial time series data used in management accounting because of inflation and growth in the economy. Thus, it is a pervasive issue in the proper development of a regression analysis.

2. **Outliers.** As mentioned earlier, when an error in the data or an unusual or nonrecurring business condition affects operations for a given period, the result might be a data point that is far from the others, an outlier. Because outliers can significantly decrease the precision and reliability of the estimate, they should be corrected or adjusted (using, for example, a dummy variable) if it is clear that they are unusual or nonrecurring.

3. **Data Shift.** In contrast to the outlier, if the unusual business condition is long lasting, such as the introduction of new production technology or other permanent change, the average direction of the data has a distinct shift that should be included in the estimate. One way to handle this is to use a dummy variable to indicate the periods before and after the shift.

## Time-Series and Cross-Sectional Regression

**Time-series regression**
is the application of regression analysis to predict future amounts, using a prior period's data.

**Cross-sectional regression**
estimates costs for a particular cost object based on information on other cost objects and other variables, where the information for all variables is taken from the same period of time.

The two examples used in this chapter, the Ben Garcia case and the WinDoor Inc. case, are both examples of what is called *time-series regression*. **Time-series regression** is the application of regression analysis to predict future amounts, using a prior period's data. In contrast, **cross-sectional regression** estimates costs for a particular cost object based on information on other cost objects and variables, where the information for all variables is taken from the same period of time. For an example of cross-sectional regression, suppose a residential home builder uses regression to estimate the cost of constructing a new home, and the builder knows that the main cost driver for building cost is the size of the home, in square feet of floor space. The builder develops a regression model using the cost of homes built previously that year as the dependent variable and the size in square feet of these homes as the independent variable. The regression equation that the builder develops is then used to predict the cost of homes to be built, based on the expected size of the new home in square feet. All of the statistical measures of reliability and precision explained above apply equally to both types of regression, except for the issue nonindependence of errors, which applies only in time-series regressions.

## Summary

Cost estimation is one of the most important activities the management accountant performs in supporting the firm's strategy. It has an important role in developing a strategic competitive position as well as in using value-chain analysis, target costing, and other planning and evaluation contexts within cost management.

To use cost estimation effectively, the management accountant develops and evaluates a cost-estimating model in six steps: (1) define the cost object, (2) determine the cost drivers, (3) collect consistent and accurate data, (4) graph the data, (5) select and apply a cost estimation method, and (6) evaluate the accuracy of the cost estimate.

This chapter presents two estimation methods. The high-low method develops a unique estimation equation using algebra and the representative low and high points in the data. Regression analysis, a statistical method, obtains a unique best-fitting line for the data. The chapter's focus is on the proper interpretation of the four key measures of the precision and reliability of the regression: $R$-squared, the $t$-value, the $p$-value, and the standard error of the estimate.

The most reliable and accurate method available to the management accountant is regression analysis, which can be solved using spreadsheet software such as Excel. An advantage of regression analysis is that it includes quantitative and objective measures of the reliability and precision of the regression estimate.

## Appendix

**LO 8-5**

*Use learning curves in cost estimation when learning is present.*

## Learning Curve Analysis

One prominent example of nonlinear cost behavior is a cost influenced by learning. When an activity has a certain labor component and repetition of the same activity or operation makes the labor more productive, the task is completed more quickly with the same or a higher level of quality. Learning can occur in a wide variety of ways, from the individual level as new employees gain experience, to the aggregate level in which a group of employees experiences improvement in productivity. We consider the latter instance in this appendix.

Costs are affected by learning in a wide variety of contexts, especially in large-scale production settings, such as the manufacture of airplanes and ships. In each case, we can model the expected improvement in productivity and use this information in the estimation of future costs. A **learning curve analysis** is a systematic method for estimating costs when learning is present.

A **learning curve analysis** is a systematic method for estimating costs when learning is present.

One of the first well-documented applications of learning curves occurred in the World War II aircraft industry.[9] Studies showed that the total time to manufacture two airplanes declined by approximately 20% of the total time without learning. In other words, the average *per-unit* time to build the first two units was 80% of the time for the first unit. For example, if the time to build the first unit is 20 hours, the *average* time to build the first two units is 16 hours ($20 \times 0.8$), or a total of 32 hours ($16 \times 2$) for two units. Without learning, it would take 40 hours ($20 \times 2$). The **learning rate** is the percentage by which average time (or total time) falls from previous levels *as output doubles*. In this example, the rate is 80%. The unit cost behavior of the learning curve is illustrated in Exhibit 8A.1. Note from the Exhibit that the effect of learning is nonlinear; learning curve analysis is an example of nonlinear cost estimation.

The **learning rate** is the percentage by which average time (or total time) falls from previous levels as output doubles.

Additional evidence of the practical importance of learning curves is the common reference to start-up costs in corporate annual reports and the financial press. A commonly accepted business principle is that new products and production processes have a period of low productivity followed by increasing productivity. Thereafter, the rate of improvement in productivity tends to decline over time until it reaches some equilibrium level where it remains relatively stable until another change in the product line or production process occurs.[10]

### EXAMPLE: LEARNING CURVES IN SOFTWARE DEVELOPMENT

SofTech, Inc., is a vendor of software for financial analysts. SofTech's development staff recently changed its development language, T-Base, to a new language, Z-Base, which permits faster development and provides certain object-oriented programming benefits. Now

[9] Frank J. Andress, "The Learning Curve as a Production Tool," *Harvard Business Review*, January–February 1954; and Charles D. Bailey and Edward V. McIntyre, "Some Evidence on the Nature of Relearning Curves," *The Accounting Review*, April 1992, pp. 368–378.

[10] As in the World War II airplane production example, the common learning rate is approximately 80%. Two conventional models are used in learning curve analysis. One measures learning on the basis of average unit cost, the other on the basis of marginal cost. Both models are conceptually and mathematically similar, although the average cost model tends to lead to lower unit costs. The average cost model is the more common, and for clarity and simplicity, it is the only model we present here. For a full explanation and comparison of the two models, see J. Chen and R. Manes, "Distinguishing the Two Forms of the Constant Percentage Learning Curve Model," *Contemporary Accounting Research*, Spring 1985, pp. 242–252.

Learning curve analysis is commonly used to improve cost estimates in situations when learning is likely to occur. Two example applications follow.

## USING THE SALES LEARNING CURVE AS A STRATEGIC CONSTRUCT

Launching a new product involves a lot more than adding a new sales force. Just as there are learning effects in many manufacturing processes, there are learning effects in bringing products to market. A sales strategy that successfully brings a new product to market involves all functions that interact with customers and attempts to understand how customers will acquire and use the product. Leslie and Holloway (2006) suggest that to properly guide resource allocation, companies utilize the sales learning curve, which models sales per person as a function of time. The more a company learns about its product and the sales process, the more efficient it becomes in selling the product. The findings of analysis show that sales typically start out slow, increase for a period,

and then finally become flat as the product matures. These changes over time can be estimated using a learning curve. The use of sales learning-curve models allows management to set more realistic expectations regarding sales, avoid excessive sales force costs, and reduce the time before a new product reaches the point of profitability by better deploying the sales force, marketing, and management resources. (Mark Leslie and Charles A. Holloway, "The Sales Learning Curve," *Harvard Business Review* 84, no. 7/8 (July–August 2006), pp. 115–123.)

## LEARNING RATES IN SURGICAL PROCEDURES

A hospital in Germany reports learning rates of over 90% for two types of common surgeries. Based on data from 1992 through 2002, researchers found a learning rate of 91% for 816 cases of knee replacement surgery, and a learning rate of 90.3% for 476 gall bladder surgeries. (Christian Ernst and Andrea Szczesny, "Cost Accounting Implications of Surgical Learning in the DRG Era—Data Evidence for a German Hospital," *Schmalenbach Business Review,* April 2005, pp. 127–166.)

**EXHIBIT 8A.1**
**Average Cost with Learning**

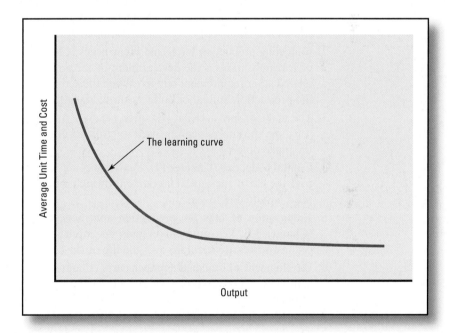

SofTech is calculating the learning time needed for its programmers to come up to speed in the new language. These estimates are important because programming costs have increased 10% to $65 per hour in the past year and are expected to rise as quickly in the coming years. For purposes of this analysis, SofTech estimates the learning rate for Z-Base to be 80% and the initial time for coding 500 lines of good code in Z-Base to be 100 hours. The time and related cost required for developing the first 4,000-line application in Z-Base can be determined by using the learning curve; see Exhibit 8A.2.

Learning rates are obtained by reviewing and analyzing historical data. The methods vary from the simple high-low method to regression analysis based on fitting a nonlinear relationship to the historical data.[11]

[11] For example, see Charles D. Bailey, "Estimation of Production Costs and Labor Hours Using an Excel Add-in," *Management Accounting Quarterly,* Summer 2000, pp. 25–31. Also, for thorough coverage of different learning models and Excel applications, see the following case and teaching note, "Instructional Case: Estimating Learning Curve Functions for Managerial Planning, Control, and Decision Making," by David E. Stout and Paul E. Juras, *Issues in Accounting Education,* May 2009, pp. 195–217.

**EXHIBIT 8A.2**
**SofTech, Inc.'s Learning Curve for Z-Base**

| Output (Multiples of 500 Lines) | Cumulative Average Time (Coding for 500 Lines) | Total Time |
|---|---|---|
| 1 =    500 lines | 100 hours | 100 hours |
| 2 = 1,000 lines | $100 \times .8 = 80$ hours | $80 \times 2 = 160$ hours |
| 3 = 2,000 lines | $80 \times .8 = 64$ hours | $64 \times 4 = 256$ hours |
| 4 = 4,000 lines | $64 \times .8 = 51.2$ hours | $51.2 \times 8 = 409.6$ hours |

Note also that a *learning rate of 1 is equivalent to no learning.* A *learning rate of .5 is best interpreted as the maximum learning rate* because the total time for actual production equals the time for a single unit. Thus, the learning rate is always a number greater than .5 and less than 1. Actual case studies reveal that the learning rate most often falls near .8.

## WHAT DECISIONS ARE INFLUENCED BY LEARNING?

Because the productivity of labor is a vital aspect of any production process, learning curve analysis can be an important way to improve the quality of a wide range of decisions. For example, when product prices are based in part on costs, learning curves could be used to determine a life-cycle plan for pricing a new product. Moreover, learning curves would be helpful in these areas:

1. **Cost-volume-profit analysis (Chapter 9).** The determination of a breakeven point might be significantly influenced by the presence of learning.[12] Failing to consider learning causes overstatement of the actual number of units required for breakeven.

2. **Budgeting production levels and labor needs (Chapter 10).** Another useful application of learning curves is the development of the annual or quarterly production plan and related labor requirement budget. When the activity or operation is affected by learning, the production and labor budgets should be adjusted accordingly.

3. **The make-or-buy decision (Chapter 11).** When the cost to make a part is affected by learning, the analysis can be used to more accurately reflect the total cost over time of the make option.

4. **Capital budgeting (Chapter 12).** Learning curves capture cost behavior more accurately over the life of the capital investment by including the expected improvements in labor productivity due to learning.

5. **Preparation of bids for production contracts; target costing and life-cycle costing (Chapter 13).** Learning curves play an important role in ensuring that the contract cost estimates are accurate over the life of the contract.

6. **Development of standard product costs (Chapters 14 and 15).** When learning occurs, standard costs change over time, and the appropriate labor costs must be adjusted on a timely basis.[13]

7. **Management control (Chapters 18 and 19).** The use of learning curves is important in properly evaluating managers when costs are affected by learning. The evaluation should recognize the pattern of relatively higher costs at the early phase of the product life cycle.

## THE GENERAL FORM OF THE LEARNING MODEL

The learning rate is usually based on an assumed doubling of output as illustrated above, but other assumptions are possible. The most general form of the learning model is as follows:

$$Y = aX^b$$

where: $Y$ = the cumulative average time per unit when producing $X$ units

$a$ = the time required for the first unit of output

$X$ = cumulative output

$b$ = the learning index

---

[12] Edward V. McIntyre, "Cost-Volume-Profit Analysis Adjusted for Learning," *Management Science,* October 1977, pp. 149–160.

[13] Jackson F. Gillespie, "An Application of Learning Curves to Standard Costing," *Management Accounting,* September 1981, pp. 63–65.

The learning rate is *Y/a,* and the learning index (*b*) can be determined from the learning rate using an algebraic approach.[14] This form of the learning model is very general and will allow consideration of other learning assumptions, in addition to the doubling-of-output base commonly used.

## LIMITATIONS OF LEARNING CURVE ANALYSIS

Although learning curve analysis can significantly enhance the ability to predict costs when learning occurs, three inherent limitations and problems are associated with the use of this method.

The first and key limitation of using learning curves is that the approach is most appropriate for labor-intensive contexts that involve repetitive tasks performed for long production runs for which repeated trials improve performance, or learning. When the production process is designed to maximize flexibility and very fast set-up times for manufacturing machinery using robotics and computer controls as many manufacturers now do, the manufacturing setting requires relatively little repetitive labor and consequently relatively little opportunity for learning.

A second limitation is that the learning rate is assumed to be constant (average labor time decreases at a fixed rate as output doubles). In actual applications, the decline in labor time might not be constant. For example, the learning rate could be 80% for the first 20,000 units, 90% for the next 35,000 units, and 95% thereafter. Such differences indicate the need to update projections based on the observed progression of learning.

Third, a carefully estimated learning curve might be unreliable because the observed change in productivity in the data used to fit the model was actually associated with factors other than learning. For example, the increase in productivity might have been due to a change in labor mix, a change in product mix, or some combination of other related factors. In such cases, the learning model is unreliable and produces inaccurate estimates of labor time and cost.

**Regression Analysis Appendix Now Online**

*The Regression Analysis Supplement (an appendix of this chapter in prior editions) is now available on the text website under "Course Wide Content." This supplement provides advanced coverage of regression analysis. The advanced coverage is not required for any of the exercises or problems at the end of Chapter 8. While the text provides comprehensive and in-depth coverage of regression analysis, some instructors and students can pursue an advanced coverage of regression analysis through the use of this supplement. While the exercises and problems in the text do not require this advanced coverage, those exercises and problems that deal with regression analysis could be addressed at an advanced level using the content provided in this online supplement.*

**Key Terms**

| | | |
|---|---|---|
| confidence interval, *273* | learning rate, *280* | *R*-squared, *272* |
| correlation, *273* | least squares regression, *269* | simple linear regression, *277* |
| cost estimation, *264* | mean absolute percentage error | standard error of the estimate |
| cross-sectional regression, *279* | (MAPE), *267* | (SE), *273* |
| dependent variable, *270* | multicollinearity, *273* | time-series regression, *279* |
| dummy variable, *272* | multiple linear regression, *277* | trend variable, *278* |
| high-low method, *267* | outliers, *270* | *t*-value, *272* |
| independent variable, *270* | *p*-value, *274* | |
| learning curve analysis, *280* | regression analysis, *269* | |

[14] To determine the learning index (*b*) for a given learning rate, first develop a linear expression for the general model by taking the natural log of both sides of the equation.

$$\ln(Y) = \ln(a) + b \times \ln(X)$$

so that:

$$b = \frac{\ln(Y) - \ln(a)}{\ln(X)} = \frac{\ln(Y/a)}{\ln(X)}$$

Thus, if we consider the changes in *Y/a* as *X* increases, the index *b* simplifies to the ratio of the learning rate to the rate of increase in output, or

$$b = \frac{\ln(\text{learning rate})}{\ln(\text{increase in output}/100)}$$

For example, to calculate the learning index for the doubling-output assumption (200%), we use:

$$b = \ln(\text{learning rate})/\ln(2)$$

And, for a learning rate of 80%, the learning index is therefore $\ln(.8)/\ln(2) = -.3219$. The index is negative because average unit labor time decreases with increasing output.

## Comments on Cost Management in Action

### Using Regression to Estimate Construction Costs

The regression model can be used by the construction contractor to estimate the construction cost to build a waste recycling plant of a given capacity. Since the model is based on the actual cost of actual construction projects, it can provide a useful means for the contractor to estimate costs. The contractor should be cautious and use only cost and capacity data that are accurate, timely, and relevant for the proposed project. Also, the contractor should consider supplementing the regression analysis with a separate estimate based on projections of labor and materials costs. Together, the two analyses should provide a solid base for estimating project costs.

**Source:** Richard K. Ellsworth, "Cost-to-Capacity Analysis for Estimating Project Costs," *Construction Accounting and Taxation,* September–October 2005, pp. 5–10.

## Self-Study Problems
(For solutions, please turn to the end of the chapter.)

### 1. Using the High-Low Method

Hector's Delivery Service uses four small vans and six pickup trucks to deliver small packages in the Charlotte, North Carolina, metropolitan area. Hector spends a considerable amount of money on the gas, oil, and regular maintenance of his vehicles, which is done at a variety of service stations and repair shops. To budget his vehicle expenses for the coming year, he gathers data on his expenses and number of deliveries for each month of the current year.

| | Total Vehicle Expenses | Total Deliveries |
|---|---|---|
| January | $145,329 | 5,882 |
| February | 133,245 | 5,567 |
| March | 123,245 | 5,166 |
| April | 164,295 | 6,621 |
| May | 163,937 | 6,433 |
| June | 176,229 | 6,681 |
| July | 180,553 | 7,182 |
| August | 177,293 | 6,577 |
| September | 155,389 | 5,942 |
| October | 150,832 | 5,622 |
| November | 152,993 | 5,599 |
| December | 201,783 | 7,433 |

**Required**   Use the high-low estimation method to determine the relationship between the number of deliveries and the cost of maintaining the vehicles.

### 2. Using Regression Analysis

George Harder is the plant manager at one of Imperial Foods Company's processing plants. George is concerned about the increase in plant overhead costs in recent months. He has collected data on overhead costs for the past 24 months and has decided to use regression to study the factors influencing these costs. He has also collected data on materials cost, direct labor-hours, and machine-hours as potential independent variables to use in predicting overhead.

George uses two regression analyses on these data, with the following results:

| | Regression 1 (materials cost and labor-hours) | Regression 2 (materials cost, labor-hours, and machine-hours) |
|---|---|---|
| *R*-squared | .65 | .58 |
| Standard error | $12,554 | $13,793 |
| Standard error as a percent of the dependent variable | 12% | 14% |
| *t*-values | | |
| Materials cost | 2.0 | −1.6 |
| Labor-hours | 4.5 | 3.8 |
| Machine-hours | | 1.4 |

**Required**   Which of the two regressions is better and why?

### 3. Using Both High-Low and Regression

John Meeks Company is a medium-size manufacturing company with plants in three small mid-Atlantic towns. The company makes plastic parts for automobiles and trucks, primarily door panels, exterior trim, and related items. The parts have an average cost of $5 to $20. The company has a steady demand for its products from both domestic and foreign automakers and has experienced growth in sales averaging between 10 and 20% over the last 8 to 10 years.

Currently, management is reviewing the incidence of scrap and waste in the manufacturing process at one of its plants. Meeks defines scrap and waste as any defective unit that is rejected for lack of functionality or another aspect of quality. The plants have a number of different inspection points, and failure or rejection can occur at any inspection point. The number of defective units is listed in the following table; management estimates the cost of this waste in labor and materials is approximately $10 per unit.

An unfavorable trend appears to exist with regard to defects, and management has asked you to investigate and estimate the defective units in the coming months. A first step in your investigation is to identify the cost drivers of defective parts, to understand what causes them, and to provide a basis on which to estimate future defects. For this purpose, you have obtained these recent data on the units produced, the units shipped, and the cost of sales since these numbers are easily available and relatively reliable on a monthly basis:

|          | Units Produced (000s) | Cost of Sales (000s) | Units Shipped (000s) | Defective Units |
|----------|-----------------------|----------------------|----------------------|-----------------|
| Jan 2012 | 55  | $  689 | 50  | 856   |
| Feb      | 58  | 737    | 53  | 1,335 |
| Mar      | 69  | 886    | 64  | 1,610 |
| Apr      | 61  | 768    | 56  | 1,405 |
| May      | 65  | 828    | 60  | 1,511 |
| Jun      | 69  | 878    | 64  | 1,600 |
| Jul      | 75  | 962    | 70  | 1,570 |
| Aug      | 81  | 1,052  | 76  | 1,910 |
| Sep      | 70  | 1,104  | 80  | 2,011 |
| Oct      | 79  | 1,224  | 89  | 2,230 |
| Nov      | 82  | 1,261  | 92  | 2,300 |
| Dec      | 70  | 1,020  | 74  | 1,849 |
| Jan 2013 | 67  | 850    | 62  | 1,549 |
| Feb      | 72  | 916    | 67  | 1,669 |
| Mar      | 85  | 1,107  | 80  | 2,012 |
| Apr      | 75  | 968    | 70  | 1,756 |
| May      | 81  | 1,037  | 76  | 1,889 |
| Jun      | 85  | 1,103  | 80  | 1,650 |
| Jul      | 92  | 1,208  | 87  | 2,187 |
| Aug      | 100 | 1,310  | 95  | 2,387 |
| Sep      | 91  | 1,380  | 101 | 2,514 |
| Oct      | 101 | 1,536  | 111 | 2,787 |
| Nov      | 105 | 1,580  | 115 | 2,310 |
| Dec      | 88  | 1,270  | 92  | 2,311 |

**Required**   Use the high-low method and regression analysis to estimate the defective units in the coming months and to determine which method provides the best fit for this purpose.

### 4. Nonlinear Regression and Learning Curves

This self-study problem illustrates how nonlinear regression can be used to estimate the learning rate, given information on output levels and average processing times. To illustrate, we reproduce below the cumulative output ($X$) and the average time per unit ($Y$) for the SofTech, Inc., illustration in Exhibit 8A.2. Using regression analysis, we now show that these learning curve data are consistent with the general learning model. The general form of the learning model is $Y = aX^b$ where $a$ = the time required for the first unit and $b$ = the learning index. Using a log transform for $Y$, the general learning model can be shown in the equivalent log-linear form (see footnote 14): $\log(Y) = \log(a) + b \times \log(X)$. The log transform is available in Excel in "Insert Function" under the Formulas tab.

The exhibit below shows that the $X$ and $Y$ values have been transformed (using log, base 10), and the results of a regression on log $X$ and log $Y$ are shown in the right two columns. Note that the regression $R$-squared is 1.0 because the data fit perfectly an 80% learning curve; the values for $Y$ were calculated using the 80% rate. Also, note that the learning index $b = -.321928$ is the learning index for a model with an 80% learning rate, as shown in footnote 14.

The value of $Y$ can now be determined for any value of $X$ using the general model. First we determine the value of the intercept, $a$. Since $\log(a) = 2.8688743$, $a$ is determined as follows: $a = 10^{2.8688743} = 739.39$. The value for $10^{2.8688743} = 739.39$ is determined using the Power function in Excel which is located in "Insert Function" under the Formulas tab. Thus, for example, the value of $Y$ for $X = 1,500$ is determined as follows:

$$Y = 739.39 \times 1,500^{-.321928} = 70.2.$$

**Log-Linear Regression of Learning Curve Data (from Exhibit 8A.2)**

| X | Y | LogX | LogY |
|------|------|---------|---------|
| 500 | 100 | 2.69897 | 2 |
| 1000 | 80 | 3 | 1.90309 |
| 2000 | 64 | 3.30103 | 1.80618 |
| 4000 | 51.2 | 3.60206 | 1.70927 |

| Regression Statistics | |
|---|---|
| Multiple $R$ | 1 |
| $R$-squared | 1 |
| Adj $R$-squared | 1 |
| Standard error | 1.677E-16 |
| Observations | 4 |

| ANOVA | |
|---|---|
| | df |
| Regression | 1 |
| Residual | 2 |
| Total | 3 |

| | Coefficients |
|---|---|
| Intercept | 2.8688743 |
| LogX | −0.321928 |

**Required**   Suppose that Virilli, Inc., a manufacturer of high-end furniture, has the following data for one of its products, where $X$ is cumulative output, and $Y$ is average unit time.

| X | Y |
|-----|----|
| 10 | 45 |
| 18 | 40 |
| 25 | 38 |
| 43 | 32 |
| 55 | 30 |
| 70 | 25 |
| 93 | 22 |
| 110 | 20 |

1. Using log-linear regression, determine the general linear model for Virilli. Specifically, determine the values of $a$ and $b$ in the model $Y = aX^b$.
2. Using the model you developed in part 1, project the value of $Y$ if output ($X$) is increased to 133.

*Please visit **http://www.mhhe.com/blocher6e** to access a narrated, animated tutorial for solving this problem.*

## Questions

8-1   Define *cost estimation* and explain its purpose.

8-2   Explain the strategic role of cost estimation.

8-3   List the two methods of cost estimation. Explain the advantages and disadvantages of each.

8-4   Explain the implementation problems in cost estimation.

8-5   What are the six steps in cost estimation? Which one is the most important? Why?

8-6   Contrast the use of regression analysis and the high-low method to estimate costs.

8-7   How is cost estimation used in activity-based costing?

8-8   Explain how to choose the dependent and independent variables in regression analysis.

8-9   What are nonlinear cost relationships? Give two examples.

8-10  List four advantages of regression analysis.

8-11  Explain what a dummy variable is and how it is used in regression analysis.

8-12  How do we know when high correlation exists? Is high correlation the same as cause and effect?

8-13  What does the coefficient of determination ($R$-squared) measure?

## Brief Exercises

8-14  Wallace Heating is attempting to estimate the production cost for heating ducts for the coming year using the high-low method. The cost driver is number of labor-hours. Wallace determines that the high and low costs are $25,830 and $18,414, respectively, and the values for the cost driver are 3,495 and 1,958 hours, respectively. What is the variable cost per hour?

8-15  Carter Dry Cleaning has developed two regression analyses for cost estimation. The accounting manager has presented statistical measures for both of these regressions. Regression A has an $R$-squared value of .53 and a $t$-value of 1.08 and Regression B has an $R$-squared of .89 and a $t$-value of 2.17. What do these statistical measures indicate about the regressions? Which regression should Carter Dry Cleaning use for cost estimation?

8-16  Williams Inc. produces fluorescent lightbulbs for commercial use. The accounting manager is attempting to estimate the total cost for the next quarter using the high-low method. He has compiled data and found the high and low costs are $10,000 and $6,000 and the associated cost drivers are 7,000 and 3,000 packs, respectively. He has also determined the variable cost to be $1.00 per pack. What is the value for $a$ (the fixed quantity)?

8-17  Grant Healthcare provides latex gloves for hospitals. Grant is forecasting costs for future production. The dependent variable is labor expense. List some possible independent variables for a regression analysis of financial data.

8-18  Smith Glass Co. produces industrial glass. Smith forecasts inspection costs using the high-low method and has compiled the following data from prior results:

|                        | 2009   | 2010   | 2011   | 2012   | 2013   |
|------------------------|--------|--------|--------|--------|--------|
| Total operating hours  | 5,683  | 3,197  | 4,105  | 5,056  | 3,586  |
| Inspection cost ($)    | 50,457 | 46,835 | 53,227 | 49,734 | 43,649 |

Which two years should Smith select for the high-low method analysis and why?

8-19  Johnson Plastics Inc. produces cases for CDs. The accounting manager has calculated a regression to determine future production costs. The regression estimate is $5,000 with an $R$-squared of .9, a $t$-value of 2.5, and a standard error of $400. Within what interval would she be reasonably (67%) confident that the actual values will fall?

8-20  Peppers Lockdown produces keys for homes and cars. As Peppers planned for next year's production, the company decided to implement a high-low system to forecast future costs. With total production of 2,500,000 keys at a total cost of $10,000, in 2012, and total production of 3,000,000 keys at a total cost of $20,000 in 2013, what is the variable cost per key?

8-21  Power Drink Inc. produces sports drinks. The accounting manager has decided to implement a high-low costing system to predict future materials handling costs. She has provided you with the following table of costs for the last five years. Which two years should be used for this method?

|                    | 2009    | 2010    | 2011    | 2012    | 2013    |
|--------------------|---------|---------|---------|---------|---------|
| Production hours   | 100,000 | 138,679 | 98,843  | 203,517 | 188,352 |
| Handling cost ($)  | 456,233 | 498,672 | 507,284 | 601,678 | 544,314 |

8-22  Jamison Construction has implemented a cost estimation system using regression analysis. The variable cost per hour of labor is $35 and the fixed cost was determined to be $125,000. If Jamison projects it will be working 200,000 hours in 2013, what is the projected total cost?

8-23  Curry Rubber manufactures rubber bands for retail companies. The accounting manager has created a regression analysis of past data. You notice that the formula has an $R$-squared of .6, a *t*-value of 2.3, and a standard error of the estimate of $200,000. The estimate for next quarter costs is $2,584,072. What do these statistics tell you about the reliability and precision of his regression analysis?

8-24   Miller Landscaping is attempting to estimate costs for future projects. Miller has compiled data and decided to use the high-low costing method. The low value is $250,000 for 5,000 hours and the high value is $400,000 for 8,000 hours. What is the variable cost per hour?

8-25   Sanders Bears produces stuffed animals. Sanders is in the process of implementing a cost forecasting system using the high-low method. The variable cost per animal is $2 and the high and low costs used were $80,000 for 30,0000 animals and $40,000 for 10,000 animals. What is the value of the fixed cost for the cost estimating equation?

8-26   Recently Walmart has offered a wireless data contract based on bandwidth used, with a minimum monthly charge of $45 for up to 5 gigabytes (GB) of use. Additional GB can be purchased at the following rates: $10 for an additional 1 GB, $25 for an additional 3 GB, and $40 for a capacity of 10 GB. What is the cost for a user who is expecting to use 9 GB?

## Exercises

[LO 8-1]   8-27   **Estimating Costs in an Uncertain Environment**   Many companies face increasingly unpredictable costs and revenues, as the recession affects demand for products and the costs of materials and labor for these products. Revenues and costs have fluctuated significantly in recent years for such cost elements as fuel, labor, commodities (agricultural commodities, metals, etc.), interest, and rent expense, among others. Dealing with the increased fluctuations requires cost estimation methods that are more sophisticated and more frequently updated. The result is that companies are including in their cost estimation additional variables and additional data for these variables. Moreover, these companies are updating their estimation models more frequently. For example, Southwest Airlines updates its revenue prediction model on a daily basis.

**Required**   Consider Southwest Airlines and the following six key areas of cost for the company. Which of these costs do you think the airline must update most frequently, and why?
1. Labor costs
2. Fuel costs
3. Maintenance spending
4. Advertising spending
5. Airport rates and charges to the airline
6. Aircraft ownership costs

[LO 8-1]   8-28   **Regression Analysis and the Insurance Industry**   Data mining, or the use of large amounts of consumer data to predict buying patterns, is widely used in certain industries to help companies select the most profitable products and services, set prices, and increase consumer demand for their products and services. Hotels, supermarkets, airlines, credit card companies, and casinos (note the example about Harrah's in the chapter, page 277) commonly use this approach, sometimes with the help of "loyalty cards" that the customer uses at checkout. Regression analysis and other analytics are then applied to the data to help the company predict buying patterns.

**Required**
1. What is the strategic role of data mining?
2. What, if any, ethical issues are of potential concern when a company uses data mining?

[LO 8-2]   8-29   Cost Classification: Match each cost to the appropriate cost behavior pattern shown in graphs (a) through (l). Any graph can fit two or more patterns.
1. The cost of lumber used to manufacture wooden kitchen tables.
2. The cost of order fillers in a warehouse. When demand increases, the number of order fillers is increased, and when demand falls off, the number is decreased.
3. The salary of the plant's quality control inspector, who inspects each batch of products.
4. The cost of water and sewer service to the manufacturing plant. The local municipality charges a fixed rate per gallon for usage up to 10,000 gallons and a higher charge per gallon for usage above that point.
5. The cost of an Internet connection of $23 per month.
6. The cost of an Internet connection of $10 per month plus $2 per hour of usage above 10 hours.

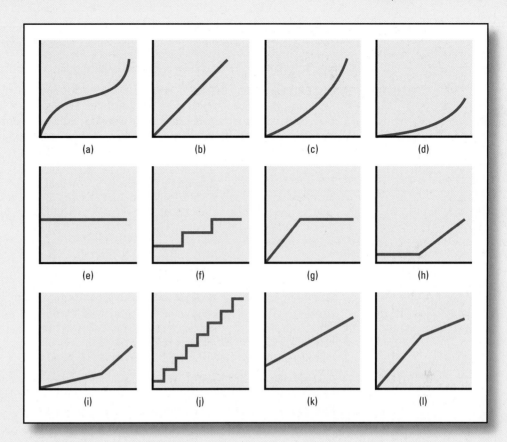

7. The cost to make copies of a given document at a printing shop, which reduces the per-copy charge for customers who make more than 100 copies of the document.

8. To discourage excess usage and to level the demand, especially in peak load times, the local electric utility increases the per-kilowatt-hour charge for each additional 5,000 kilowatt-hours' usage.

9. A clothing store in the SunnyVale Mall pays a fixed rental charge of $1,000 per month plus 2% of gross sales receipts.

10. A shoe store in the SunnyVale Mall pays 6% of gross sales receipts, up to a maximum of $3,000 per month as a rental charge.

[LO 8-2]   8-30   **Cost Relationships**   ChimneySweep provides cleaning services for residential chimneys and fireplaces. The cleaning service requires $35 in variable costs for cleaning materials. The fixed costs of labor, the company's truck, and administrative support are $165,000 per year. ChimneySweep averages 100 service calls per month.

**Required**   What is the average cost per cleaning service call?

[LO 8-2]   8-31   **Cost Relationships**   The following costs are for Optical View Inc., a contact lens manufacturer:

| Output in Units | Fixed Costs | Variable Costs | Total Costs |
|---|---|---|---|
| 250 | $4,750 | $ 7,500 | $12,250 |
| 300 | 4,750 | 9,000 | 13,750 |
| 350 | 4,750 | 10,500 | 15,250 |
| 400 | 4,750 | 12,000 | 16,750 |

**Required**
1. Graph total cost, total variable cost, and total fixed cost.
2. Graph the per-unit total cost, per-unit variable cost, and per-unit fixed cost.
3. Discuss the behavior of the fixed, variable, and total cost.

**[LO 8-2]**   8-32   **Cost Estimation; Average Cost**   Chloe's Cafe bakes croissants that it sells to local restaurants and grocery stores. The average costs to bake the croissants are $0.55 for 2,500 and $0.50 for 5,000.

**Required**   If the total cost function for croissants is linear, what will be the average cost to bake 4,200?

**[LO 8-2]**   8-33   **Cost Estimation Using Graphs**   Lawson Advertising Agency is trying to persuade Kansas City Sailboards Company to spend more on advertising. The agency's argument is that a positive linear relationship exists between advertising and sales in the sailboard industry. Sue Lawson presents these data taken from industry data for stores similar in size and market share to Kansas City Sailboards:

| Advertising Expense | Annual Sales |
|---|---|
| $2,500 | $ 95,000 |
| 3,000 | 110,000 |
| 3,500 | 124,000 |
| 4,000 | 138,000 |
| 4,500 | 143,000 |
| 5,000 | 147,000 |
| 5,500 | 150,000 |

**Required**
1. Graph annual sales and advertising expense.
2. Do the data prove Sue's point?

**[LO 8-3]**   8-34   **Analysis of Regression Results**   Wang Manufacturing uses regression analysis to predict manufacturing overhead costs based on labor-hours and/or machine-hours and has developed the three following regression equations.

| | Regression 1 | Regression 2 | Regression 3 |
|---|---|---|---|
| SE | 33,844 | 45,383 | 31,044 |
| *R*-squared | 0.55 | 0.35 | 0.58 |
| *t*-values: | | | |
| Labor-hours | 2.3 | | 1.9 |
| Machine-hours | | 1.1 | 0.8 |

**Required**   Which regression would you choose and why?

**[LO 8-3]**   8-35   **Cost Estimation; High-Low Method; MAPE**   Horton Manufacturing Inc. produces blinds and other window treatments for residential homes and offices. The owner is concerned about the maintenance costs for the production machinery, as maintenance costs for the previous fiscal year were higher than he expected. The owner has asked you to assist in estimating future maintenance costs to better predict the firm's profitability. Together, you have determined that the best cost driver for maintenance costs is machine-hours. The data from the previous fiscal year for maintenance expense and machine-hours follows:

| Month | Expense | Hours | Month | Expense | Hours |
|---|---|---|---|---|---|
| 1 | $2,625 | 1,499 | 7 | $2,865 | 1,785 |
| 2 | 2,670 | 1,590 | 8 | 2,905 | 1,805 |
| 3 | 2,720 | 1,605 | 9 | 2,780 | 1,695 |
| 4 | 2,822 | 1,655 | 10 | 2,570 | 1,410 |
| 5 | 2,855 | 1,775 | 11 | 2,590 | 1,550 |
| 6 | 3,005 | 1,880 | 12 | 2,890 | 1,405 |

**Required**
1. What is the cost equation for maintenance cost using the high-low method? Graph the data points to check for outliers.
2. Calculate the mean absolute percentage error (MAPE) for the cost equation you developed in part 1.

**[LO 8-3]**   8-36   **Cost Estimation; High-Low Method; MAPE**   Ethan Manufacturing Inc. produces floor mats for automobiles. The owner, Joseph Ethan, has asked you to assist in estimating maintenance costs.

Together, you and Joseph determine that the single best cost driver for maintenance costs is machine-hours. These data are from the previous fiscal year for maintenance expense and machine-hours:

| Month | Maintenance Expense | Machine-Hours |
|---|---|---|
| 1 | $2,600 | 1,690 |
| 2 | 2,760 | 1,770 |
| 3 | 2,910 | 1,850 |
| 4 | 3,020 | 1,870 |
| 5 | 3,100 | 1,900 |
| 6 | 3,070 | 1,880 |
| 7 | 3,010 | 1,860 |
| 8 | 2,850 | 1,840 |
| 9 | 2,620 | 1,700 |
| 10 | 2,220 | 1,100 |
| 11 | 2,230 | 1,300 |
| 12 | 2,450 | 1,590 |

**Required**

1. What is the cost equation for maintenance cost using the high-low method?

2. Calculate the mean absolute percentage error (MAPE) for the cost equation you developed in part 1.

[LO 8-3]   8-37   **The Gompertz Equation; Learning Curves**   The concept of learning curves has broad application in business, medicine, and many other fields. For example, the Gompertz equation is a mathematical model used to predict the number of deaths at a certain age. The Gompertz equation is very similar in form to that of the learning curve, except that $e$, the base of the natural logarithm, is used and there is a positive rather than a negative exponent in the equation. The Gompertz equation is as follows:

$$M(x) = Ae^{Gx}$$

Where:

$M(x)$ = the number of deaths in a population of 100,000 of those at age $x$; $M(x)$ is often called the *mortality rate.*

$A$ = the initial mortality rate at age 0.

$G$ = the exponential rate of increase in mortality for an increase in age, $x$.

$e$ = a mathematical constant, the base of the natural logarithm, which equals approximately 2.718281828.

The Gompertz equation is used to estimate the number of deaths at a given age. The equation was estimated using nonlinear regression based on 2002 U.S. census data and the following estimated equation was derived (for ages 25 through 90). The regression had a very good fit, $R$-squared of 0.97.

$$M(x) = 8.84e^{.08x}$$

**Required**

1. Use the exponential function on your calculator or the EXP function in Excel to determine the mortality rate of any age you choose between 25 and 90.

2. Think of an application or two for which an exponential equation like the Gompertz equation could be used in cost estimation.

[LO 8-3]   8-38   **Regression and Utility Rates; Sustainability**   For several years many utilities have employed regression analysis to forecast monthly utility usage by residential customers using weather forecasts, the number of holidays, the number of days in the month, and other factors. For example, the Connecticut Department of Public Utility Control (CDPUC) has determined that regression, properly used, can accurately predict natural gas usage. Most public gas utilities serving Connecticut have reported levels of accuracy from 4% to 10% using regression. One company, Dominion Natural Gas Company of Ohio, uses this approach not to forecast but to explain to customers why their natural gas bills have gone up or down compared to the prior month, and also compared to the same month of the prior year. The bill shows total MCF (thousand cubic feet of natural gas) used by the customer for that month and why the total MCF usage has changed, based on three factors:

1. Change in temperature: each degree increase in temperature causes an increase in the number of MCFs consumed. The relationship between the change in temperature and the usage of

MCF is not linear, but the monthly bill shows the average change in temperature for the month and the increase or decrease in MCF related to that change.

2. Number of billing days in the period.

3. The residual, the change in usage by the customer that is not attributable to temperature or the number of days in the billing period.

A customer of Dominion has used 13.7 MCF in December and is charged $12.50 per MCF for a total bill that month of $171.25. The following data are available to compare the current month's weather and billing period to the prior month and to the same month last year

| Usage Factors | Current Month vs. Last Month | Current Month to Last December |
|---|---|---|
| Weather | 3 degrees cooler; +2.5 MCF | 8 degrees warmer; −3.5 MCF |
| Number of billing days | 5 more days; +0.5 MCF | 1 less day; −0.1 MCF |
| Customer-controlled usage | +.9 MCF | −1.8 MCF |

### Required

1. Determine the amount of difference in the customer's bill from the prior month and from the current month last year.

2. How does Dominion's billing system affect environmental sustainability?

[LO 8-3]    8-39  **Interpreting Regression Results**    Recent research into the cost of various medical procedures has shown the impact of certain complications encountered in surgery on the total cost of a patient's stay in the hospital. The researchers used regression analysis and found the following results:

Total cost for patient = Constant, plus

> $a$ × Length of stay (measured in days), plus
>
> $b$ × Presence of one or more complications (= 1 if true, 0 if false), plus
>
> $c$ × Use of a laparoscope (= 1 if true, 0 if false)

Where:

- $a, b, c$ are coefficients of the regression model, and
- The laparoscope is an instrument somewhat like a miniature telescope with a fiber optic system which brings light into the abdomen. It is about as big around as a fountain pen and twice as long.

The research, based on 57 patients, showed the following regression results:

$R$-squared: 53%

Constant term: $3,719

Coefficients and $t$-values for independent variables:

|  | Length of Stay | Complication | Laparoscope |
|---|---|---|---|
| Coefficient | $861 | $1,986 | $908 |
| $t$-value | 10.76 | 4.89 | 2.54 |

### Required

1. What is the estimated cost for a patient whose surgery has complications and who stays in the hospital two days, and whose surgery requires a laparoscope?

2. Which, if any, dummy variables are used in this regression?

3. Comment on the statistical measures for the model.

[LO 8-3]    8-40  **Analysis of Regression Results (Continuation of 8-39)**    The following table shows additional regression results presented by the researchers in the study described in Exercise 8-39. There are two regressions. The right-hand column shows the results for all patients, including those treated with laparoscopic surgery. The left-hand column shows the results for the sample of patients who were treated without the laparoscopic surgery, and the related costs.

| | Not Laparoscopic | All Patients |
|---|---|---|
| **Coefficients for Independent Variables** | | |
| Regression intercept | $8,043 | $3,719 |
| Length of stay | | |
| Coefficient* | Not significant | 861 |
| Standard error for the coefficient | Not applicable | 80 |
| Number of complications | | |
| Coefficient | 3,393 | 1,986 |
| Standard error for the coefficient | 1,239 | 406 |
| Laparascopic | | |
| Coefficient | Not applicable | 908 |
| Standard error for the coefficient | Not applicable | 358 |
| *R*-squared | 0.11 | 0.53 |

*Note: All independent variables are significant at the level of $p = .05$ (and $t$-value $> 2$) except for the length of stay variable in the nonlaparoscopic condition. Also, the t-value for each independent variable can be calculated by dividing the coefficient of the variable by the standard error for the coefficient of that variable.

**Required**

1. Which of the two regressions has the better reliability and precision in estimating cost? Why?

2. Calculate the t-value for each of the independent variables, and interpret the values of each coefficient and the t-values for each independent variable.

[LO 8-3]   8-41   **Cost Estimation; High-Low Method**   Albedo Inc. manufactures high-end replacement telescope lenses for amateur and professional astronomers who are seeking to upgrade the performance of their telescopes. You have just become employed as a staff accountant at Albedo and Jordan Coleman, the controller, has asked you to help with maintenance cost estimation for the lens manufacturing process. You review the manufacturing process and decide that the best cost driver for maintenance costs is labor-hours. The data below are from the previous fiscal year for maintenance expense and labor-hours:

| Month | Maintenance Cost | Labor-Hours |
|---|---|---|
| 1 | $3,210 | 2,750 |
| 2 | 4,650 | 3,900 |
| 3 | 5,175 | 4,050 |
| 4 | 3,350 | 2,690 |
| 5 | 3,100 | 2,500 |
| 6 | 2,950 | 2,580 |
| 7 | 2,900 | 2,300 |
| 8 | 2,900 | 2,500 |
| 9 | 4,120 | 3,160 |
| 10 | 4,350 | 3,325 |
| 11 | 3,500 | 2,780 |
| 12 | 3,775 | 3,000 |

**Required**   What is the cost equation for maintenance cost using the high-low method?

## Problems

[LO 8-3, 8-4]   8-42   **Cost Estimation; High-Low Method**   The Jess Gilmore Company specializes in the purchase, renovation, and resale of older homes. Jess employs several carpenters and painters to do the work for him. It is essential for him to have accurate cost estimates so he can determine total renovation costs before he purchases a piece of property. If estimated renovation costs plus the purchase price of a house are higher than its estimated resale value, the house is not a worthwhile investment.

Jess has been using the home's interior square feet for his exterior paint cost estimations. Recently he decided to include the number of openings—the total number of doors and windows in a house—as a cost driver. Their cost is significant because they require time-consuming preparatory work and careful brushwork. The rest of the house usually is painted either by rollers or spray guns, which are relatively efficient ways to apply paint to a large area. Jess has kept careful records of these expenses on his last 12 jobs:

| House | Square Feet | Openings | Cost |
|-------|-------------|----------|--------|
| 1 | 2,600 | 13 | $3,335 |
| 2 | 3,010 | 15 | 3,742 |
| 3 | 2,800 | 12 | 3,100 |
| 4 | 2,850 | 12 | 3,150 |
| 5 | 4,600 | 19 | 4,700 |
| 6 | 2,700 | 13 | 3,225 |
| 7 | 2,375 | 11 | 2,920 |
| 8 | 2,450 | 11 | 2,836 |
| 9 | 2,600 | 10 | 2,945 |
| 10 | 3,700 | 16 | 4,112 |
| 11 | 2,650 | 13 | 3,210 |
| 12 | 3,550 | 16 | 3,965 |

**Required**

1. Using the high-low cost estimation technique, determine the cost of painting a 3,300-square-foot house with 14 openings. Also determine the cost for a 2,400-square-foot house with 8 openings.

2. Plot the cost data against square feet and against openings. Which variable is a better cost driver? Why?

3. What are the sustainability issues for this company, and what is the role of cost estimation in this regard?

**[LO 8-3, 8-4]**  8-43  **Cost Estimation; Machine Replacement; Ethics**  GlasTech Company manufactures glass for office buildings in Florida. As a result of age and wear, a critical machine in the production process has begun to produce quality defects. GlasTech is considering replacing the old machine with a new machine, either brand A or brand B. The manufacturer of each machine has provided GlasTech these data on the cost of operation of its machine at various levels of output:

| Output (square yards) | Machine A Estimated Total Costs | Machine B Estimated Total Costs |
|-----------------------|---------------------------------|---------------------------------|
| 2,000 | $100,000 | $140,000 |
| 4,000 | 150,000 | 200,000 |
| 8,000 | 180,000 | 230,000 |
| 15,000 | 225,000 | 280,000 |
| 30,000 | 260,000 | 300,000 |
| 48,000 | 422,000 | 370,000 |

**Required**

1. Use the high-low method to determine the cost equations for each machine. If GlasTech's output is expected to be 40,000 square yards, which machine should it purchase? At 25,000 square yards? Is the high-low method useful here? Why or why not?

2. As a cost analyst at GlasTech, you have been assigned to complete requirement 1. A production supervisor comes to you to say that the nature of the defect is really very difficult to detect and that most customers will not notice it, so he questions replacing it. He suggests that you modify your calculations to justify keeping the present machine to keep things the way they are and save the company some money. What do you say?

3. Assume that machine A is manufactured in Germany and machine B is manufactured in Canada. As a U.S.–based firm, what considerations are important to GlasTech, in addition to those already mentioned in your answer to requirement 1?

**[LO 8-3]**  8-44  **Cost Estimation; High-Low Method**  Antelope Park Amoco (APA) in Antelope Park, Alaska, has noticed that utility bills are substantially higher when the average monthly temperature is colder. The only thing in the shop that uses natural gas is the furnace. Because of prevailing low temperatures, the furnace is used every month of the year (though less in the summer months and very little in August). Everything else in the shop runs on electricity, and electricity use is fairly constant throughout the year.

For a year, APA has been recording the average daily temperature and the cost of its monthly utility bills for natural gas and electricity.

|  | Average Temperature | Utility Cost |
|---|---|---|
| January | 31°F | $760 |
| February | 41 | 629 |
| March | 43 | 543 |
| April | 44 | 410 |
| May | 46 | 275 |
| June | 50 | 233 |
| July | 53 | 220 |
| August | 60 | 210 |
| September | 50 | 305 |
| October | 40 | 530 |
| November | 30 | 750 |
| December | 20 | 870 |

**Required**    Use the high-low method to estimate utility cost for the upcoming months of January and February. The forecast for January is a near record average temperature of 10°F; temperatures in February are expected to average 40°F.

[LO 8-3, 8-4]    8-45    **Regression Analysis**    Pilot Shop is a catalog business providing a wide variety of aviation products to pilots throughout the world. Maynard Shephard, the recently hired assistant controller, has been asked to develop a cost function to forecast shipping costs. The previous assistant controller had forecast shipping department costs each year by plotting cost data against direct labor-hours for the most recent 12 months and visually fitting a straight line through the points. The results were not satisfactory.

After discussions with the shipping department personnel, Maynard decided that shipping costs could be more closely related to the number of orders filled. He based his conclusion on the fact that 10 months ago the shipping department added some automated equipment. Furthermore, he believes that using linear regression analysis will improve the forecasts of shipping costs. Cost data for the shipping department have been accumulated for the last 25 weeks. He ran two regression analyses of the data, one using direct labor-hours, and one using the number of cartons shipped. The information from the two linear regressions follows:

|  | Regression 1 | Regression 2 |
|---|---|---|
| Equation | SC = 804.3 + 15.68DL | SC = 642.9 + 3.92NR |
| *R*-squared | .365 | .729 |
| Standard error of the estimate | 2.652 | 1.884 |
| *t*-value | 1.89 | 3.46 |

where:

SC = Total shipping department costs

DL = Total direct labor-hours

NR = Number of orders shipped

**Required**

1. Identify which cost function (regression 1 or regression 2) Pilot Shop should adopt for forecasting total shipping department costs and explain why.

2. If Pilot Shop projects that 600 orders will be filled the coming week, calculate the total shipping department costs using the regression you selected in requirement 1.

3. Explain two or three important limitations of the regression you selected in requirement 1, and identify one or two ways to address the limitations. Specifically include in your discussion the effect, if any, of the global nature of Pilot Shop's business.

**(CMA Adapted)**

[LO 8-3]    8-46    **Analysis of Regression Results**    Rock 'n' Roll Heaven is an outdoor pavilion that presents musical performers throughout a six-month season, from late spring to early fall. Rock 'n' Roll presents a diverse venue of artists in a set of approximately 40 events each season. In order to better project its costs and expected attendance, Rock 'n' Roll uses regression analysis to project expected ticket sales for upcoming events for each performer. The regression results shown below are derived from the three most recent seasons. The dependent variable for Rock 'n' Roll is the number of paying ticket-holders for each event, and the independent variables are

**Five independent variables:**

1. Whether or not this particular performer appeared at Rock 'n' Roll previously (a dummy variable, 0 if no and 1 if yes).
2. The spending on advertising targeted to the performer's appearance.
3. The performer's local sales of CDs in the most recent year prior to their appearance.
4. The number of television appearances for the performer in the most recent year.
5. The number of public performances in the United States by the performer in the recent year.

| Independent Variables | Results |
|---|---|
| Regression intercept | 1,224 |
| Attendance at prior concert | |
| Coefficient | 3,445 |
| *t*-value | 4.11 |
| Spending on advertising | |
| Coefficient | 0.113 |
| *t*-value | 1.88 |
| Performer's CD sales | |
| Coefficient | 0.00044 |
| *t*-value | 1.22 |
| Television appearances | |
| Coefficient | 898 |
| *t*-value | 2.4 |
| Other public performances | |
| Coefficient | 1,233 |
| *t*-value | 3.7 |
| *R*-squared | 0.88 |
| Standard error of the estimate | 2,447 |

**Required**

1. Using the above regression, what attendance would be predicted for a performer who had appeared at Rock 'n' Roll previously, had six other public performances but no TV appearances, had local CD sales of $10 million, and for whom Rock 'n' Roll planned to spend $35,000 on advertising?

2. Evaluate the precision and reliability of the regression results shown above. What changes, if any, do you propose for the regression? Which variables should be deleted, and which do you think should be added, and why?

**[LO 8-3]**   8-47   **Correlation Analysis**   PolyChem is a large manufacturer of packaging materials for supermarkets and other retail applications; the packages are used by customers to carry away their purchases. PolyChem has succeeded for many years by providing a high-quality product and superior customer service. Recently, additional competitors have entered the market, both local and foreign, and PolyChem is finding that it must increasingly compete on price. PolyChem's strategy for dealing with the increased competition is to market its products to smaller retailers that would appreciate the firm's quality and service, as well as the firm's ability to customize the product—adding different designs and colors to the packaging material. Until recently, the firm determined product costs based on simple averages of materials purchases, plant labor, and overhead. The firm's management is now interested in improving, if possible, the accuracy of its cost information. As a start, Cheryl Greenberg, the management accountant, obtains the following sample of data (Table 1) from the plant manager, showing the machine number, the order size (quantity, in thousands), the machine setup time (in hours per unit; setup time also includes cleanup time after the order is run), run time (the operating time for the machine to produce the order), and a measure of the complexity of the order based on a subjective rating where 1 = less complex and 2 = more complex (complexity relates to the number and type of images and colors printed on the packaging material).

Cheryl wants to run some regression analyses to better understand these data and, as a first step, obtains a correlation analysis which shows the simple correlation between each of the variables in Table 1. The results are shown in Table 2. Cheryl understands that each of the correlation numbers in Table 2 is equivalent to the *R*-squared for a simple linear regression between the variable, as follows: (correlation between two variables)$^2$ = the *R*-squared for simple regression analysis between these two variables. To illustrate, note that the correlation between machine number and order quantity = −.33919. The *R*-squared for the regression between these two variables (with either as the dependent variable) is $(-.33919)^2 = .1151$. Cheryl also recalls that a negative correlation means that the two variables are inversely related—when one increases, the other decreases.

Table 1   Plant Data for PolyChem

| Machine Number | Order Size | Order Complexity | Per Unit | |
|---|---|---|---|---|
| | | | Setup Time | Run Time |
| 2 | 480 | 1 | 0.0023 | 0.0423 |
| 2 | 489 | 1 | 0.0001 | 0.0434 |
| 2 | 480 | 2 | 0.0054 | 0.0419 |
| 4 | 180 | 1 | 0.0022 | 0.0400 |
| 4 | 2160 | 1 | 0.0022 | 0.0355 |
| 4 | 1377 | 1 | 0.0023 | 0.0405 |
| 4 | 120 | 2 | 0.0042 | 0.0400 |
| 4 | 540 | 1 | 0.0026 | 0.0413 |
| 4 | 360 | 2 | 0.0142 | 0.0411 |
| 4 | 1080 | 2 | 0.0111 | 0.0376 |
| 4 | 300 | 1 | 0.0037 | 0.0430 |
| 4 | 2400 | 2 | 0.0046 | 0.0345 |
| 4 | 81 | 2 | 0.0457 | 0.0407 |
| 8 | 360 | 1 | 0.0022 | 0.0425 |
| 8 | 120 | 1 | 0.0017 | 0.0433 |
| 8 | 120 | 2 | 0.0067 | 0.0417 |
| 8 | 60 | 2 | 0.0083 | 0.0422 |
| 8 | 240 | 1 | 0.0079 | 0.0425 |
| 8 | 60 | 2 | 0.0050 | 0.0467 |

Table 2   Correlation Results for PolyChem's Plant Data

| | Number | Order Size | Complexity | Setup Time | Run Time |
|---|---|---|---|---|---|
| Number | 1.0000 | | | | |
| Order size | −0.3392 | 1.0000 | | | |
| Complexity | 0.0710 | −0.0710 | 1.0000 | | |
| Setup time | −0.0341 | −0.2028 | 0.4590 | 1.0000 | |
| Runtime | 0.3579 | −0.8118 | −0.1309 | −0.0648 | 1.0000 |

Note: Correlations with absolute value > .4 are statistically significant at $p < .10$; correlations with absolute value > .5 are statistically significant at $p < .05$.

**Required**

1. Analyze the findings in Table 2 and assess how, if at all, order size and complexity aff[...] run time. What other findings in Table 2 are of particular interest?

2. How can your analysis in 1 above help PolyChem become more competitive?

[LO 8-3]   8-48   **Regression Analysis**   United States Motors Inc. (USMI) manufactures a[...] trucks and distributes them for sale to consumers through franchised retail[...] franchise agreement, dealerships must provide monthly financial statemen[...] accounting procedures manual. USMI has developed the following financ[...] dealership that sells 1,500 new vehicles annually.

| AVERAGE DEALERSHIP FINANCIAL PROFILE | |
|---|---|
| Composite Income Statement | |
| Sales | $30,000,000 |
| Cost of goods sold | 24,750,000 |
| Gross profit | $ 5,250,000 |
| Operating costs | |
| Variable expenses | 862,500 |
| Mixed expenses | 2,300,000 |
| Fixed expenses | 1,854,000 |
| Operating income | $ 233,500 |

USMI is considering a major expansion of its dealership network. The vice president of marketing has asked Jack Snyder, corporate controller, to develop some measure of the risk associated with the addition of these franchises. Jack estimates that 90% of the mixed expenses shown are variable for purposes of this analysis. He also suggests performing regression analyses on the various components of the mixed expenses to more definitively determine their variability.

**Required**

1. Calculate the composite dealership profit if 2,000 units are sold.

2. Assume that regression analyses were performed on the separate components of the mixed expenses and that a coefficient of determination value of .60 was determined as applicable to aggregate mixed expenses over the relevant range.

   a. Define the term *relevant range*.

   b. Explain the significance of an *R*-squared value of .60 to USMI's analysis.

   c. Describe the limitations that may exist in applying the composite-based relationships to specific new dealerships that have been proposed.

   d. Define the *standard error of the estimate*.

3. The regression equation that Jack Snyder developed to project annual sales of a dealership has an *R*-squared of 60% and a standard error of the estimate of $4,500,000. If the projected annual sales for a dealership total $28,500,000, determine the approximate 95% confidence range for Jack's prediction of sales.

4. What is the strategic role of regression analysis for USMI?

**(CMA Adapted)**

[LO 8-3]   8-49   **Cost Estimation; High-Low Method; Regression Analysis; Spreadsheet Application**   Lexon, Inc., is a large manufacturer of affordable DVD players. Management recently became aware of rising costs resulting from returns of malfunctioning products. As a starting point for further analysis, Paige Jennings, the controller, wants to test different forecasting methods and then use the best one to forecast quarterly expenses for 2013. The relevant quarterly data for the previous three years follow:

| 2010 Quarter | Return Expenses | 2011 Quarter | Return Expenses | 2012 Quarter | Return Expenses |
|---|---|---|---|---|---|
| 1 | $12,500 | 1 | $12,900 | 1 | $13,300 |
| 2 | 11,300 | 2 | 12,100 | 2 | 12,300 |
| 3 | 11,600 | 3 | 11,700 | 3 | 12,100 |
| 4 | 13,700 | 4 | 14,000 | 4 | 14,600 |

The result of a simple regression analysis using all 12 data points yielded an intercept of $11,855 and a coefficient for the independent variable of $126.22. (*R*-squared = 0.44, SE = $975).

**Required**

1. Calculate the quarterly forecast for 2013 using the high-low method and regression analyses. Recommend which method Paige should use and explain why.

2. How does your analysis in requirement 1 change if Lexon manufactures its products in multiple global production facilities to serve the global market?

[LO 8-3]   8-50   **Regression; Applicants for MBA Programs; Spreadsheet Application**   Business schools have commonly observed that when job opportunities are down, those interested in business seek to enter MBA programs. To test this hypothesis, we decided to look at the number of applicants for the Graduate Management Admissions Test (GMAT), which is required for application to most MBA programs, and to

| | Unemployment Rate | Unemployment Rate for College Grads | Percentage Change in GMAT Takers |
|---|---|---|---|
| 2000 | 4.0% | 1.6% | 4% |
| 2001 | 4.6 | 2.2 | 3 |
| 2002 | 5.8 | 2.9 | 12 |
| 2003 | 6.0 | 3.1 | (7) |
| 2004 | 5.5 | 2.7 | (9) |
| 2005 | 5.1 | 2.3 | (4) |
| 2006 | 4.6 | 2 | 6 |
| 2007 | 4.7 | 2.1 | 5 |
| 2008 | 5.5 | 2.3 | 10 |

compare that to the unemployment rate. The GMAT data are only available on an annual basis, so we also use annual unemployment data. The GMAT data are from the Graduate Management Admissions Council (**www.gmac.com/gmac**) while the unemployment data are taken from the website of the U.S. Bureau of Labor Statistics (**www.bls.gov/data/home.htm**). We have data for both the total unemployment rate and the rate for college graduates 25 years of age or older. The data for 2000 through September 2008 are shown below. The unemployment rate is the median value for the 12 months in the year (or the 9 months in 2008). The percentage change (from prior year) in GMAT exam takers is from the GMAC's publication "2008 Application Trends Survey."

**Required**

1. Use regression on the above data to determine whether there is a relationship between the unemployment rate and the number of GMAT exam takers. Use both measures of unemployment and see if there is a difference in your results. State whether you expect the relationship to be positive or negative (inverse).

2. Assume that the relationship between the unemployment rate and the number of GMAT takers is a lagged relationship and a change in the unemployment rate in one year leads to a change in GMAT takers in the following year. Use regression again and compare your results to those in part 1.

[LO 8-3, 8-5]    8-51    **Learning Curves**   The Air Force Museum Foundation has commissioned the purchase of 16 Four F Sixes, pre–World War II aircraft. They will be built completely from scratch to the exact specifications used for the originals. As further authentication, the aircraft will be made using the technology and manufacturing processes available when the originals were built. Each of the 16 airplanes will be flown to Air Force and aviation museums throughout the country for exhibition. Aviation enthusiasts can also visit the production facility to see exactly how such aircraft were built in 1938.

Soren Industries wants to bid on the aircraft contract and asked for and received certain cost information about the Four F Sixes from the Air Force. The information includes some of the old cost data from the builders of the original aircraft. The available information is for the total accumulated time as the first, eighth, and thirty-second aircraft, respectively, were completed. The data reflect a learning rate of 90%.

| Output | Total Hours |
|--------|-------------|
| 1      | 250         |
| 8      | 1,458       |
| 32     | 4,724       |

**Required**

1. If Soren Industries expects that the manufacturing time will be the same as it was in 1938, how many hours will it take to build the 16 aircraft for the Air Force Museum Foundation?

2. What is the role of learning curves in Soren Industries's business for contracts such as this?

[LO 8-3, 8-5]    8-52    **Learning Curves**   The Mad Hatter (TMH) is a Newark, New Jersey, manufacturer of hats and gloves. On March 11, 2013, the company purchased a new machine to aid in producing the hat product lines. Production efficiency on the new machine increases with the workforce experience. It has been shown that as cumulative output on the new machine increases, average labor time per unit decreases up to the production of at least 3,200 units. As TMH's cumulative output doubles from a base of 100 units produced, the average labor time per unit declines by a learning rate of 80%.

TMH has developed a new style of men's hat to be produced on the new machine. One hundred of these hats can be produced in a total of 25 labor-hours. All other direct costs to produce each hat are $12, excluding direct labor cost. Direct labor cost per hour is $25. Fixed costs are $8,000 per month, and TMH has the capacity to produce 3,200 hats per month.

**Required**   TMH plans to set the selling price for the new men's hat at 200% of direct production cost. If the company is planning to sell 100 hats, what is the selling price? If the plan is to sell 800 hats, what is the selling price?

[LO 8-3, 8-5]    8-53    **Learning Curves**   Hauser Company, a family-owned business, engineers and manufactures a line of motorbikes and dirt bikes under the trade-name Trailite. The company has been in business for almost 20 years and has maintained a profitable share of the recreational vehicle market due to its reputation for high-quality products. In addition, Hauser's engineering department has kept the company in the forefront by incorporating the latest technology in the Trailite bikes. Most subassembly work for the bikes is subcontracted to reliable vendors. However, the final assembly and inspection of all products is performed at Hauser's plant. Hauser recently developed a new braking system for the Trailite Model-500 dirt bike. Because of the company's current availability of production capacity, Jim Walsh, production manager, recommended that the first lot of the new braking system be manufactured in-house rather than by subcontractors. This 80-unit production run has now been completed. The cumulative average labor-hours per unit for the braking system was 60 hours. Hauser's experience with similar products indicates that a learning curve of 80% is applicable and that the learning factor can be expected to extend only through the fourth production run (80 per batch) for a total of 320 units. Hauser's direct labor cost is $14.50 per direct labor-hour. Its management must decide whether to continue producing the braking system in its own plant or to subcontract this work. Joyce Lane, Hauser's purchasing agent, has received a proposal from MACQ, a company specializing in component assembly. MACQ has done work in the past for Hauser and has proved to be of high quality and reliable. The terms of MACQ's proposal are negotiable, and before beginning discussions with them, Joyce has decided to conduct some relevant financial analysis.

### Required

1. Hauser Company has an immediate requirement for a total of 1,000 units of the braking system. Determine Hauser's future direct labor costs to produce the required braking system units if it manufactures the units in-house.

2. A consultant has advised Joyce that the learning rate for this application might be closer to 75%. What is the effect on projected costs of using a 75% learning rate as opposed to an 80% learning rate?

3. What conditions in a manufacturing plant, if present, would offset the potential benefits of the learning curve? What is the strategic role of learning curve analysis for Hauser Company?

### (CMA Adapted)

[LO 8-3, 8-4]   8-54 **Cross-Sectional Regression; Analysis of Rankings; Spreadsheet Application**   *Bloomberg Businessweek* magazine periodically publishes a ranking of the Top Companies: Best Place to Work. The ranking gives employers, employees, and potential employees a snapshot of the overall achievements these companies have made in creating a productive and rewarding work environment. The ranking considers a number of factors (we will call these independent variables), including surveys of career service directors at U.S. colleges, surveys of the organizations themselves (on pay, benefits, and training programs, etc.), and surveys of undergraduate students. The survey data are used to create a ranking for each independent variable of the top companies. The 2009 rankings and survey data for the top 25 organizations are shown below.

| Organization/Industry | Rank | Employer Survey | Student Survey | Career Service Director Survey | Average Pay |
|---|---|---|---|---|---|
| Deloitte & Touche/Accounting | 1 | 1 | 8 | 1 | 55 |
| Ernst & Young/Accounting | 2 | 6 | 3 | 6 | 50 |
| PricewaterhouseCoopers/Accounting | 3 | 22 | 5 | 2 | 50 |
| KPMG/Accounting | 4 | 17 | 11 | 5 | 50 |
| U.S. State Dept./Government | 5 | 12 | 2 | 24 | 60 |
| Goldman Sachs/Investment banking | 6 | 3 | 13 | 16 | 60 |
| Teach for America/Nonprofit-government | 7 | 24 | 6 | 7 | 35 |
| Target/Retail | 8 | 19 | 18 | 3 | 45 |
| J.P. Morgan/Investment banking | 9 | 13 | 12 | 17 | 60 |
| IBM/Technology | 10 | 11 | 17 | 13 | 60 |
| Accenture/Consulting | 11 | 5 | 38 | 15 | 60 |
| General Mills/Consumer products | 12 | 3 | 33 | 28 | 60 |
| Abbott Laboratories/Health | 13 | 2 | 44 | 36 | 55 |
| Walt Disney/Hospitality | 14 | 60 | 1 | 8 | 40 |
| Enterprise Rent-A-Car/Transportation | 15 | 28 | 51 | 4 | 35 |
| General Electric/Manufacturing | 16 | 19 | 16 | 9 | 55 |
| Phillip Morris/Consumer products | 17 | 8 | 50 | 19 | 55 |
| Microsoft/Technology | 18 | 28 | 9 | 34 | 75 |
| Prudential/Insurance | 19 | 9 | 55 | 37 | 50 |
| Intel/Technology | 20 | 14 | 23 | 63 | 60 |
| Aflac/Insurance | 21 | 9 | 55 | 62 | 50 |
| Verizon Communications/Utilities | 22 | 15 | 37 | 49 | 40 |
| Central Intelligence Agency (CIA)/Gov't | 23 | 45 | 7 | 29 | 45 |
| Raytheon/Manufacturing | 24 | 23 | 39 | 19 | 60 |
| Nestlé/Consumer products | 25 | 20 | 31 | 44 | 50 |

**Required**

1. Using regression analysis in Excel, develop a regression model to predict company rank based on the four independent variables—employer survey rank, student survey rank, career service director rank, and average pay. Determine which, if any, of these four independent variables are significantly correlated with the overall ranking. Which is the strongest and which is the weakest independent variable, and why?

2. What are some of the limitations of the analysis you have completed in part 1 above?

[LO 8-3]    8-55    **Cost Estimation; Regression Analysis; Spreadsheet Application**    Plantcity is a large nursery and retail store specializing in house and garden plants and supplies. Jean Raouth, the assistant manager, is in the process of budgeting monthly supplies expense for 2013. She assumes that in some way supplies expense is related to sales, either in units or in dollars. She has collected these data for sales and supplies expenses for June 2010 through December 2012 and has estimated sales for 2013:

| Date | Supplies Expense | Sales Units | Sales Dollars |
|---|---|---|---|
| Jun 2010 | $2,745 | 354 | $2,009 |
| Jul | 3,200 | 436 | 2,190 |
| Aug | 3,232 | 525 | 2,878 |
| Sep | 2,199 | 145 | 1,856 |
| Oct | 2,321 | 199 | 2,168 |
| Nov | 3,432 | 543 | 2,152 |
| Dec | 4,278 | 1,189 | 2,463 |
| | | | |
| Jan 2011 | 2,310 | 212 | 1,999 |
| Feb | 2,573 | 284 | 2,190 |
| Mar | 2,487 | 246 | 1,894 |
| Apr | 2,484 | 278 | 2,134 |
| May | 3,384 | 498 | 3,210 |
| Jun | 2,945 | 424 | 2,850 |
| Jul | 2,758 | 312 | 2,265 |
| Aug | 3,394 | 485 | 2,435 |
| Sep | 2,254 | 188 | 1,893 |
| Oct | 2,763 | 276 | 2,232 |
| Nov | 3,245 | 489 | 3,004 |
| Dec | 4,576 | 1,045 | 3,309 |
| | | | |
| Jan 2012 | 2,103 | 104 | 2,195 |
| Feb | 2,056 | 167 | 2,045 |
| Mar | 3,874 | 298 | 2,301 |
| Apr | 2,784 | 398 | 2,345 |
| May | 2,345 | 187 | 1,815 |
| Jun | 2,912 | 334 | 2,094 |
| Jul | 2,093 | 264 | 1,934 |
| Aug | 2,873 | 333 | 2,054 |
| Sep | 2,563 | 143 | 1,977 |
| Oct | 2,384 | 245 | 1,857 |
| Nov | 2,476 | 232 | 2,189 |
| Dec | 3,364 | 1,122 | 3,433 |
| | | | |
| Jan 2013 (estimated) | | 180 | $1,600 |
| Feb | | 230 | 2,000 |
| Mar | | 190 | 1,900 |
| Apr | | 450 | 2,400 |
| May | | 350 | 2,300 |
| Jun | | 350 | 2,300 |
| Jul | | 450 | 2,500 |
| Aug | | 550 | 3,000 |
| Sep | | 300 | 2,500 |
| Oct | | 300 | 2,500 |
| Nov | | 450 | 3,200 |
| Dec | | 950 | 3,900 |

**Required**

1.  Develop the regression that Jean should use based on these data and use the regression procedure in Excel or an equivalent regression software program. Evaluate the reliability and precision of the regression you have chosen.

2.  What are the predicted monthly figures for supplies expense for 2013?

[LO 8-3, 8-4]    8-56    **Cross-Sectional Regression Analysis; Spreadsheet Application**    WasteTec is a large construction company that specializes in the construction of large wastewater treatment plants and recycling plants. A major cost driver in either type of facility is the capacity of the plant. For example, the capacity of a recycling plant is measured by the number of tons of water per day (TPD) that the plant can process. These plants can vary in size from a few hundred TPD to as many as several thousand TPD. Regression analysis is a useful method to estimate the cost of a new plant by using a regression equation developed from prior plant construction projects. The dependent variable of the regression is the actual construction cost of each project, while the independent variable is the TPD for the plant. Below is a sample of some recent projects and the related construction costs (in thousands).

|                    | TPD   | Cost       |
| ------------------ | ----- | ---------- |
| Commerce, CA       | 360   | $ 59,369   |
| Hudson Falls, NY   | 400   | 77,013     |
| Layton, UT         | 420   | 50,405     |
| Oxford Township, NJ| 450   | 75,779     |
| Savannah, GA       | 500   | 87,439     |
| Poughkeepsie, NY   | 506   | 57,463     |
| Panama City, FL    | 510   | 60,730     |
| Ronkonkoma, NY     | 518   | 84,457     |
| Okahuma, FL        | 528   | 88,119     |
| Spokane, WA        | 800   | 152,902    |
| Arlington, VA      | 975   | 127,021    |
| Camden, NJ         | 1,050 | 163,395    |
| York, PA           | 1,344 | 139,302    |
| Bridgeport, CT     | 2,250 | 344,852    |
| Chester, PA        | 2,688 | 448,073    |

**Required**

1.  Develop a regression model using Excel or an equivalent system to predict the cost of a proposed new plant in Babylon, New York, which will have a required capacity of 750 TPD. What is the predicted cost for the Babylon plant, using your regression?

2.  Evaluate the precision and reliability of the regression you have developed. How could it be improved?

3.  How would you incorporate sustainability issues in the analysis you have completed in parts 1 and 2 above?

[LO 8-3]    8-57    **Cost Estimating for Defense Contracting; Using the Internet**    Companies that do business with the U.S. Defense Department (e.g., The Boeing Company, Lockheed Martin Corporation, General Electric, Northrop Grumman, and General Dynamics) typically develop large multiyear proposals for large-scale defense-related projects. A key aspect of developing a successful proposal for the Department of Defense is to use proper cost estimation tools.

**Required**

1.  Review the information at the site of the International Society of Parametric Analysis (ISPA), (**www.ispa-cost.org/ISPA_PEH_4th_ed_Final.pdf**), which sets out proper estimation methods for proposals to the Department of Defense. Look especially at Chapter 3 of the ISPA's handbook. In 100 words or less describe the cost estimation methods suggested in this document for use in developing proposals for the Department of Defense. What are some examples of how cost estimation is used by defense contractors such as The Boeing Company?

2.  Review Figure 3.6 in the handbook and compare it to the related information found in this chapter.

## Solutions to Self-Study Problems

### 1. Using the High-Low Method

Begin by graphing the data to determine whether there are any unusual (i.e., seasonal) patterns or outliers in Exhibit 1 on the following page.

**EXHIBIT 1**
**Plot of Data for Hector's Delivery Service**

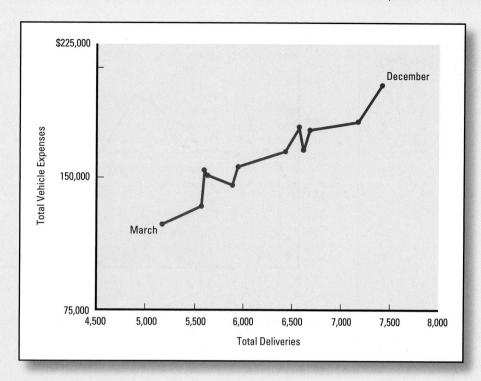

The graph shows no unusual patterns or outliers, so the high-low estimate can be determined directly from the low point (March) and the high point (December) as follows:

To determine the slope of the line (unit variable cost)

$$(\$201,783 - \$123,245)/(7,433 - 5,166) = \$34.644 \text{ per delivery}$$

To determine the intercept

$$\$201,783 - (7,433 \times \$34,644) = -\$55,726$$

$$\$123,245 - (5,166 \times \$34.644) = -\$55,726$$

The estimation equation is

$$\text{Vehicle costs} = -\$55,726 + (\$34.644 \times \text{Number of deliveries})$$

Note that the intercept is a negative number, which simply means that the relevant range of 5,166 to 7,433 deliveries is so far from the zero point (where the intercept is) that the intercept cannot be properly interpreted as a fixed cost. The estimation equation therefore is useful only within the relevant range of approximately 5,000 to 7,500 deliveries and should not be used to estimate costs outside that range.

## 2. Using Regression Analysis

All relevant criteria favor the first regression based on higher *R*-squared and *t*-values and lower standard error. Moreover, the sign on the materials cost variable in regression 2 is negative, which is difficult to explain. This variable should have a direct relationship with overhead; thus, the sign of the variable should be positive. The reason for the improvement of regression 1 over regression 2 might be that machine-hours are highly correlated with either materials costs, labor-hours, or both, thus causing multicollinearity. By excluding machine-hours as an independent variable, George reduced or removed the multicollinearity, and the regression improved as a result. He should therefore use regression 1.

## 3. Using Both High-Low and Regression

Begin by graphing the data for the number of defective units, as shown in Exhibit 2. The objective is to identify any unusual patterns that must be considered in developing an estimate.

Exhibit 2 shows that the number of defective units varies considerably from month to month and that a steady increase has occurred over the past two years. Knowing that the production level also has

**EXHIBIT 2**
**Defective Units from January 2012 to December 2013**

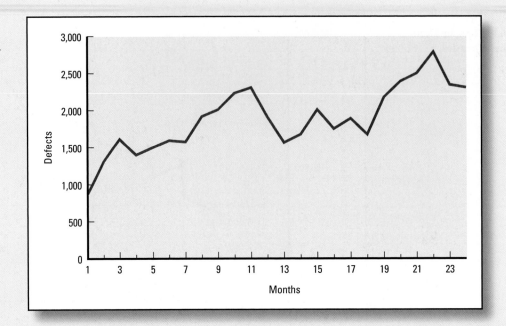

been increasing (as measured either by cost of sales, units produced, or units shipped), we now want to determine whether the relationship between defects and production level (Exhibit 3) has changed.

We begin with units produced as the independent variable, since it should have the most direct relationship with defects; the other independent variables can be tried later. The second graph (Exhibit 3) makes clear that a relationship exists between units produced and the number of defects.

The next step is to quantify this relationship with the high-low method and regression analysis. We begin with the high-low analysis. For Exhibit 3, we identify February 2012 and December 2013 as representative low and high periods, respectively.

We calculate the high-low estimate as follows (these two points are not the absolute lowest and highest points, but they produce a line that is representative of the data):

$$\text{Slope} = (2{,}311 - 1{,}335)/(88 - 58) = 32.533$$

**EXHIBIT 3**
**Defective Units vs. Production Level from January 2012 to December 2013**

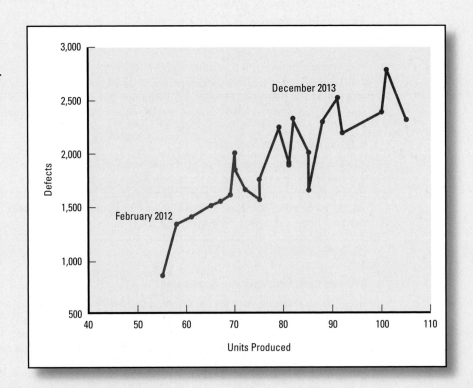

**EXHIBIT 4**
**Regressions for the Number of Defects**

| Intercept | Coefficient of Independent Variable | *t*-value for Independent Variable | *R*-squared | Standard Error of the Estimate (SE) |
|---|---|---|---|---|
| **Regression 1** | | | | |
| 103.20 | | | .883 | 161 |
| | −38.974 (units shipped) | −.44 | | |
| | −2.849 (units produced) | −.38 | | |
| | 4.702 (cost of sales) | .72 | | |
| **Regression 2** | | | | |
| 92.24 | | | .881 | 158 |
| | −2.230 (units produced) | −.309 | | |
| | 1.837 (cost of sales) | 4.54 | | |
| **Regression 3** | | | | |
| 43.95 | | | .881 | 155 |
| | 1.720 (cost of sales) | 12.77 | | |

And

$$\text{Intercept} = 2{,}311 - (32.533 \times 88) = 1{,}335 - (32.533 \times 58) = -552$$

Thus, the estimation equation is

$$\text{Number of defects} = -552 + (32.533 \times \text{Units produced})$$

The high-low estimate is subject to the limitations of subjectivity in the choice of high and low points and because it uses only those two data points to develop the estimate. Regression is performed to provide a more precise estimate. Thus, the next step is to obtain a regression analysis from the previous data and to assess the precision and reliability of the regression estimate. The regression can be completed with a spreadsheet program or any of a number of available software systems. The results for three regression analyses are presented in Exhibit 4. The dependent variable in each case is the number of defective units.

Regression 1 has the following independent variables: cost of sales, units shipped, and units produced. *R*-squared and SE are OK, but we observe that all three *t*-values are less than 2.0, indicating unreliable independent variables. Because we expect correlation among these variables and because of the low *t*-values, we suspect multicollinearity among these variables. To reduce the effect of multicollinearity, we try regression 2, which removes the variable units shipped, since that variable is likely to be least associated with defective units and has among the lowest of the *t*-values. *R*-squared for regression 2 is essentially the same as for regression 1, although SE improves very slightly, and the *t*-value for cost of sales is now OK. The results of regression 3, with the cost of sales variable only, show that SE and the *t*-value improve again while *R*-squared is unchanged. Because it has the best SE and *t*-values, and a very good *R*-squared, the third regression is the best choice.

### 4. Nonlinear Regression and Learning Curves

1. The regression solution for the Virilli case is shown below. The value of $b = -0.3394$, and the value of $a = 10^{2.02881} = 106.86$. The regression measures look good, as the *R*-squared is relatively high at .947 and the *t*-statistic for the coefficient, *b*, is 10.35. Overall these measures indicate that the regression has a good fit.

2. The value for *Y* when $X = 133$ is determined as follows.

$$Y = 106.86 \times 133^{-0.3394} = 20.33$$

| *X* | *Y* | Log*X* | Log*Y* |
|---|---|---|---|
| 10 | 45 | 1 | 1.653213 |
| 18 | 40 | 1.255273 | 1.602060 |
| 25 | 38 | 1.397940 | 1.579784 |
| 43 | 32 | 1.633468 | 1.505150 |
| 55 | 30 | 1.740363 | 1.477121 |
| 70 | 25 | 1.845098 | 1.397940 |
| 93 | 22 | 1.968483 | 1.342423 |
| 110 | 20 | 2.041393 | 1.301030 |

| Regression Statistics | |
|---|---|
| Multiple *R* | 0.97313 |
| *R*-squared | 0.94698 |
| Standard error | 0.03162 |
| Observations | 8 |

| | df | SS | MS |
|---|---|---|---|
| Regression | 1 | 0.107148 | 0.107148 |
| Residual | 6 | 0.005999 | 0.001 |
| Total | 7 | 0.113147 | |

| | Coefficient | Standard Error | *t*-Stat |
|---|---|---|---|
| Intercept | 2.02881 | 0.053959 | 37.59928 |
| Log*X* | −0.3394 | 0.032782 | −10.3522 |

*Please visit* **http://www.mhhe.com/blocher6e** *to access a narrated, animated tutorial for solving these problems.*

# CHAPTER NINE

# Short-Term Profit Planning: Cost-Volume-Profit (CVP) Analysis

**After studying this chapter, you should be able to . . .**

LO 9-1   Explain cost-volume-profit (CVP) analysis, the CVP model, and the strategic role of CVP analysis

LO 9-2   Apply CVP analysis for breakeven planning

LO 9-3   Apply CVP analysis for profit planning

LO 9-4   Apply CVP analysis for activity-based costing

LO 9-5   Understand different approaches for dealing with risk and uncertainty in CVP analysis

LO 9-6   Adapt CVP analysis for multiple products/services

LO 9-7   Apply CVP analysis in not-for-profit organizations

LO 9-8   Identify the assumptions and limitations of CVP analysis

For some companies, just about each product or service is new and different. This is true for Clear Channel Communications, Inc. (CCC; **www.clearchannel.com**), the world's largest owner of radio stations and provider of live entertainment events. CCC produces live entertainment, mostly musical entertainment, in more than 70 locations. Each show offers a new opportunity for CCC to be profitable, but careful planning is necessary to achieve success. A key part of this planning for CCC is to use cost-volume-profit (CVP) analysis, the topic of this chapter. CCC uses CVP analysis to project estimated profits for each live event, given the company's projections about attendance; that is, CVP analysis shows the relationship between volume of attendance and the event's related costs and profits.

**LO 9-1**

*Explain cost-volume-profit (CVP) analysis, the CVP model, and the strategic role of CVP analysis.*

Some of CCC's events are planned on a fixed-fee basis; that is, the entertainer is paid a fixed amount for the performance that is not tied to attendance. Other events are planned so that the entertainer receives a payment based on attendance. The fixed-fee arrangement is somewhat riskier for CCC because CCC bears the risk of low attendance and therefore low profits or losses; of course, the upside is that CCC does well if attendance is high. In contrast, the entertainer paid on the basis of attendance shares some of the risk.

For fixed-fee events, CCC uses attendance projections and CVP analysis to carefully project costs and profits, and to plan levels of advertising and other expenses. This type of short-term profit planning is critical for CCC's overall success and profitability.

## Cost-Volume-Profit Analysis

**Cost-volume-profit (CVP) analysis**

is a method for analyzing how various operating and marketing decisions will affect short-term profit.

**Cost-volume-profit (CVP) analysis** is a method for analyzing how operating decisions and marketing decisions affect short-term profit based on an understanding of the relationship between variable costs, fixed costs, unit selling price, and the output level (i.e., volume). CVP analysis has many applications:

- Setting prices for products and services.
- Introducing a new product or service.

As budget pressures mount in states across the nation and as college tuitions continue to rise, legislators and governors are increasingly demanding data proving that money given to colleges is well spent. (States spend about 11% of their general-fund budgets subsidizing higher education.) As a result, proposals—some of which are controversial—to assess "academic efficiency" are being debated among states, including Texas, Indiana, Michigan, Ohio, and California. In Texas, for example, a law passed in 2010 requires public universities to post online, among other things, the budget of each academic department. An example from Texas A&M University is presented below.

The "gains" and "losses" reported in the chart below are similar in nature to "contribution margins." Some have proposed a further "drilling down" of information to the individual professor level. Each faculty member would be assessed on criteria including the number of classes taught, the tuition brought in, and the dollar amount of research grants generated. As informed business students and taxpayers, what do you feel are the strengths and the weaknesses of trying to report "contribution-like" numbers for individual departments and/or individual instructors?

**Source:** Stephanie Simon and Stephanie Banchero, "Putting a Price on Professors," *The Wall Street Journal,* October 23, 2010 (accessed from: http://online.wsj.com/article/SB10001424052748703735804575536322093520994.html?mod=djem_jiewr_AC_domainid).

**Controversial Numbers: Cash Flow at Texas A&M**

|  | Chemistry | History | English |
|---|---|---|---|
| Funds generated | $17,451,040 | $8,681,072 | $9,258,566 |
| Faculty salaries and benefits | −$12,262,038 | −$4,042,470 | −$7,580,395 |
| **Gains** | **$ 5,189,002** | **$4,638,602** | **$1,678,171** |

|  | Oceanography | Physics and Astronomy | Aerospace Engineering |
|---|---|---|---|
| Funds generated | $3,431,130 | $10,039,564 | $4,208,388 |
| Faculty salaries and benefits | −$4,260,442 | −$11,299,763 | −$5,608,774 |
| **Losses** | **−$ 829,312** | **−$ 1,260,199** | **−$1,400,386** |

- Replacing a piece of equipment.
- Determining the breakeven point (i. e., volume level, $Q$, at which operating income = $0).
- Deciding whether to make or buy a given product or service.
- Determining the best product mix.
- Performing strategic what-if analyses.

CVP analysis is based on an explicit model of the relationships among the five factors that combine to determine the amount of short-term operating profit: variable cost per unit, total fixed costs, sales volume, selling price per unit, and sales mix.[1] The CVP model is

$$\text{Operating profit} = \text{Sales} - \text{Total costs}$$

where operating profit is profit exclusive of unusual or nonrecurring items and is *before* tax. When there are no unusual or nonrecurring items, operating profit is simply before-tax income. Since we will be looking at how costs and sales vary with volume, it is important to distinguish variable and fixed costs, and to show the above equation in the equivalent form below:

$$\text{Operating profit} = \text{Sales} - \text{Variable costs} - \text{Fixed costs}$$

Now, replacing sales with the number of units sold times the selling price per unit, and replacing variable costs with the number of units sold times the variable cost per unit, the CVP model is:

$$\text{Operating profit} = (\text{Units sold} \times \text{Selling price per unit})$$
$$- (\text{Units sold} \times \text{Variable cost per unit}) - \text{Fixed costs}$$

[1] Sales mix, by definition, is relevant to the multiproduct (or multiservice) firm. We consider this context later in the chapter.

For convenience, the CVP model is typically shown in notational form, as follows:[2]

$$\pi_B = (p \times Q) - (v \times Q) - F$$

where

$Q$ = Units sold (i.e., sales volume)

$p$ = Selling price per unit

$F$ = Total fixed costs

$v$ = Variable cost per unit

$\pi_B$ = Operating profit (i.e., profit before tax)

## Contribution Margin and Contribution Income Statement

Effective use of the CVP model requires an understanding of three additional concepts: the contribution margin, the contribution margin ratio, and the contribution income statement. The contribution margin is both a unit and a total concept. The **contribution margin per unit** is the difference between selling price per unit ($p$) and the variable cost per unit ($v$):

$$p - v = \text{Contribution margin per unit}$$

The **contribution margin per unit** is the difference between the selling price per unit ($p$) and the variable cost per unit ($v$), and is a measure of the increase in operating profit for a unit increase in sales.

The **total contribution margin** is the contribution margin per unit ($p - v$) multiplied by the number of units sold, $Q$.

The contribution margin per unit measures the increase in operating profit for each unit increase in sales. If sales are expected to increase by 100 units, operating profit should increase by 100 times the contribution margin per unit. The **total contribution margin** is the contribution margin per unit multiplied by the number of units sold.

For example, assume that Household Furnishings, Inc. (HFI), a manufacturer of home furnishings, is interested in developing a new product, a wooden TV table, that would be priced at $75 and would have variable costs of $35 per unit. Assume also that the new product will have no effect on sales of existing products. The investment would require new fixed costs of $5,000 per month ($60,000/yr). HFI expects sales of 2,400 units in the first year (2013) and 2,600 units in the second year (2014). The data for HFI are summarized in Exhibit 9.1.

The contribution margin per unit for each table would be $40 ($75 − $35). Using the contribution margin per unit, we see that if HFI expects to sell 2,400 tables in 2013, it can expect to increase total contribution margin in 2013 by $96,000 ($40 × 2,400) and operating profit by $36,000 ($96,000 − $60,000 fixed cost). In 2014 operating profit increases as sales increase by 200 units, from 2,400 to 2,600 units. Since estimated fixed costs are the same in both years, the projected increase in operating profit from 2013 to 2014 is equal to the change in total contribution margin from 2013 to 2014, that is, contribution margin per unit of $40 times the increase in units sold (200), or $8,000. These results are shown in Exhibit 9.2.

The **contribution margin ratio** is the ratio of the contribution margin per unit to the selling price per unit, $(p - v)/p$.

A measure of the profit contribution per sales dollar is the **contribution margin ratio**, which is the ratio of the contribution margin per unit to the selling price per unit, $(p - v)/p$. The contribution margin ratio for HFI's TV table is 53.33% = ($75 − $35)/$75. The ratio identifies the projected increase (or decrease) in operating profit caused by a given increase (or decrease) in sales dollars. What is the effect on operating profit of an increase

**EXHIBIT 9.1**

**Data for Household Furnishings, Inc. (HFI): TV Table**

|  | **Per Unit** | **2013** | **2014** |
|---|---|---|---|
| Fixed cost (per year) |  | $60,000 | $60,000 |
| Selling price | $75 |  |  |
| Variable cost | 35 |  |  |
| Planned production |  | 2,400 units | 2,600 units |
| Planned sales volume |  | 2,400 units | 2,600 units |

[2] Note that in Chapter 8, Cost Estimation, we used the general form of the estimation equation: $Y = a + (b \times X)$. This is a general model that is used to estimate a variety of dependent variables including cost, the effect of learning on cost, sales, and different types of operating data. Since we are interested only in revenues, costs, and profits in CVP analysis, we use a specific notation in this chapter for unit selling price ($p$), unit variable cost ($v$), and total fixed costs ($F$) in contrast to the more general notation.

**EXHIBIT 9.2**   **Contribution Income Statements for HFI's Proposed TV Table**

| | 2013 | | 2014 | | | |
| --- | --- | --- | --- | --- | --- | --- |
| | Amount | Percent | Amount | Percent | Change | Notes |
| Sales | $180,000 | 100.00% | $195,000 | 100.00% | $15,000 | |
| Variable costs | 84,000 | 46.67 | 91,000 | 46.67 | 7,000 | |
| Total contribution margin | $ 96,000 | 53.33% | $104,000 | 53.33% | $ 8,000 | 53.33% is the contribution margin ratio |
| Fixed costs | 60,000 | | 60,000 | | 0 | |
| Operating profit | $ 36,000 | | $ 44,000 | | $ 8,000 | $8,000 = 0.5333 × $15,000 |

of $15,000 in sales from 2013 to 2014? We can quickly calculate that from 2013 to 2014 estimated operating profit will increase by $8,000 ($15,000 × 0.5333).

A useful way to show the information developed in CVP analysis is to use the contribution income statement. The **contribution income statement** puts the focus on cost behavior— it separates fixed costs and variable costs. In contrast, the conventional income statement, as we used in prior chapters, puts the focus on cost type—product cost and nonproduct cost. In the contribution income statement, variable costs are subtracted from sales to get total contribution margin; fixed costs are then subtracted from total contribution margin to yield the amount of operating profit for the period. In contrast, in the conventional income statement product costs are subtracted from sales to get gross margin. From gross margin, total operating expenses are deducted to yield the amount of operating profit for the period. Exhibit 9.2 shows the contribution income statement for HFI's TV tables. Note that the sales increase of 200 units and $15,000 caused an $8,000 increase in operating profit as predicted by the contribution margin and contribution margin ratio. It is not possible to predict the change in operating profit from a given change in sales with the conventional income statement, which does not separate variable and fixed costs.

In the **contribution income statement**
variable costs are subtracted from sales to get total contribution margin; fixed costs are then subtracted from total contribution margin to yield the amount of operating profit for the period.

## Strategic Role of CVP Analysis

CVP analysis can help a firm execute its strategy by providing an understanding of how changes in its volume of sales affect costs and profits. Many firms, especially cost leadership firms, compete by increasing volume (often through lower prices) to achieve lower total costs per unit. This reduction in cost is achieved principally by spreading fixed costs over more units of output. CVP analysis provides a means to predict the effect of sales growth on operating profit. It also shows the risks in increasing fixed costs if volumes fall.

Also, CVP analysis is important in using both life-cycle costing and target costing (Chapter 13). In life-cycle costing, CVP analysis is used in the early stages of the product's cost life cycle to determine whether the product is likely to achieve the desired profitability. Similarly, CVP analysis can assist in target costing at these early stages by showing the effect on profit of alternative product designs that have different target costs.

In addition, CVP analysis can be used at later phases of the life cycle, during manufacturing planning, to determine the most cost-effective manufacturing process. Such manufacturing decisions include when to replace a machine, what type of machine to buy, when to automate a process, and when to outsource a manufacturing operation. CVP analysis is also used in the final stages of the cost life cycle to help determine the best marketing and distribution systems. For example, CVP analysis can be used to determine whether to pay salespeople on a salary basis or a commission basis for lower cost. Similarly, it can help to assess the desirability of a discount program or a promotional plan. Some of the strategic questions answered by CVP analysis are outlined in Exhibit 9.3.

CVP analysis also has a role in strategic positioning. A firm that has chosen to compete on cost leadership needs CVP analysis primarily at the manufacturing stage of the cost life cycle. The role of CVP analysis here is to identify the most cost-effective manufacturing methods, including automation, outsourcing, and total quality management. In contrast, a firm following the differentiation strategy needs CVP analysis in the early

**EXHIBIT 9.3**
**Strategic Questions Answered by CVP Analysis**

1. What is the expected level of profit at a given sales volume?
2. What additional amount of sales is needed to achieve a desired level of profit?
3. What will be the effect on profit of a given increase in sales?
4. What is the required funding level for a governmental agency, given desired service levels?
5. Is the forecast for sales consistent with forecasted profits?
6. What additional profit would be obtained from a given percentage reduction in unit variable costs?
7. What increase in sales is needed to make up a given decrease in price to maintain the present profit level?
8. What sales level is needed to cover all costs in a sales region or product line?
9. What is the required amount of increase in sales to meet the additional fixed charges from a proposed plant expansion?

phases of the cost life cycle to assess the profitability of new products and the desirability of new features for existing products. The same concepts apply for retail and service firms.

## CVP Analysis for Breakeven Planning

**LO 9-2**

*Apply CVP analysis for breakeven planning.*

We first survey the plot, then draw the model;
And when we see the figure of the house,
Then we must rate the cost of the erection;
Which, if we find outweighs ability,
What do we then but draw anew the model.

*William Shakespeare, Henry IV, Part II, Act 1*

The **breakeven point** is the point at which revenues equal total costs and operating profit is zero.

The starting point in many business plans is to determine the **breakeven point,** the point at which revenues equal total costs and operating profit is zero. This point can be determined by using CVP analysis. The CVP model is solved by inserting known (or assumed) values for unit variable cost ($v$), selling price per unit ($p$), and total fixed cost ($F$), setting desired before-tax profit ($\pi_B$) equal to zero, and then solving for $Q$. We can also determine the breakeven point in terms of sales dollars, $Y$ (where $Y = Q \times p$).

### Breakeven in Units, *Q*

Using information from Exhibit 9.2, the operating profit equation for HFI's sale of TV tables is

$$\text{Operating profit} = \text{Sales} - \text{Total variable costs} - \text{Fixed cost}$$

$$\pi_B = (p \times Q) - (v \times Q) - F$$

$$= (\$75 \times Q) - (\$35 \times Q) - \$5,000/\text{month}$$

Solving for $Q$ and letting $\pi_B = 0$, we find that the breakeven point is $Q = 125$ TV tables per month (1,500 units per year).

$$0 = [(\$75 - \$35) \times Q] - \$5,000/\text{month}$$

$$\$40 \times Q = \$5,000/\text{month}$$

$$Q = \$5,000/\text{month} \div \$40 \text{ per unit}$$

$$Q = 125 \text{ units/month}$$

The contribution to profit per TV table is measured directly by the contribution margin per unit, $p - v$, which is $40 per table. Therefore, at sales of 125 units the profit is zero, at 126 units the profit is $40, at 127 units the profit is $2 \times \$40 = \$80$, and so on. Using the contribution margin per unit gives us a quick way to estimate the change in operating profit for a change in the number of units sold. At the 128-unit level, profit is

| | |
|---|---|
| Sales: 128 units at $75/unit | $9,600 |
| Less: | |
| Variable costs: 128 at $35/unit | 4,480 |
| Contribution margin | $5,120 |
| Fixed cost per month | 5,000 |
| Operating profit | $ 120 |

## Breakeven in Dollars

We can solve for the breakeven point expressed in sales dollars either indirectly—by multiplying breakeven units by the selling price per unit, $p$, or directly—by using the equation method in a revised form, where $Y$ is the breakeven point in *sales dollars*.

This model is equivalent to the model used for breakeven in units, except that $Q$ is replaced by $Y/p$ (i.e., sales in dollars divided by selling price per unit = quantity; $Y/p = Q$), as follows:

$$\text{Operating profit} = \text{Sales} - \text{Total variable costs} - \text{Fixed cost}$$
$$0 = (p \times Q) - (v \times Q) - F$$
$$0 = [p \times (Y/p)] - [v \times (Y/p)] - F$$
$$p \times (Y/p) = [v \times (Y/p)] + F$$
$$Y = [(v/p) \times Y] + F$$

Thus, to break even the firm would have to generate sufficient sales dollars, $Y$, to cover total variable costs, $v/p \times Y$, plus total fixed cost, $F$. The quantity $v/p$ is called the variable cost ratio, which is the complement of the contribution margin ratio. That is, the variable cost ratio, $v/p$, plus the contribution margin ratio, $(p - v)/p$, will always equal 1 (i. e., 100%).

Continuing with the HFI data in Exhibit 9.2, for 2013 we have total annual variable cost ($84,000), total annual sales ($180,000), and total monthly fixed costs ($5,000). Given this information, we can obtain the ratio, $v/p = 0.4667$ ($84,000/$180,000), and then solve for breakeven in dollars, as follows:

$$Y = (0.4667 \times Y) + \$5,000/\text{month}$$
$$Y = \$9,375/\text{month}[3]$$

[3] Note that sales dollars of $9,375 per month ($Y$) equals the breakeven point in units, 125, times the selling price per unit, $75. In short, $Y = p \times Q$.

A global manufacturer of auto parts has manufacturing plants in three locations: Western Europe, Poland, and China. The firm is studying how to utilize or increase manufacturing capacity in order to reduce total manufacturing costs worldwide. The findings of the study are shown in the accompanying chart to the right.

The plants in Poland and China are highly automated, and a rapid decrease in costs in the Western Europe plant would require introducing automation and dramatically reducing labor costs. The firm also completed a competitive analysis and found that it had a key competitor in Western Europe whose plant was already automated and produced twice the volume at less the cost than the firm's plant there. Based on these findings, the company decided to retain two plants: in Poland and China. The plant in Poland would serve the European market and the one in China would serve the rest of the world. The study shows how a firm can use CVP to determine its manufacturing strategy.

**Source:** Booz Allen case study reported in: Kaj Grichnik and Conrad Winkler, *Make or Break* (New York: McGraw-Hill, 2008), p. 167.

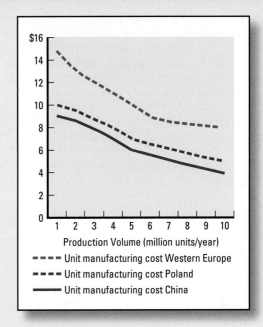

## Short-Cut Formulas

A convenient method for calculating the breakeven point in units is to use the profit equation in its equivalent algebraic form (derived by solving the model for $Q$ and noting that at breakeven, $\pi_B = 0$):

$$Q = \text{Fixed costs} \div \text{Contribution margin per unit}$$
$$= \frac{F}{p - v}$$
$$= \$5{,}000 \div (\$75 - \$35)/\text{unit} = 125 \text{ units/month}$$

The contribution margin method can also be used to obtain breakeven in dollars, using the contribution margin ratio (by solving $Y = F + [(v/p) \times Y]$), as follows:

$$Y = \frac{F}{(p - v)/p}$$

where:

$$(p - v) \div p = \text{the contribution margin ratio}$$

In the HFI example, the contribution margin ratio is 0.5333 (the same as 1 minus the $v/p$ ratio of 0.4667, as calculated above). Therefore,

$$Y = \$5{,}000 \div 0.5333 = \$9{,}375/\text{month}$$

The **CVP graph** illustrates how the levels of revenues and total costs change over different levels of sales volume expressed in units.

## CVP Graph and the Profit-Volume Graph

Breakeven analysis is illustrated graphically in Exhibit 9.4. It shows the CVP graph at the top and the profit-volume graph beneath. The **CVP graph** illustrates how the levels of revenues and total costs change over different levels of sales volume expressed in units.

Cost Planning: Own Your Own Wheels, or Just Rent?

For those who live in a large urban area, participating in a car-share program (e.g., **www.zipcar.com**) may make more sense than owning a car. For a small annual fee, the program provides a rental car that can be used for shopping excursions, travel to the regional airport, and so on. The savings over car ownership can be very significant. Assume that two programs are currently available: one has a much higher annual (fixed) fee, with a reduced hourly charge for use of a car, while the other provides just the opposite: a higher hourly charge in exchange for a reduced annual fee. Complicating the decision is the ability to rent on a daily basis from rental car agencies such as Hertz or Avis. The profit-planning (CVP) model discussed in this chapter can be used to address the relative financial attractiveness of each of these three options. For example, in terms of the car-share options, one could determine the "cost indifference point," that is, the number of rental hours per year that would yield identical total cost for each option. Similarly, a "cost indifference point," expressed in number of rental days per year, could be calculated and used to help determine whether renting on a daily basis from a rental agency makes economic sense. Of course, other factors—non-financial in nature—are likely to affect the decision as well.

**Sources:** Shivani Vora, "Test-Driving Car-Share Services," *The Wall Street Journal,* June 11, 2009, p. D2; and "An iPhone Gets Zipcar Drivers on their Way," *USA Today,* September 30, 2009, p. 3B.

**EXHIBIT 9.4**    The CVP Graph and the Profit-Volume Graph

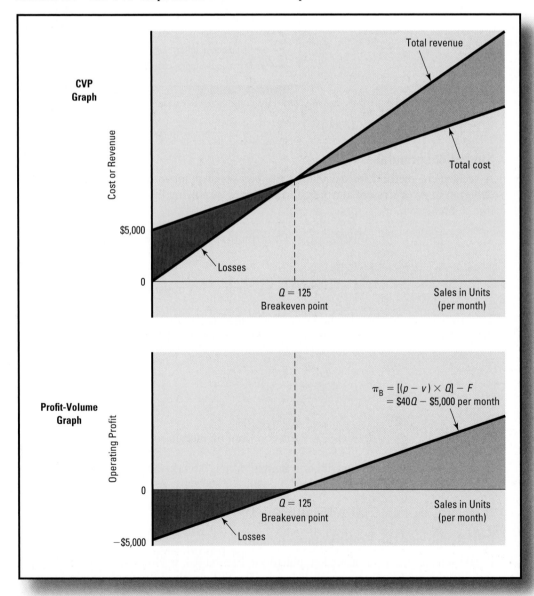

Note in the CVP graph that at sales levels lower than 125 units, the revenue line falls below the total cost line, resulting in losses. In contrast, all points above the 125-unit level show profit. Note that the slope of the total revenue line equals the selling price per unit, $p$ ($75 in our example), while the slope of the total cost line equals the slope of the variable cost line (not shown). The slope of the variable cost line is the variable cost per unit, $v$ ($35 in our example).

The **profit-volume graph** in the lower portion of the exhibit illustrates how the level of profits changes over different levels of sales volume, $Q$. At $Q = 125$ units, operating profit is zero, and positive profits appear for sales volumes greater than 125. The slope of the profit-volume line is the contribution margin per unit, $p - v$; therefore, the profit-volume graph can be used to read directly how total contribution margin and operating profit change as the sales volume, $Q$, changes. As illustrated by the profit-volume graph, the breakeven point can be expressed as the volume level that produces just enough contribution margin to cover fixed costs, $F$. Thus, at the breakeven point, total contribution margin, $Q \times (p - v)$, equals $F$.

The **profit-volume graph** illustrates how the level of operating profit changes over different levels of sales volume, $Q$.

## CVP Analysis for Profit Planning

**LO 9-3**

*Apply CVP analysis for profit planning.*

CVP analysis can be used to determine the level of sales needed to achieve a desired level of profit. Finding the desired profit involves revenue planning, cost planning, and accounting for the effect of income taxes (when planning for the desired profit *after* tax).

### Revenue Planning

CVP analysis assists managers in revenue planning, that is, determining the revenue required to achieve a desired profit level. For example, if HFI's management wants to know the sales volume necessary to achieve a pretax profit of $48,000, we substitute $60,000 for fixed costs ($F$) and $48,000 for desired pretax profit ($\pi_B$) and then solve for $Q$, as follows:

$$\pi_B = (p \times Q) - (v \times Q) - F$$
$$= Q \times (p - v) - F$$
$$Q \times (p - v) = F + \pi_B$$
$$Q = (F + \pi_B) \div (p - v)$$
$$Q = \frac{\$60,000 + \$48,000}{(\$75 - \$35)/\text{unit}} = 2,700 \text{ units per year}$$

The solution in sales dollars, $Y$, is

$$Y = p \times Q = \$75/\text{unit} \times 2,700 \text{ units/year} = \$202,500 \text{ per year}$$

### Cost Planning

For cost planning decisions, the manager assumes that the sales volume and the desired profit are known, but wants to find the value of the required variable cost per unit ($v$) or the total fixed cost ($F$) to achieve the desired operating profit at the assumed sales volume, $Q$. Three examples follow.

### *Trade-Offs between Fixed and Variable Costs—Example One (One Machine)*

To facilitate target costing, CVP analysis is used to determine the most cost-effective trade-off between different types of costs. To continue with the HFI example, assume sales of 2,700 units per year. Management is now considering the purchase of a new machine that will reduce variable cost per unit but also increase total fixed cost ($F$) by \$2,250 per month. How much must the variable cost per unit ($v$) fall to maintain the current level of operating profit, assuming that sales volume and all other factors remain the same?

$Q = 2,700$ units    $F = \$5,000 + \$2,250 = \$7,250$ per month (\$87,000 per year)

$p = \$75$        $\pi_B = \$48,000$ per year

$v =$ an unknown (previously \$35)

Now, instead of solving for $Q$ (which is given as 2,700 units), we solve for $v$, as follows:

$$Q = \frac{F + \pi_B}{p - v}$$

$$p - v = \frac{F + \pi_B}{Q}$$

$$v = p - \frac{F + \pi_B}{Q}$$

$$v = \$75 - [(\$87,000 + \$48,000) \div 2,700] = \$25$$

In effect, for sales and profits to remain unchanged with the increase in fixed costs, variable cost per unit ($v$) must fall from \$35 to \$25.

The above calculations can be obtained directly using Goal Seek under the Data/What-If Analysis tab in Excel (as circled in Exhibit 9.5). Note that the information for the HFI case is entered in the spreadsheet, and profit is calculated for the current variable cost per unit of \$35 using the following formula in cell B8: "=B3 * (B4 − B5) − B6". The Goal Seek dialog box is shown in Exhibit 9.5. To achieve the desired profit of \$48,000 by changing unit variable cost, we set Goal Seek to change cell B8, operating profit, to \$48,000 by changing cell B5, unit variable cost. Selecting OK will enter the correct value for unit variable cost, \$25, in cell B5.

### Trade-Offs between Fixed and Variable Costs—Example Two (Two Machines)

A common management decision is choosing the right equipment for the work to be done. Assume as in example one above that management is considering the purchase of a new machine and, in this case, has the choice between two machines. For example, one

**EXHIBIT 9.5**  **Using Goal Seek in CVP Analysis**

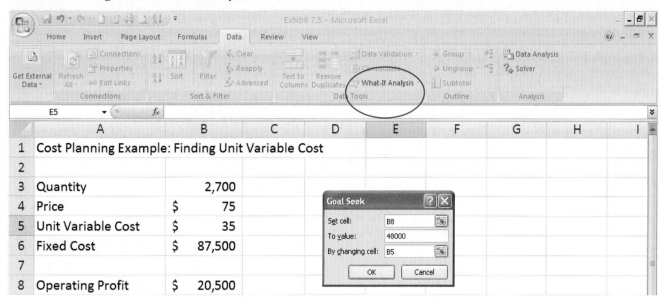

machine might have a relatively high purchase cost but lower operating costs compared to an alternative machine. So, there is an option to trade off between high fixed costs and low unit variable costs (the high fixed-cost option) versus relatively low fixed costs and relatively higher unit variable costs (the low fixed-cost option). As sales volume increases, the high fixed-cost option will be more and more attractive, since it brings a reduction in total variable costs. Breakeven analysis can help to find the level of sales (called the *indifference point*), such that having sales greater than this level will favor the high fixed-cost option, and sales less than this level will favor the low fixed-cost option.

Example two assumes that HFI can choose between two machines, either of which will complete the same operation with the same quality, but with different fixed and variable costs. Machine A has a fixed cost of $5,000 and a variable operating cost per unit of $10, while machine B has a fixed cost of $15,000 and variable operating cost per unit of $5. To find the indifference point, where the low fixed-cost (A) and high fixed-cost (B) options have the same total cost, we set the cost equations for each option equal and solve for sales quantity, $Q$, as follows:

$$\text{Cost of machine A} = \text{Cost of machine B}$$
$$\$5,000 + (\$10 \times Q) = \$15,000 + (\$5 \times Q)$$
$$Q = \$10,000 \div \$5 = 2,000 \text{ units}$$

If HFI is operating at 2,000 units or more, then machine B should be chosen, and if it is operating at below 2,000 units, then machine A should be chosen.[4] For example, at 3,000 units, the total cost of machine A is $5,000 + ($10 × 3,000) = $35,000, while the cost of machine B is $15,000 + ($5 × 3,000) = $30,000, and thus the advantage goes to machine B at this sales level.

---

[4] These conclusions ignore the risk preferences of the decision makers (i.e., they assume that decision makers are risk-neutral). Decision makers who are risk averse may not be indifferent between the two decision alternatives if expected volume is approximately 2,000 units per year. To minimize potential loss, these individuals might choose the machine with relatively lower fixed costs.

By using data from the U.S. Social Security Administration (**www.ssa .gov**), a person thinking about retiring can develop a breakeven model to determine when to apply for benefits. The question is, if one delays applying for benefits until after age 62 (the earliest one can apply for benefits), how long will it take for the total of those larger (due to applying later) payments to add up to the total that would have been received by applying earlier? Two convenient websites provide the answer: **www.metlife.com/individual/retirement/retirement-planning-tools/ social-security-decision-tool/index.html** and **www.ssa.gov/pubs/10147 .html**. For example, a person deciding whether to retire at the age of 65 or at 70 can use the analysis in the following graph. This analysis shows that retirees who survive beyond the breakeven age of 82 would receive greater lifetime benefits (not adjusted for the time value of money).

**Total Cumulative Retirement Benefits at Different Ages**

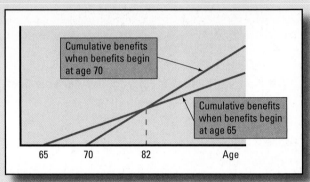

**Source:** Jonathan Clements, "Delayed Gratification When Postponing Social Security Payments Is a Smart Move," *The Wall Street Journal*, May 10, 2006, p. D1.

### *Sales Commissions and Salaries—Example Three*

Another cost planning use of CVP analysis is to determine the most cost-effective means to manage selling costs. To illustrate, HFI management is reviewing sales salaries and commissions and finds that $1,000 of the monthly $5,000 fixed costs is for sales salaries, and that $7.50 of the $35.00 variable cost per unit is a 10% sales commission. Suppose HFI management is considering a $450 increase in salary with an expected reduction in commission rate. How much must management reduce the commission rate to keep profits the same, assuming that sales volume and all other factors remain unchanged?

With the proposed changes in variable and fixed costs to accommodate the new salary and commission plan, fixed costs increase by $450 per month and variable costs decrease as a result of the decrease in the commission rate, $r$:

$$v = \text{Commision rate} \times \text{Sales price}$$
$$+ \text{ Other noncommission-based variable costs per unit}$$
$$v = (r \times \$75) + \$27.50$$

And

$$F = \text{Current monthly fixed costs} + \text{Increase in monthly salary}$$
$$F = \$5,000 + \$450 = \$5,450 \text{ per month, or } \$65,400 \text{ per year}$$

Now, we use the CVP model to solve for $v$:

$$Q = \frac{F + \pi_B}{p - v}$$

$$v = p - \frac{F + \pi_B}{Q}$$

and substituting for $v$ and $F$ with $\pi_B = \$48,000$ and $Q = 2,700$ as before:

$$(r \times \$75) + \$27.50 = \$75 - [(\$65,400 + \$48,000) \div 2,700]$$
$$r = 0.0733$$

Managing profitability for companies with different levels of fixed costs requires different strategies. Consider the example of a food and beverage company that sells mid-price dine-in gourmet soup. Its strategy is to provide quality food at reasonable prices. Hence its variable costs are high due to the usage of high quality ingredients, while selling price remains fairly mass market. As such, its contribution margin is not high, which means that in order to cover its fixed costs and to make a profit, it has to generate high volume. What can the company do in this regard? It can make sure that it locates its outlets at high consumer traffic places, thus ensuring a huge and steady stream of regular shoppers and office workers.

By contrast, consider hotels, which have relatively high fixed costs. During recessionary periods sales decrease, but fixed costs remain high. What many five-star hotels do in this situation is to offer their expensive suites and rooms at a discount to attract locals to stay for short getaways. Why are they doing this? This helps to generate contribution margin, which helps to cover fixed costs. As long as

the revenue from selling a room night is higher than the variable costs of getting the business, it results in a positive contribution margin to cover the hotel's fixed costs.

Finally, consider airlines, which need a certain "passenger load factor" to break even on their flights. The moment a decision is made to fly a plane, the costs of the fuel and landing charges are almost fixed. If insufficient paying passengers are on board the plane, the contribution margin will be less than the fixed costs, resulting in a reduction in operating income. Some airlines choose to reduce their pricing, in the hope that the resulting increase in volume will generate positive contribution margin to defray their fixed costs. Another strategy used by airlines is to cut the flight allowance of their pilots and crew, which reduces the variable costs of each flight. An outright cut in pay and headcount reduces the fixed costs of the airline as a whole. Yet another strategy is to ground some of the firm's aircraft, so that there are fewer partially filled flights that cannot recover their full costs per flight.

In this situation, the manager must reduce the commission rate from 10 to 7.33% to keep annual profit the same and pay an additional monthly salary of $450 to the salespeople.

### Including Income Taxes in CVP Analysis

The manager's decisions about costs and prices usually must include income taxes because taxes affect the amount of profit for a given level of sales. In the HFI example if we assume that the average income tax rate is 20%, to achieve the desired annual *after-tax* profit, $\pi_A$, of $48,000, HFI must generate before-tax profits of at least $60,000 [$48,000 ÷ (1 − 0.2)]. Thus, when taxes are considered, the CVP model is as follows, where the average income tax rate is $t$:

$$Q = \frac{F + \dfrac{\pi_A}{(1 - t)}}{(p - v)}$$

or

$$Q = \frac{\$60,000 + [\$48,000 \div (1 - 0.2)]}{\$75 - \$35} = 3,000 \text{ units per year}$$

This amount is an increase of 300 units over the 2,700 units required for the before-tax profit level.

## CVP Analysis for Activity-Based Costing (ABC)

**LO 9-4**

*Apply CVP analysis for activity-based costing.*

The conventional approach to CVP analysis is to use a volume-based measure, that is, a measure based on units of product manufactured and sold. The preceding discussion has assumed a volume-based approach. An alternative approach is activity-based costing (ABC). ABC identifies cost drivers for detailed-level indirect cost activities, such as machine setup, materials handling, inspection, and engineering. In contrast, the volume-based approach combines the costs of these activities and treats them as fixed costs since they do not vary in the short run with volume.

Here's how activity-based CVP differs from the traditional volume-based approach. Recall from Chapter 5 the classification of activities into four levels: unit, batch, product, and facility.

Unit-level costs are volume based, so they are treated in the same manner under volume-based and ABC-based CVP. Traditional volume-based CVP classifies the other three levels (batch, product, and facility) as indirect costs that do not vary with volume and thus are fixed costs. However, batch-level costs and product-level costs change with the number of batches or the number of product changes, and ABC-based CVP takes these possibilities into account. Facilities-level costs are not avoidable in a short-term planning horizon; these costs take many months or years to change, so facilities costs are treated as fixed costs under both volume-based and ABC-based CVP. So two activity cost levels, batch and product levels, are modeled as costs that can change in ABC-based CVP, but not in volume-based CVP analysis.

A product-level cost, such as a change in product design or features, is a cost that has a shorter planning period because these changes can be incorporated into the manufacturing process in a shorter period of time, perhaps several months to a year before the change affects total costs. If the planning period is a year or less, as has been the common assumption in this chapter, then product-level costs will normally not be considered as a cost that can change in either ABC-based or volume-based CVP for that short planning period. If the planning period is extended to several months or years (the time it takes a change in product to affect costs), then product-level changes may be included in ABC-based CVP. In contrast, many batch-level costs (product setup, inspection, purchasing, etc.) can be changed in the short term, so batch-level costs can be considered in a short-term planning horizon. Our example below uses batch-level costs to illustrate ABC-based CVP analysis.

Suppose that the cost accounting staff has been able to assign approximately $10,000 of last year's fixed costs to batch-level activities such as machine setup and inspection. This estimate was made when the firm was operating at 100 batches per year. These costs can be traced directly to each batch, although not to each unit of output. The staff has also learned that this year's production of 3,000 units is to be produced in batches of 30 units, so 100 batches will be produced again this year. We assume that batch-level costs increase in proportion to an increase in the number of batches produced during the year; that is, $100 per batch ($10,000 ÷ 100). This assumption says in effect that the ABC rate of $100 per batch is a variable cost relative to the cost driver, number of batches. Alternative assumptions are possible. For example, if we assume that *total* batch-level costs do not change with the number of batches, then total batch-level costs are fixed in the short run relative to the number of batches. This would be true for example if the firm used the same number of batches each planning period, irrespective of volume. In this case volume-based and ABC-based CVP will always produce the same calculations, and the use of the ABC-based approach to CVP does not provide additional useful information. However, we expect that for most firms the number of batches is proportional to volume—batch sizes do not change significantly—so that at least a portion of batch-level costs change in a short-term planning period as volume changes.

One possible assumption is that total batch-level costs is a mixed cost, which has a fixed component that does not vary with the number of batches and a variable component that does vary with the number of batches. Note that assuming some portion of total batch-level costs varies with the number of batches is more consistent with the idea, introduced in Chapter 5, that it is important in using ABC to distinguish activity spending and activity usage. The objective is to reduce activity spending, which means that activity costs are at least in part variable and controllable.

For simplicity, we assume here that batch-level costs vary directly with the number of batches and therefore are not a mixed cost but a pure variable cost. An example where a batch cost would be variable relative to the number of batches is a chemical processing company that uses a vat for processing chemicals, and the batch activity is the cleaning of the vat after each use. The cleaning materials (and perhaps associated labor cost) would be variable relative to the number of batches.

The activity-based CVP model can be developed in the following way.

First, we define new terms for fixed cost: $F = F^{VB} + F^{AB}$, where:

$F^{VB}$ = the volume-based fixed costs; that is, the portion of fixed costs that *does not* vary with the activity cost driver, $50,000 ($60,000 − $10,000)

$F^{AB}$ = the portion of fixed costs that *does* vary with the activity cost driver, $10,000; we assume that $10,000 is necessary for 3,000 units of output, requiring 100 production batches of 30 units each

Second, we define the following terms:

$v^{AB}$ = the cost per batch for the activity-based cost driver, $10,000 ÷ 100 = $100 per batch

$b$ = the number of units in a batch, 30 units (3,000 ÷ 100)

$v^{AB}/b$ = the cost per unit of product for batch-related costs when the batch is size $b$; $v^{AB}/b$ = $3.333 ($100.00 ÷ 30)

Third, the CVP model for activity-based costing is

$$Q = \frac{F^{VB} + \pi_B}{p - v - (v^{AB} \div b)}$$

where $\pi_B$ = $48,000 (assumed).

Fourth, substituting data from the HFI example,

$$Q = \frac{\$50,000 + \$48,000}{\$75 - \$35 - (\$100 \div 30)} = 2,673 \text{ units}$$

$$= 89.1 \text{ batches } (2,673 \div 30)$$

This method assumes that we hold batch size constant and vary the number of batches as the total volume changes. The number of batches must be a whole number, however. In this case, 90 batches are required for the 2,673 units: 89 batches of 30 units each (89 × 30 = 2,670 units) plus one additional batch. The formula to calculate an exact breakeven point using 90 batches is as follows, where the total batch-related costs for 90 batches is 90 × $100/per batch = $9,000:

$$Q = \frac{\$50,000 + \$9,000 + \$48,000}{\$75 - \$35} = 2,675 \text{ units}$$

In sum, to achieve the above output goal, the company would produce 89 full batches (30 units/batch, or 2,670 units) plus a batch of 5 units (2,675 − 2,670). At 2,675 units, the total contribution margin of $107,000 (2,675 units × $40/unit) equals total fixed costs, $107,000 (i.e., $50,000 + $9,000 + $48,000).

The solution for the activity-based model is slightly lower than for the volume-based model (2,675 units versus 2,700 units, as shown on page 315) because the ABC method allows for lower total batch-level costs. Instead of a fixed batch-level cost of $10,000 under the volume-based approach, the ABC method allows the batch-level costs to decrease (or increase) as volume decreases (or increases); in this case it decreased from $10,000 to $9,000.

To illustrate the effect of batch size on the solution, suppose that production is scheduled in smaller batches of 20 units and that batch costs continue to be $100 each. How many units must be sold now to earn $48,000? The answer is 2,800 units and 140 batches, as shown below. Note that the cost of batch-level activities has now increased substantially, from $10,000 for 100 batches to $14,000 for 140 batches because of the smaller batch size.

$$Q = (\$50,000 + \$48,000) \div (\$75 - \$35 - \$100/20)$$

$$= 2,800 \text{ units}$$

or

$$= 140 \text{ batches } (2,800 \div 20) \text{ of } 20 \text{ units each}$$

We also could determine this from the following, using $14,000 for total batch-level costs:

$$Q = \frac{\$50,000 + \$14,000 + \$48,000}{\$75 - \$35} = 2,800 \text{ units}$$

Notice that the number of units to achieve breakeven increases when the batch size is decreased. This is due directly to the increase in the total batch-level costs as batch size is decreased. CVP analysis based on ABC can provide a more comprehensive analysis of the relationships among volume, costs, and profits by considering batch-level costs.[5]

## Dealing with Risk and Uncertainty

**LO 9-5**

*Understand different approaches for dealing with risk and uncertainty in CVP analysis.*

Thus far, we have treated all inputs to the CVP model (e.g., selling price per unit, $p$) as being known with certainty. As such, the basic CVP model is said to be *deterministic* in nature. Business managers know, however, that the inputs to the CVP planning model are, at best, estimates of future values.

In the decision literature, the term "uncertainty" means that a number of different values can exist for one or more of the variables in a decision model (such as CVP), while the term "risk" is usually taken to mean the possibility of a loss or gain as a result of this uncertainty. In this section we present two broad methods for dealing with the issue of risk and uncertainty as applied to the CVP modeling process: sensitivity analysis and measures of operating risk.

**Sensitivity analysis**
is the name for a variety of methods that examine how an amount changes if factors involved in predicting that amount change.

We first discuss **sensitivity analysis,** which is the name for a variety of methods that examine how an amount (e.g., operating profit, $\pi_B$) changes if factors involved in predicting that amount (e.g., sales volume, $Q$) change. We discuss three separate approaches to sensitivity analysis: basic "what-if" analysis, construction of decision tables/decision trees, and Monte Carlo simulation analysis. CVP analysis becomes an important strategic tool when managers use it to determine the sensitivity of profits to possible changes in costs, selling price, or sales volume. If these items change significantly, the firm's strategy might also have to change. For example, if there is a risk that sales levels will fall below projected levels, management might consider reducing planned investments in fixed costs (i.e., capacity-related investments).

We conclude this section by discussing two common metrics commonly associated with CVP analysis: margin of safety (MOS) (and the MOS ratio) and degree of operating leverage (DOL).

### What-If Analysis of Sales: Contribution Margin and Contribution Margin Ratio

**What-if analysis**
is the calculation of an amount given different levels of a factor that influences that amount.

**What-if analysis** is the calculation of an amount given different levels of a factor that influences that amount. It is a common approach to sensitivity analysis when uncertainty is present. Many times it is based on the contribution margin and the contribution margin ratio. For example, the contribution margin ($40) and contribution margin ratio (0.5333) for HFI provide a direct measure of the sensitivity of HFI's profits to changes in sales volume. Each unit change in volume affects profits by $40; each dollar change in sales affects profits by $0.5333. Use of a spreadsheet such as Excel and tools such as Goal Seek can facilitate the analysis. An example of a data table for HFI is shown in

**EXHIBIT 9.6**
**What-If Sensitivity Analysis for HFI, Inc., Using a Data Table**

| Units Sold | Variable Cost per Unit | Fixed Cost | Selling Price per Unit | Operating Profit |
|------------|------------------------|------------|------------------------|------------------|
| 1,500 | $30 | $60,000 | $75 | $7,500 |
| 1,500 | 35 | 60,000 | 75 | — |
| 1,500 | 40 | 60,000 | 75 | −7,500 |
| 1,500 | 45 | 60,000 | 75 | −15,000 |

[5] See the discussion of CVP analysis for activity-based costing in Robert C. Kee, "Implementing Cost-Volume-Profit Analysis Using an Activity-Based Costing System," *Advances in Management Accounting* 10 (2001), pp. 77–94.

Exhibit 9.6; units sold, fixed cost, and price are held constant, and we examine the effect of changes in unit variable cost on profits. Goal Seek is illustrated in Exhibit 9.5.

Of course, more complicated tables can be prepared to reflect each combined result of allowing multiple variables to change. For example, we could prepare a table that shows required volume, $Q$, to break even under different combinations of total fixed cost and variable cost per unit, holding selling price per unit constant. The resulting table would have $m \times n$ cells, where $n$ = number of fixed cost values being examined and $m$ = the number of variable-cost-per-unit alternatives. Thus, if we were considering four different levels of fixed cost, $F$, and three different levels of variable cost per unit, $v$, the resulting table would have $4 \times 3 = 12$ combinations or cells in our spreadsheet. (By contrast, Exhibit 9.6 has only four result cells—operating profit under four different values of $v$, holding everything else in the CVP model constant.)

## Decision Tables/Decision Trees/Expected Value Analysis

The discussion thus far has not included probabilities in the analysis. One way to do this is to construct so-called decision tables (or decision trees) that include the following elements: a set of managerial *actions* or decisions (e.g., choice of cost structure), a set of *events* (e.g., level of demand for the company's product), and a set of *outcomes* (i.e., the financial consequence of various combinations of actions and events). Probabilities can be incorporated into the analysis by estimating a probability for each possible event. As you know from basic statistics, a probability is nothing more than the chance or likelihood that a given event will occur. The set of all possible events that could occur is referred to as a probability distribution. Collectively, the sum of these probabilities must equal 100%.

All of the preceding information can be summarized in what is called a *decision table* (or *decision tree*). From the decision table, we can calculate the *expected value* of each action (decision alternative). Again, you probably recall from statistics that an expected value is defined as the weighted average of all possible outcomes associated with each decision alternative. The weights in this calculation are equal to the outcome probabilities. The set of expected values (one for each decision alternative) along with backup information contained in the decision table can help guide the decision choice—for example, whether to choose a cost structure characterized by a greater proportion of variable costs or a greater preponderance of fixed costs.

## Monte Carlo Simulation

The discussion above refers to a simple way to incorporate outcome probabilities in a decision model. As an alternative approach, simulation analysis might be used to deal with risk and uncertainty in CVP analysis.

*Monte Carlo simulation* is a method of resampling values of factors (e.g., sales volume) in a model (e.g., CVP), according to some probability distribution, in order to generate a probability distribution of outcomes (e.g., operating profit). Thus, within the context of CVP analysis, step #1 in the simulation process is to specify the form of the probability distribution representing each factor in our CVP model.[6] The next step is to choose the number of iterations in the simulations, that is, the number of independent draws from each probability distribution. This should normally be at least 1,000. Each iteration in the context of a CVP model would produce a calculated outcome (operating income) based on input factors chosen randomly from the probability of values associated with each input factor. At the end of the simulation, we have a probability distribution on the outcome variable of interest. It is this probability distribution that shows the likelihood of various outcomes, such as the breakeven point, or generating at least $25,000 of operating income, and so on. Commercial packages (e.g., Excel add-ons, such as Crystal Ball) are available to carry out Monte Carlo simulation.[7]

---

[6] An excellent discussion of various probability distributions that are commonly used in business decision making is provided in: Chris Rodger and Jason Petch, *Uncertainty and Risk,* Business Dynamics, PricewaterhouseCoopers United Kingdom (April 1999).

[7] In addition, a free Excel add-on, to be used solely for educational (i.e., noncommercial) purposes, is available from the creator (Professor Timothy R. Mayes) at the following site: **http://clem.mscd.edu/~mayest/FIN4200/Files/BookFiles/ExcelSim%202009%20Documentation.pdf**.

A realistic example that involves uncertainty on multiple CVP model factors (inputs) is beyond the scope of this introductory discussion. However, to illustrate the basic approach of Monte Carlo simulation, we can use Excel's built-in function NORMDIST to model uncertainty around a single input to our CVP model (e.g., operating income, $\pi_B$). We will assume in this example that while $\pi_B$ is unknown, we have an estimate of the mean value and the standard deviation for $\pi_B$. Further, assume that the distribution of operating income around the mean value is normal. Given these assumptions, we might be interested in knowing the probability of at least breaking even (i.e., achieving an operating profit of at least 0).

In a blank cell, enter the following formula using the assumed sample mean and standard deviation:

$$1 - \text{NORMDIST}(0, \text{the mean, the standard deviation, TRUE})$$

NORMDIST calculates the area under the normal curve, essentially from negative infinity to the first number entered into the above formula. Since we are interested in making a probabilistic statement regarding the breakeven point (i.e., the point where $\pi_B = 0$), we enter "0" as the first number in the above formula. The other inputs to the formula tell us that the normal distribution of values will be drawn using the sample mean and standard deviation entered into the formula. "TRUE" tells Excel to return the cumulative area under the normal curve. By subtracting the NORMDIST number from 1 (i.e., 100%), we calculate the likelihood of a number (here, $\pi_B$) exceeding the first number in the NORMDIST function.

### Margin of Safety (MOS)

The margin of safety (MOS) is the amount of planned (or actual) sales above the breakeven point.

The **margin of safety (MOS)** is the amount of planned (or actual) sales above the breakeven point:

$$\text{MOS} = \text{Planned (or actual) sales} - \text{Breakeven sales}$$

Returning to the HFI example, assume that the planned sales of TV tables is 3,000 units per year; since the breakeven quantity is 1,500 units, the margin of safety is

$$\text{MOS in units} = 3,000 - 1,500 = 1,500 \text{ units}$$

or

$$\text{MOS in sales dollars} = 1,500 \times \$75 = \$112,500$$

The margin of safety also can be used as a ratio, a percentage of sales:

$$\text{MOS ratio} = \text{MOS} \div \text{Planned sales}$$
$$= 1,500 \div 3,000 = 0.5$$

What this means is that, with everything else held constant, sales volume could fall by 50% before losses start occurring.

The **margin of safety (MOS) ratio** is a useful measure for comparing the risk of two or more alternative products.

The **margin of safety (MOS) ratio** is a useful measure for comparing the risk of two or more alternative products. The product with a relatively low margin of safety ratio is the riskier of the two products and therefore usually requires more of management's attention.

### Operating Leverage

**Operating leverage** refers to the extent of fixed costs in an organization's cost structure.

In physics we refer to a lever as anything that can be used to multiply force. In profit planning we use a similar term, **operating leverage,** to refer to the extent to which the cost structure of an organization has fixed versus variable costs. The higher the relative amount of fixed costs, the higher the operating leverage, and therefore the greater the sensitivity of operating income to changes in sales volume. As such, operating leverage, similar to the physicist's lever, is used as a multiplier. We demonstrate these concepts with the following example.

Consider two firms: one has relatively low fixed costs and relatively high unit variable costs (a labor-intensive firm), and the other has relatively high fixed costs and relatively low variable costs (a highly automated firm). Sample data for two such firms are shown in Exhibit 9.7.

These two situations are compared in Exhibit 9.8A (relatively high fixed costs) and Exhibit 9.8B (relatively low fixed costs). Note that the breakeven point is the same in

**EXHIBIT 9.7**
**Contrasting Data for Automated and Labor-Intensive Firms**

|  | Automated: High Fixed Cost | Labor-Intensive: Low Fixed Cost |
|---|---|---|
| Fixed cost/year | $500,000 | $150,000 |
| Variable cost/unit | 2 | 9 |
| Selling price/unit | 12 | 12 |
| Contribution margin/unit | 10 | 3 |

**EXHIBIT 9.8A**
**CVP Graph for a Firm with Relatively High Fixed Costs**

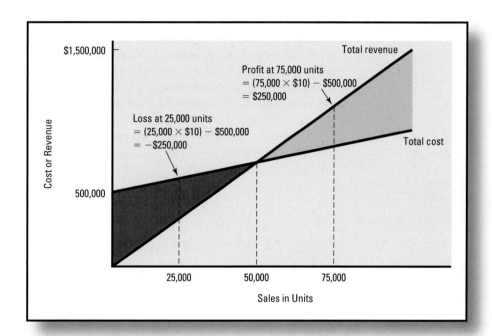

**EXHIBIT 9.8B**
**CVP Graph for a Firm with Relatively Low Fixed Costs**

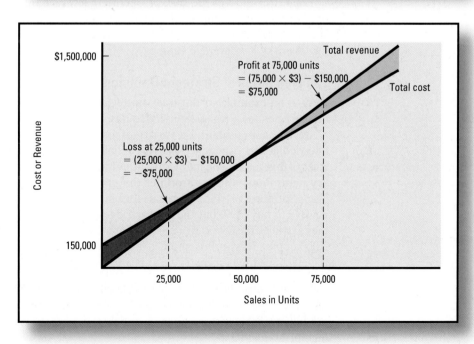

## Cost Management in Action

### Ford Motor Co. and GM: How Can They Become More Profitable?

In recent years, Detroit automakers have been struggling with declining sales and slowing profits—even losses in some recent quarterly periods. GM and Ford are particularly challenged by what investment analysts call *legacy costs*—the costs of retirement and other employee benefits. What do these retirement costs mean for operating leverage in these firms? How do you think these firms are, or should be, responding to become more competitive and profitable?

(Refer to Comments on Cost Management in Action at the end of the chapter.)

each case, 50,000 units. However, if we examine the profit at 25,000 units above breakeven or the loss at 25,000 units below breakeven, a strong contrast emerges. For the firm with relatively high fixed costs (Exhibit 9.8A), the loss at 25,000 units is relatively large, $250,000, while the profit at 75,000 units is also relatively large, $250,000. In contrast, when fixed costs are low (Exhibit 9.8B), the loss at 25,000 units is only $75,000 and the profit at 75,000 units is only $75,000.

A firm with high fixed costs (i.e., with high operating leverage) is riskier because profits are very strongly affected by the level of sales. High profits are earned beyond breakeven, but high losses result from falling below breakeven. In this context, CVP analysis is particularly important in planning the use of new manufacturing technologies that have the potential to change the relationship between fixed and variable costs.

A measure of the sensitivity of operating income to changes in sales volume is called the **degree of operating leverage (DOL)**. DOL is defined, at each volume level, $Q$, as:

**Degree of operating leverage (DOL),**
at any output level, $Q$, is the ratio of contribution margin to operating profit.

$$\text{Contribution margin} \div \text{Operating profit}$$

For the HFI data (Exhibit 9.2), the DOL for 2013 and $Q = 2,400$ units is as follows:

$$\text{DOL} = \text{Contribution margin} \div \text{Operating profit}$$
$$= \$96,000 \div \$36,000 = 2.667$$

From this volume level ($Q = 2,400$ units), operating profit would increase by 2.667% for each percentage change in sales volume. For example, a sales increase of 10% would result in a 26.67% ($= 10 \times 2.667\%$) change in operating profit (assuming everything else is held constant).

Each firm chooses the level of operating leverage that is consistent with its competitive strategy. For example, a firm with a dominant position in its market might choose a high level of leverage to exploit its advantage. In contrast, a weaker firm might choose the less risky low-leverage strategy.

### The Five Steps of Strategic Decision Making for CVP Analysis

Here is an example to illustrate strategic decision making in CVP analysis. Russ Talmadge operates a real estate service business that provides rental management services, real estate appraisal, and a variety of other services. Russ is successful because of his knowledge and experience and the reliability of his service which has gained him the trust of his customers, many of whom have been with him for several years. One of the key items in his office is a printer that prints copies of photos from his digital camera. The photos are used in appraisals and in other services. His printer was relatively inexpensive to buy ($99) but the ink cartridges are expensive—depending on the capacity of the cartridge, the cost is from $37.50 for a capacity of 500 copies to $80 for a capacity for 2,000 copies. Russ prints about 1,000 photos a month. He takes the following five steps to determine the best cartridge to buy for his printer.

1. **Determine the strategic issues surrounding the problem.** Russ's business is based on his knowledge and reliable service. The photos that are a part of his service must also be produced reliably (no printer jams or delays getting the photo to the customer) and be of high print quality.

In 2011, prices for hot-rolled steel dropped from about $900 a ton in April to about $670 a ton by mid-October. In such a turbulent environment, how do traditionally organized (and larger) steel mills (e.g., U.S. Steel or AK Steel) compare to mini-mills (such as Nucor) that operate on a reduced scale and therefore are able to more easily move on- or off-line as the market for steel fluctuates? The former companies have higher levels of fixed costs (i.e., greater operating leverage), while the structure of smaller competitors, such as Nucor, allows them to basically turn otherwise fixed costs into step or semi-variable costs. Firms with greater operating leverage are exposed to greater risk the greater the price fluctuation for products; these firms are particularly

vulnerable to price declines, similar to the decline cited above. Mini-mills are able to cushion the effect of price declines by going off-line (temporarily), a strategy that makes them more nimble competitors. An advantage of the larger mills, however, is that due to their size, when demand (and price) increases, they are able to capitalize on the increased demand. This example is yet another indicator of the general principle of the risk-reward trade-off.

**Source:** K. Evans, "High Fixed Costs Are Makings of Steel Trap," *The Wall Street Journal,* October 25, 2011 (available online at: http://online.wsj.com/article/SB10001424052970203911804576651580445851722.html).

2. **Identify the alternative actions.** Russ can purchase the high-capacity cartridge (2,000 copies) or the low-capacity cartridge (500 copies) for his printer. The high-capacity cartridge will cost 4 cents per copy ($80 ÷ 2,000) while the low-capacity cartridge will cost 7.5 cents per copy ($37.50 ÷ 500). Another option is to buy a new printer for $150 that has a cartridge costing $60 (capacity of 2,000 copies; 3 cents per copy).

3. **Obtain information and conduct analyses of the alternatives.**

**Option One: Retain current copier** The high-capacity cartridge will cost $40 per month (1,000 copies at 4 cents per copy) and the lower capacity cartridge will cost $75 per month (1,000 copies at 7.5 cents per copy). The purchase cost of the copier can be ignored since it is a sunk cost, and therefore the high-capacity cartridge will always be the low-cost option.

**Option Two: New copier** The breakeven point for the new copier (assuming Russ is using the high-capacity cartridge on his current copier) would be 15,000 copies—$150 ÷ (4 cents − 3 cents)—or, 15 months of usage.

4. **Based on Strategy and Analysis, Choose and Implement the Desired Alternative.**

**Option One** The choice of cartridge has no effect on the quality or reliability of the printer, so the choice can be made on the basis of lower cost, and in this case the high-capacity cartridge is preferred. Also, the high-capacity cartridge would mean less frequent cartridge replacement and, therefore, less chance of a potential delay when a photo is needed quickly.

**Option Two** Russ would achieve breakeven on the new copier in 15 months, not a particularly long period given the number of years he has been in business. And the addition of a new copier would give him a "backup" if one of them should fail. However, looking at a *Consumer Reports* study of copiers, Russ finds that the $150 copier does not have as high a reliability or quality rating as does his current copier. Considering the importance of quality and reliability in his business, Russ chooses option one with the high-capacity cartridge.

5. **Provide an ongoing evaluation of the effectiveness of implementation in step 4.** Russ continues to review the available printers. If he determines a way to reduce the need for photos or can print them on a color printer instead of photo paper, he may be able to reduce costs substantially. He may also be able to obtain the cartridges at lower cost from a new supplier.

## CVP Analysis with Two or More Products/Services

**LO 9-6**

*Adapt CVP analysis for multiple products/services.*

We have shown above how to calculate the CVP model for a single product. Commonly, however, a company produces or retails two or more products/services. If the multiproduct (or multiservice) company can reasonably allocate fixed costs to each product (and if there

**Sales mix**
refers to the relative proportion in which a company's products (or services) are sold.

**Weighted-average contribution margin per unit**
is an average per-unit contribution margin based on an assumed sales mix determined on the basis of physical units (not sales dollars).

**Weighted-average contribution margin ratio**
is an average contribution margin ratio at the assumed sales mix based on sales dollars (not units).

are no demand dependencies across products/services), then the company can determine its **sales mix** and construct a series of CVP models—one for each product/service.

In the absence of this, and if we are willing to assume that the company's products/services are sold in a particular mix and that this mix remains constant as total volume changes, then we can build a single CVP model for profit-planning purposes. One approach is to calculate and use in the formulas presented earlier in the chapter something called the **weighted-average contribution margin per unit,** which is determined on the basis of the contribution margin per unit for a given product weighted by the sales mix percentage for the product. Sales mix percentages are based on relative physical units (not sales dollars) for the individual products.

Assume, for example, that a company sells two products, A and B, with corresponding per-unit contribution margins of $1 and $4. If the assumed sales mix is 50:50 (1 unit of A sold for each unit of B sold), then the weighted-average contribution margin per unit would be $2.50 (i.e., [$1 $\times$ 50%] + [$4 $\times$ 50%]). If, on the other hand, the sales mix shifted to 25:75, then the weighted-average contribution margin per unit would increase to $3.25.

Of course, sales mix can also be defined on the basis of relative sales dollars. Such information can be used to calculate a **weighted-average contribution margin ratio,** which is determined on the basis of the contribution margin ratios of the individual products weighted by sales mix, as determined on the basis of relative sales dollars (not physical units). The weighted-average contribution margin ratio can then be used for breakeven and profit planning for sales volume expressed in dollars ($Y$) rather than units ($Q$).

In the two-product example presented above, assume that the sales mix based on physical units is 50:50 (as before). In addition to the assumed per-unit contribution margins ($1 and $4 for A and B, respectively), assume that the unit selling prices are $4 and $6, respectively. In this situation, the weighted-average contribution margin ratio is 50%, as follows:

$$(25\% \times 0.4) + (66.667\% \times 0.6) = 50\%$$

If the sales mix were to shift (as before) to 25:75, then the weighted-average contribution margin ratio would increase to 59.1%, as follows:

$$[25\% \times (4 \div 22)] + [66.667\% \times (18 \div 22)] = 59.1\%$$

### Weighted-Average Contribution Margin Ratio (CMR)

To illustrate, we use the example of Windbreakers, Inc., which sells light-weight sport/recreational jackets. Windbreakers has three products, Calm, Windy, and Gale. Relevant information for these products is in Exhibit 9.9. The total fixed costs for the period are expected to be $168,000, and we assume that Windbreakers's sales mix will remain constant as volume changes. As indicated in Exhibit 9.9, sales mix in dollars is 50%, 40%, and 10%, respectively, for the three products. Sales mix in terms of units is 52.63%, 39.47%, and 7.90%, respectively.

From the information in Exhibit 9.9, we can calculate the weighted-average CMR as follows:

$$0.5(0.2) + 0.4(0.25) + 0.1(0.1) = 0.21$$

**EXHIBIT 9.9**
**Sales and Cost Data for Windbreakers, Inc.**

|  | Calm | Windy | Gale | Total |
|---|---|---|---|---|
| Last period's sales | $750,000 | $600,000 | $150,000 | $1,500,000 |
| Percent of sales dollars | 50% | 40% | 10% | 100% |
| Last period's sales volume (units) | 25,000 | 18,750 | 3,750 | 47,500 |
| Percent of sales volume | 52.63% | 39.47% | 7.90% | 100% |
| Selling price per unit | $ 30 | $ 32 | $ 40 | |
| Variable cost per unit | 24 | 24 | 36 | |
| Contribution margin per unit | $ 6 | $ 8 | $ 4 | |
| Contribution margin ratio | 0.20 | 0.25 | 0.10 | |

Sometimes showing the results of a sensitivity analysis in the form of a graph is useful. The U.S. Department of Energy has used this approach to study the decision to adopt fuel cell technology for generating electricity by such large users as the Pittsburgh International Airport, AT&T Research Laboratory in Morristown, New Jersey, and Kirtland Air Force Base in New Mexico. Fuel cell technology converts natural gas to electricity in a clean and efficient manner. Fuel cells are cost effective when the cost of natural gas is relatively low and the cost of other sources of electricity is relatively high. The study produced a breakeven analysis and related sensitivity analysis showing that a breakeven line can be determined (see the following) to clearly identify the preferred technology (fuel cell or conventional sources of electricity) based on variations in the cost of natural gas and conventional electricity.

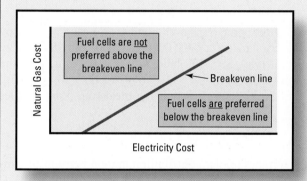

The breakeven line as shown is determined by solving the equation that sets total cost of one technology equal to that of the other. The two axes in the graph are the unit variable costs for each alternative.

To illustrate, using the data from Exhibit 9.7, we solve the equation that sets total cost of the automated factory equal to that of the labor-intensive factory. The fixed costs and volume level are assumed, and the equation is solved for the variable cost of each alternative as a function of the variable cost of the other alternative (where $Y$ = unit variable cost for the automated factory and $X$ = unit variable cost for the labor-intensive factory, volume = 50,000 units, and the remaining data are from Exhibit 9.7):

Total cost of automated factory = Total cost of labor-intensive factory

$$(Y \times 50,000) + \$500,000 = (X \times 50,000) + \$150,000$$

$$Y = X - 7$$

The sensitivity graph for these data follows. The labor-intensive factory favors the area above the line and the automated factory favors the area below the line.

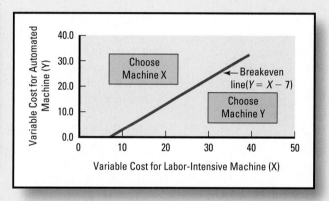

**Source:** Pacific Northwest National Laboratory, "Federal Technology Alerts: Natural Gas Fuel Cells," U.S. Department of Energy, www1.eere.energy.gov/femp/pdfs/FTA_natgas_fuelcell.pdf.

The breakeven point in dollars for all three products can be calculated as follows:

$$Y = \$168,000 \div 0.21 = \$800,000$$

This means that at the assumed sales mix (based on relative sales dollars last year) total sales of $800,000 must be generated for Windbreakers to break even. The sales for each product at the overall breakeven point are as follows:

| | |
|---|---|
| For Calm | 0.5($800,000) = $400,000 (13,334 jackets at $30) |
| For Windy | 0.4($800,000) = 320,000 (10,000 jackets at $32) |
| For Gale | 0.1($800,000) = 80,000 (2,000 jackets at $40) |
| Total | $800,000 |

The sale of jackets in the assumed sales mix produces exactly the breakeven contribution margin of $168,000:

$$\$6(13,334) + \$8(10,000) + \$4(2,000) = \$168,000$$

### Weighted-Average Contribution Margin per Unit

From the information in Exhibit 9.9 we can calculate the weighted-average contribution margin per unit as follows:

$$0.5263(\$6.00) + 0.3947(\$8.00) + 0.0790(\$4.00) = \$6.63 \text{ (rounded)}$$

Thus, the breakeven point, at the sales mix reflected in Exhibit 9.9 based on physical units, is calculated as follows:

$$Q = \$168,000 \div \$6.63 \text{ per unit (rounded)} = 25,334 \text{ (rounded)}$$

The total breakeven units of 25,334 can be broken down by product, as follows:

| | | |
|---|---|---|
| For Calm | 0.5263(25,334) = | 13,334 jackets |
| For Windy | 0.3947(25,334) = | 10,000 jackets |
| For Gale | 0.0790(25,334) = | 2,000 jackets |
| Total | = | 25,334 jackets |

Note that we could have arrived at the same breakeven numbers for each product by dividing the breakeven point in sales dollars (viz., $400,000, $320,000, and $80,000) by their respective selling prices per unit (viz., $30, $32, and $40). Finally, note that the weighted-average selling price per unit, $31.80 [(0.5 × $30) + (0.4 × $32) + (0.1 × $40)], times the total breakeven volume of 25,334 jackets equals the breakeven point in sales dollars determined previously.

### "Sales Basket" Approach

Instead of working with weighted averages (either contribution margin per unit or contribution margin ratio), we might use a "sales basket" approach to profit planning for the multiproduct firm. To do this, we construct a hypothetical "basket" of products, in which each basket consists of so many units of product #1, so many units of product #2, and so on. From this hypothetical basket of products (which now represents the standard sales mix), we could calculate either a weighted-average contribution margin per unit or a weighted-average contribution margin ratio. Profit planning then proceeds as described above. However, in this case, a two-step process is needed: first, determine the number of sales baskets needed to achieve the profit target (including breakeven), then convert the number of baskets to units of individual product based on the composition of each hypothetical sales basket.

As an example, if a hypothetical sales basket consisted of two units of Product A and three units of Product B, we would calculate the contribution margin per sales basket of five units. After solving for the number of sales baskets needed to achieve the profit target, we would convert to individual units using the following formula: 2 units of Product A and 3 units of Product B per basket. Note that, as before, we could in this case calculate the weighted-average contribution margin per unit based on the following weights: Product A, 40% (i.e., 2/5); Product B, 60% (i.e., 3/5). As such, use of the weighted-average approach versus the "sales basket" approach is a matter of personal preference: other than rounding errors, these approaches lead to the same profit-planning results.

### Value Stream Accounting and CVP

When families of products are grouped into value streams in lean accounting, there is an opportunity to use CVP for the product group rather than for a single product or for multiple products. For example, families of products, or value streams, for a consumer electronics company might include one value stream for CD players (all the different types of CD players the company sells) and another for DVD players, and other value streams for other product groups. The use of value streams simplifies the calculation of CVP and can make it more meaningful and useful. Lean accounting is covered in Chapter 17.

## CVP Analysis for Not-for-Profit Organizations

**LO 9-7**

*Apply CVP analysis in not-for-profit organizations.*

Not-for-profit organizations can also use CVP analysis. To illustrate, consider a family support agency, Orange County Family Support Center, that provides training in a classroom setting for struggling young families. The training sessions cover health care for children, financial planning, and other issues; each session involves some handout materials (books, sample medications, etc.), and a paid instructor. Orange County Family Support Center (OCFS) receives financial support from the county, whose funding is falling because of a recession in the local economy. As a result, the county commissioners have set an across-the-board budget cut of 5% for the new fiscal year. The center's funding was $735,000 last year and is projected to be approximately $700,000 next year. Its director figures that variable costs (including handout publications, medications, other materials, and some administrative costs) are $10 per visit per family for the almost 300 families who take courses at the center. All other costs are fixed, including salaries for the teachers, record-keeping costs, and facilities costs. How will the budget cut affect the level of service the center provides if we assume fixed costs cannot be changed in the short term?

To answer this question, we must determine precisely the center's activity with the associated fixed and variable costs. OCFS uses the number of families-attending-sessions, that is, the total number of times any family attends any session. The director estimates 13,500 families-attending-sessions last year and that unit variable costs are constant at $10 per family-session in the range of 10,000 to 14,000 family-sessions per year; total variable costs were therefore $135,000 ($10 × 13,500) last year. We determine total fixed costs for last year as follows:

$$\text{Funding} = \text{Total cost}$$
$$= \text{Total fixed costs} + \text{Total variable costs}$$
$$\$735,000 = \text{Total fixed costs} + \$135,000$$
$$\text{Total fixed costs} = \$600,000$$

Now the director can analyze the effect of the budget change on the center's service levels. At the $700,000 budget level expected for next year, the activity level is approximately 10,000 family-sessions. Total cost of $700,000 less fixed cost of $600,000 leaves variable costs of $100,000; thus, $100,000 ÷ $10 per family-session = 10,000 family-sessions. The director can now see that the approximate 5% cut in the budget is expected to result in an approximate 26% drop in family-sessions [26% = (13,500 − 10,000) ÷ 13,500].

## Assumptions and Limitations of CVP Analysis

**LO 9-8**

*Identify the assumptions and limitations of CVP analysis.*

### Linearity, the Relevant Range, and Step Costs

The CVP model assumes that revenues and total costs are linear over the relevant range of activity. Although actual cost behavior is not linear, we use the concept of the relevant range introduced in Chapter 3 so that within a given limited range of output, total costs are expected to increase at an approximately linear rate. The caution for the manager is therefore to remember that the calculations performed within the context of a traditional CVP model should not be used outside the relevant range.

#### *Step Costs*

As illustrated in Exhibit 9.10, the cost behavior under examination may be so "lumpy" (step costs) that an approximation via a relevant range is unworkable. Although CVP analysis can be done, it becomes somewhat more cumbersome. Exhibit 9.10 illustrates a situation with a selling price per unit of $18, a variable cost per unit of $10, an initial fixed cost of $100,000, and an incremental fixed cost of another $100,000 when output exceeds 10,000 units. The expenditure of the additional fixed cost provides capacity for up to 30,000 units. A CVP analysis requires that the manager determine the breakeven

**EXHIBIT 9.10**
**CVP Analysis with Step Cost Behavior**

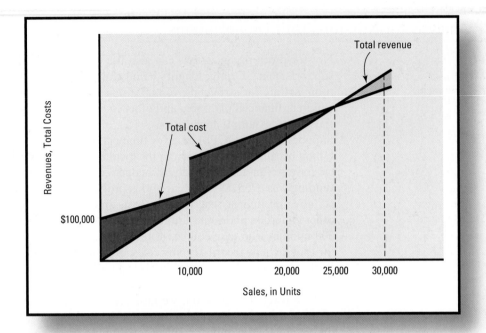

point for each range (below and above the point at 10,000 units). For these data, we find no breakeven below the 10,000 unit level of output, but the breakeven point can be obtained for the upper range as follows:

$$Q = F \div (p - v) = \$200,000 \div (\$18 - \$10) = 25,000 \text{ units}$$

## Summary

This chapter develops CVP analysis, a linear model of the relationships between costs, revenues, and sales volumes. The analysis is used for breakeven planning, revenue planning, and cost planning.

Breakeven planning determines the output level at which operating profit is zero. Breakeven analysis is used in planning and budgeting to assess the desirability of current and potential products and services. CVP analysis is also used in revenue planning to determine the sales needed to achieve a desired level of operating profit by adding desired profit to the breakeven equation. In cost planning, CVP analysis is used to find the required reduction in costs to meet desired profits or to find the required change in fixed cost for a given change in variable cost (or vice versa).

The basic CVP model can be expanded and made consistent with the traditional activity-based costing (ABC) model discussed in Chapter 5. Specifically, we expanded the CVP model to include both volume-based (short-term) fixed costs and batch-level (short-term) fixed costs.

Risk and uncertainty in CVP analysis is addressed through the use of two measures (margin of safety and degree of operating leverage) as well as through sensitivity analysis. In terms of the latter, we discussed three approaches: simple "what-if" analyses, the preparation of decision tables (or decision trees), and the use of Monte Carlo simulation.

With two or more products or services, we typically construct a CVP model by assuming that the products (or services) are sold in a predefined mix, determined either on the basis of physical units or sales dollars associated with the individual products. The assumption of a sales mix allows us to calculate and use weighted averages for the contribution margin per unit and the contribution margin ratio. Alternatively, we can use the assumed sales mix to construct a "sales basket" of items. In this case, all amounts (e.g., contribution margin) are expressed on a per-sales-basket basis.

Not-for-profit organizations also use breakeven analysis. We presented the example of a municipal family support agency's use of breakeven analysis to predict the effects of changing funding levels on the operations of this agency.

A number of limitations must be considered in using breakeven analysis. If these assumptions are violated, then the use of more sophisticated profit-planning models should be considered.

| Key Terms | | | |
|---|---|---|---|
| | breakeven point, *311* | degree of operating | sensitivity analysis, *322* |
| | contribution income | leverage (DOL), *326* | total contribution |
| | statement, *310* | CVP graph, *313* | margin, *309* |
| | contribution margin | margin of safety (MOS), *324* | weighted-average contribution |
| | per unit, *309* | margin of safety (MOS) ratio, *324* | margin per unit, *328* |
| | contribution margin ratio, *309* | operating leverage, *324* | weighted-average contribution |
| | cost-volume-profit (CVP) | profit-volume graph, *315* | margin ratio, *328* |
| | analysis, *307* | sales mix, *328* | what-if analysis, *322* |

## Comments on Cost Management in Action

### Ford Motor Co. and GM: How Can They Become More Profitable?

Ford and GM are highly leveraged auto manufacturers. The high fixed costs include high labor-related costs—both current production labor and the costs of retirement benefits for retired workers. During the 1970s and 1980s the firms made decisions that locked in high labor capacity, based on a strategy that sales volume would grow and the labor capacity would be needed. But the desired sales increases have not happened, as foreign auto manufacturers continue to increase their market share.

High operating leverage leads to faster reductions in profits when sales fall, and this is the current experience for these automakers. A recent program by GM to boost sales by offering sales discounts to customers that were equivalent to the discounts given to employees of the auto manufacturers is an example of GM's strategy to increase sales to cover these fixed costs. The firms are also looking for ways to reduce the fixed costs, and recent plant closings employee buyouts, changes in benefit plans and renewed negotiations with the United Auto Workers' union are part of that strategy. High operating leverage also means high debt levels, and the Detroit automakers are significantly affected by changes in the credit markets; in particular, the liquidity crisis and recession of 2008–2009 have affected their ability to obtain needed financing.

**Source:** Jeffrey McCracken, "Detroit's Symbol of Dysfunction: Paying Employees Not to Work," *The Wall Street Journal,* March 1, 2006, p.1; Karen Lundegaard and Joseph B. White, "Detroit Finds a Bandwagon in 'Employee Discounts,'" *The Wall Street Journal,* July 6, 2005, p.1; Joann Muller, "Carmakers in the Credit Coalmine," *Forbes,* September 26, 2008; Matthew Dolan, "Michigan Sweats GM-Chrysler Talks," *The Wall Street Journal,* October 20, 2008, p. B1.

## Self-Study Problem
(For solution, please turn to the end of the chapter.)

The following data refer to a single product, the TECHWHIZ, made by the Markdata Computer Company:

---
Sales price = $5,595
Materials cost (including purchased components) = $899
Direct labor cost = $233
Facilities cost (for a highly automated plant mainly includes rent, insurance, taxes, and depreciation) = $2,352,000 per year

---

### Required

1. What is the contribution margin per unit?

2. What is the breakeven point, in units and in dollars?

3. What is the required level of sales (in units) if the company plans to increase fixed costs by 5% (to improve product quality and appearance) and has a desired before-tax profit ($\pi_B$) of $200,000?

4. If the company's income tax rate is 22%, what unit sales are necessary to achieve an after-tax profit ($\pi_A$) of $150,000?

*Please visit http://www.mhhe.com/blocher6e to access a narrated, animated tutorial for solving this problem.*

| Questions | 9-1 | What is the underlying relationship depicted in a CVP analysis? |
|---|---|---|
| | 9-2 | What is the contribution margin ratio and how is it used? |
| | 9-3 | What are the basic assumptions of CVP analysis? |
| | 9-4 | Why do management accountants use sensitivity analysis? |
| | 9-5 | What type of risk does sensitivity analysis address? |
| | 9-6 | Why does the issue of income taxes not affect the calculation of the breakeven point? |
| | 9-7 | What is the margin of safety (MOS), and for what is it used? |
| | 9-8 | What is operating leverage, and for what is it used? |
| | 9-9 | Define degree of operating leverage (DOL). How is DOL measured? |
| | 9-10 | How is CVP analysis used to calculate the breakeven point for multiple products? |

**Brief Exercises**

9-11 Doughton Bearings produces ball bearings for industrial equipment. In evaluating the financial data from the previous year, the management accountant has determined that the company's selling price per unit is $25, while the variable cost per unit is $18. What is the contribution margin per unit?

9-12 Felton Paper produces paper for textbooks. Felton plans to produce 500,000 cases of paper next quarter to sell at a price of $100 per case. The variable cost per case, including both manufacturing and selling costs, is $80. What is the total contribution margin for next quarter?

9-13 Ford Tops manufactures hats for baseball teams. Ford has fixed costs of $175,000 per quarter and sells each hat for $20. If the variable cost per hat is $10, how many hats must Ford sell each quarter to break even?

9-14 The Cobb Clinic treats walk-in patients for various illnesses. The management accountant has estimated that the clinic has $5,000 in monthly fixed costs in addition to a $20 cost per patient visit. If the charge is $30 per visit, how many visits per month does the clinic need to break even?

9-15 Oxicon Inc. manufactures several different types of candy for various retail stores. The accounting manager has requested that you determine the sales dollars required to break even for next quarter based on past financial data. Your research tells you that the total variable cost will be $500,000, total sales will be $750,000, and fixed costs will be $75,000. What is the breakeven point in sales dollars?

9-16 Williams & Williams Co. produces plastic spray bottles and wants to earn a before-tax profit of $200,000 next quarter. Variable costs are $0.50 per bottle, fixed costs are $400,000, and the selling price is $1 per bottle. How many bottles must the company sell to meet its profit goal?

9-17 Scott Power produces batteries. Scott has determined its contribution margin to be $8 per battery and its contribution margin ratio to be 0.4. What is the effect on profits of the sale of one additional battery? Of one additional dollar of sales?

9-18 ABC Audio sells headphones and would like to earn after-tax profits of $400 every week. Each set of headphones incurs variable costs of $5 and sells for $10. Rent and other fixed costs are $200 per week; the income tax rate is 20%. How many headphones must ABC sell per week to meet its profit goal?

9-19 Franklin Cards sells greeting cards for $2 each and plans to sell 100,000 cards every quarter. The management accountant has determined the company must sell 80,000 cards every quarter to break even. What is the margin of safety (MOS), in units and in sales dollars?

9-20 May Clothing is a retail men's clothing store. May's variable cost is $20 per shirt and the sales price is $40 per shirt. May plans to sell 400,000 shirts for the year and at this level would generate a before-tax profit of $2,500,000. What is the degree of operating leverage (DOL) at this volume level?

**Exercises**

[LO 9-2, 9-3] 9-21 **Profit Planning** Connelly, Inc., a manufacturer of quality electric ice cream makers, has experienced a steady growth in sales over the past few years. Since her business has grown, Jan DeJaney, the president, believes she needs an aggressive advertising campaign next year to maintain the company's growth. To prepare for the growth, the accountant prepared the following data for the current year:

| | | |
|---|---|---|
| Variable costs per ice cream maker | | |
| Direct labor | $ | 13.50 |
| Direct materials | | 14.50 |
| Variable overhead | | 6.00 |
| Total variable costs | $ | 34.00 |

| Fixed costs | |
|---|---|
| Manufacturing | $ 82,500 |
| Selling | 42,000 |
| Administrative | 356,000 |
| Total fixed costs | $480,500 |
| Selling price per unit | $ 67.00 |
| Expected sales (units) | 30,000 |

**Required**

1. If the costs and sales price remain the same, what is the projected operating profit for the coming year?

2. What is the breakeven point in units for the coming year?

3. Jan has set the sales target for 35,000 ice cream makers, which she thinks she can achieve by an additional fixed selling expense of $200,000 for advertising. All other costs remain as in requirement 1. What will be the operating profit if the additional $200,000 is spent on advertising and sales rise to 35,000 units?

4. What will be the new breakeven point if the additional $200,000 is spent on advertising? (Prepare a contribution income statement to support your answer.) What is the percentage change in both fixed costs and in the breakeven point? What general point is illustrated by this comparison?

5. If the additional $200,000 is spent for advertising in the next year, what is the sales level (in units) needed to equal the current year's income at 30,000 units?

[LO 9-5]   9-22   **Margin of Safety (MOS)**   Harold McWilliams owns and manages a general merchandise store in a rural area of Virginia. Harold sells appliances, clothing, auto parts, and farming equipment, among a wide variety of other types of merchandise. Because of normal seasonal and cyclical fluctuations in the local economy, he knows that his business will also have these fluctuations, and he is planning to use CVP analysis to help him understand how he can expect his profits to change with these fluctuations. Harold has the following information for his most recent year. Cost of goods sold represents the cost paid for the merchandise he sells, while operating costs represent rent, insurance, and salaries, which are entirely fixed.

| | |
|---|---|
| Sales | $650,000 |
| Cost of merchandise sold | 422,500 |
| Contribution margin | 227,500 |
| Operating costs | 105,000 |
| Operating profit | $122,500 |

**Required**

1. What is Harold's margin of safety (MOS) in dollars? What is the margin of safety (MOS) ratio?

2. Of what managerial significance are the preceding measures?

3. What is Harold's margin of safety (in dollars) and operating profit if sales should fall to $500,000?

[LO 9-1, 9-2, 9-3]   9-23   **The Role of Income Taxes**   In 2013, Triad Company had fixed costs of $240,000 and variable costs of 75% of total sales revenue, earned $70,000 of net income after taxes, and had an income tax rate of 35%.

**Required**   Determine:

1. Before-tax income.

2. Total contribution margin.

3. Total sales.

4. Breakeven point in dollar sales.

[LO 9-2, 9-3]   9-24   **CVP Analysis with Income Taxes**   Cohen Company produces and sells socks. Variable costs are $6 per pair, and fixed costs for the year total $75,000. The selling price is $10 per pair.

**Required**   Calculate the following:

1. The breakeven point in units.

2. The breakeven point in sales dollars.

3. The units required to make a before-tax profit of $40,000.

4. The sales in dollars required to make a before-tax profit of $35,000.

5. The sales, in units and in dollars, required to make an after-tax profit of $25,000 given a tax rate of 30%.

**[LO 9-3]**  9-25  **Cost Planning; Machine Replacement**   Vista Company manufactures electronic equipment. It currently purchases from an outside supplier the special switches used in each of its products. The supplier charges Vista $2 per switch. Vista's CEO is considering purchasing either machine A or machine B so the company can manufacture its own switches. The projected data are as follows:

|                        | Machine A | Machine B |
|------------------------|-----------|-----------|
| Annual fixed cost      | $135,000  | $204,000  |
| Variable cost per switch | 0.65    | 0.30      |

**Required**

1. For each machine, what is the minimum number of switches that Vista must make annually for total costs to equal outside purchase cost?

2. What volume level would produce the same total costs regardless of the machine purchased?

3. What is the most profitable alternative for producing 200,000 switches per year?

4. Which of the two decision alternatives would you recommend? Why?

**[LO 9-5]**  9-26  **Degree of Operating Leverage (DOL)**   The following sales and cost data (000s) are for two companies in the transportation industry:

|                     | Company A | | Company B | |
|---------------------|-----------|-----------------|-----------|-----------------|
|                     | Amount    | Percent of Sales | Amount    | Percent of Sales |
| Sales               | $100,000  | 100%            | $100,000  | 100%            |
| Variable costs      | 50,000    | 50              | 30,000    | 30              |
| Contribution margin | $ 50,000  | 50%             | $ 70,000  | 70%             |
| Fixed costs         | 15,000    |                 | 40,000    |                 |
| Operating profit    | $ 35,000  |                 | $ 30,000  |                 |

**Required**

1. Calculate the degree of operating leverage (DOL) for each company. If sales increase from the present level, which company benefits more? How do you know?

2. Assume that sales rise 10% in the next year but that everything else remains constant. Calculate the percentage increase in profit for each company. Are the results what you expected? Explain.

3. In what sense is DOL a measure of risk?

**[LO 9-3]**  9-27  **Cost Planning: The Cost of an MBA; Time Value of Money**   The motivation for getting the MBA degree has many aspects—the prestige, greater opportunity for promotion, change of occupation, and an increase in pay. To focus just on this last motivation, suppose that you are interested in getting an MBA and are studying the various programs in the United States. You want to balance the cost of getting the degree against the future benefits in increase of pay. You have information on the cost of two MBA programs, which includes the cost of tuition, living expenses, and forgone pre-MBA salary for the two years you are in the MBA program. School A has an average cost of $100,000 and School B, a far more prestigious school at which you think your grades would qualify you to be a successful applicant, has a cost of $250,000.

**Required**   Assume that you have a five-year planning horizon, that the difference in pay for a job after both schools would remain the same for all five years, and the relevant cost of borrowing is 6%. Based on increase in pay only, how great would the increase for a job after leaving School B have to be relative to School A for you to be indifferent between the two schools? *Hint:* The present value factor for an annuity of five years at 6% is in Table 2 at the end of Chapter 12 and equals 4.212.

**[LO 9-3]**  9-28  **Cost Planning; Gasoline Prices**   In June 2008, when gasoline prices were at an all-time high, greater than $4 per gallon, Chrysler Motor Company promoted its Jeep vehicle with the offer of either $4,500 off the price of the vehicle or the guarantee that the buyer would not pay more than $2.99 per gallon of gas for the next three years (the details of the guarantee could vary by dealer).

**Required**

1. Assume that the Jeep vehicle you are interested in gets 15 mpg combined city/highway and that at the time of purchase you expected gasoline prices to average $5 per gallon over the next three years. How many miles would you have to drive the vehicle in the next three years to make the guarantee more attractive than the $4,500 discount?

2. Assume the same information as in part 1 above, except the average price of gas for the next three years is not known, but you are likely to drive 8,500 miles per year. What is the breakeven gasoline price in the coming three years so that you would be indifferent between the two options?

3. What are some important aspects of the decision that do not have to do with the price of gasoline and the $4,500 discount?

[LO 9-1, 9-2, 9-3]  9-29  **Cost Planning; High-End Copiers**   Companies that have a high demand for making copies, both color and black and white, often choose to lease a high-end copier that provides fast and reliable service at a reasonable cost. The lease is usually for three to five years and the cost to the user is $0.01 per page for black and white copies and typically $0.10 per page for color copies. These are the terms of your current three-year lease contract with Ricoh Company, which is up for renewal this month; the lease terms are expected to be the same for the next three years, if renewed.

   Hewlett-Packard Company (HP) has recently developed an innovative copier that can reduce the cost of color copies. The copier measures exactly how much color is used in a color copy, so that the price of the copy can be determined by the amount of color used rather than a fixed price per page, so the cost could be as low as $0.070 per page for a color copy. HP calls this a "flexible-pricing" approach. Assume for this example that the cost of the leased copier (three-year lease) is only the per-page charge—the initial lease cost is negligible, and the service costs would not differ between the HP copier and the copier you are using now.

   Your company is an advertising agency, Tanner and Jones, LLC, and the quality of the color copies is critical to your business success. The ability to rely on the copier at any time is also very important, as some customer requests require urgent attention. You believe that the Ricoh and HP printers are of the same reliability, but you have not had experience with the HP copier to be sure of the copy quality. The demonstration of the HP copier has shown as good or better copy quality, but you have not had three years' experience with it to know what it would be like day-to-day.

**Required**

1. Assume that your company is considering the lease of one of these HP copiers, and you expect that the average price for a color copy for your company would be $0.075 because you would carefully prioritize color copy jobs and reduce the number of copies requiring a large amount of color. You expect that training your copy center staff to properly use the new copier would cost about $12,400 for materials and lost work time. What is the breakeven number of color copies per year that would make you indifferent between the new HP copier and your current copier?

2. As in part 1 above, assume you expect that your per-copy cost for color copies with the HP copier will be $0.075, the training costs are $12,400, and you expect to make 200,000 copies per year for the next three years. In your negotiations with Ricoh concerning the new lease and the cost of color copies, what price would you bargain for?

3. Consider your choice between the copiers within the context of the competitive and business environment of Tanner and Jones. What are the issues you should consider in addition to cost of copies?

[LO 9-1, 9-3, 9-5]  9-30  **Cost Structure of Retailers; The Internet; Operating Leverage**   Today's retailers are finding that online sales and service are a necessary ingredient of their overall marketing and selling strategy because of increased competition. In certain retail sectors, consumers are moving to the Internet in large numbers for the convenience and selection they find on the Internet. Unfortunately, the investment in resources, both equipment and labor, can be huge. Some studies show that less than a third of online retailers are profitable on Internet sales. As a result, some new consulting firms, software firms, and service providers have begun to provide e-commerce solutions for retailers.

**Required**

1. How does a consulting firm, service provider, or software firm help a retailer reduce cost and become more competitive for Internet sales? What is the role of operating leverage in the retailer's decision to outsource online sales and service?

2. What role, if any, does globalization play in a retailer's efforts to reduce costs on Internet sales?

[LO 9-3] 9-31 **Structuring Sales Commissions** Questar Electronics, a producer of a wide range of consumer products, is facing increasing competitive pressures from foreign producers. In response, Questar is reexamining its overall management control system, including the way the company compensates members of its sales force. Below are highly condensed data for two representative products that Questar sells:

|  | Alpha | Omega |
|---|---|---|
| Selling price per unit | $ 100 | $ 125 |
| Variable manufacturing cost per unit | 80 | 10 |
| Manufacturing contribution margin | $ 20 | $ 15 |

**Required**

1. Under the assumption that salespeople are paid commissions equal to 10% of sales, which of the company's products will likely be more aggressively promoted? Why?

2. Can you suggest an alternative incentive plan, one that would better align employee and corporate interests (i.e., one that would motivate more goal-congruent behavior)?

[LO 9-6] 9-32 **Multiple Product CVP** Smith Company can produce two types of carpet cleaners, Brighter and Cleaner. Data on these two products are as follows:

|  | Brighter | Cleaner |
|---|---|---|
| Sales volume in units | 400 | 600 |
| Unit sales price | $750 | $1,000 |
| Unit variable cost | 300 | 450 |

The number of machine-hours to produce one unit of Brighter is 1 while the number of machine-hours for each unit of Cleaner is 2. Total fixed costs for the manufacture of both products are $264,000.

**Required**

1. Using a spreadsheet, determine the breakeven point in total units for Smith Company, based on the assumption that the sales mix (on the basis of relative sales volume in units) stays constant. Use the weighted-average contribution margin approach.

2. At this breakeven level, how many units of each product are envisioned?

3. What is the overall breakeven point in sales dollars? (Use both an indirect approach, based on your answer to (2) above, and a direct approach, based on the weighted-average contribution margin ratio and the assumption that sales mix based on relative sales dollars stays constant.)

4. Of what potential managerial value is the information related to machine-hour consumption of the two products?

[LO 9-2, 9-3, 9-5] 9-33 **CVP Analysis** Lawn Master Company, a manufacturer of riding lawn mowers, has a projected income for 2013 as follows:

| | | |
|---|---|---|
| Sales | | $46,000,000 |
| Operating expenses: | | |
| Variable expenses | $32,200,000 | |
| Fixed expenses | 7,500,000 | |
| Total expenses | | 39,700,000 |
| Operating profit | | $ 6,300,000 |

**Required**

1. Determine the breakeven point in sales dollars.

2. Determine the required sales in dollars to earn a before-tax profit of $8,000,000.

3. What is the breakeven point in sales dollars if the variable cost increases by 12%?

[LO 9-1, 9-5] 9-34 **Contribution Income Statements Using Excel; Sensitivity Analysis; Goal Seek**

**Required**

1. Using the data from 2013 in Exhibit 9.1, create an Excel spreadsheet to provide a sensitivity analysis of the effect on operating profit of potential changes in demand for HFI, Inc. Use Exhibits 9.2 and 9.6 as a guide. Assume that two-thirds of fixed costs are manufacturing-related; the remaining

one-third are selling-related. The variable manufacturing cost per unit is $30, while the variable selling cost per unit is $5. (*Hint:* Calculate the DOL for 2013 at a sales volume of 2,400 units. How does this figure help interpret your sensitivity analysis results?)

2. Use the Goal Seek tool within Excel to determine the sales price per unit that would allow HFI to earn an operating profit of $100,000, assuming that all the other cost information is the same as in Exhibit 9.1. Use Exhibit 9.5 as a guide.

**[LO 9-5]**   9-35   **CVP Analysis, DOL, and Margin of Safety (MOS)**   As noted in the text, the *margin of safety* (MOS) represents the amount by which sales (either actual or budgeted) can fall before the organization experiences a loss. On the other hand, the *margin of safety ratio* (MOS%) is the percentage by which sales can fall before a loss is experienced. This ratio is defined as MOS divided by budgeted or actual sales. Both measures are rough indicators of *risk*. Use the definition of MOS% and your algebraic skills to respond to the following requirement.

**Required**   Demonstrate, using separate equations for MOS% and DOL that MOS% and DOL are functionally related. Specifically, show that MOS% = 1 ÷ DOL. Of what interpretive or managerial value is this finding?

**[LO 9-5]**   9-36   **Further Analysis—Degree of Operating Leverage (DOL)**   Based on your reading of the text and your algebraic skills, respond to the following two requirements.

**Required**

1. In reading the text, you should have come to the conclusion that the DOL at any output level, $Q$, is defined as the ratio of contribution margin (CM) to operating income (OI). Further, your subsequent study of DOL indicates that DOL can be interpreted, at any output level, $Q$, as the percentage change in OI for each percentage change in sales volume. From the stated definition of DOL (as the ratio of CM to OI), show the mathematical derivation of the above conclusion, thereby solidifying your understanding of the concept of DOL.

2. As indicated above in requirement 1, the DOL (at any output level, $Q$) is measured as the ratio of CM to OI. The text also makes reference to the point that the notion of "operating leverage" is a risk-related measure that has something to do with the extent to which fixed costs make up an organization's cost structure. You are puzzled by the juxtaposition of these two comments. Reconcile these comments by showing that DOL can be defined in terms of fixed costs ($F$). Of what interpretive or managerial value is the resulting equation?

# Problems

**[LO 9-1, 9-2, 9-3]**   9-37   **CVP Analysis; Strategy**   Hank's Western Wear is a western hat retailer in Lubbock, Texas. Although Hank's carries numerous styles of western hats, each hat has approximately the same price and invoice (purchase) cost, as shown in the following table. Sales personnel receive large commissions to encourage them to be more aggressive in their sales efforts. Currently, the Lubbock economy is really humming, and sales growth at Hank's has been great. The business is very competitive, however, and Hank, the owner, has relied on his knowledgeable and courteous staff to attract and retain customers who otherwise might go to other western wear stores. Because of the rapid growth in sales, Hank is also finding the management of certain aspects of the business, such as restocking of inventory and hiring and training new salespeople, more difficult.

| | |
|---|---:|
| Sales price | $ 45.00 |
| Per unit variable expenses | |
|    Purchase cost | 25.50 |
|    Sales commissions | 4.50 |
| Total per unit variable costs | $ 30.00 |
| Total annual fixed expenses | |
|    Advertising | $ 22,000 |
|    Rent | 18,000 |
|    Salaries | 185,000 |
| Total fixed expenses | $225,000 |

**Required**

1. Calculate the annual breakeven point, both in terms of units and in terms of sales dollars. (Show calculations.)

2. If Hank's sells 20,000 hats, what is its before-tax income or loss? Support your answer by constructing a contribution income statement.

3. If Hank's sells 32,000 hats, what is its margin of safety (MOS) and margin of safety ratio (MOS%)? Of what interpretive value are these two measures?

4. Hank is considering the elimination of sales commissions completely and increasing salaries by $106,500 annually. What would be the new breakeven point in units? What would be the before-tax income or loss if 20,000 hats are sold with the new salary plan?

5. Identify and discuss the strategic and ethical issues in the decision to eliminate sales commissions (see requirement 4). How do these strategic concerns affect Hank's decision?

[LO 9-2, 9-3, 9-4, 9-6]    9-38 **Profit-Planning: Multiple Products**    Most businesses sell several products at varying prices. The products often have different unit variable costs. Thus, the total profit and the breakeven point depend on the proportions in which the products are sold. Sales mix is the relative contribution of sales among various products sold by a firm. Assume that the sales of Jordan, Inc., for a typical year are as follows:

| Product | Units Sold | Sales Mix |
|---------|-----------|-----------|
| A | 18,000 | 80% |
| B | 4,500 | 20 |
| Total | 22,500 | 100% |

Assume the following unit selling prices and unit variable costs:

| Product | Selling Price per Unit | Variable Cost per Unit | Contribution Margin per Unit |
|---------|------------------------|------------------------|------------------------------|
| A | $ 80 | $ 65 | $15 |
| B | 140 | 100 | 40 |

Fixed costs are $400,000 per year. Assume that the sales mix, expressed in terms of relative physical units sold, is constant as sales volume changes.

**Required**

1. Determine the breakeven point in total units and the breakdown of the total breakeven point into sales (in units) of each of the two products, A and B. Use the weighted-average contribution margin approach.

2. Use the Goal Seek function in Excel to determine the overall breakeven point (in units) for the company.

3. Determine the breakeven point in total units and the breakdown of the total breakeven point into sales (in units) of each of the two products, A and B. Use the "sales basket" approach. (Assume that each "basket" consists of four units of A and one unit of B.)

4. Determine the overall breakeven point in terms of sales dollars based on the weighted-average contribution margin ratio (CMR). (*Hint:* The weights for calculating the weighted-average CMR are based on relative sales dollars, not units, of the two products.) Breakdown the total breakeven point in sales dollars into sales dollars for Product A and sales dollars for Product B.

5. Explain the following statement: "For the multiproduct firm, there is no breakeven point independent of the sales-mix assumption."

6. Assume the original facts except that now fixed costs are expected to be $40,000 higher than originally planned. How does this expected increase in fixed cost affect the breakeven point? How does the percentage change in the breakeven point compare to the percentage increase in fixed costs? What general conclusion might you draw on the basis of these calculations?

[LO 9-1, 9-2, 9-3, 9-5]    9-39 **CVP Analysis**    Horton Manufacturing Inc. (HMI) is suffering from the effects of increased local and global competition for its main product, a lawn mower that is sold in discount stores throughout the United States. The following table shows the results of HMI's operations for 2013.

| | |
|---|---|
| Sales (11,000 units @ $90) | $990,000 |
| Less variable costs (11,000 @ $63) | 693,000 |
| Contribution margin | $297,000 |
| Less fixed costs | 324,000 |
| Operating profit (loss) | ($ 27,000) |

**Required**

1. Compute HMI's breakeven point in both units and dollars. Also, compute the contribution margin ratio.

2. What would be the required sales, in units and in dollars, to generate a pretax profit of $30,000?

3. Assume a combined income tax rate of 40%. What would be the required sales volume, in both units and in dollars, to generate an after-tax profit of $25,000? (Round the number of units up to a whole number.)

4. Prepare a contribution income statement as a check for your calculations in requirement 3 above.

5. The manager believes that a $60,000 increase in advertising would result in a $135,000 increase in annual sales. If the manager is right, what will be the effect on the company's operating profit or loss?

6. Refer to the original data. The vice president in charge of sales feels that a 10% reduction in price in combination with a $50,000 increase in advertising will cause unit sales to increases by 20%. What effect would this strategy have on operating profit (loss)?

7. Refer to the original data. During 2013, HMI saved $5 of unit variable costs per lawn mower by buying from a different manufacturer. However, the cost of changing the plant machinery to accommodate the new part cost an additional $30,000 in fixed cost per year. Was this a wise change? Why or why not?

[LO 9-3, 9-7]  9-40  **CVP Analysis**  The Brenham Hospital's Cardiac Diagnostic Screening Center (CDSC) is contemplating purchasing a blood gases analysis machine at a cost of $800,000. Useful life for this machine is 10 years. The screening center currently serves 4,000 patients per year, 35% of whom need blood gases analysis data as part of their diagnostic tests. The blood samples are presently sent to a private laboratory that charges $125 per sample. In-house variable expenses are estimated to be $75 per sample if CDSC purchases the analysis machine.

**Required**

1. Determine the indifference point between purchasing the machine or using the private laboratory.

2. Use the Goal Seek function in Excel to determine the indifference point calculated in requirement 1 above.

3. Determine how many additional patients would be needed so that CDSC would be indifferent between purchasing the analysis machine and the $125 lab charge.

4. Determine the amount of the private laboratory charge so that CDSC would be indifferent as to purchasing the analysis machine or using the private laboratory, assuming the current service level of 4,000 patients per year.

5. What other considerations are relevant to this decision?

[LO 9-2, 9-3]  9-41  **CVP Analysis in a Professional Service Firm**  Lang and Thomas, a local CPA firm, has been asked to bid on a contract to perform audits for three counties in its home state. Should the firm be awarded the contract, it must hire one new staff member at a salary of $41,000 to handle the additional workload. (Existing staff are fully scheduled.) The managing partner is convinced that obtaining the contract will lead to additional new profit-oriented clients from the respective counties. Expected new work (excluding the three counties) is 800 hours at an average billing rate of $75.00 per hour. Other information follows about the firm's current annual revenues and costs:

| | |
|---|---|
| Firm volume in hours (normal) | 30,750 |
| Fixed costs | $ 470,000 |
| Variable costs | $30.00/hr |

Should the firm win the contract, these audits will require 900 hours of expected work.

**Required**

1. If the managing partner's expectations are correct, what is the lowest bid the firm can submit and still expect to increase annual net income? What would be the hourly billing rate for the county audit job at the breakeven level?

2. If the contract is obtained at a price of $32,000, what is the minimum number of hours of new business in addition to the county work that must be obtained for the firm to break even on total new business? What is the margin of safety (MOS) regarding the county audit job proposal?

[LO 9-1, 9-2, 9-3, 9-5, 9-6]  9-42  **CVP Analysis; Sensitivity Analysis; Multiple Products**  GoGo Juice is a combination gas station and convenience store located at a busy intersection. Recently a national chain opened a similar store only a block away; consequently, sales have decreased for GoGo. In an effort to reclaim lost sales, GoGo has implemented a promotional effort; for every $10 purchase at GoGo, the customer receives a $1 coupon that can be redeemed toward the purchase of gasoline. The average gasoline customer purchases 15 gallons of gasoline at $2.50/gal. The results of an average month, prior to this coupon promotion, are shown below.

Not included in the information presented below is the monthly cost of printing the coupons, which is estimated to be $500. Coupons are issued on the basis of total purchases regardless of whether the purchases are paid in cash or paid by redeeming coupons. Assume that coupons are distributed to customers for 75% of the total sales. Also assume that all coupons distributed are used to purchase gasoline.

| | Sales | Cost of Sales (per unit or % of retail) |
|---|---|---|
| Gasoline | $100,000 | $1.875 per gallon |
| Food and beverages | 60,000 | 60% |
| Other products | 40,000 | 50% |

| | Other Costs |
|---|---|
| Labor—station attendants | $10,000 |
| Labor—supervision | 2,500 |
| Rent, power, supplies, interest, and misc. | 40,000 |
| Depreciation (pumps, computers, counters, fixtures, and building) | 7,500 |

### Required

1. If GoGo Juice implements the promotional coupon effort, calculate the profit (loss) before tax if the sales volume remains constant and the coupons are used to purchase gasoline. Assume the sales mix remains constant. Prepare a contribution income statement to support your answer.

2. Calculate the breakeven sales (in dollars) for GoGo Juice if the promotional effort is implemented. Assume that the product mix remains constant. Use the weighted-average contribution margin ratio approach to generate your answer. (*Hint:* Sales mix for this purpose is defined on the basis of relative sales dollars, not units.)

3. Based on the assumed sales mix (determined on the basis of relative sales dollars, not units), determine the breakdown of total breakeven sales dollars across the three product lines: gas; food and beverages; and other products. (Round your answers to whole dollars.)

4. Disregarding your responses to requirements 1 and 2, assume the weighted-average contribution margin ratio, after implementation of the coupon program, is 35%. Calculate the profit (loss) before tax for GoGo Juice, assuming sales increase 20% due to the new program. Assume that the sales mix in terms of relative sales dollars remains constant.

5. GoGo Juice is considering using sensitivity analysis in combination with cost-volume-profit (CVP) analysis. Discuss the use of sensitivity analysis in conjunction with CVP analysis. Include in your discussion at least three factors that make sensitivity analysis prevalent in decision making.

6. Provide a brief description of the methods that can be used to deal with uncertainty, as discussed in the chapter.

[LO 9-1, 9-2, 9-3, 9-8]   **9-43   CVP Analysis; Commissions; Ethics**   Marston Corporation manufactures pharmaceutical products sold through a network of sales agents in the United States and Canada. The agents are currently paid an 18% commission on sales; that percentage was used when Marston prepared the following budgeted income statement for the fiscal year ending June 30, 2013.

**MARSTON CORPORATION**
**Budgeted Income Statement**
**For the Year Ending June 30, 2013**
**($000 omitted)**

| | | |
|---|---|---|
| Sales | | $26,000 |
| Cost of goods sold | | |
| Variable | $11,700 | |
| Fixed | 2,870 | 14,570 |
| Gross profit | | $11,430 |
| Selling and administrative costs | | |
| Commissions | $ 4,680 | |
| Fixed advertising cost | 750 | |
| Fixed administrative cost | 1,850 | 7,280 |
| Income before interest and taxes | | $ 4,150 |
| Fixed interest cost | | 650 |
| Income before income taxes | | $ 3,500 |
| Income taxes (30%) | | 1,050 |
| Net income | | $ 2,450 |

Since the completion of the income statement, Marston has learned that its sales agents are requiring a 5% increase in their commission rate (to 23%) for the upcoming year. As a result, Marston's president has decided to investigate the possibility of hiring its own sales staff in place of the network of sales agents and has asked Tom Markowitz, Marston's controller, to gather information on the costs associated with this change.

Tom estimates that Marston must hire eight salespeople to cover the current market area, at an average annual payroll cost for each employee of $80,000, including fringe benefits expense. Travel and entertainment expense is expected to total $600,000 for the year, and the annual cost of hiring a sales manager and sales secretary will be $150,000. In addition to their salaries, the eight salespeople will each earn commissions at the rate of 10% of sales. The president believes that Marston also should increase its advertising budget by $500,000 if the eight salespeople are hired.

### Required

1. Determine Marston Corporation's breakeven point in sales dollars for the fiscal year ending June 30, 2013, if the company hires its own sales force and increases its advertising costs. Prove this by constructing a contribution income statement.

2. If Marston continues to sell through its network of sales agents and pays the higher commission rate, determine the estimated volume in sales dollars that would be required to generate the same net income before tax as projected in the budgeted income statement.

3. Describe the general assumptions underlying breakeven analysis that may limit its usefulness.

4. What is the indifference point in sales for the firm to either accept the agents' demand or adopt the proposed change? Which plan is better for the firm? Why?

5. What are the ethical issues, if any, that Tom should consider?

### (CMA Adapted)

[LO 9-2, 9-5]   **9-44   CVP Analysis; Uncertainty/Sensitivity Analysis**   Don Carson and two colleagues are considering opening a law office in a large metropolitan area to make inexpensive legal services available to people who cannot otherwise afford these services. They intend to provide easy access for their clients by having the office open 360 days per year, 16 hours each day from 7:00 a.m. to 11:00 p.m. A lawyer, paralegal, legal secretary, and clerk-receptionist would staff the office for each of the two 8-hour shifts.

To determine the feasibility of the project, Don hired a marketing consultant to assist with market projections. The consultant's results show that if the firm spends $500,000 on advertising the first year, the number of new clients expected each day would have the following probability distribution:

| Number of New Clients per Day | Probability |
|:---:|:---:|
| 10 | 0.10 |
| 20 | 0.30 |
| 40 | 0.40 |
| 60 | 0.20 |

Don and his associates believe these numbers to be reasonable and are prepared to spend the $500,000 on advertising. Other pertinent information about the operation of the office follows.

The only charge to each new client would be $30 for an initial consultation. The firm will accept on a contingency basis all cases that warrant further legal work, with the firm earning 30% of any favorable settlements or judgments. Don estimates that 20% of new client consultations will result in favorable settlements or judgments averaging $15,000 each. He does not expect repeat clients during the first year of operations.

The hourly wages for the staff are projected to be $185 for the lawyer, $50 for the paralegal, $30 for the legal secretary, and $20 for the clerk-receptionist. Fringe benefit expense will be 40% of the wages paid. A total of 400 hours of overtime is expected for the year; this will be divided equally between the legal secretary and the clerk-receptionist positions. Overtime will be paid at one and one-half times the regular wage, and the fringe benefit expense will apply to the full wage.

Don has located 6,000 square feet of suitable office space that rents for $48 per square foot annually. Associated expenses will be $22,000 for property insurance and $32,000 for utilities. The group must purchase malpractice insurance expected to cost $180,000 annually.

The initial investment in office equipment will be $60,000; this equipment has an estimated useful life of four years. The cost of office supplies has been estimated to be $10 per expected new client consultation.

**Required**

1. Determine how many new clients must visit the law office that Don and his colleagues are considering for the venture to break even in the first year of operations. (For purposes of this calculation, treat all labor costs as fixed with respect to number of new clients.)

2. Using the probability information provided by the marketing consultant, determine whether it is feasible for the law office to achieve breakeven operations. Specifically, calculate and interpret the expected value of new clients for year 1, based on the probability data given above.

3. Explain how Don and his associates could use sensitivity analysis to assist in this analysis.

4. Assume, for purposes of this question, that the distribution of new clients is normally distributed around a mean of 3,649.087, with a standard deviation of operating income equal to $5,000,000. Use the NORMDIST function in Excel to respond to the following questions.

    a. What is the probability that the firm will at least break even for year 1 (based on number of new clients added)?

    b. What is the probability that the firm will generate a minimum of $3,235,760 of pretax income on the basis of new clients added in year 1?

    c. Assume now that the mean value of new clients in year 1 is 12,600, with a standard deviation of $5,000,000 (in terms of operating income). Assume, as above, that the distribution of operating income is thought to be normally distributed around the mean value. Given these assumptions, what is the probability of generating operating income of at least $8,235,760 in year 1 based on the number of new clients added?

    d. Assume the facts stated in part (c) above, except that the standard deviation of operating income is $2,500,000. Given these assumptions, what is the probability of generating at least $8,235,760 of operating income in year 1 based on the number of new clients added? How does this result compare to the one obtained above in (c)?

**(CMA Adapted)**

[LO 9-1, 9-2, 9-3]  9-45  **CVP Analysis; Strategy; Critical Success Factors**   Garner Strategy Institute (GSI) presents executive-level training seminars nationally. Eastern University (EU) has approached GSI to present 40 one-week seminars during 2013. This activity level represents the maximum number of seminars that GSI is capable of presenting annually. GSI staff would present the week-long seminars in various cities throughout the United States and Canada.

Terry Garner, GSI's president, is evaluating three financial options for the revenues from Eastern: accept a flat fee for each seminar, receive a percentage of Eastern's profit before tax from the seminars, and form a joint venture to share costs and profits.

Estimated costs for the 2013 seminar schedule follow.

|  | **Garner Strategy Institute** | **Eastern University** |
|---|---|---|
| Fixed costs for the year: | | |
| Salaries and benefits | $200,000 | N/A* |
| Facilities | 48,000 | N/A* |
| Travel and hotel | 0 | $210,000 |
| Other | 70,000 | N/A* |
| Total fixed costs | $318,000 | $210,000 |
| Variable costs per participant: | | |
| Supplies and materials | 0 | $47 |
| Marketing | 0 | 18 |
| Other site costs | 0 | 35 |

*Eastern's fixed costs are excluded because the amounts are not considered relevant for this decision (i.e., they will be incurred whether or not the seminars are presented). Eastern does not include these costs when calculating the profit before tax for the seminars.

EU plans to charge $1,200 per participant for each one-week seminar. It will pay all variable marketing, site costs, and materials costs.

**Required**

1. Assume that the seminars are handled as a joint venture by GSI and EU to pool costs and revenues.

    a. Determine the total number of seminar participants needed to break even on the total costs for this joint venture. Show supporting computations.

b. Assume that the joint venture has an effective income tax rate of 30%. How many seminar participants must the joint venture enroll to earn an after-tax income of $169,400? Show supporting computations.

2. Assume that GSI and EU do not form a joint venture, but that GSI is an independent contractor for EU. EU offers two payment options to GSI: a flat fee of $9,500 for each seminar, or a fee of 40% of EU's profit before tax from the seminars. Compute the minimum number of participants needed for GSI to prefer the 40% fee option over the flat fee. (Round answer up to nearest whole number.) Show supporting computations.

3. What are the strategic and implementation issues for GSI to consider in deciding whether to enter into the joint venture? For Eastern?

**(CMA Adapted)**

[LO 9-1, 9-2, 9-3, 9-5]   9-46 **CVP Analysis; Strategy; Uncertainty**   Computer Graphics (CG) is a small manufacturer of electronic products for computers with graphics capabilities. The company has succeeded by being very innovative in product design. As a spin-off of a large electronics manufacturer (ElecTech), CG management has extensive experience in both marketing and manufacturing in the electronics industry. A long list of equity investors is betting that the firm will really take off because of the growth of specialized graphic software and the increased demand for computers with enhanced graphics capability. A number of market analysts say, however, that the market for the firm's products is somewhat risky, as it is for many high-tech start-ups because of the number of new competitors entering the market, and CG's unproven technology.

CG's main product is a circuit board (CB3668) used in computers with enhanced graphics capabilities. Prices vary depending on the terms of sale and the size of the purchase; the average price for the CB3668 is $100. If the firm is able to take off, it might be able to raise prices, but it also might have to reduce the price because of increased competition. The firm expects to sell 150,000 units in the coming year, and sales are expected to increase in the following years. The future for CG looks very bright indeed, but the company is new and has not developed a strong financial base. Cash flow management is a critical feature of the firm's financial management, and top management must watch cash flow numbers closely.

At present, CG is manufacturing the CB3668 in a plant leased from ElecTech using some equipment purchased from ElecTech. CG manufactures about 70% of the parts in this circuit board.

CG management is considering a significant reengineering project to significantly change the plant and manufacturing process. The project's objective is to increase the number of purchased parts (to about 55%) and to reduce the complexity of the manufacturing process. This would also permit CG to remove some leased equipment and to sell some of the most expensive equipment in the plant.

The per-unit manufacturing costs for 150,000 units of CB3668 follow:

| | Current Manufacturing Costs | Proposed Manufacturing Costs |
|---|---|---|
| Materials and purchased parts | $ 6.00 | $ 15.00 |
| Direct labor | 12.50 | 13.75 |
| Variable overhead | 25.00 | 30.00 |
| Fixed overhead | 40.00 | 20.00 |
| Manufacturing information for CB3668: | | |
|   Number of setups | 3,000 | 2,300 |
|   Batch size | 50 | 50 |
|   Cost per setup | $ 300 | $ 300 |
|   Machine-hours | 88,000 | 55,000 |

General, selling, and administrative costs are $10 variable cost per unit and $1,250,000 fixed; these costs are not expected to differ for either the current or the proposed manufacturing plan.

**Required**

1. Compute the contribution margin per unit and the breakeven point in units for CB3668, both before and after the proposed reengineering project. Assume all setup costs are included in fixed overhead.

2. Determine the number of sales units at which CG would be indifferent as to the current manufacturing plan or the proposed plan.

3.  Use Goal Seek in Excel to confirm your answer to requirement 2 above.

4.  Explain briefly (a) what CG's strategy is, (b) what you think it should be, and (c) why.

5.  Should CG undertake the proposed reengineering plan? Using a spreadsheet, support your answer with sensitivity analysis and a discussion of short-term and long-term considerations.

**[LO 9-1, 9-2, 9-4]    9-47  CVP Analysis; ABC Costing**    Using the information in Problem 9-46, complete the following:

**Required**

1.  Compute the breakeven point in units for both the current and the proposed manufacturing plans, assuming that total setup costs vary with the number of batches and that the batch size is fixed (other than for the last batch, in most cases). Assume that setup costs are the only costs that vary with the number of batches.

2.  As a check on your calculations above in requirement 1, prepare a contribution income statement at the exact breakeven point for both the current plan and the proposed plan.

3.  Compare your solution above to that for Problem 9-46 and interpret the difference.

**[LO 9-1, 9-2, 9-3, 9-5, 9-6]    9-48  Multiple Product CVP Analysis; Sensitivity Analysis**    Headlines Publishing Company (HPC) specializes in international business news publications. Its principal product is *HPC-Monthly*, which is mailed to subscribers the first week of each month. A weekly version, called *HPC-Weekly*, is also available to subscribers over the web at a higher cost. Sixty percent of HPC's subscribers are nondomestic customers. The company experienced a fast growth in subscribers in its first few years of operation, but sales have begun to slow in recent years as new competitors have entered the market. HPC has the following cost structure and sales revenue for its subscription operations on a yearly basis. All costs and all subscription fees are in U.S. dollars.

| | |
|---|---|
| **Fixed Cost** | |
| $306,000 per year | |
| **Variable Costs** | |
| Mailing | $0.60 per issue |
| Commission | 3.00 per subscription |
| Administrative | 1.50 per subscription |
| **Sales Mix Information (based on number of subscriptions)** | |
| HPC-Weekly | 20% |
| HPC-Monthly | 80 |
| **Selling Price** | |
| HPC-Weekly | $47 per subscription |
| HPC-Monthly | 19 per subscription |

**Required**    Use the above data to determine the following:

1.  Contribution margin per unit for weekly and for monthly subscriptions.

2.  Contribution margin ratio for weekly and for monthly subscriptions.

3.  HPC's breakeven point in sales units and sales dollars. Use the weighted-average contribution margin approach and show calculations. (*Hint:* When calculating the weighted-average contribution margin per unit, the weights in the calculation are based on relative units sold. When calculating the weighted-average contribution margin ratio, the weights are based on relative sales dollars, not units, of the individual products.) At the overall breakeven point in units, what is the breakeven amount (in units) for each individual product? What is the breakeven amount (in sales dollars) for each product?

4.  Explain the following quote: "For the multiproduct (or multiservice) firm, there is no breakeven point independent of the sales-mix assumption."

5.  Prepare a data table for the breakeven volume and percentage change in the breakeven point from the base case (requirement 3, above) for 1% absolute changes in sales mix for *HPC-Weekly* over the range 15% to 25%.

6.  What sales level (in total units) at the assumed sales mix is required to reach a before-tax profit of $75,000?

7. Given the assumed sales mix, what sales volume (in total units) is required to generate an after-tax profit, $\pi_A$, equal to 10% of sales dollars? (Show calculations.)

8. What are the critical success factors for HPC? For its domestic subscribers? For its international subscribers?

[LO 9-1, 9-2, 9-3, 9-5] 9-49 **CVP Analysis; Strategy; Sensitivity Analysis; Sustainability**   SolarFlex is a small but very innovative manufacturer of cutting-edge solar panels. A significant portion of the company's success is due to technologically superior product design. SolarFlex has invented a flexible photovoltaic panel that utilizes solar energy much more efficiently than traditional panels. Due to its flexible properties, SolarFlex's panels are also very resistant to weathering and the normal wear and tear associated with traditional panels. This has made SolarFlex panels especially popular among certain green-minded companies and individual consumers. SolarFlex's management team is made up of a number of high-profile executives that have extensive experience in the energy industry. Many equity investors and analysts believe the firm is poised to experience exponential growth in the coming years because of the growing popularity of environmentally friendly products and green engineering. However, a number of key industry experts warn that the market for SolarFlex's new technology is much riskier than what many believe. They point out that the market is always risky for high-tech start-ups, especially those with new and unproven technology.

The regular price for SolarFlex's main product, the Flex 1000 panel, is $600. The firm expects to sell 380,000 units in the coming year, and sales are expected to increase during the following years.

Right now SolarFlex produces its Flex 1000 panel at a small factory it recently purchased and uses some equipment it purchased from a leading industry manufacturer. The rest of the equipment is on lease. Currently, SolarFlex manufactures about 62% of the parts in its photovoltaic panels.

SolarFlex's management team has decided that it must reconfigure its manufacturing process in order to remain competitive. They decide to implement a plan to increase the number of purchased parts (to about 82%) and to reduce the complexity of the manufacturing process. This would allow SolarFlex to remove the leased equipment and to raise some cash by selling some of the purchased equipment currently used in the plant.

The per-unit manufacturing costs for 380,000 units of Flex 1000 follow:

|  | Current Manufacturing Costs | Proposed Manufacturing Costs |
| --- | --- | --- |
| Materials and purchased parts | $180 | $195 |
| Direct labor | 55 | 62.5 |
| Variable overhead | 70 | 80 |
| Fixed overhead | 90 | 55 |

General, selling, and administrative variable costs are $25 per unit and total fixed costs are $2,050,000; these costs are not expected to differ for either the current or the proposed manufacturing plan.

**Required**

1. Compute the contribution margin per unit and the breakeven point in units for the Flex 1000 panel, both before and after the proposed reengineering project.

2. Determine the number of sales units at which SolarFlex would be indifferent between the current manufacturing plan and the proposed plan.

3. Explain briefly (a) SolarFlex's strategy, and (b) if SolarFlex should undertake the proposed reengineering plan. Using a spreadsheet, support your answer with a sensitivity analysis and a discussion of both short-term and long-term considerations. Your sensitivity analysis should show the amount of projected operating income under each plan as volume goes from 0 units to 900,000 units per year, in increments of 100,000 units.

4. Using the results obtained from the sensitivity analysis conducted in (3) above, construct (in a single graph) the profit-volume equation for each of the two decision alternatives.

5. Calculate and interpret the degree of operating leverage (DOL) for each decision alternative at $Q = 400,000$ units and at $Q = 600,000$ units.

[LO 9-1, 9-2, 9-3, 9-5] 9-50 **CVP Analysis; Sustainability; Uncertainty; Decision Tables**   With gasoline prices increasing rapidly in recent years, consumers have moved to high miles-per-gallon (mpg) vehicles, in particular hybrid autos that rely on a battery as well as a gasoline engine for even greater mpg. The new vehicles save money on gas but also reduce the motorist's "carbon footprint" in an environment of global warming. To encourage the purchase of fuel-efficient vehicles such as hybrids, the government may provide incentives, including income-tax credits, which represent dollar-for-dollar reductions in the income tax liability of the individual in the year of purchase.

As both a cost-conscious and an environmentally conscious consumer, you are currently evaluating whether to purchase a hybrid vehicle. Assume that you have narrowed your decision down to two choices: a gasoline-powered vehicle or its equivalent hybrid (e.g., Ford Escape versus Escape hybrid). Relevant information regarding each of these two vehicles is as follows:

| Auto | Cost | Tax Credit | Mpg |
|------|------|-----------|-----|
| Gasoline model | $17,000 | n/a | 23.0 |
| Hybrid model | 19,000 | $500 | 27.0 |

Assume, further, that you plan to keep your auto for four years and that, based on recent experience, will likely drive the car 15,000 miles per year (60,000 miles in total).

### Required

1. Generate a cost function for each decision alternative, where the dependent variable, $Y$, is "lifetime cost" and the independent variable, $X$, is "lifetime miles driven."

2. Calculate the breakeven price for gas (per gallon) between the gasoline-powered model and the hybrid model. (Ignore the time value of money in your calculation.)

3. Prepare a graph for lifetime cost ($Y$) for each of the two autos as a function of price per gallon of gas ($X$), based on 60,000 lifetime miles for each auto. Use the following values of $X$ (price per gallon of gas) to generate each cost function: $2.75, $3.00, $3.25, $3.50, $3.75, $4.00, $4.25, $4.50, $4.75, and $5.00. Properly label each graph, including the points of intersection. What can you conclude based on the graph you prepared?

4. This decision problem is similar to the choice-of-cost structure (variable vs. fixed) discussed in the chapter. Here, the issue is whether to pay an upfront premium (extra fixed cost) for the hybrid model, in exchange for lower variable costs over the life of the vehicle. In a typical CVP model, we were able, at any output level ($X$), to calculate a measure of profit sensitivity, which we called the degree of operating leverage (DOL). In the present context, which involves only costs for each vehicle over a four-year period, we cannot calculate DOL, but we might calculate an analogous measure: the ratio of % change in lifetime cost to % change in miles. Refer to this as a pseudo-DOL. Calculate this pseudo measure for each decision alternative, from a base of 60,000 lifetime miles. To calculate the percentage change figures, use 62,000 miles. What information is conveyed in the two measures you calculated?

5. The preceding calculations give you some of the information you need to make your decision. However, being the inquisitive type, you want more information. For example, you are wondering whether, in the present context (i.e., decision choice), the price of gas (per gallon) has much of an impact on the financial consequence regarding choice of automobile. To explore this issue further you decide to construct a decision table. As pointed out in the text, a decision table discloses combinations of actions (here, choice of automobile), and events (here, lifetime miles driven, and mpg performance of each auto). Prepare a decision table that discloses the breakeven point in gas price for 50,000 miles, 60,000 miles, and 70,000 miles for each of five situations regarding the difference in initial cost (after rebate) between the gasoline-powered model and the hybrid model. Construct your table based on the following initial cost differences between the two: $2,500; $2,000; $1,500 (the base case, based on original data); $1,000; and, $500. (*Hint:* With five different initial cost differences and three alternatives for lifetime miles driven, your decision table should disclose 15 (i.e., $5 \times 3$) breakeven points in terms of price per gallon of gas.) Interpret a couple of points from the decision table you constructed.

6. The following probabilities ($p$) apply to the set of possible events (price of gas, per gallon) listed above in requirement 3: 0.05; 0.05; 0.05; 0.05; 0.15; 0.25; 0.15; 0.10; 0.10; and, 0.05. Your decision consists of one of two actions: buy the hybrid model, or buy the gasoline-powered model. Given this set of probabilities and events, calculate the expected value of the lifetime cost associated with each action (decision choice) under the assumption that lifetime miles driven = 60,000. For each action, the expected value of lifetime cost, $E(a_i)$, is the weighted average of outcomes (lifetime costs), where the weights for each outcome are the outcome's probability.

7. As noted in the preceding analyses, in some plausible scenarios the lifetime cost of each of the two decision alternatives is very close—in some cases they are practically indistinguishable. What non-financial (qualitative) factors and other quantitative factors (beyond those considered above) might be relevant to your decision? Explain.

## Solution to Self-Study Problem

### Breakeven Analysis

1. Contribution margin per unit = $5,595 − $899 − $233 = $4,463
2. Breakeven

   In units:

   $$Q = (F + \pi_B) \div (p - v)$$
   $$Q = \$2,352,000 \div \$4,463 = 527 \text{ units}$$

   In dollars:

   $$p \times Q = \$5,595 \times 527 = \$2,948,565$$

   Or

   $$p \times Q = \frac{F + \pi_B}{(p - v) \div p} = \frac{\$2,352,000}{0.797676} = \$2,948,565$$

3. New level of fixed costs = $2,352,000 (1 + 0.05) = $2,469,600

   Let the required sales volume, in units, equal $Q$. Then,

   $$Q = (F + \pi_B) \div (p - v)$$
   $$Q = (\$2,469,600 + \$200,000) \div \$4,463$$
   $$= 598 \text{ units}$$

4. Incorporate an income tax rate of 22% and desired after-tax profit ($\pi_A$) of $150,000:

   $$Q = \{\$2,352,000 + [\$150,000 \div (1 - 0.22)]\} \div \$4,463$$
   $$= 570 \text{ units}$$

*Please visit **http://www.mhhe.com/blocher6e** to access a narrated, animated tutorial for solving this problem.*

# CHAPTER TEN

# Strategy and the Master Budget

**After studying this chapter, you should be able to . . .**

LO 10-1   Describe the role of budgets in the overall management process

LO 10-2   Discuss the importance of strategy and its role in the master budgeting process

LO 10-3   Outline the budgeting process

LO 10-4   Prepare a master budget and explain the interrelationships among its supporting schedules

LO 10-5   Deal with uncertainty in the budgeting process

LO 10-6   Identify unique characteristics of budgeting for service companies

LO 10-7   Understand alternative approaches to budgeting (viz., zero-base, activity-based, time-driven activity-based, and kaizen budgeting)

LO 10-8   Discuss various behavioral considerations in budgeting

---

If you don't know where you're going, you'll end up somewhere else.

*Yogi Berra*

---

Johnson & Johnson (J&J), one of the largest manufacturers of health care products in the world, started (in 1887) as a small manufacturer of health and well-being-related products. Today, it has more than 118,000 employees and more than 250 operating companies in 60 countries. J&J sells its products in more than 175 countries. Surveys conducted over the years by *Business Week, Forbes, Fortune,* and other business journals repeatedly rank J&J as one of the most innovative and well-managed firms in the world.

How does J&J do it? It relies on a comprehensive formal planning, budgeting, and control system in formulating and implementing strategy, coordinating and monitoring operations, and reviewing and evaluating performance. Every January, each operating unit reviews and revises its 5- and 10-year plans from the previous year and prepares the budget for the coming year as well as a two-year plan. The budgeting process is not completed until the approval of the profit plan in December.

Johnson & Johnson is not unique. Growth and long-term profitability are results of a well-formulated strategy with good planning and implementation of the strategy. Firms need to plan for success. Budgeting is a common tool that organizations use for planning and controlling what they must do to serve their customers and succeed in the marketplace. This chapter provides a detailed discussion of the budgeting process and both the role and limitations of this process in the overall management of an organization.

## Role of Budgets

**LO 10-1**

*Describe the role of budgets in the overall management process.*

A **budget** is a detailed plan for the acquisition and use of financial and other resources over a specified period of time—for example, a year, month, or quarter. A budget includes both financial and nonfinancial aspects of planned operations and projects The budget for a period is both a guideline for operations and a projection of the operating results for the budgeted period. The process of preparing one or more budgets is called **budgeting.**

**How Important Are the Topics of "Budgets" and "Planning Systems" to Management Accounting Practice?**

How important are the topics of short-term planning/budgeting to the current practice of management accounting?

The Institute of Management Accountants (IMA) (**www.imanet.org**) collected survey data from a large sample of corporate accountants to identify important work activities of management accountants and the knowledge, skills, and abilities (KSAs) needed for successful practice in today's workplace. The survey instrument included 41 different topics or areas of management accounting practice. "Short-range planning/budgeting" received an overall importance ranking of 4 (of 41). However, there were differences in the perceived importance of this knowledge area in terms of entry-level practice between manufacturing and service sectors. In terms of the former, "short-range planning/budgeting" was rated 16th out of 41 knowledge areas, while for the service sector the entry-level importance ranking was 4th. Thus, the topic of budgeting is important in general to management accounting practice but is especially important for graduates who intend to secure an entry-level position in the service sector.

How important is the topic of budgeting from an international perspective? Cooper (2006) surveyed over 1,600 members of the Chartered Institute of Management Accountants (**www.cimaglobal.com**) regarding the perceived importance of 37 business topics. Respondents used a four-point scale to rate the importance of each topic (1 = of critical importance to 4 = of little or no importance). The top seven items, in decreasing order of perceived importance, are as follows: budgeting, 1.48; decision making, 1.51; forecasting, 1.54; implementing and controlling plans, 1.67; preparation of accounts, 1.71; information technology and systems, 1.72; and working capital management, 1.73.

One important conclusion from both of the above citations is the increased emphasis on the *planning function* in business organizations of all types.

**Sources:** Z. U. Khan, S. T. Cianciolo, and E. Peacock, "A Plan for Reengineering Management Accounting Education Based on the IMA's Practice Analysis," *Management Accounting Quarterly* (Winter 2000), pp. 1–6; P. Cooper, "Adapting Management Accounting Knowledge Needs to Functional and Economic Change," *Accounting Education: An International Journal* 15, no. 3 (2006), pp. 287–300.

A **budget**
is a detailed plan for the acquisition and use of financial and other resources over a specified period of time—typically a fiscal year.

**Budgeting**
is the process of preparing one or more budgets.

Budget preparations allow management time to anticipate and develop strategies for dealing with problems the organization might face in the coming periods. This extra time enables the organization to minimize the adverse effects that anticipated problems could have on operations. Budgets can help managers identify current and potential bottlenecks in operations. Critical resources can then be acquired to ease any bottlenecks and prevent such bottlenecks from becoming obstacles to attaining budgetary goals.

Budgets also serve as a mechanism through which top management communicates expectations throughout the entire organization. An integrated set of budgets allows each subunit to see how that subunit fits into the overall plan for the period covered by the budget. The manufacturing division knows, for example, that it needs to complete the production of so many units of a given product before a certain date if the marketing division schedules the delivery of that product to customers for various dates.

A budget can also be a motivating device. With the expected activities and operating results clearly delineated in the budget, employees know what is expected of them; this in turn can motivate employees to work to attain the budgeted goals. To enhance the role of the budget as a motivating device, many organizations have employees participate in the budgeting process, thus helping employees embrace the budget as their own.

Completion of a budget for all units of an organization facilitates the coordination of activities across subunits within the organization. For example, budgets show the effect of sales volumes on required purchases of materials, on production levels, the level of administrative support needed, and the level and type of sales/customer service support required for the budgetary period. In short, coordination across functional areas of the organization (sales, production, purchasing, etc.) is an important managerial responsibility. Budgeting is a tool that can be used to help achieve the requisite level of coordination of organizational activities.

Budgets also provide authority to acquire and use resources. The authorization function of budgets is especially important for government and not-for-profit organizations because budgeted amounts, sometimes referred to as *appropriations,* often serve both as approval of activities and as a ceiling for expenditures.

At the end of an operating period, the budget for the period can serve as a basis for assessing performance by reporting and interpreting variances between actual and budgeted spending and operating results. The budget represents the specific results expected of the firm's divisions and employees for the period against which actual performance can be compared.[1]

## Strategy and the Master Budget

**LO 10-2**

*Discuss the importance of strategy and its role in the master budgeting process.*

### Importance of Strategy in Budgeting

An organization's strategy is the path it chooses for attaining its long-term goals and mission. The importance of strategy in planning and budgeting cannot be overemphasized. Too often organizations view the budget for the coming period as a continuation of the budget for the current period with at best a scant attempt to link the budget to their strategy. A budget should start with a careful review and study of the organization's strategic plan. The objective is to build a budget to achieve the organization's strategic goals and objectives. Ignoring the strategic plan can result in not adequately funding the projects and initiatives that are critical to achieving success in this regard.

### Strategic Goals and Long-Term Objectives

**A long-range plan**
identifies required actions over a 5- to 10-year period to attain the firm's strategic goal(s).

**Capital budgeting**
is a process for evaluating, selecting, and financing long-term projects and programs.

**Strategic budget expenditures**
are planned spending on projects and initiatives that lead to long-term value and competitive advantage.

Strategy provides the framework within which a long-range plan for the organization is developed. A **long-range plan** identifies required actions over a 5- to 10-year period to attain the strategic goal(s) specified by the organization.

Long-range planning often entails **capital budgeting,** which is a process for evaluating, selecting, and financing major projects and programs such as purchases of new equipment, construction of a new factory, and addition of new products. Capital budgets are prepared to bring an organization's capabilities into line with the needs of its long-range plan and long-term sales forecast. An organization's capacity is a result of capital investments made in prior budgeting periods.[2]

The strategic goals and objectives of the organization are, ultimately, accomplished through a focused set of initiatives and projects. Put another way, it is this set of initiatives and projects that creates value for the organization. As such, it is important that the organization's annual budgeting process give prominence to a particular class of capital-budgeting expenditures: **strategic budget expenditures,** including those related to *sustainability.* Because such expenditures lead to long-term value creation and competitive advantage, it is important that they be clearly indentified and, to the extent possible, protected.

[1] Analysis of actual versus budgeted results is the essence of the traditional model of financial control and is covered in Chapters 14, 15, and 16.

[2] Capital budgeting is the subject of Chapter 12.

## Short-Term Objectives and the Master Budget

**A master budget**
is an aggregation of all subunit budgets into an integrated plan of action for the budget period.

**Operating budgets**
are plans for all phases of operations and include production, purchasing, personnel, and marketing budgets.

**Financial budgets**
identify sources and uses of funds for budgeted operations and capital expenditures.

Short-term objectives are goals for the coming period, which can be a month, a quarter, a year, or any length of time desired by the organization for planning purposes. These objectives serve as the basis for preparing the **master budget** for a period. Thus, the master budget is an aggregation of all subunit budgets into an integrated plan of action for the budget period. The culmination of the master budgeting process is the production of a set of budgeted (pro forma) financial statements (income statement, balance sheet, and cash flow statement).

The master budget comprises both operating budgets and financial budgets. **Operating budgets** are plans that identify resources needed to implement strategic projects and to carry out budgeted activities such as sales and customer service, production, purchasing, marketing, and research and development, as well as the acquisition of these resources. For a manufacturer, operating budgets include production, purchasing, personnel, and marketing budgets. The set of operating budgets culminates in a budgeted income statement. **Financial budgets** identify sources and uses of funds for the budgeted operations, including strategic projects and initiatives. Financial budgets include the cash budget, budgeted statement of cash flows, the budgeted balance sheet, and the capital expenditures (including strategic expenditures) budget.

Exhibit 10.1 illustrates the relationships among strategic goals, long-term objectives and plans, short-term goals, operations, and controls for an organization. By *controls,* we mean

**EXHIBIT 10.1**

**The Relationships Among Strategic Goals, Long-Term Objectives, Master Budgets, and Operations**

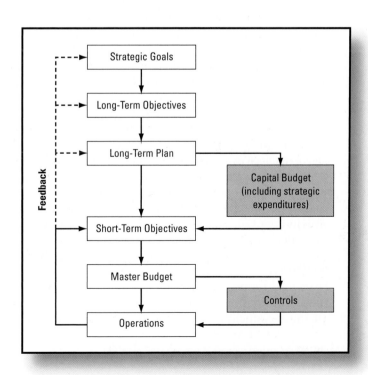

the set of procedures used to monitor the progress of the organization in terms of accomplishing its stated goals and objectives and implementing corrective action(s) if needed.[3]

## The Budgeting Process

**LO 10-3**

*Outline the budgeting process.*

The traditional budgeting process can range from the informal simple processes small firms use that take only days or weeks to complete to elaborate, lengthy procedures large firms or governments employ that span months from start to final approval. The process usually includes the formation of a budget committee; determination of the budget period; specification of budget guidelines (including the preparation of initial budget proposals); budget negotiation, review, and approval; and budget revision.

### Budget Committee

The budget committee oversees all budget matters and often is the highest authority in an organization for all matters related to the budget. The committee sets and approves the overall budget goals for all major business units, coordinates budget preparation, resolves conflicts and differences that may arise during budget preparation, approves the final budget, monitors operations as the year unfolds, and reviews the operating results at the end of the period. A typical budget committee includes the chief executive officer (CEO) or one or more vice presidents, heads of strategic business units, and the chief financial officer (CFO).

### Budget Period

A budget usually is prepared for a set time, most commonly for the fiscal year with subperiod budgets for each of the constituent quarters or months. However, in practice firms seldom have budgets for only one year. The budgets for the years beyond the coming year, however, usually contain only essential operating data. For example, Johnson & Johnson has only skeleton budgets for its 5- and 10-year budgets. Having a long-term budget in parallel with the master budget allows alignment of strategic goals and short-term operations.

### Budget Guidelines

In a traditional budgeting process the budget committee is responsible for providing initial budget guidelines that set the tone for the budget and govern its preparation. The committee issues budget guidelines after careful consideration of the general outlook of the economy and the market; the organization's strategic goals, long-term plan, and strategic projects and the expected operating results of the current period; specific corporate decisions or policies such as mandates for downsizing, reengineering, pollution control, and special promotions; and short-term objectives. Each responsibility center (or subunit) (e.g., department, division, or region) prepares its initial budget proposal based on the budget-preparation guidelines of the organization.

### Negotiation, Review, and Approval

The executives of budget units examine initial budget proposals. The examination includes determining adherence to the budget guidelines and verifying that the budget goals can be reasonably attained and are in line with the goals of the immediately higher organizational unit.

As budget units complete their budgets, the budgets go through successively higher levels of the organization until they reach the top level, at which point the combined unit budgets become the organization's budget. After a final review, the budget committee gives its approval. The CEO then approves the entire budget, which eventually is submitted to the board of directors.

### Revision

Procedures for budget revisions vary among organizations. For organizations that allow budget revisions only under special circumstances, obtaining approval to modify a budget can be difficult. Not all events, however, unfold as predicted in a budget. Strictly

---

[3] The topic of control is addressed in Parts 3 and 4 of the text.

implementing a budget as prescribed, even when the actual events differ significantly from those expected, certainly is not a desirable behavior. In such cases, managers should be encouraged not to rely on the budget as the absolute guideline in operations.

---

The finest plans are often spoiled through the pettiness of those who are supposed to carry them out, since even emperors can do nothing without the support of their soldiers and hangers-on.

*Bertolt Brecht*

---

The strategic role of budgeting for a hypothetical company, Kerry Window Systems, Inc., is given below. This is followed by a detailed example of preparing a master budget for this company.

## Comprehensive Budgeting Example: Kerry Window Systems, Inc. (KWS)

KWS is a manufacturer of aluminum window frames and storm window frames. Kerry's product is sold to a glass manufacturer that inserts the glass panes and then sells the completed windows to retailers. KWS sells an upscale window, made in strong aluminum, which is priced somewhat higher than the vinyl windows sold by competitors. In fact, Kerry's prices are similar to high-end wooden windows. To compete in this portion of the market, KWS stresses manufacturing quality and offers the final customer a comprehensive warranty against defects. Many view KWS as having among the best windows available.

With winter heating costs going up, there has been strong demand for storm windows, especially for older homes. Also, many families who are finding it more difficult to move up to a larger home as they had planned are remodeling or adding rooms to their existing homes, thus increasing demand for Kerry's windows. The result of these economic forces is that KWS is growing very fast. Another factor affecting KWS is that the business is very seasonal, as the building and remodeling season is limited to those months with good weather. KWS's manufacturing process is year-round, but its sales are seasonal. As the company grows, this means negative cash flows at certain times of the year. KWS management is particularly concerned about maintaining its product lines, and this must be done in a business environment in which available credit is hard to find, a consequence of the mortgage loan losses at many financial institutions in recent years. The owners of this business will use a comprehensive budgeting system to facilitate planning and decision making for KWS. A discussion of the five steps the company will take follows.

### The Five Steps of Strategic Decision Making for Kerry Window Systems, Inc.

1. **Determine the strategic issues surrounding the problem.** KWS operates in an industry that is very competitive and seasonal. Cash flow management is a common issue in the industry, particularly for fast-growing companies. Cost-cutting measures would damage the KWS brand at this stage of the company's growth, so the company depends on financing from a variety of sources.

2. **Identify the alternative actions.** The company can raise financing through additional short- or long-term debt, or the sale of stock.

3. **Obtain information and conduct analyses of the alternatives.** The company's stock price has remained steady in the prior several months, reflecting in part the market's overall concern for the industry and uncertainty about the degree of success that will be achieved by KWS's recent growth. The availability for debt is limited by the current poor conditions in the banking industry.

4. **Based on strategy and analysis, choose and implement the desired alternative.** KWS is in a difficult situation regarding cash flow management. The use of the master budget, paying *particular attention* to the cash budget, is crucial for the company's continued success. Forecasting sales and costs, using the tools explained in Chapter 8, is also particularly important for KWS. With accurate budgets, the company thinks it will be able to more effectively project cash needs and have a plan in place for providing the needed financing when necessary. Comprehensive and carefully prepared financial plans and cash budgets are great tools to have in approaching a bank for financing; these tools can help the company make its case for the needed financing.

5. **Provide an ongoing evaluation of the effectiveness of implementation in step 4.** As the company matures and its growth rate slows, and as conditions in the banking industry improve, the focus on financing can shift to other issues, such as advancing and protecting the company's competitive position in the market, improving profitability, and developing effective management and control systems.

In the next section of this chapter we provide an overview of the master budgeting process for a one-year period for KWS.

## Master Budget

**LO 10-4**

*Prepare a master budget and explain the interrelationships among its supporting schedules.*

A master budget is a comprehensive budget for a specific period. It consists of a capital budget and a set of interrelated operating and financial budgets. Exhibit 10.2 delineates the relationships among components of a master budget for a hypothetical manufacturing firm.

**EXHIBIT 10.2**
**The Master Budget for a Manufacturer**

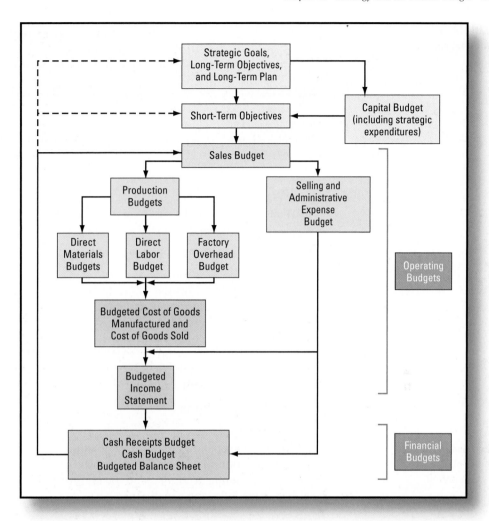

## Sales Budget

A **sales budget** shows forecasted sales, in units and dollars, for an upcoming period.

The **sales budget** shows forecasted sales, in units and dollars, for an upcoming period. Because of its effect on other budgets, the sales budget is sometimes referred to as the cornerstone of the entire master budget.

The starting point in preparing a sales budget is the sales forecast. An inaccurate sales forecast can render the entire budget a futile exercise and, when inaccurate, can impose costly expenses on the firm as well as its suppliers.[4]

Sales forecasting by its nature is, in part, subjective. To reduce subjectivity in forecasts, many firms generate more than one independent sales forecast before preparing the sales budget for the period. The following factors should be considered in sales forecasting:[5]

[4] At the end of its fiscal year on July 29, 2000, Cisco reported $1.2 billion in inventory. The firm reported in early February 2001 that it had inventories of $2.5 billion—an increase of more than 100% in six months, despite the fact that Cisco's sales grew only 25% during that same period. The increase in inventory led Cisco's suppliers to suffer a similar fate. The inventory of Solectron, one of Cisco's major suppliers, went up from $1.8 billion in February 2000 to $4.5 billion at year-end. Flextronics, another supplier to Cisco, reported increases in inventories from $470 million at the end of 1999 to $1.73 billion at the end of 2000. Much of Solectron's and Flextronics' inventory was intended for Cisco. "Cisco's (sales) forecasts were wrong . . . and these guys are feeling its pain." At a cost of 1% per month, the increases in inventory added tremendous financial burdens to these firms and increased Cisco's costs. Fred Vogelstein, "Valley Talk Missed Earnings: The Contagion IS Spreading and Oracle May Be Next," *Fortune*, March 5, 2001, p. 42.

[5] *Time* magazine attributes the use of an advanced data mining system to perform sales forecasting as one reason for Walmart's success. "By analyzing years' worth of sales data—and then cranking in variables such as the weather and school schedules—the [advanced data mining] system could predict the optimal number of cases of Gatorade, in which flavors and sizes, a store in Laredo, Texas, should have on hand on Friday before Labor Day. Then, if the weather forecast suddenly called for temperatures 5° hotter than last year, the delivery truck would automatically show up with more." Bill Saporito, "Can Walmart Get Any Bigger?" *Time*, January 13, 2003, p. 43.

**EXHIBIT 10.3**
Sales Budget

| | | | | |
|---|---|---|---|---|
| **KERRY WINDOW SYSTEMS, INC.** | | | | |
| **Sales Budget** | | | | |
| **For the Quarter Ended June 30, 2013** | | | | |
| | **April** | **May** | **June** | **Quarter** |
| Sales in units | 20,000 | 25,000 | 35,000 | 80,000 |
| Selling price per unit | × $30 | × $30 | × $30 | × $30 |
| **Gross sales revenue** | **$600,000** | **$750,000** | **$1,050,000** | **$2,400,000** |

- Current sales levels and sales trends of the past few years.
- General economic and industry conditions.
- Competitors' actions and operating plans.
- Pricing policies.
- Credit policies.
- Advertising and promotional activities.
- Unfilled back orders.

Exhibit 10.3 illustrates the sales budget for Kerry Window Systems, Inc. for the first quarter of the 2013 fiscal year. Kerry forecasts a selling price of $30 per unit. The next step is for Kerry to prepare its manufacturing budgets for the quarter.

## Manufacturing Budgets

### Production Budget

A **production budget**
shows planned production for
a given period.

A **production budget** shows planned production for a given period. For manufacturers, planned production in a given period depends on budgeted sales, the desired units of finished goods ending inventory, and the units of finished goods beginning inventory, as described in the following equation:

$$\begin{array}{ccc} \text{Budgeted} & \text{Budgeted} & \text{Desired ending} & \text{Beginning} \\ \text{production} = & \text{Sales} & + & \text{inventory} & - & \text{inventory} \\ \text{(in units)} & \text{(in units)} & \text{(in units)} & \text{(in units)} \end{array}$$

To illustrate, Kerry expects to have 5,000 units on hand at the beginning of the quarter, April 1. The firm's policy is to have on hand at the end of each month inventory equal to 30% of the following month's predicted sales. Kerry expects its total sales in May 2013 to be 25,000 units. The desired ending inventory on April 30, therefore, is 7,500 units, as shown in step 1. Step 2 shows that 22,500 units are to be manufactured in April.

Step 1. Determine the desired ending inventory (April 30):

| | |
|---|---|
| Expected sales in May | 25,000 units |
| × Desired percentage of next month's sales to be on hand on April 30 | × 30% |
| Desired ending inventory (April 30) | 7,500 units |

Step 2. Calculate budgeted production for April:

| | |
|---|---|
| Budgeted sales for April | 20,000 units |
| + Desired ending inventory (April 30) | + 7,500 units |
| Total number of units needed in April | 27,500 units |
| − Beginning inventory (April 1) | − 5,000 units |
| Budgeted production for April | 22,500 units |

Exhibit 10.4 shows Kerry's production budget for the first quarter of 2013. This budget is based on the sales budget (Exhibit 10.3) and the expected sales in July (40,000, assumed).

**EXHIBIT 10.4**
**Production Budget**

**KERRY WINDOW SYSTEMS, INC.**
**Production Budget**
**For the Quarter Ended June 30, 2013**

| | April | May | June | Quarter |
|---|---|---|---|---|
| Budgeted sales (units) | 20,000 | 25,000 | 35,000 | 80,000 |
| Add: Desired ending inventory of finished units | 7,500 | 10,500 | 12,000* | 12,000 |
| Total units needed | 27,500 | 35,500 | 47,000 | 92,000 |
| Less: Beginning inventory of finished units | 5,000† | 7,500 | 10,500 | 5,000 |
| **Budgeted production (units)** | **22,500** | **28,000** | **36,500** | **87,000** |

*Assumed, based on anticipated sales in July.
†Assumed.

Most of the quarterly amounts are simply the sums of the appropriate monthly figures. For example, in Exhibit 10.3 the budgeted sales for the quarter, 80,000 units, is the sum of the budgeted sales in April (20,000 units), May (25,000 units), and June (35,000 units). The desired ending inventory of the quarter, however, is the desired ending inventory of June, the end of the quarter, not the sum of the desired ending amount in each of the three months. The amount of beginning inventory for the quarter is the beginning inventory of the first month of the quarter. These two amounts refer to specific times in the quarter, not the amount for the entire period.

Before finalizing a production budget, the production manager reviews the feasibility of the budgeted production in view of the available facilities and other activities scheduled for the same period. In the event that budgeted production exceeds the maximum capacity available, management needs to either revise the budgeted sales level or find alternatives to satisfy the demand. If the available capacity exceeds the budgeted production level, the budget allows management ample time to find alternative uses of the idle capacity or to schedule other activities such as preventive maintenance and trial runs of new production processes.

The sales budget for the quarter shows that Kerry expects increasing sales. When sales vary over periods, management can either change the production level as needed, as Kerry did, or choose to maintain a stable production level and schedule the entire quarter's production evenly at 29,000 units per month.

Maintaining a constant production level enables the firm to keep a constant employment level. However, manufacturing excess units during slow periods builds up inventory that is costly to hold. The new manufacturing environment and increasing use of just-in-time (JIT) production-scheduling methods have led many companies to adjust production activity to changes in anticipated sales volume (and mix). JIT requires a more flexible workforce with broader skills to move the employee to the work center needed for immediate production. As well, JIT involves deploying relatively more temporary and contract laborers to match labor supply with the short-term demand for products and services.

### Direct Materials Usage Budget and Direct Materials Purchases Budget

A **direct materials usage budget** shows the amount and budgeted cost of direct materials required for production.

The information in the production budget becomes the basis for preparing several manufacturing-related budgets. One is the **direct materials usage budget** (Exhibit 10.5), which shows the amount and budgeted cost of direct materials required for production. The last line of the production budget (Exhibit 10.4) shows the number of units of the product that Kerry plans to manufacture in April: 22,500 units. This amount is reflected in line 1 of Exhibit 10.5, Kerry's direct materials usage budget. Assume that the product specification requires 3 pounds of aluminum alloy for each unit of the product, which is entered into line 2 of Exhibit 10.5. Therefore, Kerry needs a total of 67,500 pounds of aluminum (line 3) to produce the 22,500 units budgeted in April. The remainder of the direct materials usage budget (Exhibit 10.5, part B) identifies the cost of direct materials for the budget period, which can be completed only after Kerry prepares the direct materials purchases budget for the month (Exhibit 10.6). Finally, assume that Kerry uses a FIFO cost flow assumption.

**EXHIBIT 10.5**   Direct Materials Usage Budget

| | | | | | | |
|---|---|---|---|---|---|---|
| | | **KERRY WINDOW SYSTEMS, INC.** | | | | |
| | | Direct Materials Usage Budget | | | | |
| | | For the Quarter Ended June 30, 2013 | | | | |
| Line | Item | April | May | June | Quarter | Calculation |
| **A.** | **Production Requirements** | | | | | |
| 1. | Budgeted production | 22,500 | 28,000 | 36,500 | 87,000 | * |
| 2. | Pounds of aluminum alloy for one unit of product | × 3 | × 3 | × 3 | × 3 | |
| 3. | **Total pounds of aluminum alloy needed in production** | 67,500 | 84,000 | 109,500 | 261,000 | |
| **B.** | **Cost of Direct Materials** | | | | | |
| 4. | Pounds of aluminum alloy from beginning inventory | 7,000 | 8,400 | 10,950 | 7,000 | |
| 5. | Cost per pound (FIFO basis) | × $ 2.40 | × $ 2.45 | × $ 2.50 | × $ 2.40 | |
| 6. | Total cost of aluminum alloy beginning inventory | $ 16,800 | $ 20,580 | $ 27,375 | $ 16,800 | (4) × (5) |
| 7. | Total cost of aluminum alloy purchases | + 168,805 | + 216,375 | + 284,310 | + 669,490 | † |
| 8. | Total cost of aluminum alloy available | $185,605 | $236,955 | $311,685 | $686,290 | (6) + (7) |
| 9. | Desired ending inventory of aluminum alloy in units | 8,400 | 10,950 | 10,800‡ | 10,800 | † |
| 10. | Cost per unit (FIFO basis) | × $ 2.45 | × $ 2.50 | × $ 2.60 | × $ 2.60 | † |
| 11. | Aluminum alloy ending inventory | − $ 20,580 | − $ 27,375 | − $ 28,080 | − $ 28,080 | (9) × (10) |
| 12. | **Total cost of aluminum alloy used in production** | $165,025 | $209,580 | $283,605 | $658,210 | (8) − (11) |

* = Exhibit 10.4
† = Exhibit 10.6
‡ = Assumed

**EXHIBIT 10.6**
**Direct Materials Purchases Budget**

| | | KERRY WINDOW SYSTEMS, INC. | | | |
| | | Direct Materials Purchases Budget | | | |
| | | For the Quarter Ended June 30, 2013 | | | |
| Line | Item | April | May | June | Quarter |
|------|------|------:|----:|-----:|--------:|
| 1. | Total direct materials needed in production (from part A of Exhibit 10.5), in lbs. | 67,500 | 84,000 | 109,500 | 261,000 |
| 2. | Add: Desired direct materials ending inventory | + 8,400 + | 10,950 + | 10,800* + | 10,800 |
| 3. | Total direct materials needed | 75,900 | 94,950 | 120,300 | 271,800 |
| 4. | Less: Direct materials beginning inventory | − 7,000 − | 8,400 − | 10,950 − | 7,000 |
| 5. | **Total Direct materials purchases** | **68,900** | **86,550** | **109,350** | **264,800** |
| 6. | Purchase price per pound | × $ 2.45 × | $ 2.50 × | $ 2.60 | |
| 7. | **Total cost of direct materials purchases** | **$168,805** | **$216,375** | **$284,310** | **$669,490†** |

*Assumed, based on estimated production in July.
†$669,490 = $168,805 + $216,375 + $284,310

**A direct materials purchases budget**

shows the physical amount and cost of planned purchases of direct materials.

A **direct materials purchases budget** shows the amount of direct materials, such as raw materials or component parts, to be purchased during the period (in both units and cost) to meet the production and ending materials inventory requirements. A direct materials purchases budget starts with the amount of direct materials needed in production for the current period, which was determined in Line 3 of Exhibit 10.5. Kerry needs 67,500, 84,000, and 109,500 pounds of aluminum alloy to meet the production needs for April, May, and June, respectively.

The company's policy is to have in ending materials inventory each period an amount equal to 10% of the next period's production needs (line 2). Line 3 of Exhibit 10.5 shows that Kerry needs 84,000 pounds of aluminum alloy for the budgeted production in May. Thus, Kerry needs to maintain 8,400 pounds of aluminum alloy on hand at the end of April (10% of 84,000), as shown in line 2 of Exhibit 10.6. (Assume that direct materials needed for production in July = 108,000 lbs.) The sum of lines 1 and 2 (Exhibit 10.6) is the total amount of direct materials needed for April, 75,900 pounds.

Kerry expects to have 7,000 pounds of aluminum alloy on hand at the beginning of April (March's ending inventory). Subtracting the quantity expected to be on hand on April 1 from the total amount needed for April, we see that Kerry must purchase 68,900 pounds in April (line 5 of Exhibit 10.6) to meet the expected needs in April. These steps summarize the calculations in Exhibit 10.6:

| | |
|---|---|
| Total amount of direct materials needed in production during the month | Line 1 |
| + Required direct materials inventory at the end of the month | + Line 2 |
| = Total direct materials needed for the month | = Line 3 |
| − Direct materials on hand at the beginning of the mouth | − Line 4 |
| = Direct materials to be purchased during the month | = Line 5 |

Kerry's purchasing department estimates the cost of aluminum alloy to be $2.45 per pound in April. Thus, the total cost for the 68,900 pounds to be purchased in April is $168,805, as shown in line 7 of Exhibit 10.6.

At the beginning of April, assume that Kerry has on hand 7,000 pounds of aluminum alloy. At a cost of $2.40 per pound, the total cost of the beginning inventory is $16,800 (Exhibit 10.5, line 6). Adding the purchase cost of $168,805 in April (line 7 of Exhibit 10.6), the total cost of the direct materials available in April is $185,605 (line 8 of Exhibit 10.5). Under FIFO, Kerry's cost of ending inventory in April is priced at the most recent purchase price paid, which is $2.45 per pound, or $20,580 (line 11 of Exhibit 10.5). Subtracting the cost of ending inventory, $20,580, from the total cost of direct materials available, $185,605, the total cost of direct materials to be used in April is $165,025 (line 12 of Exhibit 10.5).

Following the same procedure, Kerry completes the purchase budgets for May and June. June's direct materials ending inventory of 10,800 pounds is based on the 36,000 units to be manufactured in July (3 pounds per unit $\times$ 36,000 (assumed units) = 108,000 pounds and 10% $\times$ 108,000 = 10,800 pounds).

### *Direct Labor Budget*

To prepare the direct labor budget, Kerry would take information from its production budget. Each firm needs a requisite number of employees with the required skills to carry out production activity, as budgeted. The direct labor budget enables the personnel department to plan for the hiring and repositioning of employees. A good labor budget helps the firm avoid emergency hiring, prevent labor shortages, and reduce or eliminate the need to lay off workers.

**Manufacturing cells** represent sets of machines, typically laid out in in the form of a semicircle, needed to produce a particular product or part.

Some firms have stable employment policies or labor contracts that prevent them from hiring and laying off employees in direct proportion to their production needs. A direct labor budget enables the firm to identify circumstances when it can either reschedule production or plan temporary employee reassignments to perform other tasks. One manifestation of lean manufacturing is the use of manufacturing cells. **Manufacturing cells** represent sets of machines, typically laid out in the form of a semicircle, needed to produce a particular product or part. Organizations that use cellular manufacturing systems can use the direct labor budget to plan for maintenance, minor repairs, installation, testing, learning and growth, or other activities.

A company usually prepares a direct labor budget for each type (or class) of labor; for instance, Kerry has skilled and semiskilled factory workers. The production process uses 0.5 hour of semiskilled labor and 0.2 hour of skilled labor for each unit. The hourly wages are $8 and $12 for semiskilled and skilled laborers, respectively. Exhibit 10.7 illustrates the direct labor budget for the first quarter of 2013.

### *Factory Overhead Budget*

A factory overhead budget includes all production costs other than direct materials and direct labor. Some firms, such as Kerry, separate factory overhead into variable and fixed costs. Exhibit 10.8 shows Kerry's factory overhead budget for the first quarter of 2013. Note that variable overhead cost is assumed related to the number of direct labor-hours (DLH) worked.

### *Cost of Goods Manufactured and Cost of Goods Sold Budgets*

The cost of goods manufactured budget and the cost of goods sold budget are prepared next. Exhibits 10.4 through 10.8 provide the data needed to complete these budgets for each of the months and for the quarter. Exhibit 10.9 shows a combined cost of goods manufactured and cost of goods sold budget for the first quarter of 2013 for Kerry. The company's finished goods inventory on April 1 shows a per-unit cost of $18.

Information from the cost of goods manufactured budget and the cost of goods sold budget for a period appear in two other budgets for the same period. The budgeted income statement uses the cost of goods sold figure to determine the gross margin for the period, and the balance sheet includes the finished goods ending inventory in total assets. These two pro forma financial statements are discussed later.

## Merchandise Purchases Budget

A merchandise purchases budget **budget** of a firm shows the amount of merchandise it needs to purchase during the period.

A merchandising firm does not have a production budget; instead, it prepares a merchandise purchases budget. A firm's **merchandise purchases budget** shows the amount of merchandise it needs to purchase during the period. The basic format of a merchandise purchases budget is the same as the production budget. Instead of budgeted production as shown in Exhibit 10.4, however, the last items in a merchandise purchases budget are budgeted purchases.

**EXHIBIT 10.7**
**Direct Labor Budget**

| | KERRY WINDOW SYSTEMS, INC.<br>Direct Labor Budget<br>For the Quarter Ended June 30, 2013 | | | |
|---|---|---|---|---|
| Line | April | May | June | Quarter |
| **Semiskilled Labor** | | | | |
| 1. Budgeted production (Exhibit 10.4) | 22,500 | 28,000 | 36,500 | 87,000 |
| 2. Semiskilled direct labor-hours per unit | × 0.5 × | 0.5 × | 0.5 × | 0.5 |
| 3. Total semiskilled direct labor-hours needed | 11,250 | 14,000 | 18,250 | 43,500 |
| 4. Hourly wage rate of semiskilled labor | × $ 8 × | $ 8 × | $ 8 × | $ 8 |
| 5. Total wages for semiskilled labor | $ 90,000 | $112,000 | $146,000 | $348,000 |
| **Skilled Labor** | | | | |
| 6. Budgeted production (Exhibit 10.4) | 22,500 | 28,000 | 36,500 | 87,000 |
| 7. Skilled direct labor-hours per unit | × 0.2 × | 0.2 × | 0.2 × | 0.2 |
| 8. Total skilled direct labor-hours needed | 4,500 | 5,600 | 7,300 | 17,400 |
| 9. Hourly wage for skilled labor | × $12 × | $12 × | $12 × | $12 |
| 10. Total wages for skilled labor | $ 54,000 | $ 67,200 | $ 87,600 | $208,800 |
| 11. **Total cost for direct manufacturing labor  (5 + 10)** | **$144,000** | **$179,200** | **$233,600** | **$556,800** |
| 12. Total direct manufacturing labor-hours (3 + 8) | 15,750 | 19,600 | 25,550 | 60,900 |

**EXHIBIT 10.8**
**Factory Overhead Budget**

| | KERRY WINDOW SYSTEMS, INC.<br>Factory Overhead Budget<br>For the Quarter Ended June 30, 2013 | | | | |
|---|---|---|---|---|---|
| | Rate<br>Per DLH* | April | May | June | Quarter |
| Total direct labor-hours (Exhibit 10.7) | | 15,750 | 19,600 | 25,550 | 60,900 |
| Variable factory overhead: | | | | | |
| Supplies | $0.12 | $ 1,890 | $ 2,352 | $ 3,066 | $ 7,308 |
| Indirect labor | 1.00 | 15,750 | 19,600 | 25,550 | 60,900 |
| Fringe benefits | 3.00 | 47,250 | 58,800 | 76,650 | 182,700 |
| Power | 0.20 | 3,150 | 3,920 | 5,110 | 12,180 |
| Maintenance | 0.08 | 1,260 | 1,568 | 2,044 | 4,872 |
| **Total variable factory overhead** | **$4.40** | **$ 69,300** | **$ 86,240** | **$112,420** | **$ 267,960** |
| Fixed factory overhead: | | | | | |
| Depreciation | | $ 30,000 | $ 30,000 | $ 40,000[†] | $ 100,000 |
| Factory insurance | | 2,500 | 2,500 | 2,500 | 7,500 |
| Property taxes | | 900 | 900 | 900 | 2,700 |
| Supervision | | 8,900 | 8,900 | 8,900 | 26,700 |
| Power | | 1,250 | 1,250 | 1,250 | 3,750 |
| Maintenance | | 750 | 750 | 750 | 2,250 |
| **Total fixed factory overhead** | | **$ 44,300** | **$ 44,300** | **$ 54,300** | **$ 142,900** |
| **Total factory overhead** | | **$113,600** | **$ 130,540** | **$166,720** | **$ 410,860** |
| Less: Depreciation | | 30,000 | 30,000 | 40,000 | 100,000 |
| **Cash disbursements for factory overhead** | | **$ 83,600** | **$ 100,540** | **$126,720** | **$ 310,860** |

*Direct labor-hour.
[†]Kerry purchased equipment in January for $200,000, to be delivered and installed in May (see item 5 on page 368). Exhibit 10.8 includes one month of depreciation expense for this asset (June).

**EXHIBIT 10.9**
Cost of Goods Manufactured
and Cost of Goods Sold Budget

**KERRY WINDOW SYSTEMS, INC.**
**Cost of Goods Manufactured and Cost of Goods Sold Budget**
**For the Quarter Ended June 30, 2013**

|  | April | May | June | Quarter |
|---|---|---|---|---|
| Direct materials (Line 12, Exhibit 10.5) | $165,025 | $209,580 | $283,605 | $ 658,210 |
| Direct labor (Line 11, Exhibit 10.7) | 144,000 | 179,200 | 233,600 | 556,800 |
| Total factory overhead (Exhibit 10.8) | 133,600 | 130,540 | 166,720 | 410,860 |
| Total cost of goods manufactured | $422,625 | $519,320 | $683,925 | $1,625,870 |
| Finished goods beginning inventory | 90,000* | 140,875 | 194,745 | 90,000 |
| Total cost of goods available for sale | $512,625 | $660,195 | $878,670 | $1,715,870 |
| Finished goods ending inventory† | 140,875 | 194,745 | 224,852 | 224,852 |
| **Cost of goods sold** | **$371,750** | **$465,450** | **$653,818** | **$1,491,018** |

*Finished goods beginning inventory, April 1, 5,000 units (Exhibit 10.4) at $18 per unit.
†Computations for cost per unit and finished goods ending inventory (FIFO basis):

| Cost of goods manufactured | $422,625 | $519,320 | $683,925 |
|---|---|---|---|
| Budgeted production (Exhibit 10.4, last line) | ÷   22,500 | ÷   28,000 | ÷   36,500 |
| Manufacturing cost per unit | $18.7833 | $18.5471 | $18.7377 |
| Desired ending inventory (Exhibit 10.4, line 2) | ×   7,500 | ×   10,500 | ×   12,000 |
| Finished goods ending inventory, FIFO basis | $140,875 | $194,745 | $224,852 |

## Selling and Administrative Expense Budget

The selling and administrative expense budget is then prepared. As shown in Exhibit 10.10, Kerry's selling and administrative expense budget for the first quarter of 2013 includes all the planned expenditures for selling and administrative expenses. This budget serves as a guideline for selling and administrative activities during the budget period.

Many selling and administrative expenditures are the result of sales and marketing activities and programs. Firms are known to reduce or eliminate selling and administrative expenses to increase operating income for the period. For example, in an attempt to increase operating income and to show good control of operating expenses, the manager of a retail business proposes to decrease customer service expenditures by $15 million from $20 million to $5 million. Although reduced customer services are likely to lead to decreases in sales, the budgeted total saving in expenditures exceeds the budgeted decrease in earnings for the year and the firm expects its budgeted operating income for the year to increase by $11 million as a result. Decreases in customer services, however, will likely have negative effects on the firm's reputation as well as its future sales.

Note that we have subdivided the total selling and administrative expense budget into *total expenses* (for income statement purposes) and *total cash expenses* (for preparing the cash budget for the period). Noncash expenses for Kerry include estimated bad debts expense (assumed equal to 5% of sales made on open account) plus depreciation expense. Thus, in April total budgeted noncash expenses amount to $36,000, as follows: estimated bad debts expense, $9,000; depreciation expense—selling, $20,000; and, depreciation expense—administrative, $7,000.

## Cash Receipts (Collections) Budget

The cash receipts budget provides details regarding anticipated collections of cash from operations for an upcoming period. Cash receipts from investing and financing activities are shown elsewhere on the cash budget. Kerry has three different sources of cash receipts from operations: (1) cash sales, (2) bank credit card sales, and (3) collection of credit sales (i.e., sales made by the company on "open account").

Past history indicates that, on average, cash plus bank credit card sales for Kerry represent 70% of gross sales revenue; the balance each month is credit sales to customers on open account. Kerry estimates that the breakdown between cash and bank credit card

**EXHIBIT 10.10**   Selling and Administrative Expense Budget

| KERRY WINDOW SYSTEMS, INC.<br>Selling and Administrative Expense Budget<br>For the Quarter Ended June 30, 2013 | | | | |
| --- | --- | --- | --- | --- |
| | **April** | **May** | **June** | **Quarter** |
| **Selling expenses** | | | | |
| Variable selling expenses: | | | | |
| Sales commissions (given) | $ 30,000 | $ 37,500 | $ 52,500 | $120,000 |
| Delivery expenses (given) | 2,000 | 2,500 | 3,500 | 8,000 |
| Bad debts expense (allowance method)* | 9,000 | 11,250 | 15,750 | 36,000 |
| Total variable selling expenses | $ 41,000 | $ 51,250 | $ 71,750 | $164,000 |
| Fixed selling expenses: | | | | |
| Sales salaries (given) | $ 8,000 | $ 8,000 | $ 8,000 | $ 24,000 |
| Advertising (given) | 50,000 | 50,000 | 50,000 | 150,000 |
| Delivery expenses (given) | 6,000 | 6,000 | 6,000 | 18,000 |
| Depreciation (given) | 20,000 | 20,000 | 20,000 | 60,000 |
| Total fixed selling expenses | $ 84,000 | $ 84,000 | $ 84,000 | $252,000 |
| Total selling expenses | $125,000 | $135,250 | $155,750 | $416,000 |
| **Administrative expenses (all fixed)** | | | | |
| Administrative salaries | $ 25,000 | $ 25,000 | $ 25,000 | $ 75,000 |
| Accounting and data processing | 12,000 | 12,000 | 12,000 | 36,000 |
| Depreciation | 7,000 | 7,000 | 7,000 | 21,000 |
| Other administrative expenses | 6,000 | 6,000 | 6,000 | 18,000 |
| Total administrative expenses | $ 50,000 | $ 50,000 | $ 50,000 | $150,000 |
| **Total selling and administrative expenses** | **$175,000** | **$185,250** | **$205,750** | **$566,000** |
| Less: noncash expenses (bad debts expense + depreciation) | $ 36,000 | $ 38,250 | $ 42,750 | $117,000 |
| **Cash disbursements for selling and administrative expenses** | **$139,000** | **$147,000** | **$163,000** | **$449,000** |

*Estimated bad debts = gross sales in a month × 30% × 5%:

| | | | | |
| --- | --- | --- | --- | --- |
| Gross sales revenue (Exhibit 10.3) | $600,000 | $750,000 | $1,050,000 | $2,400,000 |
| % credit sales in a month | 30% | 30% | 30% | 30% |
| Estimated % of credit sales that are uncollectible | 5% | 5% | 5% | 5% |
| Estimated bad debts expense | $9,000 | $11,250 | $15,750 | $36,000 |

sales is 60% cash/40% credit card. The bank charges a 3% service fee to process credit card sales. In the cash receipts budget, estimated collections of bank credit card sales are reflected *net* of this service fee.

In terms of credit sales, Kerry e-mails invoices to its customers on the first of each month. Credit terms are 2/10, n/eom. This means that customers who pay within 10 days receive a 2% discount; otherwise, the account is due on or before the end of the month (eom). *(Discounts for early payment of credit sales are recorded on the income statement as deductions from gross sales to arrive at net sales.)* These customers can access their accounts anytime on Kerry's website to find out the status of their accounts. Eighty percent of these customers pay within the month; of these, 60% pay within the discount period. Seventy-five percent of the remaining balances at the end of the month pay within the following month. The remaining accounts are likely bad debts. (As indicated previously, the company uses the allowance method to account for bad debts expense. *Bad debts expense is included on the income statement as a noncash component of variable selling expenses.*) Most payments are made via electronic transfer of funds.

Gross sales revenue was $400,000 in February and $450,000 in March of 2013.

Given the preceding information, and the gross sales revenues reported in Exhibit 10.3, the accountant for Kerry can now prepare the cash receipts budget for the quarter ended

June 30, 2013 (see Exhibit 10.11). Information from the last line of this budget is then incorporated into the cash budget for the quarter.

## Cash Budget

Having adequate cash on hand at all times is crucial for an organization's survival and growth. This applies to for-profit enterprises, government entities, and not-for-profit organizations (schools, hospitals, etc.). A **cash budget** brings together the cash effects of all budgeted activities. A cash budget depicts the organization's cash position during the budget period. By preparing a cash budget, management can take steps to ensure having sufficient cash on hand to carry out the planned activities, allow sufficient time to arrange for additional financing that may be needed during the budget period (and thus avoid high costs of emergency borrowing), and plan for investments of excess cash on hand to earn the highest possible return.

A cash budget includes all items that affect cash flows. The cash budget pulls data from almost all parts of the master budget. Preparing a cash budget requires a careful review of all budgets to identify all revenues, expenses, and other transactions that affect cash. A cash budget generally includes three major sections: (1) net cash flows from *operating activities;* (2) net cash flows from *investing activities;* and (3) net cash flows from *financing activities.*

The cash budget can thus be prepared to parallel the statement of cash flows that is prepared for financial-reporting purposes. This statement (and related budget) provides information about how the company generated cash (so the reader can judge whether those sources are predictable or transitory), and what the company did with the cash it had at its disposal. In short, the cash budget (and related statement of cash flows) provides the user with information regarding the cash-management ability of the company.

Although not represented in the present example, it is possible to secure a cash discount on payment of accounts payable within a discount period. (This opportunity mirrors the allowance of a cash discount on collection of accounts receivable within a discount period, as reflected in Exhibit 10.11.) From a cash-management perspective, it is

**EXHIBIT 10.11   Cash Receipts Budget—Operating Activities**

| KERRY WINDOW SYSTEMS, INC. Cash Receipts Budget—Operating Activities For the Quarter Ended June 30, 2013 | | | | | |
|---|---|---|---|---|---|
| **Sales Data** | **March** | **April** | **May** | **June** | **Quarter** |
| Cash and bank credit card sales (70% of total sales) | $315,000 | $420,000 | $525,000 | $ 735,000 | $1,680,000 |
| Credit sales (30% of total sales) | 135,000 | 180,000 | 225,000 | 315,000 | 720,000 |
| Gross sales revenue (Exhibit 10.3) | $450,000 | $600,000 | $750,000 | $1,050,000 | $2,400,000 |
| | | | | | |
| Cash received from cash sales | | | | | |
| (60% of cash plus bank credit card sales) | | $252,000 | $315,000 | $441,000 | $1,008,000 |
| Cash received from bank credit card sales | | | | | |
| (40% of cash and bank credit card sales × 97%) | | 162,960 | 203,700 | 285,180 | 651,840 |
| Collections of accounts receivable: | | | | | |
| From credit sales the month before this month: | | | | | |
| Within cash discount period | | | | | |
| (Prior month's credit sales × 80% × 60% × 98%) | | 63,504 | 84,672 | 105,840 | 254,016 |
| After the cash discount period | | | | | |
| (Prior month's credit sales × 80% × 40%) | | 43,200 | 57,600 | 72,000 | 172,800 |
| From credit sales two months before this month | | | | | |
| (75% of 20% of credit sales two months prior) | | 18,000 | 20,250 | 27,000 | 65,250 |
| **Total cash receipts, net of bank service charge (3%)** | | **$539,664** | **$681,222** | **$931,020** | **$2,151,906** |

important to take advantage of such early payment discounts. The opportunity cost of not doing this is:

[Discount %/(1 − Discount %)] × [365/no. of extra days allowed if discount is not taken]

For example, if purchase terms are 2/10, net 30, then the opportunity cost of not taking the cash discount is approximately 37.25%.

Cash flows from operating activities reflect cash flows from the company's transactions and events related to its main operating activity. Cash flows from investing activities provide information regarding the net cash effect of acquisitions and divestitures of investments and long-term assets. Cash flows from financing activities provide information regarding the net effect of issuances of, payments toward, and retirements of borrowings (debt) and equity.

Exhibit 10.12 shows the cash budget of Kerry for the quarter ended June 30, 2013. In addition to reviewing the information illustrated in Exhibits 10.3 through 10.11 to identify

**EXHIBIT 10.12   Cash Budget**

**KERRY WINDOW SYSTEMS, INC.**
**Cash Budget**
**For the Quarter Ended June 30, 2013**

| | April | May | June | Quarter |
|---|---|---|---|---|
| **Cash balance, beginning of period** | $ 75,000 | $ 84,781 | $ 91,916 | $ 75,000 |
| **Cash flow from operations:** | | | | |
| Operating cash inflows (cash receipts from cash sales, credit card sales, and collections of accounts receivable, Exhibit 10.11) | $539,664 | $681,222 | $ 931,020 | $2,151,906 |
| Operating cash outflows: | | | | |
| Purchases of direct materials: | | | | |
| From current month purchases (60% of current month's purchases, Exhibit 10.6) | $101,283 | $129,825 | $ 170,586 | $ 401,694 |
| From purchases made last month (40% of last month's purchases, Exhibit 10.6) | 62,000* | 67,522 | 86,550 | 216,072 |
| Total cash payments for direct materials purchases | $163,283 | $197,347 | $ 257,136 | $ 617,766 |
| Direct labor (Exhibit 10.7, line 11) | 144,000 | 179,200 | 233,600 | 556,800 |
| Factory overhead (Exhibit 10.8, last line) | 83,600 | 100,540 | 126,720 | 310,860 |
| Selling and administrative expenses (Exhibit 10.10, last line) | 139,000 | 147,000 | 163,000 | 449,000 |
| Total operating cash outflows | $529,883 | $624,087 | $ 780,456 | $1,934,426 |
| Net cash flow from operations | $ 9,781 | $ 57,135 | $ 150,564 | $ 217,480 |
| | | | | |
| **Investing activities:** | | | | |
| Equipment purchase | $ -0- | $200,000 | $ -0- | $ 200,000 |
| Cash balance before financing activities | $ 84,781 | $(58,084) | $ 242,480 | $ 92,480 |
| | | | | |
| **Financing activities:** | | | | |
| Bank borrowing beginning of month | | $150,000 | | $ 150,000 |
| Payments (i.e., cash outflows): | | | | |
| Repayment of principal (@ end of month) | | | (150,000) | (150,000) |
| Interest (paid end of month; 1% per month) | | | (1,500) | (1,500) |
| Net effect of financing activities | $     0 | $150,000 | $(151,500) | $ (1,500) |
| **Ending cash balance** | $ 84,781 | $ 91,916 | $ 90,980 | $ 90,980 |

*March purchases = $155,000 (assumed)

items that involve either cash inflow or cash outflow, management must gather additional information about the firm's operating characteristics and policies to complete the cash budget. The following are relevant operating characteristics and policies of Kerry that affect the availability of cash or the requirement to expend cash during the budget period:

1. The firm expects to have $75,000 cash on hand on April 1 and has a requirement of maintaining a minimum cash balance of $50,000 each month.
2. Kerry purchases direct materials with a term of n/30. The firm pays 60% of its purchases in the month of purchase and the remainder in the following month.
3. All expenses and wages are paid as incurred.
4. The firm purchased $155,000 of direct materials in March.
5. Equipment purchased in January for $200,000 will be delivered in May, terms COD. Depreciation deductions will commence in June.
6. The firm has a revolving 30-day account at 1% per month with the First National Bank for all temporary financing needs. The account must be drawn in increments of $50,000 with repayment occurring no sooner than 30 days. All borrowings take place at the beginning of the month while repayments (and interest payments) occur at the end of the month.

## Budgeted Income Statement

The budgeted (pro forma) income statement describes the expected net income for an upcoming period. In the event that the budgeted income for the period falls short of the prespecified goal, management can investigate, during the budget-negotiation process, actions to improve operating results.

Once the budgeted income statement has been approved, it can be used as the benchmark against which the performance of the period is evaluated. Exhibits 10.3, 10.9, and 10.10 provide information needed to prepare the budgeted income statement for the period (Exhibit 10.13).

**EXHIBIT 10.13**
**Budgeted Income Statement**

| KERRY WINDOW SYSTEMS, INC. Budgeted Income Statement For the Quarter Ended June 30, 2013 | | | | |
|---|---|---|---|---|
| | **April** | **May** | **June** | **Quarter** |
| Gross sales revenue (Exhibit 10.3) | $600,000 | $750,000 | $1,050,000 | $2,400,000 |
| Less: Cash discounts for early payment of credit sales (last month's credit sales × 80% × 60% × 2%) | $ 1,296 | $ 1,728 | $ 2,160 | $ 5,184 |
| Bank service charge (3% of bank credit-card sales) | $ 5,040 | $ 6,300 | $ 8,820 | $ 20,160 |
| Net sales | $593,664 | $741,972 | $1,039,020 | $2,374,656 |
| Less: Cost of goods sold (Exhibit 10.9) | 371,750 | 465,450 | 653,818 | 1,491,018 |
| Gross profit | $221,914 | $276,522 | $ 385,202 | $ 883,638 |
| Selling and administrative expenses (Exhibit 10.10) | 175,000 | 185,250 | 205,750 | 566,000 |
| Net operating income | $ 46,914 | $ 91,272 | $ 179,452 | $ 317,638 |
| Less: Interest expense (Exhibit 10.12) | 0 | 0 | 1,500 | 1,500 |
| Income before income taxes | $ 46,914 | $ 91,272 | $ 177,952 | $ 316,138 |
| Less: Income taxes (@30%) | 14,074 | 27,382 | 53,386 | 94,841 |
| **Net income** | **$ 32,840** | **$ 63,890** | **$ 124,566** | **$ 221,297** |

## Budgeted Balance Sheet

The last step in a budget-preparation cycle usually is to prepare the budgeted (pro forma) balance sheet. The starting point in preparing a budgeted balance sheet is the expected financial position at the beginning of the budget period. Exhibit 10.14 presents the expected balance sheet as of March 31, 2013, the beginning of the current budget period.

The budgeted balance sheet incorporates the effects of all operations and cash flows during the budget period and shows projected balances at the end of the budget period. Exhibit 10.15 shows the budgeted balance sheet at the end of the budget period. For example, the amount of cash in Exhibit 10.15, $90,980, is taken from the ending cash balance of the cash budget for the period (Exhibit 10.12). The ending balance of direct materials, $28,080, is from Exhibit 10.5. The gross amount for Buildings and Equipment, $969,750, is the sum of the beginning balance in the Building and Equipment account reported in Exhibit 10.14, $769,750, and the purchase of new equipment during the budget period, $200,000, as shown in the cash budget for May and, again, for the quarter (Exhibit 10.12).

**EXHIBIT 10.14**
**Beginning-of-Budget-Period Balance Sheet**

| KERRY WINDOW SYSTEMS, INC. | | | |
|---|---|---|---|
| Balance Sheet | | | |
| March 31, 2013 | | | |
| **Assets** | | | |
| Current assets: | | | |
| Cash (Exhibit 10.12) | | $ 75,000 | |
| Net accounts receivable* | | 146,250 | |
| Direct materials inventory (Exhibit 10.5) | | 16,800 | |
| Finished goods inventory (Exhibit 10.9) | | 90,000 | |
| Total current assets | | | $328,050 |
| Property, plant and equipment: | | | |
| Land (given) | | $ 40,000 | |
| Buildings and equipment, gross | $769,750 | | |
| Less: Accumulated depreciation | 168,000 | 601,750 | |
| Total property, plant, and equipment | | | 641,750 |
| Total assets | | | $969,800 |
| **Liabilities and Stockholders' Equity** | | | |
| Current liabilities: | | | |
| Accounts payable (Exhibit 10.12) | | $ 62,000 | |
| Income taxes payable | | 0 | |
| Total liabilities | | | $ 62,000 |
| Stockholders' equity: | | | |
| Common stock (given) | | $303,300 | |
| Retained earnings (given) | | 604,500 | |
| Total stockholders' equity | | | 907,800 |
| Total liabilities and stockholders' equity | | | $969,800 |

**\*Net accounts receivable, March 31, 2013:**

| | | |
|---|---|---|
| Gross accounts receivable: | | |
| From credit sales made in February (20% [a]) | $ 24,000 | |
| From credit sales made in March (100% of March's credit sales) | 135,000 | |
| Gross accounts receivable, end of March | | $159,000 |
| Less: Allowance for doubtful accounts: | | |
| For February's credit sales (5%) | $6,000 | |
| For March's credit sales (5%) | 6,750 | 12,750 |
| Net accounts receivable, March 31, 2013 | | $146,250 |

[a] That is, a total of 20% of each month's credit sales will be collected or written off in the second month following the month of sale.

**EXHIBIT 10.15**
Budgeted Balance Sheet,
June 30, 2013

| KERRY WINDOW SYSTEMS, INC. Budgeted Balance Sheet June 30, 2013 | | | |
|---|---|---|---|
| **Assets** | | | |
| Current assets: | | | |
| Cash (Exhibit 10.12) | | $ 90,980 | |
| Net accounts receivable[a] | | 333,000 | |
| Direct materials inventory (Exhibit 10.5, line 11) | | 28,080 | |
| Finished goods inventory (Exhibit 10.9) | | 224,852 | |
| Total current assets | | | $ 676,912 |
| Property, plant, and equipment: | | | |
| Land (Exhibit 10.14) | | $ 40,000 | |
| Buildings and equipment, gross | $969,750 | | |
| Less: Accumulated depreciation[b] | 349,000 | 620,750 | |
| Total property, plant and equipment | | | 660,750 |
| Total assets | | | **$1,337,662** |
| | | | |
| **Liabilities and Stockholders' Equity** | | | |
| Current liabilities: | | | |
| Accounts payable[c] | | $113,724 | |
| Income tax payable (Exhibit 10.13) | | 94,841 | |
| Total liabilities | | | $ 208,565 |
| Stockholders' equity: | | | |
| Common stock (Exhibit 10.14) | | $303,300 | |
| Retained earnings[d] | | 825,797 | |
| Total stockholders' equity | | | 1,129,097 |
| Total liabilities and stockholders' equity | | | **$1,337,662** |

[a] Ending balance of accounts receivable, net of allowance for bad debts:

| | | |
|---|---|---|
| Gross A/R: | | |
| From sales made in May (20%) | $ 45,000 | |
| From sales made in June (100%) | 315,000 | $360,000 |
| Less: Allowance for doubtful accounts: | | |
| From May's sales (5%) | $ 11,250 | |
| From June's sales (5%) | 15,750 | 27,000 |
| Net accounts receivable, June 30, 2013 | | $333,000 |

[b] Accumulated depreciation, beginning of quarter (Exhibit 10.14)

| | | |
|---|---|---|
| | | $168,000 |
| Plus: Depreciation expense for the quarter ending June 30, 2013: | | |
| Factory (Exhibit 10.8) | $ 100,000 | |
| Selling (Exhibit 10.10) | 60,000 | |
| Administrative (Exhibit 10.10) | 21,000 | 181,000 |
| Accumulated depreciation, June 30, 2013 | | $349,000 |

[c] End-of-quarter balance in accounts payable:

| | |
|---|---|
| Direct materials purchases in June (Exhibit 10.6) | $284,310 |
| Payments made in month of purchase (June), 60% | 170,586 |
| Accounts payable balance, June 30, 2013 | $113,724 |

[d] End-of-quarter balance in retained earnings:

| | |
|---|---|
| Beginning-of-quarter balance (Exhibit 10.14) | $604,500 |
| Plus: net income for quarter (Exhibit 10.13) | 221,297 |
| Retained earnings balance, June 30, 2013 | $825,797 |

## Uncertainty and the Budgeting Process

**LO 10-5**

*Deal with uncertainty in the budgeting process.*

The preceding section provides an overview of the master budgeting process, which culminates in a set of pro forma (i.e., budgeted) financial statements. As you can imagine, the validity of these statements is jointly affected by the validity of the underlying budgeting model and by the accuracy of the forecasted data going into the component budgets. Such data, because they are forecasts, are subject to various levels of uncertainty. Spreadsheet software (such as Excel) can be used to deal with uncertainty associated with the budget-preparation process. This software can be used to perform *what-if analysis, sensitivity analysis,* and *scenario analysis.* Each of these techniques is a way for managers to better understand and therefore deal with uncertainty and the budgeting process.

## What-If Analysis

The intent of what-if analysis is to examine how a change in one or more budgetary items affects another variable or budget of interest. For example, management of Kerry might use Excel to address the following questions:

- What would be the resulting impact on cash flow, or operating income, if management were able to increase product selling price by 8% while holding other factors constant?
- What would be the net effect on operating profit if Kerry were to engage in a one-year product-promotion campaign that would cost $75,000 and that would increase sales by 20%?
- Assume Kerry can invest in a new manufacturing technology. If direct labor costs, as a result of this investment, were to decrease by 8%, what would be the net impact on the company's short-term operating income?
- What would be the impact on operating income of a 7% increase in raw material costs accompanied by a commensurate percentage increase in selling price per unit?
- What would be the cash flow impact of investing in a program to better assess the financial wherewithal of potential customers if this investment reduced estimated bad debts expense by 50%?

An example of conducting a what-if analysis for Kerry is presented in Exhibit 10.16.[6] In this simple example the analysis responds to the following question: What would be the impact on the production schedule for each month of the quarter if the targeted ending inventory level were decreased from 30% to 20% of the following month's projected sales? As can be seen, budgeted production levels for Kerry are relatively insensitive to changes in the targeted level of ending inventory. A similar analysis could be performed in terms of other budgeted items of interest, for example, the effect of the proposed change of targeted ending finished goods inventory on budgeted operating income or on budgeted cash flow from operations.

## Sensitivity Analysis

As you might imagine, the pro forma financial statements that are produced as part of the master budgeting process assume a given operating strategy and scenario (state of the economy, level of product demand, achieved selling prices, etc.). Software, such as Excel, can be used to provide information about the sensitivity of the pro forma financial statements to various assumptions made in preparing the component budgets. In fact, one can think of sensitivity analysis as a tool (or method) that budget planners use to determine the extent to which a change in the forecasted value of one or more budgetary

**EXHIBIT 10.16**
**Results of What-If Analysis**

| Decision Variable: Targeted Ending Inventory, Finished Goods | | | | |
|---|---|---|---|---|
| | | Budgeted Production (units) (Exhibit 10.4) | | |
| | | April | May | June |
| Original assumption | 30% | 22,500 | 28,000 | 36,500 |
| Revised assumption | 20% | 20,000 | 27,000 | 36,000 |
| Percentage change | (33%) | (11.1%) | (3.6%) | (1.4%) |

[6] An Excel spreadsheet containing all of the budgets and the pro forma financial statements from this chapter is available from your instructor. Note to instructor: This file is available at the Online Learning Center (OLC). Please go to: **www.mhhe.com/blocher6e**.

Budgeting and Sensitivity Analysis—The Need for
Incorporating Contingencies into the Planning Process

In early 2006 Ford Motor Co. adopted an aggressive restructuring plan, dubbed the "Way Forward," in a move to return the company to profitability and help ensure the long-term viability of the company. This plan included the shuttering of a number of manufacturing plants and a significant reduction in both the blue-collar and white-collar workforce of the company. A previously adopted restructuring plan failed to deliver on promises, particularly in terms of forecasted pretax profits envisioned in that plan. The earlier plan failed, in large part, because it was based on predictions of lower gas prices and higher prices for new vehicles—neither of which materialized. As well, the previous plan underestimated the strength of Ford's Asian competitors and failed to anticipate the move by General Motors to provide

employee pricing and zero-rate financing for its customers. In short, the previous plan failed to incorporate a number of strategically important contingencies and environmental constraints.

The effects of these contingencies and eventualities can, and should, be incorporated formally into the planning/budgeting process. As explained in the text, dedicated software (e.g., SAP, Oracle, SAS) for communicating plans and information across areas and people now exists. The use of such software will not prevent various business pressures that firms experience, but it can help these firms develop appropriate contingency plans.

**Source:** J. McCracken, "'Way Forward' Requires Culture Shift at Ford," *The Wall Street Journal,* January 23, 2006, pp. B1, B3.

inputs affects individual budgets and the set of pro forma financial statements produced as part of the master budgeting process.

An example of sensitivity analysis for Kerry is provided in Exhibit 10.17. Management of the company is unsure about both the level of sales demand and product selling price. In addition to a best-guess estimate (Exhibit 10.3) used to prepare the master budget, management elicits from the marketing manager both high-end (optimistic) and low-end (pessimistic) estimates for both sales volume (in units) and selling price per unit. High-end and low-end estimated selling prices per unit were $35 and $25, respectively, while high-end and low-end estimates of sales volume were 17,500 and 22,500. Exhibit 10.17 provides estimated net operating income for a single month, April 2013, for Kerry under nine different scenarios, that is, combinations of selling price and sales volume.[7] Note that in this analysis all other budgetary inputs (e.g., total fixed costs and variable cost per unit) are held constant.

One of the primary advantages of conducting sensitivity analysis is the ability to isolate risks associated with particular components of operations and to develop contingency plans for dealing with these risks. To the extent that the output variable of interest (operating income, for example) is sensitive to changes in input factors (e.g., sales volume), management needs to know this. The ability to isolate these important factors is

**EXHIBIT 10.17**
**Results of Sensitivity Analysis: April 2013**

| Selling Price per Unit | Sales Volume (units) | Budgeted Net Operating Income | % Change from Master Budget Amount |
|---|---|---|---|
| $25.00 | 17,500 | $(67,877) | (244.6)% |
| 25.00 | 20,000 | (50,746) | (208.2) |
| 25.00 | 22,500 | (33,249) | (170.9) |
| 30.00 | 17,500 | 17,575 | 37.5 |
| **30.00** | **20,000** | **46,914** | **N/A** |
| 30.00 | 22,500 | 76,619 | 163.3 |
| 35.00 | 17,500 | 103,028 | 219.6 |
| 35.00 | 20,000 | 144,574 | 308.2 |
| 35.00 | 22,500 | 186,487 | 397.5 |

[7] Note, however, that these results are not generated from the actual underlying model depicted in the chapter. That is, the data were generated for illustrative purposes only.

the primary planning benefit of performing sensitivity analysis as part of the master budgeting process.

In the present case (Exhibit 10.17), we see significant sensitivity of budgeted net operating income as a function of both sales volume and selling price. In fact, if the realized selling price can be set no higher than $25 per unit, our analysis shows that it is virtually impossible with the current cost structure for Kerry to earn a profit. This situation would prompt managers to develop contingency plans to deal with this less-than-favorable situation.

### Scenario Analysis

Both analyses described above assumed that certain inputs to the budget-planning model (e.g., selling price per unit) could be changed independently of other inputs (e.g., sales volume). Therefore, to the extent that the variables in our planning model are interrelated (e.g., a change in selling price leads to a change in sales demand), the preceding methods are deficient. In addition, the number of possible combinations of variables—even in a simplified real-life situation—can be exceedingly large, which makes the preceding approach ungainly.

To address both of the above limitations we might create and examine a small number of realistic scenarios (that is, combinations of planning-model inputs). For each scenario we could recalculate a budgetary figure of interest, such as operating income or operating cash flow.

At a minimum, we might prepare for management a set of budgets based on a "best-case scenario," a "worst-case scenario," and a "most-likely scenario." The best-case scenario would reflect the most optimistic (but realistic) values for selling price, sales volume, and so on, while the worst-case scenario would reflect just the opposite, that is, the most pessimistic (but realistic) combination of inputs in our budgeting model.

The range of outcomes for the scenarios we create gives us an idea of how bad or good things might be; the range of possible outcomes (e.g., budgeted operating income) provides a rough measure of risk. Assuming the numbers in Exhibit 10.17 reflect realistic scenarios, we see a most optimistic outcome of $186,487, a most pessimistic outcome of −$67,877, and a most likely outcome of $46,914.

Three concluding points regarding scenario analysis seem appropriate: (1) it is possible to enhance the analysis by assigning subjective probabilities to each of the various scenarios (in turn, we could calculate an expected value of operating income); (2) the process of identifying realistic scenarios is complicated in practice and therefore suggests the need for a cross-functional team; and (3) the most sophisticated way to handle uncertainty in the budgeting process is through the use of Monte Carlo simulation.

## Budgeting in Service Companies

**LO 10-6**

*Identify unique characteristics of budgeting for service companies.*

Service companies have different operating characteristics, operating environments, and considerations than those of manufacturing and merchandising firms. This section examines special considerations in budgeting for service companies.

### Budgeting in Service Industries

Similar to budgeting for manufacturing or merchandising firms, budgeting for service firms consists of an integrated set of plans for an upcoming period. The difference is in the absence of production or merchandise purchase budgets and their ancillary budgets. A service organization achieves its budgeted goals and fulfills its mission through providing services. Therefore, an important focal point in its budgeting is personnel planning. A service firm must ensure that it has personnel with the appropriate skills to perform the services required for the budgeted service revenue.

As an example, AccuTax, Inc., provides tax services to small firms and individuals. It expects to have the following revenues from preparing tax returns for the year ended August 31, 2013:

| | | |
|---|--:|--:|
| Tax returns for business firms | | $1,000,000 |
| Individual tax returns: | | |
| Simple returns | $1,640,000 | |
| Complex returns | 1,200,000 | 2,840,000 |
| Total revenues | | $3,840,000 |

The firm has 2 partners, 8 senior consultants, and 20 consultants. On average, a partner works 50 hours a week and is paid $250,000 a year. Both senior consultants and consultants are expected to work 40 hours a week and are paid, respectively, $90,000 and $60,000 a year. The annual compensation for supporting staff is $40,000 per full-time equivalent. The number of supporting staff varies with the size of the firm. In general, one supporting staff person is needed for every 2 partners, one for every 4 senior consultants, and one for every 10 consultants. After allowing for vacation, sickness, and continuing education days, the weeks per year available to work with clients are 40 weeks for each partner, 45 weeks for each senior consultant, and 48 weeks for each consultant. All partners and senior consultants are full-time professional staff members. The firm estimates the following required professional staff times for each hour spent to complete a tax return:

| | Business Return | Complex Individual | Simple Individual |
|---|---|---|---|
| Partner | 0.4 hour | 0.1 hour | — |
| Senior consultant | 0.6 hour | 0.4 hour | 0.1 hour |
| Consultant | — | 0.5 hour | 0.9 hour |

General and administrative expenses are estimated as $150,000 per year, plus 10% of the total payroll. The firm charges $250 per hour for business returns, $100 per hour for individual returns with complicated tax matters, and $50 per hour for simple individual tax returns. The budgeted revenues and the total hours for each of the returns for the coming year are as follows:

| | Budgeted Revenue | | Hourly Charge Rate | | Required Hours |
|---|--:|:-:|--:|:-:|--:|
| Business returns | $1,000,000 | ÷ | $250 | = | 4,000 |
| Individual returns: | | | | | |
| Simple returns | 1,640,000 | ÷ | 50 | = | 32,800 |
| Complex returns | 1,200,000 | ÷ | 100 | = | 12,000 |
| Total | $3,840,000 | | | | 48,800 |

The following table shows the professional staff requirements for the budgeted revenue:

| | Total Hours | Partner | Senior Consultant | Consultant |
|---|--:|--:|--:|--:|
| Business returns | 4,000 | 1,600 | 2,400 | — |
| Complex individual returns | 12,000 | 1,200 | 4,800 | 6,000 |
| Simple individual returns | 32,800 | — | 3,280 | 29,520 |
| Total hours | 48,800 | 2,800 | 10,480 | 35,520 |
| Hours per week (given) | | ÷ 50 | ÷ 40 | ÷ 40 |
| Number of weeks worth of work | | 56 | 262 | 888 |
| Weeks per year/professional staff (given) | | ÷ 40 | ÷ 45 | ÷ 48 |
| Number of professional staff members needed | | 1.4 | 5.8 | 18.5 |

**EXHIBIT 10.18**
**Budgeted Operating Income with No Change in Staffing**

| ACCUTAX, INC. | | | |
|---|---|---|---|
| Budgeted Income Statement | | | |
| For the year ended August 31, 2013 | | | |
| Revenue | | | $3,840,000 |
| Payroll expenses: | | | |
| Partners | 2 × $250,000 = | $ 500,000 | |
| Senior consultants | 8 × $ 90,000 = | 720,000 | |
| Consultants | 20 × $ 60,000 = | 1,200,000 | |
| Supporting staff | 5* × $ 40,000 = | 200,000 | 2,620,000 |
| General and administrative expenses | $150,000 + (10% × $2,620,000) = | | 412,000 |
| Operating income | | | $ 808,000 |

*5 = (2/1) + (8/4) + (20/10) = 1 + 2 + 2

The budget shows that AccuTax has sufficient professional staff to support the expected activity. Assuming AccuTax plans no change in personnel and maintains the same staff level, its budgeted operating income will be $808,000, as shown in Exhibit 10.18.

## Alternative Budgeting Approaches

**LO 10-7**

*Understand alternative approaches to budgeting (viz., zero-base, activity-based, time-driven activity-based, and kaizen budgeting).*

Over the years alternative approaches have been proposed to facilitate budget preparation and improve operations. When used properly these approaches—zero base, activity-based, time-driven activity-based, and kaizen budgeting—improve budget effectiveness.

### Zero-Base Budgeting (ZBB)

**Zero-base budgeting (ZBB)**
is a budgeting process that requires managers to prepare budgets from a zero base.

**Zero-base budgeting (ZBB)** requires managers to prepare budgets each period from a zero base. A typical budgeting process is incremental in nature in the sense that it starts with the current budget. The process assumes that most, if not all, current activities and functions will continue into the budget period. Thus, the primary focus in a typical budgeting process is on changes to the current operating budget.

In contrast, ZBB allows no activities or functions to be included in the budget unless managers can justify their needs. ZBB requires budgeting teams to perform in-depth reviews of all budget items. Such a budgeting process encourages managers to be aware of activities or functions that have outlived their usefulness or have been a waste of resources.

The amount of work and time needed to apply a true ZBB to all aspects of operations of an organization can be monumental. An organization may find it practically impossible to review and examine all of its activities from the zero-budget level every year. As an alternative, the organization can schedule ZBB periodically or perform ZBB for different divisions each year. For example, the highway department of a state government could adopt a rotating five-year ZBB process. All divisions of the department would be subject to in-depth review of their activities every fifth year, not every year as true ZBB requires, with the process applied to different divisions each year.

### Activity-Based Budgeting (ABB)

**Activity-based budgeting (ABB)**
is a budgeting process based on activities and cost drivers of operations.

**Activity-based budgeting (ABB)** is an extension of the traditional form of activity-based costing (ABC).[8] ABB starts with the budgeted output and segregates costs required for the budgeted output into homogeneous activity cost pools such as unit, batch, product-sustaining, customer-sustaining, and facility-sustaining activity pools. Traditional budgeting and ABB are conceptually very different. Proponents of ABB maintain that use of this approach can lead to more accurate budgets pertaining to support activities, including factory (manufacturing) overhead.

[8] Chapter 5 discusses the traditional form of ABC.

For the majority of organizations, budgeting revolves around the chart-of-accounts structure. As a consequence, costs are budgeted on a departmental basis using descriptive accounts (salaries, depreciation, marketing, etc.). However, budgets expressed in these terms tell us little about the drivers of success for the organization. ABB attempts to fill this information void by focusing on the activities and associated resources needed to satisfy the projected level of customer demand.

ABB begins by budgeting activity requirements based on estimated product demand for the upcoming budget period. It then budgets the cost of resources needed to perform the set of budgeted activities needed to meet this demand. In so doing, a better match of the supply of and the demand for resources is effected. For example, management can budget intelligently for additional resources in specific areas or can plan to redeploy resources from one area of the organization to another. These insights would be difficult, if not impossible, to achieve in a traditional budgeting environment.

Of particular interest to most organizations today is the budgeting for labor (head count). How does the organization cut costs or manage its human capital when everyone appears fully employed? Which employees are involved in value-added activities, and which employees are performing non-value-added activities? What opportunities are there for redeploying people to activities within the organization that are value-added and strategically aligned? The application of ABB allows the organization to address these critical issues.

Exhibit 10.19 illustrates an ABB for the factory overhead budget of the quarter ended June 30, 2013, for Kerry Window Systems, Inc. In addition to data used in Exhibit 10.8, the ABB for Kerry used data given in Part A of Exhibit 10.19.

The result of an activity-based costing by Kerry suggests that factory overhead cost varies with hours of semiskilled labor ($0.60 per hour), hours of skilled labor ($0.20 per hour), machine-hours ($3.20 per hour), number of batches ($1,700 per batch), and number of products ($5,000 each). In addition, there is a $50,000 facility-level cost per month. The firm has a standard batch size of 2,500 units and expects to operate 6,650, 8,220, and 10,510 machine-hours, respectively, in April, May, and June.

**EXHIBIT 10.19**
Factory Overhead Budget Using Activity-Based Budgeting (ABB)

**KERRY WINDOW SYSTEMS, INC.**
**Factory Overhead Budget (Activity-Based Budgeting)**
**For the Quarter Ended June 30, 2013**

| | | April | May | June | Quarter |
|---|---|---|---|---|---|
| **A: Data** | | | | | |
| Units of output (Exhibit 10.4) | | 22,500 | 28,000 | 36,500 | 87,000 |
| Direct labor-hours: | | | | | |
| Semiskilled (Exhibit 10.7, Line 3) | | 11,250 | 14,000 | 18,250 | 43,500 |
| Skilled (Exhibit 10.7, Line 8) | | 4,500 | 5,600 | 7,300 | 17,400 |
| Machine-hours (given) | | 6,650 | 8,220 | 10,510 | 25,380 |
| Number of batches (@ 2,500/batch) | | 9 | 11.2 | 14.6 | 34.8 |
| Number of products | | 5 | 6 | 7 | 18 |
| | Activity | | | | |
| **B: Activity-Based Budget (ABB)** | Cost Rate* | | | | |
| Overhead cost pools: | | | | | |
| Semiskilled-hour-related | 0.60 | $ 6,750 | $ 8,400 | $ 10,950 | $ 26,100 |
| Skilled-hour-related | 0.20 | 900 | 1,120 | 1,460 | 3,480 |
| Machine-hour-related | 3.20 | 21,280 | 26,304 | 33,632 | 81,216 |
| Batch-related | 1,700 | 15,300 | 19,040 | 24,820 | 59,160 |
| Product-related | 5,000 | 25,000 | 30,000 | 35,000 | 90,000 |
| Facility/per month | 50,000 | 50,000 | 50,000 | 50,000 | 150,000 |
| Total budgeted factory overhead | | $119,230 | $134,864 | $155,862 | $409,956** |

*These data are assumed but in general are calculated for each cost pool as budgeted resource spending for an upcoming period divided by the practical capacity of resources (labor, utilities, equipment, etc.) supplied.
**The total budgeted overhead for Kerry under ABB ($409,956) differs slightly from the total overhead under traditional costing ($410,860—see Exhibit 10.8) due to rounding of activity cost rates in Exhibit 10.19.

**EXHIBIT 10.20**
**Traditional versus Activity-Based Budgeting (ABB)**

|  | Traditional Budgeting | Activity-Based Budgeting (ABB) |
|---|---|---|
| Budgeting unit | Expressed as the cost of functional areas or spending categories | Expressed as the cost of activities and cost drivers |
| Focus on | Input resources | High-value-added activities |
| Orientation | Historical | Continuous improvement and capacity management |
| Roles of suppliers and customers | Does not formally consider suppliers and customers in budgeting | Coordinates with suppliers and considers the needs of customers |
| Control objective | Maximize managers' performance | Synchronize activities with level of demand |
| Budget base | Descriptive accounts in departmental budgets | Value-added versus non-value-added activities |

Starting with five products in April, Kerry plans to introduce one additional product each month.

Exhibit 10.20 contrasts traditional budgeting and ABB. As noted therein, firms with traditional costing systems usually prepare budgets for departmental units such as cutting, assembling, and finishing using volume-based drivers, as Kerry did for the budget shown in Exhibit 10.8. Note that for Kerry the traditional budget for April was $113,600 compared with $119,230 under ABB. Aggregations of resource costs into functional units obscures relationships between resource consumption and output and complicates decisions regarding resource planning. As a result, traditional cost systems emphasize allocations of indirect costs to products via a broadly averaged and simplified volume-based measure, such as labor-hours, machine-hours, units of materials used, or output units. Such allocations generally do not represent resource demands (or resource consumption) of the organization's outputs and customers. Of course, some resources come in discontinuous amounts. For example, it may not be possible to hire one-third of a person. Thus, the last step in ABB is for managers to decide whether to round up (and incur some idle-capacity costs) or to round down (which may adversely affect customer-service levels).

ABB facilitates continuous improvement. The process of preparing a budget under ABB highlights opportunities for cost reduction and elimination of wasteful activities. ABB facilitates the identification of high-value-added activities and the reduction or elimination of low-value-added activities. In contrast, history often is the underlying guidance in a traditional budget.

## Time-Driven Activity-Based Budgeting

As discussed in Chapter 5, time-driven activity-based costing (TDABC) is an alternative to traditional ABC.[9] To build a TDABC system management needs to provide only two estimates for each department or business process: (1) the total cost and amount of resources supplied for a period, and (2) the amount of resource capacity, measured in time, that is consumed by the organization's cost objects (products, services, and customers).

In stage one of the two-stage TDABC process, cost rates are calculated. For example, for an activity defined as *packaging activity,* we would divide the cost of resources supplied for this activity (labor, systems, etc.) by the amount of resources supplied, measured in *time* (e.g., minutes). In stage two, costs are then allocated to cost objects by multiplying estimated cost rates (e.g., $2 per minute) by the time requirements of the cost object (for example, 4.0 minutes to package a standard, nonhazardous product that is shipped by air). Resource demands, and therefore allocated costs, of more complicated packaging activities can be captured through the use of time equations.

[9] R. S. Kaplan and S. R. Anderson, *Time-Driven Activity-Based Costing: A Simpler and More Powerful Path to Higher Profits* (Boston: Harvard Business School Press, 2007).

**Time-driven activity-based budgeting (TDABB)**
represents budgets prepared in conjunction with a TDABC system.

**Time-driven activity-based budgeting (TDABB)** is a method of budget preparation used in conjunction with TDABC. As with activity-based budgeting (ABB), TDABB works backwards from forecasted sales volume (and mix) to calculate in a straightforward way resource spending needed to support production and sales plans. That is, the organization will have to estimate resource requirements in each process and department if the production and sales forecasts for the coming period are to be realized. To generate these estimates, time equations (discussed in Chapter 5) for each major activity or process can be used to extend the basic approach described above. All of this detail can be supplied by the organization's enterprise resource planning (ERP) system. In sum, TDABC models can be used to streamline, and therefore significantly reduce the cost of, activity-based budgeting (ABB) processes. The resulting system allows managers to more accurately plan for the level of capacity needed to accomplish short-term profit goals.

### Resource Capacity Planning

**Practical capacity**
is the measure of capacity used to estimate cost-driver rates under ABC and TDABC systems.

In both ABC and TDABC systems, we calculate cost-driver rates (e.g., the cost to ship an item, or the cost to process a customer order). As we argued in Chapter 5, these rates are best defined by dividing budgeted resource costs by the **practical capacity** of resources supplied for each activity or process. The use of this level of capacity allows us to estimate the cost of unused capacity at the end of each period for each activity or process. This estimate is defined as the difference between the total cost of resources *supplied* and the cost of resources *used* (or planned to be used) during the period, where the latter is defined as the product of the activity-cost rate (based on practical capacity) and the actual activity units used (or planned to be used) during the period.

A question arises as to what the appropriate treatment of unused capacity costs should be. Such costs should not be assigned to customers served or products produced during the period. To do so would overestimate the resource demands of these cost objects. Rather, these costs should be assigned to the level (product line, department, or a given manager) within the organization where the decision to acquire the capacity was made. For example, if the excess capacity was acquired to meet the anticipated demands of a given customer or market segment, then the cost of unused capacity, as a lump-sum amount, should be assigned to these segments.

The primary benefit of reporting the cost of unused capacity for each activity or resource is that this information can be used to manage the demand for and supply of capacity (e.g., personnel) within the organization. For example, if excess capacity is identified during the budgeting process, then management can take steps to reduce spending in these areas or to find alternative uses for this available capacity. This insight in large part distinguishes both ABB and TDABC budgeting from traditional budgeting practices.

### Kaizen (Continuous-Improvement) Budgeting

**Kaizen budgeting**
is a budgeting approach that incorporates continuous-improvement expectations in the budget.

**Kaizen budgeting** is a budgeting approach that incorporates continuous-improvement expectations in the budget. A kaizen budgeting approach adjusts required resource demands based on targeted efficiency and productivity gains. As such, it is an excellent complement to both traditional and activity-based budgeting systems.

A kaizen budget decrease is not the same as the budget cuts we often see firms or governments make when facing a budget crunch because of diminishing profits, decreasing sales, or declining tax revenues. A budget cut often is a reluctant passive response to a mandate that is accomplished by reducing productive activities or services. In contrast, kaizen budgeting promotes active engagement in reforming or altering practices. A decrease in cost in a kaizen budget is a result of performing the same activity more efficiently and with higher quality; it is not a result of arbitrary elimination of activities or components.

Kaizen budgeting is not limited to internal improvements. Some firms expect and demand continuous improvements from their suppliers and explicitly incorporate consequent effects in budgeted production cost and manufacturing schedules. For example,

Citizen Watch demands that its suppliers decrease costs a minimum of 3% per year and includes this decrease in its own budget. Suppliers keep any cost savings in excess of 3%.[10]

## Behavioral Issues in Budgeting

**LO 10-8**

*Discuss various behavioral considerations in budgeting.*

A budget can be successful only if those responsible for its implementation make it happen. To encourage a successful budgeting process, management must consider a number of behavioral issues, as discussed below.

### Budgetary Slack

**Budgetary slack,** or padding the budget, is the practice of managers knowingly including a higher amount of expenditures (or lower amount of revenue) in the budget than they actually believe will occur. When the actual cost (or revenue) amounts are realized and compared to "budgeted" figures, an appearance of successful effort is indicated.

**Budgetary slack** is the "cushion" managers intentionally build into budgets to help ensure success in meeting the budget.

Managers often justify such practices as insurance against uncertain future events. After all, no one knows exactly how the future will unfold. Budgetary slack, however, wastes resources and could lead employees to make half-hearted efforts to meet or exceed the budget.

### Goal Congruence

**Goal congruence** is a term that refers to the degree of consistency between the goals of the firm, its subunits, and its employees. In general, a firm's goals should be as consistent as possible with the goals of its employees. A budget devoid of considerations for goal congruence is not likely to achieve the most desirable results. A budget that aligns the firm's goals with those of its employees has a much better chance to realize successful operations and attain desirable results. As discussed below, there are at least three major factors that affect the level of goal congruence achieved: (1) the extent to which employees participate in the budgeting process; (2) the level of difficulty embedded in the budget; and (3) whether and how compensation is linked to budgeted performance.

**Goal congruence** is consistency between the goals of the firm, its subunits, and its employees.

### Authoritative or Participative Budgeting?

Budgeting processes can be either top down or bottom up. In a top-down budgeting process, top management prepares budgets for the entire organization, including those for lower-level operations. This process often is referred to as *authoritative budgeting.* A *participative budgeting* process, on the other hand, is a bottom-up approach that involves the people affected by the budget, including lower-level employees, in the budget-preparation process.

Authoritative budgeting provides better decision-making control than does participative budgeting. Top management sets the overall goals for the budget period and prepares a budget for operating personnel to attain the goals. An authoritative budget, however, often lacks the commitment ("buy-in") of lower-level managers and employees responsible for implementing it.

A participative budget is a good communication device. The process of preparing a budget often gives top management a better grasp of the problems their employees face and provides the employees a better understanding of the dilemmas that top management deals with. A participative budget also is more likely to gain employee commitment to fulfill budgetary goals. Unless properly controlled, however, a participative budget can lead to easy budget targets or targets not in compliance with the organization's overall strategy.

An effective budgeting process often combines both top-down and bottom-up budgeting approaches. Subunits prepare their initial budgets based on the budget guidelines issued by the firm's budget committee. Senior managers review and make suggestions to the proposed budget before sending it back to the divisions for revisions. The final budget

---

[10] Robin Cooper, *Citizen Watch Company, Ltd.,* Harvard Business School case 9–194033. © 1993 by the President and Fellows of Harvard College.

**EXHIBIT 10.21**
**Budget Difficulty and Effort**

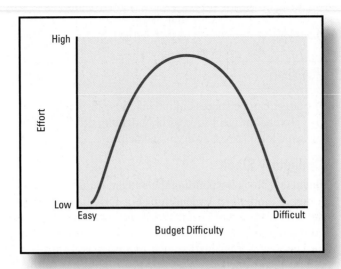

usually is reached after several rounds of negotiations. For this reason, this is generally referred to as a *negotiated budgeting* process.

## Difficulty Level of the Budget Target

An easy budget target may fail to encourage employees to give their best efforts. A budget target that is very difficult to achieve can, however, discourage managers from even trying to attain it. Exhibit 10.21 depicts research findings on the relationship between the level of employee effort and level of difficulty of budget targets. Ideally, budget targets should be challenging yet attainable. But what is a challenging and attainable budget target?

Research by Merchant and Manzoni suggests that a "highly achievable target," that is, one achievable by most managers 80 to 90% of the time, serves quite well in the vast majority of organizations, especially when accompanied by extra rewards for performances exceeding the target.[11] According to Merchant (1990), the advantages of using such a target include:

1. Increasing managers' commitment to achieving the budget target.
2. Maintaining managers' confidence in the budget.
3. Decreasing the cost of organizational control.
4. Reducing the risk that managers will engage in harmful "earnings management" practices or violate corporate ethical standards.
5. Allowing effective and efficient managers greater operating flexibility.
6. Improving the predictability of earnings or operating results.
7. Enhancing the usefulness of a budget as a planning and coordinating tool.

## Linkage of Compensation and Budgeted Performance

**Fixed-performance contract**
is an incentive compensation plan whereby compensation is a function of actual performance compared to a fixed (budgeted) target.

Traditionally, budgets have played a role in determining employee and executive compensation. The traditional model is that such compensation would be at least partially a function of the difference between actual performance (sales, operating profit, net income, etc.) and budgeted performance for a given budget period, usually a year. This type of compensation plan is sometimes referred to as a **fixed-performance contract** because actual performance is compared to a fixed (budgeted) target.

[11] K. A. Merchant, "How Challenging Should Profit Budget Targets Be?" *Management Accounting,* November 1990, pp. 46–48; K. A. Merchant, *Rewarding Results: Motivating Profit Center Managers* (Cambridge, MA: Harvard Business School Press, 1989); and K. A. Merchant and J. Manzoni, "The Achievability of Budget Targets in Profit Centers: A Field Study," *The Accounting Review,* July 1989, pp. 539–58.

Recent economic volatility (demand volatility, exchange-rate volatility, volatility of market prices, etc.) has motivated a growing number of companies (including UPS, Unilever, Statoil, Norton Lilly International, and American Century Investments) to fundamentally rethink their budgeting-and-planning processes. To some CFOs, this means increasing the frequency of budget revisions and forecasts—so-called "rolling forecasts." In fact, a 2011 survey of the CFOs of 200 large companies (sales > $2 billion per year) found that the use of rolling forecasts, as a complement to traditional budgeting practices, is becoming an established leading practice. To others it means simplification: tracking a small set of high-level strategic performance indicators rather than thousands of line items (as is the case with a traditional master budget). To still others, it means routinely conducting scenario analysis (as described previously in this chapter)—what some have referred to as "perpetual planning." And, in order to make the budgeting process more meaningful, a growing number of companies are working to more actively engage lower-level managers and employees in the budgeting process—a combination of top-down and bottom-up effort. Other companies (such as the publisher Houghton Mifflin Harcourt) are incorporating more macroeconomic factors into the sales-forecasting component of budgeting. Changes in the nature and form of budgets is also causing CFOs to reconsider employee compensation systems. Rather than tying incentive compensation to performance relative to a static budget, companies are experimenting with systems where compensation is a function of performance compared to peer companies. The informed management accountant needs to be continually updated on new developments and contemporary refinements to traditional budgeting practices.

**Source:** K. O'Sullivan, "From Adversity, Better Budgets," *CFO* (June 2010), pp. 45–48; R. Banham, "Let It Roll: More Companies Are Abandoning Budgets in Favor of Rolling Forecasts," *CFO* (May 2011), pp. 43–47; and, PricewaterhouseCoopers LLP, *Financial planning: Realizing the value of budgeting and forecasting* (2011) (available at: www.pwc.com/us/en/increasing-finance-function-effectiveness/publications/financial-planning-realizing-the-value-of-budgeting-and-forecasting.jhtml).

While this traditional model may work well in some situations, we know that its usage can have dysfunctional consequences. That is, significant incentive (and ethical) issues arise when compensation is linked to a fixed-performance target. For example, such a reward system provides incentives for managers to submit biased information in their budgets. Budgetary slack, discussed earlier, is one example. In addition, the use of fixed targets reinforced by incentives motivates some managers to **game the performance measure,** that is, to take actions that make the performance indicator look better but do not increase the value of the firm. Finally, some would argue that the use of fixed budget targets unfairly rewards managers when actual performance is affected by factors, such as macroeconomic conditions, that are beyond the control or influence of the manager. In short, critics of the conventional fixed-performance model linked to compensation contend that this process is fundamentally flawed. At least two alternatives have been proposed as a way to deal with this problem: the use of linear compensation plans and the use of rolling forecasts combined with relative performance indicators.

**Gaming the performance measure**
is a result of non-value-adding actions taken by managers to improve indicated performance.

### Use of Linear Compensation Plans[12]

Essentially, this option would sever the relationship between budgets and managerial compensation. In its place, incentive compensation would be based on a linear compensation plan. This strategy has two characteristics: (1) managerial reward is independent of budgeted targets, and (2) managerial reward is a linear function of actual performance: the greater the performance, the greater the managerial reward (both monetary and nonmonetary). In other words, this incentive system rewards people for what they actually *do*, not for what they do relative to what they *say* they can do. However, from a practical standpoint this strategy may be difficult to implement because of the use of budgeted targets in determining managerial rewards.

[12] This section draws on the following source: Michael C. Jensen, "Corporate Budgeting Is Broken—Let's Fix It," *Harvard Business Review* (November 2001), pp. 94–101.

### *Use of Rolling Forecasts and Relative Performance Results*[13]

The displeasure with respect to current budgeting practices is perhaps best epitomized by a group referred to as the Beyond Budgeting Roundtable (BBRT—see: **www.bbrt.org** and **www.project.bbrt.org**). Instead of fixed-performance contracts, the BBRT recommends the use of *relative performance (improvement) contracts* and *rolling financial forecasts.*

**Relative performance contracts** reward managers for performance based on comparison of actual results with specified benchmarks, not budgeted targets.

**Relative performance (or relative improvement) contracts** essentially reward managers for how their business units perform relative to some appropriate benchmark performance, not a fixed budget target. For example, an operating unit or division might be evaluated on the basis of its return on investment (ROI) for a period relative to the market or to best-in-class performance. Some organizations benchmark actual performance to the top quartile of their peer group. This change in incentive, at least conceptually, avoids much of the dysfunctional consequences associated with traditional budgeting systems. Units and managers are motivated to achieve to their highest level because their compensation/reward is tied to how they performed relative to a prespecified (external or internal) benchmark. In essence, this represents radical decentralization and significant reliance on self-regulation. Employees and operating managers in this model are vested with significant decision authority and are asked to use their own best judgment to achieve superior results, without being constrained by the plan embodied in a budget.

A **rolling financial forecast** provides a constant planning horizon with the use of regularly updated forecasts.

In addition to the use of relative performance contracts, the BBRT model calls for the use of **rolling financial forecasts** rather than the annual master budget (described earlier in this chapter). These forecasts are updated regularly, for example every quarter, to provide a constant planning horizon (e.g., five quarters into the future). Of particular note is the fact that these forecasts are separated from performance evaluation and control. They are prepared for a small set of key performance indicators (e.g., cash flow, sales, and number of customer orders) and serve as a high-level view of future performance. Their use is designed to allow employees to adapt to changing environments (including competitive threats) and to achieve the level of radical decentralization envisioned by the BBRT.

[13] This discussion draws on the following source: Jeremy Hope and Robin Fraser, *Beyond Budgeting: How Managers Can Break Free from the Annual Performance Trap* (Boston: Harvard Business School Press, 2003).

## Summary

An organization's budget is a quantitative plan that identifies the resources required and commitments to fulfill the organization's goals for the budget period. Budgeting allows management to plan ahead, communicate the plan and performance expectations to all divisions and employees, and, when properly implemented, motivate employees. A budget can also serve as a basis for performance evaluation.

Strategy helps a firm to be more focused in its operations and to take advantage of its strengths and opportunities. A firm executes its strategy through long-range plans and master budgets. An annual master budget is an extension of the organization's long-range plan to fulfill organizational goals and objectives.

The master budget for a manufacturer includes sales, production, direct materials, direct labor, factory overhead, selling, and administration expense budgets, as well as a cash budget, and budgeted financial statements.

A service firm prepares a budget following set procedures just as a manufacturing or merchandising firm does. A major difference between budgets for service firms and those for manufacturing or merchandising firms is the absence of a production budget or merchandise purchases budget for service firms. The budgeting procedures and all other budget items are essentially the same for both service and manufacturing or merchandising firms.

Budgets, by definition, are forward-looking and include estimates for key inputs such as sales volume, sales mix, total fixed (capacity-related) costs, variable cost per unit, and selling price per unit. What-if analysis can be performed to determine the effects of alternative scenarios (states of nature) and alternative plans. Sensitivity analysis allows us to determine the extent to which resulting budgets are affected by changes in the input factors. Together, these analyses allow the budget analyst to deal with uncertainty that is inherent in the budgeting process.

Refinements or alternatives to traditional budgeting practices include zero-base budgeting (ZBB), activity-based budgeting (ABB), time-driven activity-based budgeting (TDABB), and kaizen budgeting. By requiring budgets that start from a zero base each period, ZBB attempts to achieve a more realistic allocation of resources within the organization. ABB and TDABB are both extensions to modern cost-allocation systems, as discussed in Chapter 5. Kaizen budgeting incorporates continuous improvements into budgets that are produced.

In some quarters (e.g., BBRT) there is growing dissatisfaction, indeed frustration, with traditional budgeting practices, such as those described in this chapter. Critics contend that incentive compensation/employee reward should not be a function of the difference between budgeted and actual performance, a widespread approach in practice. In place of the annual fixed-performance contract these critics suggest either that a linear compensation plan based on actual results be used or that budgets be replaced altogether with rolling forecasts and relative-performance contracts.

## Key Terms

activity-based budgeting (ABB), *375*

budget, *351*

budgetary slack, *379*

budgeting, *351*

capital budgeting, *352*

cash budget, *366*

direct materials purchases budget, *361*

direct materials usage budget, *360*

financial budgets, *353*

fixed-performance contract, *380*

gaming the performance measure, *381*

goal congruence, *379*

kaizen budgeting, *378*

long-range plan, *352*

manufacturing cells, *362*

master budget, *353*

merchandise purchases budget, *362*

operating budgets, *353*

practical capacity, *378*

production budget, *358*

relative performance contracts, *382*

rolling financial forecast, *382*

sales budget, *357*

strategic budget expenditures, *352*

time-driven activity-based budgeting (TDABB), *378*

zero-base budgeting (ZBB), *375*

## Self-Study Problems

(For solutions, please turn to the end of the chapter.)

### 1. Master Budget

Hansell Company's management wants to prepare budgets for one of its products, duraflex, for July 2013. The firm sells the product for $80 per unit and has the following expected sales (in units) for these months in 2013:

| April | May | June | July | August | September |
|-------|-------|-------|-------|--------|-----------|
| 5,000 | 5,400 | 5,500 | 6,000 | 7,000 | 8,000 |

The production process requires 4 pounds of dura-1000 and 2 pounds of flexplas. The firm's policy is to maintain an ending inventory each month equal to 10% of the following month's budgeted sales, but in no case less than 500 units. All materials inventories are to be maintained at 5% of the production needs for the next month, but not to exceed 1,000 pounds. The firm expects all inventories at the end of June to be within the guidelines. The purchase department expects the materials to cost $1.25 per pound and $5.00 per pound for dura-1000 and flexplas, respectively.

The production process requires direct labor at two skill levels. The rate for labor at the K102 level is $50 per hour and for the K175 level is $20 per hour. The K102 level can process one batch of duraflex per hour; each batch consists of 100 units. The manufacturing of duraflex also requires one-tenth of an hour of K175 workers' time for each unit manufactured.

Variable manufacturing overhead is $1,200 per batch plus $80 per direct labor-hour. The company uses an actual cost system with a LIFO cost-flow assumption.

**Required** On the basis of the preceding data and projections, prepare the following budgets:

a. Sales budget for July (in dollars).

b. Production budget for July (in units).

c. Production budget for August (in units).

d. Direct materials purchases budget for July (in pounds).

e. Direct materials purchases budget for July (in dollars).

f. Direct manufacturing labor budget for July (in dollars).

### 2. Cash Budget and Budgeted Income Statement

Hansell Company expects its trial balance on June 30 to be as follows:

**HANSELL COMPANY**
**Budgeted Trial Balance**
**June 30, 2013**

| | Debit | Credit |
|---|-------|--------|
| Cash | $ 40,000 | |
| Accounts receivable | 80,000 | |
| Allowance for bad debts | | $ 3,500 |
| Inventory | 25,000 | |
| Plant, property, and equipment | 650,000 | |
| Accumulated depreciation | | 320,000 |
| Accounts payable | | 95,000 |
| Wages and salaries payable | | 24,000 |
| Note payable | | 200,000 |
| Stockholders' equity | | 152,500 |
| Total | $795,000 | $795,000 |

Typically, cash sales represent 20% of sales while credit sales represent 80%. Credit sales terms are 2/10, n/30. Hansell bills customers on the first day of the month following the month of sale. Experience has shown that 60% of the billings will be collected within the discount period, 25% by the end of the month after sales, 10% by the end of the second month after the sale, and 5% will ultimately be uncollectible. The firm writes off uncollectible accounts after 12 months.

The purchase terms for materials are 2/15, n/60. The firm makes all payments within the discount period. Experience has shown that 80% of the purchases are paid in the month of the purchase and the remainder are paid in the month immediately following. In June 2013, the firm budgeted purchases of $25,000 for dura-1000 and $22,000 for flexplas.

In addition to variable overhead, the firm has a monthly fixed factory overhead of $50,000, of which $20,000 is depreciation expense. The firm pays all manufacturing labor and factory overhead when incurred.

Total budgeted marketing, distribution, customer service, and administrative costs for 2013 are $2,400,000. Of this amount, $1,200,000 is considered fixed and includes depreciation expense of $120,000. The remainder varies with sales. The budgeted total sales for 2013 are $4 million. All marketing and administrative costs are paid in the month incurred.

Management desires to maintain an end-of-month minimum cash balance of $40,000. The firm has an agreement with a local bank to borrow its short-term needs in multiples of $1,000 up to $100,000 at an annual interest rate of 12%. Borrowings are assumed to occur at the end of the month. Bank borrowing at July 1 = $0.

**Required**

1. Prepare the cash budget for July 2013.
2. Prepare the budgeted income statement for July 2013.

*Please visit http://www.mhhe.com/blocher6e to access a narrated, animated tutorial for solving these problems.*

## Questions

10-1   Describe at least three benefits that an organization can expect to realize from budgeting.

**(CMA Adapted)**

10-2   Differentiate master, operating, and financial budgets.

10-3   Many accountants believe that the most important benefit of the master budgeting process is the end result: a set of pro forma financial statements. What is the rationale for this view?

10-4   Some critics of budgeting believe that budgets are effective tools for planning but not for control purposes. What is the essence of this argument?

10-5   Why is the sales budget considered the cornerstone of the organization's master budget?

10-6   In addition to the sales budget, what information does a firm need to complete its materials purchases budget?

10-7   List the major components of a cash budget.

10-8   What is zero-base budgeting (ZBB)?

10-9   Define the term *budgetary slack*. Why is it common to find slack in budgets?

10-10   How does the use of a time-driven activity-based costing (TDABC) system facilitate the preparation of budgets for an organization?

10-11   What is the essence of a fixed-performance contract and what dysfunctional consequences can occur through the use of this type of incentive system?

10-12   Distinguish between a linear-preformance contract and a fixed-performance contract in terms of motivational/incentive effects.

10-13   Define the terms *relative performance contract* and *rolling financial forecast*. What role for these is envisioned by critics of the traditional budgeting process?

## Brief Exercises

10-14   Kraft Bakeries introduced in 2013 a new line of frozen apple pie. For 2013, sales by quarter were as follows: 11,000 units; 16,000 units; 15,000 units; and 20,000 units. Because of aggressive marketing and promotion, the company expects that sales for each quarter of 2014 will be 25% higher than the respective quarter in 2013. The selling price per unit in 2014 is expected to be $4. What are the expected sales, in units and dollars, for the second quarter of 2014? For the third quarter of 2014?

10-15   Resco, a local retail establishment, expects to make inventory purchases as follows for the first quarter of 2013: January, $5,500; February, $6,500; and March, $8,000. Prior experience shows that 25% of a given month's purchases are paid in the month of purchase with the balance paid in the following month. No purchase discounts apply. What is the total expected cash disbursement for February? For March?

10-16   Ajax Manufacturing produces a single product, which takes 8.0 pounds of direct materials per unit produced. We are currently at the end of the first quarter of the year and there are 50,000 pounds of material on hand. The company's policy is to maintain an end-of-quarter inventory of materials equal to 25% of the following quarter's material requirements for production. How many units of product were produced in the first quarter of the year? Under the assumption that production will increase by 10% in the second quarter, what are the direct materials requirements (in pounds) for planned production in the second quarter?

10-17  Grey Manufacturing Company expects sales to total 13,000 in the first quarter, 12,000 units in the second quarter, and 15,000 in the third quarter of the current fiscal year. Company policy is to have on hand at the end of each quarter an amount of inventory equal to 10% of the following quarter's sales. Given this information, how many units should be scheduled for production in the second quarter?

10-18  Easy Clean operates a chain of dry cleaners. It is experimenting with a continuous-improvement (i.e., kaizen) budget for operating expenses. Currently, a typical location has operating expenses of $10,000 per month. Plans are in place to achieve labor and utility savings. The associated operational changes are estimated to reduce monthly operating costs by a factor of 0.99 beginning in January. What is the estimated operating cost for January? For June? For December?

10-19  Campbell's Wholesale Company is preparing monthly cash budgets for the fourth quarter of 2013. Monthly sales revenue in this quarter is estimated as follows: October, $30,000; November, $24,000; and December, $20,000. All sales are made on open credit with 70% collected in the month of sale and 30% collected in the following month. What is the estimated total cash collected in November? December?

10-20  Royal Cigar Company is preparing a budget for cash collections. Its sales for November and December are estimated as $90,000 and $100,000 respectively. Past practice indicates that sales in any given month are collected as follows: month of sale, 75%; month following the month of sale, 20%; uncollectible accounts, 5%. The company allows a 2% discount for cash collections in the month of sale. What is the net cash estimated to be collected in December?

10-21  The George Company has a policy of maintaining an end-of-month cash balance of at least $30,000. In months where a shortfall is expected, the company can draw in $1,000 increments on a line of credit it has with a local bank, at an interest rate of 12% per annum. All borrowings are assumed for budgeting purposes to occur at the beginning of the month, while all loan repayments (in $1,000 increments of principal) are assumed to occur at the end of the month. Interest is paid at the end of each month. For April, an end-of-month cash balance (prior to any financing and interest expense) of $18,000 is budgeted; for May, an excess of cash collected over cash payments (prior to any interest payments and loan repayments) of $22,000 is anticipated. What is the interest payment estimated for April (there is no bank loan outstanding at the end of March)? What is the total financing effect (cash interest plus loan transaction) for May?

10-22  If the December 1 balance in the Direct Materials (DM) Inventory account was $37,000, the December 31 balance was $39,500, and $150,000 of DM were issued to production during December, what was the amount of DM purchased during the month?

10-23  A company is formulating its marketing expense budget for the last quarter of the year. Sales in units for the third quarter amounted to 4,000; sales volume for the fourth quarter is expected to increase by 10%. Variable marketing expenses per unit sold amount to approximately $0.05, paid in cash in month of sale. Fixed marketing expenses per month amount to $10,000 of salaries, $5,000 of depreciation (delivery trucks), and $2,000 of insurance (paid monthly). What is the total budgeted marketing *expense* for the fourth quarter of the year? What is the estimated *cash payment* for marketing expenses for the fourth quarter?

## Exercises

[LO 10-4]  10-24  **Production and Materials Purchases Budgets**  White Corporation's budget calls for the following sales for next year:

| | | | |
|---|---|---|---|
| Quarter 1 | 90,000 units | Quarter 3 | 68,000 units |
| Quarter 2 | 76,000 units | Quarter 4 | 96,000 units |

Each unit of the product requires 3 pounds of direct materials. The company's policy is to begin each quarter with an inventory of product equal to 5% of that quarter's estimated sales requirements and an inventory of direct materials equal to 20% of that quarter's estimated direct materials requirements for production.

**Required**  Determine the production and materials purchases budgets for the second quarter.

[LO 10-4]  10-25  **Budgeted Cash Receipts and Cash Payments**  Timpco, a retailer, makes both cash and credit sales (i.e., sales on open account). Information regarding budgeted sales for the last quarter of the year is as follows:

|  | October | November | December |
|---|---|---|---|
| Cash sales | $100,000 | $120,000 | $ 80,000 |
| Credit sales | 100,000 | 150,000 | 90,000 |
| Total | $200,000 | $270,000 | $170,000 |

Past experience shows that 5% of credit sales are uncollectible. Of the credit sales that are collectible, 60% are collected in the month of sale; the remaining 40% are collected in the month following the month of sale. Customers are granted a 1.5% discount for payment within 10 days of billing. Approximately 75% of collectible credit sales take advantage of the cash discount.

Inventory purchases each month are 100% of the *cost* of the following month's projected sales. (The gross profit rate for Timpco is approximately 30%.) All merchandise purchases are made on credit, with 25% paid in the month of purchase and the remainder paid in the following month. No cash discounts for early payment are in effect.

**Required**

1. Calculate the budgeted total cash receipts for November and December.
2. Calculate budgeted cash payments for November and December (budgeted total sales for January of the coming year = $200,000).

[LO 10-4]  10-26  **Cash Disbursements Budget**  Bond Company budgets the following purchases of direct materials for the first quarter of the year:

|  | January | February | March |
|---|---|---|---|
| Budgeted purchases | $150,000 | $120,000 | $90,000 |

All purchases of direct materials are made on credit. On average, the company pays 80% of its purchases in the month of sales, and the remainder in the following month.

**Required**

1. For the months of February and March, what are the estimated cash payments for purchases of direct materials under the assumption that there is no (cash) discount for early payment?
2. For the months of February and March, what are the estimated cash payments for purchases of direct materials under the assumption that the purchase terms are 2/15, net 30? The company's policy is to take advantage of all cash discounts for early payment.
3. Provide an economic argument as to why it is good (economic) policy to take advantage of early payment discounts, as in (2) above.

[LO 10-4]  10-27  **Cash Budget—Financing Effects**  You are a relatively recent hire to Hartz & Co., a local manufacturer of plumbing supply products. You have been asked to prepare, for a presentation to the company's management, a condensed cash flow statement for the months of November and December 2013.

Assume the cash balance at November 1 will be $75,000. It is the company's policy to maintain a minimum cash balance of $50,000 at the end of each month. Cash receipts (from cash sales and collection of accounts receivable) are projected to be $525,000 for November and $450,000 for December. Cash disbursements (sales commissions, advertising, delivery expense, wages, utilities, etc.) prior to financing activity are scheduled to be $450,500 in November and $550,000 in December.

Borrowing, when needed, is done at the beginning of the month in increments of $1,000. The annual interest rate on any such loans is estimated to be 12%. Interest on any outstanding loans is paid in cash at the end of the month. Repayments of principal (if any) are assumed to occur at the end of the month. As of November 1, the company has a $50,000 short-term loan from the local bank. This loan is payable at the end of November.

**Required**  Use the preceding information to prepare the cash budget for November and December. (*Hint:* The December 31 cash balance should be $50,480.)

**[LO 10-4]**   10-28   **Cash Budget**   Marsha, Inc., has the following budgeted data for 2013:

| | |
|---|---:|
| Cash balance, beginning | $ 15,000 |
| Collections from customers | 145,000 |
| Direct materials purchases | 25,000 |
| Expenses: | |
|   Operating expenses | 50,000 |
|   Payroll | 75,000 |
|   Income taxes | 6,000 |
| Other: | |
|   Machinery purchases | 30,000 |

Operating expenses include $20,000 depreciation for buildings and equipment. All purchases of materials are paid for in the period of purchase. The company requires a minimum cash balance of $25,000.

**Required**   Compute the amount the company needs to finance or the excess cash available for Marsha to invest.

**[LO 10-4]**   10-29   **Budgeting Cash Receipts: Cash Discounts Allowed on Receivables**   Yeopay Plumbing Supply accepts bank charge cards and offers established plumbers charge accounts with terms of 1/eom, n/45. Yeopay's experience is that 25% of its sales are for cash and bank credit cards. The remaining 75% are on credit. Of the cash sales, 40% pay cash and the remaining 60% pay with bank credit cards. Yeopay receives payments from the bank on credit card sales at the end of the day. However, Yeopay has to pay 3% for these services. An aging schedule for accounts receivable shows the following pattern on credit sales:

20% pay in the month of sale.
50% pay in the first month following the month of sale.
15% pay in the second month following the month of sale.
12% pay in the third month following the month of sale.
 3% are never collected.

All accounts not paid by the end of the second month following the month of sale are considered overdue and are subject to a 2% monthly late charge. Yeopay has prepared the following sales forecasts:

| | |
|---|---:|
| June | $60,000 |
| July | 80,000 |
| August | 90,000 |
| September | 96,000 |
| October | 88,000 |

**Required**
1. Use Excel to prepare a schedule of cash receipts for September and October.
   a. At the top of a new spreadsheet, create an "Original Data" section with four subheads: Sales Data, Sales Breakdown and Terms, Breakdown of Cash/Bank Credit Card Sales, and collection of Credit Sales.
   b. Enter all pertinent data listed above.
   c. Create a new section to calculate cash receipts for September with rows for Cash Sales, Bank Credit Card Sales, Collections of Accounts Receivable (4 rows), Total Cash Receipts, and columns for: Total Sales; Percentage of Sales for cash/bank credit card sales versus credit sales; Payment Percentage for the proportions collected (i.e., percentage collected to allow for cash discounts or late charges); and Cash Receipts.
   d. Program your spreadsheet to perform all necessary calculations for determining cash receipts for September. Do not type in any amounts. All the amounts you enter into this new section should derive from data from the Original Data section using a formula.
   e. Verify the accuracy of your spreadsheet by calculating the total cash receipts in September: $86,082.

f. Create a new section titled October. Program your spreadsheet to perform all necessary calculations for determinations of cash receipts for October and verify the accuracy of your spreadsheet by showing that the total cash receipts for October is $88,141.

2. What is the appropriate accounting treatment for the bank service fees and the cash discounts allowed on collection of receivables?

[LO 10-4]    10-30 **Cash Receipts and Payments**    Information pertaining to Noskey Corporation's sales revenue follows:

| | November 2012 (Actual) | December 2012 (Budgeted) | January 2013 (Budgeted) |
|---|---|---|---|
| Cash sales | $ 80,000 | $100,000 | $ 60,000 |
| Credit sales | 240,000 | 360,000 | 180,000 |
| Total sales | $320,000 | $460,000 | $240,000 |

Management estimates 5% of credit sales to be uncollectible. Of collectible credit sales, 60% is collected in the month of sale and the remainder in the month following the month of sale. Purchases of inventory each month include 70% of the next month's projected total sales (stated at cost) plus 30% of projected sales for the current month (stated at cost). All inventory purchases are on account; 25% is paid in the month of purchase, and the remainder is paid in the month following the month of purchase. Purchase costs are approximately 60% of the selling price.

**Required**    Determine for Noskey:

1. Budgeted cash collections in December 2012 from November 2012 credit sales.

2. Budgeted total cash receipts in January 2013.

3. Budgeted total cash payments in December 2012 for inventory purchases.

**(CPA Adapted)**

[LO 10-2]    10-31 **Purchase Discounts**    It is typically beneficial for companies to take advantage of early-payment discounts allowed on purchases made on credit. To see why this is the case, determine the effective rate of interest associated with *not* taking advantage of the early-payment discount for each of the following situations. Assume in each case that payment is made on the 30th day of the billing cycle.

**Required**

1. What is the opportunity cost of not taking advantage of the discount associated with purchases made under the following terms: 2/10, n/30? (Show calculations.)

2. What is the opportunity cost of not taking advantage of the discount associated with purchases made under the following terms: 1/10, n/30? (Show calculations.)

3. What is the appropriate accounting treatment for purchase discounts?

[LO 10-4, 10-5]    10-32 **Accounts Receivable Collections and Sensitivity Analysis**    Papst Company is preparing its cash budget for the month of May. The following information is available concerning its accounts receivable:

| | |
|---|---|
| Actual credit sales for March | $130,000 |
| Actual credit sales for April | $160,000 |
| Estimated credit sales for May | $210,000 |
| Estimated collections in the month of sale | 25% |
| Estimated collections in the first month after the month of sale | 60% |
| Estimated collections in the second month after the month of sale | 10% |
| Estimated provision for bad debts (made in the month of sale) | 5% |

The firm writes off all uncollectible accounts at the end of the second month after the month of sale.

**Required**    Create an Excel spreadsheet and determine for Papst Company for the month of May:

1. The estimated cash receipts from accounts receivable collections.

2. The gross amount of accounts receivable at the end of the month.

3. The net amount of accounts receivable at the end of the month.

4. Recalculate requirements (1) and (2) under the assumption that estimated collections in the month of sale = 60% and in the first month following the month of sale = 25%.

5. What are the benefits and likely costs of moving to the situation described above in (4)?

[LO 10-5]   10-33   **What-If Analysis**   As the management accountant for the Tyson Company you have been asked to construct a *financial planning model* for collection of accounts receivable and then to perform a what-if analysis in terms of the assumption regarding estimated uncollectible accounts. You are provided with the following information:

*Collection Pattern for Credit Sales:* 65% of the company's credit sales are collected in the month of sale, 30% in the month following the month of sale, and 5% are uncollectible.

*Credit Sales:* January 2013, $100,000; February 2013, $120,000; March 2013, $110,000.

**Required**

1. What is meant by the term *what-if analysis*?

2. Generate a spreadsheet model regarding estimated bad debts expense under the following assumptions regarding the rate of uncollectible accounts: 1%, 3%, 5% (base case), and 8%. Prepare an estimate of bad debts expense for each of three months, January through March, and for the quarter as a whole.

3. What is the value to Tyson Company of creating a model and then performing the what-if analysis described above?

[LO 10-5]   10-34   **Profit Planning and Sensitivity Analysis**   You are currently trying to decide between two cost structures for your business: one that has a greater proportion of short-term fixed costs and another that is more heavily weighted to variable costs. Estimated revenue and cost data for each alternative are as follows:

|  | Cost Structure | |
| --- | --- | --- |
|  | **Alternative #1** | **Alternative #2** |
| Selling price per unit | $  100 | $  100 |
| Variable cost per unit | 85 | 80 |
| Short-term fixed costs/year | 40,000 | 45,000 |

**Required**

1. What sales volume, in units, is needed for the total costs in each cost-structure alternative to be the same?

2. Suppose your profit goal for the coming year is 5% of sales (i.e., operating profit ÷ sales = 5%). What sales level in units is needed under each alternative to achieve this goal?

3. Suppose again that your profit goal for the coming year is 5% of sales. What sales volume in dollars is needed under each alternative to achieve this goal?

[LO 10-5]   10-35   **Scenario Analysis**   As part of the process of preparing the master budget for the coming year, you've been asked to perform what-if analyses, in the form of scenarios, on the original planning assumptions regarding Product A produced by your company. The following are the base-line planning data for the coming year for this product:

| | |
| --- | --- |
| Sales volume (annual, in units) | 2,500 |
| Selling price per unit | $  1,500 |
| Variable cost per unit | $  1,000 |
| Fixed costs (per year) | $200,000 |

**Required**

1. Define what is meant by the terms *what-if analysis* and *scenario analysis.*

2. Based on the baseline planning data, what is the budgeted operating income for Product A for the coming year?

3. Determine the estimated operating income under each of the following scenarios (for each scenario you should report both the new budgeted operating income and the percentage change in operating income from the baseline budgeted result):

a. Selling price per unit is 10% higher than planned, while fixed costs per year are also 10% higher than planned.

b. Variable cost per unit is 5% higher than planned, while fixed costs are lower by this same percentage.

c. Selling price per unit is 10% higher than planned, while volume is decreased by 8%.

[LO 10-6] 10-36 **Cash Budgeting: Not-for-Profit Context** *(contributed by Helen M. Savage)* Tri-County Social Service Agency is a not-for-profit organization in the Midwest. Use the following information to complete the *cash budget* for the year ending December 31, 2013.

- The Board of Trustees requires that Tri-County maintain a minimum cash balance of $8,000.
- If cash is short, the agency may borrow from an endowment fund enough to maintain the $8,000 minimum. (An "endowment fund" is an investment fund set up by a nonprofit entity [e.g., church, university, or hospital] and used either for ongoing operations or for purposes specified by the donor(s) to the fund. Such donations are generally tax deductible for the donors.) Repayment must be made as soon as possible. No interest is charged.
- It is anticipated that the year 2013 will begin with an $11,000 cash balance.
- Contract revenue is received evenly during the year.
- Mental health income is expected to grow by $5,000 in the second and third quarters, but not change in the fourth quarter.

**Required**

1. Within the context of a not-for-profit organization, what is an *endowment fund*?
2. Complete the cash budget for 2013, for each quarter and the year as a whole, using the template that follows.
3. Determine the amount that the agency will owe the *endowment fund* at year-end.
4. Does the borrowing indicate a problem? What options would the agency have to increase revenues?
5. Do you think that a requirement to pay interest on the borrowings would have a positive impact on the agency's activities? Why or why not?

**Cash Budget for Tri-County Social Service Agency**
**2013 (in thousands)**

| | Quarters | | | | |
| | I | II | III | IV | Year |
|---|---|---|---|---|---|
| Cash balance, beginning | $ 11 | ? | ? | ? | $ 11 |
| Receipts: | | | | | |
|   Grants | $ 80 | $ 70 | ? | ? | $ 300 |
|   Contracts | ? | ? | ? | ? | $ 80 |
|   Mental health income | $ 20 | ? | ? | ? | $ 105 |
|   Charitable donations | $250 | ? | $200 | $400 | ? |
| Total cash available | ? | $473 | $333 | ? | ? |
| Less disbursements: | | | | | |
|   Salaries and benefits | ? | $342 | ? | ? | $1,365 |
|   Office expenses | $ 70 | ? | $ 71 | $ 50 | $ 256 |
|   Equipment purchases & maintenance | $2 | $4 | $ 6 | ? | $ 17 |
|   Specific assistance | $ 20 | $ 15 | $ 18 | ? | $ 73 |
|     Total disbursements | ? | ? | ? | ? | ? |
| Excess (defic.) of cash available over disbursements | $ (46) | ? | ? | $112 | ? |
| Financing: | | | | | |
|   Borrowings from endowment fund | ? | ? | $112 | ? | ? |
|   Repayments | ? | $ (39) | ? | ? | ? |
|     Total financing effects | ? | ? | ? | ? | ? |
| Cash balance, ending | ? | ? | ? | ? | ? |

[LO 10-6] 10-37 **Budgeting: Not-for-Profit Context** *(contributed by Helen M. Savage)* Catholic Charities Regional Agency serves several contiguous counties in Ohio. The finance committee of its board of directors monitors financial activity for the agency. This oversight includes decisions regarding the investment of excess funds and the management of endowment funds. These decisions are relevant to the annual budget preparation since the investment accounts serve as a source of needed funds and/or a use of excess funds.

As a Catholic Charities agency, the regional organization must adhere to guidelines adopted by the U.S. Council of Catholic Bishops. Visit the council's website at **http://www.usccb.org/finance/srig.htm** and review its *Socially Responsible Investment Guidelines,* which discuss basic principles for investments and the stated investment policy of the organization.

**Required**

1. What is the meaning of the word *stewardship*? Should the religious or philosophical position of an organization affect decisions that are made as part of the budgeting process?

2. How should a board of directors for this organization apply these principles in making investment decisions tied to the annual budget?

3. Would you, as a board member, ignore such principles to increase investment gains? Why or why not?

4. If the agency's monies are managed by an investment firm, should the board request information about the stocks included in individual investment funds to verify compliance with the stated investment policy of the organization?

**[LO 10-6]   10-38   Budgeting for a Service Firm**   Refer to the AccuTax, Inc., example in the chapter. One of the partners is planning to retire at the end of the year. May Higgins, the sole remaining partner, plans to add a manager at an annual salary of $90,000. She expects the manager to work, on average, 45 hours a week for 45 weeks per year. She plans to change the required staff time for each hour spent to complete a tax return to the following:

|  | Business Return | Complex Individual Return | Simple Individual Return |
|---|---|---|---|
| Partner | 0.3 hour | 0.05 hour | — |
| Manager | 0.2 hour | 0.15 hour | — |
| Senior consultant | 0.5 hour | 0.40 hour | 0.2 hour |
| Consultant | — | 0.40 hour | 0.8 hour |

The manager is salaried and earns no overtime pay. Senior consultants are salaried but receive time and a half for any overtime worked. The firm plans to keep all the senior consultants and adjust the number of consultants as needed including employing part-time consultants, who also are paid on an hourly basis. Higgins has also decided to have five supporting staff at $40,000 each. All other operating data remain unchanged. The manager will share 10% of any profit over $500,000 before bonus.

**Required**

1. What is the budgeted total cost for overtime hours worked by senior consultants?

2. How many full-time consultants should be budgeted?

3. Determine the manager's total compensation and total pretax operating income for the firm, assuming that the revenues from preparing tax returns remain unchanged.

**[LO 10-7, 10-8]   10-39   Budgetary Slack and Zero-Base Budgeting (ZBB)**   Bob Bingham is the controller of Atlantis Laboratories, a manufacturer and distributor of generic prescription pharmaceuticals. He is currently preparing the annual budget and reviewing the current business plan. The firm's business unit managers prepare and assemble the detailed operating budgets with technical assistance from the corporate accounting staff. The business unit managers then present the final budgets to the corporate executive committee for approval. The corporate accounting staff reviews the budgets for adherence to corporate accounting policies but not for reasonableness of the line items within the budgets.

Bob is aware that the upcoming year for Atlantis could be a difficult one because of a major patent expiration and the loss of a licensing agreement for another product line. He also knows that during the budgeting process slack is created in varying degrees throughout the organization. Bob believes that this slack has a negative effect on the firm's overall business objectives and should be eliminated where possible.

**Required**

1. Define the term *budgetary slack*.

2. Explain the advantages and disadvantages of budgetary slack from the point of view of (a) the business unit manager who must achieve the budget, and (b) corporate management.

3. Bob Bingham is considering implementing zero-base budgeting (ZBB) in Atlantis Laboratories.

   a. Define *zero-base budgeting.*

   b. Describe how *zero-base budgeting* could be advantageous to Atlantis Laboratories in controlling budgetary slack.

   c. Discuss the disadvantages Atlantis Laboratories might encounter in using ZBB.

**(CMA Adapted)**

[LO 10-7]   **10-40   Activity-Based Budgeting (ABB)**   OFC Company of Kansas City prints business forms and other specialty paper products, such as writing paper, envelopes, note cards, and greeting cards. Its Business Services division offers inventory-management services and desktop delivery on request. The division uses an activity-based costing (ABC) system. The budgeted usage of each activity cost driver and cost-driver rates for January 2013 for the Business Services division are:

| Activity | Cost Driver | Budgeted Activity | Cost-Driver Rate |
|---|---|---|---|
| Storage | Cartons in inventory | 400,000 | $0.4925/carton/month |
| Requisition handling | Requisitions | 30,000 | 12.50 |
| Pick packing | Lines | 800,000 | 1.50 |
| Data entry | Lines | 800,000 | 0.80 |
| | Requisitions | 30,000 | 1.20 |
| Desktop delivery | Per delivery | 12,000 | 30.00 |

For the month, the division expects to make 11,700 deliveries to deliver 1,170,000 cartons to customers.

**Required**

1. What is the total budgeted cost for each activity and for the Business Services division in January 2013?

2. Assume, in contrast to requirement 1, that activity-related information was not available. Rather, the only information available is that the budgeted fixed costs for the month are $1,000,000, and that the budgeted variable cost per carton is estimated as $1.30. What is the budgeted total cost for the month using this single volume-based approach? Compare and comment on the difference in your answers to requirements 1 and 2.

3. Dories Supply Chain Management Company offers to install an electronic order-processing system that transmits customer requisitions via the Internet to the Business Services division for immediate pick, packing, and delivery. No requisition handling and data entry will be needed once the system is fully functional. How much savings can the Business Services division expect from switching to the new system before considering the payment to Dories? What would be necessary in order for the company to be able to realize these estimated cost savings? Can you estimate the amount of savings if the firm uses a single cost rate (based on the number of cartons delivered) to determine the budgeted cost for the division?

[LO 10-7]   **10-41   Activity-Based Budgeting (ABB) with Continuous Improvements**   OFC Company (Exercise 10-40) has decided to implement a continuous-improvements program to enhance operational efficiency. After a careful study, management and employees agree that the firm will be able to reduce cost rates for batch-level activities by 2% and unit-level activities by 1% per month during the first year of the program starting February 2013. The firm has decided to delay the implementation of the program for customer-sustaining and facility-level activities until 2014. The firm expects the amount of cost-driver usage in each of the next two months to be the same as those in January. (Use 4 decimal points for all cost rates.)

**Required**

1. Identify unit-level and batch-level activities.

2. What are the total budgeted costs for each activity and for the division as a whole in February and March?

3. Identify three factors that are likely to be critical for a successful kaizen program.

4. What are primary criticisms regarding kaizen budgeting?

[LO 10-7]   **10-42   Time-Driven Activity-Based Budgeting (TDABB)**   The company for which you work recently implemented time-driven activity-based costing (TDABC) in conjunction with its ERP system. Management is pleased with the revised product and customer cost information that the TDABC system produces. It is now wondering how this system can be used for budgeting purposes. You have been asked to provide an example of using time-driven activity-based budgeting, given the following information:

1. There are two resources (departments): indirect labor and computer support.

2. There are two primary activities that these resources support: handling production runs and product-level support.

3. Indirect labor support is consumed as follows:
   a. To handle production runs: 10 hours/run
   b. To support products: 500 hours/product

4. Computer support is consumed as follows:
   a. To handle production runs: 0.4 hr./run
   b. To support products: 50 hours/product

5. Resource practical capacity levels:
   a. Indirect labor: 20,000 hours per quarter
   b. Computer support: 500 hours per quarter

6. Cost of supplying resources:
   a. Indirect labor: $1,000,000 per quarter
   b. Computer support: $500,000 per quarter

### Required

1. Calculate the budgeted resource cost per hour (at practical capacity) for each of the two resources, *indirect labor support* and *computer support.*

2. Determine the budgeted cost-driver rates for each of the two activities, *handle production runs* and *support products.*

3. Suppose that the total cost of resources supplied for the quarter just ended was exactly as budgeted (i.e., $1,500,000), but that only 18,000 indirect labor-hours were used along with 450 computer hours. Calculate, for each resource, the cost of unused capacity. How should this cost be handled for internal reporting purposes?

4. After implementing a TQM program, the company was able to implement process-efficiency changes, the end result of which was a 10% reduction in the indirect labor time associated with the activity handling production runs. Re-estimate the indirect labor cost component of the cost to handle a production run. Also, recalculate the cost of unused capacity for indirect labor assuming the original facts but with the 10% efficiency gain. Assume that in the original case facts, 16,000 of the 18,000 hours relate to the activity handling production runs (while the remaining 2,000 hours relate to the activity product-level support).

[LO 10-7]    10-43 **Rolling Financial Forecasts**    You are given the following budgeted and actual data for the Grey Company for each of the months January through June of the current year.

In December of the prior year, sales were forecasted as follows: January, 100 units; February, 95 units; March, 100 units; April, 110 units; May, 120 units; June, 125 units. In January of the current year, sales for the months February through June were reforecasted as follows: February, 90 units; March, 100 units; April, 105 units; May, 110 units; June, 120 units. In February of the current year, sales for the months March through June were reforecasted as follows: March, 95 units; April, 105 units; May, 105 units; June, 120 units. In March of the current year, sales for the months April through June were reforecasted as follows: April, 105 units; May, 100 units; June, 110 units. In April of the current year, sales for the months May and June were reforecasted as follows: May, 90 units; June, 105 units. In May of the current year, sales for June were reforecasted as 105 units.

Actual sales for the six-month period were as follows: January, 98 units; February, 95 units; March, 92 units; April, 108 units; May, 98 units; June, 100 units.

### Required

1. For each of the months January through June, inclusive, prepare a rolling forecast of sales volume. (*Hint:* There will be only one forecasted number for January—this is the forecast done in December. For February, there will be two forecasts: one done in December and a second done in January. For June, there will be six forecasts, one for each of the preceding six months.)

2. For each of the months March through June, determine the three-month forecast error rate, defined as 1 minus the absolute percentage error. For example, the forecast error rate for March's sales is found by dividing the *absolute value* of the forecast error for this month by the actual sales volume for the month. The *forecast error* for any month (e.g., March) is defined as the difference

between the actual sales volume for the month and the sales volume for that month forecasted three months earlier (e.g., December).

[LO 10-7]   10-44  **Kaizen Budget/Activity-Based Budgeting (ABB)**   Refer to text Exhibit 10.19 (the ABB for Kerry Window Systems, Inc.). As the management accountant for Kerry you have been asked to evaluate the possibility of implementing a continuous-improvement (i.e., kaizen) budgeting system. Assume that budgeted cost-driver usage data in Part A of Exhibit 10.19 will continue over the foreseeable future.

**Required**

1. Recalculate the budgeted factory overhead costs for June under the assumption that, starting in May, each budgeted activity cost rate decreases by 0.5% relative to the preceding month.
2. In general, what are the anticipated benefits of using a kaizen approach to budgeting?
3. What do you envision as the principal concerns or limitations regarding the use of kaizen budgeting?
4. Provide some examples of how, in the Kerry example, the company would be able to realize the budgeted cost savings referenced above in requirement 1.

[LO 10-7]   10-45  **Resource Capacity Planning/ABC**   Two years ago, in conjunction with revitalization efforts regarding the downtown area of Metro City, you and your partner purchased a local eatery. Though moribund at the time, you were able (through your hard work and dedicated efforts) to resurrect the establishment. In fact, the last few months appear to have been quite successful from a financial standpoint.

However, your establishment now faces a new competitor—an eatery located only several blocks away from yours. You and your partner are now evaluating strategic options as to how to deal with this new competition. Your facility is capable of serving 200 meals a day. (Because your clientele consists almost exclusively of college-age students, the basic menu is the same for "lunch" and "dinner." Currently, your business does not serve breakfast.)

You and your partner have (finally!) taken time to "go over the books" (i.e., financial records) carefully. Your investigation yields the following information:

    a. The primary variable cost is food (that is, the total food cost varies in response to changes in the number of meals served).

    b. Fixed operating expenses (salaries, depreciation, etc.) average approximately $1,100 per day.

    c. The average number of meals served per day over the past three months was 175.

Given the above facts, and lacking any formal study of accounting, you calculate the budgeted fixed operating cost as $6.29 per meal (i.e., $1,100 ÷ 175 meals per day). In response, in an attempt to fully recover your costs, you and your partner are contemplating a price increase.

**Required**

1. Given the competitive situation, what is the likely result of the decision to raise prices? Explain.
2. Suggest and defend an alternative approach for allocating budgeted fixed operating costs to each meal.

[LO 10-8]   10-46  **Budgetary Pressure and Ethics**   Midwest Industries produces and distributes industrial chemicals in its Belco Division, which is located in Michigan's upper peninsula. Belco's earnings increased sharply in 2013, and bonuses were paid to the management staff for the first time in three years. Bonuses are based in part on the amount by which reported income exceeds budgeted income.

Maria Gonzales, vice president of finance, was pleased with reported earnings for 2013 and therefore thought that pressure to "show" financial results would subside. However, Tom Lin, Belco's division manager, told Gonzales that he "saw no reason why bonuses for 2014 should not be double those of 2013." As a result, Gonzales felt pressure to increase reported income to exceed budgeted income by an even greater amount, a situation that would ensure increased bonuses.

Gonzales met with Bill Wilson of P&R, Inc., a primary vendor of Belco's manufacturing supplies and equipment. Gonzales and Wilson have been close business contacts for many years. Gonzales asked Wilson to identify all of Belco's purchases of perishable supplies as "equipment" on sales invoices issued by P&R. The reason Gonzales gave for her request was that Belco's division manager had imposed stringent budget constraints on operating expenses, but not on capital expenditures. Gonzales planned to capitalize (rather than expense) the cost of perishable supplies and then include them in the equipment account on the balance sheet. In this way, Gonzales could defer the recognition of expenses to a later year. This procedure would increase reported earnings, which in turn would lead to higher bonuses (in the short run). Wilson agreed to do as Gonzales had asked.

While analyzing the second quarter financial statements, Gary Wood, Belco's director of cost accounting, noticed a large decrease in supplies expense from a year ago. Wood reviewed the Supplies Expense account and noticed that only equipment, not supplies, had been purchased from P&R, a major source for such supplies. Wood, who reports to Gonzales, immediately brought this to the attention of Gonzales.

Gonzales told Wood of Lin's high expectations and of the arrangement made with Wilson (from P&R). Wood told Gonzales that her action was an improper accounting treatment for the supplies purchased from P&R. Wood requested that he be allowed to correct the accounts and urged that the arrangement with P&R be discontinued. Gonzales refused the request and told Wood not to become involved in the arrangement with P&R.

After clarifying the situation in a confidential discussion with an objective and qualified peer within Belco, Wood arranged to meet with Lin, Belco's division manager. At that meeting, Wood disclosed the arrangement Gonzales had made with P&R.

**Required**

1. Explain why the use of alternative accounting methods to manipulate reported earnings is unethical, if not illegal.

2. Is Gary Wood, Belco's director of cost accounting, correct in saying that the supplies purchased from P&R, Inc., were accounted for improperly? Explain.

3. Assuming that the agreement of Gonzales with P&R was in violation of the IMA's *Statement of Ethical Professional Practice* (**www.imanet.org**), discuss whether Wood's actions were appropriate or inappropriate.

**(CMA Adapted)**

[LO 10-4] 10-47 **Comprehensive Profit Plan**   Spring Manufacturing Company makes two components identified as C12 and D57. Selected budgetary data for 2013 follow:

|  | Finished Components | |
| --- | --- | --- |
|  | **C12** | **D57** |
| Requirements for each finished component: | | |
| RM 1 | 10 pounds | 8 pounds |
| RM 2 | 0 | 4 pounds |
| RM 3 | 2 pounds | 1 pound |
| Direct labor | 2 hours | 3 hours |
| Product information: | | |
| Sales price | $150 | $220 |
| Sales (units) | 12,000 | 9,000 |
| Estimated beginning inventory (units) | 400 | 150 |
| Desired ending inventory (units) | 300 | 200 |

|  | Direct Materials Information | | |
| --- | --- | --- | --- |
|  | **RM1** | **RM2** | **RM3** |
| Cost per pound | $ 2.00 | $ 2.50 | $ 0.50 |
| Estimated beginning inventory in pounds | 3,000 | 1,500 | 1,000 |
| Desired ending inventory in pounds | 4,000 | 1,000 | 1,500 |

The firm expects the average wage rate to be $25 per hour in 2013. Spring Manufacturing uses direct labor-hours to apply overhead. Each year the firm determines the overhead application rate for the year based on the budgeted output for the year. The firm maintains negligible work-in-process inventory and expects the cost per unit for both beginning and ending finished products inventories to be identical.

| | Factory Overhead Information |
|---|---|
| Indirect materials—variable | $ 10,000 |
| Miscellaneous supplies and tools—variable | 5,000 |
| Indirect labor—variable | 40,000 |
| Supervision—fixed | 120,000 |
| Payroll taxes and fringe benefits—variable | 250,000 |
| Maintenance costs—fixed | 20,000 |
| Maintenance costs—variable | 10,080 |
| Depreciation—fixed | 71,330 |
| Heat, light, and power—fixed | 43,420 |
| Heat, light, and power—variable | 11,000 |
| Total | $580,830 |

| | Selling and Administrative Expense Information |
|---|---|
| Advertising | $ 60,000 |
| Sales salaries | 200,000 |
| Travel and entertainment | 60,000 |
| Depreciation—warehouse | 5,000 |
| Office salaries | 60,000 |
| Executive salaries | 250,000 |
| Supplies | 4,000 |
| Depreciation—office | 6,000 |
| Total | $645,000 |

The effective income tax rate for the company is 40%.

**Required**  Prepare an Excel spreadsheet that contains the following schedules or statements for 2013:

1. Sales budget
2. Production budget
3. Direct materials purchases budget (units and dollars)
4. Direct labor budget
5. Factory overhead budget
6. Cost of goods sold and ending finished goods inventory budgets
7. Selling and administrative expense budget
8. Budgeted income statement

[LO 10-2, 10-4]  10-48  **Comprehensive Profit Plan**  (Use information in Problem 10-47 for Spring Manufacturing Company.) C12 is a mature product. The sales manager believes that the price of C12 can be raised to $160 per unit with no effect on sales quantity. D57 is a new product introduced last year. Management believes D57 has great potential and is considering lowering the price to $180 to expand market size and gain market share. The lowering of D57's price is likely to double the total units of D57 sold.

**Required**

1. Amend the spreadsheet you constructed in Problem 10-47 to incorporate the changes outlined above. What effect do the changes have on the firm's after-tax operating income?
2. Would you recommend that the firm execute this strategy? Explain.

[LO 10-2, 10-4, 10-7]  10-49  **Comprehensive Profit Plan (Kaizen Budgeting)**  (Use information in Problem 10-47 for Spring Manufacturing Company.) Spring Manufacturing Company has had a continuous improvement (kaizen) program for the last two years. According to the kaizen program, the firm is expected to manufacture C12 and D57 with the following specifications:

| Cost Element | C12 | D57 |
|---|---|---|
| Raw material 1 | 9 pounds | 7 pounds |
| Raw material 2 | -0- | 3.6 pounds |
| Raw material 3 | 1.8 pounds | 0.8 pounds |
| Direct labor | 1.5 hours | 2 hours |

The company specifies that the variable factory overhead is to decrease by 10% while the fixed factory overhead is to decrease by 5%, except for depreciation expenses. The company does not expect the price of the raw materials to change. However, the hourly wage rate is likely to be $30.

**Required**

1. What is the budgeted after-tax operating income if the company can attain the expected operation level as prescribed by its kaizen program?

2. What are the benefits of Spring Manufacturing Company adopting a continuous-improvement program? What are the limitations?

[LO 10-4]    10-50    **Budget for a Merchandising Firm**    Kelly Company is a retail sporting goods store that uses an accrual accounting system. Facts regarding its operations follow:

- Sales are budgeted at $220,000 for December and $200,000 for January, terms 1/eom, n/60.
- Collections are expected to be 60% in the month of sale and 38% in the month following the sale. Two percent of sales are expected to be uncollectible and recorded in an allowance account at the end of the month of sales. Bad debts expense is included as part of operating expenses.
- Gross margin is 25% of sales.
- All accounts receivable are from credit sales. Bad debts are written off against the allowance account at the end of the month following the month of sale.
- Kelly desires to have 80% of the merchandise for the following month's sales on hand at the end of each month. Payment for merchandise is made in the month following the month of purchase.
- Other monthly operating expenses to be paid in cash total $22,600.
- Annual depreciation is $216,000, one-twelfth of which is reflected as part of monthly operating expenses.

Kelly Company's statement of financial position at the close of business on November 30 follows:

---

**KELLY COMPANY**
**Statement of Financial Position**
**November 30, 2013**

**Assets**

| | |
|---|---:|
| Cash | $    22,000 |
| Accounts receivable (net of $4,000 allowance for doubtful accounts) | 76,000 |
| Inventory | 132,000 |
| Property, plant, and equipment (net of $680,000 accumulated depreciation) | 870,000 |
| Total assets | $1,100,000 |

**Liabilities and Stockholders' Equity**

| | |
|---|---:|
| Accounts payable | $  162,000 |
| Common stock | 800,000 |
| Retained earnings | 138,000 |
| Total liabilities and equity | $1,100,000 |

---

**Required**

1. What is the total of budgeted cash collections for December?
2. How much is the book value of accounts receivable at the end of December?
3. How much is the income (loss) before income taxes for December?
4. What is the projected balance in inventory on December 31, 2013?
5. What are budgeted purchases for December?
6. What is the projected balance in accounts payable on December 31, 2013?

**(CMA Adapted)**

**[LO 10-4]**   10-51  **Retailer Budget**   D. Tomlinson Retail seeks your assistance in developing cash and other budget information for May, June, and July. The store expects to have the following balances at the end of April:

| | |
|---|---|
| Cash | $ 5,500 |
| Accounts receivable | 437,000 |
| Inventories | 309,400 |
| Accounts payable | 133,055 |

The firm follows these guidelines in preparing its budgets:

- **Sales.** All sales are on credit with terms of 3/10, n/30. Tomlinson bills customers on the last day of each month. The firm books receivables at gross amounts and collects 60% of the billings within the discount period, 25% by the end of the month, and 9% by the end of the second month. The firm's experience suggests that 6% is likely to be uncollectible and is written off at the end of the third month.

- **Purchases and expenses.** All purchases and expenses are on open account. The firm pays its payables over a two-month period with 54% paid in the month of purchase. Each month's units of ending inventory should equal 130% of the next month's cost of sales. The cost of each unit of inventory is $20. Selling and administrative expenses, of which $2,000 is depreciation, equal 15% of the current month's sales.

Actual and projected sales follow:

| Month | Dollars | Units | Month | Dollars | Units |
|---|---|---|---|---|---|
| March | $354,000 | 11,800 | June | $342,000 | 11,400 |
| April | 363,000 | 12,100 | July | 360,000 | 12,000 |
| May | 357,000 | 11,900 | August | 366,000 | 12,200 |

**Required**

1. Prepare schedules showing budgeted purchases for May and June.
2. Prepare a schedule showing budgeted cash disbursements during June.
3. Prepare a schedule showing budgeted cash collections during May.
4. Determine gross and net balances of accounts receivable on May 31.

**(CMA Adapted)**

**[LO 10-2, 10-4, 10-5]**   10-52  **Budgeting for Marketing Expenses; Strategy**   You have been recruited by a former classmate, Susanna Wu, to join the finance team of a company that she founded recently. The company produces a unique product line of hypoallergenic cosmetics and relies for its success on an aggressive marketing program. The company is in a start-up phase and therefore has no significant history of expenses and revenues upon which to rely for budgeting and planning purposes. Given the restriction on available funds (most of the available capital has been used for new-product development and to recruit a management team), the control of costs, including marketing costs, is thought by the management team to be essential for the short-term viability of the company.

You have held a number of intensive discussions with Susanna and John Thompson, director of marketing for the firm. They have asked you to prepare an estimated budget for marketing expenses for a month of operations.

You are provided with the following data, which represent average actual monthly costs over the past three months:

| Cost | Amount |
|---|---|
| Sales commissions | $120,000 |
| Sales staff salaries | 40,000 |
| Telephone and mailing | 38,000 |
| Rental—office building | 25,000 |
| Gas (utilities) | 12,000 |
| Delivery charges | 70,000 |
| Depreciation—office furniture | 8,000 |
| Marketing consultants | 25,000 |

Your discussions with John and Susanna indicate the following assumptions and anticipated changes regarding monthly marketing expenses for the coming year:

- Sales volume, because of aggressive marketing, should increase by 10%.
- To meet competitive pressures, sales prices are expected to decrease by 5%.
- Sales commissions are based on a percentage of sales revenue.
- Sales staff salaries, because of a new hire, will increase by 10%, regardless of sales volume.
- Because of recent industrywide factors, rates for telephone and mailing costs, as well as delivery charges, are expected to increase by 6%. However, both of these categories of costs are variable with sales volume.
- Rent on the office building is based on a two-year lease, with 18 months remaining on the original lease.
- Gas utility costs are largely independent of changes in sales volume. However, because of industrywide disruptions in supply, these costs are expected to increase by 15%, regardless of changes in sales volume.
- Depreciation on the office furniture used by members of the sales staff should increase because of new equipment that will be acquired. The planned cost for this equipment is $30,000, which will be depreciated using the straight-line (SL) method, with no salvage value, over a five-year useful life.
- Because of competitive pressure, the company plans to increase the cost of marketing consultants by $5,000 per month.

**Required**

1. Use the preceding information to develop an Excel spreadsheet that can be used to generate a monthly budget for marketing expenses. (Use the built-in function "SLN" to calculate monthly depreciation charges for the new equipment to be purchased.) What is the percentage change, by line item and in total, for items in your budget?

2. The management team is worried about the short-term financial position of the new company. Given the strain on available cash, the president has expressed a desire to keep marketing expenses over the next few months to a maximum of $350,000. Discussions with the marketing department indicate that telephone and mailing costs are the only category, in the short run, that can reasonably bear the planned-for reduction in marketing costs. The budget you have prepared includes an assumed 6% increase in telephone and mailing costs. What must this percentage change (positive or negative) be in order to achieve targeted monthly marketing costs? (*Hint:* Use the Goal Seek function in Excel, which is found under Data, then What-If Analysis.)

3. Comment on the use of the budget in this situation for cost-control purposes.

## Problems

[LO 10-5]   10-53   **Profit Planning and What-If Analysis**   As a newly hired management accountant, you have been asked to prepare a profit plan for the company for which you work. As part of this task, you've been asked to do some what-if analyses. Following is the budgeted information regarding the coming year:

| | |
|---|---|
| Selling price per unit | $ 80.00 |
| Variable cost per unit | 64.00 |
| Fixed costs (per year) | 900,000 |

**Required**

1. What is the breakeven volume, in units and dollars, for the coming year?

2. Assume that the goal of the company is to earn a pretax (operating) profit of $360,000 for the coming year. How many units would the company have to sell to achieve this goal?

3. Assume that, of the $64 variable cost per unit, the labor-cost component is $20. Current negotiations with the employees of the company indicate some uncertainty regarding the labor-cost component of the variable cost figure presented above. What is the effect on the breakeven point in units if selling price and fixed costs are as planned, but the labor cost for the coming year is 4% higher than anticipated? What if labor costs are 6% higher than anticipated? What if labor costs turn out to be 8% higher than anticipated? (Show calculations.)

4. Assume now that management is convinced that labor costs will be 5% higher than originally planned when the budget for the year was put together. What selling price per unit must the

company charge to maintain the budgeted ratio of contribution margin to sales? (*Hint:* Use the Goal Seek function in Excel to answer this question.)

5. Explain the role of what-if analysis in the budgeting process.

**[LO 10-4, 10-5]**   10-54   **Cash Flow Analysis; Sensitivity Analysis**   CompCity, Inc., sells computer hardware. It also markets related software and software-support services. The company prepares annual forecasts for sales, of which the first six months of 2013 are given below.

In a typical month, total sales are broken down as follows: cash sales, 25%; VISA® credit card sales, 55%; and 20% open account (the company's own charge accounts). For budgeting purposes, assume that cash sales plus bank credit card sales are received in the month of sale; bank credit card sales are subject to a 3% processing fee, which is deducted daily at the time of deposit into CompCity's cash account with the bank. Cash receipts from collection of accounts receivable typically occur as follows: 25% in the month of sale, 45% in the month following the month of sale, and 27% in the second month following the month of sale. The remaining receivables generally turn out to be uncollectible.

CompCity's month-end inventory requirements for computer hardware units are 30% of the following month's estimated sales. A one-month lead time is required for delivery from the hardware distributor. Thus, orders for computer hardware units are generally placed by CompCity on the 25th of each month to ensure availability in the store on the first day of the month needed. These units are purchased on credit, under the following terms: n/45, *measured from the time the units are delivered to CompCity.* Assume that CompCity takes the maximum amount of time to pay its invoices. On average, the purchase price for hardware units runs 65% of selling price.

|   | | **COMPCITY, INC.** | | |
|---|---|---|---|---|
|   | | **Forecasted Sales (units and dollars)** | | |
|   | | **January–June, 2013** | | |
|   | **No. of Units** | **Hardware Sales** | **Software/Support Sales** | **Total Revenue** |
| January | 120 | $ 360,000 | $140,000 | $ 500,000 |
| February | 130 | 390,000 | 160,000 | 550,000 |
| March | 90 | 270,000 | 130,000 | 400,000 |
| April | 100 | 300,000 | 125,000 | 425,000 |
| May | 110 | 330,000 | 150,000 | 480,000 |
| June | 120 | 360,000 | 140,000 | 500,000 |
| Totals | 670 | $2,010,000 | $845,000 | $2,855,000 |

**Required**

1. Calculate estimated cash receipts for April 2013 (show details).

2. The company wants to estimate the number of hardware units to order on January 25th.

   a. Determine the estimated number of units to be ordered.

   b. Calculate the dollar cost (per unit and total) for these units.

3. Cash planning in this line of business is critical to success. Management feels that the assumption of selling price per unit ($3,000) is firm—at least for the foreseeable future. Also, it is comfortable with the 30% rate for end-of-month inventories. It is not so sure, however, about (a) the CGS rate (because of the state of flux in the supplier market), and (b) the level of predicted sales in March 2013. Discussions with marketing and purchasing suggest that three outcomes are possible for each of these two variables, as follows:

| Outcome | March Sales | CGS% |
|---|---|---|
| Optimistic | 100 units | 60% |
| Expected | 90 units | 65 |
| Pessimistic | 80 units | 70 |

The preceding outcomes are assumed to be independent, which means that there are nine possible combinations (3 × 3). You are asked to conduct a sensitivity analysis to determine the range of possible cash outflows for April 10<sup>th</sup>, under different combinations of the above. Assume, for simplicity, that sales volume for April is fixed. Complete the following table:

| Scenario | March Sales (units) | CGS % | Cash Payment April 10 |
|---|---|---|---|
| 1 | 100 | 60% | $_____ |
| 2 | 100 | 65 | _____ |
| 3 | 100 | 70 | _____ |
| 4 | 90 | 60 | _____ |
| 5 | 90 | 65 | _____ |
| 6 | 90 | 70 | _____ |
| 7 | 80 | 60 | _____ |
| 8 | 80 | 65 | _____ |
| 9 | 80 | 70 | _____ |
| | Maximum = ? | | |
| | Minimum = ? | | |
| | Range = ? | | |

4. As part of the annual budget process, CompCity, Inc., prepares a cash budget by month for the entire year. Explain why a company such as CompCity would prepare monthly cash flow budgets for the entire year. Explain the role of *sensitivity analysis* in the monthly planning process.

**(CMA Adapted)**

[LO 10-5, 10-6]    10-55    **Budgeting Customer Retention and Insurance-Policy Renewal; Sensitivity Analysis**    National Insurance Company underwrites property insurance for homeowners. You have been charged with the responsibility of developing a portion of the monthly budget for the coming 12-month period for the company.

You have collected the following driver volumes, consumption rates, unit resource costs, and other data needed to prepare your 12-month budget for those active policyholders whose policy runs from January to December:

| | |
|---|---|
| Number of active policyholders beginning of month #1 | 100,000 |
| Average monthly premium per policy | $100.00 |
| Monthly midterm cancellation rate | 0.50% |
| Policy renewal rate | 85.00% |

**Required**

1. Prepare, in good form, a monthly budget for customer retention and insurance premium revenue for the period January through December. Columns in your budget should represent months, while the rows in your budget should consist of the following: number of active policyholders at the beginning of the month; midterm cancellation rate (%); number of active policyholders at the end of the month; average number of active policyholders during the month; average monthly premium per policy; and total premiums earned per month from active policyholders. How many policies are projected to be renewed at the end of the year?

2. Within the context of budgeting, what do we mean by the term *what-if analysis*?

3. Recreate the original 12-month budget you prepared in (1) above to reflect what will happen if the policy-renewal rate falls to 80% and the monthly midterm cancellation rate increases to 0.75%. Of what potential significance is the analysis you just performed?

4. What other information or data would be included in the full budget prepared each month for the company?

[LO 10-6]    10-56    **Budgeting Insurance Policy Volume and Monthly Revenues**    National Auto Insurance Company underwrites automobile coverage for the consumer market. As part of the annual planning process, National Auto requires monthly estimates for the number of policies in force and the amount of premium revenue associated with this volume of business. You have been asked to prepare these estimates for the coming six-month period. Past experience indicates that number of policies outstanding during a given month is influenced both by macro factors [e.g., market size (total number of households) and market growth rate] and company-specific factors (e.g., market share, cancellation rate experience).

At the beginning of January for the new budget year, the number of households is estimated as 100 million; further, past experience indicates that this will increase by approximately

0.05% per month. Your own research indicates that approximately 80% of households have one or more cars. On average, each household owns 2.2 cars. Because of legal requirements, the average percentage of cars insured is high—your best estimate is that this number is 85% and growing by 0.1% per month. Current market share of National Auto in the consumer market is approximately 10%. Over the past 24 months, the rate of increase in market share for National Auto has been 0.005% per month. Because of aggressive levels of customer service, National Auto has been able to keep its monthly cancellation rate below average, to approximately 0.125%. Average monthly premium paid per auto insured for the coming year is assumed to be $100.

**Required**

1. For each of the months January–June in the coming year, prepare a budget broken down in three parts:

   a. Market size and volume.

   b. Volume for National Auto Insurance (number of policies outstanding).

   c. Premium revenues generated.

   For (a) above, you should have seven rows of data, as follows: total number of households (i.e., market size); percentage of households owning one or more cars; number of cars owned per household; percentage of car owners with insurance; total number of insured cars (marketwide); market share of National Auto; and number of autos insured by National Auto, end of the month. For (b) above, your budget should have four rows, as follows: number of cars insured, beginning of the month; cancellations during the month; number of insured autos, end of the month; and average number of insured autos during the month. For (c) above, your budget should have the following three rows: average number of cars insured during the month; average insurance premium per car per month; total monthly premium revenue.

2. What additional real-life refinements do you envision for the budgets you prepared above in (1)? What additional budgets would you anticipate preparing for the company if you were in charge of the budget-preparation process?

3. The budgets you prepared above in (1) can be referred to as *driver-based budgets.* List some of the pros and the cons of such budgets, relative to traditional budgeting practices.

[LO 10-6]   10-57   **Budgets for a Service Firm**   Triple-F Health Club (Family, Fitness, and Fun) is a not-for-profit family-oriented health club. The club's board of directors is developing plans to acquire more equipment and expand club facilities. The board plans to purchase about $25,000 of new equipment each year and wants to establish a fund to purchase the adjoining property in four or five years. The adjoining property has a market value of about $300,000.

The club manager, Jane Crowe, is concerned that the board has unrealistic goals in light of the club's recent financial performance. She has sought the help of a club member with an accounting background to assist her in preparing a report to the board supporting her concerns.

The member reviewed the club's records, including this cash-basis income statement:

**TRIPLE-F HEALTH CLUB**
**Income Statement (Cash Basis)**
**For Years Ended October 31 (in thousands)**

|  | 2014 | 2013 |
|---|---|---|
| Cash revenues: |  |  |
| Annual membership fees | $355.0 | $300.0 |
| Lesson and class fees | 234.0 | 180.0 |
| Miscellaneous | 2.0 | 1.5 |
| Total cash revenues | $591.0 | $481.5 |
| Cash expenses: |  |  |
| Manager's salary and benefits | $ 36.0 | $ 36.0 |
| Regular employees' wages and benefits | 190.0 | 190.0 |
| Lesson and class employees' wages and benefits | 195.0 | 150.0 |
| Towels and supplies | 16.0 | 15.5 |
| Utilities (heat and light) | 22.0 | 15.0 |
| Mortgage interest | 35.1 | 37.8 |
| Miscellaneous | 2.0 | 1.5 |
| Total cash expenditures | $496.1 | $445.8 |
| Increase in cash | $ 94.9 | $ 35.7 |

- Other financial information as of October 31, 2014:

  Cash in checking account, $7,000.

  Petty cash, $300.

  Outstanding mortgage balance, $360,000.

  Accounts payable arising from invoices for supplies and utilities that are unpaid as of October 31, 2014, and due in November 2014, $2,500.

- No other unpaid bills existed on October 31, 2014.

- The club purchased $25,000 worth of exercise equipment during the current fiscal year. Cash of $10,000 was paid on delivery, with the balance due on October 1. This amount had not been paid as of October 31, 2014. An additional $25,000 (cash) of equipment purchases is planned for the coming year.

- The club began operations in 2010 in rental quarters. In October 2010, it purchased its current property (land and building) for $600,000, paying $120,000 down and agreeing to pay $30,000 plus 9% interest annually on the unpaid loan balance each November 1, starting November 1, 2011.

- Membership rose 3% in 2014. The club has experienced approximately this same annual growth rate since it opened and this rate is expected to continue in the future.

- Membership fees increased by 15% in 2014. The board has tentative plans to increase these fees by 10% in 2015.

- Lesson and class fees have not been increased for three years. The board policy is to encourage classes and lessons by keeping the fees low. The members have taken advantage of this policy, and the number of classes and lessons has increased significantly each year. The club expects the percentage growth experienced in 2014 to be repeated in 2015.

- Miscellaneous revenues are expected to grow at the same rate as in 2014.

- Operating expenses expected to increase:

  Hourly wage rates and the manager's salary: 15%.

  Towels and supplies, utilities, and miscellaneous expenses: 25%.

### Required

1. Prepare a cash budget for 2015 for the Triple-F Health Club.
2. Identify any operating problems that this budget discloses for the Triple-F Health Club. Explain your answer.
3. Is Jane Crowe's concern that the board's goals are unrealistic justified? Explain your answer.

**(CMA Adapted)**

[LO 10-2, 10-4, 10-5, 10-6]

**10-58  Budgeting and Sustainability**   Neat-and-Clean handles both commercial laundry and individual customer dry cleaning. The company's dry-cleaning process involves emitting a pollutant into the air. In addition, the commercial laundry and dry cleaning services produce sediments and other elements that must receive special treatment before disposal. David Duncan, Neat-and-Clean's owner, is concerned about the cost of dealing with increasingly stringent laws and environmental regulations. Recent legislation in the state requires Neat-and-Clean to reduce the amount of its air pollution emissions.

Variable processing costs per 5-pound batch of laundry for Neat-and-Clean are estimated as follows (on average):

| Product | Selling Price | Materials (per pound of laundry) | Labor (per 5 lb. batch) | Electricity (per 5 lb. batch) | Budgeted Batches per Year* |
|---|---|---|---|---|---|
| Commercial | $25.00 | $1.00/lb. | $4.00/5 lb. batch | $1.50/5 lb. batch | 7,500 |
| Individual | 20.00 | 0.50/lb. | 4.00/5 lb. batch | 1.00/5 lb. batch | 3,000 |

*Business is relatively smooth throughout the year.

The materials that are currently being used for dry-cleaning purposes have an unfortunate effect: excessive emissions that can be considered toxic in nature. The company can switch to a more environmentally friendly cleaning compound, which is currently selling at a price equal to $2.25 per pound of laundry. (For simplicity, assume that this cost applies to both commercial and individual laundry.) The owner is hesitant to switch over to the new cleaning compound because of the increase in processing cost per load of laundry. At the same time, he is acutely aware that in a neighboring town, a competitor business was subjected to a $60,000 fine by the relevant state authority. As such, Duncan is concerned that if he doesn't switch to the new compound his business may be subject to a similar fine.

**Required**

1. Based solely on the data provided above, does it make financial sense for Duncan to switch to the more environmentally friendly cleaning compound? (Assume for this question that other costs are unaffected by this decision. Also, assume a one-year planning horizon.)

2. Independent of your answer to requirement 1 above, assume that Duncan "wants to do the right thing," both for his employees and the environment. As such, he chooses to switch to the new cleaning compound. The seller of this compound has suggested that, consistent with continuous-improvement (kaizen) budgeting, it may be possible to reduce both labor costs and electricity costs by 1% per month starting with month #1 in a 12-month planning horizon. How close to being indifferent between incurring the fine and incurring the increased processing costs would Neat-and-Clean be after one year? (Show calculations.)

3. Use Goal Seek in Excel to answer each of the following questions, independently:

    a. What is the monthly cost-reduction rate (%) that would equate the net increase in year-one processing costs with the amount of the anticipated fine ($60,000)?

    b. What is the cost per pound for the new compound that would equate the anticipated fine ($60,000) with year-one processing costs, assuming no kaizen budgeting plan (i.e., no reduction in the labor and electricity processing costs over time)? What conclusion can you draw based on this analysis?

4. What options (i.e., operational changes) secure the cost savings referenced above in requirement 2?

5. What other considerations (both qualitative and quantitative) might affect the ultimate decision by David Duncan?

[LO 10-8]   10-59   **Ethics in Budgeting/Budgetary Slack**   Norton Company, a manufacturer of infant furniture and carriages, is in the initial stages of preparing the annual budget for 2013. Scott Ford recently joined Norton's accounting staff and is interested in learning as much as possible about the company's budgeting process. During a recent lunch with Marge Atkins, sales manager, and Pete Granger, production manager, Scott initiated the following conversation:

**Scott:**   Since I'm new around here and am going to be involved with the preparation of the annual budget, I'd be interested to learn how the two of you estimate sales and production numbers.

**Marge:**   We start out very methodically by looking at recent history, discussing what we know about current accounts, potential customers, and the general state of consumer spending. Then, we add that usual dose of intuition to come up with the best forecast we can.

**Pete:**   I usually take the sales projections as the basis for my projections. Of course, we have to make an estimate o f what this year's closing inventories will be, and that sometimes is difficult.

**Scott:**   Why does that present a problem? There must have been an estimate of closing inventories in the budget for the current year.

**Pete:**   Those numbers aren't always reliable since Marge makes some adjustments to the sales numbers before passing them on to me.

**Scott:**   What kind of adjustments?

**Marge:**   Well, we don't want to fall short of the sales projections so we generally give ourselves a little breathing room by lowering the initial sales projection anywhere from 5 to 10%.

**Pete:**   So you can see why this year's budget is not a very reliable starting point. We always have to adjust the projected production rates as the year progresses and, of course, this changes the ending inventory estimates. By the way, we make similar adjustments to expenses by adding at least 10% to the estimates; I think everyone around here does the same thing.

**Required**

1. Marge Atkins and Pete Granger have described the use of *budgetary slack.*

    a. Explain why Marge and Pete might behave in this manner, and describe the benefits they expect to realize from the use of budgetary slack.

    b. Explain how the use of budgetary slack can adversely affect Marge and Pete personally, and the organization as a whole.

2. As a management accountant, Scott Ford believes that the behavior described by Marge and Pete may be unethical and that he may have an obligation not to support this behavior. By citing the specific standards from the IMA's "Statement of Ethical Professional Practice" (**www.imanet.org**), explain why the use of budgetary slack may be unethical.

**(CMA Adapted)**

[LO 10-2, 10-8]   10-60   **Criticisms of Traditional Budgeting/Incentive Issues**   As noted in the chapter, some individuals allege that the practice of tying managerial rewards to budgeted performance has dysfunctional consequences, including (but not limited to) gaming behavior. Search the Internet and pertinent literature (e.g., Michael C. Jensen, "Corporate Budgeting Is Broken—Let's Fix It," *Harvard Business Review,* November 2001, pp. 94–101) to further explore the issue of negative incentive effects associated with traditional budgeting practices. What alternatives are suggested to correct these negative consequences?

## Solutions to Self-Study Problems

### 1. Master Budget

a.

**HANSELL COMPANY**
**Sales Budget**
**For July 2013**

| | |
|---|---:|
| Budgeted sales in units | 6,000 |
| Budgeted selling price per unit | × $   80 |
| Budgeted sales | $480,000 |

b.

**HANSELL COMPANY**
**Production Budget (in units)**
**For July 2013**

| | |
|---|---:|
| Desired ending inventory (July 31) (The higher of 500 and 7,000 × 0.1) | 700 |
| Budgeted sales for July 2010 | + 6,000 |
| Total units needed for July 2010 | 6,700 |
| Beginning inventory (July 1) (The higher of 500 and 6,000 × 0.1) | − 600 |
| Units to manufacture in July | 6,100 |

c.

**HANSELL COMPANY**
**Production Budget (in units)**
**For August 2013**

| | |
|---|---:|
| Desired ending inventory (The higher of 500 and 8,000 × 0.1) | 800 |
| Budgeted sales | + 7,000 |
| Total units needed | 7,800 |
| Beginning inventory (Aug 1) | − 700 |
| Units to manufacture in August | 7,100 |

**d.**

### HANSELL COMPANY
#### Direct Materials Purchases Budget (in pounds)
#### For July 2013

| | Direct Materials | |
| --- | --- | --- |
| | **Dura-1000**<br>**(4 lb. each)** | **Flexplas**<br>**(2 lb. each)** |
| Materials required for budgeted production (6,100 units of duraflex) | 24,400 | 12,200 |
| Add: Target inventories (lower of 1,000 or 5% of August production needs) | + 1,000 | + 710 |
| Total materials requirements | 25,400 | 12,910 |
| Less: Expected beginning inventories (lower of 1,000 or 5% of July needs) | − 1,000 | − 610 |
| Direct materials to be purchased | 24,400 | 12,300 |

**e.**

### HANSELL COMPANY
#### Direct Materials Purchases Budget (in dollars)
#### For July 2013

| | **Budgeted Purchases Pounds** | **Expected PurchasePrice per Unit** | **Total** |
| --- | --- | --- | --- |
| Dura-1000 | 24,400 | $1.25 | $30,500 |
| Flexplas | 12,300 | 5.00 | 61,500 |
| Budgeted purchases | | | $92,000 |

**f.**

### HANSELL COMPANY
#### Direct Manufacturing Labor Budget
#### For July 2013

| Direct Labor Class | Direct Labor-Hours per Batch | Number of Batches | Total Hours | Rate per Hour | Total |
| --- | --- | --- | --- | --- | --- |
| K102 | 1 | 61* | 61 | $50 | $ 3,050 |
| K175 | 10 | 61* | 610 | 20 | 12,200 |
| Total | | | 671 | | $15,250 |

* No. of units ÷ 100 units/batch = 6,100/100 = 61 batches

## 2. Cash Budget and Budgeted Income Statement

### HANSELL COMPANY
#### Cash Budget
#### For July 2013

| | | |
| --- | --- | --- |
| **Cash balance, beginning (given)** | | $ 40,000 |
| **Cash flow from operations:** | | |
| July cash sales | $480,000 × 20% = | $ 96,000 |
| Collections of receivables from credit sales in June: | | |
| Within the discount period | (5,500 × $80) × 80% × 60% × 98% = | $206,976 |
| After the discount period | (5,500 × $80) × 80% × 25% = | 88,000 |

*(continued)*

| | | | |
|---|---|---:|---:|
| Collections of receivables from credit sales in May | $(5,400 \times \$80) \times 80\% \times 10\% =$ | 34,560 | $425,536 |
| Cash Disbursements: | | | |
| Materials purchases: | | | |
| June purchases | $(\$25,000 + \$22,000) \times 20\% \times 98\% =$ | $ 9,212 | |
| July purchases | $\$92,000 \times 80\% \times 98\% =$ | 72,128 | $ 81,340 |
| Direct manufacturing labor | | | 15,250 |
| Variable factory overhead | $(\$1,200 \times 61) + (\$80 \times 671) =$ | | 126,880 |
| Fixed factory overhead | $\$50,000 - \$20,000 =$ | | 30,000 |
| Variable marketing, customer services, and administrative expenses | $[(\$2,400,000 - \$1,200,000) \div \$4,000,000] \times \$480,000 =$ | | 144,000 |
| Fixed marketing, customer services, and administrative expenses | $(\$1,200,000 - \$120,000) \div 12 =$ | | 90,000 |
| Total cash flow from operations | | | ($ 61,934) |
| **Investment activities:** | | | |
| Purchases of investments and other long-term assets | | $ 0 | |
| Sales of investments and other long-term assets | | $ 0 | $ 0 |
| **Financing activities:** | | | |
| Repayment of existing debt, end of month | | $ 0 | |
| Interest payments, end of month | | $ 0 | |
| New borrowing, end of month | | $ 62,000 | $ 62,000 |
| **Cash balance, July 31, 2013** | | | $ 40,066 |

## HANSELL COMPANY
### Budgeted Income Statement
### For July 2013

| | | | |
|---|---|---:|---:|
| Sales | | | $480,000 |
| Cost of goods sold, LIFO basis* | $\$46.50 \times 6,000 =$ | | 279,000 |
| Gross margin | | | $201,000 |
| Selling and administrative expenses: | | | |
| Variable (see cash budget, above) | | $144,000 | |
| Fixed | $\$1,200,000 \div 12 =$ | 100,000 | 244,000 |
| Operating income (loss) before tax | | | ($ 43,000) |

\* Actual manufacturing cost per unit; July:

| | | | |
|---|---|---:|---:|
| Direct materials: | | | |
| Dura-1000 | $4 \text{ lb.} \times \$1.25 =$ | $ 5.00 | |
| Flexplas | $2 \text{ lb.} \times \$5.00 =$ | 10.00 | $ 15.00 |
| Direct labor: | | | |
| K102 labor | $0.01 \text{ hour} \times \$50 =$ | $ 0.50 | |
| K175 labor | $0.1 \text{ hour} \times \$20 =$ | 2.00 | 2.50 |
| Factory overhead: | | | |
| Batch-related | $(61 \times \$1,200)/6,100 =$ | $ 12.00 | |
| DLH-related | $(\$80 \times 671)/6,100 =$ | 8.80 | |
| Fixed | $(\$50,000/6,100) =$ | 8.20 | $ 29.00 |
| Cost per unit, units produced in July | | | $ 46.50 |

*Please visit* **http://www.mhhe.com/blocher6e** *to access a narrated, animated tutorial for solving these problems.*

# CHAPTER ELEVEN

# Decision Making with a Strategic Emphasis

**After studying this chapter, you should be able to . . .**

LO 11-1  Define the decision-making process and identify the types of cost information relevant for decision making

LO 11-2  Use relevant cost analysis and strategic analysis to make special order decisions

LO 11-3  Use relevant cost analysis and strategic analysis in the make, lease, or buy decision

LO 11-4  Use relevant cost analysis and strategic analysis in the decision to sell before or after additional processing

LO 11-5  Use relevant cost analysis and strategic analysis in the decision to keep or drop products or services

LO 11-6  Use relevant cost analysis and strategic analysis to evaluate service and not-for-profit organizations

LO 11-7  Analyze the short-term product-mix decision

LO 11-8  Discuss behavioral, implementation, and legal issues in decision making

LO 11-9  Set up and solve in Excel a simple product-mix problem (appendix)

The family sedan segment of the U.S. auto market—especially the Honda Accord and Toyota Camry—experiences an intense level of competition. The competition between these two cars illustrates an important cost-management issue—striking a balance between product features and price. The two cars do not differ greatly in price, but most analysts argue that the cost and price reductions in the 1997 remake of the Camry brought it to the top of U.S. car sales.

Toyota and Honda know that a number of strategic issues are involved in developing a competitive car, including fuel economy, safety features, low-cost manufacturing methods, and a competitive price. In this chapter we will discuss how to conduct relevant cost analysis and strategic analysis of decisions about product pricing, selecting cost-effective manufacturing methods, and deciding when to keep or drop a product, among others.

Decision makers should consider both short-term and long-term effects, as well as both quantitative and qualitative effects, in making the best decision. Although the art and science of decision making has many elements, including leadership, vision, execution, and other characteristics, cost management provides two important resources to improve decisions: relevant cost analysis and strategic analysis. Relevant cost analysis has a short-term focus; strategic analysis has a long-term focus. Relevant cost analysis and strategic analysis are important parts of the manager's decision-making process. This chapter provides a framework for effective managerial decision making.

## The Five Steps of the Decision-Making Process

**LO 11-1**

*Define the decision-making process and identify the types of cost information relevant for decision making.*

In deciding among alternatives for a given situation, managers employ the five-step process outlined in Exhibit 11.1. The first step, and the most important, is to consider the organization's business environment and competitive strategy. This helps focus the decision maker on answering the right question. Strategic thinking is important to avoid decisions that might be best only in the short term. For example, a plant manager might incorrectly view

**EXHIBIT 11.1** The Decision-Making Process

*Relevant information includes both quantitative (including financial) information as well as qualitative information.

the choice as whether to make or to buy a part for a manufactured product when the correct decision might be to determine whether the product should be redesigned so the part is not needed.

The manager's second step is to specify the criteria—both quantitative and qualitative—by which the decision is to be made and to identify the alternative actions. Most often the manager's principal objective is an easily quantified, short-term, achievable goal, such as to reduce cost, improve profit, reduce error rates, improve customer satisfaction, or maximize return on investment. In short, a manager most often is forced to think of multiple objectives, both the quantifiable, short-term goals, and the more strategic, difficult-to-quantify goals.

In the third step, a manager performs an analysis in which the relevant information is developed and analyzed, using relevant cost analysis and strategic analysis. This step involves three sequential activities. The manager (1) identifies and collects relevant information about the decision, (2) makes predictions about the relevant information, and (3) considers the strategic issues involved in the decision.

Fourth, based on the relevant cost analysis and strategic analysis, the manager selects the best alternative and implements it. In the fifth and final step, the manager evaluates the performance of the implemented decision as a basis for feedback to a possible reconsideration of this decision as it relates to future decisions. The decision process is thus a feedback-based system in which the manager continually evaluates the results of prior analyses and decisions to discover any opportunities for improvement in decision making.

## Relevant Cost Analysis

### Relevant Cost Information

**Relevant costs**
are future costs that differ
between and among decision
alternatives.

**Relevant costs** for a decision are costs that should make a difference in choosing among the options available for that decision. A cost that has been incurred in the past or is committed for the future is not relevant; it is a **sunk cost** as it will be the same whichever option is chosen. Similarly, costs that have not been incurred but that would be the same whichever option is chosen are not relevant. In effect, for a cost to be relevant it must be a *cost that will be incurred in the future and will differ between/among the decision maker's options.*

**EXHIBIT 11.2**
**Relevant and Irrelevant Costs:
The Car Purchase Decision**

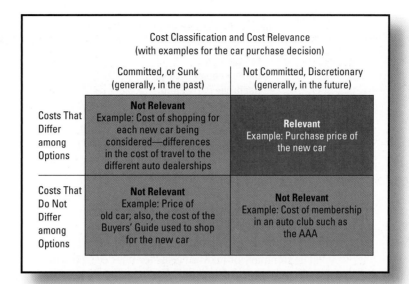

**Sunk costs**
are costs that have been incurred
in the past or are committed for
the future and are therefore
irrelevant to decision making.

For example, consider the decision to purchase a new automobile. The purchase cost of
the new auto is relevant, while the price paid previously for the current auto is irrelevant—
you can't change that. Similarly, the cost of your auto club membership, which will not
change whichever car you choose, is irrelevant. This would be true also for licenses and fees
that would be the same regardless of the car you select. Suppose further that you have narrowed your choice to two vehicles, and the dealer for one is located some distance away,
while the other dealer is nearby. The costs of travel to the different dealers are irrelevant;
they are "sunk" at the time the decision is made to travel to both dealers. Various costs
associated with the automobile purchase decision are summarized in Exhibit 11.2.

A relevant cost can be either variable or fixed. Generally, variable costs are relevant for
decision making because they differ for each option and have not been committed. In contrast, fixed costs often are irrelevant, since typically they do not differ for the options. Overall, variable costs often are relevant but fixed costs are not. As indicated by the discussion
below, the key determinant is whether a given cost is both future and differential in terms
of the decision alternative (s).

Occasionally, some variable costs are not relevant. For example, assume that a manager
is considering whether to replace or repair an old machine. If the electrical power requirements of the new and old machines are the same, the variable cost of power is not relevant.
Some fixed costs can be relevant. For example, if the new machine requires significant
modifications to the plant building, the cost of the modifications (which are fixed costs)
are relevant because they are not yet committed.

To illustrate, assume a machine was purchased for $4,200 a year ago, it is depreciated
over two years at $2,100 per year, and it has no trade-in or disposal value, either currently
or one year from now. At the end of the first year, the machine has a net book value of
$2,100 ($4,200 − $2,100) but the machine needs to be repaired or replaced. Assume that
the purchase price of a new machine is $7,000 and that this new machine is expected to
last for one year with little or no expected trade-in or disposal value at the end of the
year. The repair of the old machine would cost $3,500 and would be sufficient for another
year of productive use. The power for either machine is expected to cost $2.50 per hour.
The new machine is semiautomated, requiring a less-skilled operator and resulting in a
reduction of average labor costs from $10.00 to $9.50 per hour for the new machine. If
the firm is expected to operate at a 2,000-hour level of output for the next year, the total
variable costs for power will be $2,000 × $2.50 = $5,000 for either machine, and labor
costs will be $19,000 ($9.50 × 2,000) and $20,000 ($10 × 2,000) for the new and old
machines, respectively.

---

**Data for Machine-Replacement Example**

| | |
|---|---|
| Old machine: | |
|     Level of output | 2,000 hours/year |
|     Current net book value | $2,100 |
|     Useful life (if repaired) | 1 year |
|     Disposal value (both current and one year from now) | $0 |
|     Operating cost (labor) | $10 per hour |
|     Repair cost | $3,500 |
| New machine: | |
|     Level of output | 2,000 hours/year |
|     Purchase price | $7,000 |
|     Useful life | 1 year |
|     Disposal value (one year from now) | $0 |
|     Operating cost (labor) | $9.50 per hour |

---

The summary of relevant costs for this decision is in Exhibit 11.3, showing a $2,500 advantage for repairing the old machine. The $1,000 decrease in labor costs for the new machine is less than the $3,500 difference of replacement cost over repair cost ($7,000 − $3,500). Note that the power costs and the depreciation on the old machine are omitted because they are not relevant; they do not differ between the options. As indicated by the last column of information in Exhibit 11.3, this type of report is sometimes referred to as a *differential cost analysis.* Finally, note that the ultimate decision also will be affected by relevant nonfinancial information, including qualitative factors (e.g., reliability and quality considerations).

To show that the analysis based on total costs provides the same answer, Exhibit 11.4 shows the analysis for total costs associated with each decision alternative. Under this approach we include all costs, whether relevant or not. Thus, the Total Costs columns in Exhibit 11.4 include both power costs and the depreciation expense associated with the old machine, neither of which are relevant costs to the equipment-replacement decision under consideration. Both the relevant cost analysis reflected in Exhibit 11.3 and the total cost analysis in Exhibit 11.4 lead to the same decision. Which approach is used is largely a matter of personal preference.

**EXHIBIT 11.3**
**Relevant Cost Analysis: Equipment-Replacement Decision**

| | Relevant Costs | | Difference |
|---|---|---|---|
| | **Repair** | **Replace** | **Replace Minus Repair** |
| **Variable costs:** | | | |
|   Labor (2,000 × $10, $9.50) | $20,000 | $19,000 | $(1,000) |
| **Fixed costs:** | | | |
|   Old machine repair cost | 3,500 | | (3,500) |
|   Cost of new machine | | 7,000 | 7,000 |
| **Total costs** | $23,500 | $26,000 | $ 2,500 |

**EXHIBIT 11.4**
**Total Cost Analysis: Equipment-Replacement Decision**

| | Total Costs | | Difference |
|---|---|---|---|
| | **Repair** | **Replace** | **Replace Minus Repair** |
| **Variable costs:** | | | |
| Labor | $20,000 | $19,000 | $(1,000) |
| Power | 5,000 | 5,000 | 0 |
| **Fixed costs:** | | | |
| Old machine: | | | |
|   Depreciation | 2,100 | 2,100 | 0 |
|   Repair cost | 3,500 | | (3,500) |
| Cost of new machine | | 7,000 | 7,000 |
| **Total costs** | $30,600 | $33,100 | $ 2,500 |

## Batch-Level Cost Drivers

The above analysis has included the fixed cost associated with the purchase or repair of the machine, but has not included the fixed cost of labor for machine setup. Setup cost is a batch-level cost that varies with the number of batches and not the units or hours of output on the machine. Suppose that there will be 120 setups done during the year, irrespective of whether the machine is replaced or repaired. This sounds irrelevant, because the number of setups remains the same. But suppose further, that because the automated machine is easier to set up, it takes only one hour to set up the new machine, while the old machine takes four hours to set up. Also, assume that the automated machine requires less-skilled setup labor, so that the $9.50 per hour labor rate applies and the firm uses only the needed setup labor; there is no unused capacity in setup labor. The machine-replacement analysis should also include the differential setup time and cost as follows:

| Setup Costs for New Machine | Setup Costs for Old Machine |
| --- | --- |
| $9.50 per hour for labor | $10 per hour for labor |
| × 120 setups per year | × 120 setups per year |
| × 1 hour per setup | × 4 hours per setup |
| = $1,140 | = $4,800 |

The new machine saves $3,660 ($4,800 − $1,140) in setup labor as well as $1,000 in direct labor. The labor savings total is $4,660 ($3,660 + $1,000). This more than offsets the excess of the cost of the new machine over the cost of repair, $3,500 ($7,000 − $3,500), for a $1,160 = ($4,660 − $3,500) net benefit of replacing the machine. See the revised analysis in Exhibit 11.5.

## Fixed Costs and Depreciation

A common misperception is that depreciation of facilities and equipment is a relevant cost. In fact, depreciation is a portion of a committed cost (the allocation of a purchase cost over the life of an asset); therefore, it is sunk and irrelevant. There is an exception to this rule: when tax effects are considered in decision making. In this context, depreciation has a positive value in that, as an expense, it reduces taxable income and tax expense. If taxes are considered, depreciation has a role to the extent that it reduces tax liability. The decision maker often must consider the impact of local, federal, and sometimes international tax differences on the decision situation.

## Other Relevant Information

**Opportunity cost**
is the benefit lost when the chosen option precludes the benefits from an alternative option.

Managers should include in their decision process information such as the capacity usage of the plant. Capacity usage information is a critical signal of the potential relevance of **opportunity costs,** the benefit lost when one chosen option precludes the benefits from an alternative option. When the plant is operating at full capacity, opportunity costs are an important consideration because the decision to produce a special order or add a new product

**EXHIBIT 11.5**
**Relevant Cost Analysis:**
**Equipment-Replacement**
**Decision (including consideration**
**of setup costs)**

| | Relevant Costs | | Difference |
| --- | --- | --- | --- |
| | **Repair** | **Replace** | **Replace Minus Repair** |
| **Variable costs** | | | |
| Labor | $20,000 | $19,000 | $(1,000) |
| **Batch-level costs** | | | |
| Setup costs | 4,800 | 1,140 | (3,660) |
| **Fixed costs** | | | |
| Old machine repair cost | 3,500 | | (3,500) |
| Cost of new machine | | 7,000 | 7,000 |
| **Total costs** | $28,300 | $27,140 | $(1,160) |

line can cause the reduction, delay, or loss of sales of products and services currently offered. By definition, opportunity costs are always relevant and therefore should be included in the decision-making process.

Another important factor is the *time value of money,* which is relevant when deciding among alternatives with cash flows over an extended period of time (e.g., two or more years). These decisions are best handled by the methods described in Chapter 12.

Qualitative factors, such as differences in quality, functionality, timeliness of delivery, reliability in shipping, and service after the sale, can also strongly influence a manager's final decision and should be considered in addition to the analysis of relevant costs. Although these factors often are considered in a qualitative manner, when any factor is strategically important, management can choose to quantify it and include it directly in the analysis.

## Strategic Analysis

> The task of management is not to apply a formula but to decide issues on a case-by-case basis. No fixed, inflexible rule can ever be substituted for the exercise of sound business judgment in the decision-making process.
>
> *Alfred P. Sloan, early president and CEO of General Motors*

Alfred Sloan had an important role in developing many of the financial management tools we use today, including relevant cost analysis and strategic analysis. Sloan knew that an inflexible "run the numbers" approach would not necessarily lead to good decisions. Instead, he used a consideration of the business and competitive context of the decision, together with the use of relevant costs, which we call *strategic cost analysis.* A consideration of the business and competitive context of the decision, together with an understanding of the firm's strategy and the relevant costs ensures that each decision will help advance the firm's strategy, performance, and success.

To illustrate, a strategic decision to design the manufacturing process for high efficiency to produce large batches of product reduces overall production costs. At the same time, it might reduce the firm's flexibility to manufacture a variety of products and thus could increase the cost to produce small, specialized orders. The decision regarding cost efficiency cannot be separated from the determination of marketing strategy, that is, deciding what types and sizes of orders can be accepted.

As another example, the decision to buy rather than to make a part for the firm's product might make sense on the basis of relevant cost but might be a poor strategic move if the firm's competitive position depends on product reliability that can be maintained only by manufacturing the part in-house. A good indication of a manager's failing to take a strategic approach is that the analysis will have a product cost focus, while a strategic cost analysis also addresses broad and difficult-to-measure strategic issues. The strategic analysis directly focuses on adding value to the customer, going beyond only cost issues. (See Exhibit 11.6.)

We now consider the application of the relevant cost analysis and strategic cost analysis decision framework to four types of decisions that management accountants often deal with. The four decisions are as follows: (1) the special order decision; (2) the make, lease, or buy decision; (3) the decision to sell before or after additional processing; and (4) product-line and service-line profitability analysis.

**EXHIBIT 11.6**
**Relevant Cost Analysis versus Strategic Cost Analysis**

| Relevant Cost Analysis | Strategic Cost Analysis |
|---|---|
| Short-term focus | Long-term focus |
| Not necessarily linked to strategy | Linked to the firm's strategy |
| Product cost focus | Customer focus |
| Focused on individual product or decision situation | Integrative; considers all customer-related factors |

## Special Order Decisions

### Relevant Cost Analysis

**LO 11-2**

*Use relevant cost analysis and strategic analysis to make special order decisions.*

A special order decision occurs when a firm has a one-time opportunity to sell a specified quantity of its product or service. The order frequently comes directly from the customer rather than through normal sales or distribution channels. Special orders are infrequent and commonly represent a small part of a firm's overall business.

To make the special order decision, managers begin with a cost analysis of the relevant costs for the special order. To illustrate, consider the special order situation facing Tommy T-Shirt, Inc. (TTS). TTS is a small manufacturer of specialty clothing, primarily T-shirts and sweatshirts with imprinted slogans and brand names. TTS has been offered a contract by the business honor society, Alpha Beta Gamma (ABG), for 1,000 T-shirts printed with artwork publicizing a fund-raising event. ABG offers to pay $6.50 for each shirt. TTS normally charges $9.00 for shirts of this type for this size order.

TTS's budget of manufacturing costs for the current year is given in Exhibit 11.7. The budget is based on expected production of 200,000 T-shirts from an available capacity of 250,000. The 200,000 units are expected to be produced in 200 different batches of 1,000 units each. The three groups of cost elements are as follows:

1. **Unit-level costs** vary with each shirt printed and include the cost of the shirt ($3.25 each), ink ($0.95 each), and labor ($0.85), for a total of $5.05 per unit.
2. **Batch-level costs** vary, in part, with the number of batches produced. The batch-level costs include machine setup, inspection, and materials handling. These costs are partly variable (change with the number of batches) and partly fixed. For example, setup costs are $130 per setup ($26,000 for 200 setups) plus $29,000 fixed costs that do not change with the number of setups (e.g., setup tools or software). Setup costs for 200 batches total $55,000 ($26,000 + $29,000). Similarly, inspection costs are $30 per batch plus $9,000 fixed costs—$15,000 total [($30 × 200) + $9,000]. Materials handling costs are $40 per batch plus $7,000 fixed costs—$15,000 total [($40 × 200) + $7,000].
3. **Facilities-level costs** are fixed (in the short run) and do not vary with the number of either units produced or batches. These costs include depreciation and insurance on machinery ($315,000) and other fixed costs ($90,000), for a total of $405,000. Total fixed cost is the sum of fixed batch-level costs ($45,000) and fixed facilities-level costs ($405,000), or $450,000.

The total cost-estimation equation for TTS for the year is:

$$\text{Total cost} = \$5.05 \text{ per unit} + \$200 \text{ per batch} + \$450,000$$

**EXHIBIT 11.7**
**Budget for TTS's Manufacturing Costs**
Expected Output of 200,000 Units in 200 Batches

| Cost Element | Costs per Unit | Batch-Level Costs | | Facilities-Level |
| | | Per Batch | Fixed Costs | Costs (all fixed) |
|---|---|---|---|---|
| Shirt | $3.25 | | | |
| Ink | 0.95 | | | |
| Operating labor | 0.85 | | | |
| Subtotal | $5.05 | | | |
| Setup | | $130 | $29,000 | |
| Inspection | | 30 | 9,000 | |
| Materials handling | | 40 | 7,000 | |
| Subtotal | | $200 | $45,000 | |
| Machine-related | | | | $315,000 |
| Other | | | | 90,000 |
| Total | $5.05 | $200 | $45,000 | $405,000 |

**EXHIBIT 11.8**
**Relevant Cost Analysis of the Special Order Decision Facing TTS**

| | Relevant Unit Costs | Relevant Cost for One Batch of 1,000 Units |
|---|---|---|
| Unit-level costs: | | |
| Unprinted shirt | $3.25 | $3,250 |
| Ink and other supplies | 0.95 | 950 |
| Machine time (operator labor) | 0.85 | 850 |
| Total unit-level costs | $5.05 | $5,050 |
| Batch-level costs (that vary with the number of batches): | | |
| Setup | | 130 |
| Inspection | | 30 |
| Materials handling | | 40 |
| Total ($200/batch; $0.20/unit) | $0.20 | $ 200 |
| Total relevant costs | $5.25 | $5,250 |

The question before TTS is whether it should accept or reject the order from ABG. This order requires the same unprinted T-shirt, ink, and labor time as other shirts, for a total of $5.05 per unit. In addition, the order from ABG will require $200 of batch-level costs. Thus, as reflected in Exhibit 11.8, the relevant cost of the special order is $5.25 per unit.

To examine the short-term financial impact of accepting the order from ABG, we compare the relevant cost of $5.25 per unit to the offering price of $6.50 per unit. By accepting the order, TTS's operating income would increase by $1,250 (i.e., 1,000 units × $1.25 per unit). Thus, from a short-term financial perspective, it would be advantageous to the company to accept a selling price ($6.50 per unit) that is lower than its normal selling price ($9.00 per unit) for the special order. This conclusion assumes that the accountant has identified all relevant costs. For example, in this case there may be an additional cost to design and/or apply the special logo requested by ABG, which would raise the per-unit relevant cost above $5.25.

## Strategic Analysis

The preceding relevant cost analysis developed for TTS provides useful information regarding the effect of the special sales order on the short-term profitability of the company. At this point, it seems as if TTS should accept the special order because the order has a positive effect on operating income. But, before a decision is made, additional factors must be considered in the decision-making process. At a minimum, before making a final decision TTS also should consider the strategic factors of capacity utilization and short-term versus long-term pricing.

### Is TTS Now Operating at Full Capacity?

TTS currently has 50,000 units of excess capacity, more than enough for the ABG order. But what if TTS is operating at or near full capacity; would accepting the order cause the loss of other, possibly more profitable, sales? If so, TTS should consider the opportunity cost arising from the lost sales. Assume that TTS is operating at 250,000 units and 250 batches of activity, and that accepting the ABG order would cause the loss of sales of other T-shirts that have a higher contribution of $3.75 ($9.00 − $5.25). The opportunity cost is $3.75 per shirt, and the proper short-term financial analysis is as follows:

| | |
|---|---|
| Contribution from ABG order | $ 1,250 |
| Less: Opportunity cost of lost sales (1,000 units × $3.75) | (3,750) |
| Net contribution (loss) for the order | $(2,500) |

Exhibit 11.9 shows the short-term profit effect of accepting the ABG order at full capacity; under full capacity, the order would (due to lost sales) reduce total profits by $2,500.

Note, too, that we can define the relevant cost of the special order as the sum of out-of-pocket costs ($5,250) plus the opportunity cost of lost business ($3,750), or a total of $9,000.

**EXHIBIT 11.9**
**Special Order Decision for TTS under Full Capacity**

|  | With ABG Order | Without ABG Order |
|---|---|---|
| Sales: |  |  |
| 250,000 units at $9.00 |  | $2,250,000 |
| 249,000 at $9.00; 1,000 at $6.50 | $2,247,500 |  |
| Variable cost at $5.25 | 1,312,500 | 1,312,500 |
| Contribution margin | $ 935,000 | $ 937,500 |
| Fixed cost | 450,000 | 450,000 |
| Operating income | $ 485,000 | $ 487,500 |
| Advantage in favor of rejecting the ABG order |  | $ 2,500 |

Revenue from the special order is $6,500. Thus, by accepting the order, short-term operating income decreases by $2,500.

## Excessive Relevant Cost Pricing

The relevant cost decision rule for special orders discussed above must be used with caution: done on a regular basis, relevant cost pricing can erode normal pricing policies and lead to a loss in long-term profitability for firms such as TTS. The failure of large companies in the airline, auto, and steel industries has been attributed to their excessive relevant cost pricing because a strategy of continually focusing on the short term can deny a company a successful long term. Special order pricing decisions should not become the centerpiece of a firm's strategy.

## Other Important Strategic Factors

In addition to capacity utilization and long-term pricing issues, TTS should consider qualitative factors, such as ABG's credit history, any potential complexities in the design that might cause production problems, and other issues such as whether the sale might lead to additional sales of other TTS products. TTS, before accepting the order, might also evaluate the likely impact of the sale on the ability of the company to maintain its pricing structure with existing customers. Finally, TTS should determine whether packaging, delivery, and selling costs (e.g., sales commissions) would differ for regular versus special sales orders.

## Value Stream Accounting and the Special Order Decision

**A value stream** consists of all the activities required to create customer value for a family of products or services.

When using lean accounting (see Chapter 17 for more information on this topic) the management accountant puts families of products together in what is called a **value stream,** which consists of all the activities required to create customer value for that family of products or services. An example of a product family for a consumer electronics firm would be its group of DVD players, while another family of products would be its digital

417

televisions. An example for a service firm, a bank, would be value streams for installment loans, mortgage loans, and commercial loans. When using lean accounting, special orders are evaluated within the context of the value stream in which they are located, so the analysis of costs includes relevant costs throughout the value stream and the strategic analysis is for the entire family of products in the value stream.

## Make, Lease, or Buy Decisions

### Relevant Cost Analysis

**LO 11-3**

*Use relevant cost analysis and strategic analysis in the make, lease, or buy decision.*

Generally, a firm's products are manufactured according to specifications set forth in what is called the *bill of materials,* which is a detailed list of the components of the manufactured product. A bill of materials for the manufacture of furniture is illustrated in Chapter 4. An increasingly common decision for manufacturers is to choose which of these components to manufacture in the firm's plant and which to purchase from outside suppliers.

The relevant cost information for the make-or-buy decision is developed in a manner similar to that of the special order decision. The relevant cost of making the component consists of all avoidable costs (i.e., the costs that would be saved if the part were purchased). These costs are compared to the external purchase price for the part or component to determine the short-term financial consequence of making versus buying the part.

For example, consider Blue Tone Manufacturing, maker of clarinets and other reed-based musical instruments. Suppose that Blue Tone is currently manufacturing the mouthpiece for its clarinet but has the option to buy this piece from a supplier. The mouthpiece is plastic, while the remainder of the clarinet is made from wood. The following cost information assumes that fixed overhead costs will not change whether Blue Tone chooses to make or buy the mouthpiece (i.e., these costs are considered unavoidable):

| | | |
|---|---:|---:|
| Cost to buy the mouthpiece, per unit | | $24.00 |
| Cost to manufacture, per unit: | | |
|   Materials | $16.00 | |
|   Labor | 4.50 | |
|   Variable overhead | 1.00 | |
|     Total variable costs | $21.50 | |
|   Fixed overhead | 6.00 | |
|     Total costs | $27.50 | |
|     Total relevant costs, per unit | | $21.50 |
| Per-unit savings from continuing to make | | $ 2.50 |

In this example, while the total manufacturing cost is $27.50 per unit, the relevant per-unit cost to make the piece is $21.50. The fixed overhead cost is not relevant to this decision as long as we assume that in total this cost is unavoidable (i.e., in the short run this cost will not change regardless of the decision).

The next step is for Blue Tone to complete a strategic analysis that considers, for example, the quality of the part, the reliability of the supplier, and the potential alternative uses of Blue Tone's plant capacity. With the combined cost and strategic analysis, Blue Tone is prepared to make the decision.

### Lease vs. Purchase

A similar situation arises when a firm must choose between leasing or purchasing a piece of equipment. Such decisions are becoming ever more frequent as the cost and terms of leasing arrangements continue to become more favorable.

To illustrate the lease-or-buy decision, we use the example of Quick Copy, Inc., a firm that provides printing and duplicating services and other related business services. Quick Copy uses one large copy machine to complete most big jobs. It leases the machine from the manufacturer on an annual basis that includes general servicing. The annual lease includes both a fixed fee of $40,000 and a per copy charge of $0.02.

The copier manufacturer has suggested that Quick Copy upgrade to the latest model copier that is not available for lease but must be purchased for $160,000. Quick Copy would use the purchased copier for one year, after which it could sell it back to the manufacturer for one-fourth the purchase price ($40,000). In addition, the new machine has a required annual service contract of $20,000, which includes all repair, service, and replacement of ink cartridges. Quick Copy's options for the coming year are to renew the lease for the current copier or to purchase the new copier. The relevant information is outlined in Exhibit 11.10. The lease-or-buy decision will not (by assumption) affect the cost of paper, electrical power, and employee wages, so these costs are irrelevant and are excluded from the analysis. For simplicity, we also ignore potential tax effects of the decision and the time value of money.

The initial step in the analysis is to determine which machine produces the lowest total cost. The answer depends on the expected annual number of copies. Using cost-volume-profit analysis (Chapter 9) and Exhibit 11.11, Quick Copy's manager determines the indifference point, the number of copies at which both machines cost the same. The calculations are as follows, where $Q$ is the number of copies:

$$\text{Lease cost} = \text{Purchase cost}$$

$$\text{Annual fee} + \text{Per copy charge} = \text{Net purchase cost} + \text{Service contract}$$

$$\$40,000 + (\$0.02 \times Q) = (\$160,000 - \$40,000) + \$20,000$$

$$Q = \$100,000 \div \$0.02$$

$$= 5,000,000 \text{ copies per year}$$

As indicated in Chapter 9 (Exhibit 9.5), the Goal Seek routine in Excel can be used to solve problems such as this.

**EXHIBIT 11.10**
**Quick Copy Lease-or-Buy Information**

|  | Lease Option | Purchase Option |
|---|---|---|
| Annual lease | $40,000 | N/A |
| Charge per copy | 0.02 | N/A |
| Purchase cost | N/A | $160,000 |
| Annual service contract | N/A | $ 20,000 |
| Value at end of period | N/A | $ 40,000 |
| Expected number of copies a year | 6,000,000 | 6,000,000 |

Many consumers are becoming more environmentally conscious. One decision with substantial environmental impact is one's choice of automobile. Starting with 2013 model cars sold in the United States, that decision will be made easier through revised fuel economy and emission-rating labels mandated recently by the U.S. Department of Transportation. The redesigned sticker will show fuel efficiency in terms of a consumption rate: gallons per 100 miles driven. As well, the revised label will show estimated driving range (in miles), estimated annual fuel costs and fuel-cost savings over a five-year horizon (compared to "the average new vehicle"), the level of greenhouse gas (GHG)

emissions, and the "smog rating" (based on exhaust emissions) of the vehicle. Vehicle comparisons can be accomplished by going to www.fueleconomy.gov. In addition to GHG emissions from running an automobile, there are GHG emissions associated with the production of the fuel used to power the vehicle. While not included in the new sticker, this environmental factor can be estimated using a calculator provided at the above-referenced website.

**Source:** J. Mitchell, "Autos to Get New Fuel Labels," *The Wall Street Journal* (May 26, 2011), p. B1.

**EXHIBIT 11.11**
**The Lease-or-Buy Example**

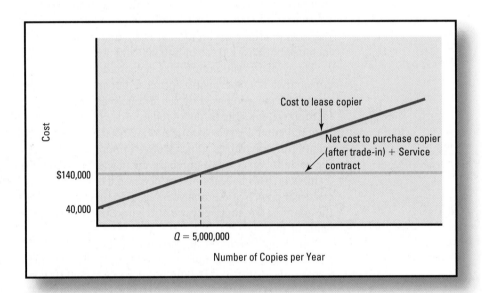

The indifference point, 5,000,000 copies, is lower than the expected annual machine usage of 6,000,000 copies. This indicates that Quick Copy will have lower costs by purchasing the new machine. Costs will be lower by $20,000:

Cost of lease − Cost of purchase

= [$40,000 + ($0.02 × 6,000,000)] − ($160,000 − $40,000 + $20,000)

= $160,000 − $140,000

= $20,000 in favor of purchase

In addition to the relevant cost analysis, Quick Copy should consider strategic factors such as the quality of the copy, the reliability of the machine, the benefits and features of the service contract, and any other factors associated with the use of the machine that might properly influence the decision.

## Strategic Analysis

The make, lease, or buy decision often raises strategic issues. For example, a firm using value-chain analysis could find that certain of its activities in the value chain can be more profitably performed by other firms. The practice of choosing to have an outside firm provide a basic service function is called *outsourcing*. Make, lease, or buy analysis has a key role in the decision to outsource by providing an analysis of the relevant costs. Many firms recently have considered outsourcing manufacturing and data processing, janitorial, or security services to improve profitability. Thomas Friedman, in his book, *The World Is Flat: A Brief History of the Twenty-First Century,* explains the breadth of outsourcing practices in the world today.[1] Even such simple activities as taking hamburger orders at the drive-thru of a fast food restaurant are being outsourced around the world.

Because of the important strategic implications of a choice to make, lease, or buy, these decisions are often made on a two- to five-year basis, using projections of expected relevant costs and taking into account the time value of money (Chapter 12) where appropriate.

## Decisions to Sell Before or After Additional Processing

### Relevant Cost Analysis

**LO 11-4**

*Use relevant cost analysis and strategic analysis in the decision to sell before or after additional processing.*

A **joint production process** is one in which multiple outputs arise, naturally, from a common resource input.

The **split-off point** is the point in the production process where products with individual identities emerge.

**Joint production costs** are those incurred prior to the split-off point; they are common (i.e., indirect) costs.

**Separable processing costs** are those incurred after the split-off point and are therefore traceable to individual products.

Another common decision concerns the option to sell a product or service before an intermediate processing step or to add further processing and then to sell the product or service for a higher price. The additional processing might add features or functionality to a product or add flexibility or quality to a service. For example, a travel agent preparing a group tour faces many decisions related to optional features to be offered on the tour, such as side-trips, sleeping quarters, and entertainment. A manufacturer of consumer electronics faces a number of decisions regarding the nature and extent of features to offer in its products.

Yet another dimension of determining appropriate product features arises in what is called a **joint production process.** As discussed in Chapter 7, a joint production process is one in which multiple outputs arise from a common resource input. From this common resource (e.g., barrel of crude oil), one gets multiple outputs. At a certain point in the process, products with individual identities emerge (e.g., diesel fuel, gasoline, aviation fuel). This point is referred to as the **split-off point.** Prior to this point, **joint production costs** are incurred; these, by definition, are not traceable to individual products. After the split-off point, **separable** (i.e., traceable) **processing costs** are incurred. Management typically has some discretion in either selling products at an intermediate stage (e.g., at the split-off point) or incurring additional processing costs and then selling the products.

As indicated in Chapter 7, for financial reporting purposes it is important to allocate joint production costs to the various outputs. Full-cost data (including allocated joint product costs) are needed to prepare balance sheets and income statements. However, these allocated costs are generally irrelevant for short-term decision-making purposes. For example, when the decision is to sell a product at the split-off point or to process it further and then sell it, the only costs and revenues relevant to the decision are those that are incremental to the decision. By the time the product has reached the split-off point, the joint costs are considered sunk, and therefore irrelevant. The only exception is that the joint costs would be relevant if the decision were whether to produce the product at all.

The analysis of features also is important for manufacturers in determining what to do with defective products. Generally, they can either be sold in the defective state to outlet stores and discount chains or be repaired for sale in the usual manner. The decision is whether the product should be sold with or without additional processing. Relevant cost analysis is again the appropriate model to follow in analyzing these situations.

To continue with the TTS example, assume that a piece of equipment used to print its T-shirts has malfunctioned, and 400 shirts are not of acceptable quality because some colors are missing or faded. TTS can either sell the defective shirts to outlet stores at a greatly reduced price ($4.50) or run them through the printing machine again. (The normal selling price per shirt is $9.00.) A second run will produce a salable shirt in most cases. The costs to run them through the printer a second time are for the ink, supplies, and labor, totaling $1.80 per shirt, plus the (assumed) setup, inspection, and materials handling costs for a batch

---

[1] Thomas L. Friedman, *The World Is Flat: A Brief History of the Twenty-First Century* (New York: Farrar, Straus, and Giroux, 2005). See also, Thomas L. Friedman, *Hot, Flat, and Crowded* (New York: Farrar, Straus, and Giroux, 2008).

A study of 328 U.S. manufacturing firms revealed that the purchasing managers at most of these firms prefer to purchase parts from outside suppliers rather than to assign the work to an internal manufacturing unit. Factors given as favoring outsourcing include the quality and speed of delivery for the external suppliers, while factors favoring insourcing include concerns for capacity utilization, overhead absorption, employee loyalty, and union contracts. The purchasing managers also tend to prefer to use a number of suppliers in order to develop multiple sourcing relationships. For example, in recent years General Motors (in its U.S. operations) had approximately 3,500 suppliers, while Toyota in Japan had only about 200. How does Toyota keep such a relatively small number of suppliers?

(Refer to Comments on Cost Management in Action at the end of the chapter.)

**EXHIBIT 11.12**
**Relevant Cost Analysis of Reprinting 400 Defective T-Shirts**

| | Reprint | Sell to Discount Store |
|---|---|---|
| **Revenue** (400 @ $9.00, $4.50) | $3,600 | $1,800 |
| **Relevant costs (assumed)** | | |
| Supplies and ink ($0.95) | 380 | |
| Labor ($0.85) | 340 | |
| Setup | 130 | |
| Inspection | 30 | |
| Materials handling | 40 | |
| Total relevant costs | $ 920 | |
| Incremental contribution margin | $2,680 | $1,800 |
| **Net advantage to reprint** | **$2,680 − $1,800 = $880** | |

of product. Thus, if TTS chooses to rework and then sell the shirts, the incremental contribution margin would be $2,680; if, on the other hand, it chooses to sell the shirts "as is" to a discounter, the incremental contribution margin would be only $1,800. Thus, there is an $880 advantage ($2,680 vs. $1,800) to reprinting the shirts. See Exhibit 11.12.

Alternatively, we could say that in terms of the decision to reprint the shirts, the revenue is $3,600 while the total cost is $2,720 (i.e., out-of-pocket costs of $920 plus opportunity costs of $1,800). Further, we could arrive at the same $880 net benefit of reprocessing the shirts by comparing the incremental revenue from further processing, $1,800 ($3,600 − $1,800) to the incremental cost of further processing, $920. Keep in mind that in terms of the decision to sell the shirts "as is" or to process them further and then sell them, the original manufacturing cost for the shirts is irrelevant—this cost is sunk and therefore the same regardless of the decision option chosen.

## Strategic Analysis

Strategic concerns arise when considering selling to discount stores. Will this affect the sale of T-shirts in retail stores? Will the cost of packing, delivery, and sales commissions differ for these two types of sales? TTS management must carefully consider these strategic issues in addition to the information provided by its relevant cost analysis.

## Product-/Service-Line Profitability Analysis

### Profitability Analysis: Keep or Drop a Product (or Service) Line

**LO 11-5**

*Use relevant cost analysis and strategic analysis in the decision to keep or drop products or services.*

An important aspect of management is the regular review of product- (and service-) line profitability. This review should address issues such as these:

- Which products (or services) are most profitable?
- Are the products priced properly?

**EXHIBIT 11.13**
Sales and Cost Data for
Windbreakers, Inc.

| | Calm | Windy | Gale | Total |
|---|---|---|---|---|
| Units sold last year | 25,000 | 18,750 | 3,750 | 47,500 |
| Revenue | $750,000 | $600,000 | $150,000 | |
| Price | $ 30.00 | $ 32.00 | $ 40.00 | |
| Relevant costs: | | | | |
|   Unit variable cost | 24.00 | 24.00 | 36.00 | |
| Unit contribution margin | $ 6.00 | $ 8.00 | $ 4.00 | |
| Nonrelevant (i.e., allocated) fixed costs | 3.60 | 3.60 | 3.60 | $171,000 |
| Operating profit per unit | $ 2.40 | $ 4.40 | $ 0.40 | |

- Which products should be promoted and advertised most aggressively?
- Which product managers should be rewarded?

This review has both a short-term and a long-term (strategic) focus. The short-term focus is addressed through relevant cost analysis. To illustrate, we use Windbreakers, Inc., a manufacturer of sport clothing. Windbreakers manufactures three jackets: Calm, Windy, and Gale. Management has requested an analysis of Gale due to its low sales and low indicated profitability (see Exhibit 11.13).

The analysis of Gale should begin with the important observation that the $3.60 allocated fixed cost per unit is irrelevant for the analysis of the short-term profitability of the three products. Under this assumption, the $171,000 total fixed costs are unavoidable in the short run. As such, they are irrelevant for this analysis. That is, no changes in product mix, including the deletion of Gale, will affect total fixed costs in the coming year. The fact that the fixed costs are irrelevant is illustrated by comparing the contribution income statements in Exhibit 11.14, which assumes that Gale is dropped, and Exhibit 11.15, which assumes that Gale is kept. The only changes caused by dropping Gale are the loss of its revenues and the elimination of variable costs. Thus, in this situation the only relevant costs for the short-term analysis are the variable costs associated with each product line. The total fixed costs are assumed unavoidable and therefore are not relevant to the assessment of the short-term profitability of each product line. Further, the results presented in Exhibit 11.16 assume that there is no effect on the sales or costs of the other

**EXHIBIT 11.14**
Contribution Income
Statement Profitability
Analysis: Gale Dropped

| | Calm | Windy | Total |
|---|---|---|---|
| Sales | $750,000 | $600,000 | $1,350,000 |
| Relevant costs: | | | |
|   Variable cost ($24 ea) | 600,000 | 450,000 | 1,050,000 |
| Contribution margin | $150,000 | $150,000 | $ 300,000 |
| Nonrelevant costs: | | | |
|   Fixed cost (unavoidable) | | | 171,000 |
| Operating profit without Gale | | | $ 129,000 |

**EXHIBIT 11.15**
Contribution Income
Statement Profitability
Analysis: Gale Retained
(all fixed costs assumed
unavoidable)

| | Calm | Windy | Gale | Total |
|---|---|---|---|---|
| Sales | $750,000 | $600,000 | $150,000 | $1,500,000 |
| Relevant costs: | | | | |
|   Variable cost ($24, 24, 36) | 600,000 | 450,000 | 135,000 | 1,185,000 |
| Contribution margin | $150,000 | $150,000 | $ 15,000 | $ 315,000 |
| Nonrelevant costs: | | | | |
|   Fixed cost (unavoidable) | | | | 171,000 |
| Operating profit with Gale | | | | $ 144,000 |

**EXHIBIT 11.16**
**Profitability Analysis: Including Traceable (i.e., avoidable) Advertising Costs**

|  | Calm | Windy | Gale | Total |
|---|---|---|---|---|
| Sales | $750,000 | $600,000 | $150,000 | $1,500,000 |
| Relevant costs |  |  |  |  |
|  Variable cost | 600,000 | 450,000 | 135,000 | 1,185,000 |
| Contribution margin | $150,000 | $150,000 | $ 15,000 | $ 315,000 |
| Other relevant costs (traceable) |  |  |  |  |
|  Advertising | 25,000 | 15,000 | 20,000 | 60,000 |
| Contribution after all relevant costs | $125,000 | $135,000 | $ (5,000) | $ 255,000 |
| Nonrelevant costs (not traceable) |  |  |  |  |
|  Fixed cost (unavoidable portion) |  |  |  | $ 111,000 |
| Operating profit |  |  |  | $ 144,000 |

two products. Thus, dropping Gale causes a reduction in total contribution margin of $4 per unit times 3,750 units of Gale sold, or $15,000, and a corresponding loss in operating profit ($15,000 = $144,000 − $129,000).

Alternatively, we could show the $15,000 reduction in operating income as the net effect of a cost savings (avoidable costs) of $135,000 and an opportunity cost (lost sales) of $150,000, as shown below:

| | | |
|---|---|---|
| Benefit: Saved variable costs of Gale | $ 135,000 | $(36 × 3,750) |
| Cost: Opportunity cost of lost sales of Gale | (150,000) | $(40 × 3,750) |
| Decrease in profit from decision to drop Gale | $ (15,000) | $ (4 × 3,750) |

Assume now that $60,000 of the $171,000 fixed costs are advertising costs to be spent directly on each of the three products: $25,000 for Calm, $15,000 for Windy, and $20,000 for Gale. That is, each of these is an avoidable cost. The remainder of the fixed costs, $110,000 ($171,000 − $60,000), are not traceable to any of the three products and are therefore allocated to each product as before. Because advertising costs are directly traceable to the individual products, and assuming that the advertising plans for Gale can be canceled without additional cost, the $20,000 of advertising costs for Gale are avoidable and therefore relevant to the decision to delete Gale.

Exhibit 11.16 shows that the total contribution margin for Gale is now a negative $5,000, providing a potential $5,000 gain by dropping Gale because of the expected $20,000 savings in avoidable advertising costs. Alternatively, management may choose to forgo the advertising for Gale and assess whether sales will fall with the loss of advertising; Gale could be profitable without advertising. We can interpret the contribution figures for Calm and Windy in the same way. The loss in deleting Calm or Windy would be $125,000 and $135,000, respectively.

### Strategic Analysis

In addition to the relevant cost analysis, the decision to keep or drop a product line should include relevant strategic factors, such as the potential effect of the loss of one product line on the sales of another. For example, some florists price cards, vases, and other related items at or below cost to better serve and attract customers to the most profitable product, the flower arrangements.

Other important strategic factors include the potential effect on overall employee morale and organizational effectiveness if a product line is dropped. Moreover, managers should consider the sales growth potential of each product. Will the decision to drop a product place the firm in a strong competitive position sometime in the future? A particularly important consideration is the extent of available production capacity. If production capacity and production resources (such as labor and machine time) are limited, consider the relative profitability of the products and the extent to which they require different amounts of these production resources.

An example of a user of the contribution income statement is STIHL, Incorporated, a manufacturer of leaf blowers, chain saws, trimmers, edgers, and many other landscaping products. STIHL uses the contribution income statement to assess the profitability of both product lines and customer groups.[2]

## Profitability Analysis: Service and Not-for-Profit Organizations

**LO 11-6**

*Use relevant cost analysis and strategic analysis to evaluate service and not-for-profit organizations.*

Triangle Women's Center (TWC) uses relevant cost analysis to determine the desirability of new services. TWC provides several services to the communities in and around a large southeastern city. It has not offered child care services but has received a large number of requests to do so in recent years. Now TWC is planning to add this service. The relevant cost analysis follows. TWC expects to hire a director ($65,000) and two part-time assistants ($30,000 each) for the child care service. TWC estimates variable costs per child at $60 per month. No other costs are relevant because none of the other operating costs of TWC are expected to change. TWC expects to receive funding of $100,000 from the United Way plus $30,000 from the city council. The analysis for the child care service's first year of operation is shown in Exhibit 11.17, which assumes that 20 children, the maximum number, will use the service.

The TWC analysis shows that the child care service will have a deficit of approximately $9,400 in the first year. Now TWC can decide whether it can make up the deficit from current funds or by raising additional funds. Relevant cost analysis provides TWC a useful method to determine the resource needs for the new program.

## Multiple Products and Limited Resources

**LO 11-7**

*Analyze the short-term product-mix decision.*

The preceding relevant cost analyses were simplified by using a single product (or service offering) and assuming sufficient resources to meet all demands. The analysis changes significantly with two or more products and limited resources. The revised analysis is considered in this section. We continue the example of Windbreakers, Inc., except that to simplify the analysis we assume that the Calm product is manufactured in a separate plant under contract with a major customer. Thus, the following analysis focuses only on the Windy and Gale products, which are manufactured in a single facility.

A key element of the relevant cost analysis is to determine the most profitable sales mix for Windy and Gale. If there are no production constraints, the answer is clear: we manufacture what is needed to meet demand for both Windy and Gale. However, when demand exceeds production capacity, management must make some trade-offs about the quantity of each product to manufacture, and therefore, what amount of demand will be unmet. The answer requires considering the production possibilities given by the production constraints. Consider two important cases: (1) one production constraint, and (2) two or more production constraints. In each of these cases, it may be necessary to incorporate demand constraints as well.

**EXHIBIT 11.17**
**Triangle Women's Center Analysis of Child Care Services**

| Relevant annual costs: | |
| --- | --- |
| Salary of director | $ 65,000 |
| Salary for two part-time assistants | 60,000 |
| Variable costs for 20 children at $60 per month each | 14,400 |
| Total relevant costs | $139,400 |
| Total funding: | |
| United Way | $100,000 |
| City council | 30,000 |
| | $130,000 |
| Expected deficit in the first year | $ 9,400 |

[2] Carl S. Smith, "Going for GPK," *Strategic Finance*, April 2005, pp. 36–39.

## Case 1: One Production Constraint

Assume that the production of Windy and Gale requires an automated sewing machine to stitch the jackets and that this production activity is a limited resource: sales demand for the two products exceeds the capacity on the plant's three automated sewing machines. Each machine can be run up to 20 hours per day five days per week, or 400 hours per month, which is its maximum capacity allowing for maintenance. This gives 1,200 (3 × 400) available hours for sewing each month. Assume further that the machine requires three minutes to assemble a Windy and two minutes to assemble a Gale.

Because only 1,200 hours of machine time are available per month and the Gale jacket requires less machine time, more Gale jackets can be made in a month than Windy jackets. The maximum number of Windy jackets is 24,000 per month (1,200 hours times 20 jackets per hour, at 3 minutes per jacket). Similarly, if the sewing machine were devoted entirely to Gale jackets, then 36,000 jackets per month could be produced (1,200 times 30 jackets per hour). This information is summarized in Exhibit 11.18.

A continuous trade-off possibility exists for the extreme situations: zero output of Windy and 36,000 of Gale or 24,000 of Windy and zero of Gale. These production and sales mix possibilities can be shown graphically; all sales-mix possibilities are represented by all possible points on the line in Exhibit 11.19. The line in Exhibit 11.19 (called an "iso-production" line) can be determined as follows:

$$\text{Slope} = -36,000 \div 24,000 = -3/2$$

$$\text{Intercept} = 36,000$$

The line in Exhibit 11.19 is thus given by

$$\text{Units of Gale} = 36,000 - (3/2 \times \text{Units of Windy})$$

To illustrate, assume that Windbreakers is producing 12,000 units of Windy so that

$$\text{Units of Gale} = 36,000 - (3/2 \times 12,000) = 18,000$$

Now that we know the production possibilities, we can determine the best product mix. Note from Exhibit 11.18 that Windy has the higher overall contribution margin, $160 per hour (20 jackets per hour × $8 per jacket). Because 1,200 machine-hours are available per month, the maximum total contribution from the production possibilities is to produce only Windy and achieve the total contribution of 1,200 × $160 = $192,000 (or $8 per unit × 24,000 units = $192,000) per month. If Windbreakers chose to produce and sell only Gale, the maximum total contribution margin would be $144,000 per month (1,200 hours × $120 per hour), a $48,000 reduction over the contribution from selling only Windy. *Thus, when there is only one production constraint and excess demand, it is generally best to focus production and sales on the product with the highest contribution per unit of scarce resource.*

**EXHIBIT 11.18**
**Windbreakers Data for the Windy and Gale Plant**
One Constraint: The Sewing Machine

| | Windy | Gale |
|---|---|---|
| Given: | | |
| Contribution margin/unit | $8 | $4 |
| Sewing time per jacket | 3 min | 2 min |
| Then, because sewing time is limited to 1,200 hours per month, we determine the contribution margin per machine-hour | | |
| Number of jackets per hour (60min/3min = 20; 60/2 = 30) | 20 | 30 |
| Contribution margin per hour (20 jackets/hr. × $8/jacket; 30 jackets/hr. × $4/jacket) | $160 | $120 |
| Also, the maximum production for each product, given the 1,200-hour constraint | | |
| For Windy: 1,200 hours × 20 jackets per hour | 24,000 | |
| For Gale: 1,200 hours × 30 jackets per hour | | 36,000 |

**EXHIBIT 11.19**
**Windbreakers Production and Sales Possibilities**
One Production Constraint—The Sewing Machine

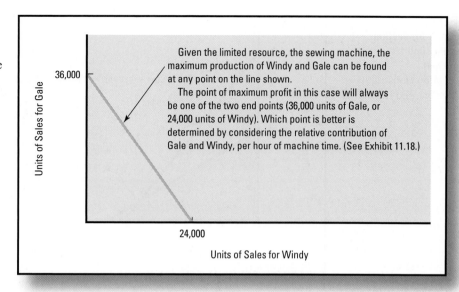

Given the limited resource, the sewing machine, the maximum production of Windy and Gale can be found at any point on the line shown.

The point of maximum profit in this case will always be one of the two end points (36,000 units of Gale, or 24,000 units of Windy). Which point is better is determined by considering the relative contribution of Gale and Windy, per hour of machine time. (See Exhibit 11.18.)

## Case 2: Two or More Production Constraints

When there are two or more production constraints, the choice of sales mix involves a more complex analysis, and in contrast to the case of one production constraint which solves for a single product, the solution can include both products when two constraints are involved. To continue with the Windbreakers case, assume that in addition to the automated sewing machine, a second production activity is required. The second activity inspects the completed jackets, adds labels, and packages the completed product. This operation is done by 40 workers, each of whom can complete the operation for the Windy jacket in 15 minutes and for the Gale jacket in 5 minutes (because of differences in material quality, less inspection time is required for the Gale jacket). This means that 4 (60 min./15 min.) Windy jackets can be completed in an hour, or 12 Gale (60 min./5 min.). Because of the limited size of the facility, no more than 40 workers can be employed effectively in the inspection and packaging process. These employees work a 40-hour week, which means 35 hours of actually performing the operation, given time for breaks, training, and other tasks. Thus, 5,600 hours (40 workers × 35 hours × 4 weeks) are available per month for inspecting and packing.

The maximum output per month for the Windy jacket is 22,400 (5,600 hours × 4 jackets per hour). Similarly, the maximum output for the Gale jacket is 67,200. All of this information is summarized in Exhibit 11.20.

The production possibilities for two constraints are illustrated in Exhibit 11.21. In addition to the production possibilities for machine time, we show the production possibilities for inspection and packing. The darker shaded area indicates the range of possible

**EXHIBIT 11.20**
**Windbreakers Data for the Windy and Gale Plant**
The Second Constraint: Inspecting and Packing

| | Windy | Gale |
|---|---|---|
| Given: | | |
| Contribution margin/unit | $8 | $4 |
| Inspection and packaging time per jacket | 15 min | 5 min |
| Then: | | |
| Number of jackets per hour | 4 | 12 |
| Contribution margin per labor-hour | | |
| (4 jackets/hr. × $8/jacket; 12 jackets/hr. × $4/jacket) | $32 | $48 |
| Also: | | |
| The maximum production for each product, given the 5,600-hour constraint | | |
| For Windy: 5,600 × 4 jackets per hour | 22,400 | |
| For Gale: 5,600 × 12 jackets per hour | | 67,200 |

**EXHIBIT 11.21**
**Windbreakers Production and Sales Possibilities (Feasible Area)**
Two Production Constraints—Sewing Machine and Inspection

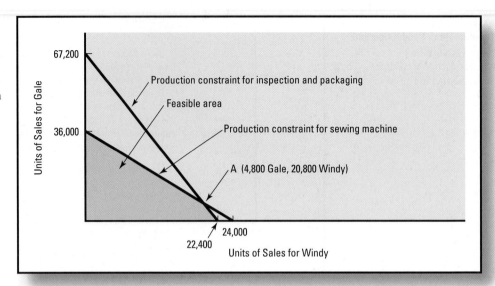

outputs (the "feasible area") for both Gale and Windy. Note that it is not possible to produce more than the 22,400 units of Windy because all 40 workers inspecting and packing full time would not be able to handle more than that number, even though the sewing machine is capable of producing 24,000 units. That is, production of more than 22,400 units of Windy is outside of the "feasible area." Similarly, although Windbreakers could pack and ship 67,200 units of Gale by having all 40 packers work full-time on that jacket, the firm could manufacture only 36,000 units of Gale because of limited capacity on the sewing machines.

The production planner can determine the best production mix by examining all of the possible production possibilities in the darker shaded area, from 36,000 on the Gale axis to point A where the constraints intersect, and then to the point 22,400 on the Windy axis. The sales mix with the highest contribution must be one of these three points: 36,000 of Gale, point A, or 22,400 units of Windy. The solution, called the *corner point analysis,* is obtained by finding the total contribution at each point and then choosing the point with the highest contribution. The solution achieved in this manner is for production at point A, 20,800 units of Windy and 4,800 units of Gale.[3] A summary analysis of these three production possibilities is presented in the following table.

| Corner Point | Windy | Gale | Contribution Margin |
|---|---|---|---|
| #1 | 0 | 0 | $      0 |
| #2 | 0 | 36,000 | 144,000 |
| #3 | 22,400 | 0 | 179,200 |
| **#4** | **20,800** | **4,800** | **$185,600** |

One way to "see" why point A represents an optimum short-term product mix is to impose on Exhibit 11.21 an iso-profit line, whose negative slope is equal to the ratio of the unit contribution margin of Gale to the unit contribution margin of Windy (i.e., −2.0). Extend this line to the right, from the origin until it just touches a point in the feasible region. This particular iso-profit line determines the optimum profit given the stated constraints and product contribution margins.

[3] The point A, 20,800 for Windy (W) and 4,800 for Gale (G), is obtained by solving the following two equations simultaneously:

$$15W + 5G = 336,000 \text{ minutes of inspection time (i.e., 40 workers} \times 35 \text{ hours per worker per week}$$
$$\times 4 \text{ weeks per month} \times 60 \text{ minutes per hour)}$$

$$3W + 2G = 72,000 \text{ minutes of sewing time (i.e., 3 machines} \times 400 \text{ hours per machine per month}$$
$$\times 60 \text{ minutes per hour)}$$

Linear programming, a mathematical method, permits the solution of much larger problems involving many products and both production and demand constraints. A linear program technique to solve the Windy and Gale case is shown in the appendix to this chapter. This technique uses the Solver function of Microsoft Excel.

## Behavioral and Implementation Issues

### Consideration of Strategic Objectives

**LO 11-8**

*Discuss behavioral, implementation, and legal issues in decision making.*

A well-known problem in business today is the tendency of managers to focus on short-term goals and neglect the long-term strategic goals because their compensation is based on short-term accounting measures such as net income. Many critics of relevant cost analysis have raised this issue. As noted throughout the chapter, it is critical that the relevant cost analysis be supplemented by a careful consideration of the firm's long-term, strategic goals. Without strategic considerations, management could improperly use relevant cost analysis to achieve a short-term benefit and potentially suffer a significant long-term loss. For example, a firm might choose to accept a special order because of a positive relevant cost analysis without properly considering that the nature of the special order could have a significant negative impact on the firm's image in the marketplace and perhaps a negative effect on sales of the firm's other products. The important message for managers is to keep the strategic objectives in the forefront in any decision situation.

### Predatory Pricing Practices

**Predatory pricing**

exists when a company has set prices below average variable cost and plans to raise prices later to recover the losses from the lower prices.

The Robinson Patman Act, administered by the U.S. Federal Trade Commission, addresses pricing that could substantially damage competition in an industry. This is called **predatory pricing,** which the U.S. Supreme Court defined in a 1993 decision, *Brooke Group Ltd. vs. Brown & Williamson Tobacco Corp.* (B&W), as a situation in which a company has set prices below average variable cost and plans to raise prices later to recover the losses from lower prices. This law is relevant for short-term *and* long-term pricing since it could require a firm to justify significant price cuts. However, the Court in the *Brooke* decision concluded that on the basis of economic theory, predatory pricing does not work and concluded in favor of B&W, the defendant in the case. The Court's reasoning has stood the test of time, because all 37 predatory pricing cases since its 1993 decision have been found in favor of the defendant. In spite of this, some economists and lawyers in 1999–2000 believed that economic theories of competition had changed since 1993. On the basis of these new theories, they took issue with the aggressive pricing practices of American Airlines, especially at the Dallas–Fort Worth airport, where a number of competing carriers had been driven to financial distress. In 2001 their suit against American was thrown out by a federal judge, causing some to argue this is the end of suits regarding predatory pricing. Another example of the failure of a predatory pricing suit is the case of a small chain of convenience stores, in which activity-based costing assisted the defendant to support its position that it was not selling gasoline below cost.[4]

A variation on the issue of predatory pricing is the recent increase in the number of countries levying fines against global firms for "dumping" their products at anticompetitive prices. A recent World Trade Organization report shows the number of cases per year increased by 100% from 1995 to 2000 and then decreased by 30% from 2000 to 2005. The U.S. antidumping laws were enacted more than 90 years ago to protect against predatory pricing by global firms exporting to the United States. The laws state that the import price cannot be lower than the cost of production or the price in the home market. Unfortunately the laws often have been used to protect uncompetitive industries in the home country. Facing increasing global pressure on the issue, U.S. congressional leaders are debating the need to reform the U.S. law.[5]

[4] Dan Carney, "Predatory Pricing: Cleared for Takeoff," *BusinessWeek,* May 14, 2001, p. 50; Thomas L. Barton and John B. MacArthur, "Activity-Based Costing and Predatory Pricing," "The Case of the Petroleum Retail Industry," *Management Accounting Quarterly,* Spring 2003, pp. 1–5. Note that price fixing, in which firms collude to set higher prices, differs from predatory pricing as described above.

[5] Paul Magnusson, "A U.S. Trade Ploy That Is Starting to Boomerang," *BusinessWeek,* July 29, 2002, pp 64–65; "The WTO Rules Against a Globally Unpopular U.S. Legislation," *Business Standard,* February 13, 2003; "Steel Wire Imports May Have Violated Antidumping Laws," *The Wall Street Journal,* March 18, 2003, p. A12; Murray Hiebert, "When It Comes to Law, China Buys American," *The Wall Street Journal,* February 17, 2006, p. B1.

## Replacement of Variable Costs with Fixed Costs

Another potential problem associated with relevant cost analysis is that managers who are evaluated on their ability to reduce controllable variable costs will have the incentive to replace variable costs with fixed costs. This happens if mid-level and lower-level managers realize that because top managers rely on relevant cost analysis, upper management might overlook fixed costs. Lower-level managers might choose to upgrade or increase fixed assets in order to reduce variable costs, although this might increase fixed costs significantly. For example, a new machine might replace direct labor. The overall costs increase because of the cost of the new machine, although variable costs under the manager's control decrease and the contribution margin increases. Management's proper goal is to maximize contribution margin and to minimize fixed operating costs at the same time. Managers should use relevant cost analysis as a tool to maximize contribution and must also develop methods to manage fixed costs.

## Proper Identification of Relevant Factors

Also, managers can fail to properly identify relevant costs. In particular, untrained managers commonly include irrelevant, sunk costs in decision making.[6] Similarly, many managers fail to see that allocated fixed costs are irrelevant. When fixed costs are shown as fixed cost per unit many managers tend to improperly find them relevant. It is easier for these managers to see the fixed cost as irrelevant when it is given in a single sum; it is more difficult to see unit fixed costs as irrelevant.

These are illustrations of the pervasive biases present in many managers' decision making. Effective use of relevant cost analysis requires careful identification of relevant costs, those future costs that differ among decision alternatives, and correctly recognizing sunk costs and unavoidable fixed costs as irrelevant in the short term.

[6] For a comprehensive coverage of decision-making biases, see John S. Hammond, Ralph L. Keeney, and Howard Raiffa, "The Hidden Traps in Decision Making," *Harvard Business Review,* September–October 1998, pp. 47–58; also D. L. Heerema and R. L. Rogers, "Is Your Cost Accounting System Benching Your Team Players?" *Management Accounting,* September 1991, pp. 35–40, gives useful illustrations of the improper use of relevant cost analysis in the automobile industry, the military, and elsewhere. Prospect theory suggests that people underweigh alternatives that are uncertain in comparison to alternatives known to be certain. The theory has been offered as a potential explanation of the tendency people have to include sunk costs in decision making. See D. Kahneman and A. Tversky, "Prospect Theory: An Analysis of Decision under Risk," *Econometrica,* March 1979, pp. 263–92; and Glen Whyte, "Escalating Commitment to a Course of Action: A Reinterpretation," *Academy of Management Review,* 1986, pp. 311–21.

## Summary

Relevant cost analysis uses future costs that differ for the decision maker's options. The principle of relevant cost analysis can be applied in a number of specific decisions involving manufacturing, service, and not-for-profit organizations. The decisions considered in the chapter include

- The special order decision for which the relevant costs are the direct manufacturing costs and any incremental fixed costs.
- The make, lease, or buy decision for which the relevant costs are the direct manufacturing costs and any avoidable fixed costs.
- The decision to sell a product before or after additional processing for which the relevant costs are the incremental (i.e., avoidable) processing costs.
- The decision to keep or drop a product or service line for which the relevant costs are the direct costs and any fixed costs that change if the product or service is dropped.
- The decision of a not-for-profit organization to offer a service.

Strategic analysis complements relevant cost analysis by having the decision maker consider the qualitative and strategic issues involved in the situation.

When two or more products or services are involved, another type of decision must be made: to determine the correct product mix. The solution depends on the number of production activities that are at full capacity. With one production constraint, the answer is to produce and sell as much as possible of the product that has the highest contribution margin per unit of time on the constrained activity. With two or more constrained activities, the analysis uses graphical and quantitative methods (such as linear programming—see the appendix) to determine the optimum short-term product (or service) mix.

A number of key behavioral, implementation, and legal issues must be considered in using relevant cost analysis. Many who use the approach fail to give sufficient attention to the firm's long-term, strategic objectives. Too strong a focus on relevant costs can cause the manager to overlook important opportunity costs and strategic considerations. Other issues include the tendency to replace variable costs with fixed costs when relevant cost analysis is used in performance evaluation and the pervasive tendency of people not to correctly view fixed costs as sunk but to view them as somehow controllable and relevant.

## Appendix

**LO 11-9**

*Set up and solve in Excel a simple product-mix problem.*

**Linear programming**
is a mathematical technique that can be used to solve constrained optimization problems, such as the optimum short-term product (or service) mix.

**Solver**
is an analytical tool available on the Data tab in Excel that can be used to solve linear programming problems.

# Linear Programming and the Product-Mix Decision

This appendix explains how **linear programming** can be used to solve product-mix decisions such as the Windbreakers case illustrated in the chapter. Linear programming is particularly useful when the product-mix decision involves multiple constraints and three or more products. A number of linear programming tools are available; we use the **Solver** function of Microsoft Excel because of its wide availability. Solver will appear as an option on Excel's Data tab.

The first step in using Solver is to enter the data for the problem into an Excel spreadsheet, in the form shown in Exhibit 11A.1.

Column A: Shows the product names.

Column B: These are the "decision cells"; initially, you can simply enter a zero in cells B5 and B6.

Columns C, D, and E: These contain data inputs.

Columns F, G, and H: These contain formulas based on the data in columns, C, D, and E; for example, cell F5 = B5 × C5; cell G5 = B5 × D5; cell F7 = SUM(F5:F6); cell G7 = SUM(G5:G6); and cell H7 = SUM(H5:H6). The target cell (i.e., the cell to be optimized) is F7.

**EXHIBIT 11A.1**
**Enter Data for the Windy and Gale Example**

| | A | B | C | D | E | F | G | H |
|---|---|---|---|---|---|---|---|---|
| 1 | Windy and Gale Example | | | | | | | |
| 2 | | | | Per-Unit Resource Consumption | | | Capacity Usage | |
| 3 | | Sales | CM | Sewing | Inspection/ | Total | Sewing | Inspect/Pack |
| 4 | Product | (units) | per Unit | Department | Packaging | CM | Time | Time |
| 5 | Windy | - | $8 | 3 | 15 | $0 | 0 | 0 |
| 6 | Gale | - | $4 | 2 | 5 | $0 | 0 | 0 |
| 7 | | | | | | $0 | 0 | 0 |

The second step in using Solver is to enter the Solver parameters as shown in the dialog box in Exhibit 11A.2. The dialog box appears by selecting Solver from the Data tab. Note that the target cell is total contribution margin, located in cell F7. The "By Changing Variable Cells" section includes those cells representing the total sales of Windy and Gale. The constraints for sewing time and inspect and pack time are then entered in the "Subject to the Constraints" section as shown. Next, select the Simplex LP as the "Solving Method." Finally, select Solve in the dialog box, at which point a dialog box labeled "Solver Results" appears. Highlight the supplemental reports you want (if any), and then click "OK." The LP solution now appears, as shown in Exhibit 11A.3.

Notice that cells B5 and B6 in Exhibit 11A.3 now show the solution values for the two products, and the cells in columns F, G, and H show the total contribution margin ($185,600) and total use of the two constraints.

**EXHIBIT 11A.2**
**Entering Solver Parameters for the Windy and Gale Example**

**EXHIBIT 11A.3**
**Solver Solution for the Windy and Gale Example**

| | A | B | C | D | E | F | G | H |
|---|---|---|---|---|---|---|---|---|
| 1 | Windy and Gale Example | | | | | | | |
| 2 | | | | Per-Unit Resource Consumption | | | Capacity Usage | |
| 3 | | Sales | CM | Sewing | Inspection/ | Total | Sewing | Inspect/Pack |
| 4 | Product | (units) | per Unit | Department | Packaging | CM | Time | Time |
| 5 | Windy | 20,800 | $8 | 3 | 15 | $166,400 | 62,400 | 312,000 |
| 6 | Gale | 4,800 | $4 | 2 | 5 | $19,200 | 9,600 | 24,000 |
| 7 | | | | | | $185,600 | 72,000 | 336,000 |

**EXHIBIT 11A.4**
**Sensitivity Report (Windy and Gale Example)**

| | A B | C | D | E | F | G | H |
|---|---|---|---|---|---|---|---|
| 1 | Microsoft Excel 14.0 Sensitivity Report | | | | | | |
| 4 | Variable Cells | | | | | | |
| 5 | | | Final | Reduced | Objective | Allowable | Allowable |
| 6 | Cell | Name | Value | Cost | Coefficient | Increase | Decrease |
| 7 | $B$5 | Windy (units) | 20,800 | 0 | $8.00 | 4.0000 | 2.0000 |
| 8 | $B$6 | Gale (units) | 4,800 | 0 | $4.00 | 1.3333 | 1.3333 |
| 10 | Constraints | | | | | | |
| 11 | | | Final | Shadow | Constraint | Allowable | Allowable |
| 12 | Cell | Name | Value | Price | R.H. Side | Increase | Decrease |
| 13 | $G$7 | Time | 72,000 | 1.3333 | 72,000 | 62,400 | 4,800 |
| 14 | $H$7 | Time | 336,000 | 0.2667 | 336,000 | 24,000 | 156,000 |

Exhibit 11A.4 shows the "Sensitivity Report" for the final solution, which contains information regarding both the variable cells and the constraints. In terms of the variable cells, the following information is provided: final values (i.e., the optimum solution—here, number of units of each product), objective coefficients (here, the contribution margin per unit for each product), and allowable increase and allowable decrease (the optimum solution holds as long as the objective function coefficients are within these ranges). In terms of the constraints, the following information is provided: the final value of each constraint (i.e., the amount of the constraint used in the optimum solution); the "shadow price" for each constraint (i.e., the amount we'd be willing to pay for each additional unit of the constrained resource in question); and, allowable increase and decrease for each constraint (i.e., the range of values over which the indicated shadow prices hold).

Not shown here is the "Answer Report" and the "Limits" report. The former shows the optimum solution amount (here, $185,600), the final values (i.e., optimum product mix), and whether each constraint is binding (in which case it might pay to relax the constraint) or not. The latter shows the optimum solution (total contribution margin generated, as well as optimum product mix) as well as the value of the objective function with each product in and out of the solution.

## Key Terms

joint production process, *421*
joint production costs, *421*
linear programming, *431*
opportunity cost, *413*

predatory pricing, *429*
relevant costs, *410*
separable processing costs, *421*
Solver, *431*

split-off point, *421*
sunk costs, *410*
value stream, *417*

## Comments on Cost Management in Action

### Trends in Make-or-Buy Strategies

Toyota Motor Company is able to maintain a small number of suppliers by using two key strategies. First, it develops a hierarchy of suppliers: Toyota deals directly with approximately 200 suppliers, which are called the *top-tier suppliers*. These 200 suppliers in turn deal with second-tier suppliers who provide products and services to those at the top tier. These second-tier suppliers in turn deal with third-tier suppliers. In this way, Toyota delegates the responsibility for managing the supply function in a way that motivates suppliers at each tier to work effectively with those above and below it in the supply chain. Second, Toyota distinguishes two types of suppliers, general and specialty. Toyota has relatively simple relationships with those in the general category of suppliers but develops close financial and technological ties with the specialty suppliers. The objective is to recognize the strategic importance of the specialty suppliers and to develop strong relationships with them to ensure success.

In a recent change the airline carriers are beginning to manufacture replacement parts for their fleets, rather than purchase the replacement parts from the manufacturers. For example, Continental Airlines can manufacture a flight deck door for a Boeing 767 for $150 in contrast to the purchase price from Boeing of $960. Similarly, American Airlines manufactures air filters for its Boeing 777 fleet for $33, in contrast to the Boeing price of $132. For the air carriers, it is definitely cheaper to make than to buy.

Other trends include a move by some firms to return some manufacturing back to domestic factories, as the cost of shipping product from China and other countries has increased dramatically with recent increases in fuel prices. In another reversal of outsourcing, the financial services industry, suffering through historic losses in 2008, has cut back in 2008 by one-half the amount of 2007 outsourcing in which computer services, customer services, and other banking activities are "off-shored."

**Sources:** "Machete Time," *BusinessWeek,* April 9, 2001, pp. 42–43; Melanie Trottman, "To Cut Costs: Airlines Make More of Their Own Parts; Jettisoning a $719 Toilet Seat," *The Wall Street Journal,* Tuesday May 3, 2005, p. B1; Timothy Aeppel, "Stung by Soaring Transport Costs, Factories Bring Jobs Home Again," *The Wall Street Journal,* June 13, 2008, p. 1; and "In a Pinch," *The Economist,* October 11, 2008, p. 86.

## Self-Study Problems
(For solutions, please turn to the end of the chapter.)

### 1. Special Order Pricing

HighValu Inc. manufactures a moderate-price set of lawn furniture (a table and four chairs) that it sells for $225. It currently manufactures and sells 6,000 sets per year. The manufacturing costs include $85 for materials and $45 for labor per set. The overhead charge per set is $35, which consists entirely of fixed costs.

HighValu is considering a special purchase offer from a large retail firm, which has offered to buy 600 sets per year for three years at a price of $150 per set. HighValu has the available plant capacity to produce the order and expects no other orders or profitable alternative uses of the plant capacity.

**Required**   Should HighValu accept the offer? Discuss both financial and nonfinancial considerations.

### 2. The Make-or-Buy Decision

Assume that HighValu Inc., as described, currently purchases the chair cushions for its lawn set from an outside vendor for $15 per set. HighValu's chief operations officer wants an analysis of the comparative costs of manufacturing these cushions to determine whether bringing the manufacturing in-house would save the firm money. Additional information shows that if HighValu were to manufacture the cushions, the materials cost would be $6 and the labor cost would be $4 per set and that it would have to purchase cutting and sewing equipment, which would add $10,000 to annual fixed costs.

**Required**   Should HighValu make the cushions or continue to purchase them from the vendor? Consider financial as well as nonfinancial factors.

### 3. Product Profitability Analysis

Consider again the Windbreakers firm described in the text. Suppose that Windbreakers determines that dropping the Gale product line will release production capacity so that it can manufacture additional units of Windy. Assume that, as described in the text, the two production constraints are the automated sewing machine and the inspection-and-packing operation. The automated sewing machine can make 20 Windys or 30 Gales per hour. As before, the inspection operation requires 15 minutes for a Windy (4 per hour) and 5 minutes for a Gale (12 per hour). Currently, 3,750 Gales and 18,750 Windys are being manufactured and sold. Sales projections show that sales of Windy could be increased to 30,000 units if additional capacity were available.

#### Required

1. If Windbreakers deletes Gale entirely, how many units of Windy can it manufacture with the released capacity?
2. What is the dollar effect on operating income if Windbreakers drops the production and sale of Gale and uses the released capacity for Windy?
3. What other factors should Windbreakers consider in its decision to drop Gale and use the released capacity to produce additional units of Windy?

*Please visit* **http://www.mhhe.com/blocher6e** *to access a narrated, animated tutorial for solving these problems.*

Questions    11-1   What are relevant costs? Provide several examples for the decision to repair or replace a piece of equipment.

11-2   List at least four different decisions for which the relevant cost analysis model can be used effectively.

11-3   What is the relevant cost when determining whether or not to process a product further?

11-4   List four to six strategic factors that are often important in the make-or-buy decision.

11-5   How do short-term evaluations affect a manager's incentives and performance?

11-6   List four or five important limitations of relevant cost analysis.

11-7   How do strategic factors affect the proper use of relevant cost analysis?

11-8   List some of the behavioral, implementation, and legal problems to be anticipated in the use of relevant cost analysis.

11-9   How does the presence of one production constraint affect the relevant cost analysis model? Two or more production constraints?

11-10   What is the relationship, if any, between the relevant cost analysis method and cost-volume-profit analysis (discussed in Chapter 9)?

Brief Exercises    11-11   Purchase price is $35 for a part that can be manufactured for $33; the $33 manufacturing costs include $5 per unit fixed cost. What is the savings to make rather than to buy?

11-12   Adams Furniture receives a special order for 10 sofas for a special price of $3,000. The materials and direct labor for each sofa are $100. In addition, the setup, supervision, and other overhead costs are $150 per sofa. Should Adams accept the special order? Why or why not? Would it make a difference to your answer if Adams is at full capacity and its current line of sofas sell for $500 each?

11-13   Wings Diner has a box lunch that it sells on football game days at the local university. Each box lunch sells for $6, which includes $2.50 variable costs and $2.50 fixed costs, plus a $1 markup. What is the lowest price Wings can sell its box lunch so that Wings will still make a profit?

11-14   Williams Auto has a machine that installs tires. The machine is now in need of repair. The machine originally cost $10,000 and the repair will cost $1,000, but the machine will then last two years. The variable (labor) cost of operating the machine is $0.50 per tire. Instead of repairing the old machine, Williams could buy a new machine at a cost of $5,000 that would also last two years; the labor cost per tire would be reduced to $0.25 per tire. Should Williams repair or replace the machine if it expects to install 10,000 tires in the next two years?

11-15   Jamison Health Care is trying to decide if it should eliminate its orthopedic care division. In the last year, the orthopedic division had a contribution margin of $100,000 and allocated overhead costs of $200,000, of which $90,000 could be eliminated if the division were dropped. Should Jamison keep the division?

11-16   ElecPlus Batteries has two different products, AAA and AA batteries. The AA batteries have a contribution margin of $1 per package, and the AAA batteries have a contribution margin of $2 per package. ElecPlus has a capacity for 1 million batteries per month, and both batteries require the same amount of processing time. If a special order for 10,000 AAA batteries exceeds the monthly capacity, should ElecPlus accept the special order?

11-17   Jackson Inc. disposes of other companies' toxic waste. Currently Jackson loads the waste by hand into the truck, which requires labor of $20 per load. Jackson is considering a machine that would reduce the amount of time needed to load the waste. The machine would cost $200,000, but would reduce labor cost to $5 per load. Should Jackson buy the machine if it averages 10,000 loads per year?

11-18   Durant Co. manufactures glass bottles for dairy products. The contribution margin is $0.10 per bottle. Durant just received notification that one of its orders for 100,000 bottles contained misprinted labels, and thus had to recall and reprint the bottle labels. If it will cost $0.05 per bottle to reprint the labels and $1,000 to reship the bottles, what will the net contribution margin be after the recall?

11-19   Lance's Diner has a hot lunch special each weekday and Sunday afternoon. Food and other variable costs for the lunch are $3.50, and the daily fixed costs are $1,000. Lance has an average of 500 customers per day. What is the lowest price Lance should charge for a special group of 200 that wants to come on Saturday for a family reunion? What should be the lowest price Lance charges on a normal weekly basis?

11-20   Sweet Dream Hotel has labor costs that are mostly fixed, including registration desk, maintenance, and general repairs and cleaning. The housekeeping staff is hired in sufficient numbers to clean the rooms that need cleaning, so that housekeeping is a variable cost for the number of occupied rooms. Which of these costs is relevant for determining the price of a room?

# Exercises

[LO 11-2]   11-21   **Special Order; Opportunity Costs**   Grant Industries, a manufacturer of electronic parts, has recently received an invitation to bid on a special order for 20,000 units of one of its most popular products. Grant currently manufactures 40,000 units of this product in its Loveland, Ohio, plant. The plant is operating at 50% capacity. There will be no marketing costs on the special order. The sales manager of Grant wants to set the bid at $9 because she is sure that Grant will get the business at that price. Others on the executive committee of the firm object, saying that Grant would lose money on the special order at that price.

| Units | 40,000 | 60,000 |
|---|---|---|
| Manufacturing costs: | | |
| Direct materials | $ 80,000 | $120,000 |
| Direct labor | 120,000 | 180,000 |
| Factory overhead | 240,000 | 300,000 |
| Total manufacturing costs | $440,000 | $600,000 |
| Unit cost | $    11 | $    10 |

**Required**
1.  Why does the unit cost decline from $11 to $10 when production level rises from 40,000 to 60,000 units?
2.  Is the sales manager correct? What do you think the bid price should be?
3.  List some additional factors Grant should consider in deciding how much to bid on this special order.
4.  What would the total opportunity cost be if by accepting the special order the company lost sales of 5,000 units to its regular customers? Assume the above facts plus a normal selling price of $20 per unit.

[LO 11-2]   11-22   **Special Order**   Alton Inc. is working at full production capacity producing 20,000 units of a unique product. Manufacturing costs per unit for the product are

| Direct materials | $ 9 |
|---|---|
| Direct labor | 8 |
| Manufacturing overhead | 10 |
| Total manufacturing cost per unit | $27 |

The unit manufacturing overhead cost is based on a $4 variable cost per unit and $120,000 fixed costs. The nonmanufacturing costs, all variable, are $8 per unit, and the sales price is $45 per unit. Sports Headquarters Company (SHC) has asked Alton to produce 5,000 units of a modification of the new product. This modification would require the same manufacturing processes. SHC has offered to share the nonmanufacturing costs equally with Alton. Alton would sell the modified product to SHC for $35 per unit.

**Required**   Set up an Excel spreadsheet to answer the following questions.
1.  Should Alton produce the special order for SHC? Why or why not?
2.  Suppose that Alton Inc. had been working at less than full capacity to produce 16,000 units of the product when SHC made the offer. What is the minimum price that Alton should accept for the modified product under these conditions? Explain.
3.  Use Goal Seek to determine the minimum price that Alton should accept for the special sales order.

[LO 11-2]   11-23   **Special Order; Use of Opportunity Cost Information**   Sharman Athletic Gear Inc. (SAG) is considering a special order for 15,000 baseball caps with the logo of East Texas University (ETU) to be purchased by the ETU alumni association. The ETU alumni association is planning to use the caps as gifts and to sell some of the caps at alumni events in celebration of the university's recent national championship by its baseball team. Sharman's cost per hat is $3.50, which includes $1.50 fixed cost related to plant capacity and equipment. ETU has made a firm offer of $35,000 for the hats, and Sharman, considering the price to be far below production costs, decides to decline the offer.

**Required**
1.  Did Sharman make the wrong decision? Why or why not?
2.  Consider the management decision-making approach at Sharman that resulted in this decision. How was opportunity cost included or not included in the decision? What decision biases are apparent in this decision?

[LO 11-2]  11-24 **Special Order**  Earth Baby Inc. (EBI) recently celebrated its tenth anniversary. The company produces organic baby products for health-conscious parents. These products include food, clothing, and toys. Earth Baby has recently introduced a new line of premium organic baby foods. Extensive research and scientific testing indicate that babies raised on the new line of foods will have substantial health benefits. EBI is able to sell its products at prices higher than competitors' because of its excellent reputation for superior products. EBI distributes its products through high-end grocery stores, pharmacies, and specialty retail baby stores.

Joan Alvarez, the founder and CEO of EBI, recently received a proposal from an old business school classmate, Robert Bradley, the vice president of Great Deal Inc. (GDI), a large discount retailer. Mr. Bradley proposes a joint venture between his company and EBI, citing the growing demand for organic products and the superior distribution channels of his organization. Under this venture EBI would make some minor modifications to the manufacturing process of some of its best-selling baby foods and the foods would then be packaged and sold by GDI. Under the agreement EBI would receive $3.10 per jar of baby food and would provide GDI a limited right to advertise the product as manufactured for Great Deal by EBI. Joan Alvarez set up a meeting with Fred Stanley, Earth Baby's CFO, to discuss the profitability of the venture. Mr. Stanley made some initial calculations and determined that the direct materials, direct labor, and other variable costs needed for the GDI order would be about $2 per unit as compared to the full cost of $3 (materials, labor, and overhead) for the equivalent EBI product.

**Required**  Should Earth Baby Inc. accept the proposed venture from GDI? Why or why not?

[LO 11-3]  11-25 **Make or Buy; Continuation of Exercise 9-25 (Chapter 9)**  Vista Company manufactures electronic equipment. In 2012, it purchased the special switches used in each of its products from an outside supplier. The supplier charged Vista $2 per switch. Vista's CEO considered purchasing either machine A or machine B so the company could manufacture its own switches. The CEO decided at the beginning of 2013 to purchase Machine A, based on the following data:

|  | Machine A | Machine B |
|---|---|---|
| Annual fixed cost | $135,000 | $204,000 |
| Variable cost per switch | 0.65 | 0.30 |

**Required**
1. For machine A, what is the indifference point between purchasing the machine and purchasing from the outside vendor?
2. At what volume level should Vista consider purchasing Machine B?
3. Use the Goal Seek function in Excel to determine the volume-indifference level you calculated above in requirement 2.

[LO 11-5, 11-7]  11-26 **Sell or Process Further; Product Mix**  Cantel Company produces cleaning compounds for both commercial and household customers. Some of these products are produced as part of a joint manufacturing process. For example, GR37, a coarse cleaning powder meant for commercial sale, costs $1.60 a pound to make and sells for $2.00 per pound. A portion of the annual production of GR37 is retained for further processing in a separate department where it is combined with several other ingredients to form SilPol, which is sold as a silver polish, at $4.00 per unit. The additional processing requires ¼ pound of GR37 per unit; additional processing costs amount to $2.50 per unit of SilPol produced. Variable selling costs for this product average $0.30 per unit. If production of SilPol were discontinued, $5,600 of costs in the processing department would be avoided. Cantel has, at this point, unlimited demand for, but limited capacity to produce, product GR37.

**Required**
1. Calculate the minimum number of units of SilPol that would have to be sold in order to justify further processing of GR37.
2. Assume that the cost data reported for GR37 are obtained at a level of output equal to 5,000 pounds, which is the maximum that the company can produce at this time. Prepare comparative income statements under each of the following scenarios: (a) all available capacity is used to produce GR37, but no SilPol; (b) 4,000 units of SilPol are produced, with the balance of capacity devoted to the production and sale of GR37; (c) 8,000 units of SilPol are produced, with the balance of capacity devoted to the production and sale of GR37; and (d) 10,000 units of SilPol are produced, with the balance of capacity devoted to the production and sale of GR37.

**(CMA Adapted)**

**[LO 11-5]** 11-27 **Product-Profitability Analysis** Barbour Corporation, located in Buffalo, New York, is a retailer of high-tech products known for its excellent quality and innovation. Recently the firm conducted a relevant cost analysis of one of its product lines that has only two products, T-1 and T-2. The sales for T-2 are decreasing and the purchase costs are increasing. The firm might drop T-2 and sell only T-1.

Barbour allocates fixed costs to products on the basis of sales revenue. When the president of Barbour saw the income statement, he agreed that T-2 should be dropped. If this is done, sales of T-1 are expected to increase by 10% next year; the firm's cost structure will remain the same.

|  | T-1 | T-2 |
|---|---|---|
| Sales | $200,000 | $260,000 |
| Variable cost of goods sold | 70,000 | 130,000 |
| Contribution margin | $130,000 | $130,000 |
| Expenses: |  |  |
| Fixed corporate costs | 60,000 | 75,000 |
| Variable selling and administration | 20,000 | 50,000 |
| Fixed selling and administration | 12,000 | 21,000 |
| Total expenses | $ 92,000 | $146,000 |
| Operating income | $ 38,000 | $(16,000) |

**Required**

1. Find the expected change in annual operating income by dropping T-2 and selling only T-1.

2. By what percentage would sales from T-1 have to increase in order to make up the financial loss from dropping T-2?

3. What is the required percentage increase in sales from T-1 to compensate for lost margin from T-2, if total fixed costs can be reduced by $45,000?

4. What strategic factors should be considered?

**[LO 11-7]** 11-28 **Product-Mix Decision** Sandalwood Company produces various lines of high-end carpeting in its Asheville, North Carolina, plant. This question pertains to two different grades of carpet in its Symphony line: commercial and residential. The former sells for $16 per square yard, while the latter sells for $25 per square yard (wholesale). Variable manufacturing costs are $10 per square yard and $15 per square yard for the commercial and residential grade products, respectively. On average, it takes 12 labor-hours to produce 100 square yards of commercial carpeting, and 18 labor-hours to produce 100 square yards of residential carpeting. The number of available labor-hours at the plant is limited to 4,600 hours per week. Current sales forecasts indicate that weekly sales for the commercial line and the residential line, respectively, are 30,000 square yards and 8,000 square yards. Fixed manufacturing costs, allocated to products on the basis of 4,600 labor-hours per week, amount to $1.50 and $2.25 for each square yard of commercial versus residential carpet, respectively.

**Required**

1. What is the gross profit (margin) for each of the two products, in total and per square yard?

2. What is the contribution margin for each of the two products, in total and per square yard?

3. Given the labor constraint and the product demand constraints, what is the optimum product mix, on a weekly basis, for each of the two products? (Show calculations.)

4. In general, what is the rule to be followed when attempting to determine the optimum short-term product (or service) mix?

5. What is the primary role of the management accountant in terms of addressing the short-term product- (or service-) mix problem?

**[LO 11-1, 11-3]** 11-29 **Solar Panels: Lease vs. Buy?** As indicated in the Real-World Focus feature on page 418, consumers (including businesses and local governments) interested in using solar power generally have an option to purchase or lease the solar panels. To adequately address the questions below, you will have to first do some research on the web. Please remember to document the website (or other source) from which you obtain information related to this exercise.

**Required**

1. In general, what are the relevant costs associated with the lease decision and the purchase decision in regard to the acquisition of solar panels?

2. What are the primary nonfinancial considerations associated with both the decision to use solar energy and the choice to lease versus purchase? Address this question from the standpoint of individual consumers, businesses, and society at large (i.e., the environment).

**[LO 11-2, 11-3, 11-4, 11-5, 11-7]**   11-30  **Relevant Cost Exercises**   Each of the following situations is independent

a. **Make or Buy**   Terry Inc. manufactures machine parts for aircraft engines. CEO Bucky Walters is considering an offer from a subcontractor to provide 2,000 units of product OP89 for $120,000. If Terry does not purchase these parts from the subcontractor, it must continue to produce them in-house with these costs:

|  | Costs per Unit |
| --- | --- |
| Direct materials | $28 |
| Direct labor | 18 |
| Variable overhead | 16 |
| Allocated fixed overhead | 4 |

**Required**   Should Terry Inc. accept the offer from the subcontractor? Why or why not? Include a consideration of both financial and nonfinancial factors.

b. **Disposal of Assets**   A company has an inventory of 2,000 different parts for a line of cars that has been discontinued. The net book value (NBV) of this inventory is $50,000. The parts can be either remachined at a total additional cost of $25,000 and then sold for $30,000 or sold as-is for $2,500.

**Required**   What should it do? Include a consideration of both financial and nonfinancial factors.

c. **Replacement of an Asset**   An uninsured boat costing $90,000 was wrecked the first day it was used. It can be either sold as-is for $9,000 cash and replaced with a similar boat costing $92,000 or rebuilt for $75,000 and be brand new as far as operating characteristics and looks are concerned.

**Required**   What should be done? Include a consideration of both financial and nonfinancial factors.

d. **Profit from Processing Further**   Deaton Corporation manufactures products A, B, and C from a joint process. Joint costs are allocated on the basis of relative sales value at the end of the joint process. Additional information for Deaton Corporation follows:

|  | A | B | C | Total |
| --- | --- | --- | --- | --- |
| Units produced | 12,000 | 8,000 | 4,000 | 24,000 |
| Joint costs | $144,000 | $ 60,000 | $36,000 | $240,000 |
| Sales value before additional processing | 240,000 | 100,000 | 60,000 | 400,000 |
| Additional costs for further processing | 28,000 | 20,000 | 12,000 | 60,000 |
| Sales value if processed further | 280,000 | 120,000 | 70,000 | 470,000 |

**Required**

1. Define the following terms: joint production process; joint production costs; separable processing costs; and split-off point.
2. Which, if any, of products A, B, and C should be processed further and then sold? (Show calculations.)
3. Why do accountants allocate to individual products joint/common costs in a joint manufacturing process?

e. **Make or Buy**   Eggers Company needs 20,000 units of a part to use in producing one of its products. If Eggers buys the part from McMillan Company for $90 instead of making it, Eggers could not use the released facilities in another manufacturing activity. Forty percent of the fixed overhead will continue irrespective of CEO Donald Mickey's decision. The cost data are

| Cost to make the part: | |
| --- | --- |
| Direct materials | $35 |
| Direct labor | 16 |
| Variable overhead | 24 |
| Fixed overhead | 20 |
|  | $95 |

**Required**   Determine which alternative is more attractive to Eggers and by what amount. What non-financial factors might bear upon the ultimate decision?

f. **Selection of the Most Profitable Product**   DVD Production Company produces two basic types of video games, Flash and Clash. Pertinent data for DVD Production Company follow:

|  | Flash | Clash |
|---|---|---|
| Sales price | $250 | $140 |
| Costs |  |  |
| Direct materials | 50 | 25 |
| Direct labor ($25/hr.) | 100 | 50 |
| Variable factory overhead* | 50 | 25 |
| Fixed factory overhead* | 20 | 10 |
| Marketing costs (all fixed) | 10 | 10 |
| Total costs | $230 | $120 |
| Operating profit | $ 20 | $ 20 |

*Based on labor-hours: 2 DLHs per unit of Flash, and 1 DLH per unit of Clash.

The DVD game craze is at its height so that either Flash or Clash alone can be sold to keep the plant operating at full capacity. However, labor capacity in the plant is insufficient to meet the combined demand for both games. Flash and Clash are processed through the same production departments.

**Required**
1. What is the meaning and importance of the statement that "Flash and Clash are processed through the same production departments"?
2. Which product should be produced? Briefly explain your answer.

g. **Special Order Pricing**   Barry's Bar-B-Que is a popular lunch-time spot. Barry is conscientious about the quality of his meals, and he has a regular crowd of 600 patrons for his $5 lunch. His variable cost for each meal is about $2, and he figures his fixed costs, on a daily basis, at about $1,200. From time to time, bus tour groups with 50 patrons stop by. He has welcomed them since he has capacity to seat 700 diners in the average lunch period, and his cooking and wait staff can easily handle the additional load. The tour operator generally pays for the entire group on a single check to save the wait staff and cashier the additional time. Due to competitive conditions in the tour business, the operator is now asking Barry to lower the price to $3.50 per meal for each of the 50 bus tour members.

**Required**   Should Barry accept the $3.50 price? Why or why not? What if the tour company were willing to guarantee 200 patrons (or four bus loads) at least once a month for $3.00 per meal?

## Problems

**[LO 11-2]**   **11-31**   **Special Order; Strategy; International**   Williams Company, located in southern Wisconsin, manufactures a variety of industrial valves and pipe fittings that are sold to customers in nearby states. Currently, the company is operating at about 70% capacity and is earning a satisfactory return on investment.

Glasgow Industries Ltd. of Scotland has approached management with an offer to buy 120,000 units of a pressure valve. Glasgow Industries manufactures a valve that is almost identical to Williams's pressure valve; however, a fire in Glasgow Industries's valve plant has shut down its manufacturing operations. Glasgow needs the 120,000 valves over the next four months to meet commitments to its regular customers; the company is prepared to pay $21 each for the valves.

Williams's product cost for the pressure valve, based on current attainable standards, is

| | |
|---|---|
| Direct materials | $ 6 |
| Direct labor (0.5 hr. per valve) | 8 |
| Manufacturing overhead (1/3 variable) | 9 |
| Total manufacturing cost | $23 |

Additional costs incurred in connection with sales of the pressure valve are sales commissions of 5% and freight expense of $1 per unit. However, the company does not pay sales commissions on special orders that come directly to management. Freight expense will be paid by Glasgow.

In determining selling prices, Williams adds a 40% markup to product cost. This provides a $32 suggested selling price for the pressure valve. The marketing department, however, has set the current selling price at $30 to maintain market share.

Production management believes that it can handle the Glasgow Industries order without disrupting its scheduled production. The order would, however, require additional fixed factory overhead of $12,000 per month in the form of supervision and clerical costs.

If management accepts the order, Williams will manufacture and ship 30,000 pressure valves to Glasgow Industries each month for the next four months. Shipments will be made in weekly consignments, FOB shipping point.

**Required**
1. Determine how many additional direct labor hours will be required each month to fill the Glasgow order.
2. Prepare an analysis showing the impact on operating profits of accepting the Glasgow order.
3. Calculate the minimum unit price that Williams's management could accept for the Glasgow order without reducing operating income.
4. Use the Goal Seek function in Excel to calculate the minimum unit selling price you calculated above in requirement 3.
5. Suppose now that if the Glasgow order were accepted sales of 5,000 units per month to regular customers would be precluded (at a selling price of $30 per unit). All other facts are as given above. What is the revised breakeven selling price per unit for the Glasgow special sales order?
6. Identify the strategic factors that Williams should consider before accepting the Glasgow order.
7. Identify the factors related to international business that Williams should consider before accepting the Glasgow order.

**(CMA Adapted)**

[LO 11-2]  11-32  **Special Order**   Award Plus Co. manufactures medals for winners of athletic events and other contests. Its manufacturing plant has the capacity to produce 10,000 medals each month; current monthly production is 7,500 medals. The company normally charges $175 per medal. Variable costs and fixed costs for the current activity level of 75% follow:

| | Current Product Costs |
|---|---|
| Variable costs | |
| Manufacturing | |
| Labor | $ 375,000 |
| Material | 262,500 |
| Marketing | 187,500 |
| Total variable costs | $ 825,000 |
| Fixed costs | |
| Manufacturing | $ 275,000 |
| Marketing | 175,000 |
| Total fixed costs | $ 450,000 |
| Total costs | $1,275,000 |

Award Plus has just received a special one-time order for 2,500 medals at $100 per medal. For this particular order, no variable marketing costs will be incurred. Cathy Senna, a management accountant with Award Plus, has been assigned the task of analyzing this order and recommending whether the company should accept or reject it. After examining the costs, Senna suggested to her supervisor, Gerard LePenn, who is the controller, that they request competitive bids from vendors for the raw materials since the current quote seems high. LePenn insisted that the prices are in line with other vendors and told her that she was not to discuss her observations with anyone else. Senna later discovered that LePenn is a brother-in-law of the owner of the current raw materials supply vendor.

**Required**
1. Calculate both the old (i.e., prior to the special order) average cost per unit and the recalculated average cost per unit, including the effect of the special sales order. Are either of these two figures relevant for evaluating whether to accept or reject the special order? Explain.
2. Based on a short-term financial analysis, determine if Award Plus Co. should accept the special order and why.

3. What is the breakeven selling price per unit for the special sales order?

4. Discuss at least three other considerations that Cathy Senna should include in her analysis of the special order.

5. Explain how Cathy Senna should try to resolve the ethical conflict arising out of the controller's insistence that the company avoid competitive bidding.

**(CMA Adapted)**

[LO 11-2]   11-33  **Special Order**   Green Grow Inc. (GGI) manufactures lawn fertilizer and because of its very high quality often receives special orders from agricultural research groups. For each type of fertilizer sold, each bag is carefully filled to have the precise mix of components advertised for that type of fertilizer. GGI's operating capacity is 22,000 one-hundred-pound bags per month, and it currently is selling 20,000 bags manufactured in 20 batches of 1,000 bags each. The firm just received a request for a special order of 5,000 one-hundred-pound bags of fertilizer for $125,000 from APAC, a research organization. The production costs would be the same, although delivery and other packaging and distribution services would cause a one-time $2,000 cost for GGI. The special order would be processed in two batches of 2,500 bags each. The following information is provided about GGI's current operations:

| Sales and production cost data for 20,000 bags, per bag: | |
| --- | --- |
| Sales price | $38 |
| Variable manufacturing costs | 15 |
| Variable marketing costs | 2 |
| Fixed manufacturing costs | 12 |
| Fixed marketing costs | 2 |

No marketing costs would be associated with the special order. Since the order would be used in research and consistency is critical, APAC requires that GGI fill the entire order of 5,000 bags.

**Required**

1. What is the total relevant cost of filling this special sales order?

2. What would be the change in operating income if the special order is accepted?

3. What is the breakeven selling price per unit for the special sales order (that is, what is the selling price that would result in a zero effect on operating income)?

4. Prepare comparative income statements, contribution format, for both the current situation and assuming the special order is accepted at the breakeven price determined in requirement 3 above.

5. Suppose that after GGI accepts the special order, it finds that unexpected production delays will not allow it to supply all 5,000 units from its own plants and meet the promised delivery date. It can provide the same materials by purchasing them in bulk from a competing firm. The materials would then be packaged in GGI bags to complete the order. GGI knows the competitor's materials are very good quality, but it cannot be sure that the quality meets its own exacting standards. There is not enough time to carefully test the competitor's product to determine its quality. What should GGI do?

[LO 11-2]   11-34  **Special Order; ABC Costing (Continuation of Problem 11-33)**   Assume the same information as for Problem 11-33, except that the $12 fixed manufacturing overhead consists of $8 per unit batch-related costs and $4 per unit facilities-level fixed costs. Also, assume that each new batch causes increased costs of $5,000 per batch; the remainder of the batch-level costs consists of tools and supervision labor that do not vary with the number of batches. The remainder of fixed costs do not vary with the number of units produced or the number of batches.

**Required**

1. Calculate the relevant unit and total cost of the special order, including the new information about batch-related costs.

2. If accepted, how would the special order affect GGI's operating income? (Show calculations.)

[LO 11-3]   11-35  **Make or Buy**   Martens, Inc., manufactures a variety of electronic products. It specializes in commercial and residential products with moderate-to-large electric motors such as pumps and fans. Martens is now looking closely at its production of attic fans, which included 10,000 units in the prior year (see the table below). These costs included $100,000 of allocated fixed manufacturing overhead. Martens has capacity to manufacture 15,000 attic fans per year.

Martens believes demand in the coming year will be 20,000 attic fans. The company has looked into the possibility of purchasing the attic fans from another manufacturer to help it meet this demand. Harris Products, a steady supplier of quality products, would be able to provide up to 9,000 attic fans per year at a price of $46 per fan delivered to Martens's facility.

For each unit of product that Martens sells, regardless of whether the product has been purchased from Harris or is manufactured by Martens, there is an additional selling and administrative cost of $20, which includes an allocated $6 fixed cost per unit. The following is based on the production of 10,000 units in the prior year.

| | | |
|---|---:|---:|
| Selling price per unit | | $72.00 |
| Costs per unit: | | |
|   Electric motor | $ 6.00 | |
|   Other parts | 8.00 | |
|   Direct labor ($15/hr.) | 15.00 | |
|   Manufacturing overhead | 15.00 | |
|   Selling and administrative cost | 20.00 | 64.00 |
| Profit per unit | | $ 8.00 |

**Required**

1. Assuming Martens plans to meet the expected demand for 20,000 attic fans, how many should it manufacture and how many should it purchase from Harris Products? Explain your reasoning with calculations.

2. Independent of requirement 1 above, assume that Beth Johnson, Martens's product manager, has suggested that the company could make better use of its fan department capacity by manufacturing marine pumps instead of fans. Johnson believes that Martens could expect to use the production capacity to produce and sell 25,000 pumps annually at a price of $60 per pump. Johnson's estimate of the costs to manufacture the pumps is presented below. If Johnson's suggestion is not accepted, Martens would sell 20,000 attic fans instead. Should Martens manufacture pumps or attic fans? Information on the sales price and costs for the marine pumps follows.

| | | |
|---|---:|---:|
| Selling price per pump | | $60.00 |
| Cost per unit: | | |
|   Electric motor | $ 5.50 | |
|   Other parts | 7.00 | |
|   Direct labor ($15/hr.) | 7.50 | |
|   Manufacturing overhead | 9.00 | |
|   Selling and administrative cost | 20.00 | 49.00 |
| Profit per pump | | $11.00 |

3. What are some of the long-term considerations in Martens's decisions in requirements 1 and 2 above?

**[LO 11-3, 11-5, 11-8]**    11-36   **Make or Buy; Strategy**   GianAuto Corporation manufactures parts and components for manufacturers and suppliers of parts for automobiles, vans, and trucks. Sales have increased each year based in part on the company's excellent record of customer service and reliability. The industry as a whole has also grown as auto manufacturers continue to outsource more of their production, especially to cost-efficient manufacturers such as GianAuto. To take advantage of lower wage rates and favorable business environments around the world, GianAuto has located its plants in six different countries.

Among the various GianAuto plants is the Denver Cover Plant, one of GianAuto's earliest plants. The Denver Cover Plant prepares and sews coverings made primarily of leather and upholstery fabric and ships them to other GianAuto plants where they are used to cover seats, headboards, door panels, and other GianAuto products.

Ted Vosilo is the plant manager for the Denver Cover Plant, which was the first GianAuto plant in the region. As other area plants were opened, Ted was given the responsibility for managing them in recognition of his management ability. He functions as a regional manager, although the budget for him and his staff is charged to the Denver Cover Plant.

Ted has just received a report indicating that GianAuto could purchase the entire annual output of Denver Cover from suppliers in other countries for $60 million. He was astonished at the low outside price because the budget for Denver Cover Plant's operating costs for the coming year was set at $82 million. He believes that GianAuto will have to close operations at Denver Cover to realize the $22 million in annual cost savings.

Denver Cover's budget for operating costs for the coming year follows:

**DENVER COVER PLANT**
**Budget for Operating Costs**
**For the Year Ending December 31, 2013**
**(000s omitted)**

| | | |
|---|---:|---:|
| Materials | | $32,000 |
| Labor | | |
|    Direct | $23,000 | |
|    Supervision | 3,000 | |
|    Indirect plant | 4,000 | 30,000 |
| Overhead | | |
|    Depreciation—equipment | $ 5,000 | |
|    Depreciation—building | 3,000 | |
|    Pension expense | 4,000 | |
|    Plant manager and staff | 2,000 | |
|    Corporate allocation | 6,000 | 20,000 |
| Total budgeted costs | | $82,000 |

Additional facts regarding the plant's operations are as follows:

- Due to Denver Cover's commitment to use high-quality fabrics in all its products, the purchasing department placed blanket purchase orders with major suppliers to ensure the receipt of sufficient materials for the coming year. If these orders are canceled as a result of the plant closing, termination charges would amount to 15% of the cost of direct materials.

- Approximately 400 plant employees will lose their jobs if the plant is closed. This includes all direct laborers and supervisors as well as the plumbers, electricians, and other skilled workers classified as indirect plant workers. Some would be able to find new jobs, but many would have difficulty doing so. All employees would have difficulty matching Denver Cover's base pay of $14.40 per hour, the highest in the area. A clause in Denver Cover's contract with the union could help some employees; the company must provide employment assistance to its former employees for 12 months after a plant closing. The estimated cost to administer this service is $1 million for the year.

- Some employees would probably elect early retirement because GianAuto has an excellent plan. In fact, $3 million of the 2013 pension expense would continue whether Denver Cover is open or not.

- Ted and his staff would not be affected by closing Denver Cover. They would still be responsible for managing three other area plants.

- Denver Cover considers equipment depreciation to be a variable cost and therefore uses the units-of-production method to depreciate its equipment. The company uses the straight-line method to depreciate its building.

**Required**

1. Explain GianAuto's competitive strategy and how this strategy should be considered with regard to the Denver Cover Plant decision. Identify the key strategic factors that should be considered in the decision.

2. GianAuto Corporation wants you to prepare an analysis of whether to close the Denver Cover Plant. In your analysis, use the above financial information, and include consideration of global competition and GianAuto's competitive strategy.

**(CMA Adapted)**

[LO 11-3]   11-37   **Make or Buy**   The Midwest Division of the Paibec Corporation manufactures subassemblies used in Paibec's final products. Lynn Hardt of Midwest's profit planning department has been assigned the task of determining whether Midwest should continue to manufacture a subassembly component, MTR-2000, or purchase it from Marley Company, an outside supplier. Marley has submitted a bid to manufacture and supply the 32,000 units of MTR-2000 that Paibec will need for 2013 at a unit price of $17.30. Marley has assured Paibec that the units will be delivered according to Paibec's production specifications and needs. The contract price of $17.30 is applicable only in 2013, but Marley is interested in entering into a long-term arrangement beyond 2013.

Lynn has submitted the following information regarding Midwest's cost to manufacture 30,000 units of MTR-2000 in 2012:

| | |
|---|---:|
| Direct materials | $195,000 |
| Direct labor | 120,000 |
| Factory space rental | 84,000 |
| Equipment leasing costs | 36,000 |
| Other manufacturing costs | 225,000 |
| Total manufacturing costs | $660,000 |

Lynn has collected the following information related to manufacturing MTR-2000:

- Equipment leasing costs represent special equipment used to manufacture MTR-2000. Midwest can terminate this lease by paying the equivalent of one month's lease payment for each of the two years left on its lease agreement.

- Forty percent of the other manufacturing overhead is considered variable. Variable overhead changes with the number of units produced, and this rate per unit is not expected to change in 2013. The fixed manufacturing overhead costs are not expected to change whether Midwest manufactures or purchases MTR-2000. Midwest can use equipment other than the leased equipment in its other manufacturing operations.

- Direct materials cost used in the production of MTR-2000 is expected to increase 8% in 2013.

- Midwest's direct labor contract calls for a 5% wage increase in 2013.

- The facilities used to manufacture MTR-2000 are rented under a month-to-month rental agreement. Midwest would have no need for this space if it does not manufacture MTR-2000. Thus, Midwest can withdraw from the rental agreement without any penalty.

John Porter, Midwest divisional manager, stopped by Lynn's office to voice his opinion regarding the outsourcing of MTR-2000. He commented, "I am really concerned about outsourcing MTR-2000. I have a son-in-law and a nephew, not to mention a member of our bowling team, who work on MTR-2000. They could lose their jobs if we buy that component from Marley. I really would appreciate anything you can do to make sure the cost analysis shows that we should continue making MTR-2000. Corporate is not aware of materials cost increases and maybe you can leave out some of those fixed costs. I just think we should continue making MTR-2000."

**Required**

1. Prepare a relevant cost analysis that shows whether the Midwest Division should make MTR-2000 or purchase it from Marley Company for 2013.

2. Identify and briefly discuss the strategic factors that Midwest should consider in this decision.

3. By referring to the specific ethical standards for management accountants outlined in Chapter 1, assess the ethical issues in John Porter's request of Lynn Hardt.

**(CMA Adapted)**

[LO 11-3, 11-6]  11-38  **Outsourcing Call Centers**  Merchants' Bank (MB) is a large regional bank operating in 634 locations in the Southeast U.S. Until 2005, the bank operated a call center for customer inquiries out of a single location in Atlanta, Georgia. MB understood the importance of the call center for overall customer satisfaction and made sure that the center was managed effectively. However, in early 2004, it became clear that the cost of running the center was increasing very rapidly, along with the firm's growth, and that some issues were arising about the quality of the service. To improve the quality and dramatically reduce the cost of the service, MB moved its call center to Bangalore, India, to be run by an experienced outsourcing firm, Naftel, which offers similar services to other banks like MB.

The Naftel contract was for five years, and in late 2008 it was time to consider whether to renew the contract, change to another call center service provider (in India or elsewhere), or bring the call center back to Atlanta.

Some important factors to consider in the decision:

- At the time of the decision in late 2008, the value of the dollar had been increasing relative to most other currencies.

- The financial crisis of 2008 had been affecting the banking business, and the outlook for growth for MB at the time had not been as rosy as it had been for the last few years. Top management and economic advisors for the bank had basically no idea what the right forecast for the coming five years was.

- At the time of the decision, the employment rate in Atlanta had been falling to the point that there was a good supply of talented employees who could have been recruited into the call center if the center were relocated back to Atlanta.
- The bank had just completed a new headquarters building in Atlanta and had a good bit of space in the building that MB had yet to lease. The outlook for the Atlanta economy was such that MB did not expect to lease much of this space for at least three years. If the call center were returned to Atlanta, it would occupy a space that would be rented for $100,000 per year, if there were a company that wanted to lease the space.
- If renewed, the Naftel contract would cost $4,200,000 per year for the next five years.
- The cost of salaries to staff the call center in Atlanta was expected to be $2,300,000 per year, the equipment would be leased for $850,000 per year, telecommunication services were expected to cost $500,000 per year, administrative costs for the call center were expected to be $600,000 per year, and the call center's share of corporate overhead was expected to be $400,000 per year.

**Required**

1. At the time of the above facts, should MB have returned the call center to Atlanta or should it have renewed the contract with Naftel? Develop your answer for both a one-year and a five-year time horizon. Consider the strategic context of the decision as an integral part of your answer. (*Hint:* Using discounted cash flow is not required but would improve your answer; MB uses a discount rate of 6%.)

2. What are the global issues that should have been considered in the decision?

3. What ethical issues, if any, should have been considered in the decision?

[LO 11-1] 11-39 **Sustainability** If Problem 10-58 (Budgeting and Sustainability) has not already been assigned, it can be assigned here.

[LO 11-5, 11-8] 11-40 **Profitability Analysis** High Point Furniture Company (HPF) manufactures high-quality furniture for sale directly to exclusive hotels, interior designers, and select retail outlets throughout the world. HPF's products include upholstered furniture, dining tables, bedroom furniture, and a variety of other products, including end tables. Through attention to quality and design innovation, and by careful attention to changing consumer tastes, HPF has become one of the most successful furniture manufacturers worldwide. Hal Blin, the chief operating officer of HPF, is reviewing the most recent sales and profits report for the three best-selling end tables in HPFs product line—the Parker, Virginian, and Weldon end tables. Hal is concerned about the relatively poor performance of the Weldon line. He discusses the prospects for the line with HPF's marketing and sales vice-president, Joan Hunt. Joan notes that there has been no significant trend up or down in any of the end table lines, though the direction of consumer tastes would probably favor the Virginian and Parker lines. Hal and Joan agree that this may be the time for further analysis to determine whether the Weldon line should be discontinued.

**HPF Sales and Profits Report: End Tables**

| | Parker | | Virginian | | Weldon | | |
| | Per Unit | Total | Per Unit | Total | Per Unit | Total | Total |
| --- | --- | --- | --- | --- | --- | --- | --- |
| Sales units | | 150,000 | | 335,000 | | 165,000 | |
| Sales dollars | $459.00 | $68,850,000 | $365.00 | $122,275,000 | $248.00 | $40,920,000 | $232,045,000 |
| **Factory Costs** | | | | | | | |
| Labor | 125.00 | 18,750,000 | 118.00 | 39,530,000 | 62.00 | 10,230,000 | 68,510,000 |
| Raw materials | 88.50 | 13,275,000 | 66.00 | 22,110,000 | 78.00 | 12,870,000 | 48,255,000 |
| Power | 23.50 | 3,525,000 | 15.60 | 5,226,000 | 13.80 | 2,277,000 | 11,028,000 |
| Repairs | 12.25 | 1,837,500 | 12.25 | 4,103,750 | 12.25 | 2,021,250 | 7,962,500 |
| Factory equipment | 33.50 | 5,025,000 | 33.50 | 11,222,500 | 33.50 | 5,527,500 | 21,775,000 |
| Other | 14.00 | 2,100,000 | 12.50 | 4,187,500 | 13.25 | 2,186,250 | 8,473,750 |
| Total factory cost | 296.75 | 44,512,500 | 257.85 | 86,379,750 | 212.80 | 35,112,000 | 166,004,250 |
| **Selling and Administrative Expenses** | | | | | | | |
| Selling expense | 45.00 | 6,750,000 | 36.00 | 12,060,000 | 25.00 | 4,125,000 | 22,935,000 |
| Office expense | 16.80 | 2,520,000 | 16.80 | 5,628,000 | 16.80 | 2,772,000 | 10,920,000 |
| Administrative expense | 27.50 | 4,125,000 | 27.50 | 9,212,500 | 27.50 | 4,537,500 | 17,875,000 |
| Other | 6.50 | 975,000 | 6.50 | 2,177,500 | 6.50 | 1,072,500 | 4,225,000 |
| Total cost | 392.55 | 58,882,500 | 344.65 | 115,457,750 | 288.60 | 47,619,000 | 221,959,250 |
| Operating profit (loss) | $ 66.45 | $ 9,967,500 | $ 20.35 | $ 6,817,250 | $ (40.60) | $ (6,699,000) | $ 10,085,750 |

Note: Selling expense consists of fixed salaries for the sales staff, advertising, and the cost of marketing/sales management. The remaining selling and administrative expenses are also considered fixed. Power is for equipment used in manufacturing and varies with the number of units produced. The remaining factory costs (repairs, factory equipment, and other) are considered fixed costs.

**Required**

1. Using Excel or an equivalent spreadsheet, develop an analysis that can help Hal decide about the future of the Weldon line. Should the Weldon line be dropped? Why or why not?

2. Using the spreadsheet you developed in requirement 1, determine whether your answer would change if sales of Weldon are expected to fall by 80%.

3. Again using the spreadsheet in requirement 1, determine whether the Weldon line should be discontinued if the resources devoted to Weldon could be used to increase sales by 10% in each of the other two lines.

4. Again using the spreadsheet in requirement 1 and using Goal Seek in Excel or an equivalent, determine the sales increase (or decrease) in the sales of the Parker line that would be necessary to maintain the firm's overall profit in part 1 if the Weldon line were discontinued. For an illustration of Goal Seek, see Exhibit 9.5 in Chapter 9.

5. Given your answers to requirements 1 through 4 above, consider the overall competitive environment facing HPF and make your recommendations regarding the firm's strategic position and direction at this time.

[LO 11-5, 11-8]      11-41  **Profitability Analysis**   "I'm not looking forward to breaking the news," groaned Charlie Wettle, the controller of Meyer Paint Company. He and Don Smith, state liaison for the firm, were returning from a meeting with representatives of the Virginia General Services Administration (GSA), the agency that administers bidding on state contracts. Charlie and Don had expected to get the specifications to bid on the traffic paint contract, soon to be renewed. Instead of picking up the bid sheets and renewing old friendships at the GSA, however, they were stunned to learn that Meyer's paint samples had performed poorly on the road test and the firm was not eligible to bid on the contract.

Meyer's two main product lines are traffic paint, used for painting yellow and white lines on highways, and commercial paints, sold through local retail outlets. The paint-production process is fairly simple. Raw materials are kept in the storage area that occupies approximately half of the plant space. Large tanks that resemble silos are used to store the latex that is the main ingredient in its paint. These tanks are located on the loading dock just outside the plant so that when a shipment of latex arrives, it can be pumped directly from the tank truck into these storage tanks. Latex is extremely sensitive to cold. It cannot be stored outside or even shipped in the winter without heated trucks, which are very expensive for a small firm such as Meyer.

Currently, Meyer has the traffic paint contracts for the states of Pennsylvania, North Carolina, Delaware, and Virginia. Of last year's total production of 380,000 gallons, 90% was traffic paint. Of this amount, 88,000 gallons were for the Virginia contract. Each state has unique specifications for color, thickness, texture, drying time, and other characteristics of the paint. For example, paint sold to Pennsylvania must withstand heavy use of salt on roads during the winter. Paint for North Carolina highways must tolerate extended periods of intense heat during summer months.

Due to the high cost of shipping paint, most paint producers can be competitive on price only in locations fairly close to their production facilities. Accordingly, Meyer has enjoyed an advantage in bidding on contracts in the eastern states close to Virginia. However, one of their biggest competitors, Heron Paint Company of Houston, Texas, is building a new plant in North Carolina. With lower costs due to its efficient new facility and its proximity, Heron will become a major competitive threat.

Meyer's commercial paint line includes interior and exterior house paints in a wide range of colors formulated to approximate authentic colonial colors. Because of the historical association, the line has been well received in Virginia. Most of these paints are sold through paint and hardware stores as the stores' second or third line of paint. The large national firms such as Benjamin Moore or Sherwin Williams provide extensive services to paint retailers such as computerized color matching equipment. Partly because it lacks the resources to provide such amenities and partly because it has always considered the commercial paint a sideline, Meyer has never tried to market the commercial line aggressively. Meyer sells 38,000 gallons of commercial paint per year.

Charlie is worried about the future of the company. The firm's strategic goal is to provide a quality product at the lowest possible cost and in a timely fashion. After absorbing the shock of losing the Virginia contract, Charlie wondered whether the firm should consider increasing production of commercial paints to lessen the company's dependence on traffic paint contracts. Carl Bunch, who manages the day-to-day operation of the firm, believes the company can double its sales of commercial paint if it undertakes a promotional campaign estimated to cost $120,000. The average price of traffic paint sold last year was $20 per gallon. For commercial paint, the average price was $24.

Charlie Wettle has assembled the following data to evaluate the financial performance of the two lines of paint. The primary raw material used in paint production is latex. The list price for latex is $32 per pound; 450 pounds of latex are needed to produce 1,000 gallons of traffic paint. Commercial paint requires 325 pounds of latex per 1,000 gallons of paint. In addition to the cost of the latex, other variable costs are as shown below.

| | Traffic | Commercial |
|---|---|---|
| Raw materials cost per gallon of paint: | | |
| Camelcarb (limestone) | 0.76 | 1.08 |
| Silica | 0.74 | 1.04 |
| Pigment | 0.24 | 0.76 |
| Other ingredients | 0.12 | 0.06 |
| Direct labor cost per gallon | 0.92 | 1.70 |
| Freight cost per gallon | 1.56 | 0.86 |

Last year, fixed overhead costs attributable to the traffic paint totaled $170,000, including an estimated $50,000 of costs directly associated with the Virginia contract; the $50,000 can be eliminated in approximately two years. Fixed overhead costs attributable to the commercial paint are $26,000. Other fixed manufacturing overhead costs total $220,000. Charlie estimates that $80,000 of this amount is inventory-handling costs that will be avoided due to the loss of the Virginia contract. Both the remaining fixed manufacturing overhead ($140,000) and the general and administrative costs of $280,000 are allocated equally to all gallons of paint produced.

**Required**

1. Calculate the contribution margin for each type of paint and total firmwide contribution under each of the following scenarios:

   Scenario A    Current production, including the Virginia contract

   Scenario B    Without either the Virginia contract or the promotion to expand sales of commercial paint

   Scenario C    Without the Virginia contract but with the promotion to expand sales of the commercial paint

2. Determine whether scenario B or C (per requirement 1 above) should be chosen by Meyer and explain why, including a consideration of the strategic context.

[LO 11-5]    11-42  **Project Analysis; Sales Promotions**   Hillside Furniture Company makes outdoor furniture from recycled products, including plastics and wood by-products. Its three furniture products are gliders, chairs with footstools, and tables. The products appeal primarily to cost-conscious consumers and those who value the recycling of materials. The company wholesales its products to retailers and various mass merchandisers. Because of the seasonal nature of the products, most orders are manufactured during the winter months for delivery in the early spring. Michael Cain, founder and owner, is dismayed that sales for two of the products are tracking below budget. The chart below shows pertinent year-to-date data regarding the company's products.

Certain that the shortfall was caused by a lack of effort by the sales force, Michael has suggested to Lisa Boyle, the sales manager, that the company announce two contests to correct this situation before it deteriorates. The first contest is a trip to Hawaii awarded to the top salesperson if incremental glider sales are attained to close the budget shortfall. The second contest is a golf weekend, complete with a new set of golf clubs, awarded to the top salesperson if incremental sales of chairs with footstools are attained to close the budget shortfall. The Hawaiian vacation would cost $16,500 and the golf trip would cost $12,500.

| | Glider | | Chair with Footstool | | Table | |
|---|---|---|---|---|---|---|
| | **Actual** | **Budget** | **Actual** | **Budget** | **Actual** | **Budget** |
| Number of units | 2,600 | 4,000 | 6,900 | 8,000 | 3,500 | 3,300 |
| Average sales price | $80.00 | $85.00 | $61.00 | $65.00 | $24.00 | $25.00 |
| Variable costs: | | | | | | |
| Direct labor: | | | | | | |
| Hours of labor | 2.50 | 2.25 | 3.25 | 3.00 | 0.60 | 0.50 |
| Cost per hour | $11.00 | $10.00 | $ 9.50 | $ 9.25 | $ 9.00 | $ 9.00 |
| Direct material | $16.00 | $15.00 | $11.00 | $10.00 | $ 6.00 | $ 5.00 |
| Sales commission | $15.00 | $15.00 | $10.00 | $10.00 | $ 5.00 | $ 5.50 |

**Required**

1. Explain whether either contest is desirable or not. Supplement your analysis by determining the total contribution margin for the glider and the chair-with-footstool products, under each of the following two scenarios: (a) actual sales volume at actual selling prices, actual costs, and actual resource usage, and (b) actual sales volume at budgeted selling prices, budgeted resource usage, and budgeted costs.

2. Explain the strategic issues guiding your choice about these contests.

**(CMA Adapted)**

[LO 11-5, 11-7] 11-43 **Profitability Analysis; Pro Forma Income Statement** RayLok Incorporated has invented a secret process to improve light intensity and manufactures a variety of products related to this process. Each product is independent of the others and is treated as a separate profit/loss division. Product (division) managers have a great deal of freedom to manage their divisions as they think best. Failure to produce target division income is dealt with severely; however, rewards for exceeding one's profit objective are, as one division manager described them, lavish.

The DimLok Division sells an add-on automotive accessory that automatically dims a vehicle's headlights by sensing a certain intensity of light coming from a specific direction. DimLok has had a new manager in each of the three previous years because each manager failed to reach RayLok's target profit. Donna Barnes has just been promoted to manager and is studying ways to meet the current target profit for DimLok.

DimLok's two profit targets for the coming year are $800,000 (20% return on the investment in the annual fixed costs of the division) plus an additional profit of $20 for each DimLok unit sold. Other constraints on division's operations are

- Production cannot exceed sales because RayLok's corporate advertising program stresses completely new product models each year, although the models might have only cosmetic changes.

- DimLok's selling price cannot vary above the current selling price of $200 per unit but may vary as much as 10% below $200.

- A division manager can elect to expand fixed production or selling facilities; however, the target objective related to fixed costs is increased by 20% of the cost of such expansion. Furthermore, a manager cannot expand fixed facilities by more than 30% of existing fixed cost levels without approval from the board of directors.

Donna is now examining data gathered by her staff to determine whether DimLok can achieve its target profits of $800,000 and $20 per unit. A summary of these reports shows the following:

- Last year's sales were 30,000 units at $200 per unit.

- DimLok's current manufacturing facility capacity is 40,000 units per year but can be increased to 80,000 units per year with an increase of $1,000,000 in annual fixed costs.

- Present variable costs amount to $80 per unit, but DimLok's vendors are willing to offer raw materials discounts amounting to $20 per unit, beginning with unit number 60,001.

- Sales can be increased up to 100,000 units per year by committing large blocks of product to institutional buyers at a discounted unit price of $180. However, this discount applies only to sales in excess of 40,000 units per year.

Donna believes that these projections are reliable and is now trying to determine what DimLok must do to meet the profit objectives that RayLok's board of directors assigned to it.

**Required**

1. Determine the dollar amount of DimLok's present annual fixed costs.

2. Determine the number of units that DimLok must sell to achieve both profit objectives. Be sure to consider all constraints in determining your answer.

3. Without regard to your answer in requirement 2, assume that Donna decides to sell 40,000 units at $200 per unit and 24,000 units at $180 per unit. Prepare a budgeted income statement (contribution format) for DimLok showing whether her decision will achieve DimLok's profit objectives.

4. Assess DimLok's competitive strategy.

5. Identify critical success factors associated with the strategy that DimLok is pursuing.

**(CMA Adapted)**

**[LO 11-7]** 11-44 **Product-Profitability Analysis; Scarce Resources** Santana Company produces a variety of consumer electronic products. Unit selling prices and costs for three models of one of its product lines are as follows:

|  | No Frills | Standard Options | Super |
|---|---|---|---|
| Selling price | $35 | $60 | $80 |
| Direct materials | 9 | 11 | 14 |
| Direct labor ($20/hour) | 10 | 20 | 30 |
| Variable overhead | 3 | 6 | 9 |
| Fixed overhead | 3 | 6 | 6 |

Variable overhead is charged to products on the basis of direct labor dollars; fixed overhead is allocated to products on the basis of machine-hours.

**Required**

1. What is fundamentally different about the fixed versus variable overhead assigned to products? (Answer the question within the context of the relevance of this difference to the determination of short-term product mix.)

2. Calculate for each product both the gross profit per unit and the contribution margin per unit. Are either of these profitability measures useful for planning the optimum short-term product mix? Why or why not?

3. If the company has excess machine capacity but a limited amount of labor time, how should the optimum short-term product mix be determined?

4. Assume now that machine-hours, not direct labor-hours, is the limiting resource. How, if at all, would this affect the product-mix decision?

5. How can the optimum product mix be determined when there are only two products, and one or more constraints?

6. How can the optimum product mix be determined when there are more than two products, and one or more constraints?

7. What is the primary role of the management accountant in terms of planning the optimum short-term product mix?

**[LO 11-9]** 11-45 **Profitability Analysis; Linear Programming (Appendix)** Home Service Company offers monthly service plans to provide prepared meals that are delivered to customers' homes and need only be heated in a microwave or conventional oven. Home Service offers two monthly plans, premier cuisine and haute cuisine. The premier cuisine plan provides frozen meals that are delivered twice each month; the premier generates a contribution of $150 for each monthly service plan sold. The haute cuisine plan provides freshly prepared meals delivered on a daily basis and generates a contribution of $100 for each monthly plan sold. Home Service's strong reputation enables it to sell all meals that it can prepare.

Each meal goes through food preparation and cooking steps in the company's kitchens. After these steps, the premier cuisine meals are flash frozen. The time requirements per monthly meal plan and hours available per month follow:

|  | Preparation | Cooking | Freezing |
|---|---|---|---|
| Hours required: |  |  |  |
| Premier cuisine | 3 | 2 | 1 |
| Haute cuisine | 1 | 3 | 0 |
| Hours available | 80 | 120 | 45 |

For planning purposes, Home Service uses linear programming to determine the most profitable number of premier and haute cuisine meals to produce.

**Required**

1. Using the Solver function of Microsoft Excel, determine the most profitable product mix for Home Service given the existing constraints and contribution margins.

2. Generate and interpret the information contained in the "Sensitivity Report" associated with the solution in requirement 1.

3. Using the Solver function of Microsoft Excel, determine the most profitable product mix for Home Service given the existing contribution margins and all constraints except the preparation time constraint.

**(CMA Adapted)**

[LO 11-7] 11-46 **Sustainability** If not assigned previously, Problem 9-50 (CVP Analysis; Sustainability; Uncertainty; Decision Tables) can be assigned here.

[LO 11-8] 11-47 **Decision-Making Biases** Obtain from your library a copy of the following article: D. Kahneman, D. Lovallo, and O. Sibony, "Before You Make That Big Decision. . . ," *Harvard Business Review,* June 2011, pp. 51–60. In this article, the authors argue that, "Even highly experienced, superbly competent, and well-intentioned managers are fallible. . . ." (p. 60). They discuss a variety of cognitive biases associated with the decision-making process. Such biases can diminish the quality of decisions. The authors maintain that understanding these biases may decrease their effect and offer a checklist designed to facilitate decision quality control.

**Required**
1. What is meant by the term "cognitive bias"?
2. What is the specific decision-making context addressed by the authors of this article?
3. What are the three major categories of the decision quality-control checklist recommended by the authors?
4. What are the specific cognitive biases discussed by the authors of this article?

[LO 11-4, 11-7, 11-8] 11-48 **Sell-or-Process-Further Decision** Humbolt Electric manufactures electronic subcomponents that can be sold at the end of Process #1 or processed further, in Process #2, and then sold. Currently, the entire output of Process #1 can be sold at a price of $2 per unit. The output of Process #2 has in the past sold for $5.50 per unit; however, the price of this output has recently dropped to $5.10 (on average).

On the basis of an analysis of the above cost and selling price information, as well as an analysis of market trend data, the VP of marketing has suggested that output from Process #2 should be curtailed whenever the price of its output falls below $4.50 per unit. The VP of manufacturing has indicated that the total available capacity is interchangeable between the two processes. (That is, fixed manufacturing costs are largely independent of decisions regarding short-term product mix.) He recommends that, based on current prices, all sales should be from Process #2 output. His analysis follows:

| | Output of Process #1 | Output of Process #2 |
|---|---|---|
| Selling price, after deducting selling-related costs | $2.00 | $5.10 |
| Costs: | | |
| Direct materials (DM) | 1.00 | 1.50 |
| Direct labor (DL) | 0.20 | 0.40 |
| Manufacturing overhead | 0.60 | 1.20 |
| Transferred-in variable costs from Process #1 (DM + DL) | N/A | 1.20 |
| Operating profit | $0.20 | $0.80 |

Direct materials and direct labor are variable costs. All manufacturing overhead costs are fixed and are allocated to units produced based on hours of capacity used.

Total hours of capacity available are 600,000. The products are produced in batches of 60 units. Each batch of output from Process #1 requires one hour of processing, and two *additional* hours of processing per batch produced in Process #2.

**Required**
1. Develop a schematic diagram of the two-stage production process. Include in your diagram relevant revenue (selling price per unit) as well as relevant costs (per unit of output).
2. If the price of the output from Process #2 for the coming year is expected to be $5.10, should all sales be only from Process #2, as asserted by the VP of manufacturing?
3. What is the lowest acceptable price for the output from Process #2 to make it as profitable as the output from Process #1?
4. Suppose that 50% of the manufacturing overhead costs are variable. Do your answers to parts 1 and 2 above change? If so, why?
5. *Sensitivity analysis:* Calculate the contribution margin per processing hour for both Process #1 output and Process #2 output under each of the following assumptions regarding the percentage of variable overhead cost: 0%, 25%, 50%, and 100%. Perform these calculations for Process #2 output both for a selling price of $5.10 per unit and a selling price of $5.50 per unit. What general conclusion can you draw on the basis of this sensitivity analysis?

## Solutions to Self–Study Problems

### 1. Special Order Pricing

The key to this exercise is to recognize that the variable manufacturing costs of $130 ($85 for materials and $45 for labor) are the relevant ones and that the fixed overhead costs, since they will not change, are not relevant.

Thus, the correct decision is to accept the offer, since the price of $150 exceeds the variable manufacturing cost of $130. HighValu also should consider strategic factors. For example, will the three-year contract be desirable? Perhaps the market conditions will change so that HighValu will have more profitable uses of the capacity in the coming years. Will the special order enhance or diminish the firm's competitive position?

### 2. The Make-or-Buy Decision

The relevant costs for this analysis are the outside purchase cost of $15 per set versus the make costs of $10 per set ($6 for materials plus $4 for labor), and $10,000 annual fixed costs.

First, determine the amount of annual savings in variable costs for the make option compared to the external purchase price:

$$6{,}000 \text{ annual sales} \times (\$15 - \$10) = \$30{,}000 \text{ annual savings}$$

Second, compare the savings in variable costs to the additional fixed costs of $10,000 per year. The net savings, an advantage to make rather than buy, is $20,000 ($30,000 − $10,000).

HighValu also should consider relevant strategic factors, such as the quality and reliability of in-house production of the sets relative to supplier quality and reliability. Are there other, more attractive, uses of the available capacity? Are any employee jobs affected? What would be the impact of this decision on employee morale?

### 3. Product Profitability Analysis

1. To determine the number of Windys that can be manufactured if the 3,750 units of Gale are no longer produced, we consider the capacity released for each of the two constraints.

   **For the automated sewing machine:** The machine produces 20 Windys per hour or 30 Gales per hour, so that the number of Windys that could be produced from the released capacity of Gale is

   $$3{,}750 \times 20/30 = 2{,}500 \text{ Windys}$$

   **For the inspection-and-packing operation:** The operation requires 15 minutes for Windy (4 per hour) and 5 minutes for Gale (12 per hour), so the number of Windys that could be inspected and packed in the released time is

   $$3{,}750 \times 4/12 = 1{,}250 \text{ Windys}$$

   In this case, the inspection and packing is the effective limitation, so that if Gale is deleted, the firm can produce 1,250 Windys with the released capacity.

2. If 3,750 units of Gale are replaced with 1,250 units of Windy, the proper relevant cost analysis should consider the contribution margin of each product:

   |  | Windy | Gale |
   |---|---|---|
   | Unit contribution margin | $  8 | $  4 |
   | Units sold (giving up 3,750 units Gale gives 1,250 of Windy, per part 1) | 1,250 | 3,750 |
   | Total contribution margin | $10,000 | $15,000 |

   Thus, the deletion of Gale and replacement with Windy would reduce the total contribution margin by $5,000 ($15,000 − $10,000).

3. Since the effect on total contribution is significant (as shown in requirement 2), Windbreakers should continue to make Gale. Other factors to consider follow:

   a. At existing sales levels of 18,750 of Windy and 3,750 of Gale, Windbreakers is operating at full capacity; if there are additional sales opportunities for Windy, the firm should consider adding to available capacity so that the current sales of Gale can be made plus the additional sales of Windy.

The analysis of the cost benefit of additional capacity is best addressed through the techniques of capital budgeting as described in Chapter 12.

b. The effect of the loss of Gale on the firm's image and therefore the potential long-term effects on the sales of Windy.

c. The long-term sales potential for Gale. Will its sales likely exceed the current 3,750 level in future years?

*Please visit* **http://www.mhhe.com/blocher6e** *to access a narrated, animated tutorial for solving these problems.*

# CHAPTER TWELVE

# Strategy and the Analysis of Capital Investments

**LO 12-1**

*Explain the strategic role of capital-investment analysis.*

Consider the following examples of strategic investments made recently by a variety of companies and industries:

- To meet a growing middle-class market for alternatives to home-brewed alcoholic products, SABMiller (the number two brewer in the world) announced plans in early 2012 to spend up to $260 million for facilities devoted to the production of "Chibuku," a commercial alternative to home-made ("informal") beers and meant for sale in a number of African countries, including Ghana, Malawi, and Zambia. (Source: *Bloomberg Businessweek,* March 19–March 25, 2012, pp. 33–34)

- To increase its presence in what has now become the world's biggest auto market, Ford Motor Co. opened in early 2012 a $490 million production plant in the southeastern Chinese city of Chongqing. The plant will be operated on a joint-venture basis and will be capable of producing 150,000 cars per year. (Source: *The Wall Street Journal,* February 27, 2012, p. B5)

- Holiday Inn recently unveiled an ambitious three-year $1 billion overhaul of its 3,400 hotels. Capital improvements for each hotel range from new bedding, external lighting, better shower fixtures, and sleeker roadside signs to standardization of music and scents in the lobby of each hotel. The average cost of these improvements per hotel franchisee is approximately $250,000. Such improvements are targeted at making Holiday Inn more competitive with its two primary rivals, Hilton Garden Inn and Courtyard by Marriott. (Source: *The Wall Street Journal,* December 9, 2010)

- In an attempt to win business from competitors like United Parcel Service Inc. in the lucrative market for international package delivery, and to cater to the rising middle classes in India, China, and Brazil, FedEx in 2010 committed to purchasing a fleet of Boeing 777s, the largest twin-engine plane on the market. Total capital expenditures for planes, new sorting centers, and other improvements were planned at $3.2 billion for fiscal 2011. (Source: *The Wall Street Journal,* July 14, 2010)

- General Motors committed $328 million to update a factory in Flint, Michigan, to provide the capability of producing the next generation of full-size pickup trucks (Chevrolet Silverado and GMC Sierra), due in showrooms in early 2013. (Source: *Bucks County Courier Times,* Tuesday, July 2011, p. A6)

- The Shaw Group (**www.shawgrp.com**), a Fortune 500 company with over 27,000 employees worldwide, recently built a $100 million facility in Lake Charles, Louisiana, that will use modular manufacturing techniques in constructing nuclear-power plants. Rather than building a plant entirely on site, the company can now assemble large sections in the factory, to be shipped to the construction site for final assembly. A company spokesperson notes that this method is less expensive, more efficient, and safer compared to building plants on site. (Source: David M. Katz, "Captains of CapEx," *CFO,* September 2010, p. 40)

- To meet the data-security and processing-reliability demands of its core customer group, and in an attempt to expand its mainframe customer base to emerging markets such as Russia, China, and Brazil, IBM spent more than $1 billion (over a three-year period) to develop a new supercomputer (the "x9"), which can process up to 1 billion transactions per day. (Source: **www.forbes.com/technology/**)

## Strategy and the Analysis of Capital Expenditures

### Underlying Nature of Capital Expenditures

A **capital investment** is a project that involves a large expenditure of funds and expected future benefits over a number of years.

What do each of the preceding examples have in common? In each case, the organization is committing a significant amount of capital for an investment project that provides expected benefits over an extended number of years. Through such well-planned **capital investments,** business entities are able to restore profitability, regain or expand market share, respond to changing business climates, reduce costs, improve quality, and strengthen strategic business processes throughout their value chain. Examples of capital investments include: the purchase of new manufacturing equipment, the implementation of a new manufacturing technology, the installation of a computer-based recordkeeping system, the offering of new services by a governmental entity, and the expansion of a business into new territories.

Fundamentally, capital-investment decisions should support the underlying strategy of the organization. As noted in Chapter 1, firms can secure competitive advantage by pursuing either a low-cost (i.e., cost-leadership) strategy or a product-differentiation strategy. In the case of the former, we would expect the use of large, highly automated manufacturing facilities, designed to capture economies of scale, and production efficiencies associated with the use of advanced manufacturing technologies (e.g., computer-integrated manufacturing, or CIM). In the case of the latter, the organization would likely devote a greater share of its capital-investment budget to research, development, and product-promotion activities.

**Capital budgeting** is the process of identifying, evaluating, selecting, and controlling capital investments.

Given the strategic nature of capital-investment decisions, organizations generally use a formal process to plan and control such expenditures. The process of identifying, evaluating, selecting, and controlling capital investments is called **capital budgeting.**

### Chapter Overview—Where Are We Headed?

This chapter presents a discussion of the following issues related to the capital-budgeting process: the role of accounting in the capital-budgeting process; the identification of relevant financial information for the analysis of capital-expenditure projects; the use of discounted cash flow (DCF) models for making capital-budgeting decisions; handling uncertainties in the decision-making process; the use of non-DCF decision models; and, selected behavioral issues. Appendix A presents alternative templates for addressing the asset-replacement decision, while advanced issues related to the use of DCF decision models are covered in Appendix B.

## The Role of Accounting in the Capital-Budgeting Process

**LO 12-2**

*Describe how accountants can add value to the capital-budgeting process.*

You might wonder why the topic of capital budgeting is covered in an accounting textbook. You might say, "Isn't capital budgeting a finance topic?" These are legitimate questions, particularly since the theory behind modern capital-budgeting decision models comes from the field of finance. Thus, if accounting adds value to the capital-budgeting process, it must come from somewhere other than model development. Within the context of capital budgeting, accounting plays a facilitative role, helping decision makers implement the decision models developed in finance. In this chapter we consider the following four specific contributions that accounting makes to the capital-budgeting process: linkage to an organization's *master budget* (planning); linkage to *strategy* (planning) and to the organization's *balanced scorecard* (control); generation of *relevant data for investment analysis* purposes (decision making); and conducting *post-audits* (control) of capital-investment projects.

### Linkage to the Master Budget

**A capital budget**
for a given period consists of a listing of approved investment projects as well as anticipated cash outflows associated with these projects.

For any given accounting period, a listing of approved investment projects is reflected in the organization's capital budget. An organization's **capital budget** for a given period consists of a listing of approved investment projects as well as anticipated cash outflows associated with these projects. As indicated in Chapter 10, the capital budget is part of the overall planning system of the organization—called the "master budget." The master budget is part of a larger system of planning and control, which we refer to as an organization's comprehensive management accounting and control system (MACS). Such a system has strategic, operational, and management control dimensions. Accounting plays both a coordinating and a leadership role in the design of an organization's MACS. That is, accounting adds value by guiding the development and use of comprehensive planning and control systems, including an effective capital-budgeting process. As a component of the master budget, the organization's capital budget is used for both strategic and management control purposes.

### Linkage to Strategy and to the Balanced Scorecard (BSC)

**A strategic control system**
refers to the processes an organization uses to monitor the progress of the organization in terms of accomplishing the strategic goals of the organization.

In Chapter 2 we introduced you to the notion of the balanced scorecard (BSC) as a critical element of an organization's strategic control system. Recall that a **strategic control system** refers to the processes an organization uses to monitor the progress of the organization in terms accomplishing the strategic goals of the organization. The BSC can be an effective tool to communicate to employees and managers the mission and strategy of the organization. Fundamentally, a BSC represents a series of linked (i.e., cause-and-effect) relationships across four broad performance perspectives: learning and growth, customer, business processes, and, financial. Included in these four dimensions is a mixture of financial and nonfinancial, internal and external, and lead versus lagged performance indicators.

It is management's responsibility, working with individuals throughout the organization (including accountants), to develop the list of relevant performance metrics. Presumably, the BSC will include some of the performance indicators—both financial and nonfinancial—used to evaluate capital-investment proposals. Accounting's special role in this process is to collect and periodically summarize the performance metrics—both financial and nonfinancial—included within the organization's BSC.

Kaplan and Norton (2008)[1] describe a five-stage "closed-loop" management system that can be used to develop strategy, translate the strategy into operational actions, and monitor and improve the effectiveness of both. Stage 2 of this process includes the development of a strategy map and associated balanced scorecard (BSC) and the identification of a set of strategic initiatives (investments) needed to achieve

[1] Robert S. Kaplan and David P. Norton, "Mastering the Management System," *Harvard Business Review,* January 2008, pp. 63–77.

Environmentally conscious construction projects and sustainable architecture have become quite prevalent on the global landscape. However, are such investments worthwhile from an economic perspective? An increasing number of businesses and organizations are concluding that such practices can be both good for the environment and good for the "bottom line" of the organization. Buildings consume over 70% of electricity produced in the United States, 13.6% of potable water, and 40% of all raw materials produced. Thus, the potential for savings through sustainable building and green architecture are significant—both for new construction as well as for existing structures. Geothermal heating and cooling systems, vegetation-covered rooftops, passive solar heating, construction materials made from recycled materials, LED lighting, and even the use of methane gas from nearby landfills for heating and

electrical generation are some of the major investments being made today by both for-profit and not-for-profit organizations. Though typically more expensive initially, these investments pay off in the long run through dramatically reduced energy and maintenance costs, as well as reductions in carbon emissions. Some of these investments have a much shorter payback period. The Empire State Building in New York City recently completed a $13 million project to retrofit the 6,514 windows in the building. This project is expected to generate energy savings of approximately $4.4 million per year, resulting in a three-year payback period!

**Sources:** Theresa Hegel, "Green Architecture Builds Momentum," *Bucks County Courier Times* (April 17, 2011), pp. A1–A2; and Anita Hamilton, "Greening the Skyline," *Time* (April 18, 2011), p. 4.

---

A **multicriteria decision model** is one that includes more than one decision criterion.

The **analytic hierarchy process (AHP)** is a multicriteria decision technique that can combine qualitative and quantitative factors in the overall evaluation of decision alternatives.

the organization's strategic objectives. The authors define (p. 68) strategic initiatives as "discretionary projects or programs, of finite duration, designed to close a performance gap." Such programs would complement capital expenditures designed to support current operations and would include, for example, a customer-loyalty program or the implementation of a training program for Six Sigma. Strategic expenditures can also be made to support the organization's environmental-performance and/or sustainability goals. As explained in Chapter 10, this approach gives prominence to strategy-related capital expenditures by separating total investment spending into two categories: strategic capital expenditures (StratEx), and capital expenditures needed to support current operations (CapEx).

The evaluation of capital-investment projects in terms of their relationship to strategy in general, and to the BSC in particular, is an interesting problem. That is, how do organizations evaluate proposed projects in a comprehensive manner—to include both financial and nonfinancial/qualitative considerations—and to ensure that such investments support the underlying strategy of the organization? The answer to this question may lie in the use of what are called **multicriteria decision models,** which include more than a single decision criterion (such as after-tax rate of return, or projected future cash flows). One of the more popular multicriteria decision models is the analytic hierarchy process (AHP).

The **analytic hierarchy process (AHP)** is a multicriteria decision technique that can combine qualitative and quantitative factors in the overall evaluation of decision alternatives; as such, the AHP can be used for capital-budgeting purposes.[2] The AHP organizes a problem into smaller and smaller parts and then calls for the use of simple pair-wise comparisons to develop a hierarchy of decision-maker preferences. This hierarchy is then manipulated analytically to produce a final matrix representing the overall priorities of the decision alternatives relative to one another. One can then make a logical decision based on the pair-wise comparisons made between the decision alternatives (for example, choice of competing capital-budgeting projects) and the various criteria used for decision-making purposes (such as quality, cash flows, impact on brand image, and payback period). The AHP allows managers to consider both tangible and intangible factors when

---

[2] A five-step procedure for implementing the AHP in a capital-budgeting context is given in T. F. Monahan, M. J. Liberatore, and D. E. Stout, "Decision Support for Capital Budgeting: A Model for Classroom Presentation," *Journal of Accounting Education* 8 (1990), pp. 225–39, and in D. E. Stout, M. J. Liberatore, and T. F. Monahan, "Decision Support Software for Capital Budgeting," *Management Accounting*, July 1991, pp. 50–53.

## Capital Expenditure Analysis in the Public and Not-for-Profit Sectors: Expanding the Notion of Cost-Benefit Comparison

The analysis of capital expenditures is an important issue for both the public and the not-for-profit sectors of the economy. In these sectors, a cost-benefit analysis will go beyond the inclusion of economic data to include an assessment of the investment on various stakeholder groups (society, consumers, employees, etc.). Such an expanded approach is needed to estimate what is called the *total welfare gain* of a proposed program. Nonmonetary, qualitative information can therefore outweigh a negative financial assessment of a given proposal. For example, for a vaccination program to support the development of countries, nonmonetary measures could include efficiency and effectiveness measures, such as number of people immunized, number of people immunized per dollar spent, and cost per immunization. Accountants can help in the information specification, gathering, and reporting of such financial and nonfinancial data.

**Source:** Professional Accountants in Business Committee, International Federation of Accountants (IFAC), *International Good Practice Guidance: Project Appraisal Using Discounted Cash Flow* (New York: IFAC, June 2008).

constructing the decision hierarchy, thereby allowing managers to link capital-budgeting decisions to strategy.[3] This ensures that the decision will be based on more than just financial or other quantitative characteristics of proposed capital investments. Accountants can add value to the decision-making process by providing accurate information and by participating in the pair-wise comparison process.

### Generation of Relevant Financial Data for Decision-Making Purposes

In Chapter 11 we defined relevant financial information for decision making as future costs or revenues that differ between decision alternatives. At that time we made the point that accounting assumes a primary responsibility for providing managers with such information. These points apply as well to capital budgeting: managerial accountants supply decision makers with relevant *after-tax* cash flow data for analyzing the desirability of proposed capital-investment projects.

Part of the relevant financial data pertaining to capital-budgeting decisions are the income-tax consequences of proposed capital expenditures. As we point out later in this chapter, tax savings due to depreciation deductions are of paramount importance in capital-expenditure analysis.[4] Income-tax laws pertaining to the acquisition, use, and disposal of investment assets are exceedingly complex. Thus, accounting can add value by ensuring that all relevant tax-related items, especially depreciation deductions and investment tax credits, are included as part of the information set provided to managers for capital-budgeting purposes.

### Conducting Post-Audits

**A post-audit** is an in-depth review of a completed capital-investment project.

Accountants can also add value in the final stage of the capital-budgeting process. Various terms have been used to describe this stage, including post-audit, post-completion audit, project reappraisal, post-appraisal, and project review. We prefer the term **post-audit** and define this as an in-depth review of a completed capital-investment project for the purpose of comparing its realized costs and benefits (both financial and nonfinancial) with the preinvestment estimates of these items.

The use of post-audits of capital-budgeting decisions is particularly important for larger, longer-term investments and investments in new manufacturing technologies. The audit for such investments should include an analysis of both cash flow results and

---

[3] A discussion of using the AHP to link capital-budgeting decisions to strategy, within a Mission-Objectives-Strategy planning framework, is provided in M. J. Liberatore, T. F. Monahan, and D. E. Stout, "A Framework for Integrating Capital Budgeting Analysis with Strategy," *The Engineering Economist* 38, no. 1 (Fall 1992), pp. 31–43, and in M. J. Liberatore, T. F. Monahan, and D. E. Stout, "Strategic Capital Budgeting Analysis for Investments in Advanced Manufacturing Technology," *Journal of Financial and Strategic Decisions* 6, no. 2 (Summer 1993), pp. 55–72.

[4] Current rules for determining depreciation deductions are contained in IRS Publication 946, available on the web at: **www.irs.gov/publications/p946/**.

operating benefits, such as forecasted improvements in manufacturing flexibility or improved manufacturing cycle times.

In general, the value of the post-audit is in its capacity as a *feedback* and *control* mechanism for the organization. The following specific benefits are associated with capital expenditure post-audits:

- Such audits help keep projects on target by, for example, limiting the ability of managers to divert project funds (without authorization) to other uses.
- The post-audit provides a formal mechanism (feedback) for determining whether existing projects should be continued, expanded, or terminated. That is, the post-audit provides valuable information that can be used to correct problems before the success of an investment is undermined.
- The process of conducting post-audits helps improve the quality of future investment proposals; since managers know that project results will be evaluated, there is an incentive for managers to make accurate estimates rather than presenting overly optimistic estimates in an effort to get projects approved.
- The feedback from post-audits allows top management to identify the biases of individual managers; such information can be used to improve the future capital-budgeting process.

Difficulties (or problems) associated with conducting capital-investment post-audits generally fall into one of the following three categories:

1. *Organizational problems*—for example, lack of qualified personnel to perform the audit and the resentment of personnel being audited.
2. *Economic problems*—for example, the cost of conducting the audit itself.
3. *Technical problems*—for example, the inability of the accounting system to produce the needed information to perform the audit, or the inability to identify the profit stemming from a particular investment.

By anticipating the preceding problems, the management accounting team can help develop a successful capital-investment post-audit process.

The following real-life example is offered as an overview of the strategic dimensions of the capital-budgeting process. The rest of this chapter covers the technical and then behavioral factors associated with this process.

## The Five Steps of Strategic Decision Making: Cost-Benefit Analysis of a Hospital Bar-Code Technology Investment[5]

1. **Determine the strategic issues surrounding the problem.** Errors in dispensing medications represent a significant and strategically important problem for hospital pharmacies. Costs, both out-of-pocket and opportunity (reputation effects, for example), for such errors can be considerable. Thus, most hospitals attempt to control these quality-related costs. Recent advances in technology, including the use of a bar-code system, can be used by hospitals to manage the risk and costs of such errors.

2. **Identify the alternative actions.** Hospital administrators can invest in employee training and the updating of existing monitoring systems associated with the control of pharmacy dispensing errors, or they can invest in and implement a new bar-code system that is designed to virtually eliminate human errors. Because this technology is relatively new, it is very expensive. Thus, one alternative is to delay the investment for a year, at which time the price of the technology will likely be significantly lower.

3. **Obtain information and conduct analyses of the alternatives.** The hospital would have to estimate the required investment outlay for the new dispensing system, both today and approximately one year from now. It would also have to estimate ongoing operating costs

[5] This example is drawn from the following: S. M. Maviglia, J. Y. Yoo, C. Franz, E. Featherstone, W. Churchill, D. W. Bates, T. K. Gandhi, and E. G. Poon, "Cost-Benefit Analysis of a Hospital Pharmacy Bar Code Solution," *Archives of Internal Medicine* 167, no. 8 (April 23, 2007), pp. 788–94. The five steps discussed in this section constitute a higher-level aggregation of the eight key principles of project appraisal presented in *Project Appraisal Using Discounted Cash Flow* (New York: IFAC, June 2008).

associated with the new monitoring system. These costs would be compared to anticipated benefits of the system, both financial and nonfinancial in nature. Financial benefits are costs avoided by eliminating adverse effects from dispensing errors. Thus, both number of event reductions and the dollar savings per event would have to be estimated. Other, more difficult, benefits are qualitative or strategic in nature and would complement the cost-benefit analysis described above.

4. **Based on strategy and analysis, choose and implement the desired alternative.** The proposed investment would be evaluated using a discounted analysis of anticipated future cash outflows and inflows (cost savings). This analysis of financial results would be supplemented by a strategic analysis of this investment, done either informally or by using a multicriteria decision model such as the analytic hierarchy process (AHP). Finally, the cash flow analysis could be supplemented by including the effect of the option to delay the investment, which is one example of a *real option.* Given the uncertainties associated with the projected costs and benefits of this proposed investment, management would likely conduct a sensitivity analysis using, for example, a Monte Carlo simulation procedure.

5. **Provide an ongoing evaluation of the effectiveness of implementation in step 4.** Assuming the investment in the new technology is made, the hospital administrators could institute a *post-audit review* of the decision, to see how close the actual results were to the projected costs and benefits.

## Identification of Relevant Cash Flow Data for Capital-Expenditure Analysis

**LO 12-3**

*Provide a general model for determining relevant cash flows associated with capital-investment projects.*

Data for evaluating the financial consequences associated with capital-investment proposals differ from data used to prepare an organization's financial statements. The former relies on forecasted *cash flow* data, while the latter relies on the use of *accrual-accounting* amounts.

### Why Focus on Cash Flows?

Accrual-based accounting income is determined under the matching principle. As such, there is no attempt to track cash flows into and out of an organization. However, in capital budgeting the focus is on cash flows and the timing of these cash flows. This is true for two reasons. One, conceptually, the financial markets value companies according to their abilities to generate "free cash flow." Alternatively, companies are valued differently depending on their dividend-paying ability, which in turn is a function of their ability to generate free cash flow. Two, from a market perspective, the timing of cash flows generated by a company matters: a cash return to shareholders in the future does not have the same value (economic worth or buying power) as a dollar received today. In short, money has a time value.

Thus, managers strive to use capital-budgeting decision models that (a) focus on cash flow amounts, and (b) take into consideration the time value of money. The use of such decision models has the potential for increasing the value or economic worth of the firm.

### Cash Flows—A Framework for Analysis[6]

A capital investment, such as the purchase of a new machine, usually starts with a large cash outflow, followed by future benefits in the form of reductions in cash expenditures, increases in cash inflows, or both. Additional funds could also be needed to support the investment over its useful life. The following structure can be used to accumulate relevant financial information associated with a simplified capital-investment project:

1. **Project initiation**—Cash flows at this point include:

   a. Cash outflows, including installation costs, to acquire the investment and to begin operations (e.g., employee training costs, machine-testing costs).

---

[6] The framework presented here relates to a simplified investment. In a later section, we expand the framework to include an equipment-replacement decision, alternative formats of which are presented in the templates included in Appendix A.

**Net working capital** (as used in a capital budgeting context) is equal to current assets other than cash, less current liabilities.

b. Cash commitments for increases in *net* working capital (i.e., current assets other than cash − current liabilities). Here, we define **net working capital** as current assets other than cash, less current liabilities.

c. Cash inflow associated with investment tax credits, if any. (For simplicity, we assume throughout this chapter that all tax-related cash flows occur in the same year as the related transaction, in this case, year 0.)

2. **Project operation**—Cash flows during the operating stage of a capital investment include:

a. After-tax cash outflows for operating expenditures and, in some cases, additional capital investment(s) after the initial outlay.

b. Commitments for additional *net* working capital needed to support operations.

c. After-tax inflows of cash (or reductions in cash operating expenses) generated by the investment.

3. **Project disposal**—Cash flows at project disposal include:

a. Cash inflows or outflows, net of tax, related to the investment's disposal. (Assume that any such cash flow effects are realized fully in the year of asset disposal.)

b. Cash inflows from the recovery of *net* working capital.

Item 3b above requires elaboration. The proposed project initially requires an increase in net working capital (see item 1b above). When the project is terminated, this initial investment in net working capital is "recovered" (i.e., converted back into cash).

## Sample Data Set: Mendoza Company—Equipment-Purchase Decision

To illustrate the calculation of relevant cash flows, we use the following example. The Mendoza Company manufactures high-pressure pipes for deep-sea oil drilling. The company is considering purchasing a new drilling machine at a base cost of $465,000, which will improve the efficiency of its drilling operations and therefore provide increased cash operating income. The controller expects the company to be in the 34% federal income tax bracket and the state and local governments to levy a combined 6% income tax.

Installation costs associated with the new machine are expected to be $5,000, while associated testing and adjusting expenses incurred before the machine is put into production will be $10,000. After its expected useful life of four years, the company expects to sell the machine for $100,000. In conjunction with this sale, the company expects to incur machine-removal and site-clearing expenses that total $95,000, all of which are assumed to be deductible for tax purposes. Mendoza elects to use straight-line (SL) depreciation for tax purposes; a zero salvage value is used for determining depreciation charges for tax purposes. After disposing of the investment, the company feels it can reassign all but 10 employees to other divisions without incurring significant expenses. However, at the end of year 4, the company expects to spend $150,000 for relocation, retraining, and work adjustment for these 10 employees. This expense is expected to be fully deductible for income-tax purposes.

The company expects the new investment to generate $1 million of cash revenue from sales in each of the next four years. This level of sales activity is expected to require cash operating expenses, such as labor, materials, energy, and selling and administrative expenses, of $733,333 per year. Mendoza expects additional cash costs of $50,000 (pretax) in the first year of operating the new machine, including expenditures for employee training, work adjustments, and learning effects.

Mendoza Company estimates that once the proposed machine is in operation (in year 0), its inventory and accounts receivable will increase $200,000 beyond the expected increase in current liabilities. That is, the amount of *net* working capital—current assets other than cash, minus current liabilities—is expected to increase because of the sales

**EXHIBIT 12.1**
**Data for Mendoza Company**
**Capital-Investment Decision**

| MENDOZA COMPANY<br>Capital-Budgeting Data<br>Machine-Purchase Decision | |
| --- | --- |
| **New Machine** | |
| Purchase price of machine, year 0 | $465,000 |
| Machine installation cost | $5,000 |
| Testing and adjustments of new machine prior to new machine's use | $10,000 |
| Expected life of new machine | 4 years |
| Depreciation method (ignore salvage value for tax purposes) | SL |
| Estimated sales (disposal) value of equipment at end of four years | $100,000 |
| Salvage value assumed for tax-depreciation purposes | $0 |
| Estimated costs related to sale of asset at end of four years | $95,000 |
| **Other Data** | |
| Expected increase in *net* working capital, year 0 | $200,000 |
| Expected reduction in *net* working capital, end of year 4 | $200,000 |
| Annual cash sales associated with the new machine | $1,000,000 |
| Annual operating cash expenses | $733,333 |
| Pretax operating cash flow per year | $266,667 |
| Combined income-tax rate (34% + 6%) | 40% |
| Corporate headquarters allocation percentage | $0.025 per dollar of sales* |
| Additional pretax cash outlays, year 1 (employee training, etc.) | $50,000** |
| Employee pretax relocation expenses, end of year 4 | $150,000** |

*Note: The total corporate headquarters' expense is unaffected by whether or not the new machine is purchased. That is, the purchase of the new machine will not entail an increase in operating expenses at the corporate level.
**Assume that these are fully deductible for tax purposes in the year incurred.

volume associated with the new machine. The company expects to fully recover (i.e., convert to cash) the $200,000 amount at the end of the four-year life of the machine.

The purchase of the new machine is not expected to increase any corporate-level support costs. However, the new investment will increase the cost-allocation base of the division that is acquiring the machine. As such, the new investment will serve to increase the corporate-level support costs that are allocated to the division. The cost-allocation rate used for performance-assessment purposes is $0.025 per dollar of sales. As noted above, the new machine is expected to generate sales of $1 million annually. Thus, total divisional expenses will increase by $25,000 per year in each of the four years of the new machine's life. Note, however, that the total corporate headquarters' expenses are not expected to increase because of the new investment undertaken by the division.

The preceding set of facts is summarized in Exhibit 12.1. It is through the proper assemblage of such data that the accounting function can add value to the organization.

## Determining After-Tax Cash Flows for Capital-Investment Analysis

As noted above, cash flows for capital-investment analysis must be stated on an *after-tax* basis. Next, we offer an analysis of the data for the Mendoza Company regarding the capital-investment project the company is considering; a summary analysis is presented in Exhibit 12.2. For the cash flow calculations presented in the following discussion, assume that the combined income-tax rate is 40%.

### Project Initiation

**Asset Acquisition**   As shown in Exhibit 12.2, the net cost of the machine is $480,000 ($465,000 + $5,000 + $10,000). This is the depreciable basis of the asset.

**Investment in Net Working Capital**   In addition to the cost of the new asset, Mendoza Company feels that, in the year of asset acquisition (i.e., in year 0) it must commit *net* working capital (current assets other than cash, less current liabilities) to support the investment.

**EXHIBIT 12.2**
**After-Tax Cash Flow Data**

| | **MENDOZA COMPANY**<br>**After-Tax Cash Flow Data**<br>**Machine-Purchase Decision (000s)** | | | | |
|---|---|---|---|---|---|
| | | | **Years** | | |
| | **0** | **1** | **2** | **3** | **4** |
| **Project Initiation** | | | | | |
| Net cost of new machine (a) | $(480.00) | | | | |
| Commitment of net working capital | $(200.00) | | | | |
| Net initial cash outflow, after tax | $(680.00) | | | | |
| **Project Operation** | | | | | |
| Cash revenues | | $1,000.00 | $1,000.00 | $1,000.00 | $1,000.00 |
| Operating expenses: | | | | | |
|   Cash items (b) | | 783.33 | 733.33 | 733.33 | 733.33 |
|   Depreciation (c) | | 120.00 | 120.00 | 120.00 | 120.00 |
|     Total operating expenses | | 903.33 | 853.33 | 853.33 | 853.33 |
| Pretax operating income | | 96.67 | 146.67 | 146.67 | 146.67 |
| Income taxes on operating income | | 38.67 | 58.67 | 58.67 | 58.67 |
| After-tax operating income | | 58.00 | 88.00 | 88.00 | 88.00 |
| Plus: Noncash expenses | | 120.00 | 120.00 | 120.00 | 120.00 |
| After-tax cash operating income | | $ 178.00 | $ 208.00 | $ 208.00 | $ 208.00 |
| **Project Disposal** | | | | | |
| Net working capital released | | | | | $ 200.00 |
| After-tax proceeds from sale of machine (d) | | | | | 3.00 |
| After-tax employee relocation expenses (e) | | | | | (90.00) |
| Net cash flow, after tax, at project disposal | | | | | $ 113.00 |
| **Net (after-tax) cash flows** | ($680) | $178 | $208 | $208 | $321 |

Notes:
(a) Net cost of new machine = Gross purchase price + Installation cost + Testing costs
     = $465,000 + $5,000 + $10,000 = **$480,000**
(b) For year 1, amount = $733,333 + $50,000 (one-time employee training costs) = **$783,333**; for all other years, amount = **$733,333**
(c) Annual depreciation (SL basis) = Depreciable cost/Useful life in years = $480,000/4years = **$120,000** (note that for tax purposes a salvage value of $0 is assumed for purposes of calculating the annual depreciation expense on the new asset)
(d) After-tax proceeds = Net selling price + Tax effect; Net selling price = $100,000 − $95,000 = $5,000;
     Tax effect = (Net selling price − NBV) × $t$ = ($5,000 − $0) × 0.40 = $2,000 taxes due because the asset will be sold at a
         gain; thus, after-tax proceeds = $5,000 − $2,000 = **$3,000**
(e) After-tax employee relocation expense = Pretax amount × (1 − $t$) = $150,000 × 0.60 = **$90,000**

Mendoza estimates that, beyond a projected increase in current liabilities, its inventories and accounts receivable will increase by $200,000 per year during the life of the project. Thus, the excess of *additional* current assets (other than cash) over *additional* current liabilities is treated as an *additional* investment outlay in year 0. (Essentially, cash will be tied up until other working capital items are recovered.) Note in this example that we are making a simplifying assumption that the dollar investment in additional net working capital is constant. Also, note that at the end of year 4 the company expects to fully recover (i.e., convert back into cash) the $200,000 year-0 commitment of net working capital.

Not all investments require additional net working capital, however. Some investments may actually decrease net working capital. Any decreased need for net working capital should be shown as a cash inflow in the period in which the decrease takes place. Companies that adopt supply-chain management, just-in-time (JIT), and computer-integrated manufacturing (CIM) systems often experience a decreased need for net working capital.

In sum, a decrease in net working capital represents a recovery of net working capital (i.e., conversion back to cash); as such, it is treated as a non-tax-deductible cash inflow. An increase in net working capital during the year is an investment; as such, it is treated as a non-tax-deductible cash outflow.

## *Project Operation*

***After-Tax Cash Operating Receipts***  The new machine expects to generate $1 million of cash revenue per year. Such an amount, everything else held constant, will increase the annual income-tax liability of the company. That is, the after-tax amount for this taxable cash receipt is found by subtracting from the gross cash inflow of $1,000,000 the associated $400,000 increase in income-tax liability ($1,000,000 × 0.40). Thus, the after-tax cash receipt each year is only $600,000. In summary, this transaction has two cash effects: a cash *inflow,* and a cash *outflow* represented by the increased income-tax liability. This leads to the following formula that can be used to determine the after-tax effect of taxable cash receipts:

$$\text{After-tax cash receipt} = \text{Taxable cash receipt} \times (1 - \text{Tax rate})$$

***After-Tax Cash Operating Expenses***  As shown in Exhibit 12.1, the increased revenue is expected to require $733,333 of cash operating expenses per year. Assuming that these expenses are fully deductible for income-tax purposes, this annual transaction has two cash effects: a cash *outlay* of $733,333, and a reduction of income taxes in the amount of $293,333 ($733,333 × 0.40). Thus, the net effect of the expense is $440,000. In effect, the net cost to the company is only $440,000 after taking into consideration the tax savings realized because of the deductibility of the expense. This leads to the following formula that can be used to determine the after-tax effect of cash operating expenses:

$$\text{After-tax cash expense} = \text{Pretax cash expense} \times (1 - \text{Tax rate})$$

***After-Tax Cash Operating Income***  Of course, the analyst can combine cash operating revenues (or cost savings) and cash operating expenses to produce the *cash operating income* associated with the proposed investment. In the case of the Mendoza Company, the expected pretax cash operating income in year 1 would be $216,667 ($1,000,000 − $783,333). On an after-tax basis, this pretax cash operating income would yield $130,000. The following formula can be used to estimate each year's after-tax cash operating income:

$$\text{After-tax cash operating income} = \text{Pretax cash operating income} \times (1 - \text{Tax rate})$$

***Noncash Revenues***  A word of caution is needed here. Noncash revenues that have tax effects also affect cash flows because of their effect on the tax liability of the company for the year. Because the income-tax liability is determined on an accrual-accounting basis, a noncash revenue, such as a credit sale planned to be collected in the following year, does not increase cash available to the firm this year, but does increase the company's taxable income for the current year. In turn, this transaction increases the cash outflows (taxes) for the current year. Thus, a noncash revenue for the current year *decreases,* rather than increases, cash available to the firm. The amount of the decrease is the increase in taxes resulting from the noncash revenue.

For example, assume that a company at the end of the year makes a $10,000 credit sale, the amount of which will be collected in the following year. Although the company receives no cash this year from the sale, it nevertheless increases its tax liability for the current year. Therefore, for a tax-paying organization, a noncash revenue is effectively a cash *outflow,* not a cash *inflow,* in the year the revenue is recognized for tax purposes.

Note, however, that for the Mendoza Company the only information we have is for *cash* revenues and *cash* operating expenses associated with the proposed investment. As such, noncash revenues are not an issue in this example.

***Noncash Expenses***  An increase in noncash expenses (e.g., depreciation, amortization costs), on the other hand, decreases taxable income, which reduces income taxes for the current period. Thus, a noncash expense increases, rather than decreases, cash flow. The deductibility of the noncash expense for income-tax purposes reduces the tax liability that otherwise would exist.

**EXHIBIT 12.3** **Asset Classes (Recovery Periods) under MACRS**

| Class | Depreciation Method | Example |
|---|---|---|
| 3-year property | 200% declining balance | Light tools and handling equipment |
| 5-year property | 200% declining balance | Computers and peripheral equipment, office machinery, automobiles, light trucks |
| 7-year property | 200% declining balance | Office furniture, appliances, carpet, and furniture in residential rental property and any asset that does not have an assigned class |
| 10-year property | 200% declining balance | Manufacturing assets for food products, petroleum refining, tobacco |
| 15-year property | 150% declining balance | Road and shrubbery, telephone distribution plant |
| 20-year property | 150% declining balance | Multipurpose farm structures |
| 27.5-year property | Straight line | Residential rental property |
| 31.5-year property | Straight line | Nonresidential real property, office building, warehouse |

*Depreciation Calculations for Income-Tax Purposes (MACRS)* Depreciation for income-tax purposes is determined using the procedures specified in the Modified Accelerated Cost Recovery System (MACRS). MACRS assigns all depreciable assets to one of eight classes, referred to as *recovery periods.* Exhibit 12.3 describes these classes and their depreciation methods, and provides examples of assets in each class.

Exhibit 12.4 shows the depreciation rates each year for depreciable assets other than residential or nonresidential real estate. These percentages reflect the use of an accelerated depreciation method—150% or 200% of the straight-line (SL) depreciation rate, depending on the property class. Note that under MACRS disposal (salvage) value is ignored for calculating depreciation expense. With the exception of residential and nonresidential real estate properties (see the last two classes of assets in Exhibit 12.3), a half-year convention is used to determine the depreciation expense for the first and last year of the asset's recovery period.

To illustrate, the first-year depreciation for a five-year property is 20% of the asset's cost—regardless of when the asset was placed into service during the year. The depreciation deduction for the second year for this asset would be 32% of the asset's cost. This amount is determined using the double-declining-balance (DDB) approach. That is, the SL rate for an asset with a five-year recovery period would be 20% per year. In year 1 (under the half-year convention) 20% of the asset's cost would be written off, leaving 80% to be deducted over the remaining four years. For year 2, the depreciation deduction (32%) is equal to 40% of this 80%. To ensure that 100% of an asset's cost is written off over the specified recovery period, the depreciation method under MACRS ultimately reverts to the SL method. For example, the switch-over for five-year property occurs in year 4.

Taxpayers can choose to use the optional SL method in lieu of the percentages specified in the MACRS tables. Except for the midyear, or in some cases midquarter,

**EXHIBIT 12.4**
**MACRS Depreciation Rates**

| Year | 3-year | 5-year | 7-year | 10-year | 15-year | 20-year |
|---|---|---|---|---|---|---|
| 1 | 33.33 | 20.00 | 14.29 | 10.00 | 5.00 | 3.75 |
| 2 | 44.45 | 32.00 | 24.49 | 18.00 | 9.50 | 7.22 |
| 3 | 14.81 | 19.20 | 17.49 | 14.40 | 8.55 | 6.68 |
| 4 | 7.41 | 11.52* | 12.49 | 11.52 | 7.70 | 6.18 |
| 5 | | 11.52 | 8.93* | 9.22 | 6.93 | 5.71 |
| 6 | | 5.76 | 8.92 | 7.37 | 6.23 | 5.28 |
| 7 | | | 8.92 | 6.55* | 5.90* | 4.89 |
| 8 | | | 4.47 | 6.55 | 5.90 | 4.52 |
| 9 | | | | 6.56 | 5.91 | 4.46* |
| 10 | | | | 6.55 | 5.90 | 4.46 |
| 11 | | | | 3.28 | etc. | etc. |

*First year of switching to the straight-line method.

Source: http://www.irs.gov/publications/p946/

convention that affects the amount of depreciation charges for the first and last year of an asset's life, the optional SL method provides for a constant depreciation deduction per year. For example, for a three-year property subject to the midyear convention, the relevant depreciation rates would be: 16 2/3% for year 1; 33.33% for years 2 and 3; and 16 2/3% for year 4. Note that under MACRS the salvage value is ignored for depreciation calculations, including situations where the optional SL method is chosen. The use of the optional SL method may be attractive to start-up firms (because they generally are unprofitable during the early stages of the business) and to firms experiencing financial difficulties. For such situations, the firm in question may want to defer rather than accelerate its depreciation deductions.

In Exhibits 12.1 and 12.2 we made a simplifying assumption that Mendoza chose the SL method under MACRS but is not subject to the midyear convention; the latter is not currently in accordance with current tax law. However, this assumption simplifies the capital-budgeting analysis that follows. Remember, however, that in most situations a company would not choose the SL optional approach and regardless of this decision *would* be subject to the midyear (or midquarter) convention. Knowledge of detailed income-tax requirements regarding the determination of depreciation deductions is yet another way that accountants can add value to the capital-budgeting process. As shown in Exhibit 12.2, the depreciation deduction for Mendoza Company, under the simplifying assumption noted above, is $120,000 per year. Given a 40% combined tax rate, this deduction provides annual income-tax savings of $48,000.

### Project Disposal

**Investment Disposal**   At the project-disposal stage, there are potential cash flow effects that should be included in any capital-investment analysis.

In some situations there are end-of-project cash expenses that should be included on an after-tax basis. These costs include asset-removal costs, restoration costs (that is, costs needed to bring the asset, such as land, back to an original state), and any employee-related costs (e.g., severance pay, relocation costs, retraining costs).

In addition, at the end of the project's life the investment asset could, perhaps, be sold—an event that could trigger a taxable gain or loss. Any cash received from the disposal of the asset at the end of its life must be adjusted by the tax effect of the transaction. Refer to Exhibit 12.5 for a summary of the procedures used for determining the after-tax cash flow effect of an asset disposal.

In the case of the Mendoza Company (Exhibit 12.2), the after-tax cash inflow from the sale of the four-year-old asset is projected to be $3,000; that is, $5,000 net sales proceeds minus $2,000 income tax paid on the gain. In this example, and throughout the rest of this chapter, we assume that gains or losses on the disposal of depreciable assets are taxed at the same rate as ordinary income.

**Recovery of Investment in Net Working Capital**   Recall that Mendoza Company committed $200,000 of net working capital at the onset of the investment, which at the end of year 4 is no longer needed. Thus, at the end of year 4 we include a $200,000 cash inflow for the conversion of this net working capital back into cash.

---

**EXHIBIT 12.5**
**After-Tax Proceeds from an Asset Disposal**

| **Net Effect of Asset Disposal on After-Tax Cash Flow, End of Year 4** |
|---|
| **Terminology** |
| Net book value (NBV) = Original cost − Accumulated depreciation |
| Net proceeds = Selling (disposal) price of asset − Disposal costs (selling commissions, etc.) |
| Gain on disposal: If net proceeds > NBV |
| Loss on disposal: If net proceeds < NBV |
| Net cash effect (inflow): |
|     For *gain* situation: Net cash effect = Net proceeds − (Gain on disposal × Tax rate) |
|     For *loss* situation: Net cash effect = Net proceeds + (Loss on disposal × Tax rate) |

Note: Assume, for simplicity, that any tax effects are realized in full in the year of asset disposal.

### *Additional Measurement Issues*

Following are four additional measurement issues that need to be considered by accountants as they gather relevant information for the analysis of capital-expenditure proposals.

*Inflation* For simplicity, we have assumed that the annual cash revenues and cash expenses associated with the proposed project, including the recovery of net working capital at the end of the project's life, are constant in amount; that is, they are not affected by inflation. In an actual capital-budgeting analysis, however, the accountant would incorporate inflation adjustments for future cash flows. Typically, the discount rate that is used in capital-budgeting models is an inflation-adjusted rate. Thus, to achieve consistency in the discounting process, the cash flows that are being discounted should incorporate the anticipated effects of inflation.

*Opportunity Costs—Include These in Your Cash Flow Analysis* As noted in Chapter 11, opportunity costs are always relevant for decision making, including the analysis of proposed capital expenditures. Consider, for example, the decision to expand manufacturing facilities to meet projected demand for a firm's product(s). Suppose that the land on which the facilities would be built could otherwise be sold for $250,000. While an out-of-pocket cost would not be involved, there is nonetheless an economic cost of using the land for the new manufacturing facilities. In this example, the opportunity cost is equal to the after-tax amount that the firm could get by selling the land; as such, this amount should be included as a relevant cash flow for capital-budgeting purposes.

*Sunk Costs—Ignore These* In Chapter 11 it was noted that these costs, because they are historical or "down-the-drain," are irrelevant for decision-making purposes. Consider the example above. The original purchase price of the land is irrelevant to the facilities-expansion decision—it is a sunk cost. Because such costs will be the same regardless of whether or not the firm invests in the new facilities, these costs should be ignored for capital-budgeting purposes.

*Allocated Overhead Costs—Be Careful of These!* As discussed elsewhere in the text, there are various circumstances in which accountants must allocate common, or shared, costs of the organization. The requirement of generating full product cost information for financial statement purposes is one such use. However, there are certain circumstances in which the allocation of these kinds of costs should be avoided.

The basic rule here is to ask whether overhead costs (administrative and/or manufacturing) will increase if a given project is accepted, or whether these costs will be largely unaffected in total. In the former case, the *incremental* overhead should be included (as an after-tax cash outflow) for capital-budgeting purposes. In the latter case, regardless of the amount allocated to the project for accounting purposes, these costs should not be charged against the project for decision-making purposes.

In the Mendoza Company example (Exhibit 12.1) corporate headquarters' expenses are not likely to change in total if the company invests in the new machine. Thus, even though an allocation of such expenses may be appropriate for some other reason (such as full product costing), no portion of these expenses should be charged against the project for capital-budgeting purposes.

## Recap—After-Tax Cash Flow Information for the Mendoza Company Investment Proposal

After-tax cash flow information for the Mendoza Company investment proposal is summarized in Exhibit 12.2. Data in this exhibit have been divided according to the three primary stages of the proposed project: (1) project initiation, (2) project operation, and (3) project disposal.

How can managers use this information to assess the financial consequences of the proposed investment? We turn now to a discussion of various capital-budgeting decision models that can be used to answer this question.

## Discounted Cash Flow (DCF) Capital-Budgeting Decision Models

### LO 12-4

*Apply discounted cash flow (DCF) decision models for capital-budgeting purposes.*

**Discounted cash flow (DCF) models**
represent capital-budgeting decision models that incorporate the present value of future cash flows.

**Non-DCF models**
for capital budgeting are those that are not based on the present value of future cash flows.

### Types of Capital-Budgeting Decision Models

Models for evaluating capital-investment proposals fall into one of two categories: **discounted cash flow (DCF) models** and **non-DCF models.** The former category includes the net present value (NPV) model, the internal rate of return (IRR) model, and the profitability index (PI) model. The latter category includes the payback model and the accounting (book) rate of return (ARR) model. As indicated by the survey results from large firms reported in Exhibit 12.6, two of the DCF models (NPV and IRR) enjoy widespread use in practice: approximately three-quarters of such firms "always" or "almost always" use both NPV and IRR for capital-budgeting purposes.

As indicated in Exhibit 12.7, recent survey evidence from owners of small businesses (that is, those with 20 or fewer employees) suggests that such businesses do not routinely use modern (DCF) models when analyzing capital-investment proposals. Rather, these owners tend to rely on informal decision models (gut feeling) or on payback information for decision-making purposes.

**EXHIBIT 12.6**
**Relative Use of Various Capital-Budgeting Models by Large Firms**

Source: J. Graham and C. Harvey, "How Do CFOs Make Capital Budgeting and Capital Structure Decisions?" *Journal of Applied Corporate Finance* 15, no. 1 (Spring 2002), pp. 8–23; and P. A. Ryan and G. P. Ryan, "Capital Budgeting Practices of the Fortune 1000: How Have Things Changed?" *Journal of Business and Management* 8, no. 4 (Fall 2002), pp. 355–364.

| Method/Model | Percentage of Firms That "Always" or "Almost Always/Often" Use the Indicated Method | |
|---|---|---|
| | Graham & Harvey (2002) (N = 392 CFOs) | Ryan & Ryan (2002) (N = 205 CFOs) |
| Payback | 57 | 53 |
| Discounted payback | 30 | 38 |
| Accounting (book) rate of return | 20 | 15 |
| NPV | 75 | 85 |
| IRR | 76 | 77 |
| Profitability index (PI)* | 12 | 12 |

*PI = NPV per dollar invested.

**EXHIBIT 12.7**
**Relative Use of Various Capital-Budgeting Models by Small Firms**

Source: M. Daniels and J. A. Scott, "The Capital Budgeting Decisions of Small Businesses," Working paper, Erivan K. Haub School of Business, Saint Joseph's University, Philadelphia, PA, 2005.

| Decision Model | Percentage of Respondents Indicating That This Is the Primary Tool Used to Assess a Project's Viability |
|---|---|
| "Gut feeling" | 29% |
| Payback period | 22 |
| Accounting (book) rate of return | 16 |
| DCF methods (NPV/IRR) | 14 |
| Combination of methods | 12 |
| Other | 8 |

Given the prominence of DCF models in practice today, particularly for large companies, we discuss these models next, using data from the Mendoza Company. We discuss the non-DCF models (payback and accounting rate of return) in a separate section of the chapter.

## DCF Models: Specifying the Discount Rate

The discounted cash flow (DCF) models evaluate capital-investment projects by converting anticipated future cash flows to a present-value basis. That is, in evaluating capital investments, DCF models explicitly take into consideration the time value of money. This process is conceptually appealing because it is consistent with the process that investors use in assigning value to securities issued by individual firms.

Unfortunately, the terminology regarding the discounting process can be confusing. In this text, when we speak in general of the rate used to convert future cash flows to a present-value basis we use the term **discount rate.** For capital-budgeting purposes, the discount rate can be approximated as the firm's weighted-average cost of capital (WACC). The use of a firm's WACC as the discount rate for capital-budgeting purposes is, however, appropriate (as explained below) only for **average-risk projects.** In the situation where a project under consideration exhibits higher or lower risk than average, an adjustment to the firm's WACC is needed (upwards for higher-risk projects, downwards for lower-risk projects).[7] For this reason, some individuals refer to a project-specific discount rate as the **hurdle rate** for a project. They consider this the minimum acceptable rate of return. In order to accept a given capital-investment project, the projected economic return on the project must exceed the "hurdle rate."

Unless otherwise noted, for purposes of discussion assume that the appropriate discount rate used for capital-budgeting purposes is the firm's WACC. Exhibit 12.8 indicates that, in fact, the majority of companies today define the discount rate for capital-budgeting purposes as the WACC.

## Estimating the WACC

A company obtains funds (capital) from both equity and debt sources. The cost to the firm for each source of funds is the return demanded by lenders and investors who buy the

The **discount rate** is a generic term that refers to the rate used in capital budgeting for converting future cash flows to a present-value basis.

**Average-risk projects** are those that approximate the risk of the firm's existing assets and operations; the WACC is used to evaluate average-risk investment projects.

For capital-budgeting purposes, the **hurdle rate** represents the minimum acceptable rate of return on an investment; also referred to as the required rate of return.

**EXHIBIT 12.8**
**Survey Evidence Regarding the Definition of "Discount Rate" for Capital-Budgeting Purposes (N = 205)**

Source: P. A. Ryan and G. P. Ryan, "Capital Budgeting Practices of the Fortune 1000: How Have Things Changed?" *Journal of Business and Management* 8, no. 4 (Winter 2002), pp. 355–364.

| Discount Rate Definition | Percentage That Consider This to Be the Best Definition of the Discount Rate |
|---|---|
| WACC | 83.2 |
| After-tax cost of debt | 7.4 |
| Retained earnings | 1.5 |
| Cost of new equity | 1.0 |
| Other | 6.9 |
| Total | 100.0 |

[7] In the study by J. Graham and C. Harvey, "How Do CFOs Make Capital Budgeting and Capital Structure Decisions?," *Journal of Applied Corporate Finance* 15, no. 1 (Spring 2002), 60% of respondents said they used a single companywide rate for investment analysis purposes; 51% said they used a "risk-matched" rate for a given project (thereby suggesting that some companies use *both* approaches).

The **weighted-average cost of capital (WACC)** is an average of the (after-tax) cost of debt and equity capital for a firm; in general, the WACC is the appropriate discount rate to use for future cash flows associated with "average-risk" projects.

**Capital structure** refers to the means by which a company is financed; the mix between debt and equity capital.

The **yield-to-maturity** is a long-term bond yield (rate of return) expressed as an annual rate; the calculation takes into account the current market price of the bond, its par value, the coupon interest rate, and the time-to-maturity; the total performance of a bond, coupon payments as well as capital gain or loss, from the time of purchase until maturity.

The **capital asset pricing model (CAPM)** depicts the risk-return relationship for equity securities and can be used to estimate the required rate of return on equity for a given company; equal to the risk-free rate of return plus a risk premium measured as the product of β and the market-risk premium.

The **beta coefficient (β)** is a measure of the sensitivity of a given stock's return to fluctuations in the overall market; the average beta of all stocks is 1.0; betas > 1 imply greater sensitivity to market fluctuations.

The **market risk premium** is the spread between the expected rate of return on a market portfolio of securities and the risk-free rate of return; represented as $(r_m - r_f)$, where $r_m$ = return on the market and $r_f$ = risk-free rate of return.

firm's securities. A firm's **weighted-average cost of capital (WACC)**, therefore, is defined as "a composite of the cost of various sources of funds comprising a firm's capital structure."[8] You could think of the WACC as the expected rate of return that investors would demand on a portfolio consisting of all of the firm's securities.[9] The weights in determining the WACC are based on the firm's **capital structure,** that is, its mix of debt and equity capital, expressed in market-value terms.[10]

### After-Tax Cost of Debt

Because interest payments are tax deductible, we must calculate the after-tax cost of debt. Because market values are used to determine the weight attached to each type of security (including debt instruments), we need to estimate the current yield (**yield-to-maturity**) of the debt instruments in a company's capital structure. That is, we need to use the effective, not nominal, interest rate of the debt.[11] Thus, we define the after-tax cost of debt, $K_d$, as follows:

$$K_d = \text{Effective interest rate} \times (1 - t)$$

where

$t$ = marginal income-tax rate

### Cost of Common Equity

The cost of common stock (and retained earnings) is defined as the rate of return demanded by investors; that is, it is the risk-adjusted return needed to attract investors to purchase the common stock of a company. For companies whose shares of stock are listed on an exchange, the **capital asset pricing model (CAPM)** can be used to estimate this rate of return, $K_e$, as follows:

$$K_e = r_f + \beta(r_m - r_f)$$

where

$r_f$ = Risk-free rate

$r_m$ = The percentage return (dividends + capital gains) on a market portfolio of securities

$\beta$ = The firm's **beta coefficient** (an index of how the price of a particular security moves as the price of the market moves)

An intuitive explanation of the CAPM is that the expected rate of return on a given stock is a function of two factors: the current risk-free rate of return (e.g., the yield on U.S. Treasury bills), and a market risk premium equal in amount to the second component on the right-hand side of the preceding equation. Alternatively, you can view the former term as compensation for the time value of money and the second term as a premium that investors demand. This second term is a function of the sensitivity of a given stock's return to the fluctuations in the overall market (i.e., its β coefficient) and the **market risk premium** (defined as the spread between the expected rate of return on a market portfolio of securities, $r_m$, and the risk-free rate of return, $r_f$). In sum, under the CAPM the expected rate of return on a stock is equal to the risk-free rate plus the specific stock's beta coefficient times the market risk premium.

If the CAPM model is used to estimate the cost of equity capital for a company, you might want to use an alternative estimate as a check on your calculation. One such estimate is based on what is called the *constant growth, dividend discount model.* Using this model, we would estimate the cost of equity capital, $K_e$, for a company as follows:

$$K_e = (D_1 \div P_0) + g$$

---

[8] Institute of Management Accountants (IMA), *Statement Number 4A:* "Cost of Capital" (Montvale, NJ: 1984), p. 1.

[9] R. A. Brealey, S. C. Myers, and A. J. Marcus, *Fundamentals of Corporate Finance,* 7th Edition (New York: McGraw-Hill/Irwin, 2012).

[10] The rest of this section draws on the material contained in M. S. Pagano and D. E. Stout, "Estimating a Firm's Cost of Capital," *Management Accounting Quarterly* 5, no. 3 (Spring 2004), pp. 13–20.

[11] For example, the *effective interest rate* on a 10-year, 8%, $100,000 bond with semiannual interest payments that was sold for $88,448 is 10%, not 8%, since the *effective interest rate* on the bond is 10%. If the issuing firm faces a marginal income-tax rate of 40%, the after-tax cost of this security is 6%.

where

$D_1$ = Expected dividend per share one period (year) forward

$P_0$ = Current price per share of common stock

$g$  = Dividend growth rate (assumed constant to perpetuity)

### Cost of Preferred Stock

The cost of preferred stock, $K_p$, is conceptually equal to the current yield that holders (i.e., investors) of the stock demand. This is also referred to as the *dividend yield* on the share of preferred stock. That is,

$K_p$ = Current dividend on preferred stock ÷ Current market price per share

### Determining Weights

Market, not book (accounting), values are needed conceptually to determine the weights associated with each source of funds in determining the WACC. As an example, consider a company in the 40% marginal income-tax bracket. This company has outstanding: a $100,000 long-term bank loan with a 12% interest rate; $500,000 face value of 8.396%, 20-year bonds, currently selling at 90% of face value (interest on the bonds is paid semiannually; the bonds mature in 10 years); $200,000 of 15%, $20 preferred stock with a current market value of $300,000; and, 10,000 shares of $1 par value common stock that the firm sold originally for $5 per share. The common stock has a current market price of $75 per share. Assume that application of the CAPM (as described above) yields an estimated rate of return (yield) of approximately 20%. Given this information, the company's WACC is approximately 13.4%, as shown in Exhibit 12.9.

Software that calculates a company's WACC and that generates estimates of underlying common stock value for the company is available (e.g., **www.valuepro.net**). Also, from **www.ibbotson.com** you can obtain cost of capital (both cost of equity and WACC) information from a sample of U.S. industries, income-tax rate and beta information for individual U.S. stocks, and international industry data that would be of interest to U.S. investors.

The **net present value (NPV)** equals the difference between the present value of future cash inflows and the present value of future cash outflows of an investment project.

The **present value (PV)** of a future cash flow is its current equivalent value; also referred to as time-adjusted value.

## Net Present Value (NPV) Decision Model

### Determining a Project's NPV

The **net present value (NPV)** of an investment is equal to the difference between the present value of the project's cash inflows and the present value of the project's cash outflows. The **present value (PV)** of a future cash flow is its current equivalent dollar value, using an appropriate discount rate; for example, using the firm's WACC. The decision rule is to accept a proposed investment if the projected NPV of the project is positive; that is, accept a project if the PV of cash inflows is greater than the PV of cash outflows. If a project has a positive NPV, then the project adds to shareholder value.

**EXHIBIT 12.9**   Estimation of Weighted-Average Cost of Capital (WACC) (Hypothetical Example)

| Source of Funds | (1) Book Value | (2) Pretax Effective Rate of Return | (3) After-tax Rate or Expected Return | (4) Total Current Market Value | (5) Weight (Based on Market Values) | (6) = (3) × (5) Components for WACC Calculation |
|---|---|---|---|---|---|---|
| Bank loan | $100,000 | 12% | 7.20% | $  100,000 | 0.06250 | 0.4500% |
| Bonds | 500,000 | 10[a] | 6.00 | 450,000 | 0.28125 | 1.6875 |
| Preferred stock | 200,000 | 15 | 10.00[b] | 300,000 | 0.18750 | 1.8750 |
| Common stock | 50,000 | | 20.00 | 750,000 | 0.46875 | 9.3750 |
| **Total** | **$850,000** | | | **$1,600,000** | **1.00** | **13.3875%** |

Notes:

[a] The estimated effective interest rate (yield to maturity) on the bonds, 10%, was found using the YIELD function in Excel.

[b] Number of preferred shares outstanding = $200,000 ÷ $20 par value per share = 10,000 shares. Current market price per share = $300,000 ÷ 10,000 shares outstanding = $30.00. Preferred stock dividend per share = 15% × $20 par value per share = $3.00. Therefore, the current dividend yield on preferred stock = $3.00 ÷ $30.00 = 10%.

### *Determining NPV with Uniform Net Cash Inflows*

Some capital-expenditure projects are characterized by an investment outlay in year 0 followed by an annuity, that is, a uniform stream of future cash inflows. Such a project's NPV can be determined in either of two ways. Let's assume a four-year project that requires an outlay at time 0 of $555,000 and after-tax inflows of $200,000 per year. The WACC is assumed to be 10%.

#### Method 1: Annuity Table

To convert the future stream of cash inflows back to its present value, you could obtain from Appendix C, Table 2, the appropriate annuity factor for 10%, four years: 3.170. Note that this factor is simply the sum of the four present-value factors presented in Appendix C, Table 1 under the 10% column. Thus, the PV of the future annuity is $634,000 ($200,000 × 3.170), and the NPV of this project is: $634,000 − $555,000 = $79,000. This implies that the investment is expected to provide an economic return greater than 10%. Alternatively, you can say that this investment is expected to earn a 10% return on the funds invested *plus* an additional $79,000 (in current dollars).

#### Method 2: Excel Formula

You can use a built-in function in Excel to estimate a project's NPV, as indicated in the screenshot presented below. Note that the difference of $26.91 in indicated NPVs that you observe is due to rounding (to three decimal points) that took place when Table 2 was constructed.

| | A | B | C | D | E |
|---|---|---|---|---|---|
| 1 | Investment Outlay | | $555,000 | | |
| 2 | After-tax Cash Inflows: | | | | |
| 3 | Year 1 | $200,000 | | | |
| 4 | Year 2 | $200,000 | | | |
| 5 | Year 3 | $200,000 | | | |
| 6 | Year 4 | $200,000 | | | |
| 7 | Discount Rate | | 10.00% | | |
| 8 | | | | Formula in Cell B9 | |
| 9 | NPV = | $78,973.09 | =NPV(C7,B3,B4,B5,B6)-C1 | | |

### *Determining NPV with Uneven Cash Inflows*

Refer now to the cash flow data for the Mendoza Company presented in Exhibit 12.2. The net investment outlay at time zero is $680,000. The after-tax cash inflows from the proposed investment are: $178,000 (year 1), $208,000 (year 2), $208,000 (year 3), and $321,000 (year 4). Assume both here and throughout the chapter a 10% discount rate (WACC) for the Mendoza example. With this information we calculate the estimated NPV of this proposed investment as $29,240, as follows:[12]

| | A | B | C | D |
|---|---|---|---|---|
| 1 | WACC | 10.00% | | |
| 2 | After-tax Cash Flows: | | | |
| 3 | Year | CF | | |
| 4 | 0 | ($680,000) | | |
| 5 | 1 | 178,000 | | |
| 6 | 2 | 208,000 | | |
| 7 | 3 | 208,000 | | |
| 8 | 4 | 321,000 | | |
| 9 | | | Formula in Cell B10 | |
| 10 | NPV = | $29,240 | =B4 + NPV(B1,B5:B8) | |

[12] Alternatively, we could use the PV factors in Appendix C, Table 1, to determine the PV of the stream of after-tax cash inflows. From this, we would subtract the required investment outlay, $680,000, to arrive at the project's estimated NPV. It is also possible to use an array formula to calculate the NPV of a project. To do this, refer to the Excel screenshot above. First, define variable names (go to Formulas, then Define Names). For example, define cell B1 as "WACC," cells A4 through A8 as "Year," and cells B4 through B8 as "CF." Then, enter into an open cell (e.g., B10) the following formula to calculate the estimated NPV of this project: =SUM(CF/(1 + WACC)^Year). Finally, rather than hitting "Enter," you now (to enter the array formula) hit: Control + Shift + Enter. Cell B10 should now display the correct amount, $29,240 (rounded).

## Internal Rate of Return (IRR) Decision Model

The **internal rate of return (IRR)** is an estimate of the true (i.e., economic) rate of return on an investment.

The **internal rate of return (IRR)** represents an estimate of the true (i.e., economic) rate of return on an investment. Mathematically, the IRR is defined as the rate of return that produces an NPV of zero. The decision rule using the IRR model is simple: Accept an investment if its projected IRR exceeds the firm's discount rate (WACC). If a project's IRR is greater than the company's WACC, it means that the project has a positive NPV.

### *Estimating a Project's IRR: Uniform Cash Inflows (Non-Mendoza Example)*

If the project consists of an initial investment outlay followed by a stream of constant cash inflows, the project's IRR is defined as the discount rate that satisfies the following equation:

Initial investment outlay = PV of future cash inflows at a specified discount rate

= Annual after-tax cash inflow × Annuity discount factor associated with the life of the project

Using $A_{r,n}$ to denote the last term in the above equation, the equation can be restated as follows:

$A_{r,n}$ = Initial investment outlay ÷ Annual after-tax cash inflow from the investment

where

$A_{r,n}$ = Annuity factor that makes the PV of the stream of future after-tax cash inflows equal to the initial investment outlay

$n$ = Life of the project (e.g., in years)

$r$ = Discount rate

As an example, for a four-year project that has an initial investment outlay of $555,000 and annual after-tax cash inflows of $200,000, the estimated IRR for this project is determined as follows:

$$\$555,000 = \$200,000 \times A_{r,4}$$
$$A_{r,4} = \$555,000 \div \$200,000 = 2.775$$

An annuity factor of 2.775 in Appendix C, Table 2 for a project with a four-year useful life corresponds to a discount rate, $r$, of between 15% and 20%. Because this rate exceeds the firm's WACC (10.0%), the project should be accepted.[13]

### *Estimating a Project's IRR: Uneven Cash Inflows (Mendoza Company example)*

When the projected future cash inflows are not even, the project's IRR can be estimated using a trial-and-error approach. That is, a discount rate, say 10%, is chosen to begin the process. Using this discount rate, you would compute the project's NPV. If the resulting NPV at this discount rate is positive, the discount rate you chose is too low (and vice versa). Thus, a higher discount rate is chosen and the project's NPV at this new rate is determined. The process stops when the resulting NPV is close to zero: the discount rate at this point represents the project's estimated IRR. The interpolation process explained in footnote 13 can be used to generate a more accurate estimate of a project's IRR.

[13] To generate a more accurate estimate of this project's IRR, we can use the following interpolation procedure:

|  | Interest rate, $r$ | | Annuity factor, $A_{r,4}$ | |
|---|---|---|---|---|
| At lower rate | 15.00% | 15.00% | 2.855 | 2.855 |
| Target rate | ? | ? | | 2.775 |
| At higher rate | 20.00% | | 2.589 | — |
| Difference | 5.00% | — | 0.266 | 0.080 |

The difference in annuity factors between the interest rates on either side of the target annuity factor (2.775) is 0.266. This suggests that an increase of 5% in interest rates, from 15% to 20%, increases the annuity factor by 0.266. Thus, to get to 2.775 we need to increase the interest rate proportionately to the decrease in the annuity factor. That is, the annuity factor must be reduced by 30.08% (0.080/0.266). Thus, the needed increase in interest rate to decrease the annuity factor by 0.266 is 30.08% of 5%, or 1.50%. The project's estimated IRR is therefore 16.50% [i.e., 15% + (30.08% × 5.00%)]. Note that this linear interpolation process produces an *estimate* of the true IRR. The true IRR, found using the built-in Excel function, is 16.42%. See if you can reproduce this result and verify that at this discount rate the NPV of the project is zero.

Alternatively, you can use the IRR function in Excel to estimate a project's IRR. Using the cash flow data for Mendoza Company (Exhibit 12.2) we generate an IRR of 11.80%, as follows:

| ◢ | A | B | C | D | E |
|---|---|---|---|---|---|
| 1 | After-tax Cash Flows: | | | | |
| 2 | Year | CF | | | |
| 3 | 0 | ($680,000) | | | |
| 4 | 1 | 178,000 | | | |
| 5 | 2 | 208,000 | | | |
| 6 | 3 | 208,000 | | | |
| 7 | 4 | 321,000 | | | |
| 8 | | | Cell Formulas | | |
| 9 | IRR = | 11.80% | =IRR(B3:B7,0.09) | | |
| 10 | NPV = | $0.00 | =B3+NPV(B9,B4:B7) | | |
| 11 | | | | | |
| 12 | Note: in the IRR formula, 0.09 is a "guess," | | | | |
| 13 | which is needed to start the algorithim used by | | | | |
| 14 | Excel to estimate a project's IRR. | | | | |

Note that we confirm that the project's IRR is 11.80%: at this discount rate, the NPV of the project is zero. Given a WACC of 10% for the Mendoza Company, this project should therefore be accepted. Managers generally find the IRR decision rule intuitively appealing: *accept projects that provide a rate of return* (e.g., 11.8%) *that exceeds the company's WACC* (e.g., 10%).

Of course, you can also use the built-in function in Excel to estimate a project's IRR when the future cash inflows are equal (rather than using the trial-and-error procedure described above).

## The Modified Internal Rate of Return (MIRR)

Survey evidence suggests that IRR is widely used in practice, in large part because of its intuitive appeal to managers. Students in accounting should be aware of a particular controversy regarding the use of IRR for evaluating capital-budgeting projects: the reinvestment rate assumption.

Critics[14] maintain that the IRR metric ignores the reinvestment potential of intermediate positive cash flows from a project. These same critics maintain that IRR inherently assumes that such cash flows are reinvested at the IRR rate and that in most cases this rate is unrealistically high. Thus, they maintain, conventional IRR calculations build in reinvestment assumptions that make bad projects look better and good ones look great. Such practice can result in major capital-budgeting distortions.

These critics suggest that a more conservative assumption regarding the reinvestment rate of return on interim cash flows be used. In most cases, this rate is better approximated by the organization's discount rate (WACC). In response to this controversy, the **modified internal rate of return (MIRR)** can be used to assess capital-budgeting projects. As the name implies, MIRR is a modification of the conventional IRR measure. The MIRR assumes all positive cash flows are reinvested at a particular rate of return (usually at the WACC) for the remaining duration of the project.

A built-in function in Excel, MIRR, provides an estimate of a project's modified internal rate of return, as follows:[15]

**MIRR(values, finance_rate, reinvest_rate)**

**Values** is an array or a reference to cells that contain a series of payments (negative values) and income (positive values) occurring at regular periods; **finance_rate** is the discount rate (i.e., WACC) used for DCF analysis of capital-budgeting projects; and **reinvest_rate** is the

---

The **modified internal rate of return (MIRR)** is IRR adjusted to account for an assumed rate of return associated with interim project cash inflows.

---

[14] See, for example, J. C. Kelleher and J. J. MacCormack, "Internal Rate of Return: A Cautionary Tale," *The McKinsey Quarterly*, October 20, 2004 (available at **www.cfo.com/article.cfm/3304945**).

[15] See **http://office.microsoft.com/en-us/excel-help/mirr-function-HP010342696.aspx?CTT=5&origin=HA010342655**.

estimated reinvestment rate (i.e., the rate of return on the periodic cash flows provided by the project—generally, this will also be the WACC).

Based on the after-tax cash flow data for the Mendoza Company presented in Exhibit 12.2, we find an estimated MIRR of 11.16%, as follows:

| | A | B | C | D |
|---|---|---|---|---|
| 1 | WACC = | 10.00% | | |
| 2 | After-tax Cash Flows: | | | |
| 3 | Year | CF | | |
| 4 | 0 | ($680,000) | | |
| 5 | 1 | 178,000 | | |
| 6 | 2 | 208,000 | | |
| 7 | 3 | 208,000 | | |
| 8 | 4 | 321,000 | | |
| 9 | | | | Cell Formula |
| 10 | MIRR = | 11.16% | =MIRR(B4:B8,B1,B1) | |

Three points are worth making regarding the reinvestment rate controversy. One, the MIRR suffers from some of the same drawbacks as the more conventional IRR metric: relying on either can lead to an incorrect choice between mutually exclusive investments; as noted below, we deal with this issue in Appendix B. Two, a search of the Internet under "MIRR" suggests heated debate as to whether or not the conventional IRR metric has an inherent reinvestment rate assumption. Some of these arguments are arcane and embedded in mathematical theory. Students of accounting should therefore simply be aware that there are different points of view regarding this issue. Third, as noted below, in most cases (e.g., other than when capital needs to be rationed), a safe bet would be to use NPV as the financial-performance metric associated with proposed investments.

## Comparison of NPV and IRR Methods: Which to Use?

If the decision is limited to accepting or rejecting a given investment project, the NPV model and the IRR model will lead to the same conclusion. There are, however, several situations that complicate capital-budgeting decisions in the real world. Appendix B to this chapter deals with three of these issues: (1) the problem of multiple IRRs, (2) choosing between mutually exclusive projects, and (3) capital budgeting under the situation of capital rationing. Given such real-world complications, modern financial theory generally argues for the use of the NPV decision model, except in the case of capital rationing. In this case, a company's capital budget should be allocated to projects on the basis of *relative profitability,* that is, on the basis of NPV per dollar invested.[16]

## Structuring an Asset-Replacement Decision Problem

The discussion to this point has involved a straightforward decision. We now consider a slightly more complicated decision: whether to keep or replace an existing asset (such as a piece of machinery). In this case, as we stressed in Chapter 11, relevant cost and revenue data consist of future amounts that differ between the decision alternatives. Thus, to properly structure an asset-replacement problem we must identify all costs and revenues that are differential to the decision. These items are then subjected to a discounted cash flow analysis using either the NPV method or the IRR method, as discussed earlier.

At the time of initial investment (time period 0), we must calculate the after-tax proceeds (if any) from the sale of the existing asset. Exhibit 12.5 provides guidelines to accomplish this. During the life of the investment, we need to calculate *incremental* (or *differential*) after-tax operating cash flows associated with the new asset versus the existing asset. As well, we need to include in the analysis the differential tax benefit each year associated with depreciation expenses calculated on the basis of the old versus new asset. Finally, at the

[16] See, for example, Brealey et al. (2012).

termination of the life of the project, we need to calculate two amounts: (1) differential after-tax cash proceeds from the sale/disposal of the old versus the new asset, and (2) differential recovery of net working capital associated with the old versus the new asset. In short, we embrace the same perspective as used in Chapter 11: for decision-making purposes, we focus on differential revenues and differential costs. In Chapter 12, we employ the same guideline; however, in Chapter 12 the identified relevant costs and revenues are subjected to a discounting process to express all such amounts on a present-value basis.

To illustrate the preceding points, let's recast the Mendoza example (Exhibit 12.2) to reflect a machine-replacement decision. Assume that the company is currently using a machine that it purchased six years ago for $320,000. The accumulated depreciation on this machine, at the replacement date (time period 0), is $192,000. (For tax purposes, the machine is being depreciated using the straight-line method over 10 years, with zero salvage value assumed.) A used equipment broker, who charges a commission of 10% of the selling price, has secured a buyer for the old machine. The buyer is willing to pay $80,000 for the machine; however, Mendoza would have to pay all asset-removal costs, estimated to be $2,000 (pretax).

The net cash proceeds from the sale (i.e., gross selling price minus sales-related costs, such as sales commissions) would be $70,000 (i.e., $80,000 − $8,000 − $2,000). Given a net book value (NBV) of $128,000 (i.e., $320,000 − $192,000), Mendoza would realize a tax-deductible loss of $58,000 on the sale of the old machine. At a combined tax rate of 40%, this loss would result in a tax savings of $23,200. As indicated in Exhibit 12.5, the net cash effect of this entire transaction would be $93,200 (net cash proceeds of $70,000, plus tax savings due to the deductibility of the loss on the sale, $23,200).

Further, assume that if the current machine is not sold, it is expected to generate cash revenues of $400,000 and cash operating expenses of $320,000 per year over each of the next four years. At the time that the existing machine was put into service (six years ago), Mendoza committed additional working capital of $50,000, which is expected to be fully recovered four years from now, at the end of the asset's life. At that point, the net-of-sales-commission estimated sales value of the existing machine is expected to be $1,500 pretax.

The net cost of the new machine as well as the working capital commitment are the same as the amounts reflected in Exhibit 12.2. However, we now assume that if the new machine is purchased, total cash revenues are expected to be $1,400,000 per year, while operating cash expenses are expected to be $1,000,000 per year. All other information regarding the new machine is as assumed earlier. Relevant information for evaluating this machine-replacement decision for Mendoza is presented in the first screenshot in Appendix A. Panels A and B in Appendix A provide alternative presentation formats for the *differential analysis* associated with the asset-replacement decision. Each presentation format indicates an NPV of $148,536 in favor of replacing the existing machine. An advantage of the format reflected in Panel B of Appendix A is the fact that it facilitates the calculation of the investment's IRR, in this case, 20.5%. Finally, Panel C in Appendix A provides an alternative presentation format, one that reveals separately the opportunity costs associated with purchasing the new machine. This method also shows an NPV figure of $148,536. Which of these presentation formats you use is largely a matter of personal preference.

## Uncertainty and the Capital-Budgeting Process

**LO 12-5**

*Deal with uncertainty in the capital-budgeting process.*

Capital-budgeting decision models rely on estimates of key input variables, such as the discount rate, life of a proposed project, after-tax cash flows associated with a project, and alternative future states of nature (e.g., good economy vs. bad economy, high price of oil/energy vs. low price of oil/energy). By definition, these estimates and states of nature are subject to uncertainty; and the longer the time horizon for the investment, the greater is the uncertainty regarding these estimates. Management accountants, as part of the decision-making team, need to understand approaches that can be used to address this uncertainty. Here we consider two broad approaches to the problem: one, conducting sensitivity analysis as part of the capital-budgeting process; and two, incorporating real options into the analysis of proposed investments.

## Sensitivity Analysis

Decision makers want to know how sensitive their capital-budgeting decisions (e.g., whether to accept or reject a proposed investment) are to estimates of the decision inputs (e.g., discount rate). In more formal terms, this assessment process is referred to as **sensitivity analysis.**

**Sensitivity analysis**
is the process of selectively varying a key input variable, for example, the discount rate, to identify the range over which a capital-budgeting decision is valid.

In the sections that follow, we provide an overview of three types of sensitivity analysis: what-if analysis, scenario analysis, and Monte Carlo simulation. This material is followed by a discussion of the use of "real options" as a way to more formally model uncertainty in the analysis of capital-expenditure proposals.

### *What-If Analyses*

What-if questions attempt to determine the impact on project profitability of changes in the value of a single input variable. For example, we might be interested in knowing the impact on NPV if the after-tax cash flows for a project are only 90% of their projected amount. Separately, what if a given project has a three-year rather than four-year life? The more general question to be asked is: Which variables in the decision model have the greatest potential to alter the indicated profitability (and hence desirability) of an investment? Once this is known, management may want to refine its estimate of the variables that have, or variable that has, the greatest impact on project profitability.

Following is an Excel screenshot of a basic what-if analysis for a project with an investment outlay of $18 and a three-year life. The table in the screenshot shows the independent impact of changes in the discount rate and changes in the amount of annual after-tax cash flows on the estimated NPV of the investment.[17]

| | A | B | C | D |
|---|---|---|---|---|
| 1 | NPVs as a Function of Changes in After-tax Cash | | | |
| 2 | Flows and Discount Rate (Initial Cash Outflow = | | | |
| 3 | $18; Project Life = 3 years) | | | |
| 4 | | | | |
| 5 | | | Annual After-tax Cash Flows | |
| 6 | Discount Rate | $7.00 | $8.00 | $9.00 |
| 7 | 0.10 | ($0.59) | $1.89 | $4.38 |
| 8 | 0.11 | ($0.89) | $1.55 | $3.99 |
| 9 | 0.12 | ($1.19) | $1.21 | $3.62 |

In addition, the decision maker might be interested, as part of the what-if analysis, in determining the breakeven point associated with a given variable. In the preceding example, managers might feel fairly certain that the appropriate discount rate (WACC) is 11%.

**Breakeven after-tax cash flow**
equals the minimum annual after-tax cash inflows needed for an investment project to be acceptable.

A reasonable question to ask is: What is the **breakeven after-tax cash flow,** that is, the minimum annual after-tax cash inflows needed for an investment project to be acceptable? In other words, what is the annual cash inflow amount that would result in a zero NPV? The Goal Seek function in Excel can be used to answer this question.[18]

Assume a model that calculates the NPV of a three-year project with an initial investment cost of $18, annual after-tax cash inflows of $7 per year, and a discount rate of 11%. The NPV function of Excel for this example shows a projected NPV of ($0.89), as indicated below:

| | A | B | C | D | E | F |
|---|---|---|---|---|---|---|
| 1 | Original Investment Outlay | | $18.00 | | | |
| 2 | Annual after-tax cash flow | | $7.00 | | | |
| 3 | Discount rate | | 0.11 | | | |
| 4 | NPV | | ($0.89) | (=NPV(C3,C2,C2,C2)-C1) | | |

[17] Excel provides a structured way to conduct and report both one-variable and two-variable sensitivity analyses, using "Data Tables." In Excel 2010, go to: Data, then What-If Analysis, then Data Tables. The following online tutorial can be consulted: **http://office.microsoft.com/en-us/excel-help/calculate-multiple-results-by-using-a-data-table-HP010342214.aspx**.

[18] The following online tutorial for Goal Seek can be consulted: **http://office.microsoft.com/en-us/excel-help/use-goal-seek-to-find-the-result-you-want-by-adjusting-an-input-value-HP010342990.aspx**.

To find the breakeven after-tax cash flow, use the following method:

After clicking OK in the dialog box above, the following solution should appear:

|  | A | B | C | D | E | F |
|---|---|---|---|---|---|---|
| 1 | Original Investment Outlay |  | $18.00 |  |  |  |
| 2 | Annual after-tax cash flow |  | $7.37 |  |  |  |
| 3 | Discount rate |  | 0.11 |  |  |  |
| 4 | NPV |  | $0.00 | (=NPV(C3,C2,C2,C2)-C1) |  |  |

Thus, a project that costs $18 and that has an after-tax cash flow of $7.37 for each of three years will, at a discount rate of 11%, result in an NPV of $0. (See the end-of-chapter Self-Study Problem for another application of the *Goal Seek* option in Excel.)

A word of caution regarding what-if analyses is in order: the basic approach looks at the *independent effects* of individual variables. In reality, variables included in the NPV model may be related to one another. That is, a change in one variable (e.g., variable costs) might be related to a change in another variable (e.g., fixed costs). The effect of such inter-relationships cannot be captured by the use of what-if analyses, which look only at the effects of changing one variable at a time. In short, there are technical limits as to how far you can take this type of sensitivity analysis.

## Scenario Analysis

**Scenario analysis**
represents an attempt to look at how a proposed investment project would fare under different combinations of variables, called *scenarios;* a special form of sensitivity analysis that is appropriate when the variables in a decision model are interrelated.

Decision makers may be interested in how their proposed investment would look under different combinations of variables, called *scenarios.* **Scenario analysis** is a form of sensitivity analysis that does just this: It looks at the profitability of a project (e.g., its indicated NPV) according to one or more plausible scenarios.[19]

Typically, decision makers specify the expected outcomes of an investment project as the base case. The associated NPV of this project assumes a specific scenario, e.g., the market price of oil, whether the U.S. economy is in recession or expansion, the state of labor relations with a key supplier, and so forth.

One could construct a separate NPV analysis for each of several additional scenarios beyond the base case. It is common to label such scenarios with descriptive terms such as *disaster scenario* (i.e., worst-case scenario for related variables such as sales price, sales demand, and variable costs), *disappointing* (reflecting less-than-favorable values for related variables), and *optimistic* (reflecting greater-than-favorable values for a set of related variables). In generating these scenarios it is not uncommon for accountants to work with marketing managers and/or the vice president of strategic planning of the company. These individuals should be most knowledgeable about possible macro-economic and uncontrollable factors that determine various scenarios. In short, scenario analysis allows managers to examine the effects of different scenarios represented as the joint effect of a set of related variables captured in the NPV model. These scenarios are developed through the use of a cross-functional team of individuals within the organization.

## Monte Carlo Simulation[20]

As noted above, risk analysis of capital-budgeting projects using traditional spreadsheets is inherently limited. For example, scenario analysis yields only a single output value (e.g., expected NPV) for a set of inputs. Scenario analysis does not have the ability to measure an outcome's probability of occurrence, which is a key measure of risk within a modeled relationship.

Thus, risk analysis can be enhanced if managers are able to generate probabilities associated with alternative values of the outcome variable (e.g., NPV, IRR) in a capital-budgeting decision model. Spreadsheet add-ons, such as Oracle Crystal Ball,[21] are able to generate such probability distributions. Oracle Crystal Ball specifies over 30 possible probability distributions (normal, uniform, binomial, triangular, etc.) that can be used to describe each input variable (such as project life or discount rate). The end result is that this process transforms what was previously a deterministic model (e.g., NPV or IRR) into a probabilistic model that can be analyzed through **Monte Carlo simulation**. Monte Carlo simulation is an extension to scenario analysis in which a computer provides a distribution of possible outcomes (for example, project NPVs) based on repeated sampling from a distribution associated with one or more input variables in a decision model.

**Monte Carlo simulation**
is an extension to scenario analysis in which a computer provides a distribution of possible outcomes, for example, project NPVs, based on repeated sampling from a distribution associated with one or more input variables in a decision model.

A capital-budgeting simulation computes the value of an outcome variable of interest (e.g., a project's NPV) many times over. Each time it simulates the project's NPV it draws a combination of input values (sales price per unit, variable cost per unit, sales volume, etc.) based on a prespecified probability distribution associated with each of these variables. Based on these inputs, an associated NPV is generated. In essence, the simulation allows the decision maker to substitute a probability distribution for the mean value of each input variable in a decision model. When the simulation is complete, for example

---

[19] The following online tutorial for performing scenario analysis in Excel is available at: **http://office.microsoft.com/en-us/excel-help/switch-between-various-sets-of-values-by-using-scenarios-HP010072669.aspx**.

[20] This discussion draws on the following source: D. F. Togo, "Risk Analysis for Accounting Models: A Spreadsheet Simulation Approach," *Journal of Accounting Education* 22, no. 2 (2004), pp. 153–63.

[21] Crystal Ball is available from Oracle (**www.oracle.com/crystalball/**). An academic version of this software is available for student/faculty use. For an extended example of using Crystal Ball to perform Monte Carlo simulation within a capital-budgeting context consult the following: V. Clark, M. Reed, and J. Stephan, "Using Monte Carlo Simulation for a Capital Budgeting Project," *Management Accounting Quarterly* 12, no. 1 (2010), pp. 20–31. Finally, the following source can be consulted for developing limited Monte Carlo simulations within Excel: John Rozycki, "Excel-Based Monte Carlo Simulation as a Capital Budgeting Risk-Management Tool," *Journal of Financial Education* 37, no. 1/2 (2011), pp. 101–28.

As noted in the text, adjusting conventional DCF analysis of capital-budgeting proposals can be advantageous to the firm in terms of maximizing shareholder value. A related question is whether incorporating real options into net present value (NPV) analysis helps reduce the problem of "escalation of commitment." Escalation of commitment refers to the tendency of decision makers to continue to commit resources to a failing course of action—that is, negative feedback regarding an investment project that has been made. One type of real option that decision makers can consider is the "abandonment option" associated with a given investment proposal. In a laboratory (i.e., behavioral) study, Denison (2009) finds evidence that users of real options exhibit less escalation of commitment to a failing course of action than do users of NPV analysis alone. The author's study contributes to accounting practice by offering managers a way to improve firm performance by reducing escalation of commitment. Escalation of commitment is discussed later in the chapter as one of the primary behavioral issues associated with the capital-budgeting process.

**Source:** Christine A. Denison, "Real Options and Escalation of Commitment: A Behavioral Analysis of Capital Investment Decisions," *The Accounting Review* 84, no. 1 (January 2009), pp. 133–135.

after 10,000 iterations, a probability distribution of NPVs for a given investment proposal is generated. Associated output from the simulation includes the mean, maximum result, minimum result, standard deviation, skewness, and percentile probabilities. The latter are particularly important as they allow statements such as "Given the probability distributions of the variables in our capital-budgeting model, this investment proposal has a 48% probability of having a negative NPV and a 35% probability of having an NPV of at least $25,000."

## Real Options[22]

The use of DCF models, such as NPV, is recommended as the preferred method of evaluating capital-budgeting proposals, as noted in the *International Good Practice Guidance* document cited in the Real-World Focus box presented on page 483. However, these models have an inherent assumption that may not comport with reality. Specifically, these models assume passive behavior on the part of management once an investment decision has been made. Alternatively, we can describe the traditional analysis as "take it or leave it." But in reality, some investment projects are dynamic in nature. They may contain one or more options for dealing with risk and uncertainty as new information (e.g., market conditions) is revealed over time. Management might expand a project in the future if things go well or it might scale back or abandon a project altogether if things are not going well. These opportunities are collectively referred to as **real options** (or options on **real assets**). In this context, real assets represent investments in both tangible property (e.g., a new manufacturing facility) and intangible property (e.g., a new information system). Traditional capital-budgeting decision models, such as DCF models, do not explicitly incorporate options on real assets that may be embedded in a proposed investment.

Real options are analogous to financial options—puts and calls. The latter gives the holder of the option the right, but not obligation, to purchase stock at a fixed price, called the *strike price* or *exercise price,* up to the expiration date of the option; the former gives the holder of the option the right, but not obligation, to sell stock for a fixed price on or before the exercise date of the option. These financial options have value and in fact are traded between investors on an organized exchange. Financial options have value precisely because they allow investors to capitalize on new information about a company that unfolds over time. In an analogous fashion, options on real assets have value because they allow decision makers to react to favorable or unfavorable new situations by dynamically adjusting the capital-budgeting decision. Unfortunately, conventional capital-budgeting decision models, such as DCF, do not incorporate into the valuation process the value of real options. Not explicitly including the value of embedded options effectively assigns any such options a value of zero.

**Real options**
represent flexibilities and/or growth opportunities embedded in capital-investment projects.

**Real assets**
represent investments in both tangible property (e.g., a manufacturing facility) and intangible property (e.g., a new information system).

[22] The material in this section is drawn from the following two sources: D. E. Stout, Y. A. Xie, and H. Qi, "Improving Capital Budgeting Decisions with Real Options," *Management Accounting Quarterly* 9, no. 4 (Summer 2008), pp. 1–10; and, D. E. Stout, H. Qi, Y. A. Xie, and S. Liu, "Incorporating Real Options into the Capital Budgeting Process: A Primer for Accounting Educators," *Journal of Accounting Education* 26 (2008), pp. 213–30.

There are four common types of real options: (1) the option to *expand* an investment (i.e., to make follow-on investments if the immediate investment project succeeds); (2) the option to *abandon* a project on the basis of new information revealed, over time, regarding states of nature that affect projected returns to the project; (3) the option to wait and learn before investing (i.e., the option to *delay* an investment–some refer to this as an investment-timing option), or (4) the option to *scale back* the magnitude of a project (e.g., by varying output or its production methods). Items (1) and (3) are analogous to call options, while items (2) and (4) are similar in nature to put options. We discuss the topic of real options in this section of the chapter because their inclusion in the capital-budgeting process provides an additional opportunity for dealing formally with risk and uncertainty. As we demonstrate with the following example, real options may change a project's expected cash flows and risk, and for this reason should be formally considered in the analysis of capital-investment projects.

### Incorporating Real Options into the Capital-Budgeting Process

There are, in general, two approaches to incorporating real options into the analysis of long-term investment projects: the use of *scenario analysis combined with decision trees,* and the use of an *options-pricing model* (such as the Black-Scholes model). The following discussion illustrates the former approach. The latter approach is illustrated in selected finance texts, such as intermediate financial management.

For purposes of illustration, assume that XYZ Company is considering investing in the production of a new technology (e.g., hand-held communications device), the target market for which is young college graduates. The estimated investment cost for this project is $100 million. Demand for the product, and therefore the project's risk, is a function of the demand for wireless Internet connections "on-the-go." The CFO of XYZ, working with marketing, estimates a 25% chance that such demand will be high, 50% probability that demand will be medium, and 25% probability that demand will be low. Associated after-tax cash flows under each of these market scenarios are estimated as follows: $70 million, $50 million, and $5 million. For projects of this nature, a 15% discount rate is assumed.

Assume that XYZ can make the investment today (time period 0), or it can delay the decision for one year. The advantage of the delay option is that over the coming year additional information regarding consumer demand for this project will be revealed. For simplicity, assume the same investment outlay cost ($100 million) and the same projected after-tax cash flows. The difference, however, is that if XYZ delays its investment by a year, the cash inflows will also be delayed (and therefore worth less in a present-value sense). Finally, assume (and this is a strong assumption) that if the project is delayed one year, the true level of consumer demand will be revealed with certainty (or near certainty). You can see that this investment-timing option is similar to a call option on a stock. In essence, management of XYZ needs to decide whether to defer the investment one year. If the company does delay the investment, then one year from now XYZ can exercise its option to invest in the project. Note, however, that it will choose to do this only if the expected NPV at $t = 0$ is positive. In this sense, the inclusion of real options complements a traditional DCF analysis of a proposed investment, as discussed earlier in this chapter.

### Traditional (DCF) Analysis

Details regarding the proposed investment are provided in the decision tree depicted in Panel A of Exhibit 12.10. Each state of nature (level of demand in our example) in the tree is shown as a separate branch of the decision tree. The expected NPV of the project is defined as the weighted average of the three possible states of nature (outcomes), with the weights represented by the demand probabilities. Given an after-tax discount rate of 15%, the expected NPV of this investment is *negative* $0.109 million. Based on this conventional analysis, the project should not be undertaken: the project's expected rate of return is less than the weighted-average cost of capital (15%); as such, this project would not add to shareholder value.

### Investment Analysis with Investment-Timing Option

As shown above, the expected NPV of the proposed investment is slightly negative. However, that analysis of the project failed to incorporate the value of the timing (or delay) option

Flexcell International Corporation (**www.flexcellint.com**), a Swiss company producing lightweight solar panels for a wide variety of applications, recently complemented a traditional DCF analysis with a real-options analysis in conjunction with making an investment decision regarding the location of a new factory complex. Specifically, the company included in its evaluation of three different sites the value of flexibility (i.e., an investment-timing option) regarding this decision. Based on this approach, the company determined that manufacturing from its home base was more cost-effective than going abroad. (Sample calculations are available at **www.hbr.org/manufacture-at-home**.)

More recent work addresses the following strategic issue: how do we balance the competitive pressure to commit to new investments against the flexibility of keeping investment options open? That is, the value of a company's capital investments is jointly a function of the evolution of industry demand and prices and the additional investments it and its competitors make. One solution to this dilemma is to blend together real-options analysis and game theory (into "option games"). Ferreira et al. (2009) report the application of this method to decisions made by a real, but disguised, mining company that recently faced the decision whether to add new capacity in the face of demand and competitive uncertainties. The indicated choice (invest now) differed from that revealed by a conventional DCF analysis.

**Sources:** Nelson Ferreira, Jayanti Kar, and Lenos Trigeorgis, "Option Games: The Key to Competing in Capital-Intensive Industries," *Harvard Business Review* (March 2009), pp. 101–107; and Suzanne de Treville and Lenos Trigeorgis, "It May Be Cheaper to Manufacture at Home," *Harvard Business Review* (October 2010), pp. 84–87.

associated with the project. In reality, XYZ company has the option to delay, by one year, its investment in the project. This situation is analogous to having a call option on a stock. In this case, the company has the ability to "purchase" the investment next year, for the indicated price, based on the revealed level of consumer demand for the proposed product.

The essence of the approach is to estimate, as before, the NPV (at $t = 0$) of the proposed investment. What is different, however, is that the planning horizon must now be extended to four periods. Also, **in the determination of the weighted-average NPV of the project, we include only those individual scenarios that have a positive NPV.** For example, if the NPV of any scenario at $t = 1$ is negative, then this scenario is not included in the computation of the weighted-average return on the project. This is precisely because at $t = 1$ the company is assumed to possess revealed information regarding the level of consumer demand. If, for example, it is revealed at $t = 1$ that demand is going to be low, then XYZ would not be forced to exercise its option to purchase the investment. On the other hand, if at $t = 1$ the revealed level of consumer demand is high, then most likely the NPV of this scenario, at $t = 1$, would be positive. As such this scenario is included in the computation of the expected value of the proposed investment. Note, however, that in order to be able to compare our NPV analysis with the conventional approach (Panel A of Exhibit 12.10) we must bring all future cash flows (both inflows and outflows) back to time period 0. Because we assume that the investment outlay cost of $1 million is known

**EXHIBIT 12.10**

**Decision Trees: Real Options Analysis (Investment-Timing Option)**

Panel A: Expected NPV--Invest in Project Today ($t = 0$), amounts in $ millions

| | | | | | | | | |
|---|---|---|---|---|---|---|---|---|
| discount rate = | 15.00% | | | | | | | |
| | | | | Cash Inflows | | | NPV of | Weighted |
| Cash Outflow | Market Demand | | | | | | Scenario | NPV |
| $t = 0$ | (Scenario) | probability | 1 | 2 | 3 | | | |
| | high | 0.25 | $70 | $70 | $70 | | $59.83 | $14.956 |
| $100 | medium | 0.50 | $50 | $50 | $50 | | $14.16 | $7.081 |
| | low | 0.25 | $5 | $5 | $5 | | ($88.58) | ($22.146) |
| | | 1.00 | | | | | Expected NPV = | ($0.109) |

Panel B: Expected NPV--Delay Investment by One Year, Only if NPV is increased, amounts in $ millions

| | | | | | | | | | |
|---|---|---|---|---|---|---|---|---|---|
| discount rate = | 15.00% | | | | | | | | |
| risk-free rate = | 5.00% | | | | | | | | |
| cash outflow one year from the present (?) = | | $100 | | | | | | | |
| | Market Demand | | | Cash Flows | | | PV of Cash | PV of Cash | Weighted |
| | (Scenario) | probability | 1 | 2 | 3 | 4 | Outflows* | Inflows** | NPV @ $t = 0$ |
| | high | 0.25 | ($100.00) | $70 | $70 | $70 | ($95.24) | $138.98 | $10.935 |
| | medium | 0.50 | ($100.00) | $50 | $50 | $50 | ($95.24) | $99.27 | $2.016 |
| | low | 0.25 | $0.00 | $0 | $0 | $0 | $0.00 | $0.00 | $0.000 |
| | | 1.00 | | | | | | Expected NPV = | $12.951 |

*discounted at risk-free rate of interest
**discounted at weighted-average cost of capital

with certainty (or near certainty), it would be appropriate to use the risk-free rate of return to discount this amount to present value at $t = 0$. For the current example, we assume that the risk-free rate of return is 5%. All of the information pertaining to the investment-timing option analysis is presented in Panel B of Exhibit 12.10.

We see from Panel B that at $t = 1$, XYZ Company would invest in the project *only if* the revealed level of demand was either high or medium. If the company invests (at $t = 1$) in the project, then it will spend $100 million and will expect to receive either $70 million or $50 million in cash inflows for each of three years. If consumer demand turns out to be low, then no investment is made at $t = 1$. Thus, given the probabilities for the three specified levels of demand, we can proceed to calculate the weighted present value of each scenario (see cells J20:J22 in Exhibit 12.10) and finally the weighted-average NPV of the project. As shown in cell J23, this value is $12.95 million, an amount considerably higher than indicated in the conventional NPV analysis presented in Panel A of Exhibit 12.10. In short, the project's expected NPV is considerably higher after considering the existence of the investment-timing option. As indicated earlier in the chapter, the decision maker normally would, as part of the evaluation of a proposed investment, conduct a sensitivity analysis on the inputs to the decision model. This issue is pursued in Problem 12-51.

Finally, we note that the same approach as discussed above, and revealed in Exhibit 12.10, can be used to deal with other types of real options. Problem 12-52 provides an alternative example of a real option embedded in a proposed investment. The approach, however, is basically the same as that illustrated above. A decision tree can be used to represent various scenarios or states of nature (e.g., levels of consumer demand). The NPV of the proposed project can first be determined using the conventional approach and then again after incorporating the effect of the real option. The decision, from a purely financial standpoint, is a function of the NPVs of the decision alternatives. Just remember that these NPVs, for comparability purposes, are calculated at $t = 0$.

### Determinants of the Value of Real Options

As members of the decision-making team that evaluates capital-budgeting proposals, accountants should have some knowledge of the drivers or determinants of value for real options. In effect, the same factors that affect the value of financial options also affect the inherent value of real options. In this regard, we offer the following three comments:

1. *Ceteris paribus,* the value of a real option is higher if the value of the underlying asset is high relative to the exercise price of the option (for XYZ, an estimate of the value of the asset is $99.89 million, while the exercise price of the project is $100 million).

2. The farther away the expiration date is, the higher the value of an option is. (The one-year expiration period in the case of XYZ is probably considered long.)

3. Perhaps most important, the value of an option increases as the risk of the project increases. (In the case of XYZ, the value of the delay option increases as the volatility of project returns increases. In essence, when project returns are considered risky, there is greater value in delaying the decision until consumer demand levels are revealed, or at least better revealed. The delay option available to XYZ therefore provides value to the company in terms of dealing with project risk.)

# Other Capital-Budgeting Decision Models

**LO 12-6**

*Discuss and apply other capital-budgeting decision models.*

The **payback period** of an investment is the length of time required for the cumulative after-tax cash inflows from an investment to recover the initial investment outlay.

## Payback Period

The **payback period** of an investment is the length of time required for the cumulative after-tax cash inflows from an investment to recover the initial investment outlay. At that point the investor has recovered the amount of money invested in the project, hence the term *payback period.*

### Determining the Payback Period with Uniform Annual Cash Inflows

For an investment that provides uniform future after-tax cash inflows, the payback period (in years) can be determined as follows:

Payback period = Total initial capital investment ÷ Annual after-tax cash inflows

For example, assume an initial capital-investment outlay (year 0) of $1,110,000. This project is projected to have a four-year life. Each year, the investment is expected to provide an after-tax cash inflow of $387,000. Based on this information, the project has a payback period of 2.87 years (i.e., $1,110,000 ÷ $387,000).

### Determining the Payback Period with Uneven Cash Inflows (Mendoza Company example)

Refer back to Exhibit 12.2, which contains cash flow information regarding the machine-purchase decision facing the Mendoza Company. With uneven cash inflows, as is the case here, the payback period is defined as the number of years it takes for the *cumulative* after-tax cash inflows to equal the initial investment outlay ($680,000). The necessary analysis is presented in Exhibit 12.11.

The amount needed in year 4 to reach the payback period is $86,000; under the assumption that the after-tax cash inflows in year 4 occur evenly throughout the year, the payback period is 3 + ($86,000 ÷ $208,000) years = 3.41 years. If we assume, as is the case when we calculate a project's NPV or IRR, that the cash inflows occur at year-end, then the payback period for this project would be 4 years.

**EXHIBIT 12.11**
**Payback Period Calculation for the Mendoza Company Example**

| (1) | (2) | (3) |
|-----|-----|-----|
| Year | After-Tax Cash Flows (Exhibit 12.2) | Cumulative After-Tax Net Cash Flows |
| 0 | $(680,000) | $(680,000) |
| 1 | 178,000 | (502,000) |
| 2 | 208,000 | (294,000) |
| 3 | 208,000 | (86,000) |
| 4 | 208,000* | 122,000 |

*Note: For purposes of determining the payback period we have (temporarily) ignored the cash inflows expected to occur at the end of year 4. The cash flows reflected in Exhibit 12.11 are the recurring cash flows, which in the present analysis are assumed to occur evenly throughout the year.

### *Evaluation of the Payback Period Model*

*Advantages*    The principal advantage of the payback period model is that, once cash flow data have been collected, the payback period is easy to compute and comprehend. Businesspeople, particularly owners of small businesses, seem to have an intuitive understanding of payback periods.

We note, too, that the payback period addresses the issue of liquidity. Projects with shorter payback periods provide increased flexibility in the sense that they provide funds for other investment opportunities. The value of such flexibility is thought to be particularly important for evaluating large-scale investments and investments in industries characterized by high-growth and/or change.

The length of payback period can serve as a rough measure of the risk associated with a proposed investment. The longer the payback period, the more risky the project is. The underlying logic is that the farther out into the future the payback period is, the more uncertainty associated with the future cash flows. For example, the longer it takes to recover the original investment, the more likely it is that the underlying product or service will become obsolete or attract competition, making it more difficult to earn cash flows as projected. Thus, all other things equal, managers prefer projects with shorter payback periods.

*Limitations*    The use of payback period information for investment decision making is subject to four primary limitations:

1. *The model fails to consider returns over the entire life of the investment.* That is, the payback model considers cash inflows from the initiation of the project until its payback period but ignores cash flows after the payback period. Notice that in the Mendoza example the calculation ignores the significant cash inflows scheduled to occur at the end of year 4.

2. *The payback period, in its unadjusted state, ignores the time value of money.* It considers only the length of time required to recover the investment regardless of differences in the timing or pattern of cash flows. For example, as long as the payback period for each of two projects is the same, the model considers them equally desirable. This is the case even if one project generates most of its cash inflows in the early years of its payback period while the other project generates most of its cash inflows in the latter years of its payback period.

3. *The decision criterion for accepting/rejecting a project is not well defined; that is, it is subjective.* This situation can be compared to the two DCF decision models we discussed earlier in this chapter. For the NPV model, the decision rule was: accept a project if its NPV is greater than 0; for the IRR model, the decision rule was: accept a project if its IRR is greater than WACC (or otherwise specified hurdle rate).

4. *Use of the model may encourage excessive investment in short-term projects, at the expense of investments critical to long-term success.* Some investments needed to secure competitive advantage—such as an investment in computer-integrated manufacturing (CIM)—can take many years to recover the original investment. A company that fails to make such strategic investments may not be competitive in the long run.

### *Present Value (or Discounted) Payback Period*

To avoid the second criticism listed above, some companies use the present value of future cash inflows to determine the investment's payback period. Because discounted cash flows are used, the resulting payback period is referred to as the **present value payback period.** As with the NPV model, the present value of future after-tax cash inflows from an investment is estimated using the firm's WACC (or otherwise specified "hurdle rate").

As shown in Exhibit 12.12, the present value payback period for the machine-purchase investment by the Mendoza Company, if we consider only recurring after-tax cash inflows, is greater than the life of the project (4 years). If we consider the additional after-tax cash inflow of $113,00 (see Exhibit 12.2), then the present value payback period on this

The **present value payback period**

of an investment is the length of time required for the cumulative *present value* of after-tax cash inflows to recover the initial investment outlay.

**EXHIBIT 12.12**
**Present Value Payback Period for the Mendoza Company Investment Proposal**

| Year | After-Tax Cash Flow | Discount Factor @ 10% | PV of After-Tax Cash Flow | Cumulative PV of After-Tax Cash Flows |
|------|---------------------|------------------------|---------------------------|----------------------------------------|
| 0 | $(680,000) | 1.000 | $(680,000) | $(680,000) |
| 1 | 178,000 | 0.909 | 161,802 | (518,198) |
| 2 | 208,000 | 0.826 | 171,808 | (346,390) |
| 3 | 208,000 | 0.751 | 156,208 | (190,182) |
| 4 | 208,000 | 0.683 | 142,064 | (48,118) |

Note: Similar to Exhibit 12.11, we consider in Exhibit 12.12 only the recurring annual after-tax cash inflows.

proposed investment is approximately 4 years, which is the life of the project. As noted above, the unadjusted (i.e., nondiscounted) payback period is approximately 3.41 years.

Because it considers the time value of money, the present value payback model is considered superior to the unadjusted payback period model. Because it relies on the use of discounted cash inflows, this version of the payback model has an important implication: *If the discounted payback period is less than the life of the project, then the project must have a positive NPV.* This result holds because the cash inflows that accrue up to the discounted payback period are, by definition, just sufficient (in a present-value sense) to cover the initial investment outlay; any cash inflows that come after the cut-off period will ensure a positive NPV for the project.

However, the discounted payback model suffers the same weaknesses of the unadjusted payback model in other respects: use of the model for capital-budgeting decision making can motivate excessive investments in short-term projects; the model ignores investment returns beyond the (discounted) payback period; and the decision criterion under this model is not set objectively, that is, the cut-off period for determining project acceptance is set by trial and error. The second limitation is particularly important since it may lead managers to incorrectly reject some positive NPV investment opportunities.

Finally, one technical note is in order. The Mendoza example is simplified in the sense that it reflects a single cash outflow (time period 0) followed by a series of cash inflows. It is possible, however, that a project requires a series of cash outflows, beyond time period 0. To calculate the payback period in this case you should first sum these cash outflows to obtain an aggregate cash outflow for the project. To calculate the payback period you add the unadjusted cash outflows; for the discounted payback period, you would add together the present value of those cash outflows.

## Accounting (Book) Rate of Return

The **accounting (book) rate of return (ARR)** on a project is equal to some measure of accounting profit to some measure of investment in the project. One specification of the ARR is:

The **accounting (book) rate of return (ARR)** of a project is equal to some measure of accounting profit to some measure of investment in the project.

$$ARR = \text{Average annual net operating income} \div \text{Average investment}$$

Be aware, however, that there are differences in practice regarding how both the numerator and the denominator for the ARR are defined. That is, there is more than a single way to calculate the ARR of an investment.

One way to define the denominator of the ARR is to take a simple average of the book value of the net investment at the beginning of the project's life and the sum of the after-tax disposal value of the asset (if any) at the end of the project's life plus the amount of net working capital recovered at the end of the project's life.

Refer back to Exhibit 12.2 for financial information regarding the machine-purchase decision for the Mendoza Company. In this case, the average book value of the proposed investment can be calculated as follows:

Net initial investment = $680,000

End-of-project amounts recovered (Exhibit 12.2) = $203,000 (i.e, $3,000 + $200,000)

Average investment over life of project = ($680,000 + $203,000) ÷ 2 = $441,500

The proposed investment for the Mendoza Company is expected to earn an average annual net-of-tax operating income of $58,000, as follows (see Exhibit 12.2):

| Year | Operating Income After-Tax |
|------|----------------------------|
| 1 | $58,000  ($178,000 − $120,000) |
| 2 | 88,000  ($208,000 − $120,000) |
| 3 | 88,000  ($208,000 − $120,000) |
| 4 | (2,000)  ($208,000 − $120,000 − $90,000) |
| Average | $58,000 |

Thus, when the denominator of the calculation is defined as *average investment* (as calculated above), the proposed project's ARR is 13.14% ($58,000 ÷ $441,500). This result means that, on average, the proposed project returns approximately 13 cents of after-tax operating profit per year for each dollar associated with the average investment in the project.

Note, however, that some companies define the denominator of the ARR as the net original investment. Again, there are different ways to define this number. If the ARR is calculated based on this measure ($680,000), the calculated ARR for the proposed project would be 8.53%.

### *Evaluation of the Accounting (Book) Rate of Return Model*

*Advantages*   To a large extent, the ARR model uses the same kind of data routinely generated for financial reporting purposes. For this reason, the ratio is called the *accounting rate of return.* Some would argue that, relative to DCF-based outputs, ARR numbers are easier for managers to understand. Further, as indicated in Chapter 19, accounting rate of return measures are used by many companies to evaluate the financial performance of operating divisions and managers. Thus, the use of ARR for capital-budgeting purposes would be consistent with the way subsequent financial performance is typically measured.

The ARR has an additional advantage over the payback period model in that it looks at financial returns (e.g., increases in after-tax operating income) over the entire life of a project. That is, the ARR gives managers an idea of how future accounting income numbers will be affected if the project is accepted.

*Limitations*   As with the payback period model, the ARR decision model ignores the time value of money. Another limitation pertains to the use of accounting numbers in the numerator and denominator. While such numbers are useful for financial reporting purposes, financial theory tells us that cash flow information is preferable for making capital-budgeting decisions. In essence, the use of DCF decision models aligns internal decision making with the process that, in theory, investors use in valuing stocks in the financial marketplace.

As indicated above, there are multiple ways to define both the numerator and the denominator in the ARR calculation. For example, one possibility is to define the denominator simply as the net cost of the asset acquired ($480,000 in the case of the Mendoza Company). While simplifying the calculation (i.e., average investment would now be defined as ($480,000 + $0) ÷ 2 = $240,000), this approach ignores the fact that the proposed project required a commitment of net working capital during the life of the project. The treatment of after-tax proceeds from the sale of the asset at the end of the project and, for asset-replacement decisions, the after-tax proceeds from the sale of an existing asset, provide additional areas of differences in practice. In short, there is no universally accepted practice as to how the components of ARR are measured. At a minimum, this leads to comparability problems across companies and potentially within divisions of the same company.

Finally, as with the case of the payback model (and, for that matter, the discounted payback model as well), there is no objectively defined decision criterion for making project acceptance decisions. What is an acceptable ARR? Any such response is determined heuristically (i.e., subjectively, using rules of thumb).

## Behavioral Issues in Capital Budgeting

**LO 12-7**

*Identify behavioral issues associated with the capital-budgeting process.*

To this point, we have dealt mainly with technical issues associated with the capital-budgeting process. It is worth noting that the success of this process is affected by a number of behavioral considerations, as discussed below.

### Common Behavioral Problems: Cost Escalation, Incrementalism, and Uncertainty Intolerance

Studies have found that escalating commitment is common in the capital-budgeting process. In an attempt to recoup past losses, a decision maker may consider past costs or losses as relevant in making capital-budgeting decisions. For example, elimination or reduction of losses from past investments may, erroneously, be included as savings associated with a proposed investment. As indicated in Chapter 11, such amounts do not meet the test of information relevancy and as such should not be included in formal decision models, such as those used for analyzing capital-investment projects. Research suggests that escalating commitments are more likely to occur when current managers are the ones responsible for the negative results of past actions.[23]

Needed capital investments may not be pursued because of the amount of time and work required to secure their approval. Projects that cost less than those that must be approved as a capital investment are undertaken instead. As a result, managers may choose to invest in multiple small additions that require no approval from above, rather than investing in a major capital project such as computer-integrated manufacturing (CIM) or a flexible manufacturing system (FMS) that would vastly improve the firm's competitive position. Failure to make necessary capital investments can reduce the firm's competitiveness, erode its market share, and jeopardize its long-term profitability and survival.

Intolerance of uncertainty may lead managers to require short payback periods for capital investments. Once a project pays for itself, the amount of risk is substantially reduced. This makes projects with short payback periods the preferred choice for some decision makers. However, many capital investments of strategic import do not have short payback periods. These projects may require a lengthy time to install, test, adjust, train personnel, and gain market acceptance; examples include investments in new manufacturing technologies, new product development, and expansion into new territories. Requiring too short a payback period makes the acceptance of such projects unlikely, even if the firm would enjoy long-term benefits from these projects.

### Goal-Congruency Issues

Perhaps the greatest behavioral challenge in capital budgeting relates to the need to align DCF decision models (such as NPV) with models used to evaluate subsequent financial performance. Typically, accrual-based measures of profitability, such as return on investment (ROI), are used to evaluate financial performance of managers and organizational subunits. As the following example shows, managers may not be motivated to make decisions that are in the best interest of the organization when NPV is used for decision making but accrual accounting income numbers are used subsequently for performance-evaluation purposes.

Assume an investment outlay of $12,000 today that will generate, for each of three years, an increase in cash contribution margin (CM) of $5,000. Further, assume no income taxes, a three-year depreciation period for the investment, zero salvage value, and the use of straight-line depreciation. Finally, assume that the financial performance of

[23] G. Whyte, "Escalating Commitment to a Course of Action: A Reinterpretation," *Academy of Management Review*, 1986, pp. 311–21.

A manufacturer of telecommunications devices is about to review investment proposals to increase its manufacturing capacity for manufacturing one of its key components. In the past, such proposals have varied in the level of technology and the degree of computer integration required for the manufacturing process. So far, the firm has minimal experience with advanced manufacturing technology and is using semiautomated machines in key parts of its manufacturing process of the components. Over the last several years, company executives have been conscious of the growing competitive pressures that may eventually require investment in advanced manufacturing technology. As a result, the firm has been actively seeking out such investment proposals. Many proposals had been reviewed in the last few years. However, no proposals have ever passed the review stage. "The numbers just don't support it," according to one member of the review committee, who has been a staunch advocator of advanced manufacturing technologies.

The firm evaluates all major investment proposals using the net present value method with the estimated long-term (five years) cost of capital as the discount rate. In addition, the firm also uses the payback method in its analysis of investment proposals. However, a short payback period is not necessary to justify investment in a project if the project is considered to be among the best in terms of investment proposals. A review of the proposals submitted over the last few years revealed that these proposals ranked consistently higher based upon the net present value method.

You believe that it is critically important for the long-term profitability of the firm to acquire new advanced manufacturing technology. You are of the opinion that the firm will lose its competitive edge, or may not even survive, if it fails to respond to this demand. As the manager of the manufacturing process, who has submitted several unsuccessful proposals for investment in advanced manufacturing technologies, how would you modify your proposal?

(Refer to Comments on Cost Management in Action at the end of the chapter.)

the manager and subunit is evaluated each year using return on investment (ROI), defined as operating income divided by beginning-of-year (B-O-Y) book value of the asset. Given these assumptions, the following rates of return would be anticipated:

| Item | Year 1 | Year 2 | Year 3 |
|---|---|---|---|
| Cash CM | $ 5,000 | $5,000 | $5,000 |
| Less: Depreciation | 4,000 | 4,000 | 4,000 |
| Operating income | $ 1,000 | $1,000 | $1,000 |
| NBV of asset (B-O-Y) | $12,000 | $8,000 | $4,000 |
| ROI | 8.33% | 12.50% | 25.00% |

Assuming a discount rate of 11.0%, this project has a projected NPV of $218.57 (details omitted) and therefore should be accepted.

The issue, however, is whether a rational decision maker/manager would be motivated to accept the investment given the projected ROIs over the coming three years. If compensation is tied to reported ROI, there may be a disincentive to invest, in spite of the fact that accepting the project would be consistent with adding shareholder value. This disincentive would be stronger:

- If the individual were likely to be transferred out of the division (job advancement, retirement, etc.).
- If the project life is long (wherein the cash flow benefits are not realized until later in the project's life).
- If the discount rate is high.
- If the disposal of any existing assets would result in a reported loss (which would, in turn, reduce reported ROI in year 1).
- If accelerated depreciation methods are used for accounting purposes.

## Addressing the Goal-Congruency Problem

The preceding example illustrates a pervasive problem in control system design: Conflicts can arise when DCF-based models are used for decision-making purposes and accrual-based accounting income numbers are used subsequently for evaluating the financial performance of managers and organizational subunits. Top management cannot expect goal congruence under these conditions. Unfortunately, such conditions tend to characterize existing business practice.

What can organizations do, then, to better align the goals of decision makers with the goals of the overall organization? To a large extent, this issue is one of the unsolved problems in control system design. An extended discussion of these issues is presented in Chapter 19. Within the context of capital budgeting, however, three possible solutions are offered.

### *Economic Value Added (EVA®)*

> **Economic value added (EVA®)** is a measure of financial performance designed to approximate an entity's *economic profit*; calculated most often as net operating profit after taxes (adjusted for accounting "distortions") less an imputed charge based on the level of invested capital.

As will be discussed more fully in Chapter 19, **economic value added (EVA®)** is a financial-performance indicator that includes a charge for use of invested capital. That is, *economic profitability* is not indicated until the organization generates sufficient cash flow to cover *all* expenses, including an imputed charge for capital invested in the business. As such, both NPV and EVA® assume that shareholder value is created only when projects recover their capital costs. Thus, the use of EVA® for evaluation of financial performance is one way to avoid the behavioral conflict noted above.

### *Separating Incentive Compensation from Budgeted Performance*

In Chapter 10 we discussed some of the negative incentive effects of traditional budgeting systems, including those where an annual fixed-performance contract is used to determine compensation.[24] Budgeted performance, against which actual performance (income earned, ROI, etc.) is measured, is reflected in the master budgeting process and set of pro forma financial statements produced as a result of that process. Among other things, linking managerial reward to a comparison between budgeted and actual performance penalizes managers for factors that emerge during the year that are beyond their control (general price-level changes, changes in worldwide demand for and pricing of oil, etc.). It simultaneously rewards such managers for market (or industrywide) positive results. Further, linking compensation to budgeted performance encourages dysfunctional, perhaps even unethical, behaviors as managers game the performance indicator in order to make budget. As we discussed in Chapter 10, some commentators feel that relative performance indicators are superior to the fixed-performance model described above. In such a case, actual financial performance for a subunit or manager is compared to some internal or external benchmark for the purpose of determining incentive rewards and executive compensation. As such, greater degrees of goal congruence are expected to be realized.

### *Post-Audit*

Another way to achieve goal congruence in terms of the capital-budgeting process is to forgo in the evaluation process the use of accrual-based accounting income numbers altogether. Rather, top management might focus on, or at least give considerable weight to, a post-decision comparison between forecasted and realized amounts for a given investment project. As indicated earlier in this chapter, such a comparison is referred to as a *post-audit*. The principal benefit of post-audits is the collection, for performance-evaluation purposes, of the same cash inflow and outflow information used for investment decision-making purposes (e.g., NPV). In turn, this should eliminate disincentives associated with the use of different models for decision making and assessment of subsequent financial performance.

## Summary

Capital-budgeting decisions represent long-term commitments of substantial amounts of resources. As such, these decisions are of strategic concern to organizations; in a very real sense these decisions affect financial results (returns) of organizations for many years into the future.

[24] See Michael C. Jensen, "Corporate Budgeting Is Broken—Let's Fix It," *Harvard Business Review* (November 2001), pp. 94–101.

As indicated in Chapter 10, the capital budget (i.e., the allocation of capital to long-term investment projects) is a key component of an organization's overall planning system, referred to as its *master budget.* Recent advances in the field of cost management, including the balanced scorecard (BSC) and the analytic hierarchy process (AHP), can be used to help align capital investments with an organization's strategy.

Accountants can add value to the capital-budgeting process of an organization in at least four ways: (1) developing relevant financial (i.e., cash flow) and nonfinancial information for decision making; (2) designing an effective post-audit mechanism; (3) identifying appropriate methods for dealing with risk and uncertainty; and (4) educating small-business owners on the value and conceptual superiority of discounted cash flow (DCF) decision models. Conceptually, the determination of relevant financial information follows the same procedure outlined in Chapter 11: To be relevant for decision making, a given cost or revenue item must be incremental to the decision. That is, only future costs and revenues that *differ* between decision alternatives are relevant for capital expenditure analysis.

In general, managers can optimize an organization's capital budget by using the net present value (NPV) decision model, which compares the present value of cash inflows to the present value of cash outflows. Typically, the discount rate used in DCF models is the organization's weighted-average cost of capital (WACC).

Cash outflows from investments can occur at three points: (1) *project initiation*—to acquire the investment and begin operations, to provide needed net working capital for the project, and to dispose of any replaced or discarded assets; (2) *project operation*—to cover operating expenditures, any additional investments, and additional net working capital; and (3) *project disposal*—to dispose of the investment, to restore facilities, and to provide training or relocation benefits for personnel whose positions have been terminated. An investment generates net cash inflows during its existence through increases in revenues or decreases in expenses, through recovery of its investment in net working capital, and from the disposal of assets. For a profit-seeking organization, all such cash flows should be stated on an after-tax basis.

Special care needs to be exercised when analyzing asset-replacement decisions. In these cases, relevant cash flows are the differences in expected future cash flows between keeping and replacing the asset. Thus, there is a need to identify differences in working capital commitments (and recoveries), differences in tax effects associated with depreciation deductions, and differences in end-of-project salvage (terminal) values. Appendix A provides alternative formats that can be used to structure an asset-replacement decision.

Exhibit 12.13 summarizes the definitions, computation procedures, advantages, and weaknesses of the various capital-budgeting decision models covered in the chapter. Some advanced considerations in using DCF models for the analysis of capital investments are presented in Appendix B to this chapter.

The determination of a project's NPV requires the use of forecasts and assumptions. Sensitivity analysis can be used to determine how sensitive the capital-budgeting decision is with respect to these assumptions. The chapter presents three examples of sensitivity analysis: what-if analysis, scenario analysis, and Monte Carlo simulation analysis. An alternative approach to dealing with the problem of risk and uncertainty is to incorporate the existence of real options that may be embedded in a capital-investment project.

Finally, managers need to understand that the capital-budgeting process is affected by a number of important behavioral considerations. Foremost among these considerations is the conflict that arises from using DCF models for investment decision making but accrual accounting numbers (such as ROI) for subsequent appraisal of financial performance, and also from incentive conflicts associated with the use of fixed-performance contracts. The use of EVA® for performance appraisal, the use of relative performance for compensation and reward, and the use of post-audits may help reduce this conflict and achieve greater congruency between the goals of decision makers and the goals of the organization as a whole.

**EXHIBIT 12.13** **Capital Investment Decision Models**

| Model | Definition | Computation Procedure | Advantages | Disadvantages |
|---|---|---|---|---|
| Payback period | Number of years to recover the initial investment | *Uniform cash flow:* Investment *divided by* net cash flow. *Uneven cash flow:* Number of years for the cumulative cash inflow to equal the initial investment | 1. Simple to use and understand<br>2. Focuses on liquidity<br>3. Rough measure of risk | 1. Ignores timing and time value of money<br>2. Ignores cash flows beyond payback period<br>3. Decision rule = "rule of thumb" |
| Accounting (book) rate of return (ARR) | Ratio of average annual net income to the initial (or average) investment (book value) | Average net income *divided by* investment book value | 1. Data are readily available<br>2. Consistent with other financial measures<br>3. Readily interpretable by managers | 1. Ignores timing and time value of money<br>2. Uses accounting numbers, not after-tax cash flows |
| Net present value (NPV) | Difference between present value (PV) of cash inflows and PV of cash outflows | PV of after-tax cash inflows − PV of cash outflows | 1. Considers the time value of money<br>2. Focuses on after-tax cash flows<br>3. Consistent with goal of maximizing shareholder value | 1. Can possibly lead to suboptimal capital budgeting under condition of capital rationing |
| Internal rate of return (IRR) | Discount rate that makes the PV of cash inflows equal to the PV of cash outflows | For uniform cash inflows—solving for $i$ in the following equation: PV annuity factor for $i$ × Annual after-tax cash inflow = Initial investment | 1. Considers time value of money<br>2. Focuses on after-tax cash flows<br>3. Ratios are intuitively appealing to managers | 1. Inherent assumption regarding reinvestment rate could be unrealistic<br>2. Complex to compute if done manually<br>3. May not lead to optimum capital budget |
| Modified internal rate of return (MIRR) | Discount rate that makes the PV of cash inflows equal to the PV of cash outflows, under the assumption that interim cash inflows are reinvested at a specified rate | Rate at which: PV costs = PV terminal value, where the left-hand term is the PV of outlays, discounted at the WACC, and the numerator of the right-hand term is the compounded future value of the interim cash inflows, reinvested at the WACC, and the denominator is $(1 + MIRR)^n$, where $n$ = number of periods | 1. Considers the time value of money<br>2. Focuses on after-tax cash flows<br>3. Ratios are intuitively appealing to managers<br>4. Avoids overly optimistic rates of return associated with the use of IRR | 1. Complex to compute if done manually<br>2. May not lead to optimum capital budget<br>3. Discrepancy as to whether there is a reinvestment rate assumption inherent in the IRR calculation |
| Profitability index (PI) (see Appendix B) | Ratio of PV of cash inflows (or NPV) to initial investment | PV of after-tax cash inflows (or NPV) *divided by* initial investment | 1. Considers time value of money<br>2. Focuses on after-tax cash flows<br>3. Useful under conditions of capital rationing | 1. When capital budget is not limited, use could lead to suboptimal capital budget |

**LO 12-8**

*Understand and use alternative presentation formats for the asset-replacement decision.*

# Spreadsheet Templates for Conducting a DCF Analysis of an Asset-Replacement Decision

The following data, related to an equipment-replacement decision facing the Mendoza Company, are used in the three templates included in this appendix.[25]

| | A | B | C | D | E | F | G | H |
|---|---|---|---|---|---|---|---|---|
| 1 | **Input Data** | | | | | | | |
| 2 | Discount rate (WACC) = | | | | 10.00% | | | |
| 3 | Combined income tax rate = | | | | 40.00% | | | |
| 4 | **New Machine:** | | | | | | | |
| 5 | Net cost of new equipment, year 0 = | | | | $480,000 | ($465,000 + $5,000 + $10,000) | | |
| 6 | Useful life of new asset (in years) = | | | | 4 | | | |
| 7 | Estimated salvage value, Yr. 4 = | | | | - | | | |
| 8 | One-time employee training costs, Yr. 1 = | | | | 50,000 | | | |
| 9 | Working capital required, Yr. 1 = | | | | 200,000 | | | |
| 10 | Recovery of working capital, Yr. 4 = | | | | 200,000 | | | |
| 11 | After-tax proceeds, sale of machine (Yr. 4) = | | | | 3,000 | ($100,000 – $95,000 – $2,000) | | |
| 12 | After-tax employee relocation costs (Yr. 4) = | | | | 90,000 | ($150,000 × (1 - 0.40)) | | |
| 13 | Cash revenues, per year = | | | | 1,400,000 | | | |
| 14 | Cash operating costs, per year = | | | | 1,000,000 | | | |
| 15 | Recurring after-tax operating cash flows, years 1–4: | | | | 240,000 | (($1,400,000 – $1,000,000) × (1 – 0.40)) | | |
| 16 | Annual depreciation charges (SL basis) | | | | 120,000 | ($480,000 – $0) ÷ 4 years | | |
| 17 | Annual depreciation tax shield (SL basis) | | | | 48,000 | ($120,000 × 0.40) | | |
| 18 | **Existing Machine:** | | | | | | | |
| 19 | After-tax proceeds, sale of old machine (Yr. 0) = | | | | 93,200 | ($70,000 + $23,300) | | |
| 20 | Existing NBV of machine = | | | | 128,000 | ($320,000 - $192,000) | | |
| 21 | Return of working capital, Year 4 | | | | 50,000 | | | |
| 22 | Net (pretax) proceeds, sale of old machine (Yr. 4) | | | | 1,500 | (given/assumed) | | |
| 23 | After-tax proceeds, sale of old machine (Yr. 4) = | | | | 900 | ($1,500 × (1 - 0.40)) | | |
| 24 | Cash revenues, per year = | | | | 400,000 | (given) | | |
| 25 | Cash operating costs, per year = | | | | 320,000 | (given) | | |
| 26 | Recurring after-tax operating cash flows, years 1–4 | | | | 48,000 | ($400,000 - $320,000) × (1 – 0.40) | | |
| 27 | Annual depreciation charge (SL basis) = | | | | 32,000 | ($128,000 ÷ 4 years) | | |
| 28 | Annual depreciation tax shield (SL basis) = | | | | 12,800 | ($32,000 × 0.40) | | |

Panel A (below) contains the first of two alternative templates that can be used in conjunction with what we call the *differential approach* to a decision analysis. The 10% discount factors shown in cells L33:L36 were calculated using the following formula: factor = $1/(1 + 0.10)^i$, where $i$ represents year (1, 2, 3, 4). (Note: All numbers in cells I34 through I40 were determined using actual discount factors from cells L33 through L37, not the rounded values shown in column H.)

| | A | B | C | D | E | F | G | H | I | J | K | L |
|---|---|---|---|---|---|---|---|---|---|---|---|---|
| 30 | **Panel A: DCF Analysis--Differential Approach #1** | | | | | | | | | | | |
| 31 | | | | | | Amount | Year(s) | PV Factor (@ WACC) | PV of Cash Flows | | | |
| 32 | Differential After-tax Cash Inflows: | | | | | | | | | | **Discount Factors, 10%** | |
| 33 | PV of differential after-tax operating cash flows: | | | | | | | | | | Year 1 = | 0.9090909 |
| 34 | | | | Recurring operating cash flows after taxes | | $192,000 | 1-4 | 3.1698654 | $608,614 | | Year 2 = | 0.8264463 |
| 35 | | | | One-time employee training costs, after taxes | | $30,000 | 1 | 0.9090909 | ($27,273) | | Year 3 = | 0.7513148 |
| 36 | | | | Differential depreciation tax shield = | | $35,200 | 1-4 | 3.1698654 | $111,579 | | Year 4 = | 0.6830135 |
| 37 | PV of differential terminal values: | | | | | | | | | | Annuity = | 3.1698654 |
| 38 | | | | Differential working capital recovered = | | $150,000 | 4 | 0.6830135 | $102,452 | | | |
| 39 | | | | Differential after-tax proceeds, sale of machines = | | $2,100 | 4 | 0.6830135 | $1,434 | | | |
| 40 | | | | After-tax employee relocation expenses = | | $90,000 | 4 | 0.6830135 | ($61,471) | | | |
| 41 | **Net Investment:** | | | | | | | | | | | |
| 42 | Net cost of new equipment, Yr. 0 = | | | | | ($480,000) | 0 | 1.0000000 | ($480,000) | | | |
| 43 | After-tax salvage value, old machine (Yr. 0) = | | | | | 93,200 | 0 | 1.0000000 | $93,200 | | | |
| 44 | Increase in working capital, Yr. 0 = | | | | | ($200,000) | 0 | 1.0000000 | ($200,000) | | | |
| 45 | | | | | | ($586,800) | | NPV = | $148,536 | | | |

---

[25] For guidance in developing a more general Excel template for asset-replacement decisions, see R. J. Balik, "Excel Best Practices," *Managerial Finance* 35, no. 5 (2009), pp. 410–426.

Panel B (below) contains an alternative format for the "differential approach" to structuring a decision analysis. Note that the PV factors in line 67 are copied from cells L33:L36. Note also that the estimated NPV of the project (cell F71) is exactly the same as the amount contained in Panel A (cell I45).

| | A | B | C | D | E | F | G | H | I |
|---|---|---|---|---|---|---|---|---|---|
| 47 | Panel B: DCF Analysis--Differential Approach #2 | | | | | | | | |
| 48 | | | | | | | Year | | |
| 49 | | | | | <u>0</u> | <u>1</u> | <u>2</u> | <u>3</u> | <u>4</u> |
| 50 | I. Net Cash Flow at Time Investment Is Made | | | | | | | | |
| 51 | Net cost of new machine, Yr. 0 | | | | $480,000 | | | | |
| 52 | After-tax salvage value of existing machine, Yr. 0 | | | | $93,200 | | | | |
| 53 | Increase in net working capital required, Yr. 0 | | | | $200,000 | | | | |
| 54 | | | | Total | $586,800 | | | | |
| 55 | II. Differential After-tax Operating Cash Flows Over Life of the Asset: | | | | | | | | |
| 56 | One-time employee-training costs, after tax | | | | | $30,000 | | | |
| 57 | Incremental net operating cash flows, after tax | | | | | $192,000 | $192,000 | $192,000 | $192,000 |
| 58 | Incremental depreciation tax shield | | | | | $35,200 | $35,200 | $35,200 | $35,200 |
| 59 | | | | Totals | | $197,200 | $227,200 | $227,200 | $227,200 |
| 60 | III. Differential Terminal After-tax Cash Flows: | | | | | | | | |
| 61 | Differential working capital released ($200,000 – $50,000) | | | | | | | | $150,000 |
| 62 | Differential after-tax salvage value of assets ($3,000 – $900) | | | | | | | | $2,100 |
| 63 | Differential employee relocation costs, after tax ($150,000 x 0.60) | | | | | | | | $90,000 |
| 64 | | | | Total | | | | | $62,100 |
| 65 | IV. Differential Net Cash Flow (After-tax) per Year | | | | ($586,800) | $197,200 | $227,200 | $227,200 | $289,300 |
| 66 | V. NPV Determination: | | | | | | | | |
| 67 | | | PV Factors | | 1.0000000 | 0.9090909 | 0.8264463 | 0.7513148 | 0.6830135 |
| 68 | | | | | | | | | |
| 69 | | | PV of After-tax Cash Flows = | | | $735,336 | | | |
| 70 | | | Net Investment Outlay = | | | ($586,800) | | | |
| 71 | | | NPV = | | | $148,536 | | | |
| 72 | VI. IRR Estimation: | | | | | | | | |
| 73 | | | IRR = | | | 20.5% | | | |

Finally, in Panel C (below) we offer a presentation format that separately highlights opportunity costs associated with the decision to replace the existing machine. This format is, in fact, consistent with the decision models discussed in Chapter 11. Once again, we find that the NPV of the decision to replace the existing machine is $148,536.

| | A | B | C | D | E | F | G | H | I |
|---|---|---|---|---|---|---|---|---|---|
| 75 | Panel C: Analysis of Equipment-Replacement Decision--Opportunity Cost Approach | | | | | | | | |
| 76 | | | | | | Existing Machine | New Machine | | |
| 77 | | | Annual cash revenues (pretax) | | | $400,000 | $1,400,000 | | |
| 78 | | | Less: Annual cash operating costs, pretax | | | $320,000 | $1,000,000 | | |
| 79 | | | Less: Depreciation expense, SL basis | | | $32,000 | $120,000 | | |
| 80 | | | Annual pretax cash operating income | | | $48,000 | $280,000 | | |
| 81 | | | Less: Income taxes | | | $19,200 | $112,000 | | |
| 82 | | | After-tax income | | | $28,800 | $168,000 | | |
| 83 | | | Plus: Depreciation expense | | | $32,000 | $120,000 | | |
| 84 | | | After-tax cash operating income per year | | | $60,800 | $288,000 | | |
| 86 | Decision Alternatives | | | | | Amount | Year(s) | PV Factor (@ WACC) | PV of Cash Flows |
| 87 | Purchase New Machine: | | | | | | | | |
| 88 | Net incremental investment, after-tax | | | | | $480,000 | 0 | 1.0000000 | ($480,000) |
| 89 | Required investment in working capital, Yr. 0 | | | | | $200,000 | 0 | 1.0000000 | ($200,000) |
| 90 | Net-of-tax salvage value, sale of old machine (Yr. 0) a | | | | | $93,200 | 0 | 1.0000000 | $93,200 |
| 91 | Annual after-tax cash income (total) | | | | | $288,000 | 1-4 | 3.1698654 | $912,921 |
| 92 | One-time operating cash outflow, after-tax, Yr. 1 | | | | | $30,000 | 1 | 0.9090909 | ($27,273) |
| 93 | Ater-tax proceeds from sale of the asset, Yr. 4 | | | | | $3,000 | 4 | 0.6830135 | $2,049 |
| 94 | After-tax employee relocation expenses, Yr. 4 | | | | | $90,000 | 4 | 0.6830135 | ($61,471) |
| 95 | End-of-investment recovery of working capital, Yr. 4 | | | | | $200,000 | 4 | 0.6830135 | $136,603 |
| 96 | | | Net present value of this decision alternative | | | | | | $376,029 |
| 97 | Less: Opporunity Costs: | | | | | | | | |
| 98 | After-tax cash operating income, per year | | | | | $60,800 | 1-4 | 3.1698654 | $192,728 |
| 99 | After-tax salvage value of existing equipment, 4 years hence | | | | | $900 | 4 | 0.6830135 | $615 |
| 100 | Recovery of working capital, end of year 4 | | | | | $50,000 | 4 | 0.6830135 | $34,151 |
| 101 | | | | | | | | | $227,493 |
| 102 | Difference in NPV, Purchase New Machine vs. Keep Existing Machine | | | | | | | | $148,536 |

## DCF Models: *Some Advanced Considerations*

Thus far we have considered the rather simple situation where the firm is evaluating independent projects, each on a "go/no-go" basis. In such situations, the NPV method and the IRR method normally lead to the same decision as to whether the project should be accepted or rejected. However, there are some pitfalls associated with the use of IRR for capital-budgeting purposes. We deal briefly with these pitfalls below. In addition, we look briefly at the capital-budgeting decision when the firm faces a capital (funds) constraint. Except for the capital-rationing situation, the primary conclusion of this appendix is that managers should be guided by project NPVs in making capital-budgeting decisions.

### THE POTENTIAL FOR MULTIPLE IRRs

In a normal investment project, there will be a large cash outflow in year 0 of the project, followed by a series of positive after-tax cash inflows during the life of the project. In this case there is only one "sign change" in the pattern of cash flows, and as such there will be only a single IRR.

Some projects, however, have a nonnormal pattern of cash flows. For example, new machinery might require a major overhaul (cash outflow) sometime during the life of the asset. A strip-mining company might incur end-of-project reclamation costs, for example, to restore to its original state the land that was mined. In both cases, there are two sign changes in the pattern of cash flows. In each of these two cases, there can be *up to* two IRRs associated with the project—one IRR for each sign change. If there are five sign changes, then there can be *up to* five IRRs. Thus, the basic rule to "accept a project if its IRR is greater than the firm's weighted-average cost of capital" breaks down. The solution to this problem is to base the decision on the NPV of the proposed investment: *If the NPV is greater than 0, accept the project.*[26]

Alternatively, the analyst may calculate a project's MIRR (rather than IRR). Each project has a single MIRR, regardless of the nature of its cash flows. Thus, we would accept a project if its MIRR were greater than the firm's WACC.

### MUTUALLY EXCLUSIVE PROJECTS

All of the examples in the body of the chapter involve "take-it or leave-it" decisions. That is, each investment project is considered independently of other investments. The basic decision therefore is whether to accept or reject the individual project being considered. However, in the real world, almost all capital-budgeting decisions involve a choice in which the selection of one alternative precludes the selection of one or more other alternatives. For example, your university may be considering whether to build a three-story or a four-story parking garage on campus—the university can invest in one but not both alternatives. The new lot could involve the use of electronic surveillance equipment or the use of security guards. These alternatives are said to be **mutually exclusive projects** in the sense that acceptance of one investment alternative precludes the acceptance of one or more other alternatives.

**Mutually exclusive projects** represent an extreme form of project interdependence: the acceptance of one investment alternative precludes the acceptance of one or more other alternatives.

In analyzing mutually exclusive projects on a DCF basis, should the analyst use NPV or IRR? Although there are situations where NPV and IRR both give the same result regarding which of two (or more) competing investments should be chosen, there are also situations where the two methods provide different signals to managers. For discussion purposes, consider the following two examples of mutually exclusive projects:

1. Each of two projects has roughly the same initial investment outlay but different useful lives; the project with the longer life also has more distant returns and a higher NPV but a lower IRR compared to the project with the shorter life.
2. Each of two projects has the same useful life but a different initial outlay.

---

[26] For an intuitive interpretation of multiple IRRs, see: David Johnstone, "What Does an IRR (or Two) Mean?" *Journal of Economic Education* (Winter 2008), pp. 78–87.

Given the project choices listed above, modern financial theory specifies that the decision maker should choose the project with the higher NPV.[27] In the case of the first example, it can be shown that the IRR method mistakenly favors the project with the quicker payback and higher IRR in spite of the fact that the alternative project has a higher NPV. In the case of the second example, it can be shown that the IRR decision rule can mistakenly favor smaller projects with high rates of return but lower NPVs. The arguments are developed more fully in a finance textbook, such as Brealey et al. (2012).

In general, the point here is that high economic rates of return (project IRRs) are not an end in and of themselves. The shareholders of a company benefit to the extent that managers choose projects that increase share value, and this increase is accomplished by choosing among investment alternatives on the basis of projected NPVs.

## CAPITAL RATIONING (CAPITAL CONSTRAINT)

**Capital rationing**
refers to the case where investment capital for a given accounting period is limited—hence the need for these funds to be "rationed."

We stated above that, in general, decision makers should use the NPV criterion for capital-budgeting purposes. This rule states that all projects with a positive NPV should be accepted. This rule, however, assumes that the organization has access to capital markets to raise, if need be, additional capital (presumably at its WACC). For many large companies, this assumption would seem to be reasonable. But many small companies, and some larger companies as well, have either self-imposed or externally imposed constraints on their ability to raise capital. This situation is referred to as **capital rationing**; in the context of a capital constraint, the overall goal of management is to allocate in an optimal manner the investment funds (capital) it has available.

The **profitability index (PI)**
of a project is a rate-of-return measure, defined as the ratio of the NPV of a project to the original investment outlay for the project.

In fact, the situation here is similar to the constrained optimization problem we considered in Chapter 11 when we addressed the issue of determining the optimal short-run product mix. Under capital rationing, the appropriate decision rule is: Allocate capital to investment projects on the basis of the NPV per dollar of the investment capital associated with each project. This relative measure of profitability is referred to as the **profitability index (PI)** and is calculated as follows:

$$PI = NPV \div \text{Initial investment (I)}$$

Under the situation of capital rationing, managers should allocate available capital (investment funds) to projects that provide the greatest NPV per dollar of investment. Consider the following two independent projects and an after-tax discount rate of 10% for the firm attempting to set an optimum capital budget for the period:

| Project | After-Tax Cash Flows (Undiscounted) | | | | NPV | PI = NPV ÷ I |
|---|---|---|---|---|---|---|
| | Period 0 | Period 1 | Period 2 | Period 3 | | |
| 1 | $(36.00) | $20.00 | $20.00 | $15.00 | $9.98 | 0.28 |
| 2 | (50.00) | 25.00 | 25.00 | 25.00 | 12.17 | 0.24 |

If there is no capital rationing, the firm would accept both projects since the NPV of each project, at 10%, is positive. Under capital rationing, Project 1 would be preferred over Project 2, since it has the higher ratio of NPV to investment (0.28) than Project 2 (0.24). In a sense, the underlying logic is one of getting the most bang for the buck. Remember, though, that the use of PI for ranking investment projects is appropriate only under conditions of capital rationing.

---

[27] In general, the existence of two mutually exclusive projects with different useful lives requires a so-called secondary analysis. That is, one cannot rely on raw, or unadjusted, NPV estimates alone. Rather, the decision maker uses either a replacement chain (or "common life") approach or an equivalent annual annuity (EAA) to determine which of the two alternatives is preferable in a present-value sense. In the former case, we replicate the two investments out to a common ending point, defined mathematically as the least (or smallest) common multiple. For any two integers, *a* and *b,* the least common multiple is the smallest positive integer that is a multiple of both *a* and *b.* Since it is a multiple, it can be divided by *a* and *b* without a remainder. For example, the least common multiple of 3 and 4 is 12. In the latter case, we calculate the annual payments each project would provide if it were an annuity. That is, we determine the stream of constant annuity cash flow (the *equivalent annual annuity*) that has the same present value as each project's calculated NPV. The project with the higher EAA will always have the higher NPV when extended out to any common life. Therefore, when comparing projects of unequal lives, we choose the one with the higher EAA.

# Appendix C

## Present Value Tables

**TABLE 1** Present Value of $1

| Periods | 4% | 5% | 6% | 7% | 8% | 9% | 10% | 11% | 12% | 13% | 14% | 15% | 20% | 25% | 30% |
|---|---|---|---|---|---|---|---|---|---|---|---|---|---|---|---|
| 1 | 0.962 | 0.952 | 0.943 | 0.935 | 0.926 | 0.917 | 0.909 | 0.901 | 0.893 | 0.885 | 0.877 | 0.870 | 0.833 | 0.800 | 0.769 |
| 2 | 0.925 | 0.907 | 0.890 | 0.873 | 0.857 | 0.842 | 0.826 | 0.812 | 0.797 | 0.783 | 0.769 | 0.756 | 0.694 | 0.640 | 0.592 |
| 3 | 0.889 | 0.884 | 0.840 | 0.816 | 0.794 | 0.772 | 0.751 | 0.731 | 0.712 | 0.693 | 0.675 | 0.658 | 0.579 | 0.512 | 0.455 |
| 4 | 0.855 | 0.823 | 0.792 | 0.763 | 0.735 | 0.708 | 0.683 | 0.659 | 0.636 | 0.613 | 0.592 | 0.572 | 0.482 | 0.410 | 0.350 |
| 5 | 0.822 | 0.784 | 0.747 | 0.713 | 0.681 | 0.650 | 0.621 | 0.593 | 0.567 | 0.543 | 0.519 | 0.497 | 0.402 | 0.328 | 0.269 |
| 6 | 0.790 | 0.746 | 0.705 | 0.666 | 0.630 | 0.596 | 0.564 | 0.535 | 0.507 | 0.480 | 0.456 | 0.432 | 0.335 | 0.262 | 0.207 |
| 7 | 0.760 | 0.711 | 0.665 | 0.623 | 0.583 | 0.547 | 0.513 | 0.482 | 0.452 | 0.425 | 0.400 | 0.376 | 0.279 | 0.210 | 0.159 |
| 8 | 0.731 | 0.677 | 0.627 | 0.582 | 0.540 | 0.502 | 0.467 | 0.434 | 0.404 | 0.376 | 0.351 | 0.327 | 0.233 | 0.168 | 0.123 |
| 9 | 0.703 | 0.645 | 0.592 | 0.544 | 0.500 | 0.460 | 0.424 | 0.391 | 0.361 | 0.333 | 0.308 | 0.284 | 0.194 | 0.134 | 0.094 |
| 10 | 0.676 | 0.614 | 0.558 | 0.508 | 0.463 | 0.422 | 0.386 | 0.352 | 0.322 | 0.295 | 0.270 | 0.247 | 0.162 | 0.107 | 0.073 |
| 11 | 0.650 | 0.585 | 0.527 | 0.475 | 0.429 | 0.388 | 0.350 | 0.317 | 0.287 | 0.261 | 0.237 | 0.215 | 0.135 | 0.086 | 0.056 |
| 12 | 0.625 | 0.557 | 0.497 | 0.444 | 0.397 | 0.356 | 0.319 | 0.286 | 0.257 | 0.231 | 0.208 | 0.187 | 0.112 | 0.069 | 0.043 |
| 13 | 0.601 | 0.530 | 0.469 | 0.415 | 0.368 | 0.326 | 0.290 | 0.258 | 0.229 | 0.204 | 0.182 | 0.163 | 0.093 | 0.055 | 0.033 |
| 14 | 0.577 | 0.505 | 0.442 | 0.388 | 0.340 | 0.299 | 0.263 | 0.232 | 0.205 | 0.181 | 0.160 | 0.141 | 0.078 | 0.044 | 0.025 |
| 15 | 0.555 | 0.481 | 0.417 | 0.362 | 0.315 | 0.275 | 0.239 | 0.209 | 0.183 | 0.160 | 0.140 | 0.123 | 0.065 | 0.035 | 0.020 |
| 16 | 0.534 | 0.458 | 0.394 | 0.339 | 0.292 | 0.252 | 0.218 | 0.188 | 0.163 | 0.141 | 0.123 | 0.107 | 0.054 | 0.028 | 0.015 |
| 17 | 0.513 | 0.436 | 0.371 | 0.317 | 0.270 | 0.231 | 0.198 | 0.170 | 0.146 | 0.125 | 0.108 | 0.093 | 0.045 | 0.023 | 0.012 |
| 18 | 0.494 | 0.416 | 0.350 | 0.296 | 0.250 | 0.212 | 0.180 | 0.153 | 0.130 | 0.111 | 0.095 | 0.081 | 0.038 | 0.018 | 0.009 |
| 19 | 0.475 | 0.396 | 0.331 | 0.277 | 0.232 | 0.194 | 0.164 | 0.138 | 0.116 | 0.098 | 0.083 | 0.070 | 0.031 | 0.014 | 0.007 |
| 20 | 0.456 | 0.377 | 0.312 | 0.258 | 0.215 | 0.178 | 0.149 | 0.124 | 0.104 | 0.087 | 0.073 | 0.061 | 0.026 | 0.012 | 0.005 |
| 22 | 0.422 | 0.342 | 0.278 | 0.226 | 0.184 | 0.150 | 0.123 | 0.101 | 0.083 | 0.068 | 0.056 | 0.046 | 0.018 | 0.007 | 0.003 |
| 24 | 0.390 | 0.310 | 0.247 | 0.197 | 0.158 | 0.126 | 0.102 | 0.082 | 0.066 | 0.053 | 0.043 | 0.035 | 0.013 | 0.005 | 0.002 |
| 25 | 0.375 | 0.295 | 0.233 | 0.184 | 0.146 | 0.116 | 0.092 | 0.074 | 0.059 | 0.047 | 0.038 | 0.030 | 0.010 | 0.004 | 0.001 |
| 30 | 0.308 | 0.231 | 0.174 | 0.131 | 0.099 | 0.075 | 0.057 | 0.044 | 0.033 | 0.026 | 0.020 | 0.015 | 0.004 | 0.001 | 0.000 |
| 35 | 0.253 | 0.181 | 0.130 | 0.094 | 0.068 | 0.049 | 0.036 | 0.026 | 0.019 | 0.014 | 0.010 | 0.008 | 0.002 | 0.000 | 0.000 |
| 40 | 0.208 | 0.142 | 0.097 | 0.067 | 0.046 | 0.032 | 0.022 | 0.015 | 0.011 | 0.008 | 0.005 | 0.004 | 0.001 | 0.000 | 0.000 |

Note: The present value (PV) factor for N periods and rate r per period = $1 \div (1 + r)^N$. For example, the PV factor for 10%, 5 years = $1 \div (1 + 0.10)^5 = 0.621$ (rounded).

**TABLE 2  Present Value of Annuity of $1**

| Periods | 4% | 5% | 6% | 7% | 8% | 9% | 10% | 11% | 12% | 13% | 14% | 15% | 20% | 25% | 30% |
|---|---|---|---|---|---|---|---|---|---|---|---|---|---|---|---|
| 1 | 0.962 | 0.952 | 0.943 | 0.935 | 0.926 | 0.917 | 0.909 | 0.901 | 0.893 | 0.885 | 0.877 | 0.870 | 0.833 | 0.800 | 0.769 |
| 2 | 1.886 | 1.859 | 1.833 | 1.808 | 1.783 | 1.759 | 1.736 | 1.713 | 1.690 | 1.668 | 1.647 | 1.626 | 1.528 | 1.440 | 1.361 |
| 3 | 2.775 | 2.723 | 2.673 | 2.624 | 2.577 | 2.531 | 2.487 | 2.444 | 2.402 | 2.361 | 2.322 | 2.283 | 2.106 | 1.952 | 1.816 |
| 4 | 3.630 | 3.546 | 3.465 | 3.387 | 3.312 | 3.240 | 3.170 | 3.102 | 3.037 | 2.974 | 2.914 | 2.855 | 2.589 | 2.362 | 2.166 |
| 5 | 4.452 | 4.329 | 4.212 | 4.100 | 3.993 | 3.890 | 3.791 | 3.696 | 3.605 | 3.517 | 3.433 | 3.352 | 2.991 | 2.689 | 2.436 |
| 6 | 5.242 | 5.076 | 4.917 | 4.767 | 4.623 | 4.486 | 4.355 | 4.231 | 4.111 | 3.998 | 3.889 | 3.784 | 3.326 | 2.951 | 2.643 |
| 7 | 6.002 | 5.786 | 5.582 | 5.389 | 5.206 | 5.033 | 4.868 | 4.712 | 4.564 | 4.423 | 4.288 | 4.160 | 3.605 | 3.161 | 2.80 |
| 8 | 6.733 | 6.463 | 6.210 | 5.971 | 5.747 | 5.535 | 5.335 | 5.146 | 4.968 | 4.799 | 4.639 | 4.487 | 3.837 | 3.329 | 2.925 |
| 9 | 7.435 | 7.108 | 6.802 | 6.515 | 6.247 | 5.995 | 5.759 | 5.537 | 5.328 | 5.132 | 4.946 | 4.772 | 4.031 | 3.463 | 3.019 |
| 10 | 8.111 | 7.722 | 7.360 | 7.024 | 6.710 | 6.418 | 6.145 | 5.889 | 5.650 | 5.426 | 5.216 | 5.019 | 4.192 | 3.571 | 3.092 |
| 11 | 8.760 | 8.306 | 7.887 | 7.499 | 7.139 | 6.805 | 6.495 | 6.207 | 5.938 | 5.687 | 5.453 | 5.234 | 4.327 | 3.656 | 3.147 |
| 12 | 9.385 | 8.863 | 8.384 | 7.943 | 7.536 | 7.161 | 6.814 | 6.492 | 6.194 | 5.918 | 5.660 | 5.421 | 4.439 | 3.725 | 3.190 |
| 13 | 9.986 | 9.394 | 8.853 | 8.358 | 7.904 | 7.487 | 7.103 | 6.750 | 6.424 | 6.122 | 5.842 | 5.583 | 4.533 | 3.780 | 3.223 |
| 14 | 10.563 | 9.899 | 9.295 | 8.745 | 8.244 | 7.786 | 7.367 | 6.982 | 6.628 | 6.302 | 6.002 | 5.724 | 4.611 | 3.824 | 3.249 |
| 15 | 11.118 | 10.380 | 9.712 | 9.108 | 8.559 | 8.061 | 7.606 | 7.191 | 6.811 | 6.462 | 6.142 | 5.847 | 4.675 | 3.859 | 3.268 |
| 16 | 11.652 | 10.838 | 10.106 | 9.447 | 8.851 | 8.313 | 7.824 | 7.379 | 6.974 | 6.604 | 6.265 | 5.954 | 4.730 | 3.887 | 3.283 |
| 17 | 12.166 | 11.274 | 10.477 | 9.763 | 9.122 | 8.544 | 8.022 | 7.549 | 7.120 | 6.729 | 6.373 | 6.047 | 4.775 | 3.910 | 3.295 |
| 18 | 12.659 | 11.690 | 10.828 | 10.059 | 9.372 | 8.756 | 8.201 | 7.702 | 7.250 | 6.840 | 6.467 | 6.128 | 4.812 | 3.928 | 3.304 |
| 19 | 13.134 | 12.085 | 11.158 | 10.336 | 9.604 | 8.950 | 8.365 | 7.839 | 7.366 | 6.938 | 6.550 | 6.198 | 4.843 | 3.942 | 3.311 |
| 20 | 13.590 | 12.462 | 11.470 | 10.594 | 9.818 | 9.129 | 8.514 | 7.963 | 7.469 | 7.025 | 6.623 | 6.259 | 4.870 | 3.954 | 3.316 |
| 22 | 14.451 | 13.163 | 12.042 | 11.061 | 10.201 | 9.442 | 8.772 | 8.176 | 7.645 | 7.170 | 6.743 | 6.359 | 4.909 | 3.970 | 3.323 |
| 24 | 15.247 | 13.799 | 12.550 | 11.469 | 10.529 | 9.707 | 8.985 | 8.348 | 7.784 | 7.283 | 6.835 | 6.434 | 4.937 | 3.981 | 3.327 |
| 25 | 15.622 | 14.094 | 12.783 | 11.654 | 10.675 | 9.823 | 9.077 | 8.422 | 7.843 | 7.330 | 6.873 | 6.464 | 4.948 | 3.985 | 3.329 |
| 30 | 17.292 | 15.372 | 13.765 | 12.409 | 11.258 | 10.274 | 9.427 | 8.694 | 8.055 | 7.496 | 7.003 | 6.566 | 4.979 | 3.995 | 3.332 |
| 35 | 18.665 | 16.374 | 14.498 | 12.948 | 11.655 | 10.567 | 9.644 | 8.855 | 8.176 | 7.586 | 7.070 | 6.617 | 4.992 | 3.998 | 3.333 |
| 40 | 19.793 | 17.159 | 15.046 | 13.332 | 11.925 | 10.757 | 9.779 | 8.951 | 8.244 | 7.634 | 7.105 | 6.642 | 4.997 | 3.999 | 3.333 |

Note: The present value (PV) annuity factor for N periods and a rate of r per period = $(1 - (1 + r)^{-N}) \div r$. For example, for N = 5 and r = 0.10, the PV annuity factor = 3.791 (rounded).

## Key Terms

accounting (book) rate of return (ARR), *486*

analytic hierarchy process (AHP), *457*

average-risk projects, *469*

beta coefficient (β), *470*

breakeven after-tax cash flow, *477*

capital asset pricing model (CAPM), *470*

capital budget, *456*

capital budgeting, *455*

capital investment, *455*

capital rationing, *496*

capital structure, *470*

discounted cash flow (DCF) models, *468*

discount rate, *469*

economic value added (EVA®), *490*

hurdle rate, *469*

internal rate of return (IRR), *473*

market risk premium, *470*

modified internal rate of return (MIRR), *474*

Monte Carlo simulation, *479*

multicriteria decision model, *457*

mutually exclusive projects, *495*

net present value (NPV), *471*

net working capital, *461*

non-DCF models, *468*

payback period, *484*

post-audit, *458*

present value (PV), *471*

present value payback period, *485*

profitability index (PI), *496*

real assets, *480*

real options, *480*

scenario analysis, *479*

sensitivity analysis, *477*

strategic control system, *456*

weighted-average cost of capital (WACC), *470*

yield-to-maturity, *470*

## Comments on Cost Management in Action

Many benefits of advanced manufacturing technology are difficult to quantify in dollar amounts or even in numbers. To make matters worse, these benefits, more often than not, are long-term in nature, and the firm will see no immediate tangible results. A large confectionery firm rejected an automated storage and distribution facility because it did not include the benefits that better customer services would bring. Better customer services often lead to higher sales volume and market share and, eventually, higher profits. Realizing these difficulties, middle managers of a kitchen unit manufacturer, with an established reputation for innovative design, forced an investment in computer-assisted design equipment by exaggerating financial benefits—a practice that should be discouraged and disallowed!

Appraisals of investments in advanced manufacturing technology need to be evaluated in terms of quantitative analysis and strategic consideration. Advanced manufacturing technology can expand the firm's product portfolio, enhance corporate image, and increase manufacturing flexibility, in addition to potentially decreasing production time and costs. Firms need to assess both the quantifiable short-term incremental cash inflows and the long-run strategic benefits in judging an investment's merits. In addition to cash flow analysis, an investment proposal can go a long way if it also includes the investment's strategic benefits. A firm manufacturing high-pressure casings decided to convert its manufacturing operations to cell manufacturing. The firm enjoyed such unplanned benefits as a 50% reduction in inventory, a 75% improvement in quality, substantial reduction in lead times, and flexible machining with overall labor reduction. An electrical switch gear products manufacturer with sales of $32 million and a total staff of 550 invested in CAD to increase its design capacity in anticipation of a 25% growth. The firm's original expectations included reduced lead time in the drawing office and reduced number of employees and WIP inventory. The additional benefits offered more accurate and timely transfer of data that greatly improved the firm's competitive edge and propelled the firm into a new marketing position.

Based on Michael Bromwich and Al Bhimani, "Strategic Investment Appraisal," *Management Accounting,* March 1991, pp. 45–48. See also M. J. Liberatore, T. F. Monahan, and D. E. Stout, "Strategic Capital Budgeting Analysis for Investments in Advanced Manufacturing Technology," *Journal of Financial and Strategic Decisions,* Summer 1993, pp. 55–72; and M. J. Liberatore, T. F. Monahan, and D. E. Stout, "A Framework for Integrating Capital Budgeting Analysis with Strategy," *The Engineering Economist,* Fall 1992, pp. 31–43.

## Self-Study Problem

(For solution, please turn to the end of the chapter.)

### Capital Budgeting for Expanding Productive Capacity

Ray Summers Company operates at full capacity of 10,000 units per year. The company, however, is still unable to fully meet the demand for its product, estimated at 15,000 units annually. This level of demand is expected to continue for at least another four years.

To meet the demand, the firm is considering the purchase of new equipment for $580,000. This equipment has an estimated useful life of four years; estimated sales (disposal) value of this asset at the end of four years is $50,000 (pretax). The engineering division estimates that installing, testing, and training for the use of the equipment will cost $12,000. These costs are to be capitalized as part of the cost of the new equipment.

An adjacent vacant warehouse can be leased for the duration of the project for $10,000 per year, which cost would be included as part of fixed manufacturing overhead. The warehouse needs $58,000 of renovations to make it suitable for manufacturing. The renovation cost is to be capitalized as part of the cost of the new equipment. The lease terms call for restoring the warehouse to its original condition at the end of the lease. The restoration is estimated to cost $20,000, a cost that is fully deductible for tax purposes. Current pretax operating profit per unit is as follows:

|  |  |  | Per Unit |
|---|---|---|---|
| Sales price |  |  | $200 |
| Variable costs |  |  |  |
|   Manufacturing | $60 |  |  |
|   Marketing | 20 | $80 |  |
| Fixed costs |  |  |  |
|   Manufacturing | $25 |  |  |
|   Marketing and administrative | 15 | 40 | 120 |
| Operating profit before tax |  |  | $ 80 |

The new equipment would have no effect on the variable costs per unit. All current fixed costs are expected to continue with the same total amount. The per-unit fixed cost includes depreciation expenses of $5 for manufacturing and $4 for marketing and administration.

Additional fixed manufacturing costs of $140,000 (excluding depreciation on the new equipment) will be incurred each year if the equipment is purchased. The company must also hire an additional marketing manager to serve new customers. The annual cost for the new marketing manager, support staff, and office expense is estimated at approximately $100,000. The company expects to be in the 40% tax bracket for each of the next four years. The company requires a minimum after-tax rate of return of 12% on investments and for tax purposes uses straight-line depreciation with a $50,000 salvage value assumed.

**Required**

1. What is the required net initial investment outlay (year 0)?

2. What effect will the acquisition of the new equipment have on total operating profit after-tax in each of the coming four years? (Assume in each year that sales equals production.)

3. What effect will the acquisition of the new equipment have on after-tax cash inflows in each of the four years?

4. Compute the payback period of the proposed investment under the assumption that cash inflows occur evenly throughout the year.

5. Compute the book (accounting) rate of return (ARR) of the proposed investment, based on the average book value of the investment.

6. Compute the net present value (NPV) of the proposed investment under the assumption that all cash inflows occur at year-end.

7. Compute the discounted payback period of the proposed investment under the assumption that cash inflows occur evenly throughout the year.

8. Compute the internal rate of return (IRR) of the proposed investment under the assumption that all cash inflows occur at year-end.

9. Use the MIRR function in Excel to estimate the modified internal rate of return for the proposed investment.

10. Assume now that the company expects the variable manufacturing cost per unit to increase once the new equipment is in place. What is the most that the unit variable manufacturing cost can increase and still allow the company to earn the minimum rate of return on this investment? (*Hint:* Use the Goal Seek option in Excel.)

*Please visit **http://www.mhhe.com/blocher6e** to access a narrated, animated tutorial for solving this problem.*

Questions    12-1   What are the distinguishing characteristics of capital-budgeting decisions?

12-2   In what ways can accountants add value to the capital-budgeting process?

12-3   What is the analytic hierarchy process (AHP) and how can it be used in making capital-budgeting decisions?

12-4    In capital-budgeting analysis, what is meant by the *income-tax effect*? Give three examples of the tax effect pertaining to the acquisition of new factory (manufacturing) equipment.

12-5    What are the limitations of the payback period method for making capital-budgeting decisions (e.g., whether to accept or reject a proposed investment)? Does the present value payback period overcome these limitations?

12-6    Does the book (accounting) rate of return (ARR) method provide a true measure of the return on investment? How about the investment's internal rate of return (IRR)?

12-7    What should be the decision criterion when using the NPV method to evaluate capital investments? Does the IRR method use the same criterion?

12-8    List at least three important behavioral issues related to the capital-budgeting process.

12-9    "The net present value (NPV) method weighs early receipts of cash much more heavily than more distant receipts of cash." Do you agree? Why?

12-10   "Depreciation expenses have no effect on cash flows and, therefore, are not relevant in capital-expenditure analysis." Do you agree? Why or why not?

12-11   Should the firm accept the independent projects described below? Why or why not?

   a.  The firm's cost of capital is 10% and the estimated internal rate of return (IRR) of the project is 11%.

   b.  A capital investment requires a $150,000 initial investment. The firm's cost of capital is 10%, and the present value of the expected cash inflows from the project is $148,000.

12-12   Provide an intuitive explanation of the modified internal rate of return (MIRR) financial performance metric. How does MIRR differ from IRR?

12-13   (Appendix B): What decision criterion should be used to choose investment projects for a firm with unlimited funds available at a weighted-average cost of 10% (after tax)? Can the firm use the same decision criterion if it has only a limited amount of available funds, say $100 million? Explain.

12-14   (Appendix B): When analyzing a proposed capital investment, what conditions or factors may lead the results to differ between the net present value (NPV) and internal rate of return (IRR) decision models?

12-15   (Appendix B): How does the size of the initial investment affect the indicated internal rate of return (IRR) and net present value (NPV) of a proposed investment?

**Brief Exercises**

12-16   For a firm facing a marginal income-tax rate of 34%, what is the after-tax cash flow effect of: (a) a $1,000 increase in contribution margin during the year, and (b) a $500 increase in cash operating expenses?

12-17   What is the present value of $1,000 to be received two years from now, if the discount rate is: (a) 10%, (b) 14%, and (c) 20%? Use both the appropriate table in the text (Appendix C, Table 1) and the appropriate function in Excel to answer these questions.

12-18   What is the present value of a stream of 5 end-of-year annual cash receipts of $500 given a discount rate of 14%? Use both the appropriate table in the text (Appendix C, Table 2) and the appropriate function in Excel to answer this question.

12-19   Use the appropriate function in Excel to calculate the annual straight-line (SL) depreciation charge for an asset that has a $10,000 acquisition cost, a salvage value of $500, and a useful life of four years.

12-20   You are given the following information: sales, $260; expenses other than depreciation, $140; depreciation, $50; marginal income-tax rate, 35%. Calculate the net after-tax cash flow effect of the preceding information. (*Hint:* You can use either a direct or an indirect approach to arrive at the answer.)

12-21   Refer to Exhibit 12.4 in the text. What is the depreciation expense deduction in each of four years for a $10,000 asset classified under MACRS as three-year property?

12-22   A company purchases an asset that costs $10,000. This asset qualifies as three-year property under MACRS. The company uses an after-tax discount rate of 12% and faces a 40% income-tax rate. Use the appropriate present value factors found in Appendix C, Table 1, to determine the present value of the depreciation deductions for this firm over the specified four-year period.

12-23   Create an Excel spreadsheet for Exercise 12-22 and demonstrate that the PV of the depreciation deductions, when the income-tax rate is 40%, is $3,218. Given an after-tax discount rate of

12%, what tax rate would be needed in order for the PV of the depreciation deductions to equal $4,000? Use the Goal Seek function of Excel.

12-24 Given an asset with a net book value (NBV) of $25,000, what are the after-tax proceeds for a firm in the 34% tax bracket if this asset is sold for $35,000 cash? What are the after-tax proceeds for this same firm if the asset is sold for $15,000 cash? (Show calculations.)

12-25 Given the following attributes of an investment project with a five-year life, and an after-tax discount rate of 12%, calculate the net present value (NPV) and the payback period of the project: investment outlay, year 0, $5,000; after-tax cash inflows, year 1, $800; year 2, $900; year 3, $1,500; year 4, $1,800; and year 5, $3,200. (Use the built-in function of Excel to estimate the NPV of this project.)

12-26 Use the data in Exercise 12-25 and the appropriate function in Excel to estimate both the IRR and the MIRR of the proposed investment. What accounts for the difference in these two measures?

12-27 MicroTech Corporation is subject to a 35% income-tax rate. Given the following information about the firm's capital structure, calculate the corporation's weighted-average cost of capital (WACC):

| Source of Funds | Market Value | Required Rate of Return |
| --- | --- | --- |
| Long-term debt | $40 million | 7.0% |
| Preferred stock | 20 million | 9.0 |
| Common stock | 60 million | 12.0 |

## Exercises

[LO 12-3]   12-28   **Identifying Relevant Cash Flows; Asset-Purchase Decision**   This exercise parallels the machine-purchase decision for the Mendoza Company that is discussed in the body of the chapter. Assume that Mendoza is exploring whether to enter a complementary line of business. The existing business line generates annual cash revenues of approximately $5,000,000 and cash expenses of $3,600,000, one-third of which are labor costs. The current level of investment in this existing division is $12,000,000. (Sales and costs of this division are not affected by the investment decision regarding the complementary line.)

Mendoza estimates that incremental (noncash) net working capital of $30,000 will be needed to support the new business line. No additional facilities-level costs would be needed to support the new line—there is currently sufficient excess capacity. However, the new line would require additional cash expenses (overhead costs) of $400,000 per year. Raw materials costs associated with the new line are expected to be $1,200,000 per year, while the total labor cost is expected to double.

The CFO of the company estimates that new machinery costing $2,500,000 would need to be purchased. This machinery has a seven-year useful life and an estimated salvage (terminal) value of $400,000. For tax purposes, assume that the Mendoza Company would use the straight-line method (with estimated salvage value considered in the calculation).

Assume, further, that the weighted-average cost of capital (WACC) for Mendoza is 14% (after-tax) and that the combined (federal and state) income-tax rate is 40%. Finally, assume that the new business line is expected to generate annual cash revenue of $3,600,000.

**Required**   Determine relevant cash flows (after-tax) at each of the following three points: (1) project initiation, (2) project operation, and (3) project disposal (termination). For purposes of this last calculation, you can assume that the asset is sold at the end of its useful life for the salvage value used to establish the annual straight-line depreciation deductions; further, you can assume that at the end of the project's life Mendoza will fully recover its initial investment in net working capital. Also, separately identify any irrelevant cost and revenue data associated with this decision.

[LO 12-3, 12-8]   12-29   **Identifying Relevant Cash Flows; Asset-Replacement Decision**   Assume that it is January 1, 2013, and that the Mendoza Company is considering the replacement of a machine that has been used for the past three years in a special project for the company. This project is expected to continue for an additional five years (i.e., until the end of 2017). Mendoza will either keep the existing machine for another five years (eight years total), or replace the existing machine now with a new model that has a five-year estimated life. Pertinent facts regarding this decision are as follows:

| | Keep Existing Machine | Purchase New Machine |
|---|---|---|
| Purchase price of machine (including transportation, setup charges, etc.) | $150,000 | $190,000 |
| Useful life (determined at time of acquisition) | 8 years | 5 years |
| Estimated salvage value, end of 2017* | $ 20,000 | $ 25,000 |
| Expected cash operating costs, per year: | | |
| Variable (per unit produced/sold) | $ 0.25 | $ 0.19 |
| Fixed costs (total) | $ 25,000 | $ 24,000 |
| Estimated salvage (terminal) values: | | |
| January 1, 2013 | $ 68,000 | |
| December 31, 2017 | $ 12,000 | $ 22,000 |
| Net working capital committed at time of acquisition of existing machine (all fully recovered at end of project, December 31, 2017) | $ 30,000 | |
| Incremental net working capital required if new machine is purchased on January 1, 2013 (all fully recovered at end of project, December 31, 2017) | | $ 10,000 |
| Expected annual volume of output/sales (in units), over the period 2013–2017 | 500,000 | 500,000 |

*Note: These amounts are used for depreciation calculations.

Assume further that Mendoza is subject to a 40% income-tax, both for ordinary income and gains/losses associated with disposal of machinery, and that all cash flows occur at the end of the year, except for the initial investment. Assume that straight-line depreciation is used for tax purposes and that any tax associated with the disposal of machinery occurs at the same time of the related transaction.

**Required**  Determine relevant cash flows (after-tax) at each of the following three points: (1) time of purchase of the new machine (i.e., time period 0, January 1, 2013), (2) project operation (i.e., each of five years), and (3) project disposal (termination) (i.e., December 31, 2017). Separately identify any irrelevant cost and revenue data associated with this decision. Finally, determine the undiscounted net cash flow and determine whether the old machine should be replaced.

**(CMA Adapted)**

[LO 12-4, 12-5]  12-30  **Future and Present Values; Spreadsheet Application**

a. It is said (S. Branch Walker) that the Indian who sold Manhattan for $24 was a sharp sales-man. If he had put his $24 away at 6% compounded semiannually, it would now be worth over $9 billion, and he could buy most of the now-improved land back! Assume that this seller invested on January 1, 1701, the $24 he received.

**Required**

1. Use Excel to determine the balance (in billions) of the investment as of December 31, 2012, assuming a 6% interest rate compounded semiannually. (*Hint:* Use the FV function in Excel.)

2. Carry out the same calculation using an 8% annual interest rate, compounded semiannually.

3. What would be the balances for requirements 1 and 2 if interest is compounded quarterly?

4. Assume that the account consisting of this investment had a balance of $9.5 billion as of December 31, 2012. How much would the total amount be on December 31, 2018, if the annual interest rate is 8%, compounded semiannually?

b. In 2000, a star major-league baseball player signed a 10-year, $252 million dollar contract with the Texas Rangers. Assume that equal payments would have been made each year to this individual and that the owner's cost of capital (discount rate) was 12% at the time the contract was signed. What is the present value cost of the contract to the owners as of January 1, 2000, the date the contract was signed, in each of the following independent situations?

**Required**

1. The baseball player received the first payment on December 31, 2000.
2. The baseball player received the first payment on January 1, 2000, the date the contract was signed.
3. Assuming the owner is in the 45% income-tax bracket, calculate your answer for requirement 1.

[LO 12-4]    12-31    **Cash Receipts Frequency and Present-Value Consequences**    Assume that you are about to sell property (a vacant parcel of real estate) you own but otherwise have no use for. The net-of-sales-commission selling price for the property is $500,000. You are willing to finance this transaction over a 20-year period and have told the buyer that you expect a 12% pretax return on the transaction. The buyer has asked you for a payment schedule under several alternatives.

**Required**

1. What will be your periodic cash receipt, to earn a 12% return, if payments are received from the purchaser:
   a. At the end of each week?
   b. At the end of each month?
   c. At the end of each quarter?
   d. At the end of each year?
2. What general conclusion can you draw based on the calculations above in (1)?

[LO 12-3]    12-32    **Value of Accelerated Depreciation**    Freedom Corporation acquired a fixed asset for $100,000. Its estimated life at time of purchase was four years, with no estimated salvage value. Assume a discount rate of 8% and an income-tax rate of 40%.

**Required**

1. What is the present value of the tax benefits resulting from calculating depreciation using the sum-of-the-years'-digits method as opposed to the straight-line method on this asset?
2. What is the present value of the tax benefits resulting from calculating depreciation using the double-declining-balance method as opposed to straight-line method on this asset?
3. What is the present value of the tax benefits resulting from using MACRS as opposed to straight-line depreciation? The asset qualifies as a three-year asset. Use the half-year convention.

**(CPA Adapted)**

[LO 12-4]    12-33    **Weighted-Average Cost of Capital (WACC)**    You are given the following information regarding the capital structure of Micro Advantage, Inc.:
   a. Micro Advantage, Inc., issued a $5,000,000, 20-year bond a year ago at 98 with a stated rate of 9%. Today, the bond is selling at 110. If the firm's tax bracket is 30%, what is the current after-tax cost of this debt?
   b. Micro Advantage, Inc., has $5,000,000 preferred stock outstanding that it sold for $24 per share. The preferred stock has a per share par value of $25 and pays a $3 dividend per year. The current market price is $30 per share. The firm's tax bracket is 30%. What is the after-tax cost of the preferred stock?
   c. In addition to the bonds and preferred stocks described in (a) and (b) above, Micro Advantage has outstanding 50,000 shares of common stock that has a par value of $10 per share and a current market price of $170 per share. The expected after-tax market return on the firm's common equity is 20%.

**Required**    What is Micro Advantage's weighted-average cost of capital (WACC)?

[LO 12-3, 12-4]    12-34    **Determining Relevant Cash Flows; Basic Capital Budgeting**    Rockyford Company must replace some machinery that has zero book value and a current market value of $1,800. One possibility is to invest in new machinery costing $40,000. This new machinery would produce estimated annual pretax cash operating savings of $12,500. Assume the new machine will have a useful life of four years and depreciation of $10,000 each year for book and tax purposes. It will have no salvage value at the end of four years. The investment in this new machinery would require an additional $3,000 investment of net working capital. (Assume that when the old machine was purchased the incremental net working capital required at the time was $0.)

If Rockyford accepts this investment proposal, the disposal of the old machinery and the investment in the new one will occur on December 31 of this year. The cash flows from the investment will occur during the next four calendar years.

Rockyford is subject to a 40% income-tax rate for all ordinary income and capital gains and has a 10% weighted-average after-tax cost of capital. All operating and tax cash flows are assumed to occur at year-end.

**Required**  Determine:

1. The after-tax cash flow arising from disposing of the old machinery.

2. The present value of the after-tax cash flows for the next four years attributable to the cash operating savings.

3. The present value of the tax shield effect of depreciation for year 1.

4. Which one of the following is the proper treatment for the additional $3,000 of net working capital required in the current year?

   a. It should be ignored in capital budgeting because it is not a capital investment.

   b. It is a sunk cost that needs no consideration in capital budgeting.

   c. It should be treated as part of the initial investment when determining the net present value.

   d. It should be spread over the machinery's four-year life as a cash outflow in each of the years.

   e. It should be included as part of the cost of the new machine and depreciated.

**(CMA Adapted)**

[LO 12-4]  12-35  **After-Tax Net Present Value and IRR (non-MACRS rules)**  eEgg is considering the purchase of a new distributed network computer system to help handle its warehouse inventories. The system costs $60,000 to purchase and install and $30,000 to operate each year. The system is estimated to be useful for four years. Management expects the new system to reduce by $62,000 a year the cost of managing inventories. The firm's cost of capital is 10%.

**Required**

1. What is the net present value (NPV) of the proposed investment under each of the following independent situations?

   a. The firm is not yet profitable and pays no taxes.

   b. The firm is in the 30% income-tax bracket and uses straight-line depreciation with no salvage value. Assume MACRS rules do not apply.

   c. The firm is in the 30% income-tax bracket and uses double-declining-balance depreciation with no salvage value. Assume MACRS rules do *not* apply.

2. What is the internal rate of return (IRR) of the proposed investment for situations 1(a) and 1(b) above?

[LO 12-4]  12-36  **Using Arrays in Excel; NPV Analysis**  Please refer to footnote 12 and the data referenced in the footnote.

**Required**

1. Follow the directions given in footnote 12 to calculate the NPV of the referenced investment project. (*Hint:* If need be, consult the following: http://office.microsoft.com/en-us/starter-help/create-or-delete-a-formula-HP010342373.aspx?CTT=3#_Toc251333379.)

2. Repeat the procedure using a discount rate (WACC) of 10% and the following cash flows, time 0 through time 10: ($1,000), $100, $200, $300, $400, $500, $600, $700, $800, $900, $1,000. (*Hints:* The NPV should be $1,903.59; remember to use the Name Manager under the Formulas tab in Excel 2010.)

**[LO 12-4, 12-6]**　12-37　**Basic Capital-Budgeting Techniques**　Answer each independent question, (a) through (e), below.

    a. Project A costs $5,000 and will generate annual after-tax net cash inflows of $1,800 for five years. What is the payback period for this investment under the assumption that the cash inflows occur evenly throughout the year?

    b. Project B costs $5,000 and will generate after-tax cash inflows of $500 in year one, $1,200 in year two, $2,000 in year three, $2,500 in year four, and $2,000 in year five. What is the payback period (in years) for this investment assuming that the cash inflows occur evenly throughout the year?

    c. Project C costs $5,000 and will generate net cash inflows of $2,500 before taxes for five years. The firm uses straight-line depreciation with no salvage value and is subject to a 25% tax rate. What is the payback period?

    d. Project D costs $5,000 and will generate sales of $4,000 each year for five years. The cash expenditures will be $1,500 per year. The firm uses straight-line depreciation with an estimated salvage value of $500 and has a tax rate of 25%.

       (1) What is the book rate of return based on the original investment?

       (2) What is the book rate of return based on the average book value?

    e. What is the NPV for each of the projects (a) through (d) above? Assume that the firm requires a minimum after-tax return of 8% on all investments.

**[LO 12-4, 12-5, 12-6]**　12-38　**Straightforward Capital Budgeting with Taxes; Sensitivity Analysis**　Dorothy & George Company is planning to acquire a new machine at a total cost of $30,600. The machine's estimated life is six years and its estimated salvage value is $600. The company estimates that annual cash savings from using this machine will be $8,000. The company's after-tax cost of capital is 8% and its income-tax rate is 40%. The company uses straight-line depreciation (non-MACRS-based).

**Required**

1. What is this investment's net after-tax annual cash inflow?

2. Assume that the net after-tax annual cash inflow of this investment is $5,000; what is the payback period?

3. Assume that the net after-tax annual cash inflow of this investment is $5,000; what is the net present value (NPV) of this investment?

4. What are the minimum net after-tax annual cost savings that make the proposed investment acceptable (i.e., the dollar cost savings that would yield an NPV of $0)?

**(CPA Adapted)**

**[LO 12-4, 12-5, 12-6]**　12-39　**Capital Budgeting with Tax (non-MACRS Depreciation) and Sensitivity Analysis**　Gravina Company is planning to spend $6,000 for a machine that it will depreciate on a straight-line basis over 10 years with no salvage value. The machine will generate additional cash revenues of $1,200 a year. Gravina will incur no additional costs except for depreciation. Its income-tax rate is 35%.

**Required**

1. What is the payback period of the proposed investment under the assumption that the cash inflows occur evenly throughout the year?

2. What is the book rate of return (ARR) based on the initial investment outlay?

3. What is the maximum amount that Gravina Company should invest if it desires to earn an internal rate of return (IRR) of 15%?

4. What is the minimum annual (pretax) cash revenue required for the project to earn a 15% internal rate of return?

5. Prepare a single schedule to show the NPVs associated with a 10-year life under annual after-tax cash flows of $500, $1,000, and $2,000 *and* discount rates of 10%, 15%, and 20%.

**(CPA Adapted)**

**[LO 12-4, 12-5]**　12-40　**NPV; Sensitivity Analysis**　Griffey & Son operate a plant in Cincinnati and are considering opening a new facility in Seattle. The initial outlay will be $3,500,000 and should produce after-tax net cash inflows of $600,000 per year for 15 years. Due to the effects of the ocean air in Seattle, however, the plant's useful life may be only 12 years. Cost of capital is 14%.

**Required**

1. Based on an NPV analysis, should the project be accepted if a 15-year useful life is assumed? What if a 12-year useful life is used?

2. How many years will be needed for the Seattle facility to earn at least a 14% return?

**[LO 12-4, 12-5]**  **12-41** **Uneven Cash Flows; NPV; Sensitivity Analysis**  MaxiCare Corporation, a not-for-profit organization, specializes in health care for senior citizens. Management is considering whether to expand operations by opening a new chain of care centers in the inner city of large metropolises. For a new facility, initial cash outlays for lease, renovations, net working capital, training, and other costs are expected to be about $15 million in year 0. The corporation expects the cash inflows of each new facility in its first year of operation to equal the total cash outlays for the year. Net cash inflows are expected to increase to $1 million in each of years 2 and 3, $2.5 million in year 4, and $3 million in each of years 5 through 10. The lease agreement for the facility will expire at the end of year 10, and MaxiCare expects the cost to close a facility will pretty much exhaust all cash proceeds from the disposal. Cost of capital for MaxiCare is 12%.

**Required**  Compute the net present value (NPV) and the IRR for this venture. What is the breakeven selling price for this investment, that is, the price that would yield an NPV of $0? (Use the Goal Seek function in Excel to determine the breakeven selling price.)

**[LO 12-3, 12-8]**  **12-42** **Asset-Replacement Decision; NPV Analysis**  Assume a situation in which a company has an existing asset, A, that has a current net book value (original cost less accumulated depreciation to date) of $300,000. This asset has a useful life of three additional years. Its estimated disposal (sales) value both today and at the end of three years is zero. Asset B, which would replace A, could be purchased today for $600,000. If purchased, B would generate annual (cash) operating cost savings (pretax) of $280,000 for each year of its three-year useful life. In determining depreciation deductions for tax purposes, assume the straight-line method and zero salvage value for both assets. The company is subject to a combined (federal plus state) income-tax of 40%, both for operating income and gains/losses related to the sale of assets. Other than the initial outlay for asset B, assume that all cash flows (and related tax payments) occur at the end of the year. Assume a weighted-average cost of capital of 10%.

**Required**

1. Determine the relevant (i.e., *differential*) cash flows (after-tax) at each of the following three points related to this asset-replacement decision: (1) project initiation (time period 0), (2) project operation, and (3) project disposal (termination, time period 3).

2. Using the net present value (NPV) decision model, should the company replace asset A with asset B? (Show calculations.)

3. What is the weighted-average cost of capital (WACC) that would make the company indifferent between keeping or replacing asset A?

**[LO 12-3, 12-4]**  **12-43** **Cash Flow Analysis; NPV; Spreadsheet Analysis**  Lou Lewis, the president of the Lewisville Company, has asked you to give him an analysis of the best use of a warehouse the company owns.

a. Lewisville Company is currently leasing the warehouse to another company for $5,000 per month on a year-to-year basis. (*Hint:* Use the PV function in Excel to calculate the PV of this stream of monthly after-tax rental incomes.)

b. The warehouse's estimated sales value is $200,000. A commercial realtor believes that the price is likely to remain unchanged in the near future. The building originally cost $60,000 and is being depreciated at $1,500 annually. Its current net book value (NBV) is $7,500.

c. Lewisville Company is seriously considering converting the warehouse into a factory outlet for furniture. The remodeling will cost $100,000 and will be modest because the major attraction will be rock-bottom prices. The remodeling cost will be depreciated over the next five years using the double-declining-balance method. (Note: Use the VDB function in Excel to calculate depreciation charges.)

d. The inventory and receivables (net of current liabilities) needed to open and sustain the factory outlet would be $600,000. This total is fully recoverable whenever operations terminate.

e. Lou is fairly certain that the warehouse will be condemned in 10 years to make room for a new highway. The firm most likely would receive $200,000 from the condemnation.

f. Estimated annual operating data, exclusive of depreciation, are

| | |
|---|---|
| Sales (cash) | $900,000 |
| Operating expenses | $500,000 |

g. Nonrecurring sales promotion costs at the beginning of year 1 (i.e., time 0) are expected to be $100,000. (These costs are fully deductible for tax purposes.)

h. Nonrecurring termination costs at the end of year 5 are $50,000. (These costs are fully deductible for tax purposes.)

i. The after-tax discount rate for capital budgeting purposes is 14%. (To calculate the present value factor for each year, $i$, $i = 1, 5$, use the following formula: PV factor$_i$ = $(1 \div 1.14^i)$. The company is in the 40% tax bracket (federal and state combined).

### Required

1. Show how you would handle the individual items in determining whether the company should continue to lease the space or convert it to a factory outlet. Use the company's analysis form, which is set up as follows:

| | | | Cash Flows in Year | | | | | |
|---|---|---|---|---|---|---|---|---|
| Item | Description | Present Value | 0 | 1 | 2 | 3 | 4 | 5 |
| a. | | | | | | | | |
| b. | | | | | | | | |
| . | | | | | | | | |
| . | | | | | | | | |
| . | | | | | | | | |
| i. | | | | | | | | |
| Identify any item that is irrelevant. | | | | | | | | |

2. After analyzing all relevant data, compute the net present value (NPV). Indicate which course of action, based only on these data, should be taken.

[LO 12-4, 12-8]   12-44   **Machine Replacement with Tax Considerations; Spreadsheet Application**   A computer chip manufacturer spent $2,500,000 to develop a special-purpose molding machine. The machine has been used for one year, and will be obsolete after an additional three years. The company uses straight-line (SL) depreciation for this machine.

At the beginning of the second year, a machine salesperson offers a new, vastly more efficient machine. It will cost $2,000,000, will reduce annual cash manufacturing costs from $1,800,000 to $1,000,000, and will have zero disposal value at the end of three years. Management has decided to use the double-declining-balance depreciation method for tax purposes for this machine if purchased. (Note: Make sure to switch to SL depreciation in year 3 to ensure that the entire cost is written off. You may find it useful to use the VDB function in Excel to calculate depreciation charges.)

The old machine's salvage value is $300,000 now, and will be $50,000 three years from now; however, no salvage value is provided in calculating straight-line depreciation on the old machine for tax purposes. The firm's income-tax rate is 45%. The firm desires to earn a minimum after-tax rate of return of 8%.

**Required**   Using the net present value (NPV) technique, show whether the firm should purchase the new machine. (Note: Use the PV and NPV functions in Excel to calculate all present value amounts.)

[LO 12-4, 12-8]   12-45   **Equipment Replacement; MACRS**   VacuTech is a high-technology company that manufactures sophisticated instruments for testing microcircuits. Each instrument sells for $3,500; variable manufacturing cost per unit (all cash) equals $2,450. An essential component of the company's manufacturing process is a sealed vacuum chamber where the interior approaches a pure vacuum. The technology of the vacuum pumps that the firm uses to prepare its chamber for sealing has been changing rapidly. On June 1, 2012, VacuTech bought the latest in electronic high-speed vacuum pumps that can evacuate in only six hours a chamber for sealing. The company paid $400,000 for the pump. Recently, the pump's manufacturer approached VacuTech with a new pump that would reduce the evacuation time to two hours.

VacuTech's management is considering the purchase of this new pump and has asked Doreen Harris, the company controller, to evaluate the financial impact of replacing it with the new model. Doreen has gathered the following information prior to preparing her analysis:

- The new pump could be installed and placed in service on January 1, 2016. The pump's cost is $608,000; installing, testing, and debugging it will cost $12,000 (which should be capitalized). The pump would be assigned to the three-year class for depreciation under the Modified Accelerated Cost Recovery System (MACRS) and is expected to have an $80,000 salvage value when it is sold at the end of four years. Depreciation on the equipment would be recognized starting in 2016, and MACRS rates (rounded) would be as follows:

| Year 1 | 33% |
|---|---|
| Year 2 | 45 |
| Year 3 | 15 |
| Year 4 | 7 |

- The current pump is being depreciated under MACRS and will be fully depreciated by the time the new pump is placed in service. If the firm purchases the new pump, it will sell the current pump for $50,000.
- At the current rate of production, the new pump's greater efficiency will result in annual pretax cash savings of $125,000.
- VacuTech is able to sell all testing instruments that it can produce. Because of the new pump's increased speed, output is expected to increase by 30 units in 2016, 50 units in both 2017 and 2018, and 70 units in 2019. Cash-based manufacturing costs for all additional units would be reduced by $150 per unit (in addition to the $125,000 savings noted above).
- VacuTech is subject to a 40% income-tax rate. For evaluating capital-investment proposals, *management assumes that annual cash flows occur at the end of the year* and uses a 15% after-tax discount rate.

**Required**
1. Determine whether VacuTech should purchase the new pump by calculating the net present value (NPV) at January 1, 2016, of the estimated after-tax cash flows that would result from its acquisition. (Use the built-in NPV function in Excel to estimate the NPV of the proposed investment.)
2. Describe the factors, other than the net present value, that VacuTech should consider before making the pump replacement decision.

**(CMA Adapted)**

[LO 12-4, 12-5] 12-46 **Risk and NPV; Sensitivity Analysis** J. Morgan of SparkPlug Inc. has been approached to take over a production facility from B.R. Machine Company. The acquisition will cost $1,500,000, and the after-tax net cash inflow will be $275,000 per year for 12 years.

SparkPlug currently uses 12% for its after-tax cost of capital. Tom Morgan, production manager, is very much in favor of the investment. He argues that the total after-tax net cash inflow is more than the cost of the investment, even if the demand for the product is somewhat uncertain. "The project will pay for itself even if the demand is only half the projected level." Cindy Morgan (corporate controller) believes that the cost of capital should be 15% because of the declining demand for SparkPlug products.

**Required**
1. Should Morgan accept the project if its after-tax cost of capital is 12%?
2. If Cindy Morgan is correct and uses 15%, does that change the investment decision?
3. Use the built-in function in Excel to estimate the project's IRR. Use the *Goal Seek* function in Excel to calculate the maximum amount that can be invested upfront in order to generate an economic rate of return equal to the 15% rate of return specified by management as appropriate for the proposed investment.
4. Is adjusting the discount rate or the desired rate of return an effective way to deal with risk or uncertainty?

## Problems

**[LO 12-4, 12-6]**   **12-47**  **Basic Capital-Budgeting Techniques; No Taxes, Uniform Net Cash Inflows; Spreadsheets**   Irv Nelson, Inc., purchased a $500,000 machine to manufacture specialty taps for electrical equipment. Nelson expects to sell all it can manufacture in the next 10 years. To encourage capital investments, the government has exempted taxes on profits from new investments. This legislation is to be in effect in the foreseeable future. The machine is expected to have a 10-year useful life with no salvage value. Nelson uses straight-line depreciation. The net cash inflow is expected to be $120,000 each year for 10 years. Nelson uses a 12% discount rate in evaluating capital investments. Assume, for simplicity, that MACRS depreciation rules do not apply.

**Required**   Using Excel, compute for the proposed capital investment the:
1. Payback period under the assumption that cash inflows occur evenly throughout the year.
2. Book rate of return based on (a) initial investment and (b) average investment.
3. Net present value (NPV) of the proposed investment under the assumption that cash inflows occur at year-end.
4. Present value payback period of the proposed investment under the assumption that cash inflows occur evenly throughout the year.
5. Internal rate of return (IRR).
6. Modified internal rate of return (MIRR).

**[LO 12-4, 12-6]**   **12-48**  **Basic Capital-Budgeting Techniques; Uneven Net Cash Inflows with Taxes; Spreadsheet Application**   Use the same information for this problem as you did for Problem 12-47, except that the investment is subject to taxes and the pretax operating cash inflows are as follows:

| Year | Pretax Cash Inflow | Year | Pretax Cash Inflow |
|------|--------------------|------|--------------------|
| 1 | $ 50,000 | 6 | $300,000 |
| 2 | 80,000 | 7 | 270,000 |
| 3 | 120,000 | 8 | 240,000 |
| 4 | 200,000 | 9 | 120,000 |
| 5 | 240,000 | 10 | 40,000 |

Irv Nelson has been paying 30% for combined federal, state, and local income taxes, a rate that is not expected to change during the period of this investment. The firm uses straight-line depreciation. Assume, for simplicity, that MACRS depreciation rules do not apply.

**Required**   Using Excel, compute for the proposed investment the:
1. Payback period for the proposed investment under the assumption that the cash inflows occur evenly throughout the year.
2. Book rate of return based on (a) initial investment and (b) average investment.
3. Net present value (NPV).
4. Present value payback period of the proposed investment under the assumption that the cash inflows occur evenly throughout the year.
5. Internal rate of return (IRR).
6. Modified internal rate of return (MIRR).

**[LO 12-4, 12-6]**   **12-49**  **Basic Capital-Budgeting Techniques; Uneven Net Cash Inflows; MACRS**   Use the data in Problem 12-48 for Irv Nelson, Inc., and MACRS. The asset qualifies as a 5-year property.

**Required**   Compute for the investment its:
1. Payback period under the assumption that the cash inflows occur evenly throughout the year.
2. Book rate of return based on: (a) the initial investment, and (b) an average investment (calculated as a simple average of the 10 average annual book values).
3. Net present value (NPV).
4. Internal rate of return (IRR).
5. Modified internal rate of return (MIRR).

12-50  **Real Options—Basic Concepts**  This problem pertains to the XYZ Company example in the body of the chapter and the associated discussion of real options.

**Required**

1. Define the term *real option*. Provide an example of each of the four common types of real options.
2. Define the terms *put option* and *call option*. Which of the four common types of *real options* are similar to put options? Which are similar to call options?
3. Based on the stated probabilities for the individual states of nature (i.e., level of consumer demand):
   a. What is the expected value each year of the after-tax cash inflows from the proposed investment, without considering the investment delay option?
   b. What is the estimated NPV of the proposed investment, without considering the investment delay option?
4. We see from Panel B of Exhibit 12.10 that XYZ would invest in the project only if the revealed level of consumer demand was high or medium. Show calculations as to why no investment would be made if the revealed level of demand were low.
5. In Panel B of Exhibit 12.10, show for each of the three scenarios the calculation for present value (at $t = 0$) of cash inflows (cells H20:H22), present value of cash outflows (cells I20:I22), and weighted net present value (cells J20:J22). What is the interpretation of the expected NPV of the project (i.e., a *positive* $12.95 million)?

12-51  **Real Options and Sensitivity Analysis**  Refer to the XYZ Company example in the chapter. Based on the results in Panels A and B of Exhibit 12.10, management of the company decided to delay the implementation of the project for one year. Those managers are now interested in knowing how sensitive this decision is with respect to the assumptions they've made regarding the basic analysis. Therefore, they've asked you to prepare some supplementary analyses regarding Panel B of Exhibit 12.10.

**Required**

1. Holding everything else constant, what is the impact on expected NPV of the decision if the probabilities for the three scenarios change as follows: high (20%), medium (50%), low (30%). Does your decision change based on these revised assumptions? Why or why not? (Show calculations.)
2. Holding everything else constant, what is the impact on expected NPV of the decision if the probabilities for the three scenarios change as follows: high (30%), medium (40%), low (30%). Does your decision change based on these revised assumptions? Why or why not? (Show calculations.)
3. Prepare a $5 \times 3$ table containing the estimated NPV of the decision to delay for each combination of the following: risk-free rate of interest (4%, 5%, 6%) and weighted-average cost of capital (13%, 14%, 15%, 16%, and 17%). For example, one cell in your table would be the estimated NPV of the project if the risk-free rate of interest is 4% and the weighted-average cost of capital is 13%. What does your analysis suggest?

12-52  **Real Options—the Option to Abandon a Project**  You and several of your classmates have just graduated from college and are evaluating various investment opportunities, including a start-up company that would produce high-quality jackets embroidered with a college logo. If demand for this customized product is high, you expect to sell approximately 100,000 units per year, at a price per unit of $80. On the other hand, because of stiff competition in the field, a pessimistic estimate is that demand for your new product would be only 40,000 units per year at a selling price of $70. Anticipated variable costs per jacket amount to $40. Capacity-related (i.e., short-term fixed) costs other than the cost of manufacturing equipment are thought to be negligible. Manufacturing equipment (with a 10-year life, a cost of $12 million, and a zero salvage value) would have to be purchased as part of this project. Assume that for income-tax purposes your company will use straight-line depreciation over the life of the proposed investment. Your anticipated income-tax bracket for this endeavor is 33 1/3%. You are unsure of what discount rate to use for capital-budgeting purposes, but you believe the appropriate rate is somewhere between 10% and 14% on an after-tax basis.

**Required**

1. What is the anticipated after-tax cash flow for this investment for each of the two possible states of nature/scenarios?

2. Under the assumption that the two scenarios (level of product demand) are equally likely, what is the expected NPV of the proposed investment? Assume a discount rate of 12%. Based on the amount you estimated, should you invest in the project?

3. How sensitive is your decision to the assumption regarding the discount rate? To answer this question, prepare an estimated NPV for the proposed project using discount rates, in 1% increments, from 10% to 14%. Is the decision to accept or reject the investment sensitive to the discount rate used in the calculation of NPV?

4. Suppose your company could abandon the project and dispose of the manufacturing equipment for $10.4 million if demand for your product turns out to be weak. You and your colleagues would make this decision at the end of the first year of operations. Does the abandonment option change your decision as to whether to invest in the project? (Use a discount rate of 12%.)

**[LO 12-4, 12-8]** 12-53 **Equipment Replacement and Strategic Considerations**  The management of Devine Instrument Company is considering the purchase of a new drilling machine, model RoboDril 1010K. According to the specifications and testing results, RoboDril will substantially increase productivity over AccuDril X10, the machine Devine is currently using.

The AccuDril was acquired 8 years ago for $120,000 and is being depreciated over 10 years expected useful life with an estimated salvage value of $20,000. The engineering department expects the AccuDril to keep going for another three years after a major overhaul at the end of its expected useful life. The estimated cost for the overhaul is $100,000. The overhauled machine will be depreciated using straight-line depreciation with no salvage value. The overhaul will improve the machine's operating efficiency approximately 20%. No other operating conditions will be affected by the overhaul.

RoboDril 1010K is selling for $250,000. Installing, testing, rearranging, and training will cost another $30,000. The manufacturer is willing to take the AccuDril as a trade-in for $40,000. The RoboDril will be depreciated using the straight-line method with no salvage value. New technology most likely will make RoboDril obsolete to the firm in five years.

Variable operating cost for either machine is the same: $10 per hour (cash-based). Other pertinent data follow:

|  | AccuDril X10 | RoboDril 1010K |
|---|---|---|
| Units of output (per year) | 10,000 | 10,000 |
| Machine-hours | 8,000 | 4,000 |
| Selling price per unit | $100 | $100 |
| Variable manufacturing cost—cash-based (not including machine-hours) | $40 | $40 |
| Other annual expenses (tooling and supervising) | $95,000 | $55,000 |
| Disposal value—today | $25,000 | |
| Disposal value—in five years | 0 | $50,000 |

Devine Instrument Company's weighted-average cost of capital (WACC) is 12%, and it is in the 40% tax bracket. Use the PV factors (Appendix C, Table 1) for calculating the NPV of each decision alternative.

**Required**

1. Determine the effect on cash flow for items that differ for the two alternatives.

2. Compute the payback period for purchasing RoboDril 1010K rather than having AccuDril X10 overhauled in two years.

3. What is the present value of each decision alternative?

4. What other factors, including strategic issues, should the firm consider before making the final decision?

**[LO 12-5, 12-8]** 12-54 **Sensitivity Analysis; Spreadsheets**  Use the information in Problem 12-53 to answer the following questions:

**Required**

1. What is the maximum machine operating cost of the overhauled AccuDril for the replacement decision to be an incorrect financial decision? (Use the PV factors and/or PV annuity factors from Appendix C to answer this question.)

2. Use the Goal Seek function in Excel to determine the maximum amount that the annual after-tax operating costs for the new machine can be before changing the decision. (*Hint:* Set up a spreadsheet to calculate the PV of after-tax cash flows for each alternative. Use the built-in functions in Excel, NPV and/or PV, to determine the present values of these cash flows.)

3. New technologies make it possible to overhaul this machine now for $80,000. Both the overhaul cost and the undepreciated cost (book value) of the existing asset are to be depreciated over two years. The overhaul will improve its productivity by 20% and reduce the cost of a major overhaul two years from now to $30,000. All overhaul costs will be depreciated using the straight-line method. With either overhaul, the machine will have no salvage value. Either overhaul can be scheduled during regular maintenance and will not affect production. Despite the old saying, "If it ain't broke, don't fix it," should you overhaul it now or wait for two years to do the overhaul as planned originally, assuming that no funds are currently available to purchase RoboDril 1010K? (Use the built-in functions, PV and/or NPV, for your present value calculations.)

4. Performing the overhaul now also improves product quality. Management believes that the quality improvement is rather subtle and very difficult to quantify. Should the firm overhaul now?

[LO 12-4, 12-5, 12-6]   12-55   **Comparison of Capital-Budgeting Techniques; Sensitivity Analysis**   Nil Hill Corporation has been using its present facilities at its annual full capacity of 10,000 units for the last three years. Still, the company is unable to keep pace with continuing demand for the product that is estimated to be 25,000 units annually. This demand level is expected to continue for at least another four years. To expand manufacturing capacity and take advantage of the demand, Nil Hill must acquire equipment costing $995,000. The equipment will double the current production quantity. This equipment has a useful life of 10 years and can be sold for $195,000 at the end of year 4 or $35,000 at the end of year 10. Analysis of current operating data provides the following information:

|  |  |  | Per Unit |
|---|---|---|---|
| Sales price |  |  | $195 |
| Variable costs: |  |  |  |
| Manufacturing | $90 |  |  |
| Marketing | 10 | $100 |  |
| Fixed costs: |  |  |  |
| Manufacturing | $45 |  |  |
| Other | 25 | 70 | 170 |
| Pretax operating income |  |  | $ 25 |

The fixed costs include depreciation expense of the current equipment. The new equipment will not change variable costs, but the firm will incur additional fixed manufacturing costs (excluding depreciation on the new machine) of $250,000 annually. The firm needs to spend an additional $200,000 in fixed marketing costs per year for additional sales. Nil Hill is in the 30% tax bracket. Management has set a minimum rate of return of 14% after-tax for all capital investments. Assume, for simplicity, that MACRS depreciation rules do *not* apply.

**Required**

1. Assume that the equipment will be depreciated over a four-year period using the straight-line method. What effects will the new equipment have on after-tax operating income in each of the four years?

2. What effect will the new equipment have on after-tax cash inflows in each of the four years?

3. Compute the proposed investment's payback period (in years), under the assumption that after-tax cash inflows occur evenly throughout the year.

4. Compute the book rate of return (ARR) based on the average investment.

5. Compute the net present value (NPV) of the proposed investment. (Use both the built-in function in Excel (NPV) and the tables presented in Appendix C to determine the present value of after-tax cash flows.)

6. Compute the internal rate of return (IRR) of the proposed investment.

7. Compute the modified internal rate of return (MIRR) for the proposed investment.

8. Management has decided to invest in the new equipment, but is unsure of the reliability of some of the estimates and as such has asked some what-if questions. Treat each of the following two cases independently.

   a. By how much can the unit variable cost for units produced by the new equipment increase and still justify the purchase of the equipment (i.e., have the investment generate an after-tax IRR of exactly 14%, its cost of capital)?

   b. The company is anticipating an increase in competition. Management believes that, in response, it will have to reduce the selling price of the product. By how much can the firm decrease the selling price (of all units sold) and still be able to justify the purchase of the new equipment?

9. What strategic considerations might bear on this investment decision? How can such considerations be dealt with formally in the planning and decision-making process?

[LO 12-5, 12-8]   12-56   **Sensitivity Analysis; Equipment-Replacement Decision**   The Mendoza Company discussed in the chapter is now considering replacing a piece of equipment that the company uses to monitor the integrity of metal pipes used for deep-sea drilling purposes. The company's pretax WACC is estimated as 12%. The following data are pertinent to the question you've been asked to analyze:

|  | Existing Asset | Replacement |
| --- | --- | --- |
| Annual (pretax) variable operating expenses | $200,000 | (?) |
| Current purchase price | N/A | $500,000 |
| Current salvage value | $40,000 | N/A |
| Expected useful life (years) | 6 | 6 |
| Expected salvage value, end of year 6 | $10,000 | $100,000 |

**Required**

1. What is the maximum amount of annual variable operating expenses, pretax, that would make this an attractive investment from a present-value standpoint?

2. Assume now that the company expects, over the coming six years, to be subject to a combined income-tax rate of 40%, including any gain/loss realized on the sale of the existing equipment. Assume that the current book value of the existing asset is $50,000 and that the after-tax WACC for Mendoza is 10%. Finally, assume that the company will use SL depreciation, with no salvage value, for income-tax purposes. In this situation, what is the maximum amount of variable operating costs that can be incurred in order to make the proposed purchase attractive in a present-value sense?

3. What strategic considerations might affect the decision whether to invest in this new equipment?

[LO 12-4, 12-5]   12-57   **Present Value Analysis; Sensitivity Analysis; Spreadsheet Application**   Because of increased consumer demand for fuel-efficient, alternative-energy automobiles, Global Auto Company is considering investing in a new hybrid crossover vehicle. Development costs each year for a two-year period for this new vehicle are estimated as $750 million. Tooling and other setup costs in year 2 are estimated at $1 billion. Actual production and sales are estimated to begin in year 3. It is anticipated that the plant being envisioned could produce vehicles for six years. Each vehicle sold is estimated to provide $3,500 of net cash flow (pretax). The estimated salvage value of the manufacturing plant after six years of operation is thought to be $250 million. Assume that all cash flows take place at year-end, and that the pretax WACC for Global Auto is 15%. Income-tax effects can be ignored in this problem.

**Required**

1. What is the minimum volume of car sales, per year, in the six-year life of the plant that is needed to make this proposed investment acceptable using NPV as decision criterion? (Note: For calculating

present values of after-tax cash flows, use the following formula rather than the factors presented in Appendix C: $PV_i = 1 \div (1 + r)^i$, where $r$ = discount rate (WACC) and $i$ = year, 1–8. Also, use the Goal Seek function in Excel to answer this question.)

2. How does your answer in (1) change if the company's pretax WACC is 14%? 16%? Do you think the estimated NPV of this project is sensitive to the estimate of the company's discount rate?

3. What strategic considerations, including those related to risk management, would likely bear on this decision?

[LO 12-4, 12-5]  12-58  **MACRS Depreciation and Capital-Budgeting Analysis; Spreadsheet Application; Sensitivity Analysis**  You and your spouse have recently inherited money from a distant relative and are considering a number of investment opportunities, one of which would involve residential real estate. Specifically, you have an opportunity to purchase an apartment complex with 25 rental units. The total price for these units, including sales commission expense, is estimated as $500,000. You estimate that to make each unit suitable for renting, average remodeling costs of $20,000 per unit would be needed. Fifteen of the units have a single bedroom and rent for $500 per month; the remaining units contain two bedrooms and rent for $650 per month. A friend of yours who is in the business suggests that ordinary maintenance and repair costs be budgeted, annually, at 16% of rental revenue. Both the purchase price of the units and the remodeling costs qualify as 27.5-year MACRS property.

In terms of calculating depreciation expense for tax purposes, you can assume that MACRS-based deductions for the first 27 years will be the same; in year 28 one-half year of depreciation will be deducted. (The present value, at 10%, of each dollar of cost-recovery spread this way is $0.3372.) If the remodeling is undertaken and annual maintenance is done as scheduled, the investment should last at least 30 years. The estimated salvage value of the investment 30 years from now is $0. You can assume that any gain/loss on this sale will be taxed at your ordinary income-tax rate.

Assume an opportunity cost of capital of 10% for purposes of evaluating this investment proposal. You and your spouse feel that your combined income-tax rate for the foreseeable future would be approximately 40%. (Note: The required PV factors are not in Appendix C. Thus, you will need to use Excel functions to generate a PV annuity factor for 27 periods and a PV factor for period 28, at various discount rates, in order to solve this problem.)

**Required**

1. What is the estimated after-tax NPV of this proposed investment? (*Hint:* The present value of MACRS depreciation deductions for 27.5-year property is equal to the product of the tax rate, the initial investment outlay, and 0.3372.) On the basis of your analysis of after-tax cash flows, is this investment desirable? Why or why not?

2. How is the estimated NPV affected if the discount rate were 8% rather than 10%? How would your estimate change if the discount rate were 12% rather than 10%? (*Hint:* Unlike (1) above, in which you were provided a MACRS present value conversion factor, you will have to develop a 28-year depreciation schedule and associated income-tax savings based on the stated tax rate. You must then discount this 28-year stream of cash savings back to present value using both the 8% and 12% discount rates. The PV annuity factor for 27 periods and the PV factor for period 28, at various discount rates, are *not* included in Appendix C. Thus, you will have to generate these yourself, using Excel.)

3. What additional factors might you have to consider before investing in this apartment complex?

[LO 12-4, 12-5]  12-59  **Environmental Cost Management**  Myers Manufacturing, Inc., wants to build a booth for painting the boxes it makes for small transformers to be used to power neon signs. The company can choose either a solvent-based or a powder paint process. The following table summarizes the costs and investment required by each approach:

|  | Solvent Paint System | Powder Paint System |
| --- | --- | --- |
| Initial investment | $400,000 | $1,200,000 |
| Unit paint cost | $0.19 | $0.20 |
| Estimated life in years | 10 | 10 |
| Annual units | 2,000,000 | 2,000,000 |

The firm will incur additional environmental costs with the solvent paint system but not with the powder paint system. The firm estimates annual environmental costs for the solvent paint system as follows:

| | Units | Unit Cost |
|---|---|---|
| Monthly pit cleaning | 12 | $ 1,000 |
| Hazardous waste disposal | 183 | 3,000 |
| Superfund fee | 18,690 | 0.17 |
| Worker training | 2 | 1,500 |
| Insurance | 1 | 10,000 |
| Amortization of air-emission permit | 0.2 | 1,000 |
| Air-emission fee | 44.6 | 25 |
| Recordkeeping | 0.25 | 45,000 |
| Wastewater treatment | 1 | 50,000 |

The firm estimates its after-tax cost of capital to be 12%. Either system is a 10-year property under MACRS. The firm pays a total of 40% in income taxes.

**Required**
1. What is the difference in cost in today's dollar for the two systems?
2. What is the most the firm is willing to pay for the powder-based system?

(Adapted from German Boer, Margaret Curtin, and Louis Hoyt, "Environmental Cost Management," *Management Accounting* [September 1998], pp. 28–38.)

[LO 12-1] 12-60 **Research Assignment; Strategy** Obtain from your library a copy of the following article: Clayton M. Christensen, Stephen P. Kaufman, and Willy C. Shih, "Innovation Killers: How Financial Tools Destroy Your Capacity to Do New Things," *Harvard Business Review,* January 2008, pp. 98–105. The article focuses on bias against innovation that is attributable to the misuse of certain financial tools. In fact, the authors conclude (p. 104) that "managers in established corporations use analytical methods that make innovation investments extremely difficult to justify."

**Required** After reading the above-referenced article, answer the following questions:
1. According to the authors of the article, how does the use of DCF tools by managers in practice bias against innovation? What solution do the authors propose to counter this problem?
2. Define the terms *fixed costs* and *sunk costs.* According to the authors of this article, what is the bias against innovation that is created by how some decision makers view such costs? What remedies do the authors recommend for dealing with this problem?
3. The authors suggest that bias in the evaluation of innovation projects is caused, as well, by an overemphasis on (short-term) earnings per share statistics. What is the essence of this argument? What do the authors propose as a recommendation for addressing this problem?

[LO 12-1] 12-61 **Research Assignment; Sustainability** Obtain from your library or your instructor a copy of the following article: Thomas L. Barton and John B. MacArthur, "The New Hue of Green for the Management Accountant," *Strategic Finance* (March 2011), pp. 36–41. The article provides a model for evaluating investments in energy-saving technologies that are both cost-effective and environmentally friendly. The authors use an actual example (Jiminy Peak Mountain Resort, www.jiminypeak.com) to illustrate the role that management accountants can play in the evaluation of sustainability-related investment proposals. (Useful information regarding the decision to invest in renewable energy products is available at the following websites: www.eos-ventures.com;northernpower.kiosk-view.com/bolton-valley; and, articles.cnn.com/2009-02-27/tech/ski.wind.turbine_1_jiminy-peak-mountain-resort-wind-turbine-zephyr?_s=PM:TECH).

**Required** After reading the above-referenced article, answer the following questions:
1. According to the authors of the article, what was the managerial question (that is, decision) facing the management of Jiminy Peak Mountain Resort?
2. List the major relevant costs and cost savings (financial benefits) associated with the investment decision problem you identified above in requirement 1.
3. Describe any nonfinancial benefits associated with the proposed investment.

4. According to the authors, what primary role can management accountants play in terms of evaluating capital investment proposals, similar to the one faced by the management of Jiminy Peak Mountain Resort?

[LO 12-4, 12-5]   12-62 **NPV Analysis; Sensitivity Analysis; Data Tables in Excel**   This assignment is designed to introduce you to the preparation of both a one-variable and a two-variable "data table" in Excel 2010. Such tables are useful for conducting and reporting the results of a series of "what-if" analyses. Assume the following cash flows for a hypothetical five-year investment project that in time 0 would require a net investment outlay of $350,000, annual (after-tax) cash inflows of $100,000, and a 10% discount rate (weighted-average cost of capital).

**Required**

1. Consult the specified online help file (Microsoft website) regarding the preparation of "data tables." (See footnote 17.)

2. Prepare a one-variable data table where you depict NPV of the proposed investment at each of the following discount rates: 8% to 12%, in increments of 0.5%.

3. Prepare a two-variable data table where in addition to the 10 discount rates assumed in requirement 2 (above), you want to consider three possible levels of after-tax cash inflows per year: $90,000, $100,000, and, $110,000. (Thus, your table will include 10 × 3 = 30 cells.)

## Solution to Self-Study Problem

### Capital Budgeting for Expanding Productive Capacity

1. Net initial investment outlay, year 0:

| | |
|---|---:|
| Purchase price of the new equipment | $580,000 |
| Installation, testing, and training | 12,000 |
| Capitalized renovation costs for the leased warehouse | 58,000 |
| Net initial investment outlay, year 0 | $650,000 |

2. Effect of the acquisition on total after-tax operating profit, years 1 through 4:

| | | | |
|---|---|---|---:|
| Incremental sales (15,000 − 10,000) | $200 × 5,000 | | $1,000,000 |
| Cost of goods sold: | | | |
|   Variable manufacturing costs | $ 60 × 5,000 | $300,000 | |
|   Additional fixed manufacturing overhead | | | |
|   ($140,000 + $10,000) | | 150,000 | |
|   Depreciation on new equipment (SL basis) | | | |
|   ($650,000 − $50,000) ÷ 4 years* | | 150,000 | 600,000 |
| Gross margin | | | $ 400,000 |
| Marketing and administrative expenses: | | | |
|   Variable marketing expenses | $ 20 × 5,000 | $100,000 | |
|   Additional fixed marketing expenses | | 100,000 | 200,000 |
| Incremental operating profit before tax | | | $ 200,000 |
| Less: Income taxes (@40%) | | | 80,000 |
| Incremental after-tax operating profit, years 1 through 3 | | | $ 120,000 |
| | | | |
| The company can expect its after-tax operating profit in year 4 | | | |
| to increase by $108,000, as follows: | | | |
| Net operating income before restoration expenses (see above) | | | $ 120,000 |
| Less: After-tax restoration expenses: | | | |
|   Restoration expenses | | $ 20,000 | |
|   Less: Income-tax savings on restoration expenses (@40%) | | 8,000 | 12,000 |
| Incremental after-tax operating profit, year 4 | | | $ 108,000 |

*Unlike the example in the body of the chapter, we are assuming here that for tax purposes, the depreciable cost of the asset is equal to cost less estimated salvage value, an assumption that may or may not comport with current tax law.

3. The incremental after-tax cash inflow is anticipated to be $270,000 for each of the first three years and $308,000 in year 4, as follows:

| | Years 1 to 3 | Year 4 |
|---|---|---|
| After-tax operating profit (see part 2 above) | $120,000 | $108,000 |
| Add: Noncash expenses included in determination of after-tax operating profit: depreciation expense | 150,000 | 150,000 |
| Add: After-tax cash inflow from disposal of equipment | -0- | 50,000* |
| Incremental after-tax cash inflows | $270,000 | $308,000 |

*Sales (salvage) value equals net book value (NBV) of the asset. Therefore, there is no tax-related gain or loss on the transaction.

4. The (unadjusted) payback period for this investment (under the assumption that cash inflows occur evenly throughout the year) is approximately 2.4 years, as follows:

$$\text{Payback period} = \text{Initial investment} \div \text{Annual cash inflow after-tax}$$
$$= \$650,000 \div \$270,000 = 2.407 \text{ years, or 2 years and 5 months}$$

5. The accounting (book) rate of return (ARR), based on average investment, is approximately 33.4%, as follows:

$$\text{Average net operating income} = [(\$120,000 \times 3) + \$108,000] \div 4 \text{ years} = \$117,000 \text{ per year}$$
$$\text{Average investment} = (\text{Book value beginning of year 1} + \text{Book value at end of year 4}) \div 2$$
$$= (\$650,000 + \$50,000) \div 2 = \$350,000$$

Accounting rate of return (ARR) = $117,000 ÷ $350,000 = 33.43%

6. The net present value (NPV) of the proposed investment, at a 12% discount rate, is $194,428, as follows (under the assumption that cash inflows occur at year-end):

| | |
|---|---|
| PV of after-tax cash inflows, years 1 through 3, at 12%: | |
| $270,000 × 2.402 = | $648,540 |
| PV of after-tax cash inflow, year 4: $308,000 × 0.636 = | 195,888 |
| Total PV of after-tax cash inflows | $844,428 |
| Net initial investment outlay (i.e., year 0) | 650,000 |
| NPV | $194,428 |

### Alternative Solution: Using an Excel Spreadsheet

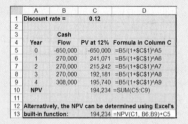

| | A | B | C | D |
|---|---|---|---|---|
| 1 | Discount rate = | | 0.12 | |
| 2 | | | | |
| 3 | | Cash | | |
| 4 | Year | Flow | PV at 12% | Formula in Column C |
| 5 | 0 | -650,000 | -650,000 | =B5/(1+$C$1)^A5 |
| 6 | 1 | 270,000 | 241,071 | =B5/(1+$C$1)^A6 |
| 7 | 2 | 270,000 | 215,242 | =B5/(1+$C$1)^A7 |
| 8 | 3 | 270,000 | 192,181 | =B5/(1+$C$1)^A8 |
| 9 | 4 | 308,000 | 195,740 | =B5/(1+$C$1)^A9 |
| 10 | NPV | | 194,234 | =SUM(C5:C9) |
| 11 | | | | |
| 12 | Alternatively, the NPV can be determined using Excel's | | | |
| 13 | built-in function: | | 194,234 | =NPV(C1, B6:B9)+C5 |

Note that the Excel-generated solutions are exact while the method based on the present value tables is an approximation because the present value factors in the tables are rounded to three decimal places.

7. Under the assumption that cash inflows occur evenly throughout the year, the discounted payback period for the proposed project is slightly more than three years, as follows:

| | A | B | C | D | E |
|---|---|---|---|---|---|
| 1 | | | | | Cumulative |
| 2 | | After-tax | Discount | PV of After- | PV of After- |
| 3 | | Cash | Factor | tax Cash | tax Cash |
| 4 | Year | Inflow | @ 12.0% | Flow | Flows |
| 5 | 0 | ($650,000) | 1.000 | ($650,000) | ($650,000) |
| 6 | 1 | $270,000 | 0.893 | $241,110 | ($408,890) |
| 7 | 2 | $270,000 | 0.797 | $215,190 | ($193,700) |
| 8 | 3 | $270,000 | 0.712 | $192,240 | ($1,460) |
| 9 | 4 | $308,000 | 0.636 | $195,888 | $194,428 |

8. Under the assumption that cash inflows occur at year-end, the estimated internal rate of return (IRR) for this investment is 25.3%, which can be determined using either a trial-and-error approach or using a built-in function for Excel, as follows:

   *Trial-and-Error:* We can surmise from 6 above that the IRR must be significantly greater than the discount rate, 12%. Thus, we might choose IRR candidates of 25% and 30% in our attempt to find a rate that produces an NPV of 0.

   |                                              | @25%      | @30%        |
   | -------------------------------------------- | --------- | ----------- |
   | PV of after-tax cash inflows (details omitted) | $653,320 | $598,120    |
   | Less: Initial investment outlay              | 650,000   | 650,000     |
   | NPV at indicated discount rate               | $ 3,320   | $ (51,880)  |

   Thus, the IRR of this project lies between 25% and 30%. By interpolation we have

   $$IRR = 25\% + [\$3,320 \div (\$3,320 + \$51,880)] \times 5\%$$
   $$= 25\% + [\$3,320 \div \$55,200] \times 5\% = 25\% + [0.06 \times 5\%] = \mathbf{25.3\%}$$

   *Excel-based formula approach:*

   |   | A      | B            | C                | D |
   | - | ------ | ------------ | ---------------- | - |
   | 1 |        | After-tax    |                  |   |
   | 2 | Year   | Cash Inflow  |                  |   |
   | 3 | 0      | ($650,000)   |                  |   |
   | 4 | 1      | $270,000     |                  |   |
   | 5 | 2      | $270,000     |                  |   |
   | 6 | 3      | $270,000     |                  |   |
   | 7 | 4      | $308,000     |                  |   |
   | 8 |        |              | Formula          |   |
   | 9 | IRR =  | 25.27%       | =IRR(B3:B7,0.12) |   |

   (**Note:** In the IRR function, the "0.12" represents an initial guess; if omitted, Excel uses 10% as the starting point in its algorithm to estimate the IRR of an investment project.)

9. The MIRR of the proposed investment is approximately 20%, as follows:

   |    | A      | B            | C                   | D |
   | -- | ------ | ------------ | ------------------- | - |
   | 1  |        | After-tax    |                     |   |
   | 2  | Year   | Cash Flow    |                     |   |
   | 3  | 0      | ($650,000)   |                     |   |
   | 4  | 1      | $270,000     |                     |   |
   | 5  | 2      | $270,000     |                     |   |
   | 6  | 3      | $270,000     |                     |   |
   | 7  | 4      | $308,000     |                     |   |
   | 8  | WACC = | 12.00%       |                     |   |
   | 9  |        |              | Formula             |   |
   | 10 | MIRR = | 19.57%       | =MIRR(B3:B7,B8,B8)  |   |

10. The most that variable costs can increase and still have the project return the minimum rate of return (12%), *holding everything else constant,* is $21.34 per unit, as follows:

    The current projected NPV of the project is $194,428; thus, the PV of future after-tax cash inflows can drop by a maximum of $194,428 (if they fell by this amount, then the IRR on the project would be exactly 12%). The amount by which the annual pretax cash flows could decrease is $106,700, as follows:

    Maximum annual decrease in annual *after-tax* cash inflows
    (through increased variable costs, using annuity factor @ 12%) = $194,428 ÷ 3.037 =   $ 64,020

    Given a 40% marginal income-tax rate, the above amount
    represents 60% (i.e., 1 − 40%) of the pretax amount;
    thus, the maximum amount that pretax income can fall = $64,020 ÷ (1 − 0.40) =   $106,700

    Therefore, the variable cost per unit can increase by $106,700 ÷ 5,000 units = $21.34 per unit. If everything else remains constant and the variable cost per unit increases by $21.34, the proposed project will yield a 12.0% return.

Alternatively, we can use the Goal Seek function in Excel to determine the maximum change in variable costs that could be realized such that the investment would yield an IRR of 12%. Use the following two-step process:

### Step 1: Set Up the Current Situation

| | A | B | C | D | E |
|---|---|---|---|---|---|
| 1 | Incremental sales per year (in units) = | | 5,000 | | |
| 2 | Selling price per unit = | | $200.00 | | |
| 3 | Variable costs per unit = | | $80.00 | | |
| 4 | Cash fixed costs per year = | | $250,000 | | |
| 5 | Marginal income tax rate = | | 0.4 | | |
| 6 | Annual depreciation deduction (SL) = | | $150,000 | | |
| 7 | Current level of after-tax operating cash flows per year = | | $270,000 | | |
| 8 | | | | | |
| 9 | Current NPV of investment proposal = | | $194,428 | (given, Part 6) | |
| 10 | PV annuity factor, 12%, 4 years = | | 3.037 | (Appendix C, Table 2) | |
| 11 | | | | | |
| 12 | Thus, decrease in annual *after-tax* cash inflows can be | | $64,020 | =C9/C10 | |
| 13 | New level of annual *after-tax* cash inflows can decrease to | | $205,980 | =C7-C12 | |
| 14 | | | | | |
| 15 | Incremental annual *pretax* cash income = | | $350,000 | =C1*(C2 C3) C4 | |
| 16 | Minus: Income taxes on above (@40%) = | | $140,000 | =C5*C15 | |
| 17 | Plus: Depreciation tax savings = | | $60,000 | =C5*C6 | |
| 18 | After-tax, annual increase in operating cash flows = | | $270,000 | =C15-C16+C17 | |

This initial spreadsheet reflects the current investment proposal and the allowable decrease in after-tax annual cash inflows (cell C12) that can occur, given the goal of generating an IRR of 12.0% on the project.

### Step 2: Use the Goal Seek Function of Excel

Next, go to the Goal Seek option under Data, What-If Analysis, then Goal Seek. Given the preceding spreadsheet, complete the Goal Seek dialog box as follows:

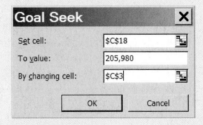

The preceding entries tell Excel to vary cell C3 (variable costs per unit) until the amount of annual cash operating profit after-tax (cell C18) has been reduced to $205,980 ($270,000 − $64,020). After clicking "OK," your spreadsheet should change to:

| | A | B | C | D | E |
|---|---|---|---|---|---|
| 1 | Incremental sales per year (in units) = | | 5,000 | | |
| 2 | Selling price per unit = | | $200.00 | | |
| 3 | Variable costs per unit = | | $101.34 | | |
| 4 | Cash fixed costs per year = | | $250,000 | | |
| 5 | Marginal income tax rate = | | 0.4 | | |
| 6 | Annual depreciation deduction (SL) = | | $150,000 | | |
| 7 | Current level of after-tax operating cash flows per year = | | $270,000 | | |
| 8 | | | | | |
| 9 | Current NPV of investment proposal = | | $194,428 | (given, Part 6) | |
| 10 | PV annuity factor, 12%, 4 years = | | 3.037 | (Appendix C, Table 2) | |
| 11 | | | | | |
| 12 | Thus, decrease in annual *after-tax* cash inflows can be | | $64,020 | =C9/C10 | |
| 13 | New level of annual *after-tax* cash inflows can decrease to | | $205,980 | =C7-C12 | |
| 14 | | | | | |
| 15 | Incremental annual *pretax* cash income = | | $243,300 | =C1*(C2-C3)-C4 | |
| 16 | Minus: Income taxes on above (@40%) = | | $97,320 | =C5*C15 | |
| 17 | Plus: Depreciation tax savings = | | $60,000 | =C5*C6 | |
| 18 | After-tax, annual increase in operating cash flows = | | $205,980 | =C15-C16+C17 | |

Thus, variable costs per unit can increase to $101.34 (or, $21.34 over the initial assumption of $80.00 per unit); if everything else other than variable cost per unit is held constant, the IRR of the project will be 12%.

*Please visit* **http://www.mhhe.com/blocher6e** *to access a narrated, animated tutorial for solving this problem.*

# CHAPTER THIRTEEN

# Cost Planning for the Product Life Cycle:
## Target Costing, Theory of Constraints, and Strategic Pricing

**After studying this chapter, you should be able to . . .**

LO 13-1   Explain how to use target costing to facilitate strategic management

LO 13-2   Apply the theory of constraints to strategic management

LO 13-3   Describe how life-cycle costing facilitates strategic management

LO 13-4   Outline the objectives and techniques of strategic pricing

Having some of the world's best-selling cars, the Camry, the Corolla, and the Prius, Toyota is among the world's most successful automakers. The reason for Toyota's success is that it is able to consistently produce high-quality cars with attractive features and competitive prices. Target costing, a method Toyota pioneered in the 1960s, is one method used to achieve high quality and desirable features at a competitive price. As we will see in this chapter, the method is a design approach in which cost management plays a large part. Using target costing, a company designs a product to achieve a desired profit while satisfying the customer's expectations for quality and product features. The balancing of costs, features, and quality takes place throughout the design, manufacturing, sale, and service of the car but has the strongest influence in the design phase. When design alternatives are being examined and selected, Toyota, like most any manufacturer, has the maximum flexibility for choosing options that affect manufacturing and all other product costs such as customer service and warranty work.

Once the design is complete, manufacturing begins. The cost consequences of the choice of features and manufacturing methods are set until the next model change, meaning cost-effective design is critical. Target costing places a strong focus on using the design process to improve the product and reduce its cost. For example, in the redesign of the Camry, Toyota made the running lamps part of the headlamp assembly and made the grill part of the bumper, which saves time and materials in manufacturing and produces a more crash-resistant bumper—a win/win for Toyota and the car buyer.

Target costing is only the first of four costing methods we will study in this chapter. Each of the methods is used for cost planning during the product (or service) life cycle. For example, target costing is used at an early phase in the product's life cycle to help create a product designed to achieve a desired profit. The other methods, which are used at different phases in the life cycle, are the theory of constraints, life-cycle costing, and strategic pricing. While once managers focused only on manufacturing costs, they now look at costs both before manufacturing (upstream) and after manufacturing (downstream) to get a comprehensive analysis of product cost and profitability over a product's cost life cycle.

**EXHIBIT 13.1**
**The Cost Life Cycle of a Product or Service**

The **cost life cycle**
is the sequence of activities within the firm that begins with research and development followed by design, manufacturing, marketing/distribution, and customer service.

The **cost life cycle** is the sequence of activities within the organization that begins with research and development followed by design, manufacturing (or providing the service), marketing/distribution, and customer service. It is the life cycle of the product or service from the viewpoint of costs incurred. The cost life cycle is illustrated in Exhibit 13.1.[1]

Of the four methods used for cost planning, target costing, the theory of constraints, and life-cycle costing are based on the product or service's cost life cycle. For example, target costing considers the role of product design (an upstream activity) in reducing costs in the manufacturing and downstream phases of the life cycle. Then, the theory of constraints can be used in the manufacturing phase to reduce manufacturing costs and to speed up delivery downstream. Next, life-cycle costing provides a comprehensive evaluation of the profitability of the different products, including costs throughout the product life cycle. The fourth method used for cost planning, strategic pricing, uses both cost life cycle and sales life cycle concepts in pricing decisions.

The **sales life cycle**
is the sequence of phases in the product's or service's life in the market from the introduction of the product or service to the market, growth in sales, and finally maturity, decline, and withdrawal from the market.

The **sales life cycle** is the sequence of phases in the product's or service's life in the market from the introduction of the product or service to the market, the growth in sales, and finally maturity, decline, and withdrawal from the market. Sales are at first small, peak in the maturity phase, and decline thereafter, as illustrated in Exhibit 13.2.

These four methods are commonly used by manufacturing firms, where new product development, manufacturing speed, and efficiency are important. Because a product with physical characteristics is involved, applications in manufacturing firms are more intuitive and easily understood. However, each method can also be used in service organizations. For example, a local government could use the theory of constraints to speed the process of billing and collection for water services and reduce the related processing costs.

**EXHIBIT 13.2**
**The Sales Life Cycle of a Product or Service**

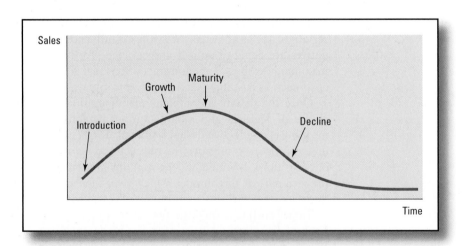

[1] The *cost life cycle* also is called a *value chain* by many writers to emphasize that each activity must add value for the ultimate consumer [Michael Porter, *Competitive Advantage* (New York: Free Press, 1985)]. Note that this concept of the value chain differs from that introduced in Chapter 2. Chapter 2 describes the industry-level value chain; the cost life-cycle concept in this chapter describes the firm-level value chain. We use the broader concept of the industry-level value chain in Chapter 2 to facilitate the strategic focus in that chapter. For a discussion of the two types of value chains, see "Value Chain Analysis for Assessing Competitive Advantage," *Statement on Management Accounting,* Institute of Management Accountants, 1996.

## Target Costing

To start this section, consider the words of Henry Ford.

Our policy is to reduce the price, extend the operations, and improve the article. You will notice that the reduction of price comes first. We have never considered costs as fixed. Therefore we first reduce the price to the point where we believe more sales result. Then we go ahead and try to make the prices. We do not bother about the costs. The new price forces the costs down. The more usual way is to take the costs and then determine the price, and although that method may be scientific in the narrow sense, it is not scientific in the broad sense, because what earthly use is it to know the cost if it tells you that you cannot manufacture at a price at which the article can be sold? But more to the point is the fact that although one may calculate what a cost is, and of course all of our costs are carefully calculated, no one knows what a cost ought to be. One of the ways of discovering is to name a price so low as to force everybody in the place to the highest point of efficiency. The low price makes everybody dig for profits. We make more discoveries concerning manufacturing and selling under this forced method than by any method of leisurely investigation.

*Henry Ford,* My Life and My Work, *1923*

**LO 13-1**

*Explain how to use target costing to facilitate strategic management.*

Henry Ford's thinking would fit well in today's corporate boardrooms, where global competition, increased customer expectations, and competitive pricing in many industries have forced companies to look for ways to reduce costs year after year while producing products with increased levels of quality and functionality.

What Ford is describing is a technique called *target costing,* in which the firm determines the allowable (i.e., target) cost for the product or service, given a competitive market price, so the firm can earn a desired profit. The formula is

Target cost = Competitive price − Desired profit

The target cost is just that, a target, and the firm has two options for managing costs to reach the target level:

1. By integrating new manufacturing technology, using advanced cost management techniques such as activity-based costing, and seeking higher productivity.
2. By redesigning the product or service. This method is beneficial for many firms because it recognizes that design decisions account for much of total product life-cycle costs. By careful attention to design, significant cost reductions are possible.

These options are not mutually exclusive, so firms may choose to employ both options in their target costing efforts to achieve increased productivity and a low-cost design.

Auto manufacturers, software developers, and other consumer product manufacturers must also have a design process that anticipates the number and types of features to include in periodic updates of a product. Target costing, based on analysis of functionality/cost trade-offs, is an appropriate management tool for these firms. With its positioning in the early, upstream phases of the cost life cycle, target costing can clearly help a firm reduce total costs (see Exhibit 13.3).

**EXHIBIT 13.3**
**Target Costing in the Cost Life Cycle**

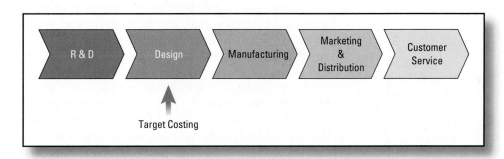

Toyota; Honda Motor Company; Boeing; Intel, Inc.; and many other firms worldwide use target costing. Many firms find it difficult to compete successfully on cost leadership or differentiation alone; they must compete on both price and functionality. Target costing uses the following five-step process to manage the trade-offs between functionality and cost:

1. Determine the market price.
2. Determine the desired profit.
3. Calculate the target cost at market price less desired profit.
4. Use value engineering to identify ways to reduce product cost.
5. Use kaizen costing and operational control to further reduce costs.

The first three steps require little additional explanation. However, the determination of desired profit can be done in a variety of ways. A common approach is to set a desired per unit profit, meaning that, if the product's price falls and target costs fall by the same dollar amount, then profits will remain the same after the price change, assuming the firm meets the new price and sales in units do not change. Another approach is to set the desired profit as a percentage of sales dollars. The section on pricing at the end of this chapter gives some additional examples of pricing methods. The following sections explain the fourth and fifth steps: the use of value engineering, kaizen costing, and operational control.

## Value Engineering

**Value engineering**
is used in target costing to reduce product cost by analyzing the trade-offs between different types of product functionality and total product cost.

**Value engineering** is used in target costing to reduce product cost by analyzing the trade-offs between different types of product functionality (different types of product features) and total product cost. An important first step in value engineering is performing a consumer analysis during the design stage to identify critical consumer preferences that define the desired functionality for the new product.

The type of value engineering used depends on the product's functionality. For one group of products—including automobiles, computer software, and many consumer electronic products such as cameras and audio and video equipment—functionality can be added or deleted relatively easily. These products have frequent new models or updates, and customer preferences change frequently. The manufacturer in effect chooses the particular bundle of features to include with each new model of the product. For automobiles, this can mean new performance and new safety features; for computer software, it might mean the ability to perform certain new tasks or analyses.

In contrast, for a product in which customer preferences are relatively stable, the functionality must be designed into the product rather than added on. These are best represented by specialized equipment and industrial products such as construction equipment, heavy trucks, and specialized medical equipment.

**Functional analysis**
is a type of value engineering in which the performance and cost of each major function or feature of the product is examined.

Target costing is more useful for products in the first group because the firm has some discretion about a larger number of features. A type of value engineering employed in these firms is **functional analysis**, a process of examining the performance and cost of each major function or feature of the product. The objective of the analysis is to determine a desired balance of functionality and cost. An overall desired level of performance achievement for each function is obtained while keeping the cost of all functions below the target cost.

In competitive industries such as computers, consumer electronics, and autos, manufacturers continuously look for ways to reduce cost and increase value throughout the value chain. Because of intense pricing pressures and increased customer expectations, target costing methods can help identify and analyze the options for competitive advantage. Going abroad is the solution for many firms but for different reasons. We look at the practices in two industries: apparel companies, and consumer electronics and computer products.

## APPAREL COMPANIES

Apparel manufacturers such as Ralph Lauren and Liz Claiborne have moved much of their product development as well as manufacturing to China. Fashion designers, fabric suppliers, button makers, and other parts of the product development process work together in the single location in China. What is the advantage to these companies?

## CONSUMER ELECTRONICS AND COMPUTER PRODUCTS

Computer and electronics companies like Apple and Hewlett-Packard have outsourced manufacturing to plants operated by contract manufacturers, such as Foxconn in China. Why is this an advantage to these companies?

(Refer to Comments on Cost Management in Action at the end of the chapter.)

Benchmarking is often used at this step to determine which features give the firm a competitive advantage. In a release of new software, for example, each desired feature of the updated version is reviewed against the cost and time required for its development. The objective is an overall bundle of features for the software that achieves the desired balance of meeting customer preferences while keeping costs below targeted levels. In another example, auto manufacturers must decide which performance and safety features to add to the new model. This decision is based on consumer analysis and a functional analysis of the feature's contribution to consumer preferences compared to its cost. For instance, improved safety air bags could be added, but target cost constraints could delay an improved sound system until a later model year. Keep in mind that regulatory requirements may also dictate which features must be added.

**Design analysis**
is a form of value engineering in which the design team prepares several possible designs of the product, each having similar features with different levels of both performance and cost.

**Design analysis** is a form of value engineering for products in the second group, industrial and specialized products. The design team prepares several possible designs of the product, each having similar features with different levels of both performance and cost. Benchmarking and value-chain analysis help guide the design team in preparing designs that are both low cost and competitive. The design team works with cost management personnel to select the one design that best meets customer preferences while not exceeding the target cost.

A useful comparison of different target costing and cost-reduction strategies in three Japanese firms, based on the field research of Robin Cooper, is illustrated in Exhibit 13.4. Note that the different market demands for functionality result in different cost-reduction approaches. Where customers' expectations for functionality are increasing, as for Nissan and Olympus, there is more significant use of target costing. In contrast, at Komatsu, the emphasis is on value engineering and productivity improvement. Note also that firms such as Nissan, which use both internal and external sourcing for parts and components,

**EXHIBIT 13.4    Target Costing in Three Japanese Firms**

| Firm/Industry | Functionality | Cost Reduction Approach | Strategy |
|---|---|---|---|
| Olympus/Cameras | Increasing rapidly; is designed in | Target costing using value engineering; the concept of distinctive functionality for the **price point**, plus supportive functionality | Heavy focus on managing functionality |
| Nissan/Auto | Rapidly increasing; easy to add or delete functionality | **Value engineering** by product and by each component of each product; then increase price or reduce functionality | Prices are set by desired customers' expectations about functionality; after functionality is set, target cost is used to find savings, especially from suppliers |
| Komatsu/Construction equipment | Static; must be designed in | **Design analysis** to determine alternative designs. **Functional analysis** to develop cost/functionality trade-offs. **Productivity programs** to reduce the remaining costs | Primary focus is on cost control rather than redesign or functionality analysis |

**Cost tables**
are computer-based databases
that include comprehensive
information about the firm's
cost drivers.

**Group technology**
is a method of identifying
similarities in the parts of
products manufactured so the
same part can be used in two
or more products, thereby
reducing costs.

**Concurrent engineering,**
or *simultaneous engineering,* is
an important method that
integrates product design with
manufacturing and marketing
throughout the product's
life cycle.

use target costing at both the product level and the component level. The overall product-level target cost is achieved when targeted costs for all components are achieved.[2]

Other cost-reduction approaches include cost tables and group technology. **Cost tables** are computer-based databases that include comprehensive information about the firm's cost drivers. Cost drivers include, for example, the size of the product, the materials used in its manufacture, and the number of features. Firms that manufacture parts of different sizes from the same design (pipe fittings, tools, and so on) use cost tables to show the difference in cost for parts of different sizes and different types of materials.

**Group technology** is a method of identifying similarities in the parts of products manufactured so the same parts can be used in two or more products, thereby reducing costs. Large manufacturers of diverse product lines, such as in the automobile industry, use group technology in this way. A point of concern in the use of group technology is that it reduces manufacturing costs but might increase service and warranty costs if a failed part is used in many different models. The combination of group technology and total quality management can, however, result in lower costs in both manufacturing and service/warranty.

**Concurrent engineering,** or *simultaneous engineering,* is an important development in the design of products that is replacing the traditional approach of product designers working in isolation on specialized components of the overall design project. In contrast, concurrent engineering relies on an integrated approach. The engineering/design process takes place throughout the cost life cycle using cross-functional teams. Information is solicited from and used at each phase of the value chain to improve the product design. For example, customer feedback in the service phase is used directly in product design. Manufacturers such as Toyota Motor Corp. and Moen, Inc., are increasingly using product design in a very flexible manner by continuously incorporating product improvements. Some experts argue that this approach has saved firms as much as 20% of total product cost.

An important part of value engineering is the use of advanced costing methods, such as ABC costing, to accurately determine the product cost for each feature of the product, each function of the product, or each design option that is being considered. ABC costing is particularly useful for helping managers in product design, purchasing, manufacturing, and marketing to work together with a common understanding of the costs of different features and options.[3]

---

Be a yardstick of quality. Some people aren't used to an environment where excellence is expected.

*Steve Jobs, former CEO of Apple, Inc.*

---

## Target Costing and Kaizen

The fifth step in target costing is to use continuous improvement (kaizen) and operational control to further reduce costs. Kaizen occurs at the manufacturing stage where the effects of value engineering and improved design are already in place; the role for cost reduction at this phase is to develop new manufacturing methods (such as flexible manufacturing systems) and to use new management techniques such as operational control (Chapters 14, 15, and 16), total quality management (Chapter 17), and the theory of constraints (next section) to further reduce costs. *Kaizen* means *continuous* improvement, that is, the ongoing search for new ways to reduce costs in the manufacturing process of a product with a given design and functionality. Toyota, for example, uses kaizen to reduce manufacturing costs on its hybrid vehicles, so that it can bring down the premium it must now charge for these vehicles.

Exhibit 13.5 shows the relationship between target costing and kaizen. Price is assumed to be stable or decreasing over time for firms for which target costing is appropriate because of intense competition on price, product quality, and product functionality. These firms respond to the competitive pressure by periodically redesigning their

---

[2] Robin Cooper and Regine Slagmulder, "Develop Profitable New Products with Target Costing," *Sloan Management Review,* Summer 1999, pp. 23–33; and Robin Cooper and Regine Slagmulder, "Target Costing for New Product Development; Component-Level Target Costing," *Journal of Cost Management,* September–October, 2001, pp. 36–43.

[3] Gary Cokins, "Integrating Target Costing and ABC," *Journal of Cost Management,* July/August 2002, pp. 13–22.

**EXHIBIT 13.5**
**Price, Cost, Kaizen, and Target Costing**

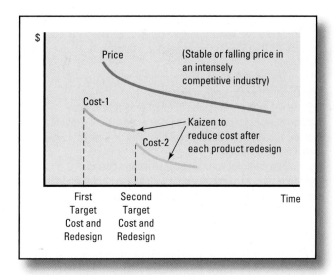

products using target costing to simultaneously reduce the product price and improve their value. Consider the two points in Exhibit 13.5 labeled first and second target cost. The time period between product redesigns is approximately the product's sales life cycle. In the time between product redesigns, the firm uses kaizen to reduce product cost in the manufacturing process by streamlining the supply chain and improving both manufacturing methods and productivity programs. Thus, target costing and kaizen are complementary methods used to continually reduce cost and improve value.

## An Illustration: Target Costing in Health Product Manufacturing

Health Products International, Inc. (HPI), is conducting a target costing analysis of a major product, a hearing aid. The HPI-2 is a reliable second-generation hearing aid that has 30% of the worldwide market. HPI-2 sells for $750 and costs $650 to produce, generating a profit of $100 per unit. A competitor has, however, recently introduced a third-generation product that incorporates a computer chip, thereby significantly improving performance. The competitor's price is $1,200. Customer analysis has revealed that cost-conscious consumers will still buy the HPI-2, but HPI can maintain market share only if the price is lowered to $600. The target profit for HPI-2, however, remains at $100, so redesigning the product and/or the manufacturing process is required.

With a price of $600 and a target profit of $100, the target cost for HPI-2 is $500. Management must find a way to reduce costs by $150 ($650 − $500), and because the product has no add-on features, design analysis is the preferred approach. The table below summarizes the three alternatives being considered.

| Alternative A | Projected Impact |
|---|---|
| Reduce R&D expenditures | ($ 50) |
| Replace microphone with one of nearly equal sensitivity | ($ 30) |
| Replace power switch with a cheaper and almost as reliable version | ($ 30) |
| Replace current inspection procedure with an integrated quality review process at each assembly station | ($ 40) |
|     Total impact | ($150) |

| Alternative B | Projected Impact |
|---|---|
| Replace the amplifier with one having slightly less power but not enough difference to be noticed by most users | ($ 50) |
| Replace microphone with one of nearly equal sensitivity | ($ 30) |
| Replace power switch with a cheaper and almost as reliable version | ($ 30) |
| Replace current inspection procedure with an integrated quality review process at each assembly station | ($ 40) |
|     Total impact | ($150) |

*(continued)*

| Alternative C | Projected Impact |
|---|---:|
| Increase R&D expenditures to develop a third-generation computer chip–based hearing aid | $ 40 |
| Replace the amplifier with one having slightly less power but not enough difference to be noticed by most users | ($ 50) |
| Replace microphone with one of nearly equal sensitivity | ($ 30) |
| Replace power switch with a cheaper and almost as reliable version | ($ 30) |
| Replace current inspection procedure with an integrated quality review process at each assembly station | ($ 40) |
| Renegotiate contract with supplier of plastic casings | ($ 20) |
| Replace plastic earpiece material with a lower quality material that will still meet user's expectations of a 6- to 10-year useful life | ($ 20) |
| Total impact | ($150) |

Manufacturing and marketing managers agreed that the design changes proposed in all the options would not significantly alter the market appeal of the current product. After a review of its alternatives, HPI chose alternative C, primarily because it included an increase in research and development expenditures that would start to position the firm to compete in the market for the new type of hearing aid. Key managers also determined that this alternative was strategically important because the new technology, while only a fraction of the market now, could be dominant in the next 10 to 15 years as prices come down on the new units and users become more aware of the benefits of the computer chip.

## An Illustration Using Quality Function Deployment (QFD)

**Quality function deployment (QFD)** is the integration of value engineering, marketing analysis, and target costing to assist in determining which components of the product should be targeted for redesign or cost reduction. It helps designers and managers break down the total product target cost into the components that make up the product. There are four steps in QFD and we will use the example of a table saw product to explain those steps.

1. Determine the customer's purchasing criteria for this product and how these criteria are ranked. For the saw, the customer criteria could be safety, performance, and economy.

2. Identify the components of the product and the manufacturing cost of each component. For simplicity, assume the components of the table saw are the motor, the saw, and the frame.

3. Determine how each component contributes to customer satisfaction. How much does the motor contribute to the customer's desired safety, performance, and economy? What about the contribution of the saw or the frame? Recognize that in actual practice there are likely to be more components and more criteria.

4. The final step is to determine the importance index of each component, by combining the information in steps one and three and then comparing this to the cost information in step 2.

To illustrate, suppose customers were asked to use a scale of 1 to 100 to rate the importance of each criterion. It is the relative rather than the absolute importance that is significant. Calculate the relative importance by dividing the score for each criterion by the total points awarded. The customer ranking and relative importance results appear in the following table.

**First: Customer Criteria and Ranking**

| | Importance | Relative Importance | |
|---|---|---|---|
| Safety | 95 | 46.3% | = 95 ÷ 205 |
| Performance | 60 | 29.3 | = 60 ÷ 205 |
| Economy | 50 | 24.4 | = 50 ÷ 205 |
| Total | 205 | 100.0% | |

---

*(margin note)*

**Quality function deployment (QFD)**

is the integration of value engineering, marketing analysis, and target costing to assist in determining which components of the product should be targeted for redesign.

Second, identify the components and both the absolute and relative cost of each:

| Second: Product Components and Cost | | |
|---|---|---|
| | Cost | Percent of Total |
| Motor | $40 | 53.3% |
| Saw | 20 | 26.7 |
| Frame | 15 | 20.0 |
| Total | $75 | 100.0% |

Third, determine the contribution of each component to satisfying customer criteria. This step usually requires a cross-functional team that may include marketing, operations, and cost management analysts. In this example, the desired criteria of safety is achieved primarily by the frame (60%) and then by the saw (30%) and motor (10%).

| Third: Determine How Components Contribute to Customer Satisfaction | | | |
|---|---|---|---|
| | Customer Criteria | | |
| **Components** | **Safety** | **Performance** | **Economy** |
| Motor | 10% | 10% | 60% |
| Saw | 30 | 50 | 10 |
| Frame | 60 | 40 | 30 |
| | 100% | 100% | 100% |

Fourth, determine the importance index for each component, which reflects the value of the component to the customer. To compute the importance index, multiply the relative importance of each criterion by each component's percentage contribution and then sum those amounts. For example, the 22.2% index for the motor is determined as follows:

$$(46.3\% \times 10\%) + (29.3\% \times 10\%) + (24.4\% \times 60\%) = 22.2\%$$

| Fourth: Determine Importance Index for Each Component | | | | |
|---|---|---|---|---|
| | Customer Criteria | | | Importance Index |
| | **Safety** | **Performance** | **Economy** | |
| **Relative importance of this criteria (step one)** | **46.3%** | **29.3%** | **24.4%** | |
| **The % contribution of each component to each customer criteria (from step 3):** | | | | |
| Motor | 10% | 10% | 60% | 22.2% |
| Saw | 30 | 50 | 10 | 31.0 |
| Frame | 60 | 40 | 30 | 46.8 |
| | 100% | 100% | 100% | 100.0% |

The importance index can now be compared to the cost information in step two to identify components where cost reductions are needed, and components where additional design features might be appropriate.

| Components | Importance Index | Relative Cost |
|---|---|---|
| Motor | 22.2% | 53.3% |
| Saw | 31.0 | 26.7 |
| Frame | 46.8 | 20.0 |
| | 100.0% | 100.0% |

The comparison above shows that far too much is being spent on the motor relative to its value to the customer. In contrast, not enough is being spent on the frame, relative to customer criteria.

This information is a guide to both the redesign of the product and the determination of the target cost for each component.

### Benefits of Target Costing

Target costing can be beneficial because it

- Orients the organization toward the customer, as design is focused on customer values.
- Reduces costs, through more effective and efficient design.
- Helps the firm achieve desired profitability on new or redesigned products.
- Can decrease the total time required for product development, through improved coordination of design, manufacturing, and marketing managers.
- Can increase communication and cooperation among departments.
- Can improve overall product quality, as the design is carefully developed and manufacturing issues are considered explicitly in the design phase.

Target costing also involves costs due to the:

- Need to develop detailed cost data.
- Time demands associated with cooperation and coordination throughout the organization.

## The Theory of Constraints

> Remember that time is money.
>
> *Benjamin Franklin*

**LO 13-2**

*Apply the theory of constraints to strategic management.*

Benjamin Franklin must be right. Most strategic initiatives undertaken by firms today focus on improving the speed of their operations throughout the cost life cycle because speed can provide a competitive edge. Customers expect quick response to inquiries and fast delivery of the product. Shorter sales life cycles in many industries mean that manufacturers are working to reduce product development and delivery time. Some of the most successful business models of recent years, such as those of Dell Inc. and **Amazon.com**, were built on speed.

In this part of the chapter, we present one of the key methods used to improve speed, the theory of constraints (TOC). Before looking closely at TOC, consider the issue of how speed is measured and improved throughout the cost life cycle, as illustrated in Exhibit 13.6. The measures are defined in different ways by different firms, depending on the nature of the firm's operations. For example, manufacturing **cycle time** (or manufacturing *lead time* or *throughput time*) is commonly defined as follows:

**Cycle time**

is the amount of time between the receipt of a customer order and the shipment of the order.

$$\text{Cycle time} = \text{Amount of time between the receipt of a customer order and the shipment of the order}$$

Recognize that some firms may define start time as the time a production batch is scheduled, the time the raw materials are ordered, or the time that production on the order is started. Similarly, the finish time of the cycle can be defined as the time that production is completed or the time the order is ready for shipping.

Another useful measure is **manufacturing cycle efficiency (MCE)**:

**Manufacturing cycle efficiency (MCE)**

is the ratio of processing time to total cycle time.

$$\text{MCE} = \frac{\text{Processing time}}{\text{Total cycle time}}$$

For example, if the processing time is 2 days and the cycle time is 10 days, then the MCE ratio is 2/10, or 20%.

**EXHIBIT 13.6** Measures of Speed and How to Improve Speed at Each Step of the Cost Life Cycle

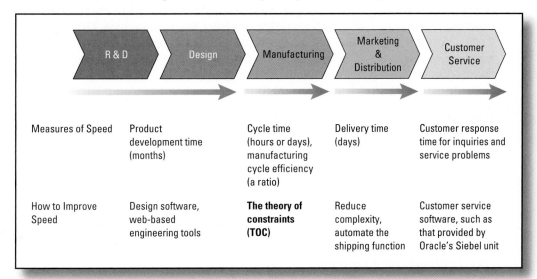

| | | Manufacturing | Marketing & Distribution | Customer Service |
|---|---|---|---|---|
| Measures of Speed | Product development time (months) | Cycle time (hours or days), manufacturing cycle efficiency (a ratio) | Delivery time (days) | Customer response time for inquiries and service problems |
| How to Improve Speed | Design software, web-based engineering tools | **The theory of constraints (TOC)** | Reduce complexity, automate the shipping function | Customer service software, such as that provided by Oracle's Siebel unit |

MCE separates total cycle time into the time required for each of the various activities: processing (value-adding work on the product), inspection, materials handling, waiting, and so on. Most firms would like to see their MCE close to 1, which reflects less time wasted on moving, waiting, inspecting, and other non-value-adding activities.[4]

The theory of constraints (TOC) was developed to help managers reduce cycle times and operating costs.[5] Prior to TOC, managers often devoted efforts to improve efficiency and speed *throughout* the manufacturing process instead of focusing attention on just those activities that were constraints (i.e., bottlenecks) in the process. **Constraints** are activities that slow a product's total cycle time. Goldratt and Cox use as an example a troop of boy scouts on a hike. The goal is to have every scout complete the hike, so the slowest hiker is the constraint and sets the overall pace for the troop. Manufacturers have learned that increased efficiency and speed with activities that are not constraints could be dysfunctional. Using resources to increase the efficiency of nonconstraints is likely to result in the buildup of work-in-process inventory for activities prior to the constraint (just as the faster scouts would be "bunched up" behind the slowest scout) and to divert attention and resources from the actual slowdown in cycle time. TOC has turned the attention to improving speed at the constraints, which causes a favorable decrease in the overall cycle time and inventory. TOC can be compared to just-in-time manufacturing (JIT) in that both are aimed at reducing cycle time and reducing inventory levels. JIT accomplishes this by methods that coordinate manufacturing processes so that materials are available just in time for the process, thereby increasing processing speed and reducing or eliminating inventory.[6]

**Constraints**
are those activities that slow the product's cycle time.

## The Use of the Theory of Constraints Analysis in Health Product Manufacturing

To illustrate the five steps of TOC, we return to our example involving Health Products International, Inc. (HPI). Suppose that HPI adopted alternative C from the list of alternatives on page 528 and is currently manufacturing both the second generation (HPI-2)

---

[4] While 100% is a theoretical maximum for MCE, many firms find their MCE ratios somewhat smaller because of delays and wasted time in the manufacturing process. For example, statistics from the auto industry show that some firms have cycle times of over 30 days and product assembly times of 1 to 2 days—an MCE of approximately 5%. Also, note that the terms used here are *manufacturing* measurements, and that similar measures are used by firms to examine the firm's progress in *filling customer orders*. For example, customer lead time (or customer cycle time) is usually defined as the time from the receipt of an order to the delivery of the product.

[5] E. Goldratt and J. Cox, *The Goal* (New York: Free Press, 1986); and E. Goldratt, *The Theory of Constraints* (New York: North River Press, 1990). See also Thomas Corbett, *Throughput Accounting* (New York: North River Press, 1998).

[6] A comprehensive comparison of TOC and JIT is provided by Bih-Ru Lea and Hokey Min, "Selection of Management Accounting Systems in Just-In-Time and Theory of Constraints-Based Manufacturing," *International Journal of Production Research*, 2003, pp. 2879–910.

and a new third generation (HPI-3) hearing aid. The prices for the HPI-2 and HPI-3 are competitive at $600 and $1,200, respectively, and are not expected to change. However, increasing cycle times have led to a backlog of orders for both products. Orders average 3,000 units for the HPI-2 and 1,800 units for the HPI-3 and new customers are told they may have to wait three or more weeks for their orders. Management is concerned about the need to improve speed in the manufacturing process and is planning to use TOC. Here are the steps HPI would take to use TOC.

## Steps in the Theory of Constraints Analysis

TOC analysis has five steps:

1. Identify the constraint.
2. Determine the most profitable product mix given the constraint.
3. Maximize the flow through the constraint.
4. Add capacity to the constraint.
5. Redesign the manufacturing process for flexibility and fast cycle time.

### Step 1: Identify the Constraint

> A **flow diagram**
> is a flowchart of the work done that shows the sequence of processes and the amount of time required for each.

The management accountant works with manufacturing managers and engineers to identify any constraint in the manufacturing process by developing a **flow diagram** of the work done. The flow diagram shows the sequence of processes and the amount of time each requires. The five processes for HPI follow, and their flow diagram is shown in Exhibit 13.7.

Process 1. Assemble earpiece.
Process 2. Test and program computer chip (product HPI-3 only).
Process 3. Install other electronics.

**EXHIBIT 13.7**
**Flow Diagram for HPI, Inc.**

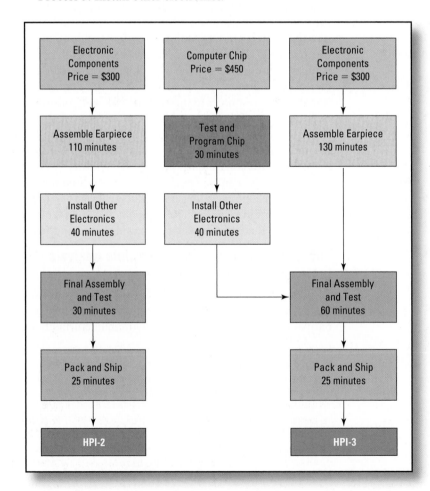

**EXHIBIT 13.8   Summary of Data for HPI, Inc., TOC Analysis**

| | HPI-2 | HPI-3 |
|---|---|---|
| Demand (per month) | 3,000 | 1,800 |
| Price | $600 | $1,200 |
| Materials cost | $300 | $750 |

| | Minutes Required for Each Product per Unit | | Number of Employees | Total Hours Available per Month |
|---|---|---|---|---|
| **Process** | **HPI-2** | **HPI-3** | | |
| 1: Assemble earpiece | 110 | 130 | 80 | 9,600 |
| 2: Test and program computer chip | 0 | 30 | 8 | 960 |
| 3: Install other electronics | 40 | 40 | 30 | 3,600 |
| 4: Perform final assembly and test | 30 | 60 | 20 | 2,400 |
| 5: Pack and ship | 25 | 25 | 18 | 2,160 |

**Step 1: Identify the Constraint (the process for which total hours required for the given demand exceeds available hours—Process 4)**

| | Hours Required | | | | |
|---|---|---|---|---|---|
| | **HPI-2** | **HPI-3** | **Total Hours** | **Hours Available** | **Slack Hours** |
| Process 1: Assemble earpiece (5,500 hrs = 3,000 × 110/60, etc.) | 5,500 | 3,900 | 9,400 | 9,600 | 200 |
| Process 2: Test and program chip | 0 | 900 | 900 | 960 | 60 |
| Process 3: Install other electronics | 2,000 | 1,200 | 3,200 | 3,600 | 400 |
| Process 4: Perform final assembly and test | 1,500 | 1,800 | 3,300 | 2,400 | (900) |
| Process 5: Pack and ship | 1,250 | 750 | 2,000 | 2,160 | 160 |

**Step 2, Part 1: Identify Most Profitable  Product = HPI-2**

| | HPI-2 | HPI-3 |
|---|---|---|
| Price | $600.00 | $1,200.00 |
| Materials cost | 300.00 | 750.00 |
| Throughput margin | $300.00 | $ 450.00 |
| Constraint time (for Process 4) | 30 | 60 |
| Throughput margin per minute | $ 10.00 | $ 7.50 |

**Step 2, Part 2: Determine the Most Profitable Product Mix**

| | HPI-2 | HPI-3 | Hours per Unit | Constraint Time (Process 4) |
|---|---|---|---|---|
| Total monthly demand | 3,000 units | 1,800 units | | |
| Constraint process time available | | | | 2,400 hours |
| Time required to meet demand for most profitable product | 3,000 units | | × 0.50 = | 1,500 hours |
| Constraint process time remaining to meet remaining demand and quantity that can be produced in the remaining time available | | 900 units | × 1.00 = | 900 hours |
| Unmet demand | -0- | 900 units | | |

Process 4. Perform final assembly and test.

Process 5. Pack and ship.

The raw materials cost for each unit is $300 for the HPI-2 and $750 for the HPI-3 ($450 for the computer chip and $300 for other electronics).

The constraint is identified by using the flow diagram to analyze the total time required for each process given the current level of demand. Exhibit 13.8 shows a summary of the data for this analysis, including the number of employees available for each process and the total time available per month for all employees (assuming a 40-hour work week in which 30 hours are available for work and 10 hours are used for breaks, training, etc.). HPI processes are very specialized, and employees are able to work only within their assigned process. Moreover, because of the specialized skills required, HPI has difficulty maintaining adequate staffing in all processes except process 5, pack and ship.

Step 1 in Exhibit 13.8 shows the total time required in each process given the current level of demand. Each of the five processes except process 4 has slack time. Therefore, the constraint occurs with process 4, perform final assembly and test. Because of inadequate time (900 hours too few) available in this process, HPI will not be able to meet the total demand for HPI-2 and HPI-3 and will delay some orders or perhaps not fill them at all. HPI must now determine which orders to fill and which not to fill. This takes us to the second step of TOC.

### Step 2: Determine the Most Profitable Product Mix Given the Constraint

The most profitable product mix is the combination of products that maximizes total profits for both products. Should we produce all 3,000 units of HPI-2 and whatever we can of HPI-3, or should we produce all 1,800 units of HPI-3 and whatever we can of HPI-2? Or some other mix? The step 2 analysis in Exhibit 13.8 provides the answer.[7]

**Throughput margin**
is a TOC measure of product profitability; it equals price less materials cost, including all purchased components and materials handling costs.

To determine the most profitable product mix, we first determine the most profitable product, given the constraint. TOC measures product profitability using the **throughput margin,** which is the product price less materials cost (which includes the costs of all materials used, purchased components, and materials-handling costs). All other manufacturing costs are excluded in determining profitability because they are assumed to be fixed and will not change regardless of which product mix is chosen.[8] Step 2, part 1, in Exhibit 13.8 shows that throughput margins for the HPI-2 and HPI-3 are $300 and $450 per unit, respectively. Although HPI-3 has the higher margin, the profitability analysis is not complete without considering the time each product requires from the constrained process 4, final assembly and test. Since HPI-3 involves twice as much constraint time as HPI-2 (60 versus 30 minutes), HPI can produce twice as many HPI-2 models for each HPI-3 produced. In effect, the relevant measure of profitability is throughput margin *per minute of time in final assembly and test,* that is, a throughput per minute of $10 for HPI-2 and $7.50 for HPI-3. This means each minute of final assembly and test used to produce HPI-2 earns $10 while each minute used to produce HPI-3 earns only $7.50. HPI-2 is the most profitable product when final assembly and test is the constraint.

The best product mix is determined in step 2, part 2, of Exhibit 13.8. Since it is the most profitable product, HPI produces all 3,000 units or demand for HPI-2 and then determines the remaining capacity in final assembly. Finally, HPI determines the number of units of HPI-3 it can produce with the remaining capacity on the constraint. Despite the demand for 1,800 units of HPI-3, only 900 can be produced with the available capacity. Thus, the optimal product mix is 3,000 units of HPI-2 and 900 units of HPI-3.

The assumption in our illustration of the TOC approach is that minimal or no inventory of HPI-3 is maintained, so that it is not possible to fill the unmet demand for HPI-3 out of inventory. This assumption is in keeping with the TOC approach which emphasizes the reduction of cost and speed of product flow by removing constraints and reducing inventory levels.

### Step 3: Maximize the Flow through the Constraint

In this step, the management accountant looks for ways to speed the flow through the constraint by simplifying the process, improving the product design, reducing setup time, and reducing other delays due to unscheduled and non-value-added activities such as inspections or machine breakdowns, among others.

---

[7] Note that the analysis in step 2, part 1, and step 2, part 2, of Exhibit 13.8 is identical to that explained in Chapter 11 under the heading of "Multiple Products and Limited Resources," for one production constraint. The determination of the optimal product mix is arrived at in the same manner. Step 2, part 2, can be solved using the Solver tool in Excel, as illustrated in Chapter 11.

[8] Note that TOC analysis assumes that factory labor is not a direct and variable cost but is a fixed cost. This assumption applies when labor is a small or an unchanging part of total cost.

### SPEEDING DELIVERY OF YOUR DRINK

Starbucks has decided to speed up drink delivery by reengineering the process of drink preparation. An 11-person team will be using lessons from the Toyota production system to reduce preparation time and improve a customer's experience. It also means that each Starbucks location could serve more drinks with the same number of workers or reduce the number of workers required to serve the same number of drinks.

### SPEED THROUGH FLEXIBILITY

Improvements in the design of auto manufacturing plants to use labor and machines more flexibly allow Honda to improve throughput and reduce costs. Flexible manufacturing improvements come through automation, flexible labor agreements, strategic outsourcing, and fast changeover times.

**Sources:** Julie Jargon, "Latest Starbucks Buzzword: 'Lean' Japanese Technique," *The Wall Street Journal,* August 4, 2009, p. A1; Kate Linebaugh, "Honda's Flexible Plants Provide Edge," *The Wall Street Journal,* September 23, 2008, p. B1.

---

**Takt time**

is the speed at which units must be manufactured to meet customer demand.

A commonly used method for identifying constraints and smoothing production flow is the use of **Takt time.** *Takt* is a German word meaning the conductor's baton, or rhythm. It is the ratio of the total time available to the expected customer demand. For example, suppose a manufacturing plant operates for eight hours per day, and that after allowing for break time, 400 minutes of manufacturing time are available per day. Also, since the average customer demand per day is 800 units, the Takt time is 30 seconds per unit:

$$\text{Takt time} = \frac{\text{Available manufacturing time}}{\text{Customer demand}}$$

$$\text{Takt time} = \frac{400 \text{ minutes}}{800 \text{ units}} = \frac{1}{2} \text{ minute or 30 seconds per unit}$$

This means that each unit must be manufactured in an average of 30 seconds to meet customer demand. To illustrate how Takt time can be used to identify constraints, consider a product that has demand of 18,000 units per week, with total operating time available per week at 75 hours. The Takt time is:

$$\frac{\text{Available time}}{\text{Demand}} = \frac{75 \text{ hr.} \times 60 \text{ min.} \times 60 \text{ seconds}}{18,000 \text{ units}}$$

$$= \frac{270,000 \text{ seconds}}{18,000 \text{ units}}$$

$$= 15 \text{ seconds per unit}$$

The plant must produce a unit each 15 seconds to keep up with demand. Assuming the manufacturing process has three operations in sequence, each requiring 15 seconds of processing time, a product will be completed every 15 seconds. Now, assume that the first operation requires 10 seconds, the second operation requires 20 seconds, and the third requires 15 seconds. The processing line is now unbalanced; the first operation moves quickly and work in process will build up at the relatively slower second operation. Furthermore, the total demand of 18,000 units cannot be met because the second process requires more than the 15 seconds of Takt time. The second operation is a constraint. In fact, the plant will only be able to meet a demand of 13,500 units (13,500 = 270,000 seconds ÷ 20 seconds) because of the slow second operation. Only when the three operations are balanced at or near the Takt time of 15 seconds will the demand be met. The goal of implementing Takt time is to balance the processing of the operations, so that the processing time of each operation is preferably a little below the overall Takt time. An operation that has a very low processing time relative to Takt time has too much capacity, making it more efficient to reduce capacity (and thus increase processing time) on that operation, as long as processing time remains below Takt time.

### Step 4: Add Capacity to the Constraint

As a longer-term measure to relieve the constraint and improve cycle time, management should consider adding capacity to the constraints by adding new or improved machines and/or additional labor.

### Step 5: Redesign the Manufacturing Process for Flexibility and Fast Cycle Time

The most complete strategic response to the constraint is to redesign the manufacturing process, including the introduction of new manufacturing technology, deletion of some hard-to-manufacture products, and redesign of some products for greater ease of manufacturing. Simply removing one or more minor features on a given product might speed up the production process significantly. The use of value engineering as described earlier might help at this point.

## The Five Steps of Strategic Decision Making for Speed and Efficiency in the Fashion Industry

Burberry Group PLC is a London-based fashion retailer with several hundred retail stores worldwide providing its famous trench coats and a variety of women's and men's fashion clothing. Burberry CEO, Angela Ahrendts, upon taking the position in July 2006, noticed that the company was making "way too much stuff." There were too many product lines—for example, 20 different versions of men's and women's polo shirts. The complexity of the large number of products resulted in delay throughout the value chain—design, manufacturing, and distribution.[9]

### The Five Steps of Strategic Decision Making for Burberry, the Fashion Retailer

1. **Determine the strategic issues surrounding the problem.**  Burberry, as a fashion retailer, competes on the basis of design and fashion innovation, a differentiation strategy.

2. **Identify the alternative actions.**  The company can continue to focus on product development, design, and innovation, with the expectation that the delays will not affect customer satisfaction or profitability. Alternatively, the company could review its product lines and look for efficiency throughout the value chain and expect to maintain the unique designs that have satisfied its customers in the past.

3. **Obtain information and conduct analyses of the alternatives.**  Ahrendts directed the CFO to prepare a report showing what amount each product contributed to overall sales. The findings were that 20% of the products produced 80% of total sales. The enterprise system, SAP, was later introduced to help determine product profitability.

4. **Based on strategy and analysis, choose and implement the desired alternative.**  Based on the CFO's information and her understanding that the firm's strategy required comprehensive, coherent product development, Ahrendts decided to reduce the number of Burberry's products by one-third and to switch from two large collections of fashion per year to five smaller collections. At the same time, she coordinated product development from London, so that all Burberry lines provided ". . . one brand and one message." The changes allowed the company to design and produce its fashions much more quickly, to adjust much more rapidly to changes in customer expectations, and to reduce costs through more efficient processes.

5. **Provide an ongoing evaluation of the effectiveness of implementation in step 4.**  The changes made the company more competitive, more profitable, and better able to meet customer expectations. However, since design and innovation are the hallmarks of the

---

[9] The information is from Burberry's 2007 annual report and from Cecilie Rohwedder, "Burberry CEO Retrenches: Fewer Items, Faster Delivery," *The Wall Street Journal*, May 24, 2007, p. B1. Other high fashion designers including Valentino, Gucci, and Zara are also changing design and manufacturing processes for greater speed and flexibility: Christina Passariello, "Logistics Are in Vogue with Designers," *The Wall Street Journal*, Friday June 27, 2008, p. B1; Kerry Capell, "Zara Thrives by Breaking All the Rules," *BusinessWeek*, October 20, 2008, p. 66; Christina Binkley, "Tracking the Trousers Cycle," *The Wall Street Journal*, August 16, 2007, p. D1.

**EXHIBIT 13.9**
**The TOC Report for an Auto Glass Manufacturer**

Source: R. J. Campbell, "Pricing Strategy in the Automotive Glass Industry," *Management Accounting,* July 1989, pp. 26–34.

| | March 2010 | | | |
| --- | --- | --- | --- | --- |
| | Style C | Style A | Style H | Style B |
| Window size | 0.77 | .073 | 7.05 | 4.95 |
| Sales volume | High | Moderate | High | Moderate |
| Units in unfilled orders | 1,113 | 234 | 882 | 23 |
| Average lead time (days) | 16 | 23 | 8 | 11 |
| Market price | $2.82 | $6.68 | $38.12 | $24.46 |
| Direct production costs | | | | |
|   Materials | 0.68 | 0.64 | 5.75 | 4.02 |
|   Scrap allowance | 0.06 | 0.05 | 0.42 | 0.34 |
|   Materials handling | 0.12 | 0.12 | 1.88 | 1.61 |
|   Subtotal | .86 | .81 | 8.05 | 5.97 |
| Throughput margin | $1.96 | $5.87 | $30.07 | $18.49 |
| Furnace hours per unit | .0062 | .0061 | .0082 | .0078 |
| Throughput margin per hour | $ 316 | $ 962 | $3,667 | $2,371 |

fashion industry and for Burberry, the company must maintain a priority on these facets of the business as well.

## Theory of Constraints Reports

When a firm focuses on improving cycle time, eliminating constraints, and improving speed of delivery, the performance evaluation measures also focus on these critical success factors. A common approach is to report throughput margin as well as selected operating data in a *theory of constraints (TOC) report.* TOC reports are useful for identifying the most profitable product and for monitoring success in achieving the critical success factors. An example of this report used by a manufacturer of automotive glass is shown in Exhibit 13.9. Note in the exhibit that window styles H and B are the most profitable because they have far higher throughput margins based on the binding constraint, hours of furnace time. The throughput margin per hour is $3,667 for style H and $2,371 for style B; in contrast, the throughput margin per hour for styles C and A is less than $1,000.

## Activity-Based Costing and the Theory of Constraints

Firms using such cost management methods as target costing and the theory of constraints may also employ activity-based costing (ABC). Like TOC, ABC is used to assess the profitability of products. The difference is that TOC takes a short-term approach to profitability analysis by emphasizing only materials related costs, while ABC costing develops a long-term analysis by including all product costs.

ABC, unlike TOC, does not explicitly include the resource constraints and capacities of production activities. Thus, ABC cannot be used to determine the best short-term product mix. ABC and TOC are thus *complementary* methods; ABC provides a comprehensive analysis of cost drivers and accurate unit costs as a basis for strategic decisions about long-term pricing and product mix. In contrast, TOC provides a useful method for improving the short-term profitability of the manufacturing plant through short-term product mix adjustments and through attention to production constraints. The differences between ABC and TOC are outlined in Exhibit 13.10.[10]

[10] For a comparison of TOC and ABC, see Robin Cooper and Regine Slagmulder, "Integrating Activity-Based Costing and the Theory of Constraints," *Management Accounting,* February 1999, p. 2; Robert Kee and Charles Schmidt, "A Comparative Analysis of Utilizing Activity-Based Costing and the Theory of Constraints for Making Product-Mix Decisions," *International Journal of Production Economics* 63 (2000), pp. 1–17; and Bih-Ru Lea, "Management Accounting in ERP Integrated MRP and TOC Environments," *Industrial Management + Data Systems* 107, no. 8 (October 2007), pp. 1188–211.

**EXHIBIT 13.10**
**Comparison of the TOC and ABC Costing Methods**

| | TOC | ABC |
|---|---|---|
| Main objective | **Short-term focus**; throughput margin analysis based on materials and materials-related costs | **Long-term focus**; analysis of all product costs, including materials, labor, and overhead |
| Resource constraints and capacities | Included explicitly; a principal focus of TOC | Not included explicitly except as shown in time-driven ABC (Chapter 5) |
| Cost drivers | No direct utilization of cost drivers | Develop an understanding of cost drivers at the unit, batch, product, and facility levels |
| Major use | Optimization of production flow and short-term product mix | Strategic pricing and profit planning |

## Life-Cycle Costing

**LO 13-3**
*Describe how life-cycle costing facilitates strategic management.*

Typically, product or service costs are measured and reported for relatively short periods, such as a month or a year. Life-cycle costing provides a long-term perspective because it considers the entire cost life cycle of the product or service (see Exhibit 13.11). It therefore provides a more complete perspective of product or service costs and profitability. For example, a product that is designed quickly and carelessly, with little investment in design costs, could have significantly higher marketing and service costs later in the life cycle. Managers are interested in the total cost, over the entire life cycle, not manufacturing costs only.

While cost management methods have tended to focus only on manufacturing costs, upstream and downstream costs can account for a significant portion of total life-cycle costs, especially in certain industries:

**Industries with High Upstream Costs**

Computer software
Specialized industrial and medical equipment
Pharmaceuticals

**Industries with High Downstream Costs**

Fashion apparel
Perfumes, cosmetics, and toiletries

### The Importance of Design

As managers consider upstream and downstream costs, decision making at the design stage is critical. Target costing, as explained earlier in this chapter, shows that although the costs incurred at the design stage may account for only a very small percentage of the

**EXHIBIT 13.11**
**Life-Cycle Costing in the Cost Life Cycle**

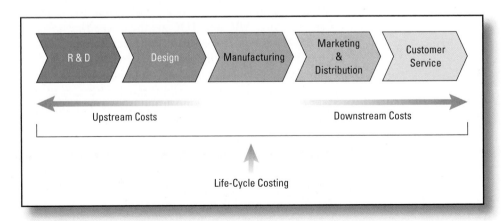

**EXHIBIT 13.12    Committed versus Incurred Costs**

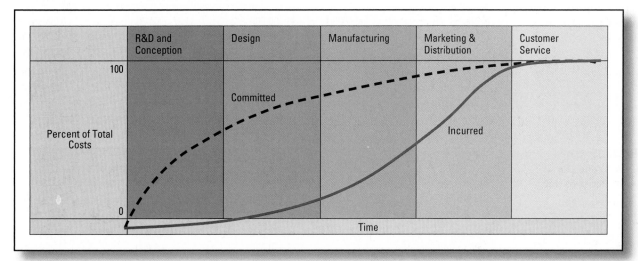

total costs over the entire product life cycle, design-stage decisions commit a firm to a given production, marketing, and service plan. Therefore, they lock in most of the remaining life-cycle costs.

This concept is illustrated in Exhibit 13.12, which shows the difference in terms of time between when costs are committed versus when those costs are actually incurred.

While Exhibit 13.12 shows the difference in timing between committing and incurring costs, Exhibit 13.13 provides an example of the effects of poor design and quality on life-cycle costs.

The critical success factors at the design stage include the following:

**Reduced time to market.** In a competitive environment where the speed of product development and the speed of delivery are critical, efforts to reduce time to market have high priority.

**Reduced expected service costs.** By careful, simple design and the use of modular, interchangeable components, the expected service costs can be greatly reduced.

**Reduced product environmental impact.** The product is designed with a focus on sustainability—low carbon footprint (use of greenhouse gasses) in manufacturing and in the later use of the product, use of recycled materials, and other means to lower the environmental impact of the product and the manufacturing of the product.[11]

**EXHIBIT 13.13**
**Value Chain Showing Upstream and Downstream Linkages for a Manufacturer**

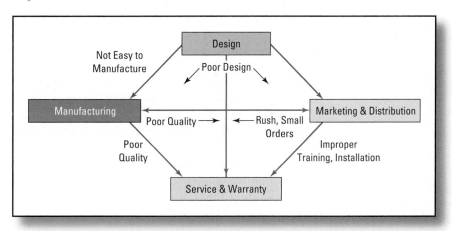

[11] John Miller, "Maersk Orders 10 Huge Ships from Daewoo," *The Wall Street Journal,* February 22, 2011, p. B3. See also, Marc J. Epstein, *Making Sustainability Work: Best Practices in Managing and Measuring Corporate Social, Environmental, and Economic Impacts* (San Francisco: Berrett-Koehler, 2008).

**EXHIBIT 13.14**
Product-Line Income
Statement for Analytical
Decisions, Inc.

|  | ADI-1 | ADI-2 | Total |
|---|---|---|---|
| Sales | $4,500,000 | $2,500,000 | $7,000,000 |
| Cost of sales | 1,240,000 | 1,005,000 | 2,245,000 |
| Gross margin | $3,260,000 | $1,495,000 | $4,755,000 |
| Research and development |  |  | 2,150,000 |
| Selling and service |  |  | 1,850,000 |
| Operating profit |  |  | $ 755,000 |

**EXHIBIT 13.15**
Life-Cycle Costing for
Analytical Decisions, Inc.

|  | ADI-1 | ADI-2 | Total |
|---|---|---|---|
| Sales | $4,500,000 | $2,500,000 | $7,000,000 |
| Cost of sales | 1,240,000 | 1,005,000 | 2,245,000 |
| Gross margin | $3,260,000 | $1,495,000 | $4,755,000 |
| Research and development | 1,550,000 | 600,000 | 2,150,000 |
| Selling and service | 1,450,000 | 400,000 | 1,850,000 |
| Operating profit | $ 260,000 | $ 495,000 | $ 755,000 |

**Improved ease of manufacture.** To reduce production costs and speed production, the design must be easy to manufacture.

**Process planning and design.** The plan for the manufacturing process should be flexible, allowing for fast setups and product changeovers, using flexible manufacturing concepts, computer-integrated manufacturing, computer-assisted design, and concurrent engineering.

### The Use of Life-Cycle Costing in a Software Firm

Consider the following application of life-cycle costing. Analytical Decisions, Inc. (ADI), provides specialized software to banks and other financial institutions. ADI has two products, each of which is used to analyze loan loss reserves and plan loan portfolios. The difference is the target markets. ADI-1 is targeted at large institutions and ADI-2 is for small banks and savings and loans. Each product is updated at least annually to improve functionality is some significant way.

Initially, ADI analyzed profitability by using a commercial software package, which provided reports like the one shown in Exhibit 13.14. This analysis shows that both products are quite profitable, even with significant R&D and selling costs. While the report shows that ADI-1 has a higher gross margin percentage than ADI-2, management has begun to realize that this simple comparison is not enough. Process analysis shows that the R&D function is carried out by project teams assigned to either ADI-1 or ADI-2 and that sales and customer-service personnel log their hours by product, making the direct assignment of the related costs to either of the two products quite simple. These results are shown in Exhibit 13.15. However, these costs are not included in the gross margin calculation.

The comparison of product profitability after including both the upstream R&D and downstream sales and service costs clearly indicates that ADI-2 is the more profitable of the two products. Additionally, the information can be further analyzed to provide a basis for management action. For example, the ratio of sales and service costs to revenue is 32.2% for ADI-1 and only 16% for ADI-2. Management should investigate further to determine whether the difference in relative spending is due to the nature of the different customers, quality issues, or some other reason, which may, in turn, reveal opportunities for cost savings.

## Strategic Pricing Using the Product Life Cycle

**LO 13-4**

*Outline the objectives and techniques of strategic pricing.*

Management accountants are involved in three pricing situations: The first is the special order decision explained in Chapter 11 in which a nonrecurring sales opportunity arises. The second context is target costing explained earlier in this chapter in which a firm faces a market price and determines how to achieve the level of costs necessary to make a profit. The third type of pricing decision—not involving special orders or market-determined prices—is the focus in this section. These are the long-term, strategic pricing decisions facing many managers. They are complex decisions involving strategic issues and careful use of cost information. To assist in these pricing decisions, the management accountant prepares cost information from the perspective of the cost life cycle, the sales life cycle, and the use of analytical pricing methods.

## Pricing Using the Cost Life Cycle

Pricing based on cost is a common approach for manufacturing and service firms. Those that compete on cost leadership use cost information to improve operating efficiency to reduce costs and price. Prices are set by the most efficient producers: the ones that are best able to reduce costs. In contrast, firms that compete on differentiation have more discretion in setting prices. The differentiated firm's goal might be to increase profits by setting an initial high price for those willing to pay, followed by lower prices for the cost-conscious customers (called *skimming*). Alternatively, the firm's goal might be to increase market share by lowering the price (called *penetration*). A third approach would be to build longer-term customer relationships by utilizing "value pricing" in which pricing is based on meeting specific customer needs. A firm's pricing policy is also influenced by patterns in the industry. For example, firms with seasonal demand (clothing, appliances, furniture, among others) usually offer discounts and promotions during the slow periods of the year. Other industries are sensitive to interest rates, stock market returns, other factors in the economy (automobiles and construction, among others), and new products or pricing policies of competitors. To deal with the complexity of the pricing decision, firms like GE Lighting, DHL, and Hewlett-Packard use web-based software systems to determine prices more quickly and accurately for different customers. The systems speed up the process of quoting prices and assist in determining the timing and location of discount programs. Thus, a number of seasonal, cyclical, economic, and other strategic factors influence the pricing policies of the firm, and cost information is only the starting point of the pricing decision. The cost information for pricing is commonly based on one of the four methods: (1) full manufacturing cost plus markup, (2) life-cycle cost plus markup, (3) full cost and desired gross margin percent, and (4) full cost plus desired return on assets.

### *Full Manufacturing Cost Plus Markup*

In this method, a firm uses the total of variable and fixed manufacturing costs and applies a markup percentage to cover other operating costs plus profit. The markup percentage could be determined by industry practice, judgment, or a desired level of profit. Suppose that a firm has a markup rate of 40% and, using ABC costing, determines the full manufacturing cost is $150. The resulting price would be $210, calculated as $150 + (150 \times 40\%)$.

### *Life-Cycle Cost Plus Markup*

The life-cycle approach to pricing uses the full life-cycle cost instead of manufacturing cost only. Suppose that in addition to manufacturing costs of $150 per unit, the example firm has selling and administrative costs of $25 per unit, for a total of $175 life-cycle cost. The firm uses a markup rate of 25% based on life-cycle costs. The calculated price is now $218.75:

$$\text{Total life-cycle costs} \times \text{Markup} = \text{Price}$$

$$\$175 \times 125\% = \$218.75$$

The life-cycle approach has the advantage that all costs are included, so that the markup percentage can be directly tied to a desired level of profit.

### *Full Cost and Desired Gross Margin Percent*

In this variation, the price is determined based upon achieving a desired gross margin percentage. To continue with the previous example, suppose that the desired gross margin is 30% of sales. Then, the price would be $214.29:

$$\text{Price} = \frac{\text{Full manufacturing cost}}{(1 - \text{Desired gross margin percentage})}$$

$$= \frac{\$150}{(1 - .3)} = \$214.29$$

This price would produce a gross margin of $214.29 − $150 = $64.29, which is 30% of sales. Alternatively, a variation of this method could be used to achieve a desired percentage return on life-cycle costs. For example, if the desired percentage return on life-cycle costs is 15%, then the price would be $205.88:

$$\text{Price} = \frac{\text{Full life-cycle cost}}{(1 - \text{Desired life-cycle margin percentage})}$$

$$= \frac{\$175}{(1 - .15)} = \$205.88$$

### *Full Cost Plus Desired Return on Assets*

Another pricing approach is to set the price to achieve a desired return on assets. Starting with the same information, now assume that the firm has $3.5 million assets committed to the production of the product and desires a 10% before-tax return on assets. Sales are expected to be 10,000 units. Using a life-cycle cost approach (a full manufacturing-cost approach could be used in a similar manner), the markup percentage would be 20%.

$$\text{Markup rate} = \frac{\text{Desired before-tax profit}}{\text{Life-cycle cost of expected sales}}$$

$$= \frac{\$3,500,000 \times 10\%}{10,000 \times \$175} = 20\%$$

And the price would then be $210:

$$\text{Price} = \text{Life-cycle cost} \times 120\% = \$175 \times 120\% = \$210$$

Each of these illustrations assumes that all sales are for the price determined. The desired price could be adjusted to reflect expected discounts or losses due to spoilage or theft.

## Strategic Pricing for Phases of the Sales Life Cycle

Strategic pricing depends on the position of the product or service in the sales life cycle. As the sales life cycle becomes shorter (only months in some industries such as consumer electronics), the analysis of the sales life cycle becomes increasingly important. In contrast to the cost life cycle just described, the sales life cycle refers to the phase of the product's or service's sales in the market, from introduction of the product or service to decline and withdrawal from the market. (Exhibit 13.2 illustrates the phases of the sales life cycle.)

> **Phase 1: Introduction.** The first phase involves little competition, and sales rise slowly as customers become aware of the new product or service. Costs are relatively high because of high R&D expenditures and capital costs for setting up production facilities and marketing efforts. Prices are relatively high because of product differentiation and the high costs at this phase. Product variety is limited.

**Phase 2: Growth.** Sales begin to increase rapidly as does product variety. The product continues to enjoy the benefits of differentiation. Competition increases, and prices begin to fall.

**Phase 3: Maturity.** Sales continue to increase but at a decreasing rate. The number of competitors and product variety both decline. Prices fall further, and differentiation is no longer important. Competition is based on cost given competitive quality and functionality.

**Phase 4: Decline.** Sales and prices decline, as do the number of competitors. Control of costs and an effective distribution network are key to continued survival.

In the first phase, the focus of management is on design, differentiation, and market- ing. The focus shifts to new product development and pricing strategy as competition develops in the second phase. In the third and fourth phases, management's attention turns to cost control, quality, and service as the market continues to become more com- petitive. Thus, the firm's strategy for the product or service changes over the sales life cycle from differentiation in the early phases to cost leadership in the final phases.

Similarly, the strategic pricing approach changes over the product or service life cycle. In the first phase, pricing is set relatively high to recover development costs and to take advantage of product differentiation and the new demand for the product. In the second phase, pricing is likely to stay relatively high as the firm attempts to build profitability in the growing market. In the latter phases, pricing becomes more competitive, and target costing and life-cycle costing methods are used as the firm becomes more a price taker than a price setter and makes efforts to reduce upstream and downstream costs.

### Strategic Pricing: Analytical and Peak Pricing Methods

Increasingly, retailers, manufacturers, and even service providers use a strategic approach to pricing in which they determine prices by what the customer is willing to bear, often using analytical methods based upon extensive data analysis of customer buying behav- ior. Consider, for example, the variability in the prices charged to fly between two destina- tions, the higher price for electricity in the middle of the day, the difference in the cost of a hotel room on a weekend versus a weekday, or the cost of peak versus off-peak minutes for a cell phone plan. Another example is the use of a "fighter brand," a low-priced ver- sion of the well-known product. The fighter brand is especially common in a recessionary environment, as consumers of high-end products look for less expensive substitutes.[12]

---

[12] Thomas H. Davenport and Jeanne G. Harris, *Competing on Analytics* (Boston: Harvard Business School Press, 2007); Josh Hyatt, "And in This Corner, the Fighter Brand," *CFO.com,* December 1, 2008; Rebecca Smith, "Electricity: The New Math," *The Wall Street Journal,* July 19, 2010, p. A6; Scott McCartney, "You Paid What for That Flight?," *The Wall Street Journal,* August 26, 2010, p. D1.

## Summary

The strategic cost management concepts introduced in the preceding chapters are extended here. First, we discuss four cost management methods used to analyze the product or service's life cycle: target costing, the theory of constraints, life-cycle costing, and strategic pricing. Target costing is a tool for analyzing the cost structure to help management identify the proper design features and manufacturing methods to allow the firm to meet a competitive price.

Target costing has five steps:

1. Determine market price.
2. Determine desired profit.
3. Calculate target cost.
4. Use value engineering to identify ways to reduce costs.
5. Use kaizen costing and operational control to further reduce costs.

The theory of constraints (TOC) is a tool that assists managers in identifying bottlenecks (constraints) and scheduling production to maximize throughput and profits. TOC analysis has five steps:

1. Identify the constraint.
2. Determine the most efficient product mix given the constraint.
3. Maximize the flow through the constraint.
4. Add capacity to the constraint.
5. Redesign the manufacturing process for flexibility and fast throughput.

Life-cycle costing assists managers in minimizing total cost over the product's or service's entire life cycle. Life-cycle costing brings a focus to the upstream (before production) activities (research and development, engineering) and downstream (after production) activities (marketing, distribution, service), as well as the manufacturing and operations that cost systems focus on. Especially important is a careful consideration of the effects of design choices on downstream costs.

Strategic pricing helps management determine the price of the product or service based on life-cycle costs or in its position in the different phases of its sales life cycle.

## Appendix

## Using the Flow Diagram to Identify Constraints

This chapter illustrated the use of the flow diagram to identify the constraint when there are two or more products being produced through a common set of processes, with no specific completion time. The flow diagram can also be useful when there is a single product or project and a specific completion time. This appendix illustrates the latter case, where the flow diagram is used to identify the processes that must be finished on time for the product or project to be completed on time.

To illustrate, suppose that a small pharmaceutical firm, Skincare Products, Inc. (SPI), manufactures an insect repellent with sunscreen. The batch production process requires mixing the active and inert ingredients in a large vat. Because of Food and Drug Administration requirements, SPI provides three inspections: (1) the raw materials it receives, (2) the mix of raw materials during the mixing process, and (3) the final product. The first and second inspections check the materials for correct chemical content and potency; the third inspection focuses on correct weight or item count. The manufacturing process has six processes, which are illustrated in Exhibit 13A.1, a flow diagram of the work done.

The exhibit shows the sequence of processes and the amount of time required for each and is used to identify the constraints. Computer techniques do this for large networks, but the constraints for a smaller one such as Exhibit 13A.1 can be identified by visual

**EXHIBIT 13A.1**

**Flow Diagram for Skincare Products, Inc.**

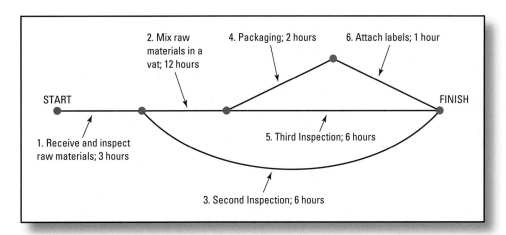

inspection. As defined earlier, a *constraint* is any process that delays the entire manufacturing process. The amount of the delay is often called *slack time*. Processes that can be delayed without delaying the finish time for the entire process are called *nonconstraints* or simply *slack* processes since the processes have some slack time in which to be completed. The constraints for SPI are shown in the following table:

| Process | Required Time (hours) |
|---|---|
| 1 – Receive and inspect raw materials | 3 |
| 2 – Mix raw materials in vat | 12 |
| 5 – Perform third inspection | 6 |

The total time for the entire manufacturing process cannot be less than the total time of these three processes added together (3 + 12 + 6 = 21 hours) since these processes must follow in sequence and cannot overlap. The remaining processes—3, 4, and 6—are not constraints and can be delayed one or more hours without delaying the entire production process. The amount of the delay can be determined as follows. Process 3 requires 6 hours and must be finished while processes 2 and 5 are being completed, but because processes 2 and 5 require 18 hours (12 + 6) and process 3 requires only 6 hours, process 3 has 12 hours (18 − 6) of slack time. Similarly, since processes 4 and 6 together require only 3 hours (2 hours plus 1 hour, respectively) and must be completed during process 5 (which requires 6 hours), in effect 3 hours of slack exist for processes 4 and 6 combined. Often the constraint processes (1, 2, and 5 in this case) are called critical processes since they cannot be delayed without delaying the entire batch of product. Also, the sequence of critical processes is often called the *critical path*.

| Key Terms | | | |
|---|---|---|---|
| | concurrent engineering, *526* | functional analysis, *524* | Takt time, *535* |
| | constraints, *531* | group technology, *526* | throughput margin, *534* |
| | cost life cycle, *522* | manufacturing cycle | value engineering, *524* |
| | cost tables, *526* | efficiency (MCE), *530* | |
| | cycle time, *530* | quality function | |
| | design analysis, *525* | deployment (QFD), *528* | |
| | flow diagram, *532* | sales life cycle, *522* | |

**Comments on Cost Management in Action**

**Why Go Abroad?**

In competitive industries such as apparel, consumer electronics, and computers, manufacturers continuously look for ways to reduce cost and increase value throughout the value chain. These industries have chosen to locate extensive manufacturing operations and/or partners in Latin America and China to reduce cost and to benefit from innovative manufacturing methods and facilities. Wage costs are lower and, using target costing and value engineering, manufacturing processes are built around modular manufacturing methods that reduce the number of parts in the product, speeding the manufacturing process and reducing costs.

**Consumer Electronics and Computer Products**   Why is outsourcing manufacturing to foreign plants an advantage to Apple and Hewlett-Packard? The contract manufacturers' manufacturing experience and technology give them a cost advantage. Foxconn and the other contract manufacturers also can focus on the manufacturing process rather than the entire product value chain. Moreover, they gain economies of scale by manufacturing similar products for different clients. The use of contract manufacturing is an important part of the strategy to achieve target costs while maintaining product leadership in design and customer service. These arrangements are not, however, without risks in terms of both supply and reputation.

**Apparel Companies**   Liz Claiborne and Ralph Lauren are saving lots of time and money by outsourcing many phases of the product development, from design to manufacturing, to plants in China. Having the product development and manufacturing in one place has helped the firms introduce new products more quickly and has also allowed them to deliver their product more quickly around the world.

**Sources:** Gabriel Kahn, "Making Labels for Less," *The Wall Street Journal,* August 13, 2004, p. B1; Justin Scheck, "Dell Plans to Sell Factories in Effort to Cut Costs," *The Wall Street Journal,* September 5, 2008, p1; Jason Dean and Ting-I Tsai, "Suicides Spark Inquiries; Apple, H-P to Examine Asian Supplier After String of Deaths at Factory," *The Wall Street Journal (Online),* May 26, 2010; Aries Poon, Loretta Chao, and Yukari Iwatani Kane, "Factory Blast Roils Tech Supply Chain; China's Hon Hai Closes Product Polishing Workshops," *The Wall Street Journal (Online),* May 24, 2011.

## Self-Study Problem
(For solution, please turn to the end of the chapter.)

### Best Brand Lighting Inc.

Best Brand Lighting Inc. (BBL) manufactures lighting fixtures. The two major markets for BBL products are major retailers, including Home Depot, Walmart, and Kmart, and specialty lighting stores. The former sell primarily to homeowners, and the latter primarily to electrical contractors.

Although its standard sizes and models typically are sold to the large retailers, BBL sells its products with more specialized features and sizes only to the specialty stores. Thus, the design and manufacturing costs of the products going to the specialty stores are slightly higher. The products in both markets have similar sales life cycles of about two years.

Because of the difference in consumers, BBL has a larger marketing cost for the products sold to the large retailers—advertising in major media to attract homeowners. In contrast, the marketing for the specialty shops consists mainly of catalogs and advertisements in trade publications resulting in a lower overall marketing cost. The sales policies also differ somewhat for the two markets. Sales to specialty stores are priced higher but include significant discounts and attractive return policies. In contrast, sales to the major retailers have restrictive return policies and offer little, if any, discount.

BBL management is interested in an in-depth analysis of the profitability of its two markets. As a first step, it has asked for the average costs and other data for all BBL products:

|  | **Major Retailers** | **Specialty Stores** |
| --- | --- | --- |
| Design costs | $   0.80 | $   1.10 |
| Manufacturing costs | 5.20 | 5.90 |
| Marketing costs | 0.95 | 0.10 |
| Returns | 0.05 | 0.95 |
| Discounts | 0.10 | 0.95 |
| Average price | 10.55 | 12.50 |
| Total market ($000) in |  |  |
| BBL's sales region | 188,000 | 32,000 |
| Current unit sales ($000) | 9,200 | 8,000 |

**Required**   Using the methods discussed in this chapter, analyze BBL's two market segments. What questions would you want to ask management and which fact-finding studies would be appropriate to support this analysis?

*Please visit* **http://www.mhhe.com/blocher6e** *to access a narrated, animated tutorial for solving this problem.*

## Questions

13-1 What is target costing?

13-2 Explain the two methods for reducing total product costs to achieve a desired target cost. Which is more common in the consumer electronics industries? In the specialized equipment manufacturing industries?

13-3 What does the term *sales life cycle* mean? What are the phases of the sales life cycle? How does it differ from the cost life cycle?

13-4 Do pricing strategies change over the different phases of the sales life cycle? Explain how.

13-5 Do cost management practices change over the product's sales life cycle? Explain how.

13-6 What does the concept of *value engineering* mean? How is it used in target costing?

13-7 For what types of firms is target costing most appropriate and why?

13-8 What is life-cycle costing? Why is it used?

13-9 Name the five steps of the theory of constraints and explain the purpose of each. Which is the most important step and why?

13-10 What does the term *constraint* mean in the theory of constraints analysis?

13-11 What is the role of the flow diagram in the theory of constraints analysis?

13-12 What is the main difference between activity-based costing and the theory of constraints? When is it appropriate to use each one?

13-13 For what types of firms is the theory of constraints analysis most appropriate and why?

13-14 How important is product design in life-cycle costing? Why?

13-15 For what types of firms is life-cycle costing most appropriate and why?

13-16 Explain the difference in intended application between strategic pricing and life-cycle costing.

13-17 How is Takt time calculated and what is it used for?

13-18 Distinguish pricing based on the cost life cycle and pricing based on the sales life cycle and give an example method for each.

13-19 At what phase in the product sales life cycle will prices likely be the highest: introduction, growth, maturity, or decline?

## Brief Exercises

13-20 The market price for a product has been $50 per unit, but competitive pressures have reduced the market price to $45. The firm manufactures 10,000 of these products per year at a manufacturing cost of $38 per unit (including $22 fixed cost and $16 variable cost per unit). Other selling and administrative costs for the product are $8 per unit. What is the firm's target manufacturing cost for this product if the profit per unit is to remain unchanged?

13-21 The firm in 13-20 above ignores competitive prices because it has a differentiated product. It uses full-manufacturing-cost-based pricing with a 40% markup. What is the firm's price?

13-22 The firm in 13-20 above ignores competitive prices because it has a differentiated product. It uses cost life-cycle-based pricing with a 10% markup. What is the firm's price?

13-23 If customer demand is 200,000 units per month, and available manufacturing capacity is 6,000 hours per week, what is the Takt time for this firm?

13-24 If a customer order is placed on May 1, the company expects to begin processing it on May 10, and the order is shipped on May 20, the cycle time is then how many days long?

13-25 If Toyota Motor Company receives an order on May 1, begins production on May 19, and ships the order on May 20 immediately following production, then what is the manufacturing cycle efficiency (MCE) ratio?

13-26 Comdex Inc. manufactures parts for the telecom industry. One of its products that currently sells for $160 is now facing a new competitor that offers the same product for $140. The parts currently cost Comdex $130. Comdex believes it must reduce its price to $140 to remain competitive. What is the target cost of the product if Comdex desires a 25% profit on sales dollars?

13-27 Why do prices at theme parks in Orlando, Florida, remain high despite seasonal and economic cyclical ups and downs? What type of strategic pricing is used by these theme parks?

## Exercises

[LO 13-1] 13-28 **Target Costing** MaxiDrive manufactures a wide variety of parts for recreational boating, including a gear and driveshaft part for high-powered outboard boat engines. Original equipment manufacturers such as Mercury and Honda purchase the components for use in large, powerful outboards. The part sells for $610, and sales volume averages 25,000 units per year. Recently, MaxiDrive's major competitor reduced the price of its equivalent unit to $550. The market is very competitive, and Maxi-Drive realizes it must meet the new price or lose significant market share. The controller has assembled these cost and usage data for the most recent year for MaxiDrive's production of 25,000 units:

| | Budgeted Quantity | Budgeted Cost | Actual Quantity | Actual Cost |
|---|---|---|---|---|
| Materials | | $ 6,500,000 | | $ 7,000,000 |
| Direct labor | | 2,500,000 | | 2,625,000 |
| Indirect labor | | 2,500,000 | | 2,400,000 |
| Inspection (hours and cost) | 920 | 300,000 | 1,000 | 350,000 |
| Materials handling (number of purchases and cost) | 3,500 | 500,000 | 3,450 | 485,000 |
| Machine setups (number and cost) | 1,400 | 750,000 | 1,500 | 725,000 |
| Returns and rework (number of times and cost) | 300 | 80,000 | 500 | 130,000 |
| | | $13,130,000 | | $13,715,000 |

**Required**

1. Calculate the target cost for maintaining current market share and profitability.
2. Can the target cost be achieved? How?

[LO 13-1]    13-29    **Target Costing; Spreadsheet Application**    Bowman Specialists Inc. (BSI) manufactures specialized equipment for polishing optical lenses. There are two models—one (A–25) principally used for fine eyewear and the other (A–10) for lenses used in binoculars, cameras, and similar equipment.

The manufacturing cost of each unit is calculated, using activity-based costing, for these manufacturing cost pools:

| Cost Pools | Allocation Base | Costing Rate |
|---|---|---|
| Materials handling | Number of parts | $2.25 per part |
| Manufacturing supervision | Hours of machine time | $23.50 per hour |
| Assembly | Number of parts | $2.55 per part |
| Machine setup | Each setup | $44.60 per setup |
| Inspection and testing | Logged hours | $35.00 per hour |
| Packaging | Logged hours | $15.00 per hour |

BSI currently sells the A–10 model for $1,050 and the A–25 model for $725. Manufacturing costs and activity usage for the two products follow:

| | A–10 | A–25 |
|---|---|---|
| Direct materials | $143.76 | $66.44 |
| Number of parts | 121 | 92 |
| Machine-hours | 6 | 4 |
| Inspection time | 1 | 0.6 |
| Packing time | 0.7 | 0.4 |
| Setups | 2 | 1 |

**Required**

1. Calculate the product cost and product margin for each product.
2. A new competitor has entered the market for lens-polishing equipment with a superior product at significantly lower prices, $825 for the A–10 model and $595 for the A–25 model. To try to compete, BSI has made some radical improvements in the design and manufacturing of its two products. The materials costs and activity usage rates have been decreased significantly:

| | A–10 | A–25 |
|---|---|---|
| Direct materials | $78.65 | $42.45 |
| Number of parts | 110 | 81 |
| Machine-hours | 5 | 2 |
| Inspection time | 1 | 0.5 |
| Packing time | 0.7 | 0.2 |
| Setups | 1 | 1 |

Calculate the total product costs with the new activity usage data. Can BSI make a positive gross margin with the new costs, assuming that it must meet the price set by the new competitor?

3. Assume the information in requirement 2, but that BSI management is not satisfied with the gross margin on the A–10 after the cost improvements. BSI wants a $50 gross margin on A–10. Suppose you are able to change the number of parts to reduce costs further to achieve the desired $50 margin. How much would the number of parts have to change to provide the desired gross margin? [*Hint:* Use the Excel *Goal Seek* function.]

4. What cost management method might be useful to BSI at this time, and why?

[LO 13-1]    13-30   **Target Costing in a Service Firm**    Take-a-Break Travel Company offers spring break travel packages to college students. Two of its packages, a seven-day, six-night trip to Cancun and a five-day, four-night trip to Jamaica, have the following characteristics:

| Package Specifications | Cancun | Jamaica | Cost Data |
|---|---|---|---|
| Oceanfront room; number of nights | 6 | 4 | $30/night |
| Meals: | | | |
| Breakfasts | 7 | 5 | $5/ea |
| Lunches | 7 | 5 | $7/ea |
| Dinners | 6 | 0 | $10/ea |
| Scuba diving trips | 4 | 2 | $15/ea |
| Water skiing trips | 5 | 2 | $10/ea |
| Airfare (round trip from Miami) | 1 | 1 | $175 (Cancun), $250 (Jamaica) |
| Transportation to and from airport | 1 | 1 | $15 (Cancun), $10 (Jamaica) |

The Cancun trip sells for $750, and the Jamaica trip sells for $690.

**Required**

1. What are the current profit margins on both trips?

2. Take-a-Break's management believes that it must drop the price on the Cancun trip to $710 and on the Jamaica trip to $650 in order to remain competitive in the market. Recalculate profit margins for both packages at these price levels.

3. Describe two ways that Take-a-Break Travel could cut its costs to get the profit margins back to their original levels.

[LO 13-1]    13-31   **Target Costing Using Quality Function Deployment (QFD)**    Rick's is a popular restaurant for fine dining. The owner and chef, Rick Goetz, is pleased with his success and is now considering expanding his existing restaurant or perhaps opening a second restaurant. Before making his decision, Rick wants to find out more about his competitive position. There are three other restaurants that compete directly with him on food quality and price. Rick knows that his profitability depends on his ability to provide a satisfying meal at the market price. His first step was to gather some information about his customers, using an independent market research firm, which informed him that his customers were looking for taste, comfort (the ambiance, service, and overall presentation of the food), and enjoyment (the distinctiveness of the dining experience, a degree of excitement). He was surprised to find that comfort and enjoyment ranked highest.

**First: Customer Criteria and Ranking**

| | Importance | Relative Importance |
|---|---|---|
| Taste | 45 | 15.0% |
| Comfort | 95 | 31.7% |
| Enjoyment | 160 | 53.3% |
| Total | 300 | 100.0% |

Next, he worked with his key wait staff and chefs to try to identify the three main components, and related cost, of the service Rick's provided:

**Second: Components and Cost**

| Components | Cost | Percent of Total |
|---|---|---|
| Menu and food preparation | $ 8 | 30.77% |
| Wait staff | 12 | 46.15 |
| Food ingredients | 6 | 23.08 |
| Total | $ 26 | 100.00% |

Having the customer criteria and components, Rick now again worked with his staff to assess how each component contributed to the desired customer criteria.

**Third: Determine How Components Contribute to Customer Satisfaction**

| Components | Customer Criteria | | |
|---|---|---|---|
| | **Taste** | **Comfort** | **Enjoyment** |
| Menu and food preparation | 30% | 20% | 45% |
| Wait staff | 30 | 60 | 35 |
| Food ingredients | 40 | 20 | 20 |
| | 100% | 100% | 100% |

**Required**

1. Using the information Rick has developed, determine the importance index for each component (menu and food preparation, wait staff, and food ingredients).

2. Compare your findings in requirement 1 to the cost of the components. What conclusions can you draw from this comparison?

[LO 13-2]    13-32    **Manufacturing Cycle Efficiency**    Waymouth Manufacturing operates a contract manufacturing plant located in Dublin, Ireland. The plant provides a variety of electronics products and components to consumer goods manufacturers around the world. Cycle time is a critical success factor for Waymouth, which has developed a number of measures of manufacturing speed. Waymouth has studied the matter and found that competitive contract manufacturers have manufacturing cycle times (MCE) of about 40%. When last calculated, Waymouth's MCE was 35%.

Key measures from the recent month's production, averaged over all the jobs during that period, are as follows:

| Activity | Average Time |
|---|---|
| New product development | 30 hours |
| Materials handling | 2 |
| Order setup | 6 |
| Machine maintenance | 3 |
| Order scheduling | 1 |
| Inspection of completed order | 5 |
| Pack and move to storage or ship | 2 |
| Manufacturing assembly | 24 |
| Order taking and checking | 3 |
| Receiving and stocking raw materials | 6 |
| Inspection of raw materials | 2 |

**Required**    Determine the manufacturing cycle efficiency (MCE) for the recent month. What can you infer from the MCE you calculated?

[LO 13-2]    13-33    **Takt Time**    Johnson Electronics manufactures a power supply used in a variety of electronic products including printers, modems, and routers. The demand for the part is 8,400 units per week. The production of the power supply requires six different manufacturing operations, each in sequence and each having the following processing times. The net available time to work is 70 hours per week, using two shifts.

| Operation | Processing Time |
|---|---|
| Operation 1 | 25 sec |
| Operation 2 | 22 sec |
| Operation 3 | 30 sec |
| Operation 4 | 24 sec |
| Operation 5 | 34 sec |
| Operation 6 | 28 sec |

**Required**

1. What is the Takt time for this product?
2. Is the processing line properly balanced for this product? Why or why not?
3. What is the strategic role of Takt time, and how is it implemented by the cost management analyst?

[LO 13-3]   13-34 **Life-Cycle Costing; Service Department**   In the chapter we illustrated the use of the life-cycle concept for both the cost and sales life cycle of a company's product lines. It can also be useful to extend the cost life cycle to the service department. In Chapter 7 we were interested in the allocation of service department costs to product lines. Here we are interested in managing the costs of a service department over its life cycle. The information technology department (IT) is a good example. The costs incurred in IT have the following phases:

1. Acquire IT assets, including computers, hubs, cables, and other assets.
2. Acquire software and deploy IT for the desired application and functionality.
3. Maintain management and operations of the IT assets.
4. Provide user support.
5. Retire the assets on a planned schedule and replace as needed.

**Required**   How can life-cycle costing help in the management of the IT department?

[LO 13-4]   13-35 **Pricing**   Williams Inc. produces a single product, a part used in the manufacture of automobile transmissions. Known for its quality and performance, the part is sold to luxury auto manufacturers around the world. Because this is a quality product, Williams has some flexibility in pricing the part. The firm calculates the price using a variety of pricing methods and then chooses the final price based on that information and other strategic information. A summary of the key cost information follows. Williams expects to manufacture and sell 50,000 parts in the coming year. While the demand for Williams's part has been growing in the past two years, management is not only aware of the cyclical nature of the automobile industry but also concerned about market share and profits during the industry's current downturn.

|  | Total Costs |
| --- | --- |
| Variable manufacturing | $ 4,680,000 |
| Variable selling and administrative | 855,650 |
| Plant-level fixed overhead | 2,345,875 |
| Fixed selling and administrative | 675,495 |
| Batch-level fixed overhead | 360,000 |
| Total investment in product line | 22,350,000 |
| Expected sales (units) | 50,000 |

**Required**

1. Determine the price for the part using a markup of 45% of full manufacturing cost.
2. Determine the price for the part using a markup of 25% of full life-cycle cost.
3. Determine the price for the part using a desired gross margin percentage to sales of 40%.
4. Determine the price for the part using a desired life-cycle cost percentage to sales of 25%.
5. Determine the price for the part using a desired before-tax return on investment of 15%.
6. Determine the contribution margin and operating profit for each of the methods in requirements 1 through 5. Which price would you choose, and why?

[LO 13-4]   13-36 **Pricing Military Contracts**   The Pentagon is constantly seeking ways to procure the most effective combat equipment and systems at the lowest possible cost. A key element in most procurement contracts is a fixed fee based on a percentage of the full cost for the contract, plus a percentage fixed fee that is incentive based. The latter is based on meeting contract deadlines and meeting or exceeding other contract performance measures. An actual Pentagon contract with Boeing involved a 10% fixed fee on cost incurred and another 5%-of-incentive award.

**Required**   Evaluate the compensation plan for this contract, with the fixed fee of 10% and the incentive fee of 5%. What do you think is the role of the incentive fee, and do you think it is too large or too small?

[LO 13-4]   13-37 **Life-Cycle Pricing**   Matt Simpson owns and operates Quality Craft Rentals, which offers canoe rentals and shuttle service on the Nantahala River. Customers can rent canoes at one station, enter the river there, and exit at one of two designated locations to catch a shuttle that returns them to their vehicles at the station they entered. Following are the costs involved in providing this service each year:

|  | Fixed Costs | Variable Costs |
|---|---|---|
| Canoe maintenance | $ 2,300 | $2.50 |
| Licenses and permits | 3,000 | 0 |
| Vehicle leases | 5,400 | 0 |
| Station lease | 6,920 | 0 |
| Advertising | 6,000 | 0.50 |
| Operating costs | 21,000 | 0.50 |

Quality Craft Rentals began business three years ago with a $21,000 expenditure for a fleet of 30 canoes. These are expected to last seven more years, at which time a new fleet must be purchased.

**Required**   Matt is happy with the steady rental average of 6,400 per year. For this number of rentals, what price should he charge per rental for the business to make a 20% life-cycle return on investment?

## Problems

[LO 13-1]   13-38 **Target Costing in a Service Firm**   UR Safe Systems installs home security systems. Two of its systems, the ICU 100 and the ICU 900, have these characteristics:

| Design Specifications | ICU 100 | ICU 900 | Cost Data |
|---|---|---|---|
| Video cameras | 1 | 3 | $150/ea. |
| Video monitors | 1 | 1 | $75/ea. |
| Motion detectors | 5 | 8 | $15/ea. |
| Floodlights | 3 | 7 | $8/ea. |
| Alarms | 1 | 2 | $15/ea. |
| Wiring | 700 ft. | 1,100 ft. | $0.10/ft. |
| Installation | 16 hrs. | 26 hrs. | $20/hr. |

The ICU 100 sells for $810 installed, and the ICU 900 sells for $1,520 installed.

**Required**
1. What are the current profit margins on both systems?
2. UR Safe's management believes that it must drop the price on the ICU 100 to $750 and on the ICU 900 to $1,390 to remain competitive in the market. Recalculate profit margins for both products at these price levels.
3. Describe two ways that UR Safe could cut its costs to get the profit margins back to their original levels.

[LO 13-1]   13-39 **Target Costing; Review of Chapter 11**   Morrow Company is a large manufacturer of auto parts for automakers and parts distributors. Although Morrow has plants throughout the world, most are in North America. Morrow is known for the quality of its parts and for the reliability of its operations. Customers receive their orders in a timely manner and there are no errors in the shipment or billing of these orders. For these reasons, Morrow has prospered in a business that is very competitive, with competitors such as Delphi, Visteon, and others.

Morrow just received an order for 100 auto parts from National Motors Corp., a major auto manufacturer. National proposed a $1,500 selling price per part. Morrow usually earns 20% operating margin as a percent of sales. Morrow recently decided to use target costing in pricing its products. An examination of the production costs by the engineers and accountants showed that this part was assigned a standard full cost of $1,425 per part (this includes $1,000 production, $200 marketing, and $225 general and administration costs per part). Morrow's Value Assessment Group (VAG) undertook a cost reduction program for this part. Two production areas that were investigated were the defective unit rate and the tooling costs. The $1,000 production costs included a normal defective cost of $85 per part. Group leaders suggested that production changes could reduce defective cost to $25 per part.

Forty-five tools were used to make the auto part. The group discovered that the number of tools could be reduced to 30 and less expensive tools could be used on this part to meet National's product specifications. These changes saved an additional $105 of production cost per part. By studying other problem areas, the group found that general and administration costs could be reduced by $50 per unit through use of electronic data interchange with suppliers and just-in-time inventory management.

In addition, Morrow's sales manager told the group that National might be willing to pay a higher selling price because of Morrow's quality reputation and reliability. He believed National's proposed price was a starting point for negotiations. Of course, National had made the same offer to some of Morrow's competitors.

**Required**
1. What should be Morrow's target cost per auto part? Explain.
2. As a result of the Value Engineering Group's efforts, determine Morrow's estimated cost for the auto part. Will Morrow meet the target cost for the part? Do you recommend that Morrow take the National offer? Explain your reasons.

**(Adapted from a problem by Joseph San Miguel)**

[LO 13-1]   13-40 **Target Costing; Health Care**   VIP-MD is a health maintenance organization (HMO) located in North Carolina. Unlike the traditional fee-for-service model that determines the payment according to the actual services used or costs incurred, VIP-MD receives a fixed, prepaid amount from subscribers. The per member per month (PMPM) rate is determined by estimating the health care cost per enrollee within a geographic location. The average health care coverage in North Carolina costs $368 per month, which is the same amount irrespective of the subscriber's age. Because individuals are demanding quality care at reasonable rates, VIP-MD must contain its costs to remain competitive. A major competitor, Doctors Nationwide, is entering the North Carolina market in early 2013 with a monthly premium of $325. VIP-MD wants to maintain its current market penetration and hopes to increase its enrollees in 2013. The latest data on the number of enrollees and the associated costs follow:

| Age | Enrollment in 2013 | Projected Enrollment in 2014 | Average Monthly Cost in 2013 |
|---|---|---|---|
| 1–4 | 45,688 | 48,977 | $ 11,147,872 |
| 5–14 | 82,456 | 84,663 | 10,059,632 |
| 15–19 | 95,873 | 95,887 | 8,436,824 |
| 20–24 | 66,246 | 67,882 | 9,539,424 |
| 25–34 | 133,496 | 132,554 | 26,432,208 |
| 35–44 | 166,876 | 175,446 | 38,882,108 |
| 45–54 | 85,496 | 90,889 | 22,741,936 |
| 55–64 | 99,624 | 101,923 | 28,691,712 |
| 65–74 | 156,288 | 161,559 | 48,918,144 |
| 75–84 | 67,895 | 72,465 | 33,132,760 |
| 85 years and older | 23,499 | 26,849 | 24,086,475 |
| | 1,023,437 | 1,059,094 | $262,069,095 |

**Required**
1. Calculate the target cost required for VIP-MD to maintain its current market share and profit per enrollee in 2013.
2. Costs in the health care industry applicable to VIP-MD and Doctors Nationwide are expected to increase by 6% in the coming year, 2014. VIP-MD is planning for the year ahead and is expecting all providers, including VIP-MD and Doctors Nationwide, to increase their rates by $15, to $340. Calculate the new target cost assuming again that VIP-MD wants to maintain the same profit per enrollee as in 2013.

[LO 13-1]   13-41 **Target Cost; Warehousing**   Caldwell Supply, a wholesaler, has determined that its operations have three primary activities: purchasing, warehousing, and distributing. The firm reports the following operating data for the year just completed:

| Activity | Cost Driver | Quantity of Cost Driver | Cost per Unit of Cost Driver |
|---|---|---|---|
| Purchasing | Number of purchasing orders | 1,000 | $150 per order |
| Warehousing | Number of moves | 8,000 | 30 per move |
| Distributing | Number of shipments | 500 | 80 per shipment |

Caldwell buys 100,000 units at an average unit cost of $10 and sells them at an average unit price of $20. The firm also has a fixed operating cost of $250,000 for the year.

Caldwell's customers are demanding a 10% discount for the coming year. The company expects to sell the same amount if the demand for price reduction can be met. Caldwell's suppliers, however, are willing to give only a 2% discount.

**Required** Caldwell has estimated that it can reduce the number of purchasing orders to 680 and can decrease the cost of each shipment $3 with minor changes in its operations. Any further cost saving must come from reengineering the warehousing processes. What is the maximum cost (i.e., target cost) for warehousing if the firm desires to earn the same amount of profit next year?

[LO 13-1]  13-42  **Target Costing; International**  Harpers, Ltd., is a U.K. manufacturer of casual shoes for men and women. It has sustained strong growth in the U.K. market in recent years due to its close attention to fashion trends. Harpers's shoes also have a good reputation for quality and comfort. To expand the business, Harpers is considering introducing its shoes to the U.S. market, where comparable shoes sell for an average of $90 wholesale, more than $16 above what Harpers charges in the United Kingdom (average price, £45). Management has engaged a marketing consultant to obtain information about what features U.S. consumers seek in shoes if they desire different features. Harpers also has obtained information on the approximate cost of adding these features:

| Features Desired in the United States | Cost to Add (in U.S. $) | Importance Rating (5 is most important) |
|---|---|---|
| Colorfast material | $4.50 | 3 |
| Lighter weight | 6.75 | 5 |
| Extra-soft insole | 3.00 | 4 |
| Longer-wearing sole | 3.00 | 2 |

The current average manufacturing cost of Harpers's shoes is £34 (approximately $56 U.S.), which provides an average profit of £11 ($18 U.S.) per pair sold. Harpers would like to maintain this profit margin; however, the firm recognizes that the U.S. market requires different features and that shipping and advertising costs would increase approximately $10 U.S. per pair of shoes.

**Required**
1. What is the target manufacturing cost for shoes to be sold in the United States?
2. Which features, if any, should Harpers add for shoes to be sold in the United States?
3. Strategically evaluate Harpers's decision to begin selling shoes in the United States.

[LO 13-1]  13-43  **Target Costing; Quality Function Deployment (QFD)**  Ranger Yacht manufactures a line of family cruiser/racing sailboats. The boats are well known for their quality, safety, and performance. Ranger hired Matthew Perry, a well-known sailboat designer and racer, to design a new sailboat, the M33. The M33 will have advanced materials in the hull and rigging to enhance the safety and performance of the boat and also to improve its overnight comfort. Safety and comfort are the two most important boat-buying criteria of Ranger's customers, rated at 33% and 32% respectively, on a 100-point scale. The other two criteria are performance (20%) and styling (15%). The overall length of the boat is about 33 feet; its two sleeping areas have room for five or six people. Ranger projects a sale price of approximately $200,000 and estimates the costs of manufacturing the M33 as shown in Table 1.

Table 1

| Component | Target Cost | Percentage of Total |
|---|---|---|
| Hull and keel | $ 36,000 | 30% |
| Standing rig | 18,000 | 15 |
| Sails | 20,000 | 17 |
| Electrical | 16,000 | 13 |
| Other | 30,000 | 25 |
| Total | $120,000 | 100% |

A team of engineers and sales managers studied the projected cost and identified how each component of the planned boat contributed to satisfying the customers' criteria. The results of this study, based on careful estimates, are shown in Table 2. For example, the estimates show that 30% of the customers' desire for safety is satisfied by the construction of the hull and keel, another 30% by the standing rig, and so on.

Table 2

| Component | Criteria | | | |
|---|---|---|---|---|
| | **Safety** | **Styling** | **Performance** | **Comfort** |
| Hull and keel | 30% | 40% | 50% | 30% |
| Standing rig | 30 | 20 | 20 | 10 |
| Sails | 10 | 10 | 30 | 10 |
| Electrical | 20 | 10 | — | — |
| Other | 10 | 20 | — | 50 |
| | 100% | 100% | 100% | 100% |

**Required**

1. Using the information in Table 2 developed by the team of engineers and sales managers, together with the customer criteria, determine which components of the boat are most important to customers, and why.

2. Take your findings in requirement 1 and compare them against the target cost figures in Table 1. What conclusions can you draw from this comparison?

[LO 13-1]   13-44   **Target Costing; Quality Function Deployment**   Bridal Photography Inc. (BPI) specializes in preparing wedding pictures, including a large book of photos for the wedding couple. Each BPI couple works directly with a single BPI photographer who helps the couple plan the photos to be made on the wedding day, select the wedding photo book, and choose the photos it is to contain. The standard fee for each wedding is $6,000, which includes all of the firm's services including the book of wedding photos. BPI is experiencing increased competition, especially based on price. BPI wants to protect its reputation and to continue to expand its business, and for this purpose has decided to use Quality Function Deployment (QFD) to better understand the cost and value trade-offs in its business. As a first step, BPI defined the four key "buying criteria" that couples use in choosing and evaluating photographers: (1) fast service, (2) great photos at the wedding, (3) quality of the photo finishing (color, clarity . . . ), and (4) the quality of the photo book. A select sample of prior customers was asked to rate these criteria and, on a 300-point scale, provided scores of 30, 120, 60, and 90, respectively.

The BPI accounting records showed the average weekly cost of $5,000 could be traced to four activities: (1) planning meeting in which the couple and the photographer determined what types of photos were desired, set dates for the photography and proofs, etc., (2) photography on the wedding day, (3) preparation of proofs from which the couple would select the photos to be used in the book, and (4) preparation of the final photos and the wedding photo book. The average costs of the four activities were $800, $2,400, $600, and $1,200, respectively.

As a final step, BPI managers, photographers, and staff worked together to determine an estimate of the contribution of each of the four activities to achieving the buying criteria. The results were as follows:

| Activity/ Criteria | Fast Service | Good Photos | Finishing | Book Quality |
|---|---|---|---|---|
| Planning meeting | 30% | 40% | - | 35% |
| Take photos | 5 | 60 | - | 15 |
| Prepare proofs | 35 | - | 50% | - |
| Prepare photo book | 30 | - | 50 | 50 |
| | 100% | 100% | 100% | 100% |

**Required**

1. Determine which activities are most valuable to the wedding couple and compare this finding to the cost of the activities. Which activities should be given greater attention in time and cost, and which should be given less time and cost?

2. Indicate some business and competitive issues that should be taken into account in considering your answer to requirement 1 above.

[LO 13-2]　13-45　**Theory of Constraints; Strategy**　Colton Furniture Co. is a small but fast-growing manufacturer of living room furniture. Its two principal products are end tables and sofas. The flow diagram for the manufacturing at Colton follows. Colton's manufacturing involves five processes: cutting the lumber, cutting the fabric, sanding, staining, and assembly. One employee cuts fabric and two do the staining. These are relatively skilled workers who could be replaced only with some difficulty. Two workers cut the lumber, and two others perform the sanding operation. There is some skill to these operations, but it is less critical than for staining and fabric cutting. Assembly requires the lowest skill level and is currently done by one full-time employee and a group of part timers who provide a total of 175 hours of working time per week. The other employees work a 40-hour week, with 5 hours off for breaks, training, and personal time. Assume a four-week month and that by prior agreement, none of the employees can be switched from one task to another. The current demand for Colton's products and sales prices are as follows, although Colton expects demand to increase significantly in the coming months if it is able to successfully negotiate an order from a motel chain.

|  | End Tables | Sofas |
|---|---|---|
| Price | $250 | $450 |
| Current demand (units per month) | 400 | 150 |

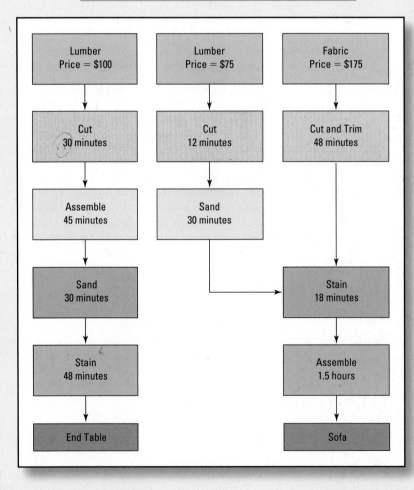

**Required**

1. What is the most profitable production plan for Colton? Explain your answer with supporting calculations.

2. How would you apply the five steps of the theory of constraints to Colton's manufacturing operations? What would you recommend for each step?

[LO 13-2]　13-46　**Theory of Constraints**　Chemical Products Company (CPC) produces a variety of chemicals, primarily adhesives, lubricants, and polymers for industrial use by manufacturers to produce plastics and other compounds. Don Leo, the production vice president, has been informed of a disturbing trend of increasing customer complaints regarding late deliveries from the Canton, Kentucky, plant. The Canton plant is one of the firm's newest and most modern plants and is dedicated to the manufacture of two products, Polymer 1 and Polymer 2. Don has downloaded some incomplete recent information about the Canton plant onto his laptop; he plans to analyze the information in the hour or so he has before his next meeting of the CPC executive committee. He is concerned that some comments will be made about the problems at Canton, and he wants to have an idea of how to respond. Because CPC views Polymer 1 and Polymer 2 as very promising in terms of both sales and profit potential, the news of these problems is likely to spark some comment. The data downloaded by Don are as follows:

| Activity | Number of Hours Required for Each Product | | Number of Hours Available per Week |
| --- | --- | --- | --- |
| | Polymer 1 | Polymer 2 | |
| Filtering | 2 | 4 | 320 |
| Stripping | 2 | 3 | 320 |
| Reacting | 3 | 5 | 320 |
| Final filtering | 2 | 1 | 160 |
| Mixing | 3 | 3 | 320 |
| Other information | | | |
| Current sales demand (per week) | 60 | 40 | |
| Price | $145 | $185 | |

Don has sketched the following flow diagram for the Canton plant. He believes it is relatively accurate because of his frequent contact with the plant.

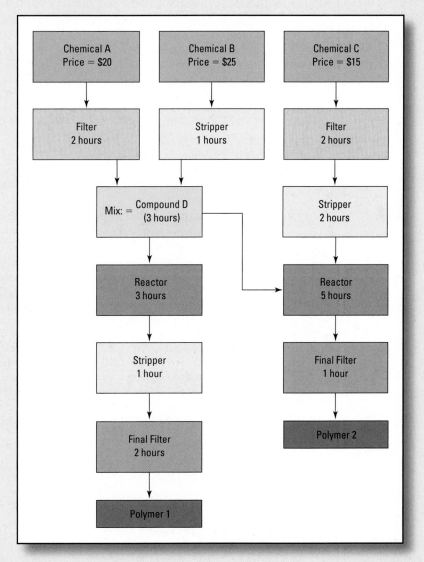

**Required** Prepare a set of notes that Don can use in the executive meeting if questions come up about the problems at the Canton plant.

[LO 13-2] 13-47 **Theory of Constraints for a Restaurant** Taylor's is a popular restaurant that offers customers a large dining room and comfortable bar area. Taylor Henry, the owner and manager of the restaurant, has seen the number of patrons increase steadily over the last two years and is considering whether and when she will have to expand its available capacity. The restaurant occupies a large home, and all the space in the building is now used for dining, the bar, and kitchen, but space is available to expand the restaurant. The restaurant is open from 6 p.m. to 10 p.m. each night (except Monday) and has an average of 24 customers enter the bar and 50 enter the dining room during each of those hours. Taylor has noticed the trends over the last two years and expects that within about four years the number of bar customers will increase by 50% and the dining customers will increase by 20%. Taylor is worried that the restaurant will be not be able to handle the increase and has asked you to study its capacity. In your study you consider four areas of capacity: the parking lot (which has 80 spaces), the bar (54 seats), the dining room (100 seats), and the kitchen. The kitchen is well staffed and can prepare any meal on the menu in an average of 12 minutes per meal. The kitchen when fully staffed is able to have up to 20 meals in preparation at a time, or 100 meals per hour (60 min./12 min. × 20 meals). To assess the capacity of the restaurant, you obtain the additional information:

- Diners typically come to the restaurant by car with an average of 3 persons per car, while bar patrons arrive with an average of 1.5 persons per car.
- Diners on the average occupy a table for an hour while bar customers usually stay for an average of two hours.
- Due to fire regulations, all bar customers must be seated.
- The bar customer typically orders two drinks at an average of $7 per drink; the dining room customer orders a meal with an average price of $22; the restaurant's cost per drink is $1, and the direct costs for meal preparation are $5.

**Required** (Note: When calculating capacity usage, you may round numbers up to the nearest whole digit.)

1. a. Given the current number of customers per hour, what is the amount of excess capacity in the bar, dining room, parking lot, and kitchen?

   b. Calculate the expected total throughput margin for the restaurant per hour, day, and month (assuming a 26-day month).

2. a. Given the expected increase in the number of customers, determine if there is a constraint for any of the four areas of capacity. What is the amount of needed capacity for each constraint?

   b. If there is a constraint, reduce the demand on the constraint so that the restaurant is at full capacity (assume some customers would have to be turned away). Calculate the expected total throughput margin for the restaurant per hour, day, and month (assuming a 26-day month).

3. Taylor has obtained construction estimates. To increase the capacity of her bar to 80 seats and dining room to 120 seats and kitchen to 25 meals at the same time would cost $250,000 which she could finance for $5,000 per month for the next four years. There would be no change to the parking lot. Given your analysis above, prepare a brief recommendation to Taylor regarding expanding the restaurant.

[LO 13-3] 13-48 **Life-Cycle Costing** Tim Waters, the COO of BioDerm, has asked his cost management team for a product-line profitability analysis for his firm's two products, Xderm and Yderm. The two skin care products require a large amount of research and development and advertising. After receiving the following statement from BioDerm's auditor, Tim concludes that Xderm is the more profitable product and that perhaps cost-cutting measures should be applied to Yderm.

|  | Xderm | Yderm | Total |
|---|---|---|---|
| Sales | $3,000,000 | $2,000,000 | $5,000,000 |
| Cost of goods sold | (1,900,000) | (1,600,000) | (3,500,000) |
| Gross profit | $1,100,000 | $ 400,000 | $1,500,000 |
| Research and development |  |  | (900,000) |
| Selling expenses |  |  | (100,000) |
| Profit before taxes |  |  | $ 500,000 |

**Required**

1. Explain why Tim may be wrong in his assessment of the relative performance of the two products.

2. Suppose that 80% of the R&D and selling expenses are traceable to Xderm. Prepare life-cycle income statements for each product. What does this tell you about the importance of accurate life-cycle costing?

3. Consider again your answers in requirements 1 and 2 with the following additional information. R&D and selling expenses are substantially higher for Xderm because it is a new product. Tim has strongly supported development of the new product, including the high selling and R&D expenses. He has assured senior managers that the Xderm investment will pay off in improved profits for the firm. What are the ethical issues, if any, facing Tim as he reports to top management on the profitability of the firm's two products?

[LO 13-3]   13-49   **Life-Cycle Costing; Health Care; Present Values**   Cure-all, Inc., has developed a drug that will diminish the effects of aging. Cure-all has spent $1,000,000 on research and development and $2,108,000 for clinical trials. Once the drug is approved by the FDA, which is imminent, it will have a five-year sales life cycle. Laura Russell, Cure-all's chief financial officer, must determine the best alternative for the company among three options. The company can choose to manufacture, package, and distribute the drug; outsource only the manufacturing; or sell the drug's patent. Laura has compiled the following annual cost information for this drug if the company were to manufacture it:

| Cost Category | Fixed Costs | Variable Cost per Unit |
|---|---|---|
| Manufacturing | $5,000,000 | $68.00 |
| Packaging | 380,000 | 20.00 |
| Distribution | 1,125,000 | 6.50 |
| Advertising | 2,280,000 | 12.00 |

Management anticipates a high demand for the drug and has benchmarked $235 per unit as a reasonable price based on other drugs that promise similar results. Management expects sales volume of 3,000,000 units over five years and uses a discount rate of 10%.

If Cure-all chooses to outsource the manufacturing of the drug while continuing to package, distribute, and advertise it, the manufacturing costs would result in fixed costs of $1,350,000 and variable cost per unit of $74. For the sale of the patent, Cure-all would receive $300,000,000 now and $25,000,000 at the end of every year for the next five years.

**Required**   Determine the best option for Cure-all. Support your answer.

[LO 13-2]   13-50   **Constraint Analysis; Flow Diagram (Appendix)**   Silver Aviation assembles small aircraft for commercial use. The majority of its business is with small freight airlines serving areas whose airports do not accommodate larger planes. The remainder of Silver's customers are commuter airlines and individuals who use planes in their businesses, such as the owners of larger ranches. Silver recently expanded its market into Central and South America, and the company expects to double its sales over the next three years.

To schedule work and track all projects, Silver uses a flow diagram. The diagram for the assembly of a single cargo plane is shown in Exhibit 1. The diagram shows four alternative paths with the critical path being *ABGEFIJ*. Bob Peterson, president of Coastal Airlines,

**EXHIBIT 1   Flow Diagram for Plane Assembly**

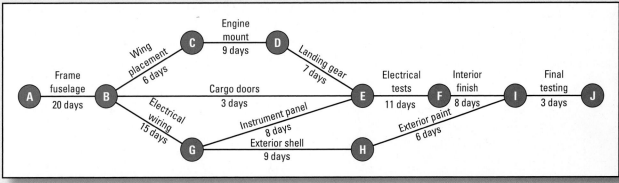

**EXHIBIT 2**
**Crash Cost Listing**

| Activity | | Expected Activity Times | | Direct Cost | | Added Crash Cost per Reduced Day |
|---|---|---|---|---|---|---|
| | | Regular | Accel. | Regular | Accel. | |
| AB | Frame fuselage | 20 days | 16 days | $12,000 | $16,800 | $1,200 |
| BC | Wing placement | 6 | 5 | 3,600 | 5,000 | 1,400 |
| CD | Engine mount | 9 | 7 | 6,600 | 8,000 | 700 |
| DE | Landing gear | 7 | 5 | 5,100 | 6,700 | 800 |
| BE | Cargo doors | 3 | 3 | 1,400 | 1,400 | — |
| BG | Electrical wiring | 15 | 13 | 9,000 | 11,000 | 1,000 |
| GE | Instrument panel | 8 | 6 | 5,700 | 8,300 | 1,300 |
| EF | Electrical tests | 11 | 10 | 6,800 | 7,600 | 800 |
| GH | Exterior shell | 9 | 7 | 4,200 | 5,200 | 500 |
| FI | Interior finish | 8 | 7 | 3,600 | 4,000 | 400 |
| HI | Exterior paint | 6 | 5 | 3,600 | 4,000 | 400 |
| IJ | Final testing | 3 | 2 | 3,500 | 4,400 | 900 |
| | | | | $65,100 | $82,400 | |

recently placed an order with Silver Aviation for five cargo planes. During contract negotiations, Bob agreed to a delivery time of 13 weeks (five work days per week) for the first plane with the balance of the planes being delivered at the rate of one every 4 weeks. Because of problems with some of the aircraft that Coastal is currently using, Bob contacted Grace Vander, sales manager for Silver Aviation, to ask about improving the delivery date of the first cargo plane. Grace replied that she believed the schedule could be shortened by as much as 10 work days or 2 weeks, but the cost of assembly would increase as a result. Bob said he would be willing to consider the increased costs, and they agreed to meet the following day to review a revised schedule that Grace would prepare.

Because Silver Aviation previously assembled aircraft on an accelerated basis, the company has a list of costs for this purpose. Grace used the data shown in Exhibit 2 to develop a plan to cut 10 working days from the schedule at a minimum increase in cost to Coastal Airlines. Upon completing her plan, she reported to Bob that Silver would be able to cut 10 working days from the schedule for an associated increase in cost of $6,600. Grace's Exhibit 3 shows an accelerated assembly schedule for the cargo plane starting from the regularly scheduled days and cost.

**Required**

1. Is Grace's plan satisfactory? Why or why not?

2. Revise the accelerated assembly schedule so that Coastal Airlines will take delivery of the first plane ahead of schedule at the least incremental cost to Coastal.

3. Calculate the incremental costs that Bob will have to pay for this revised accelerated delivery.

4. How might Silver Aviation use the information in Exhibits 1 and 2 to its competitive advantage?

**(CMA Adapted)**

[LO 13-1, 13-3]    13-51    **Research Assignment; Sustainability and the Supply Chain**    Obtain from your library a copy of the following article: Hau L. Lee, "Don't Tweak Your Supply Chain—Rethink It End to End," *Harvard Business Review,* October 2010, pp. 62–69. The article discusses the ways in which organizations might change the way they interact with supply chain members as they work toward improving their social and environmental impact.

**EXHIBIT 3**
**Accelerated Plane Assembly Schedule**

| Activity Accelerated | Additional Cost per day | Total Direct Cost |
|---|---|---|
| | | $65,100 |
| HI by one day | $ 400 | 65,500 |
| FI by one day | 400 | 65,900 |
| GH by two days | 500 | 66,900 |
| CD by two days | 700 | 68,300 |
| EF by one day | 800 | 69,100 |
| DE by two days | 800 | 70,700 |
| BG by one day | 1,000 | 71,700 |

**Required**   After reading the above-referenced article, answer the following questions:

1. Why are organizations asking supply chain partners about their environmental and social performance?

2. Generally speaking, who are the stakeholders that have an interest in improved environmental and social responsibility? In developing your response, think in terms of the extended supply chain.

3. Define the term *structural change.* According to the authors of this article, why should companies undertake broader structural changes than most currently do?

4. What role can management accountants play when improved environmental and social responsibility becomes a goal of an organization?

## Solution to Self-Study Problem

### Best Brand Lighting Inc.

A thorough analysis will require a good deal more inquiry of management and fact finding than is available from the limited information provided earlier, but a few useful observations can be made.

1. Encourage BBL to consider increasing the effort put into design to reduce manufacturing costs and to reduce the relatively high rate of product returns in the specialty segment. The cost of design appears low relative to manufacturing and downstream costs, especially in the specialty segment. Inquire about which types of design approaches are being used. Urge BBL to adopt concurrent engineering-based methods, especially because of the relatively short market life cycles in the industry.

2. Consider additional analysis of pricing. Because of BBL's strong acceptance in the specialty segment and because the differentiation strategy is likely to be important in that segment, a price increase might yield higher profits with little or no loss in market share.

   Cost leadership appears to be the appropriate strategy in the major retail segment; inquire what methods the company is using to reduce overall product costs in this segment.

   Also, investigate further the rate of customer returns for each product. Is this due to design problems or problems in sales management?

3. Consider a further analysis of marketing expenses. Would an increase in marketing effort in the major retailer segment improve sales in this segment?

4. Consider the need to perform a detailed analysis by product category within each market segment. A detailed analysis might uncover important information about opportunities to reduce cost and add value within the products' value chain.

5. Because of the relatively short sales life cycles, consider whether target costing could be used effectively at BBL. How intense is the level of competition in the industry, and to what extent are trade-offs made between functionality and price in the development and introduction of each new product? If the level of competition is very intense, and trade-offs between functionality and price are key strategic decisions, target costing should be a useful management tool.

6. Investigate the costing system. Is it activity based? How accurate are the cost figures that it develops?

*Please visit* **http://www.mhhe.com/blocher6e** *to access a narrated, animated tutorial for solving this problem.*

# Operational-Level Control

The objective of the four chapters in Part Three is to present some key tools used to evaluate the performance of mid-level managers and operating personnel, what we refer to as *operational control.* By its nature, operational control focuses on short-term financial and relevant nonfinancial performance. The performance of high-level managers (i.e., *management control*) is examined in Part Four. The essence of control is a comparison of actual performance to budgeted or expected performance.

In **Chapters 14** through **16** we cover traditional *financial-control* models, that is, models based on the use of standard costs and flexible budgets. The flexible budget allows a comparison of expected financial performance to the actual performance for a given period. The use of flexible budgets and standard costs provides a number of ways to break down and explain what we call the total operating-income variance for the period—that is, the difference between actual operating profit and budgeted operating profit for the period. Since profit is a function of five factors (sales volume, selling price, variable cost per unit, sales mix, and total fixed costs), the total operating-income variance can be broken down into components associated with each of these five factors.

In **Chapter 14** we begin by defining the total operating-income variance and then breaking this total variance down into a sales volume variance and a total flexible-budget variance. We show how the latter variance can, for a manufacturing company, be broken down into a selling-price variance and component variances related to two direct manufacturing costs (labor and materials). Chapter 14 also looks at relevant nonfinancial performance indicators that are useful supplements to the variances calculated earlier in the chapter.

**Chapter 15** focuses on the variances that arise from differences between budgeted and actual indirect manufacturing costs (i.e., manufacturing overhead). As with Chapter 14, we use flexible budgets and standard costs to further break down the total flexible-budget variance for the period. Chapter 15 also deals with the issue of recording standard overhead costs and associated variances for a period, the application of overhead variance analysis in conjunction with ABC systems, and decision rules associated with the variance-investigation decision. Chapter 15 also includes a discussion of resource-capacity planning issues.

**Chapter 16** completes the operating-income variance analysis by looking in more detail at the sales volume variance. Specifically, we show how the total sales volume variance can be broken down into components based on market size and market share, among others. Chapter 16 also looks at various measures of operating productivity.

Part Three closes with a study, in **Chapter 17**, of the management and control of quality, including topics of cost of quality (COQ), Six Sigma, lean manufacturing, and lean accounting. These topics are presented from the standpoint of how cost-management systems can be refined to support strategic initiatives on the part of management.

# CHAPTER FOURTEEN

# Operational Performance Measurement:
## Sales, Direct-Cost Variances, and the Role of Nonfinancial Performance Measures

**After studying this chapter, you should be able to . . .**

LO 14-1 Explain the essence of control systems in general and operational control systems in particular

LO 14-2 Explain the total operating-income variance for a given period

LO 14-3 Develop a general framework for subdividing the total operating-income variance into component variances

LO 14-4 Develop standard costs for product costing, performance evaluation, and control

LO 14-5 Record manufacturing cost flows and associated variances in a standard cost system

LO 14-6 Discuss major operating functions and the need for nonfinancial performance indicators

Schmidt Machinery, the example company for this chapter and the next, is a well-established (hypothetical) firm that produces a high-quality line of all-weather furniture for use on patios and decks and in sunrooms. Product XV-1 is a lightweight but durable lounge chair. Because of its very high quality and reputation for design innovation, Schmidt's products are sold largely by catalog, and over the firm's website; a few high-end retailers also carry the brand. The company currently has few direct competitors in this country, but there are a growing number of competitors from Europe and Asia. At present, the falling dollar has helped Schmidt maintain its domestic sales and to have some opportunities for foreign sales, but management is concerned that the foreign competitors will soon be able to reduce price and compete effectively. For this reason, the company is looking for ways to better manage its costs and to improve manufacturing efficiency.

The underlying business of Schmidt can conceptually be broken down into four major processes: operating processes, customer-management processes, innovation processes, and regulatory/social processes. Schmidt desires to design and implement a comprehensive management accounting and control system that enables it to successfully meet competitive threats in a sustainable manner. As a start, the company has decided to focus on a control system associated with its operating processes—*operational control,* for short.

The topic of operational control systems, as part of a more comprehensive management accounting and control system, is the subject of Part Three of the text. In this chapter we introduce you to the notion of *financial control,* which begins at the end of a period (e.g., month or quarter) by comparing actual operating income to budgeted income. This difference, which we call a variance, can then be broken down into component variances related to costs, sales volume, sales price, and sales mix.

In this chapter we focus on the determination of the sales volume variance and what is called the *total flexible-budget variance.* The latter variance can be further broken down into a sales price variance and component variances associated with two direct manufacturing costs: labor and materials. In Chapter 15 we extend the analysis to include a breakdown and analysis of variances associated with indirect manufacturing costs (i.e., manufacturing overhead costs). In Chapter 16 we provide a further discussion of sales-related and productivity variances. Finally, in Chapter 17 we look at the issue of operational control from the standpoint of quality initiatives and how management accounting systems can be refined to support such initiatives. In all four chapters we make the point that in order to develop a comprehensive management accounting and control system, we need to supplement financial-performance indicators with relevant nonfinancial measures of performance. Thus, operational control systems can be thought of as including both financial and nonfinancial performance metrics.

## Management Accounting and Control Systems

**LO 14-1**

*Explain the essence of control systems in general and operational control systems in particular.*

**Control**
refers to the set of procedures, tools, and systems organizations use to reach their goals.

A **management accounting and control system**
is an organization's core performance-measurement system.

**Operational control**
focuses on short-term operating performance.

**Financial control**
consists of a comparison between actual and budgeted financial results.

**Variances**
are the differences between budgeted and actual financial amounts.

In business we use the term **control** in a general sense to refer to the set of procedures, tools, and systems organizations use to ensure that progress is being made toward accomplishing the goals and objectives of the organization. In accounting, we refer to an organization's **management accounting and control system** as its core performance-measurement system, one that includes both planning and evaluation (feedback) components.

Comprehensive management accounting and control systems can be subdivided for discussion purposes into management control systems and operational control systems. In this text we use the term **operational control** to refer to the subset of an organization's overall management accounting and control system that focuses on *short-term operational performance.* That is, operational control focuses on the control of basic business processes (or activities) that are performed to produce and deliver to customers the organization's outputs (goods or services).

There are fundamentally two performance dimensions covered by operational control systems: financial and nonfinancial. Thus, an effective operational control system will include performance indicators of both types.

By convention, **financial control** is accomplished by comparing actual to budgeted financial amounts. Thus, budgets are useful in the financial-control process because they provide the standard against which actual financial results can be compared. Differences between budgeted amounts and actual financial results are referred to as **variances.** In this text, we use the labels F and U to refer, respectively, to favorable and unfavorable variances. Favorable variances are those that increase short-term operating income, while unfavorable variances have the opposite effect.

The following example provides a broad overview of the tasks involved in developing an effective operational control system for Schmidt Machinery Company.

### Developing an Operational Control System: The Five Steps of Strategic Decision Making for Schmidt Machinery

1. **Determine the strategic issues surrounding the problem.** Schmidt is a differentiated manufacturer, selling a high-priced product to those who value its quality, design, and functionality. With the growth of foreign competition and the possibility of price competition in the coming years, Schmidt is now looking for ways to maintain its profitability and quality by improving operational efficiency.

2. **Identify the alternative actions.** One approach, as explained in Chapter 13, would be to use target costing in the context of product redesign aimed at reducing the cost while maintaining the quality of the product that Schmidt produces. Another approach

would be to implement an operational control system. Thus, the company is currently considering whether to implement such a system, either in conjunction with or in lieu of the target-costing procedures discussed in Chapter 13.

3. **Obtain information and conduct analyses of the alternatives.** An operational control system, if fully implemented, will capture both financial and nonfinancial performance data. Financial data include budgeted results (sales volume, sales mix, selling prices, variable cost per unit, and total fixed costs). Budgeted costs on a per-unit basis are referred to as *standard costs.* To experiment with a new financial control system, Schmidt develops standard costs for the production of one of its products, XV-1 (see Exhibit 14.5 on page 571). Product design engineers have been asked to consider the possibility of redesigning XV-1 and to estimate the potential savings from the redesign.

4. **Based on strategy and analysis, choose and implement the desired alternative.** Management decides that a product redesign would be too risky at this point, jeopardizing the quality image of the company. So the firm chooses to proceed with the development and implementation of an operational control system associated with product XV-1.

5. **Provide an ongoing evaluation of the effectiveness of implementation in step 4.** As the competitive environment becomes clearer, including changes in the value of the dollar, management should continue to review its approach on how to continue to deliver its differentiated product profitably. In the future, therefore, the company will evaluate each of the following options: the management and control of quality (Chapter 17), productivity analysis (Chapter 16), and the theory of constraints (Chapter 13).

## Short-Term Financial Control

**LO 14-2**

*Explain the total operating-income variance for a given period.*

The **total operating-income variance**
of a period is the difference between the actual operating income of the period and the budgeted operating income for the period; also referred to as the **master (static) budget variance** for the period.

An important short-term financial goal for a company is to achieve the budgeted operating income for the period. At the end of a period, management wants to know whether the planned operating income was attained. The difference between the actual operating income and the master budget operating income is called the **total operating-income variance**. This variance is also referred to as the **master (static) budget variance** for the period.

Consider the analysis of operations for Schmidt Machinery Company presented in Exhibit 14.1. The bottom line of column (2) shows that the budgeted operating income for October 2013 is $200,000, while column (1) reports that the firm actually earned an operating income of $128,000 for the period. This difference is the total operating-income variance for the period, $72,000 unfavorable [column (3)].

In addition to the operating-income variance, Exhibit 14.1 reports the difference between the master (static) budget and the actual result for units sold, sales dollars,

**EXHIBIT 14.1**

**Comparison of Actual and Budgeted Operating Income**

| | SCHMIDT MACHINERY COMPANY Analysis of Operating Income For October 2013 | | | | |
|---|---|---|---|---|---|
| | **(1) Actual Operating Income** | | **(2) Master (Static) Budget** | | **(3) Variances** |
| Units | 780 | | 1,000 | | 220U* |
| Sales | $639,600 | 100% | $800,000 | 100% | $160,400U |
| Variable costs | 350,950 | 55 | 450,000 | 56 | 99,050F† |
| Contribution margin | $288,650 | 45% | $350,000 | 44% | $ 61,350U |
| Fixed costs | 160,650*** | 25 | 150,000** | 19 | 10,650U |
| Operating income | $128,000 | 20% | $200,000 | 25% | **$ 72,000U** |

*U denotes an *unfavorable* effect on operating income.
**Budgeted fixed factory overhead cost = $120,000; budgeted fixed selling and administrative expense = $30,000.
***Actual fixed factory overhead cost = $130,650; actual fixed selling and administrative cost = $30,000.
†F denotes a *favorable* effect on operating income.

variable cost per unit, and total fixed costs. For example, we see from Exhibit 14.1 that actual units sold, 780 units, is 220 units less than the sales units in the master budget, a 22% shortfall.

Exhibit 14.1 also reports that total variable costs in October were $99,050 less than budget; we refer to this difference as a favorable variance. This result may lead us to conclude that the primary reason for Schmidt's failure to be effective in earning its budgeted operating income is the shortfall in sales, not its failure to control variable costs. The shortfall is so large that even with a good control of expenses, as evidenced by the substantial favorable variance in total variable costs, the firm still failed to achieve its budgeted operating income for the month.

That conclusion is misleading. Direct comparisons between the actual operating results and the master (static) budget amounts for total variable costs can be meaningless. In this instance, the variable expenses in the master budget are for operations at a higher level than that actually attained. Variable expenses for 780 units should be less than the variable expenses for 1,000 units. Schmidt should not credit its management for having good control of variable expenses based only on the fact that the variable costs incurred are below the master budgeted amount for the period.

The total operating-income variance ($72,000 unfavorable for Schmidt in October) reveals only whether the firm achieved the budgeted operating income for the period; it does not identify causes for the deviation or help the firm identify courses of action to reduce or eliminate similar deviations in the future. The firm needs to conduct additional analyses to learn the reason for missing the target. Flexible budgets and standard costs can be used to break down and explain the total operating-income variance for a period. It is to this process of variance decomposition that we now turn.

## Flexible Budgets and Profit-Variance Analysis

**LO 14-3**

*Develop a general framework for subdividing the total operating-income variance into component variances.*

### The Flexible Budget

The budget prepared prior to the beginning of a period, as discussed in Chapter 10, is a *master budget* for the period; it lays out expectations and provides blueprints of operations for the coming period. This budget is referred to as a *static budget* because it is developed for only a single output level.

The master budget is useful for initial planning and coordination of activities for a given period. Operating conditions, however, seldom turn out exactly the way they were expected or forecasted when the master budget was prepared. Whenever the output (e.g., sales volume) attained differs from the budgeted output, the organization needs to revise the master budget before assessing short-run financial performance. This revised budget is referred to as a *flexible budget.*

The **flexible budget** is a budget that adjusts revenues and costs to the actual output level achieved.

A **flexible budget** is a budget that adjusts revenues and expenses to the actual output level achieved. Changes in output (for example, units manufactured or sold for a manufacturing firm, number of patient-days for a hospital, or number of students for a school district) change the firm's expected revenues and expenses. For financial control purposes, a firm prepares a flexible budget at the end of a period when the total work done or the actual output level for the period is known.

Flexible budgets are useful for assessing short-term financial performance. The data for Schmidt Machinery Company in Exhibit 14.1 show that the period's operating income is $72,000 less than the budgeted amount. On receiving the report, management would likely raise the following questions:

1. Why was operating income less than expected?
2. Why have expenses gone from 75 to 80% of sales? Can management do something to prevent the same thing from happening next year?
3. Why were short-term fixed costs $10,650 more than expected?

**EXHIBIT 14.2** **Operating-Income Variances (Single-Product Example)**

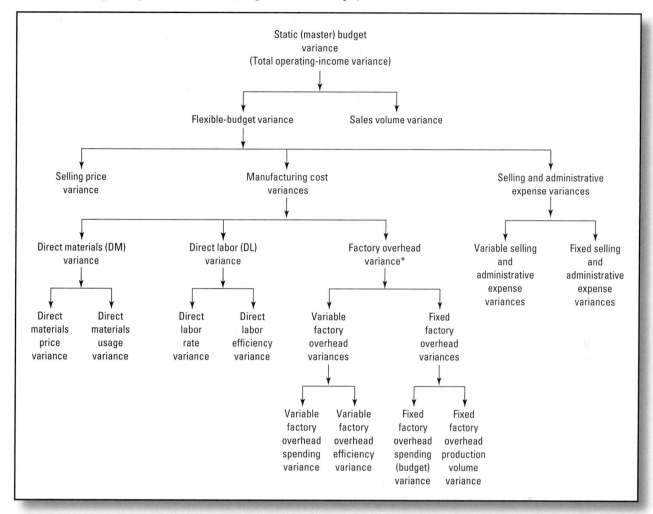

*The decomposition of this variance is covered in Chapter 15.

4. Were the disappointing financial results attributable to changes in:

   a. Units sold?

   b. Sales price?

   c. Sales mix?

   d. Production costs?

   e. Selling and general expenses?

    Preparing a flexible budget allows management to adjust the original budget to the output level achieved and to answer these questions. That is, the use of flexible budgets and standard costs (discussed later in this chapter) allows us to subdivide the total operating-income variance for the period into component variances related to each of the five factors that combine to determine short-run operating profit, namely, selling price, sales volume, sales mix, variable cost per unit, and total fixed costs. A framework for subdividing the total operating-income variance into component variances is presented in Exhibit 14.2. This exhibit gives you an overall picture of the variance-decomposition process. All of the component variances that can be calculated, when summed, equal the total operating-income variance for the period. The ability to explain this overall variance is the essence of the traditional financial control model.

**EXHIBIT 14.3**
**Flexible and Master Budgets for Schmidt Machinery Company**

| | (1)<br>Flexible Budget | | (2)<br>Master (Static) Budget | |
|---|---:|---:|---:|---:|
| Units | 780 | | 1,000 | |
| Sales ($800/unit) | $624,000 | 100.00% | $800,000 | 100.00% |
| Variable expenses ($450/unit) | 351,000 | 56,25 | 450,000 | 56.25 |
| Contribution margin ($350/unit) | $273,000 | 43.75% | $350,000 | 43.75% |
| Fixed expenses | 150,000 | 24.04 | 150,000* | 18,75 |
| Operating income | $123,000 | 19.71% | $200.000 | 25.00% |

*Budgeted fixed factory overhead cost = $120,000; budgeted fixed selling and administrative expenses = $30,000.

Flexible budgets differ from the master budget only in terms of the number of units embodied in the budget. Exhibit 14.3 illustrates the flexible budget for Schmidt for October 2013. Schmidt developed this flexible budget in three steps:

Step 1. **Determine the output of the period.** Schmidt manufactured and sold 780 units. The flexible budget, therefore, would be based on an output level of 780 units.

Step 2. **Use the selling price and the variable cost per unit data from the master budget to calculate the budgeted sales revenues and budgeted variable expenses, respectively, for the output of the period and to compute the flexible budget contribution margin.** The selling price per unit and variable cost per unit in the master budget are $800 and $450, respectively. Thus, at 780 units:

| | |
|---|---:|
| Flexible budget total sales = 780 units × $800 per unit | $624,000 |
| Flexible budget total variable expenses = 780 units × $450 per unit | 351,000 |
| Flexible budget contribution margin = 780 units × $350 per unit* | $273,000 |

*$800 − $450 (total variable cost per unit consists of manufacturing costs of $400 plus $50 of selling and administrative expenses).

Alternatively, the flexible budget contribution margin can be computed by multiplying actual sales volume by the budgeted contribution margin per unit:

$$780 \text{ units} \times \$350 \text{ per unit} = \$273,000$$

Step 3. **Determine the budgeted amount of fixed cost and then compute the flexible-budget operating income.** Schmidt Company has determined that the manufacturing and selling of 780 units is within the same operating range as the master budget operating level. Thus, the total fixed cost for the flexible budget is $150,000, and the flexible-budget operating income is:

$$\$273,000 - \$150,000 = \$123,000$$

Note that the amount of fixed costs in a flexible budget may differ from the amount in the master budget if the actual operating level is substantially different from the operating level anticipated by the firm at the time it prepared the master budget.

In summary, total sales and total expenses for a flexible budget are calculated using these formulas:

$$\text{Total sales} = \text{Actual number of units sold} \times \text{Budgeted selling price per unit}$$

$$\text{Total variable expenses} = \text{Actual number of units sold} \times \text{Budgeted variable cost per unit}$$

$$\text{Total fixed expenses} = \text{Amount of fixed expenses in the master budget}$$

An organization can prepare a budget for different levels of output or activity. In this text we use the term *pro forma* when referring to budgets prepared for multiple output levels. We use the term *flexible budget* in a more limited sense, that is, the budget based on the actual activity level achieved during a period.

## Sales Volume Variance and the Total Flexible-Budget Variance

With the help of a flexible budget, we can now separate the $72,000U total operating-income variance (Exhibit 14.1) into two components: a *total flexible-budget variance* and a *sales volume variance*. The details for this decomposition are shown in Exhibit 14.4.

### *Sales Volume Variance*

**Sales volume variance**
for each income statement item is the difference between the flexible budget amount for that item and the amount for that item reflected in the master budget for the period.

The **sales volume variance** of a period is the difference between the flexible-budget amount and the amount in the master (static) budget of the period for the corresponding income statement item. A sales volume variance measures the effect of changes in sales volume on revenue, expenses, contribution margin, or operating income of the period. Column (4) of Exhibit 14.4 shows the sales volume variances for October 2013.

The master budget [column (5)] shows that Schmidt planned to sell 1,000 units in October 2013. However, actual sales in October were only 780 units. Column (3) shows the budget for this sales volume. The difference between the flexible and the master budgets is the sales volume variance. Thus, the sales volume variance is 220 unfavorable in terms of units and $77,000 unfavorable in terms of operating income [column (4)].

Note that the sales volume variance in terms of operating income is normally the same as the contribution margin sales volume variance. This is because, as noted above, fixed expenses in the master budget and in the flexible budget usually are the same. Thus, an alternative way to compute the sales volume variance is to multiply the master budget contribution margin per unit (here $350) by the difference between the actual units sold and the units in the master (static) budget.

$$\begin{matrix} \text{Sales} \\ \text{volume variance in} \\ \text{terms of operating} \\ \text{income} \end{matrix} = \left( \begin{matrix} \text{Actual units} \\ \text{sold} \end{matrix} - \begin{matrix} \text{Units budgeted} \\ \text{to be sold} \end{matrix} \right) \times \begin{matrix} \text{Master budget contribution} \\ \text{margin per unit} \end{matrix}$$

$$= (780 - 1,000) \text{ units} \times \$350/\text{unit}$$

$$= \$77,000U$$

**EXHIBIT 14.4**
**Breakdown of Total Operating-Income Variance**

| | (1)<br>Actual | (2)<br>Flexible-Budget<br>Variances | (3)<br>Flexible<br>Budget | (4)<br>Sales Volume<br>Variances | (5)<br>Master (Static)<br>Budget |
|---|---|---|---|---|---|
| Units | 780 | 0 | 780 | 220U | 1,000 |
| Sales | $639,600 | $15,600F | $624,000 | $176,000U | $800,000 |
| Variable costs | 350,950 | 50F | 351,000 | 99,000F | 450,000 |
| Contribution margin | $288,650 | $15,650F | $273,000 | $ 77,000U | $350,000 |
| Fixed costs | 160,650 | 10,650U | 150,000** | 0 | 150,000** |
| Operating Income | $128,000 | $ 5,000F | $123,000 | $ 77,000U | $200,000 |

**SCHMIDT MACHINERY COMPANY**
**Analysis of Financial Results**
**For October 2013**

**Analysis of Total Operating-Income Variance**

Total operating-income variance*
= $128,000 − $200,000 = $72,000U

Flexible-budget variance
= $128,000 − $123,000
= $5,000F

Sales volume variance
= $123,000 − $200,000
= $77,000U

*Also called the *total master (static) budget variance.*
**Budgeted fixed factory overhead cost = $120,000; budgeted fixed selling and administrative expense = $30,000.

The sales volume variance expressed in terms of operating income shows that, holding everything else constant, a sales volume decrease of 220 units would decrease operating income by $77,000. The sales volume variance may be a result of one or more of the following:[1]

1. The market for the product has changed. The total demand for the product grew (declined) at a rate higher than expected.
2. The firm lost market share to competitors.
3. The firm failed to set a proper goal for the period.
4. The firm set an inappropriate selling price for the product.
5. The marketing and promotion programs were not effective.

Each of these causes may be a result of one or more contributing factors. For example, a firm might have lost market share because of quality problems that led to customers' dissatisfaction, shifts in customer preferences and tastes, ineffective advertising, reduction in the number of sales calls or salespeople, or products not available due to production problems, among others. The proper response to a sales volume variance depends on the cause of the variance.

### Flexible-Budget (FB) Variances

**Flexible-budget (FB) variances**
refer to differences between actual and flexible-budget amounts on the income statement.

**Flexible-budget (FB) variances** refer to differences between actual and flexible-budget amounts. As indicated in column (2) of Exhibit 14.4, for any income statement item a

$$\text{Flexible-budget variance} = \text{Actual results} - \text{Flexible-budget results}$$

Thus, there are flexible-budget variances for sales, variable costs, fixed costs, and operating income.

The **total flexible-budget variance**
for a period is the difference between the flexible-budget operating income and the actual operating income for the period.

The **total flexible-budget variance** of a period is the difference between the flexible-budget operating income and the operating income actually earned during the period. In Exhibit 14.4, we see that the total flexible-budget variance for October is $5,000 favorable, as follows:

$$\begin{aligned}\text{Total flexible-budget variance} &= \text{(Actual) operating income earned} - \text{Flexible-budget operating income} \\ &= \$128,000 - \$123,000 \\ &= \$5,000\text{F}\end{aligned}$$

The total flexible-budget variance for the period can be broken down into a selling price variance, a total variable cost flexible-budget variance, and a total fixed cost flexible-budget variance. As shown by the details that follow, in the present case the $5,000 favorable flexible-budget variance consists of a $15,600 favorable selling price variance, a $50 total variable cost variance, and a $10,650 unfavorable fixed cost variance.

***Selling Price Variance***   As the name implies, the selling price variance reflects the effect on operating income of a difference between actual and budgeted selling prices. Thus, the **selling price variance** can be determined by taking the difference between actual sales revenues for a period and the sales revenue in the flexible budget for the period. The difference between these two amounts, if any, results from deviations of the actual selling price per unit from the budgeted selling price per unit:

**Selling price variance**
is the difference between the actual sales revenue for a period and the sales revenue in the flexible budget for the period.

$$\text{Actual sales revenue} = \text{Units sold} \times \textit{Actual} \text{ selling price per unit}$$

$$\text{Flexible budget sales revenue} = \text{Units sold} \times \textit{Budgeted} \text{ selling price per unit}$$

---

[1] For a multiproduct firm (not considered in this chapter), the sales volume variance can be decomposed into a pure volume variance and a sales-mix variance. This topic is covered in Chapter 16. Also, in Chapter 16 we discuss how to separate the pure sales volume variance into market-size and market-share components.

In the above, both sales revenue figures are for the actual number of units sold during the period. The difference between these two sales revenue amounts is due solely to the difference between actual and budgeted selling price per unit. For this reason we refer to this difference as the selling price variance for the period.

$$\text{Selling price variance} = \text{Actual sales revenue} - \text{Flexible budget sales revenue}$$

$$= \left(\substack{\text{Units} \\ \text{sold}} \times \substack{\text{Actual selling} \\ \text{price per unit}}\right) - \left(\substack{\text{Units} \\ \text{sold}} \times \substack{\text{Budgeted selling} \\ \text{price per unit}}\right)$$

$$= \left(\substack{\text{Actual selling} \\ \text{price per unit}} - \substack{\text{Budgeted selling} \\ \text{price per unit}}\right) \times \substack{\text{Units} \\ \text{sold}}$$

$$= \text{Selling price variance}$$

Exhibit 14.4 shows that in October 2013 Schmidt sold 780 units of XV-1 for $639,600, or $820 per unit. The budgeted selling price, however, was $800 per unit. Using the budgeted selling price of $800 per unit, the total sales revenue in the flexible budget for 780 units actually sold is $624,000. The difference, $15,600, is a result of the actual selling price per unit being $20 higher than the budgeted selling price per unit for each of the 780 units sold, as shown here:

$$\text{Selling price variance} = \text{Actual sales revenue} - \text{Flexible budget sales revenue}$$

$$= (\$639,600 - \$624,000) = \$15,600 \text{ F}$$

$$\text{Selling price variance} = \left(\substack{\text{Actual selling} \\ \text{price per unit}} - \substack{\text{Budgeted} \\ \text{selling price per unit}}\right) \times \substack{\text{Units} \\ \text{sold}}$$

$$= (\$820 - \$800) \times 780 \text{ units}$$

$$= \$15,600\text{F}$$

The **total variable cost flexible-budget variance** is the difference between the total variable cost incurred during a period and the total variable cost in the flexible budget for the period.

***Variable Cost Flexible-Budget Variances***   The **total variable cost flexible-budget variance** is the difference between the total variable cost incurred during a period and the total variable cost in the flexible budget for the period. Thus, this variance reflects the deviation of the actual variable cost incurred during the period from the standard variable cost for the output of the period.

Note in Exhibit 14.4 that Schmidt incurred $350,950 total variable costs in October 2013 to produce and sell 780 units of XV-1. Budgeted variable costs per unit for Schmidt are referred to as *standard costs* and are reflected on the standard cost sheet illustrated as Exhibit 14.5. The standard variable manufacturing cost is $400 per unit (including $140 for

**EXHIBIT 14.5**
**Standard Cost Sheet, Product XV-1**

| SCHMIDT MACHINERY COMPANY | | | | |
|---|---|---|---|---|
| Standard Cost Sheet | | | | |
| Product: XV-1 | | | | |
| **Descriptions** | **Quantity** | **Unit Cost** | **Subtotal** | **Total** |
| Direct materials: | | | | |
| Aluminum | 4 pounds | $25 | $100 | |
| PVC | 1 pound | 40 | 40 | |
| Direct labor | 5 hours | 40 | 200 | |
| Variable factory overhead | 5 hours | 12 | 60 | |
| Total variable manufacturing cost | | | | $400 |
| Fixed factory overhead* | 5 hours | 24 | 120 | 120 |
| Standard manufacturing cost per unit | | | | $520 |
| Standard variable selling and administrative expense per unit | | | | $ 50 |

*Budgeted fixed factory overhead cost = $120,000.

direct materials, $200 for direct labor, and $60 for variable manufacturing overhead). For 780 units, the total standard variable manufacturing cost is therefore $312,000 ($400 per unit × 780 units). In addition, the standard variable selling and administrative expense is $50 per unit, or $39,000 in total ($50 per unit × 780 units). This brings the total budgeted variable cost for manufacturing and selling 780 units to $351,000 ($312,000 + $39,000). The difference between the actual variable cost incurred during the period and the total variable cost in the flexible budget for the units manufactured and sold during the period is the *total variable cost flexible-budget variance,* which in the present case is $50 favorable (see Exhibit 14.4):

$$\text{Total variable cost flexible-budget variance} = \text{Total variable cost incurred} - \text{Total flexible budget variable cost}$$

$$= \$350{,}950 - [(\$140 + \$200 + \$60 + \$50) \times 780 \text{ units}]$$

$$= \$350{,}950 - (\$450 \times 780)$$

$$= \$350{,}950 - \$351{,}000$$

$$= \$50\text{F}$$

***Further Analysis of the Total Variable Cost Flexible-Budget Variance*** The total variable cost flexible-budget variance is the sum of flexible-budget variances of all variable costs and expenses, including flexible-budget variances for direct materials, direct labor, variable overhead, and variable selling and administrative expenses.

$$\begin{array}{c}\text{Total variable}\\\text{cost flexible-}\\\text{budget}\\\text{variance}\end{array} = \begin{array}{c}\text{Total direct}\\\text{materials}\\\text{flexible-budget}\\\text{variance}\end{array} + \begin{array}{c}\text{Total direct}\\\text{labor flexible-}\\\text{budget}\\\text{variance}\end{array} + \begin{array}{c}\text{Total variable}\\\text{overhead}\\\text{flexible-budget}\\\text{variance}\end{array} + \begin{array}{c}\text{Total variable selling}\\\text{and administrative}\\\text{expenses flexible-}\\\text{budget variance}\end{array}$$

More detailed information regarding the total variable cost flexible-budget variance is provided in Exhibit 14.6. The $50 favorable total variable cost flexible-budget variance may not in and of itself be of concern to the management of Schmidt Machinery Company. However, this seemingly insignificant net variance could be the result of large but

**EXHIBIT 14.6**
**Comparison of Actual Variable Costs and Flexible-Budget Variable Costs**

| SCHMIDT MACHINERY COMPANY<br>October 2013 | | | |
|---|---|---|---|
| **Product XV-1** | | | |
| **Units Manufactured: 780** | | | |
| **Actual Results** | | | |
| Direct materials: | | | |
| Aluminum | 3,630 pounds at $26 per pound | $94,380 | |
| PVC | 720 pounds at $41 per pound | 29,520 | $123,900 |
| Direct labor | 3,510 hours at $42 per hour | | 147,420 |
| Variable factory overhead | | | 40,630 |
| Total variable cost of goods manufactured | | | $311,950 |
| Variable selling and administrative expenses | | | 39,000 |
| Total variable costs for the period | | | $350,950 |
| **Flexible Budget** | | | |
| Budgeted variable cost of goods manufactured: | | | |
| Standard variable manufacturing cost per unit (from Exhibit 14.5) | | $400 | |
| Number of units manufactured | | × 780 | $312,000 |
| Budgeted variable selling and administrative expenses (780 × $50) | | | 39,000 |
| Total budgeted variable costs for 780 units | | | $351,000 |
| Total variable cost flexible-budget variance for the period | | | $    50F* |

*F denotes a *favorable* variance.

offsetting component variances. For this reason, we can decompose this net variance using a two-step process. Step one is to calculate a flexible-budget variance for each variable cost, as shown in Exhibit 14.8. For example, the total direct labor cost variance for October was $8,580F. Step two is to use the following model to break down (decompose) this variable cost variance into its price and quantity components.

***General Model for the Analysis of Variable Cost Variances***    Any purely variable cost is a function of two factors, price (P) and quantity (Q). Thus, any flexible-budget variance for a given variable cost, such as direct materials or direct labor, should be able to be decomposed into a *price* (rate) *variance* and a *quantity* (efficiency) *variance*. A general model for the analysis of variable cost flexible-budget variances is provided in Exhibit 14.7.

We note that the price variance for direct materials can be calculated either at the time materials are purchased or at the time materials are issued to production. If the former is

**EXHIBIT 14.7**
**General Model for Analyzing Variable Cost Variances**

Legend:
AQ = Actual quantity of the resource (e.g., DM) purchased or used
AP = Actual cost per unit of the resource (e.g., per lb.)
SP = Standard cost per unit of the resource
SQ = Standard quantity of the resource that should have been used to produce the output for the period = Units of output × Standard resource input per unit of output

the case, then AQ in Exhibit 14.7 means "actual quantity of materials *purchased*" and the resulting variance is referred to as a *materials purchase-price variance*. Regardless of when the price variance for materials is calculated, the quantity variance is calculated at the end of the period, once production is known. The term AQ in the materials quantity variance *always* refers to the actual quantity of materials consumed for a given period's output.

We now apply the general model to the analysis of variable cost flexible-budget variances for the Schmidt Machinery Company, October 2013.

*Direct Materials Variances*    As indicated in Exhibit 14.7, the direct materials flexible-budget variance *for each material* is the difference between the actual direct materials cost and the total standard direct materials cost for a period's output. This variance reflects efficiency (or inefficiency) in buying and in using direct materials. Attaining efficiency in buying and using materials requires good controls over both the price paid for the materials and the quantity of the materials used in production. Since price and usage can move in opposite directions, we must analyze a total variance for each raw material by breaking the variance down into its price and quantity components.

Exhibits 14.8 and 14.9 illustrate an analysis of direct materials costs using the October 2013 operating data of the Schmidt Company. In this example, there are two direct materials: aluminum and PVC. We illustrate here the analysis of the flexible-budget variance for aluminum. Exhibit 14.8 (top portion) shows that Schmidt used 3,630 pounds of aluminum at a total cost of $94,380 to manufacture 780 units of XV-1. The standard cost sheet reported in Exhibit 14.5 indicates that the standard cost for one unit of XV-1 is 4 pounds of aluminum at $25 per pound. For October, the total flexible-budget cost for aluminum, given an output of 780 units, is $78,000. (See the middle section of Exhibit 14.8.)

**Direct Materials Flexible-Budget Variance**    The **direct materials flexible-budget variance** for each material is the difference between the total direct material cost incurred and the flexible-budget amount for this period's output. Schmidt spent $94,380 for aluminum (Exhibit 14.8, top portion). Thus, the total flexible-budget variance for aluminum for October is $16,380 unfavorable ($94,380 − $78,000). This same approach can be used to calculate the total flexible-budget variance for PVC, $1,680F (Exhibit 14.8, bottom portion).

The **direct materials flexible-budget variance** for each material is the difference between total direct materials cost incurred and the flexible-budget amount for this period's output.

574

**EXHIBIT 14.8**
A Detailed Comparison of
Actual Variable Costs and
Flexible-Budget Variable Costs

| SCHMIDT MACHINERY COMPANY | | | |
|---|---|---|---|
| October 2013 | | | |

**Product XV-1**

**Units Manufactured: 780**

**Actual Variable Costs Incurred**
Direct materials:

| | | | |
|---|---|---|---|
| Aluminum | 3,630 pounds* at $26 per pound | $94,380 | |
| PVC | 720 pounds at $41 per pound | 29,520 | $123,900 |
| Direct labor | 3,510 hours at $42 per hour | | 147,420 |
| Variable factory overhead | | | 40,630 |
| Total variable cost of goods manufactured | | | $311,950 |
| Variable selling and administrative expenses | | | 39,000 |
| Total variable costs incurred | | | $350,950 |

**Flexible Budget for Variable Costs**
Direct materials:

| | | | |
|---|---|---|---|
| Aluminum | 780 units × 4 pounds × $25 = | $78,000 | |
| PVC | 780 units × 1 pound × $40 = | 31,200 | $109,200 |
| Direct labor | 780 units × 5 hours × $40 = | | 156,000 |
| Variable factory overhead | 780 units × 5 hours × $12 = | | 46,800 |
| Total standard variable cost of goods manufactured | | | $312,000 |
| Variable selling and administrative expenses | | | 39,000 |
| Total flexible-budget variable costs | | | $351,000 |

**Variable Cost Flexible-Budget Variances**
Direct materials:

| | | | |
|---|---|---|---|
| Aluminum | $94,380 − $78,000 = $16,380U[†] | | |
| PVC | 29,520 − 31,200 = 1,680F[‡] | | $14,700U |
| Direct labor | 147,420 − 156,000 = | | 8,580F |
| Variable factory overhead | 40,630 − 46,800 = | | 6,170F |
| Variable manufacturing cost flexible-budget variance | | | $     50F |
| Variable selling and administrative expense variance | | | 0 |
| Variable cost flexible-budget variance (see Exhibit 14.6) | | | $     50F |

*Assume that lbs. purchased = lbs. used.
[†]U denotes an *unfavorable* variance.
[‡]F denotes a *favorable* variance.

## Further Analysis of the Direct Materials Flexible-Budget Variance

The **direct materials price variance (PV)**
for each material is the
difference between the actual
and standard cost per unit of
direct material multiplied by
the quantity of direct materials
used during the period.

*Price Variance*  The **direct materials price variance (PV)** for each material is the difference between the actual and the standard cost per unit of direct material multiplied by the quantity of the direct materials used during the period.[2] Exhibit 14.8 shows that in October Schmidt Machinery Company paid $26 per pound for the 3,630 pounds of aluminum used in production. The standard cost sheet (Exhibit 14.5) specifies the standard price for aluminum is $25 per pound. Thus, the actual price paid is $1 per pound more than standard. For the 3,630 pounds used, the price variance is $3,630 unfavorable (column (1) – column (2), Exhibit 14.9). Alternatively,

$$\begin{matrix} \text{Direct} \\ \text{material sprice} \\ \text{variance} \end{matrix} = \begin{pmatrix} \text{Actual price paid} \\ \text{for one unit of} \\ \text{direct material} \end{pmatrix} - \begin{matrix} \text{Standard price} \\ \text{for one unit of} \\ \text{direct material} \end{matrix} \times \begin{matrix} \text{Total number of units} \\ \text{of the direct material} \\ \text{used in production} \end{matrix}$$

$$\begin{aligned} PV &= (AP - SP) \times AQ \\ &= (\$26 - \$25) \text{ per pound} \times 3{,}630 \text{ pounds} \\ &= \$1 \text{ per pound} \times 3{,}630 \text{ pounds} \\ &= \$3{,}630 \text{ Unfavorable} \end{aligned}$$

[2] As we discuss later in this chapter, for control purposes it is preferable to calculate the materials price variance at the time materials are purchased. In this case, we use the more specific term *materials purchase-price variance*. See Exhibit 14.11 and the related discussion.

**EXHIBIT 14.9**
**Direct Materials Flexible-Budget Variance—Aluminum**

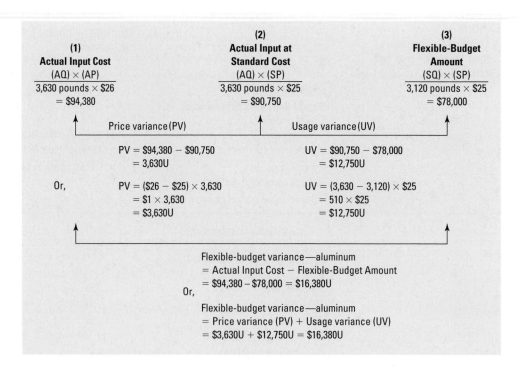

*Interpreting the Direct Materials Price Variance (PV)*   A direct materials price variance (PV) can result from failure to take purchase discounts, unexpected price change of materials, changes in freight costs, variation in grades of materials, or other causes. The purchasing department is often the office most likely to provide an explanation or have the responsibility for materials price variances.

Care must be taken in interpreting direct materials price variances. A favorable direct materials price variance could lead to excessively high manufacturing costs if the low-cost materials are of poor quality. Downstream costs such as scrap, rework, schedule disruptions, or field-service costs could exceed the price savings from lower materials prices. A firm with a differentiation strategy is likely to fail when it pursues favorable price variances through purchases of low-quality materials. A firm that competes on low cost also is likely to be adversely affected if the quality of its products is below customer expectations or it increases downstream costs.

Carrying costs and additional materials-handling costs can exceed the savings from low purchase prices. A firm with a cost-effective purchasing department that has several warehouses full of materials and supplies purchased in bulk at low prices could have a higher total overall cost than a firm that buys in small quantities as needed and maintains only a minimum amount of direct materials on hand, even though the firm paid higher purchase prices for these materials.

**Materials usage ratio** is the ratio of quantity used over quantity purchased.

In addition to price variances, many firms also use usage ratios in evaluating the performance of purchasing departments. A **materials usage ratio** is the ratio of quantity used over quantity purchased. A low materials usage ratio suggests that the purchasing department purchased for materials inventory rather than the operational needs of the period. Such a move can be costly if the firm considers all costs. In this case, the benefit of any favorable price variance should be evaluated along with the cost of inventory storage of the surplus purchases.

The **direct materials usage variance (UV)** for each raw material is the difference between the actual raw material units used during the period and the standard units that should have been used for the output of the period, multiplied by the standard cost per unit of the direct material.

*Usage Variance*   The **direct materials usage variance (UV)** refers to the efficiency with which each raw material was used during the period. For each raw material this variance is calculated as the difference between the actual raw material units used during the period and the standard units that should have been used for the output of the period, multiplied by the standard cost per unit of the direct material. This variance is also referred to as an *efficiency* or *quantity variance*.

In October 2013 Schmidt Machinery Company used 3,630 pounds of aluminum to manufacture 780 units of XV-1. According to the standard cost sheet (Exhibit 14.5), each unit of XV-1 requires 4 pounds of aluminum. The total standard quantity of aluminum for the 780 units manufactured during the period, therefore, is 3,120 pounds (780 units × 4 pounds per unit). This says that the 3,630 pounds of aluminum used in production is 510 pounds more than the total standard quantity for the 780 units of XV-1 manufactured during the period. At the standard price of $25 per pound, the usage variance this period for aluminum is $12,750 unfavorable (column (2) – column (3), Exhibit 14.9). Alternatively,

$$\begin{matrix} \text{Direct} \\ \text{materials} \\ \text{usage variance} \end{matrix} = \begin{pmatrix} \text{Total quantity} & \text{Total standard quantity of} \\ \text{of the direct} & - & \text{the direct material for} \\ \text{material used} & & \text{the units manufactured} \end{pmatrix} \begin{matrix} \text{Standard cost per} \\ \times \text{ unit of the direct} \\ \text{material} \end{matrix}$$

$$\begin{aligned} UV &= (AQ - SQ) \times SP \\ &= (3{,}630 - 3{,}120) \text{ pounds} \times \$25 \text{ per pound} \\ &= 510 \text{ pounds} \times \$25 \text{ per pound} \\ &= \$12{,}750 \text{ Unfavorable} \end{aligned}$$

*Interpreting the Direct Materials Usage Variance*  A significant direct materials usage variance suggests that operations consumed a significantly different amount of direct materials than the amount specified for the output of the period. This variance measures efficiency in using direct materials and can result from the efforts of production personnel, substitutions of materials or production factors, variation in the quality of direct materials, inadequate training or inexperienced employees, poor supervision, or other factors.

**Direct Labor Variances**  As indicated in Exhibit 14.7, a direct labor flexible-budget variance is a result of the total direct labor cost of a period being different from the total standard direct labor cost for the output of the period. As with the direct materials flexible-budget variance, a direct labor flexible-budget variance also can be divided into two components: a rate (price) and an efficiency (quantity) variance. As shown in Exhibit 14.8, the total direct labor flexible-budget variance for October 2013 is $8,580F. The procedure for further analysis of this variance is similar to the procedure discussed above for direct materials. Exhibit 14.10 shows calculations of the direct labor rate variance and the direct labor efficiency variance for Schmidt Machinery Company for October 2013.

**EXHIBIT 14.10**
**Direct Labor Flexible-Budget Variance—Schmidt Machinery Company October 2013**

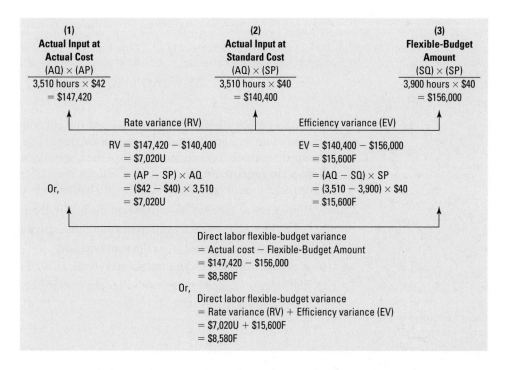

**Direct labor rate variance (RV)** is the difference between the actual and the standard wage rate multiplied by the actual direct labor hours worked during the period.

**Direct Labor Rate Variance**   The **direct labor rate variance (RV)** is the difference between the actual and the standard wage rate multiplied by the actual direct labor hours worked during the period. As indicated in the top portion of Exhibit 14.8, Schmidt Machinery Company paid an average wage rate of $42 per hour for 3,510 direct labor hours in October. The standard cost sheet, however, calls for a wage rate of $40 per hour. Thus, the firm paid $2 per hour more than the standard hourly rate. With 3,510 total hours actually worked, the total direct labor rate variance is $7,020 unfavorable (Exhibit 14.10, column (1) − column (2)). Alternatively,

$$\frac{\text{Direct labor}}{\text{rate variance}} = \left(\begin{array}{c}\text{Actual hourly} \\ \text{wage rate paid}\end{array} - \begin{array}{c}\text{Standard hourly} \\ \text{wage rate}\end{array}\right) \times \begin{array}{c}\text{Total direct labor} \\ \text{hours worked}\end{array}$$

$$RV = (AP - SP) \times AQ$$
$$= (\$42 - \$40) \text{ per direct labor-hour} \times 3,510 \text{ direct labor hours}$$
$$= \$7,020U$$

A direct labor rate variance reflects the effect on operating income when the actual hourly wage rate during the period deviates from the standard hourly wage rate. This could result from not using workers with the skill level specified in the standard cost sheet for the work performed or from using an out-of-date standard.

The personnel department usually is responsible for direct labor rate variances. Production, however, could be responsible for the variance if it chooses to use employees with a different skill level than that specified in the standard cost sheet.

The **direct labor efficiency variance (EV)** is the difference between the actual hours worked and the standard hours allowed for the units manufactured, multiplied by the standard wage rate.

**Direct Labor Efficiency Variance**   A **direct labor efficiency variance (EV)** occurs when the total direct labor hours worked deviates from the total standard direct labor hours allowed for the actual output of the period. It is calculated by multiplying the difference between the actual and the standard allowed hours by the standard hourly wage rate, as follows:

$$\begin{array}{c}\text{Direct labor} \\ \text{efficiency} \\ \text{variance}\end{array} = \left(\begin{array}{c}\text{Total direct} \\ \text{labor hours} \\ \text{worked}\end{array} - \begin{array}{c}\text{Total standard direct} \\ \text{labor hours allowed for} \\ \text{the output of the period}\end{array}\right) \times \begin{array}{c}\text{Standard} \\ \text{direct labor} \\ \text{hourly rate}\end{array}$$

As indicated in the upper panel of Exhibit 14.8, Schmidt Machinery Company used 3,510 direct labor hours to manufacture 780 units of XV-1 in October 2013. The standard cost sheet (Exhibit 14.5) allows five direct labor hours for one unit of XV-1. The total standard hours allowed for 780 units of XV-1, therefore, is 3,900 hours (780 × 5). Thus, Schmidt used 390 fewer direct labor hours than the standard hours allowed this period. At a standard wage rate of $40 per hour, the total direct labor efficiency (quantity) variance is $15,600 favorable (column (2) − column (3), Exhibit 14.10). Alternatively,

$$\frac{\text{Direct labor}}{\text{efficiency variance}} = \left(\begin{array}{c}3,510 \text{ actual} \\ \text{hours}\end{array} - \begin{array}{c}3,900 \text{ standard} \\ \text{hours allowed}\end{array}\right) \times \$40 \text{ per hour}$$

$$EV = (AQ - SQ) \times SP$$
$$= \$15,600F$$

A direct labor efficiency variance reflects the effect on operating income of using an amount of direct labor hours during the period that differs from the standard hours allowed during the period. This variance usually is the responsibility of the production department. Besides the employees' efficiency or inefficiency in carrying out their tasks, however, several other factors—including these—can lead to a direct-labor efficiency variance (EV):

1. Employees or supervisors are new on the job or are inadequately trained.
2. Employees' skill levels are different from those specified in the standard cost sheet.
3. Batch sizes are different from the standard size.
4. Materials are different from those specified.
5. Machines or equipment are not in proper working condition.
6. Supervision is inadequate.
7. Scheduling is poor.

***Timing of Variance Recognition*** Identification of variances helps managers to be aware of deviations from expected performance. For maximum control, managers should recognize variances at the earliest feasible time.

As noted earlier, a direct materials price variance can be identified either at the *time of purchase* or at the *time the materials are issued to production.* The discussion in the chapter to this point has assumed that the price variance for materials is calculated at the time of production. By contrast, recognition of the price variance at point of purchase allows the firm to take proper actions preventing the continuation of an unfavorable price variance or attaining the most benefit from favorable price variances. As indicated in the top half of Exhibit 14.11, when the materials price variance is calculated at point of purchase, *actual quantity* (AQ) in the variance calculation formula refers to the quantity of materials *purchased.* In this case, the materials price variance is referred to by the more descriptive term, *materials purchase-price variance.*

**EXHIBIT 14.11**

**Analyzing Direct Materials Variances When the Quantity Purchased and Quantity Used During a Period Are Different**

As well, recognizing materials price variances at the time of purchase lets the firm carry all units of the same material at one price—the standard cost of the material. Using one price for the same materials greatly simplifies accounting work. For example, such a firm needs to maintain subsidiary ledgers for materials only in terms of quantity.

If a price variance is not recorded until the materials are issued to production, then AQ in the price variance formula refers to the quantity of materials *used* in production and the direct materials are carried on the books at their actual purchase prices.

Regardless of when a direct materials price variance is recognized, the number of units of raw materials actually consumed in production is used to compute the direct materials usage variance, as shown in the lower portion of Exhibit 14.11.

## Standard Costs

**LO 14-4**

*Develop standard costs for product costing, performance evaluation, and control.*

A **standard cost** is a carefully determined cost a firm or organization sets for an operation— the cost the firm or organization should incur for the operation under relatively efficient conditions. A standard cost usually is expressed on a per-unit-of-output basis. Standard costs are incorporated into budgets and as such can be used to monitor and control operations and to evaluate performance.

A **standard cost** is the cost a firm should incur for an operation.

### Standard Costs versus a Standard Cost System

A standard cost prescribes expected performance. A complete standard cost for a product or service includes carefully established standards for each cost element, including manufacturing, selling, and administrative expenses, as illustrated earlier in Exhibit 14.5. Although the discussions in this and the next chapter focus on standard cost systems for manufacturing operations, these concepts and procedures can be applied to service contexts as well.

A **standard cost system** is one in which standard, not actual, costs flow through the formal accounting records.

It is useful to distinguish between standard costs and a **standard cost system**. The latter refers to an accounting system in which standard costs, and associated standard cost variances, are recorded in the formal accounting system. The flow of direct manufacturing costs in the accounting records is illustrated in the next section of this chapter.[3] Note, however, that standard costs can be used for control purposes outside of the formal accounting system. That is, at the end of the accounting period accountants can compare actual and standard costs and analyze variances using the procedures discussed in the previous section of this chapter, regardless of whether standard costs are incorporated formally in the accounting system.

A standard cost system can be applied in either a job-order or a process cost context. Because of the repetitive nature of operations, it is generally simpler to establish standards in conjunction with a process cost system. Also, the use of standard costs in a process cost system greatly simplifies the determination of equivalent-unit costs: the standard (predetermined) costs serve as the cost per equivalent unit for direct materials, direct labor, and manufacturing overhead.

### Types of Standards

Firms have different expectations for the proper level at which to set their standards. Differences in expectations lead to two basic types of standards: ideal, and currently attainable.

#### Ideal Standards

An **ideal standard** reflects maximum efficiency in every aspect of the operation.

An **ideal standard** reflects maximum efficiency in every aspect of an operation. By definition, ideal standards are difficult, but not impossible, to achieve. They assume peak operating efficiency and the absence of any production disruptions. That is, ideal standards

---

[3] Journal entries for recording standard indirect manufacturing costs (i.e., manufacturing overhead), as well as associated standard cost variances, are presented in Chapter 15.

# Cost Management in Action

## Is Two Minutes and Twenty Seconds Enough for a Brake Part?

At Westinghouse Air Brake Company in Chicago, workers are expected to "feed" a conveyor belt a finished part at fixed intervals. Having done this successfully, the workers in that work cell are rewarded with a $1.50 per hour bonus for that day's work. The bonus, a 12.5% increase in pay for the same hours, is a significant boost to the regular pay of $12 per hour and an effective incentive for most workers at the plant.

The speed of the conveyor changes from time to time to reflect changes in customer demand. When demand falls, the rate slows, and vice versa. The firm installed the bonus plan upon the recommendations of consultants and specialists in *kaizen* (continuous improvement). The bonus plan allowed Westinghouse to improve productivity in the plant by over 10 times the 1991 level. This seems to be a win-win situation for Westinghouse and Westinghouse workers. Do you see any problems?

(Refer to Comments on Cost Management in Action at the end of the chapter.)

assume perfection across all operations. As such, the use of ideal standards can lead to undue stress on employees that, in turn, may lead to decreases in morale and ultimately decreases in productivity.

As an alternative to the use of ideal standards, some organizations employ what are referred to as **continuous-improvement standards.** Such standards, as a function of time (e.g., months), become progressively tighter (i.e., more difficult to achieve). The use of this approach is somewhat analogous to the Japanese use of kaizen costing.

Organizations that use ideal standards often modify performance evaluation and reward structures so that employees are not frustrated by frequent failures to attain the standards. Organizations can, for example, use progress toward an ideal standard rather than deviations from it as the primary benchmark in their performance evaluation and reward systems.

> A **continuous-improvement standard** is one that gets progressively tighter over time.

### Currently Attainable Standards

A **currently attainable standard** sets the performance expectation at a level that a person with proper training and experience can attain most of the time without having to exert extraordinary effort. A currently attainable standard emphasizes normality and allows for some imperfections and inefficiencies.

Suppose that a firm sets the standard for the amount of plywood needed to produce 1,000 tabletops at 525 sheets of plywood, although two tabletops can be cut from one sheet. The additional 25 sheets allow for such things as less-than-ideal input quality, occasional maladjustment of the equipment used in production, worker fatigue, and varying experience and skill levels of the personnel involved in production. By using a standard that allows for normal fluctuations in relevant manufacturing factors, employees exerting reasonable effort usually can meet the standard.

> A **currently attainable standard** sets the performance criterion at a level that a person with proper training and experience can attain most of the time without having to exert extraordinary effort.

### Selection of Standards

Which standards—ideal or currently attainable—should a firm use? There is no single answer for all situations.

Firms struggling for survival in intensely competitive industries may choose to use ideal (or continuous-improvement) standards to motivate employees to put forth their best efforts. Ideal standards are not effective, however, if frequent failures in meeting the standards discourage employees or lead them to ignore the standards.

Currently attainable standards, however, may have built into them some degree of inefficiency. Allowing some inefficiencies is strategically unwise if the firm operates in an intensely competitive environment. For example, a standard that allows 25 additional sheets of plywood conveys to production that it has attained acceptable performance as long as it does not make more than 25 mistakes for every 500 sheets of plywood it cuts.

## Standard-Setting Procedures

A firm can use either an authoritative or a participative procedure in setting standards. An **authoritative standard** is determined solely or primarily by management. In contrast, a **participative standard** calls, throughout the standard-setting process, for active participation of employees affected by the standard. A firm uses an authoritative process to

> An **authoritative standard** is determined solely or primarily by management.

> A **participative standard** calls for active participation throughout the standard-setting process by employees affected by the standard.

Record oil prices in 2008 have motivated firms to rethink their supply-chain strategies. Each $10 increase in the cost of a barrel of crude oil is thought to translate to an increase of $0.04 per mile in transportation costs. Supply-chain tactics that were previously considered essential for success—moving factories offshore where labor is cheaper, and making quick and frequent deliveries to retailers to keep inventories low—are now being reexamined. In this environment it becomes increasingly important to minimize the length of the journey from distribution center to retailer—the final leg of the supply chain—and to ship in large quantities to take advantage of economies of scale. Thus, to cut fuel use, firms are moving factories closer to the markets they serve, shipping larger lot sizes less frequently, using third-party trucking services (i.e., outsourcing), adopting cheaper and sometimes slower modes of transportation, and adding warehouses. Such cost-cutting strategies are particularly important for makers of products with low margins and long life cycles—products such as packaged goods and chemicals. One result of implementing these strategies is an observed increase in inventory levels.

**Source:** David Simchi-Levi, Derek Nelson, Narenda Mulani, and Jonathan Wright, "Crude Calculations: Why High Oil Prices Are Upending the Way Companies Should Manage Their Supply Chains," *The Wall Street Journal*, October 22, 2008, p. R8.

ensure proper consideration of all operating factors, to incorporate management's desires or expectations, or to expedite the standard-setting process. Firms using an authoritative process in standard setting, however, should keep in mind that a standard is useless if ignored by employees.

By contrast, participative standards are thought to produce important behavioral effects. For example, employees are more likely to accept standards they helped to determine. Participation also reduces the chance that employees will view the standard as unreasonable and increases the likelihood that they will buy into or adopt it as their own.

## Establishing Standard Costs

Establishing a standard cost often is a joint effort of management, product-design engineers, industrial engineers, management accountants, production supervisors, the purchasing department, the personnel department, and (as noted above) employees affected by the standard.

### Establishing the Standard Cost for Direct Materials

A standard cost for direct materials of a product has three facets: quality, quantity, and price. The first step in establishing a standard cost is to specify the quality of the direct materials. The quality of direct materials determines the quality of the product and affects many phases of the manufacturing process, including the quantity of direct materials needed or used in manufacturing, the prices of direct materials, processing time, and the extent and frequency of supervision needed to complete manufacturing. Once a firm determines the quality of the direct materials, management accountants work with the industrial engineering and production departments to set the standard for the quantity of direct materials needed to manufacture the product.

Quality, quantity, and at times the timing of purchases can all affect price standards of materials. In a competitive environment, many companies emphasize long-term relationships with selected suppliers that are reliable in delivering quality materials on time. For a firm that emphasizes long-term benefits and the reliability of its supply chain, the price standard needs to be revised only when a change occurs in the underlying long-term factors that affect material prices.

### Establishing the Standard Cost for Direct Labor

Direct labor costs vary with types of work, product complexity, employee skill level, nature of the manufacturing process, and the type and condition of the equipment to be used. After considering these factors, industrial engineering, production, personnel, labor union representatives, and management accountants jointly determine the quantity standard for direct labor.

The personnel department determines the standard wage rate for the type and skill level of employees needed for the manufacturing process. The standard labor rate for either direct or indirect labor includes not only the wage paid but also the fringe benefits provided to employees and the required payroll taxes associated with wages and salaries. Fringe benefits include health and life insurance, pension plan contributions, and paid vacations. Payroll taxes include unemployment taxes and the employer's share of an employee's Social Security assessment.

**Overtime premium** refers to the *excess* wage rate over the standard hourly wage rate.

A question normally arises as to how overtime premiums are treated, both for product costing and for subsequent variance-analysis purposes. In many cases, **overtime premiums** are treated as part of factory overhead. This is true when production (or service) scheduling is random or when the overtime is caused by taking on more jobs than can be handled during a standard workweek. In this case, the overtime premium should be spread over production in general—that is, over all output for the period. In other cases, however, the overtime premium might be attributed to a specific job, client, or customer—for example, a rush order. In this case, the premium can be traced and, therefore, should be treated as part of direct labor cost. Such excess payments would typically appear as part of the direct labor rate variance for the period.

## Standard Cost Sheet

A **standard cost sheet** specifies the standard cost of manufacturing and selling one unit of a product.

A **standard cost sheet** specifies the standard costs (including both price and quantity) for all manufacturing cost elements (i.e., direct materials, direct labor, and factory overhead) required in the production of one unit of a product. Exhibit 14.5, discussed earlier, shows a standard cost sheet for Schmidt Machinery Company for manufacturing one unit of XV-1. The standard cost for one unit of XV-1 includes 4 pounds of aluminum at $25 per pound, 1 pound of PVC at $40 per pound, 5 hours of direct labor at $40 per hour, and factory overhead of $36 ($12 + $24) per direct labor-hour. Also included on the standard cost sheet for product XV-1 is the budgeted variable selling and administrative expense of $50 per unit.

**EXHIBIT 14.12    Standard Manufacturing Cost Flows (Direct Labor and Direct Materials)\***

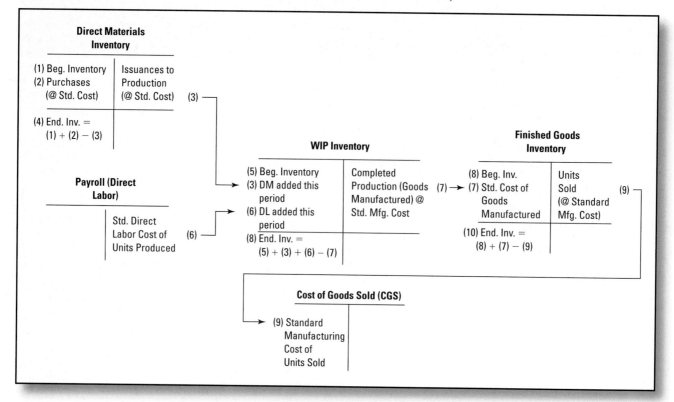

\*The accounting for standard *manufacturing overhead costs* is covered in Chapter 15.

## Recording Cost Flows and Variances in a Standard Cost System

**LO 14-5**

*Record manufacturing cost flows and associated variances in a standard cost system.*

Standard cost systems use the same accounts for inventory and for recording manufacturing costs that actual or normal costing systems use. Thus, they have accounts such as Materials Inventory, Accrued Payroll, Factory (manufacturing) Overhead, Work-in-Process Inventory, Finished Goods Inventory, and Cost of Goods Sold. Manufacturing costs flow through inventory and manufacturing cost accounts in ways that are similar to cost flows in an actual or a normal cost system. Of course, standard cost systems have standard costs instead of actual or normalized costs flowing through the accounts.

Another difference is the use of variance accounts in standard cost systems. Firms that use a standard cost system have a separate ledger account for each variance. Favorable variances will have *credit* balances while unfavorable variances will have *debit* balances. The end-of-period disposition (closing) of these variance accounts is covered in Chapter 15. A diagramatic representation of the cost-recording process for a standard cost system is given in Exhibit 14.12.

### Direct Materials Cost

A firm that uses a standard cost system *and that recognizes material price variances at point of purchase* records purchases of direct materials as follows:

|  | Account | Amount |
|---|---|---|
| *Debit:* | Materials Inventory | Total standard cost of the purchased materials |
|  | Direct Materials Purchase-Price Variance *(if unfavorable)* | Amount of *unfavorable* variance |
| *Credit:* | Cash or Accounts Payable | Purchase cost of materials |
|  | Direct Materials Purchase-Price Variance *(if favorable)* | Amount of *favorable* variance |

To illustrate, on October 7, Schmidt Machinery Company purchased 3,630 pounds of aluminum at $26 per pound, as shown in Exhibit 14.6 and Exhibit 14.8. The terms of purchase were 1/EOM, n/180. The standard cost sheet (Exhibit 14.5) lists the cost at $25 per pound. The firm records all cash discounts when earned.[4] The journal entry for the purchase is as follows:

| Date | Account | Amount | |
|------|---------|--------|---|
| Oct. 7 | Materials Inventory (3,630 × $25) | 90,750 | |
| | Materials Purchase-Price Variance—Aluminum (3,630 × $1) | 3,630 | |
| |    Accounts Payable (3,630 × $26) | | 94,380 |
| | Purchase of 3,630 pounds of aluminum at $26 per pound. | | |
| | Terms 1/EOM, n/180; standard price is $25 per pound. | | |

The purchase price Schmidt agreed to pay is $3,630 higher than the total standard cost for 3,630 pounds of aluminum—an unfavorable direct materials purchase-price variance. Schmidt records the unfavorable variance by *debiting* the variance account.

The journal entry at the end of the month to record the issuance of direct materials, after the output for the month could be determined, takes the following form:

| | Account | Amount |
|---|---------|--------|
| *Debit:* | Work-in-Process Inventory | Total standard quantity of materials, at standard cost, for the output of the period |
| | Direct Materials Usage Variance *(if unfavorable)* | Amount of *unfavorable* variance |
| *Credit:* | Materials Inventory | Total quantity of materials used, at standard cost |
| | Direct Materials Usage Variance *(if favorable)* | Amount of *favorable* variance |

As shown in Exhibit 14.9, during October the production department consumed 3,630 pounds of aluminum for the production of 780 units of XV-1. Thus, the end-of-month journal entry is:

| Date | Account | Amount | |
|------|---------|--------|---|
| Oct. 31 | Work-in-Process Inventory (780 × 4 = 3,120; 3,120 × $25) | 78,000 | |
| | Direct Materials Usage Variance—Aluminum | | |
| | (3,630 − 3,120 = 510; 510 × $25) | 12,750 | |
| |    Materials Inventory (3,630 × $25) | | 90,750 |
| | Issued 3,630 pounds of aluminum to production for the | | |
| | manufacture of 780 units of XV-1. Standard usage is | | |
| | 4 pounds per unit of XV-1. | | |

## Direct Labor Cost

The cost of the units manufactured is increased by direct labor costs. To accomplish this, the Work-in-Process Inventory account is debited for the total standard direct labor cost

[4] If, for example, payment were made before the end of October, the appropriate journal entry would be:

| | | |
|---|---|---|
| Dr. Accounts Payable ........................................................................................ | $94,380.00 | |
|   Cr. Cash ($94,380 × 0.99) ................................................................................ | | $93,436.20 |
|   Cr. Purchase Discounts Taken ........................................................................ | | $   943.80 |

for the units manufactured. An associated credit entry is made to the Accrued Payroll account for the total direct labor wages incurred for the period.

| | Account | Amount |
|---|---|---|
| *Debit:* | Work-in-Process Inventory | Total number of standard hours, at the standard hourly wage rate, for the units manufactured |
| | Direct Labor Rate or Efficiency Variance *(if unfavorable)* | Amount of variance |
| *Credit:* | Accrued Payroll | Actual wage expense |
| | Direct Labor Rate or Efficiency Variance *(if favorable)* | Amount of variance |

The difference between the amount debited (the amount that *should have been incurred* for the units manufactured) and the amount credited (the total amount of direct labor wages incurred) is the total direct labor flexible-budget variance for the period; as shown in Exhibit 14.10, this total variance can be broken down into a labor rate variance and a labor efficiency (quantity) variance. Each of these two component variances is entered into its own account.

During October, Schmidt spent 3,510 direct labor-hours for $147,420 to complete the production of 780 units of XV-1, or $42 per hour. The standard (Exhibit 14.5) calls for 5 direct labor-hours per unit of XV-1 at $40 per hour. Thus, the end-of-month journal entry is:[5]

| Date | Account | Amount | |
|---|---|---|---|
| Oct. 31 | Work-in-Process Inventory (780 × 5 = 3,900; 3,900 × $40) | 156,000 | |
| | Direct Labor Rate Variance (3,510 × [$42 − $40 = 2]) | 7,020 | |
| |     Direct Labor Efficiency Variance (390 × $40) | | 15,600 |
| |     Accrued Payroll (3,510 × $42) | | 147,420 |
| | Used 3,510 direct labor-hours to manufacture 780 units of XV-1. | | |
| | Standard cost allows 5 hours per unit of XV-1 at $40 per hour | | |

## Completion of Production

Upon completion of production, the total standard cost of the units manufactured is transferred out of the Work-in-Process Inventory account and into the Finished Goods Inventory account. The standard cost sheet (Exhibit 14.5) specifies that the total standard manufacturing cost per unit of XV-1 is $520. The following journal entry, on October 31, records the completion of 780 units of XV-1 during October:

| Date | Account | Amount | |
|---|---|---|---|
| Oct. 31 | Finished Goods Inventory (780 × $520) | 405,600 | |
| |     Work-in-Process Inventory | | 405,600 |
| | Completed 780 units of XV-1 at standard manufacturing | | |
| | cost per unit of $520. | | |

Exhibit 14.13 summarizes cost flows through ledger accounts in a standard cost system. (The recording of manufacturing overhead costs, including overhead cost variances, is covered in Chapter 15.)

---

[5] When the liability is paid (extinguished), Schmidt would simultaneously debit the Accrued Payroll account and credit Cash for $147,420.

**EXHIBIT 14.13**
**Partial Cost Flows and General Ledger Entries in a Standard Cost System**

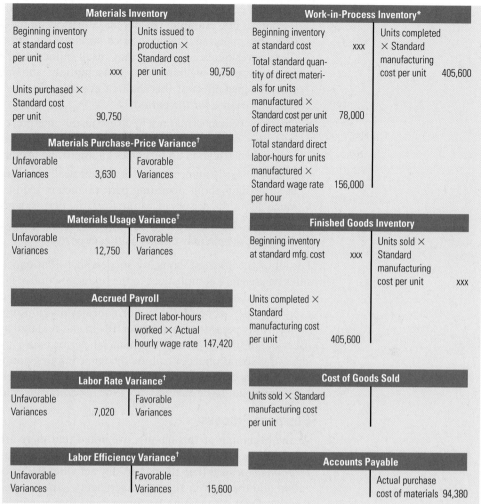

*A full accounting would include debits for manufacturing overhead costs as well—a topic covered in Chapter 15.
†The end-of-period disposition (closing) of those accounts is covered in Chapter 15.

## The Strategic Role of Nonfinancial-Performance Indicators

**LO 14-6**

*Discuss major operating functions and the need for nonfinancial performance indicators.*

Thus far, this chapter has focused on the use of flexible budgets, standards, and various operating-income variances to assess short-run financial performance. However, long-term organizational success will not likely be achieved if the focus of the accounting and control system is solely on short-run financial performance indicators. This section explains some of the limitations of short-term financial performance indicators and introduces you to the use of nonfinancial performance indicators as part of a comprehensive management accounting and control system.

### Limitations of Short-Term Financial-Performance Indicators

When put into perspective, and interpreted carefully, the financial-control model discussed thus far in the chapter can be useful for organizations as they strive for competitive advantage. However, management accountants need to recognize the following major limitations of the use of standard costs and variance analysis for operational control purposes:

- Because of the short-term nature of the performance indicators, employees and decision makers may take actions that improve short-term financial performance at the expense of long-term performance; that is, they may induce behavior that is not goal-congruent. For example, favorable labor rate variances may be realized by employing substandard labor. The use of such labor may, however, result in a deterioration of product or service quality, which could result in eroding market shares and long-term profitability.

- Focusing on individual variances may result in optimizing local, but not global, performance. For example, the purchase of nonstandard raw materials may result in a favorable materials purchase-price variance for the purchasing manager. However, those lower-quality materials may result in increased scrap and other quality-related costs, increased machine-hour consumption, and increased labor (i.e., processing) costs. The net effect of this chain of events could very well be an unfavorable flexible-budget variance for the period.
- Operating personnel may not be able to readily interpret or act upon financial-performance indicators, such as the cost variances discussed earlier in this chapter. That is, they may not find such information useful guides for improving operating performance.
- Financial performance indicators are basically backward-looking measures. They tell us something about operating performance in the past but do not necessarily tell us much about the drivers of future financial performance.
- From a systems-design standpoint, the construction, application, and use of a standard cost system may entail significant costs.

For all of the above reasons, we suggest that nonfinancial operating performance measures be used as a complement to the financial-control information achieved through the use of standard costs, flexible budgets, and resulting variances. A fuller discussion of expanding the scope of the performance-evaluation model, in the form of a balanced scorecard, is presented in Chapter 18. In the remainder of this chapter we provide an overview of the role that nonfinancial performance indicators can play in terms of achieving operational control. As the name implies, nonfinancial performance indicators are measures expressed in terms other than dollars. These performance indicators focus on, or relate to, basic *business processes,* as described below.

## Business Processes

At the beginning of this chapter, we noted that there are multiple business processes in which many, if not most, organizations engage. Common business processes include: *operating processes* (i.e., the day-to-day activities that produce the outputs of the organization and that deliver them to customers); *customer-management processes* (i.e., activities that focus on creating customers and then expanding and deepening relationships with these customers); *innovation processes* (i.e., activities designed to produce new processes, services, and products); and, *social/regulatory processes* (i.e., activities related to the organization's environmental and community responsibilities, as well as its legal responsibilities, at both local and national levels).

Organizations succeed by managing the set of activities associated with each of these four classes of business processes. Thus, an effective operational control system would establish specific objectives for each of the four business processes and then monitor performance by developing one or more key performance measures for each specified objective. For example, in the innovation-process category, management might specify the following two critical objectives: (1) manage the development-cycle cost, and (2) reduce new-product development time. To monitor performance of the former, the organization might compare actual spending versus budgeted spending on each project at each development stage. To monitor performance in terms of the latter objective, management might collect information as to the development-cycle time (elapsed time from initial concept to the time the product in question comes to market) and/or the number of projects delivered on time (i.e., according to plan). In the space below, we provide a more detailed discussion of the use of both financial and nonfinancial performance indicators for improving operating processes. The monitoring of customer-management processes, the innovation process, and social/regulatory processes is covered in greater detail in Chapter 18.

## Operating Processes

As noted above, operating processes include all activities such as acquiring raw materials from suppliers, producing outputs (i.e., services or products), and delivering products or services to customers. Depending on the strategy the organization is pursuing, it would likely give differential weight to each of the following operating-process objectives: time, cost, and quality. For each of these critical dimensions on which the organization could compete, the management accountant would help to identify a series of specific objectives and associated measures, similar to the example given above. In the remainder of this section, we provide an extended discussion of a particular operating strategy: the switch from a conventional manufacturing process to a just-in-time (JIT) process.

The goal of the discussion is to illustrate the expansion of a management accounting system for control of an operating process.

## Just-in-Time (JIT) Manufacturing

**Just-in-time (JIT) manufacturing** is a process in which production at any stage of the process does not take place until an order is received.

A JIT manufacturing process is one in which production at any stage of a process does not take place until an order, from an internal or external customer, is received. In this sense, the underlying system is sometimes referred to as demand-pull. One implication of JIT manufacturing is the reduction, if not elimination, of inventory buffer stocks (which, many would argue, serve as a cushion for poor-quality outputs). When inventory stocks are kept to a minimum, quality at each stage of the production process is expected. Obviously, the adoption of a JIT philosophy, with a focus on the elimination of waste and inefficiency, is a strategic choice made by management. What are the costs and benefits associated with a move to JIT? The management accountant can help answer this question.

### Costs of Implementing JIT

Organizations make investments in four general categories: people, tangible assets (e.g., equipment and machinery), information systems, and developing organizational processes/culture. In concept, a JIT system is straightforward: reduce inventories, eliminate waste, and produce only to order. In reality, however, the successful implementation of a JIT system, as an operating process, can require significant resources—to educate and train employees, to reconfigure the production layout (e.g., to a cellular approach), and to monitor operating performance in the new environment (i.e., to revise the organization's management accounting and control system). The organization's management accounting system can help by identifying and reporting to management the sources of delay, error, and waste in the system. While conventional systems monitor labor and materials usage, with large-batch production, the focus on a JIT system would be on measures such as defect rates, cycle times, percent of on-time deliveries, and machine up-times.

### Benefits of Implementing JIT

A switch from a conventional to a JIT manufacturing system provides the following key benefits, all of which could be estimated by the organization's management accounting system:

- Reduction in out-of-pocket inventory-carrying costs. Under JIT, the clerical process of recording and monitoring inventory levels (raw materials, work-in-process inventory, and finished goods) is significantly reduced. This results in both labor savings as well as reduced information-processing costs.

Thirty or so years ago, U.S. companies learned from their Japanese competitors the benefits of moving to just-in-time production and inventory systems. Such systems are characterized by lean inventory holdings, outsourcing of supply, and purchasing from a limited set of suppliers—in the extreme, a single supplier. While these systems do result in significant cost savings, they also decrease the amount of control a company has over its supply chain.

The record-setting earthquake and tsunami that hit Japan in March 2011 has exposed in dramatic fashion the risk to U.S. companies of supply-chain disruption. Companies in the durable manufacturing sector (e.g., Boeing) and in the computer technology sector (e.g., Dell) were particularly adversely affected by supply shortages following these events in Japan. One consequence of these raw material shortages was an increase in the lead time of producers such as Boeing and Dell, with an attendant risk of lost future business. Even Japan's manufacturers were adversely affected by the events of 2011. Sharp Corporation in 2009 completed a "factory within a factory" wherein key suppliers were located within Sharp's own manufacturing facility, further enhancing the risk position of the company.

In response, many companies (both in the United States and abroad) are now reexamining their lean inventory techniques. Some have referred to these modified inventory systems as "just in case." To reduce risk, some Japanese manufacturing is now being moved abroad. Other companies (such as Terex Corp.) are executing fixed-purchase agreements with their suppliers, in effect guaranteeing to purchase a set number of parts over a given period (e.g., a three-month period). Such agreements help reduce the risk that suppliers face when business takes a downturn. In short, practical considerations (political unrest, natural disasters, oil embargoes, etc.) have caused many companies to explore new methods of handling supply-chain risk.

**Sources:** D. Wakabayashi, "Sharp's New Plant Reinvents Japan Manufacturing Model," *The Wall Street Journal* (December 1, 2009), p. A1; T. Black and S. Ray, "Downsides of Just-in-Time Inventory," *Bloomberg Businessweek* (March 24, 2011) (http://www.businessweek.com/magazine/content/11_14/b4222017701856.htm); C. Dawson, "Even Japan Inc. Looks Offshore," *The Wall Street Journal* (April 11, 2011), p. A1; T. Aeppel, "For Lean Factories, No Buffer," *The Wall Street Journal* (April 29, 2011), p. A1; and, D. M. Katz, "All in the Timing," *CFO* (June 2011), pp. 33–35.

- Reduction in inventory-related opportunity (holding) costs. All assets that are held require that capital be tied up (i.e., not available for an alternative use). Reductions in inventory result in reductions in imputed costs associated with holding inventory.
- Possible increases in sales, market share, and profitability.
  ° Increases in product/service *quality* can result in increased sales and market share for the organization, particularly if the organization is pursuing a differentiation strategy.
  ° Reductions in cycle/processing time (i.e., faster customer-response times) may also lead to increased sales and market share for the organization.
- Decreased production costs. Improvements in product/service quality are reflected in manufacturing costs. For example, under JIT, we would anticipate reductions in defect-related quality costs (e.g., a reduction in the cost of reworking defective outputs).

The preceding discussion focuses on financial performance indicators associated with a strategic move to JIT manufacturing. Such indicators, in a mature management accounting system, should be supplemented with relevant nonfinancial operating performance indicators, discussed below.

**Customer-response time (CRT)** is a measure of operating performance defined as the elapsed time between the time a customer places an order and the time the customer receives the order.

Exhibit 14.14 provides an example of a model (**customer-response time**) that the management accountant can use to monitor and report to management time-based performance in conjunction with the adoption of a JIT production system. This model would be particularly useful for an organization that competes on the basis of time. You notice that the total customer-response time (CRT) in this model can be broken down into three major elements: receipt time, manufacturing lead (cycle) time, and delivery time. Cycle time (or, manufacturing lead time) represents the total time from the start of production to the time the product is finished. As you see from Exhibit 14.14, cycle time can be further broken down into manufacturing wait time and actual processing (manufacturing) time. Behind each of these times we would envision one or more activities that are being performed. An activity analysis, similar to the analysis required in conjunction with the implementation of an ABC system (Chapter 5) can be performed to motivate improvements in these time-based measures. The main point, however, is that the CRT model is

**EXHIBIT 14.14**
**Model of Customer-Response Time (CRT)**

* Also called *manufacturing (production) cycle time.*
† Also called *processing time.*

but one example of a nonfinancial performance indicator that could be used as part of an operational control system.

### Processing Cycle Efficiency (PCE)

**Processing cycle efficiency (PCE)**

is a measure of operating performance defined as the ratio of processing time to total manufacturing time.

An alternative (and complementary) measure of operating process efficiency is called **processing cycle efficiency (PCE)**. PCE is a method of assessing process efficiency, based on the relationship between *actual processing time* and *total production time*. In formula form, we can define PCE as:

PCE = Processing time/Total manufacturing time

PCE = Processing time/(Processing time + Moving time + Storage time + Inspection time)

Alternatively, we can view PCE as the ratio of value-added time to the sum of value-added time + non-value-added time. The notion of value-added and non-value-added is precisely the same as we saw in Chapter 5: the classifications are viewed from the standpoint of the customer. That is, an external, not internal, perspective is taken when classifying activities as value-added or non-value-added. Notice that increases in performance are reflected by increases in PCE. The optimum situation is when PCE equals 1.

### Advantages of Nonfinancial Measures of Business-Process Performance

Nonfinancial performance measures complement the financial measures discussed earlier in the chapter and in conjunction with the JIT example presented above. Both types of measures are useful in terms of building a comprehensive management accounting and control system. As well, both types of measures can be incorporated into an organization's strategic management system, such as its balanced scorecard (BSC). That is to say, the two groups of measures complement one another.

Relative to financial measures, nonfinancial performance measures have the following advantages:

* Such measures are often easy to quantify and understand. That is, they are readily understandable by operating personnel. This is a significant benefit when building an effective operational control system.

* They direct attention to basic business *processes* and hence focus attention on the precise problem areas that need attention.

* Nonfinancial performance measures can be useful indicators of *future* financial performance. That is, these measures can be viewed as the drivers of future financial performance.

| Summary |
|---------|

This chapter is the first of four that together address the topic of operational control. We define operational control systems as a subset of an organization's overall (i.e., comprehensive) management accounting and control system. A modern operational control system consists of *both* financial and nonfinancial performance indicators. Financial control is achieved through the use of flexible budgets, standard costs, and associated variances for reporting and interpreting the short-term financial results of operations. A comprehensive operational control system will also include performance indicators associated with basic business processes (operating, customer, innovation, and regulatory/social).

For any given period (e.g., a month or a quarter), an organization will typically realize an actual amount of operating income that differs from the operating income reflected in its master (static) budget. Any such difference is referred to as the *total operating-income variance* for the period. Other terms used to describe this amount are the *static budget variance* or the *master budget variance* for the period. This total variance is a function of five factors: sales volume, selling price per unit, variable cost per unit, total fixed costs, and sales mix. Through the use of flexible budgets and standard costs, we are able at the end of the period to subdivide the total operating-income variance into amounts associated with each of these five factors. This variance-decomposition process is the essence of the short-term financial control model discussed in the chapter. Exhibit 14.15 provides a summary of the variance-decomposition process we conducted for the Schmidt Machinery Company for October 2013. Our goal in this regard was to explain the $72,000U operating-income variance for the month.

**EXHIBIT 14.15**  Variance Decomposition Summary: Schmidt Machinery Company Example, October 2013

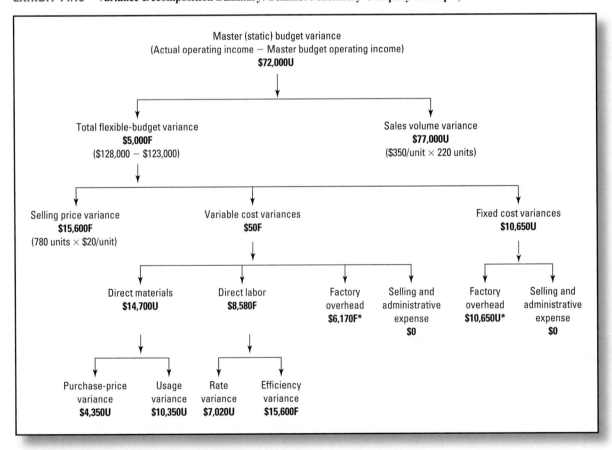

*Decomposition (breakdown) of these variances is covered in Chapter 15.

In this chapter, we assume a single product/output and show how to calculate the sales volume variance and the total flexible-budget variance for any given operating period. As can be seen in Exhibit 14.15, the total flexible-budget variance can be subdivided into a series of fixed cost variances and variable cost variances. All variable cost variances can then be subdivided into a price (rate) component and a quantity (efficiency) component. In Chapter 15 we continue the variance-decomposition process by calculating and interpreting variances for indirect manufacturing costs. In Chapter 16 we take a further look at sales variances (e.g., by introducing sales mix into the analysis) and to complement the analysis we look at various productivity indexes.

When standard costs are incorporated into the formal accounting system, the organization is said to be using a standard cost system. The standard cost for each product is reflected on what is called a standard cost sheet. Except for the inclusion of standard cost variances (e.g., materials purchase-price variance), the recording of manufacturing costs under a standard cost system parallels the process we discussed earlier in the text for job-cost and process-cost systems. (We leave until Chapter 15 the accounting issue of how standard cost variances are disposed of at the end of an accounting period.)

In this chapter we discuss major classes of business processes, including operating processes. Each business process consists of a number of activities. Thus, the control of operating processes focuses on managing these activities, a point we made earlier in the text (Chapter 5) in our discussion of ABC. This implies the use of nonfinancial operating performance indicators as a complement to the financial indicators discussed earlier in the chapter. We argue that an effective operational control system includes both financial and nonfinancial performance indicators. One example of an operating process is the production/manufacturing process. The chapter concludes with an extended discussion of one manufacturing strategy: just-in-time (JIT) production. As an example of how nonfinancial performance indicators of operating performance can be constructed to support the organization's strategy, we discuss the following two time-related metrics: customer-response time (CRT) and process cycle efficiency (PCE).

## Key Terms

authoritative standard, *581*
continuous-improvement standard, *581*
control, *564*
currently attainable standard, *581*
customer-response time (CRT), *590*
direct labor efficiency variance (EV), *578*
direct labor rate variance (RV), *578*
direct materials flexible-budget variance, *574*
direct materials price variance (PV), *575*

direct materials usage variance (UV), *576*
financial control, *564*
flexible budget, *566*
flexible-budget (FB) variance, *570*
ideal standard, *580*
just-in-time (JIT) manufacturing, *589*
management accounting and control system, *564*
master (static) budget variance, *565*
materials usage ratio, *576*
operational control, *564*
overtime premium, *583*

participative standard, *581*
processing cycle efficiency (PCE), *591*
sales volume variance, *569*
selling price variance, *570*
standard cost, *580*
standard cost sheet, *583*
standard cost system, *580*
total flexible-budget variance, *570*
total operating-income variance, *565*
total variable cost flexible-budget variance, *571*
variances, *564*

## Comments on Cost Management in Action

### Is Two Minutes and Twenty Seconds Enough for a Brake Part?

The improvement in plant productivity brought about by the bonus system and conveyor belt system at Westinghouse Air Brake Company was just what was needed to save the old Chicago plant. Without these improvements, the business would likely have gone overseas. However, the increased demand on workers' attention and effort caused stress. Workers found themselves operating two or more machines, each of which could operate at a different speed. Workers were usually in constant motion. To decrease stress, the machines were located close together in U-shaped cells when the plant was renovated. This allowed the workers to operate the machines more efficiently, and reduced the time required to move parts around the plant.

An unfortunate side effect of the system is that workers often would set aside a half-dozen or more finished parts to have some to feed the conveyor belt if there was a distraction or disruption of any kind. The few extra finished parts each worker set aside added up to a substantial amount for the plant. Plant managers frowned upon this hidden inventory practice and were constantly on the lookout for it.

**Source:** Timothy Aeppel, "Factory Lifts Productivity, But Staff Finds It's No Picnic," *The Wall Street Journal,* May 18, 1999, p. A10.

## Self-Study Problems
(For solutions, please turn to the end of the chapter.)

### 1. Sales Volume and Flexible-Budget (FB) Variances/JIT Manufacturing

Solid Box Fabrications manufactures boxes for workstations. The firm's standard cost sheet prior to October and actual results for October 2013 are as follows:

| | Budget Information | | Actual Results October 2013 |
|---|---|---|---|
| | Standard Price and Variable Costs per Unit | Fixed Costs | |
| Units | | | 9,500 |
| Sales | $50.00 | | $551,000 |
| Variable costs: | | | |
| Direct materials | | | |
| 5 pounds at $2.40 per pound = | $12.00 | | 48,000 lbs.* × $3 = $ 144,000 |
| Direct labor | | | |
| 0.5 hour at $14 per hour = | 7.00 | | 4,800 hours × $16 = 76,800 |
| Manufacturing overhead | 2.00 | | 19,000 |
| Selling and administrative | 5.00 | | 55,100 |
| Total variable cost | $26.00 | | $ 294,900 |
| Contribution margin | $24.00 | | $ 256,100 |
| Fixed costs: | | | |
| Manufacturing (factory) overhead | | $50,000 | $  55,000 |
| Selling and administrative | | 20,000 | 24,000 |
| Total fixed costs | | $70,000 | $  79,000 |
| Operating income | | | $ 177,100 |

*Assume that #lbs. purchased = #lbs. issued to production (i.e., a JIT inventory policy).

In preparing the master budget for October 2013, the firm recognized that several items on the standard cost sheet would change. For example, the selling price of the product would increase by 8%. Suppliers have notified the firm that starting October 1, materials prices would be 5% higher. The labor contract prescribes a 10% increase, starting October 1, on wages and benefits. Fixed manufacturing costs will increase $5,000 for insurance, property taxes, and salaries. Fixed selling and administrative expenses will increase as follows: $2,000 in managers' salaries, and $2,000 for advertising during October 2013. The unit sales for October 2013 are expected to be 10,000 units. Solid Box Fabrications uses JIT systems in all of its operations including materials acquisitions and product manufacturing.

**Required**
1. Prepare the master (static) budget and pro forma budgets for 9,500 units and 11,000 units for October 2013.
2. Calculate and label as favorable or unfavorable the static (master) budget variance (total operating-income variance) for October 2013. Break this variance down into the sales volume variance and the total flexible-budget variance for the period.
3. Compute and label as favorable or unfavorable each of the following variances for October 2013: selling price variance; total variable cost flexible-budget (FB) variance; and total fixed cost variance.
4. Break down the total direct materials flexible-budget variance and the total direct labor flexible-budget variance into their price (rate) and quantity (efficiency) components. Label each component variance as favorable or unfavorable.
5. Define what is meant by a just-in-time (JIT) manufacturing process. What are the primary benefits, both financial and nonfinancial, of a JIT system compared to a conventional manufacturing process?

## 2. Direct Materials Price and Usage Variances, Direct Labor Rate and Efficiency Variances, and Journal Entries

Chemical, Inc., has set the following standards for direct materials and direct labor for each 20-pound bag of Weed-Be-Doom:

|  | Per Bag |
|---|---|
| Direct materials: 25 pounds XF–2000 @ $0.08/lb. | $2.00 |
| Direct labor: 0.05 hour @ $32/hr. | 1.60 |

The firm manufactured 100,000 bags of Weed-Be-Doom in December and used 2,700,000 pounds of XF–2000 and 5,200 direct labor-hours. During the month the firm purchased 3,000,000 lbs. of XF–2000 at $0.075 per pound and incurred a total payroll of $182,000 for direct labor. The firm records purchases at standard cost and therefore recognizes material price variances at point of purchase.

**Required**

1. Compute the price and usage variances for direct materials, and the rate and efficiency variances for direct labor.

2. Prepare journal entries to record the preceding events.

*Please visit http://www.mhhe.com/blocher6e to access a narrated, animated tutorial for solving these problems.*

**Questions**

14-1   What is the difference between a master budget, pro forma budgets, and a flexible budget?

14-2   Explain how standard costs and flexible budgets can be used for short-term profit analysis, i.e., for financial control purposes.

14-3   Explain what is meant by the term "management by exception." What is the relationship between the process of standard cost variance analysis and management by exception?

14-4   Should the performance of a division be deemed less than satisfactory if all of its variances are "unfavorable"? Explain.

14-5   Explain the possible causes for direct materials *price* and direct materials *usage* variances. Who in the organization normally has influence over or responsibility for each of these variances?

14-6   Explain some of the possible causes of direct labor *rate* (price) and direct labor *efficiency* (quantity) variances. Who normally has responsibility for or influence over each of these variances?

14-7   Will overtime premiums affect direct labor variances? If so, which ones?

14-8   Which of the following should a firm use as the standard in assessing production efficiencies: standards based on ideal performance, standards based on attainable performance, or standards based on the average of recent historical performance? Explain.

14-9   Discuss behavioral concerns in establishing and implementing a standard cost system.

14-10   This chapter deals with control systems associated with business processes, such as operating processes. Provide a definition and some examples of operating processes. In what other processes would an organization engage in the normal course of business?

14-11   Describe how a just-in-time (JIT) manufacturing system is fundamentally different from a conventional manufacturing system. List two primary financial benefits associated with a shift to JIT manufacturing. What effect does the adoption of JIT have on the design of management accounting and control systems?

14-12   One of the purported benefits of moving to a JIT system is improvements in customer-response time (CRT). Define the following terms: *total customer-response time; manufacturing (production) cycle time; cycle-time efficiency; value-added time;* and *non-value-added time.*

**Brief Exercises**

14-13   The Ace Company sells a single product at a budgeted selling price per unit of $20. Budgeted fixed manufacturing costs for the coming period are $10,000, while budgeted fixed marketing expenses for the period are $24,000. Budgeted variable costs per unit include $2 of selling expenses (commission) and $4 of manufacturing costs. What is the budgeted operating income if the anticipated sales volume for the period is (a) 10,000 units, and (b) 15,000 units?

14-14   The Baldwin Company, in its master budget for 2013, predicted total sales of $160,000, variable costs of $48,000, and fixed costs of $52,000 ($24,000 manufacturing and $28,000 nonmanufacturing). Actual sales revenue for 2013 turned out to be $180,000. Actual costs were as follows: variable, $54,000, and fixed, $50,000. What was the total static budget (operating-income) variance for 2013? Was this total variance favorable (F) or unfavorable (U)?

14-15    Chapman, Inc., sells a single product, Zud, which has a budgeted selling price of $24 per unit and a budgeted variable cost of $12 per unit. Budgeted fixed costs for the year amount to $45,000. Actual sales volume for the year (47,000) fell 3,000 units short of budgeted sales volume. Actual fixed costs were $46,000. With everything else held constant, what impact did the shortfall in volume have on profitability for the year?

14-16    Davidson Corp. produces a single product: fireproof safety deposit boxes for home use. The budget going into the current year anticipated a selling price of $55 per unit. Because of competitive pressures, the company had to cut selling prices by 10% during the year. Budgeted variable costs per unit are $32, and budgeted total fixed costs are $156,000 for the year. Anticipated sales volume for the year was 10,000 units. Actual sales volume was 5% less than budget. What was the sales price variance for the year? Label this variance F (favorable) or U (unfavorable), as appropriate.

14-17    Edwards and Bell market a single line of home computer, dubbed the XL-98. The master budget for the coming year contained the following items: sales revenue, $400,000; variable costs, $250,000; fixed costs, $100,000. Actual results for the year were as follows: sales revenue, $350,000; variable costs, $225,000; fixed costs, $95,000. The flexible-budget operating income for the year was $35,000. What is the total static (master) budget variance in operating profit for the period? What portion of the total static (master) budget variance is attributable to actual sales volume being different from planned sales volume? What portion is due to a combination of selling price and costs (variable cost per unit and total fixed costs) being different from budgeted amounts?

14-18    Refer to Exhibit 14.8 and the accompanying discussion in the text. Demonstrate that the materials usage variance for PVC during October 2013 was $2,400F.

14-19    Refer to Exhibit 14.8 and the accompanying discussion in the text. Demonstrate that the purchase-price variance for PVC during October 2013 was $720U.

14-20    Refer to Exhibit 14.8 and the accompanying discussion in the text. Demonstrate that the flexible-budget variance for PVC during October 2013 was $1,680F.

14-21    Mom's Apple Pie Company uses a standard cost system. The standard direct labor time for each pie is 10 minutes. During the most recent month, the company produced and sold 6,000 pies. The standard direct labor rate is $8 per hour; the actual labor rate per hour for the month was $8.40. The company used a total of 980 labor-hours. What was the direct labor efficiency (usage) variance for the month? (Show calculations.)

14-22    Refer to the data in 14-21 above. What was the direct labor rate (price) variance for the month? (Show calculations.)

## Exercises

[LO 14-1, 14-4]    14-23    **Financial versus Operational Control; Behavioral Considerations in the Standard-Setting Process**    You have been assigned to a strategic leadership committee that has been charged by the CEO with developing and implementing a comprehensive management accounting and control system. At the first planning session that you attended the subject of financial control systems arose, but there was some uncertainty regarding the nature of such systems and some of the behavioral considerations that might have to be made in the design process. You have been asked by the chair of the committee to prepare a short written document that could be used as the basis of discussion at the next meeting. Specifically, you have been asked to: define and distinguish between operational control and financial control and how such systems relate to an organization's management accounting and control system; explain the theory behind the use of flexible budgets, standard costs, and variance analysis as elements of a financial control system; and provide input regarding how standards/budgets for performance evaluation should be set (i.e., whether authoritative standards, or participative standards, or a consultative approach should be used in the standard-setting process). Compose your response as requested.

[LO 14-1, 14-6]    14-24    **Financial versus Nonfinancial Performance Indicators for Operational Control**    As indicated in the text, both financial and nonfinancial performance indicators play important roles in an organization's overall operational control system. Explain, concisely, the relative advantage of each type of performance indicator. That is, what role would each type of performance indicator play in helping to ensure that operations are in control? (*Hint:* Think about this issue both from the standpoint of managers and from the standpoint of operating personnel.)

[LO 14-1, 14-4, 14-6]    14-25    **Behavioral and Strategic Considerations**    Chen, Inc., produces a line of soy-based products, including a premium soy-milk that comes in different flavors. This company, founded by Alan Chen, has been doing business in the United States for the past 15 years. In the face of competition associated with recent entrants into this line of business, the controller of the company,

Rosita Chang, implemented a standard cost system to better control costs of the soy-milk product line. Financial reports for tracking performance are issued monthly, and any unfavorable cost variances are investigated by management.

Recently, the production manager of the soy-milk line complained to Chang that the standards were unrealistic, that they have a negative impact on motivation (because the system focuses only on unfavorable variances), and that, because of global forces of supply and demand, they quickly become out of date. The production manager noted that his recent switch to a newly available homogenizing agent resulted in higher material-acquisition costs but decreased labor-hours to produce the soy-milk. These two changes, when combined, had a negligible effect on manufacturing cost per unit. However, the monthly performance reports continued to show a favorable labor variance (despite evidence that the workers were slowing down or slacking off a bit) and an unfavorable materials variance.

**Required**

1. Describe several ways that a standard cost system could improve (i.e., strengthen) an overall management control system.

2. Give at least two reasons how a standard cost system could have a negative impact on employee motivation.

3. Explain strategic issues regarding the decision to adopt a standard costing system, particularly in light of competitive forces confronting this company. (*Hint:* Think in terms of the costs and benefits associated with the use of standard costs as part of a comprehensive management accounting and control system.)

**(CMA Adapted)**

[LO 14-1, 14-2, 14-3]  14-26 **Flexible Budgets and Operating-Income Variance Analysis; Spreadsheet Application**  The following information is available for Brownstone Products Company for the month of July:

|  | Actual | Master Budget |
|---|---|---|
| Units | 3,800 | 4,000 |
| Sales revenue | $53,200 | $60,000 |
| Variable manufacturing costs | 19,000 | 16,000 |
| Fixed manufacturing costs | 16,000 | 15,000 |
| Variable selling and administrative expenses | 7,700 | 8,000 |
| Fixed selling and administrative expenses | 10,000 | 9,000 |

**Required**

1. Set up a spreadsheet to compute the July sales volume variance and the flexible-budget variance for the month in terms of both contribution margin and operating income.

2. Discuss implications of these variances on strategic cost management for Brownstone.

3. Create an electronic spreadsheet that will allow the firm to prepare pro forma budgets for activities within its relevant range of operations and prepare flexible budgets when sales are:

   a. 3,750 units.

   b. 4,150 units.

**(CMA Adapted)**

[LO 14-2, 14-3]  14-27 **Master (Static) Budget Variance and Components**  As the new accountant for Cohen & Co., you've been asked to provide a succinct analysis of financial performance for the year just ended. You obtain the following information that pertains to the company's sole product.

|  | Actual | Master (Static) Budget |
|---|---|---|
| Units sold | 40,000 | 45,000 |
| Sales | $380,000 | $450,000 |
| Variable costs | $210,000 | $270,000 |
| Fixed costs | $145,000 | $135,000 |

**Required**

1. What was the actual operating income for the period?

2. What was the company's master budget operating income for the period?

3. What was the total master (static) budget variance, in terms of operating income, for the period? Is this variance favorable (F) or unfavorable (U)? Why?

4. From the information given above, are you able to decompose the total master (static) budget variance into a total flexible-budget variance and a sales volume variance? Why or why not?

5. Define the meaning of the total flexible-budget variance and the sales volume variance.

**[LO 14-2, 14-3]**  14-28  **Flexible Budget and Operating-Income Variances**  Assume that Schmidt Machinery Company (Exhibit 14.1) manufactured and sold 950 units for $835 each in June. During this month the company incurred $475,000 total variable expenses and $180,000 total fixed expenses.

**Required for the Month of June:**

1. Prepare a flexible budget for the production and sale of 950 units.

2. Compute for June:

   a. The sales volume variance, in terms of operating income.

   b. The sales volume variance, in terms of contribution margin.

3. Calculate for June:

   a. The total flexible-budget (FB) variance.

   b. The total variable cost flexible-budget variance.

   c. The total fixed cost flexible-budget (FB) variance.

   d. The selling price variance.

**[LO 14-3]**  14-29  **Direct Materials and Direct Labor Variances**  Schmidt Machinery Company (Exhibit 14.5) used 3,450 pounds of aluminum in June to manufacture 920 units. The company paid $28.50 per pound during the month to purchase aluminum. On June 1, the company had 50 pounds of aluminum on hand. At the end of June, the company had only 30 pounds of aluminum in its warehouse. Schmidt used 4,200 direct labor-hours in June, at an average cost of $41.50 per hour.

**Required**  Compute for June, Schmidt Machinery Company's

1. Purchase-price and usage variances for aluminum.

2. Direct labor rate and efficiency variances.

**[LO 14-3]**  14-30  **Standard Labor Rate and Labor Efficiency Variance**  Maxwell's direct labor costs for the month of January follow:

| | |
|---|---|
| Direct labor hourly rate paid | $28.50 |
| Total standard direct labor-hours for units produced this period | 11,000 |
| Direct labor-hours worked | 10,800 |
| Direct labor rate variance | $16,000 favorable |

**Required**  Compute these (show calculations):

1. Standard direct labor wage rate per hour in January.

2. Direct labor efficiency variance.

**[LO 14-3]**  14-31  **Generating a Flexible Budget; Spreadsheet Application**  Crane Corporation's master (static) budget for the year is shown below:

| | | |
|---|---|---|
| Sales (60,000 units) | | $1,860,000 |
| Cost of goods sold: | | |
|    Direct materials | $166,000 | |
|    Direct labor | 450,000 | |
|    Overhead (variable overhead | | |
|    applied at 40% of direct labor cost) | 240,000 | 856,000 |
| Gross profit | | $1,004,000 |
| Selling expenses: | | |
|    Sales commissions (all variable) | $167,400 | |
|    Rent (all fixed) | 40,000 | |
|    Insurance (all fixed) | 30,000 | |
| General expenses: | | |
|    Salaries (all fixed) | 92,000 | |
|    Rent (all fixed) | 77,000 | |
|    Depreciation (all fixed) | 50,000 | 456,400 |
| Operating income | | $   547,600 |

**Required**

1. During the year the company actually manufactured and sold 55,000 units of product. Prepare an Excel spreadsheet that contains a flexible budget for this level of output.

2. Suppose, however, that the actual level of output had been 65,000 units of output. Rerun your spreadsheet to generate a flexible budget for this level of output.

3. Of what relevance is the notion of "relevant range" when preparing pro forma budgets or a flexible budget for control purposes?

[LO 14-3, 14-4]   14-32   **Behavioral Considerations and Continuous-Improvement Standards**   At a recent seminar you attended, the invited speaker was discussing some of the advantages and disadvantages of standard costs in terms of evaluating performance and motivating goal-congruent behavior on the part of employees. One criticism of standard costs in particular caught your attention: the use of conventional standard costs may not provide appropriate incentives for improvements needed to compete effectively with world-class organizations. The speaker then discussed so-called "continuous-improvement standard costs." Such standards embody systematically lower costs over time. For example, on a monthly basis, it might be appropriate to budget a 1% reduction in per-unit direct labor cost.

Assume that the standard wage rate into the foreseeable future is $30 per hour. Assume, too, that the budgeted labor-hour standard for October 2013 is 1.50 hours and that this standard is reduced each month by 1%. During December of 2013 the company produced 10,000 units of XL-10, using 14,800 direct labor-hours. The actual wage rate per hour in December was $32.00.

**Required**

1. Prepare a table that contains the standard labor-hour requirement per unit and standard direct labor cost per unit for the four months, October 2013 through January 2014.

2. Compute the direct labor efficiency variance for December 2013. (Show calculation.)

3. What behavioral considerations apply to the decision to use continuous-improvement standards?

[LO 14-3, 14-4]   14-33   **Flexible Budget and Operating-Income Variances**   RTI Company's master budget calls for production and sale of 18,000 units for $81,000; variable costs of $30,600; and fixed costs of $20,000. During the most recent period, the company incurred $32,000 of variable costs to produce and sell 20,000 units for $85,000. During this same period, the company earned $25,000 of operating income.

**Required**

1. Determine the following for RTI Company:

   a. Flexible-budget operating income.

   b. Flexible-budget variance, in terms of contribution margin.

   c. Flexible-budget variance, in terms of operating income.

   d. Sales volume variance, in terms of contribution margin.

   e. Sales volume variance, in terms of operating income.

2. Explain why the contribution margin sales volume variance and the operating income sales volume variance for the same period are likely to be identical.

3. Explain why the contribution margin flexible-budget variance is likely to differ from the operating income flexible-budget variance for the same period.

[LO 14-4]   14-34   **Applicability of Standard Cost Systems**   Portfolio management is a powerful concept in finance and marketing. The marketing application of the concept is to develop and manage a balanced portfolio of products. Market share and market growth can be used to classify products for portfolio purposes, and the product classifications often are extended to the organizational units that make the product. The market share/growth classifications can be depicted as follows:

|  | Market Share | |
| --- | --- | --- |
| **Market Growth Rate** | **High** | **Low** |
| High | Rising star | ? |
| Low | Cash cow | Dog |

The question mark is the classification for products that show high growth rates but have small market shares, such as new products that are similar to their competitors. A rising star is a high-growth, high-market-share product that tends to mature into a cash cow. A cash cow is a slow-growing established product that can be milked for cash to help the question mark and introduce new products. The dog is a low-growth, low-market-share item that is a candidate for elimination or segmentation. Understanding where a product falls within this market share/ growth structure is important when applying a standard cost system.

**Required**

1. Discuss the major advantages of using a standard cost accounting system.
2. Describe the types of information that are useful in setting standards and the conditions that must be present to support the use of standard costing.
3. Discuss the applicability or nonapplicability of using standard costing for a product classified as (a) a cash cow, and (b) a question mark.
4. What are some primary criticisms of using standard cost systems in today's manufacturing environment?

**(CMA Adapted)**

[LO 14-4]    14-35    **Determining Standard Direct Materials Cost**    Agrichem manufactures Insect-Be-Gone. Each bag of the product contains 60 pounds of direct materials. Twenty-five percent of the materials evaporate during manufacturing. The budget allows the direct materials to be purchased at $2.50 a pound under terms of 2/10, n/30. The company's stated policy is to take all available cash discounts. Determine the standard direct materials cost for one bag of Insect-Be-Gone.

[LO 14-4]    14-36    **Ethical Considerations**    A number of ethical issues arise in the design of management control systems. For example, such issues might arise when an individual's performance relative to budget or standard cost affects the individual's compensation or reward. Assume you are the cost accountant for a manufacturing firm. The reward system at your firm is such that the purchasing manager earns a financial reward when a significant favorable materials purchase-price variance is realized. Suppose, too, that this manager has an opportunity to get an extremely low price on raw materials that the manager knows are of substandard quality. Finally, assume that the purchasing manager believes that any problems attributable to the low-grade materials are not likely to surface until the product from which these materials is made has been in use for a while by consumers.

**Required**

1. Access the IMA's *Statement of Ethical Professional Practice* (**www.imanet.org**). Which, if any, of the IMA standards contained in the statement are at issue in this case, either from the standpoint of the purchasing manager or of the cost accountant?
2. Assume you are the cost accountant at the manufacturing plant where the preceding scenario takes place. According to the IMA's *Statement of Ethical Professional Practice,* what are your obligations in this situation?

[LO 14-4]    14-37    **Standard Costs and Ethics**    Ohio Apple Orchards (OAO), Inc., produces an organic, super-premium apple juice that it markets to specialty food outlets. OAO purchases its apples from a select group of farmers located in the Midwest. Recently, a graduate of the local university, Susanna Wu, joined the staff of OAO. Among Susanna's first responsibilities was the charge to develop and implement a standard costing system for OAO, this in response to competition arising from new and aggressive entrants to the organic foods market. Susanna discussed her task with the controller of the company, Mary Whitman, who indicated that unrefined apple juice would cost $1.50 per liter, the price she intended to pay her college pal, Bill O'Neal, who had since graduation been operating his own apple orchard at a loss. Because of favorable weather conditions during the most recent growing season, the price for comparable apple juice in the region dropped to $1.10 per liter. Mary felt that the $1.50 price, if maintained throughout the current year, would be sufficient to make Bill's operation profitable—at last.

**Required**    Is Mary's behavior regarding the cost information she provided to Susanna ethical? Support your answer by reference to the Institute of Management Accountant's *Statement* of *Ethical Professional Practice* (**www.imanet.org**).

**(CMA Adapted)**

[LO 14-5]    14-38    **Journal Entries**    Use the data in Exhibit 14.5. On October 7, Schmidt Machinery Company purchased 720 pounds of PVC at $41 per pound. On October 9, Schmidt's production department used 720 pounds of PVC for the 780 units of XV-1 it manufactured.

**Required**    Make the necessary journal entries to record the purchase and usage of PVC during October.

[LO 14-3, 14-5]   14-39   **Direct Materials Variances—Journal Entries**   Steinberg Company had the following direct materials costs for the manufacturing of product T in March:

| | |
|---|---|
| Actual purchase price per pound | $7.50 |
| Standard direct materials allowed for units of product T produced | 2,100 pounds |
| Decrease in direct materials inventory | 100 pounds |
| Direct materials used in production | 2,300 pounds |
| Standard price per pound of material | $7.25 |

**Required**
1. What was Steinberg's direct materials purchase-price variance and its direct materials usage variance for March? (Show calculations.)
2. Give the appropriate journal entries for March.

[LO 14-5]   14-40   **Journal Entries in a Standard Cost System**   Boron Chemical Company produces a synthetic resin that is used in the automotive industry. The company uses a standard cost system. For each gallon of output, the following direct manufacturing costs are anticipated:

| | |
|---|---|
| Direct labor: 2 hours at $25.00 per hour | $50.00 |
| Direct materials: 2 gallons at $10.00 per gallon | $20.00 |

During December of 2013, Boron produced a total of 2,500 gallons of output and incurred the following direct manufacturing costs:

Direct labor: 4,900 hours worked @ an average wage rate of $19.50 per hour
Direct materials:
   Purchased: 6,000 gallons @ $10.45 per gallon
   Used in production: 5,100 gallons

Boron records price variances for materials at the time of purchase.

**Required**   Give journal entries for the following events and transactions:
1. Purchase, on credit, of direct materials.
2. Direct materials issued to production.
3. Direct labor cost of units completed this period.
4. Direct manufacturing cost (direct labor plus direct materials) of units completed and transferred to Finished Goods Inventory.
5. Sale, for $150 per gallon, of 2,000 gallons of output. (*Hint:* You will need two journal entries here.)

[LO 14-6]   14-41   **Control of Operating Processes; Nonfinancial Performance Indicators**   This chapter deals with the design of effective control systems associated with business, including operating, processes. As indicated in the text, a comprehensive management accounting and control system will have both financial indicators and nonfinancial performance indicators. Financial indicators can include the operating-income variances that can be calculated each period by using standard costs and flexible budgets. This question deals with the use of nonfinancial performance indicators as a complement to the financial-performance indicators that are useful for controlling operating processes.

**Required**
1. List and define the primary business processes in which organizations engage in their attempt to meet customer expectations.
2. Fundamentally, control systems (including management accounting and control systems) collect information regarding the extent to which specified objectives are being accomplished. For each of the operating processes identified in (1), provide a listing of possible objectives that the organization might pursue. For each listed objective, provide one or more relevant *nonfinancial performance indicators* (performance metrics) that the organization's management accounting and control system might collect and report to management.

[LO 14-6]   14-42   **JIT and Process Cycle Efficiency (PCE)**   Zodiac Sound Co. manufactures audio systems, both made-to-order and more mass-produced systems that are typically sold to large-scale manufacturers of electronics equipment. For competitive reasons, the company is trying to increase its processing cycle efficiency (PCE) measure. As a strategy for improving its PCE performance, the company is considering a switch to JIT manufacturing. While the company managers have a fairly good feel for the cost of implementing JIT, they are unsure about the benefits of such a move, both in financial and nonfinancial terms. To help inform the ultimate decision regarding a move to a JIT system, you've been asked to provide some input. Fortunately, you've recently attended a continuing professional education (CPE) workshop on the costs and benefits of moving to JIT and therefore feel comfortable responding to management's request.

**Required**
1. Define the terms *value-added time, non-value-added time,* and *process cycle efficiency (PCE).* Conceptually, how are activities included in the first two categories determined? (That is, how does one know what activities are considered "value-added"?)

2. Define the terms *cycle time* and *processing (manufacturing) time.* How can processing time be broken down further?

3. Given the estimated data below, calculate and interpret the PCE for both the current manufacturing process and the proposed process after implementing JIT:

| Activity | Current System | After JIT Implementation |
|---|---|---|
| Storage | 60 minutes | 20 minutes |
| Inspection | 30 minutes | 15 minutes |
| Moving | 45 minutes | 15 minutes |
| Processing | 60 minutes | 30 minutes |

4. What is the percentage change in average PCE anticipated under JIT?

5. What additional nonfinancial performance indicators might management monitor in conjunction with the move to JIT?

## Problems

**[LO 14-2, 14-3]**   14-43   **Master Budget, Flexible Budget, and Profit-Variance Analysis; Spreadsheet Application**   Going into the period just ended, Ortiz & Co., manufacturer of a moderately priced espresso maker for retail sale, had planned to produce and sell 3,900 units at $100 per unit. Budgeted variable manufacturing costs per unit are $50. Ortiz pays its salespeople a 10% sales commission, which is the only variable nonmanufacturing cost for the company. Fixed costs are budgeted as follows: manufacturing, $50,000; marketing, $36,000.

Actual financial results for the period were disappointing. While sales volume was up (4,000 units sold), actual operating profit was only $20,000 for the period. Fixed manufacturing costs were as budgeted, but fixed marketing expenses exceeded budget by $4,000. Actual sales revenue for the period was $390,000, and actual variable costs were $70 per unit (the actual sales commission was 10% of sales revenue generated).

**Required**
1. Develop an Excel spreadsheet that is able to produce a profit-variance report similar to the one presented in text Exhibit 14.4.

2. Use the spreadsheet you developed in (1) and the data presented above to complete the profit-variance report for the period. Below the table you create, show separately the following variances:

   a. Total master (static) budget variance (i.e., the total operating-income variance for the period).

   b. Total flexible-budget variance.

   c. Flexible-budget variance for total variable costs, plus the flexible-budget variance for:

   (1) Variable manufacturing costs.

   (2) Variable nonmanufacturing costs.

   d. Flexible-budget variance for total fixed costs, plus the flexible-budget variance for:

   (1) Fixed manufacturing costs.

   (2) Fixed nonmanufacturing costs.

3. Provide a concise interpretation for each of the variances calculated above in (2).

4. Using the variances you calculated above in (2) and, in as much detail as the data allow, prepare a separate summary report similar to text Exhibit 14.2.

**[LO 14-3]**   14-44   **Materials Purchase-Price Variance and Foreign Exchange Rates**   Applied Materials Science (AMS) purchases its materials from several countries. As part of its cost-control program,

AMS uses a standard cost system for all aspects of its operations including materials purchases. The company establishes standard costs for materials at the beginning of each fiscal year.

Pat Butch, the purchasing manager, is happy with the result of the year just ended. He believes that the purchase-price variance for the year will be favorable and is very confident that his department has at least met the standard prices. The preliminary report from the controller's office confirms his jubilation. Following is a portion of the preliminary report:

| | |
|---|---|
| Total quantity purchased | 36,000 kilograms |
| Average price per kilogram | $50 |
| Standard price per kilogram | $60 |
| Budgeted quantity per quarter | 4,000 kilograms |

In the fourth quarter, the purchasing department increased purchases from the budgeted normal volume of 4,000 to 24,000 kilograms to meet the increased demands, which was a result of the firm's unexpected success in a fiercely competitive bidding. The substantial increase in the volume to be purchased forced the purchasing department to search for alternative suppliers. After frantic searches, it found suppliers in several foreign countries that could meet the firm's needs and could provide materials with higher quality than that of AMS's regular supplier. The purchasing department, however, was very reluctant to make the purchase because the negotiated price was $76 per kilogram, including shipping and import duty.

The actual cost of the purchases, however, was much lower because of currency devaluations before deliveries began, which was a result of the financial turmoil of several countries in the region.

Patricia Rice, the controller, does not share the purchasing department's euphoria. She is fully aware of the following quarterly purchases:

| | First Quarter | Second Quarter | Third Quarter | Fourth Quarter |
|---|---|---|---|---|
| Quantity | 4,000 | 4,000 | 4,000 | 24,000 |
| Purchase price (per kilogram) | $68 | $69 | $73 | ? |

**Required**

1. Calculate purchase-price variances for the fourth quarter and for the year. How much of the price variance is attributable to changes in foreign currency exchange rates?

2. Evaluate the purchasing department's performance.

[LO 14-3]   14-45   **Joint Direct Materials Variance**   Benderboard produces corrugated board containers that the nearby wine industry uses to package wine in bulk. Benderboard buys kraft paper by the ton, converts it to heavy-duty paperboard on its corrugator, and then cuts and glues it into folding boxes. The boxes are opened and filled with a plastic liner and then with the wine.

Many other corrugated board converters are in the area and competition is strong. Benderboard is eager to keep its costs under control. The company has used a standard cost system for several years. Responsibility for variances has been established. For example, the purchasing agent is responsible for the direct materials price variance, and the general supervisor answers for the direct materials usage variance.

Recently, the industrial engineer and the company's management accountant participated in a workshop sponsored by the Institute of Management Accountants at which there was some discussion of variance analysis. They noted that the workshop proposed that the responsibility for some variances was properly dual. The accountant and engineer reviewed Benderboard's system and were not sure how to adapt the new information to it.

Benderboard has the following standards for its direct materials:

Standard direct materials cost per gross of finished boxes = 4½ tons of kraft paper at $10 per ton = $45.00

During May, the accountant assembled the following data about direct materials:

Finished product: 5,000 gross of boxes
Actual cost of direct materials used during month: $300,000 for 25,000 tons
Direct materials put into production (used): 25,000 tons
Benderboard began and finished the month of May with no inventory

**Required**   Determine the following for Benderboard:

1. Direct materials price variance, calculated at point of production.

2. Direct materials efficiency (usage) variance.

3. Direct materials joint price-quantity variance (defined as: [AP − SP] × [AQ − SQ]).

**(CMA Adapted)**

[LO 14-3, 14-4]   **14-46   Standard Cost Sheet and Use of Variance Data**   ColdKing Company is a small producer of fruit-flavored frozen desserts. For many years, its products have had strong regional sales because of brand recognition; however, other companies have begun marketing similar products in the area, and price competition has become increasingly important. Janice Wakefield, the company's controller, is planning to implement a standard cost system for ColdKing and has gathered considerable information from her coworkers about production and materials requirements for ColdKing's products. Janice believes that the use of standard costs will allow the company to improve cost control, make better pricing decisions, and enhance strategic management.

ColdKing's most popular product is raspberry sherbet. The sherbet is produced in 10-gallon batches, each of which requires 6 quarts of good raspberries and 10 gallons of other ingredients. The fresh raspberries are sorted by hand before they enter the production process. Because of imperfections in the raspberries and normal spoilage, one quart of berries is discarded for every four accepted. The standard direct labor time for sorting to obtain one quart of acceptable raspberries is 3 minutes. The acceptable raspberries are then blended with the other ingredients; blending requires 12 minutes of direct labor time per batch. After blending, the sherbet is packaged in quart containers. Janice has gathered the following price information:

- ColdKing purchases raspberries for $4.00 per quart. All other ingredients cost $2.25 per gallon.

- Direct labor is paid at the rate of $15 per hour.

- The total packaging cost (labor and materials) for the sherbet is $0.50 per quart.

**Required**

1. Develop the standard cost for the direct cost components of a 10-gallon batch of raspberry sherbet. For each direct cost component, the standard cost should identify the following:

   a. Standard quantity.

   b. Standard rate (or price).

   c. Standard cost per batch.

2. As part of the implementation of a standard cost system at ColdKing, Janice plans to train those responsible for maintaining the standards to use variance analysis. She is particularly concerned with the causes of unfavorable variances.

   a. Discuss the possible causes of unfavorable materials price variances, identify the individuals who should be held responsible for them, and comment on the implications of these variances on strategic cost management.

   b. Discuss the possible causes of unfavorable labor efficiency variances, identify the individuals who should be held responsible for them, and comment on the implications of these variances on strategic cost management.

**(CMA Adapted)**

[LO 14-4]   **14-47   Standard Cost System—Behavioral Considerations**   Mark-Wright Inc. (MWI) is a specialty frozen food processor located in the midwestern states. Since its founding in 1982, MWI has enjoyed a loyal local clientele willing to pay premium prices for the high-quality frozen foods prepared from special recipes. In the last two years, MWI has experienced rapid sales growth in its operating region and has had many inquiries about supplying its products on a national basis. To meet this growth, MWI expanded its processing capabilities, which resulted in increased production and distribution costs. Furthermore, MWI has been encountering pricing pressure from competitors outside its normal marketing region.

Because MWI desires to continue its expansion, Jim Condon, CEO, has engaged a consulting firm to assist the company in determining its best course of action. The consulting firm concluded that, although premium pricing is sustainable in some areas, MWI must make some price concessions if sales growth is to be achieved. Also, to maintain profit margins, the company must reduce and control its costs. The consulting firm recommended using a standard cost system that would facilitate a flexible budgeting system to better accommodate the changes in demand that can be expected when serving an expanding market area.

Jim met with his management team and explained the consulting firm's recommendations. He then assigned the team the task of establishing standard costs. After discussing the situation with their respective staffs, the management team met to review the matter.

Jane Morgan, purchasing manager, noted that meeting expanded production would necessitate obtaining basic food supplies from sources other than MWI's traditional ones. This would entail increased raw materials and shipping costs and could result in supplies of lower quality. Consequently, the processing department would have to make up these increased costs if current cost levels are to be maintained or reduced.

Alan Chen, processing manager, countered that the need to accelerate processing cycles to increase production, coupled with the possibility of receiving lower-grade supplies, could result in a slip in quality and a higher product rejection rate. Under these circumstances, per-unit labor utilization cannot be maintained or reduced, and forecasting future unit labor content becomes very difficult.

Tina Lopez, production engineer, advised that failure to properly maintain and thoroughly clean the equipment at prescribed daily intervals could affect the quality and unique taste of the frozen food products. Jack Reid, vice president of sales, stated that if quality could not be maintained, MWI could not expect to increase sales to the levels projected.

When the management team reported these problems to Jim, he said that if agreement could not be reached on appropriate standards, he would arrange to have the consulting firm set the standards, and everyone would have to live with the results.

**Required**

1. With respect to a standard cost system, list:

   a. Its major advantages.

   b. Its disadvantages.

2. Identify those who should participate in setting standards and describe the benefits of their participation.

3. Explain the general features and characteristics associated with the introduction and operation of a standard cost system that make it an effective tool for cost control.

4. What could the consequences be if Jim Condon, CEO, has the outside consulting firm set MWI's standards?

**(CMA Adapted)**

[LO 14-3, 14-5]  14-48  **Standard Cost in Process Costing; All Variances and Journal Entries**   Dash Company adopted a standard costing system several years ago. The standard costs for the prime costs (i.e., direct materials and direct labor) of its single product are

| Material | (8 kilograms × $5.00/kg) | $ 40.00 |
| Labor | (6 hours × $18.20/hr.) | 109.20 |

All materials are added at the beginning of processing. The following data were taken from the company's records for November:

| In-process beginning inventory | None |
| In-process ending inventory | 800 Units, 75% complete as to direct labor |
| Units completed | 5,600 Units |
| Budgeted output | 6,000 Units |
| Purchases of materials | 50,000 Kilograms |
| Total actual direct labor costs | $600,000 |
| Actual direct labor-hours | 36,500 Hours |
| Materials usage variance | $1,500 Unfavorable |
| Total materials variance | $750 Unfavorable |

**Required**

1. Compute for November (show calculations):

   a. The labor efficiency variance.

   b. The labor rate variance.

   c. The actual number of kilograms of material used in the production process during the month.

   d. The actual price paid per kilogram of material during the month.

   e. The amount of direct material cost and direct labor cost transferred to the Finished Goods account.

   f. The total amount of direct material and direct labor cost in the Work-in-Process Inventory account at the end of November.

2. Prepare journal entries to record all transactions including the variances in requirement 1.

**(CMA Adapted)**

**[LO 14-3, 14-6]**    14-49  **Flexible Budget and Operating-Profit Variances**   Phoenix Management helps rental property owners find renters and charges the owners one-half of the first month's rent for this service. For August 2013, Phoenix expects to find renters for 100 apartments with an average first month's rent of $700. Budgeted cost data per tenant application for 2013 follow:

- Professional labor: 1.5 hours at $20 per hour.
- Credit checks: $50.

  Phoenix expects other costs, including lease payment for the building, secretarial help, and utilities, to be $3,000 per month. On average, Phoenix is successful in placing one tenant for every three applicants.

  Actual rental applications in August 2013 were 270. Phoenix paid $9,500 for 400 hours of professional labor. Credit checks went up to $55 per application. Other support costs in August 2013 were $3,600. The average first monthly rentals for August 2013 were $800 per apartment unit for 90 units.

**Required**

1. Prepare a profit-variance report similar to text Exhibit 14.4. Compute the total flexible-budget variance and the sales volume variance for Phoenix's operations in August 2013.

2. Determine the professional labor rate and labor efficiency variances for August 2013.

3. What nonfinancial factors should Phoenix consider in evaluating the effectiveness and efficiency of professional labor?

**[LO 14-1, 14-3, 14-6]**    14-50  **Standard Costing; Variance Analysis; Strategic Considerations**   In a *Wall Street Journal* article, the author notes that various retailers in the United States (e.g., Meijer, Inc., Gap, Inc., Office Depot, Inc., and Toys "R" Us, Inc.) are turning to consulting firms, such as Accenture, to develop engineered labor standards for cashiers and other retail workers. Monitoring labor-hour consumption (i.e., labor efficiency) under such standards involves timing from the first scan of an item in a customer's purchase to the production of a sales receipt for the customer. A commentator for Meijer, Inc., states that the system now in use had enabled the company to more efficiently staff stores while concomitantly increasing customer-service ratings. A representative from another client of Accenture states that the new system allows the retailer to determine how many workers to schedule at a given time, resulting in a labor-cost reduction of approximately 8%. Engineered standards were developed many years ago in a manufacturing environment, at places such as Westinghouse, by time-and-motion study experts. Unlike factory workers, however, most retail clerks deal directly with customers. This raises interesting questions as to whether and how the use of such monitoring (i.e., control) systems affects customer relations, including customer satisfaction. Uncertainties associated with nonstandard transactions or events are also thought to have negative motivational effects on employees whose performance is assessed using such engineered standards. (**Source:** Vanessa O'Connell, "Stores Count Seconds to Cut Labor Costs," *The Wall Street Journal*, November 13, 2008, pp. A1, A15. For additional information regarding "workforce-management systems," go to the website of Accenture, Ltd. (**www.accenture.com/home.asp**) and search under "Operations Workforce Optimization.")

**Required**

1. The article refers to the terms *engineered labor standards* and *time-and-motion studies.* Define each of these two terms.

2. Define the terms *labor rate variance* and *labor efficiency variance.* Which of these two variances is the basis for monitoring a cashier's performance, as described in the above-referenced article?

3. What cashier activities might invalidate cashier time measures? What recommendation(s) do you have for addressing this problem?

4. As described in the chapter, any control/monitoring system is likely to have behavioral consequences. In the present context, what employee morale and customer-service problems might arise from the system that was implemented? What steps do you think a retailer, such as those described in the article, can take to monitor this situation?

5. How can information about cashier time-management be used strategically by a retailer? For example, how can such information be used to lower labor costs for retail stores? For which types of firms would such detailed information likely be of greater value?

[LO 14-1, 14-2, 14-3, 14-6]   **14-51   Master Budgets; Flexible Budgets; Profit-Variance Analysis**   As part of its comprehensive planning and control system, Menendez Company uses a master budget and subsequent variance analysis. You are given the following information that pertains to the company's only product, XL-10, for the month of December.

**Required**

1. Using text Exhibit 14.4 as a guide, complete the missing parts of the following profit report for December.

| | Actual Results | Flexible-Budget Variance | Flexible Budget | Sales Volume Variances | Master (Static) Budget |
|---|---|---|---|---|---|
| Unit sales | 50,000 | —— | —— | —— | 40,000 |
| Sales | $ 450,000 | —— | —— | —— | $400,000 |
| Variable costs | $ 375,000 | —— | —— | —— | 280,000 |
| Contribution margin | $ 75,000 | —— | —— | —— | $120,000 |
| Fixed costs | 65,000 | —— | —— | —— | 75,000 |
| Operating income | $ 10,000 | —— | —— | —— | $ 45,000 |

2. Based on your completed profit report, determine the dollar amount and label (F or U) each of the following variances for December:
   a. Total master (static) budget variance.
   b. Total flexible-budget variance.
   c. Sales volume variance, in terms of operating income.
   d. Sales volume variance, in terms of contribution margin.
   e. Selling price variance.

3. Explain what is meant by the labels "favorable" and "unfavorable" in terms of a profit-variance report of the type you just prepared for the Menendez Company.

4. What information is contained in the total flexible-budget variance for the period? Include in your answer a short discussion of the component variances that can be calculated to explain the causes of the total flexible-budget variance.

5. Some individuals have recently criticized the use of standard costs and flexible budgets to perform the kinds of variance analyses covered in this chapter. Provide an overview of the arguments for and against the use of standard costs and flexible budgets for operational control purposes.

[LO 14-1, 14-2, 14-3, 14-4, 14-6]   **14-52   Summary Problem: All Variances; Spreadsheet Application**   Funtime, Inc., manufactures video game machines. Recently, market saturation and technological innovations have begun to cause pricing pressures that, in turn, are having a negative effect on profits. To stem the slide in profits until new products can be introduced, top management is turning its attention to both manufacturing economics and increased production. To realize these objectives, management has developed an incentive program to reward production managers who contribute to an increase in the number of units produced and a decrease in costs.

The production managers have responded to the pressure of improving manufacturing in several ways that increase the number of completed units beyond normal production levels. The assembly group puts together video game machines that require parts from both the printed circuit boards (PCB) and the reading heads (RH) groups. To attain increased production levels, the PCB and RH groups began rejecting parts that previously would have been tested and modified to meet manufacturing standards. Preventive maintenance on machines used to produce these parts has been postponed; only emergency repair work is being performed to keep production lines moving. The maintenance department is concerned about serious breakdowns and unsafe operating conditions.

The more aggressive assembly group production supervisors have pressured maintenance personnel to attend to their machines rather than those of other groups. This has resulted in machine downtime in the PCB and RH groups that, when coupled with demands for accelerated parts delivery by the assembly group, has led to more frequent rejection of parts and increased friction among departments.

Funtime operates under a standard cost system. The standard costs per video game machine are as follows:

| Cost Item | Standard Cost per Unit | | Total |
| --- | --- | --- | --- |
| | Quantity | Cost | |
| Direct materials: | | | |
| Housing unit | 1.0 | $20 | $ 20 |
| Printed circuit boards | 2.0 | 15 | 30 |
| Reading heads | 4.0 | 10 | 40 |
| Direct labor: | | | |
| Assembly group | 2.0 hours | 10 | 20 |
| PCB group | 1.0 hour | 11 | 11 |
| RH group | 1.5 hours | 12 | 18 |
| Total standard cost per unit | | | $139 |

Funtime prepares monthly performance reports based on standard costs. The following is the contribution report for May 2013 when production and sales both reached 2,200 units.

**FUNTIME, INC.**
**Contribution Report**
**For the Month of May 2013**

| | Budget | Actual | Variance |
| --- | --- | --- | --- |
| Units | 2,000 | 2,200 | 200F |
| Revenue | $400,000 | $396,000 | $ 4,000U |
| Variable costs: | | | |
| Direct materials | $180,000 | $220,400 | $40,400U |
| Direct labor | 98,000 | 112,260 | 14,260U |
| Total variable costs | 278,000 | 332,660 | 54,660U |
| Contribution margin | $122,000 | $ 63,340 | $58,660U |

Funtime's top management was surprised by the unfavorable contribution margin variance in spite of the increased sales in May. Constance Brown, the firm's cost accountant, was asked to identify and report on the reasons for the unfavorable contribution margin as well as the individuals or groups responsible for them. After her review, Constance prepared the following usage report:

**FUNTIME, INC.**
**Usage Report**
**For the Month of May 2013**

| Cost Item | Quantity | Actual Cost |
| --- | --- | --- |
| Direct materials: | | |
| Housing units | 2,200 units | $ 44,000 |
| Printed circuit boards | 4,700 units | 75,200 |
| Reading heads | 9,200 units | 101,200 |
| Direct labor: | | |
| Assembly | 3,900 hours | 31,200 |
| Printed circuit boards | 2,400 hours | 31,060 |
| Reading heads | 3,500 hours | 50,000 |
| Total variable cost | | $332,660 |

Constance reported that the PCB and RH groups supported the increased production levels but experienced abnormal machine downtime, causing idle time that required the use of overtime to keep up with the accelerated demand for parts. This overtime was charged to direct labor. She also reported that the production managers of these two groups resorted to parts rejections, rather than testing and modifying them, as was done routinely in the past. Constance determined that the assembly group met management's objectives by increasing production while utilizing fewer-than-standard hours.

**Required**

1. Set up an Excel spreadsheet to calculate the following variances:

   a. Direct materials price variance, calculated at point of production.

   b. Direct materials usage variance.

   c. Direct labor efficiency variance.

   d. Direct labor rate variance.

   e. Selling price variance.

   f. Sales volume variance, in terms of contribution margin.

2. Determine the components of the $58,660 unfavorable variance between budgeted and actual contribution margin during May 2013.

3. Identify and briefly explain the behavioral factors that could promote friction among the production managers and between them and the maintenance manager.

4. Evaluate Constance Brown's analysis of the unfavorable contribution results in terms of the report's completeness and its effect on the behavior of the production groups.

**(CMA Adapted)**

[LO 14-1, 14-4, 14-6]    14-53    **Production Planning and Control Strategy**    This is a story about manufacturing performance at one plant of a large company. It begins with Kristen Reynolds, a relatively new plant manager, coming to visit Bryan Simpkins, the plant's head of manufacturing. Kristen and Bryan work for ITR Incorporated, a manufacturer of lighting fixtures with plants located in six countries and worldwide sales. The plant that Kristen and Bryan manage is located in Canada near Hamilton, Ontario. It is the one plant in ITR's system that focuses on custom orders that require special materials, setup, and assembly. The other five plants supply ITR's high-volume, standardized products. Because of changes in the residential and commercial construction industries, the demand for custom orders at the Ontario plant has been increasing steadily. Unfortunately, the plant has not been filling these orders as quickly as Kristen would like. Many solid customers are waiting days or weeks longer for their orders than they did a year ago; moreover, some ITR salespeople have begun to be evasive when customers ask how soon their orders can be filled. Kristen does not know how this is affecting sales or customer goodwill.

> **Kristen:** Hi, Bryan. It's good to see you. I hope all is well with you and the family.
>
> **Bryan:** Going great—though I just learned that Jimmy will have to have braces on his teeth. I don't even want to think of how much that will cost.
>
> **Kristen:** Hey, I've been through that too. No fun. (pause) Bryan, I haven't visited the plant operations in some time. Would you take me for a quick tour?
>
> **Bryan:** Let's go.

Bryan and Kristen first visit an operation where a skilled worker is operating a machine that molds a metal frame on which multiple light fixtures will later be installed. They watch as the worker (his name badge says Ed) completes the last of a batch of 15 frames. Kristen asks how long this batch took him, and he says 82 minutes. "I know this exactly because I have productivity standards to meet, and I must record my time on all jobs. My standard is 6 minutes per item, so I beat my goal." Ed then examines each frame and finds that one has a bad twist and must be rejected; this takes about 10 minutes. He then pushes a button near the machine that calls another worker to remove the defective frame. Meanwhile, Ed loads the 14 good ones on a cart and moves them to the next manufacturing station. Bryan and Kristen note that many frames are already waiting at the next station.

The worker who was called to remove the defective frame tags it, writes up the potential cause(s) for the defect, and then moves the frame to the area of the plant designated for scrap and rework. Kristen and Bryan look at the defect report and note that it indicates two possibilities, which will be studied further by another worker assigned to the scrap and rework area. The two possibilities are poor-quality materials, as determined by apparent weaknesses in portions of the framing material, and poor work quality (Ed could have damaged the frame accidentally by banging it against one of the roof support beams located next to his work area). Kristen and Bryan note that Ed's workstation area is indeed pretty cramped.

They move to another workstation, which has no operator. By asking a worker at the adjacent station, they determine that the station is down because the machine needs repair. "Joe usually works that station, but he is helping out in the shipping department until his machine is repaired."

They move to another workstation that looks very busy. An order marked "urgent" is waiting at this station, while Dan, the operator, quickly finishes another order. Bryan asks Dan why he has not started the urgent order, and Dan explains that he cannot afford to stop the machine and set it up for another order. This would cost him some time that would lower his productivity on the current job. Dan explains that it is important that he get the items done in the current order quickly, within a standard level of productivity, or production supervisors will be coming to call. Dan says he sees the urgent sign and is working quickly to get to it. He says he might even delay lunch to start it.

To investigate some of the things they observed, Kristen and Bryan next visit the purchasing department. Here they find that the frame material Ed used was purchased from a relatively new vendor at an unbelievably low price. The purchasing department manager approved the purchase because other purchases in the month had gone over budget and this was a way to help meet the budget. The budget is a predetermined amount that the purchasing department is expected to spend each month. Plant policy requires an investigation of any large variances from the budget.

Next, Kristen and Bryan inquire about Joe's machine. A check at the job scheduler's desk shows that the workstation had been in use constantly for the last few weeks. Joe said that he noticed a funny noise but had not reported it because he had some jobs to finish and his productivity is measured by how quickly he finished them. His time between jobs is not measured, but doing jobs quickly is important. Bryan asks the job scheduler why Ed's work area is so crowded since there appears to be plenty of room elsewhere in the plant. The job scheduler says that he is not sure, but that it probably has to do with the fact that each production department is charged a certain amount of plant overhead based on the amount of square feet of space that department occupies. Thus, the department manager for whom Ed works is likely to have reduced the space as much as possible to reduce these overhead charges.

As the story ends, Bryan and Kristen are looking for an answer to how urgent orders are scheduled and moved through the plant.

**Required**    Consider the manufacturing processes observed in ITR's Ontario plant. What recommendations do you think Bryan and Kristen should make?

[LO 14-1, 14-4, 14-6]    14-54    **Research Assignment: Service-Based Innovation; Strategy**    Obtain from your library (or course pack, as appropriate) a copy of the following article: L. McCreary, "Kaiser Permanente's Innovation on the Front Lines," *Harvard Business Review* (September 2010), pp. 92–97. One usually thinks of "innovation" in terms of new technologies or new products. This article focuses on a different type of innovation: service-based innovation. In a larger sense, it deals with the issue of improving health care delivery.

**Required**    After reading the above-referenced article, answer the following questions:
1. In general, how does this article relate to the material covered in Chapter 14?
2. Describe the Innovation Consultancy and its role in the larger organization, Kaiser Permanente (KP).
3. Provide a brief description of the "human-centered design" methodology employed by the Innovation Consultancy arm of KP.
4. Discuss four concrete examples of improvements in health care delivery (innovations in service-based practice) resulting from the method described in requirement 3 above.

[LO 14-1, 14-4, 14-6]    14-55    **Research Assignment: Supply-Chain Management; Strategy**    Obtain from your library (or course pack, as appropriate) a copy of the following article: S. New, "The Transparent Supply Chain," *Harvard Business Review* (October 2010), pp. 76–82.

**Required**    After reading the above-referenced article, answer the following questions:
1. In general, how does this article relate to the material covered in Chapter 14?

2. What is meant by the term "provenance," as used in this article? According to the article, what is motivating the need for businesses to provide greater transparency of their supply chains?

3. Provide several examples of leading-edge technology that can be used by businesses to provide consumers and other stakeholders information regarding a product's provenance.

## Solutions to Self-Study Problems

### 1. Sales Volume and Flexible-Budget (FB) Variances/JIT manufacturing

1. Master and pro forma budgets:

| | Master (Static) Budget | Pro Forma Budgets | |
|---|---|---|---|
| Units | 10,000 | 9,500 | 11,000 |
| Sales ($54/unit) | $540,000 | $513,000 | $594,000 |
| Variable costs: | | | |
|   Direct materials ($12.60/unit) | $126,000 | $119,700 | $138,600 |
|   Direct labor ($7.70/unit) | 77,000 | 73,150 | 84,700 |
|   Manufacturing overhead | 20,000 | 19,000 | 22,000 |
|   Selling and administrative | 50,000 | 47,500 | 55,000 |
|   Total variable cost ($27.30/unit) | $273,000 | $259,350 | $300,300 |
| Contribution margin ($26.70/unit) | $267,000 | $253,650 | $293,700 |
| Fixed costs: | | | |
|   Manufacturing | $ 55,000 | $ 55,000 | $ 55,000 |
|   Selling and administrative | 24,000 | 24,000 | 24,000 |
|   Total fixed costs | $ 79,000 | $ 79,000 | $ 79,000 |
| Operating income | $188,000 | $174,650 | $214,700 |

2. Total master (static) budget variance = Actual operating income − Master budget operating income

= $177,100 − $188,000 = **$10,900U**

Sales volume variance, in terms of operating income = Flexible-budget operating income − Master (static) budget operating income

= $174,650 − $188,000 = **$13,350U**

or = Standard cm/unit × (Actual sales volume − Master budgeted sales volume)

= ($54.00 − $27.30)/unit × (9,500 − 10,000) units = **$13,350U**

Total flexible-budget variance = Actual operating income − Flexible-budget operating income

= $177,100 − $174,650 = **$2,450F**

3. Selling price variance = Actual sales revenue − Flexible-budget sales revenue

= $551,000 − $513,000 = **$38,000F**

or = AQ × (AP − SP) = 9,500 units × ($58.00 − $54.00)/unit = **$38,000F**

Total variable cost flexible-budget variance = Actual total variable costs − Flexible-budget total variable costs

= $294,900 − $259,350 = **$35,550U**

or AQ × (AP − SP) = 9,500 units × ($31.0421 − $27.30)/unit = **$35,550U**

Total fixed cost flexible-budget variance = Actual fixed costs − Flexible-budget fixed costs

= $79,000 − $79,000 = **$0**

**Check:** Total flexible-budget variance = Selling price variance + Total variable cost flexible-budget variance + Total fixed cost flexible-budget variance

$2,450F = $38,000F + $35,550U + $0

4. Direct materials purchase-price variance, direct materials usage variance, direct labor rate variance, and direct labor efficiency variance

**Direct Materials**

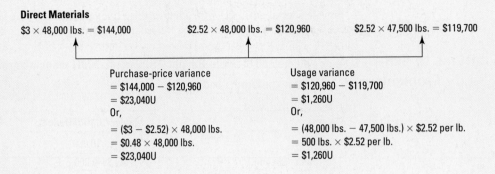

$3 × 48,000 lbs. = $144,000          $2.52 × 48,000 lbs. = $120,960          $2.52 × 47,500 lbs. = $119,700

Purchase-price variance
= $144,000 − $120,960
= $23,040U
Or,
= ($3 − $2.52) × 48,000 lbs.
= $0.48 × 48,000 lbs.
= $23,040U

Usage variance
= $120,960 − $119,700
= $1,260U
Or,
= (48,000 lbs. − 47,500 lbs.) × $2.52 per lb.
= 500 lbs. × $2.52 per lb.
= $1,260U

**Direct Labor**

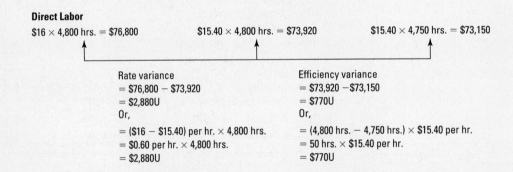

$16 × 4,800 hrs. = $76,800          $15.40 × 4,800 hrs. = $73,920          $15.40 × 4,750 hrs. = $73,150

Rate variance
= $76,800 − $73,920
= $2,880U
Or,
= ($16 − $15.40) per hr. × 4,800 hrs.
= $0.60 per hr. × 4,800 hrs.
= $2,880U

Efficiency variance
= $73,920 − $73,150
= $770U
Or,
= (4,800 hrs. − 4,750 hrs.) × $15.40 per hr.
= 50 hrs. × $15.40 per hr.
= $770U

5. A just-in-time (JIT) process is one in which products, components, and subassemblies are produced only when needed—that is, on a so-called demand-pull basis. Based originally on the Toyota production system, this philosophy requires a commitment to total quality (to ensure smooth flowing of the production line), elimination of waste and inefficiency, and a minimization of inventory holdings. In effect, the JIT philosophy reflects a new business model for the organization, as follows:

> Make only what you've sold, rather than stockpiling large quantities of goods that may remain in inventory for an extended period of time. Make use of raw materials as soon as they are delivered. Deliver to customers finished goods shortly after rolling off the assembly line.

Financial benefits from implementing a JIT manufacturing strategy include: increased sales/market share (especially for companies embracing a differentiation strategy), reduction in inventory-holding costs (both out-of-pocket costs and opportunity costs), and decreased quality-related costs (e.g., internal failure costs and external failure costs). Nonfinancial benefits associated with JIT manufacturing systems include: faster cycle times, reductions in inventory turnover ratios, improvements in defect rates, increased uptime for machinery and equipment, and improvements in on-time deliveries to customers. Of course, to obtain these benefits, the organization generally must make sizable investments in employee training, information systems, and a reconfigured plant layout (e.g., a move to *cellular manufacturing*).

## 2. Direct Materials Price and Usage Variances, Direct Labor Rate and Efficiency Variances, and Journal Entries

### 1. Variance Calculations

**Direct Materials—XF–2000**

Total standard quantity of direct materials for the product manufactured (SQ)
= 100,000 bags × 25 pounds of XF–2000 per bag = 2,500,000 pounds

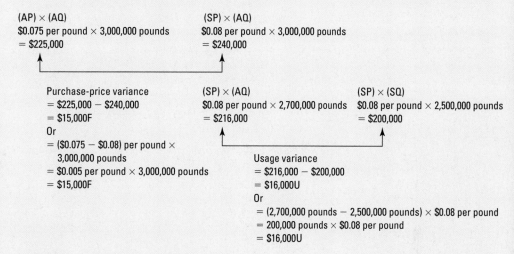

(AP) × (AQ)
$0.075 per pound × 3,000,000 pounds
= $225,000

(SP) × (AQ)
$0.08 per pound × 3,000,000 pounds
= $240,000

Purchase-price variance
= $225,000 − $240,000
= $15,000F
Or
= ($0.075 − $0.08) per pound ×
   3,000,000 pounds
= $0.005 per pound × 3,000,000 pounds
= $15,000F

(SP) × (AQ)
$0.08 per pound × 2,700,000 pounds
= $216,000

(SP) × (SQ)
$0.08 per pound × 2,500,000 pounds
= $200,000

Usage variance
= $216,000 − $200,000
= $16,000U
Or
= (2,700,000 pounds − 2,500,000 pounds) × $0.08 per pound
= 200,000 pounds × $0.08 per pound
= $16,000U

**Direct Labor**

Actual wage rate per direct labor-hour (AP)
= $182,000 ÷ 5,200 hours = $35 per hour
Total standard direct labor-hours for the product manufactured (SQ)
= 100,000 bags × 0.05 hours per bag = 5,000 hours

(AP) × (AQ)
$35/hr. × 5,200 hours
$182,000

(SP) × (AQ)
$32/hr. × 5,200 hours
$166,400

(SP) × (SQ)
$32/hr. × 5,000 hours
$160,000

Rate variance
= $182,000 − $166,400
= $15,600U
Or
= ($35 − $32) per hr. × 5,200 hrs.
= $3 per hr. × 5,200 hrs.
= $15,600U

Efficiency variance
= $166,400 − $160,000
= $6,400U
Or
= (5,200 hours − 5,000 hours) × $32 per hr.
= 200 hrs. x $32 per hr.
= $6,400U

### 2. Journal Entries

| | | |
|---|---|---|
| Materials Inventory (3,000,000 × $0.08) | 240,000 | |
|    Materials Purchase-Price Variance (3,000,000 × $0.005) | | 15,000 |
|    Accounts Payable (3,000,000 × $0.075) | | 225,000 |
| Purchased 3,000,000 pounds of XF–2000 at $0.075/per pound. | | |

| | | |
|---|---:|---:|
| Work-in-Process Inventory ($0.08 × 2,500,000) | 200,000 | |
| Materials Usage Variance (200,000 × $0.08) | 16,000 | |
|     Materials Inventory (2,700,000 × $0.08) | | 216,000 |
| Issued 2,700,000 pounds of XF–2000 for the production | | |
| of 100,000 bags of Weed-Be-Doom. | | |

| | | |
|---|---:|---:|
| Work-in-Process Inventory (5,000 × $32) | 160,000 | |
| Labor Rate Variance (5,200 × $3) | 15,600 | |
| Labor Efficiency Variance (200 × $32) | 6,400 | |
|     Accrued Payroll (5,200 × $35) | | 182,000 |
| Direct labor wages for the manufacturing of 100,000 bags | | |
| of Weed-Be-Doom for 5,200 hours at $35 per hour. | | |

*Please visit* **http://www.mhhe.com/blocher6e** *to access a narrated, animated tutorial for solving these problems.*

# CHAPTER FIFTEEN

# Operational Performance Measurement:
## Indirect-Cost Variances and Resource-Capacity Management

**After studying this chapter, you should be able to . . .**

LO 15-1 Distinguish between the product-costing and control purposes of standard costs for manufacturing overhead

LO 15-2 Calculate and properly interpret standard cost variances for manufacturing overhead using flexible budgets

LO 15-3 Record overhead costs and associated standard cost variances

LO 15-4 Dispose of standard cost variances at the end of a period

LO 15-5 Apply standard costs to service organizations

LO 15-6 Analyze overhead variances in a traditional activity-based costing (ABC) system

LO 15-7 Understand decision rules that can be used to guide the variance-investigation decision

LO 15-8 Formulate the variance-investigation decision under uncertainty (appendix)

In this chapter we continue the discussion from Chapter 14 by examining production volume and other indirect-cost variances that organizations use to monitor short-term financial performance. We expand the discussion of standard costs, flexible budgets, and variance analysis and apply these concepts to both traditional and ABC systems. Of particular interest is how such measures can be used to help manage resource capacity. This chapter deals as well with recording standard overhead costs and with the end-of-period disposition of standard cost variances. We address the issue of applying standard cost systems to service organizations and conclude the chapter by discussing the variance-investigation decision. The appendix provides a conceptual model for dealing with the variance-investigation decision under uncertainty.

## Standard Overhead Costs: Planning versus Control

**LO 15-1**

*Distinguish between the product-costing and control purposes of standard costs for manufacturing overhead.*

As pointed out in Chapter 14, standard costs can be used alone for control purposes, or they can be incorporated formally into the accounting records for both product-costing and control purposes. In Chapter 14 we used a flexible budget at the end of the period to calculate various revenue and cost variances, which helped explain why actual operating income for the period differed from operating income reflected in the master (static) budget. For *cost-control purposes,* we calculated a total flexible-budget variance and then proceeded to explain this total variance by calculating a selling price variance, fixed cost

**EXHIBIT 15.1**
**Variable Manufacturing Overhead: Product-Costing versus Control Purposes**

variances (for both manufacturing and nonmanufacturing costs), and a total flexible-budget variance for direct manufacturing costs.[1] We then subdivided the variance for direct labor and direct materials into price and efficiency components. The breakdown of the flexible-budget variance for factory overhead was left for Chapter 15. However, before looking at standard cost variances associated with manufacturing (factory) overhead, we need to differentiate the product-costing and cost-control purposes of standard costs used for factory overhead.

For *variable* factory overhead the underlying model for cost-control and product-costing purposes is the same, as illustrated in Exhibit 15.1. Recall that the Schmidt Machining Company uses direct labor-hours as the activity variable for applying overhead costs. Other allocation bases, such as number of machine-hours, could have been used by the company.

We reproduce as Exhibit 15.2 the manufacturing cost portion of the standard cost sheet for the Schmidt Machinery Company presented in Chapter 14 (Exhibit 14.5). As you can see, the standard variable overhead rate per unit is $60 (5 standard direct labor-hours/unit × $12 standard variable overhead cost per direct labor-hour). It is this amount that is charged to production for the period (product-costing purpose) and that is used in the flexible budget (cost-control purpose) in Exhibit 14.8. In short, the graph depicted in

**EXHIBIT 15.2**
**Standard Manufacturing Cost Sheet (partial reproduction of Exhibit 14.5)**

| | | | | |
|---|---|---|---|---|
| **SCHMIDT MACHINERY COMPANY** | | | | |
| **Standard Manufacturing Cost Sheet** | | | | |
| **Product: XV-1** | | | | |
| **Descriptions** | **Quantity** | **Unit Cost** | **Subtotal** | **Total** |
| Direct materials: | | | | |
|   Aluminum | 4 pounds | $25 | $100 | |
|   PVC | 1 pound | 40 | 40 | |
| Direct labor | 5 hours | 40 | 200 | |
| Variable factory overhead | 5 hours | 12 | 60 | |
| Total variable manufacturing cost | | | | $400 |
| Fixed factory overhead | 5 hours | 24 | 120 | 120* |
| Standard manufacturing cost per unit | | | | $520 |

*Total budgeted fixed overhead = 1,000 units × $120/unit = $120,000.

[1] As you recall, in order to explain the total operating-income variance for the period, we also calculated a sales volume variance. Further analysis of this variance is covered in Chapter 16. Please refer back to Exhibit 14.15 for a summary of the variance-decomposition process used by Schmidt each period to explain the total operating-income variance for the period.

**EXHIBIT 15.3**
**Fixed Manufacturing Overhead Costs: Product Costing versus Control**

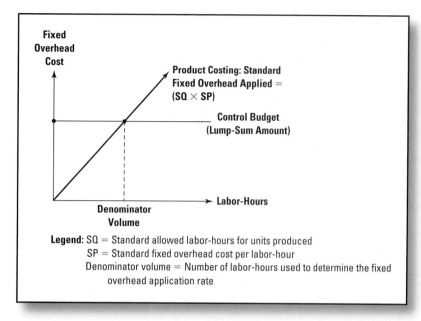

Legend: SQ = Standard allowed labor-hours for units produced
SP = Standard fixed overhead cost per labor-hour
Denominator volume = Number of labor-hours used to determine the fixed overhead application rate

Exhibit 15.1 for variable overhead cost is similar in form to what we could have prepared in Chapter 14 for either direct materials cost or direct labor cost. This makes sense because all three are variable costs.

The situation for fixed costs, however, is different, as reflected in the graph presented as Exhibit 15.3. For cost-control purposes, we see that budgeted (lump-sum) fixed overhead costs are used—see the horizontal line in Exhibit 15.3. At the end of the period, this budgeted amount is compared to the actual fixed overhead cost incurred. The resulting difference is called a *spending variance.* The spending variance for fixed overhead, along with the spending variance for nonmanufacturing fixed costs, is used to explain a portion of the total master budget variance for the period (see Exhibit 14.15).

For product-costing purposes, however, we must "unitize" fixed overhead costs.[2] As indicated in Exhibit 15.3, for product-costing purposes we treat fixed overhead costs *as if* they were variable costs. In the Schmidt Machinery Company case total fixed costs (see Chapter 14) for October 2013 are budgeted at $150,000. In this chapter, we expand the discussion further and break these costs into $120,000 for fixed overhead and $30,000 for fixed selling and administrative expenses. For our example of fixed overhead variances, the standard fixed overhead rate per unit produced is $120 (i.e., 5 standard direct labor-hours per unit × $24 standard fixed overhead cost per labor-hour). Thus, budgeted fixed overhead for the month is $120,000 (i.e., $120/unit × 1,000 units).

## Variance Analysis for Manufacturing Overhead Costs

**LO 15-2**

*Calculate and properly interpret standard cost variances for manufacturing overhead using flexible budgets.*

We assume that Schmidt Machinery Company uses a standard cost system. Thus, at the end of each period the accountant for the company prepares an analysis of the total standard cost variance for both variable and fixed overhead costs. In each case, the goal will be to explain the difference between the actual cost incurred and the cost charged to production (units produced) for the period. As shown later, these variances are recorded at the end of the period in separate variance accounts.

For product-costing purposes, the total overhead variance for the period (also called the total under/overapplied overhead) is equal to the difference between actual overhead

[2] This holds for what is called the *absorption* or *full-cost approach* to product costing, which is currently required for external reporting and for federal income-tax purposes in the United States. An alternative product-costing approach called *variable costing* treats fixed production costs as period costs. Variable costing is covered in Chapter 18. Income-tax rules regarding inventory valuation are contained in IRC Section 263 ("Uniform Capitalization Rules"). Treasury Regulation 1.263 requires that indirect (manufacturing) costs be "reasonably allocated" to outputs.

cost incurred and the standard overhead cost applied to production. For Schmidt, the total overhead variance for October 2013 is $30,880U, as follows:

Total overhead variance = Total actual overhead − Total applied overhead

= (Total variable overhead + Total fixed overhead) − (Total overhead application rate × Standard labor-hours allowed for this period's production)

= ($40,630 + $130,650) − [$36/hour × (780 units × 5 hours/units)]

= $171,280 − $140,400 = $30,880U (i.e., $30,880 *under*applied overhead)

As explained below, the total overhead variance for the period can be subdivided into a set of variable overhead cost variances and a set of fixed overhead cost variances.

## Variable Overhead Cost Analysis

We provide in Exhibit 15.4 a graphical representation of the process used to decompose the **total variable overhead variance** for the period. As indicated in Exhibit 14.8, this variance for the Schmidt Machinery Company in October 2013 is $6,170F, which is the difference between actual variable overhead costs incurred ($40,630) and the standard variable overhead costs charged to production during October [$46,800 = (780 units × 5 standard labor-hours per unit) × $12 standard variable overhead cost per labor-hour]. Note that these figures are obtained from Exhibit 14.8. Note, too, that this total variance, from a product-costing standpoint, could be called *total over/underapplied variable overhead cost* for the period, a point consistent with Exhibit 15.1. Because in October the actual variable overhead costs were less than the variable overhead costs assigned to production, we call the $6,170 figure *over*applied variable overhead.

### Cost Control: Breakdown of the Total Variable Overhead Variance

We see from Exhibit 15.4 that the total variable overhead cost variance for a period ($6,170F in our example) can be broken down into a **variable overhead spending variance** and a **variable overhead efficiency variance,** as follows:

$$\begin{aligned}
\text{Variable overhead} &= \text{\emph{Actual} variable overhead} - \text{\emph{Budgeted} variable overhead} \\
\text{spending variance} &\quad \text{based on inputs (e.g., actual labor-hours worked)} \\
&= (AQ \times AP) - (AQ \times SP) \\
&= AQ \times (AP - SP)
\end{aligned}$$

The **total variable overhead variance**
is the difference between actual variable overhead cost incurred and the standard variable overhead cost applied to production; also called *over- or underapplied variable overhead* for the period.

**Variable overhead spending variance**
is the difference between actual variable overhead cost incurred and the flexible budget for variable overhead based on *inputs* for the period (e.g., actual labor-hours worked).

**Variable overhead efficiency variance**
is the difference between the flexible budget for variable overhead based on *inputs* (e.g., actual labor-hours worked) and the flexible budget for variable overhead based on *outputs* (i.e., standard allowed labor-hours for units produced).

**EXHIBIT 15.4**
**Schmidt Machinery Company Variance Analysis: Variable Manufacturing Overhead**

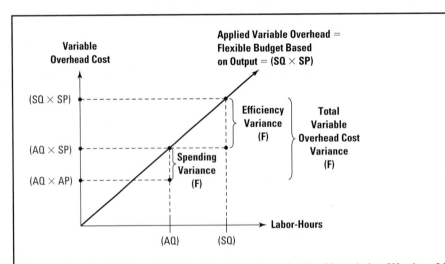

**Legend:** SQ = Standard direct labor-hours allowed for units produced = 5 hours/unit × 780 units = 3,900 hours
SP = Standard variable overhead cost per labor-hour = $12 (see Exhibit 15.2)
AQ = Actual labor-hours worked = 3,510 hours (Exhibit 14.6)
AP = Actual variable overhead cost per labor-hour worked = $40,630 ÷ 3,510 = $11.5755 (rounded)
Total variable overhead variance = Spending variance + Efficiency variance
F = A favorable effect on operating income

From Exhibit 14.8 we see that Schmidt used 3,510 labor-hours in October 2013 to produce 780 units; total variable overhead cost incurred for the month was $40,630. Based on a standard variable overhead cost per direct labor-hour of $12 and an actual variable overhead rate of $11.5755 per labor-hour ($40,630 ÷ 3,510 labor-hours), the variable overhead spending variance for the month is calculated as follows:

$$= \$40,630 - (3,510 \text{ labor-hours} \times \$12/\text{labor-hour})$$
$$= \$40,630 - \$42,120 = \$1,490\text{F}$$

Or

$$= 3,510 \text{ labor-hours} \times (\$11.5755 - \$12)/\text{labor-hour} = \$1,490\text{F (rounded)}$$

Next, we calculate the variable overhead efficiency variance, as follows:

$$\begin{array}{c}\text{Variable overhead} \\ \text{efficiency variance}\end{array} = \begin{array}{c}\textit{Budgeted} \text{ variable overhead} \\ \text{based on inputs}\end{array} - \begin{array}{c}\text{Standard variable overhead} \\ \textit{applied} \text{ to production}\end{array}$$
$$= (AQ \times SP) - (SQ \times SP)$$
$$= SP \times (AQ - SQ)$$

As implied by the graph in Exhibit 15.1, the amount of standard overhead cost applied to production (product-costing purpose) and the flexible budget based on output (cost-control purpose) for variable overhead is always equal. Thus, the second term on the right-hand side of the above equation could have been expressed as "budgeted variable overhead based on outputs."

The standard for direct labor is 5 hours per unit. Thus, the variable overhead efficiency variance for October 2013 is:

$$= \$42,120 - [(780 \text{ units} \times 5 \text{ labor-hours/unit}) \times \$12/\text{labor-hour}]$$
$$= \$42,120 - \$46,800 = \$4,680\text{F}$$

Or

$$= \$12.00/\text{labor-hour} \times (3,510 - 3,900) \text{ labor-hours} = \$4,680\text{F}$$

In sum, the above procedures have been used to break down the total variable overhead cost variance for October ($6,170F) into a variable overhead spending variance ($1,490F) and a variable overhead efficiency variance ($4,680F).

## Interpretation and Implications of Variable Overhead Variances

In traditional accounting systems, such as the system used by Schmidt Machinery Company, only a single activity variable (e.g., direct labor-hours or machine-hours) is used to assign manufacturing overhead costs to outputs. Further, as illustrated above, traditional systems use this single activity variable for cost-control purposes. That is, the flexible budget for such companies is based on a single, usually volume-related, activity variable. This simple approach requires careful interpretation of the resulting standard cost variances for variable overhead. While the formulas for these variances may look the same as those covered in Chapter 14 for direct labor and direct materials costs, the meaning and interpretation of these variances is not the same. In short, the imperfect relationship between variable factory overhead costs and the chosen activity variable (e.g., direct labor-hours) that a company uses to allocate these costs to outputs requires careful interpretation of variable overhead variances.

### Variable Overhead Spending Variance

This variance is attributable to actual spending for variable overhead items *per unit of the activity variable* being different from the standard variable overhead cost per unit of the activity variable. In the Schmidt Machinery Company example for October 2013, the budgeted spending for variable overhead cost per direct labor-hour is $12. The actual variable overhead cost per direct labor-hour was approximately $11.5755 ($40,630 ÷ 3,510 hours). Thus, spending for variable overhead items during the period per direct labor-hour worked was less than standard; for this reason the resulting variable overhead spending variance for the period ($1,490) is labeled *favorable.* The key to understanding this is to remember that the variable overhead application rate refers to the standard variable overhead cost per unit of the activity variable used for product-costing purposes and for constructing the flexible budget for cost-control purposes.

If the variable overhead spending variance is considered "material" or "significant," a follow-up analysis of individual variable overhead items is indicated. Essentially, managers of the Schmidt Machinery Company may want to know *why* spending for variable overhead items per labor-hour worked during the period was different from expectations. To answer this question, a follow-up analysis of each variable overhead cost component is required.

Perhaps the clearest example pertains to electricity costs for the factory. The electricity bill each month is a function of both *quantity* of kilowatt hours consumed and the *price* paid per kilowatt hour. Thus, if there is a spending variance for factory electric costs for the period, we can break down this variance into *price* and *efficiency* components in exactly the same way we did in Chapter 14 where we subdivided the total direct labor or direct materials flexible-budget variance for the period into price (rate) and efficiency (quantity) components.

### Variable Overhead Efficiency Variance

Care needs to be exercised when interpreting this variance. Simply put, the variable overhead efficiency variance reflects efficiency or inefficiency in the use of the activity variable used to apply variable overhead costs to products. In the case of Schmidt Machinery Company, this variable is direct labor-hours. Thus, to the extent that the incurrence of variable overhead cost for Schmidt is related to the number of direct labor-hours worked and the company during a given period uses a nonstandard amount of labor-hours, it will incur both a direct labor efficiency variance (Chapter 14) and a variable overhead efficiency variance (Chapter 15). For October 2013, Schmidt used 3,510 direct labor-hours to produce 780 units of output. The standard labor-hours allowed for this level of output was 3,900 hours (780 units × 5 labor-hours per unit). Thus, the company worked 390 fewer labor-hours than standard for the period. *If* variable overhead is incurred at the rate of $12 per labor-hour worked, then this 390-hour saving would translate to a savings of $4,680 of variable overhead costs.

The variable overhead efficiency variance is therefore related to efficiency or inefficiency in the use of whatever activity variable is used to apply variable overhead for product-costing purposes (and for constructing the flexible budget for cost-control purposes). This reinforces the need to choose the proper activity variable for allocating variable overhead costs. Also, whoever is responsible for controlling the use of this activity variable would be responsible for controlling the variable overhead efficiency variance. In the case of the Schmidt Machinery Company, this would most likely be the production supervisor.

## Fixed Overhead Cost Analysis

The **total fixed overhead variance** is the difference between the actual fixed overhead cost incurred and the fixed overhead cost applied to production based on a standard fixed overhead application rate; also called *over- or underapplied fixed overhead* for the period.

We provide in Exhibit 15.5 a graphical representation of the process used to decompose the **total fixed overhead variance** for the Schmidt Machinery Company for October 2013. For product-costing purposes, the total variance is $37,050U, which is the difference between actual fixed overhead costs incurred ($130,650, assumed) and the standard fixed overhead costs charged to production during October ($93,600 = 780 units × 5 standard labor-hours per unit × $24 standard fixed overhead rate per labor-hour—see Exhibit 15.2). Note, too, that this total variance, from a product-costing standpoint, could be called *total over- or underapplied fixed overhead cost* for the period. When the actual fixed overhead costs are greater than the fixed overhead costs assigned to production, as they were for the month of October, we call the $37,050 figure *under*applied fixed overhead.

### The Production Volume (Denominator) Variance

As noted earlier in footnote 2, for federal income-tax and U.S. GAAP purposes companies must report inventories on a full (absorption) cost basis. This means that in addition to

As we saw in Chapter 5, ABC systems attempt to associate activity costs with cost objects (products, services, etc.). Can recent thinking regarding ABC system design facilitate product-mix decisions? This is precisely the question addressed by Baxendale et al. (2005) in a field study conducted at a 70-unit retirement and assisted-living facility. The facility had 10 two-bedroom units, 41 one-bedroom units, and 19 studio units and delivered four levels of care: short-term (i.e., temporary) care, care-free living, semi-assisted living, and assisted living. The combination of unit-type and care-type resulted in a total of nine cost objects (e.g., an assisted living, one-bedroom unit = 1 cost object).

Given the nature of care, labor-hours (of different types) were used as the activity variables for the ABC system. A key objective of the study was to determine for each of the seven major activities the amount of unused capacity. To do this, the authors had to estimate the

monthly *practical capacity* of each activity. For each of the seven major activities the authors then estimated the *intensity of usage* factor for each of the nine cost objects. Activity costs and the cost of unused capacity for each of the nine activities could then be estimated. The authors next constructed a monthly income statement by service offering.

Data from the monthly income statement plus a set of constraints (e.g., total number of two-bedroom units available) allowed the authors to develop a computer model for determining the optimal short-term product mix for the facility. This model was executed using the Solver function in Excel and relied crucially on the availability of the cost of unused capacity for each of the seven activities.

**Source:** S. J. Baxendale, M. Gupta, and P. S. Rau, "Profit Enhancement Using an ABC Model," *Management Accounting Quarterly* 6, no. 2 (Winter 2005), p. 20.

**EXHIBIT 15.5**
**Schmidt Machinery Company Variance Analysis: Fixed Manufacturing Overhead**

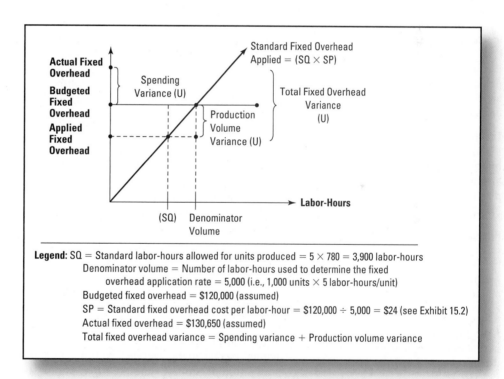

Legend: SQ = Standard labor-hours allowed for units produced = 5 × 780 = 3,900 labor-hours
Denominator volume = Number of labor-hours used to determine the fixed overhead application rate = 5,000 (i.e., 1,000 units × 5 labor-hours/unit)
Budgeted fixed overhead = $120,000 (assumed)
SP = Standard fixed overhead cost per labor-hour = $120,000 ÷ 5,000 = $24 (see Exhibit 15.2)
Actual fixed overhead = $130,650 (assumed)
Total fixed overhead variance = Spending variance + Production volume variance

absorbing variable manufacturing costs, each unit produced must also absorb a share of fixed factory overhead costs. In turn, this requires that fixed overhead costs be "unitized" for product-costing purposes. The following four-step process can be used for this purpose.

*Step 1: Determine budgeted total fixed factory overhead* Fixed manufacturing overhead costs, by definition, do not vary in the short run in response to changes in output or activity. As such, these costs are often referred to as *capacity-related* manufacturing support costs. Thus, once an organization has determined its capacity for an upcoming period (e.g., one year), it constructs a budget for capacity-related costs. In the case of Schmidt Machinery Company, the capacity-related manufacturing costs are estimated at $120,000 per month.

Capacity in the airline industry is measured by "available seat miles" (essentially, number of seats offered multiplied by miles flown). The cost of providing this capacity, in the form of different types of airplanes, is significant. The existence of these capacity-related costs is a major cause of the profitability swings that are associated with the airline industry. Too much capacity leads to operational risk (e.g., failure to achieve breakeven status); too little capacity results in significant opportunity costs, particularly when the economy strengthens. Put differently, airline carriers want full flights, but not so full that they have to turn away high-yielding business travelers. Managing capacity in the airline industry is therefore critical to the financial well-being of airline carriers.

**Source:** S. Carey, "Increases in Airline Capacity Stir Worries That Turnaround Will Stall," *The Wall Street Journal,* September 25, 2010, p. B3.

---

**Fixed overhead application rate**
is a term used for product-costing purposes; the rate at which fixed overhead is charged to production per unit of activity (or output).

**Denominator activity level (denominator volume)**
is the output (activity) level used to establish the predetermined fixed overhead application rate; generally defined as *practical capacity.*

**Theoretical capacity**
is a measure of capacity (output or activity) that assumes 100% efficiency; maximum possible output (or activity).

**Practical capacity**
is theoretical capacity reduced by normal output losses due to personal time, normal maintenance, and so on.

**Budgeted capacity utilization**
represents planned (forecasted) output for the coming period, usually a year.

**Normal capacity**
represents expected average demand per year over an intermediate-term, for example, the upcoming three to five years.

**FASB ASC 330-10-30**
GAAP financial reporting guidance regarding the determination of overhead allocation rates and the treatment of abnormal idle-capacity variances.

*Step 2: Choose an appropriate activity measure for applying fixed factory overhead*
For product-costing purposes, capacity-related manufacturing costs are assigned to outputs based on one or more activity measures (machine-hours, labor-hours, etc.). Usually, this is the same activity measure used to apply variable overhead costs to outputs. The Schmidt Machinery Company uses direct labor-hours as the activity measure for assigning fixed overhead costs to production (output).

*Step 3: Choose a denominator activity level* In order to unitize fixed overhead costs for product-costing purposes, we must choose some level of output (activity) over which the budgeted fixed overhead costs for the period (in this case, $120,000 per month) can be spread. The Schmidt Machinery Company uses 5,000 direct labor-hours per month (i.e., 1,000 units × 5 direct labor-hours per unit) for this purpose. The general term used to describe the level of output (activity) used to establish the standard **fixed overhead application rate** (here, $24 per labor-hour) is **denominator activity level** or **denominator volume**. Several alternatives exist for defining the denominator activity level: two "supply-based" alternatives, and two "demand-based" alternatives.

*Supply-Based Definitions of Capacity* The denominator activity level can be defined in terms of output capacity supplied. In this regard it is useful to think in terms of two alternatives: **theoretical capacity** (the maximum level of activity or output based on available capacity), or **practical capacity** (theoretical capacity reduced by normal employee breaks, machine downtime for maintenance, and other "expected" loss of output). As a rough rule of thumb, you might think of practical capacity as somewhere in the neighborhood of 80% to 85% of theoretical capacity. Thus, the notion of practical capacity is not rigidly defined.

*Demand-Based Definitions of Capacity* It is also possible to define capacity in terms of the demand for the organization's output. For example, we could use **budgeted capacity utilization** (the expected level of activity or output for the upcoming period, usually a year), or **normal capacity** (the average level of demand for the company's product projected over an intermediate-level number of years into the future, say, three to five years).

Given these choices, which activity level should be chosen when determining the fixed overhead application rate? The answer is partly subjective. This is due largely to the fact that the resulting product-cost information can be used for different purposes, ranging from product-pricing decisions, to performance-evaluation purposes, to tax and external reporting requirements in accounting. In terms of the latter, generally accepted accounting principles (GAAP) (FASB ASC 330-10-30: Inventory-Overall-Initial Measurement [previously, *SFAS No. 151:* Inventory Costs—An Amendment of ARB No. 43, Chapter 4]) require that allocation of fixed production overhead to products be based on the *normal capacity* of the production facilities. According to **FASB ASC 330-10-30**, normal capacity is the production expected to be achieved over a number of periods or seasons under normal circumstances, taking into account the loss of capacity resulting from planned maintenance. According to this financial reporting standard, some variation in production levels from period to period is expected and establishes the range of normal capacity. As noted in footnote 2, current income-tax requirements specify only that methods used to allocate indirect costs to inventory should result in reasonable allocations across outputs. Additional guidance for income-tax purposes regarding the use of alternative denominator-volume levels for determining income under the absorption-costing approach is given in Treasury Regulation Section 1.471-11: Inventories of Manufacturers.

Note that different definitions of the denominator volume will result in different fixed overhead application rates, different amounts of fixed overhead costs charged to production, and therefore different amounts for the production volume variance (discussed below). Depending on how variances are disposed of at the end of the year, the financial statements can be affected by the choice of denominator activity level.[3]

Our position is that *for internal reporting purposes practical capacity* be used as the denominator level for setting the fixed overhead allocation rate. We maintain this position for several reasons. One, though not necessarily controlling, the use of practical capacity is consistent with current federal income-tax requirements in the United States. Two, relative to budgeted output, the use of practical capacity volume provides more uniform data over time, which facilitates decision making on the part of management. (That is, managers do not have to continually reevaluate decisions based on changing product-cost data over time.) Third, the use of practical capacity in the denominator is logically consistent with the numerator in the fixed overhead rate calculation. That is, the numerator represents the costs of the capacity supplied and the denominator represents, in practical terms, the amount of capacity supplied.[4] Fourth, and perhaps most important, the use of practical capacity means that current customers and current production will not be burdened with the cost of unused capacity, which would be the case if budgeted output were used and budgeted output is less than practical capacity. From a pricing standpoint, this can help managers avoid the so-called death-spiral effect discussed in Chapter 5 (ABC and ABM). Finally, the resulting production volume variance data (discussed below) can be interpreted, loosely, as the *cost of unused capacity* and therefore can be used for **resource-capacity planning** purposes. This information can facilitate decisions by management as to the appropriate *supply* of capacity-related resources (and associated costs).

**Resource-capacity planning** refers to ensuring an adequate but not excessive supply of capacity-related resources.

*Step 4: Calculate the predetermined fixed overhead application rate* The last step in the process is to divide budgeted fixed factory overhead for the period by the denominator activity level. For Schmidt, this calculation results in a rate of $24 per direct labor-hour, as reported in Exhibit 15.2. Thus, for product-costing purposes each unit produced is assigned $120 of fixed factory overhead (i.e., $24/labor-hour × 5 labor-hours).

In summary, for product-costing purposes a company must choose an activity level over which it spreads budgeted fixed manufacturing costs for a given period. If the company actually operates at the level assumed when the application rate was determined, it will have assigned to production an amount exactly equal to the budgeted fixed overhead for the period. If, on the other hand, the company operates at any level of activity other than the denominator activity level, then it will have applied to production an amount greater or lesser than budgeted fixed overhead. It is this over- or underapplied budgeted fixed overhead that we call the **fixed overhead production volume variance** for the period.

**Fixed overhead production volume variance** is the difference between budgeted fixed overhead for the period and the standard fixed overhead applied to production (using the predetermined fixed overhead allocation rate).

Refer back to Exhibit 15.5. The line emanating from the origin represents the standard fixed overhead cost applied to production. The slope of this line is equal to the fixed

---

[3] As explained later in this chapter, there are different ways of disposing of standard cost variances at the end of the year. One of these methods is to restate cost of goods sold (CGS) and ending inventory amounts to actual costs by recalculating, at year-end, the actual fixed overhead cost per unit of output. Another approach is to allocate (prorate) variances to the ending inventory and CGS accounts. Under either of these approaches, the denominator activity level chosen at the beginning of the year for product-costing purposes during the year will have little or no effect on the financial statements for the year. The choice of denominator volume will, however, affect financial statements when standard cost variances are written off in their entirety to CGS. In short, in some cases the choice of denominator volume will affect an organization's financial statements for the year.

[4] We note that practical capacity can change over time due to changes in manufacturing layout, improvements in worker efficiencies, and so on.

### Managing Capacity Cost through Investments in Flexible Manufacturing

Because automobile manufacturers face high degrees of *operating leverage* (i.e., relatively high levels of capacity-related costs), volume of output is critical to financial success. Further, the ability to quickly adapt production facilities to changes in consumer demand can lead to competitive advantage for an automaker. Smart players in this market are therefore making significant investments in what are called *flexible manufacturing plants,* which enable a company to quickly shift outputs and therefore maintain adequate use of available capacity. Honda alone has, over the past 10 years, invested over $400 million to convert its East Liberty, Ohio, plant to a flexible manufacturing facility that relies heavily on the use of advanced robotics,

which enables the company to reduce setup and changeover costs (and time). How does Honda benefit? When gas prices are relatively low, the company can almost seamlessly switch production to large vehicles, such as its Ridgeline pickup truck. When gas prices are high, that same productive capacity can be easily converted to the production of smaller, more fuel-efficient automobiles. This type of production process stands in stark contrast to traditional manufacturing facilities that are configured to produce a significant volume of a single vehicle type.

**Source:** K. Linebaugh, "Honda's Flexible Plants Provide Edge," *The Wall Street Journal,* September 23, 2008, p. B1.

overhead application rate, which in the case of Schmidt Machinery Company is $24 per labor-hour (or, $120/unit). You will note that the only situation where the total fixed overhead applied exactly equals budgeted fixed overhead is when the output (activity) for the period is 5,000 standard allowed hours (or, equivalently, 1,000 units produced). The production volume variance is therefore defined as the difference between budgeted fixed factory overhead cost and the standard fixed overhead cost applied to production. For October, this variance for the Schmidt Machinery Company is $26,400U, as follows:

$$\text{Production volume variance} = \text{Budgeted fixed factory overhead cost} - \text{Standard fixed overhead cost assigned to production}$$

$$= \$120,000 - [(780 \text{ units produced} \times 5 \text{ labor-hours/unit}) \times \$24 \text{ per labor-hour}]$$

$$= \$120,000 - \$93,600 = \$26,400U$$

Or

$$= SP \times (\text{Denominator activity hours} - SQ)$$

$$= \$24/\text{labor-hour} \times [5,000 \text{ labor-hours} - (780 \text{ units} \times 5 \text{ labor-hours/unit})]$$

$$= \$24/\text{labor-hour} \times (5,000 - 3,900) \text{ labor-hours} = \$26,400U[5]$$

### Fixed Overhead Spending (Budget) Variance

**Fixed overhead spending (budget) variance**
is the difference between budgeted and actual fixed factory overhead costs for a period.

Refer to Exhibit 15.5. We see that, in general, the **fixed overhead spending (budget) variance** is defined as the difference between budgeted and actual fixed factory overhead for the period. For Schmidt Machinery Company, the fixed overhead spending (budget) variance for October was $10,650U, as follows:

$$\text{Fixed overhead spending variance} = \text{Actual fixed overhead} - \text{Budgeted fixed overhead}$$

$$= \$130,650 - \$120,000$$

$$= \$10,650U$$

Note that this is the amount reported in the profit-variance report contained in Exhibits 14.15 and 15.7.

---

[5] Given the way costs are applied to outputs under a standard cost system, the fixed overhead production volume variance can also be calculated as: Standard fixed overhead rate/unit × (Denominator volume, in units − Actual units produced). In the above example, we would have: $120/unit × (1,000 units − 780 units) = $26,400 underapplied. This approach to calculating the fixed overhead production volume variance would, in fact, be the approach used by a company that produces a single product.

## Interpretation of Fixed Overhead Variances

### Production (Denominator) Volume Variance

This variance is an artifact of unitizing fixed overhead costs for product-costing purposes. As indicated in Exhibit 15.5, in and of itself this variance has no meaning for cost-control purposes. However, as we indicated earlier in this chapter, if practical capacity is used to establish the fixed overhead application rate, then the production volume variance can be viewed as a rough measure of capacity utilization.[6] This is because the variance reflects differences between available capacity and actual capacity usage. In short, the reporting of production volume variances over time provides decision makers with information that can be used to manage *spending* on capacity-related resources. For example, consistently reported underapplied fixed overhead (i.e., unfavorable production volume variances) may signal the need to reduce spending on capacity-related costs or motivate action to better utilize the capacity that does exist.

You will note that if the fixed overhead allocation rate were based on expected (budgeted) output, then the cost of unused capacity would be hidden, that is, charged to the units actually produced during the period. To the extent that selling prices are based on indicated costs and budgeted output is less than practical capacity, the use of budgeted output could lead to successively increasing charges (and, therefore, selling prices) over time, a situation referred to as the **death-spiral effect**. In this case, fixed overhead costs get allocated over successively lower outputs.

The **death-spiral effect** is the continual raising of selling prices in an attempt to recover fixed costs, in spite of successive decreases in demand.

When practical capacity is used to calculate the fixed overhead application rate, the cost of unused capacity becomes visible to management through the amount and direction of the production volume variance. To avoid misinterpretations, yet communicate information regarding capacity usage, some companies prefer to report the fixed overhead production volume variance in physical terms only.

Finally, we note the importance of not placing too much emphasis on individual variances because of the interrelatedness of these performance indicators. For example, a production department in a manufacturing facility can generate a favorable fixed overhead production volume variance by overproducing for the period, that is, producing more units than needed to meet sales and target ending inventory requirements. Such practice, of course, runs counter to the JIT philosophy. In this case, a financial performance indicator (production volume variance) might be accompanied by one or more nonfinancial performance indicators (e.g., inventory turnover or spoilage/obsolescence rates).

### Fixed Overhead Spending (Budget) Variance

Fixed overhead spending variances typically arise when the budget procedure for the organization fails to anticipate or incorporate changes in spending for fixed overhead costs. For example, a budget that inadvertently neglects scheduled raises for factory managers, changes

---

[6] For a finer decomposition (breakdown) of the fixed overhead production volume variance, and a discussion of the implications of this breakdown for both managerial accounting and financial-reporting purposes, consult the following: K. Snead, D. Stott, and A. Garcia, "The Causes of Misapplied Capacity-Related Manufacturing Costs and Corresponding Reporting Implications: A Conceptual Perspective," *Journal of Accounting Education* 28 (2010), pp. 85–102.

in property taxes on factory buildings and equipment, or purchases of new equipment creates unfavorable spending variances for fixed manufacturing overhead.

Unfavorable fixed overhead spending variances can also result from excessive spending due to improper or inadequate cost controls. Events such as emergency repairs, impromptu replacement of equipment, or the addition of production supervisors for an unscheduled second shift all would result in unfavorable fixed overhead spending variances for the period.

## Alternative Analyses of Overhead Variances

In the discussion above, we separated the total variable overhead variance and the total fixed overhead variance each into two components. Such an analysis is referred to as a *four-variance analysis of factory overhead.* A general model for performing a four-variance analysis, which combines Exhibits 15.4 and 15.5, is given as Exhibit 15.6. Not all companies, however, want or need to analyze factory overhead costs in this level of detail. Furthermore, a company's chart of accounts may not separate total overhead into its fixed and variable components. In the following sections we discuss alternative, less-detailed, ways to analyze overhead variances.

### *Three-Variance Subdivision of the Total Overhead Variance*

As shown in the top portion of Exhibit 15.6, the three-variance analysis of manufacturing overhead separates the total overhead variance into three components: total spending variance, variable overhead efficiency variance, and fixed overhead production volume variance. That is, in a three-variance analysis, the variable overhead spending variance and the fixed overhead spending variance are combined into a single overhead variance. Thus, the total overhead variance for the period, $30,880U, can be subdivided into a total spending variance, $9,160U ($10,650 unfavorable fixed overhead spending variance + $1,490 favorable variable overhead spending variance), a favorable variable overhead efficiency variance, $4,680, plus an unfavorable production volume variance of $26,400.

**EXHIBIT 15.6**
**General Model: Four-Variance Analysis of Total Overhead Cost Variance**

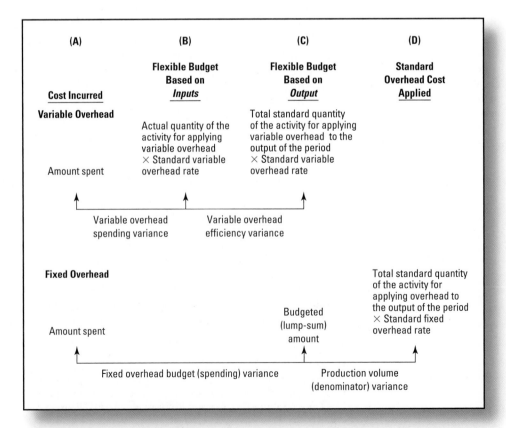

### *Two-Variance Subdivision of the Total Overhead Variance*

Companies that do not separate fixed from variable overhead costs for product-costing perform what is called a two-variance analysis of the total overhead variance. That is, the total overhead variance for the period is broken down into a **total flexible-budget variance for overhead** and a production volume variance (which pertains only to the product-costing purpose of standard costing, as described above). A two-variance breakdown of the total overhead variance is represented in the bottom portion of Exhibit 15.6.

The **total flexible-budget variance for overhead** is equal to the difference between the total actual factory overhead cost for a period and the flexible budget for total overhead based on *output.*

For the Schmidt Machinery Company, the total overhead variance in October, as before, is $30,880U. This variance is broken down as follows:

> Flexible-budget variance
> = Total actual factory overhead cost − Flexible budget for total factory overhead based on output (i.e., based on allowed labor-hours for units produced)
> = (Actual fixed overhead + Actual variable overhead) − [Budgeted fixed overhead + (Standard allowed labor-hours × Standard variable overhead rate per labor-hour)]
> = ($130,650 + $40,630) − [$120,000 + ($12.00/hr. × 3,900 hrs.)]
> = $171,280 − $166,800 = $4,480U

Note that $4,480 is the net amount of the two overhead flexible-budget variances contained in Exhibit 14.15: a total variable overhead cost variance of $6,170F, plus a total fixed overhead cost variance of $10,650U.

The second variance in a two-variance breakdown of the total overhead cost variance ($30,880U) is the production volume variance, as follows:

$$\text{Production volume (denominator) variance} = \text{Flexible budget for overhead based on } \textit{output} - \text{Applied factory overhead}$$

$$= \$166,800 - (3,900 \text{ hrs.} \times \$36.00/\text{hr.}) = \$26,400U$$

Note that the production volume variance is exactly the same as the amount calculated under the four-variance and the three-variance breakdown.

## Summary of Overhead Variances

Exhibit 15.7 provides a summary of the various approaches to the analysis of overhead variances. In each case, the total variance to be explained for the Schmidt Machinery Company for October 2013 is $30,880U. The fixed overhead production volume variance ($26,400U) relates to the product-costing use of standard costs. That is, this variance will occur only if a company uses a standard cost *system* and defines product cost as full manufacturing cost. The other variances can be calculated regardless of whether the firm uses a standard cost system.

Before leaving this discussion, it is important to point out some alternative terminology for the variances to which we referred in the preceding sections. When standard costs are incorporated formally into the accounting records (that is, when a standard cost *system* is used), we have already indicated that the total overhead variance for the period can also be referred to as *total over- or underapplied overhead.* Also, note that the production volume variance is also referred to as the *capacity variance,* the *idle-capacity variance,* the *denominator-level variance,* the *output-level overhead variance,* or simply, the *denominator variance.* The spending variance for variable overhead is sometimes referred to as a *price variance* or a *budget variance.* The total flexible-budget variance for overhead (and by extension the total flexible-budget variance for fixed overhead and the total flexible-budget variance for variable overhead) is sometimes referred to as a *controllable variance.* This latter term is more descriptive of the use of standard costs and related variances for cost-control purposes. For this reason, the production volume variance is sometimes referred to as the *noncontrollable overhead variance.* The important point is that, unfortunately, this is an area where the terminology is not standard. Therefore, you need to keep the above-listed alternatives in mind in any given situation.

**EXHIBIT 15.7**   **Schmidt Machinery Company, Overhead Variance Analyses, October 2013**

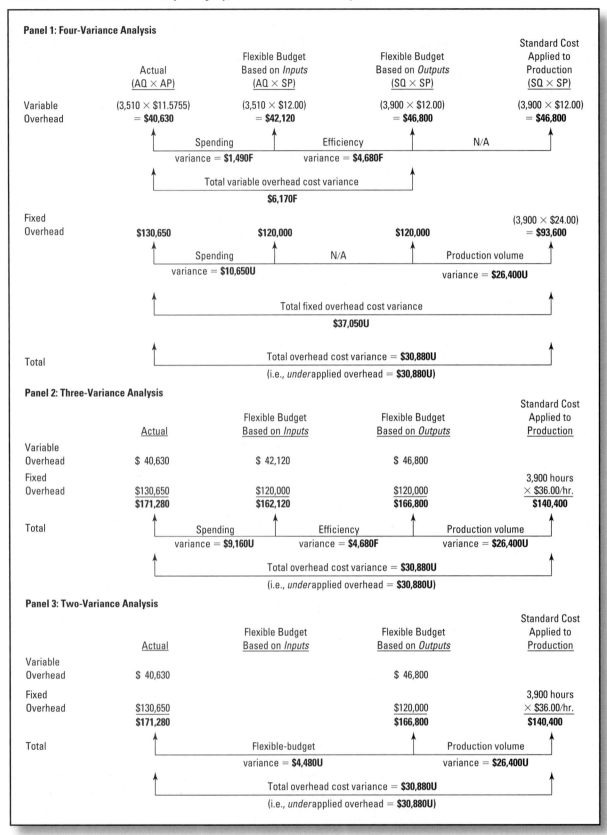

### Supplementing Financial Results with Nonfinancial Performance Indicators

As is the case for the material presented in Chapter 14, the cost variances covered in this chapter are directed at what might be called short-term *financial control*. These variances are calculated through the use of standard cost information and the use of flexible budgets. The overall intent of these variances is to tell management whether the organization is meeting its short-term financial goals. In the case of for-profit entities, financial control looks at the drivers of short-term profit, for example, the organization's ability to control costs for a given level of sales. Students of accounting should keep in mind, however, that financial control should be viewed as part of a larger and more comprehensive management accounting and control system.

The cost variances we cover in Chapters 14 and 15 are inherently limited because they relate only to *short-term* financial performance. As such, they are subject to the same criticisms as any other short-term performance measure. That is, the amount of variance can, at least to some extent, be manipulated in the short run. For example, production volume variances can be decreased by increasing production (thereby absorbing more fixed overhead costs into inventory). Spending variances for fixed overhead items can be affected by managerial choice: cutting so-called discretionary spending on short-term fixed overhead will lead to favorable (short-run) spending variances for fixed overhead costs.

We know, too, that financial measures (such as the cost variances discussed in this chapter and in Chapter 14) don't tell us what is wrong with a process or operation. They can tell us that perhaps something is wrong (because the financial results are not as expected), but we generally need to rely on an accompanying analysis of nonfinancial performance indicators to determine *why* operations are not proceeding as planned. For example, we might monitor quality, customer-response time, the ability to meet production schedules, employee motivation, employee safety, and the organization's commitment to ethical, social, and environmental commitments. In short, if a subunit of an organization is evaluated solely on the basis of its short-term financial performance (e.g., cost control), employees of that unit may ignore the unmeasured attributes of performance, such as quality and manufacturing cycle time. It is precisely for this reason that the notion of a balanced scorecard (BSC) as a strategic management system is of value. We discussed the BSC in Chapter 2 and will discuss it in greater detail in Chapter 18.

Finally, there is a question as to the appropriate role of financial-performance data for operating personnel. Certainly, managers of operating units require periodic financial-performance results. At the operational level, however, employees are probably better served with nonfinancial performance data, presumably on as close to a real-time basis as possible. These nonfinancial measures are likely predictors (i.e., leading indicators) of financial performance. As well, they are expressed in terms that operating personnel can understand. Examples would include actual machine-hours consumed per unit produced, actual energy consumption (e.g., kilowatt-hours) per machine-hour, amount of indirect materials consumed per unit (or batch) of output, percentage of first-pass yields, and so on.

## Recording Standard Overhead Costs

**LO 15-3**

*Record overhead costs and associated standard cost variances.*

### Journal Entries and Variances for Overhead Costs

As noted above and in Chapter 14, a standard cost *system* incorporates standard product costs in the formal accounting records (raw materials, WIP inventory, finished goods inventory, and cost of goods sold). As in the case of direct materials and direct labor, the standard overhead cost of the output of the period is charged to production, while actual overhead costs are recorded separately, in descriptive accounts such as Utilities Payable, Accumulated Depreciation, and Salaries Payable.

Assume that for October 2013, the Schmidt Machinery Company incurred the following variable overhead costs: utilities, $30,000, and indirect materials, $10,630. These actual overhead costs would be recorded as incurred, in entries such as the following:

| | | |
|---|---|---|
| Manufacturing Overhead | 40,630 | |
| Utilities Payable | | 30,000 |
| Indirect Materials Inventory | | 10,630 |

At the end of the month (process cost system) or at the completion of one or more jobs (job-order cost system), the WIP inventory account must be charged for the standard variable overhead cost of the 780 units produced. The standard variable overhead rate is $12 per labor-hour and the standard number of labor-hours per unit is 5. Thus, for October 2013 the appropriate journal entry would be:

| | | |
|---|---|---|
| WIP Inventory [(780 units × 5 hrs./unit) × $12.00/hr.] | 46,800 | |
| Manufacturing Overhead | | 46,800 |

At this point, you can see that the balance in the Factory Overhead account ($46,800 cr. + $40,630 dr. = $6,170F) is the total variable overhead variance for the period.

Assume now, for simplicity, that the actual fixed overhead cost for October 2013 consisted of only two items: $100,000 supervisory salaries plus $30,650 of depreciation expense. The journal entry to record actual fixed overhead costs for the month would be:

| | | |
|---|---|---|
| Manufacturing Overhead | 130,650 | |
| Accumulated Depreciation | | 30,650 |
| Salaries Payable | | 100,000 |

Recall that the standard fixed overhead rate is $24 per standard labor-hour allowed, or equivalently, $120 per unit produced (since there are 5 standard labor-hours per unit produced). The journal entry to charge production with standard fixed overhead cost would be:

| | | |
|---|---|---|
| WIP Inventory [(780 units × 5 hrs./unit) × $24/hr.] | 93,600 | |
| Manufacturing Overhead | | 93,600 |

Similar to entries we made in Chapter 14 for direct materials and direct labor, we would then use the following journal entry to transfer the standard overhead cost of completed production from WIP Inventory to Finished Goods Inventory:

| | | |
|---|---|---|
| Finished Goods Inventory ($180/unit × 780 units) | 140,400 | |
| WIP Inventory | | 140,400 |

After these entries are posted to the ledger, the Manufacturing Overhead account contains the net overhead balance for the period, $30,880 debit (i.e., net unfavorable variance). The component variances calculated using one of the approaches described above could be calculated at this point and used to close out the $30,880 balance in the Manufacturing Overhead account.

Assume that Schmidt Machinery Company uses the four-variance approach for overhead analysis. The appropriate journal entry to simultaneously close out the balance in the Manufacturing Overhead account ($30,880 debit) and record the standard overhead cost variances for October 2013 would be as follows:

| | | |
|---|---|---|
| Production Volume Variance | 26,400 | |
| Fixed Overhead Spending Variance | 10,650 | |
| Manufacturing Overhead | | 30,880 |
| Variable Overhead Spending Variance | | 1,490 |
| Variable Overhead Efficiency Variance | | 4,680 |

## End-of-Period Disposition of Variances

**LO 15-4**

*Dispose of standard cost variances at the end of a period.*

### Variance Disposition

For interim purposes (e.g., preparation of monthly or quarterly financial statements), the standard cost variances calculated in this chapter and in Chapter 14 are typically not disposed of. That is, the variance accounts are carried forward on the balance sheet under the assumption that, over the course of the year, favorable and unfavorable interim variances will offset one another. If interim financial statements are prepared, the cost variances can be shown in a temporary (i.e., holding) account on the balance sheet awaiting ultimate disposition at the end of the year.

At the end of the year, the appropriate treatment for standard cost variances depends on the size (materiality) of the net variance. Assume, for example, that variance data for Schmidt Machinery from Chapters 14 and 15 relate to the fiscal year, not just the month of October. These cost variances are as follows:

| Variance | Source | Amount |
|---|---|---|
| DM purchase price variance | Exhibit 14.15 | $ 4,350U |
| DM quantity variance | Exhibit 14.15 | 10,350U |
| DL rate variance | Exhibit 14.15 | 7,020U |
| DL efficiency variance | Exhibit 14.15 | 15,600F |
| Variable overhead spending variance | Exhibit 15.7, Panel 1 | 1,490F |
| Variable overhead efficiency variance | Exhibit 15.7, Panel 1 | 4,680F |
| Fixed overhead spending variance | Exhibit 15.7, Panel 1 | 10,650U |
| Fixed overhead volume variance | Exhibit 15.7, Panel 1 | 26,400U |
| Net standard manufacturing cost variance for the year | | $37,000U |

### *Net Variance Considered Immaterial*

If the net manufacturing cost variance of $37,000U is not considered to be material, then an appropriate treatment at year-end would be to close all variances to cost of goods sold. If the net variance is favorable, then it is closed out by crediting (i.e., reducing) cost of goods sold. If, as in the present case, the net standard cost variance is unfavorable, the Cost of Goods Sold account is debited (i.e., increased) by the amount of the net variance. The following journal entry closes out the net unfavorable variance of $37,000 to cost of goods sold:

| | | |
|---|---|---|
| Cost of goods sold | 37,000 | |
| Direct labor efficiency variance | 15,600 | |
| Variable overhead efficiency variance | 4,680 | |
| Variable overhead spending variance | 1,490 | |
| Direct materials purchase price variance | | 4,350 |
| Direct materials quantity variance | | 10,350 |
| Direct labor rate variance | | 7,020 |
| Fixed overhead spending variance | | 10,650 |
| Fixed overhead volume variance | | 26,400 |

As indicated in the text, FASB ASC 330-10-30 (paragraphs 1–8) provides financial reporting guidance both for estimating "normal capacity" (which is the required denominator for the fixed overhead rate calculation), and for dealing with abnormal amounts of idle capacity expense, which must be written off to the income statement (and therefore not included as part of inventory cost). Abnormally low production could be caused, for example, by significantly reduced product demand, labor and material shortages, and unplanned facility or equipment downtime. Ewer et al. (2010) provide four examples of how this accounting treatment might be ameliorated. One possibility involves a write-down of the depreciable cost of plant assets that are considered permanently impaired (thereby reducing future cost allocations to inventory). This example of dealing with the cost of idle capacity reinforces differences between cost data for internal (i.e., managerial) purposes and cost data for external (financial-reporting) purposes. Accountants need to be cognizant of the need to generate "different costs for different purposes."

**Source:** S. R. Ewer, C. Keller, and S. K. Olson, "No Equivocating: Expense Those Idle Capacity Costs," *Strategic Finance,* June 2010, pp. 55–59.

---

**EXHIBIT 15.8**
**Annual Income Statement with Write-Off of the Net Manufacturing Cost Variance**

**SCHMIDT MACHINERY COMPANY**
**Income Statement**
**For 2013**

| | | |
|---|---|---|
| Sales (Exhibit 14.4), at standard selling price | $624,000 | |
| **Add: Selling price variance (Exhibit 14.4)** | 15,600F | |
| Net sales, at actual selling price | | $639,600 |
| Cost of goods sold (at standard: 780 units × $520/unit) (Exhibit 15.2) | $405,600 | |
| **Add: Net manufacturing cost variance** | +37,000U* | |
| Total cost of goods sold | | 442,600 |
| Gross margin | | $197,000 |
| Selling and administrative expenses ($39,000 variable + $30,000 fixed) | | 69,000 |
| Operating income (before disposition of sales volume variance) | | $128,000 |

*$50F net variable cost variance (Exhibit 14.8) + $37,050U net fixed cost variance (Exhibit 15.7, Panel 1). Note that in this example the actual variable selling and administrative expense per unit equaled the standard cost ($50 per unit), and that the actual fixed selling and administrative expenses for the period equaled the budgeted amount, $30,000. That is, there were no cost variances for selling and administrative expenses.

Under the assumption that the results for October represent annual results for the Schmidt Machinery Company, its condensed income statement for 2013 is reflected in Exhibit 15.8. As noted above, this treatment of the net variance for the period is appropriate when the amount involved is considered immaterial.

However, some accountants argue that any variance that results from inefficiencies that could in the judgment of management have been avoided, regardless of amount, should be written off against cost of goods sold rather than carried forward on the balance sheet as is the case with the proration method discussed below. Not to do this implies that asset values reflected on the balance sheet (i.e., inventories) necessarily contain the cost of inefficiencies, a situation that some accountants would dismiss as improper.

### Net Variance Considered Material in Amount

If the net manufacturing cost variance is considered material in amount, the net variance should be allocated to the Inventory and Cost of Goods Sold (CGS) accounts. *This allocation should be based on the relative amount of this period's standard cost in the end-of-period balance of each affected account.* This means that the direct materials price variance from Chapter 14 will be apportioned to five accounts—Materials Inventory, the Materials Quantity Variance, WIP Inventory, Finished Goods Inventory, and CGS—based on the amount of this period's standard direct materials cost in each account at the end of the period. The direct materials quantity variance would be allocated only to WIP Inventory, Finished Goods Inventory, and CGS accounts. This is because the materials efficiency variance occurs *after* materials are issued to production.

Note that, as a practical matter, some companies allocate the price variance only to ending inventory and CGS accounts. This is, in fact, standard practice for problems on the Uniform CPA exam.

Any labor-cost variances and variable overhead variances would be allocated to WIP Inventory, Finished Goods Inventory, and CGS accounts on the basis of this period's standard labor and standard variable overhead costs, respectively, in these accounts at year-end. The fixed overhead spending variance should be allocated to four accounts: WIP Inventory, Finished Goods Inventory, CGS, and the Production Volume Variance. The Production Volume Variance, if allocated, would then be apportioned among WIP Inventory, Finished Goods Inventory, and CGS.

Some companies take a simpler approach to the variance-allocation decision. For example, they may use the total end-of-period account balances, rather than this period's standard cost in each end-of-period account, to allocate the net manufacturing cost variance. Other companies, in particular those that have minimal ending inventories, choose to write off against CGS the net variance, regardless of its size, because most of the variance would be allocated to CGS anyway. Thus, under this approach the error of not allocating a portion of the variance to inventories, as well as CGS, is thought to be minimal.

Finally, note that FASB ASC 330-10-30 requires that for external reporting purposes any abnormal amount of "idle capacity cost" (what we have called the *fixed overhead production volume variance*) must be written off on the current period's income statement. One implication of this reporting requirement is that the amount of fixed overhead allocated to each unit of production is not increased as a consequence of abnormally low production or an idle plant.

### The Effects on Absorption Costing Income of Denominator-Level Choice in Allocating Fixed Overhead

**Managing earnings**
refers to the manipulation of reported income.

Before leaving this section, we discuss one additional topic, principally because it deals with the issue of **managing earnings** through the selection of the denominator level used to establish the fixed-overhead application rate. We noted earlier in this chapter that alternative denominator-volume levels lead to different (fixed) overhead application rates, which in turn lead to different product costs, and ultimately to different levels of the fixed overhead production volume variance. The accounting disposition of the production volume variance essentially provides management with an opportunity to smooth, or manage, income as determined under absorption costing.

Under absorption (i.e., full) costing, a portion of fixed manufacturing overhead costs are either absorbed into or released from inventory, depending on the relationship between production volume and sales volume during the period. For example, for a given level of sales, the production of extra units shifts fixed overhead costs to the balance sheet (inventory) so that reported profit increases with increases in production.

633

The opposite is true if inventory is decreasing. For a given level of sales, decreases in production require not only this period's fixed overhead to be released as an expense on the income statement, they also imply the release of some previously capitalized fixed overhead costs (from inventory). Thus, for a given level of sales, absorption-costing income decreases as production decreases.

Note, however, a key point: The amount of fixed overhead costs absorbed or released is affected by the denominator level chosen for the predetermined overhead rate. Thus, the effect of a change in inventory can be intensified or reduced based on how the fixed overhead production volume variance is disposed of at the end of the period. Specifically, this ability to affect reported income is confined to the situation where the production volume variance is written off entirely to cost of goods sold (CGS), as follows:

- If inventory is *increasing,* choosing a *lower* denominator-volume level will *enhance* the increase in absorption costing income due to the deferral of fixed overhead in inventory.
- If inventory is *decreasing,* choosing a *higher* denominator level will *moderate* the decrease in absorption-costing income due to the release of fixed overhead into CGS.

Thus, it is through the interaction of how the fixed overhead rate is set and how the resulting production volume variance is accounted for that provides management an opportunity to manage earnings under absorption costing. The above points suggest that managers can increase short-run operating income by: (1) choosing larger denominator levels if they expect inventory to decrease, or (2) choosing smaller denominator levels if they expect inventory to increase. Note, however, that if the fixed overhead production volume variance is prorated based on the units creating the variance, then the denominator-level choice has no effect on absorption-costing income. This is because prorating this variance effectively changes the budgeted overhead application rate to the actual overhead application rate.

## Standard Costs in Service Organizations

**LO 15-5**

*Apply standard costs to service organizations.*

As noted in Chapter 14, a standard cost system facilitates planning (i.e., budget preparation) and short-term financial control (through standard-cost variance analysis) and aids managers in making decisions such as product pricing and resource management. These benefits, however, are not limited to manufacturing companies. All organizations can potentially benefit from the use of a standard cost system.

Most costs in a service organization are short-term fixed (i.e., capacity-related) costs. The bulk of labor costs are for professional personnel who usually are paid a monthly salary. Variations from one period to the next for salaried personnel should be small or nonexistent. Other overhead costs for these organizations often consist of expenses related to facilities and equipment and are therefore fixed in the short run. Other service-sector companies have minimal labor relative to capacity-related costs. Examples include the airline industry, the shipping industry, and much of the telecommunications industry. The predominance of capacity-related costs for such companies increases the importance of monitoring fixed-cost spending variances and idle-capacity variances.

Furthermore, service organizations have varied measures of output. Exhibit 15.9 lists some measures of output often used by service organizations. As shown in the exhibit, hospitals use patient-days to measure output, colleges and universities use credit-hour

**EXHIBIT 15.9**
**Output Measures for Selected Service Organizations**

| Organization | Output Measure |
|---|---|
| Airline | Revenue-producing passenger miles |
| Hospital | Patient-days |
| Hotel | Occupancy rate or number of guests |
| Accounting, legal, and consulting firms | Professional staff hours |
| Colleges and universities | Credit hours |
| Primary and secondary schools | Number of students |

**EXHIBIT 15.10**
**Standard Cost Sheet
for a Hospital**

Source: Based on Table 14 in *Managerial Cost Accounting for Hospitals* (Chicago: American Hospital Association, 1980), p. 97.

| LANCASTER COUNTY HOSPITAL | | | |
|---|---|---|---|
| Standard Cost Sheet for Pediatrics Floor | | | |
| **Direct Expenses** | **Rate/Price** | **Amount** | **Fixed** |
| Salaries and wages: | | | |
| Supervisors | | | $9,000 |
| RNs | $30.00 per hour | 1.3 hours per patient-day | |
| LPNs | 20.00 per hour | 1.7 hours per patient-day | |
| Nursing assistants | 13.00 per hour | 0.9 hour per patient-day | |
| Supplies—Inventory | 0.20 per unit | 10 units per patient-day | |
| Supplies—Noninventory | | | 300 |
| Pediatrician fees | $ 200 per hour | 0.5 hour per patient-day | |
| Other direct expenses | | | 250 |
| **Transferred Expenses** | | | |
| Housekeeping | $10.00 per hour | 48 hours + 0.4 hour per patient-day + 1.50 hours per patient discharge | |
| Laundry | $ 0.50 per pound | 500 pounds + 15 pounds per patient-day + 30 pounds per discharge + 50 pounds per surgery | |
| **Allocated Expenses** | | | |
| Personnel | $ 0.16 per hour | 242 hours + 3.9 hours per patient-day | |
| Other administrative and general | $ 6.00 per hour | 118 hours + 0.05 hour per patient-day + 1.5 hours per patient discharge | |

production to show their outputs, and so on. However, these output measures seldom are perfect indicators of the outputs of service organizations. For example, Exhibit 15.10 provides a standard cost sheet for a hospital. Patients or their families are likely to place different values on the same number of patient-days, depending on the results of treatments. A patient who is cured of an illness is likely to be more pleased with the care received than is the family of a patient who died of the same disease, although the number of patient-days was identical for both. In addition, the amount and type of work performed by a service organization to complete an output unit often varies from one client to the next or from one patient-day to another. The amounts and types of work performed for two patients with identical heart diseases during their 10-day stays can be vastly different although the number of patient-days is identical and their illnesses are the same.

The differences in operating characteristics between service organizations and typical manufacturing companies make it a necessity to modify standard cost systems before applying them to service organizations.

## Overhead Cost Variances in Traditional ABC Systems

**LO 15-6**

*Analyze overhead variances in a traditional activity-based costing (ABC) system.*

The manufacturing environment has evolved over the last few decades and many new management techniques have been developed during this period to emphasize continual improvement, total quality management, and managing activities rather than cost. These emphases have changed product costing, strategic and operational decisions, and cost-determination methods, as discussed in the preceding chapters. They also influence the ways in which many firms use standard cost systems as management tools, including the preparation of flexible budgets, the selection of performance-evaluation criteria, and the implication of reported variances.

### ABC-Based Flexible Budgets for Control

Because a number of different activities influence factory overhead costs, the accountant needs to carefully select the activity measure, or measures, that will be used to construct the flexible budget for control purposes. The Schmidt Machinery Company, as illustrated thus far in the chapter, uses a single, volume-based, activity measure (direct labor-hours) for allocating overhead costs to outputs and for determining standard cost variances for control purposes.

As described in Chapter 5, more modern cost systems, such as activity-based costing (ABC) systems, apply manufacturing support (i.e., factory overhead) costs to outputs on the basis of multiple activities performed for each product produced. That is, ABC attempts to assign manufacturing support costs to products on the basis of the resource demands, or resource consumption, of each output. To accomplish this, ABC systems use a broader set of activity measures, both volume-related and non-volume-related, in the cost-allocation process.

Cooper has developed a framework, in the form of a hierarchy, for classifying different types of activity measures used in ABC systems.[7] Cooper's framework classifies manufacturing support costs as unit-based, batch-level, product-level, or facilities-level. Unit-based measures are related to output volume and include machine-hours, direct labor-hours, units of output, and units of raw materials. Batch-level activity measures include the number of production setups, the number of times materials and parts are moved during the manufacturing process, and the number of receipts of materials. Product-level activity measures typically relate to engineering support activities and can include things such as number of products, number of processes, number of engineering change orders (ECOs), and number of schedule changes. At the top of the cost hierarchy are facilities-level costs, which are related to the capacity or ability to produce, rather than the variety of outputs, the number of batches produced, or the volume of output.

Exhibit 15.11 illustrates a traditional flexible (control) budget prepared for a company that applies factory overhead cost to outputs on the basis of standard direct labor-hours, similar in nature to the example discussed thus far in this chapter. The master budget in this exhibit is based on a planned output of 3,000 units for the period (1,500 standard labor-hours). The flexible budget is based on the actual output of the period, 2,000 units (or, equivalently, 1,000 standard labor-hours). The company in this example spent 1,200 direct labor-hours to manufacture the 2,000 units. Exhibit 15.12 shows a typical financial report for manufacturing costs incurred during the period.

In contrast, Exhibit 15.13 illustrates a flexible budget for the period prepared under traditional ABC. This representation specifies that manufacturing costs are assigned to outputs on the basis of multiple activity measures. In the present example, three different volume-related activity measures are used (units produced, direct labor-hours, and machine-hours) as well as one non-volume-related activity (number of production setups). Note that there is a single facility-level cost, insurance, that essentially has no well-defined activity variable. Because this cost is not related to volume of output, or number of batches, or number of products, it is allocated to products using a systematic, but essentially arbitrary, method, such as square feet in the factory devoted to the production of each product.

Compared to the simpler control budget presented in Exhibit 15.11, the ABC-based flexible budget presented in Exhibit 15.13 provides more accurate representation of the

**EXHIBIT 15.11   Master Budget and Traditional Flexible Budget for Control**

| Cost Elements | | | Flexible Budget for 2,000 Units | Master Budget for 3,000 Units |
|---|---|---|---|---|
| Variable | Fixed | Cost Item | (1,000 standard direct labor-hours) | (1,500 standard direct labor-hours) |
| $20/unit | | Direct materials | $ 40,000 | $ 60,000 |
| 30/Direct labor-hour | | Direct labor | 30,000 | 45,000 |
| 2/Direct labor-hour | | Indirect material | 2,000 | 3,000 |
| 5/Direct labor-hour | | Repair and maintenance | 5,000 | 7,500 |
| | $ 5,000 | Receiving | 5,000 | 5,000 |
| | 30,000 | Insurance | 30,000 | 30,000 |
| | 75,000 | Setup | 75,000 | 75,000 |
| | | Total | $187,000 | $225,500 |

[7] R. Cooper, "Cost Classification in Unit-Based and Activity-Based Manufacturing Cost Systems," *Journal of Cost Management for the Manufacturing Industry,* Fall 1990, pp. 4–14. The use of these cost classifications results in what can be considered "traditional" ABC systems, which (as we discuss in Chapter 5) can be contrasted with time-driven ABC (TDABC) systems.

**EXHIBIT 15.12**
**Traditional Financial Performance Report**

| Generally Accepted Accounting Principles | | | |
|---|---|---|---|
| | **Actual Cost** | **Flexible Budget Based on Output** | **Flexible-Budget Variance** |
| Direct materials | $ 50,000 | $ 40,000 | $10,000U |
| Direct labor | 36,000 | 30,000 | 6,000U |
| Indirect materials | 3,000 | 2,000 | 1,000U |
| Repair and maintenance | 6,500 | 5,000 | 1,500U |
| Receiving | 3,000 | 5,000 | 2,000F |
| Insurance | 30,000 | 30,000 | — |
| Setup | 50,000 | 75,000 | 25,000F |
| Total | $178,500 | $187,000 | $ 8,500F |

**EXHIBIT 15.13** **Representation of Manufacturing Costs under a Traditional ABC System**

| Data | Activity Measure | Cost Function Variable | Fixed | Flexible (Control) Budget | Master (Static) Budget |
|---|---|---|---|---|---|
| **Operating Data** | | | | | |
| Output | Number of units | | | 2,000 units | 3,000 units |
| Standard Direct labor-hours | | | | 1,000 hours | 1,500 hours |
| Standard Machine-hours | | | | 300,000 hours | 450,000 hours |
| Number of setups | | | | 2 setups | 3 setups |
| **Cost Data** | | | | | |
| Direct materials | Number of units | $20/unit | — | $ 40,000 | $ 60,000 |
| Direct labor | Direct labor-hours | $30/hour, 0.5 hour/unit | — | 30,000 | 45,000 |
| Indirect materials | Direct labor-hours | $2/direct labor-hour | — | 2,000 | 3,000 |
| Repair and maintenance | Machine-hours | $0.01/machine-hour | $ 3,000 | 6,000 | 7,500 |
| Receiving | Number of setups | $1,500/setup | 500 | 3,500 | 5,000 |
| Setup | Number of setups | $25,000/setup | — | 50,000 | 75,000 |
| Insurance | Facility-level | | $30,000 | 30,000 | 30,000 |
| Total | | | | $161,500 | $225,500 |

**EXHIBIT 15.14** **Financial-Performance Report Using a Traditional ABC Model**

| | Cost Incurred | Flexible (Control) Budget | Flexible-Budget Variance |
|---|---|---|---|
| Direct materials | $ 50,000 | $ 40,000 (2,000 units × $20 per unit) | $10,000U |
| Direct labor | 36,000 | 30,000 (2,000 units × 0.5 labor-hour per unit × $30 per labor-hour) | 6,000U |
| Indirect materials | 3,000 | 2,000 (1,000 labor-hours × $2 per labor-hour) | 1,000U |
| Repair and maintenance | 6,500 | 6,000 [(300,000 machine-hours × $0.01 per machine-hour) + $3,000] | 500U |
| Receiving | 3,000 | 3,500 [(2 setups × $1,500 per setup) + $500] | 500F |
| Insurance | 30,000 | 30,000 ($30,000 per period) | — |
| Setup | 50,000 | 50,000 (2 setups × $25,000 per setup) | — |
| Total | $178,500 | $161,500 | $17,000U |

manufacturing costs that should have been incurred for the production of 2,000 units. A financial-performance report for the period, based on the ABC flexible budget, is presented in Exhibit 15.14.

The total manufacturing cost flexible-budget variance for the period, based on a traditional costing system, is $8,500, favorable (Exhibit 15.12). In contrast, the ABC approach yields a $17,000 unfavorable variance for the same period (Exhibit 15.14). Exhibit 15.15 compares these short-run financial-performance reports.

**EXHIBIT 15.15**
**Financial-Performance Reports: Comparison of Traditional and ABC Approaches**

| | Variance | | |
| --- | --- | --- | --- |
| | **Traditional** | **Activity-Based** | **Difference** |
| Direct materials | $10,000U | $10,000U | — |
| Direct labor | 6,000U | 6,000U | — |
| Indirect materials | 1,000U | 1,000U | — |
| Repair and maintenance | 1,500U | 500U | $ 1,000 |
| Receiving | 2,000F | 500F | 1,500 |
| Insurance | — | — | — |
| Setup | 25,000F | — | 25,000 |
| Total | $ 8,500F | $17,000U | $25,500 |

Exhibit 15.15 demonstrates that cost variances identified using a traditional approach (single activity for applying factory overhead) can be misleading. Substantial differences are found in variances for repair and maintenance, receiving, and setups. The traditional costing approach in our example considers repair and maintenance as a cost that varies with direct labor-hours. In contrast, the ABC approach identifies repair and maintenance as a mixed cost with the variable portion of the cost varying with machine-hours. As a result, the cost variance for repair and maintenance decreases from $1,500 unfavorable to $500 unfavorable. The traditional costing approach considers both receiving and setups as fixed costs while the ABC approach classifies these two overhead costs as variable, batch-related costs. As illustrated in Exhibit 15.15, the difference in the net variance between these two approaches is $25,500.

### Flexible-Budget Analysis under Traditional ABC When There Is a Standard Batch Size for Production Activity

When production occurs in a standard (i.e., predetermined) batch size, the accountant can modify the preceding traditional ABC analysis to provide more detailed information regarding the cause of any observed overhead cost variances. In the sections below we discuss these procedures within the context of production-related setup costs.

#### Fixed Setup Costs in a Traditional ABC System

The short-term fixed cost component of setup costs is controlled using the same procedures discussed previously in this chapter. That is, the difference between actual fixed setup costs and budgeted fixed setup costs is called a *spending* (or *flexible-budget*) *variance*. And the difference between the fixed setup costs allocated to production and budgeted fixed setup costs is called a *production volume variance*. The only complicating factor in terms of calculating the latter is the possible need to convert actual units produced to standard number of batches. This is necessary only when setup-related support costs are allocated on the basis of *setup hours* (not number of setups). We make this conversion by dividing actual output by the standard (i.e., budgeted or planned) batch size.

#### Variable Setup Costs in a Traditional ABC System

If output is produced in a standard batch size, we must first convert (as we did above for fixed setup-related costs) the actual output of the period to number of standard batches allowed. We then convert this to the standard allowed setup hours. This latter figure, when multiplied by the standard variable setup cost per setup hour gives us the flexible budget for variable setup overhead costs. As we did earlier in the chapter, we then define the total flexible-budget variance for variable setup overhead cost as the difference between actual variable setup costs and the flexible budget for variable setup overhead costs. Finally, this total flexible-budget variance is decomposed into a *spending variance* and an *efficiency variance* using the procedures discussed earlier.

#### Interpretation of Setup-Related Standard Cost Variances

Management accountants can add value to their organization by accompanying cost-variance data with plausible explanations for these variances. This holds true regardless of whether the organization in question is using a traditional cost system or a traditional

As indicated elsewhere in this chapter, the issue of capacity-resource management is important for a wide range of industries and companies. There are real and significant costs of having excess capacity (i.e., idle capacity and overspending on resources) and insufficient capacity (which results in opportunity costs). Because capacity-related costs tend to be fixed in the short term (and therefore not easily changed), the management of capacity-related spending is of strategic importance to many organizations. Recently, so-called German accounting (GPK) and resource consumption accounting (RCA) have been proposed as alternatives to traditional cost-management systems used in the United States. Among other things, proponents of these systems maintain that such systems provide more decision-relevant information, including information regarding capacity management and resource spending. Both GPK and RCA include the use

of a large number of resource cost centers (far more than the number used in conventional ABC systems), the breakdown of costs into (short-term) fixed and variable components, the use of replacement cost depreciation, a sophisticated ERP system for processing a large volume of data, and the use of practical (or even theoretical) capacity for setting cost-allocation rates. As a student of accounting you should be aware of these alternative cost-information systems.

**Sources:** Carl S. Smith, "Going for GPK—Stihl Moves toward This Costing System in the U.S.," *Strategic Finance*, April 2005, pp. 36–39; Brian Mackie, "Merging GPK and ABC on the Road to RCA," *Strategic Finance*, November 2006, pp. 33–39; B. Douglas Clinton and Sally A. Webber, "RCA at Clopay," *Management Accounting Quarterly*, October 2004, pp. 21–26; Kip R. Krumwiede, "Rewards and Realities of German Cost Accounting," *Strategic Finance* (April 2005), pp. 27–34; Anton van der Merwe and David E. Keyes, "The Case for Resource Consumption Accounting," *Strategic Finance*, April 2002, pp. 1–6.

ABC system. *Fixed-spending variances* for setup activities are likely to be relatively small but could arise if new setup equipment were leased or if the leasing charge actually incurred on setup equipment was different from the planned amount. They might also occur if salaries paid to supervisors or engineers allocated to setup activity are different from those planned. The production volume variance for fixed setup costs can be viewed roughly as a measure of capacity utilization. One limitation of this interpretation, however, is the fact that it does not consider the income effect of reduced output. That is, lower-than-anticipated output volume could have been sold at a higher-than-budgeted selling price, thereby resulting in a net increase to short-term operating profit.

The *variable setup spending variance* exists because the actual variable cost per setup hour was different from the budgeted cost per setup hour. The interpretation of this variance follows the interpretation discussed earlier in this chapter. That is, this variance is partly due to the fact that the actual quantity of individual resources (e.g., energy) was different per setup hour than planned and/or the prices paid for these items were different from planned amounts. The *variable setup efficiency variance* is due to the actual number of setup hours, for the actual output of the period, being different from the standard setup hours allowed. This variance could be due to batch size being different from the planned size and/or a different number of setup hours per batch compared with standard.

## Extension of ABC Analysis: GPK and RCA

**GPK** and **resource consumption accounting (RCA)** are two other sophisticated cost-management systems that are being proposed as alternatives to ABC systems. Both GPK and RCA can be used to allocate indirect (i.e., support) costs across the value chain. Both of these systems rely on a significant number of cost centers and cost-allocation pools—far more than are typically found in an ABC system. As such, both GPK and RCA are usually paired with an enterprise resource planning (ERP) system that tracks and maintains detailed information regarding resources and activities associated with business processes.

GPK is a German cost-management system that attempts to establish a strong relationship between resources consumed and the appropriate cost driver. Notably, GPK distinguishes between flexible and short-term fixed (capacity-related) resources. In contrast, ABC systems typically embrace a long-term or strategic time horizon. Thus, GPK is proposed as a tool for managing short-run financial performance. RCA on the other hand, can loosely be thought of as a combination of ABC and GPK. Therefore, it is a mix of activity-based and direct assignment based on resource consumption. Proponents of RCA maintain that RCA provides increased product-cost accuracy because it only includes the cost of resources used.

**GPK**
is a detailed German cost accounting system, roughly translated as *flexible standard costing.*

**Resource consumption accounting (RCA)**
is a comprehensive cost-management system represented as a cross between GPK and ABC.

Implementation results for RCA and GPK to date suggest that these systems are more effective in large organizations that have highly routine and repetitive operations. Such a context would seem conducive to the construction of the many resource cost pools characteristic of RCA and GPK. It will be interesting to see whether these systems for short-term planning and cost control will gain acceptance in the United States. As indicated in Chapter 5, some U.S. companies have been reluctant to implement a traditional ABC system because of the perceived complexity. RCA and GPK systems would seem to be even more complex. Thus, additional experimentation in the United States is needed before we are able to draw a conclusion regarding the role of these systems. It may be the case that there is room for both ABC systems and more detailed systems such as RCA and GPK. The former may yield relevant information for strategic decision making, while the latter may be used for short-term financial control.

## Investigation of Variances

**LO 15-7**

*Understand decision rules that can be used to guide the variance-investigation decision.*

Identifying and reporting cost variances are the first steps in reducing variances and improving financial performance. Not all variances call for investigation and corrective action, however. In general, the proper response to a variance depends on the causes and the degree of controllability of the variance.

### Causes and Controllability

The causes of variances and the controllability of variances fall into two categories: random and systematic. **Random variances** are beyond the control of management, either technically or financially, and are often considered as *uncontrollable variances*. Many standards are point estimates of long-term average performance. Small variances in either direction occur in operations, and firms usually cannot benefit from investigating or responding to them. For example, prices of goods or services acquired in open markets fluctuate with, among other factors, supply and demand at the time of acquisition and the amount of time allowed to acquire the goods or services. These variances are essentially random and require no management action.

**Random variances**
are variances beyond the control of management, either technically or financially, and often are considered as uncontrollable variances.

**Systematic variances,** by contrast, are persistent and are likely to recur until corrected. They usually are controllable by management or can be eliminated or reduced through actions of management. Systematic variances that are material in amount require prompt corrective action. Among causes for systematic variances are errors in prediction, modeling, measurement, and implementation. Each of these factors has its own implications regarding the need for further investigation or proper managerial action to correct the variance. Exhibit 15.16 classifies variances according to controllability, causes, and indicated action.

**Systematic variances**
are variances that, until corrected, are likely to continue.

**Prediction errors** result from inaccurate estimation of the amounts of variables included in the standard-setting process. For example, management expected a 5% price increase for a direct material when the price increased 10%, or it expected to have adequate $25-per-hour workers available when a shortage forced the firm to hire workers at $35 per hour.

A **prediction error**
is a deviation from the standard because of inaccurate estimations.

**EXHIBIT 15.16** **Cause of Variance and Indicated Corrective Action**

| Controllability | Cause | Corrective Action | Example |
|---|---|---|---|
| Uncontrollable (random) | Random error | None | Overtime wages paid to make up time lost by employees ill with the flu<br>Materials lost in a fire |
| Controllable (systematic) | Prediction error | Modify standard-setting processes | Increases in materials prices faster than expected |
|  | Modeling error | Revise model or modeling process | Failure to consider learning-curve effect in estimating product costs<br>Not allowing for normal materials lost |
|  | Measurement error | Adjust accounting procedure | Bonus attributed to the period paid, not in the period earned<br>Costs assigned to wrong jobs |
|  | Implementation error | Take proper actions to correct the causes | Failure to provide proper training for the task |

**Modeling errors**
are failures in not including all relevant variables or including wrong or irrelevant variables.

**Modeling errors** result from failing to include all relevant variables or from including wrong or irrelevant ones in the standard-setting process. For example, a modeling error occurs when a firm uses the production rate of experienced workers as a standard, although most of its workers are new hires with little or no experience. The unfavorable direct labor efficiency variance that the firm experiences is a result of modeling error, not of inefficient operations. The standard of making 100 gallons of output from every 100 gallons of input material is a modeling error when the manufacturing process has a 5% normal evaporation rate. Corrective actions for both prediction and modeling errors require the firm to change its standard and the standard-setting process.

**Measurement errors**
are uses of incorrect numbers because of improper or inaccurate accounting systems or procedures.

**Measurement errors** are uses of incorrect numbers because of improper or inaccurate accounting systems or procedures. Including bonuses for extraordinary productivity as a cost of the period in which the bonuses are paid rather than the period in which they are earned is a measurement error. Charging overhead incurred for setups based on direct production labor-hours rather than the number of setups is a measurement error. Corrective actions for measurement errors include redesigning the firm's accounting system or procedures.

**Implementation errors**
are deviations from the standard due to operator errors.

**Implementation errors** are deviations from the standard due to operator errors. Unfavorable materials usage variances from using materials of lesser quality than those specified by the standard are implementation errors. The direct labor rate or efficiency variance in an operation that assigned workers with a different skill level than the one called for in the standard is an implementation error. Setting a cutting machine to cut tubes in lengths of 2 feet 9.7 inches, instead of 2 feet 10 inches as required, is an implementation error.

Some implementation errors are temporary and disappear in subsequent periods in the normal course of operations. Other implementation errors could be persistent and reappear until the firm takes proper corrective action. An incorrectly set cutting machine continues to manufacture products with wrong lengths until the problem is corrected. Use of wrong or excessive materials in production, on the other hand, might occur in one or only a few production runs.

## Role of Control Charts

Managers and employees can use control charts to identify random versus systematic variances. A control chart plots measures of an activity or event over time; this widely used tool helps managers identify out-of-control variances. A control chart has a horizontal axis, a vertical axis, a horizontal line at the level of the desirable characteristic, and one or two additional horizontal lines for the allowable range of variation. The horizontal axis represents time intervals, batch numbers, or production runs. The vertical line denotes scales for the characteristic of interest, such as the amount of the cost variance. Upper and lower limits indicate the allowable range of the variance. Variances within these limits are deemed random and no further action is needed unless a pattern emerges.

It is management's responsibility to set upper and lower control limits in control charts. When the control limits are established using a statistical procedure, the chart is called a **statistical control chart**. Please see Chapter 17 for a fuller discussion of the use of control charts.

A **statistical control chart** sets control limits using a statistical procedure.

The chapter appendix examines a cost-benefit approach to the variance-investigation decision.

## Summary

Establishing standard overhead application rates requires selection of appropriate activity measures. These rates can be determined using relatively simple procedures (e.g., a single, volume-related activity measure) or more sophisticated procedures, such as ABC. Recently, both GPK and RCA systems have been proposed as alternatives to ABC systems. The resulting standard-cost data can be used both for product-costing purposes and, through their inclusion in flexible budgets, control purposes.

For control purposes, actual overhead costs (both variable and fixed) are compared to flexible-budget costs. A summary of the overhead cost variances realized by the Schmidt Machinery Company for October 2013 is presented in Exhibit 15.17. This exhibit is a variant of the model presented earlier in Exhibit 15.7. Both exhibits are general in nature

**EXHIBIT 15.17**
**Overhead Variance Analysis Summary: Schmidt Machinery Company, October 2013**

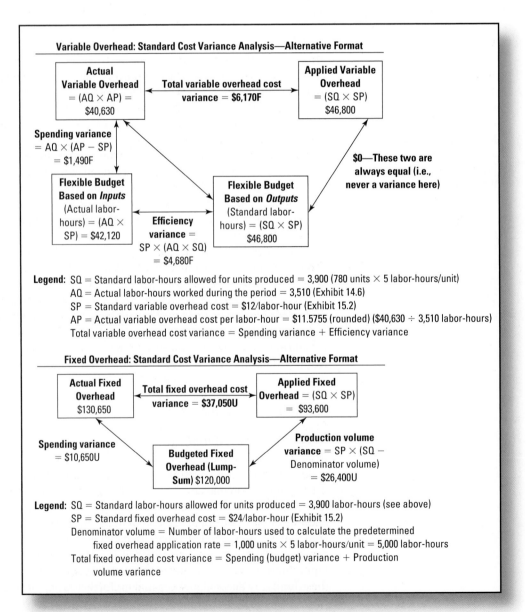

and therefore can be used in a four-variance, a three-variance, and a two-variance approach to subdivide the total overhead variance for the period. Feel free to use whichever of the two models you find more appealing.

As indicated in the top portion of Exhibit 15.17, the *total variable overhead cost variance* (also referred to as the total *variable overhead flexible-budget variance* or the *total over- or underapplied variable overhead cost* for the period) is calculated as the difference between actual variable overhead cost for the period and the flexible budget for variable overhead based on *output* (i.e., based on allowed activity for the number of units manufactured during the period). Variable overhead spending and efficiency variances are components of the total variable overhead cost variance. The variable overhead efficiency variance reflects efficiency or inefficiency in the use of the activity measure used to construct the flexible budget; in the case of the Schmidt Machinery Company, this activity measure is direct labor-hours. The spending variance for variable overhead reflects the fact that during the period spending on variable overhead items, per direct labor-hour, was different from planned spending. As such, this variance reflects both price effects and usage (efficiency) effects. The ability to disentangle these effects, however, requires detailed information about budgeted prices and budgeted quantities of individual variable overhead items.

The bottom portion of Exhibit 15.17 indicates a *total fixed overhead cost variance* for the period, which is also called the *total over- or underapplied fixed overhead for the period.* This variance can be decomposed into a fixed overhead spending variance and a production volume variance. The former variance is defined as the difference between the actual fixed overhead costs and the budgeted (lump-sum) fixed overhead costs for the period. If management desires, this total variance can be broken down on a line-item basis. The fixed overhead production volume variance exists only because of the product-costing need to assign a share of fixed overhead costs to each unit produced. To do this, the accountant develops a fixed overhead allocation rate, which is defined as budgeted fixed overhead cost divided by an assumed level of activity, called the *denominator volume.* If the denominator volume is defined as *practical capacity,* then the resulting production volume variance can be thought of as a rough (and admittedly incomplete) measure of the capacity utilization. Some organizations choose to report the fixed overhead production volume variance in physical terms only.

You should remember that, in practice, different terms are used to describe the same overhead variance. Thus, you are advised in constructing any performance reports to clearly define the meaning of each variance contained in the report.

If a company uses a standard cost system, it records inventory and CGS amounts at standard cost. In such a system, variances from standard cost are recorded in separate accounts. At the end of the year, the company can dispose of standard-cost variances by charging them to CGS. Alternatively, the company can prorate the variances among the cost of goods sold, ending work-in-process inventory, and ending finished goods inventory. For materials price variances, the proration should include the materials ending inventory and materials usage variance. Generally accepted accounting principles (viz., FASB ASC 330-10-30—available at **www.fasb.org**) provide guidance for disposing of fixed overhead production volume variances for external reporting purposes.

Uses of standard cost systems are not limited to manufacturing operations; service firms and other organizations also can benefit from using them. Because operating characteristics of service firms often differ from those of manufacturing firms, modifications might be needed and emphases could be different when using standard costs in a service organization.

Changes in manufacturing environments in recent years have motivated changes in cost systems. Increasingly, companies are using systems with multiple activity measures, both volume-based and non-volume-based. Flexible budgets based on ABC systems provide more accurate data for cost-control purposes. The use of practical capacity for establishing ABC rates yields relevant information regarding the existence and cost of unused capacity. This information can be used over time for resource-capacity planning. For operational control purposes, financial results such as the cost variances reported in this chapter (and in Chapter 14), should be accompanied by relevant nonfinancial performance indicators.

Standard cost variances can be thought of as information signals. Whether to investigate a particular variance is a function of the assumed cause of the variance. Causes of variances can be random or systematic. The former generally require no follow-up, while the latter require some type of intervention by managers. Control charts can be used to isolate random versus nonrandom variances. The appendix discusses the variance-investigation decision under uncertainty.

# APPENDIX

**LO 15-8**

*Formulate the variance-investigation decision under uncertainty.*

## Variance-Investigation Decisions under Uncertainty

Investigation of variances costs time and money. Managers must weigh the anticipated costs of investigation against the anticipated benefits in deciding whether to investigate a particular variance. The purpose of investigation is to determine the underlying cause of the variance in order to take appropriate corrective action.

As noted in the chapter, the states of nature underlying a variance can be either *random* or *systematic.* The alternative actions available to management when facing a variance are either to conduct an investigation or to take no action. With two possible states of nature and two courses of action, there are four combinations, each of which entails a different "cost" to the organization. These four combinations follow:

**IR** **I**nvestigate and conclude that the reported variance is a **r**andom fluctuation. No further action is needed.

**IN** **I**nvestigate and conclude that the reported variance is a result of systematic (i.e., **n**onrandom) causes. Management may need to take corrective action.

**NR** Do **n**ot investigate and the reported variance is a result of **r**andom variations.

**NN** Do **n**ot investigate and the reported variance is a result of systematic (i.e., **n**onrandom) causes.

### PAYOFF TABLE

The cost to the firm for different courses of action and states of nature is likely to be different. Exhibit 15A.1 shows the consequences of alternative management actions under different states of nature. The cost of an investigation is represented as $I$. When the variance is the result of a nonrandom factor, the cost to the firm to correct the variance is $C$. The cost of correction includes the cost to correct the nonrandom factor that led to the variance and the cost of the process being out of control until the variance is corrected. If management decides not to investigate the reported variance and the variance is systematic and persistent, the firm suffers a total cost equal to $L$ (the present value of all losses the firm will suffer before the next decision point).

The decision not to investigate is correct when the variance is a random occurrence. In this situation, the firm wastes no resources at all; it will, however, suffer a loss of $L$ if the reported variance is the result of a nonrandom cause.

Management should also estimate the likelihood that the operation (e.g., raw material usage) is in control or out of control, based on its understanding of the state of nature of the operation. Being "in control" implies that the reported variance is in all likelihood a random phenomenon. Being "out of control" suggests that the reported variance is the result of one or more systematic causes. The estimated probabilities of the states of

**EXHIBIT 15A.1**
**Payoff Table for Variance-Investigation Decision**

| Management Action | States of Nature | |
|---|---|---|
| | **Random** | **Nonrandom** |
| Investigate | *I* | *I* + *C* |
| Do not investigate | none | *L* |

**EXHIBIT 15A.2**
**Payoff Table: Assumed Data**

| Management Action | States of Nature (probability) | | Expected Value (Cost) |
| | Random (90%) | Nonrandom (10%) | |
|---|---|---|---|
| Investigate | $1,000 | $6,000 | $1,500 |
| Do not investigate | 0 | 30,000 | 3,000 |

nature enable management to compute the expected costs for each alternative action. These expected costs then serve as the input to the variance-investigation decision.

Assume that upon receiving a variance report, management estimates the probability to be 90% that the reported variance is a random fluctuation. The cost to conduct an investigation is approximately $1,000. Corrective actions, if needed, will likely cost the firm approximately $5,000, including the loss realized from the process being out of control until the underlying problem is corrected. Assume that the firm will suffer losses with a present value of $30,000 if it conducts no investigation and if the variance stemmed from a nonrandom cause. Exhibit 15A.2 summarizes this cost-related information.

Management has a 90% chance of finding that the variance is merely a random fluctuation and that an investigation, if conducted, would be a waste of time and resources. However, there is a 10% chance that the variance results from one or more nonrandom factors that should be corrected to avoid further losses. With the cost of investigation, $1,000, and the cost of corrective action, $5,000, the firm's total cost will be $6,000 if the investigation finds that the cause of the variance is nonrandom. The expected value (cost) of the decision to investigate is, therefore, $1,500, as follows:

$$E(\text{Investigate}) = (\$1,000 \times 90\%) + (\$6,000 \times 10\%) = \$1,500$$

The states of nature in Exhibit 15A.2 suggest a 90% chance that the variance is random. The firm incurs no cost if it decides not to investigate. However, there is a 10% chance that the variance is a result of one or more nonrandom factors. The firm is likely to suffer a total loss of $30,000 if the variance is a result of one or more nonrandom factors and management allows the variance to continue by conducting no investigation. Thus, the expected cost of the decision to not investigate the cause of the variance is $3,000, as follows:

$$E(\text{Do not investigate}) = (\$0 \times 90\%) + (\$30,000 \times 10\%) = \$3,000$$

The $1,500 expected cost of investigation is lower than the $3,000 expected cost of not investigating. Thus, according to the payoff table, the firm would incur a lower cost (on average) if it were to conduct an investigation to find the cause of the reported variance and then take appropriate action based on the finding of the investigation.

## INDIFFERENCE PROBABILITY

**Indifference probability** is the probability regarding states of nature that makes management indifferent between courses of action (such as whether or not to investigate the cause of a reported variance).

In a form of sensitivity analysis, managers can use a payoff table to determine the probability, called the **indifference probability,** that would make the decision-maker indifferent between investigating and not investigating the cause of the reported variance. As long as the probability for a nonrandom variance is at or below the indifference probability, then according to the payoff table the preferred action is *not* to investigate the cause of the reported variance.

Let $p$ be the probability for a nonrandom variance to occur. Then the probability of a random variance is $1 - p$. Exhibit 15A.3 shows the payoff table.

The expected costs of management actions can be represented as follows:

$$E(\text{Investigate}) = [I \times (1 - p)] + [(I + C) \times p]$$

and

$$E(\text{Do not investigate}) = L \times p$$

**EXHIBIT 15A.3**
**Using a Payoff Table to Determine Indifference Probability**

| Management Action | States of Nature | |
| | Random (1 − *p*) | Nonrandom (*p*) |
|---|---|---|
| Investigate | *I* | *I* + *C* |
| Do not investigate | 0 | *L* |

If the expected cost of each action is the same, it makes no difference to the firm which course of action is taken. That is, for management to be indifferent to either course of action (to investigate or not to investigate), the expected costs must be equal. Therefore, at the indifference point:

$$[I \times (1 - p)] + [(I + C) \times p] = L \times p$$

Simplifying the above equation, we get

$$I + (C \times p) = L \times p$$

Rewritten,

$$p = \frac{I}{L - C}$$

For data presented in Exhibit 15A.2, the indifference probability is 4%:

$$p = \frac{\$1,000}{\$30,000 - \$5,000} = 4\%$$

This result suggests that if the probability is 4% for the cause of variance to be one or more nonrandom factors, it makes no difference (in terms of expected cost) which course of action management takes. The expected final cost of taking either course of action will be the same. The optimal action is to conduct an investigation when the probability for nonrandom factors exceeds 4%. If the probability for a nonrandom cause is below 4%, the optimal action is not to investigate.

## EXPECTED VALUE OF PERFECT INFORMATION (EVPI)

The **expected value of perfect information (EVPI)** represents the maximum amount a rational decision maker would be willing to pay for "perfect information."

We can use the preceding framework to calculate what is referred to as the **expected value of perfect information (EVPI)**, which we define as the maximum amount that a rational manager would pay for *perfect information*. In turn, perfect information is defined as knowledge (i.e., certainty) of whether the process under consideration is in control or out of control (thereby requiring an intervention). In this decision context, EVPI can be thought of as the difference between the expected cost with perfect information and the expected cost without perfect information. To calculate the former, we need to choose for each possible state of nature the *best* course of action (decision) and then multiply the associated "cost" for this decision by the probability of that state of nature occurring. We then sum these resulting expected costs to get the expected cost with perfect information. Thus,

EVPI = Expected cost with perfect information − Expected cost without perfect information

= Expected cost with perfect information − Expected value of cost-minimizing choice under uncertainty

= Maximum amount a rational manager would pay for perfect information

Based on the data from Exhibit 15A.2:

EVPI = [($0 × 0.90) + ($6,000 × 0.10)] − Expected cost without perfect information

= $600 − $1,500 = $900

That is, management would be willing to pay up to $900 for perfect information. This amount represents the long-run (or average) decrease in expected cost.

## Key Terms

budgeted capacity
utilization, *622*
death-spiral effect, *625*
denominator activity level, *622*
denominator volume, *622*
expected value of perfect
information (EVPI), *646*
FASB ASC 330-10-30, *622*
fixed overhead application
rate, *622*
fixed overhead production
volume variance, *623*
fixed overhead spending
(budget) variance, *624*

GPK, *639*
implementation error, *641*
indifference probability, *645*
managing earnings, *633*
measurement error, *641*
modeling error, *641*
normal capacity, *622*
practical capacity, *622*
prediction error, *640*
random variances, *640*
resource-capacity
planning, *623*
resource consumption
accounting (RCA), *639*

statistical control chart, *642*
systematic variances, *640*
theoretical capacity, *622*
total fixed overhead
variance, *620*
total flexible-budget variance
for overhead, *627*
total variable overhead
variance, *618*
variable overhead efficiency
variance, *618*
variable overhead spending
variance, *618*

## Comments on Cost Management in Action

### How Do We Account for Inventory Changes?

The authors of this paper provide a method to incorporate both planned and unplanned changes in inventory levels (essentially, capacity usage) into the profit-variance model discussed in Chapters 14 and 15 of the text. As such, their reporting framework overcomes an inherent limitation of the basic model, which assumes that inventory changes are zero (or, insignificant in amount so that, for analytical purposes, they can be ignored).

How does the revised model presented by Balakrishnan and Sprinkle work? Essentially, we need to make two changes to the model presented in the text: one, prepare a flexible budget based on output (actual sales volume and mix) and the *budgeted* change in inventory; and two, include in all columns of the profit-variance report the cost of planned unused capacity. The difference between the master (static) budget column and the new flexible-budget column is the sales volume variance, the difference between the two flexible-budget columns is equal to the inventory change variance, and the difference between the actual column and the flexible budget based on the actual change in inventory is the redefined flexible-budget variance. In each of the four columns of the variance-analysis report, the cost of unused capacity is divided between planned and unplanned idle capacity. (For additional details, refer to the original article.)

What additional insight does the revised model provide to managers? The authors argue that the revised profit-variance analysis is superior for three reasons: (1) the framework highlights the profit effects of producing for inventory; (2) the framework helps management disentangle the effects on profit of planned versus unplanned (i.e., *a priori* unanticipated circumstances) changes in inventory; and (3) flexible-budget cost variances are computed using *production* volume, not *sales* volume. As such, the revised format can better assist managers in managing capacity-related costs. Finally, the revised reporting format facilitates performance evaluation by separating the profit impact attributable to planned and unplanned changes in inventory, sales volume, and capacity utilization.

Interested readers should also consult Snead et al. (2010), who provide a detailed treatment of the fixed overhead production volume variance. In particular, these authors offer a framework that can be used to partition this total variance into components related to each of the following underlying causes: capacity that is not explicitly planned to be used; capacity currently unused, but acquired explicitly to accommodate future projected growth needs; and capacity not currently used but available to cover short-term seasonality effects. As such, both Balakrishnan and Sprinkle (2002) and Snead et al. (2010) offer enhancements to the basic variance-analysis framework presented in this chapter.

**Sources:** R. Balakrishnan and G. B. Sprinkle, "Integrating Profit Variances and Capacity Costing to Provide Better Managerial Information," *Issues in Accounting Education* 17, no. 2 (May 2002), pp. 149–61; K. Snead, D. Stott, and A. Garcia, "The Causes of Misapplied Capacity-Related Manufacturing Costs and Corresponding Reporting Implications," *Journal of Accounting Education,* June 2010, pp. 85–102.

## Self-Study Problems

(For solutions, please turn to the end of the chapter.)

### 1. Analysis of the Total Overhead Cost Variance

Simpson Manufacturing has the following standard cost sheet for one of its products:

|  |  | Total |
|---|---|---|
| Direct materials | 5 pounds at $2 per pound | $ 10 |
| Direct labor | 2 hours at $25 per hour | 50 |
| Variable factory overhead | 2 hours at $5 per hour | 10 |
| Fixed factory overhead | 2 hours at $20 per hour | 40 |
| Cost per unit |  | $110 |

The company uses a standard cost system and applies factory overhead based on direct labor-hours and determines the factory overhead rate based on a practical capacity of 400 units of the product.

Simpson has the following actual operating results for the year just completed:

| | | |
|---|---|---|
| Units manufactured | 360 | |
| Direct materials purchased and used | 1,800 pounds | $19,800 |
| Direct labor incurred | 750 hours | 20,250 |
| Variable factory overhead incurred | | 4,800 |
| Fixed factory overhead incurred | | 15,800 |

Before closing the periodic accounts, the (standard cost) entries in selected accounts follow:

| Account | Debit (total) | Credit (total) |
|---|---|---|
| Work-in-process inventory | $153,000 | $134,640 |
| Finished goods inventory | 134,640 | 111,690 |
| Cost of goods sold | 111,690 | |

**Required**

1. Determine for the period the following items:

   a. Flexible budget for variable overhead cost based on output for the period.

   b. Total variable overhead cost applied to production during the period.

   c. Total budgeted fixed overhead cost.

   d. Total fixed overhead cost applied to production during the period.

2. Compute the following variances using a four-variance analysis:

   a. Total variable overhead cost variance.

   b. Variable overhead spending variance.

   c. Variable overhead efficiency variance.

   d. Total underapplied or overapplied variable overhead.

   e. Fixed overhead spending variance.

   f. Fixed overhead production volume variance.

   g. Total fixed overhead cost variance.

   h. Total underapplied or overapplied fixed overhead.

3. Compute the following variances using three-variance analysis:

   a. Overhead spending variance.

   b. Overhead efficiency variance.

   c. Fixed overhead production volume variance.

4. Compute the total overhead flexible-budget variance and the fixed overhead production volume variance using a two-variance analysis.

5. Using a single overhead account (e.g., Factory Overhead), make proper journal entries for:

   a. Incurrence of overhead costs.

   b. Application of overhead costs to production.

   c. Identification of overhead variances assuming that the firm uses the four-variance analysis identified in requirement 2.

   d. Close all overhead cost items and their variances of the period if:

      (1) The firm closes all variances to the Cost of Goods Sold account.

      (2) The firm prorates variances to the inventory accounts and the Cost of Goods Sold account.

## 2. Variance Investigation (Appendix)

David Smiley is the manager of Photobonics Manufacturing. He notices that the operation in the last four weeks has had an unfavorable materials usage variance of $25,000. He is trying to decide whether to investigate this variance. If he investigates and discovers that the process is out of control (i.e., not due to a random occurrence and therefore not likely to correct itself), corrective actions will likely cost the firm $5,000. The cost of investigation is expected to be $2,500. The company would suffer an esti-mated total loss (in present-value terms) of $55,000 if the out-of-control operation continues. Smiley estimates the probability the operation is out of control is 60%.

**Required**

1. What are the expected costs of investigating and of not investigating? Should the operation be investigated? Why or why not?

2. What is the indifference probability that the operation is out of control?

3. What is the *expected value of perfect information (EVPI)* in this case?

*Please visit* **http://www.mhhe.com/blocher6e** *to access a narrated, animated tutorial for solving these problems.*

## Questions

**15-1** "As long as the total actual factory overhead cost is not significantly different from the total standard applied factory overhead cost for the period, there is no need to conduct further analyses of the factory overhead variance." Do you agree? Why or why not?

**15-2** What is the difference between the applied variable overhead cost and the total variable over-head cost in the flexible budget? What is the difference between the applied factory overhead cost and the total flexible budget cost for fixed overhead?

**15-3** List causes that could lead to a variable overhead *spending* variance.

**15-4** List causes that could lead to a variable overhead *efficiency* variance.

**15-5** List causes that could lead to a fixed overhead *spending* variance.

**15-6** List causes that could lead to a *fixed overhead production volume* variance.

**15-7** Would the choice of denominator level affect the amount of the fixed factory overhead budget variance? Fixed overhead production volume variance? Explain.

**15-8** What are the justifications for using practical capacity as the denominator volume when calcu-lating the fixed overhead application rate?

**15-9** Why do some firms choose to use a two-variance analysis instead of a three-variance or a four-variance analysis of the total overhead cost variance for the period?

**15-10** Explain two available treatments for disposing of overhead cost variances at the end of a period.

**15-11** What provisions of GAAP (viz., FASB ASC 330-10-30, previously *SFAS No. 151*—available at **www.fasb.org**) pertain to the issue of end-of-period disposition of overhead cost variances? Be specific.

**15-12** What factors should be considered in determining whether or not to investigate a variance?

**15-13** "The direction of a variance (favorable or unfavorable) is irrelevant in decisions regarding whether or not to investigate the variance." Do you agree? Why or why not?

## Brief Exercises

**15-14** Sipple Furniture's master budget for the year includes $360,000 for fixed supervisory salaries. Practical capacity, which is used to set the fixed overhead allocation rate, is 500 units per month. Supervisory salaries are expected to be incurred uniformly throughout the year. During August, the company produced 250 units, incurred production supervisory salaries of $29,000, and reported underapplied fixed overhead of $14,000 for supervisory salaries. What is Sipple Furniture's supervisory salaries budget (spending) variance for August?

**15-15** Baxter Corporation's master budget calls for the production of 5,000 units per month and $144,000 indirect labor costs for the year. Baxter considers indirect labor as a component of variable over-head cost. During April, the company produced 4,500 units and incurred indirect labor costs of $10,100. What amount would be reported in April as a flexible-budget variance for indirect labor?

**15-16** Patel and Sons, Inc., uses a standard cost system to apply overhead costs to units produced. Practical capacity for the plant is defined as 50,000 machine-hours per year, which represents 25,000 units of output. Annual budgeted fixed overhead costs are $250,000 and the budgeted variable overhead cost rate is $4 per unit. Factory overhead costs are applied on the basis of standard machine-hours allowed for units produced. Budgeted and actual output for the year was 20,000 units, which took 41,000 machine-hours. Actual fixed overhead costs for the year amounted to $245,000 while the actual variable overhead cost per unit was $3.90. What was (a) the fixed overhead spending (budget) variance for the year, and (b) the fixed overhead production volume variance for the year?

**15-17** Refer to the data in 15-16. Given this information, what was (a) the variable overhead spending variance for the year, and (b) the variable overhead efficiency variance for the year?

15-18    Refer to the data in 15-16. Provide the correct summary journal entries for actual and applied overhead costs (both variable and fixed) for the year. Assume that the company uses a single account, Factory Overhead, to record both actual and applied overhead. Also, assume that the only variable overhead cost was electricity and that actual fixed overhead consisted of depreciation of $150,000 and supervisory salaries of $95,000.

15-19    Refer to your answers to 15-16 and 15-17 and the journal entries made in conjunction with 15-18. Given this information, provide the appropriate journal entries: (a) to record the overhead cost variances for the period (thereby closing out the balance in the Factory Overhead account), and (b) to close the variance accounts to the CGS account at the end of the period.

15-20    As an extension of 15-19, assume that at the end of the year management of Patel and Sons, Inc., decides that the overhead cost variances should be allocated to WIP Inventory, Finished Goods Inventory, and CGS using the following percentages: 10%, 20%, and 70%, respectively. Provide the proper journal entry to close out the manufacturing overhead variances for the year.

15-21    Refer to the information in 15-16. Calculate and label the following overhead variances for the year: (a) total overhead cost variance, (b) total flexible-budget variance, and (c) fixed overhead production volume variance.

15-22    Refer to the variances you calculated in conjunction with 15-21 and to the information in 15-16 and 15-18. Give the appropriate journal entries to record: (a) actual overhead costs for the year and applied overhead costs for the year (both variable and fixed), and (b) the three manufacturing cost variances calculated in 15-21.

15-23    Refer to the journal entries made in 15-22. Provide an appropriate end-of-year closing entry for each of the following two independent situations: (a) the net overhead cost variance is closed entirely to Cost of Goods Sold, and (b) the net overhead variance is allocated among WIP Inventory, Finished Goods Inventory, and CGS using the following percentages: 10%, 20%, and 70%, respectively.

## Exercises

[LO 15-1]    15-24    **Flexible-Overhead Budgets for Control; Spreadsheet Application**    Johnny Lee, Inc., produces a line of small gasoline-powered engines that can be used in a variety of residential machines, ranging from different types of lawnmowers, to snowblowers, to garden tools (such as tillers and weed-whackers). The basic product line consists of three different models, each meant to fill the needs of a different market. Assume you are the cost accountant for this company and that you have been asked by the owner of the company to construct a flexible budget for manufacturing overhead costs, which seem to be growing for this company faster than revenues are growing. Currently, the company uses machine-hours (MH) as the basis for assigning both variable and fixed factory overhead costs to products.

Within the relevant range of output, you determine that the following fixed overhead costs per month should occur: engineering support, $15,000; insurance on the manufacturing facility, $5,000; property taxes on the manufacturing facility, $12,000; depreciation on manufacturing equipment, $13,800; indirect labor costs: supervisory salaries, $14,800; setup labor, $2,400; materials handling, $2,500. Variable overhead costs are budgeted at $21 per machine-hour, as follows: electricity, $8; indirect materials: Material A = $1, Material B = $4; maintenance labor, $6; and, manufacturing supplies, $2.

### Required

1. Use an Excel spreadsheet to prepare a flexible budget for Johnny Lee, Inc., for each of the following monthly levels of machine-hours: 4,000; 5,000; and 6,000. (*Hint:* Provide in the spreadsheet a separate line for each of the overhead costs for the company.)

2. Generate an equation to represent, within the relevant range, the manufacturing overhead costs per month for Johnny Lee, Inc.

3. Generate a graphical representation of the monthly overhead cost function (within the relevant range) for Johnny Lee, Inc.

[LO 15-2, 15-3, 15-4]    15-25    **Journal Entries for Factory Overhead Costs and Standard Cost Variances; Spreadsheet Application**
Refer to the information for Johnny Lee, Inc., in Exercise 15-24. Assume that in a given month the standard allowed machine-hours for output produced were 5,500. Also, assume that the denominator activity level for setting the predetermined overhead rate is 6,550 machine-hours per month.

Actual fixed overhead costs for the month were as follows: engineering support, $15,500 (salaries); factory insurance, $5,500; property taxes, $12,000; equipment depreciation, $13,800; supervisory salaries, $14,800; setup labor, $2,200; materials-handling labor, $2,400. The actual variable overhead cost per machine-hour worked was equal to the standard cost except for the following two items: electricity, $8.50 per machine-hour; manufacturing supplies, $2.10 per machine-hour. The company used 5,600 machine-hours in December.

The company uses a single overhead account, Factory Overhead, and performs a two-way analysis of the total overhead cost variance each month.

**Required**

1. Calculate the (a) flexible-budget variance, and (b) the fixed overhead production volume variance for the month. (*Hint:* The total overhead variance for the month is $16,660U.)

2. Provide summary journal entries to record actual overhead costs and standard overhead cost applied to production during the month.

3. Provide the journal entry to record the two overhead cost variances for the month.

4. Assume that the variances calculated above represent net variances for the year. Give the required journal entry to close these variances to the Cost of Goods Sold (CGS) account.

[LO 15-1, 15-2]    15-26    **Graphical Analysis—Variable Overhead Cost Variances**    You are in charge of making a presentation to operating managers regarding the meaning of the total overhead variance that appears each month on their performance reports. The controller suggested that a graphical presentation might be an effective way to communicate the essential points to your audience. As such, she provided you with this partially completed graph. This graph represents a situation where: (1) machine-hours are used to apply variable overhead costs to products, and (2) there is both an unfavorable variable overhead spending variance and an unfavorable variable overhead efficiency variance for the period in question. The controller also indicated that she would like you to use the following notation for some of the items to be included in your chart: actual number of machine-hours worked during the period = AQ; standard number of machine-hours allowed for the output of the period = SQ; actual variable overhead cost per machine-hour worked during the period = AP; and standard variable overhead cost per machine-hour = SP.

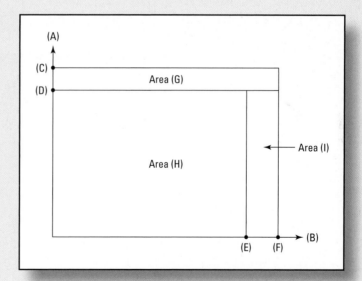

**Required**    Based on the preceding assumptions and information, properly label the following components of the above graph:

1. (A) = ?
2. (B) = ?
3. (C) = ?
4. (D) = ?
5. (E) = ?
6. (F) = ?
7. Area (G) = ?
8. Area (H) = ?
9. Area (I)  = ?
10. Sum of areas (G), (H), and (I) = ?

**[LO 15-1, 15-2]**    15-27    **Graphical Analysis—Fixed Overhead Cost Variances**    (Continuation of 15-26) The controller is satisfied with the graphical representation you prepared in conjunction with 15-26. She thinks this graphical representation of variable overhead variances will be well received by operating managers of the company. As such, she asks you to prepare an accompanying graph for fixed overhead variances. She indicates that you should assume the following in constructing your graph: (1) fixed overhead is applied to production on the basis of standard machine-hours allowed for the output of the period (the standard total overhead cost per machine-hour is $10, while the standard *variable* overhead cost per machine-hour is $6); (2) during the example case, there was a favorable production volume variance and an unfavorable spending (budget) variance for fixed overhead. Based on these assumptions, the controller has asked you to complete the following graph.

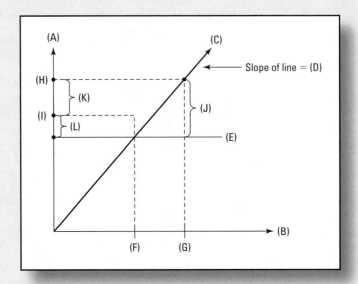

**Required**

1. (A) = ?
2. (B) = ?
3. (C) = ?
4. (D) = ?
5. (E) = ?
6. (F) = ?
7. (G) = ?
8. (H) = ?
9. (I)  = ?
10. Vertical distance (J)  = ?
11. Vertical distance (K) = ?
12. Vertical distance (L) = ?

**[LO 15-1, 15-2]**    15-28    **Flexible Budget and Variances for Depreciation**    Clark Company's master budget includes $360,000 for equipment depreciation. The master budget was prepared for an annual volume of 120,000 chargeable hours. This volume is expected to occur uniformly throughout the year. During September, Clark performed 9,000 chargeable hours, and the firm recorded $28,000 of depreciation expense.

**Required**

1. Determine the flexible-budget amount for equipment depreciation in September.
2. Compute the spending variance for the depreciation expense on equipment.
3. Calculate the fixed overhead production volume variance for the depreciation expense. What is the interpretation of this variance?
4. List possible reasons for the spending variance.

**[LO 15-1, 15-2]** 15-29 **Fixed Overhead Rate; Denominator Level; Two-Variance Analysis** Overhead information for Cran-Mar Company for October follows:

| | |
|---|---:|
| Total overhead incurred | $30,000 |
| Budgeted fixed overhead | $7,125 |
| Total standard overhead rate per machine-hour (MH) | $4.90 |
| Standard variable overhead rate per MH | $3.00 |
| Standard MHs allowed for the units manufactured | 3,600 |

**Required**
1. What is the standard fixed factory overhead rate per machine-hour?
2. What is the denominator activity level that was used to establish the fixed overhead application rate?
3. Prepare a diagram such as the one in Exhibit 15.7, Panel 3, to calculate the following overhead variances for October:
   a. Total flexible-budget variance for factory overhead.
   b. Fixed overhead production volume variance.
   c. Total factory overhead cost variance.

**[LO 15-1, 15-2]** 15-30 **Performance Reporting: The Use of Standard Cost Variance Information** You have been hired recently as the cost accountant for the consumer products division of Zobel Manufacturing Company. The production manager of one of the product lines in this division has expressed concern and dismay over the nature of the periodic reports used to evaluate her performance. In a recent conversation with you she stated: "I feel that the cost accounting reports used to evaluate the financial performance of my product line are misleading and unfair. I have been a line manager for over 15 years and, as such, know how to produce a good product! Because of competitive pressures, our line has even been able to cut raw material costs. It doesn't appear to me that the financial reports we get from accounting reflect these improvements. As well, the reports always contain only negative information—what you guys call *cost variances*. I am frustrated that the managers above use these reports to evaluate my performance and the performance of my product line."

Following is a typical report that is provided to the line manager in question:

**ZOBEL MANUFACTURING COMPANY**

**Consumer Products Division**

**Performance Report: Product Line X**

**December 2013**

| | Actual Cost | Master Budget | Cost Variance |
|---|---:|---:|---:|
| Direct materials | $15,390 | $14,000 | $1,390U |
| Direct labor | 25,680 | 24,500 | 1,180U |
| Factory overhead | 21,500 | 20,000 | 1,500U |
| Totals | $62,570 | $58,500 | $4,070U |

Note: U = unfavorable

**Required** Identify and discuss at least three changes to the monthly performance report that would make the information in the report more informative and less threatening to the operating managers.

**(CMA Adapted)**

**[LO 15-2, 15-3]** 15-31 **Variable Overhead Variances; Journal Entries** The Platter Valley factory of Bybee Industries manufactures field boots. The cost of each boot includes direct materials, direct labor, and manufacturing overhead. The firm traces all direct costs to products, and it assigns overhead based on direct labor-hours.

The company budgeted $15,000 variable overhead and 2,500 direct labor-hours to manufacture 5,000 pairs of boots in March 2013.

The factory used 2,700 direct labor-hours in March 2013 to manufacture 4,800 pairs of boots and spent $15,600 on variable overhead during the month.

**Required**
1. Compute the flexible-budget variance, the spending variance, and the efficiency variance for variable overhead for March.
2. Provide appropriate journal entries to record the variable overhead spending and efficiency variances.
3. Comment on the factory's operation in March 2013 with regard to variable overhead cost.

**[LO 15-2, 15-3]**    15-32    **Fixed Overhead Cost Variances; Journal Entries**    (Continuation of Exercise 15-31) For March 2013 the Platter Valley factory of Bybee Industries budgeted $90,000 of fixed overhead. Its practical capacity is 2,500 direct labor-hours per month (to manufacture 5,000 pairs of boots).

The factory spent 2,700 direct labor-hours in March 2013 to manufacture 4,800 pairs of boots. The actual fixed overhead incurred for the month was $92,000.

**Required**

1. Compute the spending (budget) variance and the fixed overhead production volume variance for March.

2. Compute the fixed overhead flexible-budget variance.

3. Provide appropriate journal entries to record the fixed overhead spending and fixed overhead production volume variances for March.

4. Comment on the factory's results in March 2013 with regard to fixed overhead costs.

**[LO 15-2]**    15-33    **Three-Variance and Four-Variance Analysis of Factory Overhead**    (Continuation of Exercises 15-31 and 15-32) The Platter Valley factory of Bybee Industries uses a three-variance analysis of the total factory overhead variance.

**Required**

1. Use the data given in Exercises 15-31 and 15-32 to compute the total overhead spending variance, the efficiency variance, and the fixed overhead production volume variance.

2. Use your answers for requirement 1 of Exercises 15-31 and 15-32 to determine the spending variances (both variable and fixed), the efficiency variance, and the fixed overhead production volume variance.

**[LO 15-2]**    15-34    **Two-Variance Analysis of the Factory Overhead Variance**    (Continuation of Exercises 15-31 and 15-32) The Platter Valley factory of Bybee Industries uses a two-variance analysis of the total factory overhead variance.

**Required**

1. Use the data given in Exercises 15-31 and 15-32 to compute the total flexible-budget variance and the fixed overhead production volume variance for March.

2. Use your answers for requirement 1 of Exercises 15-31 and 15-32 and determine the flexible-budget variance and the fixed overhead production volume variance for March.

3. What information is contained in each of the variances in a two-variance breakdown of the total overhead variance?

**[LO 15-2]**    15-35    **Factory Overhead Variances; Spreadsheet Application**    J & J Job Shop had the following operating data for its operations in 2013:

| | |
|---|---|
| Budgeted fixed overhead | $21,000 |
| Standard variable overhead application rate | $3 per MH |
| Fixed overhead incurred | $21,400 |
| Variable overhead incurred | $32,500 |
| Practical capacity (5,000 units) | 10,000 MH |
| Actual machine-hours (MH) worked | 9,800 |
| Units produced | 4,700 |

**Required**    Build an Excel spreadsheet for the J & J Job Shop that computes the following:

1. Variable overhead spending variance.

2. Variable overhead efficiency variance.

3. Fixed overhead spending (budget) variance.

4. Fixed overhead production volume variance.

5. Overhead spending variance using a three-variance analysis.

6. Overhead flexible-budget (controllable) variance using a two-variance analysis.

**[LO 15-1, 15-2]**    15-36    **Overhead at Two Activity Levels; Four-Variance versus Two-Variance Analysis**    Patrick Company applies factory overhead based on machine-hours. The company had the following budget for its operation in 2012, which was at 85% level of theoretical capacity:

| | |
|---|---|
| Standard machine-hours (MH) | 21,250 |
| Variable factory overhead | $61,250 |
| Total factory overhead rate per MH | $14.00 |

Patrick budgeted its operation for 2013 at 90% of theoretical capacity. The standard calls for 2 machine-hours per unit manufactured. During 2013 Patrick used 23,000 machine-hours to manufacture 11,000 units. The company incurred $12,000 more factory overhead cost than the flexible-budget amount for the units manufactured, of which $5,000 was due to fixed factory overhead.

**Required**

1. What is the budgeted fixed factory overhead at an 85% level of operation? At a 100% level of operation?

2. What was the standard variable factory overhead rate and the standard fixed factory overhead rate in 2013? (Assume no change in the variable overhead rate. For the variable overhead rate, round your answer to four decimal places.)

3. What is the total factory overhead flexible-budget amount for 2013? (Assume no cost change from 2012.)

4. Compute the following four overhead variances for Patrick Company:
   a. Variable overhead spending variance.
   b. Variable overhead efficiency variance.
   c. Fixed overhead spending variance.
   d. Fixed overhead production volume variance.

5. Compute the following two overhead variances for Patrick Company:
   a. Total flexible-budget variance.
   b. Fixed overhead production volume variance.

[LO 15-1, 15-2]  15-37  **Factory Overhead Analysis—Two, Three, and Four Variances; Spreadsheet Application**  Walkenhorst Company's machining department prepared its 2013 budget based on the following data:

| | |
|---|---|
| Practical capacity | 40,000 units |
| Machine-hours per unit | 2 |
| Variable factory overhead | $3.00 per machine-hour |
| Fixed factory overhead | $360,000 |

The department uses machine-hours to apply factory overhead. In 2013, the department used 85,000 machine-hours and $625,000 in total manufacturing overhead to manufacture 42,000 units. Actual fixed overhead for the year was $375,000.

**Required**  Set up an Excel spreadsheet to determine for the year:
1. The variable, fixed, and total factory overhead application rates.
2. The flexible budget for overhead cost based on output achieved in 2013.
3. The fixed overhead production volume variance.
4. The total overhead spending variance.
5. The overhead efficiency variance.
6. The variable and fixed overhead spending variances.

[LO 15-6]  15-38  **Traditional ABC Costing**  Alden Company uses a two-variance analysis for overhead variances. Practical capacity is defined as 32 setups and 32,000 machine-hours to manufacture 6,400 units for the year. Selected data for 2013 follow:

| | | |
|---|---|---|
| Budgeted fixed factory overhead: | | |
|   Setup | $ 64,000 | |
|   Other | 200,000 | $264,000 |
| Total factory overhead incurred | | $480,000 |
| Variable factory overhead rate: | | |
|   Per setup | | $600 |
|   Per machine-hour | | $5 |
| Total standard machine-hours allowed for the units manufactured | | 30,000 hours |
| Machine-hours actually worked | | 35,000 hours |
| Actual total number of setups | | 28 |

**Required**

1. Compute (a) the total overhead spending variance, (b) the overhead efficiency variance, and (c) the total overhead flexible-budget variance for 2013.

2. Assume that the company includes all setup costs as variable factory overhead. The budgeted total fixed overhead, therefore, is $200,000, and the standard variable overhead rate per setup is $2,600. What are the (a) overhead spending, (b) efficiency, and (c) flexible-budget variances for the year?

3. Assume that the company uses only machine-hours as the activity measure to apply both variable and fixed overhead, and that it includes all setup costs as variable factory overhead. What is the (a) overhead spending variance, (b) efficiency variance, and (c) flexible-budget variance for the year?

[LO 15-6]   15-39  **ABC and Practical Capacity; Spreadsheet Application**   The XYZ Manufacturing Company produces two products, S-101 and C-110. You have obtained the following information regarding the annual manufacturing support (i.e., factory overhead) costs associated with the manufacturing process used to produce these two products:

| Cost Pools | Budgeted Costs | Activity Measure (Cost Driver) | Practical Capacity | Budgeted Activities for the Coming Year | |
|---|---|---|---|---|---|
| | | | | S-101 | C-110 |
| Setup activity | $ 250,000 | Setup hours | 5,000 | 2,500 | 2,350 |
| Packing and shipping | 50,000 | Number of shipments | 2,000 | 1,200 | 775 |
| Inspection | 30,000 | Number of batches | 1,000 | 250 | 700 |
| Machining | 750,000 | Units produced | 150,000 | 100,000 | 40,000 |
| Purchase ordering | 40,000 | Number of orders | 300 | 50 | 110 |
| Total | $1,120,000 | | | | |

Estimated production for the coming year: S-101 = 100,000 units; C-110 = 40,000 units.

**Required**
1. Prepare an Excel spreadsheet that provides activity-based costing (ABC) cost-allocation rates based on budgeted activity units for the coming year. (a) What is the budgeted manufacturing support cost per unit of S-101? (b) What is the budgeted manufacturing support cost per unit of C-110?

2. Using your spreadsheet, recalculate the activity-based costing (ABC) cost-allocation rates, this time based on practical capacity as the denominator activity level. (a) What is the budgeted manufacturing support cost per unit of S-101? (b) What is the budgeted manufacturing support cost per unit of C-110?

3. Compute, for each cost pool listed above, the difference between the budgeted cost for the year and the total cost allocated to production. How do you interpret these variances (differences)?

[LO 15-7, 15-8]   15-40  **Use of Payoff Tables (Appendix); Spreadsheet Application**   Past experience indicates a 75% probability that a reported overhead cost variance is not due to a specific cause (i.e., is attributable to random fluctuations). Past experience also shows that the average cost to investigate the underlying cause of a variance is $1,200 and that the cost to correct an out-of-control process is, on average, $3,800. If the underlying variance is systematic and management decides not to investigate the cause of the variance, the costs are thought to be significant: $28,000.

**Required**   Set up an Excel spreadsheet to answer the following questions:
1. Given the preceding information, what is the expected value of investigating the reported variance?

2. Prepare a payoff table that summarizes the above information. (*Hint:* Your table should include cells for combinations of management actions (investigate vs. do not investigate) and states of nature (systematic cause vs. random event), plus cells to represent the expected cost of each management action.

3. Given the above information, what is the probability level, $p$, for nonrandom variance that makes management indifferent between the two courses of action: investigate versus do not investigate? (*Hint:* You can use the formula in the text to calculate $p$. You could also use the Goal Seek function from the Tools menu in Excel to calculate this number.)

## Problems

[LO 15-2]   15-41  **Capacity Levels and Fixed Overhead Rates**   At its Sutter City plant, Yuba Machine Company manufactures nut shellers, which it sells to nut processors throughout the world. Since its inception, the family-owned business has used actual factory overhead costs in costing factory output. On December 1, 2013, Yuba began using a predetermined factory overhead application rate to determine manufacturing costs on a more timely basis. The following information is from the 2013–2014 budget for the Sutter City plant:

| Plant maximum (theoretical) capacity | 100,000 DLHs |
|---|---|
| Variable overhead costs | $3.00 per DLH |
| Fixed overhead costs: | |
|   Salaries | $ 80,000 |
|   Depreciation and amortization | 50,000 |
|   Other expenses | 30,000 |
| Total fixed factory overhead | $160,000 |

Based on these data, the predetermined factory overhead application rate was established at $4.60 per direct labor-hour (DLH).

A variance report for the Sutter City plant for the six months ended May 31, 2014, follows. The plant incurred 40,000 DLHs, which represents one-half of the company's *practical capacity* level.

| | Variance Report | | |
|---|---|---|---|
| | **Actual Costs** | **Applied*** | **Variance†** |
| Total variable factory overhead | $120,220 | $120,000 | $ (220) |
| Fixed factory overhead: | | | |
|   Salaries | $ 39,000 | $ 32,000 | $ (7,000) |
|   Depreciation and amortization | 25,000 | 20,000 | (5,000) |
|   Other expenses | 15,300 | 12,000 | (3,300) |
| Total fixed factory overhead | $ 79,300 | $ 64,000 | $(15,300) |

*Based on 40,000 direct labor-hours (DLHs).
†Favorable (Unfavorable).

Yuba's controller, Sid Thorpe, knows from the inventory records that one-quarter of this period's applied fixed overhead costs remain in the work-in-process and finished goods inventory accounts. Based on this information, he has included $48,000 of fixed overhead (i.e., three-quarter's of the period's applied fixed overhead) as part of the cost of goods sold in the following interim income statement:

### YUBA MACHINE COMPANY
### Interim Income Statement
### For Six Months Ended May 31, 2014

| Sales | $625,000 |
|---|---|
| Cost of goods sold | 380,000 |
| Gross profit | $245,000 |
| Selling expense | 44,000 |
| Depreciation expense | 58,000 |
| Administrative expense | 53,000 |
| Operating income | $ 90,000 |

### Required

1. Define the term *maximum (theoretical) capacity* and explain why it might not be a satisfactory basis for determining the fixed factory overhead application rate. What other capacity levels can be used to set the fixed overhead allocation rate? Explain.

2. Prepare a revised variance report for Yuba Machine Company using *practical capacity* as the basis for determining the fixed overhead application rate.

3. Determine the effect on Yuba's reported operating income of $90,000 at May 31, 2014, if the fixed factory overhead rate was based on practical capacity rather than on maximum capacity.

4. What capacity level should companies use to determine the factory overhead application rate? Why?

**(CMA Adapted)**

[LO 15-2, 15-4]   15-42  **Ethics and Overhead Variance**   New Millennium Technologies uses a standard cost system and budgeted 50,000 machine-hours to manufacture 100,000 units in 2013. The budgeted total fixed factory overhead was $9,000,000. The company manufactured and sold 80,000 units in 2013 and would report a loss of $9,600,000 after charging the production volume variance to cost of goods sold (CGS) of the period.

Bob Evans, VP–Finance, believes that the denominator activity level of 50,000 machine-hours is too low. The maximum capacity of the firm is between 5,000,000 and 6,000,000 machine-hours. Bob considers a denominator level at half the low-end capacity to be reasonable. Furthermore, he believes that the unfavorable production volume variance should be capitalized (rather than written off against the current period's earnings) because the demand for the firm's products has been increasing rapidly. A conservative projection of the firm's sales places the total sales at a level that will require at least 5 million machine-hours in less than 5 years. Bob was able to show a substantial improvement in operating income after revising the cost data. He used the revised operating results in briefing financial analysts.

**Required**

1. Compute the net effect on operating income of the two changes made regarding fixed factory overhead.

2. Is it ethical for Bob to make the changes? (Consult **www.imanet.org**.)

3. Do the provisions of GAAP regarding inventory costing (i.e., FASB ASC 330-10-30, previously *SFAS No. 151*—available at **www.fasb.org**) bear upon the current issue? If so, how?

4. How does the choice of the denominator volume level in setting (fixed) overhead application rates provide managers with an opportunity to manage earnings?

[LO 15-2, 15-4]   15-43  **Income Statement Effects of Alternative Denominator Activity Levels; Spreadsheet Application**

At a recent board meeting of the Grayson Manufacturing Company, several individuals in attendance expressed concern that they could not understand how the choice of an activity level for determining overhead application rates for the company could affect reported operating profits. The controller, Susanna Wu, told members of the board that, in fact, companies have some latitude in how overhead application rates are set. For example, she told the board that companies can spread budgeted fixed overhead for the period over budgeted (forecasted) activity, normal capacity, practical capacity, or even theoretical (maximum) capacity. All of this didn't resonate well with members of the board, who basically saw the discussion as just another example of how accounting can be used to "manage income" (i.e., "cook the books"). The chair of the finance committee of the board asked Susanna to generate a concise report that would illustrate, in concrete terms, the issues involved. In turn, you have been asked to prepare this report, which will be distributed to attendees at the next meeting of the finance committee. These committee members are adept at using spreadsheets and therefore have requested that your report be distributed to them electronically.

Based on your subsequent discussions with the controller, you come up with the following information that is pertinent to your task:

a. Basis for applying overhead costs to units produced = standard machine-hours.

b. Budgeted fixed overhead (total) = $350,000/year.

c. Standard number of machine-hours per unit produced = 2.0.

d. Sales data: units sold = 11,500; unit selling price = $100.

e. Standard variable manufacturing cost per unit produced = $60.25.

f. Beginning inventory = $0 (0 units).

g. Budgeted operating costs: variable = $4.95/unit sold; fixed = $65,000/year.

h. Actual number of units produced during the year = 12,250.

i. Capacity levels (in machine-hours): theoretical capacity = 30,000 hours; practical capacity = 27,000 hours; normal capacity = 25,000 hours; budgeted (forecasted) usage = 24,000 hours.

**Required**

1. Develop an Excel spreadsheet to calculate the amount of the fixed overhead production volume variance under each of the following denominator activity levels that can be used to set the fixed overhead allocation rate: (a) theoretical capacity; (b) practical capacity; (c) normal capacity; and (d) budgeted capacity usage.

2. Determine the end-of-year balance in the Finished Goods Inventory account (at standard manufacturing cost) under each of the following denominator activity levels for establishing the fixed overhead allocation rate: (a) theoretical capacity; (b) practical capacity; (c) normal capacity; and, (d) budgeted capacity usage.

3. Assume that the practice of the company at the end of the year is to close any standard cost variances to cost of goods sold (CGS). What is the amount of operating profit that would be reported for each of the following choices for defining the denominator activity level for purposes of calculating the fixed overhead allocation rate: (a) theoretical capacity; (b) practical capacity; (c) normal capacity; and, (d) budgeted capacity usage?

4. What conclusions can be drawn based on the preceding analyses you conducted? That is, what is the bottom-line information you would like to convey to members of the finance committee?

5. How do the provisions of GAAP regarding inventory costing (i.e., FASB ASC 330-10-30, previously *SFAS No. 151*) affect the decision as to how the fixed overhead production volume variance (also known as the idle capacity variance) is handled at the end of a period?

**[LO 15-2, 15-4]** 15-44 **Managing Earnings; Denominator Capacity Level; Ethics** Any given cost-information system is a function of a number of design choices. For product-costing purposes, one such design choice relates to how overhead, particularly fixed manufacturing overhead, application rates are determined. As controller for your company, you have been asked to prepare a written presentation for an upcoming meeting of the board of directors of your company. In preparing this assignment, assume that board members are reasonably knowledgeable about financial-reporting issues, but not necessarily about the intricacies of cost accounting systems. As you construct your document, feel free to consult outside references in addition to the material in your text. You can assume that this document is meant as a formal presentation to members of the board. Thus, your writing should be concise, clear, and reflective of proper grammar and construction.

**Required** Prepare, in proper form, a memo for the board that addresses the following issues:
1. Explain how manufacturing overhead rates are constructed in conventional cost accounting systems. Speak separately about fixed versus variable overhead application rates. What key choices must be made in establishing these rates? In answering this question, you might want to discuss differences (if any) between current IRS (income tax) requirements and internal reporting purposes, and between financial reporting requirements (e.g., FASB ASC 330-10-30, previously *SFAS No. 151*—available at **www.fasb.org**) and internal reporting purposes.

2. Your company uses a standard cost system. As such, at the end of each period it must "clean up" the accounts by disposing of any standard cost variances that occurred for the period. You need to educate members of the board about how the variances for fixed manufacturing overhead are disposed of at the end of the period. In your answer, pay particular attention to the following two financial-reporting issues: (a) the requirements of FASB ASC 330-10-30, and (b) how, under absorption costing, reported earnings can be "managed" by choice of the denominator volume used to establish the fixed overhead application rate.

3. Access the Institute of Management Accountant's *Statement of Ethical Professional Practice* (**www.imanet.org/about_ethics_statement.asp**). Which of the stated standards relate directly to the issue of setting (fixed) overhead application rates and the decision as to how any resulting production volume variances are disposed of for financial-reporting purposes? Be specific.

**[LO 15-2, 15-4, 15-6]** 15-45 **Research Assignment: Strategy; Resource-Capacity Planning; Time-Driven ABC** Obtain from your library a copy of the following article: Robert S. Kaplan and David P. Norton, "Mastering the Management System," *Harvard Business Review* (January 2008), pp. 63–77. The authors of this article propose a five-stage management system designed to balance strategy and operations, that is, short-term operational concerns with long-term (strategic) priorities. In general, stage three of the process deals with what the authors call *dynamic budgeting* to include resource and capacity planning. It is this issue that is the subject of the present research assignment. (*Note:* The following additional source, available for download from the Harvard Business Publishing website, may also be helpful: Robert S. Kaplan, "Resource Capacity Planning in the Strategy Execution System," *Balanced Scorecard Report,* Reprint No. B0809A [2008].)

**Required** After reading the above-referenced article(s), please respond to the following questions:
1. Provide an overview of the five-step cycle that comprises the management system proposed by the authors of this article.

2. Stage 3 of the proposed system focuses on "Planning Operations," a significant component of which deals with planning resource capacity. Describe the process of resource-capacity planning within the context of the five-stage management cycle proposed by the authors. For example, discuss the linkage of Stage 3 to both Stage 2 and Stage 4 of the management cycle.

3. The authors indicate that their preferred tool for resource-capacity planning is time-driven activity-based costing (TDABC). Provide a brief overview of TDABC, including how this implementation differs from traditional ABC models. (*Hint:* In addition to the article, refer to Chapter 5 of the text.)

4. Refer to the Towerton Financial example presented on pages 70–71 of the article. How did this organization use TDABC results to determine the level of resource capacity (people and computing) needed to implement its strategy?

**[LO 15-2, 15-4]** 15-46 **Research Assignment: Control of Capacity-Related Manufacturing Costs; Strategy** Obtain from your library (or instructor or course pack, as appropriate) a copy of the following article: K. Snead, D. Stott, and A. Garcia, "The Causes of Misapplied Capacity-Related Manufacturing Costs and Corresponding Reporting Implications: A Conceptual Perspective," *Journal of Accounting Education* 28 (2010), pp. 85–102.

**Required** After reading the above-referenced article, answer the following questions:
1. In general, how does this article relate to the material covered in Chapter 15?
2. What do the authors of this article mean when they use the term "misapplied" manufacturing overhead costs?
3. Into what components do the authors feel the production volume variance should be decomposed? How are each of the component variances calculated and interpreted?
4. According to the authors, what is the connection between the variance-decomposition model proposed by the authors and the managerial control of capacity-related costs?
5. What do the authors of this article indicate are the financial-reporting consequences of their proposed framework?

**[LO 15-1, 15-2, 15-3]** 15-47 **Four-Variance Analysis of Total Overhead Cost Variance** Franklin Glass Works has the capacity to manufacture 200,000 units for the year ended November 30, 2013. The standard cost sheet specifies two direct labor-hours (DLHs) for each unit manufactured. Total factory overhead was budgeted at $900,000 for the year with a fixed overhead rate of $3 per unit. Both fixed and variable overhead are assigned to products on the basis of standard DLHs. The actual data for the year ended November 30, 2013, follow:

| | |
|---|---|
| Units manufactured | 198,000 |
| Direct labor-hours (DLHs) worked | 440,000 |
| Variable factory overhead incurred | $352,000 |
| Fixed factory overhead incurred | $575,000 |

**Required**
1. Determine the following for the year just completed:
   a. Total standard hours allowed for the units manufactured.
   b. Variable overhead efficiency variance.
   c. Variable overhead spending variance.
   d. Fixed overhead spending variance.
   e. Total fixed overhead cost applied to units manufactured.
   f. Production volume variance.
2. Prepare appropriate journal entries for the four-variance analysis. Assume the company uses only two overhead accounts, one for variable overhead, the other for fixed overhead.
3. Provide a concise explanation of each of the four overhead variances you calculated.

**[LO 15-4]** 15-48 **Proration of Variances** Butrico Manufacturing Corporation uses a standard cost system, records materials price variances when raw materials are purchased, and prorates all variances at year-end. Variances associated with direct materials are prorated based on the balances of direct materials in the appropriate accounts, and variances associated with direct labor and manufacturing overhead are prorated to Finished Goods Inventory and CGS on the basis of the relative direct labor cost in these accounts at year-end.

The following Butrico information is for the year ended December 31:

The company had no beginning inventories and no ending work-in-process (WIP) inventory. It applies manufacturing overhead at 80% of standard direct labor cost.

| | |
|---|---|
| Finished goods inventory at 12/31: | |
|     Direct materials | $ 87,000 |
|     Direct labor | 130,500 |
|     Applied manufacturing overhead | 104,400 |
| Raw materials inventory at 12/31 | 65,000 |

Cost of goods sold for the year ended 12/31:

| | |
|---|---:|
| Direct materials | $348,000 |
| Direct labor | 739,500 |
| Applied manufacturing overhead | 591,600 |
| Direct materials price variance (unfavorable) | 10,000 |
| Direct materials usage variance (favorable) | 15,000 |
| Direct labor rate variance (unfavorable) | 20,000 |
| Direct labor efficiency variance (favorable) | 5,000 |
| Actual manufacturing overhead incurred | 690,000 |

**Required**

1. Compute the amount of direct materials price variance to be prorated to finished goods inventory at December 31.

2. Compute the total amount of direct materials cost in finished goods inventory at December 31, after all materials variances have been prorated. (*Hint:* The correct amount is $85,732.)

3. Compute the total amount of direct labor cost in finished goods inventory at December 31, after all variances have been prorated. (*Hint:* The correct amount is $132,750.)

4. Compute the total cost of goods sold for the year ended December 31, after all variances have been prorated. (*Hint:* The correct amount is $1,681,678.)

5. How, if at all, would the provisions of GAAP regarding inventory costing (i.e., FASB ASC 330-10-30, previously *SFAS No. 151*—available at **www.fasb.org**) bear upon the end-of-period variance-disposition question?

6. Under absorption costing, explain how reported earnings can be managed by the method used to dispose of (fixed) overhead cost variances at the end of the period.

**(CMA Adapted)**

**[LO 15-1, 15-2, 15-3, 15-4]**    15-49    **Four-Variance Analysis; Journal Entries**    Edney Company employs a standard cost system for product costing. The standard cost of its product is

| | |
|---|---:|
| Raw materials | $14.50 |
| Direct labor (2 direct labor-hours × $8) | 16.00 |
| Manufacturing overhead (2 direct labor-hours × $11) | 22.00 |
| Total standard cost | $52.50 |

The manufacturing overhead rate is based on a normal capacity level of 600,000 direct labor-hours. (Normal capacity is defined as the level of capacity needed to satisfy average customer demand over a period of two to four years. Operationally, this level of capacity would take into consideration sales trends, and both seasonal and cyclical factors affecting demand.) The firm has the following annual manufacturing overhead budget:

| | |
|---|---:|
| Variable | $3,600,000 |
| Fixed | 3,000,000 |
| | $6,600,000 |

Edney spent $433,350 direct labor cost for 53,500 direct labor-hours to manufacture 26,000 units in November. Costs incurred in November include $260,000 for fixed manufacturing overhead and $315,000 for variable manufacturing overhead.

**Required**

1. Determine each of the following for November:
   a. The variable overhead spending variance.
   b. The variable overhead efficiency variance.
   c. The fixed overhead spending (budget) variance.
   d. The fixed overhead production volume variance.
   e. The total amount of under- or overapplied manufacturing overhead.

2. Provide appropriate journal entries to record actual overhead costs, standard overhead costs applied to production, and all four overhead variances.

3. Give the appropriate journal entry to close all overhead variances to the cost of goods sold (CGS) account. (Assume the variances you calculated above are for the year, not the month.)

4. How, if at all, would the provisions of GAAP regarding inventory costing (FASB ASC 330-10-30, previously *SFAS No. 151*—available at **www.fasb.org**) bear upon the end-of-period variance-disposition question?

5. Explain how reported earnings under absorption costing can be managed by the method used to dispose of (fixed) overhead cost variances at the end of the period.

**(CMA Adapted)**

[LO 15-2, 15-4]   15-50   **Research Assignment: Control of Overhead Costs; Strategy**   Obtain from your library (or instructor or course pack, as appropriate) a copy of the following article: K. P. Coyne, S. T. Coyne, and E. J. Coyne, Jr., "When You've Got to Cut Costs Now: A Practical Guide to Reducing Overhead by 10%, 20%, or (wince) 30%," *Harvard Business Review* (May 2010), pp. 74–82.

**Required**   After reading the above-referenced article, answer the following questions:
1. In general, how does this article relate to the material covered in Chapter 15?

2. The authors state (p. 75) that "administrative cost-reduction opportunities follow similar patterns everywhere." What two major conclusions do the authors offer, based on the accumulated experience in implementing successful cost-cutting programs?

3. The authors of this article also state (p. 75) that cost-reduction goals typically require "ten or more actions." For each of the three classifications of cost-reduction goals discussed in the article, provide examples of specific actions that managers can pursue in an attempt to meet the stated cost-reduction goal.

4. Provide a concise summary of the authors' recommended approach for determining the "right level of overhead."

[LO 15-5, 15-6]   15-51   **ABC Data; Capacity-Resource Planning; Nonfinancial Performance Indicators**   National Computer (a fictitious company) competes at the retail level on the basis of customer service. It has invested significant resources in its Customer Service Department. Recently, the company has installed a traditional activity-based costing (ABC) system to provide better-quality cost information for pricing, decision making, and customer-profitability analysis. Most of the costs of running the Customer Service Department are considered committed (i.e., short-term fixed) costs (principally, personnel and equipment costs). The budgeted cost for the upcoming period is $1 million. Activity analysis, recently conducted when the ABC system was implemented, revealed the following information:

| Activities | Percentage of Employee Time | Estimated (Budgeted) Cost-Driver Quantity |
| --- | --- | --- |
| Handling customer orders | 80% | 8,000 customer orders |
| Processing customer complaints | 10 | 400 customer complaints |
| Conducting customer credit checks | 10 | 500 credit checks |

**Required**
1. Based on the preceding information, calculate the activity-cost driver (ABC) rates for each of the three activities performed by the Customer Service Department. Assume that during the period actual cost-driver activity levels are exactly as planned. Under this situation, what is the total cost assigned to each of the three activities? For each activity, what is the cost of unused capacity?

2. Suppose that during the upcoming period, activities (i.e., cost-driver quantities) are exactly as budgeted. Suppose, too, that the practical capacity level for each of these activities is 10,000 customer orders, 500 customer complaints, and 500 credit checks. Using cost-driver rates based on practical capacity levels for each activity, what is the cost assigned to each of the three activities? Also, what is the unused capacity and the associated cost of unused capacity for each activity?

3. What actions might the management of National Computer take in response to the analysis conducted in response to (2) above?

4. What nonfinancial performance indicators do you recommend National Computer monitor in terms of its Customer Service Department? In general, how are these indicators chosen? (That is, how do you justify the items you are recommending?)

**[LO 15-2, 15-4, 15-6]**  15-52  **Managing Resource Capacity through Traditional Activity-Based Costing (ABC)**  This assignment deals with the application of a traditional ABC system to the problem of measuring and managing the cost of capacity. As controller for Zen Company, you've been asked to provide input regarding the appropriate level of resource capacity needed to support the strategic initiatives of the company, as indentified in the company's strategic planning system (e.g., its balanced scorecard system and associated strategy maps—see Chapter 18).

Because of the focus of the company on exceptional customer service, you've decided to run a pilot test by focusing on a single activity: *handling customer orders.* During the most recent year, total resource costs of this activity were $500,000. You've determined that, during the year, 7,000 customer orders were handled by the company. Observations of the process and your own interviews with knowledgeable personnel indicate that the current level of resource spending in this area provides the capacity to efficiently process approximately 10,000 customer orders. (That is, the practical capacity of resources supplied is 10,000 customer orders.) An analysis of past accounting data and the application of the cost-estimation techniques covered in Chapter 8 suggest that resource spending for this activity in the coming year will be approximately $560,000. The company expects to handle 8,000 customer orders during the coming year. Your basic task is to determine how the use of ABC data can facilitate decisions regarding the appropriate level of spending to support the customer-ordering process.

**Required**
1. Distinguish between short-term variable costs and short-term fixed (i.e., capacity-related) costs. For many organizations today, including the Zen Company, which type of costs characterize support costs, such as the cost of handling customer orders?

2. ABC fundamentally deals with the issue of assigning costs to activities, then activity-based costs to outputs such as products, services, or customers. From the start, however, you are a bit bewildered: which data at your disposal should be used to calculate the cost of handling a customer order? Show calculations. Include in your answer an explanation of the term *practical capacity* and a short discussion of what is referred to as the *death-spiral effect.*

3. How can the use of ABC data assist managers in managing spending on resource capacity? (*Hint:* Be sure to address the issue of the *cost of unused capacity.*) Why is the management of resource capacity costs of strategic importance to companies such as Zen?

4. Assume that Zen, in an effort to improve the process of handling customer orders, implements a TQM or other initiative, the effect of which is to increase the number of orders that can be handled efficiently. As a result, the practical capacity of the process increases to approximately 14,000 orders per year. Has the cost of handling a customer order changed in response to the TQM initiative? (Assume a total cost, as before, of $560,000.) Assume, as before, that the company in the coming year expects to process 8,000 customer orders. After the TQM implementation, what is the estimated cost of unused capacity?

5. What strategies are available to managers for reducing or eliminating unused capacity?

6. What recommendation would you make to management regarding how the cost of unused capacity should be assigned?

**[LO 15-5]**  15-53  **Two-Variance Analysis: Service Company Example**  International Finance Incorporated issues letters of credit to importers for overseas purchases. The company charges a nonrefundable application fee of $3,000 and, on approval, an additional service fee of 2% of the amount of credit requested.

The firm's budget for the year just completed included fixed expenses for office salaries and wages of $500,000, leasing office space and equipment of $50,000, and utilities and other operating expenses of $10,000. In addition, the budget also included variable expenses for supplies and other variable overhead costs of $1,000,000. The company estimated these variable overhead costs to be $2,000 for each letter of credit approved and issued. The company approves, on average, 80% of the applications it receives.

During the year, the company received 600 requests and approved 75% of them. The total variable overhead was 10% higher than the standard amount applied; the total fixed expenses were 5% lower than the amount budgeted.

In addition to these expenses, the company paid a $270,000 insurance premium for the letters of credit issued. The insurance premium is 1% of the amount of credits issued in U.S. dollars. The actual amount of credit issued often differs from the amount requested due to fluctuations in exchange rates and variations in the amount shipped from the amount ordered by importers. The strength of the dollar during the year decreased the insurance premium by 10%.

**Required**

1. Calculate the (a) variable, and (b) fixed overhead rates for the year.
2. Prepare an analysis of the overhead variances for the year just completed. (a) What is the total controllable (i.e., flexible-budget) variance for the period? (b) What is the overhead volume variance for the period? (*Hint:* These two should sum to $88,000U.)

[LO 15-6]   15-54   **ABC versus Traditional Approaches to Control of Batch-Related Overhead Costs**   The Bangor Manufacturing Company makes mechanical toy robots that are typically produced in batches of 250 units. Prior to the current year, the company's accountants used a standard cost system with a simplified method of assigning manufacturing support (i.e., overhead) costs to products: all such costs were allocated to outputs based on the standard machine-hours allowed for output produced. You have recently joined the accounting team and are developing a proposal that the company adopt an ABC system for both product-costing and control purposes. To illustrate the benefit of such a system in terms of the latter, you decide to put together an analysis of batch-related overhead costs. You chose these costs because a previous investigation indicated that there is both a variable component to these costs (materials plus power) plus a fixed component (depreciation and salaries). Last year's budget indicated that the variable overhead cost per setup hour was $20 and that the fixed overhead production setup costs per year were $20,000. Output was budgeted at 10,000 units for the year. Typically a batch takes four hours of setup time. For cost-control purposes, assume that the flexible budget is based on the budgeted number of setup hours for the output of the period.

You have also collected data regarding actual results for the past year. Specifically, the company produced (and sold) 9,000 toy robots, which were produced in an average batch size of 200 units. The actual setup hours per batch last year turned out to be 4.25 hours and the actual variable overhead cost per setup hour was $19. Actual fixed setup-related overhead costs were $21,000 last year.

Your discussion with the company controller indicates that under the previous accounting system, all setup-related overhead costs were allocated to production based on machine-hours. The standard machine-hours allowed per unit produced was 1.50 hours. The denominator activity level assumed for applying fixed manufacturing support costs to units produced was 15,000 machine-hours.

**Required**

1. Under the ABC approach, what was the (a) spending variance and (b) production volume variance last year for the *fixed* setup-related overhead costs described above? How would you explain these results to management?
2. Under the ABC approach, what was the (a) spending variance and (b) efficiency variance last year for the *variable* setup-related overhead costs described above? How would you explain these results to management?
3. Write a brief statement outlining the projected costs and benefits of using an ABC approach for the day-to-day control of the overhead costs referred to above as compared to the use of a more traditional cost system.
4. The Bangor Manufacturing Company is currently experiencing severe cost-based pressure from foreign competitors. As such, top management of the company is interested in improving the existing financial-control system in the organization. What other recommendation might you have for management in this regard? That is, what do you recommend to accompany the type of financial analysis referred to above?

[LO 15-7, 15-8]   15-55   **Decision Making under Uncertainty (Appendix)**   The manager of Computech must decide whether to initiate an advertising campaign for the firm's newest multimedia computer chip. There has been some discussion among division managers about the chip's market condition. The marketing department assesses the probability of having a strong market to be 0.40.

The manager, with the help of the marketing staff, has estimated the profits she believes the firm could earn:

| | |
|---|---|
| Profits with advertising: | |
| Strong market | $21 million |
| Weak market | 9 million |
| Profits without advertising: | |
| Strong market | 16 million |
| Weak market | 10 million |

**Required**
1. Should the firm undertake the advertising campaign? Why or why not?
2. What is the probability level regarding the state of the market that will render the manager indifferent as to the courses of action?
3. What is the maximum amount the firm should pay to obtain perfect information regarding the state of the market, assuming such information is available?

[LO 15-7, 15-8]   15-56 **Variance Investigation under Uncertainty (Appendix)**   The internal auditor of Xenon Company estimates the probability of its internal control procedure being in control to be 75%. She estimates the cost to conduct an investigation to find areas for improvement to be about $20,000 and the cost to revise and improve the internal control procedure to be approximately $60,000. The present value of savings from having the new procedure is expected to be $240,000.

**Required**
1. Construct a payoff table for the company to use in determining its best course of action.
2. What is the expected cost to the firm if it conducts an investigation? If it does not investigate? Should the firm investigate? Why or why not?
3. What is the expected value of perfect information? Note: The expected value of perfect information (EVPI) is defined as the *maximum* value the manager would pay to have knowledge (i.e., certainty) of whether the process is in control or out of control. In the present context, the EVPI can be thought of as the difference between the expected cost with perfect information and the expected cost without perfect information. (To calculate the former, we need to choose for each possible state of nature the best course of action [decision] and then multiply the associated "cost" by the probability of that state of nature occurring. We then sum these resulting expected costs to get the *expected cost with perfect information.*) (*Hint:* For this problem, the expected cost under perfect information is $15,000.)

[LO 15-1, 15-2]   15-57 **All Manufacturing Variances**   Eastern Company manufactures special electrical equipment and parts. The company uses a standard cost system with separate standards established for each product.

The transformer department manufactures a special transformer. This department measures production volume in terms of direct labor-hours (DLHs) and uses a flexible-budget system to plan and control departmental overhead costs.

Standard costs for the special transformer are determined annually in September for the coming year. The standard cost of a transformer at its Decatur plant for the year just completed is $67 per unit, as shown here:

| Direct materials: | | |
|---|---|---|
| Iron | 5 sheets × $2 | $10 |
| Copper | 3 spools × $3 | 9 |
| Direct labor | 4 labor-hours × $7 | 28 |
| Variable overhead | 4 labor-hours × $3 | 12 |
| Fixed overhead | 4 labor-hours × $2 | 8 |
| Total | | $67 |

Overhead rates were based on practical capacity of 4,000 DLHs per month. Variable overhead costs are expected to vary with the number of DLHs actually used.

During October, the plant produced 800 transformers. This number was below expectations because a work stoppage occurred during labor contract negotiations. When the contract was settled, the department scheduled overtime in an attempt to reach expected production levels. The following costs were incurred in October:

| **Direct Material** | |
|---|---|
| Iron | Purchased 5,000 sheets at $2.00/sheet and used 3,900 sheets |
| Copper | Purchased 2,200 spools at $3.10/spool and used 2,600 spools |
| **Direct Labor** | |
| Regular time | 2,000 labor-hours at $7.00 and 1,400 labor-hours at $7.20 |
| Overtime | 600 of the 1,400 labor-hours were subject to overtime premium. The total overtime premium of $2,160 is included in variable overhead in accordance with company accounting practices. |
| **Factory Overhead** | |
| Variable | $12,000 |
| Fixed | $8,800 |

**Required**

1. What is the most appropriate time to record any variance of actual materials prices from standard? Explain.
2. What is the total direct labor rate (price) variance for October?
3. What is the total direct labor efficiency variance for October?
4. What is the total direct materials purchase price variance for October?
5. What is the total direct materials usage variance for October?
6. What is the variable overhead spending variance for October?
7. What is the variable overhead efficiency variance for October?
8. What is the budget (spending) variance for fixed overhead for October?
9. What is the fixed overhead production volume variance for October?

**(CMA Adapted)**

## Solutions to Self–Study Problems

### 1. Analysis of the Total Overhead Cost Variance

| | |
|---|---:|
| 1. a. Units manufactured during the period | 360 |
| Standard direct labor-hours allowed per unit produced | × 2 |
| Total standard direct labor-hours allowed for the units manufactured | 720 |
| Standard variable factory overhead rate per direct labor-hour | × $5.00 |
| Flexible budget for variable factory overhead for the units produced | $3,600 |
| | |
| b. The total variable factory overhead applied to production (same as the flexible budget for variable overhead based on output) | $3,600 |
| | |
| c. Practical capacity (units) | 400 |
| Standard direct labor-hours per unit | × 2 |
| Total standard direct labor-hours at practical capacity | 800 |
| Standard fixed factory overhead rate per direct labor-hour (given) | × $20 |
| Total budgeted fixed factory overhead for the period | $16,000 |
| | |
| d. Total standard direct labor-hours for the units manufactured (from 1a) | 720 |
| Standard fixed factory overhead rate per direct labor-hour | × $20 |
| Total fixed factory overhead applied | $14,400 |

2. a, b, and c.

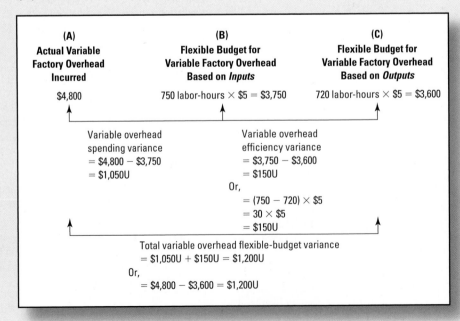

d. Total underapplied variable factory overhead = Total variable overhead flexible-budget variance = $1,200

e, f, and g.

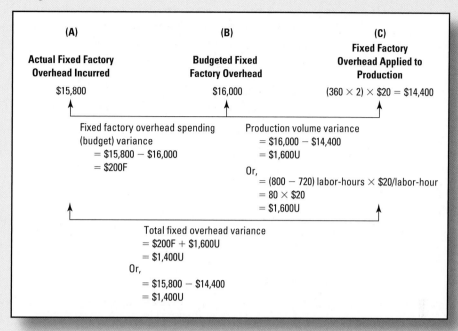

h. Total underapplied fixed factory overhead = Total fixed overhead variance = $1,400U

3. a. $\dfrac{\text{Factory overhead}}{\text{spending variance}} = \dfrac{\text{Variable factory overhead}}{\text{spending variance}} + \dfrac{\text{Fixed factory overhead}}{\text{spending variance}}$

$= \$1,050U + \$200F$

$= \$850U$

b. $\dfrac{\text{Factory overhead}}{\text{efficiency variance}} = \dfrac{\text{Variable factory overhead}}{\text{efficiency variance}} = \$150U$

c. Fixed overhead production volume variance = $1,600U

4. $\dfrac{\text{Factory overhead}}{\text{controllable (flexible-budget) variance}} = \dfrac{\text{Factory overhead}}{\text{spending variance}} + \dfrac{\text{Factory overhead}}{\text{efficiency variance}}$

$= \$850U + \$150U$

$= \$1,000U$

Fixed overhead production volume variance is $1,600U, the amount identified in both four-variance and three-variance analyses.

| 5. a. | Factory Overhead | 20,600 | |
| | Cash, Prepaid accounts, Accumulated depreciation; or sundry payable accounts | | 20,600 |
| b. | Work-in-Process Inventory | 18,000 | |
| | Factory Overhead | | 18,000 |
| c. | | | |
| | Variable Factory Overhead Spending Variance | 1,050 | |
| | Variable Factory Overhead Efficiency Variance | 150 | |
| | Fixed Overhead Production Volume Variance | 1,600 | |
| | Factory Overhead | | 2,600 |
| | Fixed Factory Overhead Spending Variance | | 200 |

*(Continued)*

d.(1)

| | | | |
|---|---|---|---|
| Cost of Goods Sold | | 2,600 | |
| Fixed Factory Overhead Spending Variance | | 200 | |
| Variable Factory Overhead Spending Variance | | | 1,050 |
| Variable Factory Overhead Efficiency Variance | | | 150 |
| Fixed Overhead Production Volume Variance | | | 1,600 |

d.(2) Ending balances at standard cost:

| | | |
|---|---|---|
| Work-in-Process Inventory ($153,000 − $134,640) | $ 18,360 | |
| Finished Goods Inventory ($134,640 − $111,690) | 22,950 | |
| Cost of Goods Sold (CGS) | 111,690 | |
| Total | $153,000 | |

| Account | Standard Cost | Percent of Total | Proration of Net Variance | Adjusted Cost |
|---|---|---|---|---|
| Work-in-Process Inventory | $ 18,360 | 12% | $2,600 × 0.12 = $ 312 | $ 18,672 |
| Finished Goods Inventory | 22,950 | 15 | 2,600 × 0.15 = 390 | 23,340 |
| Cost of Goods Sold | 111,690 | 73 | 2,600 × 0.73 = 1,898 | 113,588 |
| Total | $153,000 | 100% | $2,600 | $155,600 |

| | | |
|---|---|---|
| Cost of Goods Sold | 1,898 | |
| Work-in-Process Inventory | 312 | |
| Finished Goods Inventory | 390 | |
| Fixed Factory Overhead Spending Variance | 200 | |
| Variable Factory Overhead Spending Variance | | 1,050 |
| Variable Factory Overhead Efficiency Variance | | 150 |
| Fixed Overhead Production Volume Variance | | 1,600 |

## 2. Variance Investigation (Appendix)

### Courses of Action

$A_1$: Investigate to determine the cause(s) of the efficiency variance.
$A_2$: Do not investigate.

### States of Nature

$S_1$: The operation is in control (operates normally).
$S_2$: The operation is out of control.

### Cost and Probability

$I$ = Cost of investigation = $2,500
$C$ = Cost of corrective action, if the process is found to be out-of-control = $5,000
$L$ = Losses from being out of control with no corrective action taken = $55,000
$P$ = Probability of the operation being in control = 40%

| | Payoff Table | |
|---|---|---|
| | **States of Nature** | |
| **Management Action** | **In Control\* (0.40)** | **Out of Control† (0.60)** |
| Investigate | $2,500 | $2,500 + $5,000 |
| Do not investigate | 0 | $55,000 |

\* That is, the variance is due to random, not systematic, factors.
† That is, the variance is not due to random factors.

1. $E$(investigate) $= (40\% \times \$2,500) + (60\% \times \$7,500) = \$5,500$

$E$(do not investigate) $= 60\% \times \$55,000 = \$33,000$

The expected total cost to the firm will be lower if Smiley investigates the variance and takes proper action to correct the cause of the variance, if the investigation finds the operation to be out of control.

2. Smiley is indifferent to the alternative courses of action if the probability of the process *not* being in control ($p$) is at a level that renders the expected cost of investigating and the expected cost of not investigating equal.

$$E(\text{Investigate}) = E(\text{Do not investigate})$$

$$([I \times (1 - p)] + [(I + C) \times p]) = L \times p$$

$$p = I/(L - C)$$

$$p = \$2,500/(\$55,000 - \$5,000)$$

$$p = 0.05$$

Therefore, if the probability that the process is out of control is 5% (i.e., there is a 5% probability that the observed variance has a nonrandom cause), the company would be indifferent between conducting an investigation and not conducting an investigation. If the probability, $p$, of a nonrandom variance is less than 0.05, then the optimal action is *not* to conduct an investigation.

3. EVPI $= [(\$0 \times 0.40) + (\$7,500 \times 0.60)] -$ Expected cost without perfect information

$$= \$4,500 - \$5,500 = \underline{\underline{\$1,000}}$$

Thus, the manager would be willing to pay up to \$1,000 for perfect information. This amount represents the long-run (or average) decrease in expected cost.

*Please visit* **http://www.mhhe.com/blocher6e** *to access a narrated, animated tutorial for solving these problems.*

# Operational Performance Measurement: Further Analysis of Productivity and Sales

## After studying this chapter, you should be able to . . .

LO 16-1  Explain the strategic role of the flexible budget in analyzing productivity and sales

LO 16-2  Calculate and interpret the measures for total productivity, partial operational productivity, and partial financial productivity

LO 16-3  Use the flexible budget to calculate and interpret the sales quantity, sales mix, market size, and market share variances

LO 16-4  Use the flexible budget to analyze sales performance over time

This chapter covers the measures of performance for both productivity (employee output per labor-hour or other measure of input) and sales growth. Productivity and sales growth can both be measured on many dimensions, and a comprehensive analysis of these many dimensions is often the key to tracking performance and attaining strategic goals. Productivity and sales growth have been much in the news since the onset of the recession in 2008. Organizations responded to falling sales by reducing their workforce, the short-term effect of which was to improve productivity. Productivity increased dramatically in 2009 and 2010. Labor costs fell by 2% in 2010—the largest decrease since 1948. The cost savings of workforce reductions were far greater than the lost revenues from sales declines, and company profits increased. A recent survey of 700 chief financial officers shows that 70% report an improvement in productivity over the last few years.[1]

As an example of the relevance of productivity and sales growth measures, the period 2008–2011 was a challenge for the auto industry worldwide; sales fell by 30% or more at many auto companies. The recession's effect on unemployment, the increase in gasoline prices, the March 2011 earthquake and tsunami in Japan, and the 2011 flooding in Thailand had a dramatic effect on the industry worldwide. This period also saw both GM and Chrysler go through bankruptcy and move from unprofitable to profitable companies. Dramatic reductions in output and labor costs led the way. In fact, by late 2011, labor and benefits costs per hour at the "Detroit Big Three" averaged $55, which was very close to that of Japanese rivals. What a change! In 2007, for example, GM paid $1,400 more in labor costs per vehicle than Toyota. After its bankruptcy reorganization, GM's labor costs had come down significantly. In just three years, the Detroit automakers have come close to parity in productivity with other worldwide automakers.[2]

---

[1] "More, Better, Faster—But How?" *CFO*, November 2011, p. 14. Reflecting the cyclical and seasonal nature of productivity, U.S. measures of productivity worsened in early 2011 and then improved again in the summer of 2011 (*The Fiscal Times,* November 3, 2011); "A Jump in Labor Costs," *Bloomberg Businessweek,* August 29, 2011, p. 16; David Wessel and James R. Hagerty, "Flat U.S. Wages Help Fuel Rebound in Manufacturing (Productivity)," *The Wall Street Journal,* May 29, 2012, p. 1.

[2] Data from the Center for Automotive Research, a nonprofit research group, as cited on **Cars.com**, October 14, 2011. See also, Bill Vlasic, "With New Labor Contracts, Detroit Protects Turnaround," *The Wall Street Journal,* October 28, 2011, pp. B1–2; "A Jump in Labor Costs," *Bloomberg Businessweek,* August 29, 2011, p. 16; "How America Started Selling Cars Again," *Time,* December 19, 2011, pp. 31–41.

The measurement of productivity and sales growth turns out to be an extension of the operational-level performance measures introduced in Chapters 14 and 15—standard costing and the flexible budget, nonfinancial operational performance measures, and resource-capacity planning. This chapter extends Chapters 14 and 15 through coverage of an extension of the flexible budget—productivity measures and additional sales variance measures. Other methods for improving efficiency and financial control are covered elsewhere in the text (see Chapter 1 for summary) including: target costing, benchmarking. business process improvement, and total quality management.

## The Strategic Role of the Flexible Budget in Analyzing Productivity and Sales

**LO 16-1**

*Explain the strategic role of the flexible budget in analyzing productivity and sales.*

The strategic role of sales analysis is to better understand the reasons behind an increase (or decrease) in total sales dollars over the budgeted amount, or an increase (decrease) over the prior year. The key question for a competitive analysis is how the change in sales has affected the firm's profitability and growth in desired market areas. Is the firm meeting strategic sales goals? Are sales increasing in profitable or unprofitable product lines? To begin to answer these questions, the total amount of change in sales is decomposed into many components, each of which holds some answers about these strategic questions. For example, the total dollar change in sales over (or under) the budget can be explained in terms of changes in selling prices and changes in the volume of units sold. A change in prices or volume will affect total sales. The decomposition of total sales into these two variances, the selling price and volume variances, is illustrated using the flexible budget in Chapter 14. Chapter 16 now takes one of these two variances, the volume variance, and further decomposes it into elements that explain the effect of changes in product mix (the proportion of total sales for each of the products), the size of the markets for the firm's products, and the firm's share in these markets. The further analysis allows managers to see how changes in product mix and market size/share affect profits. The decomposition of the sales variances uses the flexible budget in two ways: (1) analyzing differences between actual sales and the master budget sales (as in the approach in Chapter 14) and (2) analyzing changes in sales over the prior year.

The strategic role of productivity analysis is to assist management in identifying the drivers of productivity and to implement methods that improve productivity and profitability. The good news is that in most countries productivity has been increasing in recent years. In the United States since 2001, productivity in the private, nonfarm business sector has increased an average of 2.7% per year in contrast to the average of 1.5% annual rate in the prior two decades. The economic downturn of 2007–2008 took its toll, however, as figures for 2007 and 2008 show a decline to 1.4% in both of those years. However, productivity increased again in 2009 and 2010 as labor costs decreased in those two years. Also, productivity has differed substantially across industries, depending on the industry's ability to control waste and labor costs and to develop product and manufacturing process innovations. For example, some of the industries that have been slow to innovate relative to other industries include furniture manufacturing, printing, and food manufacturing.

The key determinants of productivity for most organizations are:

1. Control of waste.
2. Product and manufacturing process innovation.
3. Fluctuations in demand due to changes in the business cycle or for other reasons.

First, the control of waste is achieved through efforts in work flow management and quality. A good example is the Toyota Production System (TPS) which has helped Toyota to become one of the most productive automakers in the world.[3] The main elements of TPS are (1) a long-term focus on relationships with suppliers and coordination with these suppliers; (2) an emphasis on balanced, continuous flow manufacturing with stable production levels; (3) continuous improvement in product design and manufacturing processes with the objective of eliminating waste; and (4) flexible manufacturing systems (FMS) in which different vehicles are

---

[3] Taiichi Ohno, *Toyota Production System: Beyond Large Scale Production*, Productivity Inc., 1988.

produced on the same assembly line and employees are trained for a variety of tasks. The focus on waste and balanced production flows is also called *lean manufacturing.*

Product and process innovation is the second key determinant of competitiveness in productivity, often achieved through the implementation of information technology. Third, it is important to understand that productivity in a firm or industry is greatly influenced by the business cycle. Higher productivity is usually seen when a firm is coming out of a low point in the business cycle, as the firm stretches existing resources to meet demand, and then productivity growth slows as resources are added. So it is always important to analyze productivity within the larger context of the competitive environment and business cycle in which the firm operates. While many of the examples to follow are in the manufacturing context, the topic of productivity applies as well in service companies where labor costs are a high proportion of total costs. There are examples of productivity analysis in the service industries in the end-of-chapter problems.

## Analyzing Productivity

**LO 16-2**

*Calculate and interpret the measures for total productivity, partial operational productivity, and partial financial productivity.*

The single best measure of a country's average standard of living is productivity: the value of output of goods and services a country procures per worker. The more workers produce, the more income they receive, and the more they can consume. Higher productivity results in higher standards of living.

*Martin Neil Baily and Matthew J. Slaughter*
*Former Members of the U.S. President's*
*Council of Economic Advisers*

**Productivity**
is the ratio of output to input.

Baily and Slaughter, writing in *The Wall Street Journal,* note that productivity is key to the success of a country, a company, and an individual worker.[4] **Productivity** is measured as the ratio of output to input.

$$\text{Productivity} = \frac{\text{Output}}{\text{Input}}$$

A firm that spends five days to manufacture 100 units has a productivity of 20 units per day. A social service worker who processes 75 cases over a four-week period has a productivity of 3.75 cases per day. A firm that uses 24.5 pounds of material for each unit manufactured is more productive than a firm that uses 25 pounds of the same materials to manufacture one unit of the same product. To improve productivity, firms need to know the productivity levels of their operations.

**Operational productivity**
is the ratio of output units to input units.

**Financial productivity**
is the ratio of output to input with either the numerator or the denominator a dollar amount.

A measure of productivity can be either an operational or a financial productivity measure. **Operational productivity** is the ratio of output units to input units. Both the numerator and the denominator are physical measures. **Financial productivity** is also a ratio of output to input, except that either the numerator or the denominator is a dollar amount. For example, the number of tables made from a sheet of plywood involves operational productivity; the number of tables per dollar cost of plywood reflects financial productivity.

**Partial productivity**
focuses on the relationship between input factors and output.

A productivity measure may include all production factors or focus on a single factor or part of the production factors that the firm uses in manufacturing. A productivity measure that focuses on the relationship between one input factor and the output attained is a **partial productivity** measure. The following are examples of partial productivity:

- Direct materials productivity (output/units of materials).
- Workforce productivity (output per labor-hour or output per person employed).
- Process productivity (output per machine-hour or output per kilowatt-hour).

**Total productivity**
includes all input resources in the computation of the ratio of output attained to input resources consumed.

A productivity measure that includes all input resources used in production is a **total productivity** measure. The number of tables manufactured per dollar of manufacturing

[4] Martin Neil Baily and Matthew J. Slaughter, "What's Behind the Recent Productivity Slowdown," *The Wall Street Journal,* December 13–14, 2008, p. A15.

costs is a total productivity measure because the denominator, manufacturing costs, includes all manufacturing costs incurred to make the tables. Exhibit 16.1 summarizes productivity measures.

Exhibit 16.2 presents selected production data of Erie Precision Tool Company in 2012 and 2013 for manufacturing drill bits. The manufacturing costs include total fixed factory overhead and other operating expenses of $300,000 per year and variable manufacturing costs consisting of metal alloy (direct materials) and direct labor-hours.

The firm earned $1,100,000 operating income in 2013, a 17% increase over the $940,000 earned in 2012. Without examining the operating data in detail, management would probably be happy with the improvement. The increase in operating income, however, compares unfavorably to the improvement in total sales. The total sales in 2013 are 120% of the total sales in 2012. With the fixed factory overhead and fixed operating expenses remaining unchanged at $300,000 each year, the increase in operating income should have been more than the 20% increase in total sales. The lower increase in operating income is a result of a higher-than-proportional increase in the firm's variable costs for direct materials and direct labor. The total variable costs increased 32% [($1,000,000 − $760,000)/$760,000] while the total sales increased only 20%.

Several factors could have contributed to the increase in direct materials and direct labor costs, including increases in the number of units manufactured and sold, changes in the amounts and/or the proportions of the inputs used in production, and increases in the unit cost of resources. The firm should identify factors that caused the changes so that management can decrease manufacturing costs and increase operating income.

**EXHIBIT 16.1   Productivity Measures**

|  | Partial Productivity | | Total Productivity | |
|---|---|---|---|---|
|  | **Operational** | **Financial** | **Total Units of Output** | **Sales Value of Output** |
| Numerator (output) | Units of output | Units of output | Units of output | Sales value of output |
| Denominator (input) | Units of input | Dollar value of input | Dollar value of input | Dollar value of input |
| Productivity measure (output/input) | Units of output per unit of input | Units of output per dollar value of input | Units of output per dollar value of input | Dollar value of output per dollar value of input |

**EXHIBIT 16.2**
**Operating Data of Erie**
**Precision Tool Company**

| | | |
|---|---|---|
| **ERIE PRECISION TOOL COMPANY** | | |
| **Operating Data** | | |
| | **2013** | **2012** |
| Units manufactured and sold | 4,800 | 4,000 |
| Total sales ($500 price per unit) | $2,400,000 | $2,000,000 |
| Direct materials (25,000 pounds at $24/pound in 2012 and 32,000 pounds at $25/pound in 2013) | 800,000 | 600,000 |
| Direct labor (4,000 hours at $40 per hour in 2012 and 4,000 hours at $50/hour in 2013) | 200,000 | 160,000 |
| Fixed factory overhead and fixed operating expenses | 300,000 | 300,000 |
| Operating income | $1,100,000 | $ 940,000 |

Productivity measurements discussed in this chapter examine the effect of a firm's productivity on its operating income. Increased productivity decreases costs and increases operating income. Changes in the productivity of different resources, however, do not always occur in the same direction or at an equal rate. A firm's productivity or use of direct materials can improve while its direct labor productivity might deteriorate. For instance, a furniture manufacturer increased materials productivity by reducing waste due to improper cutting of lumber. However, to reduce improper cutting of lumber, workers spent more labor-hours to cut the boards carefully. The labor-hour productivity decreased. Management needs to know the changes in productivities of individual production resources, which partial productivities provide.

## Partial Productivity

A partial productivity measure depicts the relationship between output and one of the required input resources used in producing the output.

$$\text{Partial productivity} = \frac{\text{Number of units manufactured}}{\text{Number of units or cost of a single input resource}}$$

For example, partial productivity of the direct materials for the Erie Precision Tool Company in 2012 is 0.16 units of output per pound of material, as computed here:

$$\text{Partial productivity of direct materials in 2012} = \frac{4,000}{25,000} = 0.16 \text{ units/pound}$$

### *Partial Operational Productivity*

Firms often use benchmarks in assessing productivity. Among benchmarks often used are past productivity measures of the firm, productivity of another firm in the same industry, the industry standard or average, or benchmarks established by the top management as the goal for the firm to attain. Sources of benchmarking information include industry and national associations focused on productivity and quality such as the American Production and Inventory Control Society (**www.apics.org**), the American Productivity & Quality Center (**www.apqc.org**), and the American Society for Quality (**www.asq.org**). In this example, we use Erie Precision Tool Company's productivity level in 2012 as the benchmark to assess productivity in 2013.

A comparison of partial productivity from 2012 to 2013 shows that the partial productivity of direct materials decreased. The firm manufactured 0.16 units in 2012 but only 0.15 units in 2013 from 1 pound of direct materials, a 6.25% decrease in productivity. See Exhibit 16.3 for calculations. Partial productivity of direct labor, however, improved in 2013. The firm manufactured one unit for each direct labor-hour in 2012 and 1.2 units per hour in 2013, a 20% increase in productivity.

Changes in productivity also can be examined by computing the amount of input resources that the firm would have used in 2013 had it maintained the 2012 partial

**EXHIBIT 16.3**
Partial Productivity of Erie
Precision Tool Company

| ERIE PRECISION TOOL COMPANY | | |
|---|---|---|
| Partial Productivity—Direct Materials and Direct Labor | | |
| | Partial Operational Productivity | |
| | **2013** | **2012** |
| Direct materials | 4,800/32,000 = 0.15 | 4,000/25,000 = 0.16 |
| Direct labor | 4,800/4,000 = 1.20 | 4,000/4,000 = 1.00 |
| | Partial Financial Productivity | |
| | **2013** | **2012** |
| Direct materials | 4,800/$800,000 = 0.006 | 4,000/$600,000 = 0.0067 |
| Direct labor | 4,800/$200,000 = 0.024 | 4,000/$160,000 = 0.025 |

**EXHIBIT 16.4**
Changes in Operational Partial
Productivity of Erie Precision
Tool Company

| | ERIE PRECISION TOOL COMPANY | | | | |
|---|---|---|---|---|---|
| | Effects of Changes in Operational Partial Productivity of Direct Materials and Direct Labor | | | | |
| | **(1)** | **(2)** | **(3)** | **(4)** | **(5)** |
| | | 2012 Partial | = (1) ÷ (2) | Input | = (3) − (4) |
| | 2013 | Operational | 2013 Output at | Used in | Savings (Loss) |
| Input Resource | Output | Productivity | 2012 Productivity | 2013 | in Units of Input |
| Direct materials | 4,800 | 0.16 | 30,000 | 32,000 | (2,000) |
| Direct labor | 4,800 | 1.00 | 4,800 | 4,000 | 800 |

productivity, as shown in Exhibit 16.4. In this case, the 4,800 units manufactured and sold in 2013 would have required only 30,000 pounds of direct materials (4,800 ÷ 0.16). The decreased partial productivity required the use of an additional 2,000 pounds in 2013 (32,000 − 30,000). Similarly, the firm would have used 4,800 direct labor-hours in 2013 had it had the same direct labor partial productivity in 2013 as in 2012. The firm saved the cost for 800 hours of direct labor (4,800 − 4,000) when its partial productivity in 2013 for direct labor increased from 1.0 to 1.2.

### Partial Financial Productivity

The bottom panel of Exhibit 16.3 reports the partial financial productivities of direct materials and direct labor. The partial financial productivity indicates the number of units of output manufactured for each dollar the firm spent on the input resource. The partial financial productivity for direct materials is determined by dividing the output (4,000 units in 2012 and 4,800 units in 2013) by the cost of the resource for the year (cost of direct materials: $600,000 in 2012 and $800,000 in 2013). The partial financial productivities are 0.0067 in 2012 and 0.006 in 2013, a decrease in productivity from 2012 to 2013 of 10% [(0.0067 − 0.006) ÷ 0.0067].

The direct labor partial *financial* productivity is 0.025 for 2012 and 0.024 for 2013, a decrease of 4% [(0.025 − 0.024) ÷ 0.025]. This result is in conflict with the direct labor partial *operational* productivity reported earlier (20% improvement). These results suggest that although employee productivity per hour increased, the cost increase due to higher hourly wages more than offset the gain in productivity per hour.

Factors that may contribute to the difference in manufacturing costs between two operations are differences in output level, input cost, or productivity. Panel 1 of Exhibit 16.5 shows how the flexible budget can be used for determining the effects of each of these factors. Point A is the actual operating results of 2013. The amounts for all three factors at point A are the actual 2013 figures: units of output, productivity, and input cost. Point B is the cost to manufacture the 2013 output at the *2012 productivity level* and 2013 input cost. The only difference between points A and B is in productivity. Thus, any difference between points A and B is attributable to changes in productivity between 2013 and 2012.

**EXHIBIT 16.5** **Partitioning Partial Financial Productivity Using the Flexible Budget**

**ERIE PRECISION TOOL COMPANY**
**Partitioning Partial Financial Productivity into Productivity Change and Input Price Change**

**Panel 1: Flexible Budget Framework**

|  | A | B | C | D |
|---|---|---|---|---|
| Output | 2013 | 2013 | 2013 | 2012 |
| Productivity | 2013 | 2012 | 2012 | 2012 |
| Input Cost | 2013 | 2013 | 2012 | 2012 |

Productivity Change ⟵→ Input Price Change ⟵→ Output Change

**Panel 2: Operating Data for Partitioning Partial Financial Productivity**

|  | Actual 2013 Operating Results | 2013 Output at *2012 Productivity* and 2013 Input Cost | 2013 Output at 2012 Productivity and *2012 Input Cost* | Actual 2012 Operating Results |
|---|---|---|---|---|
| Output units | 4,800 | 4,800 | 4,800 | 4,000 |
| Input units and costs |  |  |  |  |
| Direct materials | 32,000 × $25 = $ 800,000 | 30,000 × $25 = $750,000 | 30,000 × $24 = $720,000 | 25,000 × $24 = $600,000 |
| Direct labor | 4,000 × $50 = 200,000 | 4,800 × $50 = 240,000 | 4,800 × $40 = 192,000 | 4,000 × $40 = 160,000 |
| Total | $1,000,000 | $990,000 | $912,000 | $760,000 |

**Panel 3: Partitioning Productivity and Input Price Changes**

|  | **2013 Operations** | | | **2012 Operations** |
|---|---|---|---|---|
|  | 2013 output/ (2013 input × 2013 input costs) | 2013 output/(2012 input for 2013 output × 2013 input costs) | 2013 output/(2012 input for 2013 output × 2012 input costs) | 2012 output/ (2012 input × 2012 input costs) |
| Direct materials | 4,800/$800,000 = 0.006 | 4,800/$750,000 = 0.0064 | 4,800/$720,000 = 0.006667 | 4,000/$600,000 = 0.006667 |
| Direct labor | 4,800/$200,000 = 0.024 | 4,800/$240,000 = 0.0200 | 4,800/$192,000 = 0.025000 | 4,000/$160,000 = 0.025000 |

Productivity Change ⟵→ Input Price Change ⟵→ Output Change

|  | | | |
|---|---|---|---|
| Direct materials | 0.0060 − 0.0064 = 0.0004U | 0.006400 − 0.006667 = 0.000267U | 0.006667 − 0.006667 = 0 |
| Direct labor | 0.0240 − 0.0200 = 0.0040F | 0.02000 − 0.025000 = 0.005000U | 0.025000 − 0.025000 = 0 |

**Panel 4: Summary of Results**

**Productivity Change from 2012 to 2013**

|  | Productivity Change | | Input Price Change | | Output Change | | Total Change |
|---|---|---|---|---|---|---|---|
| Direct materials | 0.0004U | + | 0.000267U | + | 0 | = | 0.000667U |
| Direct labor | 0.0040F | + | 0.005000U | + | 0 | = | 0.001000U |

**Change as Percent of 2012 Productivity (2012 Productivity shown in Exhibit 16.3)**

|  | Productivity Change | | Input Price Change | | Output Change | | Total Change |
|---|---|---|---|---|---|---|---|
| Direct materials | 6%U | + | 4%U | + | 0% | = | 10%U |
| Direct labor | 16%F | + | 20%U | + | 0% | = | 4%U |

Point C is the cost to manufacture the 2013 output at the 2012 productivity level and *2012 input cost.* The only difference between points B and C is in the unit cost of the input resource in each of the years: point B uses the 2013 cost per unit for the input resource while point C uses the 2012 cost per unit for the input resource. The difference between the amounts in points B and C, if any, results from the difference in unit cost of the input resource.

Point D is the cost to manufacture the *2012 output* at 2012 productivity and 2012 unit cost of the input resource. Any difference in the costs between points C and D is because of different output levels between these two points. The output is then divided by the total cost of the required resource to manufacture the output. Because the total cost of the required resource in each of the years is determined using the same productivity level (2012 productivity) and the same unit cost of the input resource (2012 cost per unit of the input resource), the total cost of the required resource in each of the years is in proportion to their respective output levels. As a result, the ratios of output to input (costs) at points C and D are always identical, and the change in productivity for output change from 2012 to 2013 is always equal to zero. The column for point D is included for completeness, to show the total change from the actual results of 2012 to the actual results of 2013; the change in productivity from 2012 to 2013 is the result of two changes only: the change in input prices and the change in materials or labor productivity.

The analysis shows that, of the 10% decrease in partial financial productivity of direct materials (from 0.0067 to 0.006, Exhibit 16.3), 6% (0.0004/0.0067, bottom of panel 4, Exhibit 16.5) is attributable to productivity change. The remaining 4% (bottom of panel 4, Exhibit 16.5) reflects the price change in the cost per pound of direct materials ($24 in 2012 to $25 in 2013).

The 2013 financial partial productivity of direct labor is 4% lower than that of 2012 (from 0.025 to 0.024, Exhibit 16.3). The lower partial financial productivity of direct labor in 2013 is not due to decreased productivity of direct labor in 2013, however. The partial productivity of direct labor increased by 16% (bottom of panel 4, Exhibit 16.5). The $10 increase in wages ($40 per hour in 2012 and $50 per hour in 2013) more than offsets the gain in labor productivity. As a result, total direct labor cost increased and the partial financial productivity decreased by 4%.

### Partial Productivity: Operational versus Financial

Both the numerator and the denominator of a partial operational productivity measure are physical units. Using physical measures makes partial operational measures easy for operational personnel to understand and use in operations. The fact that an operational productivity measure is unaffected by price changes or other factors also makes it easier to benchmark.

Partial financial productivity has the advantage of considering the effects of both cost and quantity of an input resource on productivity. At the management level, the effect of cost, not merely the physical quantity, is the main concern. In addition, partial financial productivity can be used in operations that use more than one production factor. Partial operational productivity, on the other hand, measures only one input resource at a time.

### Limitations of Partial Productivity Analysis

A partial productivity measure has several limitations. First, it measures only the relationship between an input resource and the output; it ignores any effect that changes in other manufacturing factors have on productivity. An improved partial productivity measure could have been obtained by decreasing the productivity of one or more other input resources. For example, Erie Precision Tool Company can improve its partial productivity of direct labor by speeding up labor usage, though waste of direct materials might increase. Or, it can boost direct materials partial productivity through reduction in direct materials waste by using more labor-hours to cut each piece of material carefully. Management accountants call this the cross-substitution of factors of input.

A second limitation is that partial productivity ignores any effect that changes in other production factors have on productivity. For example, increases in materials quality are likely to raise the partial productivity of direct materials as well as direct labor. Erie Precision Tool Company might have workers with more experience or higher skill in

2013 than those in 2012. As a result, the partial productivity of labor increased in 2013. The average hourly wage rate for workers with more experience or higher skill will be higher. Is it worthwhile for the firm to make the trade-off? Unfortunately, an analysis of operational partial productivity cannot provide an answer.

Third, the analysis and interpretation of partial productivity should include effects that changes in the firm's operating characteristics have on the productivity of the input resource. For example, installation of high-efficiency equipment can also improve direct labor partial operational productivity.

Fourth, an improved partial productivity does not necessarily mean that the firm or division operates efficiently. As computed for example in Exhibit 16.5, an improvement simply means productivity is better than last year.

### Partial Productivity, the Flexible Budget, and Standard Costs (Review of Chapter 14)

It is common for productivity analysis as illustrated above to use the year-to-year analytical framework. The analysis could also be based upon a budget or standard, and then the analysis would be very much like the application of the flexible budget in Chapter 14. For example, in Exhibit 16.5, panel 2, the differences in total costs for each of the points A, B, C, and D represent differences in cost very much like the variances calculated in Chapter 14. The difference is that in Chapter 14 we compared actual performance to the master budget using the flexible budget to distinguish volume and flexible-budget variances. Note that the volume variance in dollars in Exhibit 16.5, panel 2 is $152,000 ($912,000 − $760,000); this is the increased cost for producing 800 more units at standard productivity and price. Now, look back to page 569 to review the calculation of the sales volume variance in Exhibit 14.4. The volume variance for variable expense of $99,000 in column 4 of Exhibit 14.4 is calculated in the same way as the volume variance in Exhibit 16.5, panel 2; the only difference is that the benchmark in Exhibit 14.4 is the master budget, and the benchmark in Exhibit 16.5 is the prior year results. Similarly, the flexible-budget variances for labor and materials in Chapter 14 are computed in a way similar to the computation of the input price and productivity variances in Exhibit 16.5, panel 2.

In effect, the use of the flexible budget in Chapters 14 and 16 is quite similar, but there are different objectives. The flexible budget in Chapter 14 was used to identify the volume and flexible-budget variances for materials and labor, *for changes in volume relative to the master budget.* In contrast, the flexible budget is used in Exhibit 16.5 to identify changes in input prices and productivity *from year to year* (rather than in comparison to the master budget). The variances in Chapter 14 calculate the effect of differences in usage or price for a given level of good output, at a standard level of input. Chapter 14 works with the materials or labor standard of a certain number of materials units or labor-hours *per unit of output,* while productivity analysis looks at the inverse: the number of units of output *per unit or materials or labor input.*

Both standard cost analysis (Chapter 14) and productivity analysis (Chapter 16) are widely used and have different objectives. Standard cost analysis focuses on meeting standards of materials and labor usage, while productivity analysis analyzes changes in productivity over time.

### Total Productivity

Total productivity is the ratio of output to the total cost of all input resources used to produce the output.

$$\text{Total productivity} = \frac{\text{Units or sales value of output}}{\text{Total cost of all input resources}}$$

Total productivity is a financial productivity measure. The numerator can be either the number of units or the sales value of the output attained. The denominator is the total dollar amount of all direct (variable cost) resources used in the production of the output.

The first panel of Exhibit 16.6 shows the computation of Erie Precision Tool Company's total productivity of variable manufacturing costs for 2012 and 2013. The computation of

Sometimes it takes real savvy to understand what the productivity numbers really mean. For example, when a company reduces its workforce, very often there is a shift in work responsibilities. K&S Machine Shop in High Point, North Carolina, cut 40 jobs in 2009. As a result, top managers now are often required to design the parts requested in new orders and to set up these orders on the plant's machines. Similarly, a Greensboro, North Carolina, advertising firm cut back positions that provided general support such as answering the phone and greeting visitors at the office door. These tasks are now shared by the professional staff. So the increased productivity for these companies has come at a price. Productivity has increased in operations, but there are negative effects on other types of work.

Productivity measures provided by government and trade organizations are subject to bias and errors. The measures are constantly updated and revised, as the underlying wage cost and output data

are updated. Economists advise it may take several months of updates to get solid figures for productivity in any given prior period. Moreover, economists have argued that the manner in which productivity is calculated can be misleading. For example, the different ways of counting imported parts (used in assembling finished products here in the United States) in the determination of manufacturing output can bias the productivity numbers.

**Required**

As a management accountant and consultant who advises companies on operational efficiency and strategy, how would you explain the importance of these productivity measurement issues to your clients?

(Refer to Comments on Cost Management in Action at the end of the chapter.)

**EXHIBIT 16.6**

**Total Productivity for Erie Precision Tool Company**

| ERIE PRECISION TOOL COMPANY Total Productivity | | |
|---|---|---|
| **Panel 1: Total Productivity in Units** | **2013** | **2012** |
| (a) Total units manufactured | 4,800 | 4,000 |
| (b) Total variable manufacturing costs incurred | $1,000,000 | $ 760,000 |
| (c) Total productivity: (a) / (b) | 0.004800 | 0.005263 |
| (d) Decrease in productivity: 0.005263 − 0.004800 = 0.000463, or 8.8% (0.000463 ÷ 0.005263) | | |
| **Panel 2: Total Productivity in Sales Dollars** | | |
| (a) Total sales | $2,400,000 | $2,000,000 |
| (b) Total variable manufacturing costs incurred | $1,000,000 | $ 760,000 |
| (c) Total productivity: (a) / (b) | $ 2.4000 | $ 2.6316 |
| (d) Decrease in productivity: $2.6316 − $2.4000 = $0.2316, or 8.8% ($0.2316 ÷ $2.6316) | | |

total productivity involves three steps: First, determine the output of each period: 4,000 units in 2012 and 4,800 units in 2013. Second, calculate the total variable costs incurred to produce the output: $760,000 in 2012 and $1,000,000 in 2013 (Exhibit 16.5, panel 2). Third, compute the total productivity by dividing the amount of output by the total cost of variable input resources: 0.005263 in 2012 and 0.004800 in 2013.

The total productivity indicates that for every thousand dollars of variable cost incurred in 2012, the firm manufactured 5.263 units of output. The total productivity in 2013 is 0.0048, indicating that the firm manufactures 4.8 units for every thousand dollars of variable cost.

The total productivity of all resources required to manufacture the output is often used in assessing production operations. Achieving higher productivity by making more units is an important first step for a successful firm.

### Limitations of Total Productivity

Total productivity measures the combined productivity of all operating factors. As such, use of a total productivity measure in performance evaluations decreases the possibility of manipulating some of the manufacturing factors to improve the productivity measure of other manufacturing factors.

However, total productivity is a financial productivity measure. Personnel at the operational level may have difficulty linking financial productivity measures to their day-to-day operations. Furthermore, deterioration in total productivity can result from increased costs of resources that were beyond the manager's control, or decreased productivity of some of the input resources that were outside the control of the manager. Ambiguity in the relationship between the controllability of operations and a performance measure based on total productivity could defeat the purpose of having a productivity measurement.

In addition, productivity measures can ignore the effects of changes in demand for the product, changes in selling prices of the goods or services, and changes in special purchasing or selling arrangements on productivity. For example, a special arrangement to sell products at a discount price decreases the productivity in dollars of output per input unit. Alternatively, a special purchase of materials increases financial productivity. Neither of these actions can be attributed to a loss or gain in productivity.

## Analyzing Sales: Comparison with the Master Budget

In comparing the master budget to actual results for sales, this section uses the flexible budget to help answer strategic questions about sales performance. Are sales increasing at the expected rate? Are sales as profitable as expected? How much success has the firm had at increasing its share of the market in its industry? What factors have contributed to the increase or decrease in sales growth and profitability? These questions can be answered by further analyzing the sales variances first introduced in Chapter 14. For a quick review, look at Exhibit 14.4 on page 569 and note that the comparison of actual sales with budgeted sales, using the flexible budget, identifies the two variances to explain the difference between actual and budgeted sales dollars. These two variances are the sales volume variance (measured in sales dollars rather than contribution) and the selling price variance. The sales volume variance is due to a change in units sold times budgeted selling price. Budgeted unit sales were 1,000 units in this example, budget price was $800, the actual sales in units were 780 units, and total actual sales dollars were $639,600. The actual price received was $639,600/780, or $820, a $20 improvement over the budgeted price. The sales volume variance of $176,000 (U) is computed in Exhibit 14.4 as follows:

$$\text{Sales volume variance} = \text{Budgeted sales price} \times \text{Change in sales volume}$$

$$\$176,000 \text{ (U)} = \$800 \times (1,000 - 780) = \$800,000 - \$624,000$$

We use the (U) after the variance to indicate it is unfavorable, because unit sales were below budget. The selling price variance is completed in a similar fashion. Note that it is favorable because of the $20 increase in price.

$$\text{Selling price variance} = \text{Actual sales units} \times \text{Change in price}$$

$$\$15,600 \text{ (F)} = 780 \times (\$820 - \$800) = \$15,600 = \$639,600 - \$624,000$$

The favorable selling price variance reflects the positive effect on profits of an increase in selling price over the budget. For simplicity, this example has assumed a single product, so the sales price and sales volume variances are easy to interpret. The more common case is there are two or more products. The selling price variance could then be computed for each product in a manner similar to the above. Management would also investigate whether a change in the price of one product might be associated with or caused by a change in the price of another product. A more complete coverage of pricing issues is provided in Chapter 13.

When there are multiple products, the sales volume variance could also be computed for each product in a manner similar to the above. Also, the volume variance can be partitioned into two further parts, one that relates to the mix, or proportion, of products in total sales, and the other to the total quantity of sales. The further analysis allows managers to see how changes in product mix and total quantity affect profits. While the selling price variance is measured in sales dollars (as we have shown above), when the volume variance is partitioned into the quantity and mix variances, these three variances are commonly measured in terms of *contribution margin,* as we will see below.

## Sales Volume Variance Partitioned into Sales Quantity and Sales Mix Variances

### Sales Quantity Variance

**LO 16-3**

*Use the flexible budget to calculate and interpret the sales quantity, sales mix, market size, and market share variances.*

**Sales quantity variance**

focuses on deviations between the number of units sold and the number of units budgeted to be sold and measures the effect of these deviations on operating results.

One contributing factor to the sales volume variances of firms with multiple products is the difference between the budgeted and the actual sales units—the sales quantity variance. The **sales quantity variance** focuses on deviations between the number of units sold and the number of units budgeted to be sold and measures the effect of these deviations on contribution and income. A product's sales quantity variance is the product of three elements:

1. The difference in *total units of all products* between the actual units sold and the units budgeted to be sold.
2. The budgeted sales mix ratio of the product. The sales mix for a product is its sales in units as percent of total sales in units.
3. The budgeted contribution margin per unit of the product.

With the focus of a sales quantity variance being the difference in total units between the actual units sold and the budgeted units, we use the budgeted amounts for the other two elements, sales mix and contribution margin per unit, to compute the sales quantity variance.

$$
\begin{array}{c}\text{Sales}\\\text{quantity}\\\text{variance of}\\\text{a product}\end{array} = \left(\begin{array}{c}\text{Total units}\\\text{of all}\\\text{products}\\\text{sold}\end{array} - \begin{array}{c}\text{Budgeted}\\\text{total units}\\\text{of all}\\\text{products}\end{array}\right) \times \begin{array}{c}\text{Budgeted}\\\text{sales mix}\\\text{of the}\\\text{product}\end{array} \times \begin{array}{c}\text{Budgeted}\\\text{contribution}\\\text{margin per unit}\\\text{of the product}\end{array}
$$

Notice that the calculation of the sales quantity variance for a product uses the budgeted sales mix and the budgeted contribution margin per unit of the product. However, the difference in quantity is the difference between the total number of units sold and the total number of units budgeted to be sold for all of the firm's products.

### Sales Mix Variance

**Sales mix**

is the relative proportion of sales of each product to total sales.

**Sales mix variance**

is the effect that changes in the relative proportions of products from the budgeted proportions have on the total contribution margin or operating income of the period.

The second component of the volume variance is the sales mix variance. **Sales mix** is the relative proportion of a product's sales to total sales. A product's **sales mix variance** is the effect that a change in the relative proportion of the product from the budgeted proportion has on the total contribution margin of the period. It is calculated by multiplying the difference between budgeted and actual sales mix by the number of total units sold and the budgeted contribution margin per unit:

$$
\begin{array}{c}\text{Sales mix}\\\text{variance of}\\\text{a product}\end{array} = \left[\begin{array}{c}\text{Actual sales}\\\text{mix of the}\\\text{product}\end{array} - \begin{array}{c}\text{Budgeted sales}\\\text{mix of the}\\\text{product}\end{array}\right] \times \begin{array}{c}\text{Total}\\\text{units}\\\text{sold}\end{array} \times \begin{array}{c}\text{Budgeted contribution}\\\text{margin per unit of}\\\text{the product}\end{array}
$$

### Illustration of the Calculation of the Sales Quantity and Sales Mix Variances

The calculations for the sales quantity and sales mix variances can be illustrated using information from the Schmidt Machinery Company (used in Chapter 14). Assume that, as in Chapter 14, we have product XV-1 but that now in addition we have product FB-33. These are the only two products sold by Schmidt Machinery. In contrast to the results for the month of October 2013 used in Chapter 14, we are now considering budgeted and actual results for the month of December 2013; the budgeted information is shown in Exhibit 16.7 and the actual information is shown in Exhibit 16.8. Note in comparing Exhibits 16.7 and 16.8 that there is no difference in prices, variable costs, or fixed costs; the only differences are in units sold. This allows us to focus strictly on the sales quantity

**EXHIBIT 16.7**
**Master Budget for Schmidt Machinery**

**SCHMIDT MACHINERY COMPANY**
**Master Budget**
**For the Month Ended December 31, 2013**

|  | XV-1 | | FB-33 | | Both Products |
|---|---|---|---|---|---|
|  | Total | Per Unit | Total | Per Unit | Total |
| Units | 1,000 | | 3,000 | | 4,000 |
| Sales | $800,000 | $800 | $1,800,000 | $600 | $2,600,000 |
| Variable costs | 450,000 | 450 | 960,000 | 320 | 1,410,000 |
| Contribution margin | $350,000 | $350 | $ 840,000 | $280 | $1,190,000 |
| Fixed costs | 150,000 | | 450,000 | | 600,000 |
| Operating income | $200,000 | | $ 390,000 | | $ 590,000 |

**EXHIBIT 16.8**
**Income Statements for Two Products**

**SCHMIDT MACHINERY COMPANY**
**Income Statement**
**For the Month Ended December 31, 2013**

|  | XV-1 | | FB-33 | | Both Products |
|---|---|---|---|---|---|
|  | Total | Per Unit | Total | Per Unit | Total |
| Units | 1,600 | | 3,400 | | 5,000 |
| Sales | $1,280,000 | $800 | $2,040,000 | $600 | $3,320,000 |
| Variable costs | 720,000 | 450 | 1,088,000 | 320 | 1,808,000 |
| Contribution margin | $ 560,000 | $350 | $ 952,000 | $280 | $1,512,000 |
| Fixed costs | 150,000 | | 450,000 | | 600,000 |
| Operating income | $ 410,000 | | $ 502,000 | | $ 912,000 |

and sales mix variances for these two products. To begin the analysis we calculate the budgeted and actual sales mix, as follows:

| Product | Units Sold | Actual Sales Mix | Budgeted Sales Mix | Budgeted Sales |
|---|---|---|---|---|
| XV-1 | 1,600 | 32% = 1,600/5,000 | 25% = 1,000/4,000 | $1,000 |
| FB-33 | 3,400 | 68  = 3,400/5,000 | 75  = 3,000/4,000 | 3,000 |
| Total | 5,000 | 100% | 100% | $4,000 |

The calculation of the mix and quantity variances for each product are illustrated in Exhibit 16.9, using the flexible budget. Panel 1 of Exhibit 16.9 shows the flexible budget framework that is used to calculate the variances. Note that the master budget is in the right-hand column C while column A has the actual sales mix, and B has the budgeted sales mix. The difference between columns B and C is the budgeted (column C) and actual (column B) total units sold. Panel 2 of Exhibit 16.9 shows the calculation of the mix and quantity variances for product XV-1, while panel 3 shows the calculations for product FB-33. Panel 4 shows the total for both products, and panel 5 shows the summary of the results for each product and in total. Note that the sales quantity variance plus the sales mix variance for each product equals the sales volume variance for that product. Also, the volume variance calculated here can be reconciled to the volume variance as determined directly from the comparison of actual and budgeted results in Exhibits 16.8 and 16.7, respectively. Since actual sales price equals budget sales price in this example, the selling price variance equals zero, and since the volume variance plus the selling price variance is the total sales variance, the entire difference between actual and budget contribution margin is the volume variance ($1,512,000 − $1,190,000 = $322,000). See panel 4 of Exhibit 16.9.

**EXHIBIT 16.9   Sales Mix and Quantity Variances**

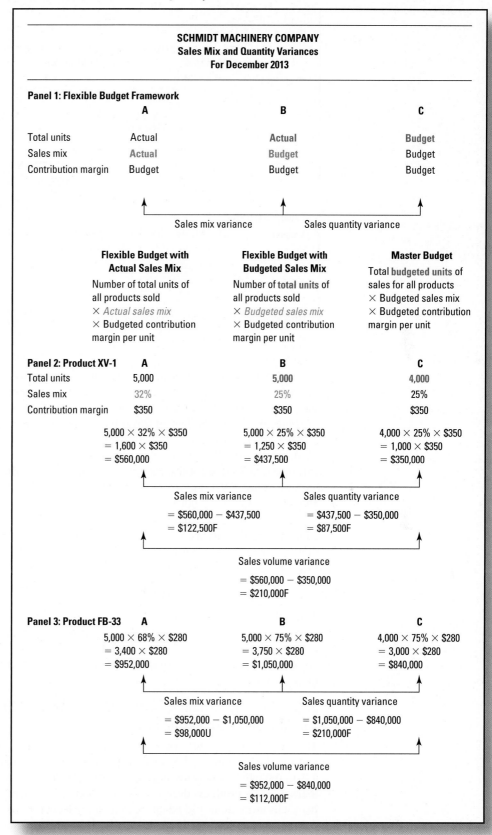

**SCHMIDT MACHINERY COMPANY**
**Sales Mix and Quantity Variances**
**For December 2013**

**Panel 1: Flexible Budget Framework**

|  | A | B | C |
|---|---|---|---|
| Total units | Actual | **Actual** | **Budget** |
| Sales mix | Actual | Budget | Budget |
| Contribution margin | Budget | Budget | Budget |

Sales mix variance   Sales quantity variance

| **Flexible Budget with Actual Sales Mix** | **Flexible Budget with Budgeted Sales Mix** | **Master Budget** |
|---|---|---|
| Number of total units of all products sold × Actual sales mix × Budgeted contribution margin per unit | Number of **total units** of all products sold × Budgeted sales mix × Budgeted contribution margin per unit | Total **budgeted units** of sales for all products × Budgeted sales mix × Budgeted contribution margin per unit |

**Panel 2: Product XV-1**

|  | A | B | C |
|---|---|---|---|
| Total units | 5,000 | 5,000 | 4,000 |
| Sales mix | 32% | 25% | 25% |
| Contribution margin | $350 | $350 | $350 |

| 5,000 × 32% × $350 | 5,000 × 25% × $350 | 4,000 × 25% × $350 |
|---|---|---|
| = 1,600 × $350 | = 1,250 × $350 | = 1,000 × $350 |
| = $560,000 | = $437,500 | = $350,000 |

Sales mix variance
= $560,000 − $437,500
= $122,500F

Sales quantity variance
= $437,500 − $350,000
= $87,500F

Sales volume variance
= $560,000 − $350,000
= $210,000F

**Panel 3: Product FB-33**

|  | A | B | C |
|---|---|---|---|
|  | 5,000 × 68% × $280 | 5,000 × 75% × $280 | 4,000 × 75% × $280 |
|  | = 3,400 × $280 | = 3,750 × $280 | = 3,000 × $280 |
|  | = $952,000 | = $1,050,000 | = $840,000 |

Sales mix variance
= $952,000 − $1,050,000
= $98,000U

Sales quantity variance
= $1,050,000 − $840,000
= $210,000F

Sales volume variance
= $952,000 − $840,000
= $112,000F

**EXHIBIT 16.9** Continued

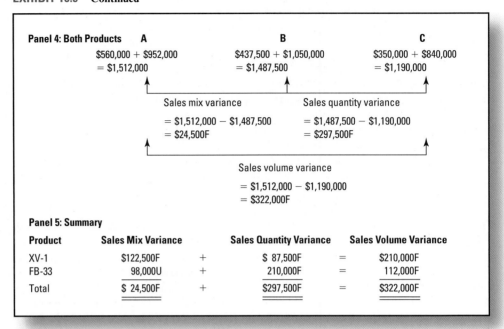

**Panel 4: Both Products**

|  | A | B | C |
|---|---|---|---|
|  | $560,000 + $952,000 | $437,500 + $1,050,000 | $350,000 + $840,000 |
|  | = $1,512,000 | = $1,487,500 | = $1,190,000 |

Sales mix variance
= $1,512,000 − $1,487,500
= $24,500F

Sales quantity variance
= $1,487,500 − $1,190,000
= $297,500F

Sales volume variance
= $1,512,000 − $1,190,000
= $322,000F

**Panel 5: Summary**

| Product | Sales Mix Variance | | Sales Quantity Variance | | Sales Volume Variance |
|---|---|---|---|---|---|
| XV-1 | $122,500F | + | $ 87,500F | = | $210,000F |
| FB-33 | 98,000U | + | 210,000F | = | 112,000F |
| Total | $ 24,500F | + | $297,500F | = | $322,000F |

The analysis has partitioned the volume variance into meaningful components. For example, with the information in Exhibit 16.9, managers would note that the change in sales mix in favor of a higher proportion of sales of XV-1 (this product increased to 32% of total sales over a budget of 25%) has a net positive effect on contribution and profit because XV-1 has a higher unit contribution than FB-33 (XV-1's contribution per unit is $350, while FB-33's contribution is $280, from Exhibit 16.8). The favorable quantity variance reflects that total sales units were greater than the number indicated in the master budget (for XV-1, an increase of 600 units = 1,600 − 1,000; for FB-33, an increase of 400 units = 3,400 − 3,000).

Note that the mix, quantity, and volume variances can be calculated on the basis of contribution margin (as we have done above), or on the basis of total sales units or sales dollars. For example, if we were to use sales dollars to complete the analysis in Exhibit 16.9, then the sales mix variance for XV-1 would have been:

$$(1,600 − 1,250) \times \$800 = \$280,000$$

rather than as is currently calculated, based on contribution margin:

$$(1,600 − 1,250) \times \$350 = \$122,500$$

Both methods are used in practice, but the contribution margin method is more commonly used.

### Sales Quantity Variance Partitioned into Market Size and Market Share Variances

Two contributing factors of the sales quantity variance are changes in the market size and the firm's share of the market. As the total global market for its products increases, a firm is likely to sell more units. Conversely, the firm is likely to sell fewer units when the market for its products decreases. Also, when a firm's share of the market increases, the firm sells more units and when market share decreases, sales fall.

At the time Schmidt prepared the budget for December 2013 the firm expected that the total global market for both its products, XV-1 and FB-33, would be 40,000 units per month and that Schmidt would have 10% of the total global market. The master budget data for December is shown in Exhibit 16.7. Exhibit 16.8 shows the actual operations of the month. Exhibit 16.9 shows that the firm had a favorable total sales quantity variance of $297,500, an amount which can be attributed to both a change in market size and a change in market share.

### *Market Size Variance*

**Market size variance**
is the effect of changes in market size on a firm's total contribution margin.

Market size is the total units for the industry. The **market size variance** measures the effect of changes in market size on a firm's total contribution margin. As the market size expands, firms are likely to sell more units. Conversely, as the market size contracts, firms are likely to sell fewer units. In computing the market size variance, the focus is on the change in market size: the difference between the actual and budgeted market sizes (units). When determining the market size variance of a firm, we assume that the firm maintains the budgeted market share and the budgeted average contribution margin per unit. The equation for computing a market size variance follows:

$$\begin{array}{c}\text{Market} \\ \text{size} \\ \text{variance}\end{array} = \left(\begin{array}{c}\text{Actual} \\ \text{market size} \\ \text{(in units)}\end{array} - \begin{array}{c}\text{Budgeted} \\ \text{market size} \\ \text{(in units)}\end{array}\right) \times \begin{array}{c}\text{Budgeted} \\ \text{market} \\ \text{share}\end{array} \times \begin{array}{c}\text{Weighted-average} \\ \text{budgeted contribution} \\ \text{margin per unit}\end{array}$$

The first term on the right side of the equation is the focus of the variance: the difference in market size (in units) between the actual and the budgeted market size. The second term is the budgeted market share. The product of the first two terms is the effect of the change in market size on unit sales if the firm maintains the budgeted market share. To estimate the effect on contribution of the change in sales units, we multiply the number of units by contribution margin per unit, the last term in the equation. Notice that the contribution margin per unit is the weighted-average budgeted contribution margin per unit of all of the firm's products in the same market, not the contribution margin per unit of an individual product. The weighted-average budgeted contribution margin per unit for a firm is determined by dividing the total units of the firm into the total contribution margin of the firm. Some managers refer to this contribution margin as the *composite contribution margin per unit.* Schmidt Machinery Company budgeted to sell 4,000 units of XV-1 and FB-33 to earn a total contribution margin of $1,190,000, as shown in Exhibit 16.7. Thus, the weighted-average budgeted contribution per unit is $297.50 ($1,190,000/4,000 units).

The firm budgeted to sell 4,000 units and expected the total market to be 40,000 units. The budgeted market share is 10% of the total market. The total market for December 2013 turned out to be 31,250 units; the total market size decreased. Panel 1 of Exhibit 16.10 shows the calculation of Schmidt's market size variance, which is $260,312.50 unfavorable.

**EXHIBIT 16.10**
**Market Size and Market Share Variances**

**SCHMIDT MACHINERY COMPANY**
**Market Size and Share Variances**
**For December 2013**

**Panel 1: Market Size Variance**
= **Difference in market size × Budgeted market share × Weighted-average budgeted contribution margin per unit**
= (31,250 − 40,000) × 10% × $297.50 = $260,312.50U

**Panel 2: Market Share Variance**
= **Difference in market share × Actual market size × Weighted-average budgeted contribution margin per unit**
= (16% − 10%) × 31,250 × $297.50 = $557,812.50F

**Panel 3: Reconciliation**

| | |
|---|---|
| Market size variance | $260,312.50U |
| Market share variance | 557,812,50F |
| Sales quantity variance | $297,500.00F |

The actual market size of the industry (31,250 units) is a decrease of 8,750 units from the budgeted market size of 40,000 units. If the firm maintained its budgeted market share of 10%, the 8,750 units decrease in market size would have decreased Schmidt's total sales by 875 units. With a weighted-average contribution margin of $297.50 per unit, the decrease in units (875) would have decreased Schmidt's total contribution margin and operating income by $260,312.50.

### Market Share Variance

Market share is a firm's proportion of a particular market. The market share of a firm is a function of its core competitive competencies and competitive environment and reflects the firm's competitive position. A successful firm maintains or increases its market share. A firm experiencing continuous erosion in its market share would likely experience financial difficulties.

**Market share variance**

measures the effect of changes in market share on total contribution margin and operating income.

The **market share variance** compares a firm's actual market share to its budgeted market share and measures the effect of the difference in market shares on the firm's total contribution margin and operating income. Three items are involved in determining the market share variance: the difference between the firm's actual and budgeted market share, the total actual market size, and the weighted-average budgeted contribution margin per unit. Notice that the computation uses the *actual,* not budgeted, total market size and the *budgeted,* not actual, weighted-average contribution margin per unit. The product of these three factors—the difference in market shares, total actual market size, and weighted-average budgeted contribution margin per unit—is the market share variance. The equation is:

$$\begin{matrix} \text{Market} \\ \text{share} \\ \text{variance} \end{matrix} = \begin{pmatrix} \text{Actual} & & \text{Budgeted} \\ \text{market} & - & \text{market} \\ \text{share} & & \text{share} \end{pmatrix} \times \begin{matrix} \text{Total actual} \\ \text{market size} \\ \text{(in units)} \end{matrix} \times \begin{matrix} \text{Weighted-average} \\ \text{budgeted contribution} \\ \text{margin per unit} \end{matrix}$$

Panel 2 of Exhibit 16.10 shows the calculation of the market share variance for Schmidt Machinery Company's December 2013 operations.

Although the total market for the industry decreased to 31,250, Schmidt's total units sold are higher than the budgeted sales for the period. Its market share increased from the budgeted 10% to 16% (5,000 units ÷ 31,250 units = 16%)—an increase of 6%. With the actual total market size being 31,250 units, the 6% increase in the market share increased Schmidt's total sales by 1,875 units. At a budgeted weighted-average contribution margin of $297.50 per unit, the increase of 1,875 units increased its total contribution margin and operating income by $557,812.50.

Together, the market size variance and market share variance equal the sales quantity variance of the period. Panel 3 of Exhibit 16.10 confirms this result. For December 2013, the total of these two variances is $297,500 favorable, which equals the sales quantity variance reported in Exhibit 16.9.

Exhibit 16.11 shows the calculation of the market size and market share variances using a flexible budget framework. The results are the same as in Exhibit 16.10. Remember that market share and market size variances explain the firm's sales quantity variance. The total variance in Exhibit 16.11, the difference between points A and C, is the total sales quantity variance for both products. Point A of Exhibit 16.11 is the budgeted total contribution margin that the firm would have earned from the actual number of units sold. Starting from the industry's total market size, the total number of units sold by the firm is the product of the industry's total actual market size and the firm's actual market share:

$$31,250 \text{ units} \times 16\% = 5,000 \text{ units}$$

The weighted-average budgeted contribution margin per unit is $297.50. Therefore, the total budgeted contribution margin from 5,000 actual sales units is $1,487,500, as shown at point A of panel 2.

Point B is the budgeted total contribution margin the firm would have earned, given the actual market size, had it maintained the budgeted market share. With the actual

**EXHIBIT 16.11**   **Analyzing Market Size and Share Variances Using Columnar Form**

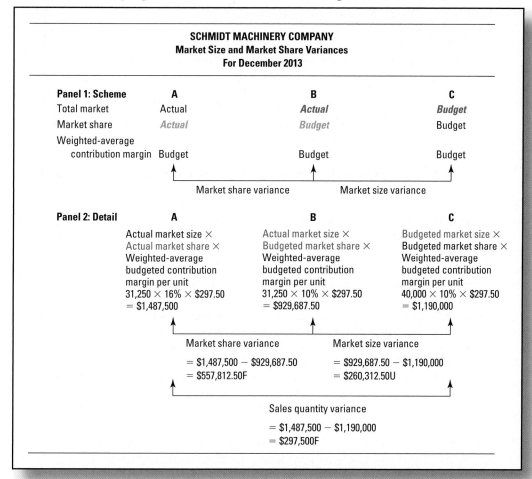

market size of 31,250, the firm would have sold 3,125 total units if it had maintained its budgeted market share of 10%. At the weighted-average budgeted contribution margin of $297.50 per unit the total contribution margin would be $929,687.50. The only difference between point A and point B is in market share. The $557,812.50 difference ($1,487,500 − $929,687.50) between these two points, therefore, is a market share variance. This variance is favorable because the actual market share is 16%, as opposed to the budgeted 10%.

Point C is the master budget. The budgeted total units of sales in the master budget is the product of the budgeted market size and the budgeted market share:

$$40,000 \times 10\% = 4,000 \text{ units}$$

At the weighted-average budgeted contribution margin of $297.50 per unit the total budgeted contribution margin in the master budget is

$$4,000 \text{ units} \times \$297.50 \text{ per unit} = \$1,190,000$$

The only difference between point B and point C is in the total market size: actual market size at Point B and budgeted market size at point C. The difference, therefore, is a market size variance, which is $260,312.50. The variance is unfavorable because the actual market size is smaller than the budgeted market size anticipated at the time when the firm prepared the master budget for December 2013. The various components of sales performance are summarized in Exhibit 16.12.

Note that the market share and market size variances can be calculated on the basis of contribution margin (as we have done above) or on the basis of total sales units or sales

**EXHIBIT 16.12**
**Components of Sales Variances**

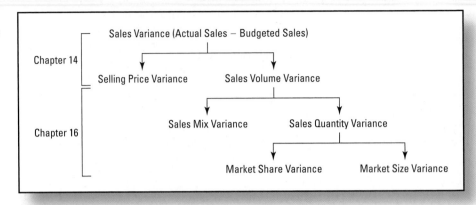

dollars. All three methods are used in practice, but the contribution margin method is most common, and therefore is the one we use in this chapter.

### The Five Steps of Strategic Decision Making for Schmidt Machinery

Schmidt Machinery is a well-established firm that produces very high-quality all-weather furniture which is used on patios and decks and in sunrooms. Product XV-1 is a light-weight but durable lounge chair and FB-33 is a lightweight and durable table. Because of its very high quality and reputation for design innovation, Schmidt's products are sold largely by catalog and over the firm's website; a few high-end retailers also carry the brand. The firm has few direct competitors in the United States, but there are a growing number of competitors from Europe and Asia. Also, the decline of the dollar against other currencies in prior years helped Schmidt maintain its domestic sales and to have some opportunities for foreign sales. However, the global economic recession and a recent rise in the dollar has reduced sales worldwide. While Schmidt's sales have increased, the company is concerned that the recession will deepen and that sales of its products will eventually be affected. Schmidt is facing questions such as which production lines to close and which product advertising to increase or decrease should that happen. Schmidt knows that the XV-1 product has a larger percentage of its sales overseas than FB-33 but Schmidt is not sure which of its two products should be supported at this difficult time.

1. **Determine the strategic issues surrounding the problem.** Schmidt is a differentiated manufacturer, selling a high-priced product to those who value its quality, design, and functionality. With the growth of foreign competition and the increased price competition, Schmidt is now looking for ways to maintain its profitability by determining an effective marketing strategy for its two products.

2. **Identify the alternative actions.** The question facing Schmidt is whether to scale back production and marketing of one or both of its products.

3. **Obtain information and conduct analyses of the alternatives.** Schmidt calculates the sales quantity and market share and market size variances as illustrated in Exhibits 16.10 and 16.11. Schmidt also conducts further economic analysis which shows that, in the coming years, the dollar will likely rise against other currencies and that the worldwide recession will continue to show lower and lower levels of consumer spending.

4. **Based on strategy and analysis, choose and implement the desired alternative.** Based on an analysis of the quantity, market share, and market size variances for both products, which show an unfavorable market size variance but a favorable market share variance and a favorable quantity variance, and with the negative news about the dollar and the global recession, Schmidt decides to make contingency plans for the possible reduction in the production and sales of the FB-33 product. One reason is the lower unit contribution of the FB-33 product. The second reason is that while the global recession will affect sales worldwide, and XV-1 has a greater share of worldwide sales, Schmidt expects that the recession will have the greatest negative impact on sales in the United States and thus a relatively greater impact on FB-33.

5. **Provide an ongoing evaluation of the effectiveness of implementation in step 4.** As the global economic environment becomes more predictable, including potential changes in the value of the dollar, management should continue to review its planning for the two products. Also, management should consider obtaining additional information about the market size for each product (for example, by country or region), so that the company can further partition the market share and market size variances for each product.

## Analyzing Sales: Comparison with Prior Year Results

**LO 16-4**

*Use the flexible budget to analyze sales performance over time.*

A common application of sales performance analysis is to partition the difference between the current period's profit and the prior year's profit. The analytical framework, based on the flexible budget, is the same as for the analysis of the master budget immediately above. For example, suppose that Schmidt Machinery has another month of operations to consider, the month of January 2014. We use the actual data for December, as used in the prior section, and analyze the change in sales performance from December to January. The relevant information is shown in Exhibit 16.13. We assume that fixed costs do not change, and since unit variable costs have not changed, the only changes to analyze in this example are changes in units sold and prices for the two products.

Notice that the December 2013 data is the same as shown in Exhibit 16.8, with product contribution margins for XV-1 of $350 ($800 − $450) and for FB-33, $280 ($600 − $320). The contribution margins in January 2011 are $355 and $270 for XV-1 and FB-33, respectively. Our first step is to calculate the income statements for January and December, as shown in Exhibit 16.14.

### Analysis of Selling Price and Volume Variances

The next step is to decompose the total difference in contribution margin (or difference in operating income) of $4,950 ($1,512,000 − $1,507,050; or also $912,000 − $907,050) by calculating the selling price and volume variances for January, as shown in Exhibit 16.15.

The selling price variance is a net unfavorable variance of $28,050, composed of a favorable selling price variance for XV-1 of $7,650 and an unfavorable selling price

**EXHIBIT 16.13**
**Schmidt Machinery Company Actual Data**

|  | January 2014 | December 2013 |
|---|---|---|
| Sales units | 5,100 | 5,000 |
| Sales mix for each product |  |  |
| XV-1 | 30% | 32% |
| FB-33 | 70% | 68% |
| Price |  |  |
| XV-1 | $805 | $800 |
| FB-33 | 590 | 600 |
| Variable cost per unit |  |  |
| XV-1 | 450 | 450 |
| FB-33 | 320 | 320 |

**EXHIBIT 16.14**
**Comparative Income Statements for Schmidt Machinery Company**

|  | January 2014 | December 2013 |
|---|---|---|
| Sales XV-1 | $1,231,650 | $1,280,000 |
| Sales FB-33 | 2,106,300 | 2,040,000 |
| Total sales | 3,337,950 | 3,320,000 |
| Less variable costs | 1,830,900 | 1,808,000 |
| Contribution margin | 1,507,050 | 1,512,000 |
| Less fixed costs | 600,000 | 600,000 |
| Operating income | $ 907,050 | $ 912,000 |

**EXHIBIT 16.15**   **Selling Price and Volume Variances for January 2014**

| | January 2014 | Sales Price Variance | Flexible Budget | Sales Volume Variance | December 2013 |
|---|---|---|---|---|---|
| Sales | | | | | |
| XV-1 | $1,231,650 | $ 7,650 | $1,224,000 | $(56,000) | $1,280,000 |
| FB-33 | 2,106,300 | (35,700) | 2,142,000 | 102,000 | 2,040,000 |
| Total sales | 3,337,950 | (28,050) | 3,366,000 | 46,000 | 3,320,000 |
| Variable costs | | | | | |
| XV-1 | 688,500 | – | 688,500 | (31,500) | 720,000 |
| FB-33 | 1,142,400 | – | 1,142,400 | 54,400 | 1,088,000 |
| Total variable costs | 1,830,900 | | 1,830,900 | 22,900 | 1,808,000 |
| Contribution margin | | | | | |
| XV-1 | 543,150 | 7,650 | 535,500 | (24,500) | 560,000 |
| FB-33 | 963,900 | (35,700) | 999,600 | 47,600 | 952,000 |
| Total contribution margin | 1,507,050 | $(28,050) | $1,535,100 | $ 23,100 | 1,512,000 |
| Fixed costs | 600,000 | | | | 600,000 |
| Operating income | $ 907,050 | | | | $ 912,000 |

variance for FB-33 of $35,700. The selling price variance for XV-1 is due to the price increase of $5: $7,650 = 5,100 × .3 × $5. The selling price variance for FB-33 is due to the price decline of $10: $35,700 = 5,100 × .7 × $10.

The sales volume variance is a net favorable variance of $46,000. The volume for XV-1 fell by 70 units [(.32 × 5,000) − (.3 × 5,100)], at a price of $800 each, or $56,000 unfavorable. In contrast, the sales of FB-33 increased by 170 units [(.7 × 5,100) − (.68 × 5,000)], at a price of $600 each, or $102,000.

The flexible budget column in the center of Exhibit 16.15 is determined from January sales in units (including January sales mix), December prices, and December unit variable costs. For example, the flexible budget for sales of the two products is:

XV-1:   $1,224,000 = 5,100 units × 30% mix × $800

FB-33:  $2,142,000 = 5,100 units × 70% mix × $600

The flexible budget for variable costs for the two products is determined in a similar way:

XV-1:      $688,500 = 5,100 units × 30% mix × $450

FB-33:  $1,142,400 = 5,100 units × 70% mix × $320

In this case, since January unit variable costs are the same as December unit variable costs, the flexible budget for variable costs is the same as the total actual variable cost for January.

Overall, the analysis of sales data for January shows that the relatively small selling price changes are associated with significant changes in volume and selling price variances. For product XV-1, where price increased, there was a significant favorable selling price variance but a much larger unfavorable volume variance. The case for product FB-33 is somewhat different: the price decrease caused a significant unfavorable selling price variance, but a much larger favorable volume variance. Total sales increased by $17,950 ($46,000 − $28,050; or equivalently, $3,337,950 − $3,320,000) which is the net effect of the selling price and volume variances for both products. However, variable costs increased by $22,900 ($1,830,900 − $1,808,000) due to the increase in volume; that is, the increase in sales of 100 units caused an increase in total variable cost (170 units increase for FB-33 at $320 each, less 70 units reduction in volume for XV-1 at $450 each). The net effect is a relatively small reduction in total contribution and operating income of $4,950 ($912,000 − $907,050).

## Analysis of Mix and Quantity Variances

The above analysis can be enhanced by computing the mix and quantity variances for each product, as illustrated in Exhibit 16.16.

**EXHIBIT 16.16**
**Sales Mix and Quantity Variances by Product Line**

| | Sales Mix Variance | Sales Quantity Variance | Volume Variance |
|---|---|---|---|
| XV-1 | $(35,700)U | $11,200F | $(24,500)U |
| FB-33 | 28,560F | 19,040F | 47,600F |
| Contribution margin | $ (7,140)U | $30,240F | $ 23,100F |

The mix variances are determined as follows:

Change in mix × Units sold in January 2014 × December 2013 unit contribution

XV-1:  (.3 − .32) × 5,100 × $350 = $35,700 unfavorable

FB-33:  (.7 − .68) × 5,100 × $280 = 28,560 favorable

The quantity variances are determined as follows:

Change in total units sold × December 2013 sales mix × December 2013 contribution margin

XV-1:  (5,100 − 5,000) × .32 × $350 = $11,200 favorable

FB-33:  (5,100 − 5,000) × .68 × $280 = $19,040 favorable

Note that the total of the mix and quantity variances equals the volume variance for each product, as expected. In effect, the analysis of the change in operating income from December 2013 to January 2014 is very similar to the analysis for a comparison with the master budget, and the interpretation of the variances is also similar. In the period-to-period analysis, the interpretation focuses on changes from the prior period, instead of on variances between performance and the master budget.

## Analysis of Variable Cost Variances

The above approach can also be extended to analyze the changes in unit variable costs. This would involve calculating price and usage variances for materials and labor, much like the procedures used in Chapter 14. Again, the flexible budget based on actual output and prior year actual unit variable costs would provide the desired framework. For example, if the unit variable cost in January for product XV-1 was $460 rather than $450 as shown in Exhibit 16.13, and assuming that the unit variable cost for XV-1 was $450 in December, then we can calculate a variable cost variance as follows for January:

Variable cost flexible-budget variance = ($460 − $450) × 5,100 × .3 = $15,300U

The variable cost flexible-budget variance could also then be partitioned into the six variances for usage and price of materials and labor, and usage and spending for variable overhead. The partition would be done in the same manner as explained and illustrated in Chapters 14 and 15.

## Summary

Productivity is the ratio of output to input. Improvements in productivity enable firms to do more with fewer resources. A productivity measure is often compared to the performance of a prior period, another firm, the industry standard, or a benchmark in assessing a firm's productivity.

Partial productivity is the ratio of output level attained to the amount of an input resource used in the operation. The higher the ratio, the better. A partial operational productivity is the required physical amount of an input resource to produce one unit of output. The partial financial productivity of an input resource is the number of units or the value of output manufactured for each dollar spent on the input resource. A partial financial productivity measure can be separated into changes in productivity, input price, and output. The productivity change is the difference between the actual amount used and the expected amount of input resources to manufacture the output. The input price change accounts for the effects of the difference between the budgeted (or benchmark) and the actual prices for the input resource on the operating income of the period.

Total productivity measures the relationship between the output achieved and the total input costs and is usually a financial productivity measure.

Measures of productivity are applicable to all organizations including service firms and not-for-profit organizations. However, imprecise measures for output, or lack of definite relationships between output and input resources may limit the usefulness of productivity measures for some service or not-for-profit organizations.

Increasing global competition and rapid changes in technologies require management to be constantly alert to changes in resource productivity. Management must be aware of levels and changes in its productive factors, such as materials, labor, energy, and processes.

To effectively evaluate sales performance, management must be fully informed of the effects of changes in selling prices, sales volumes, sale mixes, market sizes, and market shares on the firm's sales.

The sales volume variance reflects the difference in contribution margin or operating income between a flexible budget and the master budget. The sales volume variance for a single product firm can be determined by multiplying the budgeted contribution margin per unit of the product times the difference between the number of units sold and the budgeted units to be sold. The sales volume variance of firms with multiple products can be separated into sales mix and sales quantity variances. The sales mix variance is the product of three components: (1) the difference between the actual sales mix (defined as the ratio of the units of the product to the total units of all products) and the budgeted sales mix, (2) the total number of units of all products sold during the period, and (3) the product's budgeted contribution margin.

A product's sales quantity variance has three elements: (1) the difference between the firm's total actual units sold and budgeted sales units, (2) the product's budgeted sales mix, and (3) the budgeted contribution margin. The product of these three elements is the product's sales quantity variance. A sales quantity variance assesses the difference between the units sold and budgeted sales and measures the effect of this difference on total contribution margin and operating income.

A sales quantity variance can be separated further into market size and market share variances. A market size variance assesses the effect of changes in the industry's total market size on the firm's total contribution margin and operating income. A market size variance is the product of three factors: (1) the difference between the actual and the budgeted total market size (in number of units), (2) the firm's budgeted market share, and (3) the weighted-average budgeted contribution margin per unit. The market size variance is favorable if the actual total market size is larger than the market size expected when the master budget was prepared. A market share variance measures the effect of changes in the firm's market share on its operating income. A market share variance is the product of three elements: (1) the actual total number of units in the market (actual market size), (2) the difference between the firm's actual and budgeted market share, and (3) the weighted-average budgeted contribution margin per unit.

Sales performance can be analyzed from either of two benchmarks: the master budget or the prior period. The period-to-period analysis also uses the flexible budget, and the same variances are calculated, with similar interpretations.

## Key Terms

| | | |
|---|---|---|
| financial productivity, *672* | partial productivity, *672* | sales quantity variance, *681* |
| market share variance, *686* | productivity, *672* | total productivity, *672* |
| market size variance, *685* | sales mix, *681* | |
| operational productivity, *672* | sales mix variance, *681* | |

## Comments on Cost Management in Action

### Productivity: Not So Easy to Measure

The examples of the machine shop and the advertising firm indicate that when jobs are cut, some work is spread among remaining employees. The result is that the productivity of the remaining employees is likely to suffer. For example, the managers in the machine shop now have less time to develop proposals for new work or to attend to other management functions. Similarly, the time lost by the advertising professionals will mean more distractions and less progress on serving current clients or seeking new clients. These work losses are not directly measured in the productivity statistics.

The measurement issues that economists advise about are important issues. Managers rely on the productivity statistics to guide them, along with other considerations, in determining when and where to add capacity to their operations. New investment is likely to be drawn to areas with higher productivity. Productivity statistics are also used as benchmarks to help managers assess the performance of their own operations. Timely and reliable productivity data are valuable also for strategic decisions—when to add new products and when to add or cut the workforce.

**Sources:** Peter Whoriskey, "Economists Offer More Pessimistic View on Manufacturing in Upcoming Report," *The Washington Post*, March 19, 2012; Justin Lahart, "Portion of Recent Gains Could Be an Illusion," *The Wall Street Journal*, May 6, 2010, p. A16; Alexander Kowalski and Ilan Kolet, "Productivity Is Not the Savior You Think It Is," *Bloomberg Businessweek*, October 24, 2011, pp. 13–14.

## Self-Study Problems

(For solutions, please turn to the end of the chapter.)

### 1. Productivity Variances

Carlson Automotive Company manufactures fuel-injection systems. It manufactured and sold 60,000 units in 2012 and 64,000 units in 2013 at $25 per unit. In 2012, the firm used 75,000 pounds of alloy TPX–45 at $7.20 per pound and used 10,000 direct labor-hours at an hourly wage rate of $30. In 2013, the firm used 89,600 pounds of alloy TPX–45 at $6.80 per pound and used 10,847 direct labor-hours at an hourly wage rate of $32. The total amount of all other expenses remains the same at $450,000 each year. Jerry Olson, CEO, was disappointed that although the total sales increased in 2013, operating income declined from $210,000 in 2012 to $193,616 in 2013.

**Required**   Analyze the following:
1. Partial operational productivity of direct material and direct labor for both 2012 and 2013.
2. Partial financial productivity of direct material and direct labor for both 2012 and 2013.
3. Detailed partition of partial financial productivity.
4. Total productivity for 2012 and 2013 as measured in both units and sales dollars.

### 2. Sales Variances

Springwater Brewery has two main products: premium and regular ale. Its operating results and master budget for 2013 (000s omitted) follow:

| | Operating Results of 2013 | | | Master Budget for 2013 | | |
|---|---|---|---|---|---|---|
| | **Premium** | **Regular** | **Total** | **Premium** | **Regular** | **Total** |
| Barrels | 180 | 540 | 720 | 240 | 360 | 600 |
| Sales | $28,800 | $62,100 | $90,900 | $36,000 | $43,200 | $79,200 |
| Variable expenses | 16,200 | 40,500 | 56,700 | 21,600 | 27,000 | 48,600 |
| Contribution margin | $12,600 | $21,600 | $34,200 | $14,400 | $16,200 | $30,600 |
| Fixed expenses | 10,000 | 5,000 | 15,000 | 10,000 | 5,000 | 15,000 |
| Operating income | $ 2,600 | $16,600 | $19,200 | $ 4,400 | $11,200 | $15,600 |

Pam Kuder, CEO, expected the total industry sales to be 1,500,000 barrels during the period. After the year, Mark Goldfeder, the controller, reported that the total sales for the industry were 1,600,000 barrels.

**Required**   Calculate the following:
1. Selling price variances for the period for each product and for the firm.
2. Sales volume variances for the period for each product and for the firm.
3. Sales quantity variances for each product and the firm.
4. Sales mix variances for the period for each product and for the firm.
5. The sum of the sales quantity variance and sales mix variance. Also, verify that this total equals the sales volume variance.
6. Market size variance.
7. Market share variance.
8. The sum of market size variance and market share variance. Also, verify that this total equals the sales quantity variance.

*Please visit* **http://www.mhhe.com/blocher6e** *to access a narrated, animated tutorial for solving these problems.*

**Questions**

16-1   What is productivity? What does it measure?

16-2   Discuss why improving productivity is important for a firm that competes on a cost leadership strategy.

16-3   List benchmarks or criteria often used in assessing productivity, and discuss their advantages and disadvantages.

16-4   What is operational productivity? Financial productivity?

16-5   What is partial productivity? Total productivity?

16-6   "A financial productivity measure contains more information than an operational productivity measure does." Do you agree?

16-7   "A total productivity measure encompasses all partial productivity measures." Do you agree?

16-8   "Partial productivity measures should be calculated only for high-value-added activities." Do you agree?

16-9   Why do manufacturing personnel prefer operational productivity measures to financial productivity measures?

16-10  "A productivity measure such as machine-hour productivity is more important in a JIT environment than in a non-JIT environment." Do you agree?

16-11  Which of the following statements is true? (a) The lower the partial productivity ratio, the greater the productivity, (b) productivity improves when partial productivity increases, (c) prices of inputs are incorporated in the partial operational productivity ratio, (d) the partial productivity ratio measures the number of outputs produced per multiple input, and (e) more than one of the above is true.

16-12  List important measures in assessing marketing effectiveness.

16-13  What are the components of the sales variance?

16-14  Distinguish between a selling price variance and a sales volume variance.

16-15  What is the difference between a sales quantity variance and a sales volume variance?

16-16  "As long as a firm sells more units than the units specified in the master budget, it will not have an unfavorable sales volume variance." Do you agree? Why?

16-17  What are the relationships among a selling price variance, a sales mix variance, a sales quantity variance, and a sales volume variance?

16-18  Distinguish between market size variance and market share variance.

16-19  "A favorable sales quantity variance indicates that the marketing manager has done a good job." Do you agree? Can you give an example in which a market size variance or market share variance is opposite to that of the sales quantity variance?

16-20  What are the relationships between market size variance, market share variance, sales quantity variance, and sales volume variance?

16-21  "An improvement in earnings growth can be achieved at the expense of market share (an unfavorable market share variance)." Do you agree?

**Brief Exercises**  Use the following information for brief exercises 16-22 through 16-24. CompuWorld sells two products, R66 and R100, and calculates sales variances using contribution margin. Pertinent data for the current year follow:

| | Budgeted | | Actual | |
|---|---|---|---|---|
| | R66 | R100 | R66 | R100 |
| Selling price | $ 50 | $160 | $ 55 | $ 155 |
| Variable cost per unit | 40 | 90 | 43 | 95 |
| Contribution margin | $ 10 | $ 70 | $ 12 | $ 60 |
| Fixed cost per unit | 6 | 30 | 5 | 25 |
| Operating income | $ 4 | $ 40 | $ 7 | $ 35 |
| Sales in units | 1,200 | 400 | 1,000 | 1,000 |

16-22  What is the R66 sales quantity variance?
    a. $400F                d. $3,000F
    b. $1,000F            e. $3,600F
    c. $1,200F

16-23  What is the R100 sales mix variance?
    a. $20,000F           d. $40,000F
    b. $30,000F           e. $70,000F
    c. $35,000F

16-24  What is the total sales volume variance?
    a. $10,000F           d. $22,000F
    b. $12,400F           e. $40,000F
    c. $13,000F

Use the following information for brief exercises 16-25 through 16-27. C. W. McCall sells a goldplated souvenir mug; McCall expects to sell 1,600 units for $45 each to earn a $25 contribution margin per unit. Janice McCall, president, expects the year's total market to be 32,000 units. For the year just completed, the local college won the national hockey championship, and as a result the total actual market was 100,000 units. C. W. McCall sells 3,000 units and calculates sales variances using contribution margin.

16-25  What is the market share variance?
    a. $8,000U            d. $50,000U
    b. $11,200U          e. $70,000U
    c. $40,000U

16-26  What is the market size variance?
    a. $51,000F           d. $85,000F
    b. $68,000F           e. $119,000F
    c. $71,400F

16-27  What is the firm's sales volume variance?
    a. $35,000F           d. $85,000F
    b. $49,000F           e. $135,000F
    c. $51,000F

16-28  Darwin, Inc., provided the following information:

| | |
|---|---|
| Budgeted production | 10,000 units |
| Actual production | 9,500 units |
| Budgeted input | 9,750 gallons |
| Actual input | 8,950 gallons |

**Required**  What is the partial operational productivity ratio?
a.  0.97 unit per gallon.
b.  1.02 units per gallon.

c. 1.06 units per gallon.

d. 1.12 units per gallon.

e. None of the above.

## Exercises

**[LO 16-1]**   16-29   **Productivity and Strategy; Manufacturing**   To maintain profit growth, several manufacturing companies have responded to the recession by cutting jobs. Harley-Davidson reduced its workforce by 1,400 in 2010 and by an additional 1,600 in 2011. As sales have declined, the company has reduced labor capacity at many plants. The same is true at General Electric, Texas Instruments, Coca-Cola, and many other companies that have reduced capacity at certain plants, closed selected plants entirely, or dropped product lines. In many of these companies, the profits are held as cash, and the companies are holding off on making any new investments until economic conditions improve. Some analysts say the companies are just shrinking their operations to match the decline in expected future demand; the companies are profitable but smaller.

**Required**

1. Do the recent actions by these companies support their long-term strategies?

2. How do the productivity gains at these companies affect profits in the short-term and long-term?

**[LO 16-1]**   16-30   **Productivity; Sustainability**   Telematics is a system of sensors installed on cars and trucks that provides current information on the status and operation of many of the vehicle's parts. It can be used to show the location of the vehicle, the oil level, the condition of the brake pads, whether all lights are working, and whether a seatbelt is buckled, among many other potential measures. United Parcel Service (UPS) uses telematics on nearly one-half of its 55,000-vehicle U.S. truck fleet.

**Required**

1. Describe what you think is UPS's strategy. Does telematics support UPS's strategy, and if so, how?

2. How can telematics be used to improve productivity and sustainability at UPS?

**[LO 16-2]**   16-31   **Productivity and Quality Improvement in Retail**   Most manufacturers have long adopted quality improvement techniques to reduce or eliminate errors, defects, and waste and speed the flow of product to the consumer. Many retailers are now following the lead. For example, Best Buy was able to save approximately $20 million through a quality improvement program that streamlined the installation of appliances. Target has also adopted quality improvement as a means of reducing waste and cost in its retail operations.

**Required**   How does quality improvement as described above differ from productivity?

**[LO 16-2]**   16-32   **Partial Financial Productivity and Total Productivity**   ABC Corporation makes small parts from steel alloy sheets. Management has the flexibility to substitute direct materials for direct manufacturing labor. If workers cut the steel carefully, more parts can be manufactured from a metal sheet, but this requires additional direct manufacturing labor-hours. Alternatively, ABC can use fewer labor-hours if it is willing to tolerate more waste of direct materials. ABC decided to improve materials productivity in 2013 and the following provides information for 2012 and 2013:

|  | 2012 | 2013 |
| --- | --- | --- |
| Output units | 400,000 | 490,000 |
| Direct manufacturing labor-hours | 10,000 | 13,500 |
| Wages per hour | $26 | $24 |
| Direct materials used | 160 tons | 180 tons |
| Direct materials cost per ton | $3,375 | $3,250 |

**Required**   Carry all computations to four digits after the decimal point.

1. Compute the partial financial productivity for both labor and materials for 2012 and 2013.

2. Calculate ABC's total productivity in units per dollar in 2012 and 2013.

3. Evaluate management's decision in 2013 to improve materials productivity.

**[LO 16-2]**   16-33   **Partial Operational and Financial Productivity**   Software Solution (SOS) helps subscribers solve software problems. All transactions are made over the telephone. For the year 2012, 10 engineers, most of whom are recent graduates, handled 100,000 calls. The average yearly salary for software engineers was $45,000. Starting in 2013, the firm retained and hired only software engineers with at least two years of experience. SOS raised the engineers' salary to $60,000 per year. In 2013, eight engineers handled 108,000 calls.

**Required**
1. Calculate the partial operational productivity ratio for both years.
2. Calculate the partial financial productivity ratio for both years.
3. Did the firm make the right decision to hire only software engineers with at least two years' experience?
4. List other factors that should be considered in making the decision.

[LO 16-2]    16-34 **Productivity: Which Way to Lean?**    Lean manufacturing is what a lot of manufacturing firms are after these days. This means a renewed focus on productivity and profitability, particularly for firms that compete on a cost leadership strategy and are facing increased global low-cost competition. Adopting the right accounting approach to facilitate improvements in productivity is critical for these companies. Companies like Whirlpool, Pratt-Whitney (a unit of United Technologies), General Electric, and many other manufacturers are adopting the methods of lean manufacturing.

**Required**
1. How can productivity measures described in this chapter help a company to achieve lean manufacturing?
2. The founding principles of lean manufacturing are based in part on the Toyota Production System. Explain the Toyota Production System and list its four main elements.

[LO 16-2]    16-35 **Quality and Productivity**    Each summer the Harbour Report (**www.oliverwyman.com/ow/automotive.htm**) rates the productivity of the major automakers, including the Detroit Big 3, Toyota, Honda, and many other brands. The report is closely watched as a barometer of the future profitability of the firms. However, some have argued that the productivity reports are insufficient. For example, a company can temporarily raise its productivity by laying off or "buying out" employees. Also, some would argue that the focus on productivity fails to draw attention to other key strategic factors such as quality, design, and customer service. For example, the J.D. Power organization (**www.jdpower.com/autos**) rates the initial quality of many new cars.

**Required**    What do you think are the priorities for the auto companies: quality, productivity, customer service, design, or some other key strategic success factor? Briefly explain your answer.

[LO 16-2]    16-36 **Productivity and the Economy**    The U.S. Bureau of Labor Statistics (**www.bls.gov**) provides quarterly data for productivity in business, nonfarm business, and manufacturing industries. The Bureau also breaks down these data into industry segments. The data for the annual percentage change in productivity for the recent decade is as follows, for the category of business productivity. Capital expenditure data are maintained by the Census Bureau, **http://www.census.gov**.

| Year | Percentage Change in Productivity |
|------|-----------------------------------|
| 1997 | 1.5 |
| 1998 | 2.9 |
| 1999 | 3.3 |
| 2000 | 3.4 |
| 2001 | 2.9 |
| 2002 | 4.6 |
| 2003 | 3.7 |
| 2004 | 2.6 |
| 2005 | 1.6 |
| 2006 | 0.9 |
| 2007 | 1.5 |
| 2008 | 0.6 |
| 2009 | 2.3 |

**Required**   Economists argue that the changes in productivity are influenced by changes in the economy, for example, the economic downturn of 2000–2001 as well as the recent recession which started in 2008. Others argue that productivity is most affected by advances in and adoption of information technology, investments in research and development, and capital investment in new plant and equipment—more highly automated and efficient manufacturing facilities. The data above show that productivity was on the decline in the period 2005–2008 and improved again in 2009. In 2009, capital investment was sluggish as was the pace of innovation and adoption of information technology. Based on the above information and the data from the Census Bureau, what do you forecast the productivity change will be for 2010 and the following couple of years?

**[LO 16-2]**   16-37   **Alternative Measures of Productivity**   A common measure of productivity, as explained in this chapter and as used by many business and trade organizations including the U.S. Bureau of Labor Statistics, is the ratio of output to input, where input is typically measured in units of materials, labor-hours, or related measures. An alternative is to use the ratio of capacity available to capacity utilized. For example, the amount of capacity in the U.S. manufacturing industries has almost doubled over the last two decades. However, the rate of capacity utilization (output/capacity available) has fallen slightly over this period of time, with a steep drop in 2009 followed by slow increases in 2010 and 2011. Some would say that this measure gives a better picture of productivity than the one we have used in the chapter.

**Required**   Compare the measure of productivity based on capacity utilization with the measure used in the chapter. Which measure do you think is most useful for assessing the state of the manufacturing sector of the economy? Explain briefly.

**[LO 16-2]**   16-38   **Productivity Measures for Call Centers**   Our examples in the chapter have focused on manufacturing, where the output is units of product and the inputs are manufacturing activities or costs. The concept of productivity can be applied in a variety of settings, wherever there are inputs and outputs. For example, consider the call center for a cell phone company. Suppose the call center operates 24 hours a day every day of the week to respond to user problems and questions. To calculate productivity for the call center, we could divide the total number of calls over a period of time by the number of hours or the number of employees in the call center during that period.

**Required**   Evaluate the productivity measure identified above for the call center. Identify some alternative measures of productivity for the call center and explain your choices.

**[LO 16-3]**   16-39   **Sales Volume, Sales Quantity, and Sales Mix Variances**   The Greensboro Performing Arts Center (GPAC) has a total capacity of 7,500 seats: 2,000 center seats, 2,500 side seats, and 3,000 balcony seats. The budgeted and actual tickets sold for a Broadway musical show are as follows:

| | | Percentage Occupied | |
| --- | --- | --- | --- |
| | Ticket Price | Budgeted Seats | Actual Seats |
| Center | $70 | 90% | 95% |
| Side | 60 | 80 | 85 |
| Balcony | 50 | 85 | 75 |

The actual ticket prices are the same as those budgeted. Once a show has been booked, the total cost does not vary with the total attendance.

**Required**   Compute the following for the show (calculate mix percentage and unit contribution margin to four decimal places and round the variances to the nearest whole dollar):
1. The budgeted and actual sales mix percentages for different types of seats.
2. The budgeted average contribution margin per seat. Assume the ticket price is also the contribution margin.
3. The total sales quantity variance and the total sales mix variance.
4. The total sales volume variance.

**[LO 16-4]**   16-40   **Sales Variances; Year to Year**   Hathaway Products, Inc., produces an innovative lighting system used in restaurants and high-end retail stores to provide a pleasing, warm atmosphere. Hathaway produces two versions of the product, called Starlight and Moonlight. Sales management at Hathaway wants to complete a sales performance analysis and has collected the following information for 2012 and 2013.

|  | 2013 | 2012 |
|---|---|---|
| Sales units | 12,000 | 10,000 |
| Sales mix for each product |  |  |
| Starlight | 20% | 25% |
| Moonlight | 80% | 75% |
| Price |  |  |
| Starlight | $35.00 | $35.00 |
| Moonlight | $85.00 | $90.00 |
| Variable cost per unit |  |  |
| Starlight | $22.00 | $22.00 |
| Moonlight | $48.00 | $48.00 |
| Fixed cost | $150,000 | $150,000 |

**Required**

1. Calculate a flexible budget contribution income statement for 2013, showing the 2013 results, the 2012 results, and the flexible budget. Use Exhibit 16.15 as a guide.

2. Calculate the volume variances for each product based both on sales dollars and contribution margin.

3. Determine the sales volume variance, the sales mix variance, and the sales quantity variance for each product, based on contribution margin.

## Problems

[LO 16-2]   16-41  **Partial Operational Productivity**   Hadley Technology Inc. manufactures a scrambling device for cellular telephones. The device's main component is a delicate part, CT140. CT140 is easily damaged and requires careful handling. Once damaged, it must be discarded. The firm hires only skilled laborers to manufacture and install CT140; however, some are still damaged. Robotic instruments process all other parts. Hadley's operating data for 2012 and 2013 follow:

|  | 2013 | 2012 |
|---|---|---|
| Units manufactured | 600,000 | 800,000 |
| Number of CT140 used | 800,000 | 825,000 |
| Number of direct labor-hours spent | 150,000 | 200,000 |
| Cost of CT140 per unit | $156 | $135 |
| Direct labor wage rate per hour | $56 | $63 |

**Required**

1. Compute the partial operational productivity for 2012 and 2013.

2. On the basis of the partial operational productivity that you computed, what conclusions can you draw about the firm's productivity in 2013 relative to 2012?

[LO 16-2]   16-42  **Partial Financial Productivity**   Use the data for Hadley Technology Inc. in problem 16-41 to complete the requirements.

**Required (in your calculations use 6 significant digits after the decimal point)**

1. Compute the partial financial productivity ratios for 2012 and 2013.

2. On the basis of the partial financial productivity ratios you computed, what conclusions can you draw about the firm's productivity in 2013 relative to 2012?

3. Separate the change of the partial financial productivity ratio from 2012 to 2013 into productivity changes, input price changes, and output changes.

4. Does the detailed information provided by separating the change of the partial financial production ratio offer any additional insight into the relative productivity for 2012 and 2013?

[LO 16-2]   16-43  **Total Productivity**   Use the data for Hadley Technology Inc. in problem 16-41 for the following.

**Required**

1. Compute the total productivity ratios for 2012 and 2013.

2. On the basis of the total productivity that you computed, what conclusions can you draw about the firm's productivity in 2013 relative to 2012?

[LO 16-2]   16-44  **Partial Operational and Financial Productivity**   In the fourth quarter of 2012 Simpson Company embarked on a major effort to improve productivity. It redesigned products, reengineered manufacturing processes, and offered productivity improvement courses. The effort was completed in the last quarter of 2012. The controller's office has gathered the following year-end data to assess the results of this effort.

|  | 2013 | 2012 |
|---|---|---|
| Units manufactured and sold | 18,000 | 15,000 |
| Selling price of the product | $40 | $40 |
| Materials used (pounds) | 12,600 | 12,000 |
| Cost per pound of materials | $10 | $8 |
| Labor-hours | 5,000 | 6,000 |
| Hourly wage rate | $25 | $20 |
| Power (kwh) | 2,000 | 1,000 |
| Cost of power per kwh | $2 | $2 |

**Required (in your calculations use 6 significant digits after the decimal point)**

1. Prepare a summary contribution approach income statement for each of the two years and calculate the change in operating income.

2. Compute the partial operational productivity ratios for each production factor in 2012 and 2013.

3. Compute the partial financial productivity ratios for each production factor in 2012 and 2013.

4. On the basis of the partial operational and financial productivity you computed, what conclusions can you make about the firm's productivity in 2012 relative to 2013?

5. Separate the changes in the partial financial productivity ratio from 2012 to 2013 into productivity changes, input price changes, and output changes.

6. Discuss additional insight on the relative productivity between 2012 and 2013 from the detailed information provided by separating the change in the financial partial productivity ratios.

[LO 16-2]    16-45   **Partial Operational and Financial Productivity**    Varceles Design has decided to experiment with two alternative manufacturing approaches, identified as MF and LI, for producing men's fashions. The firm expects the total demand to be 20,000 suits. Management estimates the required input resources using different manufacturing approaches are:

|  | Materials (yds.) | Labor (hrs.) |
|---|---|---|
| MF | 300,000 | 100,000 |
| LI | 200,000 | 120,000 |

The cost of materials is $8 per yard; the cost of labor is $25 per hour.

**Required (in your calculations use 4 significant digits after the decimal point)**

1. Compute the partial operational productivity ratios for each of the production approaches. Which approach would you select based on the partial operational productivity ratios?

2. Calculate the partial financial productivity ratios for each of the production approaches. Which approach would you select based on the partial financial productivity ratios?

3. Compute the total productivity ratios for each of the production approaches. Which approach would you select based on the total productivity ratios?

[LO 16-2]    16-46   **Direct Labor Rate and Efficiency Variances; Productivity Measures; Review of Chapter 14**    Textron Manufacturing Inc. assembles industrial testing instruments in two departments, assembly and testing. Operating data for 2012 and 2013 follow:

|  | 2013 | 2012 |
|---|---|---|
| Assembly department |  |  |
| Actual direct labor-hours per instrument | 20 | 25 |
| Actual wage rate per hour | $36 | $30 |
| Standard direct labor-hours per instrument | 21 | 24 |
| Standard wage rate per hour | $35 | $28 |
| Testing department |  |  |
| Actual direct labor-hours per instrument | 10 | 12 |
| Actual wage rate per hour | $24 | $20 |
| Standard direct labor-hours per instrument | 11 | 14 |
| Standard wage rate per hour | $25 | $21 |

The firm assembled and tested 20,000 instruments in both 2012 and 2013.

**Required (in your productivity calculations use 6 significant digits after the decimal point)**

1. Calculate the direct labor rate and the efficiency variances for both departments in both years.

2. Calculate the direct labor partial operational productivity ratio for both departments in both years.

3. Calculate the partial financial productivity for both departments in both years.

4. Compare your answers for requirements 2 and 3. Comment on the results.

5. How do productivity measures offer different perspectives for the firm's strategic decisions from those of variance analysis?

[LO 16-2]   16-47   **Productivity and Market Share in the Auto Industry; Internet Exercise**   The following data were obtained from the recent financial statements for two U.S. automakers (in $millions).

|  | Ford | GM |
|---|---|---|
| Sales | $128,954 | $135,592 |
| Cost of goods sold | 122,296 | 130,508 |

**Required**

1. Calculate and interpret total productivity in dollars for the two automakers. Assume that total variable manufacturing costs are 80% of cost of goods sold for each automaker.

2. Go to the Internet for these companies and look under investor information to find the financial statements for each company. Review the sections on management's discussion and analysis and related financial statements and disclosures, and find the market size and market share information provided by these firms.

   Ford: **www.ford.com**

   GM: **www.gm.com**

[LO 16-2]   16-48   **Productivity and Ethics**   Janice Interiors installs custom interiors for luxury mobile homes. In its most recent negotiation with the union, the firm proposed to share productivity gains in direct labor equally with the union. In return, the union agreed not to demand wage increases. Most union members, however, are skeptical about management's honesty in calculating productivity measures. Nevertheless, union members voted to try the program. Kim Tomas, the management accountant responsible for determining productivity measures, collected these data at the end of 2013:

|  | 2013 | 2012 |
|---|---|---|
| Number of installations | 560 | 500 |
| Direct labor-hours | 112,000 | 99,000 |

Steve Janice, the CEO, is very anxious to demonstrate the firm's good intentions by showing the labor union a positive result. He suggests to Kim that some of the direct labor-hours are actually indirect. For example, some of the labor-hours are indirect because these hours cannot be allocated to specific types of work. Following his suggestion, Kim reclassifies 12,000 hours as indirect labor.

**Required**

1. Evaluate whether Steve's suggestion to reclassify some of the direct labor-hours as indirect labor is ethical.

2. Would it be ethical for Kim to modify her calculations?

[LO 16-2]   16-49   **Partial Operational and Financial Productivity; Medical Practice**   Integrated Medical Care (IMC) is a family medical practice with 6 physicians and a nursing staff of 8 to 10 nurses and an administrative staff that varies from 4 to 7 personnel. Rajat Patel, the chief physician at IMC, is interested in studying the efficiency of the practice as a basis to set some benchmarks for further improvement, for rewarding his staff, and for comparing the efficiency of the IMC practice to other family medical practices. He is able to get comparable data for other practices from industry sources. So that the data are consistent with the industry sources, Patel has asked Marin & Associates, his accounting firm, to develop a set of productivity measures that would satisfy this requirement. Upon investigation, Joseph Marin finds that the measures to be used are the partial financial and operational productivity measures as defined in the chapter. The following information is for the last two years for the IMC practice:

|  | 2013 | 2012 |
|---|---|---|
| Patient visits | 30,000 | 26,000 |
| Nursing hours used | 18,675 | 17,800 |
| Administrative hours used | 12,225 | 12,225 |
| Cost of nursing support per hour | $39.00 | $38.00 |

| | $25.56 | $24.00 |
|---|---|---|
| Cost of administration per hour | | |
| Industry average financial productivity | | |
| Nursing | .035 | .034 |
| Administrative | 1.120 | 1.140 |

**Required (in your calculations use 6 significant digits after the decimal point)**

1. Compute the partial financial productivity ratios for nursing and administrative support for 2012 and 2013.

2. Separate the change of the partial financial productivity ratio from 2012 to 2013 into productivity changes, input price changes, and output changes.

3. Write a brief memo from Joseph Marin to Rajat Patel interpreting the findings above.

[LO 16-3]  16-50  **Sales Variances; Flexible-Budget Variance; Review of Chapter 14**   Robinson Company has two products, A and B. Robinson's budget for August follows:

| | Master Budget | |
|---|---|---|
| | **Product A** | **Product B** |
| Sales | $240,000 | $300,000 |
| Variable cost | 140,000 | 180,000 |
| Contribution margin | $100,000 | $120,000 |
| Fixed cost | 80,000 | 40,000 |
| Operating income | $ 20,000 | $ 80,000 |
| Selling price | $    120 | $     50 |

On September 1, these operating results for August were reported:

| | Operating Results | |
|---|---|---|
| | **Product A** | **Product B** |
| Sales | $180,400 | $341,120 |
| Variable cost | 106,600 | 216,480 |
| Contribution margin | $ 73,800 | $124,640 |
| Fixed cost | 80,000 | 40,000 |
| Operating income | $ (6,200) | $ 84,640 |
| Units sold | 1,640 | 6,560 |

**Required**

1. For each product determine the following variances measured in contribution margin:
   a. Flexible-budget variance.
   b. Sales volume variance.
   c. Sales quantity variance.
   d. Sales mix variance.

2. Explain the amount of the flexible-budget variance using the amounts of the selling price and variable cost variances.

[LO 16-3]  16-51  **Sales Variances; Flexible-Budget Variance; Review of Chapter 14**   Jay Banning, CEO and a major stockholder of Banning Inc., was unhappy with its operating results in 2013. The company manufactures two environmentally friendly industrial cleaning machines used primarily in automobile repair shops, gas stations, and auto dealerships. The master budget and operating results of the year (000s omitted except for the selling price per unit) follow:

| | Actual | | Budget | |
|---|---|---|---|---|
| | **T10** | **S40** | **T10** | **S40** |
| Sales | $126,000 | $58,500 | $100,000 | $40,000 |
| Variable cost | 61,200 | 34,500 | 50,000 | 25,000 |
| Contribution | $64,800 | $24,000 | $ 50,000 | $15,000 |
| Fixed cost | 10,000 | 10,000 | 10,000 | 10,000 |
| Operating income | $ 54,800 | $14,000 | $ 40,000 | $ 5,000 |
| Units sold | 1,200 | 1,500 | | |
| Unit selling price | | | $100 | $40 |

**Required**

1. Compute the contribution margin flexible-budget variance, contribution margin sales volume variance, contribution margin sales quantity variance, and contribution margin sales mix variance for each product and for the firm.

2. Write a memo to Jay Banning about the implications of the variances that you just computed on the firm's strategy, planning, and operational control.

[LO 16-3] 16-52 **Sales Volume, Sales Quantity, and Sales Mix Variances** Classic Ice Cream operates several stores in a major metropolitan city and its suburbs. Its budget and operating data for 2013 follow:

| | | Budgeted Data | | | Actual Operating Results | |
|---|---|---|---|---|---|---|
| Flavor | Gallons | Selling Price per Gallon | Variable Costs per Gallon | Gallons | Selling Price per Gallon | Variable Costs per Gallon |
| Vanilla | 250,000 | $1.20 | $0.50 | 180,000 | $1.00 | $0.45 |
| Chocolate | 300,000 | 1.50 | 0.60 | 270,000 | 1.35 | 0.50 |
| Strawberry | 200,000 | 1.80 | 0.70 | 330,000 | 2.00 | 0.75 |
| Anchovy | 50,000 | 2.50 | 1.00 | 180,000 | 3.00 | 1.20 |

**Required (in your calculations use 4 significant digits after the decimal point)**

1. Compute these variances for the individual flavors and total sold:
   a. Sales volume.
   b. Sales mix. Extend the sales mix calculation to five decimal places.
   c. Sales quantity.
2. Assess sales in 2013 based on your analyses.

[LO 16-3] 16-53 **Market Size and Share Variances** Transpacific Airlines (TPA) budgeted 80 million passenger-miles, or 5% of the total market for the year just completed, at a contribution margin of 40 cents per mile. The budgeted average price was 52 cents per passenger mile.

The operating data for the year show that TPA flew 69.12 million passenger-miles with an average price of 48 cents per passenger-mile. The terrorist activity in the early part of the year in several countries in the region decreased the total miles flown by all airlines for the year by 10%. There is no flexible-budget variance for all costs.

**Required**

1. Assess the effects of price, sales volume, market size, and market share on the firm's operating results for the year.

2. Explain the risks posed by the global economic environment for TPA, and suggest strategies for mitigating those risks.

[LO 16-3] 16-54 **Market Size and Market Share Variances for Small Business** Diane's Designs is a small business run out of its owner's house. For the past six months, the company has been selling two products, a welcome sign and a birdhouse. The owner has been concerned about the company's marketing effectiveness. The master budget and actual results for March of this year follow:

| | Master Budget | | |
|---|---|---|---|
| | Welcome Sign | Birdhouse | Total |
| Units | 50 | 25 | 75 |
| Sales | $1,000 | $250 | $1,250 |
| Variable costs | 890 | 120 | 1,010 |
| Contribution margin | $ 110 | $130 | $ 240 |
| Fixed costs | 75 | 75 | 150 |
| Operating income | $ 35 | $ 55 | $ 90 |

| | Actual Results | | |
|---|---|---|---|
| | **Welcome Sign** | **Birdhouse** | **Total** |
| Units | 45 | 35 | 80 |
| Sales | $675 | $420 | $1,095 |
| Variable costs | 580 | 270 | 850 |
| Contribution margin | $ 95 | $150 | $ 245 |
| Fixed costs | 75 | 75 | 150 |
| Operating income | $ 20 | $ 75 | $ 95 |

The total market for welcome signs for the last six months was 3,000 budgeted and 3,000 actual. Diane expected the total market for birdhouses to be 200 units per month; the actual volume for the entire market, however, turned out to be only 175 units per month.

**Required (round to four decimal places; e.g., 33.3333%)**
1. Compare Diane's Designs' market share for welcome signs and birdhouses.
2. What is the market share contribution margin variance?
3. What is the market size contribution margin variance?
4. Explain possible reasons for these variances.

[LO 16-4]   16-55   **Market Size and Market Share Variances; Foreign Currency Fluctuations**   Tall Pines Brewery (TPB) makes two specialty beers in its microbrewery: Golden Ale and Dark Ale. Both beers sell for the same price per case in the U.S. market and in the export market. The latter market is primarily European countries. Both beers also have the same variable production costs, though the export product has slightly higher variable costs due to shipping and other distribution costs associated with the export beers. The price, cost, and market information for the two beers are shown below.

| | **Budget** | **Actual** | **Budgeted Wt Avg CM** |
|---|---|---|---|
| Sales units (cases) | | | |
| Domestic | $22,000 | $22,350 | |
| Export | 12,000 | 14,500 | |
| Total | $34,000 | $36,850 | |
| Price per case | | | |
| Domestic | $88 | $87 | |
| Export | 90 | 92 | |
| Variable cost per case | | | |
| Domestic | $62 | $62 | |
| Export | 68 | 68 | |
| Contribution margin per case | | | |
| Domestic | $26 | $25 | |
| Export | 22 | 24 | |
| Total contribution margin | | | |
| Domestic | $572,000 | $558,750 | $24.5882 |
| Export | 264,000 | 348,000 | |

| | **Industry Budget** | **Industry Actual** |
|---|---|---|
| Sales units | | |
| Domestic | $901,500 | $924,550 |
| Export | 635,400 | 645,750 |

The budget was prepared with the expectation that the currency exchange rate would be $1.29 per euro. The actual average exchange rate for the period reflected the falling dollar, at $1.42 per euro.

**Required (round all calculations to 4 decimal places after the decimal point)**
1. What is the market share variance?
2. What is the market size variance?

3. Explain possible reasons for these variances, including a consideration of the effect of the change in the currency exchange rate for the dollar and the euro.

[LO 16-4]    16-56 **Comparative Income Statements and Sales Performance Variances; Current to Prior Year**   Clippers Inc. (CI) manufactures two types of garden clippers. A light duty model called the "half-inch" is intended for clipping branches and stems up to one-half inch thick. The "one-inch" model is designed for heavier stems and branches. To boost sales, CI decided at the beginning of 2013 to reduce the price of the half-inch model to better position its price relative to some key competitors. On the other hand, CI felt that the one-inch model was technically superior to competitors' models and decided that a small price increase was appropriate. The data for the current and prior year are as follows:

|  | 2013 | 2012 |
| --- | --- | --- |
| Sales units | 7,200 | 6,500 |
| Sales mix for each product |  |  |
| Half-inch model | 50% | 30% |
| One-inch model | 50% | 70% |
| Price |  |  |
| Half-inch model | $12.00 | $14.00 |
| One-inch model | $36.00 | $32.00 |
| Variable cost per unit |  |  |
| Half-inch model | $6.00 | $6.00 |
| One-inch model | $8.00 | $8.00 |
| Fixed cost | $35,000 | $35,000 |

**Required**
1. Calculate a comparative contribution income statement for CI for 2013 that shows the volume and selling price variances for each product based on contribution margin. (*Hint:* Use Exhibit 16.15 as an example.)
2. Determine the sales mix variance and the sales quantity variance for each product, based on contribution margin.
3. Did the price change have the expected results? Why or why not?

[LO 16-4]    16-57 **Comparative Income Statements and Sales Performance Variances; Current to Prior Year**   Green Grow Inc. manufactures riding lawn mowers that it sells to the large discount stores such as Walmart, Lowes, and Home Depot. The mowers are marketed as a "value" product, with good quality at a very good price. The company's two products are the Quality mower, which in 2012 sold for $1,200 (the discounters retailed it for $1,500), and the Heavy Duty model, which Green Grow Inc. sold for $1,600 (and was retailed for $2,200). At the end of 2012, the company has come under increased price competition from other manufacturers. The company believes it must reduce its price in 2013 on both products to keep its current market share with sales of 3,500 units. The unit variable costs for the Quality product are $800 and $950 for the Heavy Duty product. Management does not believe it can reduce these variable costs for the coming year but will begin to study ways to do so for 2014. In the meantime, the company management believes it can maintain its total market share by increasing its advertising expenses by $150,000 and cutting the price on both models by 10%. Fixed costs were $550,000 in 2012 and are not expected to change in 2013, with the exception of the increase in advertising. In 2012 the sales mix was 40% for Quality and 60% for Heavy Duty, respectively. In 2013, the sales mix was 50% for Quality and 50% for Heavy Duty, respectively.

**Required**
1. Calculate a comparative contribution income statement for Green Grow Inc. for 2013 that shows the volume and selling price variances for each product based on contribution margin. (*Hint:* Use Exhibit 16.15 as an example.)
2. Determine the sales mix variance and the sales quantity variance for each product, based on contribution margin.
3. Did the price change and increase in advertising have the expected results? Why or why not?
4. What methods should Green Grow Inc. adopt to become more competitive in 2013 and 2014?

**[LO 16-4]**   16-58   **Sales and Variable Cost Variances; Current to Prior Year; Review of Chapter 14**   RJM Enterprises is a manufacturer of consumer electronics products. The industry is very competitive and RJM has seen its profits fall in recent years, including an operating loss of $18,585 in 2012. RJM was able to turn that around in 2013 by aggressively cutting costs. The summarized financial results for RJM are shown below.

|  | 2013 | 2012 |
|---|---|---|
| Gross sales: | $934,920 | $1,273,545 |
| Less variable costs |  |  |
| Materials | $550,368 | $ 746,200 |
| Labor | 329,280 | 511,875 |
| Total contribution margin | $ 55,272 | $ 15,470 |
| Fixed costs | 33,509 | 34,055 |
| Operating income | $ 21,763 | $ (18,585) |

Jim Green, the management accountant at RJM, is analyzing the company's performance for 2013, in order explain to management the specific aspects that drove the company to success. Some of the information Jim obtained is:

|  | 2013 | 2012 |
|---|---|---|
| Sales units | 39,200 | 45,500 |
| Price | $23.85 | $27.99 |
| Materials cost per unit of material | $7.80 | $8.20 |
| Materials required/unit | 1.80 | 2.00 |
| Labor required/unit | 0.60 | 0.75 |
| Wage rate ($/hour) | $14.00 | $15.00 |

Assume that RJM, for efficiency and to reduce cost, maintains little or no materials or work-in-process inventory.

**Required**
1. Determine the selling price variance for 2013 based on sales dollars. Determine the volume variance based on contribution margin.
2. Determine the variable cost variances:
   a. The usage and price variances for materials.
   b. The usage and rate variances for labor.
3. Interpret your findings in requirements 1 and 2 above.

## Solutions to Self-Study Problems

### 1. Productivity Variances

1. Operational partial productivity

|  | 2012 | | | | | 2013 | | | | |
|---|---|---|---|---|---|---|---|---|---|---|
|  | Output | | Input Resource Used | | Partial Productivity | Output | | Input Resource Used | | Partial Productivity |
| TPX–45 | 60,000 | ÷ | 75,000 | = | 0.8 | 64,000 | ÷ | 89,600 | = | 0.7143 |
| Direct labor | 60,000 | ÷ | 10,000 | = | 6.0 | 64,000 | ÷ | 10,847 | = | 5.9002 |

2. Financial partial productivity

|  | 2012 | | | | | 2013 | | | | |
|---|---|---|---|---|---|---|---|---|---|---|
|  | Units of Output | | Cost of Input Resource Used | | Partial Productivity | Units of Output | | Cost of Input Resource Used | | Partial Productivity |
| TPX–45 | 60,000 | ÷ | $540,000 | = | 0.1111 | 64,000 | ÷ | $609,280 | = | 0.1050 |
| Direct labor | 60,000 | ÷ | $300,000 | = | 0.2000 | 64,000 | ÷ | $347,104 | = | 0.1844 |

3. Separation of financial partial productivity

| | **(A)**<br>2013 Output with<br>**2013 Productivity**<br>at 2013 Input Costs | **(B)**<br>2013 Output with<br>**2012 Productivity**<br>*at 2013 Input Costs* | **(C)**<br>**2013 Output with**<br>2012 Productivity<br>*at 2012 Input Costs* | **(D)**<br>**2012 Output with**<br>2012 Productivity<br>at 2012 Input Costs |
|---|---|---|---|---|
| Direct materials | 64,000/$609,280 = 0.1050 | 64,000/$544,000 = 0.1176 | 64,000/$576,000 = 0.1111 | 60,000/$540,000 = 0.1111 |
| Direct labor | 64,000/$347,104 = 0.1844 | 64,000/$341,333 = 0.1875 | 64,000/$320,000 = 0.2000 | 60,000/$300,000 = 0.2000 |

| | Productivity change | Input price change | Output change |
|---|---|---|---|
| Direct materials | 0.1050 − 0.1176<br>= 0.0126U | 0.1176 − 0.1111<br>= 0.0065F | 0.1111 − 0.1111<br>= 0 |
| Direct labor | 0.1844 − 0.1875<br>= 0.0031U | 0.1875 − 0.2000<br>= 0.0125U | 0.2000 − 0.2000<br>= 0 |

Summary of Results:

| | Productivity<br>Change | Input<br>Price<br>Change | Total<br>Change | **Change as Percent of<br>2012 Productivity\*** | | |
|---|---|---|---|---|---|---|
| | | | | Productivity<br>Change | Input<br>Price<br>Change | Total<br>Change |
| Direct materials | | | | | | |
| TPX–45 | 0.0126U | 0.0065F | 0.0061U | 11.34%U | 5.85%F | 5.49%U |
| Direct labor | 0.0031U | 0.0125U | 0.0156U | 1.55%U | 6.25%U | 7.8%U |

\*2012 productivity: Direct materials − TPX-45    60,000 units ÷ (75,000 pounds × $7.20 per pound) = 0.111111
                 Direct labor    60,000 units ÷ (10,000 hours × $30 per hour) = 0.2
Change as Percent of 2012 productivity:

| | Productivity Change | Input Price Change | Total Change |
|---|---|---|---|
| DM − TPX–45 | 0.0126 ÷ 0.111111 = 11.34% | 0.0065 ÷ 0.111111 = 5.85% | 0.0061 ÷ 0.111111 = 5.49% |
| Direct labor | 0.0031 ÷ 0.2 = 1.55% | 0.0125 ÷ 0.2 = 6.25% | 0.0156 ÷ 0.2 = 7.8% |

4. Total productivity

| Total productivity in units | 2012 | 2013 |
|---|---|---|
| (a) Total units manufactured | 60,000 | 64,000 |
| (b) Total variable manufacturing costs incurred | $840,000 | $956,384 |
| (c) Total productivity (a) / (b) | 0.071429 | 0.066919 |
| (d) Decrease in productivity | 0.071429 − 0.066919 = 0.00451 | |

| Total productivity in sales dollars | 2012 | 2013 |
|---|---|---|
| (a) Total sales | $1,500,000 | $1,600,000 |
| (b) Total variable manufacturing costs incurred | $840,000 | $956,384 |
| (c) Total productivity (a) / (b) | $1.7857 | $1.6730 |
| (d) Decrease in productivity | $1.7857 − $1.6730 = $0.1127 | |

## 2. Sales Variances

1. Selling price variances (in 000s)

**Flexible budget sales:**

| | **Master Budget for 2013** | | | Budgeted Selling<br>Price per Unit | | Total Units<br>Sold in 2013 | | Flexible<br>Budget Sales |
|---|---|---|---|---|---|---|---|---|
| | Total Sales | | Units | | | | | |
| Premium | $36,000 | ÷ | 240 | = $150 | × | 180 | = | $27,000 |
| Regular | 43,200 | ÷ | 360 | = 120 | × | 540 | = | 64,800 |

**Selling price variances:**

| | Premium | | | Regular | | |
|---|---|---|---|---|---|---|
| | Actual | Flexible Budget | Selling Price Variance | Actual | Flexible Budget | Selling Price Variance |
| Barrels | 180 | 180 | | 540 | 540 | |
| Sales | $28,800 | $27,000 | $1,800F | $62,100 | $64,800 | $2,700U |

2. Sales volume variances (in 000s) for the period for each product and for the firm.

**Flexible budget variable expenses:**

| | Master Budget for 2013 | | | Budgeted Variable Expenses per Unit | | Total Units Sold in 2013 | | Flexible Budget Variable Expenses |
|---|---|---|---|---|---|---|---|---|
| | Total Variable Expenses | | Number of Units | | | | | |
| Premium | $21,600 | ÷ | 240 | = | $90 | × | 180 | = | $16,200 |
| Regular | 27,000 | ÷ | 360 | = | 75 | × | 540 | = | 40,500 |

**Sales volume variances:**

| | Premium | | | Regular | | |
|---|---|---|---|---|---|---|
| | Flexible Budget | Master Budget | Sales Volume Variance | Flexible Budget | Master Budget | Sales Volume Variance |
| Barrels | 180 | 240 | 60U | 540 | 360 | 180F |
| Sales | $27,000 | $36,000 | $9,000U | $64,800 | $43,200 | $21,600F |
| Variable expenses | 16,200 | 21,600 | 5,400F | 40,500 | 27,000 | 13,500U |
| Contribution margin | $10,800 | $14,400 | $3,600U | $24,300 | $16,200 | $ 8,100F |
| Fixed expenses | 10,000 | 10,000 | — | 5,000 | 5,000 | — |
| Operating income | $  800 | $ 4,400 | $3,600U | $19,300 | $11,200 | $ 8,100F |

3. Sales quantity variances for the firm and for each product. (See the solution for 4.)
4. Sales mix variances for the period for each product and for the firm (000s omitted).

**Sales mixes:**

| | Budgeted | | Actual | |
|---|---|---|---|---|
| | Total Sales in Units | Sales Mix | Total Sales in Units | Sales Mix |
| Premium | 240 | 0.40 | 180 | 0.25 |
| Regular | 360 | 0.60 | 540 | 0.75 |
| Total | 600 | 1.00 | 720 | 1.00 |

**Budgeted contribution margin per unit =**
Budgeted selling price per unit (item 1 above) − Budgeted variable cost per unit (item 2 above)

Premium = $150 − $90 = $60
Regular  = $120 − $75 = $45

**Sales mix and sales quantity variances:**

| Flexible Budget | | Master Budget |
|---|---|---|
| Total units of all products sold × **Actual sales mix** × Budgeted contribution margin per unit | ***Total units of all products sold* × Budgeted sales mix** × Budgeted contribution margin per unit | ***Total budgeted units of all products to be sold* ×** Budgeted sales mix × Budgeted contribution margin per unit |

Premium

$720 \times 0.25 \times \$60 = \$10,800 \qquad 720 \times 0.40 \times \$60 = \$17,280 \qquad 600 \times 0.40 \times \$60 = \$14,400$

Sales mix variance

$= \$10,800 - \$17,280$
$= \$6,480U$

Sales quantity variance

$= \$17,280 - \$14,400$
$= \$2,880F$

Sales volume variance

$= \$10,800 - \$14,400$
$= \$3,600U$

Total (both premium and regular)

$$\text{Sales mix variance} = \$6,480U + \$4,860F = \$1,620U$$
$$\text{Sales quantity variance} = \$2,880F + \$3,240F = \$6,120F$$

5. Verification

Sales mix variance + Sales quantity variance = Sales volume variance

| | | | | | |
|---|---|---|---|---|---|
| Premium | $6,480U | + | $2,880F | = | $3,600U |
| Regular | 4,860F | + | 3,240F | = | 8,100F |
| Total | $1,620U | + | $6,120F | = | $4,500F |

6. Market size variance. (See the solution for 7.)

7. Market share variance (000s omitted).

### Weighted-Average Budgeted Contribution Margin per Unit

| | |
|---|---|
| Master budget total contribution margin | $30,600 |
| Master budget total sales units | ÷ 600 |
| Total | $    51 |

**Market Shares:**

Budgeted: Total sales in units 600 ÷ Total sales of the industry 1,500 = 0.40
Actual:   Total sales in units 720 ÷ Total sales of the industry 1,600 = 0.45

**Market Share and Size Variances:**

| Actual total market size × **Actual market share** × Average budgeted contribution margin per unit | **Actual total market size** × **Budgeted market share** × Average budgeted contribution margin per unit | **Budgeted total market size** × Budgeted market share × Average budgeted contribution margin per unit |
|---|---|---|

$$1,600 \times 0.45 \times \$51 = \$36,720 \qquad 1,600 \times 0.40 \times \$51 = \$32,640 \qquad 1,500 \times 0.40 \times \$51 = \$30,600$$

Market share variance
= $36,720 − $32,640
= $4,080F

Market size variance
= $32,640 − $30,600
= $2,040F

Sales quantity variance = $4,080F + $2,040F = $6,120F

8.  The sum of market size variance and market share variance follows. It verifies that this total equals the sales quantity variance.

Total market size variance + Total market share variance = Total quantity variance
  $2,040F        +        $4,080F        =        $6,120F

*Please visit http://www.mhhe.com/blocher6e to access a narrated, animated tutorial for solving these problems.*

# CHAPTER SEVENTEEN

# The Management and Control of Quality

**After studying this chapter, you should be able to . . .**

LO 17-1  Discuss the strategic importance of quality

LO 17-2  Define accounting's role in the management and control of quality

LO 17-3  Develop a comprehensive framework for the management and control of quality

LO 17-4  Understand alternative approaches for setting performance expectations (Six Sigma, absolute vs. goalpost specifications, and Taguchi loss functions)

LO 17-5  Prepare and interpret relevant financial information to support quality-related initiatives

LO 17-6  Discuss the use of nonfinancial performance data to support quality-related initiatives

LO 17-7  Describe and understand techniques that can be used to detect and correct quality problems

LO 17-8  Describe lean manufacturing and changes in management accounting systems to support a change to "lean"

The competitive landscape of the world has changed dramatically. Today, high quality of products and services is a non-negotiable given. Global competition gives consumers abundant choices, and consumers today are much more cost and value conscious. Most organizations, to varying degrees, have responded with quality-related management programs, with names such as total quality management (TQM), Six Sigma, and lean management (or lean manufacturing). Organizations that fail to embrace such initiatives may find themselves at a competitive disadvantage.

This chapter attempts to answer the following question: how can cost-management systems be configured to support managerial initiatives related to quality? In the next section, we discuss the strategic importance of quality. This is followed by a discussion of accounting's role in the management and control of quality. Next, we derive a comprehensive framework (Exhibit 17.3) that can be used to manage and control quality. The remainder of the chapter discusses in detail the elements of the framework depicted in Exhibit 17.3. Throughout this chapter our task is to demonstrate how accounting can add value to the organization by providing managers with information that supports quality-related initiatives embraced by the organization.

**LO 17-1**

*Discuss the strategic importance of quality*

## The Strategic Importance of Quality

**Total quality management (TQM)** is the unyielding and continuous effort by everyone in the firm to understand, meet, and exceed the expectations of customers.

Many firms in the United States have engaged in relentless efforts to improve the quality of their products and services. In this text, we refer to such efforts collectively as **total quality management (TQM),** that is, the unyielding and continuous effort by everyone in the organization to understand, meet, and exceed the expectations of customers. In fact, continuous improvement has become a way of life for many firms and organizations, both in the United States and abroad, as evidenced by the quality standards and awards discussed below.

### Baldrige Quality Award

In 1987, Congress established the Malcolm Baldrige National Quality Award to enhance the competitiveness of U.S. businesses by promoting quality awareness, recognizing quality and performance achievements, and publicizing successful performance strategies of

U.S. organizations in the areas of manufacturing, service, small business, and—added in 1999—education and health care. Seven broad categories make up the criteria: leadership, strategic planning, customer and market focus, information and analysis, human resource focus, process management, and business results. The fierce competition to win the award is evidence of the importance U.S. organizations place on being recognized for the quality of their operations.

### ISO 9000 and ISO 14000

**ISO 9000:2000**

is a set of guidelines for quality management and quality standards developed by the International Organization for Standardization, located in Geneva, Switzerland.

**ISO 14000**

is a set of quality standards designed to minimize environmental effects of an organization's outputs.

In 1947, to standardize practices for quality management, a specialized agency (the International Organization for Standardization, **www.iso.org**) was formed. In 1987 this body adopted a set of quality standards, which were revised in 1994 and again in 2000. Thus, the current set of quality-management standards is referred to as **ISO 9000:2000**. Worldwide, ISO 9000:2000 has become a certification sought after by global organizations (including governmental entities) to gain the stamp of approval on the quality of their products and services. The ISO 9000:2000 standards focus on developing, documenting, and implementing effective procedures for ensuring consistency of operations and performance in production and service delivery processes, with an overall goal of continual improvement.

**ISO 14000** is a set of standards that relate to environmental management, that is, what an organization does to minimize harmful effects to the environment. As with ISO 9000:2000, ISO 14000 is concerned with quality management, that is, processes in place that ensure a product will have the least harmful impact on the environment, at any stage of its life cycle, either by pollution or by depleting natural resources.

### Quality and Profitability: Conceptual Linkage

Whether a company competes through a strategy of cost leadership or product differentiation, quality issues permeate every aspect of operations. A company choosing to compete through low prices is not necessarily choosing to produce low-quality products. Its low-priced products must still meet customer expectations. Similarly, a differentiation strategy will not be successful, or at least will not be as successful as it could be, if the company fails to build quality into its products and services. Thus, from top management's perspective, a key question is how best to manage and control quality and quality-related costs.

Exhibit 17.1 shows that a manufacturing firm with improved quality can achieve competitive advantage and enjoy higher profitability and a higher return on investment (ROI). Improved quality decreases product returns. Lower sales returns decrease warranty costs and repair expenses. Improved quality lowers inventory levels for raw materials, components, and finished products because the firm has more reliable manufacturing processes and schedules. Improved product quality also lowers manufacturing costs as the firm reduces or eliminates rework costs and increases productivity. Customers are likely to perceive quality products as having higher values, which allows the firm to command higher prices and enjoy a larger market share. Higher prices and greater market shares

**EXHIBIT 17.1**

**Conceptual Relationship between Improved Quality and Financial Performance**

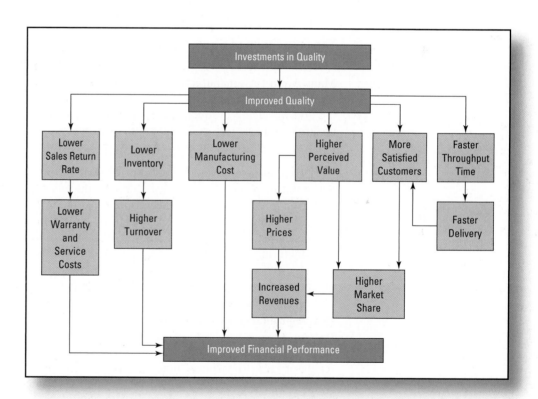

increase revenues and profits. Improved quality also decreases cycle time. Faster cycle times speed deliveries, and prompt delivery produces satisfied customers, creates new demand, and increases market shares. Higher revenues and lower costs boost net income and increase the firm's ROI.

## Accounting's Role in the Management and Control of Quality

**LO 17-2**

*Define accounting's role in the management and control of quality.*

The preceding discussion should have conveyed to you that quality initiatives, such as TQM, are management, not accounting, initiatives or prerogatives. Thus, an appropriate question to ask at this point is how accounting can add value to, or support, quality-related initiatives of management. An inspection of Exhibit 17.1 suggests that accountants can add value to the process by providing managers with relevant and timely information, of both a financial and nonfinancial nature, that supports the quality-oriented initiatives of an organization. The following example provides an overview of the process that was used to develop internal accounting procedures for measuring and managing quality in the pharmaceutical industry.

### The Five Steps of Strategic Decision Making: Improving Quality in Pharmaceutical and Medical-Product Companies[1]

Many world-class manufacturers, including producers of semiconductors and goods for the aerospace and electronics industries, have implemented effective systems for measuring and managing product quality. However, the situation in the pharmaceutical and medical-products sectors is different: historically, quality control was superseded in importance by a focus on product innovation and compelling marketing.

1. **Determine the strategic issues surrounding the problem.** Lack of effective systems for monitoring and controlling quality in the pharmaceutical and medical-products industry ("pharma" for short) is becoming costly for these firms. Over the period 2001–2007, the industry incurred more than $700 million in fines and, it is thought, suffered billions more in lost revenues. Thus, for some firms in this industry, adopting world-class manufacturing processes can create a competitive advantage—both by reducing regulatory risk and by reducing production costs. One such process is the movement to lean manufacturing coupled with Six Sigma quality-performance expectations.

2. **Identify the alternative actions.** At one level, corporate management may feel that strict regulation in the industry obviates the need for investing in a new quality-management system. At another level, executives may feel that a new quality-management and compliance-management system is needed to secure competitive advantage and reduce regulatory risk. In terms of a new system, choices need to be made as to (a) what data should be collected (e.g., qualitative vs. quantitative, including financial data regarding product quality), (b) to whom such data should be reported, (c) how often the data should be reported, and (d) how targeted performance in terms of quality (e.g., Six Sigma) should be specified. Finally, a decision needs to be made as to the methods that should be used to isolate and correct quality-related problems.

3. **Obtain information and conduct analyses of the alternatives.** Corporate management would have to estimate the required investment outlay for the new monitoring and control system, as well as ongoing operating costs associated with the system. Benefits of the new quality-management and compliance system would have to be quantified and reported over time. These costs would be compared to anticipated benefits of the new

---

[1] Background information for this example is taken from Anil G. D'souza, David J. Keeling, and Richard D. Phillips, "Improving Quality in 'Pharma' Manufacturing," *The McKinsey Quarterly,* September 2007.

system, both financial and nonfinancial in nature (e.g., improved relationship with regulators). Financial benefits would include opportunity costs as well as out-of-pocket costs, a point we made in Chapter 11.

4. **Based on strategy and analysis, choose and implement the desired alternative.**   The company in question can choose to implement a comprehensive system for managing and controlling quality. This system might consist of a cost-of-quality (COQ) reporting framework that would report, on a time-series basis using activity-based costing data, both out-of-pocket and opportunity cost information. Such data could be benchmarked against best-in-class performers (either within or external to the company). Nonfinancial performance indicators would be derived from an explicit statement of strategy and would be analyzed statistically to justify their continued use. If lean production methods are adopted, then the company must consider whether and how to change its internal reporting system to support this change in production philosophy.

5. **Provide an ongoing evaluation of the effectiveness of implementation in step 4.**   Assuming the investment in the new system is made, management could institute a post-audit review of the decision, to see how close the actual results were to the projected costs and benefits of the new system. (The topic of conducting post-audits in conjunction with capital budgeting decisions was introduced in Chapter 12.)

## Comprehensive Framework for Managing and Controlling Quality

**LO 17-3**

*Develop a comprehensive framework for the management and control of quality.*

**Quality**
is defined as customer satisfaction with the total experience of a product or service, that is, the difference between customer expectations and actual performance of the product or service.

**Design quality**
is the difference between customer expectations (for attributes, services, functionality, etc.) and product design.

**Performance quality**
is the difference between the design specifications of the product and the actual performance of the product.

**EXHIBIT 17.2**
**Dimensions of Quality**

### The Meaning of Quality

For purposes of discussion we define the term **quality** to mean the total level of customer satisfaction with the organization's product or service. Defined in this manner, we can decompose quality into two broad components: *features* and *performance.* The former component refers to the extent to which product/service design is consistent with customer expectations (in terms of product/service characteristics, attributes, or functionality)—in short, **design quality.** Outputs that fail to meet such expectations result in quality-of-design failure costs. Conceptually, you can think of design failure as the difference between the actual features of the product (or service) and the features that the customer wants. Such failures represent one component of total quality cost.

The other broad component of quality, **performance quality,** is defined as the difference between the design specifications of the product and the actual performance of the product. Thus, a personal computer whose electronic mouse consistently malfunctions or whose operating system constantly locks up relates to what can be called *performance-quality failures.*

The two broad categories of quality (and related costs) are depicted in Exhibit 17.2. The issue of Quality of Design was covered in Chapter 13 (Target Costing). In this chapter we focus on the left-hand side of Exhibit 17.2: performance quality and related costs. Exhibit 17.1 provides broad guidance for the development of a comprehensive framework (or system) for the management and control of quality. One possible framework is presented in Exhibit 17.3. This exhibit serves as the focal point around which the discussion in the rest of the chapter is built. The discussion should reinforce in your mind the

As noted earlier, some organizations have a quality orientation and embrace managerial initiatives such as TQM to support this competitive strategy. For each of the following examples, consider (1) which nonfinancial performance indicators, or controls, might be instituted to help control quality, and (2) what kinds of quality-related costs might be involved by failing to control quality:

- A study published in the November 15, 2005, issue of *Cancer* (a journal of the American Cancer Society) underscores the difficulty of improving screening rates to detect colon cancer, the third leading cause of cancer deaths.* Based on a review of patient charts from individuals associated with a California HMO, fewer than 30% of eligible patients over age 50 received any of the three types of colon-cancer tests. According to the National Committee for Quality Assurance, a Washington-based nonprofit organization that promotes health care quality, Tufts Health Plan (Waltham, MA) achieved the highest score in the nation, 72%, for colorectal cancer screening.

- UnumProvident Corporation, a disability-income insurer, paid an $8 million civil penalty and $600,000 court costs to settle a suit brought against the company by the California Department of Insurance, to resolve allegations that it cheated policyholders by improperly denying claims.† This settlement followed an earlier fine of $15 million paid by the company to the U.S. Labor Department in a multistate settlement.

- Boston Scientific Corporation recently reached an agreement with the U.S. Food and Drug Administration (FDA) in which the company committed itself to an "aggressive timeline" for resolving quality-control problems.‡ Prior to this agreement, the FDA had announced that it would withhold approval of some new products until the company resolved these issues. The FDA alleged that the company had failed to report, or delayed reporting, potential safety problems associated with its products.

- PeopleSoft, Incorporated, prior to its acquisition by Oracle, reached an agreement to pay Cleveland State University $4.25 million to settle a lawsuit over computer problems that delayed financial aid to thousands of students.§ The university claimed that students often waited months for financial aid because of computer problems that also hindered other services for more than two years.

**Sources:**
*R. L. Rundle, "Colon-Cancer Screening Rates Rise Only Slightly, Study Says," *The Wall Street Journal* (October 11, 2005), p. B1.

†D. Gullapalli, "UnumProvident Is Set to Pay $8 Million Penalty in California," *The Wall Street Journal* (October 3, 2005), p. C3.

‡"Boston Scientific Set to Fix Quality Issues," *The Wall Street Journal* (February 4, 2006), p. A2.

§"Software Firm Will Pay CSU $4.25M Settlement," *The Wall Street Journal* (February 4, 2006), p. A2.

**EXHIBIT 17.3**
**Comprehensive Framework for Managing and Controlling Quality**

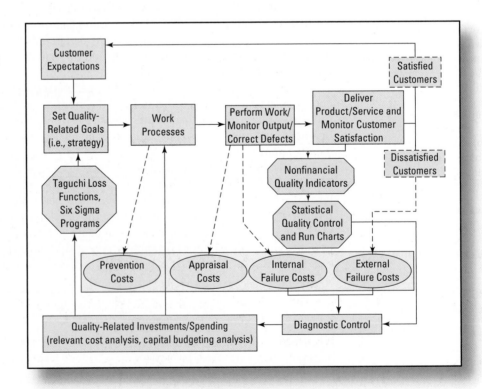

notion that management accounting systems are dynamic in nature and need to evolve over time to meet the changing information needs of top management. We now provide an overview of the primary elements of the framework.

### Knowledge of Business Processes

Because the framework presented in Exhibit 17.3 is comprehensive, it presumes knowledge of key business processes. Thus, the development and implementation of a comprehensive framework for managing and controlling quality is best thought of as a cross-functional effort, with input of managers from across the firm's internal value chain. Because of their record-keeping and reporting responsibilities, management accountants can be viewed as the key point of contact across various subunits and managers within the organization. Thus, the development of such a comprehensive system requires the management accountant to have broad business knowledge, including knowledge of fundamental business processes.

### Role of the Customer

In the past, most quality-control reporting systems had a decidedly inward focus. That is, measures and techniques were developed and used based on what the *organization* felt were appropriate to the situation. More recently, however, organizations have begun to realize a fundamental flaw in system design: failure to embrace an outward (i.e., *customer-based*) viewpoint. Thus, in the comprehensive model shown in Exhibit 17.3, we depict consumer expectations as the cornerstone of the entire framework. In this sense, then, the model can be viewed as customer-based. As well, the model attempts to capture (as "external failure costs") various costs associated with dissatisfied customers.

### Financial Component

You will notice that the reporting of quality *cost* information is a key element of the comprehensive framework shown in Exhibit 17.3. In fact, we depict cost information in four separate categories (namely, prevention, appraisal, internal failure, and external failure) to give prominence to the different types of quality costs that organizations incur. This financial approach to the management and control of quality, known as *cost of quality* (COQ), is dealt with in greater detail later in the chapter.

### Nonfinancial Performance Indicators

As illustrated in Exhibit 17.3, the financial performance indicators of our comprehensive reporting framework are complemented by both internal and external nonfinancial performance indicators. As we explain later in the chapter, nonfinancial performance indicators can be leading indicators (i.e., predictors) of future financial performance. As such, any comprehensive framework for managing and controlling quality should have a combination of both financial and nonfinancial performance indicators.

### Feedback Loops

You will notice that Exhibit 17.3 contains a number of feedback loops, designed to inform future decisions and to support an organization's overall goal of continuous improvement. Thus, for example, the entire model continually helps the organization better understand "customer expectations" and, in turn, set appropriate quality goals for the organization.

### Relevant Cost Analysis of Quality-Related Spending and Investments

As indicated in Exhibit 17.3, management accountants can provide relevant financial information that can be used by managers for evaluating quality-related spending and investment decisions. Thus, the framework presented in Exhibit 17.3 draws directly from the material covered in Chapters 11 (relevant cost analysis) and 12 (capital budgeting analysis) of the text.

### Link to Operations Management

The framework presented in Exhibit 17.3 provides a good example of cross-disciplinary inputs to a management process. As noted above, accounting has primary reporting responsibility for relevant financial and nonfinancial performance measures. The question arises, then, as to how managers, after using such information, identify and analyze quality-related problems. For this, we draw from the field of operations management techniques such as control charts, Pareto diagrams, and cause-and-effect diagrams. Management accountants should have at least cursory knowledge of these techniques.

### Breadth of the System

In the past, for many organizations (particularly manufacturers), quality was assumed to be the responsibility of production (i.e., the manufacturing process). However, as indicated by the discussion at the beginning of this chapter (and implied by the model presented in Exhibit 17.3), many organizations today are embracing a broader responsibility for quality—across all elements of the value chain. Any comprehensive framework developed to support a TQM strategy should therefore have a broad reporting perspective. You will note that the performance measures associated with Exhibit 17.3 cut across the entire value chain.

In the remaining sections of this chapter, we discuss in greater detail the elements of the conceptual framework illustrated in Exhibit 17.3.

## Alternative Approaches to Setting Quality-Related Expectations

**LO 17-4**

*Understand alternative approaches for setting performance expectations (Six Sigma, absolute vs. goalpost specifications, and Taguchi loss functions).*

As seen from Exhibit 17.3, the actual quality goals embraced by the organization are affected principally by customer demands—that is, the level of quality (including product functionality) customers are willing to pay for. In this section we first discuss the Six Sigma approach to setting quality-related performance standards. This is followed by a discussion of an alternative approach: the use of "goalpost" versus absolute conformance standards. We conclude with a discussion of Taguchi loss functions, which can be used in conjunction with absolute performance standards.

### Setting Quality Expectations: A Six Sigma Approach

**Six Sigma**

is an overall strategy to accelerate improvements and achieve unprecedented performance levels by focusing on characteristics that are critical to customers and identifying and eliminating causes of errors or defects in processes.

Six Sigma[2] has been embraced by many organizations as the guiding principle that drives improvements in products, services, and processes (e.g., product development, logistics, sales, marketing, and distribution). **Six Sigma** can perhaps best be defined as a business process-improvement approach that seeks to find and eliminate causes of defects and errors, reduce cycle times and manufacturing costs, improve productivity, better meet customer expectations, and achieve higher asset utilization and returns on investment in both manufacturing and service operations.[3]

Rudisill and Clary[4] offer the following actual examples of improvements realized by adopting Six Sigma:

- Reduction of scrap in a ball-bearing manufacturing plant and capacity assembly plant.
- Identification and reduction of unnecessary spare parts inventory for a paper cup plant.
- Reduction of defects and product variation in a textile finishing plant.
- Reduction of lead-times for product development and scale-up in a pharmaceutical company.
- Reduction of wait-time for loan approval notification (from the bank).

Six Sigma is based on a simple problem-solving methodology, **DMAIC—D**efine, **M**easure, **A**nalyze, **I**mprove, and **C**ontrol. Typically, the application of Six Sigma is done using cross-functional teams, more or less on a consulting project basis. In the design stage of the project, the Six Sigma team *defines* the problem and specifies the deliverables of the project. In the *measure* stage, the team collects relevant process-performance data. In the *analyze* stage, the team tries to uncover root causes of an underlying quality problem. This is followed by the *improve* stage, in which proposed solutions to the underlying problem(s) are generated and then implemented. Finally, in the *control* stage of the project, appropriate controls are put in place to ensure that the identified problem does not recur.

Motorola, Inc., pioneered the concept of Six Sigma as a structured approach for assessing and improving both product and service quality. Today, this approach has gained notoriety and credibility because of its adoption by firms such as Allied Signal and General Electric. The term Six Sigma actually comes from statistics: in a normal distribution, the area outside of $+/-$ six standard deviations from the mean is very, very small. From a control standpoint, we can express this area in terms of relative number of defects. One interpretation of a Six Sigma quality expectation is approximately 3.4 defects per million items produced.[5]

The move from, say, a 3-sigma to a 6-sigma quality level is dramatic. For example, suppose your bank tracks the number of errors associated with checks written on the bank by its customers. If the bank finds, say, 12 errors per 1,000 checks processed, this is

---

[2] Six Sigma is a federally registered trademark and service mark of Motorola, Inc.

[3] J. R. Evans and W. M. Lindsay, *An Introduction to Six Sigma and Process Improvement* (Mason, OH: South-Western, 2005), p. 3.

[4] F. Rudisill and D. Clary, "The Management Accountant's Role in Six Sigma," *Strategic Finance*, November 2004, pp. 35–39.

[5] As Evans and Lindsay (2005, pp. 36–38) show, this is a loose interpretation of the statistical basis for Six Sigma. That is, they show that the general specification for a $k$-sigma quality level is as follows: $k \times$ Process standard deviation = Tolerance/2.

equivalent to an error rate of 12,000 per million—somewhere between 3.5 and 4 sigma levels! As Evans and Lindsay point out,[6] a change from 3 to 4 sigma represents a 10-fold improvement in quality; a change from 4 to 5 sigma, a 30-fold improvement; and a change from 5 to 6 sigma, a 70-fold improvement. For this reason, Six Sigma is not likely the goal for all processes and operations. The appropriate quality expectation is a function of the strategic importance of the process and the anticipated costs of taking the process to an increasingly higher level of quality.

### Implementation Tips: Six Sigma[7]

Following are steps management can take to ensure the success of Six Sigma projects.

- First and foremost, *provide necessary leadership and resources.* As with many other strategic initiatives, the CEO and top-management team must exhibit strong support for the Six Sigma program. Such support can come in the form of employee training and making sure that there is appropriate buy-in for the concept on the part of key managers in the organization.

- *Implement a reward system.* Bonus and incentive schemes for the organization might have to be amended to accommodate rewards associated with reaching Six Sigma goals.

- *Provide ongoing training.* Since Six Sigma is a *process* (think of the DMAIC approach as iterative in nature), employee training should be ongoing, reinforcing the strategic importance of the process and the need for continual improvement.

- *Judiciously select early projects.* As noted above, Six Sigma principles can be applied to processes throughout the entire value chain of the organization. It is recommended, however, that top management starts with easy, nonpolitical, and noncontroversial projects that support the strategic goals of the organization. Given success with these projects, Six Sigma can then be rolled out to other more complicated and difficult projects.

- *Break up difficult projects.* Top management should try to parse complicated projects into smaller, short-term segments, each of which has its own milestone. This allows individuals to experience success along the way and to be recognized for their efforts to help the organization succeed.

- *Avoid employee layoffs.* From a motivational standpoint, it is crucial that improvements based on Six Sigma should not jeopardize the jobs of those who helped accomplish the goal. Judicious job reassignment is one strategy for dealing with this situation; layoffs should be viewed as a last resort.

[6] Ibid., p. 39.

[7] This discussion is adapted from P. C. Brewer and J. E. Eighme, "Using Six Sigma to Improve the Finance Function: Here Are Some Tips for Success," *Strategic Finance* (May 2005), pp. 27–33.

## Setting Quality Expectations: Goalpost versus Absolute Conformance Standards

**Tolerance**

refers to an acceptable range of a quality characteristic, such as thickness (measured, for example, in centimeters).

An alternative approach to defining quality expectations, or product **tolerances**, is to choose between goalpost and absolute conformance standards. One advantage of the latter is that it is consistent with the use of Taguchi loss functions for control purposes, a subject dealt with later in this section of the chapter.

### Goalpost Conformance

**Goalpost conformance**

is conformance to a quality specification expressed as a specified range around the targeted performance level.

**Goalpost conformance** is conformance to a quality specification expressed as a specified range around the targeted performance level. The target is the ideal or desirable outcome of the operation. The range around the target is referred to as the *quality tolerance*.

For example, the target for a production process to manufacture 0.5-inch sheet metal is 0.5-inch thickness for all sheet metal manufactured. Recognizing that meeting the target every time in manufacturing is difficult, a firm often specifies a tolerance range. A firm that specifies a tolerance of ± 0.05 inch meets the stated quality standard when the thickness of its products is between 0.55 inch and 0.45 inch.

This approach assumes that the customer would accept any value within the tolerance range. As such, the approach assumes that quality-related costs do not depend on the actual value of the quality characteristic, as long as this value falls within the specified range. Exhibit 17.4 depicts the goalpost conformance specifications for the sheet metal example.

**EXHIBIT 17.4**
**Goalpost Conformance**

**EXHIBIT 17.5**
**Absolute Conformance (Robust Quality Approach)**

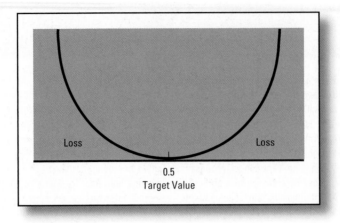

Loss                    Loss

0.5
Target Value

## Absolute Quality Conformance

**Absolute quality conformance (robust quality approach)**

requires all products or services to meet the target value *exactly,* with no variation.

**Absolute quality conformance** or the **robust quality approach** aims for all products or services to meet the target value *exactly,* with no variation. An absolute conformance requires all sheet metal to have a thickness of 0.5 inch, not 0.5 inch $\pm$ 0.05 inch or even 0.5 inch $\pm$ 0.0005 inch. Exhibit 17.5 depicts the robust quality approach. This approach assumes that the smaller the departure from the target value, the better the quality.

Variations from the target value are assumed to have negative economic consequences. As indicated in Exhibit 17.5, the "cost" of deviating from the target value is assumed to be nonlinear in nature. Thus, robustness in quality comes with meeting the exact target consistently. Any deviation from the target is viewed as a quality failure and weakens the overall quality of the product or service.

## Goalpost or Absolute Conformance?

Goalpost conformance assumes that a firm incurs no quality or failure cost or loss if all quality measures fall within the specified limits. That is, the firm suffers quality costs or losses only when the measure is outside the limits. No such quality tolerance exists in absolute conformance, which views quality costs or losses as a continuously increasing function starting from the target value. Quality costs, hidden or out-of-pocket, occur whenever the quality measure deviates from its target value.

Which of these two approaches, goalpost or absolute conformance, is better? Perhaps we can find an answer in the experience Sony had in two of its plants that manufacture color televisions.[8]

The two Sony plants manufacture the same television sets and follow the same specification for color density. The two plants, however, have adopted different types of quality conformance. The San Diego plant uses goalpost conformance, and the Tokyo plant adopts absolute conformance. On examining the operating data over the same period, Sony found that all the units produced at the San Diego plant fell within the specifications (zero defects), but some of those manufactured at the Japanese plant did not. The quality of the Japanese units, however, was more uniform around the target value, while the quality of the San Diego units was uniformly distributed between the lower and upper limits of the specification, the goalpost, as depicted in Exhibit 17.6.

The average quality cost (loss) per unit of the San Diego plant, however, was $0.89 higher than that of the Japanese plant. One reason for the higher quality cost for units produced at the San Diego plant was the need for more frequent field service. Customers are more likely to complain when the density is farther away from the target value. Although the plant in Tokyo had a higher rejection rate, it experienced lower warranty and repair costs for its products. For firms desiring to attain long-term profitability and customer satisfaction, absolute conformance may be the better approach.

The extension of absolute performance standards to estimate Taguchi quality loss functions is covered next.

[8] Evans and Lindsay, *The Management and Control of Quality,* pp. 112–13.

**EXHIBIT 17.6**

**Color Density of Sony TV Sets Manufactured in the San Diego Plant and a Japanese Plant**

Source: J. R. Evans and W. M. Lindsay, *The Management and Control of Quality,* 6th ed. (Mason, OH: South-Western, 2005), p. 113.

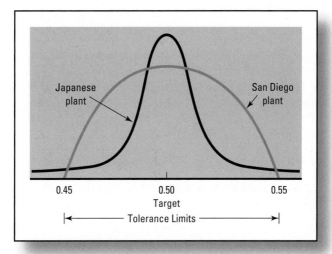

## Taguchi Quality Loss Function

Genichi Taguchi and Y. Wu proposed the absolute quality conformance approach as an *off-line* quality control.[9] Taguchi and Wu hypothesize that any variation from the exact specifications entails a cost or loss to the firm. This cost or loss can be depicted by a quadratic function similar to the one shown in Exhibit 17.5.

**Taguchi quality loss function** depicts the relationship between quality costs and level of deviation from target quality.

The **Taguchi quality loss function** depicts the cost function associated with deviation from target quality. The loss grows larger as the variation increases (a quadratic function): the total loss increases as the magnitude of a quality characteristic of the product or service moves farther away from the target value. In a quadratic function the loss quadruples when the deviation from the target value doubles. For instance, if the loss is $4 when the deviation is 0.1 from the target value, the loss will be $16 when the deviation doubles, or is 0.2 from the target value.

The total cost of deviations from the quality target includes direct costs in manufacturing and service and hidden quality costs. Direct costs are costs such as rework, warranty repair or replacement, additional production costs, and loss on disposal. The hidden quality losses include customer dissatisfaction, loss of future business, loss of market share, additional engineering costs, additional management costs, and additional inventory. Management accountants can add value to the organization by helping to estimate these various costs.

[9] Taguchi and Wu, *Introduction to Off-Line Quality Control.* See also Evans and Lindsay, *The Management and Control of Quality,* pp. 594–97, and T. L. Albright and H. P. Roth, "The Measurement of Quality Costs: An Alternative Paradigm," *Accounting Horizons,* June 1992, pp. 15–27.

### Quality Loss Function

Taguchi and Wu show that a quadratic function provides a good approximation of quality losses. For a quality characteristic with the target value $T$, the loss from having a quality characteristic $x$ can be estimated by the following quadratic function:

$$L(x) = k(x - T)^2$$

where

> $x$ = the observed value of the quality characteristic
> $T$ = the target value of the quality characteristic
> $k$ = the cost coefficient, determined by the firm's costs of failure

$k$ is a constant estimated for the quality characteristic based on the total production and service costs and hidden costs to the firm due to deviation of the quality characteristic from the target value. The value of $k$ for a particular quality characteristic can be estimated as follows:

$$k = \frac{\text{Total quality cost}}{(\text{Tolerance allowed})^2}$$

For example, assume that a company has determined that no customer will accept sheet metal deviating more than 0.05 inch from the target value in thickness, that the target thickness is 0.5 inch, and that the estimated cost to the firm is $5,000 for each rejection by a customer. The $5,000 estimated cost to the firm includes repair or replacement, processing, service costs, and other costs due to customer dissatisfaction. Then

$$k = \frac{\$5,000}{0.05^2}$$
$$k = \$2,000,000$$

If the actual thickness of a unit is 0.47, then the estimated quality cost (or loss) for the unit is

$$L(0.47) = \$2,000,000(0.47 - 0.50)^2 = \$1,800$$

If, however, the thickness is 0.46, then the estimated total loss from the deviation increases to $3,200, as follows:

$$L(0.46) = \$2,000,000(0.46 - 0.50)^2 = \$3,200$$

### Total Loss and Average Loss

Each of the losses calculated above represents the estimated loss from having one unit with the observed quality characteristic. The total loss for all the units manufactured during a period is the sum of the losses from all units whose observed value of the quality characteristic deviated from the target value.

Alternatively, the total loss due to variations in the quality characteristic can be determined by multiplying the average loss per unit by the total number of units manufactured. The average loss per unit is the expected loss due to variations in the quality characteristic. Exhibit 17.7 shows the calculations of the expected total losses in two plants identified as A and B. These two plants have different probability distributions of deviations from the target value, as noted in columns (3) and (5).

The output from plant A spreads evenly over the range from 0.46 to 0.54, with no unit falling outside the tolerance limits. In contrast, the output from plant B concentrates near the specified target value (0.50), but not all units lie within the tolerance limits.

Albright and Roth show that the expected, or average, loss per unit can be determined using variance and the square of the mean deviation from the target value, as follows:[10]

$$EL(x) = k(\sigma^2 + D^2)$$

---

[10] Albright and Roth, "The Measurement of Quality Costs," p. 23.

**EXHIBIT 17.7**
**Total Estimated Quality Losses Using a Taguchi Loss Function**

| (1) | (2) | (3) | (4) = (2) × (3) | (5) | (6) = (2) × (5) |
|---|---|---|---|---|---|
| **x** | **L(x)** | **Plant A** | | **Plant B** | |
| **Measured Thickness** | **Quality Cost (or Loss)** | **Probability** | **Weighted Loss** | **Probability** | **Weighted Loss** |
| 0.43 | $9,800 | 0 | $ 0 | 0.02 | $196 |
| 0.46 | 3,200 | 0.20 | 640 | 0.03 | 96 |
| 0.48 | 800 | 0.20 | 160 | 0.15 | 120 |
| 0.50 | 0 | 0.20 | 0 | 0.60 | 0 |
| 0.52 | 800 | 0.20 | 160 | 0.15 | 120 |
| 0.54 | 3,200 | 0.20 | 640 | 0.03 | 96 |
| 0.57 | 9,800 | 0 | 0 | 0.02 | 196 |
| Expected loss | | | $1,600 | | $824 |

where

$EL(x)$ = expected (average) loss from having a quality characteristic equal to $x$

$\sigma^2$ = variance of the quality characteristic about the target value[11]

$D$ = the deviation of the mean value of the quality characteristic from the target value

= $\bar{x} - T$

Assume that the variance is 0.0008 for plant A[12] and 0.000412 for plant B and that the value of $D$ is 0 for both plants.[13] Thus,

Plant A: $EL(x)$      = $2,000,000(0.0008 + 0) = \$1,600$
Plant B: $EL(x)$      = $2,000,000(0.000412 + 0) = \$824$

Notice the similarity in the quality characteristic between plant A and that observed in the Sony plant at San Diego (as depicted in Exhibit 17.6): all units are within and spread evenly over the specified tolerance limits. The quality characteristic of plant B is similar to that observed in the Sony plant in Japan: not all units lie within the tolerance limits, but most units cluster around the target value. Some units, however, fall outside the tolerance limits. Plant B, like the Sony plant in Japan, incurs a smaller average cost per unit. Even though all units of plant A fall within the tolerance limits while some units of plant B are outside the limits, plant B has a lower expected loss than that of plant A.

### Using Quality Loss Function (QLF) for Tolerance Determination

As demonstrated by the following example, the Taguchi quality loss function (QLF) can also be used to set tolerances for an operation. Assume a situation in which a firm can repair any rejected units that exceed the specified tolerance level. Even though such repairs

---

[11] Variance, $\sigma^2$, is computed as follows:

$\sigma^2 = \Sigma(x - \bar{x})^2\, f(x)$

where, $x$ = quality characteristic, e.g., measured thickness, as in Exhibit 17.7

    $\bar{x}$ = mean value of quality characteristic, $\bar{x} = \Sigma x f(x)$

    $f(x)$ = probability of observing quality characteristic, $x$; each value of $f(x)$ lies between 0 and 1, and all values of $f(x)$ sum to 1.

[12] For plant A,

    $\bar{x}$ = column(1) × column(3) = $\Sigma x f(x)$ = (0.46 × 0.20) + (0.48 × 0.20) + (0.50 × 0.20) + (0.52 × 0.20) +
        (0.54 × 0.20) = 0.50

and, $\sigma^2$ = [(0.46 − 0.50)$^2$ × 0.20] + [(0.48 − 0.50)$^2$ × 0.20] + [(0.50 − 0.50)$^2$ × 0.20] + [(0.52 − 0.50)$^2$ × 0.20] +
    [(0.54 − 0.50)$^2$ × 0.20]

    = 0.0008

[13] The mean value of the quality characteristic is 0.50 for plant A, as calculated in footnote 12. The target value of the quality characteristic is also 0.50. Therefore, for plant A $D$ = 0.50 − 0.50 = 0. Verify that the value of $D$ is also zero for plant B by carrying out the same procedure.

cost money, repairs that correct defects save downstream quality costs such as field repairs, warranty costs, and loss of goodwill. By contrasting the estimated repair cost with the quality cost of not detecting and repairing defects, the firm can determine an acceptable tolerance level for its outputs. Rewriting the equation for estimating the value of $k$:

$$\text{Total quality cost} = k \times (\text{Tolerance})^2$$

Let's return to our sheet metal example. Assume that the cost to the firm in question is estimated as $300 if the firm repairs the product before shipping. Assume, too, that the firm repairs all units that exceed the tolerance level for thickness. Then, this firm can determine the tolerance as follows:

$$\$300 = \$2,000,000 \times (\text{Tolerance})^2$$

Solve the equation,

$$\text{Tolerance} = 0.0122$$

Alternatively, the tolerance can be determined as shown below.

$$\text{Tolerance} = T_0 \sqrt{C_1/C_2}$$

where

$T_0$ = current (or customer) tolerance

$C_2$ = manufacturer's quality cost when the product fails to meet customer's specification

$C_1$ = manufacturer's cost to rework or scrap the unit before shipping

In the example above, the firm expects the external failure cost, $C_2$, to be $5,000; the cost to the firm to be $300 if the firm repairs, reworks, or scraps the defective unit before shipping ($C_1$); and the customer's tolerance to be 0.05. Given these assumptions, the firm would then set the tolerance at 0.0122, as follows:

$$\text{Tolerance} = 0.05\sqrt{\$300/\$5,000} = 0.0122$$

## Financial Measures and Cost of Quality (COQ)

**LO 17-5**

*Prepare and interpret relevant financial information to support quality-related initiatives.*

As indicated in Exhibit 17.3, there are two major situations in which management accountants can provide relevant financial information as part of a comprehensive framework for managing and controlling quality: relevant cost (and revenue) data for decision-making purposes, and cost-of-quality (COQ) reports.

### Relevant Cost Analysis: Decision Making

Quality-related spending (investment) affects the target level of quality and ultimately work processes and outputs—as depicted in Exhibit 17.3. In terms of spending on quality-related initiatives, we can employ the same decision framework that we presented in Chapter 11. That is, financial information relevant to quality-related decisions consists of future costs (and revenues) that differ between decision alternatives. In terms of relevant costs, we can also use the term *avoidable costs* since, by definition, these are future costs that can be avoided by choosing one decision alternative over another. As discussed in Chapter 12, long-term investments in quality are evaluated using discounted cash flow (DCF) decision models, such as net present value (NPV).

Activity and process decisions are prime examples of quality-related investments. For example, some manufacturers are moving from process layouts (batch processing) to cellular manufacturing. Other firms are embracing a just-in-time (JIT) production philosophy. Obviously, there can be significant outlay costs associated with a plant-layout change or a change in manufacturing philosophy.

At the same time, improvements in quality provide an opportunity for increasing revenues and for significant cost savings. The managerial accountant can provide decision makers with accurate estimates of costs and benefits associated with quality-related spending, such as a move to JIT. Benefits could include the contribution margin associated with increased sales (because of decreased cycle times associated with JIT production or the use of cellular manufacturing). Benefits could also include reduced spending on rework/scrap costs, lower financing costs associated with inventory reductions, reduced inventory obsolescence costs, reduced spending on inventory-recording costs, and reduced inventory-handling and storage-activity costs. Note that, as in Chapter 11, *relevant costs* include both *opportunity costs* and *out-of-pocket costs.*

## Cost-of-Quality (COQ) Reporting

Quality costs for many companies are essentially buried in the company's financial statements. For example, in the case of a manufacturer some costs appear in manufacturing (factory) overhead accounts (e.g., product testing, materials inspection, normal spoilage costs), while other quality costs are included as part of general and administrative expenses. When warranted, traditional cost accounting systems—both job-order and process—report separately the cost of abnormal spoilage.

However, as indicated in Exhibit 17.3, quality costs are associated with activities across the value chain—from the design of work processes, to production of outputs (goods and services), to delivery of outputs to customers. Thus, quality costs also include costs associated with support functions such as product design, purchasing, public relations, and customer services.

The traditional general ledger is an effective instrument for what it is designed to do: post and summarize transactions into specific account balances. But the expense data in this format (e.g., salaries, supplies, depreciation) are structurally deficient for decision support, including measuring the total **cost of quality (COQ)** for the organization. They disclose what was spent but not why or for what or for whom. Expense data must be transformed into the costs of the activities within processes that traverse the departmental cost centers reported in a general ledger system—and ultimately transformed into the cost of products, services, and customers.

Thus, an expansive view would define *cost of quality* as the cost of activities associated with the prevention, identification, repair, and rectification of poor quality, as well as opportunity costs from lost production and lost sales as a result of poor quality. For interpretive purposes, we might subdivide total COQ into the following four categories: prevention costs, appraisal costs, internal failure costs, and external failure costs. These terms are defined below. Exhibit 17.8 provides examples of the components of COQ. Consistent with the discussion in Chapter 11, we include both out-of-pocket as well as opportunity costs in the analysis of COQ.

**Cost of quality (COQ)**
is a comprehensive reporting framework for classifying quality-related costs.

**EXHIBIT 17.8**
**Examples of Quality Costs, by Category**

| Prevention Costs | Appraisal Costs |
|---|---|
| Training: | Raw materials inspection |
|   Instructor fees | Work-in-process inspection |
|   Testing equipment | Finished goods inspection |
|   Tuition for external training | Test equipment: |
|   Wages and salaries for time spent |   Depreciation |
|   on training and education |   Salaries and wages |
| Planning and execution of a quality program: |   Maintenance |
|   Salaries |   Software |
|   Cost of meetings/Quality circles | |
| Investments: | **External Failure Costs** |
|   Product redesign | Sales returns and allowances |
|   Process improvement | Warranty cost/field service |
|   Equipment maintenance | Contribution margin of canceled sales orders |
| | Contribution margin of lost sales orders* |
| **Internal Failure Costs** | Product recalls |
|   Scrap disposal (net cost) | Product liability lawsuits |
|   Rework (materials, labor, overhead) | |
|   Loss due to downgrades* | |
|   Reinspection costs | |
|   Loss due to work interruptions* | |

*Opportunity costs

## *Prevention Costs*

**Prevention costs**
are costs incurred to keep
quality defects from occurring.

**Prevention costs** are incurred to keep quality defects from occurring. Prevention costs include the following:

- **Quality training costs.** Costs incurred to conduct internal training programs and for employees to participate in external programs to ensure proper manufacturing, delivering, and servicing of products and services, and to improve quality. These costs include salaries and wages for time spent in training, instruction costs, clerical staff expenses and miscellaneous supplies, and costs expended to prepare handbooks and instructional manuals.
- **Equipment maintenance costs.** Costs to install, calibrate, maintain, repair, and inspect production equipment.
- **Supplier-assurance costs.** Costs incurred to ensure that materials, components, and services received meet the firm's quality standards. These costs include costs of selection, evaluation, and training of suppliers to conform with the requirements of total quality management (TQM).
- **Information systems costs.** Costs expended for developing data requirements and measuring, auditing, and reporting quality data.
- **Product redesign and process improvement.** Costs incurred to evaluate and improve product designs and operating processes to simplify manufacturing processes or to reduce or eliminate quality problems.
- **Quality circles.** Costs incurred to establish and operate quality control circles to identify quality problems and to offer solutions to improve the quality of products and services.

A **quality circle**
is a small group of employees
from the same work area that
meet regularly to identify and
solve work-related problems
and to implement and monitor
solutions to the problems.

## *Appraisal Costs*

**Appraisal (detection) costs**
are costs devoted to the
measurement and analysis of
data to determine conformity
of outputs to specifications.

**Appraisal (detection) costs** are costs devoted to the measurement and analysis of data to determine conformity of outputs to specifications. These costs are incurred during production and prior to deliveries to customers. Through the measurement, analysis, and monitoring of manufacturing processes and the inspection of products and services prior to delivery, firms identify defective items and ensure that all units meet or exceed customer requirements. Appraisal costs include the following:

- **Test and inspection cost.** Costs incurred to test and inspect incoming materials, work in process, and finished goods, and the cost incurred to inspect machinery; also, costs associated with field-testing of products at the site of the consumer.
- **Test equipment and instruments.** Expenditures incurred to acquire, operate, or maintain facilities, software, machinery, and instruments for testing or appraising the quality of products, services, or processes.

## *Internal Failure Costs*

**Internal failure costs**
are associated with defective
processes or defective products
detected before delivery to
customers.

**Internal failure costs** are associated with defective processes or defective products detected before delivery to customers. These costs include:

- **Costs of corrective action.** Costs for time spent to find the cause of failure and to correct the problem.
- **Rework and (net) scrap costs.** Materials, labor, and overhead costs for scrap, rework, and reinspection.
- **Process costs.** Costs expended to redesign the product or processes; unplanned machine downtime for adjustment; and lost production due to process interruption for repair or rework.
- **Expediting costs.** Costs incurred to expedite manufacturing operations due to time spent for repair or rework.
- **Reinspection and retest costs.** Salaries, wages, and expenses incurred during reinspection or retesting of reworked or repaired items.

- **Lost contribution due to increased demand on constrained resources.** Constrained resources spent on defective units increase cycle time and reduce total output. Contribution margin lost from units not produced because of the unavailability of the constrained resources reduce the operating income of the firm.

### External Failure Costs

**External failure costs**
are associated with defective/poor-quality outputs detected after being delivered to the customer.

**External failure costs** are costs associated with defective/poor-quality outputs detected after being delivered to the customer. External failure costs include the following:

- **Repair or replacement costs.** Repair or replacement of returned products.
- **Costs to handle customer complaints and returns.** Salaries and administrative overhead of the customer service department; allowances or discounts granted for poor quality; and, freight charges for returned products.
- **Product recall and product liability costs.** Administrative costs to handle product recalls, repairs, or replacements; legal costs; and settlements resulting from legal actions.
- **Lost sales and customer ill-will due to defective outputs.** Lost contribution margin on canceled orders, lost sales, and decreased market shares.
- **Costs to restore reputation.** Costs of marketing activities to minimize damages from a tarnished reputation and to restore the firm's image and reputation.

### Conformance Costs and Nonconformance Costs

**Costs of conformance**
consist of prevention costs and appraisal costs.

**Costs of nonconformance**
consist of internal failure costs and external failure costs.

Conceptually, the total cost of quality (COQ) can be categorized into conformance costs and nonconformance costs. Prevention and appraisal costs are **costs of conformance** because they are incurred to ensure that products or services meet customer expectations. Internal failure costs and external failure costs are **costs of nonconformance**. They are costs incurred because of poor-quality products or services and include opportunity costs. The total cost of quality (COQ) is the sum of conformance and nonconformance costs.

Prevention costs are usually the least expensive and the easiest among the four costs of quality for management to control. Internal and external failure costs are among the most expensive costs of quality, especially external failure costs. In a typical scenario, the cost of prevention may be $0.10 per unit, the cost of testing and replacing poor quality parts or components during production may be $5, the cost of reworking or reassembling may be $50, and the cost of field repair and other external costs may be $5,000 or higher.

Better prevention of poor quality reduces all other costs of quality. With fewer problems in quality, less appraisal is needed because the products are made right the first time. Fewer defective units also reduce internal and external failure costs as repairs, rework, and recalls decrease. By spending more on prevention and appraisal, companies spend less on internal or external failure costs. The savings alone can be substantial. Meanwhile, the firm enjoys higher perceived values of its products, increased sales and market share, and improved earnings and return on investment, as depicted earlier in Exhibit 17.1.

## COQ Reports

The purpose of reporting quality costs is to make management aware of the magnitude of these costs, to motivate continuous improvement in COQ, and to provide a baseline against which the impact of quality-improvement investments can be measured.

### Report Format

A COQ report is useful only if its recipients understand, accept, and can use the content of the report. Each organization should select and design a reporting system that (1) can be integrated into its information system, and (2) promotes the quality initiatives specified by top management. To facilitate assessment of the magnitude of quality costs and their impact, the organization should express its COQ component costs relative to net sales (or total operating costs) for the period.

**EXHIBIT 17.9    Cost-of-Quality (COQ) Matrix**

Source: J. R. Evans and W. M. Lindsay, *Managing for Quality and Performance Excellence,* 8th ed. (Mason, OH: South-Western, 2011), p. 391.

| | Design Engineering | Purchasing | Production | Finance | Accounting | Other | Totals | % of Sales |
|---|---|---|---|---|---|---|---|---|
| Prevention costs:<br>Quality planning<br>Training<br>Other | | | | | | | | |
| Appraisal costs:<br>Test and inspect<br>instruments<br>Other | | | | | | | | |
| Internal failure costs:<br>Scrap<br>Rework<br>Other | | | | | | | | |
| External failure costs:<br>Returns<br>Recalls<br>Other | | | | | | | | |
| Totals | | | | | | | | |

A cost-of-quality matrix, as illustrated in Exhibit 17.9, is a convenient and useful tool in reporting quality costs. With columns identifying functions or departments across the value chain and rows delineating COQ categories, a cost-of-quality matrix enables each department, function, process, or product line to identify and recognize the effects of its actions on the total cost of quality and to pinpoint areas of improvement.

### Illustration of a COQ Report

Exhibit 17.10 illustrates a COQ report.[14] Bally Company is a small midwestern manufacturing company with annual sales of around $9 million. The company operates in a highly competitive environment and has been experiencing increasing pressures from new and existing competitors to raise quality and lower cost. The report shows that the external failure costs for items such as warranty claims, customer dissatisfaction, and loss of market share accounted for 75% of the total COQ in year 0 ($1,770,000 ÷ $2,360,000, or 22.13% ÷ 29.5%).

[14] Adapted from "Managing Quality Improvements," *Statement of Management Accounting No. 4-R* (Montvale, NJ: Institute of Management Accountants, 1993).

**EXHIBIT 17.10**
**Cost-of-Quality (COQ) Report for Bally Company**

| | Year 2 | % of Sales | Year 0 | % of Sales | Percent Change in Cost |
|---|---|---|---|---|---|
| **Prevention Costs** | | | | | |
| Training | $ 90,000 | | $ 20,000 | | 350% |
| Quality planning | 86,000 | | 20,000 | | 330 |
| Other quality improvement | 60,000 | | 40,000 | | 50 |
| Supplier evaluation | 40,000 | | 30,000 | | 33 |
| Total | $ 276,000 | 3.07% | $ 110,000 | 1.38% | 151 |
| **Appraisal Costs** | | | | | |
| Testing | $ 120,000 | | $ 100,000 | | 20 |
| Quality performance measurement | 100,000 | | 80,000 | | 25 |
| Supplier monitoring | 60,000 | | 10,000 | | 500 |
| Customer surveys | 30,000 | | 10,000 | | 200 |
| Total | $ 310,000 | 3.44% | $ 200,000 | 2.50% | 55 |
| **Internal Failure Costs** | | | | | |
| Rework and reject | $ 55,000 | | $ 150,000 | | (63) |
| Reinspection and testing | 35,000 | | 30,000 | | 16 |
| Equipment failure | 30,000 | | 50,000 | | (40) |
| Downtime | 20,000 | | 50,000 | | (60) |
| Total | $ 140,000 | 1.56% | $ 280,000 | 3.50% | (50) |
| **External Failure Costs** | | | | | |
| Product liability insurance | $ 70,000 | | $ 250,000 | | (72) |
| Warranty repairs | 100,000 | | 120,000 | | (17) |
| Customer losses (estimated) | 600,000 | | 1,400,000 | | (57) |
| Total | $ 770,000 | 8.55% | $1,770,000 | 22.12% | (56) |
| **Total Quality Costs** | $1,496,000 | **16.62%** | $2,360,000 | **29.50%** | (37) |
| Total sales | $9,000,000 | 100.00% | $8,000,000 | 100.00% | |

To be more competitive and to increase market share, Bally began a corporatewide three-year TQM process. The firm started with substantial increases in prevention and appraisal expenditures. The investment started to pay off in year 2. Internal failure, external failure, and total quality costs have all decreased. COQ reports over time can help document these improvements.

Exhibit 17.10 compares the current year's quality costs to those of a base year. Alternative bases for comparisons can be the budgeted amounts, flexible budget costs, or long-range goals.

To better communicate results, the accountant can transform time-series data, such as the data presented in Exhibit 17.10, into one or more histograms. Based on before-and-after histograms, managers are more able to see improvement in overall COQ spending that has occurred over time. The visual representation of the histograms also enables managers to better evaluate trade-offs, such as increased spending in prevention and appraisal with the expectation of reductions in failure costs. This process of feedback and evaluation makes COQ more than just an accounting scheme—it becomes a financial investment justification tool.

## COQ and Activity-Based Costing (ABC)

An ABC system is ideally suited to the preparation of COQ reports. An ABC system identifies cost with activities and thus increases the visibility of costs of quality. Costs of activities that are the result of poor quality become clear to the organization. Traditional costing systems, in contrast, focus the cost reporting on organizational functions such as production, sales, and administration. An organization with a good ABC system in place needs only to identify costs and activities relating to COQ and classify these costs according to the COQ categories that the firm chooses to use.

## Nonfinancial Quality Indicators

**LO 17-6**

*Discuss the use of nonfinancial performance data to support quality-related initiatives.*

As seen from the preceding discussion, relevant financial data are needed to guide investment decision making and in planning and controlling quality-related costs. However, as indicated in Exhibit 17.3, *nonfinancial* performance data also play an important role in a comprehensive framework for managing and controlling quality.

### Internal Nonfinancial Quality Metrics

Organizations strive to specify internal dimensions of quality on which they must focus in order to meet customer expectations. Thus, we find the following examples of internal nonfinancial quality measures:

- Process yield (i.e., good output/total output).
- Productivity (i.e., ratio of acceptable outputs—goods or services—to resource inputs).
- Percentage of first-pass yields (i.e., percentage of initial output meeting quality standards).
- Number of defective parts produced (e.g., parts-per-million, *ppm*).
- Machine up-time (or, machine downtime).
- Trend in dollar amount of inventory held.
- Employee turnover (e.g., number of employees who voluntarily leave the company/total number of employees).
- Safety record (e.g., number of accidents per month, number of days since last accident).
- Throughput (i.e., outputs—goods or services—produced and delivered to customers).
- Production (manufacturing) lead time (i.e., difference between when an order is received by manufacturing and when that order is completed).
- Cycle-time efficiency (i.e., ratio of time spent on value-added activities to the sum of time spent on value-added and non-value-added activities; also known as *throughput time ratio* or *process cycle efficiency*).
- Throughput efficiency (i.e., the ratio of throughput to resources used).
- New product (or service) development time.

You will notice that many of the preceding metrics relate to process efficiency. Improving quality should improve many if not most of these measures. In actual practice, responsibility for implementing process changes designed to improve these measures is assigned to cross-functional teams. Further, some type of benchmark, either internal or external, is generally used as the standard against which actual performance is gauged.

### External (Customer Satisfaction) Quality Metrics

A comprehensive framework for managing and controlling quality will include a set of external, as well as internal, quality measures. These metrics are customer-based, as shown by the following examples:

- Number of defective units shipped to customers as a percentage of total units shipped.
- Number of customer complaints.
- **Customer loyalty** (measured, for example, by repeat purchases or customer retention rates or by percentage growth in business with existing customers).
- Percentage of products that experience early or excessive failure.
- Delivery delays (e.g., difference between scheduled delivery date and date requested by the customer).
- On-time delivery rate (e.g., percentage of shipments made on or before the scheduled delivery date).
- Market research information on customer preferences and satisfaction with specific product features (see, for example, the customer version of the "Loyalty Acid Test" at **http://www.loyaltyrules.com/loyaltyrules/acid_test_customer.html** for a sample customer-satisfaction survey).

**Customer loyalty**
is a measure of customer satisfaction, measured (for example) by repeat business with a customer.

What nonfinancial performance data are available to passengers of U.S. domestic airlines? How can these airlines benchmark their operating performance in terms of critical success factors? Since 1991 such data have been provided on an annual basis in what is called the *Airline Quality Rating* (AQR) report. The AQR reports for each domestic carrier monthly performance data in four major categories, based on data obtained from the U. S. Department of Transportation's monthly *Air Travel Consumer Report* (www.dot.gov/airconsumer). The *Airline Quality Rating 2011* report reflects monthly AQR scores for calendar year 2010. The AQR for an airline is based on a weighted-average of performance measures in four major areas that are important to customers, as follows:

$$AQR = \frac{(+8.63 \times OT) + (-8.03 \times DB) + (-7.92 \times MB) + (-7.17 \times CC)}{(8.63 + 8.03 + 7.92 + 7.17)}$$

where

OT = On-time arrival
DB = Denied boarding
MB = Mishandled baggage
CC = Customer complaints (12 separate items: fares, refunds, etc.)

The creators of the above model state that the AQR provides both consumers and industry watchers a means for looking at comparative quality for each airline on a timely basis, using objective, performance-based data.

AQRs for the top three (of 16) and bottom three domestic airlines for 2010 and 2009, as well as composite data (16 airlines for 2010; 18 airlines for 2009) are as follows:

| Airline | 2010 AQR | | 2009 AQR | |
| --- | --- | --- | --- | --- |
| | Score | Rank | Score | Rank |
| Air Tran | −0.48 | 1 | −0.49 | 2 |
| Hawaiian Airlines | −0.58 | 2 | −0.40 | 1 |
| JetBlue | −0.62 | 3 | −0.90 | 3 |
| Comair | −1.56 | 14 | −2.22 | 16 |
| Atlantic Southeast | −1.72 | 15 | −2.49 | 17 |
| American Eagle | −2.82 | 16 | −2.83 | 18 |
| Industry Average | −1.20 | | −1.27 | |

A separate ranking of nine major airlines (McCartney, 2011), based on two airline performance factors collected by FlightStats.com (on-time arrival and canceled flights) and three factors reported in the DOT Air Travel Consumer Report, shows AirTran, Alaskan Airlines, and Southwest at the top, with United, American, and Delta as the bottom three. (Authors' Note: In 2011, Southwest Airlines acquired AirTran. At the time of publication (2012) Southwest has begun the process of "full integration" of AirTran planes to Southwest.)

**Sources:** B. D. Bowen and D. E. Headly, *Airline Quality Rating 2011* (April 2011), available at: www.airlineinfo.com/public/2011aqr.pdf (accessed 08 November 2011); Scott McCartney, "The Big Guys Finish Last in 2010 Airline Rankings," *The Wall Street Journal* (January 13, 2011), pp. D1, D3.

- Customer response time (CRT), or the total lapse of time between when a customer places an order and when the customer actually receives the completed goods. This total time can be broken down into three components: receipt time; manufacturing lead time; and, delivery time. (See Exhibit 14.14.)

- **Net promoter score** (i.e., willingness of customers to recommend your business, defined as the difference between the percentage of "promoters" [those strongly recommending the company] and "detractors" [those who would not recommend your company plus those that are neutral]).[15]

A **net promoter score** is a measure of customer satisfaction, defined as the difference between the percentage of customers classified as "promoters" and those classified as "detractors" (those not recommending the business plus those who are neutral).

The preceding list is meant to be illustrative, not exhaustive. In practice, the actual metrics used are based on an organization's strategy. As is the case with internal quality measures, the preceding metrics require some benchmark (standard) against which actual performance for a period can be compared.

## Role of Nonfinancial Performance Measures

Internal and external nonfinancial measures of quality are important components of the framework presented in Exhibit 17.3 for a number of reasons:

- They are, for the most part, readily available (compared, for example, to the generation of activity-based costs, the preceding list of nonfinancial quality performance data are much less costly to obtain).

- Such information is relevant to operating personnel (production employees, salespersons, etc.)—that is, operating personnel understand these metrics and therefore can use them as the basis for improving operations.

[15] F. Reichheld, "The One Number You Need to Grow," *Harvard Business Review* (December 2003), pp. 46–54; and F. Reichheld, *The Ultimate Question: Driving Good Profits and True Growth* (Boston: Harvard Business Press, 2008).

- Because these measures relate to physical processes, they focus attention on precise problem areas that need attention.
- Such information is more timely than financial measures of quality—in the extreme, these measures of quality can be reported on a real-time basis (i.e., instantaneously as operations occur). Thus, nonfinancial quality indicators provide immediate short-run feedback on whether quality-improvement efforts have, in fact, succeeded in improving quality.
- These nonfinancial performance measures can be useful predictors (i.e., leading indicators) of future *financial* performance.

## Detecting and Correcting Poor Quality

**LO 17-7**

*Describe and understand techniques that can be used to detect and correct quality problems.*

As indicated in Exhibit 17.3, a comprehensive framework for managing and controlling quality relies on the use of a number of techniques for detecting poor quality and then taking appropriate corrective action. These techniques come principally from the field of operations management. In general, you can think of these techniques as embracing a single, overall goal: improving underlying business processes.

### Detecting Poor Quality

Once an appropriate set of financial and nonfinancial performance indicators has been specified, management needs to determine how to analyze the data it collects. The overall goal is to determine when the underlying process is not in control and, therefore, is in need of correction. One way to accomplish this is through the use of control charts.

A **control chart**
plots successive observations of an operation (or cost) taken at constant intervals.

A **control chart** plots successive observations of an operation (or cost), taken at constant intervals, to help determine whether a process is in control or not. The operation can be a machine, workstation, individual worker, work cell, part, process, or department. Costs can include labor, materials, energy, or any of the costs of quality discussed earlier in this chapter. Intervals can be time periods, batches, production runs, or other demarcations of the operation.

A typical control chart has a horizontal axis representing units, time intervals, batch numbers, or production runs, and a vertical axis denoting a financial or nonfinancial performance measure. The vertical measure has a specified allowable range of variations, which are referred to as *upper* and *lower limits,* respectively. As such, control charts are appropriate for use with goalpost performance standards. Exhibit 17.11 contains control charts for manufacturing 1/8-inch drill bits in three workstations: A, B, and C.

Assume that a firm has determined all drill bits must be within 0.0005 inch of the specified diameter. All units from workstation A are within the specified range ($\pm 0.0005''$), and no further investigation is necessary. Three units from workstation B are outside the specified range—an indication that the process in workstation B may not be in proper control. Management may want to investigate the cause of the aberration to prevent further quality failures. Although all units manufactured by workstation C are within the specified range acceptable to the firm, the control chart reveals that quality characteristics of workstation C are drifting upward. (Used in this manner, the control chart is often

A **run chart**
shows the trend in observations over time.

referred to as a **run chart**. A run chart shows the trend of observations over time.) Management may want to launch an investigation because the trend suggests that in the near future the operation may produce drill bits outside the control limits.

When the central line and the limits in a control chart are determined through a statistical process, the control chart is a *statistical quality control* (SQC) *chart* or *statistical process control* (SPC) *chart.* The control charts presented in Exhibit 17.11 are SQC (or SPC) charts if the line in the center, 0.125″, is determined by calculating the arithmetic mean ($\mu$, read mu) of the observations and the limits, 0.1255″ and 0.1245″, are determined based on the standard deviation ($\sigma$, read sigma) of the observations. For example, the standard deviation of the drill bits is, say, 0.00025″ and the firm has determined that variations within two standard deviations of the mean are acceptable. Thus, the limits are $\mu \pm 2\sigma$, or $0.125'' \pm 2 \times 0.00025''$, which are 0.1255″ and 0.1245″ for upper and lower limits, respectively.

**EXHIBIT 17.11**
**Control Charts for 1/8-Inch Drill Bit**

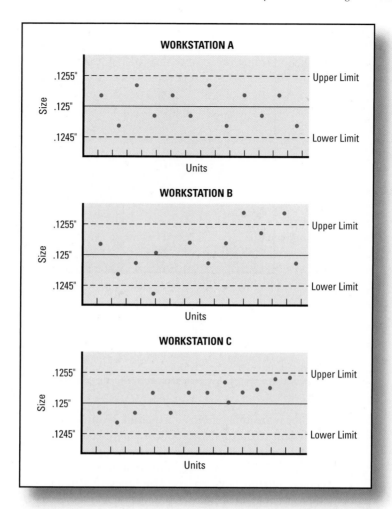

A firm sets the upper and lower control limits based on experience, technology, and customer expectations. The purpose of a control chart is to help distinguish between random and nonrandom variations. A process (or operation, or cost) is considered to be in *statistical control* if no sample observation is outside the established limits. Variations that fall within the established limits are deemed *random* variations so that no further investigation is needed. Observations outside the limits may signal quality failures or an out-of-control process.

However, for observations within the established limits to be considered random, the observations should show no apparent patterns or runs, with an approximately equal number of observations above and below the center line and most points nearing the center line. A process may be out of control if the observations show trends, cycles, clusters, or sudden shifts hugging the center line or the control limits. Posting control charts in a common area facilitates early detection of quality problems, promotes awareness of workers on the quality status of their products or services, and encourages active participation in efforts to manage and control quality.

## Taking Corrective Action

Once control charts indicate that a process may be out of control, what techniques are available for diagnostic purposes, that is, to guide corrective action? Histograms, Pareto charts (diagrams), and cause-and-effect diagrams are useful techniques for diagnosing causes of quality problems and identifying possible solutions to these problems.

### Histogram

A **histogram**
is a graphical representation of the frequency of attributes or events in a given set of data.

A **histogram** is a graphical representation of the frequency of attributes or events in a given set of data. Patterns or variations that are often difficult to see in a set of numbers

**EXHIBIT 17.12**
**Histogram of Quality Problem:**
**Contributing Factors**

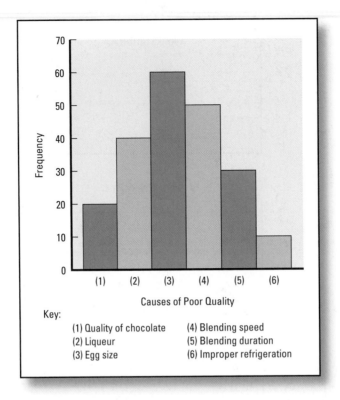

Causes of Poor Quality

Key:
(1) Quality of chocolate    (4) Blending speed
(2) Liqueur                 (5) Blending duration
(3) Egg size                (6) Improper refrigeration

become more apparent in a histogram. Exhibit 17.12 contains a histogram of factors that contribute to the quality problems identified by a company that makes chocolate mousse.

The company has experienced uneven quality in one of its products. The company has identified six contributing factors to the quality problem: substandard chocolate, improper liqueur mixture, uneven egg size, uneven blending speed, variant blending time, and improper refrigeration after production. It identified 210 batches as having poor quality. The histogram in Exhibit 17.12 suggests that variations in egg size may be the largest contributor to the quality problem, followed by uneven speed in blending ingredients.

### Pareto Diagram

**A Pareto diagram**
is a histogram of the frequency of factors contributing to a quality problem, ordered from the most to the least frequent.

A **Pareto diagram** is a histogram of factors contributing to a specified quality problem, ordered from the most to the least frequently occurring factor. Joseph Juran observed in the 1950s that a few causes usually account for most of the quality problems, thus the name Pareto.[16] See Exhibit 17.13 for the Pareto diagram associated with the chocolate mousse quality problem.

A Pareto diagram not only discloses the frequency of factors associated with a quality problem but also provides a useful visual aid. A Pareto diagram includes a curve that shows the cumulative number of causes, as shown in Exhibit 17.13. Using a Pareto diagram, management can separate the few major causes of quality problems from the many trivial ones. Thus, management can focus its efforts on areas that are likely to have the greatest impact on quality improvement. For example, the cumulative line in Exhibit 17.13 shows that improper egg size and erratic blending speed account for 110 quality problems in manufacturing chocolate mousse. To improve quality, management would most likely demand that all suppliers deliver eggs uniform in size and that operating personnel regulate the speed of blenders.

### Cause-and-Effect Diagram

**A cause-and-effect diagram**
organizes a chain of causes and effects to sort out root causes of an identified quality problem.

The **cause-and-effect,** or "fish-bone," **diagram** organizes a chain of causes and effects to sort out root causes of an identified quality problem. Karou Ishikawa discovered that for situations with myriad factors the number of factors that influenced a process or contributed

[16] V. Pareto, a nineteenth-century Italian economist, observed that 80% of the wealth in Milan was owned by 20% of its residents.

**EXHIBIT 17.13**
**Pareto Diagram of Quality Problem: Ranking of Contributing Factors**

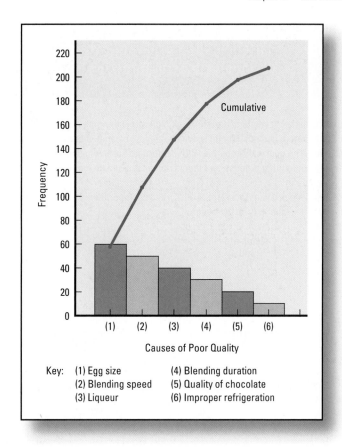

Key: (1) Egg size      (4) Blending duration
(2) Blending speed      (5) Quality of chocolate
(3) Liqueur      (6) Improper refrigeration

to a quality problem were often overwhelming. He developed cause-and-effect diagrams as an organizing aid.[17]

A cause-and-effect diagram consists of a spine, ribs, and bones. At the right end of the horizontal spine is an identified quality-related problem. The spine connects causes to an effect (i.e., to the specified quality problem). Each branch or rib pointing into the spine describes a main cause of the problem. Bones pointing to each rib are contributing factors to the cause. In Exhibit 17.14 we illustrate the general structure of a cause-and-effect diagram.

**EXHIBIT 17.14**
**Basic Cause-and-Effect ("Fish-Bone") Diagram**

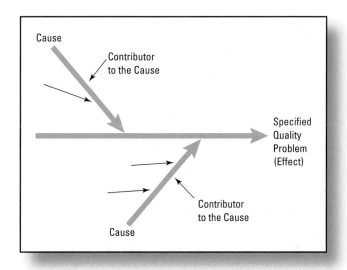

[17] K. Ishikawa, *Guides to Quality Control,* 2nd ed. (Tokyo: Asian Productivity Organization, 1986).

## Flattening the Corporate Pyramid: Creating a Lean Management Structure

As indicated in the text, lean is about eliminating waste and performing business operations and processes more efficiently. Normally, we connect the term *lean* to manufacturing. The goal in this context is to eliminate unnecessary steps in the manufacturing process that lead to increased cost and decreased manufacturing cycle (process) time. But the term can apply to management structure (e.g., layers) as well. Unnecessary layers of management get in the way of everything, including the speed with which decisions can be made. Elimination of such layers has resulted in what is called a *flatter* organization, wherein managers have broader responsibility over wider groups of employees and where decision making moves down within the organization. Entrenched practice sometimes makes it difficult for companies to eliminate managerial layers. For this reason, companies such as Toyota prefer to build plants from scratch rather than to acquire existing operations.

**Source:** Paul Glader, "It's Not Easy Being Lean," *The Wall Street Journal*, June 19, 2006, pp. B1, B3.

---

**EXHIBIT 17.15**

**Cause-and-Effect Diagram for the Chocolate Mousse Quality Problem**

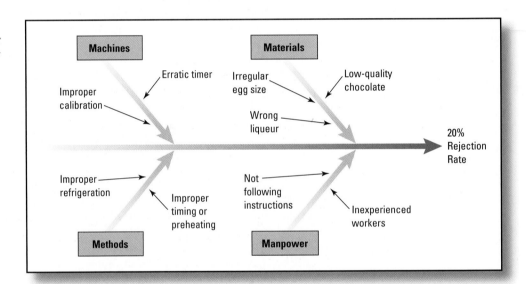

Typical main causes for quality problems in manufacturing operations are

- Machines
- Materials
- Methods
- Manpower

Some users refer to these four main categories as *4M*.

In Exhibit 17.15 we show a cause-and-effect diagram for the quality problems in the chocolate mousse example. Assume that the company identified the following main causes for the 20% rejection rate:

- Machines:

    Equipment not properly calibrated

    Timer functions erratically

- Materials:

    Suppliers delivered wrong or irregular-size eggs

    Low-quality chocolate

    Wrong liqueur used

- Methods:

    Improper refrigeration of ingredients

    Ingredients not added at proper time or in prescribed sequence

    Inappropriate preheating

- Manpower:

    New workers lack proper experience and are not given adequate training

    Workers failed to follow instructions

Many organizations have found brainstorming an effective technique in constructing cause-and-effect diagrams similar to the one presented in Exhibit 17.15.

## Lean Manufacturing and Accounting for Lean

**LO 17-8**

*Describe lean manufacturing and changes in management accounting systems needed to support a change to "lean."*

### Lean Manufacturing

The practice of total quality management (TQM), when combined with a strategic focus on productivity (Chapter 18) and an emphasis on increasing the speed of product flow and reducing inventory levels and customer lead times (the theory of constraints, Chapter 13), has led a number of companies to adopt what is called *lean manufacturing.* The goal of lean manufacturing ("lean," for short) is to increase product flow and product quality, reduce inventory, improve decision making, and increase profitability. Organizations adopting lean usually also adopt lean accounting, a new approach to costing and performance measurement that helps the organization show the financial benefits of the lean manufacturing initiative. Chapter 13 explains how lean manufacturing is related to productivity goals and measures. In Chapters 9 and 11, we show how lean accounting can play a role in the application of cost-volume-profit (CVP) analysis and short-term decision making, respectively. And in Chapter 18, we show how lean accounting plays a role in performance measurement. The objective of the discussion of lean in this chapter is to outline the strategic role of lean manufacturing and lean accounting and to illustrate the methods used to implement them. As such, the material in this section can be considered an extension of the topics covered earlier in this chapter. The primary conceptual lesson here for the management accountant is the need to reexamine and redesign cost-management systems as the underlying environment changes.

At the heart of lean manufacturing is the Toyota Production System (TPS), which has helped Toyota to become one of the most productive automakers in the world.[18] The main elements of TPS are: (1) a long-term focus on relationships with suppliers and coordination with these suppliers; (2) an emphasis on balanced, continuous-flow manufacturing with stable production levels; (3) continuous improvement in product design and manufacturing processes, with the objective of eliminating waste; and (4) flexible manufacturing systems in which different vehicles are produced on the same assembly line and employees are trained for a variety of tasks. Lean manufacturing is an approach to operations that has similar goals. The five principles of lean manufacturing are:[19]

1. *Value.* Lean starts with what is of value to the customer; rather than focus on internal standards of performance, lean measures success in terms of providing value to the customer.

2. *Value Stream.* The value stream consists of all the activities required to create customer value for a family, or group, of related products or services. Lean organizations do not focus on the cost of individual products but on the costs and profitability of the value stream. As such, the cost accounting system is greatly simplified, which gives rise to the notion of lean accounting.

[18] Taiichi Ohno, *Toyota Production System: Beyond Large Scale Production,* Productivity Inc, 1988.

[19] Institute of Management Accountants (IMA), Statements on Management Accounting, "Accounting for the Lean Enterprise: Major Changes to the Accounting Paradigm," and "Lean Enterprise Fundamentals" (**www.imanet.org/publications_statements.asp**).

3. *Pull and Flow.* A lean production process is scheduled to satisfy customer orders as they arrive at the company; this is the concept of *pull* production. The emphasis is on reducing lead time—the time it takes to process a customer's order. The company does not produce to meet a production forecast or budget; this is called the *push* approach. The push approach can result in excess inventory, especially when the inventory does not satisfy changed customer needs.

4. *Empowerment.* The lean manufacturing system has measures of performance, both financial and nonfinancial, that help the employee achieve the organization's lean goals. In the lean system these measures are collected in what is called a *box score,* which is similar to the balanced scorecard. The lean approach produces these measures frequently (daily or weekly) so that operating and management personnel have real-time information on their progress toward meeting goals.

5. *Perfection.* The lean approach emphasizes Six Sigma, continuous improvement, and elimination of non-value-added transactions (processes).

The key concepts of lean manufacturing as compared to traditional production systems are summarized in Exhibit 17.16.

## Accounting for Lean

Accounting for lean (lean accounting, for short) uses value streams to measure the financial benefits of a firm's progress in implementing lean manufacturing. Lean accounting places the firm's products and services into value streams, each of which is a group of related products or services. For example, a company manufacturing consumer electronics might have two groups of products (and two value streams)—digital cameras and video cameras—with several models in each group. Accounting for value streams significantly reduces the need for cost allocations (since the products are aggregated into value streams), which can help the firm to better understand the profitability of its process improvements and product groups.[20]

A second motivation for value-stream accounting arises from the fact that organizations implementing lean may see the operating improvements rather quickly, but traditional financial statements will not show these improvements for some time. The organization's commitment to lean manufacturing may take several months or years to complete, so that the failure to see these improvements in the financial statements for a long period could undermine the commitment and success of the effort.

There are three reasons why the improvements in financial results typically appear later than the operating improvements from implementing lean manufacturing.[21]

1. Customers will benefit from the improved manufacturing flexibility by ordering in smaller, more diverse quantities. In the short term, this means that total sales may fall, as will financial results. In the longer term, the increased value added to the customers will increase sales and the overall volume of customer demand should increase.

**EXHIBIT 17.16**
**Lean vs. Traditional Manufacturing Processes**

|  | **Traditional Production** | **Lean Manufacturing** |
|---|---|---|
| Key focus points | Reduce cost<br>Reduce idle time | Meet customer demand with short lead time<br>Reduce overproduction and inventory level |
| Manufacturing scheduling | Meet forecasted demand (push); production in batches | Meet a customer order received (pull); production is driven by the receipt of customer orders |
| Batch production | Reduce *number* of setups to reduce setup costs | Reduce setup *time* to maximize manufacturing flexibility and to reduce inventory; maximize the ability to meet diverse customer needs; the principle of one-piece flow |

[20] For a reference on the value-stream income statement see the Institute of Management Accountants, Statements on Management Accounting: "Accounting for the Lean Enterprise: Major Changes to the Accounting Paradigm," and Frances A. Kennedy and Peter C. Brewer, "Lean Accounting: What's It All About," *Strategic Finance,* November 2005, pp. 27–34.

[21] Robin Cooper and Brian Maskell, "How to Manage Through Worse-Before-Better," *MIT Sloan Management Review* (Summer 2008), pp. 58–65.

2. Improvements in productivity will create excess capacity; as equipment and facilities are used more efficiently, some will become idle. The result is no improvement in short-term financial results. When the excess capacity is reduced over time, or redeployed, the financial results will show the improvement from the cost savings.

3. Because full-cost accounting methods include all manufacturing costs as part of product cost, fixed manufacturing costs are included in the balance sheet as part of inventory until the product is sold. The decrease in inventory that results from lean means that, using full-cost accounting, the fixed costs incurred in prior periods (when inventory was increasing) flow through the income statement when inventory is decreasing.

Value-stream income statements can be adapted to separate from operating income the effects of each of the above items. An example of a value-stream income statement that addresses the third item above (viz., the effect of inventory reduction) is shown in Exhibit 17.17. Rimmer Company has two value streams, digital cameras and video cameras.

**EXHIBIT 17.17    Sample Value-Stream Income Statement**

| | **RIMMER COMPANY** Value-Stream Income Statement | | | | |
|---|---|---|---|---|---|
| | **Digital Cameras** | | **Video Cameras** | | **Total** |
| Sales | | $585,000 | | $540,000 | $1,125,000 |
| Operating costs: | | | | | |
|   Materials | $ 25,200 | | $ 12,800 | | |
|   Labor | 168,000 | | 88,000 | | |
|   Equipment related costs | 92,400 | | 48,400 | | |
|   Occupancy costs | 11,200 | | 4,800 | | |
|     Total operating costs | | 296,800 | | 154,000 | $ 450,800 |
| Less: Other value-stream costs | | | | | |
|   Manufacturing | 120,000 | | 240,000 | | |
|   Selling and administration | 10,000 | 130,000 | 10,000 | 250,000 | 380,000 |
| Value-stream profit before inventory change | | 158,200 | | 136,000 | 294,200 |
| Less: Cost of decrease in inventory | | (10,000) | | (20,000) | (30,000) |
|   Value-stream profit | | $148,200 | | $116,000 | $ 264,200 |
| Less: Nontraceable costs | | | | | |
|   Manufacturing | | | | | 155,000 |
|   Selling and administration | | | | | 54,000 |
|     Total nontraceable fixed costs | | | | | 209,000 |
| Operating income | | | | | $ 55,200 |

Assume that the operating costs and other value-stream costs are directly traceable to the two value streams, so no cost allocation is involved; the costs that cannot be traced to a value stream ($209,000 in total) are assigned only to the total company level. Note also that the recent implementation of lean has resulted in the decline in inventory, and that the prior period fixed manufacturing cost flowing through the current income statement is shown separately: $10,000 for the digital cameras stream, and $20,000 for the video cameras stream. The temporary total effect on income, $30,000, is set apart; lean managers would argue that, taking a long-term view, total operating income should be interpreted as $85,200 ($55,200 + $30,000).

## The Strategic Role of Lean Accounting

Lean manufacturing and lean accounting can play a key role in an organization's success. Lean is particularly appropriate for firms in dynamic and competitive environments, where there is product complexity and changing customer expectations. These are the types of firms that Robin Cooper describes in his study of lean enterprises—firms like Toyota, Nissan, and Sony.[22] These companies have long embraced the principles of lean, just-in-time (JIT), and continuous improvement. A commodity-based firm (agribusiness, building products, etc.) with a few homogeneous products and integrated manufacturing processes would probably focus on efficiency and many of the lean manufacturing principles but have little need for the value-stream income statement. Similarly, firms such as Coach and Tiffany that succeed on the basis of a strong differentiated brand would likely focus on performance measures that advance their brands, rather than emphasizing the principles of lean. Exhibit 17.18 provides a summary of the strategic role that can be played by the lean approach relative to full-cost accounting.

**EXHIBIT 17.18** **Summary Comparison: Traditional (Absorption) Costing vs. Lean Accounting**

| | **Full-Cost Accounting** | **Lean Accounting** |
|---|---|---|
| Key focus points | Causality; linking resources, cost drivers, and cost objects | Process flow and throughput; speed up product throughput |
| | Obtain accurate product costs | Facilitate the five principles of lean manufacturing<br>Support just-in-time (JIT) and theory-of-constraints (TOC) efforts; reduce inventory and customer lead time |
| Strategy implementation | Full-cost based; can be used to support long-term decisions | Short-term focus on reducing lead times, inventory levels, and value-stream income; value-stream goals can be linked to company strategy<br><br>Focus on day-to-day decisions |
| Cost allocation | Trace direct costs and use cost drivers for indirect costs | The goal is to avoid cost allocation; the use of the value stream, by aggregating products into product families, means that many costs can be traced directly to the value stream so that allocation is not needed |
| Nonfinancial information included? | Can be a supplement, as in a balanced scorecard | Included in the box score report that includes operational, capacity usage, and financial measures |
| Product cost detail and product-mix analysis | Individual product; product mix at the detail level | Aggregation of products; product cost at the value-stream level; analysis of average product cost within value stream |
| Reflects the financial benefits of lean manufacturing? | Only in the long term | Directly shows the financial benefits of lean efforts, through value-stream accounting and through the recognition of the cost of decreasing inventory levels |
| Product costs for pricing | Product costs may or may not play a role in pricing | Assumes that the firm is a price-taker; costs are not used in pricing |
| Reporting interval | Often monthly | Frequent; often weekly or daily |

[22] Robin Cooper describes a type of competition that differs from cost leadership and differentiation, as described by Michael Porter and explained in Chapter 1. Cooper studied firms that compete on both cost and product leadership, in very competitive environments. See *When Lean Enterprises Collide: Competing through Confrontation*, Harvard Business School Press, 1995.

## Summary

In today's globally competitive environment, with short product life cycles and rapidly changing technologies and consumer tastes, organizations can sustain long-term survival and profitability only by manufacturing quality products and rendering quality services.

A quality product or service meets or exceeds customer expectations at a price customers are willing to pay. To achieve quality products or services, many firms adopt *total quality management,* which requires continuous efforts by everyone in an organization to understand, meet, and exceed the expectations of both internal and external customers.

How can accounting add value to the organization by supporting quality-related initiatives of management? We propose, in Exhibit 17.3, a comprehensive framework that can be used to manage and control quality for a business. The framework implies an iterative or continuous process that begins and ends with the goal of meeting customer expectations. One primary role in this process for accounting is to provide relevant financial information, which informs the decision-making process. We identify two such examples: relevant cost (and revenue) data for evaluating spending and investments in quality, and the preparation of cost-of-quality (COQ) reports. Such financial information regarding quality is supplemented with internal and external nonfinancial measures of quality. To detect poor quality (i.e., out-of-control processes), these data can be analyzed using run or control charts. Histograms, Pareto diagrams, and cause-and-effect diagrams can then be used for diagnostic purposes, that is, to identify the source of quality problems in order to motivate appropriate corrective action.

Management accountants, with training and expertise in analyzing, measuring, and reporting information, can help design and implement the type of comprehensive control system depicted in Exhibit 17.3.

Recently, some companies have embraced lean manufacturing initiatives. In response, the management accounting and control systems for these organizations may have to be revised to better reflect and support such initiatives. The use of value-stream income statements was illustrated in the chapter as one possible revision. The primary conceptual lesson is the organic nature of cost-management systems: they need to change in response to changes in business strategy—a lesson that has been a primary theme throughout this text.

## Key Terms

| | | |
|---|---|---|
| absolute quality conformance, *722* | external failure costs, *729* | quality, *715* |
| appraisal (detection) costs, *728* | goalpost conformance, *721* | quality circle, *728* |
| cause-and-effect diagram, *736* | histogram, *735* | robust quality approach, *722* |
| control chart, *734* | internal failure costs, *728* | run chart, *734* |
| cost of quality (COQ), *727* | ISO 9000:2000, *712* | Six Sigma, *719* |
| costs of conformance, *729* | ISO 14000, *712* | Taguchi quality loss function, *723* |
| costs of nonconformance, *729* | net promoter score, *733* | tolerance, *721* |
| customer loyalty, *732* | Pareto diagram, *736* | total quality management (TQM), *711* |
| design quality, *715* | performance quality, *715* | |
| | prevention costs, *728* | |

## Self-Study Problems

(For solutions, please turn to the end of the chapter.)

### 1. Relevant Cost Analysis: Quality Improvement Program

An automobile manufacturer plans to spend $1 billion to improve the quality of a new model. The manufacturer expects the quality-improvement program to eliminate the need for recall and reduce the costs for other warranty repairs. The firm's experience had been, on average, 1.5 recalls for each new model at a cost of $300 per vehicle per recall. The average cost per recall, if one is needed, is expected to increase by 10% for the new model. Costs for other warranty repairs are expected to decrease from $200 to $80 per unit sold. Sales of the new model were expected to be 500,000 units without the quality-improvement program. The company believes that the well-publicized quality-improvement program will increase total sales to 650,000 units. If there is a profit of $5,000 per unit on any incremental sales attributable to the quality-improvement program, is the $1 billion expenditure justified?

## 2. Taguchi Quality Loss Function

Marlon Audio Company manufactures video tapes. The desired speed of its model SF2000 is 2 inches per second. Any deviation from this value distorts pitch and tempo, resulting in poor sound quality. The company sets the quality specification to $2 \pm 0.25$ inches per second because an average customer is likely to complain and return the tape if the speed is off by more than 0.25 inch per second. The cost per return is $36. The repair cost before the tape is shipped, however, is only $3 per tape.

### Required

1. Compute $L(x)$ if $x$ is 2.12 inches per second.

2. Estimate the tolerance for the firm to minimize its quality-related cost (loss).

## 3. Cost-of-Quality (COQ) Report

Precision Electric Instruments manufacturers fans for mini and micro computers. As a first step to focus on quality improvements, the firm has compiled the following operating data for 2013 (in thousands):

| | |
|---|---:|
| Line inspection | $ 55 |
| Training | 120 |
| Returns | 100 |
| Warranty repairs | 68 |
| Preventive equipment maintenance | 20 |
| Recalls | 157 |
| Design engineering | 67 |
| Scrap (net of salvage value) | 30 |
| Downtime | 40 |
| Product-testing equipment | 88 |
| Product liability insurance | 20 |
| Supplier evaluation | 15 |
| Rework | 35 |
| Inspection and testing of incoming materials | 25 |
| Litigation costs to defend allegation of defective products | 240 |

### Required
Prepare a cost-of-quality (COQ) report and classify the costs as prevention, appraisal, internal failure, and external failure. Express each category subtotal as a percentage of total COQ.

*Please visit http://www.mhhe.com/blocher6e to access a narrated, animated tutorial for solving these problems.*

## Questions

17-1 Provide a brief explanation of the conceptual relationship between improvements in quality and improvements in financial performance.

17-2 Define quality. For management and control purposes, define the two primary components of quality.

17-3 In what respect are traditional accounting systems deficient in terms of the goal of managing and controlling quality?

17-4 Describe the major elements of a comprehensive framework for managing and controling quality, such as the framework presented in Exhibit 17.3.

17-5 What is meant by Six Sigma? What five steps are usually associated with Six Sigma applications?

17-6 Discuss the difference between goalpost conformance and absolute quality conformance.

17-7 Taguchi argues that being within specification limits is not enough to be competitive in today's global economy. Do you agree? Why?

17-8 What functions does a cost-of-quality (COQ) report play in a quality-improvement program?

17-9 Of the four categories in a COQ report, which category of quality cost is the most damaging to the organization? Why is this the case?

17-10 From a design standpoint, what are some desirable characteristics of a cost-of-quality (COQ) reporting system? That is, if you were to design such a system from scratch, what would the key attributes of the system be?

17-11 Name and briefly describe three methods that companies can use to either identify or correct quality problems.

**Brief Exercises**

17-12 A customer places an order on January 1, 2013. Ten days later that order is received by the manufacturing department. Fifteen days later, the order is put into production. Processing (manufacturing) time is 20 days for this order. The completed order is then shipped 10 days later. For this order, what was the total customer-response time (CRT)?

17-13 On average, the manufacturing (processing) time spent per order is approximately four days. In addition, a typical order spends four days moving from process to process, three days in storage, and two days in inspection. For an average order, what is the manufacturing cycle efficiency?

17-14 For a typical order, assume the following times (in hours): storage time (in between processes), 5.0; inspection time, 1.0; move time (from process to process), 2.0; and manufacturing (processing) time, 8.0. Given this information, what is the manufacturing cycle efficiency?

17-15 Solidtronic, Inc., an OEM manufacturer, has a product specification of 75 +/− 5. The cost for warranty services is estimated as $500 per unit. What is the value of $k$, the cost coefficient, in the Taguchi loss function for this situation?

17-16 Refer to the information in 17-15. Calculate the estimated total cost when the measured quality characteristic, $x$ (e.g., circumference, measured in inches), is 78.

17-17 Refer to the information in 17-15. What is the expected loss (cost) per unit if the manufacturing process is centered on the target specification with a standard deviation of 2?

17-18 Listed below are selected items from the cost-of-quality (COQ) report for Watson Products for last month.

| Category | Amount |
|---|---|
| Rework | $ 725 |
| Equipment maintenance | 1,154 |
| Product testing | 786 |
| Field-service costs | 560 |
| Spoilage | 459 |
| Product liability insurance | 780 |
| Product repair | 695 |

What is Watson's total prevention and appraisal cost for the month?

17-19 A customer's order is delivered (received by the customer) on December 1, 2013. This order was placed with the company on September 1, 2013, and received by the manufacturing department on September 15, 2013. Actual production on the order began on October 15, 2013, and was completed November 15, 2013. Based on this information, calculate the following for this order: total customer-response time (CRT); order receipt time; manufacturing lead time (processing time); manufacturing wait time; manufacturing time; and delivery time. (*Hint:* Refer to Exhibit 14.14.) Prepare your answers in days.

17-20 In 2014 a manufacturing company instituted a total quality management (TQM) program producing the comparative report shown below:

| Summary COQ Report (in thousands) | | | |
|---|---|---|---|
| | 2013 | 2014 | % Change |
| Prevention costs | $ 200 | $ 300 | +50 |
| Appraisal costs | 210 | 315 | +50 |
| Internal failure costs | 190 | 114 | −40 |
| External failure costs | 1,200 | 621 | −48 |
| Total COQ | $1,800 | $1,350 | −25 |

On the basis of this report, which one of the following statements is *most* likely correct?

a. An increase in conformance costs resulted in a higher-quality product and, therefore, a decrease in nonconformance costs.

b. An increase in inspection costs was solely responsible for the decrease in quality costs.

c. Quality costs such as scrap and rework decreased by 48%.

    d. Quality costs such as returns and repairs under warranty decreased by 40%.

    e. Nonconformance costs increased by 50% and conformance costs decreased by approximately 47%.

17-21 Assume that a plasma TV company is working at a three-sigma level of quality in terms of each of 100 component parts in each TV it manufactures. Because of the high price associated with these TV sets, the company defines a product defect as any unit with one or more defective components. (That is, a good-quality output is defined as a TV set with zero defective parts.) On average, what is the probability of producing a unit with zero defects? (Show calculations.)

## Exercises

**[LO 17-4]** 17-22 **Six Sigma Interpretation; Spreadsheet Application** To what probabilities do each of the following sigma levels correspond, based on a standard normal curve: 3 sigma, 4 sigma, 5 sigma, and 6 sigma? (*Hint:* Use the NORMSDIST function in Excel. Note that this function returns the standard normal *cumulative* distribution function. The distribution has a mean of 0 (zero) and a standard deviation of 1.) **Check figures:** For three sigma, the two-tailed probability equals 0.27%; for six sigma, the two-tailed probability level is 0.0000002%. To what level of defects per million do each of the two-tailed probabilities correspond to? What is the point of these calculations?

**[LO 17-4]** 17-23 **Management Accounting's Role in Six Sigma** This chapter contains an overview of the Six Sigma process that many organizations are using today to improve services and products. One could get the impression from the discussion that this topic is more properly a management or an operations management issue. Respond to this position by speculating as to the appropriate role of the management accountant in the Six Sigma process. (*Hint:* Use as the basis of structuring your response the DMAIC implementation approach that is commonly associated with Six Sigma.)

**[LO 17-4]** 17-24 **Applying Six Sigma Principles to the Accounting Function** Brewer and Eighme (2005) report the results of an actual case study of applying Six Sigma principles to improve the accounting function, specifically, to improve the speed with which a subsidiary communicated quarterly financial results to its parent company (to allow preparation of consolidated financial statements). Assume you are in charge of a Six Sigma project designed to address this problem. Discuss steps you would take as project manager to address the problem, including the five steps in the *DMAIC* (design, measure, analyze, improve, and control) framework discussed in the text. (P. C. Brewer and J. E. Eighme, "Using Six Sigma to Improve the Finance Function," *Strategic Finance,* May 2005, pp. 27–33.)

**[LO 17-4]** 17-25 **Taguchi Loss Function Analysis** Flextronchip, an OEM manufacturer, has a fifth-generation chip for cell phones, with chip specification of $0.2 \pm 0.0002$ mm for the distance between two adjacent pins. The loss due to a defective chip has been estimated as $20.

**Required**

1. Compute the value of $k$ in the Taguchi loss function.
2. Assume that the quality control manager takes a sample of 100 chips from the production process. The results are as follows:

| Measurement | Frequency |
|---|---|
| 0.1996 | 2 |
| 0.1997 | 5 |
| 0.1998 | 12 |
| 0.1999 | 11 |
| 0.2000 | 45 |
| 0.2001 | 10 |
| 0.2002 | 8 |
| 0.2003 | 5 |
| 0.2004 | 2 |

    a. Calculate the estimated quality loss for each of the observed measurements.

    b. Calculate the expected (i.e., average) loss for the production process as a whole.

3. Using the data from (2) above:

    a. Determine the variance in the measured distance between two pins.

b. Calculate the expected loss of the process using the calculated variance, per the method presented by Albrecht and Roth, "The Measurement of Quality Costs: An Alternative Paradigm," *Accounting Horizons* (June 1992), pp. 15–27.

[LO 17-4]   17-26   **Using Taguchi Loss Function to Determine Tolerance**   The desired distance for Flextronchip customers is 0.2 mm between two adjacent pins. Any deviation from this value causes interference. The process of handling complaints costs the firm at least $40 per chip. The engineers of the firm expect the average customer will be likely to complain when the distance is off target by at least 0.0001. At the factory, the adjustment can be made at a cost of $1.60, which includes the labor to make the adjustment and additional testing.

**Required**   What should the tolerance be before an adjustment is made at the factory?

[LO 17-4]   17-27   **Taguchi Loss Function [$L(x)$] Analysis**   Duramold specializes in manufacturing molded plastic panels to be fitted on car doors. The blueprint specification for the thickness of a high-demand model calls for $0.1875 \pm 0.0025$ inch. It costs $120 to manufacture and $150 to scrap a part that does not meet these specifications. The thickness measure for the unit just completed is 0.1893 inch.

**Required**
1. Use the Taguchi loss function, $L(x)$, to determine:
   a. The value of the cost coefficient, $k$.
   b. The amount of loss for the unit, $L(x = 0.1893)$.
2. Assume that Duramold can eliminate the uneven thickness by adding a production worker, at the critical production point, for $6 per unit. Under this assumption:
   a. At what tolerance should the panels be manufactured? Show calculations.
   b. What should be the production specification for these panels?

[LO 17-1, 17-5]   17-28   **Graphical Depiction: Is There an Optimal Level of Spending on Quality, or Is Quality "Free"?**   Some proponents of TQM assert that quality is free, that is, that quality is a never-ending quest and that improving product/service quality will reduce a firm's total spending on quality. Others believe that after a point there are diminishing returns to additional expenditures on quality. Provide a graphical representation of each of these arguments. (*Hint:* Let the vertical axis of your graph represent $ (e.g., revenues or costs), and let the horizontal axis represent the level of quality—the higher the value on the x-axis, the greater the indicated quality level.) Supplement your graphs with appropriate explanations/interpretations.

[LO 17-5]   17-29   **COQ Histogram; Spreadsheet Application**   Genova Company classifies its costs of quality into four categories. The costs of quality (COQ) as a percentage of cost of goods sold for the last three years are as follows:

|  | 2013 | 2014 | 2015 |
| --- | --- | --- | --- |
| Prevention costs | 1.00% | 4.00% | 2.00% |
| Appraisal costs | 3.00 | 2.50 | 1.50 |
| Internal failure costs | 27.00 | 23.00 | 14.00 |
| External failure costs | 31.00 | 18.00 | 12.00 |

**Required**
1. Use a spreadsheet to prepare a histogram that shows the costs of quality (COQ) trends as a percentage of costs of goods sold.
2. Comment on the trends in cost of quality (COQ) over the three-year period from 2013 to 2015.
3. What cost of quality can the company expect as a percentage of its cost of goods sold in 2016? Explain.

[LO 17-5]   17-30   **Quality Cost Classification**

**Required**   Classify each of the following costs into one of the four quality cost (i.e., COQ) categories:
1. Materials, labor, and overhead costs of scrapped units. *internal*
2. Engineering time spent to determine the causes of failures to meet product specification.
3. Wages and salaries for the time spent by workers to gather quality measurements.
4. Information systems costs expended to develop data requirements.
5. Clerical staff expenses to coordinate training programs. *prevention*
6. Salaries for members of problem-solving teams.
7. Payment to settle a product-liability lawsuit. *external*

[LO 17-5]   17-31   **Cost of Quality (COQ) Reporting for Environmental Performance**   This chapter includes an overview of a cost-of-quality (COQ) reporting system. Such a system has, in fact, been applied in practice by a number of companies. This exercise pertains to the application of a COQ reporting framework to environmental management.

1. What motivation is there to implement an accounting and control system for environmental performance?

2. Construct a sample environmental cost-of-quality report using the four categories that comprise a traditional COQ report (i.e., prevention costs, appraisal/detection costs, internal failure costs, and external failure costs).

3. Do you think firms would be motivated to provide to shareholders information contained in the environmental COQ report you propose above in (2)? Why or why not?

[LO 17-5]   17-32   **Cost of Quality (COQ) Report: Environmental Management**   You are given the following environmental quality-related costs:

| | |
|---|---:|
| Employee training | $100,000 |
| Product design | 140,000 |
| Supplier certification | 40,000 |
| Process inspection | 320,000 |
| Depreciation—pollution-control equipment | 400,000 |
| Maintaining pollution-control equipment | 200,000 |
| Cleaning up polluted lake | 500,000 |
| Restoring land after use | 700,000 |
| Property damage claim | 600,000 |

**Required**

1. Prepare a cost of quality (COQ) report of environmental management for the year. Determine subtotals for each of the four reporting categories and express each subtotal as a percentage of total operating expenses ($10,000,000) for the year.

2. Based on the report you prepare, what conclusions can you draw regarding the company's environmental quality performance for the year?

3. Can you offer management suggestions for the design of an effective cost of quality reporting system for the environmental program? (That is, what would make for a good reporting system?)

[LO 17-5]   17-33   **Cost-of-Quality Improvement—Relevant Cost Analysis**   PIM Industries, Inc., manufactures electronics components. Each unit costs $30 before the final test. The final test rejects, on average, 5% of the 50,000 units manufactured per year. The average rejection rate of the industry is 3%. A consultant has determined that poor lighting is the most likely cause of this high rejection rate. It would cost $100,000 for new adequate lighting in the assembly department, which would be useful for 5 years. With adequate lighting that will cost an additional $5,000 in operating cost each year, the firm expects to reduce its rejection rate to no higher than the industry average.

**Required**

1. Should the firm install the lighting? (Show calculations)

2. What other considerations might affect this decision?

3. What is the primary role of the management accountant in this decision context?

[LO 17-5]   17-34   **Relevant Cost Analysis—Conversion to JIT; Spreadsheet Application**   As part of its commitment to quality, the J. J. Borden manufacturing company is proposing to introduce just-in-time (JIT) production methods. Managers of the company have an intuitive feel regarding the financial benefits associated with a change to JIT, but they would like to have some data to inform their decision making in this regard. You are provided with the following data:

| Item | Existing Situation | After Adopting JIT |
|---|---|---|
| **Manufacturing Costs as Percentage of Sales:** | | |
| Product-level support costs | 12% | 5% |
| Variable manufacturing overhead | 28 | 10 |
| Direct materials | 30 | 20 |
| Direct manufacturing labor | 22 | 15 |

*(Continued)*

**Other Financial Data:**

| | | |
|---|---|---|
| Sales revenue | $1,350,000 | $1,650,000 |
| Inventory of WIP | 180,000 | 30,000 |

**Other Data:**

| | | |
|---|---|---|
| Manufacturing cycle time | 60 days | 30 days |
| Inventory financing cost (per annum) | 10% | 10% |

**Required**   You have been asked, in conjunction with your position as the management accountant for the company, to construct an Excel spreadsheet that can be used to estimate the financial benefits associated with the adoption of JIT.

**[LO 17-3, 17-6]**   17-35   **Quality Ratings—Graduate Business Programs**   You can see from the discussion in the text that quality ratings, and quality-award programs, exist for various types of businesses and organizations. Some of you may be contemplating enrolling in an MBA program upon completion of your undergraduate studies. It might interest you, therefore, that graduate business programs in this country and abroad are ranked by a number of publications, including *The Wall Street Journal, Bloomberg BusinessWeek,* the *Financial Times,* the *Economist,* and *U.S. News & World Report.* To some extent, these sources use different measures to determine their quality rankings. Develop a list of criteria that could be used to generate quality rankings of graduate business programs.

**[LO 17-3, 17-6]**   17-36   **Spotting Quality in Business Programs**   Through its accreditation function, AACSB International (**www.aacsb.edu**) seeks continuous quality improvement in the content, delivery, and administration of management education. The AACSB in fact accredits business programs, at both the undergraduate and graduate levels, based on an overall assessment of the quality of these programs. As a student, you may have formed some thoughts regarding how to spot quality in a business-degree program. If you were in charge of developing accreditation standards for business-degree programs, what specific measures of quality would you include? That is, how would you spot quality in terms of a business-degree program?

**[LO 17-6]**   17-37   **Nonfinancial (Operational) Control Measures: Environmental Performance**   Assume that the company for which you are working is interested in implementing a comprehensive monitoring and control system regarding environmental performance. The company is convinced that improved performance in this area will lead to reduced costs, an improved corporate image, greater market share, and ultimately to greater financial returns. To supplement a number of financial-performance indicators in the area of environmental quality, the company is interested in developing a set of nonfinancial performance indicators, which (it is hoped) will motivate better environmental quality. In this regard, the company has embraced five strategic objectives: minimize hazardous materials; minimize raw/virgin materials usage; minimize energy requirements; minimize release of residues into the environment; and maximize opportunities to recycle. For each of these five strategic objectives, provide at least two relevant nonfinancial performance indicators that could lead to improved environmental performance.

**[LO 17-6]**   17-38   **Assessing the Use and Role of Nonfinancial Performance Indicators**   This question pertains to the use of nonfinancial performance indicators as part of a comprehensive management accounting and control system. You are asked to think critically about the value and challenges of using such data for performance-evaluation purposes. The following source should be accessed and read prior to answering the questions that appear below: Christopher D. Ittner and David F. Larker, "Coming Up Short on Nonfinancial Performance Measurement," *Harvard Business Review* (November 2003), pp. 88–95.

**Required**

1. What are the primary benefits of incorporating nonfinancial performance indicators as part of an overall management accounting and control system?

2. Why do the authors of this above-referenced article believe that many companies fail to realize the kinds of benefits listed above in (1)?

3. The Institute of Management Accountants (IMA) recently revised its definition of "management accounting" (see **http://www.imanet.org/PDFs/Secure/Member/SMA/SMA_DefinManAcct_0408_2.pdf**). After accessing this statement, comment on an appropriate role of the management accountant in regard to the development and use of nonfinancial performance indicators.

**[LO 17-7]** 17-39 **Pareto Diagram (Chart)** The following causes of absenteeism for a fellow student are for the year just completed:

| Cause of Absenteeism | Occurrences |
|---|---|
| Personal illness | 12 |
| Child's illness | 26 |
| Car broke down | 8 |
| Personal emergency | 32 |
| Overslept | 9 |
| Unexpected visitor | 11 |

**Required** Construct a Pareto diagram (chart). In conjunction with the framework presented in Exhibit 17.3, what role is played by the use of these diagrams?

**[LO 17-5]** 17-40 **Relevant Cost Analysis—Quality Improvements** Destin Company produces water control valves, made of brass, which it sells primarily to builders for use in commercial real estate construction. These valves must meet rigid specifications (i.e., the quality tolerance is small). Valves that, upon inspection, get rejected are returned to the Casting Department, i.e., to stage one of the four-stage manufacturing process. Rejected items are melted and then recast. As such, no new materials in Casting are required to rework these items. However, new materials must be added in the Finishing Department for all reworked valves. As the cost accountant for the company, you have prepared the following cost data regarding the production of a typical valve:

| Cost | Casting | Finishing | Inspection | Packing | Total |
|---|---|---|---|---|---|
| Direct materials | $200 | $ 12 | $-0- | $ 8 | $220 |
| Direct labor | 110 | 120 | 20 | 20 | 270 |
| Variable manufacturing overhead | 100 | 150 | 20 | 20 | 290 |
| Allocated fixed overhead | 70 | 80 | 40 | 10 | 200 |
| | $480 | $362 | $80 | $58 | $980 |

The company, spurred by intense price pressures from foreign manufacturers, recently initiated a number of quality programs. As a result, the rejection rate for valves has decreased from 5.0% to 3.5% of annual output (equal in total to 15,000 units). The reduction in reject rates has enabled the company to reduce its inventory holdings from $400,000 to $250,000. Destin estimates that the annual financing cost associated with inventory holdings is 12%.

**Required** Provide a dollar estimate of the annual cost savings associated with the recently enacted quality improvements. Show calculations.

**[LO 17-7]** 17-41 **Control Chart; Spreadsheet Application** Refer to the background information in Exercise 17-40 for the Destin Company. One of the quality improvements management instituted recently was the use of statistical control charts. Over the most recent 12-week period, you have obtained the following average cycle-time data regarding the valve-production process:

| Week | Average Manufacturing Cycle Time (minutes) |
|---|---|
| 1 | 12.5 |
| 2 | 18.0 |
| 3 | 15.0 |
| 4 | 10.0 |
| 5 | 15.5 |
| 6 | 12.8 |
| 7 | 23.5 |
| 8 | 16.5 |
| 9 | 17.5 |
| 10 | 11.0 |
| 11 | 14.5 |
| 12 | 16.0 |

**Required**

1. Use Excel to prepare a control chart from the weekly, sequential observations given above. Management has determined that the target performance level for cycle time is 14.0 minutes, and that the upper and lower control limits should be set, respectively, at 16.0 and 12.0 minutes.

2. What is the mean and what is the standard deviation of the 12 manufacturing cycle-time observations?

3. What conclusions can you draw about the process, based on the cycle-time data contained in your spreadsheet?

4. What is the primary difference between the control chart you produced and what is called a *statistical* control chart?

[LO 17-7]   17-42  **Using a Run Chart to Examine Process Stability; Spreadsheet Application**   All processes illustrate some variation (in quality, conformance to specification, etc.). One hallmark of a quality process is stability. As noted in the text, both control charts and run charts (as well as histograms) can be used to examine process stability. In this exercise you are provided with some information regarding loan processing times at a bank (for an individual loan officer) over a 20-day period. In sequential order, these data are as follows: 90, 73, 62, 88, 47, 68, 87, 68, 50, 69, 26, 78, 80, 30, 32, 73, 60, 50, 36, and 89.

**Required**

1. Use Excel to plot the above data, in time-series fashion.

2. What is meant by the term *process stability*?

3. What techniques might you use to support a conclusion as to whether or not this process is stable?

[LO 17-8]   17-43  **Benefits and Challenges of Lean**   Much discussion at your organization recently has centered on the notion of lean. In preparation for an upcoming meeting of senior managers across business functions, you have been asked to prepare an explanatory memo. Your memo should address, at a minimum, the following issues: (1) the definition of lean, (2) the strategic value of adopting lean principles for your organization, (3) anticipated costs of moving to lean, (4) implications for cost-system design, and (5) sources for additional information regarding these issues.

**Required**   Prepare, in good form, a memo for management that addresses the preceding issues. In responding to this assignment, please access and read the following Statement of Management Accounting: *Accounting for the Lean Enterprise: Major Changes to the Accounting Paradigm,* Montvale, NJ: Institute of Management Accountants, 2006 (accessible on the web at the following address: **http://www.imanet.org/PDFs/Secure/Member/SMA/SMA_LeanParadigm.pdf**).

[LO 17-8]   17-44  **Implementation of Lean Accounting**   Watlow Electric Manufacturing Company introduced lean principles in 2005 and reported a successful implementation in 2008. Watlow began with the implementation of lean principles and then adopted value-stream management (VSM) using the value-stream income statement. As expected, the use of VSM achieved better decision making (previously the firm had treated direct labor as a pure variable cost that varied with volume; after VSM it was clear that the behavior of labor costs was far more complex), reduced inventory, reduced cycle times, and improved communication and coordination among employees. It was this latter result, better communication, that surprised Watlow management, as employees began to work as teams that focused on the key success factors for the firm. The steps taken by Watlow to implement lean included:

- Identify the main value streams of the company (Watlow selected value streams consisting of 25–150 employees each; more than 90% of the company's employees were assigned to a value stream)

- Determine the key measures for achieving the company's strategic goals (these included measures of quality, safety, on-time delivery, and cost)

- The accounting system was adapted to VSM, including changes in the accounting for materials, labor, and overhead

**Required**   Given the implementation of lean as described above, what do you see as the challenges ahead for Watlow? What features of lean accounting have yet to be implemented?

[LO 17-8]   17-45  **Toyota: Keeping It Lean**   Toyota has grown to become the largest auto manufacturer in the world, with plants located around the world. In 2005–2007 the company hired 40,000 new employees to keep up with this growth. A challenge for Toyota during times of growth is to make sure that the new hires effectively become part of the company's culture, including the Toyota Production System which guides the flow of product through Toyota's plants. The new hires must also learn the Toyota Way, an eight-step method for decision making. Toyota's new managers go through extensive training at the Toyota Institute in Japan. Even veteran Toyota managers are required to go back to the Institute for training when they get a promotion. Concerned about the decline in quality in recent years, Toyota has redoubled its efforts in training and has begun to hire back some retired workers in Japan. New entry-level employees are trained at Toyota Technical Institutes located around the world.

**Required**   Why is training so important for Toyota?

[LO 17-8]   17-46   **Value-Stream Income Statement**   The Marshall Company is a large manufacturer of office furniture. The company has recently adopted lean accounting and has identified two value streams—office chairs and office tables. Total sales in the most recent period for the two streams are $245 and $310 million, respectively.

In the most recent accounting period, Marshall had the following operating costs, which were traced to the two value streams as follows (in thousands).

|                         | Chairs    | Tables   |
|-------------------------|-----------|----------|
| Operating costs:        |           |          |
| Materials               | $ 16,500  | $14,500  |
| Labor                   | 123,000   | 96,500   |
| Equipment-related costs | 44,500    | 62,800   |
| Occupancy costs         | 11,350    | 12,600   |

In addition to the traceable operating costs, the company had manufacturing costs of $116,750,000 and selling and administrative costs of $25 million that could not be traced to either value stream. Due to the implementation of lean methods, the firm has been able to reduce inventory in both value streams significantly and has calculated the fixed cost of prior period inventory that is included in the current income statement to be $5.5 million for the office chair stream and $22.5 million for the office table stream.

**Required**   Prepare the value-stream income statement for Marshall Company.

[LO 17-1]   17-47   **Ethics**   Keystone Electronics Corporation (KEC) is an eight-year-old company that has developed a process to produce highly reliable electronic components at a cost well below the established competition. In seeking to expand its overall components business KEC decided to enter the facsimile equipment business as there was a niche for lower-priced facsimile machines in a vigorously growing marketplace. The market KEC pursued consisted of small regional businesses not yet approached by the larger vendors. KEC sells its machines with a one-year warranty and has established a maintenance force to handle machine breakdowns.

As KEC customers learned of the benefits of fax transmissions, some increased their usage significantly. After six months, large-volume users began experiencing breakdowns, and the field technicians' portable test equipment was not sophisticated enough to detect hairline breaks in the electronic circuitry caused by the heavier-than-expected usage. Consequently, field technicians were required to replace the damaged components and return the defective ones to the company for further testing.

This situation caused an increase in maintenance costs, which added to the cost of the product. Unfortunately, there was no way to determine how many of the businesses would become heavy users and be subject to breakdowns. Some of the heavier-volume users began switching to the more expensive machines available from the larger competitors. Although new sales orders masked the loss of heavier-volume customers, the increased maintenance costs had an unfavorable impact on earnings. In her recent report prepared for the quarterly meeting of the board of directors, Mary Stein, KEC's assistant controller, summarized this situation and its anticipated effect on earnings.

Jim March, vice president of manufacturing, is concerned that the report does not provide any solutions to the problem. He asked Maria Sanchez, the controller, to have the matter deferred so that his engineering staff could work on the problem. He believes that the electronic components can be redesigned. This redesigned model, while more costly, could be an appropriate solution for the heavier-volume users, who should not expect a low-cost model to serve their anticipated needs. March expects that the board may decide to discontinue the product line if no immediate solution is available, and the company could miss a potentially profitable opportunity. March further believes that the tone of the report places his organization in an unfavorable light.

The controller called Stein into her office and asked her to suppress the part of the formal report related to the component failures. Sanchez asked Stein to just cover it orally at the meeting, noting that "engineering is working with marketing on the situation to reach a satisfactory solution." Stein feels strongly that the board will be misinformed about a potentially serious impact on earnings if she follows the advice of Sanchez.

**Required**

1. Refer to the IMA's *Statement of Ethical Professional Practice* (**www.imanet.org**). Explain why the request from Maria Sanchez to Mary Stein is unethical. Cite both actions and nonactions on the part of Sanchez that result in an unethical situation.

2. Identify steps that Mary Stein should follow to resolve the situation.

**(CMA Adapted)**

[LO 17-4] 17-48 **Taguchi Loss Function Analysis; Spreadsheet Application** North Platt Machinery Company manufactures a shaft that must fit inside a sleeve. The firm has just received an order of 50,000 units from Southernstar Exploration Company for $80 per unit. North Platt can manufacture the shaft at $50 per unit. Southernstar desires the diameter of the shaft to be 1.275 cm. The diameter of the shaft must not be less than 1.25 cm, in order to fit properly inside the sleeve. To be able to insert the shaft into a sleeve without the use of force, the diameter cannot be larger than 1.30 cm. A defective shaft is discarded and a replacement has to be shipped via express freight to locations around the world. North Platt estimates that the average cost of handling and shipping a replacement shaft will be approximately $70. Shown below are the diameters from a sample of 80 shafts manufactured during a trial run.

| Diameter | Number of Units | Diameter | Number of Units | Diameter | Number of Units |
|---|---|---|---|---|---|
| 1.232 | 1 | 1.273 | 6 | 1.292 | 2 |
| 1.240 | 2 | 1.274 | 7 | 1.293 | 1 |
| 1.250 | 3 | 1.275 | 18 | 1.294 | 4 |
| 1.258 | 2 | 1.276 | 8 | 1.298 | 2 |
| 1.262 | 2 | 1.277 | 5 | 1.300 | 2 |
| 1.270 | 3 | 1.280 | 2 | 1.304 | 1 |
| 1.272 | 6 | 1.288 | 2 | 1.320 | 1 |

**Required** Set up an Excel spreadsheet that uses a Taguchi loss function to determine:

1. The expected loss from this process.

2. The diameter tolerance that should be set for the manufacture of the shaft.

[LO 17-2, 17-4] 17-49 **Research Assignment; Strategy** Obtain from your library a copy of the following article: John H. Flemming, Curt Coffman, and James K. Harter, "Manage Your Human Sigma," *Harvard Business Review* (July–August 2005), pp. 107–14. The authors of this article state (p. 114): "Ask any CEO to list his or her most pressing business challenges, and you will no doubt hear concerns about customer and employee retention, authentic and sustainable growth, eroding margins, and cost efficiencies. . . . We are confident that measuring and managing two simple factors—employee and customer engagement—can lead to breakthrough improvements in all aspects of your business."

**Required** After reading the above-referenced article, answer the following questions:

1. What is the general issue addressed by the authors of this article? That is, what managerial problem are they discussing?

2. How, conceptually, is the Human Sigma approach developed by the authors of this article similar to or distinct from Six Sigma?

3. How do the authors propose to measure the effectiveness of the employee-customer encounter? What evidence do they offer regarding the predictive value of the performance metric they are proposing?

4. According to the authors, what strategies can an organization use to improve the quality of the employee-customer encounter?

## Problems

[LO 17-3, 17-5, 17-6]   17-50   **Cost-of-Quality (COQ) Analysis; Nonfinancial Performance Measures**   The Duncan Materials Company manufactures and sells synthetic coatings that can withstand high temperatures. Its primary customers are aviation manufacturers and maintenance companies. The following table contains financial information pertaining to cost of quality (COQ) in 2013 and 2014 in thousands of dollars:

|  | 2013 | 2014 |
|---|---|---|
| Sales | $15,000 | $18,750 |
| Materials inspection | 300 | 60 |
| Production inspection | 160 | 125 |
| Finished product inspection | 225 | 70 |
| Preventive equipment maintenance | 20 | 60 |
| Scrap (net) | 500 | 300 |
| Warranty repairs | 700 | 400 |
| Product design engineering | 150 | 270 |
| Vendor certification | 10 | 60 |
| Direct costs of returned goods | 250 | 80 |
| Training of factory workers | 40 | 140 |
| Product testing—equipment maintenance | 60 | 60 |
| Product testing labor | 210 | 90 |
| Field repairs | 70 | 30 |
| Rework before shipment | 240 | 180 |
| Product-liability settlement | 360 | 60 |
| Emergency repair and maintenance | 190 | 60 |

**Required**

1. Classify the cost items in the table into cost-of-quality (COQ) categories.

2. Calculate the ratio of each COQ category to revenues in each of the two years.

3. Comment on the results.

4. In addition to the financial measures listed in the table, what nonfinancial measures might Duncan Materials Company monitor in its effort to achieve overall improvements in quality?

5. Are financial or nonfinancial quality measures likely of more use to: (a) managers? (b) operating personnel? Why?

[LO 17-5]   17-51   **Cost-of-Quality (COQ) Analysis; Spreadsheet Application**   Use the data in Problem 17-50 and a spreadsheet to complete this problem. Use the spreadsheet functions to carry out all calculations. Do not hard-code or carry out calculations elsewhere and type in the calculated amounts.

1. Determine the information you'll need to generate a cost-of-quality (COQ) report and set up a spreadsheet for this information. Among the items to be included in the COQ report are proper headings of the report, revenue and cost items (cost items should be in the cost-of-quality category), and cost as a percentage of revenues for each of the two years.

2. Input the data provided in 17-50 into the spreadsheet by COQ category.

3. Enter functions or steps to calculate the total amount for each COQ category and the total COQ. Do not hard-code or type in the amounts.

4. Enter functions or steps to calculate the total cost of each COQ category as a percentage of revenues for each of the years. Use two digits after the decimal point for the percentages. Do the same for the total COQ. Do not hard-code or type in the amounts.

5. Move to another area of the spreadsheet or use a fresh sheet and title the area "Cost of Quality Trend Analysis." Enter functions or steps for the percentages; do not hard-code or type in the amounts.

6. Create a bar chart to compare the percentages of each of the COQ categories and the total COQ in 2013 and 2014.

7. Do a sensitivity analysis by making the following changes to the 2014 amounts:
   - Increase the total sales by 5%.
   - Increase total prevention cost by 6%.
   - Decrease total internal failure cost by 60%.
   - Decrease total external failure cost by 50%.

**Required**   What is the total COQ as a percentage of total sales?

**[LO 17-03, 17-5]**   17-52 **Ethics**   Jan Williams was recently hired as assistant controller of GroChem, Inc., which processes chemicals for use in fertilizers. Williams was selected for this position because of her past experience in the chemical processing field. During her first month on the job, Williams made a point of getting to know the people responsible for the plant operations and learning how things are done at GroChem.

During a conversation with the plant supervisor, Williams asked about the company procedures for handling toxic waste materials. The plant supervisor replied that he was not involved with the disposal of wastes and suggested that Williams might be wise to simply ignore the issue. This response strengthened the resolve of Williams to probe the area further, to be sure that the company was not vulnerable to litigation.

Upon further investigation, Williams discovered evidence that GroChem was using a nearby residential landfill to dump toxic wastes. It appeared that some members of GroChem's management team were aware of this situation and, in fact, may have been involved in arranging for this dumping; however, Williams was unable to determine whether her superior, the controller, was involved.

Uncertain as to how she should proceed, Williams began to consider her options by outlining the following three alternative courses of action:

1. Seek the advice of her superior, the controller.

2. Anonymously release the information to the local newspaper.

3. Discuss the situation with an outside member of the board of directors, with whom Williams is acquainted.

**Required**

1. Explain how the use of a cost-of-quality (COQ) reporting framework can facilitate better managerial control and decision making regarding environmental costs and potential liabilities.

2. Discuss why Jan Williams has an ethical responsibility to take some action in the matter of GroChem, Inc., and the dumping of toxic wastes. Refer to the specific ethical standards contained in the IMA's *Statement of Ethical Professional Practice* (**www.imanet.org**) to support your answer.

3. For each of the three alternative courses of action that Jan Williams has outlined, explain whether or not the action is consistent with the ethical standards referred to above.

4. Without prejudice to your answer to (3), assume that Jan Williams sought the advice of her superior, the controller, and discovered that the controller was involved in the decision to dump the toxic waste produced by the company. Refer to the IMA's *Statement of Ethical Professional Practice* and describe steps that Williams should take to resolve the situation.

**(CMA Adapted)**

**[LO 17-5, 17-7]**   17-53 **Cost-of-Quality (COQ) Reporting; Spreadsheet Application**   Carrie Lee, the president of Lee Enterprises, was concerned about the results of her company's new quality control efforts. "Maybe the emphasis we've placed on upgrading our quality control system will pay off in the long run, but it doesn't seem to be helping us much right now. I thought improved quality would give a real boost to sales, but sales have remained flat at about $10,000,000 for the last two years."

Lee Enterprises has seen its market share decline in recent years because of increased foreign competition. An intensive effort to strengthen the quality control system was initiated a year ago (on January 1, 2014) in the hope that better quality would strengthen the company's competitive position and reduce warranty and servicing costs. The following costs (in thousands) relate to quality and quality control over the last two years:

|  | 2013 | 2014 |
| --- | --- | --- |
| Warranty repairs | $420 | $140 |
| Rework labor | 140 | 200 |
| Supplies used in testing | 4 | 6 |
| Depreciation of testing equipment | 22 | 34 |
| Warranty replacements | 60 | 18 |
| Field servicing | 180 | 120 |
| Inspection | 76 | 120 |
| Systems development | 64 | 106 |
| Disposal of defective products | 54 | 76 |
| Net cost of scrap | 86 | 124 |
| Product recalls | 340 | 82 |
| Product testing | 98 | 160 |
| Statistical process control | — | 74 |
| Quality engineering | 56 | 80 |

**Required**

1. Prepare a spreadsheet that produces a cost-of-quality (COQ) report for both 2013 and 2014. Carry percentage computations to two decimal places.

2. Use your spreadsheet to prepare a histogram showing the distribution of the various quality costs by category. (*Note:* Your histogram should include results for both 2013 and 2014.)

3. Prepare a written evaluation to accompany the reports you have prepared in requirements 1 and 2. This evaluation should discuss the distribution of quality costs in the company, changes in this distribution that you detect have taken place over the last year, and any other information you believe would be useful to management.

4. A member of the management team believes that employees will be more conscientious in their work if they are held responsible for mistakes. He suggests that workers should do rework on their own time and that they also should pay for disposal of defective units and the cost of scraps. The proposal estimates that the firm can save another $400,000 in quality costs and the employees are less likely to make as many errors. Should the firm implement the proposal? Why or why not?

**(CMA Adapted)**

[LO 17-2, 17-5]    17-54    **Relevant Costs and Quality Improvement**    Lightening Bulk Company is a moving company specializing in transporting large items worldwide. The firm has an 85% on-time delivery rate. Twelve percent of the items are misplaced and the remaining 3% are lost in shipping. On average, the firm incurs an additional $60 per item to track down and deliver misplaced items. Lost items cost the firm about $300 per item. Last year the firm shipped 5,000 items with an average freight bill of $200 per item shipped.

The firm's manager is considering investing in a new scheduling and tracking system costing $150,000 per year. The new system is expected to reduce misplaced items to 1% and lost items to 0.5%. Furthermore, the firm expects total sales to increase by 10% with the improved service. The average contribution margin on any increased sales volume, after cost savings associated with a reduction in misplaced and lost items, is expected to be 40%.

**Required**

1. Based on a relevant-cost analysis, should the firm install the new tracking system? Show calculations.

2. What other factors does the firm's manager need to consider in making the decision?

3. Upon further investigation, the manager discovered that 80% of the misplaced or lost items either originated in or were delivered to the same country. What is the maximum amount the firm should spend to reduce the problems in that country by 90%?

[LO 17-1, 17-2, 17-3, 17-5]    17-55    **Relevant Costs and Quality Improvement**    Worrix Corporation manufactures and sells each year 3,000 premium-quality multimedia projectors at $12,000 per unit. At the current production level, the firm's manufacturing costs include variable costs of $2,500 per unit and annual fixed costs of $6,000,000. Additional selling, administrative, and other expenses, not including 15% sales commissions, are $10,000,000 per year.

The new model, introduced a year ago, has experienced a flickering problem. On average the firm reworks 40% of the completed units and still has to repair under warranty 15% of the units shipped. The additional work required for rework and repair causes the firm to add additional capacity with annual fixed costs of $1,800,000. The variable costs per unit are $2,000 for rework and $2,500, including transportation cost, for repair.

The chief engineer, Patti Mehandra, has proposed a modified manufacturing process that will almost entirely eliminate the flickering problem. The new process will require $12,000,000 for new equipment and installation and $3,000,000 for training. Patti believes that current appraisal costs of $600,000 per year and $50 per unit can be eliminated within one year after the installation of the new process. The firm currently inspects all units before shipment. Furthermore, warranty repair cost per unit will be only $1,000, for no more than 5% of the units shipped.

Worrix believes that none of the fixed costs of rework or repair can be saved and that a new model will be introduced in three years. The new technology will most likely render the current equipment obsolete.

The accountant estimates that warranty repairs now cause the firm to lose 20% of its potential business.

**Required**

1. What is the net investment cost associated with the new process?

2. What is the net financial benefit (over the next three years) from using the new process?

3. Based on financial information, should Worrix use the new process?

4. What additional factors should be considered before making the final decision?

5.  A member of the board is very concerned about the substantial amount of additional funds needed for the new process. Because the current model will be replaced in about three years, the board member suggests that the firm should take no action and the problem will go away in three years. Do you agree?

[LO 17-2, 17-5]    17-56  **Analyzing Cost-of-Quality (COQ) Reports**  Bergen Inc. produces telephone equipment at its Georgia plant. In recent years, the company's market share has been eroded by stiff competition from Asian and European competitors. Price and product quality are the two key areas in which companies compete in this market.

Jerry Holman, Bergen's president, decided to devote more resources to the improvement of product quality after learning that, in a 2011 survey of telephone equipment users, his company's products had been ranked fourth in product quality. He believed that Bergen could no longer afford to ignore the importance of product quality. Jerry set up a task force (that he headed) to implement a formal quality-improvement program. Included on the task force were representatives from engineering, sales, customer service, production, and accounting because Jerry believed that this is a companywide program and that all employees should share the responsibility for its success.

After the first task-force meeting, Sheila Haynes, manager of sales, asked Tony Reese, production manager, what he thought of the proposed program. Tony replied, "I have reservations. Quality is too abstract to be attaching costs to it and then to be holding you and me responsible for cost improvements. I like to work with goals that I can see and count! I don't like my annual bonus to be based on a decrease in quality costs; there are too many variables that we have no control over!"

Bergen's quality-improvement program has been in operation for 18 months, and the following cost report was recently issued.

As they were reviewing the report, Sheila asked Tony what he thought of the quality program now. "The work is really moving through the production department," replied Reese. "We used to spend time helping the customer service department solve its problems, but they are leaving us alone these days. I have no complaints so far. I'll be anxious to see how much the program increases our bonuses."

| Cost-of-Quality (COQ) Report by Quarter | | | | | |
|---|---|---|---|---|---|
| (in thousands) | | | | | |
| | June 30, 2013 | September 30, 2013 | December 31, 2013 | March 31, 2014 | June 30, 2014 | September 30, 2014 |
| Prevention costs: | | | | | | |
| Machine maintenance | $ 215 | $ 215 | $ 202 | $ 190 | $ 170 | $ 160 |
| Training suppliers | 5 | 45 | 25 | 20 | 20 | 15 |
| Design reviews | 20 | 102 | 111 | 100 | 104 | 95 |
| | $ 240 | $ 362 | $ 338 | $ 310 | $ 294 | $ 270 |
| Appraisal costs: | | | | | | |
| Incoming inspection | $ 45 | $ 53 | $ 57 | $ 36 | $ 34 | $ 22 |
| Final testing | 160 | 160 | 154 | 140 | 115 | 94 |
| | $ 205 | $ 213 | $ 211 | $ 176 | $ 149 | $ 116 |
| Internal failure costs: | | | | | | |
| Rework | $ 120 | $ 106 | $ 114 | $ 88 | $ 78 | $ 62 |
| Scrap (net) | 68 | 64 | 53 | 42 | 40 | 40 |
| | $ 188 | $ 170 | $ 167 | $ 130 | $ 118 | $ 102 |
| External failure costs: | | | | | | |
| Warranty repairs | $ 69 | $31 | $ 24 | $ 25 | $ 23 | $ 23 |
| Customer returns | 262 | 251 | 122 | 116 | 87 | 80 |
| | $ 331 | $ 282 | $ 146 | $ 141 | $ 110 | $ 103 |
| Total COQ | $ 964 | $1,027 | $ 862 | $ 757 | $ 671 | $ 591 |
| Total production cost | $4,120 | $4,540 | $4,380 | $4,650 | $4,580 | $4,510 |

**Required**

1.  Identify at least three factors that should be present for an organization to successfully implement a quality-improvement program.

2.  By analyzing the cost-of-quality (COQ) report presented, determine whether Bergen's quality-improvement program has been successful. (*Hint:* You might want to focus on the oldest quarter and on the most recent quarter.) List specific evidence to support your answer.

3.  Discuss why Tony Reese's current reaction to the quality-improvement program is more favorable than his initial reaction.

4.  Jerry Holman believed that the quality-improvement program was essential and that Bergen could no longer afford to ignore the importance of product quality. Discuss how Bergen could measure the opportunity cost of *not* implementing the quality-improvement program.

5.  Comment on the following statement: "COQ reports allow an organization to focus on the reduction or elimination of non-value-added costs of quality."

**(CMA Adapted)**

[LO 17-2, 17-5]   17-57   **Benefits of Switching to JIT**   You have recently been hired as the management accountant for ABC Manufacturing Technologies, Inc. The company produces a broad line of subassemblies that are used in the production of flat-screen TVs and other electronic equipment. Competitive pressures, principally from abroad, have caused the company to reexamine its competitive strategy and associated management accounting and control systems. More to the point, the company feels a pressing need to adopt JIT manufacturing, to improve the quality of its outputs (in response to ever-increasing demands by consumers of electronic products), and to better manage its cost structure.

A year ago ABC acquired, via a five-year lease, new manufacturing equipment, the annual cost of which is $500,000. To support the move to JIT, however, ABC would have to acquire new, computer-controlled manufacturing equipment, the leasing cost of which is estimated at $2 million per year for four years. If the company were to break its existing lease it would incur a one-time penalty of $240,000.

The replacement equipment is expected to provide significant decreases in variable manufacturing cost per unit, from $50 to $35. This reduction is attributed to faster set-up times with the new machine, faster processing speed, a reduction in material waste, and a reduction in direct labor expenses (because of increased automation). In addition, improvements in manufacturing cycle time and improvements in product quality are expected to increase annual sales (in units) by approximately 30% (based on a current volume of 40,000 units).

Additional financial information regarding each decision alternative (existing equipment versus replacement equipment) is as follows:

| Item | Pre-JIT | Post-JIT |
|---|---|---|
| Selling cost per unit | $ 5.00 | $ 5.00 |
| Average per-unit cost of raw materials inventory | 15.00 | 12.00 |
| Average per-unit cost of WIP inventory | 25.00 | 20.00 |
| Average per-unit cost of finished goods inventory | 40.00 | 30.00 |
| Selling price per unit | 65.00 | 65.00 |

The increased automation, including computer-based manufacturing controls, associated with the replacement equipment will greatly reduce the need for inventory holdings. The annual inventory-holding cost, based on the company's weighted-average cost of capital, is 15%. Based on engineering estimates provided to ABC by the lessor company, all inventory holdings (raw materials, WIP, and finished goods) can safely be cut in half from current levels. Currently, ABC holds, on average, four months of raw materials inventory, three months of WIP inventory, and two months of finished goods inventory—all of which are based on production requirements.

**Required**

1.  Essentially, how is a JIT manufacturing system different from a conventional system?

2.  What is an appropriate role for management accounting regarding a company's adoption of a JIT manufacturing system?

3.  Based on the information presented above, determine the annual financial benefit (including reduction in inventory carrying costs) associated with the proposed move by the company to JIT.

4.  Based on an analysis of financial considerations alone, should the company in this situation make the switch to JIT? Why or why not?

5.  What qualitative factors might bear on the decision at hand?

**[LO 17-6]** 17-58 **Environmental Performance: Meeting Stakeholder Expectations** How important to stakeholders is the environmental performance (e.g., management of greenhouse gas emissions) of publicly listed companies? This issue is addressed in the following short piece: D. C. Esty, "What Stakeholders Demand," *Harvard Business Review* (October 2007), pp. 30, 34, which can be accessed as background reading for the following set of questions.

**Required**

1. Who are the primary stakeholders that would be interested in corporate disclosures regarding environmental performance?

2. Go to the following website (**www.climatecounts.org/**) and obtain information regarding the "scorecard" that this organization has developed to rate environmental performance. What are the 22 criteria used by Climate Counts to rate corporate environmental performance?

3. In the electronics industry group, what distinguishes the environmental performance of IBM versus Apple Computer according to the scorecard used by Climate Counts?

4. Provide arguments as to likely consequences of companies that fail to meet stakeholder expectations regarding environmental performance.

5. What strategic role can the management accountant assume in regard to corporate environmental performance?

**[LO 17-6]** 17-59 **Net Promoter Score** Upon graduation, you and a friend established a computer-consultancy business. Your business has generally been successful, but you and your colleague wish to expand the business significantly over the next three years. You have always assumed that the service your firm rendered to clients was of sterling quality. However, up to this point you have not attempted to measure customer satisfaction. Recently, you prepared and sent to your clients a customer-satisfaction survey that, among other items, asked the following question: "How likely is it that you would recommend our services to a friend or business associate?" Customers responded to this question using a 10-point scale, with 10 = "Extremely Likely," 5 = "Neutral/Uncertain," and 1 = "Extremely Unlikely." You received 290 responses to this question, which were as follows:

| Score | No. of Responses | Score | No. of Responses |
|-------|------------------|-------|------------------|
| 1 | 6 | 6 | 30 |
| 2 | 8 | 7 | 16 |
| 3 | 9 | 8 | 72 |
| 4 | 21 | 9 | 70 |
| 5 | 23 | 10 | 35 |

**Required**

1. What is meant by the term *net promoter score*?

2. Given the above data (customer responses), calculate the net promoter score for your consulting firm.

3. Of what strategic importance are nonfinancial customer performance measures in general and the net promoter score in particular?

**[LO 17-7]** 17-60 **Expected Quality Cost; Confidence Intervals; Sample Size (Requires Chapter 8)** Paragon Manufacturing produces small motors for assembly in handheld tools such as chain saws and circular saws. The company recently began manufacturing a new motor, model EZ3, and forecasts an annual demand of 200,000 units for this model.

Each model EZ3 requires a housing manufactured to precise engineering specifications. Paragon purchases these housings, which are not subject to quality control inspection before entering the production process; however, Paragon performance-tests the entire motor after final assembly. During pilot production runs of the new motor, several of the housings had wrong sizes and were rejected. If the housings were too shallow, they could not be assembled correctly; if they were too deep, the motor would not operate properly.

Ross Webster, Paragon's production manager, gathered the following information during the pilot production runs:

• When housings were rejected during assembly because they were too shallow, they were replaced with new housings. This change in housings required nine minutes of additional direct labor for each affected unit.

- The units that were rejected during performance testing because the housings were too deep had to be torn down and reassembled with new housings. This operation required 1 hour and 15 minutes of additional direct labor for each affected unit.
- The supplier of the housings is willing to take back the defective housings but will refund only one-half of the price. In the future, if Paragon inspects the housings before they enter the assembly process, the supplier will refund the full price of all rejected housings.
- The costs of model EZ3 follow:

| | |
|---|---|
| Materials* | $ 44 |
| Direct labor (3 hrs. @ $12/hr.) | 36 |
| Variable overhead (@ $18/hr.) | 54 |
| Total costs | $134 |

*Includes $7.00 for housing.

- The majority of the rejections experienced during the pilot runs were related to the housings. Ross's estimate of the probability of rejections for a lot of 800 housings follows:

| Rejection during Assembly | | Rejection during Performance Testing | |
|---|---|---|---|
| Quantity | Probability | Quantity | Probability |
| 90 | 0.40 | 50 | 0.50 |
| 70 | 0.30 | 40 | 0.15 |
| 50 | 0.20 | 20 | 0.15 |
| 30 | 0.10 | 10 | 0.20 |

If Paragon decides to inspect the housings prior to assembly, Ross must select the appropriate sample size by using the following two formulas. The estimated sample size (formula 1) must be modified by the second formula (final sample size) because Ross will be sampling without replacement.

**Formula 1**

$$nc = C^2 pq/a^2$$

**Formula 2**

$$nf = \frac{nc}{1 + \dfrac{nc}{N}}$$

where:

$nc$ = first estimate of sample size
$nf$ = final sample size
$C$ = confidence coefficient
$p$ = maximum rejection rate
$q = 1 - p$
$a$ = precision level
$N$ = number of items in the population

### Required

1. Determine the maximum amount that Paragon Manufacturing would be willing to spend annually to implement quality control inspection of the housings before assembly begins. (Check figure: $509,000.)
2. For the purpose of quality control inspection, determine the sample size that Ross should select from a lot of 800 housings if the desired level is 95.5% (confidence coefficient 2.00) with a precision of 1% and rejections not to exceed 1%. (Check figure: 265 units.)
3. Without prejudice to your answer in requirement 2, for quality control inspection purposes, assume that the sample size is 240 housings and the desired level is 95.5% (confidence coefficient 2.00) with a precision of 1% and rejections not to exceed 1%. Determine whether Ross should accept or reject a lot if there are:
   a. Two defective housings in the sample.
   b. Three defective housings in the sample.

Explain your answer in each situation.

**(CMA Adapted)**

[LO 17-7]    17-61  **Constructing and Interpreting a Control Chart**    As indicated in the text, various tools from operations management and statistics are used to help support Six Sigma goals and process improvements in a lean environment. One such tool is a control chart—a key element used to assess statistical process control (SPC). You are given the following error rates for a loan-processing activity at a bank: 2.8, 2.4, 2.4, 4.2, 1.8, 2.8, 3.8, 3.4, 3.2, 3.2, 2.2, 1.6, 1.4, 1.4, 2.4, 1.8, 2.6, 2.0, 2.4, 2.4, 2.2, 2.8, and 2.4.

**Required**
1. Define the term *control chart.* What is the difference between a control chart and a run chart? What do these charts have in common?
2. Use the data on error rates to construct a control chart for the loan-processing operation. Although there are various ways to construct the chart (see any text on Operations Management or Quality Control for details), define the upper-control limit (UCL) of your chart as the mean plus 2 standard deviations; define the lower-control limit (LCL) of your chart as the mean less 2 standard deviations. (In each case, use the sample standard deviation for the data set at hand.)
3. Supply an interpretation of the control limits you established above in (2).
4. What techniques can be used to judge, using a control chart, whether a process is in *statistical* control?
5. Control charts were developed many years ago for application in the manufacturing sector. However, these charts can be used in other contexts as well. What quality measure might you collect, for use in a control chart, for each of the following nonmanufacturing settings: hospital, insurance company, hotel, and local police department?

[LO 17-8]    17-62  **Research Activity: Applying Lean Principles to Knowledge Work**    Can lean principles be applied to so-called *knowledge work*? This issue is addressed in the following article: B. R. Staats and D. M. Upton, "Lean Knowledge Work," *Harvard Business Review* (October 2011), pp. 101–10. After accessing and reading this article, respond to the following set of questions.

**Required**
1. Define what is meant by the term *lean* (or *lean management*). To date, what types of organizations have successfully applied lean? Why have these contexts proven fruitful for the application of lean?
2. According to the authors, what is meant by the term *knowledge work*? Why is it more difficult/challenging to apply lean principles to this work context?
3. Based on their own research, what do the authors claim to be the primary benefits of applying lean principles to knowledge work?
4. Based on their experience with over 1,800 projects, the authors developed six principles that they say could be used to guide the implementation of lean to knowledge work (such as software and IT-development projects). Provide an overview of each of these principles.

## Solutions to Self-Study Problems

### 1. Relevant Cost Analysis: Quality Improvement Program

| | | |
|---|---|---:|
| Cost of the quality-improvement program | | $1,000,000,000 |
| Savings from eliminating recalls | $300 × 110% × 1.5 × 500,000 = $247,500,000 | |
| Decrease in warranty-repair cost | ($200 − $80) × 500,000 =   60,000,000 | |
| Profit from increased sales | (650,000 − 500,000) × $5,000 =  750,000,000 | 1,057,500,000 |
| Increase in profit from the quality-improvement program | | $   57,500,000 |

Yes, the increase in profit from the additional sales and the decrease in costs of warranty repairs and recalls exceed the $1 billion cost-of-quality improvements.

### 2. Taguchi Quality Loss Function
1. $36 = k(0.25)^2$
   $k = \$576$
   $L(x = 2.12) = \$576 \times (2.12 - 2.0)^2 = \$8.2944$
2. $3 = \$576 \times (\text{tolerance})^2$
   Tolerance $= 0.0722$
   Therefore, the specification should be set at 2 inches $\pm$ 0.0722 inch.

### 3. Cost-of-Quality (COQ) Report

**PRECISION ELECTRIC INSTRUMENTS**
**Cost-of-Quality Report**
**For the Year 2013**

|  |  | % of Total |
|---|---|---|
| Prevention costs: |  |  |
| Training | $ 120 |  |
| Design engineering | 67 |  |
| Preventive equipment maintenance | 20 |  |
| Supplier evaluation | 15 |  |
| Total prevention costs | $ 222 | 20.6 |
| Appraisal costs: |  |  |
| Line inspection | $ 55 |  |
| Product-testing equipment | 88 |  |
| Inspection and testing of incoming materials | 25 |  |
| Total appraisal costs | $ 168 | 15.5 |
| Internal failure costs: |  |  |
| Scrap (net) | $ 30 |  |
| Downtime | 40 |  |
| Rework | 35 |  |
| Total internal failure costs | $ 105 | 9.7 |
| External failure costs: |  |  |
| Returns | $ 100 |  |
| Warranty repairs | 68 |  |
| Recalls | 157 |  |
| Product liability insurance | 20 |  |
| Litigation costs | 240 |  |
| Total external failure costs | $ 585 | 54.2 |
| Total cost of quality (COQ) | $1,080 | 100.0 |

*Please visit **http://www.mhhe.com/blocher6e** to access a narrated, animated tutorial for solving these problems.*

# PART FOUR

# Management-Level Control

A common element of Parts Three and Four is the focus on control (performance evaluation)—that is, the methods, procedures, and systems used to monitor performance to ensure that the organization is implementing its strategy. As part of a comprehensive management and accounting and control system, we discuss incentives and rewards for individuals and managers to work most effectively in implementing the organization's strategy. Part Three focuses on the level of operations (*operational control*) while Part Four focuses on the higher level, that is, *management control.*

The objective of the three chapters in Part Four is to present a variety of tools that top managers (such as CFOs) use to evaluate mid-level managers and the organization as a whole. Mid-level managers include plant managers, product-line managers, heads of research and development (R&D) departments, and regional sales managers. They all have significant responsibility in helping the organization achieve its strategic goals.

In **Chapters 18 and 19** we introduce the concept of responsibility accounting and a performance evaluation framework that consists of the following organizational subunits: cost centers, revenue centers, profit centers, and investment centers. Tied to the concept of controllability, different mechanisms are used to evaluate the short-term financial performance of each of these subunits of the organization. The coverage in Part Four of the text has a strong strategic focus since mid-level managers have a significant responsibility for achieving strategic goals, and it is critical that the performance evaluation be aligned with these strategic goals. The strategic focus is emphasized in our presentation of *comprehensive* management control systems which, like the balanced scorecard, include both financial and nonfinancial measures.

The comparison of variable costing with full costing (**Chapter 18**) is included as part of the coverage of assessing profit centers. We cover this topic in Part Four because of its importance in performance evaluation; variable costing is also extensively covered in Part Two, Planning and Decision Making, while full costing is covered in Part One.

**Chapter 19** covers investment center evaluation, including the key topics of return on investment, residual income, and EVA®. Transfer pricing, also covered in **Chapter 19,** is an important topic for the assessment of both profit centers and investment centers. When buying and selling exist between units within the organization, the determination of the transfer price will affect the performance evaluation of both the buying unit and the selling unit. Therefore, we cover the topic of transfer pricing both as an *incentive issue* (having the right incentive for the unit managers to choose to trade inside or outside the firm in a manner that achieves the firm's strategic and financial goals) and as a *motivation issue* (the choice of a transfer price should result in a fair measure of performance for both units).

Management compensation, covered in **Chapter 20,** discusses the link from performance to rewards, and the motivation that is needed for managers to achieve strategic goals. Going one step further, one can evaluate the performance of the firm as a whole, that is, of its top managers collectively. **Chapter 20** provides different ways to develop this assessment.

# CHAPTER EIGHTEEN

# Strategic Performance Measurement:

## Cost Centers, Profit Centers, and the Balanced Scorecard

**After studying this chapter, you should be able to . . .**

LO 18-1  Identify the objectives of management control

LO 18-2  Identify the types of management control systems

LO 18-3  Explain the objectives and applications of strategic performance measurement for cost centers, revenue centers, and profit centers

LO 18-4  Explain the role of variable costing and full costing in evaluating profit centers

LO 18-5  Explain the role of the balanced scorecard in strategic performance measurement

---

*It is not enough to do your best: you must know what to do, then do your best.*

*W. Edwards Deming*

---

Deming, the influential business consultant and innovator, understood the importance of performance measurement in strategy implementation. He also understood the importance of aligning managers' incentives with the organization's strategic goals. When incentives are aligned, managers are evaluated and rewarded for achieving the critical success factors that contribute to the organization's success. Many of the most successful companies use this approach, often with the help of the balanced scorecard (BSC), a key tool for aligning performance and strategic goals. The BSC has helped many organizations achieve strategic goals, including United Parcel Service (UPS), Northwestern Mutual (life insurance), Saatchi & Saatchi (advertising agency), Teach for America, and the Boston Lyric Opera.[1] At Duke Children's Hospital (DCH), an academic children's hospital within the Duke University Health System in Durham, North Carolina, the implementation of the BSC resulted in a nearly $30 million reduction in

---

[1] Robert S. Kaplan and David P. Norton, *The Strategy-Focused Organization: How Balanced Scorecard Companies Thrive in the New Business Environment* (Boston: Harvard Business School Press, 2001); Robert S. Kaplan and David P. Norton, *Strategy Maps* (Boston: Harvard Business School Press, 2004).

cost and a $50 million increase in net margin. The BSC helped UPS significantly increase its revenues. As Kaplan and Norton note:

> The Balanced Scorecard made the difference. Each organization executed strategies using the same physical and human resources that had previously produced failing performance. The strategies were executed with the same products, the same facilities, the same employees, and the same customers. The difference was a new senior management team using the Balanced Scorecard to focus all organizational resources on a new strategy. The scorecard allowed these successful organizations to build a new kind of management system—one designed to manage strategy.

The BSC is particularly important in difficult economic times, when traditional profit-based measures are distorted and difficult to benchmark against established benchmarks such as prior year earnings, industry earnings, and competitors' earnings. Moreover, the manager's objective during difficult times is to look for actions taken currently which are expected to lead to profit growth in the future. This means a refocus on nonfinancial measures that define the organization's competitive advantage—the critical success factors. Additionally, in difficult economic times, a company may need to change strategic direction, to move from a focus on product development and innovation to cost control, or to make another type of strategic change. In the recent economic decline, the firms with a strong ability to reduce costs and meet customer expectations will be more successful. Firms such as McDonald's and Walmart have continued to grow in revenue and profit during the recent recession and the current slow-growth economy because they are uniquely positioned to meet the needs of the new consumer, the economic-slump consumer.

This chapter covers the measures used to evaluate management performance. These measures include topics introduced in previous chapters, such as the balanced scorecard, the contribution income statement, cost allocation, the flexible budget, and outsourcing. These topics are covered here in the important role they play in management performance evaluation. For example, an understanding of the difference between the contribution income statement and the full-cost income statement is important in an effective analysis of performance. We begin with an explanation of the broad concepts underlying performance measurement and control.

**LO 18-1**

*Identify the objectives of management control.*

## Performance Measurement and Control

**Performance measurement** is the process by which managers at all levels gain information about the performance of tasks within the firm and judge that performance against preestablished criteria as set out in budgets, plans, and goals.

**Management control** refers to the evaluation by upper-level managers of the performance of mid-level managers.

**Operational control** refers to the evaluation of operating-level employees by mid-level managers.

**Performance measurement** is the process by which managers at all levels gain information about the performance of tasks within the firm and judge that performance against preestablished criteria as set out in budgets, plans, and goals.

Performance is evaluated at many different levels in the firm: top management, mid-management, and the operating level of individual production and sales employees. In operations, the performance of individual production supervisors at the *operating level* are evaluated by plant managers, who in turn are evaluated by executives at the *management level.* Similarly, individual salespersons are evaluated by sales managers who are evaluated in turn by upper-level sales management.

**Management control** refers to the evaluation by upper-level managers of the performance of mid-level managers. **Operational control** refers to the evaluation of operating-level employees by mid-level managers. Part Three of the text, which includes Chapters 14 through 17, covers operational-level control. Operational control is explained more fully in the introduction to Chapter 14. Part Four, which begins with this chapter and includes Chapters 18 through 20, covers management control. Since upper-level managers are more directly responsible for implementing the organization's strategy, we call control at this level *strategic performance measurement.* In contrast, control at the operating level is called *operational performance measurement.*

## Operational Control versus Management Control

In contrast to operational control, which focuses on detailed short-term performance measures, management control focuses on higher-level managers and long-term, strategic issues. Operational control has a management-by-exception approach; that is, it identifies units or individuals whose performance does not comply with expectations so that the problem can be promptly corrected. In contrast, management control is more consistent with the management-by-objectives approach, in which long-term objectives such as growth and profitability are determined and performance is periodically measured against these goals.

Management control also has a broader and more strategic objective: to evaluate the unit's overall profitability as well as the performance of its manager, to decide whether the unit should be retained or closed, and to motivate the manager to achieve top management's goals. Because of this broader focus, various objectives for management control generally have multiple measures of performance rather than a single financial or operating measure, as is sometimes true in operational control. Exhibit 18.1 is an organization chart that illustrates the different roles of management control and operational control.

## Objectives of Management Control

In a management-by-objectives approach, top management assigns a set of responsibilities to each mid-level manager. The nature of these responsibilities and, therefore, the precise nature of top management's objectives depends on the functional area involved (operations, marketing, etc.) and on the scope of authority of the mid-level manager (the extent of the resources under the manager's command).

These areas of responsibility are often called *strategic business units* (SBUs). The concept of a strategic business unit is particularly useful for diversified firms that need performance measures to manage the different business units. General Electric Company (GE) is widely cited as pioneering the concept.

A **strategic business unit (SBU)** consists of a well-defined set of controllable operating activities over which the SBU manager is responsible. Generally, managers have autonomy for making decisions and for managing the SBU's human and physical resources. In practice, a variety of terms are used for the SBU: business unit, center, division, or simply unit. For consistency throughout this text we will use the concept of *SBU* when referring to strategic performance measurement in a general sense, and the term *center* when

A **strategic business unit (SBU)** consists of a well-defined set of controllable operating activities over which an SBU manager is responsible.

**EXHIBIT 18.1**
**Organization Chart: Operational and Management Control**

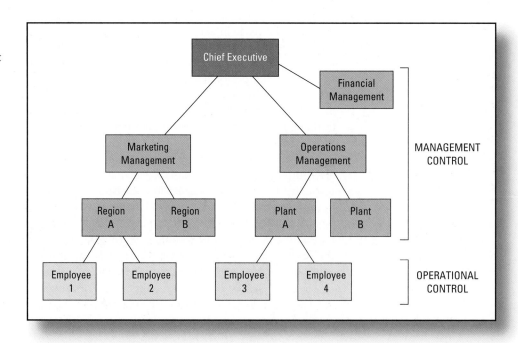

referring to the four types of SBUs covered in this chapter and the following chapter: cost centers, profit centers, revenue centers, and investment centers. Each of these centers is a type of SBU.

The objectives of management control are to:

1. *Motivate* managers to exert a high level of effort to achieve the goals set by top management.
2. Provide the right *incentive* for managers to make decisions consistent with the goals set by top management, that is, to align managers' efforts with desired strategic goals. The alignment of managers' goals with those of top management is also referred to as *goal congruence.*
3. *Determine fairly the rewards* earned by managers for their effort and skill and the effectiveness of their decision making.

A concise summary of top management's objectives is to provide fair compensation to the manager for working hard and making the right decisions, all within the context of autonomous action by the SBU manager. A common mechanism for achieving these multiple objectives is to develop an **employment contract** between the manager and top management that covers each of these points. Assuming that managers act in autonomous self-interest, the contract is designed to provide incentives for them to act independently while achieving top management's objectives and earning the desired compensation. This is called goal congruence. The contract specifies the manager's desired behaviors and the compensation to be awarded for achieving specific outcomes by using these behaviors. The contract can be written or unwritten, explicit or implied; some contracts are legal and enforceable by the courts. For clarity and effectiveness, organizations often use explicit written contracts.

An **employment contract** is an agreement between the manager and top management designed to provide incentives for the manager to act independently to achieve top management's objectives.

## Employment Contracts

An economic model called the **principal-agent model** is a prototype that contains the key elements that contracts must have to achieve the desired objectives. The model sets out three important aspects of management performance that affect the contracting relationship: uncertainty, risk aversion, and lack of observability.

The **principal-agent model** is a conceptual model that contains the key elements that contracts must have to achieve the desired objectives.

### Uncertainty

Each manager operates in an environment that is influenced by factors beyond the manager's control—operating factors such as unexpected and unpreventable machine breakdowns and external factors such as fluctuations in market prices and demands. The manager's lack of control means that there is some degree of *uncertainty* about the effectiveness of the manager's actions, independent of the efforts and abilities the manager brings to the job.

---

Risk, gentlemen! That's why we're aboard her.

*Captain James T. Kirk, U.S.S. Enterprise*

---

### Risk Aversion

The presence of uncertainty in the manager's environment means that it is important to also consider the manager's tolerance for risk. A manager's risk preferences are important in management and control because they can have unexpected and undesirable effects on the manager's behavior. Risk preferences describe the way individuals view decision options because they place a weight on certain outcomes that is different from the weight on uncertain outcomes. The risk associated with uncertain outcomes may be undesirable (or desirable) to the decision maker, irrespective of the value of the outcome itself. It is necessary to separate the value of the outcome from the positive or negative weight associated with the risk due to uncertainty. For example, it is common for managers to be averse to risk and thus to prefer a certain $50 over a 50-50 chance of winning $100.

A risk-neutral manager would see these options as equivalent. One who prefers risk would prefer to have the chance at winning the $100, but this type of risk-prone behavior is less common among managers.

There are implications for performance evaluation. For example, the risk-averse manager is most likely to be motivated by supervision and rewards that reduce risk. Moreover, risk preferences can interfere with proper decision making. For example, a risk-averse manager may choose not to take a risky action that top management would take (for example, to install a costly new machine that would probably reduce operating costs) because of the personal consequences to the manager of a potential unfavorable outcome. For proper motivation and decision making, management control systems should be designed to reduce the negative effects of risk preferences.

### Lack of Observability

The efforts and decisions made by the manager are *not observable to top management*. The manager generally possesses information not accessible to top management. Because of the manager's independent and unobservable actions, top management is able to observe only the observable outcomes of those actions, not the efforts that led to those outcomes. We assume that the manager, in addition to being risk-averse, is typically also effort-averse.

The presence of uncertainty in the job environment and the lack of observability and the existence of private information for the manager complicate the contracting relationship. Ideally, with no uncertainty and perfect observability, the manager and top management would base their contract on the amount of effort the manager is to supply. An observable effort would assure both parties of the desired effort. However, the presence of uncertainty, risk aversion, and the lack of observability mean that the contract between the manager and top management must rely on effective incentives that specifically incorporate both uncertainty and the lack of observability. This can be accomplished by understanding and applying the three principles of employment contracts:

1. Because of uncertainty in the manager's environment, the contract should recognize that other factors inside and outside the firm also influence the outcomes of the manager's efforts and abilities. Therefore, the contract should separate the outcome of the manager's actions from the effort and decision-making skills employed by the manager; that is, separate the performance of the manager from the performance of the SBU.

2. The contract must include only factors that the manager controls. This principle is similar to the first principle, which separates the manager from the SBU; this second principle excludes *known* uncontrollable factors from the contract.

3. Because of uncertainty and lack of observability, the interests of the risk-averse manager are not aligned with those of top management. The risk-averse manager might make decisions to avoid risk, when top management (because of its ability to diversify risk over the entire organization) might prefer the risky choices.

In effect, the contract between top management and the manager should recognize the manager's risk aversion and the role of uncertainty; in other words, the contract needs to recognize and apply the three principles of contracting.

In the principal-agent model illustrated in Exhibit 18.2, top management supplies compensation to the manager who operates in an environment of uncertainty. The manager supplies effort and decision-making skills as well as a degree of risk aversion. The effect of the effort and decision-making skills on the factors in the environment produces the outcomes. The outcomes are multifaceted, including financial and nonfinancial results: earnings, customer satisfaction, operating efficiency, and so on. The accountant prepares a performance report consisting of financial and nonfinancial measures of the outcomes of the manager's decisions and efforts; the performance report goes to top management, which uses it to determine the manager's pay. In this way, the principal-agent model shows the relationships among the key factors that affect the manager's performance and compensation.[2]

---

[2] The principal-agent model illustrates the concept of what is called *moral hazard*—the risk that the manager might take advantage of the firm's lack of observability to claim and receive rewards that are not earned under the employment contract.

**EXHIBIT 18.2**
**The Principal-Agent Model**

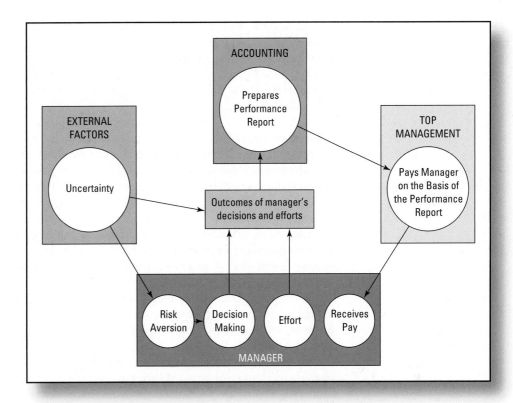

## Design of Management Control Systems for Motivation and Evaluation

**LO 18-2**

*Identify the types of management control systems.*

Developing a management control system involves clearly identifying the *who, what,* and *when* for the evaluation. We start with the *who,* that is, who is interested in evaluating the organization's performance? The four recipients of performance reports are: (1) the firm's owners, directors, or shareholders, (2) its creditors, (3) the community or governmental units affected by its operations, and (4) its employees. Each has a different view about what performance is desired.

The second aspect of management control is *what* is being evaluated. Commonly the evaluation is of the individual manager, to assess the effectiveness and efficiency of the manager's performance. Alternatively, the focus of the evaluation might be the SBU under the manager's control for the purpose of determining whether or not to expand or to divest the SBU. Rather than focusing on the individual manager, the evaluation might be directed to a team of managers. A manager's performance can be compared either with that of other managers or with the manager's own previous performance. Comparison to other managers is common, but comparison to the manager's previous performance is preferable when comparison to others is inappropriate or unfair in some way.

The third aspect of management control is *when* the performance evaluation is conducted. There are two considerations. First, the evaluation can be done on the basis of either *resources input* to the manager or *outputs* of the manager's efforts. The first approach uses the master budget (Chapter 10), while the second uses the flexible budget (Chapter 14). The focus is on inputs when measuring the outputs of the manager's efforts is difficult or the nature and extent of the manager's control over the outputs is not clear. Then the manager's evaluation is performed *ex ante,* that is, before the manager's efforts and decisions have been made. In effect, the manager negotiates with top management for the amount of resources needed. This approach is common in service and not-for-profit organizations for which the outputs are often difficult to measure. In contrast, in manufacturing, where the inputs and outputs are often relatively easy to measure, the *ex post* approach based on actual outputs is more commonly used.

**EXHIBIT 18.3**
**Sales Life Cycle**
**of Management Control**

| Stage of Product's Sales Life Cycle | Appropriate Performance Evaluation Measures |
| --- | --- |
| Early | Revenue, market penetration |
| Growth | Profitability, asset management |
| Mature | Profitability, strategy |

Another timing option is to tie the evaluation to the product life cycle. The life cycle of a product or service is the time from its introduction to its removal from the market. In the early stages of a product's sales life cycle, management focuses primarily on nonfinancial factors such as market penetration and success in developing certain customers. The appropriate performance measures at this time include revenue according to customer class and area, the number of back orders, the number of new customers, and customer satisfaction. As the product achieves market acceptance, profitability and asset management become more important, and the performance measures change. Finally, when the product is in its mature phase—when the nature of the competition is established and the future of the market is clear—the focus on profitability continues with the addition of interest in strategic issues such as customer satisfaction, information regarding product modifications, and potential new markets. Top management must choose the types of performance measures that are appropriate for the sales life-cycle stage of the product or service, as illustrated in Exhibit 18.3.

The systems for management control are of two types, formal and informal. Formal systems are developed with explicit management guidance while informal systems arise from the unmanaged, and sometimes unintended, behavior of managers and employees. Informal systems reflect the managers' and employees' reactions and feelings that result from the positive and negative aspects of the work environment. An example is the positive feelings of security and acceptance held by an employee in a company that has a successful product and offers generous employee benefits.

## Informal Control Systems

Informal systems are used in firms at both the individual and the team levels. At the individual level, employees' performance is influenced by the individual drives and aspirations they bring to the workplace; these are separate from any incentives and guidance provided by management. Such individual motivators explain performance differences between employees.

When informal systems exist at the work group or team level, shared team norms, such as a positive attitude to help the firm achieve quality goals or to improve sales, influence the performance of team members. At a broader level, organization-level norms can influence the behavior of teams and of individual employees. For example, some firms have a culture of commitment to customer service (IBM and the retailer Nordstrom); others have a culture devoted to quality (Toyota, FedEx) or innovation (3M, Apple). Management accountants must consider these informal systems to properly develop control systems that have the desired impact on employees' performance.

## Formal Control Systems

The four important formal management control systems at the individual employee level are (1) hiring policies, (2) promotion policies, (3) leadership development, and (4) strategic performance measurement systems. In each system, management sets expectations for desired employee performance. Hiring and promotion policies are critical in all companies and supplement strategic performance measurement systems. Leadership development includes training courses, readings and other media, meetings, policies, and procedures that help managers become more effective. Strategic performance measurement systems are the most common method for evaluating managers.

Less is known about formal systems for management control at the team level, although the increased emphasis on teamwork in recent years has led to the development of team-based management (TBM) programs and resources, particularly in organizations focusing

**EXHIBIT 18.4**
**Systems for Management Control**

on customer relationship management and quality management. The four management control systems are summarized in Exhibit 18.4.

## Strategic Performance Measurement

**LO 18-3**

*Explain the objectives and applications of strategic performance measurement for cost centers, revenue centers, and profit centers.*

**Strategic performance measurement**
is a system used by top management to evaluate SBU managers.

A firm is **decentralized**
if it has chosen to delegate a significant amount of responsibility to SBU managers.

**Strategic performance measurement** is a system used by top management to evaluate SBU managers. It is used when responsibility can be effectively delegated to SBU managers and adequate measures for evaluating the performance of the managers exist. Before designing strategic performance measurement systems, top managers determine when delegation of responsibility (called *decentralization*) is desirable.

### Decentralization

A firm is **decentralized** if it has chosen to delegate a significant amount of responsibility to SBU managers. In contrast, a centralized firm reserves much of the decision making at the top management level. For example, in a centralized multistore retail firm, all pricing decisions, product purchasing, and advertising decisions are made at the top management level, typically by top-level marketing and operations executives. In contrast, a decentralized retail firm allows local store managers to decide which products to purchase and the type and amount of advertising to use.

The strategic benefit of the centralized approach is that top management retains control over key business functions, ensuring a desired level of performance. Additionally, with top management involvement in most decisions, the expertise of top management can be effectively utilized, and the activities of the different units within the firm can be effectively coordinated. For many firms, however, a decentralized approach is preferable. The main reason is that top management cannot effectively manage the operations at a very detailed level; it lacks the necessary local knowledge. Decisions at lower levels in the firm must be made on a timely basis using the information at hand to make the firm more responsive to the customer. For example, the retail store manager must often make quick changes in inventory, pricing, and advertising to respond to local competition and changing customer buying habits and tastes.

Although the main reason for decentralization is the use of local or specialized knowledge by SBU managers, other important incentives exist. First, many managers would say that decentralized strategic performance measurement is more motivating because it provides them the opportunity to demonstrate their skill and their desire to achieve as well as to receive recognition and compensation for doing so. Second, because of the direct responsibility assumed by SBU managers, the decentralized approach provides a type of training for future top-level managers. Finally, most managers would agree that the decentralized approach is a better basis for performance evaluation. It is perceived to be more objective and to provide more opportunity for the advancement of hard-working, effective managers.

**EXHIBIT 18.5**
**Advantages and Disadvantages of Decentralization**

| Advantages of Decentralization | Disadvantages of Decentralization |
|---|---|
| • Uses local knowledge<br>• Allows timely and effective response to customers<br>• Trains managers<br>• Motivates managers<br>• Offers objective method of performance evaluation | • Can hinder coordination among SBUs<br>• Can cause potential conflict among SBUs |

As shown in Exhibit 18.5, decentralization has a downside as well. It can hinder coordination within the firm. The increased focus on competition also could cause increased conflict among managers, which can lead to counterproductive actions and reduced overall performance.

## Types of Strategic Business Units

The four types of strategic business units (SBUs) are cost centers, revenue centers, profit centers, and investment centers.

**Cost centers** are a firm's production or support SBUs that are evaluated on the basis of cost. Examples include a plant's assembly department, data processing department, and shipping and receiving department. When the focus is on the selling function, centers are called **revenue centers** and are defined either by product line or by geographical area. When an SBU both generates revenues and incurs the major portion of the cost for producing these revenues, it is a **profit center**. Profit center managers are responsible for both revenues and costs and therefore seek to achieve a desired operating profit. The use of profit centers is an improvement over cost and revenue centers in many firms because they align the manager's goals more directly with top management's goal to make the firm profitable.

The choice of a profit, cost, or revenue center depends on the nature of the production and selling environment in the firm. Products that have little need for coordination between the manufacturing and selling functions are good candidates for cost centers. These include many commodity products such as food and paper products. For such products, the production manager rarely needs to adjust the functionality of the product or the production schedule to suit a particular customer. For this reason, production managers should focus on reducing cost while sales managers focus on sales; this is what cost and revenue centers accomplish.

In contrast, sometimes close coordination is needed between the production and selling functions. For example, high-fashion and consumer products require close coordination so that consumer information coming into the selling function promptly reaches the design and manufacturing functions. Cost and revenue centers could fail to provide the incentive for coordination; in this case, production managers would be focusing on cost and not listening to the ever-changing demands coming from the selling function. A preferred option is to use the profit center for both the revenue and production managers so that both coordinate efforts to achieve the highest overall profit for the firm.

When a firm has many different profit centers because it has many different product lines, comparing their performance could be difficult because they vary greatly in size and in the nature of their products and services. A preferred approach is to use **investment centers,** which include assets employed by the center as well as profits in the performance evaluation. Investment centers are covered in Chapter 19.

## The Balanced Scorecard

Each of the four types of centers described above focuses on a critical financial measure of performance. Rather than focus on financial performance only, most firms use multiple measures of performance to evaluate centers, often in the form of a balanced scorecard. The balanced scorecard provides a more comprehensive performance evaluation,

**Cost centers**
are a firm's production or support SBUs that are evaluated on the basis of cost.

**A revenue center**
is defined either by product line or by geographical area and focuses on the selling function.

**A profit center**
both generates revenues and incurs the major portion of the cost for producing these revenues.

**An investment center**
includes assets employed by the SBU as well as profits in performance evaluation.

and therefore an evaluation that can be more effective in meeting the evaluation objectives of motivation, fairness, and proper incentives for the alignment of managers' performance with strategic goals.

## Cost Centers

Cost SBUs include manufacturing plants or direct manufacturing departments such as assembly or finishing and manufacturing support departments such as materials handling, maintenance, or engineering. The direct manufacturing and manufacturing support departments are often evaluated as cost centers since these managers have significant direct control over costs but little control over revenues or decision making for investment in facilities.

### Strategic Issues Related to Implementing Cost Centers

Three strategic issues arise when implementing cost centers. One is cost shifting, the second is excessively focusing on short-term objectives, and the third is the tendency of managers and top management to miscommunicate because of the pervasive problem of budget slack.

#### Cost Shifting

Cost shifting occurs when a department replaces its controllable costs with noncontrollable costs. For example, the manager of a production cost center that is evaluated on controllable costs has the incentive to replace variable costs with fixed costs. The reason for this is that the manager generally is not held responsible for increases in noncontrollable fixed costs. The net effect might be higher overall costs for the firm, although controllable costs in the manager's department might decrease. Fixed costs go up while variable costs go down. The effective use of cost centers requires top management to anticipate and prevent cost shifting by requiring an analysis and justification of equipment upgrades and any changes in work patterns that affect other departments.

#### Excessive Short-Term Focus

A second strategic issue is the broad concern that many performance measurement systems focus excessively on annual cost figures; this motivates managers to attend only to short-term costs and to neglect long-term strategic issues. This concern is an important reason why cost centers should use nonfinancial strategic considerations as well as financial information on costs.

#### Role of Budget Slack

**Budget slack**
is the difference between budgeted performance and expected performance.

A third strategic issue in implementing cost-based SBUs is to recognize both the negative and the positive roles of budget slack. **Budget slack** is the difference between budgeted and expected performance. The majority of SBUs have some amount of slack, evidenced by a budgeted cost target that is somewhat easier to attain than is reasonably expected. Managers often plan for a certain amount of slack in their performance budgets to allow for unexpected unfavorable events. However, a significant amount of slack might result from SBU managers' attempts to simply make their performance goals easier to achieve.

The positive view of slack is that it effectively addresses the decision-making and fairness objectives of performance evaluation. By limiting managers' exposure to environmental uncertainty, it reduces their relative risk aversion. The resulting evaluation therefore satisfies fairness, and the reduced risk helps the managers make decisions that are more nearly congruent with the goals of top management.

## Implementing Cost Centers in Departments
### *Production and Support Departments*

The two methods for implementing cost centers for production and support departments are the discretionary-cost method and the engineered-cost method. These two methods have different underlying cost behavior and a different focus: inputs or outputs, respectively. When costs are predominantly fixed, an input-oriented planning focus is appropriate because fixed costs are not controllable in the short term. The planning approach is taken so that top management can effectively budget for expected costs in each discretionary-cost center; the focus is on beginning-of-period planning for expected costs rather than end-of-period evaluation of the amount of costs expended. In contrast, if costs are primarily variable and therefore controllable, an output-oriented approach, based on end-of-period evaluation of controllable costs, is appropriate. The input-oriented approach is called the **discretionary-cost method** because costs are considered to be largely uncontrollable and discretion is applied at the planning stage. The output-oriented approach is called the **engineered-cost method** since costs are variable and therefore "engineered," or controllable.

Another factor in choosing between discretionary- and engineered-cost methods is the complexity of the work environment. Cost centers that have relatively ill-defined outputs (for instance, research and development) or have less well-defined goals are therefore more likely to be evaluated as discretionary-cost centers; cost centers in which the operations are well defined and the output goals are more clearly determined will take an engineered-cost approach. See Exhibit 18.6.

Cost behavior in a production department is therefore important in choosing the cost department method. As explained in Chapter 5, the behavior of an activity measure depends on the level of analysis: the facility, the product, the batch of production, or the unit of production. Similarly, when studying a cost center, we must know on which level of analysis it operates. For example, costs in the engineering department are driven primarily by product-level activity measures: the number of new products or product changes. Also, costs in the inspection department are caused primarily by batch-level activity measures: the number of production runs or setups.

Relatively few cost drivers exist at the facility level because most of its costs are fixed and do not fluctuate with changes in production level, production mix, or product. Therefore, most departments at this level are evaluated as discretionary-cost centers.

For cost departments at the unit, batch, and product levels, managers commonly implement the engineered-cost method based on the appropriate cost driver for that production activity. For example, for the engineering department where the cost driver is at the product level, the engineered-cost method uses the number of engineering changes to new and existing products as the cost driver and evaluates the performance of the engineering department on its costs for each engineering change completed. Similarly, for the

The **discretionary-cost method** considers costs largely uncontrollable and applies discretion at the planning stage; it is an input-oriented approach.

The **engineered-cost method** considers costs to be variable and therefore engineered, or controllable; it is an output-oriented approach.

**EXHIBIT 18.6**
**Cost Centers for Production and Support Departments**

| Discretionary-Cost Approach | Engineered-Cost Approach |
| --- | --- |
| Costs are mainly fixed and uncontrollable | Costs are mainly variable and controllable |
| Firms use an input-oriented planning focus | Firms use an output-oriented evaluation focus |
| Outputs are ill-defined | Outputs are well-defined |
| The focus is on planning | The focus is on evaluation |

inspection department where the cost driver is at the batch level (inspection is done for each batch), the appropriate cost center method is again the engineered-cost method, in which management reviews the cost incurred versus the number of batches inspected.

Some production departments are more difficult to classify as batch, product, or facility level. For example, the maintenance department can be viewed as a facility-level activity because much of the demand for maintenance is for plant and equipment that is not influenced by production level (units or batches). However, because the wear on equipment is greater at a higher level of production or for a larger number of batches, batch and unit cost drivers also can be appropriate. The choice of method depends in part on management's objectives. If management wants to motivate a reduction in maintenance use (because of rising maintenance costs or overall budget constraints), the engineered-cost method is appropriate since it rewards cost reduction. In contrast, if management is concerned about the low overall serviceability of plant and equipment (due perhaps to a prior lack of maintenance), the discretionary-cost method provides the proper incentive because it does not affect the manager's performance evaluation for the current use of maintenance, and thereby motivates the proper additional expenditures on maintenance.

Another option for management control of the engineering department or maintenance department is to treat each of them as profit centers and to charge users a price for their services. The effects of using a profit center method are added emphasis on cost control and an incentive for the center to provide quality service and perhaps seek markets outside the firm.

### Administrative Support Departments

Administrative support departments such as human resources, research and development, information technology services, and printing and duplicating are also commonly evaluated as cost centers. They seldom have a source of revenue, but the department managers control most of the costs, so the cost center method is appropriate. The choice of a discretionary-cost or engineered-cost method for these departments depends on the cost behavior in the department and on management's objectives, as explained earlier. The proper choice of method might change over time. For example, when cost reduction is a key objective, the human resources department might be treated as an engineered-cost center for a time. Later it might be changed to a discretionary-cost SBU to motivate managers to focus on long-term goals such as the design of new employee bonus systems.

Cost behavior in administrative support departments is often a step-cost, as illustrated in Exhibit 18.7. As clerical and/or service support personnel are added, labor

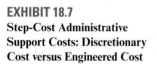

**EXHIBIT 18.7**
**Step-Cost Administrative Support Costs: Discretionary Cost versus Engineered Cost**

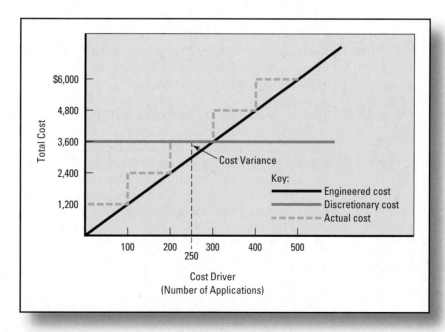

costs increase in a step-cost pattern. Suppose that one clerk is required to process 100 new employee applications per month and that each clerk is paid $1,200 per month. If the firm processes 250 applications per month, it needs three clerks at a total cost of $3,600 per month. If the discretionary-cost method is used, the supervisor of personnel management is likely to have negotiated for three clerks *at the beginning of the year,* and therefore the budget is $3,600 and there is no meaningful *ex post* evaluation. The discretionary-cost method is represented by the horizontal line in Exhibit 18.7.

Recognizing that processing each application in effect costs $12 ($1,200/100), management might choose to use an engineered-cost method that evaluates the personnel department manager by comparing the budget of $3,000 (250 applications times $12 per application) to the actual expenditure of $3,600. Because slack or overcapacity can exist due to the nature of the step-cost, an unfavorable cost variance is likely; only when the operation is exactly at one of the full-capacity points (100, 200, 300 . . .) will there be no variance. Therefore, the interpretation of the cost variances must include both the productivity of labor and the underutilization of labor due to excess capacity.

## Outsourcing or Consolidating Cost Centers

*Outsourcing* is the term used to describe a firm's decision to have a service or product currently provided by a support department supplied by an outside firm. Many firms have found that the use of an outside source is an effective way to obtain reliable product or service at a reasonable cost without the risk of obsolescence and other potential management problems. It can also enable a firm to gain access to new technologies. The cost of outsourcing is that the firm loses control over a potentially strategic resource and must rely on the outside firm's competence and continued performance. For this reason, firms analyze this decision thoroughly, select the vendors carefully, and develop precisely worded contracts. Outsourcing is an option increasingly used by many firms for their manufacturing, customer service, engineering, and other services.

Another option often used by companies is to consolidate decentralized cost centers into one or a few centralized cost centers. The goals are to reduce overall costs and to increase the overall quality of the services provided. Accounting and human resource service departments are often consolidated for these reasons.

## Cost Allocation

When the cost center is centralized, an important issue is how to allocate the jointly incurred costs of service departments, such as IT, engineering, human resources, or maintenance, to the departments using the services. The various cost allocation methods are explained in Chapter 7. The choice of method affects the amount of cost allocated to each cost center and therefore is critical in effective cost center evaluation. For example, if the cost of maintenance is allocated based on the square feet of space in each production department, the departments with more space have higher allocated costs. The incentives of such an allocation method are not clear because the production departments likely cannot control the amount of space they occupy. Alternatively, if maintenance costs are allocated on the basis of the number of maintenance jobs requested, the production departments can control their allocated maintenance costs by controlling usage.

The criteria for choosing the cost allocation method, as explained in Chapter 7, are the same as the objectives for management control: to (1) motivate managers to exert a high level of effort, (2) provide an incentive for managers to make decisions consistent with top management's goals, and (3) provide a basis for a fair evaluation of managers' performance. For example, when management wants to encourage production departments to reduce the amount of maintenance, allocation based on usage provides the desired incentive. In contrast, if management wants the departments to increase the use of maintenance to improve the serviceability of the equipment, the most effective incentive might be not to allocate the maintenance cost or perhaps to subsidize it in some way.

A useful approach to achieving the three criteria just explained is to use dual allocation. **Dual allocation** is a cost allocation method that separates fixed and variable costs. Variable costs are directly traced to user departments, and fixed costs are allocated on

**Dual allocation**
is a cost allocation method that separates fixed and variable costs. Variable costs are directly traced to user departments, and fixed costs are allocated on some logical basis.

### THE PLUS SIDE

As noted in Chapter 1 and following Thomas L. Friedman's observation in his important book, *The World Is Flat,* many of today's products and services are becoming commodities, provided by the lowest-cost global supplier. The reasons include cost savings, but often there are strategic reasons as well. The outsourcing relationship provides assistance in product innovation and product and service quality and can even save a multinational company on its global tax burden. But most important, companies say that the outsourcing relationships allow them to focus on key business processes, to enhance the firm's most competitive value-adding processes, products, and services. A recent survey of 226 global customers of outsourcing showed that 76% indicated that the top reason was cost savings, while 70% indicated that a key reason was to gain access to talent for innovation and competitive advantage.

### ON THE MINUS SIDE

Outsourcers also note that sometimes problems arise. Quality problems can develop if the projects are not planned and managed carefully. Also, security problems can arise as data and technologies are dispersed into other countries. Critical innovations and technologies can be at risk of unwanted exposure. But most important, the cost savings may not be realized as expected, because the outsourcing activity creates additional costs related to increased management supervision, increased security measures, wage increases in the host country, or unexpected additional operating costs. The recent survey of 226 global users of outsourcing indicated that top obstacles to outsourcing were establishing the cost savings (48%), lack of experience in selecting an outsourcing partner (48%), and conflict between outsourcing and company values (45%). Apparently because these were *global* companies, only 22% saw the "ethics of moving jobs offshore" as an obstacle to outsourcing.

An additional obstacle is the preference for American English by U.S. customers. Over time, this has resulted in the growth of customer service call centers in the Philippines, where there are now more call center employees for U.S. firms than any other foreign country.

### OUTSOURCING: BACK TO THE UNITED STATES

As noted in Chapter 16, productivity improvements in U.S. firms in recent years and wage increases elsewhere have led to a leveling of productivity worldwide. The result is that firms like Caterpillar, Honda, Ford Motor, and General Electric are bringing jobs back to the United States. Also, some of the smaller U.S.-based retailers that cannot maintain purchasing and quality monitoring programs overseas (as can for example Walmart and Target) are particularly looking for U.S.-based suppliers.

**Sources:** Thomas L. Friedman, *The World Is Flat: A Brief History of the Twenty-First Century* (New York: Farrar, Straus, and Giroux, 2005); PricewaterhouseCoopers Global Outsourcing Survey, 2007; John Helyar, "Outsourcing: A Passage Out of India," *Bloomberg Businessweek,* March 19, 2012, pp. 36–38; Mike Ramsey and Neal E. Boudette, "Honda Revs Up Plants in America," *The Wall Street Journal,* December 21, 2011, p. 1; Peter Coy, "A Renaissance in U.S. Manufacturing," *Bloomberg Businessweek,* May 9, 2011, pp. 11–13; Vikas Bajaj, "A New Capital of Call Centers," *The New York Times,* November 26, 2011, p. B1; Nick Leiber, "Suddenly, Made in USA Looks Like a Strategy," *Bloomberg Businessweek,* March 28, 2011, pp. 57–58; John Bussey, "Analysis: Will Costs Drive Firms Home?" *The Wall Street Journal,* May 5, 2011; Megha Bahree, "Indian Tech Firms Want to Bring Jobs to U.S., Europe," *The Wall Street Journal,* November 11, 2011, p. B5.

some logical basis. For example, the variable costs of maintenance, such as supplies, labor, and parts, can be traced to each maintenance job and charged directly to the user department. This approach is both fair and positively motivating. In contrast, the fixed costs of the maintenance department (training, manuals, equipment, etc.) that cannot be traced to each maintenance job should be allocated to the user departments using a basis that fairly reflects each department's use of the service. For example, those departments for which maintenance jobs require more expensive equipment might be allocated a higher proportion of the maintenance department's fixed costs.

To improve dual allocation, indirect costs could be traced to cost centers using activity-based costing (Chapter 5). This approach tends to produce the most accurate cost assignment and therefore would be the most motivating and fairest to the SBU managers.

## Revenue Centers

**Revenue drivers**
are the factors that affect sales volume, such as price changes, promotions, discounts, customer service, changes in product features, delivery dates, and other value-added factors.

Management commonly uses revenue drivers in evaluating the performance of revenue centers. **Revenue drivers** in manufacturing firms are the factors that affect sales volume, such as price changes, promotions, discounts, customer service, changes in product features, delivery dates, and other value-added factors. In service firms, the revenue drivers focus on many of the same factors, with a special emphasis on the quality of the service—is it courteous, helpful, and timely?

The marketing and sales departments can be viewed as both revenue and cost centers. The revenue center responsibility stems from the fact that these departments manage the revenue-generating process. These managers must therefore report revenues, typically by product line, and often also by sales area and salesperson. Top management uses the

A number of large firms, including Xerox, are outsourcing significant parts of their information technology (IT) operations. Approximately 20% of the largest U.S. firms have already outsourced this operation, according to current estimates, and the trend is for that percentage to increase. Some of the outsourcing is to application service providers (ASPs), which provide a wide range of IT services (e-mail, transaction processing, and more), often over the Internet. In other cases, the IT tasks have been taken over by large consulting firms such as Accenture and IBM. Also, a recent survey by Ernst & Young shows that an increasing number of firms in developed countries are turning to emerging market countries (e.g., India and China) for core research and development needs. Reasons include both the cost savings and the increased quality of research and innovation in the emerging countries. Why are these firms outsourcing their technology functions? How does outsourcing technology make the firm more competitive?

(Refer to Comments on Cost Management in Action at the end of the chapter.)

revenue reports to assess performance in achieving desired sales goals. Often this analysis is performed at a detailed level to determine the separate effects of changes in price, quantity, and sales mix on overall sales dollars.[3]

The marketing and sales departments also can be cost centers. In the pharmaceuticals, cosmetics, software, games and toys, and specialized electrical equipment industries, the cost of advertising and promotion is a significant portion of the total cost of producing and selling the product. The marketing and sales departments incur two types of costs: order-getting and order-filling costs. **Order-getting costs** are expenditures to advertise and promote the product. They include samples, demonstrations, advertising and promotion, travel and entertainment expenses, commissions, and marketing research. Because showing how these costs have directly affected sales is often difficult, managers frequently view order-getting costs as a discretionary-cost center and focus on planning these expenditures rather than evaluating their effectiveness. In contrast, other firms have developed extensive analyses of order-getting costs to identify the most effective activities for improving sales. Such additional analyses might consist of statistical analyses of general economic data and the firm's sales and operating data, with operational analyses consisting of ratios of sales per salesperson, sales per number of follow-ups on inquiries, and returns and allowances per product and salesperson.

A second category of marketing costs is **order-filling costs,** which include freight, warehousing, packing and shipping, and collections. These costs have a relatively clear relationship to sales volume and as a result, they can often be effectively managed as an engineered-cost center. The engineered-cost method could be implemented by using customer cost analysis as explained in Chapter 5 or by developing appropriate operating ratios—average shipping cost per item, average freight cost per sales dollar, and so on.

**Order-getting costs**
are expenditures to advertise and promote the product.

**Order-filling costs**
include freight, warehousing, packing and shipping, and collections.

## Profit Centers

The profit center manager's goal is to earn profits. A key advantage of the profit center is that it brings the manager's incentives into congruence with those of top management: to improve the firm's profitability. Moreover, the profit center should also motivate individual managers because by earning profits, the managers are contributing directly to the firm's financial success. For these reasons, the profit center meets the management control objectives of motivation and decision making explained earlier.

### Strategic Role of Profit Centers

Three strategic issues cause firms to choose profit centers rather than cost or revenue centers. First, profit centers provide the incentive for the desired coordination among the marketing, production, and support functions. The handling of rush orders is a good example. A cost center would view a rush order unfavorably because of the potential

---

[3] Sales variances are explained in Chapter 16. Also, some marketing managers have a relatively broad view of the responsibility of the marketing function, which includes responsibility for sales and cost of sales. This is suggested, for example, by the Institute of Marketing's definition: "Marketing is the management process for identifying, anticipating, and satisfying customer requirements profitably."

**EXHIBIT 18.8**
**Cost Leadership, Differentiation, and SBUs**

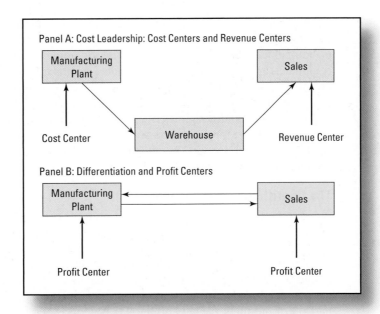

Panel A: Cost Leadership: Cost Centers and Revenue Centers

Manufacturing Plant

Sales

Cost Center

Warehouse

Revenue Center

Panel B: Differentiation and Profit Centers

Manufacturing Plant

Sales

Profit Center

Profit Center

added cost associated with the disruption of the production process, but a revenue center would view it favorably. If they are in separate cost and revenue centers, the production manager has little incentive to meet with the marketing manager to coordinate the rush order. In contrast, if the production unit is a profit unit, its manager accepts the order if it improves the center's profit, a decision consistent with the goals of both the production unit and top management.

This idea is illustrated in Exhibit 18.8. Panel A of Exhibit 18.8 shows a cost leadership firm in which a commodity is manufactured to certain standard quality and functionality specifications. These standards are common in the industry and firms compete primarily on price. In this case, the manufacturing plant's role is to provide product for sale at the lowest cost; this can be visualized as filling the warehouse, as shown in the exhibit. The warehouse might be small if the firm's supply chain management system is effective. The function of the sales organization is to sell product from the warehouse. In effect, the sales and manufacturing units are logically separate and can be evaluated simply: the plant as a cost center and the sales organization as a revenue center. These performance measures align very well with the objectives of the plant and the sales organization in this case.

In contrast, see panel B of Exhibit 18.8, which reflects a firm that competes on differentiation. The arrows shown going in both directions between the plant and the sales organization indicate that this product requires extensive coordination between manufacturing and sales. An example is fashion apparel. The design and manufacturing of the apparel must be closely coordinated with sales, since styles may change frequently, and the new style preferences must be communicated from sales to the plant in a closely coordinated way. Profit centers for both the plant and the sales organization provide the right incentive in this case, as it requires both the plant and sales management to attend to both customer preferences and manufacturing costs. An alternative approach is to organize responsibility to the product lines (responsible for both manufacturing and sales) and evaluate the product lines as profit centers, rather than to separate the manufacturing and sales functions.

A second reason that firms use profit centers rather than cost centers is to motivate managers to consider their product or service as marketable to outside customers. Production departments that provide products and services primarily for other internal departments might find that they can market their products or services profitably outside the firm, or that the firm might be able to purchase the product or service at a lower price outside the firm.

The third reason for choosing profit centers is to motivate managers to develop new ways to make profit from their products and services. For example, an increasing number of companies find that service contracts (for home entertainment equipment, business equipment, appliances, and so on) provide a significant source of profit in addition to the sale of the product. In the software industry, revenues from providing service and upgrades can be as important as the software's original sales price. Coordination between marketing, production, and design is critical for the success of these efforts, and since many of these contracts are for three years or more, the expected future costs of the service must be carefully analyzed. In a profit center, managers have the incentive to develop creative new products and services because the profit center evaluation rewards the incremental profits.

## The Contribution Income Statement

A common form of profit center evaluation is the **contribution income statement,** which is based on the contribution margin developed for each profit center and for each relevant group of profit centers. The contribution income statement is illustrated in Exhibit 18.9 for Machine Tools Inc. (MTI). MTI has two operating divisions, A and B, each of which is considered a profit center. The level of detail at which the contribution income statement is developed varies depending on management's needs. For a firm with a limited number of products, the level of detail in Exhibit 18.9 is common. For a firm with several products, a more extensive contribution income statement would be required to provide sufficient detail for management analysis.

This contribution income statement is an extension of the income statement illustrated in Exhibits 11.14 through 11.16 of Chapter 11. Chapter 11 introduces the idea of traceable fixed costs; that is, fixed costs can be traced directly to a product line or production unit. Exhibit 18.9 shows both contribution margin and contribution margin less traceable fixed costs, **contribution by profit center (CPC)**. The concept of CPC is important because it measures profit after *all* traceable costs and is therefore controllable by the profit center manager. CPC is a more complete and fair measure of performance than either contribution margin or operating income.

This chapter expands the contribution income statement by distinguishing controllable and noncontrollable fixed costs. **Controllable fixed costs** are fixed costs that the profit SBU manager can influence in approximately a year or less. That is, the manager typically budgets these costs in the annual budget; some of them involve contractual relationships for a year or less. Examples include advertising; sales promotion; certain engineering, data processing, and research projects; and management consulting. In contrast, **noncontrollable fixed costs** are those that are not controllable within a year's time; usually they include facilities-related costs such as depreciation, taxes, and insurance.

---

The **contribution income statement** is based on the contribution margin developed for each profit center and for each relevant group of profit centers.

The **contribution by profit center (CPC)** measures *all* costs traceable to, and therefore controllable by, the individual profit centers.

**Controllable fixed costs** are those fixed costs that the profit center manager can influence in approximately a year or less.

**Noncontrollable fixed costs** are those fixed costs that are not controllable within a year's time, usually including facilities-related costs such as depreciation, taxes, and insurance.

---

**EXHIBIT 18.9** Machine Tools Inc. Contribution Income Statement (000s omitted)

| | Company as a Whole | Company Breakdown into Profit Centers | | Breakdown of Division B to Product-Level Profit Centers | | | |
| --- | --- | --- | --- | --- | --- | --- | --- |
| | | Division A | Division B | Not Traceable | Product 1 | Product 2 | Product 3 |
| Net revenues | $2,000 | $600 | $1,400 | | $400 | $700 | $300 |
| Variable costs | 900 | 200 | 700 | | 100 | 350 | 250 |
| Contribution margin | $1,100 | $400 | $ 700 | | $300 | $350 | $ 50 |
| Controllable fixed costs | 250 | 100 | 150 | $ 25 | 25 | 100 | 0 |
| Controllable margin | $ 850 | $300 | $ 550 | (25) | $275 | $250 | $ 50 |
| Noncontrollable fixed costs | 400 | 120 | 280 | 20 | 10 | 130 | 120 |
| Contribution by profit center (CPC) | $ 450 | $180 | $ 270 | $(45) | $265 | $120 | $ (70) |
| Untraceable costs | 200 | | | | | | |
| Operating income | $ 250 | | | | | | |

**Controllable margin**

is determined by subtracting short-term controllable fixed costs from the contribution margin.

As illustrated in Exhibit 18.9, the firm develops a useful measure of the profit SBU manager's short-term performance by subtracting controllable fixed costs from the contribution margin to determine the **controllable margin**. In contrast, to measure the manager's performance in managing both short- and long-term costs, the CPC measure is most appropriate since it includes both short-term and long-term fixed costs.

One complication in completing the contribution income statement is that some costs that are not traceable at a detailed level are traceable at a higher level of aggregation. The untraceable costs column in the income statement represents costs traceable to division B but not traceable to any of the product lines. For example, the $25,000 controllable fixed costs might consist of the cost of advertising that was arranged at the division level to benefit all three products, so it is not traceable to any one product.

In addition to providing useful measures of the manager's performance in managing costs, the contribution income statement can be used to determine whether a profit center should be dropped or retained, much like the contribution margin analysis in Exhibit 11.16. The analysis is now enhanced because of our ability to distinguish controllable and noncontrollable fixed costs. For example, using the analysis in Exhibit 18.9, MTI can determine that if it drops product 3, the short-term effect will be to reduce profit by $50,000, the amount of the controllable margin. All costs involved in the determination of the controllable margin are avoidable within a period of one year. Taking the longer-term view, suppose that MTI could ultimately save an additional $120,000 of noncontrollable fixed costs by dropping product 3. Then, in the long term, MTI can save a net of $70,000 by dropping product 3, the amount of the contribution by CPC for product 3. The above analysis has assumed that the sales of the products are independent, that a change in sales for one product will not affect the level of sales for another product. Sales interdependencies between products must also be included in the analysis when they occur.

### The Contribution Income Statement: Variable Costing versus Full Costing

**LO 18-4**

*Explain the role of variable costing and full costing in evaluating profit centers.*

The use of the contribution income statement often is called *variable costing* because it separates variable and fixed costs. Only variable costs are included in determining the cost of sales and the contribution margin. In contrast, full costing is a cost system that includes fixed cost in product cost and cost of sales. Full costing is the conventional costing system because it is required by financial reporting standards (generally accepted accounting principles) and by the Internal Revenue Service for determining taxable income. A key reason full costing is preferred for financial reporting is that it satisfies the matching principle; that is, in determining cost of goods sold it matches the revenues of the period with the full cost of the product. The details of full-costing systems are explained in Chapters 3 through 7.

The advantage of variable costing is that it meets the three objectives of management control systems by showing separately those costs that can be traced to, and controlled by, each profit center. In this section, we see an additional reason for using variable costing. Although income determined using full costing is affected by changes in inventory levels, income using variable costing is not affected. Exhibits 18.10A and B show how using full costing affects income.

Panel 1 in Exhibit 18.10A shows the data used in the illustration, including units produced and sold and costs for two periods. Panel 2 shows both the full- and variable-cost income statements for the first of two periods. Two periods are used to show the differences for both possible cases, increasing or decreasing inventory. In the first period, inventory increases; in the second period, it decreases. Exhibit 18.10B shows the comparison of the two income statements for period 2.

In period 1, inventory increases by 40 units because production of 100 units exceeds sales of 60 units. Inventory decreases by the same amount in period 2. Using full costing, the unit product cost is $30 variable plus $40 fixed, or $70 per unit in both periods. The $70 unit cost is used to calculate the cost of goods sold on the income statements in periods 1 and 2 for full costing. The selling and administrative costs ($5 variable and $1,200 fixed) are deducted after gross margin to determine the income of $300 in period 1 and $2,300 in period 2.

The variable-costing income statement uses only variable cost to determine product cost. The cost of sales and inventory figures are determined using a variable manufacturing cost of $30 per unit. To calculate the total contribution margin, the variable selling and administrative costs of $5 per unit sold are deducted along with the $30 variable manufacturing cost per unit. The result is a total contribution margin of $3,900 in period 1 and $9,100 in period 2. In variable costing, all fixed costs (both manufacturing fixed cost of $4,000 and selling and administration fixed costs of $1,200) are deducted from the contribution margin, to get a $1,300 loss in period 1 and $3,900 income in period 2.

The difference in income in period 1 for full and variable costing is $1,600 ($300 income compared to a $1,300 loss), which is exactly the amount of fixed cost included in the increase in inventory under full costing ($1,600 = 40 units × $40 per unit fixed cost). Note that the amount of ending inventory in period 1 differs by $1,600 ($2,800 for full cost versus $1,200 for variable costing). This amount is also the difference in income for variable and full costing for both periods 1 and 2, when inventory decreases by 40 units. Note the shaded areas in Exhibit 18.10 (A and B) which show the difference of $1,600 in operating income for each period is due to the difference in the value of inventory (ending inventory for period 1 and beginning inventory for period 2, since the two periods start and end with

**EXHIBIT 18.10A**
**Comparison of Full and Variable Costing–Period 1**

| Panel 1 Data Summary | Period 1 | Period 2 | |
|---|---|---|---|
| Units | | | |
| Beginning inventory | 0 | 40 | |
| Price | $100 | $100 | |
| Sold | 60 | 140 | |
| Produced | 100 | 100 | |
| Unit variable costs | | | |
| Manufacturing | $30 | $30 | |
| Selling and administrative costs | $5 | $5 | |
| Fixed costs | | | Per unit |
| Manufacturing | $4,000 | $4,000 | $40 |
| Selling and administrative costs | $1,200 | $1,200 | |

| Panel 2 | | |
|---|---|---|

| Period 1 Income Statement | Full Costing | | Variable Costing | |
|---|---|---|---|---|
| Sales (60 × $100) | | $6,000 | | $ 6,000 |
| Less: Cost of goods sold | | | | |
| Beginning inventory | $ 0 | | $ 0 | |
| + Cost of goods produced | 7,000 | | 3,000 | |
| | (= 100 × $70) | | (= 100 × $30) | |
| = Cost of goods available for sale | 7,000 | | 3,000 | |
| − Ending inventory ($1,600 difference) | 2,800 | | 1,200 | |
| | (= 40 × $70) | | (= 40 × $30) | |
| = Cost of goods sold | | 4,200 | | 1,800 |
| Less: Variable selling and administrative costs | | N/A | | 300 |
| **Gross margin** | | **$1,800** | | |
| **Contribution margin** | | | | **$ 3,900** |
| Less: Fixed manufacturing costs | | N/A | $4,000 | |
| Less: Selling and administrative costs | | | | |
| Variable | $ 300 | | N/A | |
| Fixed | 1,200 | | $1,200 | |
| Total other costs | | 1,500 | | 5,200 |
| Operating income ($1,600 difference) | | **$ 300** | | **$(1,300)** |

Difference in ending inventory = $2,800 − $1,200 = $1,600

Difference in operating income = $300 − $(1,300) = $1,600

| Recap |
|---|
| Difference in ending inventory = $2,800 − $1,200 = $1,600 (or 40 units × $40/unit = $1,600) |
| Difference in income = $300 − $(1,300) = $1,600 |

N/A = not applicable.

**EXHIBIT 18.10B**
Comparison of Full and
Variable Costing–Period 2

| Period 2 Income Statement | Full Costing | | Variable Costing | |
|---|---|---|---|---|
| Sales (140 × $100) | | $14,000 | | $14,000 |
| Less: Cost of goods sold | | | | |
| Beginning inventory ($1,600 difference) | $2,800 | | $1,200 | |
| + Cost of goods produced (for 100 units, same as period 1) | 7,000 | | 3,000 | |
| = Cost of goods available for sale | 9,800 | | 4,200 | |
| − Ending inventory | 0 | | 0 | |
| = Cost of goods sold | | 9,800 | | 4,200 |
| Less: Variable selling and administrative | | N/A | | 700 |
| **Gross margin** | | **$ 4,200** | | |
| **Contribution margin** | | | | **$ 9,100** |
| Less: Fixed manufacturing costs | N/A | | $4,000 | |
| Less: Selling and administrative costs | | | | |
| Variable | $ 700 | | N/A | |
| Fixed | 1,200 | | $1,200 | |
| Total other costs | | 1,900 | | 5,200 |
| Operating income ($1,600 difference) | | $ 2,300 | | $ 3,900 |
| **Recap** | | | | |
| Difference in beginning inventory = $2,800 − $1,200 = $1,600 | | | | |
| Difference in income = $3,900 − $2,300 = $1,600 | | | | |

N/A = not applicable.

no inventory). A useful guide then is that *full-costing income exceeds variable-costing income (by the amount of fixed cost in the inventory change) when inventory in units increases, and variable-costing income is higher than full-costing income when inventory in units decreases.*

The important point is that variable costing is not affected by the change in inventory because all fixed costs are deducted from income in the period in which they occur; fixed costs are not included in inventory so that inventory changes do not affect income. For this reason, variable-costing income can be considered a more reliable measure and is preferable for use in strategic performance measurement. When full costing is used (as is required for financial reporting), the management accountant must use special caution in interpreting the amount of income and attempt to determine what portion of income, if any, might be due to inventory changes. This is especially important if income is used as a basis for performance evaluation, as it is in profit centers. A survey of senior financial executives showed that a majority (76%) use full costing for both financial reporting and for internal purposes such as performance evaluation and decision making; the remaining 24% used variable costing for internal purposes.

### The Contribution Income Statement and International Accounting Standards

The International Accounting Standards Board (**www.IASB.org**) is a London-based independent organization that develops and interprets international financial reporting standards (IFRSs). The mission of the IASB is to develop a single set of high quality, globally accepted accounting standards. As of April 2012, 123 countries throughout the world either permit or require IFRS for publicly held companies. The United States continues to use generally accepted accounting principles (GAAP) as developed by the U.S.-based Financial Accounting Standards Board (FASB). The FASB, under the guidance of the SEC, has developed a plan in which the FASB and the IASB will work together to complete a convergence of IFRS and GAAP. The timetable for convergence is not firmly set, but many believe it is a matter of only a few years before U.S. firms will be using IFRS or something very much like it. Some of the notable differences between GAAP and IFRS are that IFRS does not permit LIFO valuation of inventory (GAAP does), and IFRS does permit market value treatment of certain long-lived assets (GAAP does not). Experts note that the move to IFRS will certainly affect U.S.-based firms in terms of corporate taxation, international transfer pricing (Chapter 19), global investment strategies (Chapter 12), the evaluation of the performance of foreign operations and the managers of those operations (Chapters 18 and 19), and the compensation of managers of global units (Chapter 20).

The move from GAAP to IFRS will likely have wide-ranging effects and present a great deal of uncertainty to CFOs and others involved in strategic performance measurement. For example, bonus contracts written for GAAP and tax considerations based on U.S./GAAP-based taxable income will have to be rewritten for international standards. Some things to note as this change takes place:

1. Many global companies are likely to benefit from the move to IFRS as it will provide a single set of standards which will be used worldwide. Therefore, reporting entities in different countries around the world will likely have the same accounting procedures and policies. This means lower accounting costs for the company as the need for translation or reconciliation of different accounting methods is reduced, and the company is able to directly compare its financial reports from different countries.

2. A related benefit for companies is that the comparability of managers' performance evaluation reports (cost center, profit center, or investment center) will be improved. After the convergence from GAAP to IFRS, it is likely that many global managers will be evaluated according to the same accounting standards.

3. Those companies that have designed special in-company performance measures using, for example, variable-costing principles or lean-accounting principles may have already achieved the desired level of comparability in reporting across the units, and thus the switch to IFRS will not have much of an effect. The improvement in comparability will be greatest for those companies that have relied on external financial reports as a basis for performance evaluation.

### The Contribution Income Statement and Value Streams

In applications of lean accounting, products and services are grouped in families called *value streams.* The value-stream income statement shows the contribution of each of the organization's value streams in much the same way as the contribution income statement illustrated in Exhibit 18.9; each value stream is a profit center. Moreover, a unique feature of the value-stream income statement is that it shows separately the increase or decrease in profit due to a change in inventory; in effect, the value-stream income statement adjusts the full-cost income statement to contribution-based variable costing. The ability to see the inventory effect as a separate item on the income statement provides significant additional information for managers, one of the contributions of value streams in lean accounting.[4]

## Strategic Performance Measurement and the Balanced Scorecard

**LO 18-5**

*Explain the role of the balanced scorecard in strategic performance measurement.*

The sacred obligation of senior leadership:
Vision: What will it be?
Goals: What four or five things must we do to get there?
Alignment: Translate the work of each person into an alignment with the goals.

*Soichiro Honda, Founder of Honda Motor Company*

Cost, revenue, and profit centers are widely used methods to achieve strategic performance measurement. A common characteristic of these SBUs in practice is that they use little or no nonfinancial information. However, a complete strategic performance evaluation

---

[4] For more information on the value-stream income statement see Frances A. Kennedy and Peter C. Brewer, "Lean Accounting: What's It All About," *Strategic Finance,* November 2005, pp. 27–34, and Statement on Management Accounting, "Accounting for the Lean Enterprise: Major Changes to the Accounting Paradigm" (Institute of Management Accountants, 2006).

necessarily attends to all critical success factors of the business, including many nonfinancial factors. A useful approach for a complete strategic performance evaluation is to include both financial and nonfinancial factors for the SBU using the balanced scorecard. The balanced scorecard measures the SBU's performance in four key perspectives: (1) customer satisfaction, (2) financial performance, (3) internal business processes, and (4) learning and innovation. Cost, revenue, and profit centers focus on the financial dimension. The main concept of the balanced scorecard is that no single measure can properly evaluate the SBU's progress to strategic success. Rather, multiple measures typically grouped in the four key perspectives provide the desired comprehensive evaluation of the SBU's performance. Moreover, by attending directly to the firm's critical success factors, the balanced scorecard effectively aligns the performance measurement/evaluation process to the firm's strategy.

## Implementing the Balanced Scorecard and the Strategy Map for Performance Evaluation

Several issues are of concern in effectively implementing the BSC and strategy map for performance evaluation.

- The BSC and strategy map are more likely to be used in an evaluation of performance over time rather than for performance of an SBU relative to other SBUs. The reason is that the scorecard measures for one unit may not be appropriate for another SBU and, therefore, it is difficult to compare them.

- Many studies have shown that the BSC is widely used for strategic planning and often also for performance evaluation, but less often in management compensation. To effectively tie performance to strategic objectives, the BSC should also be tied to management compensation.

- The successful implementation of a balanced scorecard requires the validation of the links between measures that are assumed to improve performance throughout the scorecard. Without validation, the company cannot be sure that attention to the measures will produce the desired results. Validation involves using a causal model to test the effects of the measures on desired performance. In one study, 23% of the firms participating used the causal model approach to validate the links in the scorecard, and these companies had on average a 2.95% higher return on assets and a 5.14% higher return on equity than the other companies in the study.[5]

- Managers must be provided information on the strategic linkages in the scorecard. One study has shown that those evaluating the performance of a business relied more on the strategically linked measures than other measures when they were provided information on the strategically relevant measures. In contrast, the nonstrategically linked measures were most commonly used when the strategic linkage information was not provided.[6]

- Many large firms have installed extensive computer systems called *enterprise resource planning* systems (ERPs). They provide an information system base that stores the detailed information for the balanced scorecard. Firms without an ERP might have difficulty developing and maintaining the data needed for the scorecard.

- In contrast to financial data that are subject to financial audit and control systems, much of the nonfinancial information used in the scorecard is not subject to control or audit. Thus, the reliability and accuracy of some of the nonfinancial data could be questionable.

- The performance reviews of managers occur at regular intervals—usually every quarter or every year—which fits well with the typical firm's preparation of financial statements quarterly and annually. In contrast, the nonfinancial information is often prepared on

[5] Christopher D. Ittner and David F. Larcker, "Coming up Short on Nonfinancial Performance Measurement," *Harvard Business Review,* November 2003, pp. 88–95.

[6] Rajiv D. Banker, Hsihui Chang, and Mina J. Pizzini, "The Balanced Scorecard: Judgmental Effects of Performance Measures Linked to Strategy," *The Accounting Review,* January 2004, pp. 1–23.

a weekly or daily basis for effective use in operations and decision making. This variance in preparation cycles can complicate the nature and timing of reviews.

- Typically, all financial data used by the cost or profit SBUs are developed internally, using well-developed information systems. In contrast, some of the most valuable nonfinancial information, such as customer surveys, are developed external to the firm, which creates additional issues regarding the timeliness and the reliability of this nonfinancial information.

### Implementing Strategy Using the BSC: Six Steps to Maximize the Value of Nonfinancial Measures

In 2004, Deloitte & Touche, in collaboration with *The Economist,* surveyed 250 executives and board members of large companies in North America, Europe, and Asia. The findings were that many executives (73%) felt that their companies were under increasing pressure to measure and report nonfinancial indicators, including customer satisfaction, innovation, sustainability, and employee commitment. However, while 86% said their companies are good to excellent at measuring financial performance, only 34% responded favorably about measuring nonfinancial performance. Ittner and Larcker, writing a year earlier, found similar results, which they explained as failed implementation due to:

- Not linking the nonfinancial measures to strategy.
- Not validating the assumptions behind the links of performance measures to desired outcomes.
- Setting the wrong performance targets.
- Measuring the results incorrectly.

To address the need for more effective implementation of nonfinancial measures, Ittner and Larcker suggest the following six steps.[7]

1. **Develop a causal model** to show the links of measures to performance and desired outcomes.
2. **Gather data** to find out who maintains the nonfinancial data in the firm, with the objective of improving the consistency and accuracy and accessibility of the data to decision makers.
3. **Turn the data into information** by using regression analysis and other statistical tools, including forecasting and other analytical tools, to test the validity of the model developed in step 1 above.
4. **Continually refine the model** by monitoring internal and external events and by rebuilding the model on a timely basis.
5. **Base actions on findings.** Have the confidence in the model to follow where it leads.
6. **Assess outcomes.** Continuously assess the effectiveness of the model and of the actions taken in step 5 to produce the desired outcomes; does the model work?

## Management Control in Service Firms and Not-for-Profit Organizations

Management control in service firms and not-for-profit organizations is commonly implemented in the form of a cost center or a profit center. As do manufacturing and retail firms, these organizations choose a cost center when the manager's critical mission is to control costs; a profit center is preferred when the department manager must manage both costs and revenues or, alternatively (in a not-for-profit organization), manage costs without exceeding budgeted revenues.

The most common type of SBU in service firms and not-for-profit organizations is the cost center. For example, the performance of a bank's consumer loan department often is monitored as a cost center, as illustrated in Exhibit 18.11. Note that the structure of the

---

[7] Christopher D. Ittner and David F. Larcker, "Coming Up Short on Nonfinancial Performance Measurement."

## In Which Countries Are Companies Most Likely to Use the Balanced Scorecard?

A 2008 survey of companies from 44 countries around the globe provides evidence of the widespread use of scorecard systems. While initially developed and implemented as a North American strategic tool, the balanced scorecard and other scorecarding systems are now being used around the world. As the accompanying table shows, of the 382 respondents to a recent survey, more than half use scorecarding systems, with the highest rate of usage among South American respondents and the lowest rate among European respondents.

The five most-cited reasons for implementing a scorecarding system, in order of frequency, are: (1) need to track progress toward achieving organizational goals; (2) need to align employee behavior with an organization's strategic objectives; (3) need to communicate strategy to everyone in a clear and simple manner; (4) need to measure performance at different levels in an organization; and (5) ability to measure people, projects, and strategies.

**Use of Scorecarding Systems by Region**

| Region | Total Respondents | Percentage Using Scorecarding System |
|---|---|---|
| Africa (primarily South Africa) | 19 | 68% |
| Asia (including the Middle East) | 62 | 50 |
| Europe | 137 | 39 |
| U.S. and Canada | 135 | 55 |
| South and Central America | 28 | 79 |
| Total | 382 | 51 |

**Source:** R. Lawson, W. Stratton, and T. Hatch, "Scorecarding Goes Global: Companies around the World Are Deriving Benefits from Performance Management Tools," *Strategic Finance,* March 2008, pp. 35–41.

---

**EXHIBIT 18.11**

**Performance Report for the Consumer Loan Department**

| | |
|---|---|
| Variable costs | |
| Direct labor | $23,446 |
| Supplies | 3,836 |
| Controllable fixed costs | |
| Supervision salaries | 15,339 |
| Advertising | 6,500 |
| Fees and services | 4,226 |
| Other | 766 |
| Noncontrollable fixed costs | |
| Facilities | 650 |
| Data processing | 2,200 |
| Other | 899 |
| Total costs | $57,862 |
| Operating performance | |
| Number of accounts at end of month | 1,334 |
| Number of new accounts | 54 |
| Number of closed accounts | 22 |
| Number of transactions processed | 1,994 |
| Number of inquiries processed | 334 |

performance report is much like that of the profit center analysis in Exhibit 18.9. The difference is that the focus in Exhibit 18.11 is on costs, which are separated into variable costs such as labor and supplies, controllable fixed costs such as supervision salaries, and noncontrollable fixed costs such as data processing and facilities management. In addition, Exhibit 18.11 includes information regarding certain operating measures critical to the department's success: the number of new accounts, the number of closed accounts, the number of transactions processed, and the number of inquiries handled. This information is used to evaluate the department's performance over time and perhaps to compare its performance to that of related departments such as the mortgage loan department. Note that the report does not include the cost of funds provided for the loans since it is assumed that the department manager cannot control either the supply or the cost of those funds.

## Summary

The principal focus of management control systems is strategic performance measurement. The goal of top management in using strategic performance measurement is to *motivate the managers* to provide a high level of effort, to *guide them to make decisions that are congruent with the goals of top management,* and to provide a basis for determining *fair compensation for the managers.*

A large number of management control systems are used in practice, including both formal and informal systems and individual or team-based systems. The chapter focuses on one type of formal control system at the individual level, the strategic performance measurement system.

Strategic performance measurement systems are implemented in four different forms, depending on the nature of the manager's responsibilities: the revenue center, cost center, profit center, and investment center. Revenue, cost, and profit centers are covered in this chapter, and the investment center is covered in the following chapter, Chapter 19.

The four types of SBUs are employed in manufacturing firms as well as service firms and not-for-profit and governmental organizations. Typical cost centers in manufacturing firms are production and production-support departments. Cost centers often are evaluated as either engineered-cost centers or discretionary-cost centers. Discretionary-cost centers focus on planning desired cost levels; engineered-cost centers focus on evaluation of achieved cost levels.

The marketing and sales departments may be evaluated as revenue centers or cost centers. As a revenue center, these departments have the goal of sales growth; as a cost center, there are goals for managing order-getting and order-filling costs.

The profit center is used when the manager is responsible for both costs and revenues and when coordination between the marketing and production areas is needed: for example, in handling special orders or rush orders. Evaluation on profit provides the incentive for the departments to work together. Profit centers are also used to set a desirable competitive tone. All departments have the profit incentive to compete with other providers of the product or service, inside or outside the firm. The contribution income statement is an effective method for evaluating profit centers because it identifies each profit center's controllable costs.

The contribution income statement is used for profit centers. It has the benefit of not being affected by changes in finished goods inventory. In contrast, income as determined by the conventional income statement based on full costing is affected by inventory changes.

A key issue in the effective use of strategic performance measurement systems is the integration of strategic considerations into the evaluation. This requires an identification of the firm's critical success factors and the appropriate measurement and reporting of these factors, commonly in the form of a balanced scorecard. In many cases, a substantial portion of these factors is nonfinancial, including operating and economic data from sources external to the firm.

## Key Terms

budget slack, *773*
contribution by profit
center (CPC), *780*
contribution income
statement, *780*
controllable fixed costs, *780*
controllable margin, *781*
cost center, *772*
decentralization, *771*
discretionary-cost method, *774*

dual allocation, *776*
employment contract, *767*
engineered-cost method, *774*
investment center, *772*
management control, *765*
noncontrollable fixed
costs, *780*
operational control, *765*
order-filling costs, *778*
order-getting costs, *778*

performance
measurement, *765*
principal-agent model, *767*
profit center, *772*
revenue center, *772*
revenue drivers, *777*
strategic business unit
(SBU), *766*
strategic performance
measurement, *771*

## Comments on Cost Management in Action

### Outsourcing Technology

In a 2008 survey of CFOs, 57% reported that their firms were outsourcing a portion or all of their information technology (IT) needs. The motivation for outsourcing IT is twofold. First, it can help to dramatically reduce the firm's overall cost of IT. Second, and perhaps most important, it helps the firm to keep up with advancing technology by partnering with an application service provider or consulting firm with a high level of expertise.

How does IT make the firm more competitive? Consultants and analysts disagree on this point. Some argue that IT is a strategic resource in most industries and should be supported within the firm to achieve the desired integration of IT and business strategy. They point to Walmart, which has used IT to improve its strategic goal of low cost and low price. Similarly, ADP, Inc., and Levi Strauss have used IT to improve their competitive position through enhancements in customer service.

Others argue that the question is not *whether* to outsource but *which* of the IT activities to choose to outsource and *where* to outsource. For example, Xerox has an outsourcing arrangement with Electronic Data Systems (EDS) to handle its operational IT tasks while it maintains a partnership with the software developer Oracle to develop Xerox's strategic goals for IT. Also, IT outsourcing has gone global. Software engineers and database managers in India and the Philippines are less costly than in other areas of the world.

N. Venkatraman, a leading author on IT outsourcing, argues that IT should be viewed as a strategic SBU in either a cost, profit, investment, or service form (for Venkatraman, a "service" SBU puts customer service as top priority). Venkatraman proposes a simple formula for choosing the type of SBU based on two factors: (1) the degree to which the firm needs either operational efficiency or business capability from IT and (2) the degree of risk the firm is willing to bear. A low-risk firm that requires operational efficiency should choose the cost center; a low-risk firm that requires business capability should use a service provider. In contrast, a firm willing to accept risk and requiring business capability should choose an investment center because it will provide the desired long-term perspective for IT.

Looking at technology in the form of research and development (R&D), a recent survey by Ernst & Young shows that companies in developing countries, North America, and Western Europe expect to more than double the portion of their R&D targeted to emerging countries such as China, India, and Brazil. The improved quality of the R&D in these countries, together with the lower cost, are the key incentives.

**Sources:** John Light, "More Companies Plan to Put R&D Overseas," *The Wall Street Journal,* February 22, 2011, p. B4; John R. Hagerty, "U.S. Loses High-Tech Jobs as R&D Shifts toward Asia, *The Wall Street Journal,* January 18, 2012, p. B1; "In a Pinch: How the Financial Crisis Will Affect the Outsourcing Industry," *The Economist,* October 11, 2008, p. 86; Sarah Johnson, "Nobody Doesn't Like Outsourcing," **CFO**.com, December 11, 2008; N. Venkatraman, "Beyond Outsourcing: Managing IT Resources as a Value Center," *Sloan Management Review,* Spring 1997, pp. 51–64. For further information view the Outsourcing Institute's website at **http://outsourcing.com/.**

## Self-Study Problem

(For solution, please turn to the end of the chapter.)

### Discretionary-Cost and Engineered-Cost Methods

C. B. (Chuck) Davis is the manager of the claims processing department for Liberty Life Insurance Co. He has 12 clerks working for him to process approximately 900 claims per month. Each clerk earns a monthly salary of $2,400, including benefits. The number of claims varies somewhat, and, in recent years, it has been as low as 810 and as high as 1,020 per month. Chuck has argued with Liberty officials that his 12 clerks are not enough to handle 1,000 or more claims; he knows from a recent study of his department that it takes a well-trained clerk an average of 121 minutes to process a claim (processing time also varies widely, from as little as a few minutes to as much as several hours, depending on the claim's complexity). While Liberty management agrees that 12 clerks are not sufficient for a month with 1,000 claims, it notes that most months require that only 800 claims be processed. Management concludes, therefore, that 12 clerks are about right. Assume that each clerk works an eight-hour day except for 40 minutes of break time and that each month has an average of 22 working days. In the most recent month, January, the department processed 915 claims.

#### Required

1. What type of SBU does Liberty management appear to use for the claims processing department?

2. Assuming that Liberty uses the discretionary-cost method to implement cost centers, what is the budgeted cost in the claims department for January?

3. Assuming that Liberty uses the engineered-cost method to implement cost centers, what is the budgeted cost in the claims department for January?

4. If you were Chuck Davis, what would you use as a more effective argument to top management in requesting additional clerks?

*Please visit* **http://www.mhhe.com/blocher6e** *to access a narrated, animated tutorial for solving this problem.*

**Questions**

18-1   What is the difference between management control, performance evaluation, and operational control?

18-2   What is strategic performance measurement, and why is it important for effective management?

18-3   Does an effective performance evaluation focus on individual or team performance?

18-4   Explain the difference between informal and formal control systems. What type of control system is strategic performance measurement?

18-5   Name two types of organizational design and explain how they differ.

18-6   What are four types of SBUs, and what are the goals of each?

18-7   Since full costing is accepted for financial reporting purposes and variable costing is not, why should we be concerned about the difference between them? What is the difference, and why is it important?

18-8   What are some important behavioral and implementation issues in strategic performance measurement? How does the management accountant deal with these issues?

18-9   What is the role of cost allocation in strategic performance measurement?

18-10   Can strategic performance measurement be used for service firms and not-for-profit organizations? How?

18-11   In what situations is a cost center most appropriate? A profit center? A revenue center?

18-12   How do centralized and decentralized firms differ? What are the advantages of each?

18-13   Can the marketing department be both a revenue center and a cost center? Explain.

**Brief Exercises**

18-14   Which type of cost center has a planning focus, and which type has an evaluation focus?

18-15   What is the role of risk preference in performance evaluation?

18-16   Pepper's Automotive produces auto parts for various automotive retailers. Peppers is evaluating the exhaust system division of the company and has come up with the following data for the year: net revenues are $1,000,000, variable costs are $300,000, and fixed costs are $400,000. Of the fixed costs, controllable fixed costs are $100,000 and noncontrollable fixed costs are $300,000. What is the controllable margin and total contribution by profit center (CPC)?

18-17   Pepper's Automotive has further analyzed the exhaust division into three products: exhaust pipes, intake valves, and intake pipes. The income statement is available below. What is the change in profit in both the short run and long run by dropping intake valves from its product line?

|  | Exhaust Pipes | Intake Valves | Intake Pipes |
|---|---|---|---|
| Net revenues | $500,000 | $300,000 | $200,000 |
| Variable costs | 50,000 | 150,000 | 100,000 |
| Contribution margin | 450,000 | 150,000 | 100,000 |
| Controllable fixed costs | 50,000 | 50,000 | 0 |
| Controllable margin | 400,000 | 100,000 | 100,000 |
| Noncontrollable fixed costs | 100,000 | 150,000 | 50,000 |
| Contribution by profit center | $300,000 | $(50,000) | $ 50,000 |

18-18   Meargia Plastics is evaluating its plastic bottles division. The accounting manager has come up with the following data for the year: contribution margin of $500,000, controllable fixed costs of $200,000, and noncontrollable fixed costs of $50,000. What is the controllable margin and total contribution by profit center?

18-19   Explain the difference between the engineered-cost and discretionary-cost approaches to evaluating support departments.

18-20   Manuel Inc. produces textiles in many different forms. After recording lower than anticipated profits last year, Manuel has decided to shut down one of its divisions that is not performing well. The accounting manager has compiled the following data on the two divisions being considered for closing and has asked you to evaluate the short-term and long-term effects on profits of closing each division. Which division should be closed and why?

|  | Winter Outerwear | High-End Suits |
|---|---|---|
| Net revenues | $1,000,000 | $5,000,000 |
| Variable costs | 500,000 | 2,000,000 |
| Contribution margin | 500,000 | 3,000,000 |
| Controllable fixed costs | 0 | 2,000,000 |
| Controllable margin | 500,000 | 1,000,000 |
| Noncontrollable fixed costs | 750,000 | 1,500,000 |
| Contribution by SBU | $ (250,000) | $ (500,000) |

18-21   Calabria Healthcare supplies prescription drugs to pharmacies. As the management accountant, you are required to analyze the financial statements for this quarter. You already have analyzed the company's two divisions, Name Brand and Generic, and your supervisor wants an analysis of the comparable profitability of the SBUs. The contribution margins are $500,000 and $200,000, respectively; the controllable fixed costs are $200,000 and $50,000; and the noncontrollable fixed costs are $50,000 and $100,000. What are the total contributions by profit center (CPC) for these divisions and operating income for the company? Assume there are no untraceable fixed costs.

18-22   Phelps Glass Inc. has reported the following financial data: net revenues of $10 million, variable costs of $5 million, controllable fixed costs of $2 million, noncontrollable fixed costs of $1 million, and untraceable costs of $500,000. The accounting manager has supplied you with these data and asked you to come up with the controllable margin, total contribution, CPC, and operating income.

## Exercises

[LO 18-1]   18-23   **Risk Aversion and Decision Making**   John Smith is the production manager of Elmo's Glue Company. Because of limited capacity, the company can produce only one of two possible products. The two products are:

a. A space-age bonding formula that has a 15% probability of making a profit of $1,000,000 for the company and an 85% chance of generating $200,000 in profit.

b. A reformulated household glue that has a 100% chance of making a profit of $310,000.

John gets a bonus of 20% of the profit from his department. John has the responsibility to choose between the two products. Assume John is more risk-averse than the top management of Elmo's Glue Company.

**Required**
1. Which product will John choose? Why?
2. Is this the product Elmo's would choose? Why or why not? Assume the company is risk-neutral.
3. How can Elmo's change its reward system to have John consistently make decisions which are consistent with top management's wishes?

[LO 18-1]   18-24   **Risk Aversion; Strategy**   John Holt is the production supervisor for ITEXX, a manufacturer of plastic parts with customers in the automobile and consumer products industries. On a Tuesday morning, one of ITEXX's sales managers has just asked John to reschedule his manufacturing jobs for the rest of the week to accommodate a special order from a new customer. The catch is that getting the customer requires fast turn-around on the order and would mean not only delaying the current production schedule, but in addition running the production equipment all three shifts for the remainder of the week. This would make it impossible to complete the regularly scheduled maintenance on the equipment that John had planned for midweek. The sales manager is keen on getting the new customer, which could mean an important increase in overall sales and output at the plant. However, John is worried not only about the delay of the current jobs, but the chance that the delay in maintenance will cause one of the machines to fail, which would back up the orders in the plant for at least a week, meaning a substantial delay for the new order as well as those currently scheduled.

**Required**   Explain how you think John should resolve this problem. What would be a good policy for handling issues like this in the future?

[LO 18-1]    18-25 **Research and Development: Risk Aversion and Performance Measurement**    As the economic outlook in many countries becomes uncertain, some managers look to cut costs in research and development to provide a short-term boost to profits. The problem with this strategy is that it reduces the opportunities for new products and product improvements in the coming years, which are necessary for the long-term competitiveness of the firm. As Intel Chairman Craig Barrett says, "You cut off your future if you do not invest."

**Required**

1. What role does risk aversion play in determining the amount to invest in research and development on an ongoing basis? How might a firm manage risk aversion so as to continue the desired level of spending on research and development?

2. What type of strategic business unit would you choose to evaluate the performance of the research and development department? Explain your choice briefly.

[LO 18-2]    18-26 **Leadership Development**    Training courses and other forms of professional development are commonly used by organizations to improve managers' effectiveness in leading teams, providing the desired motivation to their employees, and leading their SBUs to success. Often these training efforts are designed to develop effective leadership behaviors. For example, a study done within Google identified the following eight behaviors of effective managers:

- Be a good coach
- Empower your team and do not micromanage
- Express interest in team members' success and personal well-being
- Be productive and results-oriented
- Be a good communicator and listen to your team
- Help your employees with career development
- Have a clear strategy for the team
- Develop and maintain key technical skills needed by all team members

**Required**    For each of the eight desired behaviors, develop one or two examples of that behavior. For example, providing constructive feedback is a behavior that a good coach would employ.

[LO 18-3]    18-27 **Departmental Cost Allocation in Profit Centers**    Elvis Wilbur owns two restaurants, the Beef Barn and the Fish Bowl. Each restaurant is treated as a profit center for performance evaluation. Although the restaurants have separate kitchens, they share a central baking facility. The principal costs of the baking area include depreciation and maintenance on the equipment, materials, supplies, and labor.

**Required**

1. Elvis allocates the monthly costs of the baking facility to the two restaurants based on the number of tables served in each restaurant during the month. In April the costs were $24,000, of which $12,000 is fixed cost. The Beef Barn and the Fish Bowl each served 3,000 tables. How much of the joint cost should be allocated to each restaurant?

2. In May total fixed and unit variable costs remained the same, but the Beef Barn served 2,000 tables and the Fish Bowl served 3,000. How much should be allocated to each restaurant? Explain your reasoning.

[LO 18-3]    18-28 **Allocation of Marketing and Administrative Costs; Profit SBUs**    Chilton Day School allocates marketing and administrative costs to its three schools based on total annual tuition revenue for the schools. In 2012 the allocations (000s omitted) were as follows:

|  | Preschool | Middle School | High School | Total |
|---|---|---|---|---|
| Tuition revenue | $1,500 | $1,800 | $2,200 | $5,500 |
| Marketing and administration | 275 | 325 | 400 | 1,000 |

In 2013, the middle and high schools experienced no change in revenues, but the preschool's tuition revenue increased to $1.9 million. Marketing and administrative costs rose to $1,250,000.

**Required**

1. Using revenue as an allocation base, how should the costs be allocated for 2013?

2. What are the shortcomings of this allocation formula?

[LO 18-3]  18-29  **Allocation of Administrative Costs**   Wical Rental Management Services manages four apartment buildings, each with a different owner. Wical's top management has observed that the apartment buildings with more expensive rental rates tend to require more of her time and also the time of her staff. The four apartment buildings incur a total annual operating expense of $7,345,733, and these operating expenses are traced directly to the apartment buildings for the purpose of determining the profit earned by the building owners. The annual management fee that Wical earns is based on a percentage of total annual operating expenses and is negotiated each year. For the current year the fee rate is 6%, and Wical has the following information for current year average rental rates and occupancy rates.

| Apartment Complex | Number of Units | Average Occupancy | Average Rent |
|---|---|---|---|
| Cape Point | 100 | 88.0% | $1,895 |
| Whispering Woods | 250 | 77.0 | 1,295 |
| Hanging Rock | 200 | 72.0 | 995 |
| College Manor | 350 | 82.0 | 895 |
| Total | 900 | | |

**Required**
1. For the current year, Wical must choose between the number of units in each complex, the average occupancy, or the total annual rental revenue in each complex to allocate the management fee. Explain your choice of method and show how much of the management fee would be allocated to each apartment building using your method.
2. What ethical issues, if any, are involved in the choice of method in requirement 1?

[LO 18-3]  18-30  **Responsibility for Inefficiency; Ethics**   General Hospital leases its diagnostic equipment from Normed Leasing, which is also responsible for maintaining the equipment. Recently the hospital's MRI machine needed repair and physicians were required to order expensive nonemergency laboratory tests for their patients to diagnose conditions that could have been diagnosed more easily (and less expensively) using the MRI machine. Rather than bill its patients for the entire costs of these tests, the hospital billed the patients for the cost of an MRI and billed the difference to Normed. Normed disputes the charge, claiming that the physicians should have postponed diagnosis of the patients' conditions until the MRI machine could be repaired.

**Required**   What issues should be addressed to determine how the charge should be handled properly? How can this situation be prevented? If appropriate, include ethical issues in your response.

[LO 18-3]  18-31  **Assigning Responsibility**   Kristen Langdon, the sales manager at a large bicycle manufacturer, has secured an order from a major department store that is due to ship on November 1. She is eager to please the department store in the hope of getting more future business. She asks Bryan Collins, the company's purchasing agent, to procure all necessary parts in time for production to begin on October 10. Bryan orders the parts from reputable suppliers, and most of them arrive by October 7. George Watkins, the production manager, begins production as scheduled on October 10, although the gears that Bryan ordered were delayed because of quality control problems at the manufacturer. Bryan assures George that the gear shipment will arrive before October 16 when those parts are scheduled to be attached to the bicycles. The shipment finally arrives on October 18 after production has been delayed for two days.

**Required**   Which department should bear the responsibility for the two days' downtime? How can similar problems be avoided in the future?

[LO 18-3]  18-32  **Outsourcing; Choice of Strategic Business Unit**   The management of office printing, duplicating, filing, and overall document storage is one of the most significant overhead costs in many companies, especially companies with large and complex product lines and/or a diverse customer base, such as the large consumer products company, Procter & Gamble (P&G). Increasingly, companies like P&G are outsourcing their overall document management activity to service providers such as Xerox, Hewlett-Packard (HP), or Canon. Xerox and HP provide the equipment, materials, and labor for the activity in what is often called "managed print services" (MPS). MPS has reduced P&G's costs significantly and also provides P&G an opportunity to better focus its efforts on strategic marketing and operational matters.

**Required**

1. What type of SBU was probably used by P&G to manage print services prior to outsourcing? What type of responsibility accounting is probably being used by P&G now, after outsourcing? Explain briefly.

2. How would the decision to outsource print services affect the sustainability objectives of a firm such as Procter & Gamble?

[LO 18-3]    18-33 **Outsourcing; Link to Strategy**  Walmart's Sam's Club has recently outsourced 10,000 jobs (about 9% of Sam's Club's workforce) to independent marketing firms. The marketing firms provide in-store product demonstrations. Most of the 10,000 jobs were part-time jobs. Industry analysts say the change was a smart move because it allowed Sam's Club to focus on other key strategic issues and to eliminate a significant portion of the high costs associated with training, hiring, and managing a part-time workforce.

**Required**

1. What type of strategy do you think Sam's Club follows, cost leadership or differentiation, and why?

2. Do you think Sam's Club's decision to outsource the product-demonstration activity is consistent with the firm's strategy? Explain briefly.

[LO 18-3]    18-34 **Cost Allocation; Sharing Cab Fare**  Suppose there are three passengers sharing a single cab ride and that passenger A's usual fare to his destination would be $12, passenger B's usual fare to her destination would be $18, and passenger C's fare would be $30. Since they are sharing the cab, and assuming no surcharge, the total cab fare is $30, rather than the $60 they would have had to pay in total individually. So there is a $30 saving to sharing the cab.

**Required**   How would you split up the total cost of the cab fare among passengers A, B, and C?

[LO 18-3, 18-5]    18-35 **Intangibles; Validating the Balanced Scorecard**  Today intangibles, such as customer relationships, account for more than half of total assets of firms in the United States though such intangibles are not recorded on the firm's balance sheet under current U.S. accounting standards. The importance of nonfinancial measures is one of the motivations for the increased use of the balanced scorecard, which includes a perspective on customer relationships. However, according to a 2005 research study, data on intangibles such as customer satisfaction can yield significant forecasts of earnings only when the data are analyzed in conjunction with financial statistics and only when tied to corporate strategy. This result is based on a wide range of customer relationship data (e.g., customer satisfaction, employee turnover, the speed of loan processing, and the average number of products and services purchased) from 115 retail banks and represents potentially useful guidance for managers wanting to know how to use nonfinancial measures effectively.

**Required**   Comment on the implications of the study for the use of the balanced scorecard relative to profit centers. We have noted in the text that it is important to validate the balanced scorecard. What does it mean to validate the scorecard in the context of the retail bank example above?

[LO 18-3]    18-36 **Managing the Research and Development Department**  Effective use of research and development (R&D) is an important part of any firm's competitive strategy. Some firms take an "incrementalist" approach to R&D, continually striving to add value to their products and services. Other firms take a quite different approach by looking only for "breakthrough" results from R&D. The breakthrough results are those that fundamentally change the nature of the products, the services, and the competition in the industry. An example of a breakthrough result is General Electric's digital X-ray technology, first sold in 1996, which uses digital imaging to replace the conventional film-based technology. Other examples include Apple's iPhone and Toyota's hybrid vehicles.

Many firms employ both strategies: one R&D department uses the incrementalist approach that focuses on continually improving existing products and another R&D department uses the breakthrough approach that develops fundamental changes. The incrementalist R&D projects help to keep the current product lines competitive while the breakthrough projects hold the promise of a successful future.

**Required**   Describe what type of SBU you would recommend for each of the two types of research and development departments and explain why.

[LO 18-3]    18-37 **Financial Reporting and SBU Performance**  Samentech Inc. operates in the highly competitive agribusiness industry. Recently, rising fuel costs have added a significant financial burden to day-to-day operations, and top management has become increasingly concerned about the financial performance of several of its business units. Business unit performance and the performance of the unit managers is evaluated using the financial information in the "Segment Reporting" section of Samentech's annual report. Samentech uses this approach to evaluation because it knows that the information is audited and therefore accurate.

Some key executives have noticed that many business unit leaders seem unwilling to cooperate and coordinate with other business units; difficulties have arisen, for example, in convincing unit managers to share certain services when the result would be to reduce total costs to the company. A recent example is the failure of the unit managers to agree to share the services of an insurance firm that offered lower rates if all units used the same insurance policy; some unit managers wanted to maintain individual insurance coverage for their units so that they had maximum flexibility in choosing the terms of the coverage.

Moreover, the financial performance of many units and for Samentech overall has been behind industry averages, and the firm's stock price has been declining as well. These issues were largely ignored in recent years because there were "more important issues" at hand. But the pace of decline in stock price has alarmed Frank Ramirez, the CFO of Samentech Inc., who believes that the lackluster performance of many of the business units may be due to inadequacies in the company's performance measurement system.

**Required**  Mr. Ramirez asks you to help him prepare a report for top management in which you:
1. Explain why Samentech Inc. should or should not use information from the company's annual financial report to evaluate leaders of business units.
2. Provide a proposed new evaluation plan for business unit leaders.
3. Explain the long-term benefits Samentech Inc. could gain if it adopts a more effective evaluation strategy for its business unit leaders.

[LO 18-3]  18-38  **Financial Incentives and Auto Repair/Inspections Companies**  Some states in the United States are finding increased pressure from citizen groups and other organizations to increase efforts to reduce carbon emissions. One of the key producers of carbon emissions is the automobile, so that some states have become more strict in implementing auto inspection procedures that include compliance with emissions standards. The goal is to reduce emissions overall in the vehicles operating in the state. Some environmental groups that support the emissions tests have suggested that the financial incentive for those inspecting vehicles is to be strict with the testing because any failed tests would require some repair that could then be performed by the inspector. However, recent research shows the unexpected—the Environmental Protection Agency (EPA) estimates that approximately 50% of inspections for which the vehicle fails to comply with state-level emission standards are allowed to pass the inspection without the repair needed for compliance. In most states, vehicle inspections are performed by auto mechanics, auto dealers, and other companies that repair autos.

**Required**  Develop a brief explanation of the finding that many inspections are not in compliance with state standards. What incentives are necessary to improve the rate of compliance? Are there ethical issues you identified in developing your answer? Are there sustainability issues you identified in developing your answer?

[LO 18-3]  18-39  **Allocation of Central Costs; Profit Centers**  Woodland Hotels, Inc., operates four resorts in the heavily wooded areas of northern California. The resorts are named after the predominant trees at the resort: Pine Valley, Oak Glen, Mimosa, and Birch Glen. Woodland allocates its central office costs to each of the four resorts according to the annual revenue the resort generates. For the current year, the central office costs (000s omitted) were as follows:

| | |
|---|---:|
| Front office personnel (desk, clerks, etc.) | $ 8,000 |
| Administrative and executive salaries | 4,000 |
| Interest on resort purchase | 3,000 |
| Advertising | 600 |
| Housekeeping | 2,000 |
| Depreciation on reservations computer | 80 |
| Room maintenance | 800 |
| Carpet-cleaning contract | 50 |
| Contract to repaint rooms | 400 |
| | $18,930 |

| | Pine Valley | Oak Glen | Mimosa | Birch Glen | Total |
|---|---|---|---|---|---|
| Revenue (000s) | $ 5,350 | $ 7,995 | $ 8,857 | $ 6,550 | $ 28,752 |
| Square feet | 55,475 | 76,599 | 41,774 | 83,664 | 257,512 |
| Rooms | 86 | 122 | 66 | 174 | 448 |
| Assets (000s) | $92,345 | $136,745 | $72,355 | $57,499 | $358,944 |

**Required**

1. Based on annual revenue, what amount of the central office costs are allocated to each resort? What are the shortcomings of this allocation method?

2. Suppose that the current method were replaced with a system of four separate cost pools with costs collected in the four pools allocated on the basis of revenues, assets invested in each resort, square footage, and number of rooms, respectively. Which costs should be collected in each of the four pools?

3. Using the cost pool system in requirement 2, how much of the central office costs would be allocated to each resort? Is this system preferable to the single-allocation base system used in requirement 1? Why or why not?

[LO 18-3, 18-4]  18-40  **Profit Centers: Comparison of Variable and Full Costing**  Yale Company manufactures hair brushes that sell at wholesale for $3 per unit. The company had no beginning inventory in 2012. These data summarize the 2012 and 2013 operations:

| | 2012 | 2013 |
|---|---|---|
| Sales | 1,800 units | 2,200 units |
| Production | 2,000 units | 2,000 units |
| Production cost | | |
|   Factory—variable (per unit) | $0.60 | $0.60 |
|     —fixed | $1,000 | $1,000 |
| Marketing—variable | $.40 | $.40 |
| Administrative—fixed | $500 | $500 |

**Required**

1. Prepare an income statement for each year based on full costing.

2. Prepare an income statement for each year based on variable costing.

3. Prepare a reconciliation and explanation of the difference each year in the operating income resulting from using the full-costing method and variable-costing method.

[LO 18-3, 18-4]  18-41  **Full versus Variable Costing**  Security Technology Inc. (STI) is a manufacturer of an electronic control system used in the manufacture of certain special-duty auto transmissions used primarily for police and military applications. The part sells for $55 per unit and had sales of 24,000 units in the current year, 2012. STI has no inventory on hand at the beginning of 2012 and is projecting sales of 26,000 units in 2013. STI is planning the same production level for 2013 as in 2012, 25,000 units. The variable manufacturing costs for STI are $16 and the variable selling costs are only $.50 per unit. The fixed manufacturing costs are $200,000 per year and the fixed selling costs are $500 per year.

**Required**

1. Prepare an income statement for 2012 and 2013 using full costing.

2. Prepare an income statement for 2012 and 2013 using variable costing.

3. Prepare a reconciliation and explanation of the difference each year in the operating income resulting from the full- and variable-costing methods.

[LO 18-3, 18-4]  18-42  **Profit Centers: Comparison of Variable and Full Costing (Underapplied Overhead)**  Mark Hancock, Inc., manufactures a specialized surgical instrument called the HAN-20. The firm has grown rapidly in recent years because of the product's low price and high quality. However, sales have declined this year due primarily to increased competition and a decrease in the surgical procedures for which the HAN-20 is used. The firm is concerned about the decline in sales and has hired a consultant to analyze the firm's profitability. The consultant has provided the following information:

| | 2012 | 2013 |
|---|---|---|
| Sales (units) | 3,200 | 2,800 |
| Production | 3,800 | 2,300 |
| Budgeted production and sales | 4,000 | 3,400 |
| Beginning inventory | 800 | 1,400 |

| Data per unit (all variable) | | |
| --- | --- | --- |
| Price | $2,095 | $1,995 |
| Direct materials and labor | 1,200 | 1,200 |
| Selling costs | 125 | 125 |
| Fixed costs | | |
| Manufacturing overhead | $700,000 | $595,000 |
| Selling and administrative | 120,000 | 120,000 |

Hancock explained to the consultant that the unfavorable economic climate in 2012 and 2013 had caused the firm to reduce its price and production levels and reduce its fixed manufacturing costs in response to the decline in sales. Even with the price reduction there was a decline in sales in both 2012 and 2013. This led to an increase in inventory in 2012, which the firm was able to reduce in 2013 by further reducing the level of production. In both years Hancock's actual production was less than the budgeted level so that the overhead rate for fixed overhead, calculated from budgeted production levels, was too low and a production volume variance was calculated to adjust cost of goods sold for the underapplied fixed overhead (the calculation of the production volume variance is explained fully in Chapter 15, and reviewed briefly below).

The production volume variance for 2012 was determined from the fixed overhead rate of $175 per unit ($700,000/4,000 budgeted units). Since the actual production level was 200 units short of the budgeted level in 2012 (4,000 − 3,800), the amount of the production volume variance in 2012 was 200 × $175 = $35,000. The production volume variance is underapplied (since actual production level is less than budgeted) and is therefore added back to cost of goods sold to determine the amount of cost of goods sold in the full-cost income statement. The full-cost income statement for 2012 is shown below:

| | | |
| --- | --- | --- |
| Sales | | $6,704,000 |
| Cost of goods sold: | | |
| Beginning inventory | $1,100,000 | |
| Cost of goods produced | 5,225,000 | |
| Cost of goods available for sale | $6,325,000 | |
| Less ending inventory | 1,925,000 | |
| Cost of goods sold: | | $4,400,000 |
| Plus underapplied production volume variance | | 35,000 |
| Adjusted cost of goods sold | | $4,435,000 |
| Gross margin | | $2,269,000 |
| Less selling and administrative costs | | |
| Variable | $ 400,000 | |
| Fixed | 120,000 | 520,000 |
| Operating income | | $1,749,000 |

**Required**

1. Using the full-cost method, prepare the income statements for 2013.

2. Using variable costing, prepare an income statement for each period, and explain the difference in operating income from that obtained in requirement 1.

3. Write a brief memo to the firm to explain the difference in operating income between variable costing and full costing.

[LO 18-5]   18-43  **Balanced Scorecard**

**Required**   Prepare Problem 2-35.

[LO 18-5]   18-44  **Balanced Scorecard**

**Required**   Prepare Problem 2-39.

[LO 18-5]   18-45  **Balanced Scorecard**

**Required**   Prepare Problem 2-43.

## Problems

[LO 18-3, 18-5]   18-46   **Profit Center Limitations**   Kenneth Merchant and Tatiana Sandino summarize clearly some of the potential limitations of profit center evaluation in the article, "Four Options for Measuring Value Creation" (*Journal of Accountancy,* August 2009, pp. 34–37). While profit centers are commonly used, these limitations are well known. Here are two of the most prominent.

1. Profit is a measure of past performance and not a measure of past or future value creation; that is, profit does not directly measure the improvement or decline in the market value of the company. The value of a public or privately held company can be measured in a variety of ways (see Chapter 20).

2. Profit as determined by U.S.-based generally accepted accounting principles (GAAP) is conservatively biased; for example, GAAP tends to use valuations based on purchase cost rather than current market values (note the section in this chapter in which we discuss international financial reporting standards (IFRS), which permit market value accounting in some situations where this treatment is not permitted under GAAP).

Merchant and Sandino propose four approaches to improving the profit center approach for strategic performance measurement:

1. Use market measures of value creation, such as stock price among others.

2. Use non-GAAP alternative measures of profit that reduce the conservative bias. Some of these measures, such as EVA®, are explained in Chapter 19.

3. Use a measure of profit that extends beyond the usual quarterly or annual statements; instead, look for long-term profit performance over 3 to 6 years or more.

4. Use a combination of measures. The balanced scorecard is one example of this approach.

### Required

1. Do you agree with Merchant and Sandino's assessment of the limitations of profit center measurement? Explain briefly.

2. Do you think the authors' proposals for improvement are practical and potentially effective?

[LO 18-3]   18-47   **Contribution Income Statement; Spreadsheet Application**   High Fashion Inc. is an upscale clothing store in New York City and London. Each store has two main departments, Men's Apparel and Women's Apparel. Marie Phelps, High Fashion's CFO, wants to use strategic performance measurement to better understand the company's financial results. She has decided to use the profit center method to measure performance and has gathered the following information about the two stores and the two departments of the New York City store:

| | |
|---|---|
| Total net sales | $3,250,000 |
| Fixed costs | |
| Partly traceable and controllable | 250,000 |
| Partly traceable but noncontrollable | 180,000 |
| Nontraceable costs | 65,000 |
| Total net sales (percent) | |
| London Store | 40% |
| New York Store | 60 |
| New York—Men's Apparel | 40 |
| New York—Women's Apparel | 60 |
| Cost of goods sold—variable (percent of sales) | |
| London Store | 55% |
| New York—Men's Apparel | 40 |
| New York—Women's Apparel | 60 |
| Variable operating costs (percent of sales) | |
| London Store | 36% |
| New York—Men's Apparel | 22 |
| New York—Women's Apparel | 32 |
| Fixed controllable costs—partly traceable (percent of total) | |
| London Store | 40% |
| New York total | 40 |
| Men's Apparel | 45 |
| Women's Apparel | 40 |
| Could not be traced to Men's or Women's Apparel | 15 |
| Could not be traced to London or New York | 20 |

| Fixed noncontrollable costs—partly traceable (percent of total) | |
| --- | --- |
| London Store | 50% |
| New York total | 40 |
|    Men's Apparel | 30 |
|    Women's Apparel | 10 |
|    Could not be traced to Men's or Women's Apparel | 60 |
|    Could not be traced to London or New York | 10 |

**Required**

1. Using this information, prepare a contribution income statement for High Fashion, showing contribution margin, controllable margin, and contribution by profit center (CPC) for both the London and New York stores and for both departments of the New York store. Using Excel is highly recommended for this problem; Excel can improve accuracy and allows for easy assessment of changed assumptions.

2. What are the global issues that are an important part of the profit center evaluation for High Fashion Inc.?

[LO 18-3]  18-48  **Allocating the Costs of the Legal Department**  Most large companies have an in-house legal staff that helps the company deal with current and pending legal matters. Often the legal staff's efforts are assisted by outside counsel, especially when specialized technical issues are involved. The legal department is growing in importance for some firms, as the firms attempt to deal with new government regulations. For management accountants, the regulatory changes have been dramatic as a result of the Sarbanes-Oxley Act of 2002, which increased the responsibilities of financial managers in publicly held firms. One portion of the act, for example, requires a company to maintain a code of ethics.

**Required**  Most companies allocate the cost of legal services to their SBUs on the basis of some measure of size, such as the total assets or total revenues of the SBU. What is the likely effect of this allocation approach on the desired motivation and behavior within the SBUs? What approach would you propose for allocating legal costs, and why?

[LO 18-3, 18-5]  18-49  **Validating the Balanced Scorecard; Spreadsheet Application**  Bernard Daisy Inc. is a chain of home supply and gardening product stores. In 2013, Daisy adopted the balanced scorecard (BSC) for evaluation of store and store manager performance. The BSC has helped Daisy to identify the critical success factors for sales and profitability. In particular, it has helped Daisy better understand its competitive environment and the drivers of success in that environment. On the advice of its chief financial officer, Daisy's board has requested that the company president conduct a study to validate the balanced scorecard. The objective of the study is to make sure that the scorecard measures being used are in fact the key measures associated with success. The following data have been obtained for the most recent quarter's results for each of the company's 30 stores, listed in order of when the store was opened (the most recent is store 30). There are five district managers, each of whom is responsible for six of the stores. In this study a store manager's success is measured by increase in sales of each store for the current quarter over the same quarter last year. The data below include the percentage change in sales and four of the measures included in the customer perspective of the company's BSC. The scorecard measures include:

1. A survey of customers; this measure is taken from a survey form that is handed to customers on a random basis as they leave the store. The customers rate the store's performance on a scale of 0 to 100, where 100 is the highest score.

2. Each district manager evaluates each store once a quarter, using also a scale from 0 to 100, where 100 is the highest score.

3. The district managers have a staff that on a random basis measures the wait time in the check-out line for customers in each store. The figures shown here are the average wait times, in seconds, for the samples taken in the most recent quarter.

4. Average number of store employees who have had one or more of the company's in-house training courses in the past quarter, as a proportion of total employees at the store.

**Required**

1. Briefly compare the benefits of the profit center approach relative to the balanced scorecard.

2. Use regression or correlation analysis in Excel to analyze the validity of the four scorecard measures in the customer perspective of the BSC; here validity means that the BSC measure contributes to an increase in sales over the prior quarter. What conclusions can you draw from your analysis?

| Store Number | Sales | Survey | Manager Review | Average Wait Time | Employee Training |
|---|---|---|---|---|---|
| 1 | −18.1% | 65 | 33 | 95 | 56 |
| 2 | −13.3 | 54 | 54 | 92 | 30 |
| 3 | 0.5 | 72 | 86 | 81 | 45 |
| 4 | −9.8 | 50 | 94 | 89 | 60 |
| 5 | −4.5 | 53 | 40 | 85 | 75 |
| 6 | 0.0 | 57 | 86 | 81 | 50 |
| 7 | 7.5 | 61 | 80 | 75 | 45 |
| 8 | 15.5 | 67 | 74 | 69 | 88 |
| 9 | 20.6 | 70 | 70 | 80 | 90 |
| 10 | 31.5 | 79 | 61 | 71 | 60 |
| 11 | 35.0 | 81 | 88 | 68 | 30 |
| 12 | 12.5 | 64 | 76 | 80 | 18 |
| 13 | −2.6 | 54 | 38 | 83 | 33 |
| 14 | 3.5 | 59 | 27 | 78 | 48 |
| 15 | 20.6 | 71 | 70 | 65 | 63 |
| 16 | 7.8 | 62 | 80 | 75 | 78 |
| 17 | 14.5 | 66 | 43 | 69 | 93 |
| 18 | 20.0 | 71 | 70 | 65 | 55 |
| 19 | 29.4 | 77 | 63 | 58 | 39 |
| 20 | 39.4 | 84 | 55 | 50 | 67 |
| 21 | 45.7 | 88 | 49 | 59 | 34 |
| 22 | 59.4 | 84 | 87 | 49 | 78 |
| 23 | 63.8 | 89 | 56 | 45 | 48 |
| 24 | 35.6 | 81 | 58 | 62 | 36 |
| 25 | 5.2 | 60 | 82 | 77 | 51 |
| 26 | 11.8 | 64 | 77 | 72 | 66 |
| 27 | 30.7 | 77 | 62 | 57 | 81 |
| 28 | 7.8 | 77 | 73 | 68 | 96 |
| 29 | 15.1 | 73 | 67 | 62 | 57 |
| 30 | 24.8 | 77 | 62 | 57 | 36 |

[LO 18-3]   18-50  **Contribution Income Statement for Profit Centers; Strategy, International**   Stratford Corporation is a diversified company whose products are marketed both domestically and internationally. Its major product lines are pharmaceutical products, sports equipment, and household appliances. At a recent meeting, Stratford's board of directors had a lengthy discussion on ways to improve overall corporate profitability without new acquisitions. New acquisitions are problematic because the company already has a lot of debt. The board members decided that they needed additional financial information about individual corporate operations to target areas for improvement. Dave Murphy, Stratford's controller, has been asked to provide additional data to assist the board in its investigation. Stratford is not a public company and, therefore, has not prepared complete income statements by product line. Dave has regularly prepared an income statement by product line through contribution margin. However, he now believes that income statements prepared through operating income along both product lines and geographic areas would provide the directors with the required insight into corporate operations. Dave has the following data available:

| | Product Lines | | | |
|---|---|---|---|---|
| | Pharmaceutical | Sports | Appliances | Total |
| Production/Sales in units | 160,000 | 180,000 | 160,000 | 500,000 |
| Average selling price per unit | $8.00 | $20.00 | $15.00 | |
| Average variable manufacturing cost per unit | 4.00 | 9.50 | 8.25 | |
| Average variable selling expense per unit | 2.00 | 2.50 | 2.25 | |
| Fixed factory overhead excluding depreciation | | | | $ 500,000 |
| Depreciation of plant and equipment | | | | 400,000 |
| Administrative and selling expense | | | | 1,160,000 |

Dave had several discussions with the division managers from each product line and compiled this information:

* The division managers concluded that Dave should allocate fixed factory overhead on the basis of the ratio of the variable costs per product line or per geographic area to total variable costs.

- Each division manager agreed that a reasonable basis for the allocation of depreciation on plant and equipment would be the ratio of units produced per product line or per geographic area to the total number of units produced.
- There was little agreement on the allocation of administrative and selling expenses, so Dave decided to allocate only those expenses that were directly traceable to the SBU; that is, manufacturing staff salaries to product lines and sales staff salaries to geographic areas. He used these data for this allocation:

| Manufacturing Staff | | Sales Staff | |
|---|---|---|---|
| Pharmaceutical | $120,000 | United States | $ 60,000 |
| Sports | 140,000 | Canada | 100,000 |
| Appliances | 80,000 | Europe | 250,000 |

- The division managers provided reliable sales percentages for their product lines by geographic area:

| | Percentage of Unit Sales | | |
|---|---|---|---|
| | United States | Canada | Europe |
| Pharmaceutical | 40% | 10% | 50% |
| Sports | 40 | 40 | 20 |
| Appliances | 20 | 20 | 60 |

Dave prepared this product-line income statement:

### STRATFORD CORPORATION
#### Statement of Income by Product Lines
#### For the Fiscal Year Ended April 30, 2013

| | Product Lines | | | | |
|---|---|---|---|---|---|
| | Pharmaceutical | Sports | Appliances | Unallocated | Total |
| Sales in units | 160,000 | 180,000 | 160,000 | | 500,000 |
| Sales | $1,280,000 | $3,600,000 | $2,400,000 | — | $7,280,000 |
| Variable manufacturing and selling costs | 960,000 | 2,160,000 | 1,680,000 | — | 4,800,000 |
| Contribution margin | $ 320,000 | $1,440,000 | $ 720,000 | — | $2,480,000 |
| Fixed costs | | | | | |
| Fixed factory overhead | $ 100,000 | $ 225,000 | $ 175,000 | — | $500,000 |
| Depreciation | 128,000 | 144,000 | 128,000 | — | 400,000 |
| Administrative and selling expense | 120,000 | 140,000 | 80,000 | $ 820,000 | 1,160,000 |
| Total fixed costs | $ 348,000 | $ 509,000 | $ 383,000 | $ 820,000 | $2,060,000 |
| Operating income (loss) | $ (28,000) | $ 931,000 | $ 337,000 | $(820,000) | $ 420,000 |

### Required

1. Prepare a contribution income statement for Stratford Corporation based on the company's geographic areas of sales.
2. As a result of the information disclosed by both income statements (by product line and by geographic area), recommend areas on which Stratford Corporation should focus its attention to improve corporate profitability.
3. What changes would you make to Stratford's strategic performance measurement system? Include the role, if any, of the firm's international business operations in your response.

**(CMA Adapted)**

[LO 18-3] 18-51 **Centralization versus Decentralization: Banking** RNB is a bank holding company for a state-wide group of retail consumer-oriented banks. RNB was formed in the early 1960s by investors who believed in a high level of consumer services. The number of banks owned by the holding company expanded rapidly. These banks gained visibility because of their experimentation with innovations such as free-standing 24-hour automated teller machines, automated funds transfer systems, and other advances in banking services.

RNB's earnings performance has been better than that of most other banks in the state. The founders organized RNB and continue to operate it on a highly decentralized basis. As the number of banks owned has increased, RNB's executive management has delegated more responsibility and authority to individual bank presidents, who are considered to be representatives of executive management. Although certain aspects of each bank's operations are standardized (such as procedures for account and loan applications and salary rates), bank presidents have significant autonomy in determining how each bank will operate.

The decentralization has led each bank to develop individual marketing campaigns. Several of them have introduced unique "packaged" accounts that include a combination of banking services; however, they sometimes fail to notify the other banks in the group as well as the executive office of these campaigns. One result has been interbank competition for customers where the market overlaps. The corporate marketing officer had also recently begun a statewide advertising campaign that conflicted with some of the individual banks' advertising. Consequently, customers and tellers have occasionally experienced both confusion and frustration, particularly when the customers attempt to receive services at a bank other than their "home" bank.

RNB's executive management is concerned that earnings will decline for the first time in its history. The decline appears to be attributable to reduced customer satisfaction and higher operating costs. The competition among the banks in the state is keen. Bank location and consistent high-quality customer service are important. RNB's 18 banks are well located, and the three new bank acquisitions planned for next year are considered to be in prime locations. The increase in operating costs appears to be directly related to the individual banks' aggressive marketing efforts and new programs. Specifically, expenditures increased for advertising and for the special materials and added personnel related to the "packaged" accounts.

For the past three months RNB's executive management has been meeting with the individual bank presidents to review RNB's recent performance and seek ways to improve it. One recommendation that appeals to executive management is to make the organization's structure more centralized. The specific proposal calls for reducing individual bank autonomy and creating a centralized individual bank management committee of all bank presidents to be chaired by a newly created position, vice president of bank operations. The individual banks' policies would be set by consensus of the committee to conform to overall RNB plans.

**Required**

1. Discuss the advantages of a decentralized organizational structure.

2. Identify disadvantages of a decentralized structure. Support each disadvantage with an example from RNB's situation.

3. Do you think the proposed more centralized structure is in the strategic best interests of RNB? Why or why not?

**(CMA Adapted)**

[LO 18-3, 18-5]    18-52    **Balanced Scorecard; Strategic Business Units; Ethics**    Pittsburgh-Walsh Company, Inc. (PWC), manufactures lighting fixtures and electronic timing devices. The lighting fixtures division assembles units for the upscale and mid-range markets. The trend in recent years as the economy has been expanding is for sales in the upscale market to increase while those in the mid-range market have been relatively flat. Over the years, PWC has tried to maintain strong positions in both markets, believing it is best to offer customers a broad range of products to protect the company against a sharp decline in either market. PWC has never been the first to introduce new products but watches its competitors closely and quickly follows their lead with comparable products. PWC is proud of its customer service functions, which have been able to maintain profitable relationships with several large customers over the years.

The electronic timing devices division manufactures instrument panels that allow electronic systems to be activated and deactivated at scheduled times for both efficiency and safety purposes. Both divisions operate in the same manufacturing facilities and share production equipment.

PWC's budget for the year ending December 31, 2013, follows; it was prepared on a business unit basis under the following guidelines:

- Variable expenses are directly assigned to the division that incurs them.

- Traceable fixed overhead expenses are directly assigned to the division that incurs them.

- Common fixed expenses are allocated to the divisions on the basis of units produced, which bears a close relationship to direct labor. Included in common fixed expenses are costs of the corporate staff, legal expenses, taxes, marketing staff, and advertising.

- The company plans to manufacture 8,000 upscale fixtures, 22,000 mid-range fixtures, and 20,000 electronic timing devices during 2013.

## PITTSBURGH-WALSH COMPANY, INC.
### Budget
### For the Year Ending December 31, 2013
### (amounts in thousands)

| | Lighting Fixtures Upscale | Lighting Fixtures Mid-Range | Electronic Timing Devices | Totals |
|---|---|---|---|---|
| Sales | $1,440 | $770 | $800 | $3,010 |
| Variable expenses | | | | |
| Cost of goods sold | 720 | 439 | 320 | 1,479 |
| Selling and admin. | 170 | 60 | 60 | 290 |
| Contribution margin | $ 550 | $271 | $420 | $1,241 |
| Fixed overhead | 140 | 80 | 80 | 300 |
| Divisional contribution | $ 410 | $191 | $340 | $ 941 |
| Common fixed expenses | | | | |
| Overhead | 48 | 132 | 120 | 300 |
| Selling and admin. | 11 | 31 | 28 | 70 |
| Operating Income | $ 351 | $ 28 | $192 | $ 571 |

PWC established a bonus plan for division management that provides a bonus for the manager if the division exceeds the planned product line income by 10% or more.

Shortly before the year began, Jack Parkow, the CEO, suffered a heart attack and retired. After reviewing the 2013 budget, Joe Kelly, the new CEO, decided to close the lighting fixtures mid-range product line by the end of the first quarter and use the available production capacity to grow the remaining two product lines. The marketing staff advised that electronic timing devices could grow by 40% with increased direct sales support. Increasing sales above that level and of upscale lighting fixtures would require expanded advertising expenditures to increase consumer awareness of PWC as an electronics and upscale lighting fixture company. Joe approved the increased sales support and advertising expenditures to achieve the revised plan. He advised the divisions that for bonus purposes, the original product-line income objectives must be met and that the lighting fixtures division could combine the income objectives for both product lines for bonus purposes.

Prior to the close of the fiscal year, the division controllers were given the following preliminary actual information to review and adjust as appropriate. These preliminary year-end data reflect the revised units of production amounting to 12,000 upscale fixtures, 4,000 mid-range fixtures, and 30,000 electronic timing devices.

## PITTSBURGH-WALSH COMPANY, INC.
### Preliminary Actual Information
### For the Year Ending December 2013
### (amounts in thousands)

| | Lighting Fixtures Upscale | Lighting Fixtures Mid-Range | Electronic Timing Devices | Totals |
|---|---|---|---|---|
| Sales | $2,160 | $140 | $1,200 | $3,500 |
| Variable expenses | | | | |
| Cost of goods sold | 1,080 | 80 | 480 | 1,640 |
| Selling and admin. | 260 | 11 | 96 | 367 |
| Contribution margin | $ 820 | $ 49 | $ 624 | $1,493 |
| Fixed overhead | 140 | 14 | 80 | 234 |
| Divisional contribution | $ 680 | $ 35 | $ 544 | $1,259 |
| Common fixed expenses | | | | |
| Overhead | 78 | 27 | 195 | 300 |
| Selling and admin. | 60 | 20 | 150 | 230 |
| Operating Income (loss) | $ 542 | $ (12) | $ 199 | $ 729 |

The controller of the lighting fixtures division, anticipating a similar bonus plan for 2014, is contemplating deferring some revenue into the next year on the pretext that the sales are not yet final and accruing, in the current year, expenditures that will be applicable to the first quarter of 2014. The corporation would meet its annual plan, and the division would exceed the 10% incremental bonus plateau in 2013 despite the deferred revenues and accrued expenses contemplated.

**Required**

1. Did the new CEO make the correct decision? Why or why not?

2. Outline the benefits that an organization realizes from profit center reporting, and evaluate profit center reporting on a variable-cost basis versus a full-cost basis.

3. Why would the management of the electronic timing devices division be unhappy with the current reporting? Should the current performance measurement system be revised?

4. Explain why the adjustments contemplated by the controller of the lighting fixtures division may or may not be unethical by citing specific standards in the Institute of Management Accountants' Standards of Ethical Conduct.

5. Develop a balanced scorecard for PWC, providing three to five perspectives and four to six measures of each perspective. Make sure your measures are quantifiable.

[LO 18-3]    18-53    **Profit Centers**    Charleston Manufacturing Company, a maker of building products for commercial and industrial construction, has four divisions: bathroom fixtures; roofing products; adhesives, paints, and other chemicals; and flooring. Each division is evaluated on its profit as determined by the annual financial report, and the profit figure is used to determine the division managers' compensation. After slow growth during a recent period of recession, the firm has begun to grow in both sales and profits in the past several months, but top management has observed that it is not growing as fast as other firms in the industry. The firm's CEO is concerned that it is losing ground in the industry at a time of improving opportunities. The CEO believes that the problem might be in the firm's performance measurement system and sets up a task force to determine how the firm should proceed.

**Required**    You are assigned to lead the task force. What are your suggestions for the CEO regarding Charleston's performance measurement system?

[LO 18-3]    18-54    **Choice of Strategic Business Unit**    Hamilton-Jones, a large consulting firm in Los Angeles, has experienced rapid growth over the last five years. To better serve its clients and to better manage its practice, the firm decided two years ago to organize into five strategic business units, each of which serves a significant base of clients: accounting systems, executive recruitment and compensation, client-server office information systems, manufacturing information systems, and real-estate consulting. Each SBU is served by a variety of administrative services within the firm, including payroll and accounting, printing and duplicating, report preparation, and secretarial support. Hamilton-Jones management closely watches the trend in the total costs for each administrative support area on a month-to-month basis. Management has noted that the costs in the printing and duplicating area have risen 40% over the last two years, a rate that is twice that of any other support area.

**Required**    Should Hamilton-Jones evaluate the five strategic business units as cost or profit centers? Why? How should the administrative support areas be evaluated?

[LO 18-3]    18-55    **Choice of Strategic Business Unit**    Martinsville Manufacturing Company develops parts for the automobile industry. The main product line is interior systems, especially seats and carpets. Martinsville operates in a single large plant that has 30 manufacturing units: carpet dyeing, seat frame fabrication, fabric cutting, and so on. In addition to the 30 manufacturing units, there are six manufacturing support departments: maintenance, engineering, janitorial, scheduling, materials receiving and handling, and information systems. The costs of the support departments are allocated to the 30 manufacturing units on the basis of direct labor cost, materials costs, or the square feet of floor space in the plant occupied by the unit. In the case of the maintenance department, the cost is allocated on the basis of square feet. Maintenance costs have been relatively stable in recent years, but the firm's accountant advises that the amount of maintenance cost is a little high relative to the industry average.

**Required**    What are the incentive effects of the current basis for allocating maintenance costs for the manufacturing units? What would be a more desirable way, if any, for allocating these costs? Explain your answer.

[LO 18-3]    18-56    **Design of Strategic Business Unit**    MetroBank is a fast-growing bank that serves the region around Jacksonville, Florida. The bank provides commercial and individual banking services, including investment and mortgage banking services. The firm's strategy is to continue to grow by acquiring smaller banks in the area to broaden the base and variety of services it can offer. The bank now has 87 strategic business units, which represent different areas of service in different locations. To support its growth, MetroBank has invested several million dollars in upgrading its information services function. The number of networked computers and of support personnel has more than doubled in the last four years and now accounts for 13% of total operating expenses. Two years ago, MetroBank decided to charge information services to the SBUs based on the head count (number of employees) in each SBU. Recently, some of the larger SBUs have complained that this method overcharges them and that some of the smaller SBUs are actually using a larger share of the total information services resources. MetroBank's controller has decided to investigate these complaints. His inquiry of the director of the information services department revealed that the larger departments generally use more services, but some small departments in fact kept him pretty busy. Based on this response, the controller is considering changing the charges for information services to the basis of actual service calls in each SBU rather than the head count.

**Required**    Is the information services department at MetroBank a profit center or a cost center? Which type of unit should it be, and why? Also, evaluate the controller's decision regarding the basis for charging information services costs to the SBUs.

[LO 18-3]    18-57    **Profit Centers: Hospitals**    Suburban General Hospital owns and operates several community hospitals in North Carolina. One of its hospitals, Cordona Community Hospital, is a not-for-profit institution that has not met its financial targets in the past several years because of decreasing volume. It has been losing market share largely because of the entrance of a new competitor, Jefferson Memorial Hospital. Jefferson has successfully promoted itself as the premier provider of quality care; its slogan is "Patients Come First." To compete with Jefferson, Cordona has developed a new department, guest services, to improve patient relations and overall customer service. Guest services personnel will be positioned throughout the hospital and at major entrances to help patients and their families get where they are going. Guest services will also be visible in the waiting rooms of high-volume areas such as cardiovascular services and women's services to help guide the patients throughout their visit. Cordona's management is wrestling with how to charge guest services to the various profit centers in the hospital.

**Required**    What are some different ways to allocate the guest service costs, and what would be the effect of each on the behavior of the managers of the different profit centers?

[LO 18-3, 18-5]    18-58    **Strategy; Balanced Scorecard**    WaveCrest Boats, Inc., located in Kinston, North Carolina, is a large manufacturer of sailboats. The company was founded by brothers Tom and Bill Green, who started it to combine their work and hobby, sailing. The Greens's boats are intended primarily for the first-time boat buyer and accordingly include a number of design features for ease of use. Some of WaveCrest's innovative designs have received the attention of other manufacturers in the industry and of sailing magazine editors. The intended market for the boats is the recreational boating enthusiast and sailing camps and clubs that are looking for a durable and easy-to-use boat.

The sailboat industry can be described as a very cyclical business and depends a great deal on overall economic conditions. Because most customers view sailing as a rather expensive recreational hobby, sales increase when the economy is at its best. Also, the adoption of a boat for racing in a given area and the requirement that competitors use that particular boat to compete have dramatically affected sales.

WaveCrest's plant occupies a single large building plus three smaller buildings for supplies, administration, and other manufacturing uses. The plant has two key manufacturing departments, each with a supervisor. The molding department develops the molds for the boats and produces the fiberglass hull for each boat. The assembly department installs the fittings, rubrail and other hardware, and packs the mast, sails, lines, and other items for shipment.

WaveCrest is currently manufacturing two boat designs, a 14-foot cat-rigged boat and a 16-foot sloop-rigged boat. The wholesale price of these boats is $4,500 and $8,950, respectively. The plant manufactures an average of 100 of the 14-foot boats and 50 of the 16-foot boats per month. The plant is staffed by six highly skilled workers in the molding department and five additional employees in the assembly department. Tom and Bill work on marketing and customer relations in addition to boat design and testing. Tom is principally responsible for design and production and has been able to create two promising new designs that the firm is market testing and considering for production, as well as some new ideas for streamlining the production process. Bill is primarily responsible for marketing and customer relations and is on the road much of the time attending boat shows and visiting sailing camps and clubs.

**Required**

1. Develop what you think is or should be WaveCrest's competitive strategy.

2. The Green brothers are interested in evaluating their performance other than using the financial report. In particular, they want to be able to evaluate their progress toward specific goals in each business area. Because they do not see much of each other as a result of Bill's travel, they also want a way to be more aware of what the other is doing and accomplishing. Someone has suggested the use of a balanced scorecard for this purpose. Based on the firm's strategy, develop three to five perspectives of a potential balanced scorecard and four to six measures for each perspective. Do you think the balanced scorecard will provide the information the brothers are seeking?

**[LO 18-3, 18-5]** 18-59 **Performance Measurement; Balanced Scorecard; Hospital** Bridgeport Hospital and Health Care Services (BHHS) in Bridgeport, Connecticut, is a part of the Yale University Health System. BHHS is a 450-bed community-teaching hospital with the following mission: "In 2001, Bridgeport Hospital and Health Care Services, as an integral part of the Yale New Haven Health System, will be the system patients choose, the system to which physicians and payers refer, and the employer of choice for health-care personnel."

To transform this mission to reality, BHHS adopted the balanced scorecard for performance measurement and a plan to implement it by the end of 2005. In the first year of the scorecard, 1999, BHHS identified 12 scorecard perspectives and 56 critical success factors across these 12 perspectives. The following year, 2000, BHHS refined the scorecard to include the following five perspectives and 35 nonquantitative critical success factors:

1. **Organizational health** (teamwork, leadership development, communications, facilities . . .).
2. **Process improvement** (reducing delays, streamlining processes, and maximizing the effective use of technology . . .).
3. **Quality improvement** (patient satisfaction, improving patient outcomes, external recognition for patient care . . .).
4. **Volume and market share growth** (expanded clinical services . . .).
5. **Financial health** (financial returns, system efficiencies . . .).

**Required**

1. Why did BHHS reduce the number of scorecard perspectives and critical success factors in 2000? The number of perspectives was further reduced to four in 2001; state which you think are the remaining four perspectives and explain why.

2. For the five perspectives in the 2000 plan, develop two to five possible measurable critical success factors that the hospital might use to measure performance toward the goals of each perspective.

3. Will the scorecard as described in the 2000 plan be effective in helping BHHS achieve its mission?

4. Develop a strategy map for BHHS, incorporating each of the five perspectives of the 2000 plan. Explain why you have developed the map in this way.

5. Would a profit center approach work for BHHS? Why or why not?

**[LO 18-3]** 18-60 **Value Streams and Profit Centers** Anderson Company is a manufacturer of very inexpensive DVD players and television sets. The company uses recycled parts and a highly structured manufacturing process to keep costs low so that it can sell at very low prices. The company uses lean accounting procedures to help keep costs low and to examine financial performance. Anderson uses value streams to study the profitability of its two main product groups, DVD players and TVs. Information about finished goods inventory, sales, production, and average sales price follows.

| | DVD Group | TV Group |
|---|---|---|
| Units | | |
| Beginning inventory | 200 | 900 |
| Price | $ 55 | $ 45 |
| Sold | 13,500 | 15,500 |
| Budgeted and actual production | 14,000 | 15,000 |

Anderson's costs for the current quarter are as follows. Note that some of the company's manufacturing and selling costs are traceable directly to the two value streams, while other costs are not traceable. Anderson considers all traceable fixed costs to be controllable by the manager of each group. Also, Anderson's value stream shows operating income determined by the full cost method; the difference from the traditional full cost income statement is that the effect on income from a change in inventory is shown as a separate item on the value-stream income statement.

| | DVD Group | TV Group | Total |
|---|---|---|---|
| Unit variable costs | | | |
|   Manufacturing | $   30 | $   16 | |
|   Selling and administrative | 5 | 5 | |
| Traceable fixed costs | | | |
|   Manufacturing | 140,000 | 255,000 | $395,000 |
|   Selling and administrative | 10,000 | 10,000 | 20,000 |
| Nontraceable fixed costs | | | |
|   Manufacturing | | | 130,000 |
|   Selling and administrative | | | 80,000 |

**Required**

1. Consider Anderson's two value streams as profit centers and use the contribution income statement (Exhibit 18.9) as a guide to develop a value-stream income statement for the company. In your solution, replace the term *controllable margin* (in Exhibit 18.9) with *value-stream income.* Be sure to include the inventory effect on profit as a separate line item in your value-stream income statement.

2. Interpret the findings of the analysis you completed in requirement 1.

3. What is the benefit of the use of value streams for evaluating profit centers relative to the use of the contribution income statement for individual product lines?

[LO 18-3]    18-61   **Cost Centers; The Finance Function; Spreadsheet Application**   The consulting firm A. T. Kearney analyzes and ranks the top offshore outsourcing locations for companies seeking to outsource the finance function. Kearney provides three measures of the attractiveness of the country as a location for outsourcing: financial attractiveness (low cost), skills availability, and business environment (that supports investment in the country). For each measure, a larger score is a better score; financial attractiveness is scored in the range from 0 to 4, while skills availability and business environment are scored from 0 to 3.

The A.T. Kearney measures are useful to a firm that is considering outsourcing its finance function and is also considering outsourcing this function to a foreign country. A firm that considers the finance function as a cost center may wish to find a location where the work can be done reliably at the lowest possible cost. Note that outsourcing would not be considered if for any reason the finance function is considered strategically critical to the company; in that case the finance function would be retained close to top management. For example, a company with a stable and cost leadership type of operation would be more likely to offshore the finance function than a company that operates in a dynamic competitive environment where financial skills are needed for many day-to-day decisions.

Note: The countries below are listed in alphabetical order. You can review the Cost Management in Action section of the chapter for more information on outsourcing.

| | Financial Attractiveness | Skills Availability | Business Environment |
|---|---|---|---|
| Brazil | 2.64 | 1.78 | 1.47 |
| Bulgaria | 3.16 | 1.04 | 1.56 |
| Chile | 2.65 | 1.18 | 1.93 |
| China | 2.93 | 2.25 | 1.38 |
| Czech Republic | 2.43 | 1.10 | 2.05 |
| Egypt | 3.22 | 1.14 | 1.25 |
| Estonia | 2.44 | 0.96 | 2.20 |
| India | 3.22 | 2.34 | 1.44 |
| Indonesia | 3.29 | 1.47 | 1.06 |
| Jordan | 3.09 | 0.98 | 1.54 |
| Latvia | 2.64 | 0.91 | 2.00 |
| Malaysia | 2.84 | 1.26 | 2.02 |
| Mexico | 2.63 | 1.49 | 1.61 |
| Philippines | 3.26 | 1.23 | 1.26 |
| Poland | 2.59 | 1.17 | 1.79 |
| Singapore | 1.65 | 1.51 | 2.53 |
| Slovakia | 2.79 | 1.04 | 1.79 |
| Thailand | 3.19 | 1.21 | 1.62 |
| United Arab Emirates | 2.93 | 0.86 | 1.92 |
| Vietnam | 3.33 | 0.99 | 1.22 |

**Required**

1. Using Excel, analyze the above measures for these 20 countries and develop a ranking for choosing the best offshore outsourcing location for the finance function. Explain briefly how you developed your ranking.

2. What are some of the strategic and global issues to consider in outsourcing the finance function?

[LO 18-3]    18-62 **Contribution Income Statement for Profit Centers**    Outdoor World Inc. (OWI) is a sporting goods retailer that specializes in bicycles, running shoes, and related clothing. The firm has become successful by careful attention to trends in cycling, running, and changes in the technology and fashion of sport clothing. In recent years however, the profit margins have begun to fall, and OWI has decided to employ a contribution income statement to further analyze the company's profitability. The company has two stores, one in Hartford, Connecticut, and the other in Boston, Massachusetts. The total sales for the two stores for the most recent year are $6,875,000 and $5,625,000 for the Hartford and Boston stores, respectively. Both stores are considered profit centers, and within each store are two profit centers: one for clothing and the other for cycles and running shoes. The breakdown of sales within the two stores is approximately 50% clothing and 50% cycles/shoes for Boston but is estimated to be 60%/40% for Hartford, due to the greater interest in cycling in the Boston area. OWI is interested in finding the profit contribution of clothing and cycling/shoes at the Hartford store but not at the Boston store.

Cost of purchases for resale averages 60% of retail value at Boston, and at Hartford the cost is 70% for clothing and 50% for cycles/shoes. Variable operating costs at each store are similar—30% of retail sales at Boston, and at Hartford operating costs are 25% of retail sales for the clothing unit and 35% for the cycle/shoes unit. OWI estimates it has a total of $1,075,000 fixed cost, of which $325,000 cannot be traced to either store; of the remaining $750,000, $400,000 is traceable to the stores and controllable by store managers and $350,000 can be traced to the stores but cannot be controlled in the short term by the store managers. These fixed costs are estimated to be traceable to the stores as follows.

| Fixed Controllable Costs | Percent of Total Cost |
|---|---|
| Boston | 45% |
| Hartford total | 40 |
|    Clothing | 50 |
|    Cycles/shoes | 30 |
|    Could not be traced to clothing or cycling at Hartford | 20 |
| Could not be traced to Boston or Hartford | 15 |

| Fixed Noncontrollable Costs | Percent of Total Cost |
|---|---|
| Boston | 40% |
| Hartford total | 50 |
|    Clothing | 55 |
|    Cycles/shoes | 35 |
|    Could not be traced to clothing or cycling at Hartford | 10 |
| Could not be traced to Boston or Hartford | 10 |

**Required**

1. Prepare a contribution income statement for OWI showing the contribution margin, controllable margin, and contribution by profit center for both the Boston and Hartford stores, and also for the clothing and cycles/shoes units of the Hartford store.

2. Interpret the contribution income statement you prepared in (1) above. What recommendations do you have for the management of OWI?

[LO 18-3]    18-63 **Choice of Strategic Business Unit**

**Required**    For each of the following cases, determine whether the business unit should be evaluated as a cost center or a profit center and explain why. If you choose cost center, then explain which type of cost center, the discretionary-cost center or the engineered-cost center.

1. A trucking firm has experienced a rapid increase in fuel costs and has only been partly successful in passing along the increased costs to customers. In recent months, fuel prices have come back

down, but the firm's management knows to expect a continued volatility in the cost of fuel. To secure the firm's profits when fuel costs are rising, the company has established an Office of Sustainability to develop and implement a strategy for reducing costs and reducing the firm's overall carbon footprint.

2. To more effectively compete in a dynamic market for consumer electronics, a manufacturer of consumer electronics products has established a new department for Innovation and Refinement that reports directly to the chief operating officer (COO). The role of the new department is to develop new products and to refine existing products that keep the firm on the leading edge of innovation in the industry. A key tool of the new department is to use predictive analytics, a type of statistical analysis that is used to analyze market trends, consumer data, and economics forecasts, to best identify the products that consumers want and what types of innovation are most likely to be valued.

3. The recent economic downturn has convinced Marshall Clothing Stores Inc. to initiate risk management practices and to locate this activity in a new department that reports directly to the chief financial officer (CFO). The objectives of risk management are to identify significant new risks that could potentially affect the company in the coming one to five years and to develop plans for adapting to the risk. For example, the company is concerned about the rapidly increasing inventories in certain departments of its stores, due to an unexpected decrease in demand in these areas. The company faces losses on selling these items at a discount.

[LO 18-3, 18-5]   18-64   **Research Assignment; Sustainability**   Read the following article by Marc J. Epstein, Adriana Rejc Buhovac, and Kristi Yuthas: "Implementing Sustainability: The Role of Leadership and Organizational Culture," *Strategic Finance*, April 2010, pp. 41–47. The article explains the use of management control systems in the context of the firm's sustainability objectives. The research for this article was funded by the Institute of Management Accounting (IMA).

The article is available in the Cases and Readings Supplement that comes with the text; it can also be accessed using the link provided on the text website.

**Required**

1. What is the difference between local and corporate decision making, and what is the significance of the difference for sustainability?

2. Study the Corporate Sustainability Model in Figure 1. Based on this study, do you think sustainability should be managed by means of a cost center, profit center, the balanced scorecard, or some other method, and why?

3. Identify two of the leading companies in the area of sustainability and explain why you think each of these companies has chosen to take a leadership role in sustainability.

4. Review Exhibit 18.4 in the text. Do you think sustainability is best managed as part of an informal or a formal type of management control system? Briefly explain your answer.

5. Explain briefly the role of leadership in sustainability management.

6. Explain briefly the role of organization culture in sustainability management.

## Solution to Self-Study Problem

### Discretionary-Cost and Engineered-Cost Methods

1. Liberty management is apparently using a cost center for its claims department because it generates no revenues. Since management has chosen not to adjust the number of clerks for the changing number of claims each month, it appears to be using a discretionary-cost method to budget these costs. That is, management has determined it is more effective to provide a reasonable resource (12 clerks) for the claims processing area and not to be concerned directly with the clerks' efficiency, the slack during slow times, or the hectic pace at peak load times. Management's view is that the work averages out over time.

2. If Liberty uses the discretionary-cost method, the budget would be the same each month and would not depend on the level of claims to be processed. The budget would include the costs to provide the number of clerks that management judges to be adequate for the job (12 clerks × $2,400 = $28,800 per month).

3. If Liberty uses the engineered-cost method, each claim that is processed has a budgeted cost based on the average time used as determined by a work flow study. Assume that each clerk works an eight-hour day except for 40 minutes of break time; the number of claims a clerk can process each month (assuming 22 working days) is

$$\frac{[(8 \text{ hours} \times 60 \text{ minutes}) - 40] \times 22 \text{ days}}{121 \text{ minutes}} = 80 \text{ claims per month}$$

The cost per claim is thus

$$\$2,400/80 = \$30 \text{ per claim}$$

The engineered-cost budget for January is

$$915 \text{ claims} \times \$30 \text{ per claim} = \$27,450$$

The unfavorable variance for January using the engineered-cost method is $1,350 ($28,800 actual expenditure less $27,450 budgeted expenditure). This unfavorable variance is best interpreted as the cost of unused capacity for processing claims. Since the capacity for processing claims is $80 \times 12 = 960$ claims, the department has unused capacity of 45 claims ($960 - 915 = 45$ claims), or approximately one-half of one clerk.

4. Chuck could make the strategic argument that the claims processing department should be staffed for peak capacity rather than for average capacity to ensure promptness and accuracy during the busy months and to provide a better basis for employee morale, which is an important factor in performance during the low-volume months as well.

*Please visit* **http://www.mhhe.com/blocher6e** *to access a narrated, animated tutorial for solving this problem.*

# CHAPTER NINETEEN

# Strategic Performance Measurement:
## Investment Centers

**After studying this chapter, you should be able to . . .**

LO 19-1 Explain the use and limitations of return on investment (ROI) for evaluating investment centers

LO 19-2 Explain the use and limitations of residual income (RI) for evaluating investment centers

LO 19-3 Explain the use and limitations of economic value added (EVA®) for evaluating investment centers

LO 19-4 Explain the objectives of transfer pricing, and describe the advantages and disadvantages of various transfer-pricing alternatives

LO 19-5 Discuss important international issues that arise in transfer pricing

As indicated in the preceding chapter, when an organization decentralizes it does so to achieve certain objectives, including maximization of shareholder value. From top management's viewpoint, one of the costs of decentralization is the need to implement an effective performance-measurement system. The traditional approach to the design of such a system is to focus on the tenet of controllability: subunits of a decentralized organization (and their managers) should, as much as possible, be evaluated only on factors they can control, or at least influence, by their actions. In previous chapters, we've looked at how top management can evaluate the financial performance of lower-level units of the organization (viz., cost centers and profit centers). This chapter covers issues related to the performance of investment centers—the highest subunit level of an organization. By definition, managers of these units exercise control over revenues, costs, and level of investment. Thus, the evaluation of financial performance of these units should logically incorporate a measure of invested capital. Such measures allow top management to compare the financial performance of different investment centers within the organization. As indicated in the vignette that follows, the task of evaluating the performance of investment units is complicated when these units exchange goods and services with one another. That is, in such situations a "transfer price" between units must be chosen to evaluate the financial performance of both the buying unit and the selling unit. Setting an appropriate transfer price is especially challenging in an international context.

## Five Steps in the Evaluation of the Financial Performance of Investment Centers in an Organization

Global Electronics, Inc. (a fictitious company), was started five years ago by a small group of entrepreneurial students. The company produces innovative electronics products that appeal to young, educated individuals. Global is pursuing a low-cost, high-volume strategy. In fact, the company has from its inception grown rapidly and now does business in all 50 states as well as selected countries abroad. Its incentive to go abroad is to reduce cost and to facilitate growth in foreign sales. The company is decentralized and organized into a series of cost centers, profit centers, and investment centers. Recently, to take advantage of income-tax opportunities, Global has established several foreign subsidiaries, which both produce and distribute the company's products. Initially, the company felt little need for a comprehensive performance-evaluation system. However, with recent growth and development, the owners of the company are looking at alternative models for evaluating the performance of the various units into which the company is divided. Business consultants with whom the owners met recently recommended the following five-step process for developing a performance-measurement system for Global.

1. **Determine the strategic issues surrounding the problem.** Global Electronics, Inc., has organized itself into a number of decentralized units, including investment centers where the managers have broad responsibility over operating decisions and level of investment in the unit. The owners of the company want to institute a performance-measurement system that would allow the owners to evaluate the performance (both financial and non-financial) of each of the investment centers it has created.

2. **Identify the alternative actions.** The first task is to choose one or more financial-performance indicators that incorporate in the measure the level of investment in each unit. Proposed alternative indicators include return on investment (ROI), residual income (RI), or economic value added (EVA®).[1] Global must also choose the time period over which financial performance will be evaluated (i.e., one year versus time-series basis). For interdivisional transfers of products and services, Global must choose an appropriate transfer-pricing system from among the following alternatives: variable cost, full cost, market price, or negotiated price. Further, the company must determine whether transfer prices will be recorded at actual, budgeted, or standard cost.[2] For evaluating the financial performance of its investment centers Global must also decide whether to use a single or a dual transfer-pricing system. Finally, Global must consider whether to supplement short-term financial performance indicators with one or more nonfinancial performance indicators.

3. **Obtain information and conduct analyses of the alternatives.** The choice of a performance-evaluation system for decentralized units, such as investment centers, has important behavioral consequences. For example, to a greater or lesser extent the aforementioned choices maintain or decrease managerial autonomy, increase or decrease managerial motivation, and result in varying degrees of goal congruency. Further, some choices as to system design are simpler (administratively) to implement and maintain. In terms of selecting the appropriate transfer-pricing method, there are significant income-tax considerations, particularly given the (now) international scope of the company's operations. To protect itself, the company is considering entering into an advance pricing agreement (APA) with the IRS regarding its transfer-pricing method to be used for both domestic and international purposes. Finally, the company is concurrently considering the introduction of a balanced scorecard (BSC) (see Chapter 18) and so management needs to consider choice of performance metric(s) in conjunction with the design of its BSC.

4. **Based on strategy and analysis, choose and implement the desired alternative.** After discussion of these issues with its consultants, the company chooses a mix of financial-performance indicators and a specific transfer-pricing system that attempts to balance implementation costs against behavioral benefits and income-tax considerations. The high-level financial-performance indicators should be linked strategically to the company's BSC. Overall, the proposed performance-evaluation system for its investment centers will help Global implement its growth strategy and determine where growth is most profitable.

5. **Provide an ongoing evaluation of the effectiveness of the step 4 implementation.** The financial performance of all strategic investment centers of the company is evaluated quarterly, in conjunction with both subunit and corporate scorecards. Further, the financial-performance metrics are benchmarked to best-in-class performance of Global's competitors. Changes to the way financial performance is evaluated, as well as potential changes

---

[1] EVA® is a registered trademark of Stern Stewart & Co.

[2] As noted in Chapter 14, standard costs are *normative*—they represent the costs that *should be* incurred under relatively efficient operating conditions.

to the transfer-pricing system used by the company, are discussed during quarterly meetings with the owners of the company.

The rest of this chapter is divided into two parts. In Part One we discuss alternatives for evaluating the financial performance of investment centers. In Part Two we discuss the issue of transfer pricing. In both cases, our approach is to discuss both the advantages and limitations of various alternatives that exist. As you will see, evaluation of the short-term *financial performance* of investment centers is important, but incomplete. Thus, a strategic analysis of the performance of an investment center must also include *nonfinancial-performance indicators,* such as those included in an entity's balanced scorecard. In fact, all of these points were considered by the management of Global in its attempt to implement a performance-evaluation system for its investment centers.

## Part One: Financial-Performance Indicators for Investment Centers

Under the notion of *controllability,* it is appropriate for top management to evaluate the profitability of each investment center in relation to the amount of capital invested in the subunit. In this regard, top management can use one or a combination of the following metrics: return on investment (ROI), residual income (RI), or economic value added (EVA®). Each of these measures is discussed in this part of the chapter. In general, we evaluate each of these alternatives on the basis of the following criteria:

- Extent to which the measure motivates a high level of effort on the part of investment center managers.
- Extent to which the use of the measure results in goal congruency (consistency between decisions made by managers and the goals of top management).
- Extent to which the measure rewards managers fairly for their effort and skill, and for the effectiveness of the decisions they make.

Please keep the preceding criteria in mind as you study the rest of this chapter.

## Return on Investment

**LO 19-1**

*Explain the use and limitations of return on investment (ROI) for evaluating investment centers.*

**Return on investment (ROI)** is some measure of profit divided by some measure of investment in the business unit.

The most commonly used measure of short-term financial performance of an investment center is **return on investment (ROI),** which is defined as some measure of profit divided by some measure of investment in the business unit. ROI is a percentage, and the larger the percentage, the better the ROI. The achieved level of ROI depends on many factors, including general economic conditions, and, in particular, the current economic conditions of the company's industry. For example, cyclical industries such as airlines and home construction have ROIs that vary significantly under differing economic conditions. In calculating ROI, "profit" (i.e., the numerator of the ratio) for an investment center (compared to the firm as a whole) is typically defined as divisional operating income. The amount of "investment" (i.e., the denominator of the ratio) is often determined by the assets of the business unit.

### Return on Investment (ROI) Equals Return on Sales (ROS) Times Asset Turnover (AT)[3]

ROI is the product of two components, return on sales and asset turnover. Since sales and profits relate to a period of time, for consistency the amount of assets used to calculate ROI is usually determined from the simple average of the value of assets at the start of the period and the value of assets at the end of the period.

$$ROI = \text{Return on sales} \times \text{Asset turnover}$$

$$ROI = \frac{\text{Profit}}{\text{Sales}} \times \frac{\text{Sales}}{\text{Assets}}$$

[3] ROI based on ROS and AT is often referred to as the *DuPont approach* since it was originated by Donaldson Brown, chief financial officer of DuPont Corporation early in the 1900s.

The figure to the right shows the relationship between asset turnover (AT) and return on sales (ROS) for a return on investment of 10%. Any point falling above the line would represent an ROI of greater than 10%, a point falling below this line would be an ROI of less than 10%. The curve shows that there are lots of different combinations of AT and ROS that will produce an ROI of 10%. Also, it is common that different industries will fall at different points of the figure. For example, restaurants typically have low ROS and higher AT so they will appear to the upper left of the figure (for example, in 2011 Einstein Noah Restaurant Group, Inc., had an ROS of 3.1% and AT of 2.1, for an ROI of 6.5%). In contrast, utilities typically have lower AT and higher ROS (for example, Duke Energy in 2011 had an ROS of 11.7% and AT of 0.23, for an ROI of 2.7%).

**Return on sales (ROS),**
or profit per sales dollar, measures the manager's ability to control expenses and increase revenues to improve profitability.

**Asset turnover (AT),**
the amount of sales dollars generated per dollar of investment, measures the manager's ability to increase sales from a given level of investment.

**Return on sales (ROS),** or profit per sales dollar, measures the manager's ability to control expenses and increase revenues to improve profitability. Return on sales is also called *profit margin.* **Asset turnover (AT),** the amount of sales dollars generated per dollar of investment, measures the manager's ability to increase sales from a given level of investment. Together, the two components of ROI tell a more complete story of the manager's performance and therefore enhance top management's ability to evaluate and compare different units within the organization. For example, research has shown that firms with different operating strategies tend also to have a different mix of return on sales versus asset turnover. Firms with high operating leverage (see Chapter 9) tend to have low asset turnover and high return on sales; those with low operating leverage and commodity-like products tend to have the highest asset turnover and the lowest return on sales. Please see the nearby Real-World Focus for an elaboration on these points. Note that for performance-evaluation purposes, a business unit can be defined variously. As illustrated in the CompuCity example that follows, business units can be defined in terms of product lines, geographic regions, or product lines within geographic regions.

### Illustration of Evaluation Using ROI

Assume that CompuCity is a retailer with three product lines: computers, software, and computer help books. The company has stores in three regions: the Boston area, South Florida, and the Midwest. Each store sells only computers, software, and books. CompuCity's profits for the Midwest region declined last year, due in part to increased price competition in the computer product line.

Because of this decline in profits, top management uses ROI to study and investigate the performance of the Midwest region. Each of the three product lines (as well as each of the three geographic regions) is considered an investment center for evaluation purposes. CompuCity knows that the markups are highest in software and lowest for computers because of price competition. Investment in each product line consists of the inventory for sale and the value of the real estate and improvements of the retail stores. Inventory is relatively low in the computer product line since merchandise is restocked quickly from the manufacturers. Inventory is also low in the book product line because about 40% of CompuCity's books are on consignment from publishers.

The current book value (recorded cost) of the real estate and store improvements is allocated to each of the three product lines in the Midwest region on the basis of square feet of floor space used. The software product line occupies the largest amount of floor space, followed by computers and books. Panel 1 of Exhibit 19.1 shows the operating income, sales, and investment information for the Midwest region of CompuCity in 2012 and 2013. Panel 2 shows the calculation of ROI, including ROS and asset turnover, for the Midwest region for both 2012 and 2013.

The data in Exhibit 19.1 indicate that Midwest region's ROI has fallen (from 14.4% in 2012 to 13.5% in 2013) due mainly to a decline in overall ROS (from 6.1% in 2012 to 5.1% in 2013). Further analysis shows that the drop in ROS is due to the sharp decline in ROS for the computer product line (from 4% in 2012 to 2% in 2013). The computer product line's decline in ROS is likely the result of the increased price competition.

The analysis also shows that software is the most profitable product line for the Midwest region (based on an ROI of 20% in 2013); this is so primarily because of the relatively high ROS (highest at 10% since the markup on software products is relatively high). In contrast, the computer and book product lines in the Midwest region have higher asset turnovers due to the lower required levels of inventory and floor space for the computer product line, and the large percentage of consignment inventory for the book product line. ROI has also improved significantly for the software product line because of the decline in investment, due either to a reduction in inventory or a decrease in floor space for software (recall that investment is allocated to the three product lines on the basis of floor space).

### *Strategic Analysis Using ROI*

Use of ROI enables CompuCity to evaluate the short-term financial performance of each of the three product lines within the Midwest region. CompuCity can set performance goals for each product line in terms of both return on sales (ROS) and asset turnover (AT). Product line managers then have very clear goals to increase sales and reduce costs, reduce inventory, and use floor space effectively. To be effective, the goals should recognize differences in the competitive factors among the product lines. For example, a lower ROS should be expected of the computer product line because of competitive pricing that affects that line.

Exhibit 19.1 data also reflect the way that competitive factors in the computer product line and business relationships regarding inventory in the computer and book product lines affect profitability. This provides a useful basis for an improved analysis, that is, for determining how the firm should position itself strategically. How should CompuCity's competitive approach be changed in view of recent and expected changes in the competitive environment? Perhaps the computer product line should be reduced and the software product line expanded. Which stores in the Midwest are successful, and why? A value-chain analysis might provide insight into strategic competitive advantage and opportunity. For example, CompuCity might find it more profitable to reduce its computer product line and replace it with a product line that is potentially more profitable, such as printers, pagers, cell phones, fax machines, supplies, and computer accessories.

## Return on Investment (ROI): Measurement Issues

If ROI is used to evaluate the relative performance of business units (such as product lines or regions, or product lines within regions), then income and investment should be determined consistently and fairly across these units.

1. Income and investment, to the extent possible, must be measured in the same way for each business unit. For example, all units to be evaluated should use the same inventory cost-flow assumption (FIFO or LIFO) and the same depreciation method.[4]
2. The measurement method must be reasonable and fair for all business units. For example, if some units have much older assets than other units, the use of net book value (NBV) for assets can significantly bias the ROI measures in favor of the older units.

---

[4] Each of the policies also has the effect of either simultaneously increasing income and increasing investment or simultaneously decreasing income and decreasing investment. Since ROI is a ratio that normally is between zero and 1, an increase in income increases ROI although investment also has increased by the same amount, and vice versa.

**EXHIBIT 19.1**  Return on Investment (ROI), Return on Sales (ROS), and Asset Turnover (AT) for CompuCity (*Midwest Region*)

**Panel 1: Operating Income, Investment, and Sales**

| Product Line | Operating Income 2012 | 2013 | Investment (Assets) 2012 | 2013 | Sales 2012 | 2013 |
|---|---|---|---|---|---|---|
| Computers | $ 8,000 | $ 5,000 | $ 50,000 | $ 62,500 | $200,000 | $250,000 |
| Software | 15,000 | 16,000 | 100,000 | 80,000 | 150,000 | 160,000 |
| Books | 3,200 | 5,000 | 32,000 | 50,000 | 80,000 | 100,000 |
| Total | $26,200 | $26,000 | $182,000 | $192,500 | $430,000 | $510,000 |

**Panel 2: Return on Sales, Asset Turnover, and Return on Investment**

| Product Line | Return on Sales (ROS) 2012 | 2013 | Asset Turnover (AT) 2012 | 2013 | Return on Investment (ROI) 2012 | 2013 |
|---|---|---|---|---|---|---|
| Computers | 4% = 8,000/200,000 | 2% = 5,000/250,000 | 4.00 = 200,000/50,000 | 4.00 = 250,000/62,500 | 16% = 8,000/50,000 | 8% = 5,000/62,500 |
| Software | 10% = 15,000/150,000 | 10% = 16,000/160,000 | 1.50 = 150,000/100,000 | 2.00 = 160,000/80,000 | 15% = 15,000/100,000 | 20% = 16,000/80,000 |
| Books | 4% = 3,200/80,000 | 5% = 5,000/100,000 | 2.50 = 80,000/32,000 | 2.00 = 100,000/50,000 | 10% = 3,200/32,000 | 10% = 5,000/50,000 |
| Total | 6.10% = 26,200/430,000 | 5.10% = 26,000/510,000 | 2.36 = 430,000/182,000 | 2.65 = 510,000/192,500 | 14.40% = 26,200/182,000 | 13.50% = 26,000/192,500 |

**EXHIBIT 19.2**
**Effect on ROI of Capitalizing Certain Costs: CompuCity (*Midwest Region*)**

| Panel 1: ROI Prior to Capitalizing Display Materials (same as Exhibit 19.1, 2013) | | |
|---|---|---|
| | **Computer Unit** | **Book Unit** |
| Assets | $62,500 | $50,000 |
| Income | $5,000 | $5,000 |
| ROI | 8% | 10% |

| Panel 2: Year-One Results—Book Unit Expenses Display Costs While the Computer Unit Capitalizes These Costs | | |
|---|---|---|
| Assets | $64,000 = $62,500 + $1,500 | $50,000 |
| Income | $6,500 = $5,000 + $1,500 | $5,000 |
| ROI | 10.16% = $6,500 ÷ $64,000 | 10% |

To illustrate the effect of an accounting policy on divisional ROIs, assume that all business units of CompuCity expense all furniture and other items used to display products; these items cost $2,000 per year. Suppose the computer product line in the Midwest region decides to capitalize these expenses. What is the short-term effect on ROI if depreciation is $500 per year on these items? The increase in the NBV of assets for the computer product line in the Midwest region is $1,500, and the net effect on income for this product line is $1,500. Exhibit 19.2 compares the computer product line (unit) to the book product line (unit) for the Midwest region before the change (Panel 1) and after the change (Panel 2).

The illustration shows that the decision to capitalize the display costs in the short run increased the computer product line's assets, income, and ROI. Although the book product line has the higher ROI when both units expense display costs, the computer product line's decision to capitalize these costs while the book product line does not has caused the computer product line to at least temporarily have the higher ROI.

### Which Assets to Include in the ROI Calculation

A common method for calculating ROI is to define investment as the net cost of long-lived assets plus working capital (i.e., current assets minus current liabilities). A key criterion for including an asset in ROI is the degree to which the business unit controls it. For example, if the unit's cash balance is controlled at the firmwide level, only a portion (or perhaps none) of the cash balance should be included in the investment amount for calculating ROI for that unit. Similarly, receivables and inventory should include only those controllable at the unit level.

Long-lived assets are commonly included in investment if they are traceable to the business unit (for shared assets, see the next section). Management problems arise, however, if the long-lived assets are leased or if some significant portion of them is idle. Leasing requires a clear firmwide policy regarding how to treat leases in determining ROI so that business unit managers are properly motivated to lease or not to lease, as is the firm's policy. In general, the leased assets should be included as investments since they represent assets used to generate income, and the failure to include them can cause a significant overstatement of ROI.

For idle assets, the main issue is again controllability. If the idle assets have an alternative use or are readily saleable, they should be included in the investment amount for ROI. Also, if top management wants to encourage the divestment of idle assets, including idle assets in the determination of ROI would motivate the desired action since divestment would reduce investment and increase ROI. Alternatively, if top management sees a potential strategic advantage to holding the idle assets, excluding idle assets from ROI would provide the most effective motivation since holding idle assets would not affect the ROI calculation.

### Measuring Investment: Allocating Shared Assets

When shared facilities, such as a common maintenance facility, are involved, management must determine a fair sharing arrangement. As in joint cost allocation (Chapter 7), top management should trace the assets to the business units that used them and allocate—on a basis that is as close to actual usage as possible—the assets that cannot be traced. For

**Assessing the ROI for Employee Training/Development Programs**

Is it possible to measure the financial return associated with employee training and development programs? Indeed, there is a cottage industry of firms devoted to helping companies answer this question (e.g., Knowledge Advisors, www.knowledgeadvisors.com; Bellevue University's Omaha's Human Capital Lab, http://humancapitallab.com; and PricewaterhouseCoopers, People and Change Practice, www.pwc.com/sg/en/people-and-change). Evidence exists that over the 10-year period 2001–2010, companies known to educate workers on a large scale generated larger stock market returns than a broad index of companies (i.e., the S&P 500). Assessing the "business case" for employee-development programs is yet another example where management accountants can add value to their organizations. For a further exploration of this topic, see Problem 19-39 in the end-of-chapter assignment material.

**Source:** David McCann, "Human Capital: Measured Response," *CFO* (June 2011), pp. 21–22, 25.

example, the investment in a vehicle maintenance facility might be allocated on the basis of the number of vehicles in each unit or on the total value of these vehicles.

Alternatively, the required capacity and therefore the investment in the joint facility are sometimes large because the user units require high levels of service at periods of high demand. In this case, the assets should be allocated according to the *peak demand* by each individual business unit; units with higher peak-load requirements would be allocated a relatively larger portion of the total investment cost. For example, a computer services department might require a high level of computer capacity because certain units within the company require a large amount of service at certain times.

### Measuring Investment: Current Values

**Historical cost**
of divisional assets is the book value of current assets plus the net book value (NBV) of long-lived assets.

**Net book value (NBV)**
is the original cost of a depreciable asset less accumulated depreciation to date on that asset.

The amount of investment is typically the **historical cost** of divisional assets, which is defined as the book value of current assets plus the net book value (NBV) of long-lived assets. **Net book value (NBV)** for a depreciable asset is the difference between the original cost of an asset and accumulated depreciation on that asset. A problem arises when long-lived assets are a significant portion of the total investment base because most long-lived assets are stated at historical cost, and price changes since their purchase can make the historical-cost figures irrelevant and misleading.

If the relatively small historical-cost value is used for investment in ROI, the result is that *ROI can be significantly overstated* relative to ROI determined with the current value of the assets. The consequence is that the use of historical-cost ROI can mislead strategic decision makers, since the inflated ROI figures can create an illusion of profitability. The illusion is removed when the assets are replaced later at their current value.

For example, a business unit that enjoys a relatively high ROI of 20% based on NBV (e.g., income of $200,000 and NBV of assets of $1,000,000) would find that *if* replacement cost of the assets were four times book value (4 × $1,000,000 = $4,000,000), the ROI after replacement would become a relatively low 5% ($200,000 ÷ $4,000,000). Strategically, the firm should have identified the low profitability of this business unit in a timely manner, but use of historical-cost ROI can delay this recognition. Thus, instead of measuring assets at historical cost (for purposes of calculating ROI) an organization may choose some measure of current value of these assets. Presumably, the resulting ROIs better inform management about the true profitability of the organization's various business units. Note, however, that if current-cost data are not currently being reported (for example, for financial accounting purposes) the organization in this case will incur additional information-gathering costs.

In addition to its strategic value, the use of current value helps to reduce the unfairness of historical-cost NBV when comparing among business units with *different aged assets*. Units with older assets under the NBV method have significantly higher ROIs than business units with newer assets because of the effect of price changes and of accumulating depreciation over the life of the assets. If the old and new assets are contributing equivalent service, the bias in favor of the unit with older assets is unfair to the manager of a unit with newer assets.

***Measures of Current Value***   The three methods for developing or estimating the current values of assets are (1) gross book value, (2) replacement cost, and (3) liquidation value. **Gross book value (GBV)** is historical cost without the reduction for accumulated depreciation. It is a rough estimate of the current value of the assets. GBV improves on NBV because it removes the bias due to differences in the age of assets and differences in depreciation methods used across different business units. However, it does not address potential price changes in the assets since the time of original purchase.

**Replacement cost** represents the current cost to replace the assets at the current level of service and functionality. In contrast, **liquidation value** is the estimated price that could be received from sale of the assets of a business unit. In effect, replacement cost is a purchase price and liquidation value is a sales price. Generally, replacement cost is higher than liquidation value.

GBV is preferred by those who value the objectivity of a historical-cost number; original purchase cost is a reliable, verifiable number. In contrast, replacement cost is preferred when ROI is used to evaluate the manager or the business unit as a continuing enterprise because the use of replacement cost is consistent with the idea that the assets will be replaced at the current cost and the business will continue. On the other hand, liquidation value is most useful when top management is using ROI to evaluate the business unit for potential disposal and the relevant current cost is the sales (i.e., liquidation) value of the assets.

To illustrate, consider CompuCity's three marketing regions, each of which for performance-evaluation purposes is considered a business unit. CompuCity has 15 stores in the Midwest, 18 in the Boston region, and 13 in South Florida. CompuCity owns and manages each store. Exhibit 19.3 shows the NBV, GBV, estimated replacement cost, and estimated liquidation value for 2013 for the stores in each region.[5]

The stores in the Boston region, where CompuCity began, are among the oldest and are located in areas where real estate values have risen considerably. The newer stores (in the Midwest and Florida) are also experiencing significant appreciation in real estate values. ROI based on NBV shows the Boston region to be the most profitable. Additional analysis based on GBV, however, shows that when considering that stores in the Boston region are somewhat older, the ROI figures for all three regions are comparable, illustrating the potentially misleading information from ROI based on NBV.

*Replacement cost* is useful in evaluating managers' performance because it best measures the investment in the continuing business: the ROI figures show that all three regions are somewhat comparable, with South Florida slightly in the lead.

**Gross book value (GBV)** is historical cost without the reduction for accumulated depreciation.

**Replacement cost** represents the current cost to replace the assets at the current level of service and functionality.

**Liquidation value** is the estimated price that could be received from the sale of the assets of a business unit.

**EXHIBIT 19.3**
**Investment Data and ROI for CompuCity in Its Three Marketing Regions (000s omitted)**

| Region | Operating Income | Measure of Assets | | | |
|---|---|---|---|---|---|
| | | Net Book Value | Gross Book Value | Replacement Cost | Liquidation Value |
| Financial data: | | | | | |
| Midwest | $26,000 | $192,500 | $250,500 | $388,000 | $ 332,000 |
| Boston region | 38,500 | 212,000 | 445,000 | 650,000 | 1,254,600 |
| South Florida | 16,850 | 133,000 | 155,450 | 225,500 | 195,000 |
| Return on investment (ROI): | | | | | |
| Midwest | | 13.5% | 10.4% | 6.70% | 7.8% |
| Boston region | | 18.2 | 8.7 | 5.9 | 3.1 |
| South Florida | | 12.7 | 10.8 | 7.5 | 8.6 |

[5] The values for net book value (NBV) and gross book value (GBV) in Exhibit 19.3 represent the simple average of beginning-of-year and end-of-year values (beginning and ending values are not shown). Replacement cost and liquidation value are estimated as of the point when ROI is calculated.

*Liquidation value* provides a somewhat different picture. The ROI based on liquidation value for the Boston region is very low relative to the other two regions. Because of the significant appreciation in real estate values of stores in the Boston region, the liquidation value for the Boston region is quite high. The replacement cost figure is lower than liquidation cost because of the assumption that if CompuCity replaces its stores in the Boston region, these stores would be located where the real estate values are lower. The analysis of liquidation-based ROIs is useful for showing CompuCity management that the real estate value of these stores could now exceed their value as CompuCity retail locations. Perhaps the company should sell these stores and relocate elsewhere in areas whose values are near those suggested by the replacement-cost figures.

## Strategic Issues Regarding the Use of ROI

The use of ROI for performance-evaluation purposes is well entrenched in business practice. However, management accountants should be aware of some of the limitations or deficiencies of using ROI to evaluate the performance of investment centers. We address four such issues: applicability of ROI as a performance indicator in the knowledge-based economy; goal-congruency problems associated with the use of any short-term financial-performance indicator, such as ROI; behavioral consequences associated with using different models for investment decision making (e.g., NPV) and subsequent performance evaluation (e.g., ROI); and incentive effects regarding new investment by the most profitable units of the organization.

### Value Creation in the New Economy

As indicated in footnote 3, the ROI metric was developed for use by industrial-age companies (DuPont, General Motors, etc.). For such companies, the ROI performance indicator served its purpose well: its use allowed top management to effectively allocate capital across business units (such as product lines or geographic territories). In short, companies in that era competed by how effectively they managed their physical assets (plant, property, and equipment). It was entirely appropriate, therefore, to evaluate business units on the basis of the amount of profit generated by the use of these physical assets.

Today's business environment is drastically different. Value creation for many companies competing in what can be called the *knowledge-based economy* consists of managing intangible, as well as tangible, assets. Examples of such assets are: the skills level of the organization's employees (i.e., human capital); distinctive processes, including supply chains; loyal customers; and innovative products and services. Thus, in today's competitive environment a broader performance-measurement and control system is demanded, such as the use of a balanced scorecard (BSC), covered in this text in Chapters 2 and 18.

### Short-Term Focus of the Metric

Somewhat related to the above, we note that ROI (and, as we shall see, residual income, or RI, as well) is a short-term measure of profitability and as such is subject to manipulation on the part of business-unit managers. ROI is a ratio. Thus, managers, particularly those whose bonuses are tied to realized ROI figures, are motivated to do whatever it takes to increase the numerator of the calculation or to decrease the denominator, or both. Some actions border on the unethical, if not illegal. Other actions (e.g., delaying needed repairs and maintenance, reducing spending on critical research and development activities or on productivity-improvement programs) can be myopic in nature. That is, they can provide a short-term boost to reported profits (i.e., to the numerator of the ROI metric), but at the expense of the long-term competitive position of the business.

On the denominator side, the use of ROI can provide further goal-congruency problems: It can discourage managers of business units from making investments that would increase the value of the organization as a whole. There are two dimensions to this problem: (1) there can be a disconnect between the method used to make capital-budgeting decisions (e.g., discounted cash flow [DCF] decision models, as discussed in Chapter 12) and the method used subsequently to evaluate managerial performance, and (2) disincentive effects related to the short-term ROI associated with new investment opportunities may exist. We explore

Gary et al. (2011) provide evidence, based on simulation analysis, regarding the return on investment (ROI) of pursuing a doctoral degree after a career start in public accounting. Specifically, the authors wanted to determine whether a Ph.D. in accounting and a subsequent career in academia could provide a financial return to the degree recipient over the course of his or her working years that would be sufficient to justify giving up a career in public accounting. The authors considered various combinations of years to complete the doctorate (4, 5, and 6 years) as well as years in public accounting prior to enrolling in a doctoral program. Further, the authors considered a number of plausible career paths in the academic community.

The simulation results suggest that it is possible, and even likely, for an individual switching from an initial career in public accounting to earn a positive return on investment via a Ph.D. degree in accounting. Not surprisingly, the authors show that expected ROI is higher for individuals who leave public accounting early in their careers and for those who spend less time in a Ph.D. program. The authors have an interactive website (www.mgt.unm.edu/roi) that can be accessed and used to estimate the ROI for a specific individual/situation.

**Source:** R. F. Gary, C. A. Denison, and M. L. Bouillon, "Can Obtaining an Accounting Ph.D. Provide a Positive Financial Return?" *Issues in Accounting Education* 26, no. 1 (2011), pp. 23–38.

these issues in the following two sections. Both situations can motivate suboptimal decision making on the part of business-unit managers.

***Decision Model and Performance Model Inconsistency*** As we demonstrated in Chapter 12, long-term investment projects should be evaluated using a discounted cash flow (DCF) decision model, such as net present value (NPV). Such a model compares the present value of expected after-tax cash flows from a project to the present value of cash outflows (investment outlays) for the project. If the NPV is positive, the project in question should be accepted because the expectation is that the project will increase the value of the organization.

In practice, the business-unit manager's financial performance may be judged using an accounting-based metric such as ROI. The use of two different metrics, one for making the investment decision (NPV) and the other for evaluating subsequent financial performance (ROI) creates an inherent and significant incentive problem: It may discourage managers from making investment decisions that add value to the organization (i.e., NPV > 0) yet have unfavorable short-term effects on the business unit's ROI. One solution to this problem is to calculate depreciation, for ROI purposes, on a present-value basis. (This issue is explored in end-of-chapter assignment 19-37.) The end result is that the use of present-value depreciation aligns the decision-making model with the model used subsequently to evaluate the financial performance of the business unit.

As demonstrated in the following section, investment disincentive effects can exist even when ROI, rather than NPV, is used to evaluate long-term investment proposals.

***ROI: Disincentive for New Investment by the Most Profitable Units*** Business units evaluated on ROI have an important disincentive that conflicts with the goals of the firm: ROI encourages units to invest only in projects that earn *higher than the unit's current ROI* so that the addition of the investment improves the unit's overall ROI. Thus, the most profitable business units (i.e., the ones with relatively high ROIs) have a corresponding disincentive to invest in any project that does not exceed their current ROI, even those projects that, on a present-value basis, are attractive to the organization as a whole.[6]

The disincentive for new investment hurts the firm strategically in two ways. First, it rejects investment projects that would be beneficial. Second, to take advantage of a unit's apparent management skill, ROI evaluation provides a disincentive for the best units to grow. In contrast, the units with the lowest ROI have an incentive to invest in new projects to improve their ROI. Management skills could be lacking in the low-ROI units, however.

---

[6] As we demonstrated in Chapter 12, an attractive project is one that has a positive estimated net present value (NPV).

**EXHIBIT 19.4**   **ROI for Boston Region's Proposed Investment**

|  | First Year | Second Year | Third Year |
|---|---|---|---|
| Depreciation expense (straight-line method) | $7,500 = $22,500/3 | $7,500 | $7,500 |
| NBV at year-end | $15,000 = $22,500 − $7,500 | $7,500 = $15,000 − $7,500 | $0 = $7,500 − $7,500 |
| Average NBV for the year | $18,750 = ($22,500 + $15,000)/2 | $11,250 = ($15,000 + $7,500)/2 | $3,750 = ($7,500 + $0)/2 |
| ROI | $13.33\% = \dfrac{\$10,000 - \$7,500}{\$18,750}$ | $22.22\% = \dfrac{\$10,000 - \$7,500}{\$11,250}$ | $66.67\% = \dfrac{\$10,000 - \$7,500}{\$3,750}$ |

The disincentive can be illustrated if we assume that CompuCity's Boston region has an option to purchase for $22,500 a telephone switch that can increase the capacity of its toll-free service number and reduce operating costs by $10,000 per year. The switch is expected to last for three years and have no salvage value. Exhibit 19.4 shows the determination of ROI for the purchase of the switch using the straight-line method of depreciation. The ROI for its purchase is expected to be 13.33% in the first year and 22.22% and 66.67% in the second and third years, respectively.[7]

Using NBV, the Boston region's ROI is currently 18.2% (Exhibit 19.3). Consequently, the manager of the Boston region might not purchase the switch because the first year's return of 13.33% is less than the current ROI for the Boston region. Buying the switch would reduce Boston's ROI from 18.16% to 17.77% [($38,500 + $10,000 − $7,500) ÷ ($212,000 + $18,750)] in the first year. In later years, the ROI from the switch would substantially exceed Boston's current ROI, but the manager might not be able (or willing) to wait for that improvement if strong pressure for current profits exists.

Moreover, from a firmwide perspective, since the rate of return on the switch in each year exceeds the firm's threshold rate of return of 12%, the Boston region should purchase it. Thus, a significant limitation of ROI is that it can cause business-unit managers to decline some investments, in conflict with firmwide interests. This situation is an excellent example of a goal-congruency problem: *The use of ROI to evaluate the short-term financial performance of business-unit managers might not motivate decisions that increase the value of the business.* One way to address this limitation is to use an alternative measure of business-unit profitability, called *residual income.*

[7] Using the discounted cash flow (DCF) methods explained in Chapter 12, the purchase of the switch has an internal rate of return (IRR) of approximately 16% ($22,500 ÷ $10,000 = 2.250; the PV annuity factor for 16% and three years is 2.246).

# Residual Income

## LO 19-2

*Explain the use and limitations of residual income (RI) for evaluating investment centers.*

**Residual income (RI)**

is a dollar amount equal to the income of a business unit less an imputed charge for the level of investment in the division.

In contrast to ROI, which is a percentage, **residual income (RI)** is a dollar amount equal to the income of a business unit less an imputed charge for the level of investment in the unit. The charge is determined by multiplying a desired minimum rate of return by the level of investment in the business unit.[8] Residual income can be interpreted as the income earned after the division has "paid" a charge for the funds invested by top management in the business unit.

The RI calculation for CompuCity is illustrated in Exhibit 19.5 using an assumed minimum rate of return of 12%. Note that since all three business units (regions) have an ROI higher than 12%, all also have a positive RI. Note, too, that in this case each unit's ranking on ROI is the same as its ranking based on RI: the Boston region unit has the highest ROI and residual income. However, this will not always be the case.

The issues regarding the measurement of investment and income for RI are the same as those discussed earlier for ROI. However, RI does have the advantage of motivating a business unit to pursue an investment opportunity as long as the investment's expected return exceeds the minimum return set by the firm. For example, using RI, the Boston region would *accept* the opportunity to purchase the telephone switch described in Exhibit 19.4 because this investment would increase the unit's residual income. The RI in the first year after the investment in the switch would be

$$\$13,310 = (\$38,500 + \$10,000 - \$7,500) - [0.12 \times (\$212,000 + \$18,750)]$$

This amounts to a $250 improvement over the unit's current RI ($13,060, from Exhibit 19.5).

An additional advantage of RI is that a firm can adjust the required rates of return for differences in risk. For example, business units with higher business risk can be evaluated at a higher minimum rate of return. The increased risk might be due to obsolete products, increased competition in the industry, or other economic factors affecting the business unit. In Exhibit 19.5 we used the same minimum rate of return (12%) when calculating the RI of each geographic region of CompuCity. However, this is not required or necessarily desirable. We could have used different rates of return for each region, in order to capture risk differences across the three regions.

Another advantage is that it is possible to calculate a different investment charge for different types of assets. For example, a higher minimum rate of return could be used for long-lived assets that are more likely to be specialized in use and thus not so readily saleable.

**EXHIBIT 19.5**
**Illustration of Residual Income Calculations for CompuCity Geographic Regions**

| | Financial Data (from Exhibit 19.3) | |
| --- | --- | --- |
| | Operating Income | Net Book Value (NBV) of Assets |
| Regions: | | |
| Midwest | $26,000 | $192,500 |
| Boston region | 38,500 | 212,000 |
| South Florida | 16,850 | 133,000 |
| Return on investment (ROI): | | |
| Midwest | 13.51% | |
| Boston region | 18.16% | |
| South Florida | 12.67% | |
| Residual income (RI): | | |
| Midwest | $2,900 = $26,000 − (0.12 × $192,500) | |
| **Boston region** | **$13,060 = $38,500 − (0.12 × $212,000)** | |
| South Florida | $890 = $16,850 − (0.12 × $133,000) | |

[8] Conceptually, the minimum desired rate of return is defined as an entity's weighted-average cost of capital (WACC). However, we are speaking here about the evaluation of an investment center, not firmwide performance. Thus, adjustments to the firm's WACC are likely appropriate when evaluating *subunit* performance.

### Time Period of Analysis: Single versus Multiperiod Perspective

Both ROI and RI are *short-term* indicators of financial performance. That is, they both generally reflect one-year performance. Because of this, some organizations choose to evaluate these performance indicators over multiple years. Trend analysis, perhaps combined with competitive benchmarking, would yield more informative indications of an investment center's financial performance. By including multiple years in the evaluation window, there may be less incentive to engage in short-term behaviors that are dysfunctional in terms of long-term profitability. Finally, in the discussion of ROI we pointed out that the use of present-value depreciation is one mechanism for achieving compatibility between the model used for long-term investment decision making and the model used subsequently to evaluate managerial performance. The use of multiyear residual income (RI) figures is thought to accomplish the same objective. Why? Because the NPV of residual incomes over the life of a project, if cash flows are exactly as predicted, will be exactly equal to the NPV of net after-tax cash flows. In short, the use of multiyear RI figures helps to achieve goal congruency.

### Limitations of Residual Income (RI)

Although the residual income measure deals effectively with the disincentive problem of ROI, it has its own limitations. A key issue is that because RI is not a percentage, it is not useful for comparing units of significantly different sizes. RI favors larger units that would be expected to have larger residual incomes, even with relatively poor performance. Moreover, relatively small changes in the minimum rate of return can dramatically affect the RI for business units of different size, as illustrated in Exhibit 19.6. Although business units A and B both have the same ROI of 15%, the RI amount differs significantly: $300,000 for business unit A, but only $22,500 for business unit B. The difference would be greater for a smaller minimum return.

ROI and RI can complement each other in the evaluation of investment centers. The advantages and limitations of each measure are summarized in Exhibit 19.7.

**EXHIBIT 19.6**  The Effect of Business Unit Size and Minimum Desired Rate of Return on Residual Income (RI)

| | Business Unit A | Business Unit B |
|---|---|---|
| Investment | $10,000,000 | $750,000 |
| Operating income | $1,500,000 | $112,500 |
| Return on investment (ROI) | 15% = $1,500,000 ÷ $10,000,000 | 15% = $112,500 ÷ $750,000 |
| Residual income (RI), at a minimum desired return of 12% | $300,000 = $1,500,000 − (0.12 × $10,000,000) | $22,500 = $112,500 − (0.12 × $750,000) |

Return on Investment and Economic Profit
When a Company Is Not Capital-Intensive

When a company's or a unit's business model doesn't call for substantial capital investment (for example, it is a "people-intensive" industry such as service industries), then ROI may be relatively high, very sensitive to small changes in investment, and highly volatile, and thus often inappropriate as a tool for comparing the performance of business units or companies. For example, two of the most innovative and successful companies, Apple and Google, are not capital-intensive firms.

One way to measure performance that is appropriate in this case is to divide annual economic profit (EVA® or residual income) by revenue, a measure that gives executives a clearer picture of absolute and relative value creation among companies, irrespective of a particular company's or business unit's absolute level of investment. ROI will always be an essential measure for management performance measurement. But in businesses with low levels of investment, replacing ROI with economic profit divided by revenue can make internal and peer comparisons much more meaningful. Examples of actual application of this financial measure are provided in the article by Dodd and Rehm listed below.

Another approach is to determine economic profit by explicitly including the cost and productivity of the personnel employed by the company. This approach is recommended for companies that are people-intensive, such as the hotel industry. Please see the reference below by Barber and Strack for additional detail regarding this approach.

**Source:** Mikel Dodd and Werner Rehm, "Comparing Performance When Invested Capital Is Low," *The McKinsey Quarterly,* November 2005 (www .mckinseyquarterly.com/); Felix Barber and Rainer Strack, "The Surprising Economics of the People Business," *Harvard Business Review,* June 2005, pp. 81–90; Jena McGregor, "The World's Most Innovative Companies," *BusinessWeek,* April 24, 2006, pp. 63–74.

**EXHIBIT 19.7** **Advantages and Limitations of ROI and Residual Income (RI)**

| | Advantages | Limitations |
|---|---|---|
| Return on investment (ROI) | • Easily understood by managers<br>• Comparable to interest rates and to rates of return on alternative investments<br>• Widely used | • Disincentive for high-ROI units to invest in projects with ROI higher than the minimum rate of return but lower than the unit's current ROI<br>• Can lead to goal-congruency problems (e.g., suboptimal investment decision making) |
| Residual income (RI) | • Supports incentive to accept all projects with ROI above the minimum rate of return<br>• Can use the minimum rate of return to adjust for differences in risk<br>• Can use a different minimum rate of return for different types of assets | • Favors large units<br>• Can be difficult to determine a minimum rate of return for organizational subunits |
| Both ROI and RI | • *Comprehensive financial measure;* includes key elements important to top management: revenues, costs, and level of investment<br>• *Comparability;* expands top management's span of control by allowing comparison of business units | • *Can mislead strategic decision making;* not as comprehensive as the balanced scorecard, which includes customer satisfaction, business processes, and learning, as well as financial measures; the balanced scorecard is linked to strategy<br>• *Measurement issues;* variations in the measurement of inventory and long-lived assets and in the treatment of nonrecurring items, income taxes, foreign exchange effects, and the use/cost of shared assets<br>• *Short-term focus;* investments with long-term benefits might be neglected; captures financial performance for only a single year; may cause goal-congruency problems within the organization<br>• Failure to capture value-creating activities (i.e., managing an organization's intangible assets) |

# Economic Value Added

**LO19-3**

*Explain the use and limitations of economic value added (EVA®) for evaluating investment centers.*

**Economic value added (EVA®)**

is an estimate of a business unit's *economic profit* generated during a given period.

**Economic value added (EVA®)** is an estimate of a business's *economic profit* generated during a given period. In its simplest form, EVA® can be defined as profit less an imputed charge for the use of assets (capital) during the period. We might depict this measure of earnings as follows:

> Sales
> Less: Operating expenses (including taxes)
> Less: Financing expense (Cost of capital × Amount of invested capital)
> _____
> EVA®

As with RI and ROI, EVA® is a potentially useful metric for evaluating the financial performance of investment units because it explicitly incorporates the level of invested capital in the measure. That is, similar to residual income (RI), no measure of return *on* investment is indicated until there is a recovery of the cost *of* capital. Similar to RI, EVA® motivates managers to increase investment as long as such investments return at least $1 beyond the cost of capital. In this sense, this use of EVA® is thought to better align the interests of shareholders and managers of a company.

On the surface, RI and EVA® look confusingly similar. There is a major difference, however. Residual income (RI) is calculated entirely using reported (i.e., GAAP-based) accounting data. As such, RI suffers from all of the limitations associated with historical-based accounting statements. By contrast, EVA® attempts to approximate economic, rather than accounting, earnings and level of invested capital.

Thus, RI and EVA® are similar in form but strikingly different in terms of measurement. The overall objective of EVA® is to provide an estimate of the *value added* to (or destroyed by) each division of an organization (or the entire organization itself) during a given period. As such, EVA® is one approach to what we call *value-based management.*

## Estimating EVA®

The equation listed above for EVA® can be expanded as follows:

$$\text{EVA}^® = \text{NOPAT} - (k \times \text{Average invested capital})$$

where NOPAT = After-tax *cash* operating income, after depreciation (that is, "the total pool of cash funds available to suppliers of capital")

= Revenues − Cash operating costs − Depreciation − Cash taxes on operating income

It is precisely because of the deduction for depreciation that the earnings figure in the computation of EVA® is referred to as *net* operating profit after tax (i.e., as NOPAT). In the above formulation, invested capital = economic capital = cash contributed by suppliers of funds to the business (or business unit).

Finally, note that in determining the imputed charge for invested capital, $k$ represents the weighted-average cost of capital (WACC).[9]

An alternative specification of EVA® is:

$$\text{EVA}^® = (r - k) \times \text{Invested capital}$$

where

$r$ = Rate of return on capital (what economists might call *cash-on-cash return*)

= NOPAT ÷ Invested capital

and

$k$ = WACC

[9] See Chapter 12 for a discussion of the calculation of the weighted-average cost of capital (WACC) for a company as a whole. As indicated in footnote 8, supra, adjustments to the firmwide WACC may be needed when estimating *divisional* discount rates.

The primary advantage of the preceding formulation is its associated interpretation:

---

If $r > k$ during a period, then shareholder value was increased during that period (i.e., EVA® was positive).

---

As seen from the above, in order to calculate EVA® for a period, we need to estimate both NOPAT and capital. Stewart, in the seminal work in the area, lists 164 possible adjustments to reported accounting data to estimate NOPAT and capital.[10] In the EVA® literature, adjustments to the capital figures reported in financial statements are referred to as *equity-equivalent (EE)* adjustments.

The actual number of adjustments in practice is typically much less than 164. Note that if no adjustments to reported accounting data are made, then the EVA® metric reduces to RI. The following table lists some common adjustments that analysts can make when estimating EVA®.

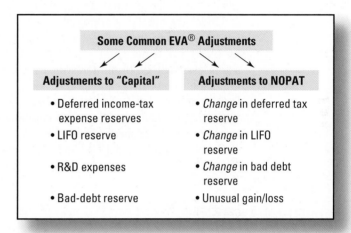

**Some Common EVA® Adjustments**

| Adjustments to "Capital" | Adjustments to NOPAT |
|---|---|
| • Deferred income-tax expense reserves | • *Change* in deferred tax reserve |
| • LIFO reserve | • *Change* in LIFO reserve |
| • R&D expenses | • *Change* in bad debt reserve |
| • Bad-debt reserve | • Unusual gain/loss |

## Alternative Approaches to Estimating EVA® NOPAT and EVA® Capital

Stewart provides two alternative ways for estimating an entity's EVA®: the *operating approach* and the *financing approach*. Which of the two methods you use is simply a matter of personal preference. If applied correctly, both yield the same estimate of EVA®.

### Financing Approach

In the financing approach, NOPAT is estimated by building up to the rate of return on capital from the standard return on equity (ROE) calculation in three steps:

1. Eliminate financial leverage (i.e., the effect of debt financing).
2. Eliminate so-called financial distortions.
3. Eliminate so-called accounting distortions.

As a result of the first two adjustments above, NOPAT will represent the total returns available to *all* providers of capital to the company. The NOPAT return therefore represents the productivity of capital employed in the business, irrespective of how investments in that capital were financed.

To calculate EVA® capital using the financing approach, you would first determine the total of interest-bearing debt plus capitalized leases. To this figure, you would add the book value of common equity (par value of stock, capital in excess of par, and retained earnings), the book value of preferred stock, and noncontrolling interests (if any). Finally, it is necessary to adjust for equity equivalents, such as the estimated present

---

[10] G. Bennett Stewart III, *The Quest for Value* (New York: Harper Collins, 1995).

value of noncapitalized leases, the balance sheet amount of deferred taxes, and the LIFO reserve (if any). The resulting figure represents an estimate of EVA® capital.

### Operating Approach

The operating approach to estimating NOPAT essentially consists of starting with (cash) sales and then subtracting depreciation and recurring cash economic expenses. Next, we deduct the amount of cash operating taxes, after which time we are left with EVA® NOPAT. In estimating the amount of cash taxes paid, we adjust reported income-tax expense by the change in the deferred tax account during the period. Note that interest expense, because it is a financing charge, is ignored in the determination of EVA® NOPAT. What this means, therefore, is that we must remove (that is, add back to income-tax expense) the assumed income-tax benefit associated with the deductibility of interest expense. Finally, to estimate EVA® NOPAT we make a number of "EE" adjustments (e.g., the effect of a change in the LIFO reserve account, and imputed interest on non-capitalized leases). The resulting profit figure should be the same as the NOPAT figure calculated under the financing approach.

Under the operating approach, EVA® capital is estimated basically by looking at the left-hand side of the entity's balance sheet. We define EVA® capital as net working capital (NWC) plus net fixed assets (NFA), where NWC is defined as (adjusted) current assets less NIBCLS (noninterest-bearing current liabilities). Typical EE adjustments that are made to reported balance sheet data include adjustments for the LIFO reserve and for the present value of noncapitalized leases. In effect, we capitalize these leases and therefore put them on a par with capitalized leases, if any, that already appear on the company's balance sheet.

Problems 19-46 and 19-47 at the end of the chapter explore the issue of estimating EVA® using the operating approach and financing approach, respectively.[11]

## Using Average Total Assets

For purposes of calculating ROI, RI, and EVA®, at what point in the accounting period are assets measured? In practice, accountants use the average of the beginning and ending balances of the year for total assets in these performance metrics. The reason is that since income is applicable to the entire year, then using a simple average of the amount of total assets for the year is consistent with the period covered by the income. For example, CompuCity's ROI for 2013 (using information from Exhibit 19.1 and assuming the investment amounts shown in the exhibit are for the year-end) would be calculated as 13.89%:

$$\text{ROI} = \frac{\$26,000}{(\$182,000 + \$192,500) \div 2} = 13.89\%$$

## Part Two: Transfer Pricing

**Transfer pricing**
is the determination of an exchange price for a product or service when different business units within a firm exchange it.

**Transfer pricing** is the determination of an exchange price for a product or service when different business units within a firm exchange it. The products can be final products sold to outside customers or intermediate products provided to other internal units. Regardless of whether business units of an organization are considered profit centers (Chapter 18) or investment centers, transfer prices are needed for performance-evaluation purposes. For example, without transfer prices it would not be possible to implement the performance metrics discussed in Part One of this chapter (i.e., ROI, RI, and EVA®).

[11] Additional guidance for estimating EVA® NOPAT and EVA® capital are provided in the following sources: G. Bennett Stewart III, *The Quest for Value* (New York: Harper Collins, 1995), and D. S. Young and S. F. O'Byrne, *EVA® and Value-Based Management: A Practical Guide to Implementation* (New York: McGraw-Hill, 2001).

## When Is Transfer Pricing Important?

Transfers of products and services between business units is most common in firms with a high degree of vertical integration. Such firms engage in a number of different value-creating activities in the value chain. Wood product, food product, and consumer product firms are examples. For instance, a computer manufacturer must determine transfer prices if it prepares the chips, boards, and other components and assembles the computer itself. (See Exhibit 2.3 in Chapter 2: Value Chain for the Computer Manufacturing Industry.) A useful way to visualize the transfer-pricing context is to create a graphic such as the one in Exhibit 19.8 that illustrates the business units involved in the transfer of products and services and identifies them as inside or outside the firm, non-domestic or domestic. Exhibit 19.8 shows the transfers for a hypothetical computer manufacturer, High Value Computer (HVC), that purchases a key component, the x-chip, from both internal and external suppliers and purchases other components from non-domestic sources. The internal unit that manufactures x-chips sells them both internally and externally. Where it is known, the transfer price is shown in Exhibit 19.8.

The management accountant's role is to help determine the proper transfer price for the internal sales of the x-chip. We begin by considering the objectives of transfer pricing.

## Objectives of Transfer Pricing

**LO 19-4**

*Explain the objectives of transfer pricing, and describe the advantages and disadvantages of various transfer-pricing alternatives.*

Transfer prices are used to accomplish certain objectives. It is against these objectives that alternative transfer-price options can be evaluated. As is the case with the financial-performance metrics discussed in Part One of this chapter, we can identify three primary objectives for transfer prices:

1. Motivate a high level of effort on the part of business-unit managers (i.e., extent to which a particular transfer-pricing method maintains autonomy of the business units).
2. Goal congruency (i.e., achieve consistency between decisions made by managers of business units and the goals of top management); for example, one important goal of transfer pricing is to minimize, within allowable limits, income-tax consequences of internal transfers of goods and services.

**EXHIBIT 19.8**
**Transfer-Pricing Context for High Value Computer (HVC) Company Example**

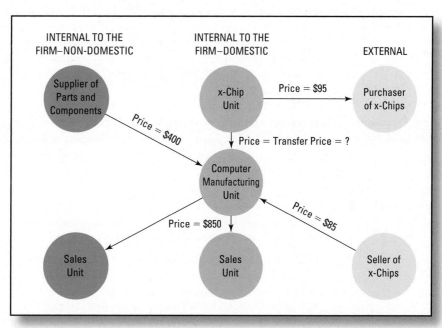

Note: "Internal to the firm" refers to interdivisional transfers of goods and/or services. In the HVC example, internal units include both domestic and non-domestic units/divisions.

3. Reward business-unit managers fairly for their effort and skill, and for the effectiveness of the decisions they make.

From a practical standpoint, specific transfer-pricing alternatives can also be evaluated in terms of implementation/administrative costs. In the next section we discuss several transfer-pricing methods, including advantages and disadvantages of each of these methods.

## Transfer-Pricing Methods

The four available methods for determining the transfer price are: variable cost, full cost, market price, and negotiated price.[12]

The **variable-cost method**
sets the transfer price equal to
the variable cost of the selling
unit.

The **variable-cost method** sets the transfer price equal to the selling unit's variable cost, with or without a markup. This method is desirable when the selling unit has excess capacity and the selling unit's variable cost is less than the external purchase price. The relatively low transfer price encourages buying internally, a situation that benefits the firm as a whole. To help ensure an internal transfer and because of equity considerations, some companies add a markup to variable cost when determining the transfer price. One alternative in this regard is to add a lump-sum amount to variable costs. Also, variable costs can be defined either as actual or as standard costs.

The **full-cost method**
sets the transfer price equal to
the variable cost plus an
allocated fixed cost for the
selling unit.

The **full-cost method** sets the transfer price equal to variable costs plus an allocated share of the selling unit's fixed costs, with or without a markup for profit. Advantages of this approach are that it is well understood and that the information for determining the transfer price is readily available in the accounting records. A key disadvantage is that it includes fixed costs, which can cause improper decision making (Chapter 11). To improve on the full-cost method, firms can use the activity-based costing (ABC) method described in Chapter 5.[13] Again, costs can be defined either as actual or as standard costs.

The **market-price method**
sets the transfer price as the
current price of the product in
the external market.

The **market-price method** sets the transfer price as the current price of the product in the external market. Its key advantage is objectivity; it best satisfies the arm's-length criterion desired for both management and for tax purposes. Further, using market prices generally (but not necessarily always) provides proper economic incentives. A key disadvantage is that the market price, especially for intermediate products, is often not available.

The **negotiated-price method**
involves a negotiation process
and sometimes arbitration
between units to determine the
transfer price.

The **negotiated-price method** involves a negotiation process and sometimes arbitration between units to determine the transfer price. This method is desirable when the units have a history of significant conflict and negotiation can result in an agreed-upon price. One could also argue that the use of negotiated transfer prices is consistent with the theory of decentralization. The primary limitation is that the method can reduce the desired autonomy of the units. Further, this method may be costly and time-consuming to implement.

**Dual pricing**
involves the use of multiple
prices for an internal transfer.

Firms can also use two or more methods, called **dual pricing**. For example, when numerous conflicts exist between two units, standard full cost might be used as the buyer's transfer price, while the seller might use market price.[14]

The advantages and limitations of each of the four methods are summarized in Exhibit 19.9.

---

[12] Administered transfer prices are also possible. In this situation the transfer price is set either by management or by an arbiter. Such "imposed" prices are sometimes used when a specified internal transaction occurs frequently. While avoiding confrontations sometimes associated with a negotiated transfer price, we note that an imposed transfer price impinges on business-unit authority and therefore the spirit of decentralization.

[13] For an explanation of the use of activity-based costing in transfer pricing, see Robert S. Kaplan, Dan Weiss, and Eyal Desheh, "Transfer Pricing with ABC," *Management Accounting*, May 1997, pp. 20–28, and Gary J. Colbert and Barry H. Spicer, "Linking Activity-Based Costing and Transfer Pricing for Improved Decisions and Behavior," *Journal of Cost Management*, May–June 1998, pp. 20–26.

[14] For an illustration of dual allocation in transfer pricing, see David W. Young, "Two-Part Transfer Pricing Improves IDS Financial Control," *Healthcare Financial Management*, August 1998, pp. 56–65.

**EXHIBIT 19.9**  **Advantages and Limitations of Alternative Transfer-Pricing Methods**

| Method | Advantages | Limitations |
|---|---|---|
| Variable cost | • Provides the proper motivation for the manager to make the correct *short-term decision,* in which the seller's fixed costs are not expected to change. When the seller's variable cost is less than the buyer's outside price, the variable cost transfer price will cause internal sourcing, the correct decision | • Inappropriate for long-term decision making in which fixed costs are relevant and prices must cover fixed as well as variable costs<br>• Unfair to seller if seller is profit or investment center (i.e., no profit recognized on the transfer) |
| Full cost | • Easy to implement<br>• Intuitive and easily understood<br>• Preferred by tax authorities over variable cost<br>• Appropriate for long-term decision making in which fixed costs are relevant, and prices must cover fixed as well as variable costs | • Irrelevance of fixed cost in short-term decision making; fixed costs should be ignored in the buyer's choice of whether to buy inside or outside the firm<br>• If used, should be standard rather than actual cost (allows buyer to know cost in advance and prevents seller from passing along inefficiencies) |
| Market price | • Helps to preserve unit autonomy<br>• Provides incentive for the selling unit to be competitive with outside suppliers<br>• Has arm's-length standard desired by taxing authorities<br>• Usually provides proper economic incentives | • Intermediate products often have no market price<br>• Should be adjusted for any cost savings associated with an internal transfer, such as reduced selling costs |
| Negotiated price | • Can be the most practical approach when significant conflict exists<br>• Is consistent with the theory of decentralization | • Need negotiation rule and/or arbitration procedure, which can reduce autonomy<br>• Potential tax problems; might not be considered arm's length<br>• Can be costly and time-consuming to implement<br>• Resulting profitability measures (e.g., ROI or RI) are partly a function of the negotiating skills of the manager, rather than the operational performance of the business unit |

## Choosing the Right Transfer-Pricing Method: The Firmwide Perspective

One aspect of transfer pricing is whether the transfer price will lead to actions that benefit the organization as a whole. Looked at differently, we might ask whether the transfer price motivates an internal transfer when this benefits the firm, and whether it motivates an external sale when such a sale is warranted (from an organizationwide perspective). To guide such a decision, three questions must be addressed:

1. Is there an outside (i.e., an external) supplier?
2. Is the seller's variable cost (or, more generally, its incremental cost) less than the external market price?
3. Is the selling unit operating at full capacity?

Exhibit 19.10 shows the influence of each of these three factors on the choice of a transfer price and on the decision to purchase inside or outside the firm.

**First: Is there an external supplier?** If not, there is no market price, and the best transfer price is based on cost or negotiated price. If there is an outside supplier, we must consider the relationship of the inside seller's variable cost (or, more generally, its incremental cost) to the market price of the external supplier by answering the second question.

**Second: Is the seller's variable cost (or, more generally, its incremental cost) less than the external market price?** If not, the seller's costs are likely far too high, and from the standpoint of the organization as a whole the buyer should buy externally. On the other hand, if the seller's incremental costs are less than the market price, we must consider the capacity in the selling unit by answering the third question.[15]

[15] We focus on variable costs in this second step because commonly the transfer-pricing issue is addressed as a short-term decision in which fixed costs are not expected to differ whether the internal transfer is made or is not made. In this case, the analysis is very much like the make-or-buy decision problem covered in Chapter 11—the fixed costs of the seller generally are irrelevant since they will not change in the short run. Thus, unless otherwise noted, in this discussion we will be using the words "incremental cost" and "variable cost" synonymously.

**EXHIBIT 19.10    Choosing the Right Transfer Price**

|  | Decision to Transfer | Transfer Price |
|---|---|---|
| **First**: Is there an external supplier? If there is **no** outside supply, then———→ | Buy internally | Cost or negotiated price |
| If there is an external supply, answer the second question; | | |
| **Second**: Is the seller's incremental cost less than the external price? | | |
| **If it is greater than the external price**, the seller must look for ways to reduce cost. If not feasible, then ————————————→ | Buy externally | No transfer price |
| If seller's incremental costs are less than the external price, answer the third question; | | |
| **Third**: Is the selling unit operating at full capacity? | | |
| **If seller has excess capacity**, then ———————————————→ | Buy internally | **Low**: Variable/incremental cost  **High**: Market price |
| If the seller is at full capacity———→ And if the contribution of the external sales to the entire firm is **greater than** the savings of the internal purchase, then————→ | Buy externally | No transfer price |
| Or if the contribution of the external sales to the entire firm is **less than** the savings of the internal purchase, then————→ | Buy internally | Market price |

**Third: Is the selling unit operating at full capacity?** That is, will the order from the internal buyer cause the selling unit to deny other sales opportunities? If not, the selling division should provide the order to the internal buyer at a transfer price somewhere between variable cost and market price. In contrast, if the selling unit is at full capacity, we must determine and compare the cost savings of internal sales versus the selling division's opportunity cost of lost sales. If the cost savings to the internal buyer are higher than the cost of lost sales to the seller, then from the standpoint of the organization as a whole, the buying unit should buy inside, and the proper transfer price should be the market price.

Determining the correct transfer price and correct transfer decision can be illustrated using the High Value Computer (HVC) case (Exhibit 19.8). HVC has the option to purchase the x-chip outside the firm for $85 or to manufacture it. Note that if the manufacturing unit of HVC purchases the x-chip from the outside supper, it must add a component to the x-chip at a variable cost of $5 to make the x-chip function as desired; this additional step is not necessary if the x-chip is purchased internally. Also, note that the x-chip production unit can sell its chip outside for $95 but there is a variable selling cost of $2 per unit; there is no selling cost for internal transfer. The relevant information is presented in the top portion of Exhibit 19.11. The lower portion of Exhibit 19.11 shows the calculation of the relevant costs for each of the two options.

A comparison of options 1 and 2 in Exhibit 19.11 shows that the firm as a whole benefits (in the short run) under option 1 when the computer manufacturing unit of HVC purchases the x-chip externally, and the x-chip product unit of HVC sells externally. The reason is that the computer manufacturing unit's savings of $30 from internal transfer ($30 = $85 outside price plus $5 for additional variable cost to add a component to the x-chip less $60 variable cost of the internal x-chip product unit) is less than the x-chip product unit's opportunity cost of lost sales, $33 ($95 less $60 manufacturing cost less $2 selling cost). The opportunity cost of the x-chip product unit is important since the unit is assumed to be working at full capacity. The $450,000 difference between the two options is due to the net difference identified above, ($33 − $30) × 150,000 = $450,000. In summary, we can answer the same three questions for HVC in the following way:

**First: Is there an outside supplier?** HVC has an outside supplier, so we must compare the internal seller's incremental costs (in this case, its variable costs) to the external seller's price.

The decline in value of Southeast Asian currencies (the Indonesian rupiah, Thai baht, Malaysian ringgit, and Sri Lanka rupee) relative to the U.S. dollar in the early 2000s appeared to be an opportunity for some Southeast Asian manufacturers to increase their exports to U.S. retailers and manufacturers. The idea is that the falling currency prices would make the Asian goods less expensive in U.S. dollars, which would increase their appeal in the United States relative to other products and thus increase demand. Nike, which has a number of manufacturing plants in Southeast Asia, says, however, that these currency changes will not have much effect on U.S. prices. Is Nike likely to miss the potential to lower prices and increase U.S. sales?

(Refer to Comments on Cost Management in Action at the end of the chapter.)

**EXHIBIT 19.11**

**Transfer-Pricing Example: The High Value Computer (HVC) Company**

Key assumptions:
   The computer manufacturing unit can buy the x-chip inside or outside the firm.
   The x-chip product unit can sell inside or outside the firm.
   The x-chip product unit is at full capacity (150,000 units).
   One x-chip is needed for each computer manufactured by HVC.
Other information:

| | |
|---|---:|
| Sales price of computer for HVC's computer manufacturing unit | $850 |
| Variable manufacturing cost of the computer manufacturing unit (excluding x-chip) ($400 parts and $250 labor) | 650 |
| Variable x-chip manufacturing cost for HVC's x-chip product unit | 60 |
| Price of x-chip from outside supplier, to HVC's computer manufacturing unit | 85 |
| Variable cost to computer manufacturing unit to add needed component to outside supplier's x-chip | 5 |
| Price of x-chip from HVC's x-chip product unit to outside buyer | 95 |
| Variable selling cost to the x-chip product unit for outside sales | 2 |

**Option 1: X-Chip Product Unit Sells Outside**

HVC manufactures 150,000 computers, using x-chips purchased for $85 from outside supplier; HVC's x-chip product unit sells 150,000 units for $95 each to an outside buyer.

| | Contribution Income Statement* (000s omitted) | | |
|---|---|---|---|
| | Computer Manufacturing Unit | X-Chip Product Unit | Total |
| Sales (price = $850, $95) | $127,500 | $14,250 | $141,750 |
| Less: Variable costs | | | |
| x-chip ($85 + $5) | 13,500 | | 13,500 |
| Other costs ($650, $60 + $2) | 97,500 | 9,300 | 106,800 |
| Contribution margin | $ 16,500 | $ 4,950 | $ 21,450 |

**Option 2: X-Chip Product Unit Sells Inside (to HVC's Computer Manufacturing Unit)**

HVC manufactures 150,000 computers, using x-chips purchased for $60 (variable cost) from the inside supplier.

| | Computer Manufacturing Unit | X-Chip Product Unit | Total |
|---|---|---|---|
| Sales (price = $850, $60) | $127,500 | $9,000 | $136,500 |
| Less: Variable costs | | | |
| x-chip ($60) | 9,000 | | 9,000 |
| Other costs ($650, $60) | 97,500 | 9,000 | 106,500 |
| Contribution margin | $ 21,000 | — | $ 21,000 |

*It is assumed that fixed costs will not differ for the two options; thus, these costs are excluded from the analysis.

**Second: Is the seller's variable cost (or, more generally, its incremental cost) less than the external market price?** For HVC, it is, so we must consider the utilization of capacity in the inside selling unit.

**Third: Is the selling unit operating at full capacity?** For HVC, it is, so we must consider the contribution of the selling unit's external sales relative to the savings from selling internally.

Again, for HVC, the contribution of the selling unit's external sales is $33 per unit, which is higher than the savings from selling internally ($30). Therefore, HVC's x-chip product unit should choose outside sales and make no internal transfers.

By way of summary, we note that from the standpoint of HVC as a whole, setting an appropriate transfer price is important because it motivates divisional actions that may either increase or decrease the total operating profits of the firm. You can see this by looking at the total contribution margins associated with each of the two options listed in Exhibit 19.11. A transfer price that motivates option 1 increases total contribution margin (and therefore operating income). In short, setting the appropriate transfer price affects the "size of the pie." We turn next to a discussion of a general model that can be used to help guide the determination of the "correct" transfer price from the standpoint of the firm as a whole. Later, we consider a second situation where the "size of the pie" (i.e., the amount of firmwide profit) is affected by the transfer price chosen: transfers between domestic and non-domestic units, each of which may be subject to its own set of income-tax rates, customs duties, and so on.

## General Transfer-Pricing Rule

The preceding discussion of decision making, and accompanying summary (Exhibit 19.10), may seem overwhelming to you in terms of detail and complexity. It may also seem as if the transfer-pricing decision can be mechanized according to a set of rules. This is certainly not the case because as we stated at the beginning of this section of the chapter, the ultimate transfer-pricing decision is a function of several considerations. One of these is the extent to which the transfer price motivates the "correct" decision from the standpoint of the firm as a whole. Thus, in interpreting Exhibit 19.10 you should understand that the stated rules relate to this issue.

In Chapter 11 we introduced you to the notion of relevant costs for decision making. One definition of such costs is the sum of out-of-pocket costs plus opportunity costs (if any). We can appeal to this same notion in the context of setting an appropriate transfer price. Thus, the essence of Exhibit 19.10 can be summarized by the following general transfer-pricing rule:

Minimum transfer price = Incremental (i.e., out-of-pocket) cost of the producing division + Opportunity cost to the organization (if any) by making an internal transfer

From the standpoint of the firm as a whole, the preceding rule will generally ensure that the optimum decision (transfer internally or not) will be motivated by the transfer price. Refer once again to the data (and two options) presented in Exhibit 19.11. We see that there is a pretax benefit to HVC as a whole if option 1 is chosen: HVC is better off, at least in the short run, if the computer manufacturing unit purchases its chips externally and the x-chip product unit sells its chips externally. As we'll see below, a transfer price based on the general rule presented above will motivate this decision:

| | | |
|---|---:|---:|
| Incremental cost of the x-chip product unit, per chip = | | $60 |
| Opportunity cost of making an internal transfer: | | |
| External sales price | $95 | |
| Less: Incremental costs: | | |
| Selling cost | 2 | |
| Variable manufacturing cost | 60 | $33 |

Thus, the minimum transfer price should be set at $93 (i.e., $60 + $33). At this price, the computer manufacturing unit at HVC would be motivated to purchase externally, at $90 per chip. By doing so, HVC as a whole would generate a total contribution margin of $21,450,000 (compared to $21,000,000, as determined under option 2).

At the same time, we should correctly view the amount indicated by the general rule as a minimum amount that the selling division should accept. In Chapter 11, we essentially saw the same thing: In deciding whether a business should accept a special (i.e., one-time) order, the minimum specified price was the sum of out-of-pocket costs plus opportunity cost (if any). (Recall the notion of *opportunity cost:* benefit forgone by taking a particular course of action.) *Minimum* within the context of the special sales order means the *floor* below which the firm would not normally consummate the deal. The same logic would apply in the transfer-pricing case. Here, opportunity cost is the contribution margin the organization forgoes, if any, by transferring internally rather than making the sale to an external party.

We conclude here by noting that estimating opportunity costs may not be an easy task, or even possible in some situations. For example, unless the product in question is traded in a purely competitive market (e.g., commodity-type products), then selling price, and therefore opportunity cost, are partly a function of the amount of internal versus external sales by the producer. These interactions complicate efforts to determine an opportunity cost associated with internal transfers. As another example, the product in question may be in the form of an intermediate product for which no organized external market exists. In such cases, the organization would have to rely on the use of one of the other transfer-pricing options.

## International Issues in Transfer Pricing

**LO 19-5**

*Discuss important international issues that arise in transfer pricing.*

Transfer pricing is perhaps the most important international tax issue faced by multinational corporations (MNCs). Most countries now accept the Organization of Economic Cooperation and Development's model treaty, which calls for transfer prices to be adjusted using the arm's-length standard, that is, to a price that unrelated parties would have set. The model treaty is widely accepted, but the way countries apply it can differ.

**The arm's-length standard** says that transfer prices should be set so they reflect the price that unrelated parties acting independently would have set.

**The comparable-price method** establishes an arm's-length price by using the sales prices of similar products made by unrelated firms.

**The resale-price method** is based on an appropriate markup using gross profits of unrelated firms selling similar products.

**The cost-plus method** determines the transfer price based on the selling unit's cost plus a gross profit percentage determined by comparing the seller's sales to those of unrelated parties.

However, worldwide support is strong for an approach to limit attempts by MNCs to reduce tax liability by setting transfer prices that differ from the arm's-length standard.

The **arm's-length standard** calls for setting transfer prices to reflect the price that unrelated parties acting independently would have set. The arm's-length standard is applied in several different ways, but the three most widely used methods are (1) the comparable-price method, (2) the resale-price method, and (3) the cost-plus method. The **comparable-price method** is the most commonly used and the most preferred by tax authorities. It establishes an arm's-length price by using the sales prices of similar products made by unrelated firms.[16]

The **resale-price method** is used for distributors and marketing units when little value is added and no significant manufacturing operations exist. In this method, the transfer price is based on an appropriate markup using gross profits of unrelated firms selling similar products.

The **cost-plus method** determines the transfer price based on the selling unit's costs plus a gross profit percentage determined by comparing the seller's sales to those of unrelated parties or to unrelated parties' sales to those of other unrelated parties.

By keeping detailed records of the determination of cost, the management accountant can assist in determining the appropriate transfer price for international transfers of goods and services. The application of modern costing techniques, such as ABC (Chapter 5), would be particularly useful in terms of justifying a particular transfer price to taxing authorities. While it is true that there are limits to the transfer price charged in multinational transactions, it is also true that minimizing worldwide tax is a legitimate business objective. By setting a (legitimate) high transfer price for goods or services transferred to a unit operating in a relatively high-tax country, a company can reduce its tax liability. Such a transfer price would increase the cost and thus reduce the income of the purchasing unit, thereby minimizing taxes for this unit. At the same time, the higher profits shown by the selling unit (as a result of the high transfer price) would be taxed at lower rates in the seller's home country. As demonstrated by the example that follows, international tax-planning opportunities associated with a firm's transfer-pricing process allow the firm to affect the "size of the pie."

### Income-Tax Planning Opportunities: International Transfer Pricing

To illustrate the tax-planning opportunities associated with the setting of international transfer prices, refer to facts presented in Exhibit 19.11 and assume the following: (1) option 2 (i.e., all transfers take place within HVC), (2) the x-chip product unit is located in Korea while the computer manufacturing unit is located in the United States; (3) the x-chip product unit incurs no fixed costs; fixed costs for the computer manufacturing unit, per year, amount to $2,000,000; and (4) income-tax rates are as follows: Korea, 40%; the United States, 30%. Under these assumptions, the amount of operating income (i.e., *pretax* profits) shown under each of the three transfer-pricing options, for both units and for HVC as a

---

[16] In this context, *unrelated* indicates that the firm has no common ownership interest.

**EXHIBIT 19.12**
HVC Unit and Total Operating
Income (000s Omitted) under
Alternative Transfer Prices

| | Transfer-Pricing Options | | |
| --- | --- | --- | --- |
| Volume = 150,000 units | Market Price ($85.00/unit) | Variable Cost ($60.00/unit) | Negotiated Price ($72.50/unit) |
| **x-Chip Product Unit (Seller):** | | | |
| Revenues | $ 12,750 | $  9,000 | $ 10,875 |
| Costs: | | | |
| Variable costs (Exhibit 19.11; $60/unit) | 9,000 | 9,000 | 9,000 |
| Operating income | 3,750 | -0- | 1,875 |
| **Computer Manufacturing Unit (Buyer):** | | | |
| Revenues (Exhibit 19.11; $850/unit) | $127,500 | $127,500 | $127,500 |
| Costs: | | | |
| Transferred-in costs (from x-chip product unit) | 12,750 | 9,000 | 10,875 |
| Variable costs (Exhibit 19.11; $650/unit) | 97,500 | 97,500 | 97,500 |
| Fixed costs (assumed) | 2,000 | 2,000 | 2,000 |
| Operating income | 15,250 | 19,000 | $ 17,125 |
| **Combined Operating Income (HVC)** | $ 19,000 | $ 19,000 | $ 19,000 |

Note: The combined operating income reflected in Exhibit 19.11 is $21,000,000, under all transfer-pricing options. To convert from contribution margin (Exhibit 19.11) to operating income (Exhibit 19.12) we are assuming that the computer manufacturing unit of HVC incurs fixed costs of $2,000,000 per year. As such, firmwide operating income reflected in Exhibit 19.12 for each transfer-pricing alternative is $19,000,000.

whole, is shown in Exhibit 19.12. The negotiated transfer price of $72.50 per unit was determined by taking a simple average of the market price per chip ($85) and the variable cost of the x-chip ($60). Thus, the highly condensed income statement presented in Exhibit 19.12 reflects the anticipated profit situation, *before tax and before customs/import duties,* for HVC as a whole.

In the preceding section, we saw that setting the appropriate transfer price (at $93 per chip) would ensure that, from HVC's perspective, a correct decision (between option 1 and option 2) would be made. It may seem from the data presented in Exhibit 19.12 that choice of transfer price is irrelevant because the "bottom lines" are all the same. However, we have to this point left out of the exhibit the effect of one crucial factor: transnational differences in income-tax rates. In HVC's case, the income-tax differential that exists in Korea and the United States provides HVC with an ability (within limits) to maximize *after-tax* firmwide profits based on choice of transfer price.

To illustrate, first focus on the bottom portion of Exhibit 19.12. What would the after-tax income statement look like for each division and for HVC as a whole given the assumed tax rates and under each of the three transfer-pricing options? The relevant calculations are presented in Exhibit 19.13. As can be seen from this exhibit, both the total amount of

**EXHIBIT 19.13**
HVC Unit and Total After-Tax
Operating Income (000s
omitted) and Income-Tax
Expense Based on Alternative
Transfer-Pricing Choices and
Assumed Tax Rates

| | Transfer Pricing Options | | |
| --- | --- | --- | --- |
| Volume = 150,000 units | Market Price ($85.00/unit) | Variable Cost ($60.00/unit) | Negotiated Price ($72.50/unit) |
| **x-Chip Product Unit (Seller):** | | | |
| Operating income (Exhibit 19.12) | $ 3,750 | $    0 | $ 1,875 |
| Less: Income taxes (@ 40%) | 1,500 | 0 | 750 |
| After-tax operating income | $ 2,250 | $    0 | $ 1,125 |
| **Computer Manufacturing Unit (Buyer):** | | | |
| Operating income (Exhibit 19.12) | $15,250 | $19,000 | $17,125 |
| Less: Income taxes (@ 30%) | 4,575 | 5,700 | 5,138 |
| After-tax operating income | $10,675 | $13,300 | $11,987 |
| **Combined (Firmwide) Amounts:** | | | |
| Income tax expense | $ 6,075 | $ 5,700 | $ 5,888 |
| After-tax operating income | $12,925 | $13,300 | $13,112 |

taxes paid and the firmwide operating income after tax are affected by the choice of transfer price. We note, too, that the extent of this effect is a function of the difference in tax rates: the larger the disparity in tax rates, all else held constant, the greater the after-tax differences observed across transfer-pricing options. In short, this is yet another example where the "size of the pie" for the firm as a whole is affected by the choice of transfer price.

## Other International Considerations

In addition to income tax, there are other considerations that bear upon the transfer-price decision in an international context. These include minimizing customs charges, using transfer prices to deal with currency restrictions of foreign countries, and dealing with the risk of expropriation of assets.

### *Risk of Expropriation*

**Expropriation**

occurs when a government takes ownership and control of assets that a foreign investor has invested in that country.

**Expropriation** occurs when a government takes ownership and control of assets that a foreign investor has invested in that country. In managing the relationship with any one country, the management accountant attempts to find a strategic balance among these sometimes conflicting objectives. When a significant risk of expropriation exists, the firm can take appropriate actions such as limiting new investment or developing improved relationships with the foreign government (e.g., by actually paying higher taxes to that government via the transfer-pricing decision).

### *Minimization of Customs Charges*

The transfer price can affect the overall cost, including customs charges (i.e., tariffs and duties) imposed on goods imported from a non-domestic (i.e., a foreign) unit. As such, issues related to these charges are similar to the income-tax considerations discussed above: In order to reduce tariffs and customs duties, firms have incentives to lower the transfer prices for products imported into a country. Such charges should be expressed on an after-tax basis if the levies are deductible in determining taxable income in the country of import.

### *Currency Restrictions*

As a foreign unit accumulates profits, a problem arises in some countries that limits the amount and/or timing of repatriation of these profits to the parent company. One way to deal with these restrictions is to set the transfer price so that profits accumulate at a relatively low rate. This issue therefore provides managers and the management accountant with additional planning opportunities in certain circumstances.

## Advance Pricing Agreements

An **advance pricing agreement (APA)**

is an agreement between the Internal Revenue Service (IRS) and a firm that establishes an agreed-upon transfer price.

An **advance pricing agreement (APA)** is an agreement between the Internal Revenue Service (IRS) and a firm that establishes an agreed-upon transfer price. The APA usually is obtained before the firm engages in the transfer. The APA program's goal is to resolve transfer-pricing disputes in a timely manner and to avoid costly litigation. The program supplements the dispute resolution methods already in place: administrative (IRS), judicial, and treaty mechanisms.

---

## Summary

Return on investment (ROI) and residual income (RI) are two of the most commonly used and well-understood measures for evaluating the short-term financial performance of investment centers.

ROI, which is defined as the ratio of operating income generated by the investment center to the level of investment in the investment center, has several disadvantages: a short-term focus, the difficulty in determining a unique measure for earnings and investment, and investment-disincentive effects.

RI is computed as the investment center's earnings for a period less a capital charge based on a minimum desired rate of return. RI solves some, but not all, of ROI's problems. For example, both have a short-term focus, both rely on accrual-based accounting numbers, and both focus solely on (short-term) financial performance.

The increased interest in the balanced scorecard (BSC) and in economic value added (EVA®) suggests that firms are adapting performance-appraisal systems for investment centers to include a long-term strategic focus.

When an organization's business units exchange goods or services internally (i.e., between its own business units) and management desires to assess the financial performance of these units, a transfer price must be associated with the internal transfers. The management accountant can serve an important role by overseeing the objectives of transfer pricing: performance evaluation (of management and business units), tax minimization, management of foreign currencies and risks, and other strategic objectives. Common transfer-pricing methods include variable cost, full cost, market value, and negotiated price. Cost-based transfer prices can be set either at actual or at standard cost (see Chapter 14). In setting the transfer price, management considers the availability and quality of outside supply, the internal selling unit's capacity utilization, and the firm's strategic objectives in determining the proper transfer price. A general transfer-pricing guideline specifies that the minimum transfer price to the selling division is the sum of out-of-pocket costs plus opportunity costs to the seller (if any). As was the case in the "special sales order" decision covered in Chapter 11, this rule provides a floor or minimum transfer price. Some companies use dual pricing in which two separate transfer prices are used to price an internal transfer.

Perhaps the most important aspect in determining a transfer price for international transfers is minimizing international taxes. With the efforts of various international groups, each country monitors transfer prices used in international trade. The most common transfer-pricing methods used for international trade include the comparable-price method, the resale-price method, and the cost-plus method. A U.S. firm can determine the acceptability (to various countries) of its transfer-pricing method by requesting what is called an *advance pricing agreement* (APA) from the IRS.

## Key Terms

advance pricing agreement (APA), *838*
arm's-length standard, *836*
asset turnover (AT), *814*
comparable-price method, *836*
cost-plus method, *836*
dual pricing, *830*
economic value added, (EVA®), 826

expropriation, *838*
full-cost method, *830*
gross book value (GBV), *819*
historical cost, *818*
liquidation value, *819*
market-price method, *830*
negotiated-price method, *830*
net book value (NBV), *818*

replacement cost, *819*
resale-price method, *836*
residual income (RI), *823*
return on investment (ROI), *813*
return on sales (ROS), *814*
transfer pricing, *828*
variable-cost method, *830*

## Comments on Cost Management in Action

### Foreign Currency Translation, Transfer Pricing, and Profits

Nike is probably correct that U.S. prices for its products and those of its competitors will not change much. The reason is that the cost elements of its products from Southeast Asia affected by the falling local currencies, primarily labor costs, represent only a modest portion of the total product cost. Most of the cost of these manufactured products is for materials, which are imported from the United States and elsewhere outside Southeast Asia. Thus, the effect of the falling Southeast Asian currencies on *total* product cost is likely to be small; Nike estimates it to be 10% or less although some currencies have fallen to less than half of their previous value to the dollar.

Moreover, Southeast Asian manufacturers find that they have increased financing costs and sometimes reduced financing availability when the local currency falls and the raw materials from the United States and elsewhere become more expensive. For some of these manufacturers, the total operating and financing cost (in U.S. dollars) might even increase.

From a transfer-pricing perspective, the dramatic change in currency value presents real problems in performance evaluation. Should the local manufacturing unit be responsible for costs in U.S. currency or in terms of the local currency? Are the currency fluctuations controllable by the local managers? The answers to these questions are difficult and complex, but many companies expect their local managers to take steps to mitigate the negative effects of currency fluctuations by buying or selling options or other financial instruments, for example.

**Source:** Based on Jonathan Moore and Moon Ihlwan, "Cheaper Exports? Not So Fast," *BusinessWeek,* February 2, 1998, pp. 48–49.

## Self-Study Problems
(For solutions, please turn to the end of the chapter.)

### 1. Return on Investment (ROI) and Residual Income (RI)

Selected data from an investment center of IROL, Inc., follow:

| | |
|---|---|
| Sales | $8,000,000 |
| Net book value of assets, beginning | 2,500,000 |
| Net book value of assets, end | 2,600,000 |
| Net operating income | 640,000 |
| Minimum rate of return | 12% |

**Required**
1. Calculate return on sales (ROS), asset turnover (AT), and return on investment (ROI).
2. Calculate residual income (RI).

### 2. Transfer Pricing

Johnston Chemical Company manufactures a wide variety of industrial chemicals and adhesives. It purchases much of its raw material in bulk from other chemical companies. One chemical, T-Bar, is prepared in one of Johnston's own plants. T-Bar is shipped to other Johnston plants at a specified internal price.

The Johnston adhesive plant requires 10,000 barrels of T-Bar per month and can purchase it from an outside supplier for $150 per barrel. Johnston's T-Bar unit has a capacity of 20,000 barrels per month and is presently selling that amount to outside buyers at $165 per barrel. The difference between the T-Bar unit's price of $165 and the outside firm's T-Bar price of $150 is due to short-term pricing strategy only; the materials are equivalent in quality and functionality. The T-Bar unit's selling cost is $5 per barrel, and its variable cost of manufacturing is $90 per barrel.

**Required**
1. From the standpoint of the company as a whole, should the adhesive unit purchase T-Bar inside or outside the firm? Show calculations to support your answer.
2. Based on your answer in requirement 1, what is T-Bar's proper transfer price?
3. How would your answer to requirements 1 and 2 change, if at all, if the T-Bar unit had a capacity of 30,000 barrels per month?

*Please visit http://www.mhhe.com/blocher6e to access a narrated, animated tutorial for solving these problems.*

## Questions

19-1    What is meant by the term *investment center*? How is the financial performance of investment centers measured?

19-2    What is return on investment (ROI), and how is it calculated?

19-3    What are the measurement issues to consider when using return on investment (ROI)?

19-4    What are the advantages and limitations of return on investment (ROI) as a performance measure?

19-5    What are the components of return on investment (ROI), and how is each component interpreted and used?

19-6    What are the advantages and limitations of residual income (RI) as a performance measure?

19-7    How does the concept of economic value added EVA® compare, as a measure of financial performance, to return on investment (ROI) and residual income (RI)?

19-8    What are the three methods most commonly used in international taxation to determine a transfer price acceptable to tax authorities? Explain each method briefly.

19-9    What is meant by the term *arm's-length standard,* and for what is it used?

19-10    What does *expropriation* mean, and what is the role of transfer pricing in this regard?

## Brief Exercises

19-11    Smith Branded Apparel designs T-shirts for businesses and corporations. The accounting manager has presented the latest quarter's return on sales of 10% and asset turnover of 1.5. What is the company's current return on investment (ROI)?

19-12    Williams Manufacturing uses scrap metal to produce various tools, such as drill bits, hammer heads, saw blades, and nails. The CEO has asked you to analyze the saw blades division to determine asset turnover for last quarter. You find that the saw blades division had an ROI of 20%, sales of $10 million, and operating profits of $1 million. What was the asset turnover rate for last quarter?

19-13  Scott Healthcare provides a walk-in clinic for its patients and a pharmacy for any medication prescribed by the doctor. Last year Scott generated total sales of $500,000 and $100,000 in profits. Scott also had average assets of $250,000 for the year. What are Scott Healthcare's return on sales (ROS), asset turnover (AT), and return on investment (ROI)?

19-14  Matthews Produce harvests and sells Florida oranges. Matthews has hired you to determine its return on investment (ROI) based on both net book value and gross book value. You are given that profits are $2 million, the net book value (NBV) of operating assets is $10 million, and the gross book value (GBV) of these assets is $40 million. What is ROI based on NBV and based on GBV?

19-15  Foreman Publishing Company's income for the most recent quarter was $500,000, and the average net book value (NBV) of assets during the quarter was $1.5 million. If the company has a required rate of return of 15% on investment, what was residual income (RI) for the quarter?

19-16  Tinsley Plastics manufactures plastic bottles used for beverages and household cleaners. The average net book value (NBV) of assets during the quarter is estimated as $500,000. If the required rate of return is 10% on average assets, and the firm wants to have residual income (RI) of $100,000 for this quarter, what must its profits be?

19-17  Moore Money is a financial services firm specializing in fixed-income investments. You have been asked by the accounting manager to analyze the company's financial data from last quarter. You find the firm had return on investment (ROI) of 15% and asset turnover of 0.5. What was the firm's return on sales?

19-18  King Mattresses sells both mattress sets and bed frames. Last quarter total sales were $50,000 for mattress sets and $25,000 for bed frames. Return on investment (ROI) was 10% for both divisions, while asset turnover (AT) was 5 for mattress sets and 2 for bed frames. What was the amount of operating profit for each division?

19-19  Using the data from 19-18 above, compute King Mattresses's total return on sales (ROS).

19-20  Felton Co. produces rubber bands for commercial and home use. Felton reported $1 million residual income (RI) with $20 million net book value (NBV) of assets and $5 million in operating income for the year. What was the required rate of return?

## Exercises

[LO 19-1]   19-21  **Return on Investment (ROI); Comparisons of Three Investment Centers (Divisions)**

**Required**   Fill in the blanks:

|  | Division | | |
|---|---|---|---|
|  | X | Y | Z |
| Sales | $1,500,000 | $750,000 | $ _____ |
| Operating income | 150,000 | 75,000 | _____ |
| Investment (assets) | 600,000 | _____ | 2,500,000 |
| Return on sales | _____ | _____ | 0.5% |
| Asset turnover | _____ | _____ | 1.5 |
| Return on investment | _____ | 1% | _____ |

[LO 19-1]   19-22  **Return on Investment (ROI); Different Measures for Total Assets; Spreadsheet Analysis**   Alex Chunn, Inc., has the following financial data for 2013 for its three regional divisions:

|  | | Historical Cost | | Current Cost | |
|---|---|---|---|---|---|
| Region | Operating Income | Net Book Value | Gross Book Value | Replacement Cost | Liquidation Value |
| North Atlantic | $65,000 | $250,000 | $450,000 | $990,000 | $350,000 |
| Mid Atlantic | 40,000 | 290,000 | 310,000 | 380,000 | 445,000 |
| South Atlantic | 30,000 | 100,000 | 180,000 | 650,000 | 980,000 |

**Required**   Prepare an Excel spreadsheet that will calculate return on sales (ROS) for each division for 2013. The sales in the North, Mid, and South Atlantic regions are $2,350,000, $1,450,000, and $500,000, respectively. Calculate investment (asset) turnover (AT) and return on investment (ROI) for each of the four measures of investment.

[LO 19-1]   **19-23   Return on Investment (ROI); Return on Sales (ROS); Asset Turnover (AT)**   Liz Raiborn, Inc., has the following financial results for the years 2013 through 2015 for its three regional divisions:

|  | 2013 | 2014 | 2015 |
|---|---|---|---|
| **Revenue** | | | |
| Southwest | $14,900 | $22,000 | $26,000 |
| Midwest | 6,700 | 7,000 | 7,200 |
| Southeast | 12,400 | 13,000 | 13,300 |
| Total | $34,000 | $42,000 | $46,500 |
| **Net Operating Income** | | | |
| Southwest | $ 1,100 | $ 1,200 | $ 1,350 |
| Midwest | 1,250 | 1,600 | 1,550 |
| Southeast | 1,000 | 1,200 | 1,600 |
| Total | $ 3,350 | $ 4,000 | $ 4,500 |
| **Average Total Assets** | | | |
| Southwest | $14,000 | $14,200 | $16,800 |
| Midwest | 4,700 | 4,200 | 4,200 |
| Southeast | 5,300 | 5,600 | 5,600 |
| Total | $24,000 | $24,000 | $26,600 |

**Required**   Calculate return on sales (ROS), asset turnover (AT) and return on investment (ROI) for each division and for the firm as a whole for each of the three years 2013, 2014, and 2015.

[LO 19-1]   **19-24   Target Sales Price; Return on Investment (ROI)**   Schwenn Products, a bicycle manufacturer, uses normal volume as the basis for setting prices. That is, it sets prices on the basis of long-term volume predictions and then adjusts these prices only for large changes in pay rates or materials prices. You are given the following information:

| | |
|---|---|
| Materials, wages, and other variable costs | $300 per unit |
| Fixed costs | $200,000 per year |
| Target return on investment (ROI) | 25% |
| Normal volume | 1,500 units per year |
| Investment (average total assets) | $1,000,000 |

**Required**

1. What sales price is needed to attain the 25% target ROI?
2. What ROI rate will be earned at sales volumes of 2,000 and 1,000 units, respectively, using the sales price you determined in requirement 1?

[LO 19-1]   **19-25   ROI; Goal-Congruency Issues**   As indicated in the chapter, return on investment (ROI) is well entrenched in business practice. However, its use can have negative incentive effects on managerial behavior. For example, assume you are the manager of an investment center and that your annual bonus is a function of achieved ROI for your division. You have the opportunity to invest in a project that would cost $500,000 and that would increase annual operating income of your division by $50,000. (This level of return is considered acceptable from top management's standpoint.) Currently, your division generates annual operating profits of approximately $600,000, on an asset base (i.e., level of investment) of $4,000,000.

**Required**

1. What is the current return on investment (ROI) being realized by your division (i.e., before considering the new investment)?
2. What would happen to the near-term ROI of your division after adding the effect of the new investment?

3. As manager of this division, given your incentive-compensation plan, would you be motivated to make the new investment? Why or why not?

4. Can you offer any recommendations for improving the design of the incentive-compensation plan under which you are working? That is, can you think of a plan that would result in increased goal congruency between your incentives and the goals of the company?

**[LO 19-1, 19-2]**  19-26  **Return on Investment (ROI) and Residual Income (RI)**   Consider the following data (in millions) from Trident Financial, Inc., which has two main divisions: mortgage loans, and consumer loans:

|  | Mortgage Loans | Consumer Loans |
|---|---|---|
| Average total assets | $2,000 | $20,000 |
| Operating income | $400 | $2,500 |
| Return on investment (ROI) | 20% | 12.5% |

**Required**

1. Based on ROI, which division is more successful? Why?

2. Trident uses residual income (RI) as a measure of the financial performance of its divisions. What is the RI for each division if the minimum desired rate of return is: (a) 10%, (b) 15%, and (c) 20%? Which division is more successful under each of these rates?

**[LO 19-1, 19-2, 19-3]**  19-27  **ROI; Residual Income; EVA®**   Heather Smith Cosmetics (HSC) manufactures a variety of products and is organized into three divisions (investment centers): soap products, skin lotions, and hair products. Information about the most recent year's operations follows. The information includes the value of intangible assets including research and development, patents, and other innovations that are not included on HSC's balance sheet. Were these intangibles to be included in the financial statements (as they are for EVA®), the increase in the balance sheet and the increase in after-tax operating income would be as given below.

| Division | Operating Income | Average Total Assets | Value of Intangibles | Intangibles' Effect on Income |
|---|---|---|---|---|
| Soap products | $3,250,000 | $60,000,000 | $1,500,000 | $1,000,000 |
| Skin lotions | 2,750,000 | 33,000,000 | 8,000,000 | 6,000,000 |
| Hair products | 5,000,000 | 55,000,000 | 1,000,000 | 700,000 |
| Minimum desired rate of return | 5.00% | | | |
| Cost of capital | 4.00% | | | |

**Required**

1. Calculate the return on investment (ROI) for each division.

2. Calculate the residual income (RI) for each division.

3. Calculate EVA® for each division and comment on your answers for ROI, RI, and EVA®.

**[LO 19-2, 19-3]**  19-28  **Economic Profit and Employee Productivity; Service Industries**   A recent *Harvard Business Review* article points out a new way to calculate economic profit that could be more appropriate for service firms and other "people-intensive" companies. Instead of focusing on investment and return on investment, the focus is on employee productivity, both in terms of generating revenues and reducing costs.

The approach is to first determine economic profit in the conventional way, except that we ignore taxes, so that economic profit is before tax, as follows:

$$\text{Economic profit} = \text{Operating profit} - \text{Capital charge}$$

Assume the following information for a hotel chain that wishes to adopt the new method. The firm has $100 million in operating profit, $1 billion in investment, and uses a cost of capital rate of 5%, so the capital charge is $50 million and the economic profit is $50 million. Relevant calculations are contained in Part 1 of the following schedule.

---

**Part 1: Economic Profit (in thousands, except cost of capital rate)**

| | |
|---|---:|
| Revenue | $500,000 |
| Operating costs: | |
|    Personnel costs | 300,000 |
|    Other costs | 100,000 |
| Operating profit | $100,000 |
| Operating profit before personnel costs (OPBP) | $400,000 |
| Investment (capital) | $1,000,000 |
| Cost of capital, rate | 0.05 |
| Capital charge | $   50,000 |
| Economic profit = Operating profit − Capital charge | $   50,000 |

**Part 2: Economic Profit Calculated Using Employee Productivity**

| | |
|---|---:|
| Number of employees | 10,000 |
| Employee productivity: | |
|    Operating profit before personnel cost per employee ($400,000/10,000) | $40 |
|    Capital charge per employee ($50,000/10,000) | 5 |
|      Employee productivity | $35 |
| Less personnel cost per employee | 30 |
| Economic profit per employee = Productivity − Cost | $ 5 |
| Total economic profit, all employees | $50,000 |
| Note: All numbers in thousands except for number of employees | |

The next step is to decompose economic profit using employee productivity. To do this we first determine operating profit before personnel costs (OPBP):

$$OPBP = \text{Operating profit} + \text{Personnel costs}$$
$$\$400,000 = \$100,000 + \$300,000$$

Employee productivity can be determined by calculating OPBP less capital charge, per employee. For this example, since there are 10,000 employees, OPBP is $40,000 per employee and the capital charge is $5,000 per employee, so that productivity is $35,000 per employee. The next step is to determine personnel cost per employee, $30,000, and subtract that from employee productivity to obtain economic profit per employee, $5,000 (i.e., $35,000 − $30,000). Total economic profit for all employees is thus $5,000 × 10,000, or $50 million, the same amount as determined in the conventional way. The value of the decomposition of economic profit into employee productivity and personnel costs per employee is that it provides measures that the hotel chain can benchmark to other hotel chains. It also provides a direct measure of the profit that is being generated per employee relative to the average personnel cost for each employee. Measures of revenue per employee and personnel cost per employee are widely used in the hospital, health and human services, and other people-oriented service industries.

**Source:** Felix Barber and Rainer Strack, "The Surprising Economics of the People Business," *Harvard Business Review,* June 2005, pp. 81–90.

**Required**   Use the above approach and assume a chain of residential care facilities employs 15,000 people, has a cost of capital of 6%, and has the following information (000s).

| | |
|---|---:|
| Revenue | $600,000 |
| Operating costs | |
|    Personnel costs | 360,000 |
|    Other costs | 150,000 |
| Operating profit | $ 90,000 |
| Investment | $1,000,000 |

Determine the productivity per employee, personnel costs per employee, and economic profit per employee.

[LO 19-1, 19-2, 19-3]   19-29   **Return on Investment (ROI) for Innovative Companies**   A survey by *BusinessWeek* and the Boston Consulting Group identified the world's 25 most innovative companies, looking at three dimensions of innovation: process innovation, product innovation, and business model innovation.

The top five companies were Apple, Google, 3M, Toyota, and Microsoft. The top-25 companies were great performers over the 10-year period 1995–2005. The 25 companies had an average return on sales of 3.4% in comparison to 0.40% for the Standard & Poor's 1200 Global Stock Index. The top 25 stock returns, based on increase in stock price and dividends over this 10-year period, averaged a 14.3% annual return, in contrast to the 11.1% return for the S&P Global 1200. These companies are surpassing the Global 1200 companies in part because of superior innovation.

**Required** What are the issues to consider in calculating the return on investment (ROI), residual income (RI), and economic value added (EVA®) for a highly innovative company?

[LO 19-4] 19-30 **Transfer-Pricing Issues** When transfer prices are based on actual cost, a supplying division often has no incentive to reduce cost. For example, a design change that would reduce the supplying division's manufacturing cost would benefit only downstream divisions if the transfer price is based on a markup over cost.

**Required** What can or should be done to provide the supplying division an incentive to reduce manufacturing costs when the transfer price is cost-based?

[LO 19-4] 19-31 **General Transfer-Pricing Rule** Scottsdale Manufacturing is organized into two divisions: Fabrication and Assembly. Components transferred between the two divisions are recorded at a predetermined transfer price. Standard variable manufacturing cost per unit in the Fabrication Division is $500. At the present time, this division is working to capacity. Fabrication estimates that the units it produces could be sold on the external market for $650. The product under consideration is viewed as a commodity-type product, with no differentiating features or characteristics.

**Required**
1. What roles are played by transfer prices? That is, why are transfer prices needed?
2. Use the general transfer-pricing rule presented in the chapter to determine an appropriate transfer price. Why (or in what sense) is the amount you calculated considered an appropriate transfer price?
3. What if the Fabrication Division had excess capacity? How would this change the indicated transfer price? Why is the amount you determined considered an appropriate transfer price?
4. Are there any downsides of using the general transfer-pricing rule to determine the transfer price for internal transfers?

[LO 19-4] 19-32 **Transfer Pricing; Decision Making** Truball Inc., which manufactures sports equipment, consists of several operating divisions. Division A has decided to go outside the company to buy materials since division B informed it that the division's selling price for the same materials would increase to $200. Information for division A and division B follows:

| | |
|---|---|
| Outside price for materials | $150 |
| Division A's annual purchases | 10,000 units |
| Division B's variable costs per unit | $140 |
| Division B's fixed costs, per year | $1,250,000 |
| Division B's capacity utilization | 100% |

**Required**
1. Will the company benefit if division A purchases outside the company? Assume that division B cannot sell its materials to outside buyers.
2. Assume that division B can save $200,000 in fixed costs if it does not manufacture the material for division A. Should division A purchase from the outside market?
3. Assume the situation in requirement 1. If the outside market value for the materials drops $20, should division A buy from the outside? Explain.

[LO 19-4] 19-33 **Transfer Pricing; Decision Making** Using the information from requirement 1 of exercise 19-32, assume that division B could sell 10,000 units outside for $215 per unit with variable marketing costs of $10. Should division B sell outside or to division A? Explain.

[LO 19-5] 19-34 **Transfer Pricing; International Taxation**   Crain Company has a manufacturing subsidiary in Singapore that produces high-end exercise equipment for U.S. consumers. The manufacturing subsidiary has total manufacturing costs of $1,500,000, plus general and administrative expenses of $350,000. The manufacturing unit sells the equipment for $2,500,000 to the U.S. marketing subsidiary, which sells it to the final consumer for an aggregate of $3,500,000. The sales subsidiary has total marketing, general, and administrative costs of $200,000. Assume that Singapore has a corporate tax rate of 33% and that the U.S. tax rate is 46%. Assume that no tax treaties or other special tax treatments apply.

**Required**   What is the effect on Crain Company's total corporate-level taxes if the manufacturing subsidiary raises its price to the sales subsidiary by 20%?

## Problems

[LO 19-1] 19-35 **Return on Investment (ROI); Different Measures for Total Assets**   Ready Products, Inc., operates two divisions, each with its own manufacturing facility. The accounting system reports the following data for 2013:

**HEALTH CARE PRODUCTS DIVISION**
Income Statement for the Year
Ended December 31, 2013 (000s)

| | |
|---|---:|
| Revenues | $600 |
| Operating costs | 470 |
| Operating income | $130 |

**COSMETICS DIVISION**
Income Statement for the Year
Ended December 31, 2013 (000s)

| | |
|---|---:|
| Revenues | $600 |
| Operating costs | 400 |
| Operating income | $200 |

Ready estimates the useful life of each manufacturing facility to be 15 years. As of the end of 2013, the plant for the health care division is four years old, while the manufacturing plant for the cosmetics division is six years old. Each plant had the same cost at the time of purchase, and both have useful lives of 15 years with no salvage value. The company uses straight-line depreciation and the depreciation charge is $70,000 per year for each division. The manufacturing facility is the only long-lived asset of either division. Current assets are $300,000 in each division.

An index of construction costs, replacement costs, and liquidation values for the manufacturing facilities for the period that Ready has been operating is as follows:

| | | | Liquidation Value | |
|---|---|---|---|---|
| Year | Cost Index | Replacement Cost | Health Care | Cosmetics |
| 2007 | 80 | $1,000,000 | $800,000 | $ 800,000 |
| 2008 | 82 | 1,000,000 | 800,000 | 800,000 |
| 2009 | 84 | 1,100,000 | 700,000 | 700,000 |
| 2010 | 89 | 1,150,000 | 600,000 | 700,000 |
| 2011 | 94 | 1,200,000 | 600,000 | 800,000 |
| 2012 | 96 | 1,250,000 | 600,000 | 900,000 |
| 2013 | 100 | 1,300,000 | 500,000 | 1,000,000 |

**Required**
1. Compute return on investment (ROI) for each division using the historical cost of divisional assets (including current assets) as the investment base. Interpret the results.
2. Compute ROI for each division, incorporating current-cost estimates as follows:
   a. Gross book value (GBV) of long-lived assets, plus book value of current assets.
   b. GBV of long-lived assets restated to current cost using the index of construction costs, plus book value of current assets.

    c. Net book value (NBV) of long-lived assets restated to current cost using the index of construction costs, plus book value of current assets.

    d. Current replacement cost of long-lived assets, plus book value of current assets.

    e. Current liquidation value of long-lived assets, plus book value of current assets.

3. Which of the measures calculated in requirement 2 would you choose to (a) evaluate the performance of each division manager, and (b) decide which division is most profitable for the overall firm? What are the strategic advantages and disadvantages to the firm of each measure for both (a) and (b)?

**[LO 19-1]**    **19-36 Return on Investment (ROI) and Incentive/Goal-Congruency Issues; Spreadsheet Application**
Assume the purchase of new equipment (e.g., delivery trucks) used in a product-delivery service (such as UPS or FedEx). This equipment is needed to improve delivery service and respond to recent environmental goals embraced by the company. The cost of the new equipment is $1 million; the expected useful life of these assets is five years. Estimated salvage value at the end of five years is $0. The company in question will depreciate these assets over a five-year period using straight-line depreciation. The anticipated increase in operating income (before depreciation deductions) attributable to the use of the new equipment is $300,000. Ignore taxes.

**Required**
1. Generate, using an Excel spreadsheet, a schedule of the year-by-year ROIs associated with this investment opportunity. For purposes of these calculations, define the investment base (denominator of the ROI ratio) as average net book value (NBV) of the assets during the year.
2. Generate a second schedule showing the year-by-year ROIs for this investment opportunity under the assumption that the denominator in the ROI calculation is defined as the gross book value of the assets to be acquired.
3. Why do the results differ in (1) and (2) above? What behavioral issue is associated with the use of (1) versus (2) above?
4. What impact would the use of an accelerated depreciation method have on the conclusions above in (1) and (2)? For example, prepare a new schedule of annual ROIs under the assumption that the double-declining-balance depreciation method is used. (Assume a switch to straight-line depreciation in year 4. Thus, the total depreciation charge over the five-year period should be $1 million.)
5. Would the use of the residual income (RI) measure of financial performance eliminate the behavioral issue raised above? Why or why not? For the options specified above in parts 1, 2, and 4, show the year-by-year RIs for this investment, based on a weighted-average cost of capital (WACC) of 10%. For each of the four options, base the imputed interest charge each year on a simple average of beginning-of-year and end-of-year asset values.

**[LO 19-1]**    **19-37 Return on Investment (ROI); Present-Value Depreciation; Spreadsheet Application**    As indicated in the chapter, there are goal-congruency problems associated with the use of ROI as an indicator of business-unit financial performance. One such problem relates to the bias against accepting new investments because of the adverse effect on a business unit's ROI metric. Assume, for example, that a manager of a business unit can invest in a new, depreciable asset costing $30,000 and that this asset has a three-year life with no salvage value. Cash inflows associated with this investment are projected to be as follows: $12,000, $14,400, and $17,280. (Ignore taxes.) This scenario leads to an estimated internal rate of return (IRR) of 20%. Assume that the minimum required rate of return is 15%.

**Required**
1. Demonstrate, using the IRR function in Excel, that the IRR on this proposed investment is indeed 20%.
2. Calculate the year-by-year ROI (accounting rate of return) on this proposed investment, using each year as the denominator of your calculation the beginning-of-year book value of the asset. Assume the asset will be depreciated using the straight-line method. What incentive effects can you anticipate based on the data you generated?
3. Recalculate the year-by-year ROI (accounting rate of return) on this proposed investment, this time using "present value" depreciation (defined as the change in the present value of the asset during the period). Use the project's anticipated IRR (20%) as the discount factor in your calculations. As in (2) above, define the denominator of your calculation as the beginning-of-year book value of the investment. (*Hint:* Your depreciation figures should be $6,000, $9,600, and $14,400, respectively, for years 1, 2, and 3.) What incentive effects do you anticipate based on your calculations?

4. Calculate for each of three years the residual income (RI) for this proposed investment. RI is defined as income after (present-value) depreciation and after a capital charge assessed on beginning-of-year book value of the asset. For purposes of these calculations assume a 10% cost of capital (discount rate). Use the built-in function in Excel to estimate the NPV of the proposed investment. (*Hint:* Your answer should be approximately $5,800.) At a discount rate of 10%, determine the net present value (NPV) of the residual income (RI) figures you estimated. What is the potential value of using multiyear RI figures determined with present-value depreciation?

[LO 19-1]    19-38 **Return on Customer; Review of Chapter 5**    The concept of return on investment (ROI) has been adapted widely for a variety of uses. One recent development is to extend customer profitability analysis to include the concept of "return on customer." In Chapter 5, we presented an approach for using activity-based costing (ABC) to determine the full cost of serving a customer, including product and service, thereby determining the net profit from serving that customer. The analysis was further extended in Chapter 5 to calculate a measure of the expected value of the customer based on expected future sales. That value was called *customer lifetime value (CLV),* which is the net present value of all estimated future profits from the customer. For example, assume a customer is expected to produce profits of $20,000 per year for each of the next three years. Using a discount rate of 6%, the CLV for this customer is 2.673 × $20,000 = $53,460. (The PV annuity factor, 2.673, is obtained from Appendix C, Chapter 12.)

Return on customer (ROC) can be measured as the increase in customer value plus the current year profit on the customer, relative to the prior year value of the customer. The first step in calculating ROC is to determine the customer lifetime value (CLV) at the end of each year. CLV can rise or fall, as our projections of future profits from the customer increase or decrease. Suppose we have the following information for customer Y:

> Customer lifetime value at the end of 2012 = $2,000,000
> Customer lifetime value at the end of 2013 = $2,500,000
> Profit on sales to customer Y during 2013 = $250,000

ROC for customer Y for 2013 is determined as follows:

$$ROC = \frac{\text{Profit from customer Y in 2013} + \text{Change in CLV from 2012 to 2013}}{\text{CLV for customer Y in 2012}}$$

$$\text{ROC for customer Y} = \frac{\$250,000 + (\$2,500,000 - \$2,000,000)}{\$2,000,000}$$

$$= 37.5\%$$

ROC gives management a way to further analyze the profitability of a given customer. The goal is to attract and retain high-ROC customers.

**Required**    Assume customer X has a CLV at the beginning of the year of $150,000, a CLV at the end of the year of $75,000, and that profits from sales to X were $25,000 during the year. Customer Z has a CLV at the end of the year of $100,000, a CLV at the beginning of the year of $50,000, and profits from sales this year of $10,000. Determine the ROC for each customer and interpret the results for these two customers.

[LO 19-1]    19-39 **Research Assignment; Strategy**    Obtain from your library a copy of the following article: Laurie Bassie and Daniel McMurrer, "Maximizing Your Return on People," *Harvard Business Review* (March 2007), pp. 115–123. The authors of this article state (p. 123): "Globalization has left only one true path to profitability for firms operating in high-wage, developed nations: to base their competitive strategy on exceptional human capital management (HCM) . . . managing human capital by instinct and intuition becomes not only inadequate, but reckless. The most competitive companies will be those that manage their employees like the assets they are."

**Required**    After reading the above-referenced article, answer the following questions:
1. What is the general issue addressed by the authors of this article? That is, what managerial problem are they discussing?
2. The authors develop a framework that, they assert, can be useful for increasing the long-term value of investments in human capital. What are the two major factors in the authors' framework? How can the framework be used by managers as part of a comprehensive management accounting and control system?

3. The authors provide three examples of how their evaluation/assessment framework was used in practice to assess the quality of an organization's HCM. For each example, indicate how organizational performance was defined, and how the evaluation framework proposed by the authors was used to improve that performance. (That is, what principal results were achieved?)

[LO 19-1]   19-40  **Research Assignment: Employee Wellness Programs; Sustainability**   What is the return on investment (ROI) on investments in corporate wellness programs? What are the nonfinancial returns on such investments? The following article addresses the notion of "sustainability" in a slightly different context—sustainability of the organization's workforce: Leonard L. Berry, Ann M. Mirabito, and William B. Baun, "What's the Hard Return on Employee Wellness Programs?" *Harvard Business Review* (December 2010), pp. 104–12. (Obtain a copy of this article from your library, your instructor, or your coursepack.) After reading the article, respond to the following questions.

**Required**

1. How do the authors of this article define *workplace wellness*?

2. What evidence of financial returns on employee wellness programs is offered by the authors of this article?

3. What do the authors of this article cite as important nonfinancial performance indicators associated with corporate wellness programs?

4. Based on their examination of the literature and their own consulting experience, the authors identify the "six pillars of a successful, strategically integrated wellness program." Provide an overview of each of these six pillars.

[LO 19-1]   19-41  **Return on Investment (ROI) and Sustainability; Internet-Based Research**   One of the three underlying precepts of sustainability is economic performance (balanced with social and environmental performance). This question pertains to the application of ROI as part of a performance-management system related to corporate sustainability. To answer the following questions you'll have to search appropriate sites on the Internet.

**Required**

1. Define the term *corporate sustainability*.

2. What is the connection between the goal of corporate sustainability and the design of cost-management systems?

3. Based on your research, what are some primary financial returns associated with corporate investments in sustainability projects (all of which have a direct impact on the ROI associated with such projects)?

4. Based on your research, provide at least five examples of relevant nonfinancial performance indicators associated with corporate sustainability projects.

[LO 19-1]   19-42  **Performance Evaluation; Strategy Map; Review of Chapter 18; Correlation Analysis**   Maydew Manufacturing Inc. is a large manufacturer of lawn and garden equipment including mowers, edgers, tillers, related equipment, and accessories. The firm has been very successful in recent years, and sales have grown more than 10% in each of the last five years. The firm is organized into 15 investment centers based on product-line groups. Return on investment (ROI) and residual income (RI) calculations have been made for each of the last four years and used in management compensation for the last two years. Recently Maydew's top management has contracted with MM&PC, a large consulting firm, to review the performance-measurement process at the firm. One of MM&PC's key recommendations has been to consider the implementation of the balanced scorecard (BSC) both for performance measurement and for strategic management. As a step in this direction, MM&PC has asked Maydew for some data on ROI and other measures being considered for the BSC to analyze the relationships among these data. It is hoped that the analysis will help MM&PC develop a strategy map for the firm. The following data show the most recent year's ROI for each investment center and the average for the last three years for training hours per employee in the center, customer retention rate in the unit (customers are primarily large department store chains and other distributors of lawn and garden equipment), the QSV score, and the defect rate (per thousand products). The QSV score is a measure of the Quality-Service-Value of the investment center made by an analysis of a variety of operating data including the results of onsite inspection of each unit by key operating executives and other measures of operating performance (the highest score is 10, and the lowest is 0).

| Manager | ROI | Training Hours per Employee | Customer Retention | QSV Score | Defect Rate |
|---------|------|------|------|------|------|
| 1 | 21.3 | 98 | 99.3 | 7 | 3.3 |
| 2 | 15.4 | 122 | 98.2 | 8 | 4.7 |
| 3 | 9.6 | 67 | 86.7 | 6 | 11.2 |
| 4 | 12.4 | 88 | 84.5 | 9 | 13.7 |
| 5 | 18.6 | 92 | 91.4 | 8 | 2.1 |
| 6 | 4.5 | 33 | 90.7 | 4 | 28.9 |
| 7 | 8.8 | 49 | 88.9 | 6 | 1.2 |
| 8 | 22.6 | 77 | 93.5 | 10 | 12.4 |
| 9 | 11.8 | 102 | 95.5 | 9 | 8.0 |
| 10 | 14.6 | 95 | 91.1 | 6 | 7.4 |
| 11 | 16.5 | 87 | 92.7 | 6 | 2.8 |
| 12 | 12.1 | 80 | 86.4 | 8 | 4.9 |
| 13 | 6.2 | 66 | 80.2 | 4 | 15.3 |
| 14 | 1.3 | 50 | 78.0 | 4 | 22.8 |
| 15 | 9.7 | 78 | 85.5 | 7 | 30.5 |

**Required**

1. Using the concept of the strategy map, consider how the nonfinancial factors (training hours, customer retention, QSV score, and defect rate) affect ROI. Which of these variables has the greatest influence on ROI? Use regression and correlation analysis to address this requirement.

2. Explain which two managers you would rate as the best overall and which you would rate as the worst overall, and give reasons why.

[LO 19-1, 19-2]  19-43  **Return on Investment (ROI); Residual Income (RI)**   Consolidated Industries is a diversified manufacturer with business units organized as divisions, including the Reigis Steel Division. Consolidated monitors its divisions on the basis of both unit contribution and return on investment (ROI), with investment defined as average operating assets employed. All investments in operating assets are expected to earn a minimum return of 9% before income taxes.

Reigis's cost of goods sold is considered to be entirely variable; however, its administrative expenses do not depend on volume. Selling expenses are a mixed cost with 40% attributed to sales volume. The 2013 operating statement for Reigis follows. The division's operating assets employed were $80,750,000 at November 30, 2013, unchanged from the year before.

### REIGIS STEEL DIVISION
#### Operating Statement
#### For the Year Ended November 30, 2013
#### (000s omitted)

| | | |
|---|---:|---:|
| Sales revenue | | $35,000 |
| Less expenses: | | |
| Cost of goods sold | $18,500 | |
| Administrative expenses | 3,955 | |
| Selling expenses | 2,700 | 25,155 |
| Income from operations, before tax | | $ 9,845 |

**Required**

1. Calculate Reigis Steel Division's unit contribution if it produced and sold 1,484,000 units during the year ended November 30, 2013.

2. Calculate the following performance measures for 2013 for Reigis:

   a. Pretax ROI, based on average operating assets employed.

   b. Residual income (RI), calculated on the basis of average operating assets employed.

3. Reigis management is presented the opportunity to invest in a project that would earn an ROI of 10%. Is Reigis likely to accept the project? Why or why not?

4. Identify several items that Reigis should control if it is to be fairly evaluated as a separate investment center within Consolidated Industries using either ROI or RI performance measures.

**(CMA Adapted)**

[LO 19-1, 19-2]  19-44  **Calculating Return on Investment (ROI) and Residual Income (RI); Comparing Results**   Blackwood Industries manufactures die machinery. To meet its expansion needs, it recently (2011) acquired one of its suppliers, Delta Steel. To maintain Delta's separate identity, Blackwood reports Delta's operations as an investment center. Blackwood monitors all of its investment centers on the basis of return on investment (ROI). Management bonuses are based on ROI, and all investment centers are expected to earn a minimum 10% return before income taxes.

Delta's ROI has ranged from 14% to 18% since 2011. The company recently had the opportunity for a new investment that would have yielded a 13% ROI. However, division management decided against the investment because it believed that the investment would decrease the division's overall ROI.

The 2013 operating statement for Delta follows. The division's operating assets were $15,000,000 at the end of 2013, a 5% increase over the 2012 year-end balance.

| DELTA DIVISION Operating Statement for Year Ended December 31, 2013 (000s omitted) | | |
| --- | --- | --- |
| Sales | | $25,000 |
| Cost of goods sold | | 16,600 |
| Gross profit | | 8,400 |
| Operating expenses: | | |
| Administration | $2,340 | |
| Selling | 3,610 | 5,950 |
| Operating income | | $ 2,450 |

**Required**

1. Calculate the following performance measures for 2013 for the Delta division:

   a. Return on average investment in operating assets.

   b. Residual income (RI) calculated on the basis of average operating assets.

2. Which performance measure (ROI or RI) should Blackwood Industries use to provide the proper incentive for each division to act autonomously in the firm's best interests? Would Delta's management have been more likely to accept the capital investment opportunity if RI had been used as a performance measure instead of ROI? Explain.

3. What type of strategic performance measurement do you recommend for the Delta division? Explain.

[LO 19-2]  19-45  **Residual Income (RI); Performance Evaluation Time Horizon; Spreadsheet Application**   As referenced in the five-step process presented at the beginning of this chapter, one issue that confronts top management is selection of an appropriate time period for evaluating the financial performance of the company's investment centers. This exercise demonstrates why, in conjunction with residual income (RI), it is desirable to evaluate financial performance over a multi-year period. The primary point is that, by doing so, top management is better able to align manager goals and incentives with organizational goals.

Assume, as covered in Chapter 12, that your company uses the net present value (NPV) method to evaluate capital investment opportunities. Generally speaking, this means that a long-term investment project will be undertaken if the present value of future net cash flows (after-tax) is positive when discounted at the firm's weighted-average cost of capital (WACC). The following facts pertain to an investment opportunity that is available to the manager of one of the investment centers in your company. Investment outlay cost, time period 0, equals $800,000. This amount relates to an asset with a five-year life, and no salvage value, that will be depreciated using the straight-line (SL) method. The investment is expected to increase cash inflows by $300,000 per year. Assume a discount rate of 10%, both for purposes of calculating NPV and for calculating annual residual income (RI) figures.

**Required**

1. Use Excel to prepare a schedule that contains annual cash-flow data, annual operating income amounts, and annual residual income (RI) figures. What is the estimated NPV of the proposed investment? What is the present value (PV) of the stream of expected residual incomes (RIs) from this investment?

2. From a behavioral perspective, what is the primary implication of the analysis you conducted above in (1)?

[LO 19-3]  19-46  **EVA® NOPAT and EVA® Capital: Operating Approach**  You are provided with the following financial statement information from Nimrod, Inc. for its most recent fiscal year.

**Statement of Financial Position (Balance Sheet)**
**End of Year (000s)**

| | |
|---|---:|
| **Assets** | |
| Cash | $   35 |
| Net accounts receivable (A/R) | 190 |
| Inventory | 190 |
| Other current assets | 95 |
| Total current assets | $ 510 |
| Property, plant, and equipment (net) | 605 |
| Other long-term assets | 120 |
| Total assets | $1,235 |
| **Liabilities and Stockholders' Equity** | |
| Short-term debt (@10%) | $  100 |
| Accounts payable | 150 |
| Income taxes payable | 20 |
| Other current liabilities | 200 |
| Total current liabilities | $ 470 |
| Long-term debt (8%) | 150 |
| Other long-term liabilities | 120 |
| Total liabilities | $ 740 |
| Deferred income taxes | 70 |
| Common equity | 425 |
| Total liabilities and shareholders' equity | $1,235 |

The statement of income for the company for the year just ended is as follows:

**Statement of Income**
**Most Recent Year (000s)**

| | |
|---|---:|
| Net sales | $2,000 |
| Cost of goods sold (CGS) | 1,670 |
| Gross margin | 330 |
| Less: SG&A costs | 185 |
| Depreciation | 35 |
| Other operating expenses | 50 |
| Total expenses | 270 |
| Net operating profit | 60 |
| Less: Interest expense | 22 |
| Plus: Other income | 12 |
| Income before tax | 50 |
| Less: Income tax (@ 40%) | 20 |
| Net profit after tax | $   30 |

Assume a weighted-average cost of capital (WACC) of 10.7% and an income-tax rate of 40%.

**Required**

1. Prepare, using the *operating approach,* an estimate of EVA® NOPAT. In addition to the above data, you discovered the following: increase during the year of the LIFO reserve, $2; imputed interest expense on noncapitalized leases, $4; and increase in deferred tax liability during the year, $5. (*Hint:* The correct answer is $53; the amount of cash taxes paid on operating profit during the year is $25.) What is the rationale for the various adjustments you made to the company's reported income statement?

2. Prepare, using the *operating approach,* an estimate of EVA® capital. (*Hint:* The correct answer is $925.) In addition to the above information, you note the following: end-of-year value of the LIFO reserve, $10; and present value of noncapitalized leases, $50. What is the rationale for the adjustments you made to reported balance sheet amounts in order to estimate EVA® capital?

3. Given the company's WACC, what is the estimated EVA® for the year? How do you interpret this figure?

[LO 19-3]  19-47  **EVA® NOPAT and EVA® Capital: Financing Approach**  Refer to the preceding problem for reported financial statement data for Nimrod, Inc.

**Required**

1. Prepare, using the *financing approach,* an estimate of EVA® NOPAT. In addition to the above data, you discover the following: increase during the year of the LIFO reserve, $2; imputed interest expense on noncapitalized leases, $4; and increase in deferred tax liability during the year, $5. (*Hint:* The correct answer is $53.) What is the rationale for the various adjustments you made to the company's reported income statement?

2. Prepare, using the *financing approach,* an estimate of EVA® capital. (*Hint:* The correct answer is $925.) In addition to the above information, you note the following: end-of-year value of the LIFO reserve, $10; and present value of noncapitalized leases, $50. What is the rationale for the adjustments you made to reported balance sheet amounts in order to estimate EVA® capital?

3. Given the company's WACC, what is the estimated EVA® for the year? How do you interpret this figure?

[LO 19-3]  19-48  **EVA®; Shareholder Value Analysis and Sustainability; Internet-Based Research**  Increasing shareholder value is a key objective for many profit-seeking organizations. As indicated in the chapter, EVA® is meant to approximate "economic income" and in this sense can be viewed as a measure of shareholder value added by the firm during a period. Increasingly, managers are realizing that shareholder value is enhanced by creating value for employees, customers, suppliers, the community, and other stakeholders. This problem asks you to consider how EVA®, as a measure of economic value created during a period, can be used to guide and justify sustainability-related investments.

**Required**

1. How is economic value added (EVA®) for any accounting period estimated? How does this financial performance metric differ from both conventional accounting income and from residual income (RI)?

2. Given the definition of EVA® you provided in (1) above, provide some thoughts as to how EVA® can be used as part of a comprehensive performance-management system to assess and justify corporate investments in sustainability-related projects.

3. Search the Internet to see whether you can identify an example of how an actual company used EVA® to support a sustainability-related investment project or program (i.e., one that dealt with social or environmental performance).

4. Explain how EVA®, as a financial performance metric, can be used as part of a larger strategic management system.

[LO 19-4]  19-49  **General Transfer-Pricing Rule; Goal Congruence**  National Motors, Inc., is divided, for performance-evaluation purposes, into several divisions. The Automobile Division of National Motors purchases most of its transmission systems from another unit of the company. The Transmission Division's incremental cost for manufacturing a standard transmission is approximately $900 per unit. This division is currently working at 75% of capacity. The current market price for a standard transmission is approximately $1,250.

**Required**

1. Using the general guideline equation presented in the chapter, what is the minimum price at which the Transmission Division would sell its output to the Automobile Division?

2. Suppose now that National Motors requires that whenever divisions with excess capacity sell their output internally to other divisions of the company, they must do so at the incremental cost of the supplying (producing) division. Evaluate this transfer-pricing rule vis-à-vis each of the following objectives: autonomy, goal congruency, performance evaluation of the divisions, and motivation/incentive effects.

3. If the two divisions of National Motors were to negotiate a transfer price, what is the likely range of possible prices? Evaluate the use of a negotiated transfer price using the same objectives listed above in (2).

4. Which, in your opinion, is the preferable transfer-pricing method—(2) or (3) above? Why?

**(CMA Adapted)**

[LO 19-4]  19-50  **Transfer-Pricing Methods**  Mylar Corporation started as a single plant to produce its major components and then assembled its main product into electric motors. Mylar later expanded by developing outside markets for some components used in its motors. Eventually, the company reorganized into four manufacturing divisions: bearing, casing, switch, and motor. Each manufacturing division operates as an autonomous unit, and divisional performance is the basis for year-end bonuses.

Mylar's transfer-pricing policy permits the manufacturing divisions to sell either externally or internally. The price for goods transferred between divisions is negotiated between the buying and selling divisions without any interference from top management.

Mylar's profits for the current year have dropped although sales have increased, and the decreased profits can be traced almost entirely to the motor division. Jere Feldon, Mylar's chief financial officer, has learned that the motor division purchased switches for its motors from an outside supplier during the current year rather than buying them from the switch division, which is at capacity and has refused to sell to the motor division. It can sell them to outside customers at a price higher than the actual full (absorption) manufacturing cost that has always been negotiated in the past with the motor division. When the motor division refused to meet the price that the switch division was receiving from its outside buyer, the motor division had to purchase the switches from an outside supplier at an even higher price.

Jere is reviewing Mylar's transfer-pricing policy because he believes that suboptimization has occurred. Although the switch division made the correct decision to maximize its division profit by not transferring the switches at actual full manufacturing cost, this was not necessarily in Mylar's best interest because of the price the motor division paid for them. The motor division has always been Mylar's largest division and has tended to dominate the smaller divisions. Jere has learned that the casing and bearing divisions are also resisting the motor division's expectation to use the actual full manufacturing cost as the negotiated price.

Jere has requested that the corporate accounting department study alternative transfer-pricing methods to promote overall goal congruence, motivate divisional management performance, and optimize overall company performance. Three transfer-pricing methods being considered follow. The one selected will be applied uniformly across all divisions.

- Standard full manufacturing costs plus markup.
- Market selling price of the products being transferred.
- Outlay (out-of-pocket) costs incurred to the point of transfer plus opportunity cost to the seller, per unit.

**Required**

1. Discuss the following:

   a. The positive and negative motivational implications of employing a negotiated transfer-price system for goods exchanged between divisions.

   b. The motivational problems that can result from using actual full (absorption) manufacturing costs as a transfer price.

2. Discuss the motivational issues that could arise if Mylar Corporation decides to change from its current policy of covering the transfer of goods between divisions to a revised transfer-pricing policy that would apply uniformly to all divisions.

3. Discuss the likely behavior of both buying and selling divisional managers for each transfer-pricing method listed above, if it were adopted by Mylar.

**(CMA Adapted)**

[LO 19-4]    19-51    **Transfer Pricing; Decision Making**    Phoenix Inc., a cellular communication company, has multiple business units, organized as divisions. Each division's management is compensated based on the division's operating income. Division A currently purchases cellular equipment from outside markets and uses it to produce communication systems. Division B produces similar cellular equipment that it sells to outside customers but not to division A at this time. Division A's manager approaches division B's manager with a proposal to buy the equipment from division B. If it produces the cellular equipment that division A desires, division B would incur variable manufacturing costs of $60 per unit.

---

**Relevant Information about Division B**

Sells 50,000 units of equipment to outside customers at $130 per unit
Operating capacity is currently 80%; the division can operate at 100%
Variable manufacturing costs are $70 per unit
Variable marketing costs are $8 per unit
Fixed manufacturing costs are $580,000

**Income per Unit for Division A (assuming parts purchased externally, not internally from division B)**

| | | |
|---|---:|---:|
| Sales revenue | | $320 |
| Manufacturing costs: | | |
|    Cellular equipment | 80 | |
|    Other materials | 10 | |
|    Fixed costs | 40 | |
| Total manufacturing costs | | 130 |
| Gross margin | | 190 |
| Marketing costs: | | |
|    Variable | 35 | |
|    Fixed | 15 | |
| Total marketing costs | | 50 |
| Operating income per unit | | $140 |

**Required**

1. Division A wants to buy all 25,000 units from division B at $75 per unit. Should division B accept or reject the proposal? How would your answer differ if (a) Division A requires all 25,000 units in the order to be shipped by the same supplier, or (b) Division A would accept partial shipment from division B?

2. What is the range of transfer prices over which the divisional managers might negotiate a final transfer price? Provide a rationale for the range you provide.

[LO 19-4]  19-52  **Transfer Pricing; Strategy**  Federated Manufacturing Inc. (FMI) produces electronic components in three divisions: industrial, commercial, and consumer products. The commercial products division annually purchases 10,000 units of part 23–6711, which the industrial division produces for use in manufacturing one of its own products. The commercial division is growing rapidly. The commercial division is expanding its production and now wants to increase its purchases of part 23–6711 to 15,000 units per year. The problem is that the industrial division is at full capacity. No new investment in the industrial division has been made for some years because top management sees little future growth in its products, so its capacity is unlikely to increase soon.

    The commercial division can buy part 23–6711 from Advanced Micro Inc. or from Admiral Electric, a customer of the industrial division now purchasing 650 units of part 88–461. The industrial division's sales to Admiral would not be affected by the commercial division's decision about part 23–6711.

| | |
|---|---:|
| **Industrial division:** | |
|   Data on part 23–6711: | |
|     Price to commercial division | $185 |
|     Variable manufacturing costs | 155 |
|     Price to outside buyers | 205 |
|   Data on part 88–461: | |
|     Variable manufacturing costs | $ 65 |
|     Sales price | 95 |
| **Other suppliers of part 23–6711:** | |
|   Advance Micro Inc., price | $200 |
|   Admiral Electric, price | 210 |

**Required**

1. What is the proper decision regarding where the commercial division should purchase the additional 5,000 parts and what is the correct transfer price?

2. Assume that the industrial division's sales to Admiral will be canceled if the commercial division does not buy from Admiral. What would be the unit cost to FMI in this case, and would the desired transfer price change?

3. What are the strategic implications of your answer to requirement 1? How can FMI become more competitive in one or more of its divisions?

[LO 19-4]  19-53  **Strategy; Strategic Performance Measurement; Transfer Pricing**  Ajax Consolidated has several divisions; however, only two transfer products to other divisions. The mining division refines toldine, which it transfers to the metals division where toldine is processed into an alloy and is sold to customers for $150 per unit. Ajax currently requires the mining division to transfer its total annual output of 400,000 units of toldine to the metals division at total (actual) manufacturing cost plus 10%. Unlimited quantities of toldine can be purchased and sold on the open market at $90 per unit. The mining division could sell all the toldine it produces at $90 per unit on the open market, but it would incur a variable selling cost of $5 per unit.

Brian Jones, the mining division's manager, is unhappy transferring the entire output of toldine to the metals division at 110% of cost. In a meeting with Ajax management, he said, "Why should my division be required to sell toldine to the metals division at less than market price? For the year just ended in May, the contribution margin on metals was more than $19 million on sales of 400,000 units while the mining division's contribution was just over $5 million on the transfer of the same number of units. My division is subsidizing the profitability of the metals division. We should be allowed to charge the market price for toldine when we transfer it to the metals division."

The following is the detailed unit cost structure for both the mining and metals divisions for the fiscal year ended May 31, 2013:

| | Cost per Unit | |
| --- | --- | --- |
| | **Mining Division** | **Metals Division** |
| Transfer price from mining division | — | $ 66 |
| Direct material | $12 | 6 |
| Direct labor | 16 | 20 |
| Manufacturing overhead | 32* | 25† |
| Total cost per unit | $60 | $117 |

*Manufacturing overhead in the mining division is 25% fixed and 75% variable.
†Manufacturing overhead in the metals division is 60% fixed and 40% variable.

**Required**

1. Explain whether transfer prices based on cost are appropriate as a divisional performance measure and why.

2. Using the market price as the transfer price, determine the contribution margin for both divisions for the year ended May 31, 2013.

3. If Ajax were to institute the use of negotiated transfer prices and allow divisions to buy and sell on the open market, determine the price range for toldine that both divisions would accept. Explain your answer.

4. Identify which of the three types of transfer prices—cost-based, market-based, or negotiated—is most likely to elicit desirable management behavior at Ajax and thus benefit overall operations. Explain your answer.

[LO 19-4]  19-54  **Transfer Pricing; Ethics**  Target Manufacturing, Inc., is a multinational firm with sales and manufacturing units in 15 countries. One of its manufacturing units, in country X, sells its product to a retail unit in country Y for $200,000. The unit in country X has manufacturing costs of $100,000 for these products. The retail unit in country Y sells the product to final customers for $300,000. Target is considering adjusting its transfer prices to reduce overall corporate tax liability.

**Required**

1. Assume that both country X and country Y have corporate income-tax rates of 40% and that no special tax treaties or benefits apply to Target. What would be the effect on Target's total tax burden if the manufacturing unit raises its price from $200,000 to $240,000?

2. What would be the effect on Target's total taxes if the manufacturing unit raised its price from $200,000 to $240,000 and the tax rates in country X and country Y are 20% and 40%, respectively?

3. Comment on any ethical issues you observe in this case.

[LO 19-5]  19-55  **Transfer Pricing—International Example**  A subsidiary company located in country A purchases $100 worth of goods. It then repackages, exports, and sells those goods to the parent company, located in country B, for $200. The parent company sells the goods for $300. Therefore, both entities have a $100 profit. Assume that the income-tax rate in country A is 20%, while the tax rate in country B is 60%.

**Required**

1. Given the above facts and assumptions, what is the company's combined (i.e., worldwide) after-tax income *per unit* for this transaction? (Show calculations.)

2. Consider now a transfer-pricing approach in which the subsidiary sells the goods to the parent company for $280, and the parent company then sells the goods for $300. What is the revised worldwide (i.e., combined) after-tax profit *per unit* for this transaction? (Show calculations.)

3. What is the effect of the transfer-pricing decision when the income tax rates for the two countries in question are equal?

4. What limitations exist regarding the setting of transfer prices for multinational transfers?

[LO 19-5]   19-56 **Transfer Pricing; International Considerations; Strategy**   As indicated in the chapter, determining the appropriate transfer price in a multinational setting is a very complex problem, with multiple strategic considerations. Consider as an example a U.S. company with a subsidiary in Italy and a subsidiary in Ireland. The Italian subsidiary produces a product at a cost of $1,000 per unit. This unit is then sold to the Irish subsidiary, which adds $100 of cost to each unit. The unit is then shipped to the U.S. parent company, which adds an additional $100 of cost to each unit. The unit is then sold to a U.S. customer for $2,000. Assume that the tax rate in Italy is 30%, the tax rate in Ireland is 15%, and the tax rate in the United States is 35%.

**Required**

1. Define the term *transfer price*. Why is the issue of transfer pricing of strategic concern to organizations?

2. Fundamentally, what creates income-tax planning opportunities as regards the determination of transfer pricing in a multinational setting? Where could one go to obtain information regarding stated income-tax rates for various countries?

3. Assume that the transfer price associated with the sale to the Irish subsidiary is $1,200, and that the transfer price for the sale to the U.S. parent company is $1,600. Under this situation, what is the income tax paid by each of the following: (a) the Italian subsidiary, (b) the Irish subsidiary, (c) the U.S. parent company, and (d) the consolidated entity (i.e., worldwide tax paid)?

4. Assume now that the transfer price associated with the sale to the Irish subsidiary is $1,100, and that the transfer price for the sale to the U.S. parent company is $1,800. Under this situation, what is the income tax paid by each of the following: (a) the Italian subsidiary, (b) the Irish subsidiary, (c) the U.S. parent company, and (d) the consolidated entity (i.e., worldwide tax paid)?

5. What considerations, including qualitative factors, bear on the transfer-pricing decision in a multinational context?

[LO 19-5]   19-57 **Transfer Pricing; Strategy**   Better Life Products (BLP), Inc., is a large U.S.-based manufacturer of health care products; it specializes in cushions, braces, and other remedies for a variety of health problems experienced by elderly and disabled persons. BLP knows that its industry is price-competitive and hopes to compete through rapid growth, primarily within the United States, where it has a well-established brand image. Because of the competitive industry conditions, BLP is focusing on cost and price reductions as a principal way to attract customers. Because of rising domestic production costs, lower production costs in other countries, and a modest increase in global demand for its products, BLP manufactures some of these products outside the United States. Much of the materials for use by foreign manufacturers is shipped from the United States to the foreign manufacturer, which assembles the final product. In this way, BLP takes advantage of the foreign country's lower labor costs. For this purpose, BLP has formed three divisions, one in the United States to purchase and perform limited assembly of the raw materials; one a foreign division to complete the manufacturing, especially of the labor-intensive components of manufacturing; and one a marketing and sales division in the United States. Sales of BLP's products are approximately 80% in the United States, 10% in Canada, and 10% worldwide. The foreign divisions tend to focus only on manufacturing because of the specialized nature of the products and because of BLP's desire to have the U.S. sales division coordinate all sales activities. BLP now has 18 U.S. divisions and 23 foreign divisions operating in this manner.

Foreign divisions' shipments to the United States are subject to customs duties according to the U.S. Tariff Code, which adds to BLP's cost of the foreign-based manufacturing. However, the code requires U.S. companies to pay duty on only the value added in foreign countries. For example, a product imported from an Argentine company to BLP pays customs on only the amount of the product's cost resulting from labor incurred in Argentina. To illustrate, a product with $10 of materials shipped from the United States to Argentina that incurs $10 of labor costs in Argentina is charged a tariff based on the $10 of labor costs, not the $20 of total product cost. Thus, for tariff purposes, having as small a portion of total product cost from the foreign country as possible is advantageous to BLP.

BLP division managers, including those of the foreign manufacturing facilities, are evaluated on the basis of profit. Jorge Martinez is the manager of the manufacturing plant in Argentina; his compensation from BLP is based on meeting profit targets.

BLP uses a transfer-pricing approach common in the industry to allow each of the company's divisions to determine the transfer pricing autonomously through interdivision negotiations. In recent years, however, top management has played an increased role in such negotiations. In particular, when the divisions determine a transfer price that can lead to increased taxes, foreign exchange exposure, or tariffs, the corporate financial function becomes involved. This has meant that the transfer prices charged by foreign divisions to U.S. sales divisions have fallen to reduce the value added by the foreign country and thereby reduce the tariffs. To avoid problems with U.S. and Argentine government agencies, the transfer prices have been reduced slowly over time.

One effect of this transfer-pricing strategy has been the continued decline of the foreign divisions' profitability. Jorge and others have difficulty meeting their profit targets and personal compensation goals because of the continually declining transfer prices.

### Required

1. Assess BLP's manufacturing and marketing strategies. Are they consistent with each other and with what you consider to be the firm's overall business strategy?
2. Assess BLP's performance-measurement system. What changes would you suggest and why?

[LO 19-5] 19-58 **Strategic Performance Measurement** With the multinational company (MNC) becoming a significant business structure throughout the world, a growing problem is developing in the analysis of the MNC's financial results. When the incidents in this problem occurred, the U.S. dollar was strengthening considerably relative to other currencies. Besides causing economic problems in many developing countries, it also created a problem in the proper evaluation of a multinational's subsidiaries and their contribution to its total results.

Security System Corporation provides financial services for dealers and consumers in a variety of construction and consumer product areas. The firm is searching for the proper method to evaluate its subsidiaries. Of concern is each subsidiary's contribution to the company's overall earnings and how to evaluate whether the specific goals developed by the subsidiary's management have been met.

In search of answers, the company is concerned with the following concepts:

- Analysis of results: In local currency or U.S. dollars?
- Management's explanation of variances: In local currency or U.S. dollars?
- What should the time frames be for comparative data: Plan or forecast?

The company has six distinctive business segments in the new-residential-housing market: consumer appliance market, commercial nonresidential construction, consumer aftermarket, home furnishings market, automotive market, and capital goods market. Last year the company achieved 30% of its revenues and 35% of its earnings from its international subsidiaries. However, years ago, when one British pound sterling equaled US$2.33 (whereas now it's one pound = US$1.62), the company achieved 35% of its revenue—but more significantly, 47% of its earnings—from its international subsidiaries. During the past five years, although the U.S. dollar equivalent of earnings from the international subsidiaries has declined from 47% of the total to 35%, most operations have reported significant, steady year-to-year gains when expressed in the local currency.

All operations report their monthly financial data to the company's world headquarters in U.S. dollars. They use the existing exchange rate at the close of business on the last day of the month. The company reports the exchange based on accounting guidelines (except for one or two special situations). The comparisons of the monthly financial data are made against a financial plan that uses a predetermined exchange rate for the various months of the year.

Over the past five years, as the U.S. dollar has fluctuated against foreign currencies, the company has analyzed the financial results of its operations totally in U.S. dollars. It then compares these results to a fixed-plan exchange rate.

The company establishes exchange rates to be used each year, many times optimistically, and then sets an earnings per share (EPS) target on that basis. If the dollar strengthens even more, the company misses its targets and prepares statements showing that a particular group missed its planned targets when, in fact, all of the group's operations could have exceeded their local currency plans but are losing on the comparison because of unfavorable exchange-rate effects.

**Required** How should the firm measure its results to enhance its competitive position? How can it safeguard its overall EPS target if it uses local currencies in the reporting system? Where does the responsibility for the U.S.-dollar-denominated goals lie?

**(CMA Adapted)**

## Solutions to Self-Study Problems

### 1. Return on Investment (ROI) and Residual Income (RI)

1. ROS = Operating income ÷ Sales

   = $640,000 ÷ $8,000,000

   = 0.08

   AT = Sales ÷ Average investment

   = $8,000,000 ÷ [($2,500,000 + $2,600,000) ÷ 2]

   = 3.137 times

   ROI = ROS × AT

   = 0.08 × 3.137

   = 25.1%

2. RI = Operating income − (Average investment × Minimum rate of return)

   = $640,000 − ([($2,500,000 + $2,600,000) ÷ 2] × 0.12)

   = $334,000

### 2. Transfer Pricing

1. Since the T-Bar unit is at full capacity and the contribution on outside sales of $70 (= $165 − $5 − $90) is higher than the $60 cost saving of inside production (= $150 − $90), the T-Bar unit should sell outside and the adhesive unit should purchase T-Bar for $150 outside the firm.

2. From the standpoint of the company as a whole, the correct decision is induced if we appeal to the general transfer-pricing rule. The minimum transfer price, from the firm's standpoint, is the sum of out-of-pocket costs of the T-Bar division ($90) plus the opportunity cost, if any, incurred because of an internal transfer ($70 = $165 − $90 − $5), or a total of $160. At this amount, the adhesive division will be motivated to purchase externally (at $150/unit) and the T-Bar unit will be indifferent between selling internally (contribution margin per unit = $160 − $90 = $70) and selling externally (contribution margin per unit = $165 − $90 − $5 = $70). Because of the latter, we say that $160 represents a minimum transfer price.

3. If the T-Bar unit has excess capacity, it can sell T-Bar both internally and externally. The correct transfer price is then the price that will cause the adhesive unit to purchase internally; that is, any price between variable cost of the seller ($90) and the outside market price to the adhesive unit ($150). The units might agree on a price by considering what is a fair return to each unit and in effect split the profit on the sale between them. The actual outcome of the negotiations for the transfer price depends on a number of factors, including the negotiation skills of the two managers.

*Please visit http://www.mhhe.com/blocher6e to access a narrated, animated tutorial for solving these problems.*

# CHAPTER TWENTY

# Management Compensation, Business Analysis, and Business Valuation

After studying this chapter, you should be able to . . .

LO 20-1    Identify and explain the types of management compensation

LO 20-2    Identify the strategic role of management compensation and the different types of compensation used in practice

LO 20-3    Explain the three characteristics of a bonus plan: the base for determining performance, the compensation pool from which the bonus is funded, and the bonus payment options

LO 20-4    Describe the role of tax planning and financial reporting in management compensation planning

LO 20-5    Apply the different methods for business analysis and business valuation

---

There's no praise to beat the sort you can put in your pocket.

*Moliére*

---

The goals of this chapter are to determine how to compensate managers, how to analyze a firm's overall performance, and how to estimate the economic value of the firm. We have emphasized strategy throughout the book. How do we quantitatively assess the firm's success in achieving its strategy and fairly compensate management for this success? Fundamentally, all measures of the firm's value are predictions of future performance—an assessment of the future value of the current ownership in the firm. Choosing a method for predicting future value is a difficult task, as Bill Barker, a writer for The Motley Fool (**www.fool.com**) says: "I don't think there is any method that anyone will think is the perfect one. If you ask 10 investors what the Holy Grail method would be, you'd get 10 different answers." In this spirit, we consider a number of different valuation methods in this chapter.

## Part One: Management Compensation

**LO 20-1**

*Identify and explain the types of management compensation.*

Recruiting, motivating, rewarding, and retaining effective managers are critical to the success of all firms. Effective management compensation plans are an important and integral part of the determination of a strategic competitive advantage and are important concerns of the management accountant.

## TRENDS IN CEO PAY

CEO pay has increased significantly over the last decade. For example, the total compensation of the top five executives of 1,500 of the largest U.S. companies increased from an average of 4.8% of the firm's earnings in 1993 to 12.1% of the firm's earnings in 2000–2002. After a substantial fall in 2001–2003, CEO pay began to increase again in 2004–2005, by 3.7% in 2004 and 2005 and 5% in 2007. However, CEO pay fell in 2008 and fell again by 0.9% in 2009 as a consequence of the recession. In a sharp reversal, pay was up by 11% in 2010, reflecting in part the improvement in some measures of the state of the economy. However, in 2011, the increase was only 1.4%, a result of greater pressure by shareholders on corporate boards. Other factors influencing CEO pay at this time include: (1) increased oversight of CEO compensation by corporate boards and federal agencies (oversight especially for those firms receiving federal assistance) and (2) stringent disclosure rules of the SEC.

## SEC DISCLOSURE RULES

SEC rules require significant disclosure of executive compensation. The SEC requires a company to disclose:

- A total compensation amount for executives.
- A breakdown of compensation to include stock options, both the number of shares and the value of the shares involved in these options.
- Exactly what payments an executive would receive if there were a change in the executive's role in the company.
- The above information for each executive.

The objective of the disclosures (required since 2006) is to provide investors with a clearer and more complete understanding of the compensation of the firm's key executives. On the other hand, some have pointed out that firms' compensation disclosures are so complex that many investors are left confused and frustrated.

In January 2011 the SEC adopted a "say on pay" rule that requires companies to have nonbinding shareholder votes on executive pay. While companies can ignore the results of the vote, board members are likely to consider voter reaction in determining pay policies.

**Sources:** PricewaterhouseCoopers, "2007Global Equity Incentives Survey" (www.pwc.com/extweb/pwcpublications.nsf/docid/eeace28ff7a0b05e852573b700758d02); Claudia Deutsch, "A Brighter Spotlight, Yet the Pay Rises," *The New York Times,* April 6, 2008, Business Section, p. 1; Joann S. Lublin, "Adding It Up," *The Wall Street Journal,* April 10, 2006, p. R1; Kara Scannell, "SEC Ready to Require More Pay Disclosures," *The Wall Street Journal,* June 3, 2009, p. C1. See also: http://www.sec.gov/answers/execomp.htm); Joann S. Lublin, "CEO Pay in 2010 Jumped 11%," *The Wall Street Journal,* May 9, 2011, p. B1; Jessica Holzer, "Split SEC Adopts 'Say on Pay' Rule," *The Wall Street Journal,* January 26, 2011, p. C3; Scott Thurm, "CEO Pay Lags Behind 2011 Results, "*The Wall Street Journal,* March 26, 2012, pp. B1–2.

## Types of Management Compensation

**Management compensation plans**
are policies and procedures for compensating managers.

**A salary**
is a fixed payment.

**A bonus**
is based on the achievement of performance goals for the period.

**Benefits** (perks)
include automobile/parking, membership in a fitness club, tickets to entertainment events, and other extras paid for by the firm.

**Management compensation plans** are policies and procedures for compensating managers. Compensation includes one or more of the following: salary, bonus, and benefits. **Salary** is a fixed payment; a **bonus** is based on the achievement of performance goals for the period. **Benefits** include automobile/parking, membership in a fitness club, life insurance, medical benefits, tickets to entertainment events, and other extras paid for by the firm. Benefits are often also referred to as *perks*.

Compensation can be paid currently (usually an annual amount paid monthly, twice a month, or weekly) or deferred to future years. Salary and benefits are typically awarded currently; bonuses are either paid currently or deferred, though a wide variety of plans is found in practice.

The compensation plans for high-level managers are generally explained in the firm's proxy statements and must be approved by the shareholders. Base salary usually is an annual amount paid throughout the year, although it can also include predetermined future cash payments and/or stock awards. Perks are commonly awarded on an annual basis, although they can include future payments or benefits. Base salary and perks are negotiated when the manager is hired and when compensation contracts are reviewed and renewed. They are not commonly influenced by the manager's current performance, as is bonus pay. Recent studies of top executives at public companies show that bonus pay is the fastest growing part of total compensation.

## Strategic Role and Objectives of Management Compensation

**LO 20-2**

*Identify the strategic role of management compensation and the different types of compensation used in practice.*

The strategic role of management compensation has three aspects: (1) the strategic conditions facing the firm, (2) the effect of risk aversion on managers' decision making, and (3) certain ethical issues.

**EXHIBIT 20.1**
**Compensation Plans Tailored for Different Strategic Conditions**

| Product Sales Life Cycle Phase | Salary | Bonus | Benefits |
|---|---|---|---|
| Product introduction | High | Low | Low |
| Growth | Low | High | Competitive |
| Maturity | Competitive | Competitive | Competitive |
| Decline | High | Low | Competitive |

### Design the Compensation Plan for Existing Strategic Conditions

The compensation plan should be grounded in the strategic analysis of the firm: its competitive strengths and weaknesses and critical success factors. As the strategic conditions facing the firm change over time, the compensation plan should also change. For example, the firm's strategy changes as its products move through the different phases of the sales life cycle: product introduction, growth, maturity, and decline (Chapter 13). As a firm's product moves from the growth phase to the maturity phase, the firm's strategy also moves from product differentiation to cost leadership. When this happens, the compensation plan should change in response to the new strategy. Exhibit 20.1 illustrates how the mix of salary, bonus, and perks might change as the firm and its products move through different phases of the sales life cycle.

Note in Exhibit 20.1 that the mix of the three parts of total compensation changes as strategic conditions change. For example, in the mature phase of the product's life cycle, when competition is likely to be the highest and the firm is interested in maintaining an established market and controlling costs, a balanced compensation plan of competitive salary, bonus, and benefits is needed to attract, motivate, and retain the best managers. In contrast, during the growth phase, when the need for innovation and leadership is the greatest, the emphasis is on relatively large bonuses to effectively motivate managers. In effect, top management considers the specific strategic conditions facing the firm as a basic consideration in developing the compensation plan and making changes as strategic conditions change.

### Risk Aversion and Management Compensation

The manager's relative risk aversion can have an important effect on decision making (see Chapter 18, "Employment Contracts"). Risk aversion is the tendency to prefer decisions with predictable outcomes over those that are uncertain. It is a relatively common decision-making characteristic of managers. A risk-averse manager is biased against decisions that have an uncertain outcome, even if the expected outcome is favorable.

For example, a risk-averse manager might cancel a planned investment in new equipment that would reduce operating costs if there is a chance that nonoperating costs from installation problems, employee training needs, or other reasons might increase. In contrast, the firm's top management and shareholders might not see the risk of additional nonoperating costs as significant relative to the potential for a long-term reduction in operating costs. The difference in perspective comes about because the outcome of the decision, while likely to have a relatively small impact on the firm and therefore on top management and shareholders, is likely to directly and significantly impact the manager's current bonus.

Compensation plans can manage risk aversion effectively by carefully choosing the mix of salary and bonus in total compensation. The higher the proportion of bonus in total compensation, the higher the incentive for the manager to avoid risky outcomes. To reduce the effect of risk aversion, a relatively large proportion of salary should be in total compensation, with a smaller portion in bonus. Determining the proper balance between salary and bonus must consider all three compensation objectives.

### Ethical Issues

There is a common concern that executive pay is too high and that lower-level employees are not properly compensated relative to the very high salaries and bonuses of top executives, particularly during periods of corporate downsizing and falling earnings. High executive compensation is unjust, some argue, and compensation plans are unethical. Others point out that most executives are worth their high compensation because they bring far greater value to the firm than the cost of their compensation. Shareholders and bondholders who see their investments appreciate and attribute this to the executive are likely to see the compensation plans as just and ethical. For example, when Mark Hurd left as CEO of Hewlett-Packard (HP) in August 2010 (to become copresident and a director of a key rival, Oracle Corp.), HP's stock price began to fall relative to Oracle, and as of May 2011, HP stock had fallen by more than 50% relative to Oracle stock. Some have called this the "Hurd Effect," a measure of the value of Mark Hurd to HP.[1] For further discussion of ethics and executive compensation, see the Real-World Focus item on page 865.

Sometimes the management compensation plan provides an incentive for unethical action. Notable examples include Kenneth Lay, CEO of Enron; Andrew Fastow, CFO of Enron; Scott Sullivan, CFO of WorldCom; and Dennis Kozlowski, CEO of Tyco International. Each of these executives was convicted of or admitted to illegal activities that have harmed their companies and the companies' shareholders. In all these cases, the incentive to increase cash or stock option–based compensation was present. Also, a recent study of 1,200 corporations found evidence that private inside information of top executives was used to time the exercise of their stock options, because of a significant pattern of rising stock prices prior to the exercise of the options followed by a pattern of falling stock prices following the exercise of the stock options.[2]

## Objectives of Management Compensation

The firm's key objective is to develop management compensation plans that support its strategic objectives, as set forth by management and the owners. The objectives of management compensation are therefore consistent with the three objectives of management control as defined in Chapter 18:

1. To motivate managers to exert a high level of effort to achieve the goals set by top management.
2. To provide the incentive for managers, acting autonomously, to make decisions consistent with the goals set by top management.
3. To determine fairly the rewards earned by managers for their effort and skill and the effectiveness of their decision making.

In Chapters 18 and 19, these objectives were used to develop performance measurement systems (e.g., cost, revenue, profit, and investment centers). In this chapter, the objectives are used to develop effective management compensation plans.

The first objective is to motivate managers to exert a high level of effort to achieve the firm's goals. A performance-based compensation plan is best for this purpose. For example, a bonus plan that rewards the manager for achieving particular goals is appropriate. The goals could be financial or nonfinancial, current or long term.

The second objective is to provide the appropriate incentive for managers to make decisions that are consistent with the firm's objectives. The firm's objectives are identified in the strategic competitive analysis from which its critical success factors (CSFs) are derived. CSFs include customer satisfaction, quality, service, product development, and

---

[1] "The Mark Hurd Effect," *Bloomberg Businessweek,* May 16, 2011, p. 38. A similar case is reported for Black & Decker, whose stock fell by 8% the day Joseph Galli, its chief executive, departed; see "Power Drain," *BusinessWeek,* May 17, 1999, p. 50. See also, Robert B. Reich, "CEOs Deserve Their Pay," *The Wall Street Journal,* September 14, 2007, p. A13. Reich makes the point that those with the skills necessary to be a successful CEO, to deliver competitive advantage for the company, are very hard to find. As noted above, there is strong evidence that some CEOs can have a significant effect on a company's stock price. However, other research has an alternative explanation for the decline in stock price after a CEO's retirement. The research has shown evidence of potential manipulation of the company's earnings (and therefore stock price) in the few years prior to a CEO's departure, because of CEO retirement bonuses tied to earnings. See Paul Kalyta, "Compensation Transparency and Managerial Opportunism: A Study of Supplemental Retirement Plans," *The Accounting Review,* April 2009, pp. 405–23.

[2] Eli Bartov and Partha Mahanram, "Private Information, Earnings Manipulations, and Executive Stock-Option Exercises," *The Accounting Review,* October 2004, pp. 889–920. See also, Scott Patterson and Serena Ng, "Executives' Stock Deals Preceded Price Drops," *The Wall Street Journal,* June 4, 2009, p. C1.

innovation in production and distribution. Firms attend to CSFs by making them part of the manager's compensation.

For example, McDonald's rewards managers who develop its CSFs—quality, service, cleanliness, and value—in addition to the conventional financial performance measures (earnings, growth in sales). International Paper Company includes nonfinancial factors such as quality, safety, and minority employee development as factors in management compensation plans. Research has shown that successful firms with clear strategic goals specified in CSFs include these factors in their compensation plans.[3]

In developing compensation plans, the management accountant works with other financial professionals to achieve fairness by making the plan simple, clear, and consistent. Fairness also means that the plan focuses only on the controllable aspects of the manager's performance. For example, compensation should not be affected by expenses that cannot be tied directly to the manager's unit. Similarly, the manager's performance evaluation should be separate from that of the unit because economic factors beyond the manager's control are likely to affect the unit's performance. Fairness in this sense is often achieved by basing the manager's compensation on performance relative to prior years or to agreed-upon goals rather than on comparison to the performance of other managers.

## Bonus Plans

As a general view, remuneration by fixed salaries does not in any class of functionaries produce the maximum amount of zeal.

*John Stuart Mill, English philosopher and economist, 1806–1873*

As stated earlier, bonus compensation is the fastest growing element of total compensation and often the largest part. A wide variety of bonus pay plans can be categorized according to three key aspects:

- The **base of the compensation,** that is, how the bonus pay is determined. The three most common bases are (1) stock price, (2) cost, revenue, profit, or investment center–based performance, and (3) the balanced scorecard.
- **Compensation pools,** that is, the source from which the bonus pay is funded. The two most common compensation pools are earnings in the manager's own SBU and a firmwide pool based on the firm's total earnings.
- **Payment options,** that is, how the bonus is to be awarded. The two common options are cash and stock (typically common shares). The cash or stock can either be awarded currently or deferred to future years. Stock can either be awarded directly or granted in the form of stock options.

### Bases for Bonus Compensation

**LO 20-3**

*Explain the three characteristics of a bonus plan: the base for determining performance, the compensation pool from which the bonus is funded, and the bonus payment options.*

The key objective in determining the base for compensation is to align managers' incentives with the strategic goals of the company. Bonus compensation can be determined on the basis of stock price, strategic performance measures (cost, revenue, profit, or investment center), or the balanced scorecard (critical success factors). For example, when the manager's unit is publicly held, its stock price is a relevant base. When stock price is used, the amount of the bonus could depend on the amount of the increase in stock price or on whether the stock price reaches a certain predetermined goal. When an accounting measure or CSF is used, the amount of the bonus can be determined in any

---

[3] C. Ittner and D. Larcker, "Total Quality Management and the Choice of Information and Reward Systems," *Journal of Accounting Research* (1995 Supplement), pp. 1–34; R. Bushman, R. Indjejikian, and A. Smith, "CEO Compensation: The Role of Individual Performance Evaluation," *Journal of Accounting and Economics,* April 1996; and Antonio Davila and Mahan Venkatachalam, "The Relevance of Non-Financial Performance Measures for CEO Compensation: Evidence from the Airline Industry," *Review of Accounting Studies* 9 (2004), pp. 443–64.

one of three ways: by (1) comparison of current performance to that of prior years, (2) comparison of performance to a predetermined budget, or (3) comparison of the manager's performance to that of other managers. A limitation of the first two methods, comparison to prior years or to budget, is that the economic situation of the manager's unit may have changed significantly from the prior year or from the time the budget target was set, thereby making the budget or prior year amount an unfair basis for evaluation and compensation. A problem with the third method is that it does not take into account the different economic circumstances of the different managers, some of whom may be in units that are in favorable economic times while others are not. The firm chooses its compensation plan to achieve the best balance of motivation and fairness from these options.

The choice of a base comes from a consideration of the compensation objectives, as outlined in Exhibit 20.2. A common choice is to use cost, revenue, profit, or investment centers because they are often a good measure of economic performance; therefore, they

**EXHIBIT 20.2**   **Advantages and Disadvantages of Different Bonus Compensation Bases Relative to Compensation Objectives**

|  | Motivation | Right Decision | Fairness |
|---|---|---|---|
| Stock price | (+/−) Depends on whether stock and stock options are included in base pay and bonus <br> (+) Aligns management compensation with shareholder interests | (+) Consistent with shareholder interests. | (−) Might lack controllability |
| Strategic performance measures (cost, revenue, profit, and investment centers) | (+) Strongly motivating if noncontrollable factors are excluded | (+) Generally a good measure of economic performance <br> (−) Typically has only a short-term focus <br> (−) If bonus is very high, creates an incentive for inaccurate reporting | (+) Intuitive, clear, and easily understood <br> (−) Measurement issues: differences in accounting conventions, cost allocation methods, and financing methods |
| Balanced scorecard (critical success factors) | (+) Strongly motivating if noncontrollable factors are excluded <br> (+) Aligns management compensation with shareholder interests | (+) Consistent with management's strategy <br> (−) Can be subject to inaccurate reporting of financial and nonfinancial measures | (+) If carefully defined and measured, CSFs are likely to be perceived as fair <br> (−) Potential measurement issues, as above |

Key: (+) means the base has a positive effect on the objective.
   (−) means the base has a negative effect on the objective.

are motivating and perceived to be fair. As many firms move to a more strategic approach to cost management, however, the use of CSFs and scorecard-based measures in compensation is likely to increase.

Once the base is chosen the firm also must choose a method for calculating the amount of the bonus based on the actual level of performance relative to the target. The most common approach is a simple linear calculation, that is, the greater the amount that performance exceeds the target (prior year, budget, or that of other managers), the greater the amount of the bonus. For example, if the bonus formula is 10% of profit over budget, and actual and budgeted profit are $200,000 and $100,000 respectively, then the amount of the bonus would be $10\% \times (\$200,000 - \$100,000) = \$10,000$.

The base for the bonus is likely to have multiple targets. As noted in the section "Objectives of Management Compensation" above, it is common to have management control systems with the balanced scorecard or some combination of financial and operating measures. In this case there are multiple bases for the performance measurement. The issue then is to determine a weighting for the multiple measures—which measures have the greatest priority? A common solution is to provide a numerical weight (as illustrated in many of the books and cases on the balanced scorecard), while a popular alternative is to have top management state the priorities in a ranking or general way at the beginning of the period and then, at the end of the period (at the time of the performance evaluation), assess the overall performance of the manager by considering all of the performance measures simultaneously, without quantitative weights. This more subjective approach is favored by some who feel that top management needs the flexibility to apply their judgment to assess the overall performance of the manager based upon the multiple measures.

## Bonus Compensation Pools

**A unit-based pool** is a basis for determining a bonus according to the performance of the manager's unit.

A manager's bonus can be determined by the so-called **unit-based pool** that is based on the performance of the manager's unit. For example, the bonus pool might be determined as the amount of the unit's earnings that are more than 5% of the investment in the unit. The appeal of the unit-based pool is the strong motivation for effective managers to perform and to receive rewards for their effort; the upside potential to the individual manager is very motivating.

**A firmwide pool** is a basis for determining the bonus available to all managers through an amount set aside for this purpose.

Alternatively, the amount of bonus available to all managers is often a **firmwide pool** set aside for this purpose. A firmwide pool, for example, might be the amount of firmwide earnings that are more than 5% of firmwide investment. Each unit manager's bonus is then drawn from this common pool. As an example of a firmwide compensation pool, the investment-banking firm Goldman Sachs bases its bonus pool on revenues. Because of declining revenues, the firm's bonus pool has declined each year during the period 2009–2011.[4]

When the bonus pool is unit-based, the amount of the bonus for any one manager is independent of the performance of the other managers. In contrast, when a firmwide pool is used, each manager's bonus depends in some predetermined way on the firm's performance as a whole. The sharing arrangements vary widely, although a common arrangement is for all managers to share equally in the firmwide bonus pool. Generally, the firmwide pool provides an important incentive for coordination and cooperation among units within the firm since all managers share in the higher overall firm profits that result from cross-unit efforts. Moreover, those who think executive pay is too high often argue that pay linked to overall firm performance is preferable since all managers share in this success. We summarize the advantages and disadvantages of each approach to bonus pools in Exhibit 20.3.

## Bonus Payment Options

In recent years, the use of different payment options for bonus compensation plans has greatly increased. In the competition for top executives, firms are developing innovative ways to attract and retain the best.

---

[4] Colin Barr, "Goldman's Shrinking Bonus Pool," **Fortune.cnn.com**, April 19, 2011.

**EXHIBIT 20.3**   **Advantages and Disadvantages of Different Bonus Pools Relative to Compensation Objectives**

| | Motivation | Right Decision | Fairness |
|---|---|---|---|
| Unit-based | (+) Strong motivation for an effective manager—the upside potential<br>(−) Unmotivating for manager of economically weaker units | (−) Provides the incentive for individual managers *not* to cooperate with and support other units when needed for the good of the firm | (−) Does not separate the performance of the unit from the manager's performance |
| Firmwide | (+) Helps to attract and retain good managers throughout the firm, even in economically weaker units<br>(−) Not as strongly motivating as the unit-based pool | (+) Effort for the good of the overall firm is rewarded—motivates teamwork and sharing of assets among units | (+) Separates the performance of the manager from that of the unit<br>(+) Can appear to be more fair to shareholders and others who are concerned that executive pay is too high |

Key: (+) means the pool has a positive effect on the objective.
    (−) means the pool has a negative effect on the objective.

We look at the four most common payment options:

1. **Current bonus** (cash and/or stock) based on current (usually annual) performance, the most common bonus form.
2. **Deferred bonus** (cash and/or stock) earned currently but not paid for two or more years. Deferred plans are used to avoid or delay taxes or to affect the manager's future total income stream in some desired way. This type of plan can also be used to retain key managers because the deferred compensation is paid only if the manager stays with the firm.
3. **Stock options** confer the right to purchase stock at some future date at a predetermined price. Stock options are used to motivate managers to increase stock price for the benefit of the shareholders. Some firms require executives to own a significant amount of stock in the company.
4. **Performance shares** grant stock for achieving certain performance goals over two years or more.

The current and deferred bonus plans generally focus the manager's attention on short-term performance measures, most commonly on accounting earnings. In contrast, stock options and performance shares focus attention directly on shareholder value. See the advantages and disadvantages of the four plans in Exhibit 20.4 (page 868).

As shown in Exhibit 20.4, all four bonus plans are subject to significant limitations, just as there are significant limitations to the responsibility accounting systems covered in Chapters 18 and 19. In particular, it is difficult to measure economic performance using one or even a few financial measures. Thus, it is difficult to align performance rewards with the desired motivation for managers. Moreover, bonus plans based on simple measures can be relatively easy for managers to manipulate—by making discretionary accounting changes, estimating or timing transactions, and so on. Many have argued for multiple measures (as in a balanced scorecard) and longer term payouts to better capture the relationship between economic performance and the rewards to managers. These are certainly useful approaches. Overall, one realizes that the design of effective compensation plans is a very challenging task.

## Tax Planning and Financial Reporting

**LO 20-4**

*Describe the role of tax planning and financial reporting in management compensation planning.*

In addition to achieving the three main objectives of compensation plans, firms attempt to choose plans that reduce or avoid taxes for both the firm and the manager. By combining salary, bonus, and perks, accountants can maximize potential tax savings for the firm and delay or avoid taxes for the manager. For example, many perks (club memberships, company car, entertainment) are deductible to reduce the firm's tax liability but are not considered income to the manager (and therefore not taxed).

**EXHIBIT 20.4**  **Advantages and Disadvantages of Bonus Payment Options Relative to Compensation Objectives**

| | Motivation | Right Decision | Fairness |
|---|---|---|---|
| Current bonus | (+) Strong motivation for current performance; stronger motivation than for deferred plans | (−) Short-term focus<br>(−) Risk-averse manager avoids risky but potentially beneficial projects | (+/−) Depends on the clarity of the bonus arrangement and the consistency with which it is applied<br>(−) Difficult to measure economic performance in one or a few financial measures<br>(−) Simple measures are easily manipulated by managers |
| Deferred bonus | (+) Strong motivation for current performance, but not as strong as for the current bonus plan since the reward is delayed<br>(+) Tax advantages of deferred compensation (see next section) | Same as for current bonus | Same as for current bonus |
| Stock options | (+) Unlimited upside potential is highly motivating<br>(−) Delay and uncertainty in reward reduces motivation | (+) Incentive to consider longer-term issues<br>(+) Provides better risk incentives than for current or deferred bonus plans<br>(+) Consistent with shareholder interests | (−) Uncontrollable factors affect stock price<br>Also, same as for current bonus |
| Performance shares | Same as for stock options | (+) Incentive to consider long-term factors that affect stock price<br>(+) Consistent with the firm's strategy, when critical success factors are used<br>(+) Consistent with shareholder interests when earnings per share is used | (+/−) Depends on the clarity of the bonus arrangements and the consistency with which it is applied<br>(−) Difficult to measure economic performance in one or a few financial measures<br>(−) Simple measures are easily manipulated by managers |

Key: (+) means the payment option has a positive effect on the objective.
  (−) means the payment option has a negative effect on the objective.

In contrast, although salary is a deductible business expense for the firm, it is taxable income for the manager. Bonus plans have a variety of tax effects as outlined in Exhibit 20.5. Tax planning is complex and dynamic and therefore an integral part of compensation planning. Exhibit 20.5 suggests general relationships; a thorough coverage of tax planning is beyond the scope of this text.

Firms also attempt to design compensation plans that have a favorable effect on the firm's financial report. For example, present accounting rules do not require current recognition of certain types of compensation, such as deferred compensation. A thorough coverage of financial reporting rules regarding management compensation is not attempted here. Exhibit 20.5 provides an overview of the issues.

## Management Compensation in Service Firms

Although most compensation plans are used by manufacturing or merchandising firms, an increasing number of service firms, especially financial and professional service firms, are using these plans. A good example is the compensation plan for the architectural and engineering design firm, Short-Elliott-Hendrickson, Inc. (SEH).[5] SEH provides professional

[5] Mark Pederson and Gary A. Lidgerding, "Pay-for-Performance in a Service Firm," *Management Accounting,* November 1995, pp. 40–43. A similar balanced scorecard–based system, designed for public accounting firms, is described by Michael Hayes in "Pay for Performance," *Journal of Accountancy,* June 2002, pp. 24–28.

Many companies today are looking for ways to better align the interests of shareholders, directors, and executives.

### DIRECTORS' COMPENSATION

Coca-Cola Company, for example, requires its board members

> ... to own Company stock, thereby creating a direct linkage with corporate performance. The Board suggests that within five years of joining the Board, such ownership should be in an amount at least equal in value to four times the annual Board cash compensation. To facilitate this objective, the Company will provide a mechanism by which a Board member can or must accept some or all of his or her Board compensation in Company stock. Directors are prohibited from engaging in strategies using puts, calls, equity swaps or other derivative securities in order to hedge or offset any decreases in the market value of any directly or indirectly owned shares.

The Coca-Cola Company has long had a focus on linking directors' performance to the Company's market performance. Warren Buffet, a long-time Coke investor, and recently appointed to the board, has argued that this plan better aligns the interests of investors, directors, and managers: Directors of the company are subject to the same risks facing investors.

### CEO COMPENSATION

Recent reports in *The New York Times* (2010 CEO pay) and *Bloomberg Businessweek* (2009 CEO pay) indicate that there appears to be relatively little correlation between CEO total compensation and the change in stock returns for their companies. Total compensation is of course a combination of cash awards and bonuses, and in 2010 in particular the portion of total pay in cash awards increased. So while it is not clear whether bonuses do or do not align performance with rewards, the evidence does not appear to support it. While there is an extensive body of academic research on CEO pay and performance, the finding of little or no relationship between pay and performance is common. See particularly the paper by Jensen and Murphy cited below.

**Sources:** Coca-Cola Corporate Governance Statement: http://www.thecoca-colacompany.com/investors/governance/guidelines.html; Pradnya Joshi, "We Knew They Got Raises. But This?" *The New York Times,* July 3, 2011, p. B1; Jessica Silver-Greenberg and Alexis Leondis, "How Much Is a CEO Worth?" *Bloomberg Businessweek,* May 10, 2010, p. 70; Michael Jensen and Kevin J. Murphy, "CEO Incentives—It's Not How Much You Pay, But How," *Journal of Applied Corporate Finance,* Winter 2010, pp. 64–76; Roger Lowenstein, "Is Any CEO Worth $189,000 per Hour?" *Bloomberg Businessweek,* February 20, 2012; David McCann, "Execs to Cash in Despite Market Woes," CFO.com, December 9, 2011.

---

**EXHIBIT 20.5    Tax and Financial Report Effects of Compensation Plans**

| | | | Tax Effect* | |
|---|---|---|---|---|
| | | **Financial Statement Effect** | **On the Firm** | **On the Manager** |
| Salary | | Current expense | Current deduction | Currently taxed |
| Bonus | Current | Current expense | Current deduction | Currently taxed |
| | Deferred | Deferred expense | Deferred deduction | Deferred tax |
| | Stock options—nonqualified plans | Stock options must be expensed when granted (e.g., using an options pricing model) and the expense taken against current income | Deduction when expensed | Taxed as ordinary income when exercised |
| | Stock options—qualified plans | As above | No deduction | Taxed as capital gains when stock is sold if held 18 months from exercise date |
| | Performance shares | As above | Deferred deduction | Deferred tax |
| Perks | Certain retirement plans | Current expense | Current deduction | Deferred tax |
| | Other perks | Current expense | Current deduction | Never taxed |

*The tax law regarding deferred compensation has changed as a result of the American Jobs Creation Act of 2004. The law places restrictions on the deferral of taxes under these compensation plans. See, for example, Anne Tergesen, "Rethink that Deferred Comp Plan Now," *BusinessWeek,* June 30, 2008, pp. 66–67.

---

services in a variety of markets, each of which is organized as a profit center: airport planning, water resources, waste management, municipal services, structural engineering, architecture, and others. SEH has developed a compensation plan for managers of each profit center. The plan uses a balanced scorecard approach that focuses on three areas: (1) financial results, (2) client satisfaction, and (3) improvement in the process of developing and providing the services. Management considers the financial results area to be the most important and has developed the following three criteria for evaluating managers and each profit center: profitability, efficiency, and collection of accounts receivable.

What does a company do when its stock price falls and its executive stock options are no longer attractive? If the firm does not move quickly, it can lose key executives to other employers that offer a more attractive compensation package. With the inevitable ups and downs of the stock market, firms are likely to face this problem at one point or another. What should a firm do when its stock options "go bad?"

(Refer to comments on Cost Management in Action at the end of the chapter.)

**EXHIBIT 20.6    Management Compensation Plan for the Water Resources Group of SEH, Inc.**

| 1. Profit Multiplier (ratio: net revenues to direct labor dollars) | | 2. Staff Utilization (ratio: chargeable time to total time) | | 3. Collection of Accounts | | | |
|---|---|---|---|---|---|---|---|
| | | | | **Percentage of Accounts Receivable > 90 Days** | | **Days Revenue Unbilled** | |
| Actual | 88% | Actual | 79% | Actual | 14% | Actual | 50 days |
| Goal | 95 | Goal | 83 | Goal | 10 | Goal | 45 days |
| Variance | 7% | Variance | 4% | Variance | 4% | Variance | 5 days |
| Multiply by | | Multiply by | | Multiply by | | Divide by | |
| weight of | 3 | weight of | 3 | weight of | 2 | goal | 45 days |
| Weighted | | Weighted | | Weighted | | Percent | |
| variance | 21% | variance | 12% | variance | 8% | variance | 11% |
| Less | 100 | Less | 100 | Less | 100 | Less | 100 |
| **Score** | **79%** | | **88%** | | **92%** | | **89%** |

1. **Profitability** is measured by the *profit multiplier,* the ratio of net revenues to direct labor dollars.

2. **Efficiency** is measured by *staff utilization,* which is determined from the ratio of direct labor-hours chargeable (to clients) to total hours worked less vacation and holiday time.

3. **Collection of accounts receivable** is measured by two ratios:

   a. The percentage of accounts receivable over 90 days, a measure of the ability to collect customer accounts.

   b. Average days of unbilled work outstanding, a measure of the ability to complete assignments and bill promptly for them.

As shown in Exhibit 20.6, SEH's compensation plan is based on three criteria and four measures (two measures for collection of accounts). Note that the Water Resources Group fell short of its target in each of the three areas with scores of 79% for the profit multiplier, 88% for staff utilization, and 92% and 89%, respectively, for each of the two measures of collection of accounts. The advantage of this compensation plan is that it clearly places responsibility for results on the three criteria that are important to SEH's strategy and is therefore consistent with the objectives of management compensation. The objectives of motivation and correct decision making are achieved since the managers of SEH's profit centers have clear, attainable goals consistent with the firm's strategy. The objective of fairness is achieved by focusing on ratios rather than total profits, which increases comparability among managers.

## Part Two: Business Analysis and Business Valuation

**LO 20-5**

*Apply the different methods for business analysis and business valuation.*

In this second part of the chapter, we examine the evaluation of the firm as a whole. The goal of strategic cost management is the success of the firm in maintaining competitive advantage, so we evaluate the firm's overall performance as well as the performance of individual managers. Business valuation is particularly important in difficult economic times, when failing companies are acquired by stronger companies and analysts must value the acquired company—the price paid in the acquisition. Also, as some companies fall short of meeting their financial goals due to the weakening economy and the market value of the company falls, business valuation provides top management a means to assess the risk of takeover by a venture capital firm or other set of investors. In response, the Institute of Management Accountants has provided an updated *Statement on Management Accounting,* "Business Valuation" (Institute of Management Accountants, 2009).

We take a broad approach that includes both the process of evaluating a firm's overall performance and the process of determining an overall value for the firm; ultimately, the objective of the firm's managers is to improve the overall value of the firm.

**Business analysis** uses the balanced scorecard, financial ratio analysis, and economic value added as benchmarks to evaluate the firm's overall performance. In contrast, **business valuation** values the firm by estimating its total market value, which can then be compared to the market value for prior periods or for comparable firms.[6]

**Business analysis**
uses the balanced scorecard, financial ratio analysis, and economic value added to evaluate the firm's overall performance.

**Business valuation**
values the firm by estimating its total market value, which can then be compared to the market value for prior periods or for comparable firms.

## Business Analysis

Business analysis includes a set of tools used to evaluate the firm's competitiveness and financial performance. The objective is a comprehensive evaluation. Business analysis begins with a careful strategic and competitive analysis of the firm, including SWOT (strengths-weaknesses-opportunities-threats) analysis and strategic positioning analysis, tools that are explained in Chapters 1 and 2. Then we consider tools used to implement strategy, including the balanced scorecard. Finally, we move to financial ratios and other measures, including some that were used in Chapter 19 to measure the performance of individual SBU managers. We put all these tools together to complete a comprehensive business analysis of the firm.

Because business analysis for any company is comprehensive and extensive, we can only present a summary of some of the highlights of the analysis. We use an example of a firm that manufactures cleaning products, EasyKleen Company; summarized information for the firm is shown in Exhibit 20.7. The information includes the firm's balance sheet and income statement, additional financial information, the statement of operating cash flows, and calculation of free cash flow. The following shows a brief example of how the balanced scorecard, financial ratio analysis, and EVA® can be used for a business analysis of EasyKleen.

### The Balanced Scorecard

The use of the balanced scorecard to evaluate the firm is similar to the use of critical success factors (CSFs) in evaluating and compensating the individual manager. When evaluating the firm using CSFs, the management accountant uses benchmarks from industry information and considers how the CSFs have changed from prior years. A favorable evaluation results when the CSFs are superior to the benchmarks and to prior years' performance. For example, assume that EasyKleen has three CSFs, one each from the three key performance categories:

1. Return on total assets (financial performance).
2. Number of quality defects (business processes).
3. Number of training hours for plant workers (learning and growth).

A target level of performance is set for each CSF based on a study of the performance of the best firms in the industry. The benchmark is set at 90% of the best performance in

---

[6] A thorough presentation of business analysis and valuation goes beyond the scope of this text. Excellent references include the following texts: Krishna G. Palepu and Paul M. Healy, *Business Analysis and Valuation: Using Financial Statements,* 5th ed. (Mason, OH: South-Western, 2013), and K.R. Subramanyam and John J. Wild, *Financial Statement Analysis,* 10th ed. (New York: McGraw Hill, 2009).

**EXHIBIT 20.7**
**Selected Financial Information**

| EASYKLEEN COMPANY | | |
|---|---|---|
| Summary of Selected Financial Information | | |
| For the Year Ended December 31, 2013 | | |
| **Financial Statements** | **2013** | **2012** |
| Current assets | | |
| Cash | $   50,000 | $ 70,000 |
| Accounts receivable | 100,000 | 80,000 |
| Inventory | 50,000 | 60,000 |
| Total current assets | $ 200,000 | $210,000 |
| Long-lived assets | 200,000 | 180,000 |
| Total assets | $ 400,000 | $390,000 |
| Current liabilities | $   50,000 | $ 60,000 |
| Long-term debt | 150,000 | 200,000 |
| Total liabilities | $ 200,000 | $260,000 |
| Shareholders' equity | 200,000 | 130,000 |
| Total liabilities and equity | $ 400,000 | $390,000 |
| Sales | $1,000,000 (50% are credit sales) | |
| Cost of sales | 500,000 | |
| Gross margin | $ 500,000 | |
| Operating expense | 300,000 | |
| Operating income | $ 200,000 | |
| Income tax (50%) | 100,000 | |
| Net income | $ 100,000 | |
| **Additional Financial Information** | | |
| Depreciation expense | $30,000 | |
| Capital expenditures | $50,000 | |
| Dividends | $30,000 | |
| Year-end share price | $ 16.25 | |
| Number of outstanding shares | 50,000 | |
| Interest expense | $10,000 ($5,000 after-tax) | |
| Training expenses | $30,000 ($15,000 after-tax; 26 hours per employee) | |
| Quality defects | 350 ppm (parts per million) | |
| Weighted-average cost of capital (WACC) | 6% | |
| **Cash Flow from Operations** | | |
| Net income | $100,000 | |
| Depreciation expense | 30,000 | |
| Decrease (increase) in accounts receivable | (20,000) | |
| Decrease (increase) in inventory | 10,000 | |
| Increase (decrease) in current liabilities | (10,000) | |
| Total cash flow from operations | $110,000 | |
| **Free Cash Flow** | | |
| Cash flow from operations | $110,000 | |
| Less: Capital expenditures | 50,000 | |
| Less: Dividends | 30,000 | |
| Free cash flow | $ 30,000 | |

the industry, and EasyKleen is evaluated on its overall performance, as illustrated in Exhibit 20.8.

EasyKleen management sees from the balanced scorecard that the firm met its goal in the financial area but fell short in both the operations and human resources areas. The scorecard is a guide for directing attention to achieving desired goals.

## Financial Ratio Analysis

Financial ratio analysis uses financial statement ratios to evaluate the firm's performance. Two common measures of performance are liquidity and profitability. *Liquidity* refers to

**EXHIBIT 20.8**   **Balanced Scorecard**

| | | EASYKLEEN COMPANY<br>Balanced Scorecard<br>For the Year Ended December 31, 2013 | | |
|---|---|---|---|---|
| **Category** | **CSF** | **Target Performance** | **Actual Performance*** | **Variance** |
| Financial Performance | Return on total assets | 22% | 25.3% | 3.3% (exceeded) |
| Operations | Quality defects | 300 ppm | 350 ppm | 50 ppm (unmet) |
| Learning and Growth | Training hours | 32 hours per employee | 26 hours per employee | 6 hours (unmet) |

*See Exhibit 20.9 for return on assets and Exhibit 20.7 for quality defects and training hours.

the firm's ability to pay its current operating expenses (usually for a year or less) and maturing debt. The six key measures of liquidity are the accounts receivable turnover, the inventory turnover, the current ratio, the quick ratio, and two cash flow ratios. The higher these ratios the better and the higher the evaluation of the firm's liquidity. The four key profitability ratios are gross margin percent, return on assets, return on equity, and earnings per share. The six liquidity ratios and four profitability ratios are explained in other finance and accounting texts and are not covered here. Instead, we show how each of the ratios is calculated for EasyKleen Company in Exhibit 20.9. The information is taken from Exhibit 20.7 and assumes that the benchmark level of performance is 90% of the best in the industry.

As Exhibit 20.9 indicates, EasyKleen had a very good year financially. It met seven of its ten goals. Profitability is the strongest area; it exceeded three of four ratios substantially; only the earnings per share target was unmet by a small margin. The liquidity goals were largely met, although receivables turnover and cash flow from operations fell short. This points to the need to improve the collection of receivables, which would improve both of these ratios. Overall, the financial ratio analysis shows that EasyKleen performed quite well.

### *Economic Value Added*

Economic value added (EVA®) is a business unit's income after taxes and after deducting the cost of capital. The cost of capital is usually obtained by calculating a weighted average of the cost of the firm's two sources of funds, borrowing and selling stock. EVA® focuses

**EXHIBIT 20.9**   **Financial Ratio Analysis**

| | | | | |
|---|---|---|---|---|
| | EASYKLEEN COMPANY<br>Financial Ratio Analysis<br>For the Year Ended December 31, 2013 | | | |
| **Ratio** | **Benchmark** | **Actual** | | **Percent<br>Achievement** |
| **Liquidity Ratios** | | | | |
| Accounts receivable turnover (Credit sales/Average receivables) | 7 | 5.56 = $500,000 ÷ [($100,000 + $80,000) ÷ 2] | | 79% (unmet) |
| Inventory turnover (Cost of sales/Average inventory) | 8 | 9.09 = $500,000 ÷ [($50,000 + $60,000) ÷ 2] | | 114% (met) |
| Current ratio (Current assets/Current liabilities) | 2 | 4 = $200,000 ÷ $50,000 | | 200% (met) |
| Quick ratio (Cash and receivables/Current liabilities) | 1 | 3 = ($50,000 + $100,000) ÷ $50,000 | | 300% (met) |
| **Liquidity: Cash Flow Ratios** | | | | |
| Cash flow ratio (Cash flow from operations/Current liabilities) | 2.5 | 2.2 = $110,000 ÷ $50,000 | | 88% (unmet) |
| Free cash flow ratio (Free cash flow/Current liabilities) | .5 | .6 = $30,000 ÷ $50,000 | | 120% (met) |
| **Profitability Ratios** | | | | |
| Gross margin percent (Gross profit/Net sales) | 35% | 50% = $500,000 ÷ $1,000,000 | | 143% (met) |
| Return on assets (Net income/Average total assets) | 22% | 25.3% = $100,000 ÷ [($400,000 + $390,000) ÷ 2] | | 115% (met) |
| Return on equity (Net income/Average shareholders' equity) | 44% | 60.6% = $100,000 ÷ [($200,000 + $130,000) ÷ 2] | | 138% (met) |
| Earnings per share (Net income/Weighted–average number of shares outstanding) | $2.15 | $2.00 = $100,000 ÷ 50,000 | | 93% (unmet) |

managers' attention on creating value for shareholders. By earning higher profits than the firm's cost of capital, the firm increases its internal resources available for dividends and/or to finance its continued growth, which increases stock price and adds shareholder value.

The calculation of EVA® is described fully in Chapter 19. Here we take a simple example such that the only adjustments to income are training expenses and interest expense and the only adjustment to invested capital is training expense. In effect, we are assuming for simplicity that there are no "equity equivalents" such as noncapitalized leases or deferred taxes, the firm uses FIFO for inventory, cost of goods sold equals the cash paid for inventory, and all operating expenses and taxes are paid in cash.

$$
\begin{aligned}
\text{EVA}^® ={}& \text{EVA}^® \text{ net income} - (\text{Cost of capital} \times \text{EVA}^® \text{ Invested capital}) \\
={}& \text{Net income} + \text{Training expenses after tax} + \text{Interest expense after tax} \\
& - 0.06 \times (\text{Average total assets} + \text{Training expenses} - \text{Current liabilities}) \\
={}& (\$100,000 + \$15,000 + \$5,000) - 0.06 \times [(\$400,000 + \$390,000) \div 2 \\
& + \$30,000 - \$50,000] \\
={}& \$97,500
\end{aligned}
$$

The EVA® of $97,500 for EasyKleen is a very positive value relative to net income and invested capital. It indicates the firm's strong profitability and, in particular, its significant contribution to shareholder value.[7]

## Business Valuation

This section examines how to value the company, to arrive at a single dollar figure for the company. Some might argue the value of the company and changes in its value are the most useful measures of the firm's success. Certainly these measures are relevant for the owners of the firm and interested investors.

Initially we take the approach of the owner, shareholder, or interested investor and calculate the value of the firm's shareholder equity. Later, we consider the broader question of what one would pay to purchase the entire company—debt, equity, and assets.

There are four approaches to measuring the value of shareholders' equity: the book value method, the market value method, the discounted cash flow method, and the multiples-based method. A fifth measure, enterprise value, estimates the acquisition value of a firm. The first and easiest is to obtain the book value of the firm's shareholder equity from the balance sheet. For EasyKleen, the book value of equity is $200,000 in 2013. An advantage of the book value measure is its clarity, accessibility, and objectivity. A limitation is that it reflects book values only, and therefore does not reflect the market value of the firm's assets or liabilities and may not include key intangible assets. In many cases the book value of the firm's equity is relatively small and undervalues the firm's equity.

A second approach is to obtain the market value of the firm's common equity, directly from the current market value of the firm's shares. Here for simplicity we assume that all of EasyKleen's shareholders are common shareholders; there is no preferred stock.

The firm's market value is determined by multiplying the number of outstanding shares by the current market price of the shares. For the EasyKleen Company, the value is:

$$\text{Number of shares} \times \text{Share price}$$
$$= 50,000 \times \$16.25 = \$812,500$$

The market value method has the advantage of providing a clear and objective measure of equity which reflects the current value of the company. This measure is often called the firm's *market capitalization.*

---

[7] If the EVA® for future periods is projected and then the discounted value of each of these future EVA® values is taken, the sum is what is called market value added (MVA). MVA is an estimate of the difference between the market value of a company and the amount of invested capital. It is interpreted just as EVA®; the difference is that it aggregates the net present value of all future projected EVA® amounts. MVA helps explain a company's market performance (and value) by linking it to projected returns on capital.

For nonpublic firms a relevant stock price is not available, and one of the other methods is needed to evaluate the firm.[8]

The third method for obtaining the value of the firm is to obtain the present value of the firm's cash flows; this is called the *discounted cash flow (DCF) method.* It is one of the most commonly used methods in equity valuation. Economic and accounting theory say that the equity value of an investment should be the present value of future dividends from the investment, and the DCF method is the most consistent with that.

## The Discounted Cash Flow Method

The discounted cash flow (DCF) method measures the firm's equity value as the discounted present value of its net cash flows. The DCF method is based on the same concepts used in Chapter 12 for capital-budgeting decisions. Cash flows a year or more into the future are discounted to consider the time value of money; cash flows in recent periods are more valuable than cash flows in distant periods.

There are four steps in the application of the DCF method.[9]

1. **Forecast free cash flows over a finite horizon (usually five years).** Free cash flow refers to cash flows available for investing and financing activities of the company and is calculated as operating cash flow less capital expenditures and less dividends paid. For EasyKleen, free cash flow in 2013 is equal to $30,000. For this illustration, we assume that free cash flows will also be $30,000 in 2014 and will increase by $10,000 in each of the next four years. These cash flow assumptions are shown in Exhibit 20.10.

2. **Forecast free cash flows beyond the finite horizon, using some simplifying assumption.** For EasyKleen, we make the conservative forecast that free cash flows after 2018 will continue at the rate of $70,000 per year (the same as year 2018), and we also assume that these cash flows will continue indefinitely.

3. **Discount free cash flows at the weighted-average cost of capital (WACC), the firm's cost of capital weighted for both debt and equity.** The weighted-average cost of capital (WACC) for EasyKleen is given as 6%. The derivation of WACC is explained in Chapter 12 and is not duplicated here. The present value of free cash flows is determined using the WACC of 6%, as illustrated in Exhibit 20.10. The sum of the present values for the first five years is $205,700.

The present value of the cash flows from 2019 on are determined using the discount factor for an annuity with a continuing life, which is the inverse of the discount rate

**EXHIBIT 20.10**
**DCF Valuation of the EasyKleen Company**

| Years | Free Cash Flow | Present Value Factor (for 6%) | Present Value of Cash Flows |
|---|---|---|---|
| 2014 | $30,000 | 0.943 | $ 28,290 |
| 2015 | 40,000 | 0.890 | 35,600 |
| 2016 | 50,000 | 0.840 | 42,000 |
| 2017 | 60,000 | 0.792 | 47,520 |
| 2018 | 70,000 | 0.747 | 52,290 |
| Total present value of cash flows in the planning period ⟶ | | | $ 205,700 (A) |
| 2019+ | $70,000 | 16.667 | $1,166,690 (B) |
| Total present value of 2019+ years' cash flows 0.747 | | | 871,517 (C) = (B) × 0.747 |
| Plus: Marketable securities and investments | | | 0 (D) |
| Less: Market value of debt (assumed = book value) | | | 150,000 (E) |
| Value of the firm's equity | | | $ 927,217 = (A) + (C) + (D) − (E) |

[8] The valuation of privately held businesses is examined in David S. Jenkins and Gregory Kane, "A Contextual Analysis of Income- and Asset-Based Approaches to Private Equity Valuation," *The Accounting Review,* March 2006, pp. 19–35.

[9] The steps shown here are guided by the steps illustrated in the text by Krishna G. Palepu and Paul M. Healy, *Business Analysis and Valuation: Using Financial Statements,* 5th ed. (Mason, OH: South-Western, 2013).

The price-earnings ratio (PE) is the ratio of a company's stock price to current earnings per share (EPS). The numerator of this ratio, stock price, fluctuates often, sometimes dramatically, due to fluctuations in the company's stock price and the overall stock market. A company's earnings also fluctuate, though usually not with the volatility of the stock price. The chart below shows the PE ratio for the S&P 500 firms from 1881 to 2011. If you take the very long view, the price-earnings ratio for the S&P 500 has averaged about 16 over the last 130 years (17 over the last 50 years), with the lowest point in 1920 and the highest in 1999. Sometimes PE ratios will fall while earnings are holding steady; the market is saying it is not sure of the sustainability of those earnings. At other times, the market shows "irrational exuberance" and the PE ratios increase dramatically. A key take-away is that the price-earnings ratio will vary significantly as economic conditions change. Also, the ratio will differ significantly from industry to industry; as of late 2011, the highest PE ratios were in the health care and consumer products industries, while the lowest were in the commodities and financial sectors. Thus, use caution when using the PE ratio in business valuation.

Another key issue concerning the PE ratio is that the denominator, earnings per share (EPS), can be significantly influenced by management through the repurchase of shares. A common practice in recent years, repurchasing shares can help executives meet the EPS targets used in bonus payments.

**Sources:** Data from Robert Shiller, Yale University; see also Nelson D. Schwartz, "As Layoffs Rise, Stock Buybacks Consume Cash," *The New York Times,* November 22, 2011, p. 1; "Companies Bet Big on Themselves," *Bloomberg Businessweek,* November 21, 2011, pp. 55–56.

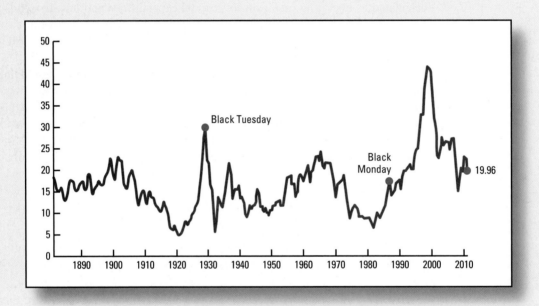

$(1/0.06 = 16.667)$.[10] This gives a discounted value for these six-year-plus cash flows of $1,166,690. To discount this amount back from the beginning of 2019 to the present, we discount $1,166,690 by the fifth year discount factor (0.747) to arrive at the discounted value of the continuing (six-year-plus) cash flows, $871,517.

4. **Calculate the value of equity.** To determine the firm's *net valuation,* we now add the discounted value of the planning period cash flows and the discounted value of the six-year-plus cash flows to the value of current nonoperating investments such as marketable securities, and we subtract the market value of long-term debt. The net valuation for the firm's equity is then $927,217. If the cash flow estimates are reliable, the DCF method provides a useful measure in determining the firm's value.

[10] Typically, the firm's cash flows are assumed to continue indefinitely, and thus the discount factor for an annuity is used in perpetuity (continuing life). This assumption is consistent with the idea that the firm is an ongoing entity with little or no likelihood of bankruptcy. If a shorter period is desired, the appropriate discount factor from the annuity table can be used for the desired number of years. For example, if the desired period, after the planning period, is from the 6th year to the 20th year, the discount factor is found in the annuity table for 15 years (6 through 20), or 9.712. The factor 9.712 is then used in place of the factor 16.667 in the analysis in Exhibit 20.10.

## Multiples-Based Valuation

A common and easy-to-apply approach to valuing a business is to use the ratio of stock price to some financial measure—usually sales, earnings, or cash flow. For example, the earnings-based multiple computes value as the product of expected annual accounting earnings times a multiplier. The earnings multiplier is similar to the price-to-earnings (PE) ratio, that is, the ratio of stock price to earnings per share. The difference is that the earning multiplier adjusts the PE ratio to recognize that future earnings should be discounted to determine the company's value. The earnings multiplier has important limitations. The accounting treatment of inventory, depreciation, and other important components of earnings might not be comparable to that of other firms in the industry. When earnings are not comparable, determining a relevant and useful multiplier is difficult.

If the earnings multiplier is not available for a given firm, an average or representative value is taken from the earnings multipliers of other firms in the industry. This multiplier can then be adjusted upward to recognize a firm with future profit potential not recognized in current earnings or vice versa. Assume that the relevant earnings multiplier for EasyKleen is 8.5. Then the value of EasyKleen using this method is determined as follows:

$$\text{Earnings multiplier} \times \text{Earnings}$$
$$= 8.5 \times \$100,000 = \$850,000$$

The earnings multiplier is easy to apply and can provide a useful evaluation of the firm, subject to the limitations noted. The sales-based multiple and the cash flow–based multiples are applied in a similar fashion.

In practice, the management accountant and analyst commonly use two or more of the valuation techniques and evaluate the assumptions in each to arrive at an overall valuation. In the case of EasyKleen, a valuation of approximately $900,000 is reasonable, given the range of measures obtained.

## Enterprise Value

The methods we have considered thus far determine the value of the firm's equity. Enterprise value (EV) is another measure of what the market says the company is worth, but this time in an acquisition. In an acquisition, an acquirer would "buy" not only the firm's equity, but also the firm's debt, cash, and cash equivalents. So EV is measured as the market value of the firm's equity (market capitalization) plus debt, and less cash (cash is subtracted because it is available after the acquisition to pay off debt or for other uses):

$$\text{EV} = \text{Market capitalization} + \text{Debt} - \text{Cash}$$

EV is used by investors and shareholders when an acquisition is being considered.

## An Illustration of the Five Steps of Strategic Decision Making in the Valuation of a Fashion Retailer

Arizona Sunrise, Inc. (ASI) is a retailer of women's fashion clothing with 455 stores in the United States and 55 in Canada, an increase of 62 stores over the prior year. The company is growing fast because of its unique fashion styles and the quality of its clothing. ASI products are priced at levels slightly higher than competitive brands, but production and selling costs are somewhat higher as well, thus sales have grown very fast, but earnings and cash flows have trailed behind. In some recent quarterly periods, cash flow from operations has been low and in some cases even negative. Bettman, PLC, a similar retailer located in London, is also known for its fashion-wise designs and product quality. Bettman has expressed an interest in buying ASI, both because of ASI's recent success and because the fall in the dollar relative to the British pound in recent years has effectively reduced the purchase cost in U.K. currency. Bettman would maintain the ASI brand name for at least a few years and at least initially would maintain the local store management. In the longer term, Bettman's plan is to integrate the two product lines into a single global brand. Bettman plans to purchase ASI in a cash transaction but is not sure what value to place on ASI.

### *The Five Steps of Strategic Decision Making for Arizona Sunrise, Inc.*

1. **Determine the strategic issues surrounding the problem.** Both firms involved in the case are differentiators based on quality and style. The key business issue is how the combined firms will be more or less competitive than the separate firms. Bettman's plan to move the two firms to a larger, global brand, could help the firm establish a presence globally, thereby improving its opportunity for further growth. The immediate issue is to determine the purchase price of ASI.

2. **Identify the alternative actions.** Bettman can use a variety of methods to value ASI, as described above: discounted cash flows, multiples of earnings, and enterprise value, among other methods.

3. **Obtain information and conduct analyses of the alternatives.** Bettman performs a discounted cash flow analysis based on ASI's projected free cash flow for the next five years and projects a value of $24 billion. A valuation based on the earnings multiple yielded a smaller value of $14 billion, the current market value of ASI's equity was $16 billion, and the enterprise value was calculated to be $15 billion.

4. **Based on strategy and analysis, choose and implement the desired alternative.** The analysis produced a wide range of valuations, but a cluster of them was around $15 billion. Moreover, enterprise value is particularly appropriate for valuing a purchase because it takes into account ASI's debt and cash equivalents available to the purchaser. Bettman also considers the strategic advantages and disadvantages of the purchase and is persuaded to make an offer of $15 billion because the acquisition of ASI could help Bettman establish a stronger brand globally, thereby improving its opportunity for further growth and profitability.

5. **Provide an ongoing evaluation of the effectiveness of implementation in step 4.** If Bettman purchases ASI, it will need to complete the implementation through a plan for integrating the two businesses operationally, financially, and strategically. This will be a key management goal for the first few years after the acquisition. Bettman is required by international financial accounting standards to regularly assess the value of the acquisition, and if the value of the acquisition should fall, Bettman must write the asset down to the new fair market value.

If the purchase is not completed, Bettman should continue to look for firms like ASI that would help Bettman obtain the global presence that is central to its strategy.

## Summary

In this chapter we discussed management compensation and the evaluation of a business. The first part introduces the objectives and methods for compensating managers. The three principal objectives for management compensation, which follow directly from the objectives for management control, are the *motivation* of the manager, the *incentive* for proper decision making, and *fairness* to the manager.

The three main types of compensation are *salary, bonus,* and *benefits.* The bonus is the fastest growing part of total compensation and often the largest part. The three important factors in the development of a bonus plan are the base for computing the bonus (cost, revenue, profit, investment center, stock price, and the balanced scorecard), the source of funding for the bonus (the business unit or the entire firm), and the payment options (current and deferred bonus, stock options, and performance shares). The development of an executive compensation plan is a complex process involving these three factors and the three types of compensation, as well as the objectives of management control.

Tax planning and financial reporting concerns are important in compensation planning because of management's desire to reduce taxes and report financial results favorably. Thus, accountants must consider taxes and financial reporting issues when they develop a compensation plan for managers.

Management compensation plans are used in service and not-for-profit organizations as well. The chapter illustrates an actual example for a professional services firm.

The second part of the chapter considers the evaluation of the entire firm in contrast to the previous two chapters and the first part of this chapter that focused on the individual manager. The evaluation of the firm is important for investors and as one part of an overall assessment of the performance of top management. The common evaluation methods include the balanced scorecard, financial ratio analysis, and economic value added. Methods used to directly value a business include the market value method, the discounted cash flow method, the multiples-based method, and enterprise value.

## Key Terms

| | | |
|---|---|---|
| benefits, *861* | firmwide pool, *866* | salary, *861* |
| bonus, *861* | management compensation | unit-based pool, *866* |
| business analysis, *871* | plans, *861* | |
| business valuation, *871* | | |

## Comments on Cost Management in Action

### When Good Options Go Bad

When a company's stock price falls and its executive stock options no longer look attractive, it has a number of choices. One is to simply re-price the options to a lower price that is more in keeping with the lower market price of the firm's stock. Another choice is to grant new options that have a lower exercise price to replace the old.

A common way to re-price options is to backdate the options to a time when the stock price was somewhat lower; the result is that the exercise price is lower and the options are now again "in the money." Re-pricing options is legal as long as it is clearly communicated to shareholders and in the company's financial and tax reports. Illegal backdating has been identified at a number of large public companies and criminal penalties imposed. Because the legal issues regarding backdating were clarified in the Sarbanes-Oxley Act of 2002, instances of illegal backdating are now rare. A continuing issue, however, is the practice of timing stock option grants. *Spring-loading* is the term used to refer to the case in which grants are given prior to expected good news, while *bullet-dodging* refers to the practice of granting options after bad news. These practices are associated with an upward trend in stock prices after the grant date.

Another approach is for the executive to hedge his or her own stockholding or stock options by buying "put" (right-to-sell) options on the firm's stock in the open market. If the stock price falls dramatically, the executive can still sell the stock or exercise the options at the relatively favorable ("put") price. This practice is very much like that engaged in by global firms to hedge their exposure to foreign exchange fluctuations.

The problem with executives hedging their stock holdings and options is that it undermines the principle of pay for performance. Through hedging, the executive can effectively protect against a fall in the stock. Hedging reduces the risk of stock ownership and therefore reduces the incentive for executives to take steps to sustain the firm's stock price.

**Sources:** Brian J. Hall and Thomas A. Knox, "Underwater Options and the Dynamics of Executive Pay-to-Performance Sensitivities," *Journal of Accounting Research,* May 2004, p. 365; "GE: When Execs Outperform the Stock," *BusinessWeek,* April 17, 2006, p. 74; David Yermack, "Good Timing: CEO Stock Option Awards and Company News Announcements," *Journal of Finance,* June 1997, pp. 449–76.

## Self-Study Problems
(For solutions, please turn to the end of the chapter.)

### 1. Management Compensation Plan

Davis-Thompson-Howard & Associates (DTH) is a large consulting firm that specializes in the evaluation of governmental programs. The lawyers, accountants, engineers, and other specialists at DTH evaluate both the performance of existing programs and the success of potential new government programs. DTH obtains most of its consulting engagements by completing proposals in open bidding for the services desired by governmental agencies. The competition for these proposals has increased in recent years, and as a result DTH's yield (the number of new engagements divided by proposals) has fallen from 49% a few years ago to only 26% in the most recent year. The firm's profitability has fallen as well. DTH has decided to study its management compensation plan as one step among the many it will take in attempting to return the firm to its previous level of profitability.

DTH has six regional offices, two located near Washington, D.C., and the others near large metropolitan areas where most of their clients are located. Each office is headed by an office manager who is one of the firm's professional associates. The firm's services in these offices are classified into financial and operational audit services, educational evaluation, engineering consulting, and financial systems. The Washington offices tend to provide most of the financial and audit services, and the other offices offer their own mix of professional services. No two offices are alike since each has adapted to the needs of its regional client base. DTH's objective is to be among the three most competitive firms in its areas of service and to increase its revenues by at least 10% per year.

DTH's compensation plan awards each office a bonus based on (1) the increase in billings over the prior year and (2) the number of net new clients acquired in the current year. The office manager has the authority to divide the office bonus as appropriate, although these same two criteria are generally used to allocate it to the office professionals. Top management is not aware of any problems with the compensation plan; there have been no significant complaints.

One observation by the CEO might suggest a reason for the firm's decline in yield of proposals. It has been losing out particularly on large new contract proposals that require a large number of staff and a significant professional travel commitment. These are jobs for which it would be necessary to coordinate two or more DTH offices. The CEO notes that DTH has as many regional offices as most of its competitors, which now seem to be winning a larger share of these contracts.

**Required**    Discuss the pros and cons of DTH's compensation plan. Is it consistent with the company's objectives and competitive environment?

## 2. Business Valuation

WebSmart is a relatively new Internet company that sells educational products on the web. The firm focuses on students preparing for college entrance exams. The key competitive advantage at WebSmart is its highly regarded publication, *Guide to Competitive Colleges,* which is sold widely in bookstores and on **Amazon.com**. The firm has grown rapidly and now is seeking additional venture capital investment to allow it to improve its operations and provide additional advertising and promotion. One of the venture capital firms that WebSmart approached has asked WebSmart to provide an estimate of the firm's value. Relevant financial information about WebSmart from the most recent financial statement follows. WebSmart owns no significant fixed assets, but operates out of leased space. WebSmart management knows that the median stock price-to-sales multiple in the industry is approximately 7.

| | |
|---|---:|
| Total assets per most recent financial statements | $1,450,000 |
| Total book value of equity, per most recent financial statements | 1,200,000 |
| Estimated market value of *Guide to Competitive Colleges* | 1,350,000 |
| Net income | (85,000) |
| Cash flow from operations | (165,000) |
| Total revenues | $  600,000 |

**Required**    Develop an estimate of the value of WebSmart and explain your reasoning.

*Please visit http://www.mhhe.com/blocher6e to access a narrated, animated tutorial for solving these problems.*

## Questions

20-1    Identify and explain the three objectives of management compensation.

20-2    Explain the three types of management compensation.

20-3    Explain how a manager's risk aversion can affect decision making and how compensation plans should be designed to deal with risk aversion.

20-4    Explain how management compensation can provide an incentive to unethical behavior. What methods can be used to reduce the chance of unethical activities resulting from compensation plans?

20-5    From a financial reporting standpoint, what form of compensation is most desirable for the firm?

20-6    From a tax-planning standpoint, what form of compensation is least desirable for the manager? For the firm?

20-7    List the three bases for bonus incentive plans; explain how they differ and how each achieves or does not achieve the three objectives of management compensation.

20-8    Identify and explain the six financial ratios used to evaluate liquidity as part of the firm's business analysis.

20-9    What are the two types of bonus pools for bonus incentive plans? How do they differ, and how does each achieve or not achieve the three objectives of management compensation?

20-10   List the four types of bonus payment options and explain how they differ. How does each achieve or not achieve the three objectives of management compensation?

20-11   Develop arguments to support your view as to whether executive pay in the United States is (or is not) too high.

20-12   Explain the different business valuation methods. Which method do you think is superior and why?

20-13   What type of management compensation is the fastest growing part of total compensation? Why do you think this is the case?

20-14   Why do you think it is important for a management accountant to be able to complete an evaluation of the firm that is separate from an evaluation of individual managers?

20-15   How does the firm's management compensation plan change over the life cycle of the firm's products?

## Brief Exercises

20-16   Sticky Fingers Inc. produces scotch tape and masking tape. Last year's annual report has been compiled, and you are in charge of business analysis for the year. The company had a goal for inventory turnover of 6, cost of goods sold of $400,000, beginning inventory of $50,000, and ending inventory of $70,000. What was the actual inventory turnover, and at what percent did the firm achieve its goal?

20-17   Tinsley Inc. is an industry-leading cardboard manufacturer. You have been asked to determine a market value for the firm's equity. The firm has 100,000 shares outstanding, earnings per share of $2.50 last year, and a stock price of $25. What is the market value?

20-18   Jamison Auto Parts produces replacement parts for automobiles. Last year Jamison had EVA® net income of $200,000, cost of capital of 10%, and EVA® capital of $750,000. Determine the firm's economic value added.

20-19   Moore Heel is a shoe manufacturing company. Moore has hired you to value the company based on the discounted cash flow method. You have determined that the present value of the company's cash flows is $400,000, marketable securities total $150,000, and the market value of debt is $250,000. What is the value of the firm?

20-20   Smith Co. is a firm specializing in financial advice for retired individuals. After some analysis, you have determined that an earnings multiplier of 7 is appropriate for this type of business. Smith's most recent earnings totaled $250,000 and earnings per share was $4.50. What is the value of the firm based on the earnings multiplier?

20-21   Johnson Healthcare is a health care firm specializing in products for the disabled. Johnson plans to maintain a 10% gross profit margin. After analyzing last year's data, you found that Johnson had gross profit of $250,000 and net sales of $1,500,000. What was the gross profit margin, and by what percentage did the firm achieve its goal?

## Exercises

[LO 20-1, 20-2]   20-22   **Compensation; Strategy; Market Value**   Jackson Supply Company is a publicly owned firm that serves the medical supply needs of hospitals and large medical practices in six southeastern states. The firm has grown significantly in recent years, as the areas it serves have grown. Jackson has focused on customer service and has developed an excellent reputation for speed of delivery and overall quality of service. The company ensures that customer service is each manager's main focus by making it count for 50% of the management bonus. The firm measures specific indicators of customer service monthly; progress toward these measures as well as others is used to determine each manager's bonus. In the past several months, top management has noticed that although most managers are meeting or exceeding their customer service goals and receiving bonuses accordingly, the firm's stock price has been lagging while competitive firms' stock prices have been rising steadily.

**Required**   What modification, if any, should Jackson Supply Company make to its management compensation plan?

[LO 20-1, 20-2]   20-23   **Evaluating an Incentive Pay Plan; Strategy**   Anne-Marie Fox is the manager of a new and used boat dealership. She has decided to reevaluate the compensation plan offered to her sales representatives to determine whether the plan encourages the dealership's success. The representatives are paid no salary, but they receive 20% of the sales price of every boat sold, and they have the authority to negotiate the boats' prices as far down as their wholesale cost if necessary.

**Required**   Is this plan in the dealership's strategic best interest? Why or why not?

**[LO 20-1, 20-2, 20-3]**   20-24   **Alternative Compensation Plans**   ADM, Inc., an electronics manufacturer, uses growth in earnings per share (EPS) as a guideline for evaluating executive performance. ADM executives receive a bonus of $5,000 for every penny increase in EPS for the year. This bonus is paid in addition to fixed salaries ranging from $500,000 to $900,000 annually.

Cygnus Corporation, a computer components manufacturer, also uses EPS as an evaluation tool. Its executives receive a bonus equal to 40% of their salary for the year if the firm's EPS is in the top third of a list ranking the EPS for Cygnus and its 12 competitors.

**Required**
1. Why are companies such as ADM, Inc., and Cygnus Corporation switching from stock option incentives to programs more like the ones described? What does the use of these plans by the two firms say about each firm's competitive strategy?
2. What are the weaknesses of incentive plans based on EPS?

**[LO 20-2]**   20-25   **Performance Evaluation and Risk Aversion**   Jill Lewis is the office manager of PureBreds, Inc. Her office has 30 employees whose collective job is to process applications by dog owners who want to register their pets with the firm. There is never a shortage of applications waiting to be processed, but random events beyond Lewis's control (e.g., employees out sick) cause fluctuations in the number of applications that her office can process. Jill is aware that it is important that the applications be processed quickly and accurately.

Alex Zale, the district manager to whom Jill reports, bases his evaluation of Jill on the number of applications that are processed.

**Required**
1. If Jill is risk-averse, how should Alex compensate her? Why?
2. What is a disadvantage of an evaluation method that is based only on the number of processed applications?
3. List at least two ways that Alex could measure how accurately Jill's office is processing the applications.

**[LO 20-2]**   20-26   **Performance Evaluation and Risk Aversion**   Heartwood Furniture Corporation has a line of sofas marketed under the name NightTime Sleepers. Heartwood management is considering several compensation packages for Amy Johnson, NightTime's general manager. Amy's duties include making all investing and operating decisions for NightTime.

**Required**
1. Amy is risk-neutral and prefers to receive the maximum reward for her hard work. Do you recommend compensation based on flat salary, an ROI-based bonus, or a combination of both? Why?
2. If Amy does not make investing decisions for NightTime, is ROI still a good performance measure? If so, then explain why. If not, suggest an alternative.
3. Heartwood Furniture plans to evaluate Amy by comparing NightTime's ROI to the ROI of Stiles Furniture, which operates in a business environment similar to that of NightTime. Both companies have the same capabilities, but Stiles uses a significantly different manufacturing strategy than NightTime.
   a. Would evaluating Amy with this benchmark be fair?
   b. Would using residual income instead of ROI offer any advantages for Heartwood?

**[LO 20-3]**   20-27   **Bonus Compensation Base and Pool**   There are three components to a bonus plan: the base of the bonus compensation (earnings, revenues), the bonus pool (firmwide or unit-based), and the payment options (cash, stock options). It is common in many industries, including the financial services industry, to use a firmwide pool and revenue as the base for bonus compensation.

**Required**
1. What are some alternative bases for compensation pools, in addition to revenue?
2. What effect do you expect the use of revenues, rather than some other base, to have on both the motivation of managers and the total bonuses paid to managers? Comment on the effectiveness of the revenue base relative to other options for the bonus compensation base.
3. Explain the likely motivational effects of the use of the firmwide bonus plan for firms in the financial services industry.
4. Do you consider the firmwide revenue plan for bonus compensation to be a fair method for determining bonuses? Why or why not?

[LO 20-3]   20-28   **Compensation and Trust**   Bill George, a Harvard Business School professor, notes the increasing lack of trust many now have for the executive compensation plans in place in many corporations. Writing in *Bloomberg Businessweek* (September 13, 2010, p. 56), he suggests six policies which, if followed by regulators and the compensation committees on corporate boards, would rebuild trust in corporate pay policies:

1. Provide full transparency for compensation policies and actual practices.
2. Create policies that reward long-term performance.
3. Reward executives for their performance, not the company's stock price.
4. Lengthen the time horizon for bonuses.
5. Use approaches that include qualitative measures like strategy implementation, research milestones, and leadership development.
6. Boost fairness between executives and workers.

**Required**

1. Which of George's suggestions do you think are critical to rebuilding shareholders' and others' trust in corporate compensation policies? Explain briefly.
2. Can you think of another suggestion for improving shareholders' trust in corporate executive pay policies and practices? Explain your choice(s) briefly.

[LO 20-3]   20-29   **Compensation at Nonpublic Companies**   The executive compensation programs of the largest public companies often include the types of equity-based compensation such as stock options and performance shares as described in this chapter. Smaller nonpublic companies often have the same types of strategic goals and want to provide the same types of compensation plans as do the larger public companies but do not have the equity types of compensation to offer since the firms do not have publicly traded stock.

**Required:**

1. What are the advantages of equity-based compensation such as stock options and performance shares?
2. What types of compensation can nonpublic companies offer that would provide the desired incentives that equity-based compensation offers?

[LO 20-3]   20-30   **Compensation in Tough Economic Times**   During an economic recession companies are under pressure to reduce costs, and a significant part of total cost for most companies is salaries and wages, including both executive compensation and employee compensation.

**Required**   Review the types of compensation we have covered in this chapter and explain which types of compensation you would reduce if needed to help a company through difficult economic times.

[LO 20-4]   20-31   **International Accounting Standards and Bonus Compensation**   The International Accounting Standards Board (www.IASB.org) is a London-based independent organization that develops and interprets international financial reporting standards (IFRS). The mission of the IASB is to develop a single set of high quality, globally accepted accounting standards. As of April 2012, 123 countries throughout the world either permit or require IFRS for publicly held companies in their country. The U.S. continues to use generally accepted accounting principles (GAAP) as developed by the U.S.-based Financial Accounting Standards Board (FASB). The FASB, under the guidance of the SEC, has developed a plan in which the FASB and the IASB work together to complete a convergence of IFRS and GAAP. The timetable for convergence is not firmly set, but many believe it will be a matter of only a few years before U.S. firms will be using IFRS or something very much like it. Some of the notable differences between GAAP and IFRS are that IFRS does not permit LIFO valuation of inventory (GAAP does), and IFRS does permit market value treatment of certain long-lived assets (GAAP does not). Experts note that the move to IFRS will certainly affect U.S.-based firms in terms of corporate taxation, international transfer pricing (Chapter 19), global investment strategies (Chapter 12), and the evaluation of the performance of foreign operations and the managers of those operations (Chapters 18 and 19).

**Required**   How is the move from GAAP to IFRS likely to affect the development of compensation plans in U.S.-based firms?

[LO 20-5]   20-32   **Business Analysis**   Williams Company is a manufacturer of auto parts having the following financial statements for 2012–2013.

## Balance Sheet
### December 31, 2013 and 2012

|  | 2013 | 2012 |
|---|---|---|
| Cash | $ 260,000 | $ 135,000 |
| Accounts receivable | 150,000 | 225,000 |
| Inventory | 385,000 | 175,000 |
| Total current assets | $ 795,000 | $ 535,000 |
| Long-lived assets | 1,640,000 | 1,500,000 |
| **Total assets** | $2,435,000 | $2,035,000 |
| Current liabilities | $ 200,000 | $175,000 |
| Long-term debt | 900,000 | 800,000 |
| Shareholder equity | 1,335,000 | 1,060,000 |
| **Total debt and equity** | $2,435,000 | $2,035,000 |

## Income Statement
### For the years ended December 31, 2013 and 2012

|  | 2013 | 2012 |
|---|---|---|
| Sales | $3,500,000 | $3,600,000 |
| Cost of sales | 2,500,000 | 2,600,000 |
| Gross margin | 1,000,000 | 1,000,000 |
| Operating expenses* | 500,000 | 450,000 |
| Operating income | 500,000 | 550,000 |
| Taxes | 175,000 | 192,500 |
| Net income | $ 325,000 | $ 357,500 |

## Cash Flow from Operations

|  | 2013 | 2012 |
|---|---|---|
| Net income | $325,000 | $357,500 |
| Plus depreciation expense | 60,000 | 50,000 |
| +Decrease (-inc) in Accounts receivable and Inventory | (135,000) | — |
| +Increase (-dec) in Current liabilities | 25,000 | — |
| Cash flow from operations | $275,000 | $407,500 |

*Operating expense includes depreciation expense.

Additional financial information, including industry averages for 2013, where appropriate:

|  | 2013 | 2012 | Industry 2013 |
|---|---|---|---|
| Capital expenditures | $ 200,000 | $ 100,000 |  |
| Income tax rate | 35% | 35% | 35.0% |
| Depreciation expense | $ 60,000 | $ 50,000 |  |
| Dividends | $ 50,000 | $ 50,000 |  |
| Year-end stock price | $ 2.25 | $ 2.75 | 25.00 |
| Number of outstanding shares | 1,800,000 | 1,800,000 |  |
| Sales multiplier |  |  | 1.50 |
| Free cash flow multiplier |  |  | 18.00 |
| Earnings multiplier |  |  | 9.00 |
| Cost of capital | 5.0% | 5.0% |  |
| Accounts receivable turnover |  |  | 11.10 |
| Inventory turnover |  |  | 10.50 |
| Current ratio |  |  | 2.30 |
| Quick ratio |  |  | 1.90 |
| Cash flow from operations ratio |  |  | 1.20 |
| Free cash flow ratio |  |  | 1.10 |
| Gross margin percentage |  |  | 30.0% |
| Return on assets (net book value) |  |  | 20.0% |
| Return on equity |  |  | 30.0% |

**Required** Calculate and interpret the financial ratios (per Exhibit 20.9) for Williams for 2012 and 2013. Since the calculation of many ratios requires the average balance in an account (e.g., average receivables is required in calculating receivables turnover), you may assume that the balances in these accounts in 2012 are the same as those in 2011.

[LO 20-5] 20-33 **Business Valuation** Refer to the information in Exercise 20-32.

**Required** Develop a business valuation for Williams Company for 2013 using the following methods: (1) book value of equity, (2) market value of equity, (3) discounted cash flow (DCF), (4) enterprise value, and (5) all the multiples-based valuations for which there is an industry average multiplier. For the calculation of the DCF valuation, you may use the simplifying assumption that free cash flows will continue indefinitely at the amount in 2013.

[LO 20-5] 20-34 **Business Valuation** Five different analysts have submitted valuations for a private technology firm that is the subject of a possible acquisition. The valuations are as follows:

| Analyst | Valuation |
|---------|-----------|
| 1 | $26,331,000 |
| 2 | 38,803,000 |
| 3 | 65,000,000 |
| 4 | 27,000,000 |
| 5 | 17,000,000 |

**Required** The value of having multiple analyst reports is that one can develop a range of possible valuations and select a final valuation that seems appropriate. What valuation would you choose for this technology company? Explain your reasoning.

## Problems

[LO 20-3] 20-35 **Compensation; Net Present Value** Glee Candy Co. makes chewy chocolate candies at a plant in Winston-Salem, North Carolina. Brian Bishop, the production manager at this facility, installed a packaging machine last year at a cost of $400,000. This machine is expected to last for 10 more years with no residual value. Operating costs for the projected levels of production are $95,000 annually.

Brian has just learned of a new packaging machine that would work much more efficiently in Glee's production line. This machine would cost $520,000 installed, but the annual operating costs would be only $30,000. This machine would be depreciated over 10 years with no residual value. He could sell the current packaging machine this year for $180,000.

Brian has worked for Glee for seven years. He plans to remain with the firm for about two more years, when he expects to become a vice president of operations at his father-in-law's company. Glee pays Brian a fixed salary with an annual bonus of 5% of net income for the year.

Assume that Glee uses straight-line depreciation and has a 10% required rate of return. Ignore income-tax effects.

**Required**
1. As the owner of Glee, would you want Brian to keep the current machine or purchase the new one?
2. Why might Brian not prefer to make the decision that the owner of Glee desires?

[LO 20-3] 20-36 **Compensation; Benefits; Ethics** DuMelon Publishing Inc. is a nationwide company headquartered in Boston, Massachusetts. The firm's benefits are a significant element of employee compensation. All professional employees at DuMelon receive company-paid benefits including medical insurance, term life insurance, and paid vacations and holidays. They also receive a set reimbursement amount of $250 per day maximum for travel expenses when they conduct business for DuMelon. DuMelon offers a 25% match for money the professionals deposit in the company-sponsored 401(k) plan.

These benefits vary, depending on the employee's salary and level in the company. For example, the amount of vacation days increases as a professional is promoted to higher levels. The maximum amount that can be contributed to the 401(k) plan also increases as the employee's salary increases, subject to an overall limitation provided by tax laws.

When a DuMelon employee attains the position of vice president of a function, such as operations or sales, that person qualifies for a special class of additional benefits: a company car, a larger office with decoration allowances, and access to the executive suite at the Boston office. (The executive suite features a dining room and lounge for the executives' use.) The perks also include total reimbursement for all business travel expenses.

**Required**

1. Explain the implications for employee behavior and performance of DuMelon's two levels of benefits for professional employees, including ethical issues.

2. Suppose that the policy for benefits is not applied strictly at DuMelon. As a result, the following instances have occurred:

   a. The company has occasionally paid the travel expenses of VPs' spouses. Company policy is unclear as to whether this is allowed.

   b. Some VPs have special-ordered their company-provided vehicles, which on average costs the company an additional $23,000 for each car.

   c. Passes to the executive suite have been lent to other DuMelon professionals.

   d. Some of the vice presidents have offices that are much larger than those of other vice presidents. No apparent factors determine who gets the larger offices.

   How might these situations affect the behavior of vice presidents and other professionals at DuMelon? What are the underlying implications for cost control of benefits? Use specific examples when applicable.

[LO 20-3]   20-37   **Incentive Pay in the Hotel Industry**   Kristin Helmud is the general manager of Highland Inn, a local mid-priced hotel with 100 rooms. Her job objectives include providing resourceful and friendly service to the hotel's guests, maintaining an 80% occupancy rate, improving the average rate received per room to $88 from the current $85, achieving a savings of 5% on all hotel costs, and reducing energy use by 10% by carefully managing the use of heating and air conditioning in unused rooms and by carefully managing the onsite laundry facility, among other means. The hotel's owner, a partnership of seven people who own several hotels in the region, want to structure Kristin's future compensation to objectively reward her for achieving these goals. In the past, she has been paid an annual salary of $72,000 with no incentive pay. The incentive plan the partners developed has each of the goals weighted as follows:

| Measure | Percent of Total Responsibility |
|---|---|
| Occupancy rate (also reflects guest service quality) | 20% |
| Operating within 95% of expense budget | 30 |
| Average room rate | 30 |
| Energy use | 20 |
| | 100% |

If Kristin achieves all of these goals, the partners determine that her performance should merit a bonus of $30,000. The partners also agree that her salary will need to be reduced to $60,000 because of the addition of the bonus.

The goal measures used to compensate Kristin are as follows:

| | |
|---|---|
| *Occupancy goal:* | 29,200 room-nights = 80% occupancy rate × 100 rooms × 365 days |
| Compensation: | 20% weight × $30,000 target reward = $6,000 |
| | $6,000 ÷ 29,200 = $0.2055 per room-night |
| *Expense goal:* | 5% savings |
| Compensation: | 30% weight × $30,000 target reward = $9,000 |
| | $9,000 ÷ 5 = $1,800 for each percentage point saved |
| *Room rate goal:* | $3 rate increase |
| Compensation: | 30% weight × $30,000 target reward = $9,000 |
| | $9,000 ÷ 300 = $30.00 for each cent increase |
| Energy use goal: | 10% savings |
| Compensation: | 20% weight × $30,000 target reward = $6,000 |
| | $6,000 ÷ 10 = $600 for each percentage point saved |

Kristin's new compensation plan will thus pay her a $60,000 salary plus 20.55 cents per room-night sold plus $1,800 for each percentage point saved in the expense budget plus $30 for each cent increase in average room rate plus $600 for each percentage point saved in energy use. The minimum potential compensation would be $60,000 and the maximum potential compensation for Kristin would be $60,000 + $30,000 = $90,000.

**Required**
1. Based on this plan, what will Kristin's total compensation be if her performance results are

   a. 30,000 room-nights, 5% saved, $3.00 rate increase, and 8% reduction in energy use?

   b. 25,000 room-nights, 3% saved, $1.15 rate increase, and 5% reduction in energy use?

   c. 28,000 room-nights, 0% saved, $1.00 rate increase, and 2% reduction in energy use?

2. Comment on the expected effectiveness of this plan. In what way, if at all, would you change the compensation weights?

[LO 20-3]   20-38 **Incentive Pay Formula Development**   Use the concepts in Problem 20-37 to complete the following requirements.

**Required**
1. Design an incentive pay plan for a restaurant manager whose goals are to serve 300 customers per day at an average price per customer of $6.88. The restaurant is open 365 days per year. These two goals are equally important. The incentive pay should be $12,800 if the manager achieves all goals. Assume the manager's salary is $68,000.

2. Calculate the manager's total compensation if the restaurant serves 280 customers per day at an average price of $6.75.

[LO 20-3]   20-39 **Compensation Pools; Residual Income; Review of Chapter 19**   Wilson Brands Inc. (WBI) is a retailer of consumer products. The company made two acquisitions in previous years to diversify its product lines. In 2011, WBI acquired a consumer electronics firm producing computers. WBI now (2013) has three divisions: consumer electronics, office supplies, and computers. The following information (in thousands) presents operating revenue, operating income, and invested assets of the company over the last three years.

|  | Revenue | Income | Assets |
|---|---|---|---|
| **Consumer Electronics** |  |  |  |
| 2011 | $155,780 | $16,750 | $84,550 |
| 2012 | 125,480 | 9,500 | 90,450 |
| 2013 | 110,650 | 6,850 | 98,450 |
| **Office Supplies** |  |  |  |
| 2011 | 48,750 | 2,100 | 22,500 |
| 2012 | 45,660 | 2,340 | 21,900 |
| 2013 | 49,800 | 2,250 | 19,500 |
| **Computers** |  |  |  |
| 2011 | 100,500 | 2,350 | 21,450 |
| 2012 | 95,400 | 1,650 | 22,550 |
| 2013 | 114,350 | 2,675 | 23,100 |

The number of executives covered by WBI's current compensation package follows:

|  | 2011 | 2012 | 2013 |
|---|---|---|---|
| Consumer Electronics | 300 | 350 | 375 |
| Office Supplies | 40 | 40 | 37 |
| Computers | 120 | 140 | 175 |

The current compensation package is an annual bonus award. Senior executives share in the bonus pool, which is calculated as 10% of the company's annual residual income. *Residual income* is defined as operating income minus an interest charge of 6% of invested assets.

**Required**
1. Use asset turnover, return on sales, and return on investment (ROI) to explain the differences in profitability of the three divisions.

2. Compute the bonus amount to be paid during each year; also compute individual executive bonus amounts.

3. If the bonuses were calculated by divisional residual income, what would the individual bonus amounts be?

4. Discuss the advantages and disadvantages of basing the bonus on WBI's residual income compared to divisional residual income.

[LO 20-3]   20-40  **Compensation; Strategy**   Mobile Business Incorporated (MBI) is a worldwide manufacturing company that specializes in high technology products for the aerospace, automotive, and plastics industries. State-of-the-art technology and business innovation have been key to the firm's success over the last several years. MBI has 10 manufacturing plants in six foreign countries. Its products are sold worldwide through sales representatives and sales offices in 23 countries. Performance information from these plants and offices is received weekly and is summarized monthly at the Toronto headquarters.

The company's current bonus compensation plan focuses on giving rewards based on the utilization of capital within the company (i.e., management of inventory, collection of receivables, and use of physical assets). The board of directors is concerned, however, with the short-term focus of this plan.

Some employees believe that the company's current compensation plan does not reflect its stated goals of maintaining and enhancing its global position through innovative products.

**Required**   Develop a bonus package that considers MBI's strategic goals and the global environment in which it operates.

[LO 20-3]   20-41  **Executive Compensation; Teams; Strategy; Ethics**   Universal Air Inc. supplies instrumentation components to airplane manufacturers. Although only a few competitors are in this market, the competition is fierce.

Universal uses a traditional performance incentive plan to award middle-management bonuses on the basis of divisional profit. Recently, Charles Gross, chief executive officer, concluded that these objectives might be better served with new performance measures. On January 1, 2013, he assigned his executive team of top-level managers to develop these new measures.

The executive team conducted a customer survey. Although Universal has always prided itself on being on the technological forefront, the survey results indicated technology to be a low priority for customers, who were more concerned with product quality and customer service. As a result, the executive team developed 30 new criteria to measure middle-management performance and directed the controller to develop the necessary monthly reports and graphs to report on these new measures. Then the executive team announced to middle managers that these new indicators would be used to evaluate their performance. The managers were not enthusiastic and complained that some measures were influenced by the performance of other departments that they could not control. Over the next few months, customer complaints increased, and a major customer chose a competitor over Universal.

Upon seeing these results, Charles decided to review the new process. In a meeting with executive and middle managers, he emphasized that the new measures should help balance the company's performance between increased customer value and improved operating process efficiency. He set up two cross-functional teams of executives and middle managers to develop a second set of new measures: one to evaluate new product development and the other to evaluate the customer order and fulfillment process. Both teams are to focus on cost, quality, and scheduling time.

Richard Strong, quality inspection manager, is the brother-in-law of John Brogan, cost accounting manager. On June 1, John telephoned Sara Wiley, the purchasing manager at Magic Aircraft Manufacturing Inc., one of Universal's major customers. Brogan said, "Listen Sara, we're jumping through all these hoops over here to measure performance, and management seems to be changing the measures every day. It was so easy before, getting a bonus based on the bottom line; now we have to worry about things out of our control based on how the customer perceives our performance. Would you do me a favor? If you have any complaints, please have your people call me directly so I can forward the complaint to the right person. All that really matters is for all of us to make money." In actuality, Richard was the only person to whom John reported the customer complaints that Sara offered.

**Required**

1. For Universal Air Inc. to remain competitive, should it implement the second set of new performance measures? Identify for the company:

a. At least three customer value-added measures.

b. At least three process-efficiency measures.

2. Identify at least three types of employee behaviors that Universal can expect by having middle management participate in the development of the second set of new performance measures.

3. Describe what executive management at Universal should do to ensure the effectiveness of the cross-functional teams.

4. Referring to the specific standards for ethical conduct by a management accountant (Chapter 1), consider whether John Brogan's behavior is unethical.

**(CMA Adapted)**

[LO 20-3]  20-42  **Executive Compensation**  Jensen Corporation is a holding company with several diversified divisions operating throughout the United States. Jensen's management allows the divisions to operate on an autonomous basis in most areas; however, the corporate office becomes involved in determining some division strategies related to capital budgeting, development of marketing campaigns, and implementation of incentive plans. The area of incentive plans has often been a problem to Jensen because many of the companies it has acquired already had such plans in place. These plans are not easily changed without causing discontent among the managers. Jensen has striven for consistency among its divisions with regard to bonus and incentive plans, but this has not always been achievable.

The restaurant division operates a chain of vegetarian restaurants, Hobbit Hole, in the eastern United States. Jensen acquired it approximately three years ago and has made very few changes to it. The restaurant's reputation was well established and, aside from nominal changes in marketing strategy, the chain has been allowed to operate in much the same manner as it did before its acquisition. In addition to a base salary, Hobbit Hole unit managers participate in the restaurant's profits. This incentive plan was in place when Jensen acquired the chain; although the profit percentage might vary among restaurant units, the overall plans are basically the same. The unit managers are satisfied with this incentive strategy, and Jensen's management does not believe that changes are necessary.

Jensen's motel division was formed 15 years ago when Jensen purchased a small group of motels in the Midwest. Since that time, the division has grown significantly as the company has acquired motels throughout the country using the name Cruise and Snooze Inns. Since its initial motel purchase, Jensen has implemented its own incentive program for unit managers in the individual motels. The incentive program provides annual bonuses based on the achievement of specific goals that are not necessarily finance oriented but pertain to areas such as improved quality control and customer service. This program requires administrative time, but Jensen believes that the results have been satisfactory.

**Required**

1. Hobbit Hole's restaurant unit managers are covered by a profit participation incentive plan. Discuss the following for this incentive plan:

   a. Its benefits to Jensen Corporation.

   b. The incentive effects that it could cause, if any.

2. The Cruise and Snooze Inns' motel unit managers participate in an incentive program based on goal attainment. Discuss the following for this type of incentive plan:

   a. Advantages to Jensen Corporation.

   b. Disadvantages to Jensen Corporation.

3. Having two different types of incentive plans for two operating divisions of the same company raises questions.

   a. Describe the potential negative incentive effects of having different types of incentive plans for Hobbit Hole and Cruise and Snooze Inns.

   b. Present the rationale that Jensen Corporation can give to the unit managers of Hobbit Hole and Cruise and Snooze Inns to justify having different incentive plans for two operating divisions of the same company.

**(CMA Adapted)**

[LO 20-3]  20-43  **Compensation; Regression Analysis; Spreadsheet Application**  Many people ask, "Are executives worth their very high pay?" As noted in the chapter, this is a difficult question to answer because the benefits an effective executive brings to the company are hard to measure. One thing we can do, however, is to see if *changes* in executive pay are correlated with changes in company performance. If pay increases when company performance increases, and vice versa, then this would be an indication that pay practices are aligned with the interests of shareholders. To study this question, we have data (from *The New York Times,* April 10, 2011) for the 30 highest paid chief executive officers (CEOs) in the United States. The data below include 29 of these 30 CEOs (because he was a new CEO in 2010, the change in compensation could not be determined for the fourth-ranked CEO, Michael D. White of DirecTV; therefore, he is not included):

| | | % Change from 2009 to 2010 | |
| | | Total Compensation | Total Return |
| **CEO** | **Company** | | |
|---|---|---|---|
| Phillipe Dauman | Viacom | 140 | 30 |
| Ray Irani | Occidental Petroleum | 142 | 22 |
| Lawrence Ellison | Oracle | (17) | 16 |
| John Lundgren | Stanley Black & Decker | 253 | 32 |
| Brian Roberts | Comcast | 13 | 33 |
| Robert Iger | Disney | 30 | 22 |
| Alan Mulally | Ford Motor | 48 | 68 |
| Samuel Palmisano | IBM | 19 | 14 |
| David Farr | Emerson Electric | 233 | 35 |
| Howard Schultz | Starbucks | 45 | 25 |
| William Welden | Johnson & Johnson | (5) | (1) |
| Louis Camalleri | Philip Morris | (16) | 27 |
| Randall Stephenson | AT&T | — | 11 |
| Miles White | Abbot Laboratories | (9) | (8) |
| George Buckley | 3M | 41 | 7 |
| Louis Chenevert | United Technologies | 9 | 16 |
| Robert Kelly | Bank of New York | 73 | 9 |
| Muhtar Kent | Coca-Cola | 30 | 18 |
| Robert Stevens | Lockheed Martin | (7) | (4) |
| John Chambers | Cisco | 106 | 5 |
| James Hackett | Anadarko Petroleum | (20) | 23 |
| James Mulva | ConocoPhillips | 25 | 38 |
| Ivan Seidenberg | Verizon | 5 | 19 |
| Andrew Liveris | Dow Chemical | 13 | 26 |
| Paul Jacobs | Qualcomm | 1 | 2 |
| John Stumpf | Wells Fargo | (6) | 16 |
| Susan Ivey | Reynolds American | 4 | 30 |
| Rupert Murdoch | News Corp. | (6) | 33 |
| James M. Cracchiolo | Ameriprise Financial | (8) | 50 |

In the above table, the change in compensation is measured as the percentage change in total compensation from 2009 to 2010; total return (our measure of company performance) is measured by the percentage change in stock price plus dividends.

**Required** Using regression and/or correlation analysis, examine the above data and determine whether there is a significant relationship between the change in compensation for these executives and the change in the company's performance. That is, from your analysis, does it appear that the CEOs' pay is aligned with shareholder interests? Comment briefly on your findings.

**[LO 20-3]** 20-44 **Compensation; Regression Analysis** A recent study of the airline industry examined whether a performance for a selected nonfinancial measure was a significant predictor of CEO compensation. A sample of 35 firms was taken and regression obtained to determine the potential relationship between selected financial and nonfinancial independent variables and three dependent variables: (a) CEO cash compensation, (b) CEO compensation in the form of options granted during the year, and (c) total CEO compensation (a + b).

The independent variables were:

- Passenger load (PL), the proportion of seats filled to the seats available.
- Stock price return (RT), the increase in stock price plus dividends over the year relative to beginning of year.
- Return on assets (ROA), income over total assets.
- Sales.

- Stock price volatility (V), the standard deviation of daily stock price changes in the company's stock price.
- CEO ownership (CEO), the percentage of the company's outstanding shares owned by the CEO.
- CEO tenure (CEO-T), the number of years the CEO has been on the job.
- Ratio of book value of the company to the market value of the company (BM), a measure of the market value of the company.

The table below shows the three dependent variables, the eight independent variables, and the significance (*p*-value) of the independent variable in each equation. For example, in the regression with the dependent variable, cash compensation (Regression One), the PL variable is significant at the .01 level, RT is significant at the .01 level, and the ROA variable is not significant. The authors of the study hypothesized that there would be a positive significant relationship between CEO compensation and the one nonfinancial variable, passenger load.

|  | Regression One* | Regression Two* | Regression Three* |
|---|---|---|---|
| Passenger load (PL) | 0.01 | NS | NS |
| Stock return (RT)* | 0.01 | 0.01 | 0.01 |
| Return on assets (ROA) | NS | NS | NS |
| Sales* | 0.01 | 0.01 | 0.01 |
| Stock price volatility (V) | NS | NS | 0.05 |
| CEO ownership % (CEO)† | 0.01 | 0.01 | 0.01 |
| CEO tenure (CEO-T) | 0.01 | NS | 0.05 |
| Book value to Market Value (BM) | NS | 0.05 | NS |
| R squared | 69.3% | 11.0% | 50.0% |

*Dependent variables were transformed using the natural logarithm.
†This variable had a significant negative coefficient, indicating an inverse relationship with the dependent variable.
NS means that the variable is not significant at $p = .05$ or less.

**Required**  Review the three regressions above and develop a brief explanation for each of the following:
1. Which of the three regressions would you most rely on, and why?
2. What do the regression results tell you about the relationships of the independent variables to the three dependent variables?
3. Were the authors of the study correct about their expectation regarding the PL variable?
4. How would you use this information in designing compensation plans for executives in the airline industry?

[LO 20-5]  **20-45  Business Analysis; Spreadsheet Application**  Blue Water Yachts is a small company founded by two businesspeople who are friends and avid sailors. At present, they are interested in expanding the business and have asked you to review its financial statements.

Blue Water Yachts sells approximately 100 to 150 sailboats each year, ranging from 14-foot dinghies to 20-foot sailboats. Their sales prices range from $2,000 to more than $10,000. The company has a limited inventory of boats consisting primarily of one or two boats from each of the four manufacturers that supply Blue Water. The company also sells a variety of supplies and parts and performs different types of service. Most sales are on credit.

The company operates from a large building that has offices, storage, and sales for some of the smaller sailboats. The larger sailboats are kept in a fenced area adjacent to the main building, and an ample parking area is nearby. This year Blue Water purchased a boat lift to haul boats. The lift has brought in revenues for boat repairs, hull painting, and related services, as well as the boat hauls.

The balance sheet and income statement for Blue Water Yachts for 2008 through 2013 follow. The increase in net fixed assets in the recent two years is due to improvements in the building, paving of the parking area, and the purchase of the lift.

The company obtains its debt financing from two sources: a small savings and loan for its short-term funds, and a larger commercial bank, also for short-term loans, but principally for long-term financing. The terms of the loan agreement with the bank include a restriction that its current ratio must remain higher than 1.5.

**Required**  Evaluate the liquidity and profitability of Blue Water Yachts using selected financial ratios. Assess the company's overall profitability, liquidity, and desirability as an investment. Use a spreadsheet to improve the speed and accuracy of your analysis.

## BLUE WATER YACHTS COMPANY
### Comparative Balance Sheet
#### For the Years Ended December 31,

| | 2008 | 2009 | 2010 | 2011 | 2012 | 2013 |
|---|---|---|---|---|---|---|
| Cash | $ 23,260 | $ 21,966 | $ 18,735 | $ 28,426 | $ 43,692 | $ 31,264 |
| Accounts receivable | 99,465 | 102,834 | 112,903 | 125,663 | 104,388 | 142,009 |
| Allowance for bad debts | (9,304) | (8,786) | (8,824) | (11,266) | (7,282) | (12,506) |
| Inventory | 35,009 | 56,784 | 61,792 | 67,884 | 58,994 | 95,774 |
| Other current assets | 11,894 | 12,894 | 9,024 | 11,006 | 18,923 | 22,903 |
| Total current assets | $160,324 | $185,692 | $193,630 | $221,713 | $218,715 | $279,444 |
| Property and equipment | 262,195 | 282,008 | 299,380 | 368,565 | 405,269 | 498,626 |
| Accumulated depreciation | (65,984) | (93,442) | (122,892) | (158,099) | (187,227) | (226,307) |
| Total assets | $356,535 | $374,258 | $370,118 | $432,179 | $436,757 | $551,763 |
| Accounts payable | $ 82,635 | $ 78,127 | $ 63,346 | $ 56,256 | $ 40,189 | $ 49,544 |
| Taxes payable | 11,630 | 10,983 | 11,780 | 14,083 | 3,738 | 15,632 |
| Short-term loans | 59,876 | 56,980 | 37,583 | 41,093 | 49,594 | 76,962 |
| Accrued payroll payable | 5,227 | 4,598 | 3,649 | 4,224 | 4,774 | 4,779 |
| Total current liabilities | $159,368 | $150,688 | $116,358 | $115,656 | $ 98,295 | $146,917 |
| Long-term debt | 158,173 | 172,388 | 179,490 | 214,997 | 229,471 | 262,258 |
| Equity | 38,994 | 51,182 | 74,270 | 101,526 | 108,991 | 142,588 |
| Total liabilities and equity | $356,535 | $374,258 | $370,118 | $432,179 | $436,757 | $551,763 |

## BLUE WATER YACHTS COMPANY
### Comparative Statement of Income and Operating Cash Flow
#### For the Years Ended December 31,

| | 2008 | 2009 | 2010 | 2011 | 2012 | 2013 |
|---|---|---|---|---|---|---|
| Sales | $767,580 | $724,878 | $777,480 | $929,478 | $764,610 | $938,857 |
| Returns and allowances | 38,379 | 35,645 | 40,334 | 45,998 | 32,887 | 46,380 |
| Cost of sales | 473,908 | 441,298 | 458,015 | 545,778 | 453,669 | 530,597 |
| Gross margin | $255,293 | $247,935 | $279,131 | $337,702 | $278,054 | $361,880 |
| Depreciation expense | $ 29,075 | $ 27,458 | $ 29,450 | $ 35,207 | $ 29,128 | $ 39,080 |
| Interest expense | 18,597 | 19,557 | 20,998 | 21,475 | 24,889 | 28,993 |
| Salaries and wages | 81,923 | 73,664 | 77,846 | 95,764 | 92,903 | 99,447 |
| Accounting and legal | 9,304 | 8,786 | 9,323 | 11,834 | 13,108 | 11,380 |
| Administration expense | 79,666 | 75,234 | 80,693 | 96,469 | 87,995 | 97,441 |
| Other expense | 12,630 | 18,927 | 15,763 | 22,903 | 18,934 | 22,662 |
| Total expense | $231,195 | $223,626 | $234,073 | $283,652 | $266,957 | $299,003 |
| Net income | $ 24,098 | $ 24,309 | $ 45,058 | $ 54,050 | $ 11,097 | $ 62,877 |
| Cash flow from operations (adjustments to net income) | | | | | | |
| Depreciation | | $ 27,458 | $ 29,450 | $ 35,207 | $ 29,128 | $ 39,080 |
| Decrease (increase) in receivables | | (3,887) | (10,031) | (10,318) | 17,291 | (32,397) |
| Decrease (increase) in inventory | | (21,775) | (5,008) | (6,092) | 8,890 | (36,780) |
| Decrease (increase) in other current assets | | (1,000) | 3,870 | (1,982) | (7,917) | (3,980) |
| Increase (decrease) in current liabilities | | (8,680) | (34,330) | (702) | (17,361) | 48,622 |
| | | $ 16,425 | $ 29,009 | $ 70,163 | $ 41,128 | $ 77,422 |

[LO 20-5]   20-46 **Business Valuation**   Refer to the information in Problem 20-45 for the Blue Water Yachts Company.

**Required**   Develop a business valuation for Blue Water Yachts Company for 2013 using the book value of equity method and the multiples-based method. Assume that the industry average earnings multiple is 8 and the industry average multiple on operating cash flow is 6. Which of the methods would you use and why?

[LO 20-5]   20-47 **Business Analysis**   Brooks Plumbing Products, Inc. (BPP) manufactures plumbing fixtures and other home improvement products that are sold in Home Depot and Walmart as well as hardware stores. BPP has a solid reputation for providing value products, good quality, and a good price. The company has been approached by an investment banking firm representing a third company, Garden Specialties Inc. (GSI), that is interested in acquiring BPP. The acquiring firm (GSI) is a retailer of garden supplies; it sees the potential synergies of the combined firm and is willing to pay BPP shareholders $38 cash per share for their stock, which is greater than the current stock price; the stock has traded at about $35 in recent months. Summary financial information about BPP follows.

**Required**   Evaluate BPP as a company using financial ratio analysis. Since the calculation of some ratios requires the averaging of balances, you may assume that the balances in 2011 are the same as those in 2012.

### BROOKS PLUMBING PRODUCTS, INC.
#### Selected Financial Information

| | 2013 | 2012 | 2013 Industry Average |
|---|---|---|---|
| Cash | $ 79,919,778 | $ 3,456,227 | |
| Accounts receivable | 56,778,465 | 87,294,771 | |
| Inventory | 39,665,416 | 59,883,645 | |
| Long-lived assets | | | |
|   Gross book value | 167,278,377 | 143,778,377 | |
|   Net book value | 100,620,809 | 95,887,302 | |
|   Replacement cost | 170,587,409 | 188,465,338 | |
|   Liquidation value | 68,734,002 | 67,335,209 | |
| Current liabilities | 119,045,766 | 120,995,274 | |
| Long-term debt | 31,997,364 | 37,885,302 | |
| Shareholder equity | 125,941,338 | 87,641,369 | |
| Capital expenditures | 23,500,000 | 12,990,336 | |
| Sales | 667,534,771 | 638,776,465 | |
| Cost of sales | 498,657,788 | 477,491,001 | |
| Operating expense* | 102,667,355 | 134,765,229 | |
| Income tax rate | 38% | 38% | 38.0% |
| Depreciation expense | $ 18,766,493 | $ 15,664,254 | |
| Dividends | $ 2,750,000 | $ 1,250,000 | |
| Year-end stock price | $ 35.78 | $ 22.99 | |
| Number of outstanding shares | 25,689,554 | 22,763,554 | |
| Sales multiplier | | | 1.40 |
| Free cash flow multiplier | | | 8.80 |
| Earnings multiplier | | | 13.50 |
| Cost of capital | 5.2% | 5.2% | |
| Accounts receivable turnover | | | 5.50 |
| Inventory turnover | | | 8.60 |
| Current ratio | | | 1.90 |
| Quick ratio | | | 1.10 |
| Cash flow from operations ratio | | | 1.40 |
| Free cash flow ratio | | | 1.10 |
| Gross margin percentage | | | 33.0% |
| Return on assets (net book value) | | | 19.0% |
| Return on equity | | | 28.0% |
| Earnings per share | | | $ 2.33 |

*Operating expense includes depreciation expense

**[LO 20-5]**   20-48 **Business Valuation**   Refer to the information in Problem 20-47.

**Required**
1. Develop a business valuation for 2013 using the market value method, the book value method, and the multiples-based methods.
2. Determine an estimated value for BPP using the discounted free cash flow method, assuming that the 2013 amount of free cash flow continues indefinitely.
3. Which of the methods would you use and why?
4. Is the GSI offer a good one? Why or why not?
5. What would be the effect of sustainability issues, if any, in the acquisition BPP by GSI?

[LO 20-5]    20-49    **Business Analysis and Business Valuation**    JJP Autoparts, Inc., a manufacturer of auto parts, experienced a decline in earnings in the recent year and has consulted its accounting firm for an analysis of the firm's financial statements. Additionally, the company knows that its market value has fallen from the prior year, since the share price has fallen from $5.50 at the end of 2012 to $2.34 at the end of 2013. So, JJP also want an analysis of the firm's change in value. The comparative balance sheet and income statement for 2013 follow:

| Balance Sheet | 2013 | 2012 |
| --- | --- | --- |
| Cash | $   453,680 | $   455,675 |
| Accounts receivable | 38,756 | 34,885 |
| Inventory | 156,754 | 134,665 |
| Total current assets | 649,190 | 625,225 |
| Long-lived assets | 452,541 | 445,287 |
| **Total assets** | $1,101,731 | $1,070,512 |
| Current liabilities | $   219,884 | $   265,448 |
| Long-term debt | 350,000 | 350,000 |
| Shareholders' equity | 531,847 | 455,064 |
| **Total debt and equity** | $1,101,731 | $1,070,512 |
| **Income Statement** | | |
| Sales | $1,588,364 | $1,455,634 |
| Cost of sales | 1,289,665 | 1,109,886 |
| Gross margin | 298,699 | 345,748 |
| Operating expenses | 174,855 | 133,874 |
| Operating income | 123,844 | 211,874 |
| Tax expense | 47,061 | 80,512 |
| Net income | $     76,783 | $   131,362 |

Note: The amounts for operating expense above include depreciation expense of $43,997 in 2012 and $42,746 in 2013.

Additional relevant information about JJP is that it uses a cost of capital rate of 5.7%. Also it incurred capital expenditures of $100,000 in 2012 and $50,000 in 2013; there were no cash dividends in either year. The number of outstanding shares is 653,554, the same in both years. Industry data, the average values for firms in the autoparts industry, follow:

| | |
| --- | --- |
| Sales multiplier | 2.20 |
| Free cash flow multiplier | 8.80 |
| Earnings multiplier | 21.00 |
| Accounts receivable turnover | 8.80 |
| Inventory turnover | 7.00 |
| Current ratio | 2.00 |
| Quick ratio | 1.10 |
| Cash flow from operations ratio | 1.40 |
| Free cash flow ratio | 1.10 |
| Gross margin percentage | 30.0% |
| Return on assets (net book value) | 18.0% |
| Return on equity | 24.0% |
| Earnings per share | $1.15 |

**Required:**

1. Calculate and interpret the liquidity, cash flow, and profitability ratios for JJP for 2012 and 2013. In your calculations, you may assume that the balance sheet values for 2012 are the same as for the prior year, 2011.

2. Develop and interpret a business valuation for JJP for 2012 and 2013 using the methods you think appropriate.

[LO 20-5]    20-50    **Research Assignment; Business Valuation**    Read the following article by Joel Litman and Mark L. Frigo, "When Strategy and Valuation Meet," *Strategic Finance*, August 2004, pp. 31–39. The article provides a comprehensive discussion of how business strategy and business valuation are interrelated and provides five lessons based on an understanding of this interrelationship.

The article is available in the Cases and Readings Supplement that comes with the text or it may be accessed using the link found on the text website.

**Required**

1. Explain briefly the different skills required by a business strategy expert and a business valuation expert.

2. Explain why a great product seldom ensures a great business.

3. Explain why being "different" is not central to strategy.

4. Explain the difference between a great company and a great stock.

5. Explain when and why growth is not necessarily a good thing.

## Solution to Self-Study Problems

### 1. Management Compensation Plan

DTH's goal is to increase its business by at least 10% a year in a very competitive environment. The compensation plan is consistent with this goal because it rewards increases in revenues and new clients. It is likely, however, that under the current plan, each office is focusing only on the client base in its own region.

A problem occurs when DTH must make proposals that require joint cooperation and participation among two or more offices. The compensation plan does not have an incentive for cooperation. In fact, it could be a distraction and reduce the potential for a substantial bonus for any given office to develop a proposal for a large contract in which other offices might benefit. The cost of the proposal would be borne by the office, and the benefits would accrue to other offices as well as the originating office. The cost of the proposal for large contracts must therefore be shared among the offices in some way, or any one office will not have the incentive to spend the time and money necessary to develop a large proposal.

In addition to sharing the cost of the proposal, DTH should consider having a firmwide proposal development group for these large projects. The individual offices would then be charged for the cost of this group, perhaps in proportion to the fees received from large contracts in that office. Clearly, the firm is losing the larger contracts, and the compensation and proposal development plans must provide the needed incentive for each office to go after them aggressively.

Another alternative is to go to a firmwide compensation pool that would provide a direct and strong incentive for each office to cooperate in developing new business. A disadvantage of this approach is that it would reduce the motivation for each office to seek business in its own region because the revenues from these individual efforts would be shared firmwide.

Another issue concerning the current compensation plan is the office manager's discretion to divide the office bonus among the professionals in the office. Although no one has complained, a lower-level professional is unlikely to complain about the office manager's bonus decisions. The equity of this system should be reviewed to ensure that each office manager is using this discretion in a fair and appropriate way.

### 2. Business Valuation

Since WebSmart is a relatively new company currently showing losses and negative cash flows, the earnings-multiple and discounted cash flow approaches are not suitable. Moreover, since the company is not public, there is no current stock price. This leaves two possibilities: the book value of equity method and the revenues-multiple method. The book value of equity is given at $1,200,000. In contrast, the revenue multiple would estimate value at $4,200,000 = 7 \times $600,000. Alternatively, WebSmart could use projected revenues in the multiple calculation. Moreover, it could use projected cash flows in a cash flow multiple or discounted cash flow calculation, since cash flow would presumably be positive in the coming years.

Also, the firm has an asset, the *Guide to Competitive Colleges,* which has a market value of $1,350,000, so any valuation would have to be higher than that figure. Overall, this is a difficult firm to value; the range from $1,350,000 to $4,200,000 is a very wide range. Also, there is significant uncertainty about future cash flows, which are critical to the overall valuation.

*Please visit **http://www.mhhe.com/blocher6e** to access a narrated, animated tutorial for solving these problems.*

# A

**abnormal spoilage**   An unacceptable unit that should not arise under efficient operating conditions

**absolute quality conformance (robust quality approach)**   Conformance that requires all products or services to meet the target value *exactly* with no variation

**accounting (book) rate of return (ARR)**   Equals the ratio of some measure of accounting profit to some measure of investment in the project

**activity**   A specific task or action of work done

**activity analysis**   The development of a detailed description of the specific activities performed in the firm's operations

**activity-based budgeting (ABB)**   A budgeting process that is based on activities and associated activity costs to support production and sales

**activity-based costing (ABC)**   A costing approach that assigns resource costs to cost objects based on activities performed for the cost objects

**activity-based management (ABM)**   Uses activity analysis and activity-based costing to help managers identify the value of activities and to make strategic performance management decisions—adding and deleting products, adjusting process capacities, adjusting prices, removing costs and complexities, and more

**activity consumption cost driver**   Measures how much of an activity a cost object uses

**actual costing system**   A costing process that uses actual costs incurred for direct materials, direct labor, and factory overhead

**actual factory overhead**   Costs incurred in an accounting period for indirect materials, indirect labor, and other indirect factory costs, including factory rent, insurance, property tax, depreciation, repairs and maintenance, power, light, heat, and employer payroll taxes for factory personnel

**additional processing costs**   Costs that occur after the split-off point and can be identified directly with individual products; also called *separable costs*

**advance pricing agreement (APA)**   An agreement between the Internal Revenue Service (IRS) and a firm that establishes an agreed-upon transfer price

**allocation bases**   The cost drivers used to allocate costs

**analysis of variance table***   A table that separates the total variance of the dependent variable into both error and explained variance components

**analytic hierarchy process (AHP)**   A multicriteria decision technique that can combine qualitative and quantitative factors in the overall evaluation of decision alternatives

**appraisal (detection) costs**   Costs devoted to the measurement and analysis of data to determine conformity of outputs to specifications

**arm's-length standard**   A transfer price set to reflect the price that unrelated parties acting independently would have set

**asset turnover (AT)**   The amount of sales dollars generated per dollar of investment; measures the manager's ability to increase sales from a given level of investment

**authoritative standard**   A standard determined solely or primarily by management

**average cost**   The total of manufacturing cost (materials, labor, and overhead) divided by the number of units of output

**average cost method**   A method that uses units of output to allocate joint costs to joint products

**average-risk projects**   Projects that approximate the risk of the firm's existing assets and operations; the WACC (weighted-average cost of capital) is used in DCF (discounted cash flow) models to evaluate average-risk investment projects

# B

**backflush costing**   A method that charges current production costs (using standard costs) directly to finished goods inventory without accounting for the flows in and out of work-in-process

**balanced scorecard (BSC)**   An accounting report that includes the firm's critical success factors in four areas: (1) financial performance, (2) customer satisfaction, (3) internal processes, and (4) learning and growth

**batch-level activity**   An activity performed for each batch of products or services

**benchmarking**   A process by which a firm identifies its critical success factors, studies the best practices of other firms (or other business units within a firm) for achieving these critical success factors, and then implements improvements in the firm's processes to match or beat the performance of those competitors

**benefits (perks)**   Special benefits for the employee, such as automobile/parking, membership in a fitness club, tickets to entertainment events, and other extras paid for by the firm

**beta coefficient (β)**   A measure of the sensitivity of a given stock's return to fluctuations in the overall market; the average beta of all stocks is 1.0; a beta coefficient greater than 1 implies greater sensitivity to market fluctuations, while a beta less than 1 implies lower sensitivity of return to fluctuations in the overall market

**bill of materials**   A detailed list of the components of the manufactured product

**bonus**   Compensation based on the achievement of performance goals for the period

**book rate of return**   The ratio of some measure of accounting profit to some measure of investment in the project; also called *accounting rate of return (ARR)*

**breakeven after-tax cash flow**   The minimum annual after-tax cash inflows needed for an investment project to be acceptable (in a present value sense)

**breakeven point**   The point at which revenues equal total costs and operating profit is zero

---

*Key term appears in Regression Analysis Supplement online at **www.mhhe.com/blocher6e**.

**budget** A detailed plan for the acquisition and use of financial and other resources over a specified period of time—typically a fiscal year

**budget slack** The difference between budgeted performance and expected performance

**budgetary slack** The "cushion" managers intentionally build into budgets to help ensure success in meeting the budget

**budgeted capacity utilization** The planned (forecasted) output for the coming period, usually a year

**budgeting** The process of preparing one or more budgets

**business analysis** Evaluates the firm's overall performance by using one or more of the following methods: balanced scorecard, financial ratio analysis, and economic value added

**business intelligence** An approach to strategy implementation in which the management accountant uses data to understand and analyze business performance

**business process improvement (BPI)** A management method by which managers and workers commit to a program of continuous improvement in quality and other critical success factors

**business valuation** Values the firm by estimating its total market value, which can be compared to the market value for prior periods or for comparable firms

**by-products** Products in a joint production process whose total sales values are minor in comparison with the sales value of the joint products

# C

**capital asset pricing model (CAPM)** Model that depicts the risk-return relationship for equity securities and that can be used to estimate the required rate of return on equity for a given company; equal to the risk-free rate of return plus a risk premium measured as the product of $\beta$ and the market-risk premium

**capital budget** A listing of approved investment projects as well as anticipated cash outflows associated with these projects for a given period

**capital budgeting** A process of identifying, evaluating, selecting, and controlling an organization's capital (long-term) projects and programs

**capital investment** A project that involves a large expenditure of funds and expected future benefits over a number of years

**capital rationing** The case where investment capital for a given accounting period is limited—hence the need for these funds to be "rationed"

**capital structure** The means by which a company is financed; the mix between debt and equity capital

**cash budget** A schedule depicting the effects on cash of all budgeted activities

**cause-and-effect diagram** A diagram that organizes a chain of causes and effects to sort out root causes of an identified quality problem; also called a *"fish-bone" diagram*

**comparable-price method** Establishes an arm's-length price by using the sales prices of similar products made by unrelated firms

**concurrent engineering** An engineering method that integrates product design with manufacturing and marketing throughout the product's life cycle; also called *simultaneous engineering*

**confidence interval (CI)** In regression analysis, the CI refers to a range around the regression line within which the management accountant can be confident the actual value of the predicted cost will likely fall

**constraints** Those activities that slow the product's total cycle time

**continuous improvement** (The Japanese word is *kaizen*) A management technique in which managers and workers commit to a program of continuous improvement in quality and other critical success factors

**continuous-improvement standard** A standard that gets progressively tighter over time

**contract manufacturing** The practice of having another manufacturer (sometimes a direct competitor) manufacture a portion of the firm's products

**contribution by profit center (CPC)** measures profit after traceable costs and is therefore a performance measure that is controllable by the profit center manager

**contribution income statement** Focuses on variable costs and fixed costs, in contrast to the conventional income statement, which focuses on product costs and nonproduct costs

**contribution margin income statement** An income statement based on contribution margin that is developed for each profit center and for each relevant group of profit centers

**contribution margin per unit** The difference between the selling price per unit ($p$) and the variable cost per unit ($v$); it is a measure of the change in operating profit for a unit change in sales

**contribution margin ratio** The ratio of the contribution margin per unit to the selling price per unit, $(p - v) \div p$

**control** The set of procedures, tools, and systems that organizations use to reach their goals

**control chart** A graph that depicts successive observations of an operation (or cost) taken at constant intervals

**controllable cost** A cost that a manager or employee has discretion in choosing to incur or can significantly influence the amount of within a given, usually short, period of time

**controllable fixed costs** Fixed costs that the profit center manager can influence in approximately a year or less

**controllable margin** A margin determined by subtracting short-term controllable fixed costs from the contribution margin

**conversion cost** Direct labor and overhead combined into a single amount

**core competencies** Skills or competencies that the firm employs especially well

**correlation** A given variable tends to change predictably in the same or opposite direction for a given change in the other, correlated variable

**cost** Incurred when a resource is used for some purpose

**cost allocation** The process of assigning indirect costs to cost pools and cost objects

**cost assignment** The process of assigning costs to cost pools or from cost pools to cost objects

**cost center** A firm's production or support unit that is evaluated on the basis of cost

**cost driver** A factor that causes or relates to a change in the cost of an activity

**cost driver analysis** The examination, quantification, and explanation of the effects of cost drivers

**cost element**   An amount paid for a resource consumed by an activity and included in a cost pool

**cost estimation**   The development of a well-defined relationship between a cost object and its cost drivers for the purpose of predicting the cost

**costing**   The process of accumulating, classifying, and assigning direct materials, direct labor, and factory overhead costs to products, services, or projects

**cost leadership**   A competitive strategy in which a firm outperforms competitors in producing products or services at the lowest cost

**cost life cycle**   The sequence of activities within the firm that begins with research and development, followed by design, manufacturing, marketing/distribution, and customer service

**cost management**   the development and use of cost management information

**cost management information**   The information developed and used to implement the organization's strategy. It consists of financial information about costs and revenues, and nonfinancial information about customer retention, productivity, quality, and other key success factors for the organization

**cost object**   Any product, service, customer, activity, or organizational unit to which costs are accumulated for some management purpose

**cost of capital**   A composite of the cost of various sources of funds comprising a firm's capital structure

**cost of goods manufactured**   The cost of goods that were finished and transferred out of the Work-in-Process Inventory account during a given period

**cost of goods sold**   The cost of the product transferred to the income statement when inventory is sold

**cost of quality (COQ)**   A comprehensive reporting framework for classification of quality-related costs

**cost of quality (COQ) report**   A report that shows the costs of prevention, appraisal, and internal and external failures

**cost-plus method**   A method that determines the transfer price based on the selling unit's cost plus a gross profit percentage determined by comparing the seller's sales to unrelated parties

**cost pools**   The meaningful groups into which costs are collected

**costs of conformance**   The sum of prevention and appraisal costs

**costs of nonconformance**   The sum of internal failure costs and external failure costs

**cost tables**   Computer-based databases that include comprehensive information about the firm's cost drivers

**cost-volume-profit (CVP) analysis**   A short-term profit-planning model; that is, a method for analyzing how various operating decisions and marketing decisions will affect short-term profit

**critical success factors (CSFs)**   Measures of those aspects of the firm's performance that are essential to its competitive advantage and therefore to its success

**cross-sectional regression**   A method of cost estimation for a particular cost object based on information on other cost objects and variables, where the information for all variables is taken from the same period of time

**currently attainable standard**   A level of performance that workers with proper training and experience can attain most of the time without extraordinary effort

**customer cost analysis**   Identifies cost activities and cost drivers related to servicing customers

**customer lifetime value (CLV)**   The net present value of all estimated future profits from a given customer

**customer loyalty**   A measure of customer satisfaction, measured (for example) by repeat purchases or customer retention rates, or by percentage growth in business with existing customers

**customer profitability analysis**   Identifies customer service activities, cost drivers, and the profitability of individual customers or customer group

**customer-response time (CRT)**   A measure of operating performance defined as the elapsed time between the time the customer places an order and the time the customer receives the order

**CVP graph**   A diagrammatic representation of how revenues and total costs change over different levels of sales volume expressed in units

**cycle time**   The amount of time between receipt of a customer order and shipment of the order

# D

**death-spiral effect**   Continual raising of selling prices in an attempt to recover fixed costs, in spite of successive decreases in demand; generally described as one of the dangers of cost-plus pricing

**decentralized**   A firm that has chosen to delegate a significant amount of decision authority and responsibility to subunit managers

**degree of operating leverage (DOL)**   A measure, at any level of sales volume, of the sensitivity of operating profit to changes in volume; defined as the ratio of contribution margin to operating profit

**degrees of freedom***   Represents the number of independent choices that can be made for each component of variance

**denominator activity level**   The output (activity) level used to establish the predetermined fixed overhead application rate; generally defined as *practical capacity;* also called the *denominator volume*

**denominator volume**   The output (activity) level used to calculate the predetermined fixed overhead application rate; generally defined as *practical capacity;* also called the *denominator activity level*

**departmental overhead rate**   An overhead rate calculated for a single production department

**dependent variable**   In cost estimation, the cost to be estimated

**design analysis**   A form of value engineering in which the design team prepares several possible designs of the product, each having similar features with different levels of both performance and cost

**design quality**   The difference between customer expectations (for attributes, services, functionality, etc.) and actual product design

---

*Key term appears in Regression Analysis Supplement online at **www.mhhe.com/blocher6e**.

**desired rate of return** The minimum rate of return the investing firm requires for an investment (also called the *"hurdle rate"*); for average-risk projects, this is defined as the weighted-average cost of capital (WACC)

**differential cost** A cost that differs for each decision option and is therefore relevant

**differentiation** A competitive strategy in which a firm succeeds by developing and maintaining a unique value for the product (or service) as perceived by consumers

**direct cost** A cost conveniently and economically traced directly to a cost pool or a cost object

**direct labor cost** The labor used to manufacture the product or to provide the service

**direct labor efficiency variance (EV)** The difference between the actual direct labor-hours worked and the standard direct labor-hours allowed for the units manufactured, multiplied by the standard wage rate per hour

**direct labor rate variance (RV)** The difference between the actual and standard hourly wage rate multiplied by the actual direct labor-hours worked during the period

**direct materials cost** The cost of the materials in the product and a reasonable allowance for scrap and defective units

**direct materials flexible-budget variance** For each material, the difference between total direct materials cost incurred and the flexible-budget amount for the units manufactured during the period

**direct materials price variance (PV)** For each direct material, the difference between the actual and standard unit price of the material multiplied by the actual quantity used during the period

**direct materials purchases budget** A plan that shows the physical amount and cost of planned purchases of direct materials

**direct materials usage budget** A plan that shows the amount and budgeted cost of direct materials required for production

**direct materials usage variance (UV)** For each material, the difference between the actual direct material units used during the period and the number of standard units that should have been used for the output of the period, multiplied by the standard cost per unit of the direct material

**direct method** Service department cost allocation accomplished by using the service flows *only to production departments* and determining each production department's share of that service

**discounted cash flow (DCF) models** Represent capital-budgeting decision models that incorporate the present value of future after-tax cash flows

**discount rate** A generic term that refers to the rate used in capital budgeting for converting future cash flows to a present-value basis

**discretionary-cost method** Used when costs are considered largely uncontrollable; apply discretion at the planning stage; an input-oriented approach

**dual allocation** A cost allocation method that separates fixed and variable costs and traces variable service department costs to the user departments; fixed costs are allocated based on either equal shares among departments or a predetermined budgeted proportion

**dual pricing** involves the use of multiple prices for an internal transfer or cost allocation, one based on variable cost and one based on fixed cost

**dummy variable** Used in a regression model to represent the presence or absence of a condition

**Durbin-Watson (DW) statistic*** A measure of the extent of nonlinearity in the regression

# E

**economic value added (EVA®)** A measure of financial performance designed to approximate an entity's *economic profit;* calculated most often as net operating profit after taxes (adjusted for accounting "distortions") less an imputed charge based on the level of invested capital

**effective operation** The attainment of the goal set for the operation

**employment contract** An agreement between the manager and top management, designed to provide incentives for the manager to act autonomously to achieve top management's objectives

**engineered-cost method** An output-oriented method that considers costs to be variable and therefore controllable

**enterprise risk management (ERM)** A framework and process that firms use to manage the risks that could negatively or positively affect the company's competitiveness and success

**equivalent units** The number of units that could have been produced given the amount of work actually performed on both completed and partially completed units; used in conjunction with process costing

**executional cost drivers** Factors that the firm can manage in the short term to reduce costs such as workforce involvement, design of the production process, and supplier relationships

**expected value of perfect information (EVPI)** The maximum amount that a rational decision maker would be willing to pay for "perfect information"

**expropriation** A situation in which a government takes ownership and control of assets that a foreign investor has invested in that country

**external failure costs** Costs associated with defective/poor-quality outputs detected after being delivered to the customer

# F

**facility-level activity** An activity performed to support operations of products in general

**factory overhead** All the indirect manufacturing costs commonly combined into a single cost pool in a manufacturing firm

**factory overhead applied** The amount of overhead assigned to a cost object using a predetermined factory overhead rate

**FASB ASC 330-10-30** GAAP financial reporting guidance regarding the determination of overhead allocation rates and the treatment of abnormal idle-capacity variances

**FIFO method** A process costing method for calculating the unit cost that includes only costs incurred and work performed during the current period

---

*Key term appears in Regression Analysis Supplement online at **www.mhhe.com/blocher6e**.

**financial budgets**   A plan that identifies sources and uses of funds for budgeted operations and capital expenditures for the coming period

**financial control**   The comparison between actual and budgeted financial results

**financial productivity**   The ratio of output to the dollar amount of one or more input factors

**Finished Goods Inventory**   The cost of goods that are ready for sale

**firmwide pool**   A basis for determining the bonus available to all managers through an amount set aside for this purpose

**fixed cost**   The portion of the total cost that does not change with a change in the quantity of output within the relevant range

**fixed overhead application rate**   A term used for product-costing purposes; the rate at which fixed overhead is charged to production per unit of activity (or output)

**fixed overhead production volume variance**   The difference between budgeted fixed overhead and the standard fixed overhead applied to production (using the predetermined fixed overhead allocation rate); also called the *production volume variance*

**fixed overhead spending (budget) variance**   The difference between budgeted and actual fixed factory overhead costs for a period

**fixed-performance contract**   An incentive compensation plan whereby compensation is a function of actual performance compared to a fixed (budgeted) target

**flexible budget**   A budget that adjusts revenues and costs to the actual output level achieved

**flexible-budget (FB) variance**   The difference between actual and flexible-budget amounts on the income statement

**flow diagram**   A flowchart of the work done that shows the sequence of processes and the amount of time required for each

**F-statistic***   In a regression analysis, the ratio of the mean square for the regression (explained variance) to mean square error; used to evaluate the statistical reliability of the regression model

**full-cost method**   A transfer price set equal to the variable cost plus allocated fixed cost for the selling unit

**functional analysis**   A type of value engineering in which the performance and cost of each major function or feature of the product is examined

# G

**gaming the performance measure**   Non-value-adding actions taken by managers to improve indicated performance

**goal congruence**   The consistency between the goals of the firm and the goals of its employees. It is achieved when the manager acts independently in such a way as to simultaneously achieve top management's objectives

**goalpost conformance**   Conformance to a quality specification expressed as a specified range around a targeted performance level

**GPK**   Detailed German cost accounting system, roughly translated as *flexible-standard costing;* an extension of ABC

**gross book value (GBV)**   An asset's historical (i.e., acquisition) cost without the reduction for accumulated depreciation

**group technology**   A method of identifying similarities in the parts of products manufactured so the same part can be used in two or more products, thereby reducing costs

# H

**high-low method**   A method using algebra to determine a *unique* cost estimation line between representative high and low points in a given data set

**high-value-added activity**   Something that, in the eyes of the consumer, adds value to a product or service

**histogram**   A graphical representation of the frequency of attributes or events in a given set of data

**historical cost**   The book value of current assets plus the net book value (NBV) of long-lived assets

**hurdle rate**   The minimum acceptable rate of return on an investment for capital-budgeting purposes, also referred to as the *required rate of return;* for average-risk projects, the hurdle rate is defined as the weighted-average cost of capital (WACC)

# I

**ideal standard**   A standard that reflects perfect implementation and maximum efficiency in every aspect of the operation

**implementation error**   A deviation from standard due to operator errors

**independent variable**   A cost driver used to estimate the value of the dependent variable

**indifference probability**   The probability regarding states of nature that makes management indifferent between alternative courses of action (such as whether or not to investigate the cause of a reported variance)

**indirect cost**   A cost that is not conveniently or economically traceable to a specific cost pool or cost object

**indirect labor cost**   Supervision, quality control, inspection, purchasing and receiving, and other labor-related manufacturing support costs; a component of total manufacturing overhead

**indirect materials cost**   The cost of materials used in manufacturing that are not easily or economically traceable to the finished product; a component of total manufacturing overhead

**internal accounting controls**   A set of policies and procedures that restrict and guide activities in the processing of financial data with the objective of preventing or detecting errors and fraudulent acts

**internal failure costs**   Costs associated with defective processes or defective products detected before delivery to customers

**internal rate of return (IRR)**   An estimate of the true (i.e., economic) rate of return on an investment

**investment center**   A business unit that includes in its financial-performance metric the level of assets (capital) employed by the unit as well as profit generated by that unit

*Key term appears in Regression Analysis Supplement online at **www.mhhe.com/blocher6e**.

**ISO 9000:2000** A set of guidelines for quality management and quality standards developed by the International Organization for Standardization, located in Geneva, Switzerland

**ISO 14000** A set of quality standards designed to minimize environmental effects of an organization's outputs

# J

**job costing** A product costing system that accumulates and assigns costs to a specific job

**job cost sheet** A cost sheet that records and summarizes the costs of direct materials, direct labor, and factory overhead for a particular job

**joint production costs** Costs incurred prior to the split-off point; common (i.e., indirect) costs

**joint production process** Multiple outputs that arise from a common resource input

**joint products** Products from the same production process that have relatively substantial sales values

**just-in-time (JIT) manufacturing** A process in which production at any stage of the process does not take place until an order is received

**just-in-time (JIT) system** A comprehensive production and inventory system that purchases or produces materials and parts only as needed and just in time to be used at each stage of the production process

# K

**kaizen budgeting** A budgeting approach that incorporates continuous improvement expectations in the budget

**kanban** A set of control cards used to signal the need for materials and products to move from one operation to the next in an assembly line

# L

**lean accounting** The accounting technique that uses value streams to measure the financial benefits of a firm's progress in implementing lean manufacturing

**learning curve analysis** A systematic method for estimating costs when learning is present

**learning rate** The percentage by which average time (or total time) falls from previous levels, as output doubles

**least squares regression** A cost-estimation method in which the variable and fixed cost coefficients are found by minimizing the sum of the squares of the estimation errors

**life-cycle costing** A method used to identify and monitor the costs of a product throughout its life cycle

**linear programming** A mathematical technique that can be used to solve constrained optimization problems, such as the optimum short-term product (or service) mix

**liquidation value** The estimated price that could be received from the sale of the assets of a business unit

**long-range plan** A plan that identifies actions required during the 5- to 10-year period covered by the plan to attain the firm's strategic goals

**low-value-added activity** Consumes time, resources, or space, but adds little to satisfying customer needs

# M

**management accounting** A profession that involves partnering in management decision making, devising planning and performance management systems, and providing expertise in financial reporting and control to assist management in the formulation and implementation of an organization's strategy

**management accounting and control system** An organization's core performance-measurement system

**management compensation plans** Policies and procedures for compensating managers

**management control** The system used by upper-level managers to evaluate the performance of mid-level managers

**managing earnings** The manipulation of reported income

**manufacturing cells** A set of machines, typically laid out in the form of a semicircle, needed to produce a particular product or part

**manufacturing cycle efficiency (MCE)** The ratio of processing time to total cycle time

**margin of safety (MOS)** The amount of planned (or actual) sales above the breakeven point

**margin of safety ratio (MOS%)** The margin of safety (in units or in dollars) divided by breakeven sales (in units or in dollars)

**market-price method** A transfer price set as the current price of the product in the external market

**market risk premium** The spread between the expected rate of return on a market portfolio of securities and the risk-free rate of return; represented as $(r_m - r_f)$, where $r_m$ = return on a market portfolio of securities and $r_f$ = risk-free rate of return

**market share variance** A comparison of the firm's actual market share to its budgeted market share and measurement of the effect of changes in the firm's market share on its total contribution margin and operating income

**market size variance** A measure of the effect of changes in the total market size on the firm's total contribution margin and operating income

**master budget** An aggregation of all subunit budgets into an integrated plan of action for the budget period

**master (static) budget variance** The difference between actual operating income and the master budget operating income for a period; also called the *total operating-income variance*

**Materials Inventory** Materials used in the manufacturing process or to provide the service

**materials requisition** A department supervisor uses this to request materials for production

**materials usage ratio** The ratio of the quantity used to the quantity purchased

**mean absolute percentage error (MAPE)** A measure of cost-estimation accuracy, calculated as the mean (average) absolute percentage prediction error

**mean squared variance*** The ratio of the amount of variance of a component in a regression model to the number of degrees of freedom for that component

**measurement errors** Incorrect numbers resulting from improper or inaccurate accounting systems or procedures

**merchandise purchases budget** A plan that shows the amount of merchandise the firm needs to purchase during the budget period

**mixed cost** A cost that includes both variable and fixed cost components

**modeling error** A deviation from the standard because of the failure to include all relevant variables or because of the inclusion of wrong or irrelevant variables in the standard-setting process

**modified internal rate of return (MIRR)** The internal rate of return (IRR) of a capital investment adjusted to account for an assumed rate of return associated with interim project cash inflows

**Monte Carlo simulation (MCS)** An extension to scenario analysis in which a computer provides a distribution of possible outcomes, for example, project NPVs, based on repeated sampling from a distribution associated with one or more input variables in a decision model

**multicollinearity** The condition when two or more independent variables are highly correlated with each other

**multicriteria decision model** A model that includes more than one decision criterion

**multiple linear regression** Used to describe regression applications having two or more independent variables

**multistage ABC** The assignment of resource costs to certain activities which in turn are assigned to other activities before being assigned to the final cost objects

**mutually exclusive projects** An extreme form of project interdependence: the acceptance of one investment alternative precludes the acceptance of one or more other alternatives

# N

**negotiated-price method** The determination of a transfer price through a negotiation process and sometimes arbitration between units

**net book value (NBV)** An asset's historical (acquisition) cost less accumulated depreciation

**net present value (NPV)** Equals the difference between the present value of future cash inflows and the present value of future cash outflows of an investment project

**net promoter score** A measure of customer satisfaction, defined as the difference between the percentage of customers classified as "promoters" and those classified as "detractors" (those not recommending the business plus those who are neutral)

**net realizable value (NRV)** The estimated sales value of the product at the split-off point; determined by subtracting the separable processing and selling costs beyond the split-off point from the ultimate sales value of the product

**net working capital** As used within the context of capital budgeting, current assets other than cash (CA − Cash) less current liabilities (CL)

**network diagram** A flowchart of the work done that shows the sequence of processes and the amount of time required for each

**nonconstant variance*** The condition when the variance of the error terms in a regression model is not constant over the range of values for the independent variable

**noncontrollable fixed costs** Costs that are not controllable within a year's time, usually including facilities-related costs such as depreciation, taxes, and insurance

**non-DCF models** Capital-budgeting models that are not based on an analysis of the present value of future cash flows

**non-value-added activity** An activity that does not contribute to customer value or to the organization's needs

**normal capacity** The expected average demand per year over an intermediate term, for example, the upcoming three to five years

**normal costing system** A costing process that uses actual costs for direct materials and direct labor and applies factory overhead to various jobs using a predetermined application rate

**normal spoilage** An unacceptable unit that occurs under efficient operating conditions; spoilage that is inherent in the manufacturing process

**NORMDIST** A function in Excel that calculates the area under the normal curve

# O

**operating budgets** Plans that identify resources needed to support operating activities and the acquisition of these resources

**operating leverage** The extent to which fixed costs characterize a cost structure

**operating risk** The risk that operations will not provide sufficient margin to cover (short-term) fixed costs

**operation costing** A hybrid costing system that uses job costing to assign direct materials costs to jobs and process costing to assign conversion costs to products or services

**operational control** The monitoring of short-term operating performance; takes place when mid-level managers monitor the activities of operating-level managers and employees

**operational productivity** The ratio of output to the number of units of an input factor

**opportunity cost** The benefit lost when choosing one option precludes receiving the benefits from an alternative option

**order-filling costs** Expenditures for freight, warehousing, packing and shipping, and collections

**order-getting costs** Expenditures to advertise and promote the product

**outliers** Unusual (i.e., abnormal) data points that strongly influence a regression analysis

---

*Key term appears in Regression Analysis Supplement online at **www.mhhe.com/blocher6e**.

**overapplied overhead** The excess of applied overhead over actual factory overhead cost for a period

**overhead** All the indirect costs commonly combined into a single cost pool

**overhead application** A process of allocating overhead costs to cost objects

**overtime premium** The *excess* wage rate over the standard hourly wage rate

# P

**Pareto analysis** A management tool that shows 20% of a set of important cost drivers are responsible for 80% of the total cost incurred

**Pareto diagram** A histogram of the frequency of factors contributing to a quality problem, ordered from the most to the least frequent

**partial productivity** A productivity measure that focuses only on the relationship between one of the inputs and the output attained

**participative standard** Active participation throughout the standard-setting process by employees affected by the standards

**payback period** The length of time (in years) required for the cumulative after-tax cash inflows from an investment to recover the initial investment outlay

**performance evaluation** The process by which managers at all levels gain information about the performance of tasks within the firm and judge that performance against preestablished criteria as set out in budgets, plans, and goals

**performance measurement** A measurement that identifies items that indicate the work performed and the results achieved by an activity, process, or organizational unit

**performance quality** The difference between the design specifications of the product and the actual performance of the product

**period costs** All nonproduct expenditures for managing the firm and selling the product; also referred to as *selling, general, and administrative (SG&A) expenses*

**periodic inventory system** A method that involves a count of inventory at the end of each accounting period to determine the ending balance in inventory

**perpetual inventory system** A method that updates the finished goods inventory account for each purchase or sales transaction

**physical measure method** A method that uses a physical measure such as pounds, gallons, yards, or units of volume produced at the split-off point to allocate the joint costs to joint products

**planning and decision making** Budgeting and profit planning, cash flow management, and other decisions related to operations

**plantwide overhead rate** A single overhead rate used throughout the entire production facility

**post-audit** An in-depth review of a completed capital-investment project

**practical capacity** Theoretical capacity reduced by normal output losses due to personal time, normal maintenance, and

so on; the measure of capacity used to estimate cost-driver rates under ABC and TDABC systems

**predatory pricing** Exists when a company has set prices below average variable cost and plans to raise prices later to recover the losses from the lower prices

**predetermined factory overhead rate** An estimated rate used to apply factory overhead cost to a cost object

**prediction error** A deviation from a standard because of an inaccurate estimation of the amounts for variables used in the standard-setting process

**preparation of financial statements** Requires management to comply with the financial reporting requirements of regulatory agencies

**present value (PV)** Equals future cash flows expressed in terms of current purchasing power; also referred to as time-adjusted value

**present value payback period** The length of time required for the cumulative *present value* of after-tax cash inflows to recover the initial outlay for an investment

**prevention costs** Costs incurred to keep quality defects from occurring

**prime costs** The sum of direct materials and direct labor

**principal-agent model** A conceptual model that contains the key elements that contracts must have to achieve the desired objectives

**process costing** A costing system that accumulates product or service costs by process or department and then assigns them to a large number of nearly identical products

**processing cycle efficiency (PCE)** A measure of operating performance defined as the ratio of processing time to total manufacturing time (or, the ratio of value-added time to total time)

**product costs** Under GAAP, the costs necessary to complete the product (direct materials, direct labor, and factory overhead)

**production budget** A budget showing planned output (production) for an upcoming period

**production cost report** A report that summarizes the physical units and equivalent units of a department, the costs incurred during the period, and the costs assigned to units completed and to units in ending work-in-process inventories

**production volume variance** Represents the over- or underapplied budgeted fixed overhead for the period, that is, the difference between the fixed overhead costs applied to production and the (lump-sum) budgeted fixed overhead for the period; also called *fixed overhead production volume variance*

**productivity** The ratio of output to input

**product-level activity** An activity performed to support the production of a specific product or service

**profit center** A business unit whose manager is responsible for revenues and expenses, but not the level of invested capital, in the unit

**profitability index (PI)** A rate-of-return measure, defined as the ratio of the NPV of a project to the original investment outlay for the project; useful for project-selection purposes when capital funds are limited and therefore need to be rationed

**profit-volume graph** Illustrates how the level of operating profit changes over different levels of output volume

*p*-value Measures the risk that a particular independent variable has only a chance relationship to the dependent variable

# Q

**quality**   Defined as customer satisfaction with the total experience of a product or service, that is, the difference between customer expectations and actual performance of the product or service

**quality circle**   A small group of employees from the same work area that meets regularly to identify and solve work-related problems, and to implement and monitor solutions to these problems

**quality function deployment (QFD)**   The integration of value engineering, marketing analysis, and target costing to assist in determining which components of the product should be targeted for redesign

# R

**random variances**   Variances beyond the control of management, either technically or financially, that often are considered as uncontrollable variances

**rank-order correlation**   A statistic that measures the degree to which two sets of numbers tend to have the same order or rank

**real assets**   Investments in both tangible property (e.g., a manufacturing facility) and intangible property (e.g., a new information system); can be contrasted with real options

**real options**   Flexibilities and/or growth opportunities embedded in capital-investment projects; can be contrasted with financial options, which are traded on an organized exchange

**reciprocal flows**   The flow of services back and forth between service departments

**reciprocal method**   A cost allocation method that considers all reciprocal flows between service departments through simultaneous equations

**regression analysis**   A statistical method for obtaining the unique cost-estimating equation that best fits a set of data points

**relative performance contracts**   Assessment of performance based on comparison of actual results with specified benchmarks, not budgeted targets; contrast with fixed-performance contracts

**relevant cost**   A future cost that differs between and among decision alternatives; an avoidable cost

**relevant range**   The range of the cost driver in which the actual value of the cost driver is expected to fall, and for which the relationship between the cost and the cost driver is assumed to be approximately linear

**replacement cost**   The current cost to replace the assets at the current level of service and functionality

**resale-price method**   A transfer-pricing method based on an appropriate markup based on gross profits of unrelated firms selling similar products

**residual income (RI)**   A dollar amount equal to the income of a business unit less an imputed charge for the level of investment in the division

**resource**   An economic element applied or used to perform activities

**resource-capacity planning**   Procedures used to ensure adequate but not excessive supply of capacity-related resources

**resource consumption accounting (RCA)**   A comprehensive and fully integrated management accounting approach that provides managers with decision support information based on an operational view of the organization

**resource consumption cost driver**   An activity or characteristic that consumes resources

**return on investment (ROI)**   Some measure of profit divided by some measure of investment in a business unit

**return on sales (ROS)**   A firm's profit per sales dollar; measures the manager's ability to control expenses and increase revenues to improve profitability

**revenue center**   A business unit with responsibility for sales, defined either by product line or by geographical area, that focuses on the selling function

**revenue drivers**   The factors that affect sales volume, such as price changes, promotions, discounts, customer service, changes in product features, delivery dates, and other value-added factors

**rework**   A produced unit that must be reworked into a good unit that can be sold in regular channels

**risk preferences**   The way individuals differentially view decision options, because they place a weight on *certain* outcomes that differs from the weight they place on *uncertain* outcomes

**robot**   A computer-programmed and controlled machine that performs repetitive activities

**robust quality approach**   See *absolute quality conformance*

**rolling financial forecast**   A constant planning horizon with the use of regularly updated forecasts

*R*-squared   A number between zero and one. Often it is described as a measure of the explanatory power of the regression; that is, the degree to which changes in the dependent variable can be predicted by changes in the independent variable

**run chart**   A chart that shows trends in observations over time

# S

**salary**   A fixed payment

**sales budget**   A schedule showing forecasted sales, in units and dollars, for an upcoming period

**sales life cycle**   The sequence of phases in a product's or service's life in the market—from the introduction of the product or service to the market, to growth in sales, and finally maturity, decline, and withdrawal from the market

**sales mix**   The relative proportion in which a company's products (or services) are sold

**sales mix variance**   The product of the difference between the actual and budgeted sales mix multiplied by the actual total number of units of all products sold, and by the budgeted contribution margin per unit of the product

**sales quantity variance**   The product of three elements: (1) the difference between the budgeted and actual total sales quantity, (2) the budgeted sales mix of the product, and (3) the budgeted contribution margin per unit of the product. It measures the effect of the change in the number of units sold from the number of units budgeted to be sold

**sales value at split-off method**   A method that allocates joint costs to joint products on the basis of their relative sales values at the split-off point

**sales volume variance**   The difference between the flexible-budget amount for that item and the amount for that item reflected in the master budget for the period for each income statement item

**schedule of cost of goods manufactured and sold**   A schedule that shows the manufacturing costs incurred, the change in the work-in-process inventory, the cost of goods sold, and the change in finished goods inventory during the period

**scenario analysis**   Represents an attempt to look at how a proposed investment project would fare under different combinations of variables, called *scenarios;* a special form of sensitivity analysis that is appropriate when the variables in a decision model are interrelated

**scrap**   Residual output that has little or no value

**selling price variance**   The difference between the total actual sales revenue and the total flexible-budget sales revenue for the units sold during a period

**sensitivity analysis**   The process of selectively varying a key input variable, for example, the discount rate, to identify the range over which a capital-budgeting decision is valid

**separable processing costs**   Costs incurred after the split-off point, traceable to individual products

**simple linear regression**   Used to describe regression applications having a single independent variable

**Six Sigma**   An overall strategy to accelerate improvements and achieve unprecedented performance levels by focusing on characteristics that are critical to customers and identifying and eliminating causes of errors or defects in processes

**Solver**   An analytical tool available on the Data Tab in Excel which can be used to solve linear programming problems

**split-off point**   The point in the production process at which individual products can be separately identified

**spoilage**   An unaccepted unit that is discarded or sold for disposal value

**standard cost**   The cost a firm should incur for an operation

**standard cost sheet**   A listing of the standard price and quantity of each manufacturing cost element for the production of one unit of a product

**standard cost system**   One in which standard, not actual, costs flow through the formal accounting records

**standard error of the estimate (SE)**   A measure of the dispersion of the actual observations around the regression line; as such it provides a measure of the accuracy of the regression's estimates

**static budget variance**   (See *master budget variance*)

**statistical control charts**   Charts that set control limits using a statistical procedure

**step cost**   A cost that varies with the cost driver, but in discrete steps; also called *semi-fixed cost*

**step method**   A cost allocation method that uses a sequence of steps in allocating service department costs to production departments

**strategic budget expenditures**   Planned spending on projects and initiatives that lead to long-term value and competitive advantage

**strategic business unit (SBU)**   A well-defined set of controllable operating activities over which an SBU manager is responsible

**strategic control system**   The processes an organization uses to monitor its progress in terms of accomplishing the strategic goals of the organization

**strategic cost management**   The development of cost management information to facilitate the principal management function, strategic management

**strategic management**   The development and implementation of a sustainable competitive position

**strategic performance measurement**   An accounting system used by top management for the evaluation of SBU managers

**strategy**   A plan for using resources to achieve sustainable goals within a competitive environment

**strategy map**   A graphical representation of the organization's value proposition; used to depict the series of causes and effects embodied in the four perspectives of an organization's balanced scorecard

**structural cost drivers**   Strategic plans and decisions that have a long-term effect with regard to issues such as scale, experience, technology, and complexity

**sunk costs**   Costs that have been incurred in the past or committed for the future and are therefore irrelevant for decision-making purposes

**sustainability**   The balancing of the company's short- and long-term goals in all three dimensions of performance—social, environmental, and financial

**SWOT analysis**   A systematic procedure for identifying a firm's critical success factors: its internal strengths and weaknesses, and its external opportunities and threats

**systematic variances**   Variances that, until corrected, are likely to recur; also called *nonrandom variances*

# T

**Taguchi quality loss function**   Depicts, in the form of a quadratic function, the relationship between quality costs and level of deviation from target quality

**Takt time**   The speed at which units must be manufactured to meet customer demand

**target costing**   The desired cost for a product as determined on the basis of a given competitive price, so the product will earn a desired profit

**theoretical capacity**   A measure of capacity (output or activity) that assumes 100% efficiency; maximum possible output (or activity)

**theory of constraints (TOC)**   An analysis of operations that improves profitability and cycle time by identifying the bottleneck in the operation and determining the most profitable product mix given the bottleneck

**throughput margin**   A TOC measure of product profitability; it equals price less materials cost, including all purchased components and materials handling costs

**time-driven activity-based budgeting (TDABB)**   An approach to budgeting wherein budgets are prepared in conjunction with a time-driven activity-based cost (TDABC) system

**time-driven activity-based costing (TDABC)**   The assignment of resource costs directly to cost objects using the cost per time unit of supplying the resource, rather than first assigning costs to activities and then from activities to cost objects

**time-series regression**   The application of regression analysis to predict future amounts, using prior periods' data

**time ticket**   A sheet showing the time an employee worked on each job, the pay rate, and the total cost chargeable to each job

**tolerance**  An acceptable range of a quality characteristic, such as thickness (measured, for example, in centimeters)

**total contribution margin**  The contribution margin per unit $(p - v)$ multiplied by the number of units sold, $Q$

**total fixed overhead variance**  The difference between actual fixed overhead costs for the period and the standard fixed overhead costs charged to production for the period; this variance can be broken down into a fixed overhead spending variance and a fixed overhead production volume variance

**total flexible-budget (FB) variance**  The difference between the flexible-budget operating income and the actual operating income for the period

**total manufacturing cost**  The sum of materials used, labor, and overhead for the period

**total flexible-budget variance for overhead**  The difference between the total actual overhead for a period and the flexible budget for total overhead based on *output*

**total operating-income variance**  The difference between the actual operating income of the period and the master budget operating income projected for the period; also referred to as the *master (static) budget variance* for the period

**total productivity**  A measure including all input resources in computing the ratio of the output attained and the input used to attain the output

**total quality management (TQM)**  The unyielding and continuous effort by everyone in the organization to understand, meet, and exceed customer expectations

**total variable cost flexible-budget variance**  The difference between actual variable cost incurred and the total variable costs in the flexible budget for the period

**total variable overhead variance**  The difference between actual variable overhead cost incurred and the standard variable overhead cost applied to production; also called *over-* or *underapplied variable overhead* for the period

**transfer pricing**  The determination of an exchange price for a product or service when different business units within a firm exchange it; used to evaluate the financial performance of profit and investment centers

**transferred-in costs**  The costs of work performed in the earlier department that are transferred into the present department

**trend variable**  A variable in a regression model that takes on values of 1, 2, 3, . . . for each period in sequence

**$t$-value**  A measure of the reliability of each of the independent variables; that is, the degree to which an independent variable has a valid, stable, long-term relationship with the dependent variable

**two-stage cost assignment**  A procedure that assigns a firm's resource costs to cost pools and then to cost objects

# U

**underapplied overhead**  The amount that actual factory overhead exceeds the factory overhead applied for a given accounting period

**unit-based pool**  A basis for determining a bonus according to the performance of the manager's unit

**unit cost**  The total manufacturing cost (materials, labor, and overhead) divided by the number of units of output

**unit-level activity**  An activity performed for each unit of the cost object

**units accounted for**  The sum of the units transferred out and ending inventory units

**units to account for**  The sum of the beginning inventory units and the number of units started during the period

# V

**value activities**  Firms in an industry perform activities to design, manufacture, and provide customer service

**value-added activity**  An activity that contributes to customer value and satisfaction or satisfies an organizational need

**value chain**  An analytic tool firms use to identify the specific steps required to provide a product or service to the customer

**value-chain analysis**  A strategic analysis tool used to identify where value to customers can be increased or costs reduced, and to better understand the firm's linkages with suppliers, customers, and other firms in the industry

**value engineering**  Used in target costing to reduce product cost by analyzing the trade-offs between different types of product functionality and total product cost

**value stream**  A group of related products; useful for preparing profitability reports as part of lean accounting; all the activities required to create customer value for a family of products or services

**variable cost**  The change in total cost associated with each change in the quantity of the cost driver

**variable-cost method**  In transfer pricing, the transfer price equals the variable cost (either actual or standard) of the selling unit

**variable expense flexible-budget variance**  The difference between the actual variable expenses incurred and the total standard variable expenses in the flexible budget for the units sold during the period

**variable overhead efficiency variance**  The difference between the flexible budget for variable overhead based on *inputs* (e.g., actual labor-hours worked) and the flexible budget for variable overhead based on *outputs* (i.e., standard allowed labor-hours for units produced)

**variable overhead spending variance**  The difference between actual variable overhead cost incurred and the flexible budget for variable overhead based on *inputs* for the period (e.g., actual labor-hours worked)

**variances**  The differences between budgeted and actual amounts, for either financial or nonfinancial measures

# W

**weighted-average contribution margin per unit**  An average per-unit contribution margin based on an assumed sales mix determined on the basis of physical units (not sales dollars)

**weighted-average contribution margin ratio**   An average contribution margin ratio at the assumed sales mix based on sales dollars (not units)

**weighted-average cost of capital (WACC)**   An average of the (after-tax) cost of debt and equity capital for a firm; in general, the WACC is the appropriate discount rate to use for future cash flows associated with "average risk" projects

**weighted-average method**   A method for calculating unit cost under process costing that includes all costs, both those incurred during the current period and those incurred in the prior period that are shown as the beginning work-in-process inventory of the current period

**what-if analysis**   The calculation of an amount given different levels for a factor that influences that amount

**work cells**   Small groups of related manufacturing processes organized in clusters to assemble parts of finished products

**Work-in-Process Inventory**   Contains all costs put into the manufacture of products that are started but not complete at the financial statement date

**working capital**   The difference, at any balance sheet date, between total current assets (CA) and total current liabilities (CL); contrast with *net working capital* (as used within the context of capital budgeting)

# Y

**yield-to-maturity**   A long-term bond yield (rate of return) expressed as an annual rate; the calculation takes into account the current market price of the bond, its par value, the coupon interest rate, and the time-to-maturity; the total performance of a bond, coupon payments as well as capital gain or loss, from the time of purchase until maturity

# Z

**zero-base budgeting (ZBB)**   A budgeting process that requires managers to prepare budgets each period from a base of zero

Page numbers followed by n refer to notes.